Medical Risks

Editorial Committee

Representatives of the Association of Life Insurance
Medical Directors of America:

John O. Alden, M.D.
Paul S. Entmacher, M.D.
John J. Hutchinson, M.D.
John C. Robinson, M.D.
Richard B. Singer, M.D., Chairman

Representatives of the Society of Actuaries:

John A. Bevan, F.S.A.
Edward A. Lew, F.S.A.
Ernest J. Moorhead, F.S.A.
Charles A. Ormsby, F.S.A.

Project Director:

Louis Levinson, F.S.A.

Medical Risks: Patterns of Mortality and Survival

A Reference Volume Sponsored by
The Association of Life Insurance Medical Directors of America
and The Society of Actuaries

Editors:

Richard B. Singer, M.D.
Louis Levinson, Fellow of the Society of Actuaries

Lexington Books
D.C. Heath and Company
Lexington, Massachusetts
Toronto

Library of Congress Cataloging in Publication Data

Main entry under title:

Medical risks.

    Includes index.
    1. Mortality—Tables. 2. Death—Causes—Tables. 3. Life expectancy—Tables.
4. Medical statistics. I. Singer, Richard B. II. Levinson, Louis. III. Association
of Life Insurance Medical Directors of America. IV. Society of Actuaries.
[DNLM: 1. Mortality—Tables. HB1321 M489]

RA407.M4	312'.2	74-31609
ISBN 0-669-98228-5		

Published simultaneously in Canada

Printed in the United States of America

International Standard Book Number: 0-669-98228-5

Library of Congress Catalog Card Number: 74-31609

Life is short, the art long,
opportunity fleeting,
experience treacherous,
judgment difficult.

Hippocrates — *Aphorisms*

Contents

Medical Risks: Patterns of Mortality and Survival

Errata Sheet, First Printing (1976, White Cover)

Page	Line	Change line or entry to read (correction in bold face):
vii	9	Chapter 4 **Physical, Toxic, and Other Risks**, John C. Robinson, M.D. 33
xi	8	**Physical, Toxic, and Other Risks** (Chapter 4); Cerebrovascular Disease (Chapter 6); Other Cardiovascular Diseases (Chapter. . . . .
xi	21	Philip G. Sullivan, M.D., **M.P.H.**
xv	43	(§626), Dr. Benjamin Burrows (§422), Dr. **Laurence** B. Ellis (§353), Dr. Jack A. End (§321), Dr. Paul S. Entmacher. . . . .
12	27	$\sum\limits_{0}^{t-1} d_{x+t}/\ell_x$
12	Table 2-3	(Change annual withdrawal rates for five successive intervals to read:) (i=1) **.0510**, (2) **.0456**, (3) **.0370**, (4) **.0187**, (5) **.0170** (Change footnote to read:) *Withdrawal rate $= W_{x+t}/(\ell_{x+t} - \frac{1}{2} d_{x+t})$
29	18	LL=**(200) (0.48)=96** per cent, and the upper confidence limit, UL=**(200) (1.84)=368** per cent (see Table 3-3).
30		(Paste new page with corrected Table 3-3 and text over existing page.)
31	1	In this example d′, MR as **100 per cent**, and q′ are **within** the 95 per cent confidence limits on a percentage basis and therefore do not. . . . .
31	3-4	fall below the lower 90 per cent confidence limit of **5.4, the lower confidence limit of 108 per cent exceeds the expected mortality ratio of 100 per cent**, and q′ falls below the lower confidence limit of **0.0108** for the mortality rate
31	8	1−0.020=0.980, the 95 per cent confidence limits based on 10 deaths are **0.9632 to 0.9904** (see the corresponding confidence. . . . .
48	12	in the United States, due mainly to a **twentyfold** increase in mortality from lung cancer. The corresponding death rate. . . . .
111	23	section to aortic valve prostheses. Four prosthetic **valves,** Bjork-Shiley, Braunwald-Cutter, Lillehei-Kaster and Smeloff-. . . . .
111	Last	I. J. Warkany and H. Kalter, "**Congenital** Malformations," New Eng. J. Med., 265:993-1001 (1961).
118	13	tension in the absence of **variant** beats (pairs or runs, bigeminy, bundle branch block after atrial premature beats, or T. . . . .
3-43	Table 309c	(Change subheading for lower half of table to read:) Patients with Angiogram, no operations (See §**307** - Series 2)
3-118	Table 353c	(Change mortality rate q_o, Males, Class III (Better), Age 40-49:) **.026**
3-148	2	Prevalence, Incidence, and Mortality in the Framingham Study, Ann. Int. Med., 71:89-105 **(1969).**
3-172	10	(5) Methods of follow-up were not described. Average follow-up was **7.8** years.

Contributors

John O. Alden, M.D.

Member, Mortality Monograph Committee (joint committee of the Association of Life Insurance Medical Directors of America and the Society of Actuaries); Treasurer, Association of Life Insurance Medical Directors of America; Medical Director, Life Division, Aetna Life and Casualty, Hartford, Connecticut.

John A. Bevan, F.S.A.

Member, Mortality Monograph Committee (joint committee of the Association of Life Insurance Medical Directors of America and the Society of Actuaries); Actuary, Connecticut General Life Insurance Company, Hartford, Connecticut.

Paul S. Entmacher, M.D.

Coronary Heart Disease (Chapter 7); Endocrine and Metabolic Diseases (Chapter 16).

Member, Mortality Monograph Committee (joint committee of the Association of Life Insurance Medical Directors of America and the Society of Actuaries); Vice President and Chief Medical Director, Metropolitan Life Insurance Company, New York, New York.

Jerzy Gajewski, M.D., Ph.D.

Genitourinary Diseases (Coauthor, Chapter 14).

Associate Medical Director, John Hancock Mutual Life Insurance Company, Boston, Massachusetts.

Herbert S. Gardner, F.S.A.

Project assistance: preparation and review of abstracts.

Cesar I. Gonzales, M.D.

Genitourinary Diseases (Coauthor, Chapter 14).

Associate Medical Director, John Hancock Mutual Life Insurance Company, Boston, Massachusetts.

William E. Huckabee, M.D.

Respiratory Diseases (Coauthor, Chapter 12).

Associate Medical Director, John Hancock Mutual Life Insurance Company, Boston, Massachusetts.

John J. Hutchinson, M.D.

Neuropsychiatric Disorders (Chapter 6); Systemic Disorders (Chapter 15).

Member, Mortality Monograph Committee (joint committee of the Association of Life Insurance Medical Directors of America and the Society of Actuaries); Vice President, New York Life Insurance Company, New York, New York.

x

Wilmer A. Jenkins, F.S.A.

Project assistance: preparation and review of abstracts.

Past President, Society of Actuaries.

Harold S. Kost, M.D.

Respiratory Diseases (Coauthor, Chapter 12).

General Medical Director, John Hancock Mutual Life Insurance Company, Boston, Massachusetts.

Louis Levinson, F.S.A.

Methodology (Coauthor, Chapter 2); Coeditor.

Project Director, Mortality Monograph Committee (joint committee of the Association of Life Insurance Medical Directors of America and the Society of Actuaries).

Edward A. Lew, F.S.A.

Interpretation of Comparative Mortality and Survival Data (Coauthor, Chapter 3); Cancer (Coauthor, Chapter 5); Hypertension (Coauthor, Chapter 8).

Member, Mortality Monograph Committee (joint committee of the Association of Life Insurance Medical Directors of America and the Society of Actuaries); Past President, Society of Actuaries.

Ernest J. Moorhead, F.S.A.

Member, Mortality Monograph Committee (joint committee of the Association of Life Insurance Medical Directors of America and the Society of Actuaries); Past President, Society of Actuaries.

C. Perry Norton, M.D.

Arrhythmias and ECG Abnormalities (Coauthor, Chapter 10).

Associate Medical Director, New England Mutual Life Insurance Company, Boston, Massachusetts.

William J. November, F.S.A.

Project assistance: preparation and review of abstracts.

Charles A. Ormsby, F.S.A.

Member, Mortality Monograph Committee (joint committee of the Association of Life Insurance Medical Directors of America and the Society of Actuaries); Senior Vice President, John Hancock Mutual Life Insurance Company, Boston, Massachusetts; Past President, Home Office Life Underwriters Association.

Michael J. Rich, F.S.A.

Genitourinary Diseases (Coauthor, Chapter 14).

Assistant Actuary, John Hancock Mutual Life Insurance Company, Boston, Massachusetts.

James W. Richhart, F.S.A.

Respiratory Diseases (Coauthor, Chapter 12).

Assistant Actuary, John Hancock Mutual Life Insurance Company, Boston, Massachusetts.

John C. Robinson, M.D.

Miscellaneous Risk Factors (Chapter 4); Cerebrovascular Disease (Chapter 6); Other Cardiovascular Diseases (Chapter 11); Digestive System Diseases (Chapter 13).

Secretary, Mortality Monograph Committee (joint committee of the Association of Life Insurance Medical Directors of America and the Society of Actuaries); Chief Medical Director, Travelers Insurance Company, Hartford, Connecticut.

Richard B. Singer, M.D.

Plan and Scope of the Study (Chapter 1); Methodology (Coauthor, Chapter 2); Interpretation of Comparative Mortality and Survival Data (Coauthor, Chapter 3); Cancer (Coauthor, Chapter 5); Hypertension (Coauthor, Chapter 8); Congenital and Valvular Heart Disease (Coauthor, Chapter 9); Arrhythmias and ECG Abnormalities (Coauthor, Chapter 10); Coeditor.

Chairman, Mortality Monograph Committee (joint committee of the Association of Life Insurance Medical Directors of America and the Society of Actuaries); Second Vice President and Director of Medical Research, New England Mutual Life Insurance Company, Boston, Massachusetts.

Philip G. Sullivan, M.D.

Congenital and Valvular Heart Disease (Coauthor, Chapter 9).

Associate Medical Director, New England Mutual Life Insurance Company, Boston, Massachusetts.

Edward H. Wells, F.S.A.

Project assistance: preparation and review of abstracts.

Frank G. Whitbread, F.S.A.

Project assistance: preparation and review of abstracts.

Preface

The idea for this volume had its origin in a proposal put forward to the Executive Council of the Association of Life Insurance Medical Directors of America in 1965. The idea had been discussed in the Board of Life Insurance Medicine and the Publications Committee of the Association, and both groups voted to recommend the proposal, which was accordingly presented by the respective Chairmen (Dr. Singer for the Board of Life Insurance Medicine and Dr. Entmacher for the Publications Committee). The substance of the proposal was for the Association to sponsor the preparation and publication of a volume of reference tables of comparative mortality and survival data. Such data were known to exist in many published articles scattered throughout the medical literature. If such articles could be retrieved, critically evaluated, and useful data presented on a comparative basis within a uniform format, it was thought that the resulting tables would be of value not only to medical directors, underwriters, and actuaries in the life insurance industry but also to many workers in the health sciences.

Following discussion in the Executive Council, the President of the Association, Dr. John C. Talbot, appointed an ad hoc committee to explore the feasibility of the proposal and to prepare recommendations. The committee consisted of Dr. Paul S. Entmacher, Dr. John J. Hutchinson, Dr. John C. Robinson, and Dr. Richard B. Singer as Chairman. Pursuant to a unanimous recommendation to undertake the project, these members were reappointed as an Editorial Committee to supervise the preparation of the volume. The Committee enlarged itself by inviting three Fellows of the Society of Actuaries to join in the project, thus providing badly needed actuarial expertise. These new members were Edward A. Lew, Ernest J. Moorhead, and Charles A. Ormsby. After conducting a search, the Committee invited Dr. Henry J. Bakst, Professor of Preventive Medicine at Boston University Medical School, to direct the work of preparation of the volume under the general supervision of the Committee. It was recognized that the time and effort involved would be beyond the collective capacity of the Committee members themselves, all of whom had full-time responsibilities in their individual company positions. Funds were made available through the efforts of Dr. Albert L. Larson, President of the Association in 1966-67. Thirty of the largest insurance companies contributed a total of $41,750 specifically for the support of the project.

Financial support was made available to Dr. Bakst as Principal Investigator through an institutional grant to Boston University. Funds were used to search the medical literature, to evaluate promising articles, and to commence preparation of trial tables. The Editorial Committee contributed articles and experimented with different models of tabular format to suit the variety of data presented in the articles. Work commenced in January 1968 and continued for 19 months when it had to be suspended because of the pressure of Dr. Bakst's administrative duties. His subsequent appointment as Dean made it necessary for Dr. Bakst to submit his resignation, which was accepted by the Editorial Committee in early 1970 with the utmost reluctance and regret. After instituting a search for a suitable replacement, the Committee, through a stroke of good fortune, was able to appoint as Project Director a Fellow of the Society of Actuaries, Louis Levinson, retired Chief Actuary and Vice President of a large insurance company, with a long-time interest in mortality classes. This appointment was made in June 1970, and preparation of the tables was completed through the unstinting efforts of the Project Director, with limited assistance from a part-time staff, a group of volunteer retired actuaries, and individual members of the Committee.

A change in the organizational relationship of the Editorial Committee came about in 1968 when the respective Presidents, Dr. William Purdy of the Association of Life Insurance Medical Directors of America and Morton Miller, F.S.A., of the Society of Actuaries entered into an agreement to set up a standing Liaison Committee, to plan, organize, and circulate mortality studies of mutual interest to the two organizations. The Editorial Committee was now recognized as a joint committee in charge of a mortality study under the aegis of the Liaison Committee. The actuaries on the Editorial Committee were now officially appointed as representatives of the Society of Actuaries, and the appointment of the medical director members was reconfirmed by the Association. In 1970 the Treasurer of the Association, Dr. John O. Alden, was appointed as a member of the Committee, and a new representative of the Society of Actuaries, John A. Bevan, F.S.A., was also appointed. The name of the Committee was changed to the Mortality Monograph Committee. Additional financial support needed to complete the project was provided on an annual basis through the budget of one of the Mortality Committees of the Society of Actuaries. The total cost of preparation of the volume eventually came to $109,000 in round figures, of which about 40 per cent came from the companies originally solicited by the Association and 60 per cent from the companies which subsidized the annual mortality study work of the Society of Actuaries.

Additional details on table construction, methodology, and interpretation may be found in the first three chapters of this volume. The work of preparation of the tables and their descriptive text was carried out by or under the direction of the Project Director, with the assistance of, as noted above, members of the Committee and the retired actuaries' group, and a very small part-time staff. The draft of each abstract was revised until it met the approval of the Project Director and Chairman, and then the draft was sent to all Committee members for review and comment. After selection of and consultation with the publisher, Lexington Books, the Mortality Monograph Committee made the decision to assume responsibility for typesetting the tables, a decision that contributed to the economy and accuracy of the process. Production of the tables was an exceedingly complex operation, and it was a great advantage in the training of the compositors, and in the correction of errors to have the typesetting and proofreading spread out over a period of many months, with close contact between Committee staff and those actually engaged in the composition work. The cost of the composition work was included in the Committee budget. The Committee also assumed responsibility for the preparation of the Chapter material; most of the writing was done by individual Committee members and the Project Director, although the assistance of medical or actuarial colleagues was obtained for some portions. Because of the pressure of time chapter drafts were not sent to all Committee members for review, as was the case with the abstracts. This responsibility was delegated to the Project Director and Chairman, who were designated as editors of the volume.

There is a long tradition of cooperation between these two sponsoring organizations, both dependent in their professional activities on the availability of suitable mortality data in the preparation and production of mortality studies. Extensive studies based on life insurance experience were jointly undertaken and published between 1914 and 1960. The present volume continues this tradition of making contribution to scientific knowledge of mortality in relation to body build, blood pressure, and other medical characteristics. At the same time this volume breaks new ground in two ways. For the first time the bulk of the data presented is drawn from sources outside insured populations, thus covering many patient groups and conditions not likely to be found among persons who have been issued life insurance. Also, for the first time a technical publisher has been chosen, instead of the printing being carried out by the joint committee supervising the study, or by the Society of Actuaries, as was the case with the *Impairment Study 1951* and the *Build and Blood Pressure Study 1959.* It is the hope of the Mortality Monograph Committee, the Association, and the Society that this volume may prove to be useful to clinical investigators, physicians in a variety of medical and surgical specialties, epidemiologists, statisticians, and public health specialists, as well as those in the life insurance industry.

March, 1976   R.B.S.

Acknowledgments

Many, many individuals and organizations have given help and encouragement to this enterprise. In what is at best only a partial and imperfect recognition of the assistance it has received, the Mortality Monograph Committee desires to express its very great appreciation to the following:

——— the Association of Life Insurance Medical Directors of America, its Executive Council, the Society of Actuaries, its Board of Governors and Executive Director, and the respective presidents and officers of these two professional bodies, for their confidence in and support of the project, especially the necessary financial support of the project from 1968 to 1976;

——— to Louis Levinson, Project Director, and the late Dr. Henry J. Bakst for their leadership, expertise, and thousands of hours of toil that brought the project to a successful completion;

——— to the executives of those companies that responded to the 1967 appeal by the Association for funds to support the project—Aetna Life Insurance Company, Bankers Life Company, The Canada Life Assurance Company, Connecticut General Life Insurance Company, Connecticut Mutual Life Insurance Company, Equitable Life Insurance Company of Iowa, The Equitable Life Assurance Society of the United States, the Great-West Life Assurance Company, Hartford Life and Accident Insurance Company, Jefferson Standard Life Insurance Company, John Hancock Mutual Life Insurance Company, The Life Insurance Company of Virginia, The Lincoln National Life Insurance Company, London Life Insurance Company, The Manufacturers Life Insurance Company, Massachusetts Mutual Life Insurance Company, Metropolitan Life Insurance Company, The Mutual Life Insurance Company of New York, The National Life & Accident Company, New England Mutual Life Insurance Company, New York Life Insurance Company, Pan-American Life Insurance Company, The Penn Mutual Life Insurance Company, Phoenix Mutual Life Insurance Company, Pilot Life Insurance Company, The Prudential Insurance Company of America, Southwestern Life Insurance Company, State Mutual Life Assurance Company of America, Sun Life Assurance Company of Canada, and The Travelers Insurance Company;

——— to Herbert S. Gardner, Wilmer A. Jenkins, William J. November, Edward H. Wells, and Frank G. Whitbread, all Fellows of the Society of Actuaries, who volunteered their skills and donated their time in the preparation and review of many of the abstracts;

——— to Burpee W. Shaw, assistant to the Project Director, for his work on the abstracts, including extremely thorough computation checking in most of the tables, and to Janet R. Pettengill, assistant to the Chairman, for literature search, drafting of text, computation, and indefatigable work in supervising manuscript copy preparation, printed copy production, proofreading and correction of the abstracts, and index preparation;

——— to Linda A. Sampieri, Manager, Secretarial Department, New England Mutual Life Insurance Company for offering the typography service to the Committee, to Frederick H. Harrison and Phyllis B. Elgart for their interest, enthusiasm and skill in translating the manuscript tables into a high-quality finished product, and to the typesetters trained by them;

——— to all those who, at one time or another, assisted in literature search, drafting and checking of abstracts, evaluation of articles, and editorial tasks, including Ellen Chase, Cynthia M. Clancy, Frederic W. Corwin, Jr., Gordon T. Darwin, Karen Dennison, Dr. Robert B. Dickerson, Harry Don, Dr. Robert B. Downes, Diane Gipson, Eugenie A. Holness, Davis Kinsman, Elizabeth A. Leach, Elizabeth Singer Maule, Dorothy A. Murray, William J. Petrillo, Sharon Poizner, John U. O'Sullivan, Judy F. Thorpe, and Theodore Yonge;

——— to Joseph C. Sibigtroth, F.S.A., and Dr. John J. Hutchinson for making available results of the 1972 New York Life Single Impairment Study for inclusion in the volume, and to Charles A. Schwab and staff for careful review of the tabular data and drafting of descriptive text;

——— to all of the authors of articles who generously responded to the Committee's request for data additional to those contained in the published article, including Dr. John W. Barch (§902), Dr. Gilbert W. Beebe (§230), Dr. Murray F. Bell (§326), Dr. John J. Bergan (§625), Dr. Yvonne Bishop (§80), Dr. David J. Breithaupt (§251), Dr. Fred A. Bryan, Jr., (§626), Dr. Benjamin Burrows (§422), Dr. Lawrence B. Ellis (§353), Dr. Jack A. End (§321), Dr. Paul S. Entmacher (§376), Dr. Zdenek Hrubec (§303), Dr. William B. Kannel (§380), Dr. Robert J. Keehn (§285), Dr. Harry Kessler (§250), Dr. Irving I. Kessler (§906), Edward A. Lew, F.S.A., (§304), Jess L. Mast (§902), Dr. Brian MacMahon (§905), Dr. Howard M. McCue, Jr., (§322), Dr. Roger S. Mitchell (§410), Dr. Max H. Myers (§100-§190), Cecil J. Nesbitt, F.S.A., (§785), Barton S. Pauley, F.S.A., (§352, §501, §506), Dr. Sidney Pell (§321), Dr. W. Kenneth Poole (§626), Charles A. Schwab (§326), Dr. Richard B. Singer (§306, §349, §368, §399), Paul Sorlie (§380), Dr. Helen B. Taussig (§330), Eve Weinblatt (§313), Dr. Jack P. Whisnant (§209), Dr. Robert J. Wineman (§626);

——— to Michael McCarroll, Vice President and General Manager, and the editorial and production staff of Lexington Books for taking all of this material and making a book out of it.

PART I
TEXT

1

Plan and Scope of the Study
Richard B. Singer, M.D.

This book is a compilation of mortality and survival statistics in relation to *risk factors* identified in groups of people under follow-up observation. The term "risk factors" is used here to include the history or presence of a specific disease, or continued exposure to a hazardous occupation or habit, or the presence of an abnormal finding on physical examination, or an abnormal medical test result. Almost all of these risks are medical in nature.

The purpose of the book is to make available, in a single volume, tables of comparative mortality and survival data for the convenient reference use of the clinician, the clinical investigator, the counselor in health hazard appraisal, the epidemiologist, and those involved in risk selection for life insurance. To accomplish this purpose it has been necessary to carry out a number of steps:

(1) *To search and retrieve* source material of potential value;
(2) *To evaluate* over 2,000 articles, rejecting a majority of these as unsuitable;
(3) *To request* additional information from the authors in some cases;
(4) *To derive* intermediate data and comparative indices of mortality and survival by performing and checking many thousands of computations;
(5) *To arrange* the results under broad disease categories;
(6) *To utilize a standardized format*, each unit of which consists of one or more tables with attached citations and explanatory text;
(7) *To interpret* the results through a series of chapters on Life Table Methodology, the major disease categories, and application of the tabular data.

Preparation of this reference volume has proceeded in accordance with the plan as originally conceived and outlined above, but the magnitude of the task and the time required to complete it far exceeded original expectations (see the brief history of the project given in the preface). Several factors combined to create unusual difficulties that had to be overcome. For example, many decisions on Life Table Methodology and Tabular Formats had to be developed through a lengthy process of trial and error, even though the original concept of table design was clear and not significantly altered in the course of the work.

The methods employed by authors of articles dealing with follow-up studies were found to be so varied as to make it often difficult and sometimes impossible to present their results in terms of the comparative mortality and survival indices adopted as a standard for this volume. In some cases articles had to be abandoned after a great deal of effort had been expended in trying to produce a satisfactory version of the data. It was necessary to make a critical evaluation of several articles for each one that was eventually considered to be an acceptable source of data. In the search and retrieval process the sophisticated techniques of the MEDLARS type of computerized search proved to be of limited value because of the very low specificity of the lists provided and the inadequacy of key words used in coding.

Each set of tables was subjected to a lengthy process of preparation and critical revision; although time-consuming, this did produce more accurate and comprehensible reference data. Such difficulties are not unexpected in a project for which there were no precedents to serve as guidelines, but they did result in a prolongation of the time required for completion to more than twice the number of years originally estimated.

Source Material

The scope of the project was intended to be as comprehensive as time and manpower limitations permitted. Setting apart readily available major insurance studies[1,2] the Committee aimed to retrieve and develop data on as wide a range as possible of diseases and risk factors. Another limitation was set with respect to date of publication: with few exceptions only articles published since 1950 have been utilized. However, a major limitation on comprehensiveness was imposed by the difficulty of finding good, published follow-up studies for a great many diseases. Certain diseases are represented in the volume with many tabular abstracts of articles of high quality, for example, 15 abstracts on coronary heart disease and 11 on diabetes mellitus. In contrast, only eight abstracts each could be prepared for *all* respiratory diseases and *all* geni-

4

tourinary diseases, despite a computer search of recent medical literature through the National Library of Medicine, although a "miscellaneous" abstract in each major category does include limited data on a number of diseases. It is apparent that some specific diseases and some categories of disease are much more likely than others to have attracted the attention of investigators to conduct and report follow-up studies. Cardiovascular diseases and cancer are the two categories with the most comprehensive coverage. These are the two leading categories of cause of death, and there is actually a rough proportionality between numbers of deaths and numbers of abstracts in the major disease categories. It should be noted, however, that cause of death statistics are misleading as to the prevalence and prognosis in many diseases. A few valuable sources of mortality data have been deliberately bypassed because of their current availability.[1,2] These are, of course, cited at appropriate points in this volume as an aid for further reference by the interested reader.

At the outset, files of committee members contained articles which readily demonstrated the availability of useful follow-up studies in the medical literature.[3] Four different search procedures were employed in locating additional articles containing valuable mortality and survival data:

(1) Regular scanning of approximately 100 medical and a few professional insurance journals by Committee members and others trained to do this searching;
(2) Investigation of the discussion and bibliography of each article for further articles that might be of value;
(3) A search of the Index Medicus and Current Bibliography of Epidemiology (CUBE), when the latter became available;
(4) Listings made available through the National Library of Medicine as the result of computerized search processes (MEDLARS and MEDLINE).

Experience showed that the first two methods of searching listed above were the most effective and productive. Systematic scanning of the journals that were considered the most likely to contain articles with mortality and survival data did yield a significant number of articles each year. Almost all of the journals were published in the United States, Great Britain, Canada, with a few from Australia, New Zealand, South Africa, and the Scandinavian countries. The levels of mortality in relation to age and sex tend to be similar in the white population of all of these countries and in Western Europe, and follow-up studies would therefore tend to be more comparable, one with another, than would follow-up studies made in most other countries. Our systematic searching procedures were therefore confined to the most productive English language journals. When an article containing valuable data was found, it frequently happened that the authors had made a review of the recent literature on the condition reported, and a bibliography of these articles was therefore a productive source of additional articles.

A major difficulty was encountered in the attempt to utilize customary methods of bibliographic searching of the medical literature. Subject classifications in the printed indices of medical literature, and key words used in the computer indexing turned out to be relatively nonspecific for the subject matter desired for this volume. Representatives of the Committee met with officials of the National Library of Medicine in a number of conferences designed to produce the best possible set of instructions for this search program, but a satisfactory solution could not be found. For example, many articles coded for "follow-up" as a subheading or key word do not contain mortality or survival data. Most articles coded under "mortality" deal with mortality by cause in the general population and have nothing to do with follow-up studies or survival curves for a group defined by a common medical risk at time of diagnosis. Many articles that do present mortality follow-up present such limited data in numbers of cases and deaths that they could not be utilized. Nevertheless, searching of this type was carried out in those categories of disease where relatively few articles had been located by other means, and sometimes an additional article or two was located. Occasionally an article "popped up" in the listing which really did not belong in the category of diseases being searched. This was an unexpected bonus.

Yet another method was employed in the search for well-executed mortality studies. There were several agencies or institutions discovered which are heavily involved in follow-up studies on a continuous or intermittent basis. The Mayo Clinic has had an extraordinarily complete set of medical records from the beginning of its operation. A separate department of vital statistics has aided members of the Clinic staff in the preparation of many valuable reports of follow-up studies based on Clinic records. Registries are maintained by health or professional organizations on a number of special diseases, such as chronic renal failure (Renal Transplant and Hemodialysis Registries), cystic fibrosis, etc. Published reports and additional data from these registries have provided source material for several tables.

The Follow-up Agency is a branch of the Federal government affiliated with the National Research Council and National Academy of Sciences. This agency conducts follow-up studies based on medical records of the Veterans Administration and medical records of the Army, Navy, or Air Force. The End Results Section of the National Cancer Institute is engaged in a continuous process of receiving, compiling, and analyzing mortality statistics received from nine cancer registries located at different points in the United States. Four major reports have been published to date on the survival data.

The Committee approached all of these agencies or registries for bibliographic lists and sometimes additional data, and officials were invariably most cooperative in their response. The very extensive cancer tables in this volume are based on detailed data made available by Dr. Myers, Head, End Results Section, National Cancer Institute, in a form that was much more useful to the Committee than the survival results as published in the various reports of the End Results Group.

Despite the best efforts of the Committee to make coverage of the literature as complete as possible, undoubtedly some articles containing valuable data were not detected and therefore not included among the published abstracts.

Evaluation of Articles

It was an easy task to reject articles as unsuitable because they did not contain follow-up data of the type desired. Many of these were articles in which the title or key words reproduced in the search listing appeared potentially hopeful, but a quick review of the article revealed otherwise. Some of the acceptable articles were also readily identified because they contained a sufficient volume of data presented in the form of Life Tables or graphs of survival curves. However, another group of articles required very careful study and sometimes experimentation before a decision could be made. These articles contained data presented in a great variety of forms. One reviewer might think that the article was unsuitable, but another some times was able to discover a method of processing the data to yield comparative mortality and survival results suitable for this monograph. Guidelines for clear-cut acceptance or rejection of articles in this category were extremely difficult to develop.

In quite a few instances articles were considered to be provisionally acceptable, provided that additional data could be obtained from the authors. If tabular data were at a minimum in the article and the principal results were in terms of survival curves, it was found that the figures taken off the graphs for survival rates at accepted intervals were not very accurate. In such cases the actual survival rates were requested. In other cases, it was necessary to have data regarding the age distribution, or age and sex distribution, in order to make calculations of the expected mortality and survival, as a base line against which to compare the observed mortality and survival. This concept of comparative mortality and survival has been basic to the entire process of table preparation. In many cases the Committee received prompt cooperation from the authors. Unfortunately, in other cases files were no longer available or no reply was received. In the latter event if the requested data were essential to the calculation of expected rates, it was necessary to abandon the article.

Table Construction

Conventional methodology of Life Table construction was, of course, well known to members of the Committee as a model for construction of tables for this monograph. This methodology is described in Chapter 2. However, as more articles were reviewed and efforts were made to construct tables from a great variety of presentations of data, a number of questions arose and had to be answered by a lengthy process of experimentation. A system of notation for the mathematical symbols had to be developed that would be easily learned and followed by the nonmathematical reader. The same was true for the general design of the tables. Many different designs had to be developed to accommodate the various ways in which data were presented in the articles. For some articles or reports, particularly the cancer data, the life table data were so voluminous that excessive number and size of the tables became a consideration. In order to condense life table data from an annual basis to intervals of two or five or ten years, it was necessary to choose among possible alternative methods of calculation. These alternatives and the manner in which they affect the mortality and survival ratios are set forth in the next two chapters. The tables themselves make clear which type of calculation has been used through appropriate use of the mathematical symbols.

After the methodological problems were resolved a procedure was set up for table construction in which the Project Director assigned recommended articles to one of the Committee Members, or to one of a group of retired actuaries who had volunteered to aid the project, or made the initial draft himself. Several individuals were involved in the construction of most of the tables as they were sent from one to another for review and revision. In addition, a descriptive text had to be prepared to accompany the tables. These descriptions also went through several revisions. When a satisfactory draft had finally been produced, it was circulated to all members of the Committee. Such review ordinarily elicited useful comments and corrections which were incorporated into the final, approved set of tables. Table copy, ready for the printers, was also prepared under the direct supervision of the Committee.

Table Arrangement

Each unit or abstract of the Mortality and Survival data consists of one or more tables, together with the citation for the article or articles abstracted and an accompanying descriptive text. The arrangement of the tables and text follows a format that is as standardized as possible, but considerable variation has been imposed by the nature of the presentations in the original articles. Whenever the original data have been sufficiently complete, a Life Table methodology has been used, with the data divided into two related tables. The first table, entitled "Observed Data and Comparative Experience in. . .," contains observed data from the source article, including number of entrants, number exposed to risk, sometimes number withdrawn or lost, number of observed deaths, and number of "expected deaths," a derived rather than an observed quantity. The right-hand part of the table contains the indices of comparative mortality and survival: the mortality ratio, the survival ratio, and the excess death rate. All of these quantities are defined and explained in Chapter 2.

The second member of the pair of Life Tables is entitled "Derived Mortality and Survival Data." The columns on the left-hand side of this table contain the mortality rates and survival rates calculated from the data given for each interval of time of the follow-up study. Corresponding "expected" mortality and survival rates are given in the right-hand part of this table, based on population or other appropriate standard mortality tables, with rates dependent on the age and sex distribution of the group under study. Such standard or expected rates are necessary for the calculation of expected deaths and the indices of comparative mortality and survival. When data are not available for various intervals within the follow-up period of study, other tabular formats have been utilized. Sometimes results have been presented in articles in terms of graphs of survival curves; these, too, have been converted to tabular data. Other tables have been developed to give mortality by cause of death, incidence and prevalence data, distribution of entrants by age and sex, and other results. Each abstract bears an appropriate section number and title.

A uniform order has been followed for the text: *Reference, Subjects Studied, Follow-up, Results,* and sometimes *Comments*. When additional data have been supplied by the authors, this fact is indicated under the *Reference*. Important descriptive characteristics for the group under study are given in the first section of the text. The information includes such factors as the location and period of time for the study, the criteria used for selection of the group and for exclusion of certain cases, the age and sex distribution, and related matters. The methods employed in follow-up, the completeness of follow-up, and the terminal date are given in the *Follow-up* part of the text. The *Results* part of the text is generally the longest part. It contains a narrative description of the important mortality and survival results as contained in the tables. Although terms like "heavy mortality" and "severe excess mortality" are used, this is basically a factual description of the data. Any extended interpretation of the tabular results is generally reserved for the chapter material, or occasionally for the *Comments* portion of the text. This last portion may also contain a brief description of other results reported in the article which were not used to develop tables for the abstract.

The tabular abstracts are arranged in nine major categories of disease or other risk factors, with each major category subdivided into a number of subcategories. A very simplified and pragmatic classification has been adopted, which takes into account the nature of the available material, rather than existing systems of disease classification, which tend to be complex and very detailed. Abstracts have been given consecutive section numbers within each subcategory. One hundred numbers are available for each of eight major categories and 200 for the Systemic Disorders. Smaller numbers are thus reserved for each subcategory, according to the availability of actual or potential abstracts for the subcategory. The major categories are as follows:

1-99	Physical, Toxic, and Other Risk Factors
100-199	Cancer
200-299	Neuropsychiatric Disorders
300-399	Cardiovascular Diseases
400-499	Respiratory Diseases
500-599	Digestive System Diseases
600-699	Genitourinary Diseases
700-899	Systemic Disorders
900-999	Endocrine and Metabolic Diseases

There are some data available on various diseases which are limited in nature, usually permitting no more than one or two lines of data and therefore hardly justifying a separate abstract. Such data have been collected from various sources and placed in an appropriate table under each major disease category, generally the last abstract in the category. These combination tables should therefore be consulted for possible data, in addition to the appropriate subcategory where individual abstracts are located.

Interpretation

There is one chapter of interpretive text for each of the major categories except the cardiovascular diseases, with a chapter for each of its five subcategories. As a result there are 14 chapters of text of this type. In these chapters an attempt is made to review the mortality and survival data of the available abstracts in perspective, and to relate the various diseases one to another and to cause of death statistics. Attention may be called to major diseases for which no follow-up studies could be located in the medical literature. Trends in mortality and the potential effects of new treatment methods are sometimes commented on where appropriate material is available. References are also given to recent articles and other sources which can provide the reader with further information on diseases in which he has a particular interest. However, limitations of space permit only the briefest review of the entire disease category, with a great many diseases not covered at all. The major focus in each of these chapters is naturally on the data contained in the tables.

This initial chapter on the "Plan and Scope of the Study" is followed by a chapter on "Methodology" and another on "Interpretation of Comparative Mortality and Survival Data." The chapter on Methodology is designed for the reader who wishes a detailed explanation of the methods used in constructing the tables. Definitions are given for all of the life table symbols used. These are usually consistent with general actuarial practice, but an effort has been made to simplify them as much as possible. An explanation of the mathematical formulas and symbols used in the volume is given in Chapter 2. The reader will also find an important reference table in Chapter 3 giving statistical confidence limits (levels of probable random variability) by number of deaths observed or expected. In order to conserve space no confidence limits have been included with the tabular data. However, with the number of deaths given it is not difficult for the user of this volume to extract from Chapter 3 the confidence limits to assess the statistical significance of any increased mortality ratio or excess death rate.

Chapter 3 contains a review of the purpose, design, execution, and reporting of follow-up studies, with some examples. Various types of standard mortality tables are described. Choosing the most appropriate standard mortality and survival rates is a necessary part of the interpretation of the significance of indices of comparative mortality and survival. Other topics considered include examples of reporting follow-up data and limitations inherent in the interpretation of such studies. It is recommended that each user of the tables as a reference source should read the contents of Chapter 3 with care before attempting to interpret the tabular data.

Applications of comparative mortality and survival data are probably familiar to potential users of this volume. In clinical medicine any physician might desire information on prognosis more detailed than that found in a textbook of medicine in order to counsel a patient with a chronic disease, and comparative survival rates would be an appropriate way[4] in which to couch such advice. Mortality and survival statistics are used in other applications in medicine: in the planning of clinical trials in order to obtain conclusive results;[5] in any study of the natural history of disease or of the results of a particular form of treatment; in "health hazard appraisal" for individual preventive medical care;[6] and in the management and care of the individual patient.[7] In Public Health there are obvious applications concerned with epidemiology and vital statistics; of growing importance is the use of mortality data in a variety of ways in connection with the analysis of health practices and health resource planning.[8,9] Mortality data are also an indispensable tool in the development of risk selection procedures to be used in life underwriting and life insurance medicine.[10,11,12,13] Any extensive discussion of these applications is beyond the scope of this volume.

References

1. *1951 Impairment Study*. Chicago: Society of Actuaries (1954).

2. *Build and Blood Pressure Study 1959*, Volumes I and II. Chicago: Society of Actuaries (1960).

3. R.B. Singer, "The Usefulness of Mortality and Survival Data in Existing Medical Literature." *Trans. Stud. Coll. Physicians Phila.*, 36:147-157 (1969).

4. M.C. Sheps, "Shall We Count The Living or the Dead?" *New Eng. J. Med.*, 259:1210-1214 (1958).

5. Coronary Drug Project Research Group, "Clofibrate and Niacin in Coronary Heart Disease." *J. Am. Med. Assoc.*, 231:360-381 (1975).

6. L.C. Robbins and J.H. Hall, *How to Practice Prospective Medicine*. Indianapolis, Ind.: Methodist Hospital (1970).

7. R.A. Rosati et al., "A New Information System for Medical Practice." *Arch. Int. Med.*, 135:1017-1024 (1975).

8. P. Braun, "The Center for The Evaluation of Clinical Procedures." *Proc., Medical Section, Am. Life Ins. Assoc.*, 2:11-27 (1974).

9. J.P. Bunker, F. Mosteller and B. Barnes, eds., *Costs, Risks and Benefits of Surgery*. New York, Oxford University Press (in press 1976).

10. E.V. Higgins, "Cancer—The Challenger." *Ann. Life Ins. Med.*, 1:145-171 (1962).

11. H. Blackburn and R.W. Parlin, "Antecedents of Disease, Insurance Mortality Experience." *Ann. N.Y. Acad. Sci.*, 134:965-1017 (1966).

12. R.B. Singer, "Comparative Mortality—Keystone of Medical Selection." Presented at Life Insurance Medicine Seminar, January 15-19, 1973, sponsored by the Board of Life Insurance Medicine.

13. R.D.C. Brackenridge, *Medical Selection of Life Risks*. London, England: The Undershaft Press (in press 1976).

2

Methodology
Louis Levinson, F.S.A., and Richard B. Singer, M.D.

The material contained in this monograph has been compiled chiefly from papers published in medical journals reporting experience with respect to mortality and survival observed in a variety of impairments. Data from other sources, such as studies of life insurance experience and publications by agencies of the federal government, have also been employed.

A variety of methods is utilized by the authors of such source articles in presenting data; to achieve some uniformity in the abstracts it has been necessary in many cases to derive rates and ratios indirectly from the results reported. Methods used in such cases are described later in this chapter; at this point it should be noted that regular principles of life table construction and of comparative mortality have been employed in these translations[1,2,3,4] and, accordingly, the essential character of the data reported on has been preserved.

For readers not familiar with the methods commonly used in the life table and in mortality studies, a brief résumé of the life table and of the principal functions appearing in the monograph may be helpful. Fuller expositions on this subject may be found in various references[4,5,6,7,8,9,10] and in the monographs by Gershenson,[11] Spiegelman,[12] Chiang,[13] and Benjamin and Haycocks.[14]

The Life Table

Life tables (called also "tables of mortality" or "mortality tables" and sometimes "survival tables"), customarily arranged according to age, are compact models of mortality and survival experience describing rates of death and survival among a given collection of persons in a specific period of time. The basic feature of a life table is the *annual rate of mortality*—the proportion of deaths which occur in a year among a collection of lives exposed to the risk of death. This rate is identified by the symbol q, with the age to which it applies indicated in a subscript. Thus, q_x or q_{40} represents the proportion of lives aged x or 40 years who die within one year. The persons in the collection who do not die are survivors and their *annual rate of survival*, designated p, is complementary to q, that is, $p + q = 1$, since the annual rate of mortality plus the annual rate of survival represents the totality of the life contingencies of the year. Subscripts corresponding to those modifying q indicate the age over which survival obtains—p_x or p_{40}, which represent annual rates of survival applicable to lives x or 40 years of age.

The lives whose experience is presented in a life table possess some degree of homogeneity. Almost all life tables, therefore, have some common feature (supplemental to age) which distinguishes the experience of the lives investigated from that of other collections of lives. The abstracts contained in this volume, for the most part, comprise a catalogue of life tables reflecting experience of groups of individuals with some physical or mental disorder, a history of such disorder, or a medical impairment or untoward condition indicative of a higher than average rate of mortality. The period over which the studies generating the basic rates took place is usually one in which no extraordinary change in treatment occurred which might bias the rates produced (where such situations arose, any unusual results consequent thereon are pointed out).

Many of the tables in the monograph indicate also (in addition to age, or more frequently, age groups) experience by duration from some initial point such as the attainment of a given age, the onset of some malady, a date of diagnosis of some disorder, a date marking the commencement of treatment, etc.

In investigations designed to develop a complete life table with respect to the experience at some age, enumeration of the lives subject to the risk of death and of the deaths occurring within a year among the lives counted at that age yield the *annual rate of mortality*—the proportion of the persons at the age under consideration living at the beginning of the year who die during the year. This procedure repeated for each age within the range of ages subject to study produces a series of rates of mortality and of survival.

Once the rates of mortality for the successive ages within the age range under study have been determined, other features of the life table can be developed. These secondary features are represented by rates (principally cumulative mortality, cumulative survival, excess deaths per 1000) expressed per unit or per 100 or 1000 and by quantities associated with the numbers living and dying and their interrelationships. The introduction of the number living at a given initial point enables us to evaluate these secondary functions and to lay the basis for the construction of complete life tables.

The number of persons living at a common starting point, followed with respect to survival and mortality in successive years of observation, is termed a "cohort." Assume that the members of the cohort are of the same age. Let the number of such lives at the initial point be designated ℓ_x where the subscript identifies the common age of the members of the cohort. Survivors at subsequent annual intervals will be symbolized ℓ_{x+1}, etc.

If there are no losses to observation in a cohort otherwise than by death, decreases in the numbers living on successive anniversaries represent decrements by death. The symbol d stands for the number of deaths during the year. If the age of persons dying within a given year commencing t years after the initial starting point was x + t, the number of such deaths is represented by d_{x+t}. Hence $\ell_x - d_x = \ell_{x+1}$, $\ell_{x+1} - d_{x+1} = \ell_{x+2}$, etc. Survivors at the end of a given interval represent the number living at the beginning of the interval diminished by the number dying within the interval. It should be noted that the count of the number living is taken as of the beginning of a year—of the number dying, within the year. The number surviving at the end of a year is the same as the number living at the beginning of the following year.

Table 2-1 is a five-year segment of an illustrative life table arising from a cohort of 7,294 lives all x years of age. The annual rates of mortality and survival represent the results of a study of these contingencies in the cohort. The size of the cohort, 7,294, may be equal to the number of persons who were the subject of the actual study and hence the source of the mortality and survival rates, but if a larger or smaller number of lives were taken as the size of the cohort, relations of the several functions of the life table would be unchanged if the rates of survival and mortality remained the same.

Cumulative Survival Rate—First ("Direct") Method

The quotient ℓ_{x+t}/ℓ_x (where ℓ_x represents the number of persons in a cohort and ℓ_{x+t} their survivors t years later) represents the t-years *cumulative survival rate* P_t (age x being understood from the context). This function indicates the proportion of the original number who continue alive t years after the initial point, and the method has been described as the "direct method."[2] The difference between the initial number of lives, ℓ_x, and the ℓ_{x+t} t-year survivors denotes losses by death (this exposition thus far is limited to death as the only decrement). Accordingly, $\ell_x - \ell_{x+t} = d_x + d_{x+1} \cdots + d_{x+t-1}$ from which $\ell_x - (d_x + d_{x+1} + d_{x+2} \cdots + d_{x+t-1})$ is equal to 1_{x+t}, yielding, in turn, the equation

$$\ell_{x+t}/\ell_x = P_t = 1 - \sum_0^{t-1} d_{x+t}\Big/\ell_x,$$

when both sides are divided by ℓ_x.

Cumulative Survival Rate—Second ("Life Table") Method

The symbols ℓ_x and ℓ_{x+t} designate the numbers of persons living at the limiting ages of the span of ages x to x+t. Since ℓ_{x+1}/ℓ_{x+1}, ℓ_{x+2}/ℓ_{x+2}, ... $\ell_{x+t-1}/\ell_{x+t-1}$ are each equal to 1, the value of ℓ_{x+t}/ℓ_x is not changed if it is considered to be a product expressible as $(1/\ell_x)(\ell_{x+1}/\ell_{x+1})(\ell_{x+2}/\ell_{x+2}) \cdots (\ell_{x+t-1}/\ell_{x+t-1})(\ell_{x+t})$. This latter expression, in turn, may be rearranged to $(\ell_{x+1}/\ell_x)(\ell_{x+2}/\ell_{x+1})(\ell_{x+3}/\ell_{x+2}) \cdots (\ell_{x+t}/\ell_{x+t-1})$ which is equal to ℓ_{x+t}/ℓ_x after cancelling out the numerator of each term and the equal denominator of the succeeding term. The foregoing compound product may be written as $(p_x)(p_{x+1})(p_{x+2}) \cdots (p_{x+t-1})$ which is equal to $\ell_{x+t}/\ell_x = P_t$. This may be called the "life table method" of calculating cumulative survival rates.

TABLE 2-1
Life Table Annual Rates—Illustrative Cohort

	Interval	Age at	Annual Rate		No. Alive	No. Deaths
No.	Start-End	Start Year	Mortality	Survival	Start Year	During Year
i	t to t + Δ t	x+t	q_{x+t}	p_{x+t}	ℓ_{x+t}	d_{x+t}
1	0-1 yrs	x	.0894	.9106	7294	652
2	1-2	x+1	.0730	.9270	6642	485
3	2-3	x+2	.0594	.9406	6157	366
4	3-4	x+3	.0485	.9515	5791	281
5	4-5	x+4	.0416	.9584	5510	229

Table 2-2 displays cumulative survival rates by the direct and life table methods developing from the cohort of 7,294 lives and the annual mortality and survival rates presented in Table 2-1.

Cumulative survival rates shown in Table 2-2 are the same under the first and second methods. This identity holds because death is the only decrement in Table 2-2. In groups of lives in which losses to observation otherwise than by death occur, values of cumulative survival rates may not be calculated by the first method.

Withdrawals

Besides the single decrement assumption employed so far, it has also been assumed that intervals are one year in duration, that experience by individual year of age is given, and that year-by-year data are available. Actually few reports yield explicit information in these respects and, for present purposes, we shall first introduce the effect of losses to observation on the functions already referred to.

In most experience studies the members of a given original group do not all remain under observation for the entire period of study, and the totality of survivors is generally unknown. What prevents completeness of such information is the fact that some lives become lost to observation by failure to maintain contact for any one of a variety of reasons, such as change of residence. A loss to observation also occurs by reason of termination of follow-up for a given entrant. Thus an individual coming under observation as the result of the onset of an impairment within a year preceding the end of the period of study would not be includible in any mortality consequences pertaining to the second or subsequent years of observation. Such an individual comes to the termination of follow-up in the course of the first year. To all such losses the term "withdrawal" is applied and the letter w is used to designate these decrements (for a given group of lives, w_i represents subjects withdrawing in interval i). The letter u may be used on occasion to designate those who are lost track of (untraced) during an interval, if they are reported separately from the other withdrawals. Under special circumstances cases may be withdrawn from the group by reason of some other contingent event, such as recurrence of an original condition, evidence of full recovery, etc. In the customary type of life table study the two important decrements are those due to death and those due to withdrawal—either from loss to follow-up or termination of the follow-up process during the period of observation.

If withdrawals occur in the course of one year among ℓ_x persons living at the beginning of the year, the number of deaths to be observed during the year among the ℓ_x is likely to be smaller than it would have been if the withdrawals had not taken place. A rate of mortality represented by d_x/ℓ_x (where d_x denotes the *observed* number of deaths during the year) then would understate the actual experience. To correct such understatement the number subject to the risk of death during the year is commonly estimated to be the number living at the start of the year reduced by one-half the number of withdrawals taking place during the year. Symbolically, the *number exposed to the risk of death*, designated E_x, is set equal to $\ell_x - \frac{1}{2} w_x$. Other more theoretically precise methods of estimating the number exposed to risk have been considered for use,[7,13,14] but the simpler expression $(\ell_x - \frac{1}{2} w_x)$ was thought most suitable for the so-called double decrement tables in this monograph. In a few instances other methods utilized in the original articles have been retained in the calculation of rates and ratios for the tables in the abstracts.

TABLE 2-2
Illustrative Life Table—Cumulative Survival Rates

	Interval				Direct Method			Life Table Method	
		Age at	No. Alive	Cum. Deaths	Survivors	Cumulative		Annual	Cumulative
No.	Start-End	Start Year	Start Year	End Year	End Year	Surv. Rate		Surv. Rate	Surv. Rate
i	t to $t + \Delta t$	$x+t$	ℓ_{x+t}	$\sum_0^{t-1} d_{x+t}$	ℓ_{x+t+1}	$P_{t+1} = \dfrac{\ell_{x+t+1}}{\ell_x}$*		p_{x+t}	$P_{t+1} = \prod_0^t p_{x+t}$
1	0-1 yrs	x	7294	652	6642	.9106		.9106	.9106
2	1-2	x+1	6642	1137	6157	.8441		.9270	.8441
3	2-3	x+2	6157	1503	5791	.7939		.9406	.7939
4	3-4	x+3	5791	1784	5510	.7554		.9515	.7554
5	4-5	x+4	5510	2013	5281	.7240		.9584	.7240

* $\ell_{x+t+1} = \ell_x - \sum_0^{t-1} d_{x+t}$

12

When withdrawals are taken into account, annual rates of mortality and survival are computed analogously to the methods used where death is the only decrement. The proportions dying and surviving are calculated with reference to the exposed to risk as described above rather than to the number living at the beginning of the year. In such cases $q_x = d_x/(\ell_x - \frac{1}{2} w_x)$, that is, $q_x = d_x/E_x$ and $p_x = 1 - [d_x/(\ell_x - \frac{1}{2} w_x)] = 1 - d_x/E_x$. The number living at the end of the year commencing at age x years, viz. ℓ_{x+1} may be written $\ell_x - w_x - d_x$, where the last term, d_x, does not include any deaths occurring among the lives lost to observation.

Table 2-3 illustrates the functions of a double decrement table corresponding with those in the single decrement table shown in Table 2-1. The rates of mortality are those employed in the single decrement table, as a result of which it may be noted that the numbers of deaths are smaller than those in the corresponding intervals in Table 2-1.

Arrangement of the columns in Table 2-3 is somewhat unconventional in that in the actual construction of a life table, rates of mortality and withdrawal are secondary, derived from the basic elements of the experience which precede their computation, namely, the numbers of deaths, withdrawals, and persons alive and exposed to the contingencies of death or other loss to observation. The order in the table is designed to demonstrate that the rates of mortality are those exhibited in Table 2-1. Columns of the tables in the monograph are generally arranged in the order in which data are developed.

If one attempts to apply the direct method of computing a cumulative survival rate for a group of lives among whom withdrawals occur, employing the numbers exposed to risk E_{x+t}/E_x as a parallel to ℓ_{x+t}/ℓ_x, the result is not a rate of survival but a rate of continuing alive and of remaining under observation. Such a rate would be influenced by the magnitude and incidence of the withdrawals during the period of observation. The direct method, therefore, does not produce a valid cumulative survival rate in a double decrement table. Contrariwise, the life table method applied to such a table would develop a valid cumulative survival rate which is independent of any withdrawals taking place. As pointed out by Cutler and Ederer, "maximum utilization" of survival data is accomplished through use of the life table methods.[4]

Cumulative Mortality Rate

Cumulative mortality rates are complements of cumulative survival rates (i.e., $Q_i = 1 - P_i$) and have counterparts to the first and second methods of calculating the latter. Thus, if the only decrement is death in a cohort the cumulative mortality rate under the first method is

$$\sum_0^{t-1} d_{x+t}$$

and under the second, $1 - [(p_x)(p_{x+1}) \cdots (p_{x+t-1})]$.

However, under a double decrement table, where withdrawal constitutes a second decrement to death, the direct method is not an admissible process for developing this function for a reason reflecting that cited in connection with the cumulative survival rate. The cumulative mortality rate by the second method, as is the case with the cumulative survival rate, is the same as it is under a single decrement table, namely, $1 - [(p_x)(p_{x+1}) \cdots (p_{x+t-1})]$, since the complementary survival function is $[(p_x)(p_{x+1}) \cdots (p_{x+t-1})]$.

TABLE 2-3

Exposed to Risk—Illustrative Observed Cohort (Double Decrement Table)

Interval		Age at Start Year	Annual Rates		No. Alive Start Year	No. Deaths During Year	No. Withdr. During Year	Exposed to Risk
No.	Start-End		Mortality	Withdrawal				
i	t to $t + \Delta t$	$x+t$	q_{x+t}	*	ℓ_{x+t}	d_{x+t}	w_{x+t}	$E_{x+t}=\ell_{x+t}-\frac{1}{2}w_{x+t}$
1	0-1 yr	x	.0894	.0500	7294	636	356	7116.0
2	1-2	x+1	.0730	.0449	6302	450	277	6163.5
3	2-3	x+2	.0594	.0366	5575	325	200	5475.0
4	3-4	x+3	.0485	.0184	5050	243	92	5004.0
5	4-5	x+4	.0416	.0107	4715	195	50	4690.0

*Withdrawal rate = w_{x+t}/ℓ_{x+t}

Expected Experience—The Standard Life Table

The significance of the rates of mortality and survival obtained in an investigation of the experience of a class of observed lives may be gauged by comparing them with a standard of reference. Such a standard should be based on lives correspondent with those being investigated, except for the characteristic being studied and should be reasonably related to the period of study, the environments (geographical, social, etc.) surrounding the subjects and other salient features of the group under observation such as its age-sex-race composition. "Expected" results are intended to represent the mortality and survival which it is anticipated would be experienced among lives of the same age, sex, race, etc. as those under investigation but not known to be subject to the particular hazard under study nor to other special risks. General population tables constructed from vital statistics and census reports and tables based on insurance experience are commonly used as standards. Functions from a standard table are distinguished in this monograph by a prime (')—the expected rate of mortality on the standard table, for instance, is designated q', the cumulative survival rate, P', etc. Representative mortality rates from population life tables and insurance standard select tables are given in Table 3-1, Chapter 3.

In lieu of employing a standard mortality table for evaluating comparative experience a few studies reported in this volume were conducted by the process of "matched pairs." Under this method each member of a group with some characteristic being investigated (e.g., a disease) is "matched" with a person of the same age, sex, race, geographical location, occupation, marital status, medical history, etc., but free of the particular characteristic. A comparison of the mortality and survival results in the two groups provides a means of measuring the effect of the unmatched feature. To locate the individuals in the control group, the availability of voluminous data on a large population is obviously called for; this method is most successful under extensive investigations such as the American Cancer Society study of smoking (§40) and the Follow-up Agency's investigation of psychoneurosis among veterans of military service (§285).

Comparative Mortality—Cohort and Annual Exposure Methods

If we are given a life table representative of the experience in a body of lives and we wish to gain a perspective of that experience, the usual method is to seek an answer to the question, "How many persons actually died in the observed group as compared with the number who would have died if the members of the group had been subject to standard rates of mortality?" One way to answer this question is to trace the experience of the observed group, noting the number of deaths, and compare the number of deaths with those experienced among a group subject to standard rates of mortality. Two such groups followed from a common point of time and composed initially of the same number of lives represent two cohorts. A comparison of the respective numbers of deaths in the two cohorts may be made with respect to duration elapsed from the starting point. Table 2-4 displays, for a cohort of 7,294 lives, standard rates of mortality and survival, year by year survivors, and expected annual and cumulative deaths for five annual intervals commencing at a given initial point. These functions may be compared with the analogous functions in Table 2-1 and Table 2-2 for the corresponding observed cohort of 7,294 lives. Unless due adjustment is made therefor, over any interval commencing subsequently to the initial one, the numbers of the lives in the two cohorts would not be equal at the beginning of the interval so that there would be no common base of reference. In the absence of a common number exposed to risk it

TABLE 2-4
Expected Deaths — Cohort Method
(Single Decrement in Standard Cohort)

No.	Interval Start-End	Standard Rate Mortality	Standard Rate Survival	No. Alive Start of Yr.	No. Expected Deaths Annual	No. Expected Deaths Cumulative
i	t to t+Δt	q'_{x+t}	p'_{x+t}	ℓ'_{x+t}	d'_{x+t}	$\Sigma d'_{x+t}$
1	0-1 yr	.0064	.9936	7294	46.7	46.7
2	1-2	.0070	.9930	7247.3	50.7	97.4
3	2-3	.0077	.9923	7196.6	55.4	152.8
4	3-4	.0085	.9915	7141.2	60.7	213.5
5	4-5	.0093	.9907	7080.5	65.8	279.3

would be difficult to make a meaningful comparison of the deaths in the two cohorts (observed and standard) during intervals subsequent to the first. Furthermore, standard tables of mortality take account of deaths as the only decrement, while most special investigations of experience incorporate the effects of other withdrawals from observation by loss to follow-up. While this method—*the cohort comparison approach*—has some valid applications, it has the shortcomings described above when attention is focused on the annual experience either by individual years or an aggregate basis.

Ordinarily the answer to the question is obtained by what we will call the *annual exposure method*. Under this method of comparing observed with expected experience the number of deaths observed and the number which would occur if standard rates of mortality applied is determined year by year *with reference to the number of lives exposed to risk*. Thus, the number of deaths at age x+t in the observed table, d_{x+t}, is given by $(\ell_{x+t})(q_{x+t})$ or $(E_{x+t})(q_{x+t})$; if, on the other hand, those exposed to the risk of death were subject to an annual rate of mortality equal to q'_{x+t}, the expected number of deaths, d'_{x+t}, would have been $(\ell_{x+t})(q'_{x+t})$ or $(E_{x+t})(q'_{x+t})$. At age x+t+1, the observed deaths, d_{x+t+1}, would number $(\ell_{x+t+1})(q_{x+t+1})$ or $(E_{x+t+1})(q_{x+t+1})$, and the expected, $(\ell_{x+t+1})(q'_{x+t+1})$ or $(E_{x+t+1})(q'_{x+t+1})$. It should be noted that the numbers at risk are consistently those appearing in the observed table, and a different number of deaths at a particular age resulting from the application of the standard rates does not affect the number of survivors actually subject to risk at the next age.

Expected annual and cumulative deaths developed on the basis of 7,294 individuals living at a given initial point, subject only to a single decrement by death, are shown in Tables 2-4 and 2-5. As previously explained, the deaths enumerated in Table 2-4 represent those occurring in accordance with the cohort method: the deaths in each year represent the application of standard (expected) rates of mortality to the number of survivors remaining at the beginning of the year after the expected deaths of the previous year have been subtracted from the number living at the start of that year. The deaths indicated in Table 2-5, on the other hand, are developed by the annual exposure method: the numbers against which the standard rates of mortality are applied represent observed survivors—the residue after *observed* deaths have been deducted from the previous year's survivors. The numbers exposed to risk are those of a cohort of 7,294 lives subject to the single decrement of deaths each year in accordance with the observed mortality rates shown in Table 2-1.

When the observed cohort is subject to the double decrement of both deaths and withdrawals, as shown in Table 2-3, another illustration of annual and cumulative expected deaths must be provided. Table 2-6 indicates the expected deaths developing when standard rates of mortality are applied to the observed exposures shown in Table 2-3.

Indices of Comparative Mortality and Survival

In what degree the mortality and survival experience of a particular observed group differs from a standard may be judged by comparing salient features of the observed experience with those expected under the standard. The features employed in such comparisons are the annual and cumulative rates of mortality and survival, the annual and cumulative numbers of deaths, the excess rate of death and the survival index.

The *annual mortality ratio* (MR), expressed as a percentage, is one of the most important comparative mortality functions. This ratio compares the annual observed rate of mortality with that expected, i.e., MR = $100\, q_i/q'_i$ or it compares the equivalent fraction represented by the relation of the observed number of deaths to the number expected among the subjects actually exposed to the risk of death—in symbols, MR = $100\, d_i/d'_i$. The MR is frequently based on average annual rates of mortality (such average rates are described later in this chapter). The identical annual mortality ratios from d/d' and q/q' are shown in Table 2-7, utilizing observed data from Table 2-3 and expected data from Table 2-6.

TABLE 2-5
Expected Deaths — Annual Exposure Method
(Single Decrement in Observed Cohort)

Interval		Standard Rate		No. Alive	No. Expected Deaths	
No.	Start-End	Mortality	Survival	Start of Yr.	Annual	Cumulative
i	t to t + Δt	q'_{x+t}	p'_{x+t}	ℓ_{x+t}	d'_{x+t}	$\Sigma d'_{x+t}$
1	0-1 yr	.0064	.9936	7294	46.68	46.68
2	1-2	.0070	.9930	6642	46.49	93.17
3	2-3	.0077	.9923	6157	47.41	140.58
4	3-4	.0085	.9915	5791	49.22	189.80
5	4-5	.0093	.9907	5510	51.24	241.04

TABLE 2-6

Expected Deaths — Annual Exposure Method
(Double Decrement in Observed Cohort)

	Interval	Standard Rate		No. Exposed	No. Expected Deaths	
No.	Start-End	Mortality	Survival	to Risk	Annual	Cumulative
i	t to $t+\Delta t$	q'_{x+t}	p'_{x+t}	E_{x+t}	d'_{x+t}	$\Sigma d'_{x+t}$
1	0-1 yr	.0064	.9936	7116.0	45.54	45.54
2	1-2	.0070	.9930	6163.5	43.14	88.68
3	2-3	.0077	.9923	5475.0	42.16	130.84
4	3-4	.0085	.9915	5004.0	42.53	173.37
5	4-5	.0093	.9907	4690.0	43.62	216.99

TABLE 2-7
Comparative Mortality — Annual Mortality Ratios

	Interval	No. Exposed	Annual No. of Deaths		Mortality	Annual Mortality Rate		Mortality
No.	Start-End	to Risk	Observed	Expected	Ratio*	Observed	Expected	Ratio*
i	t to $t+\Delta t$	E_{x+t}	d_{x+t}	d'_{x+t}	100 d/d'	q_{x+t}	q'_{x+t}	100 q/q'
1	0-1 yr	7116.0	636	45.54	1400%	.0894	.0064	1400%
2	1-2	6163.5	450	43.14	1040	.0730	.0070	1040
3	2-3	5475.0	325	42.16	770	.0594	.0077	770
4	3-4	5004.0	243	42.53	570	.0485	.0085	570
5	4-5	4690.0	195	43.62	445	.0416	.0093	445

*Mortality ratios in excess of 200% are rounded off.

In the case of cumulative mortality the ratios to be obtained must correspond with respect to the method of deriving the cumulative mortality: the annual exposure method, giving $\Sigma d/\Sigma d'$, or the cohort method, giving Q/Q'. The cumulative ratios by these methods are contrasted in Table 2-8, again utilizing data from the double decrement tables given previously.

Corresponding ratios involving rates of survival are called the annual survival ratio, $100 p_{x+t}/p'_{x+t}$, and the cumulative survival ratio, $100 P_{x+t}/P'_{x+t}$, where P_{x+t} and P'_{x+t} are derived from the respective annual survival rates by the life table method (Table 2-2). Both annual and cumulative survival ratios for the double decrement illustration are given in Table 2-9. Cumulative survival ratios tend to decrease progressively as long as the annual survival ratio is less than unity.

Another important measure of comparative mortality is the *excess death rate per 1000 per year* (EDR), representing the number of extra deaths per 1000 exposed to risk in an indicated year, arising in the observed group over the standard group. This function may be expressed symbolically as $EDR=1000(q_i-q_i')$. Alternative, equivalent expressions are $1000(d_i-d_i')/\ell_i$ and $1000(d_i-d_i')/E_i$, depending on exposure. As in the case of the annual ratios mentioned above, average annual rates of mortality, when called for by the data available, may be used. Such average annual excess death rates may be calculated by the annual exposure method as $EDR=1000(\Sigma d-\Sigma d')/\Sigma\ell$ or $EDR=1000(\Sigma d-\Sigma d')/\Sigma E$. Excess death rates on an annual and cumulative basis have been derived from the illustrative data of the double decrement tables and are shown in Table 2-10, together with the average rate over the entire five years.

The alternate methods of computing expected deaths and associated functions develop interesting features of comparative experience. Differences resulting from the employment of the alternative methods are characteristic of the methods. The consistently higher cumulative mortality ratios by the annual exposure method over the cohort method, after the first year, shown in Table 2-8, are due to the smaller expected deaths derived from the exposure in the observed rather than the standard cohort (see Tables 2-4 and 2-5). The reader may see examples of the difference in mortality ratios by the two methods in the cancer tables in abstracts §120-§190. In the first interval, duration 0-2 years, shown in the tables, the interval mortality ratio by the annual exposure method almost invariably exceeds the cumulative mortality ratio for the interval calculated by the cohort method. The difference is due to the reduced exposure and the resulting lesser expected deaths in the second year, following the termination by death of the high proportion of first-year cancer

16

TABLE 2-8
Comparative Mortality — Cumulative Mortality Ratios
by the Annual Observed and Cohort Methods

Interval		Annual Exposure Method			Cohort Method		
		Cumul. No. of Deaths		Cumulative	Cumulative Mort. Rate		Cumulative
No.	Start-End	Observed	Expected	Mort. Ratio*	Observed†	Expected*	Mort. Ratio*
i	t to t + Δ t	Σd_{x+t}	$\Sigma d'_{x+t}$	100 $\Sigma d/\Sigma d'$	Q_{x+t}	Q'_{x+t}	100 Q/Q'
1	0-1 yr	636	45.54	1400%	.0894	.0064	1400%
2	1-2	1086	88.68	1220	.1559	.0134	1160
3	2-3	1411	130.84	1080	.2061	.0210	980
4	3-4	1654	173.37	955	.2446	.0293	835
5	4-5	1849	216.99	850	.2760	.0383	720

*Mortality ratios in excess of 200% are rounded off.

$$\dagger Q_{x+t} = 1 - \prod_x^{x+t} p_{x+t} \qquad Q'_{x+t} = 1 - \prod_x^{x+t} p'_{x+t}$$

TABLE 2-9
Comparative Survival — Annual and Cumulative Survival Ratios

Interval		Annual			Cumulative		
		Survival Rate		Survival	Survival Rate		Survival
No.	Start-End	Observed	Expected	Ratio	Observed	Expected	Ratio
i	t to t + Δ t	p_{x+t}	p'_{x+t}	100 p/p'	P_{x+t}	P'_{x+t}	100 P/P'
1	0-1 yr	.9106	.9936	91.6%	.9106	.9936	91.6%
2	1-2	.9270	.9930	93.4	.8441	.9866	85.6
3	2-3	.9406	.9923	94.8	.7940	.9790	81.1
4	3-4	.9515	.9915	96.0	.7554	.9707	77.8
5	4-5	.9584	.9907	96.7	.7240	.9617	75.3

TABLE 2-10
Comparative Mortality — Annual and Average Annual Excess Death Rates

Interval		Exposure	No. of Deaths		Excess
No.	Start-End	Person-Yrs	Observed	Expected	Death Rate
i	t to t + Δ t	E_{x+t}	d_{x+t}	d'_{x+t}	1000(d-d')/E
1	0-1 yr	7116.0	636	45.54	83
2	1-2	6163.5	450	43.14	66
3	2-3	5475.0	325	42.16	52
4	3-4	5004.0	243	42.53	40
5	4-5	4690.0	195	43.62	32
1-5	0-5 yrs	28448.5	1849	216.97	57

deaths. The cohort method does not take this situation into account, so that expected deaths are larger as a consequence and by producing a greater denominator reduce the ratio.

Intervals Other than One Year

A nominal rate of mortality may be derived for intervals shorter than one year most simply by increasing the number of deaths over the interval to the full year by proportion, and taking the ratio of the result to the number living at the beginning of the interval. Observation over short intervals (days, weeks, or months) in published articles cited in the abstracts of this volume is usually complete—rarely, in such cases, are there losses to follow-up; the lives at the start of the interval may generally be taken to be the exposed to risk. Caution is called for in extrapolating for a nominal annual rate, especially if the period of observation is short. To illustrate: if, over an interval of one week, two per cent or more of the lives exposed die, a nominal rate obtained by proportional extension of the deaths would result in a *yearly* rate of over 100 per cent—implying that more died than existed at the outset. It should be kept in mind that some bias of this kind exists as well in less extreme cases. Usually, reports of experience over short intervals betoken extremely high rates of death because of an acute condition for which annual rates would be inappropriate. In such cases functions are ordinarily computed on the basis of short intervals, so that rates may be tabulated for intervals as short as a single day or even one hour.

More often encountered in the presentation of mortality and survival experience are situations in which the source material as contained in a paper or article is limited to results at or over relatively long intervals. Represented typically in this limited form are cumulative survival rates at isolated points in the course of the follow-up period, or aggregates of deaths and exposures over intervals of varying duration. Such data are significant, but they may not clearly indicate the incidence of mortality. If it appears that distortion is not likely to be introduced by irregularities in withdrawal or in other influences, the approach taken in the preparation of tables in this volume in such cases is to "reconstruct" intermediate data by mathematical methods so as to approximate details of the foreshortened material.

If isolated cumulative survival rates constitute the source material, the general approach is to derive average annual rates of survival and death over the durations between those given. From such rates useful estimate of intervening functions may be made from which (after selecting an applicable standard basis) mortality ratios and other comparative functions may be derived. The reconstructed functions ordinarily are based on the assumption that the annual rates of survival intermediate between the given cumulative survival rates are constant. If the interval between the rates given is, say, n years, the steps in the process of developing such constant annual rates are first to compute the quotient of the given cumulative survival rates at the end and the beginning of the interval, thus obtaining the cumulative survival rate for n years, p_i (n years) = P_i/P_{i-n}. The nth root of p_i is then extracted yielding the *geometric mean annual rate of survival*, designated $\check{p}$. A complementary function $\check{q} = 1 - \check{p}$, is referred to herein for the sake of brevity as the *"geometric mean" annual rate of mortality* rather than as the "complement of the geometric mean annual rate of survival."

If the source material is presented in the form of aggregate deaths and exposures over several years, the average rate of mortality taken to apply to the constituent years of the interval is the aggregate mean denoted $\bar{q}$ and the complementary average annual rate of survival, $\bar{p}$. That is to say, the average annual mortality rate over an n-year interval for which total deaths and exposures are given may be symbolized

$$\bar{q}_i = \sum_1^n d_t \bigg/ \sum_1^n E_t.$$

If the experience is one in which no withdrawals occur, $\bar{q}$ would be given by

$$\sum_1^n d_t \bigg/ \sum_1^n \ell_t.$$

When annual rates of mortality and survival are not available or when results for several years are to be condensed, either of the averages described are substituted for them in the several formulas in which they would be inserted. The rate entering into the calculation of any function is designated in the relevant column heading.

The Survival Index. This function which appears in some tables in this volume is a type of cumulative survival ratio intended to approximate the weighted average of such ratios taken at the end of the several intervals falling within the period of observation. The index is obtained by computing at some intermediate duration within the period the cumulative survival ratio based on the average annual cumulative survival rates, observed and expected, for that duration. The index provides a single figure which reflects the general character of relative survival during the period.

18

Age Groups in Lieu of Individual Ages

For a group of diverse ages, the number of expected deaths in the group in any year in the ideal case is determined by analyzing the total exposure of the year into its constituent individual ages, by applying to the lives exposed at each respective age the corresponding probability of death from an appropriate standard table, and by a summation of the numbers developed at the individual ages. In each succeeding year the process is repeated, but age distributions of the survivors change from year to year as the individuals subject to higher rates of mortality are removed by death.

Almost without exception, experience in source material is reported in age groupings rather than according to individual ages. This arrangement has some advantages: it economizes on space, and it tends to smooth irregularities in the experience of individual ages, where erratic experience may occur by reason of the small numbers exposed. In many instances, appropriate expected data are provided in the source material and they can be incorporated in the abstracts. However, expected functions wanted are not always given; to obtain them resort is taken to estimating expected experience. If we are concerned with an age grouping as composed at commencement of observation, a reasonably satisfactory estimate of expected functions for the first year can be made by assuming a central age for the age group in the vicinity of the median. Some refinement in the selection of the central age can be achieved by giving some effect within an age group to the distribution trend in the neighboring age groups.

With duration, the experience attributable to a central age as described in the preceding paragraph tends to diverge from the more precise method of analysis of the individual ages. Divergencies on this account are generally of small moment and normally do not prejudice results to any significant extent. However, if the age grouping is composed of individuals at advanced ages and subject to high rates of mortality, deviations from the precise procedure by the central age device may be more substantial. Even in such cases the inaccuracy of the practical method is rarely sufficient to invalidate the general result actually experienced.

Some large mortality studies, the calculations for which are handled by electronic computers, permit analyses of the data by individual ages and durations. *The End Results Study*, the source for most of the data in the cancer abstracts (§100-§190), is perhaps the best illustration of such a situation. Differences between tabular cumulative survival rates supplied by the End Results Section and those appearing in the cancer tables do arise, partly from this circumstance and partly from variations in age composition of the cohort during follow-up. However, except for the oldest lives, differences are small and do not materially affect the mortality rates and ratios appearing in the tables.

Progressive Changes in Mortality and Survival Indices

In the general population, after the onset of adolescence, the risk of death increases with age (except for a period of several years in the early twenties when it declines after an earlier steep increase). While there are exceptions to this pattern of mortality among lives experiencing some diseases or morbid conditions, increases in mortality rates with advance in age are quite general. The impact on the level of mortality rates brought about by an impairment varies. While mortality levels in many impairments are perceptibly higher than standard experience, the progression of the extra mortality rates relative to a standard may increase or decrease or remain parallel to the standard over extensive age ranges. Such variations occur as well with respect to mortality ratios and EDRs. Progressions in these two functions are in great measure independent; a phenomenon encountered frequently in mortality studies is a series of mortality ratios declining as ages increase while excess death rates in the same experience increase. Similar diversity is encountered where all ages are combined and experience is presented by duration from some initial point, such as the onset of disease, the date of diagnosis, etc.

Comment with Regard to Notation Used in the Tables

Some comment may be in order with regard to the arrangement of the tables contained in the abstracts of this volume and to some of the factors entering into the preparation of the material displayed in them. These tables are composed of several columns showing life table functions in formats which are not strictly uniform. However, the salient character of the mortality and survival experienced among the subjects studied is quite consistently shown. Differences in presentation arise by reason of the variety of forms in which data in the papers and articles constituting the sources of information are presented. Without exhausting the diversity, the following may be mentioned among several forms of presentation of data: the numbers of lives observed at intervals over the follow-up period together with deaths and withdrawals over these intervals; cumulative rates of survival at varying durations and the number of persons entering observation; interval rates of mortality and the number of lives first observed; charts, diagrams, and line- or bar-graphs showing cumulative survivors at points during follow-up.

Since an objective in the arrangement of the tables in this volume is the logical presentation of the functions displayed as they are developed from the source data, differences in the order of the table columns is a necessary consequence. Reference may be made to Chapter 1 where the organization of the abstracts is described.

Generally, captions name the function listed in the respective columns of the tables together with the symbols or formulas as developed in this chapter. As examples, a set of mortality ratios may have a caption of this kind:

Mortality Ratio

Interval	Cumulative
100 d/d′	100Σd/Σd′

and the EDR column may be headed,

Excess Death Rate
1000 (d-d′)/E

However, if the source material did not yield the elements shown in the foregoing but provided means for obtaining the indicated alternative components, these column headings may read:

Mortality Ratio

Interval	Cumulative
100 $\breve{q}/\breve{q}′$	100 Q/Q′

Excess Death Rate
1000($\breve{q}$ - $\breve{q}′$)

The various forms of data presentation in the source material also dictate differing ways of extracting information not explicitly provided. Differing avenues of approach in the development of some functions have been described in this chapter. For convenience of the reader the notation employed in the abstracts and definitions of the symbols and functions are listed in the appended Glossary.

GLOSSARY OF SYMBOLS AND DEFINITIONS

SYMBOL	DEFINITION OR FORMULA
	Duration and Intervals of Follow-up
i	Subscript representing an interval in a series numbered 1, 2, 3...
t	Relation in time of starting point of an interval i to the commencement of follow-up (t = O for first follow-up interval).
Δt	Length or duration of an interval of follow-up, in years or other specified unit of time, measured from starting point t. If the starting point of an interval is at duration t, the end is at duration t + Δ t.
	Functions—Observed Basis
ℓ	Number alive at start of the indicated interval.
w	Number withdrawn alive from follow-up during the indicated interval.
u	Number lost to follow-up (untraced) during the indicated interval.
E	Number exposed to risk during the indicated interval. E = ℓ — ½w or E = ℓ — ½ (u+w).
d	Number of deaths observed during the indicated interval.
q	Rate of mortality for the indicated interval; proportion of deaths observed among ℓ or E. q = d/ℓ or q = d/E.

GLOSSARY OF SYMBOLS AND DEFINITIONS (CONTINUED)

SYMBOL	DEFINITION OR FORMULA
p	Rate of survival for the indicated interval; proportion of ℓ living at the end of the interval. $p = 1 - q$.
p_i	Interval survival rate. If more than one year. $p_i = (p_1)\,(p_2)\,(p_3)\ldots$
P	Cumulative survival rate at end of indicated interval.
P_t	Cumulative survival rate at duration t. $P = \Pi p = (p_1)\,(p_2)\,(p_3)\ldots(p_t)$.
Q	Cumulative mortality rate at end of indicated interval. $Q = 1 - P$.
Q_t	Cumulative mortality rate at duration t.

Functions—Standard or Expected Basis

q'	Rate of mortality applicable to the indicated interval on standard (expected) basis, compiled independently of the observed experience.
p'	Rate of survival applicable to the indicated interval on standard (expected) basis. $p' = 1 - q'$
d'	Number of "expected" deaths, assumed to occur during the individual interval if the standard mortality rate were operative. $d' = (\ell)\,(q')$ or $d' = (E)\,(q')$
P'	Cumulative survival rate on standard (expected) basis at the end of the indicated interval. $P' = \Pi p' = (p'_1)\,(p'_2)\,)p'_3)\ldots P'_t$ is the rate at duration t.
Q'	Cumulative mortality rate on standard (expected) basis at the end of the indicated interval $Q' = 1 - P'$. Q'_t is the rate at duration t.

Mean Rates of Mortality and Survival

$\bar{q}$	Mean aggregate annual rate of mortality based on experience of more than one interval. $\bar{q} = \Sigma d/\Sigma \ell$ or $\bar{q} = \Sigma d/\Sigma E$.
$\bar{p}$	Mean aggregate annual rate of survival. $\bar{p} = 1 - \bar{q}$
$\check{p}$	Geometric mean annual rate of survival based on experience over the indicated interval of duration Δt units of time. $\check{p} = \sqrt[\Delta t]{p_i}$. If the beginning of the interval i is at duration t, then $p_i = P_{t+\Delta t}/P_t$
$\check{q}$	Complement of $\check{p}$, referred to as "geometric mean annual mortality rate." $\check{q} = 1 - \check{p}$

Comparative Mortality and Survival Functions
Mortality Ratios

MR (annual or interval)	$100\ d/d' = 100\ q/q'$
MR (aggregate mean annual)	$100\ \Sigma d/\Sigma d'$
MR (aggregate mean annual)	$100\ \bar{q}/\bar{q}'$
MR (geometric mean annual)	$100\ \check{q}/\check{q}'$
MR (cumulative)	$100\ Q/Q'$

GLOSSARY OF SYMBOLS AND DEFINITIONS (CONTINUED)

Comparative Mortality and Survival Functions
Survival Ratios

SR (annual or interval)	$100\ p/p'$
SR (aggregate mean annual)	$100\ \bar{p}/\bar{p}'$
SR (geometric mean annual)	$100\ \breve{p}/\breve{p}'$
SR (cumulative)	$100\ P/P'$

Comparative Mortality and Survival Functions
EDR — Extra deaths per 1000 per Year*

EDR (annual or interval)	$1000\ (d-d')/E = 1000\ (d-d')/\ell = 1000\ (q-q')$
EDR (aggregate mean annual)	$1000\ (\bar{q}-\bar{q}')$
EDR (geometric mean annual)	$1000\ (\breve{q}-\breve{q}')$

*In a few instances a different unit of time, usually shorter than one year, is indicated in the table.

References

1. Joint Committee, *Medico-Actuarial Mortality Investigation, Volume 1, Introduction. Statistics of Height and Weight of Insured Persons. Rates of Mortality to be Used as a Standard of Expected Deaths. Instructions to Companies for Preparing Data and General Information*. New York: Assoc. Life Ins. Med. Dir. and Act. Soc. Am. (1912).

2. J. Berkson and R.P. Gage, "Calculation of Survival Rates for Cancer." *Proc. Staff Meetings of Mayo Clinic*, 25:270-286 (1950).

3. H.F. Dorn, "Methods of Analysis for Follow-up Studies." *Human Biology*, 22:238-248 (1950).

4. S.J. Cutler and F. Ederer, "Maximum Utilization of The Life Table Method in Analyzing Survival." *J. Chron. Dis.*, 8:699-712 (1958).

5. E. Fix and J. Neyman, "A Simple Stochastic Model of Recovery, Relapse, Death and Loss of Patients." *Human Biology*, 23:205-241 (1951).

6. A.S. Littell, "Estimation of The T-Year Survival Rate from Follow-up Studies over a Limited Period of Time." *Human Biology*, 24:87-116 (1952).

7. L. Elveback, "Actuarial Estimation of Survivorship in Chronic Disease." *J. Am. Stat. Assoc.*, 53:420-440 (1958).

8. F. Ederer, L.M. Axtell, and S.J. Cutler, "The Relative Survival Rate: A Statistical Methodology." In *End Results and Mortality Trends in Cancer*, National Cancer Institute Monograph No. 6. Bethesda, Md.: National Institutes of Health (1961), pp. 101-121.

9. E.A. Gehan, "Estimating Survival Functions from The Life Table." *J. Chron. Dis.*, 21:629-644 (1969).

10. A.C. Irwin, "Survivorship: The Estimation and Interpretation of Survival Experience." *Canad. Med. Assoc. J.*, 105:489-497 (1971).

11. H. Gershenson, *Measurement of Mortality*. Chicago: Society of Actuaries (1965).

12. M. Spiegelman, *Introduction to Demography*, rev. ed. Cambridge, Mass.: Harvard University Press (1968).

13. C.L. Chiang, *Introduction to Stochastic Process in Biostatistics*. New York: John Wiley and Sons, Inc. (1968).

14. B. Benjamin and H.W. Haycocks, *The Analysis of Mortality and Other Actuarial Statistics*. Cambridge, England: University Press (1970).

3

Interpretation of Mortality and Survival Data
Edward A. Lew, F.S.A., and Richard B. Singer, M.D.

Nature of Follow-Up Studies

A typical follow-up study is begun by carefully choosing a population having characteristics which it is desired to investigate. The population is then observed at convenient intervals over an appropriate follow-up period, the numbers of individuals exposed to risk in each interval are determined, and the deaths occurring during each interval are related to the exposed to risk in the interval to obtain the rate of mortality for the interval. Some follow-up studies are designed to observe morbidity instead of, or in addition to, mortality, in which case any clearly defined morbid event, such as an attack of acute myocardial infarction, may be substituted for the lethal event, death. However, the follow-up studies abstracted in this volume relate almost exclusively to mortality and survival. The methods used to develop the observed data in these follow-up studies were discussed in the previous chapter. For more intensive discussions of the problems encountered in follow-up studies, the reader is referred to articles by Marshall,[1] Larus,[2] Dorn,[3] Sartwell,[4] Lew,[5] and Irwin.[6]

The proximate purpose of follow-up studies is to estimate rates of mortality. These are customarily developed for time intervals reckoned from entry into the study, taking into account the varying dates of entry and dates of withdrawal from the study and in the course of the period covered by the investigation.

A *longitudinal prospective* investigation represents the classic form of a follow-up study. Such an investigation is usually designed in advance with the objective of either compiling a mortality experience or testing some hypothesis relating to the population under study, for example, does a drug reduce mortality or change some characteristic, such as serum cholesterol? The population is chosen with this specific objective in mind and the subjects followed year by year or at less frequent intervals from a predetermined current starting point. The deaths and withdrawals in each interval are carefully recorded. In some investigations it is possible to examine the subjects periodically, to record their physical condition and carry out special tests. The Framingham Study exemplifies this type of investigation. Epidemiological characteristics of the Framingham Study are described in abstract §380, and long-term mortality results in relation to blood pressures observed at the first three examinations are given in §320.

Frequently adequate records are available for a period of years going back in time so that a longitudinal prospective study can be made beginning at some time in the past. This has been typical of mortality studies made from the records of insured lives based on policies issued for a period of years prior to the date when the study is planned and begun. The investigation of Army personnel who were diagnosed as having an acute myocardial infarction during World War II and followed for 15 years on the basis of Veterans Administration records provides another example of this type of study (§303), and additional ones are to be found in the follow-up of cases of specific cardiovascular diseases that developed during the Framingham Study. Such "historical" prospective studies made possible by longitudinal observation of the entire Framingham cohort include those on coronary heart disease (§301, §302), cerebrovascular disease (§204), congestive heart failure (§381), and arterial occlusive disease as manifested by the development of intermittent claudication (§382). The term "historical prospective" study was suggested by Clark and Hopkins.[7] Another example of a carefully planned and executed investigation of mortality based on past records is the Halothane Study (§80). The primary purpose of this study was to find out whether halothane and certain other general anesthetics produced liver damage in surgical patients. Records were reviewed on a large number of operations, and all patient deaths occurring within six weeks of operation were analyzed.

An important type of prospective investigation designed to test a hypothesis is illustrated by *clinical trials*. In such investigations the population is divided into two or more groups, at least one of which serves as a control group for other groups to whom specific forms of treatment are given. As a rule, clinical studies are planned in advance, begun at a chosen date and continued until the experience demonstrates whether or not there are significant differences between the treated groups and the control group. Occasionally records will permit a type of study similar to a clinical trial to be made starting from some date in the past. If this is done, the problem of selecting an adequate control group is a rather difficult one: random samples from more widely representative populations, samples of patients with other presumably nonrelated conditions and relatives having characteristics similar to the treated group have been used. New methods for clinical trials are in the course of being developed. One method widely resorted to has been the so-called "double blind" procedure, in which a physician manages the care of a patient unaware of whether a particular treatment drug or placebo is being used. An example of this method is the Coronary Drug Research Project Study (§315), the purpose of which was to determine whether certain drugs could, by lowering serum cholesterol levels in patients who had recovered from a previous myocardial infarction, have a beneficial effect on survival.

24

The objective in abstracting most of the follow-up studies reported in this volume has been to develop a comparative mortality experience among individuals with a particular mental or physical condition or characteristic. Such factors have included a *history* of a serious acute disease such as myocardial infarction, a *chronic disease,* such as elevated blood pressure or a heart murmur, and *abnormal findings* on special tests, such as chest X-rays, electrocardiograms, and blood chemistry. Populations with medical factors or characteristics such as these have been selected in various ways, sometimes with a deliberate attempt to eliminate individuals with other significant impairments (as in most studies of insured lives) and sometimes embracing all individuals with the medical characteristic being investigated regardless of the presence of other impairments (as in most clinical studies). Accordingly, one of the key questions that must be considered is how representative is the population under study of all subjects with the characteristic being investigated.

The representativeness of the population under study depends on two major characteristics: (1) whether the individuals were born at about the same time or over a broad span of time so that their life histories involved varying biological exposures; and (2) whether the individuals experienced a specified event at about the same time prior to their entry into the study or at widely varying periods of time prior to their entry. The event may have been the onset of a disease, diagnosis of a disease, beginning of treatment, return to work, or a radical change in circumstances or habits. It is clear that the health status of individuals may have been adversely affected if their childhood and youth were spent in times of low standards of sanitation and personal hygiene, low living standards, and lack of effective medical care, whereas corresponding individuals, born some years later, may have enjoyed more favorable circumstances. Analogously, individuals who acquired harmful habits early in life may constitute a more seriously impaired group than those who took up such habits later; this is indicated in the studies of smoking habits by Hammond, which show that subjects who did not start smoking until they were past 30 constitute an entirely different group from those whose smoking began in their teens (§42).

In order to see the effects of many medical factors more clearly it is desirable to conduct follow-up studies by cohorts traced in time rather than by attained age, when the effects observed pertain to a mixture of cohorts. It is furthermore necessary to take into account the accuracy and completeness of the data, the salient characteristics of the population under study and the shortcomings of the common units used to measure mortality. Most importantly, it is essential to recognize the limitations of statistical methodology and to focus attention on the biological meaning of the findings.

Accuracy and Completeness of Observations

The prime requisite in designing mortality investigations is to define and provide practical criteria for the identification of one or more specific characteristics under consideration. It is essential that the observations recorded do, in fact, pertain to the specific characteristics which it is desired to investigate. Such factors are often in the nature of adverse deviations in a cluster of related physiological or biochemical variables which describe the disease or impairment. If the adverse deviations can be described in qualitative terms only, it is important to examine the problems involved in identifying and classifying them, particularly with respect to the time criterion for entry into the study and characterization of the severity of the condition. The time criterion may be based on the date of onset, date of diagnosis, date of first examination, date of treatment, date of return to work, or some other clearly defined time. The date of onset and the severity of chronic diseases are rather difficult to judge because overt symptoms may not appear until considerable time has elapsed. More broadly, it is helpful to know how errors in diagnosis can be made under different circumstances. If the adverse deviations can be given in numerical terms, some appreciation of the biases in measurement and of the variability of the measurements is in order.

Some of these considerations are illustrated by the Framingham Study where individuals were examined periodically and an attack of acute myocardial infarction could be confirmed by both clinical and electrocardiographic evidence (§302). The study of myocardial infarction among Army personnel was also very accurately documented in the detailed records maintained by the armed forces (§303). In the Coronary Drug Research Project patients were carefully selected and characterized, and follow-up observations were accurately made in accordance with an elaborate protocol.

Special problems arise in studies of mortality by cause. They relate to the determination of the underlying cause of death when more than one cause is reported, when historical or regional comparisons are made, and when the classifications "senility," "ill-defined cause" or "unknown cause" appear with some frequency. When more than one cause is reported, the practice since 1948 has been to take the cause designated by the certifying physician as the underlying cause. A large proportion of death certificates show more than one condition, and the underlying condition is often—particularly at the older ages—difficult to isolate and may not even exist. Over a period of years there have been major changes in the medical concept of the underlying cause of death; the designation of the underlying cause may also differ from one area to another, depending on the varying training and skills of the certifying physicians and the degree of attention given to completing death certificates. Because of such differences in certification and coding there can be appreciable differences in the reporting of deaths ascribed to many chronic diseases, notably the cardiovascular renal disorders.

Most studies abstracted in this volume have relied on the designation of causes of death as given on death certificates, where such data have been reported. In a few instances, notably Hammond's studies of cigarette smokers (§40 and §42) and the Halothane Study (§80), special efforts were made to review and improve on the designation of the cause of death cited in the death certificate. However, it should be emphasized that most of the follow-up data abstracted have been used to develop rates and ratios of total mortality, and the corresponding survival rates and ratios. These results are independent of uncertainties related to cause of death.

The completeness of observation, especially with respect to deaths, is a major determinant of the accuracy of a mortality study. The cases lost to follow-up must be kept to an absolute minimum to ensure that the mortality rates will not be biased by an undue proportion of deaths in the untraced subjects. In many investigations there is a marked self-selection at time of withdrawal from observation. In studies based on the records of insured lives there has been some tendency for those in poor health not to withdraw, whereas in many clinical studies those who became ill may have been lost to follow-up because they sought medical treatment elsewhere or migrated to warmer or dryer climates. Women have in general been more difficult to trace than men, because their surnames may be changed upon marriage, divorce or remarriage, and partly because a high proportion of women have no long-duration employment connection.

The problems of incomplete or biased follow-up were present in a number of follow-up studies reviewed in this monograph. Thus, in the follow-up of cancer patients there were grounds for presuming that those who died were traced more fully than those who survived, especially five years or more following diagnosis.

Characteristics of Population Selected for Study

With rare exceptions follow-up studies of groups having a medical condition or characteristic in common involve individuals who were not chosen randomly from all persons in the general population exhibiting the characteristic under study. Such sample populations tend to be unrepresentative in varying degrees. It is crucial to make a careful appraisal of the individuals in nonrandom populations in order to be able to put one's finger on the factors affecting the mortality experience other than those explicitly under study.

The criteria adopted for the inclusion of subjects in an investigation can have a major influence on the mortality exhibited. The individuals included may have "selected themselves" to some extent, and the marked effects of self-selection on mortality are highly visible in the distinctly lower death rates among annuitants in the early years following issue of annuity contracts. The pronounced effects of physical screening are seen clearly in the lower mortality of insured lives, particularly past mid-life during the first five years following issue of the insurance. The progressive gradations in death rates by socioeconomic status indicate the magnitude of class selection; even in employee populations engaged in nonhazardous pursuits, such as clerical occupations, death rates may vary from 30 per cent below average in the case of managerial and supervisory personnel to 10-15 per cent above average for employees at the lower socioeconomic levels.[8] This differential matches that found for variations in mortality by educational attainment, which for white males age 25 to 64 ranges from 25 per cent below average for those with some college education to 10 per cent above average for those with less than eight years of formal schooling.[9]

In typical medical, public health, and life insurance investigations selection occurs when entrants into a study are held to some specified physical standards. The mere fact that the very ill and the moribund are as a rule automatically excluded provides appreciably lower mortality for a period of time. This phenomenon was observed in the Cancer Prevention Study which comprised a population exceeding a million, where the mortality in the first year of the study was found to be comparable to that of insured lives in the first year following issue of the insurance.[10] An individual's awareness of his physical condition may also produce self-selection at time of withdrawal from a study.

Among the more noteworthy examples of selection on the mortality experienced are those in veterans with neuroses resulting in medical discharge during service in World War II (§285). In this study it was found that veterans with a history of neurosis did not show any significant excess mortality as compared with the general population, but nevertheless experienced higher mortality than corresponding veterans without a history of neurosis. This finding reflects the fact that men admitted into military service were a selected group whose underlying mortality was appreciably below that of the general population.

Systematic bias may be more difficult to detect and allow for than the kinds of selection mentioned above. Systematic bias may arise from a high degree of nonresponse or from gaps in the registers from which the subjects for a study are chosen. In the Framingham Study about 23 per cent of those initially invited to participate declined to do so, and nearly 7 per cent left Framingham before the first examination. There is evidence to suggest that the population remaining in the Framingham Study was not representative in many respects.[5] Whenever the criteria established for entry into a study cannot be complied with, whether by reason of self-selection, nonresponse, gaps in registers, or other reasons, substantial biases of an indeterminate nature can be introduced.

Nevertheless a great deal can be learned from examining the different results for a variety of populations such as hospital and private patients, regional populations, employee groups, and insured lives, even when these different populations are not broadly representative. The more we know about the characteristics of the individuals included in a study, the better we can gauge the influences responsible for any disparities in the results observed for different populations. When the results for diverse populations are of a piece, we can generalize from the findings with greater confidence and fewer reservations. When the results are dissimilar, we are on notice to look for differences and extraneous factors that may have escaped our attention.

Moreover, the findings for a variety of populations yield information as to the range of mortality likely to be encountered over a fuller spectrum of characteristics. For instance, studies of well documented diagnoses of a disease may not be as informative as investigations covering a wider range of diagnoses. This is illustrated by the findings on confirmed myocardial infarction, which condition is not infrequently missed when acute symptoms are absent or confusing, or when other serious complications are involved; the prognosis in myocardial infarction can be visualized more intelligently in the light of variations in patterns of survival in different populations and for various diagnoses associated with coronary heart disease. To be more specific, follow-up studies of myocardial infarction in hospitalized patients by their nature exclude sudden deaths which occur before the patient can be hospitalized. Only prospective studies of relatively large populations include sudden deaths and mortality in myocardial infarction; examples of such studies are the Framingham Study (§302), the study of Army personnel (§303), the study of a large population (§312), and the study of a large group covered by a health insurance plan (§313 and §314).

Measures of Comparative Mortality

The reader who consults the original articles on which abstracts in this volume have been based will discover a bewildering variety of ways of presenting the findings. In some articles life table methods have not been used. It has nevertheless been possible in such articles to approximate the exposed to risk from the data given, and relate the deaths reported to the exposed to risk in order to derive mortality rates. The accuracy of such death rates is influenced not only by the accuracy of the underlying data but also by the assumptions made if there was an estimation of the exposed to risk. In other articles life table methods were used and the results displayed in graphs of cumulative survival rates. It was then necessary to calculate death rates from the survival rates taken off the graphs, as illustrated in abstract §208. In both of these situations it was sometimes possible to obtain additional data from the authors, thus permitting more accurate calculation of the rates and ratios presented in the tables of this volume.

The objective of this monograph has been to translate the findings of the follow-up studies accepted for review into the form of (1) interval mortality and survival rates in relation to those expected; (2) proportions surviving a specified period of time and those dying within the period compared with corresponding proportions expected; (3) extra deaths per 1000 exposed to risk in relation to those expected.

In mortality investigations of insured lives, death rates deemed appropriate as a yardstick of normal mortality have as a rule been the contemporaneous death rates among lives insured at standard premium rates. In clinical studies the death rates generally chosen as a yardstick have been the contemporaneous death rates in the general population. Illustrative mortality rates of both types are given in Table 3-1, later in this chapter. In some studies of specific disease or impairments the death rates of individuals free of those diseases or impairments drawn from the same population as the cases under study have been used as the basis for expected mortality, the "mortality yardstick."

Mortality ratios and extra deaths per 1000 have been commonly used in measuring life insurance underwriting performance. They have the merit of rendering manifest even small departures from expected mortality. In some circumstances the pattern of excess mortality can be perceived more clearly from the extra deaths per 1000 than from the corresponding mortality ratios. For instance, in mortality comparisons for all ages combined it is essential to keep in mind that mortality ratios usually decrease with advancing age, so that mortality ratios for all ages combined may be materially affected by the age composition of the population under study. Also, in mortality comparisons by sex it is well to bear in mind that female death rates are normally very low at ages under 50, so that moderately high mortality ratios among females at these younger ages may represent relatively small absolute departures from expected mortality.

The proportion surviving a specified period of time provides an absolute measure of the mortality in a population. If an index of comparative survival is desired, the actual proportion surviving can be compared with the corresponding proportion in a standard cohort with annual mortality rates based on a chosen suitable yardstick of mortality. This index has been widely used in surgical follow-up and clinical studies, as the "relative survival rate", or, in the terminology of this volume, the cumulative survival ratio.[11] Its principal shortcoming lies in the insensitivity of the proportion surviving to relatively large changes in mortality, with the result that small differences in survival rates are difficult to interpret.

It should be emphasized that the plausibility of all comparative measures of mortality here considered depends on the suitability of the death rates used as the yardstick of expected mortality. Select mortality tables based on the experience of lives insured at standard premium rates are clearly appropriate for studies of insurance applicants and for guiding decisions as to how mortality risk in such applicants should be classified. Ultimate death rates among insured lives may be appropriate to use in the comparative experience of selected groups in the general population considered to have a better than average mortality—a series of private patients might be an example. General population mortality may be appropriate for unselected groups from lower or middle segments of the population such as patients in municipal or general hospitals. Examples of mortality tables commonly used as yardsticks are given in the next section.

Comment on Standard Mortality Tables

Groups of insured lives of the same attained age may be compared one with another, and with the general population to illustrate the quantitative effects of selection in reducing mortality. Table 3-1 shows mortality rates at a number of attained ages for the 1959-61 U.S. white population in comparison with those for an intercompany insured population in the

TABLE 3-1

Male and Female Mortality Rates per 1000
Population Mortality/Select Mortality/Ultimate Mortality

| Attained Age | Unselected U.S. White (1959-61) | Select (1955-60 Intercompany)* | | | Ultimate† |
		1st Yr	6th Yr	11th Yr	16th Yr Up
Male					
0	25.9	1.85	—	—	—
5	0.62	0.49	0.49	—	—
15	0.93	0.66	0.71	0.73	0.73
25	1.56	0.56	1.04	1.22	1.25
35	2.07	0.75	1.08	1.24	1.40
45	5.58	1.91	3.26	3.59	3.96
55	14.3	3.92	7.84	8.91	11.0
65	33.9	8.67	17.0	20.3	28.0
75	70.7	20.0	33.7	43.8	63.4
85	160.4	—	—	—	149.2
Female					
0	19.6	1.68	—	—	—
5	0.47	0.35	0.35	—	—
15	0.41	0.23	0.28	0.36	0.36
25	0.65	0.24	0.49	0.61	0.66
35	1.22	0.47	0.87	0.87	1.21
45	3.03	0.96	2.14	2.27	2.32
55	6.87	1.78	4.12	4.96	5.67
65	17.4	4.20	8.97	10.2	13.1
75	47.4	12.3	24.1	27.9	43.6
85	136.2	—	—	—	107.4

*Graduated rates derived from 1955-60 Select Basic Tables (TSA 1962 Reports) with Juvenile Extension.

†Ultimate Basic Tables, Intercompany Experience 1957-60 (TSA 1962 Reports).

28

first, sixth and eleventh years after issue of insurance ("select" mortality rates), and more than 15 years after issue ("ultimate" rates). The insurance experience was nearly contemporaneous with that of the population. Except at the youngest ages the general population experiences mortality rates approximately two to four times greater than those within one year after issue of standard insurance to applicants successfully passing the screening examination. There is a progressive decrease in this mortality differential with the passage of time. Thus insured men at attained age 35 were found to have an annual mortality rate of 0.75 per 1000 in the first year after policy issue, 1.08 per 1000 when the policy was issued five years previously, and 1.24 per 1000 when the policy was issued ten years previously. More than 15 years after policy issue the average rate for all men at attained age 35, the ultimate rate, was 1.40 per 1000, still substantially below the population rate, but this difference probably reflects differences in socio-economic status rather than the effects of selection.

Various types of insured groups also afford the opportunity to compare mortality rates within two years after issue with select mortality rates averaged for the first two years of policy duration after the issue of standard insurance. Such results are shown in Table 3-2 for a single company which issues an unusually large volume of individual insurance under pension agreements, about 90 per cent of which involves no screening evidence of insurability except that the applicant must be actively at work at his place of employment (AI or automatic issue).[12] Compared with standard select experience in the first two years the automatic issue mortality rates in males showed mortality ratios of 154 per cent in two age groups under 40, and somewhat in excess of 200 per cent in three age groups 40-49, 50-59 and age 60 up. Although these ratios were substantially in excess of 100 per cent, representing standard select mortality, they were nevertheless below the mortality ratios for males in the general population. Despite the fact that the automatic issue cases were without benefit of the customary examination, the requirement that they must be actively at work did provide a measurable degree of selection, as the mortality was considerably lower than in the total population. On the average the mortality of the automatic issue cases fell between select standard mortality and the mortality of applicants who qualified for substandard but not standard insurance. The "pension SD" group included high-risk examined pension cases who would have been declinable in a nonpension application. Mortality ratios for this highly impaired group ranged from 4,300 per cent in men under age 30 downward with advancing age to 520 per cent in men age 60 up (fewer than 10 deaths with mortality ratios in parentheses). The final category includes those exercising a group life insurance conversion privilege who did not qualify for standard insurance. The mortality ratios were somewhat lower than observed in the pension SD cases, but well above the ratios for the general population. This phenomenon, producing a higher mortality, is called antiselection and is partly due to a high proportion of persons with impaired health among those electing to convert their group insurance.

TABLE 3-2

Insurance Mortality Experience, Males, Early Durations (1-2 Years) Mortality Ratios* — Effect of Selection and Antiselection

Age Group	Automatic Issue† (1962-70)	All Rated (1955-64)	Pension SD• (1955-64)	Group Conversion□ (1964-69)	U.S. White■ (1959-61)
15-29	154%	220%	(4300%)	(1690%)	355%
30-39	154	345	(2200)	710	290
40-49	220	205	1570	580	335
50-59	210	225	720	520	350
60 up	205	170	(520)	555	400

*Basis of expected mortality — New England Life standard select male rates, durations 1-2 years (1955-64). Ratios in parentheses are based on fewer than 10 deaths.
†Pension applications with no screening except requirement that applicant must be actively at work at the time of application.
•Pension application, examined and underwritten, mortality risk high enough to be declinable for non-pension application.
□Applicants exercising privilege to convert group life insurance, not qualifying for standard insurance.
■U.S. White Male Mortality Rates, 1959-61

A more complete discussion of the subject may be found in an article by Lew and Seltzer.[13] Extensive mortality tables by nationality over a wide period of time have been compiled by Preston et al.[14] Examples of the effects of selection on reducing mortality are evident in the use made of a health questionnaire in the American Cancer Society prospective study (§60) and in the control group of veterans (§285).

Statistical Significance Evaluation

Inasmuch as most mortality investigations are based on relatively small numbers of deaths, it is of considerable importance to be able to estimate the statistical limits of random error of mortality rates, survival rates, and the comparative indices derived therefrom. The following approach utilizes the concept of "confidence limits" to measure the degree of reliability of mortality ratios and related variables. It follows very closely the development of the topic on pages 14-15, Volume I of the *Build and Blood Pressure Study 1959*.[15] For a more extensive discussion the reader is referred to statistical textbooks such as that of Mood and Graybill.[16]

The concept of confidence limits is found in sampling theory where repeated sample estimates are taken from a population in order to measure some particular characteristic. Confidence limits define an interval ranging above and below an observed sample estimate (such as number of deaths); both the observed value and its associated confidence limits are subject to sampling variation. Where a series of repeated sample estimates has been made and confidence limits computed for each estimate, then the "confidence level" indicates the proportion of the estimates for which the confidence limits will enclose the "true" value in the underlying population. For example, consider 10 deaths, with a mortality ratio of 200 per cent. Corresponding to a confidence level of 95 per cent, the corresponding lower confidence limit, LL= (200) (58/100)=116 per cent, and the upper confidence limit, UL= (200) (208/100)=416 per cent (see Table 3-3). Ninety-five out of 100 intervals computed in this way from similar samples of the underlying population would include the "true" mortality ratio.

If a single sample estimate is considered by itself, then, as a practical matter, the confidence level can be interpreted as the chance that the confidence limits enclosed the "true" value. If the concept of confidence limits is applied to the interpretation of mortality ratios, a mortality ratio would be considered a single sample estimate of the "true" comparative mortality of the underlying population. The confidence limits define a range extending above and below the observed ratio. The confidence level may be considered, for practical purposes, as indicating the chance that the "true" value of the mortality ratio is enclosed within the range encompassed by the confidence limits.

Confidence limits are not shown in this volume because their inclusion for each of the many mortality ratios and other indices would unduly complicate the numerous tables and expand their size. However, confidence limits for confidence levels of 90 per cent and 95 per cent may be readily computed by the use of Table 3-3 or the procedures indicated below. Confidence limits may be similarly calculated for the number of observed deaths, d, and the observed mortality rate, q, instead of the mortality ratio, MR.

When the number of deaths exceeds 35 a normal distribution may be assumed to hold approximately (the approximation is closer when d is 100 or more). The confidence limits for a confidence level of 68 per cent are then defined by the formula $CL=MR(1 \pm 1/\sqrt{d})$, where MR is the mortality ratio, d is the observed number of deaths (or policies terminated by death), and $MR/\sqrt{d}$ is the *standard deviation* of the mortality ratio under the assumption of a normal distribution. For the more stringent test with a confidence level of 95 per cent, the confidence limits are given by the formula $CL=MR(1 \pm 1.96 \, MR/\sqrt{d})$, assuming a normal distribution.

When the number of deaths is less than 36, the errors in the above formulas become appreciable. In such cases a better estimate for confidence limits can be obtained by assuming a Poisson probability distribution instead of a normal distribution. Table 3-3 gives upper and lower confidence limits directly for the number of deaths, d, according to the Poisson distribution. In the right-hand portion the table also provides similar confidence limits as a percentage in relation to the mortality ratio, mortality rate or number of deaths, any one of these taken as 100 per cent. The confidence limits by the Poisson distribution have actually been taken well above the number 36 referred to previously as a dividing line between use of the Poisson distribution and the normal distribution.

As an example of the use of Table 3-3 in determining confidence limits, let us assume d = 10 observed deaths, and an exposure of 500 person-years, giving a mortality rate, q, of 0.020. Let us further assume an expected mortality rate, q', of 0.010, from which the expected deaths, d', would be 5.0 and the mortality ratio, MR = 10/5.0 = 200 per cent. The lower (LL) and upper (UL) confidence limits may be read off for d in the left-hand portion of the table, and as a

TABLE 3-3

Confidence Limits Based on Number of Observed Deaths—Poisson Distribution

No. of Deaths Observed	Limits with respect to d				Limits relative to MR, q or d as 100%*			
	95% Limits		90% Limits		95% Limits		90% Limits	
	Lower	Upper	Lower	Upper	Lower	Upper	Lower	Upper
d	LL	UL	LL	UL	LL	UL	LL	UL
2	0.24	5.7	0.5	5.0	35%	833%	40%	400%
3	0.6	7.3	1.0	6.6	41	500	45	300
4	1.1	8.8	1.5	8.1	45	364	50	267
5	1.6	10.3	2.1	9.5	49	312	53	238
6	2.3	11.7	2.8	10.7	51	261	56	214
7	2.9	13.1	3.5	12.1	53	241	58	200
8	3.5	14.5	4.1	13.4	55	229	60	195
9	4.2	15.8	4.8	14.6	57	214	62	188
10	4.8	17.1	5.6	15.9	58	208	63	179
12	6.2	19.8	7.0	18.5	61	194	65	171
14	7.6	22.4	8.5	21.0	63	184	67	165
16	9.1	24.8	10.1	23.4	65	176	68	158
18	10.6	27.4	11.7	25.8	66	170	70	154
20	12.2	29.8	13.3	28.2	67	164	71	150
22	13.8	32.1	14.9	30.6	68	159	72	148
24	15.4	34.6	16.6	32.9	69	156	73	145
26	17.0	36.9	18.4	35.1	70	153	74	141
28	18.6	39.2	20.1	37.5	71	151	75	139
30	20.2	41.7	21.7	39.9	72	149	75	138
32	21.9	44.2	23.4	42.2	72	147	76	137
34	23.5	46.2	25.1	44.2	74	145	77	136
36	25.1	48.6	26.7	46.4	74	143	78	135
38	26.9	50.9	28.4	48.6	75	141	78	134
40	28.5	53.2	30.3	51.2	75	140	78	132
45	32.8	58.9	34.7	56.7	76	137	79	130
50	36.9	65.0	39.2	62.5	77	135	80	128
55	41.5	70.4	43.5	67.6	78	133	81	126
60	45.8	76.2	48.0	73.2	79	131	82	125
65	50.1	81.9	52.5	78.6	79	130	83	124
70	54.6	87.5	57.0	84.7	80	128	83	123
75	59.0	93.0	61.5	90.0	81	127	83	122
80	63.5	98.4	66.1	95.2	81	126	84	121
85	68.0	103.7	70.6	101.1	82	125	84	120
90	72.3	109.8	75.1	106.2	83	124	85	120
95	76.9	114.9	79.7	111.1	83	124	85	119
100	81	120	84	117	83	123	85	119
300	266	333	271	330	90	113	91	111
500	456	545	463	535	92	110	93	108
1,000	938	1,060	948	1,050	94	107	95	106
10,000	9,804	10,200	9,835	10,200	98	102	98	102

*To obtain confidence limits for a given value of mortality ratio, MR, or mortality rate, q, multiply by LL/100 or UL/100. Confidence limits for d are given directly. With d in excess of 100 calculate confidence limits by multiplying the value of MR, q or d by $(1\pm1.96$ S.D.), 95% limits, or $(1\pm1.65$ S.D.), 90% limits, where S.D.=standard deviation = $1/\sqrt{d}$.

percentage of MR, q, or d, in the right-hand portion. Both 95 per cent and 90 per cent confidence limits are shown. The confidence limits for this example would be:

	95% Confidence Limits	90% Confidence Limits
No. of deaths, d=10	4.8 to 17.1 deaths	5.6 to 15.9 deaths
Percentage of MR, q, or d	58% to 208%	63% to 179%
Mortality Ratio, MR=200%	116% to 416%	126% to 358%
Mortality rate, q=0.020	0.0116 to 0.0416	0.0126 to 0.0358

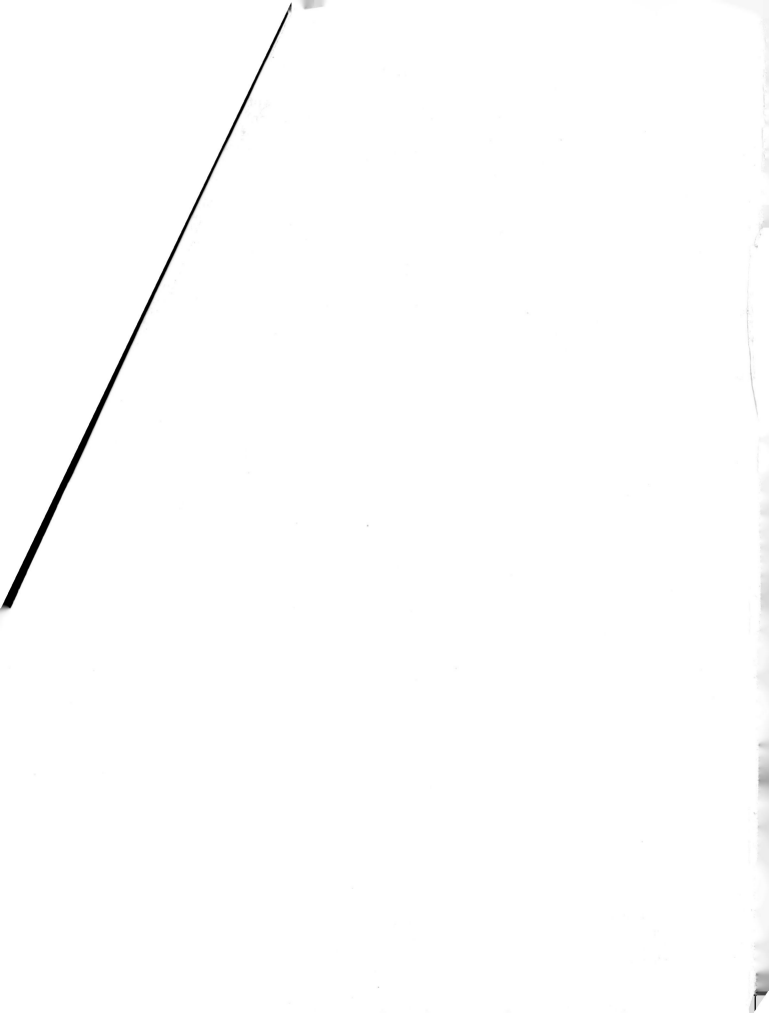

TABLE 3-?

Confidence Limits B′
Observed Deaths - ′

No. of Deaths Observed	Limits with respec 95% Limits							
	Lower	Upper						
d	LL	UL						
3	0.6	8						
4	1.1							
5	1.6							
6	2.2							
7	2.8	14.ₓ						
8	3.5	15.8						
9	4.1	17.1						
10	4.8	18.4						
11	5.5	19.7	6.2					
12	6.2	21.0	6.9					
13	6.9	22.2	7.7	₂.				
14	7.7	23.5	8.5	21.5				
15	8.4	24.7	9.2	23.1				
16	9.1	26.0	10.0	24.3				
17	9.9	27.2	10.8	25.5				
18	10.7	28.4	11.6	26.7	0.5ₓ			
19	11.4	29.7	12.4	27.9	0.60			
20	12.2	30.9	13.3	29.1	0.61			
22	13.8	33.3	14.9	31.4	0.63	1.ₓ		
24	15.4	35.7	16.5	33.8	0.64	1.49		
26	17.0	38.1	18.2	36.1	0.65	1.47		
28	18.6	40.5	19.9	38.4	0.66	1.45		
30	20.2	42.8	21.6	40.7	0.67	1.43	0.7ₓ	
32	21.9	45.2	23.3	43.0	0.68	1.41	0.73	
34	23.5	47.5	25.0	45.3	0.69	1.40	0.74	
36	25.2	49.8	26.7	47.5	0.70	1.38	0.74	1.ₓ
38	26.9	52.2	28.5	49.8	0.71	1.37	0.75	1.31
40	28.6	54.5	30.2	52.1	0.72	1.36	0.76	1.30
45	32.8	60.2	34.6	57.7	0.73	1.34	0.77	1.28
50	37.1	65.9	39.0	63.3	0.74	1.32	0.78	1.27
55	41.4	71.6	43.4	68.9	0.75	1.30	0.79	1.25
60	45.8	77.2	47.9	74.4	0.76	1.29	0.80	1.24
65	50.2	82.8	52.3	79.9	0.77	1.27	0.80	1.23
70	54.6	88.4	56.8	85.4	0.78	1.26	0.81	1.22
75	59.0	94.0	61.3	90.9	0.79	1.25	0.82	1.21
80	63.4	99.6	65.9	96.4	0.79	1.24	0.82	1.20
85	67.9	105.1	70.4	101.8	0.80	1.24	0.83	1.20
90	72.4	110.6	75.0	107.2	0.80	1.23	0.83	1.19
95	76.9	116.1	79.6	112.7	0.81	1.22	0.84	1.19
100	81.4	121.6	84.1	118.1	0.81	1.22	0.84	1.18

*The confidence limits have been calculated in accordance with the traditional formula and definition of confidence interval for the Poisson distribution, as described in *Distributions in Statistics: Discrete Distributions*, by N.L. Johnson and S. Kotz, Boston, Houghton, Mifflin & Co. (1969). We are indebted to Dr. Robert A. Lew for his assistance in the preparation of this table. When d exceeds 100, an approximation of the confidence limits that is satisfactory for most purposes can be obtained by assuming a normal distribution. The formula is: 95% limits $= d \pm 1.96\sqrt{d}$, 90% limits $= d \pm 1.65\sqrt{d}$.

N.B. To obtain the lower confidence limits, LL, for a mortality ratio, MR, or a mortality rate q, multiply MR or q by the appropriate LL factor in the right-hand portion of the table. The upper confidence limits, UL, for MR or q may similarly be computed by multiplying MR or q by the appropriate UL factor from the right-hand part of the table.

decimal ratio of MR, q or d in the right-hand portion. Both 95 per cent and 90 per cent confidence limits are shown. The confidence limits for this example, with d′ = 5.0, would be:

	95% Confidence Limits	90% Confidence Limits
No. of deaths, d = 10	4.8 to 18.4 deaths	5.4 to 17.0 deaths
Limits as ratio of d	0.48 to 1.84	0.54 to 1.70
Mortality Ratio, MR = 200%	96% to 368%	108% to 340%
Mortality Rate, q = 0.020	0.0096 to 0.0368	0.0108 to 0.0340

TABLE 3-3

Confidence Limits Based on Number of Observed Deaths - Poisson Distribution*

No. of Deaths Observed	Limits with respect to d				Limits as a Ratio of d			
	95% Limits		90% Limits		95% Limits		90% Limits	
	Lower	Upper	Lower	Upper	Lower	Upper	Lower	Upper
d	LL	UL	LL	UL	LL	UL	LL	UL
3	0.6	8.8	0.8	7.8	0.21	2.93	0.27	2.60
4	1.1	10.2	1.4	9.2	0.27	2.56	0.34	2.29
5	1.6	11.7	2.0	10.5	0.32	2.33	0.39	2.10
6	2.2	13.1	2.6	11.8	0.37	2.18	0.44	1.97
7	2.8	14.4	3.3	13.1	0.40	2.06	0.47	1.88
8	3.5	15.8	4.0	14.4	0.43	1.97	0.50	1.80
9	4.1	17.1	4.7	15.7	0.46	1.90	0.52	1.74
10	4.8	18.4	5.4	17.0	0.48	1.84	0.54	1.70
11	5.5	19.7	6.2	18.2	0.50	1.79	0.56	1.66
12	6.2	21.0	6.9	19.4	0.52	1.75	0.58	1.62
13	6.9	22.2	7.7	20.7	0.53	1.71	0.59	1.59
14	7.7	23.5	8.5	21.9	0.55	1.68	0.61	1.56
15	8.4	24.7	9.2	23.1	0.56	1.65	0.62	1.54
16	9.1	26.0	10.0	24.3	0.57	1.62	0.63	1.52
17	9.9	27.2	10.8	25.5	0.58	1.60	0.64	1.50
18	10.7	28.4	11.6	26.7	0.59	1.58	0.64	1.48
19	11.4	29.7	12.4	27.9	0.60	1.56	0.65	1.47
20	12.2	30.9	13.3	29.1	0.61	1.54	0.66	1.46
22	13.8	33.3	14.9	31.4	0.63	1.51	0.68	1.43
24	15.4	35.7	16.5	33.8	0.64	1.49	0.69	1.41
26	17.0	38.1	18.2	36.1	0.65	1.47	0.70	1.39
28	18.6	40.5	19.9	38.4	0.66	1.45	0.71	1.37
30	20.2	42.8	21.6	40.7	0.67	1.43	0.72	1.36
32	21.9	45.2	23.3	43.0	0.68	1.41	0.73	1.34
34	23.5	47.5	25.0	45.3	0.69	1.40	0.74	1.33
36	25.2	49.8	26.7	47.5	0.70	1.38	0.74	1.32
38	26.9	52.2	28.5	49.8	0.71	1.37	0.75	1.31
40	28.6	54.5	30.2	52.1	0.72	1.36	0.76	1.30
45	32.8	60.2	34.6	57.7	0.73	1.34	0.77	1.28
50	37.1	65.9	39.0	63.3	0.74	1.32	0.78	1.27
55	41.4	71.6	43.4	68.9	0.75	1.30	0.79	1.25
60	45.8	77.2	47.9	74.4	0.76	1.29	0.80	1.24
65	50.2	82.8	52.3	79.9	0.77	1.27	0.80	1.23
70	54.6	88.4	56.8	85.4	0.78	1.26	0.81	1.22
75	59.0	94.0	61.3	90.9	0.79	1.25	0.82	1.21
80	63.4	99.6	65.9	96.4	0.79	1.24	0.82	1.20
85	67.9	105.1	70.4	101.8	0.80	1.24	0.83	1.20
90	72.4	110.6	75.0	107.2	0.80	1.23	0.83	1.19
95	76.9	116.1	79.6	112.7	0.81	1.22	0.84	1.19
100	81.4	121.6	84.1	118.1	0.81	1.22	0.84	1.18

*The confidence limits have been calculated in accordance with the traditional formula and definition of confidence interval for the Poisson distribution, as described in *Distributions in Statistics: Discrete Distributions*, by N.L. Johnson and S. Kotz, Boston, Houghton, Mifflin & Co. (1969). We are indebted to Dr. Robert A. Lew for his assistance in the preparation of this table. When d exceeds 100, an approximation of the confidence limits that is satisfactory for most purposes can be obtained by assuming a normal distribution. The formula is: 95% limits = $d \pm 1.96\sqrt{d}$, 90% limits = $d \pm 1.65\sqrt{d}$.

N.B. To obtain the lower confidence limits, LL, for a mortality ratio, MR, or a mortality rate q, multiply MR or q by the appropriate LL factor in the right-hand portion of the table. The upper confidence limits, UL, for MR or q may similarly be computed by multiplying MR or q by the appropriate UL factor from the right-hand part of the table.

decimal ratio of MR, q or d in the right-hand portion. Both 95 per cent and 90 per cent confidence limits are shown. The confidence limits for this example, with $d' = 5.0$, would be:

	95% Confidence Limits	90% Confidence Limits
No. of deaths, d = 10	4.8 to 18.4 deaths	5.4 to 17.0 deaths
Limits as ratio of d	0.48 to 1.84	0.54 to 1.70
Mortality Ratio, MR = 200%	96% to 368%	108% to 340%
Mortality Rate, q = 0.020	0.0096 to 0.0368	0.0108 to 0.0340

In this example d', MR and q' are *within* the 95 per cent confidence limits on a percentage basis and therefore do not differ significantly from the estimates based on d at the 95 per cent confidence level. However, the expected deaths d', fall below the lower 90 per cent confidence limit of 5.6, the actual mortality ratio of 200 per cent exceeds the relative upper confidence limit of 179 per cent in the table, and q' falls below the lower confidence limit of .0261 for the mortality rate. On this basis the observed mortality may be said to differ significantly from the expected at the 90 per cent, but not the 95 per cent confidence level.

The confidence limits for the interval survival rate, P, are the same as those for the mortality rate, q. Since p = 1 - q = 1 - 0.020 = 0.980, the 95 per cent confidence limits based on 10 deaths are 0.9584 to 0.9884 (see the corresponding confidence limits for q above).

Calculations involved in obtaining confidence limits for the cumulative survival rate, P, are more complex, as they require a propagation of the random errors of successive interval survival rates. Methods for calculating these confidence limits are given in Chapter 12 of the monograph by Chiang[17] and the article by Cutler and Ederer.[11] It is impractical to arrange confidence limits for cumulative mortality and survival rates into a table such as Table 3-3. Complete life table data, including the annual distribution of deaths and annual mortality rates are needed to carry out these calculations. Such complete data are not available in many of the abstracts in which cumulative survival rates were the principal source of information.

It is essential to keep in mind that the statistical limits of error calculated by the formulas indicated above are valid only if the specified distribution holds and if the populations under study can be reasonably regarded as random samples. When the differences between observed and expected findings are small and within the confidence limits they may be unresolvable. In such situations it is possible that the magnitudes of the biases present could be responsible for differences greater than those between the actual and expected findings, especially when rare events are involved.

Inferences from Follow-up Studies

The aim of follow-up studies of mortality experience is to trace a sequence of events in time and endeavor to infer a cause and effect relationship between a particular condition or characteristic and the mortality experience. Sometimes multiple factors may be analyzed. The first step is to decide whether the observed mortality does, in fact, represent a real and significant departure from normality, and to estimate the magnitude of the extra mortality involved. The fundamental consideration, however, is to judge what factor or factors have been primarily responsible for the extra mortality observed.

The most serious pitfall to be avoided is that of attributing a causal relationship between events which are merely associated in time. Another major difficulty lies in the assessment of the interplay between the hypothesized causal factors and in overlooking the influence of unknown or unsuspected factors. It is necessary to bear in mind that positive findings may be spurious and negative findings may be misleading. Particular caution is in order with respect to positive correlations merely because negative correlations tend to go unreported.

The term *causal relationship* has different connotations for different people. The question in follow-up studies is to judge whether the observed higher mortality among individuals with certain characteristics can be largely attributed to those characteristics. A high degree of association between increased mortality and the characteristics does not of itself establish the existence of a causal relationship. Such a relationship requires not only a finding of consistent, strong and specific association, but also other evidence, such as a plausible biological mechanism. Alternative explanations of the relationship must be given due consideration. If the relationship is reproduced under different circumstances, and if it disappears when the characteristics under study are modified or eliminated, the argument for a causal relationship is strengthened.

The multiplicity of influences that affect mortality makes it very difficult to make the judgment that a particular set of characteristics is mainly responsible for the variation observed. This is because it is usually impracticable to control all the factors other than the one under study. In addition to numerous biological factors, including genetic traits, with which this monograph is basically concerned, the mortality observed in the follow-up studies here discussed has also been subject to the influence of socioeconomic status, diverse life styles, and environmental factors, to mention only the more important nonbiological factors at work.

To get around this fundamental difficulty, various types of matched pair analyses have been resorted to. In practice it has been feasible to control only the most important extraneous factors and to minimize the effect of other or unknown extraneous factors by assigning individuals to the test and control groups by some random process. In large scale prospective studies it has been possible to take account of a large number of factors ranging from family history, personal medical history, and physical condition to education, eating, drinking and smoking habits, and occupational exposure. Multiple factor analysis can obviously be carried much further when such detailed information is available. In both the Framingham and the American Cancer Society studies (§380, §40, §42) several multiple factor analyses were carried out. An even more powerful technique, matched group analysis, permits intensive exploration of the effects of strongly associated factors for groups of individuals in the presence of other factors on which information is available.[16]

Mortality studies and multiple factor analyses are invaluable in pointing up the characteristics which are statistically significant as possible causal factors. The real objective, however, is to uncover relationships which are biologically significant and not to rest with statistical associations.

References

1. E.W. Marshall, Jr., "The Interpretation of Mortality Statistics." *Trans. Act. Soc. Am.*, 33:74-91 (1932).

2. J. Larus, "The Interpretation of Mortality Statistics." *Proc. Home Office Life Und. Assoc.*, 18:7-20 (1939).

3. H.F. Dorn, "Methods of Analysis for Follow-up Studies." *Human Biol.*, 22:238-248 (1950).

4. P.E. Sartwell, "Retrospective Studies—A Review for the Clinician." *Ann. Int. Med.*, 81:381-386 (1974).

5. E.A. Lew, "Biostatistical Pitfalls in Studies of Athrosclerotic Heart Disease." *Fed. Proc.*, 21, Supp. (11):62-70 (1962).

6. A.C. Irwin, "Survivorship: The Estimation and Interpretation of Survival Experience." *Canad. Med. Assoc. J.*, 105:489-497 (1971).

7. V.A. Clark and C.E. Hopkins, "Time Is of The Essence." *J. Chron. Dis.*, 20:565-569 (1967).

8. "Socio-Economic Mortality Differentials." *Stat. Bull. Metropol. Life Ins. Co.*, 56:2-5 (January 1975).

9. E. Kitagawa and P.M. Hauser, "Educational Differentials in Mortality by Cause." *Demography*, 5:318-363 (1968).

10. E.C. Hammond, "Life Expectancy of American Men in Relation to Their Smoking Habits." *World Conference on Smoking*, (1967).

11. S.J. Cutler and F. Ederer, "Maximum Utilization of the Life Table Method in Analyzing Survival." *J. Chron. Dis.*, 8:699-712 (1958).

12. R.B. Singer, "Comparative Mortality—Keystone of Medical Selection." Presented at seminar sponsored by the Board of Life Insurance Medicine, Litchfield Park, Arizona (January 1973).

13. E.A. Lew and F. Seltzer, "Uses of the Life Table in Public Health." *Milbank Mem. Fund Quart.*, 48:15-37 (1970).

14. S.H. Preston, N. Keyfitz and R. Schoen, *Causes of Death—Life Tables for National Populations*. New York and London: Seminar Press (1972).

15. *Build and Blood Pressure Study 1959*. Chicago: Society of Actuaries (1960).

16. A.M. Mood et al., *Introduction to the Theory of Statistics*, 3rd ed. New York: McGraw-Hill and Co. (1974).

17. C.L. Chiang, *Introduction to Stochastic Processes in Biostatistics*. New York: John Wiley and Sons, Inc. (1968).

4

Physical, Toxic, and Other Risks
John C. Robinson, M.D.

The miscellaneous factors described in this chapter are divided into five categories: Addictions and Intoxications, Occupational Hazards, Environmental Risks, Family History, and Accidental and Other Risks. The abstracts falling under these categories have been assembled in Table 4-1, together with data on numbers of deaths occurring in the United States in 1970 from causes that have also been placed in these categories. It should be emphasized that mortality by cause of death in the general population frequently cannot be taken as an index of mortality in a particular risk factor, especially of types considered in this chapter. This is especially true of occupational diseases, environmental risks, cigarette smoking (which has arbitrarily been classified as an "environmental risk"), and family history of deaths or premature deaths due to a particular disease. A double asterisk has been used in Table 4-1 for the conditions just mentioned, and also for postsurgical mortality, to indicate that the condition is not listed among causes of death, and that deaths occurring in persons with such conditions present during life have been assigned to other causes and hence are listed elsewhere.

Approximately 140,000 deaths were reported in the United States during 1970 for the causes listed, and over 90 per cent were due to physical causes, various types of accidents, and homicide. Suicides, another type of death due to violence or poison, have been excluded from this chapter and are considered in a later chapter with mental disorders. Approximately 5,000 deaths are reported as due to alcoholism in Table 4-1. These do not include deaths classified as alcoholic cirrhosis; all cases of death attributed to cirrhosis are considered with other digestive tract diseases in Chapter 13. Alcoholism is the only example of the category of addiction and intoxication for which abstract data are available.

The previously mentioned difficulty in interpreting cause of death statistics is illustrated by occupational diseases, which are not listed as such in the list of causes. In such diseases the excess or total mortality is classified under other causes of death. For example, a patient with asbestosis has an occupational lung disease. If he dies of lung cancer, the death would be reported under that cause. If he dies of asbestosis, the death would be included with respiratory causes. Under existing methods of completing death certificates and compiling statistics by cause of death, there is no way of relating diverse causes to a particular category, such as occupational diseases.

In abstract §80 extensive data are presented for deaths occurring within six weeks postoperatively (postsurgical mortality); some of these might be listed as a separate cause of death under "Surgical and Medical Accidents." However, in the great majority of cases these deaths would come under the condition for which the operation was performed or some complication or intercurrent disease arising in the postoperative period.

A final point that should be made is the obvious one that accidental death is not a condition which can be made the subject of a follow-up study, using the accident as the starting point. Accidents and other forms of violence constitute collectively a most important cause of death, comprising about seven per cent of all deaths in the United States during 1970. However, their importance cannot be assessed through follow-up studies of the type considered in these abstracts. Accidental deaths do, however, appear in connection with occupational hazards in §20, and in various other abstracts where specific causes of death are presented.

Addictions and Intoxications

Alcoholism—Nature and Extent of the Problem. Alcoholics are excessive drinkers whose dependence upon alcohol has attained such a degree that it produces a noticeable mental disturbance or an interference with their bodily and mental health, their interpersonal relations, and their smooth social and economic functioning; or they are drinkers who show the prodromal signs of such development.[1] Alcoholism is a disease and as such merits the attention of all physicians.

The cause of alcoholism is not known, but psychologic and social factors are of great importance, including the following: the personality of the individual; the kind of alcoholic beverages consumed; the amount of alcohol consumed and the time of day during which the drinking takes place; the availability of the alcohol consumed; the attitude of the peer group toward drinking habits; and unexpected stress factors.[2] While many people drink alcohol regularly, only about 10 per cent of these people become sufficiently dependent upon it to become alcoholics.[3]

Alcoholism is regarded as one of the major problems of our time.[2] There are an estimated nine million alcoholics in the United States, about seven per cent of the entire adult population.[4] Out of 76,687 duPont employees, 922 were identified as known, suspected, or recovered alcoholics, a prevalence of 1.2 per cent (§1). Several studies suggest that

34

TABLE 4-1

Numbers of Deaths in the U.S. — 1970
Physical, Toxic and Other Causes

Hazard	Deaths in U.S. Number	% in Category	Follow-up Data
Addictions and Intoxications			
Alcoholism	4,923	(3.5%)	§1-§6
Occupational Hazards			
Accidents of Industrial Type	5,568	(3.9)	§20
Occupational Diseases	**		§20
Environmental Risks			
Environmental (Pollution)	**		—
Cigarette Smoking	**		§40-§42
Family History	**		§60, §61
Accidental and Other Risks (Excluding Suicide)	131,345	(92.6%)	
Accidental Poisoning	5,299	(3.7%)	—
Accidents, All Other	100,190	(70.7)	—
Homicide	16,848	(11.9)	—
Injuries, Other	5,427	(3.8)	—
Surgical and Medical Accidents	3,581	(2.5)	—
Post-Surgical Mortality	**		§80
Total (all listed in Cause of Death Statistics)	141,836	(7.4% of all deaths)	

**Listed elsewhere under various separate causes

serious understatement exists in the reporting of deaths associated with alcoholism.[5] In France, for example, it is said to be the third most important cause of death.[6] The death rate from alcoholic disorders, a more inclusive term than alcoholism, in 1964 approximated 8.7 per 100,000 population in the United States.[5]

Alcohol and the Liver. Alcohol is a protoplasmic poison. It acts as a central nervous system depressant but has many other pharmacological actions, both in small and acute intoxicating doses. In chronic abuse alcohol becomes an important source of energy (seven calories per gram); by oxidation and entry into the citric acid cycle it may contribute to the synthesis of body fat. It interferes with cellular metabolism.[7] There are myriad sequelae and complications of chronic alcoholism, many of which have been recently reviewed in a symposium reported in the *Annals of the New York Academy of Sciences*. Such complications include the following: fatty liver, alcoholic hepatitis and cirrhosis;[8,9] pancreatitis;[10] impairment of body defense mechanisms;[11] an increased risk of cancer of the head, neck, mouth, pharynx, esophagus and liver;[12] alcoholic heart disease (cardiomyopathy);[13,14] and increased risk associated with general anesthesia and surgery.[15] Mortality follow-up studies will be found in other parts of this volume on cirrhosis of the liver (Chapter 13), and alcoholic cardiomyopathy (Chapter 11). There are six abstracts that deal directly with mortality and survival experience among different groups of chronic alcoholics (§1-§6).

Alcoholism–Mortality. The various follow-up studies of alcoholism reported herewith include employees of a large chemical manufacturing company (§1), two groups of life insurance policyholders (§2, §3), a large group of clinic patients in Toronto (§4), and two groups of patients treated in a psychiatric hospital, one in South Africa (§5), and the other in Norway (§6). Severity is not easy to evaluate in chronic alcoholism, but it is perhaps reasonable to regard the life insurance series as including only less severe alcoholics (few severe ones would apply for insurance, and they would probably be refused insurance if they did apply). Patients hospitalized for the treatment of alcoholism were probably more severe, on the average, than the outpatients and the employees. On this basis the overall results of the six studies have been summarized in Table 4-2 with excess death rate as the measure of mortality, thus minimizing the effect of differences in age and sex composition, and entry period. The lowest levels of mortality were found in the two insurance series, with

TABLE 4-2

Mortality in Alcoholism — Results of Six Series

Abstract	Severity	Population	Ave. Age	Sex	Entry Date	Follow-up	Deaths	EDR*
§2	Least	Insured Lives	37	90% M	1940-1961	1-22 yrs	109	7.6
§3	Least	Insured Lives	42	100% M	1954-1970	1-17 yrs	73	5.5
§1	Moderate	Industrial	51	94% M	1964-1969	all 5 yrs	102	18
§4	Moderate	Clinic	45	83% M	1951-1963	1-13 yrs	738	9.5
§5	Most	Hospital	45	86% M	1959-1963	max. 7 yrs	90	19.4
§6	Most	Hospital-Discharge	<40	100% M	1925-1939	min. 23 yrs	1061	16.2

*EDR = excess death rate per 1000 per year

EDRs of 7.6 and 5.5 per 1000, respectively. The two series estimated to be the most severe alcoholics, because of the psychiatric hospital treatment, showed EDRs about three times as high—19 and 16 per 1000. The excess death rate was just as high, 18 per 1000, among the duPont employees, who included among their numbers both former and suspected alcoholics as well as those known to be alcoholics at the time of entry into the study. An intermediate EDR of 9.5 per 1000 was found in the Toronto clinic outpatients, but the authors acknowledge that mortality may have been underestimated through failure to determine deaths of patients who had left Canada prior to the date of the follow-up. Numbers of deaths ranged from 73 to 1,061, and all of the studies indicate a highly significant increased mortality risk.

Patterns of excess death rates in relation to age show an irregular tendency to higher rates at the older ages in four of the series, and a more consistent increase with advancing age in two of them (Tables 1a and 3a). There were only minor sex differences in EDR, although mortality ratios were higher among females (Tables 1a, 4a, 5a). EDR increased with duration in the Equitable Life series (Table 2a), but no consistent trend of EDR with duration was detected in comparing the other three series with experience reported by duration (Tables 3a, 5a, 6a). Excess mortality was distributed among major causes of death, including cardiovascular disease, cancer, deaths by violence, and cirrhosis (Tables 1c, 3c, 4c, 6d).

Other Addictions and Intoxications. Drug addiction apart from alcoholism has become a mounting public health problem in the past 15 to 20 years. Addicts are exposed to many unusual and potentially lethal risks, especially if they habitually take their drug by a parenteral mode of administration. Among the risks are fatal overdosage, severe hepatitis, overwhelming infection, and death by violence—accidental or by suicide or homicide. Unfortunately, reliable statistics are extremely difficult to collect, and the literature search for this volume failed to disclose any follow-up studies with useful mortality data. Hewitt and Milner have analyzed the recent trend in drug-related deaths in the United States.[16] They found a virtually constant death rate, about ten per million, from 1949 through 1958, followed by a consistent increase starting in 1959 and reaching 25 per million in 1967. It was their conclusion that changes in reporting procedures could not account for the increase in drug-related deaths, which they felt was sufficient to warrant the term "epidemic." Experimentation with drug use has become common in adolescents and young adults, but the resulting risk of addiction and the attendant risks of personal tragedy and premature death have not been measured, as far as it was possible to acertain.

Acute intoxications may be due to accidental exposure to toxic agents, such as carbon monoxide, or overdose of a drug, such as salicylate intoxication, a fairly common and often fatal therapeutic complication in young children. Some acute intoxications and chronic exposure to toxic substances, such as lead, may lead to serious medical complications with increased mortality risk. Sporadic cases of accidental exposure of this type are almost impossible to gather in numbers sufficient for a meaningful follow-up study. However, exposure on an occupational or environmental basis does provide opportunity for follow-up investigation, and these toxins are discussed later in the chapter. Some discussion of long-term effects of toxic substances may be found in monographs on toxicology, such as that of Hamilton and Hardy.[17]

Occupational Hazards

Background. Occupational hazards were as real to the primitive hunter as to the modern astronaut. The concept of occupational disease goes back to earliest civilization. The ancient Egyptians, Pliny the Elder, and Herodotus were aware of the influence of occupation on the health of workers.[18] Lead colic was known to Hippocrates, and Galen was familiar with diseases peculiar to chemists, miners, tanners, and other occupations of his day. Bernardino Ramazzini (1633-1714), the first great student of occupational disease, exhorted the Italian physicians of his day always to take a detailed occupational history whenever they had a case of illness in a working man.[17,18] Lack of general interest in this field prior to the early years of the present century has been replaced by the development of occupational medicine as an active subspecialty of preventive medicine and by increasing legislative activity to safeguard and protect the health of the worker at his place of employment. Occupational medical programs, sponsored by management, government or a labor union, are now so varied and numerous that they have an impact on the health of almost all employees in relation to their work.[19]

A major objective of occupational medicine is to prevent and deal constructively with work-related accidental injury and disease. Occupational injury is defined as an injury arising out of, and in the course of employment, resulting from the action of physically or chemically traumatizing agents at the work place. Occupational disease is a disease arising out of, and in the course of, employment, resulting from the exposure to, the absorption of, or intoxication from, harmful chemicals, microbiologic or physical agents to which the general public would not normally be exposed.[19] As previously explained, occupational diseases are not given a distinctive heading in the mortality statistics which form the basis of Table 4-1, but are scattered among other causes of death. Accidents of industrial type, causing 5,568 deaths during 1970, were responsible for about five per cent of the total of 120,065 accidental deaths for that year, excluding suicide and homicide (Table 4-1). Unsafe conditions of work always require vigilant attention in an effort to reduce accidental death and injury. The best way to deal with this is through a health and safety team approach, involving cooperation of the physician with safety engineers, toxicologists, occupational nurses, and hygienists.[19]

Mortality by Occupation. An overview of comparative mortality in many occupational groups is afforded by the most recent life insurance experience, to which 17 companies contributed data on men 20 to 59 years of age, issued insurance during 1949 to 1963 and followed between 1954 and 1964. Results of the *1967 Occupational Study* have been partially abstracted in Tables 20a and 20b for workers in 44 separate occupational categories. There was a rather wide range in average age at issue of insurance, from 26 to 42 years (Table 20a). Excess total mortality was of relatively modest proportions, less than 1.5 deaths per 1000 per year, in a majority of occupations shown. Accidental death rates were relatively high in some occupations, such as lumbering, in which those engaged in this occupation experienced 32 accidental deaths (excluding motor vehicle accidents) against 3.2 expected, with an excess death rate of 1.8 per 1000 (Table 20b). However, the accidental excess death rates were quite low, under 0.5 per 1000, in many occupations. This was true, not only for occupations wherein low rates might be expected, such as the chemical industry, but in other occupations for which more excess mortality would be anticipated. One example of such low rates were EDRs of only 0.3 per 1000 for motor vehicle accidents and 0.2 per 1000 for all other accidents among truck drivers. Motor vehicle accidental deaths have been excluded from other accidental deaths in the left-hand part of Table 20b in some occupations.

The right-hand portion of Table 20b has been reserved for two additional causes of death, selected as being of greatest interest from the standpoint of comparative mortality and varying from one occupation to another. Most of these concern major categories of disease such as cardiovascular or cancer, but others relate to less common causes such as respiratory diseases, or motor vehicle accidents, where these have been excluded from other accidental deaths. Some of these causes probably represent occupational hazards, such as respiratory diseases among miners, who have a high incidence of pneumoconioses and other associated hazards, such as cirrhosis of the liver among those involved in the handling and serving of liquor. These patterns of mortality are also of potential interest from the viewpoint of either the presence or absence of excess mortality in major causes of death. To illustrate, excess mortality due to cardiovascular diseases is unusually high among railroad engineers and conductors, but fewer coronary deaths than expected were found in men working in diverse occupations connected with shipping. The excess death rate for cancer was very small, 0.1 per 1000, in those working in the chemical industry, which has for some time been suspected as being a rich source of exposure to chemical products possessing potential carcinogenic properties. For additional details and discussion the reader is referred to the abstract or the published study, which also has a bibliography.

Occupational diseases have manifold causes and clinical manifestations. Sometimes the cause is readily apparent, such as poisoning in mercury miners. At other times it is less obvious, such as necrosis of the jaw in those engaged in the manufacturing of matches. As "phossy jaw" is slow to develop and as phosphorous affects only a small number of people exposed, many years elapsed before the cause was recognized.[7] Only recently was polyvinyl chloride linked to angiosarcoma of the liver. Infrared radiation from hot glass or metals may take up to 25 years to produce cataracts in the eyes of glass-blowers, bottle-workers, and chain-makers.[7] The lung is a frequent site of involvement for a great many occupational diseases, including silicosis, due to silicon dioxide inhalation by miners, quarrymen, stone masons and sand blasters; coal workers' pneumoconiosis (CWP), and other types of pneumoconiosis in those exposed to talc, kaolin, and other silicate compounds; asbestosis, a special type of lung disease due to a special type of silicate product; occupational asthma; industrial bronchitis; byssinosis, a disease of spinners, weavers, and others exposed heavily to the fibers of cotton, linen, and flax; pneumonitis due to a variety of toxic gases; and cancer due to exposure to a great many different substances, such as asbestos, radioactive trace elements associated with the mining of uranium and various metals, or in the production of arsenic, coal gas, and printing ink.[20] A brief discussion of some of these diseases is given in Chapter 12.

Follow-up studies have been carried out to investigate mortality in various occupational groups. A recent example is a study by McMichael, Spirtas, and Kupper on a cohort of 6,678 male rubber workers (tire manufacturing).[21] Although an overall mortality ratio of only 93 per cent was found for the actively employed workers under age 65 at entry into the study, higher mortality ratios were found for certain cases of death such as cancer of the stomach (219 per cent), and leukemia (315 per cent). For a more extensive discussion of occupational diseases the reader is referred to two of the monographs previously cited.[19,20]

Recent legislation has created the National Institute of Occupational Health and Safety, and the present trend is for expanded research into causes and methods of prevention of occupational diseases. Safety measures may be costly to enforce and may even have the effect of closing a plant, with economic hardship to the worker and the community. Where medical knowledge is incomplete great dispute is apt to arise over the importance of suspected occupational health hazards. Research, legislation, regulation, and worker attitudes are all important in future developments in occupational health. The importance of legislation justifies a brief review of the principal developments in the United States.

Along with a lack of interest by physicians in occupational medicine, little was done to safeguard the worker until 1907 when the Hours of Service Act was passed. This act specified hours and conditions of work for railroad train employees and telegraph and signal operators. In 1910 the Bureau of Mines was created. In 1911 Illinois passed a law providing compensation for industrial diseases caused by poisonous fumes, gases, and dusts, and requiring monthly examinations of workers in industries using lead, zinc, arsenic, brass, mercury and phosphorous. In 1913 the United States Department of Labor was established to foster, promote, and develop the welfare of wage earners. By 1940 workmen's compensation statutes of one sort or another were in effect in 47 of the then 48 states.

The Federal Coal Mine and Safety Act became law in 1969 giving the Bureau of Mines, the Secretary of Health, Education, and Welfare, and the National Institute of Occupational Safety and Health Board expanded powers to set standards for dust control with enforcement authority, and to set standards for work conditions that might affect the health of miners including accidents, noise control and sanitation.

The Williams-Steiger Occupational Safety and Health Act was passed in 1970 with the purpose of assuring so far as possible every working man and woman in the country safe and healthful working conditions and to preserve our human resources. The administration and enforcement of the act are vested primarily with the Secretary of Labor and the Occupational Safety and Health Review Commission. Research and review functions are vested in the Secretary of Health, Education, and Welfare. It also created the National Institute of Occupational Safety and Health which is responsible for research into the detection, cause, control and treatment of occupational disorders.

Environmental Risks

In this section an overview of hazards outside the work environment will be presented, followed by a further discussion of the risk associated with one specific type of inhaled air pollution created by personal choice, namely, tobacco smoking. Deaths associated with smoking, as with other environmental and occupational risk factors, are not listed as such in published statistics, but are divided among other causes.

With respect to respiratory hazards, at the workplace the emphasis is on providing an environment as free as possible from pollutants. Beyond this are legal requirements with respect to specific hazards with which the employer must comply. For instance, each new coal mine worker must have a chest X-ray and any miner who subsequently shows evidence of pneumoconiosis shall have the option of a transfer to another position in the mine operation with less exposure.[22] Asbestos and other workers must be watched for evidence of reaction to dust exposure. Where there is exposure to known carcinogens, the employer must, at his expense, make available periodic examinations including specific diagnostic tests.

Despite all this attention paid to hazards in the work environment, in the United States alone each year we put into the atmosphere 25 million tons of sulfur oxides, 15 million tons of hydrocarbons, 8 million tons of nitrogen oxides, and 2 million tons of other miscellaneous gases, vapors, and solids.[23] Of this 50 million tons of pollutants, 60 per cent comes from transportation, 19 per cent from industry, 12 per cent from power generation, 6 per cent from space heating, and 3 per cent from refuse incineration.

Pollution extends to other areas of the environment as well as the air: to the food that we eat (insecticide contamination in the plant food chain, heavy metal concentration in the sea food chain); to the water that we drink (sewage and industrial contamination, not adequately treated); and in one sense abuse of drugs and medications can be regarded as a kind of pollution.

It is known that we all absorb lead, asbestos, pesticides, and many other potentially toxic and even mutagenic chemicals without even being aware of their presence in our environment.[24] DDT, dieldrin, and other halogenated hydrocarbons can be stored apparently harmlessly in body fat, only to become potentially fatal if suddenly released during various forms of physiological stress such as pregnancy, lactation, starvation, intoxication, acute infection, and other disturbances.[24]

We are a nation of pill poppers. Valium has been reported as the largest selling drug on the commercial market, comprising 4 per cent of all new prescriptions and refills, a total of 3 billion tablets in 1974. Not only is the widespread use of prescription and nonprescription drugs an environmental hazard of itself, other constituants of the environment can react with certain drugs in an entirely unexpected way. DDT and parathion interfere with the action of certain drugs such as inhibiting the hypnotic action of barbiturates or enhancing and prolonging the action of other drugs.[25]

Some environmental hazards constitute a threat to the unborn fetus. If a pregnant woman is exposed to mercury, as in contaminated fish, she may or may not become ill, but her fetus is at great risk.[26] A classic example of the unsuspected effects of mercury poisoning from factory waste is that of "Minamata disease," in which disabling or fatal mercury poisoning occurred in residents in Minamata, Japan, who ate contaminated fish as a principal article of their diet.[27]

Environmental quality and protection have developed into political and economic issues as well as a health problem. The medical literature is extensive and the reader who is interested can find abundant source material in "Selected References on Environmental Quality as It Relates to Health," a monthly bibliography published by the National Library of Medicine.

Finally we come to the problem of tobacco smoke. Its effects on smokers will be the next topic discussed, but mention should be made of its effects on nonsmokers. One study has been made of the influence of tobacco smoke on the indoor atmosphere of cars, rest rooms, submarines, and other confined places.[28] It was shown that the sidestream smoke of a cigarette actually contains a greater concentration of hazardous toxins than the mainstream smoke from the butt end as puffed by the smoker. It was further found that while the respiratory uptake of carbon monoxide and nicotine was lower in the nonsmokers than the smokers, the carboxyhemoglobin levels in the nonsmokers approached 3 per cent in some instances, a level at which subtle perceptual alterations occur. Nonsmokers have become increasingly vocal in protest against the annoyance and possible hazard of exposure to the cigarette smoking of others in public places. The result has been a growing tendency to set aside separate areas for nonsmokers in restaurants, aircraft, and other public facilities.

Smoking of Tobacco—Background. In this discussion smoking refers to the smoking of tobacco. While the focus will be on cigarette smoking, pipe and cigar smoking are also included. The habitual use of tobacco is related primarily to psychological and social drives, reinforced and perpetuated by the pharmacological actions of nicotine. The start of the habit is largely determined by psychological and social factors.

In 1964 it was reported that 70 million persons in the United States, including overseas members of the Armed Forces, consumed tobacco on a regular basis. In 1962 the per capita consumption of tobacco was almost 11 pounds; the per capita consumption of cigarettes was 3,958, cigars 55, and pipe tobacco 0.6 pounds. An additional 0.8 pounds per capita was consumed as chewing tobacco and snuff. About 1950 the production of filter tip cigarettes began to increase and by 1962, 55 per cent of all cigarettes manufactured in the United States were filter tipped. These and other data in this chapter, as well as the mortality results in abstract §41 have been taken from the landmark report, *Smoking and Health,* prepared by the Advisory Committee to the Surgeon General of the Public Health Service and published in 1964.[29]

Tobacco was introduced into Spain and England early in the sixteenth century by explorers returning from the New World. Even then questions arose as to whether tobacco consumption was good for the health, bad for the health, or had no effect on the health.[29] In 1604, King James I of England is quoted as saying that smoking was "barbarous, beastly, hateful to the nose, a vile and stinking custom, harmful to the brain and dangerous to the lungs."[29] Kassel has reported on various penalties invoked in the past on smokers.[30] Tobacco smoking in Japan was forbidden by the state in 1603 and, when that did not stop the habit, it was further decreed in 1612 that anyone caught even selling tobacco would have all his property confiscated. The Sultan of Turkey introduced the death penalty for smoking in 1633. At about the same time the penalty in Russia for smoking was a beating and banishment to Siberia. Decapitation was the penalty for selling tobacco in China in 1638. During the seventeenth century to smoke in church was to risk excommunication. Smoking in public was prohibited in Germany until 1848. Early in the present century opposition movements to the consumption of tobacco began to appear. Even at that time cancer, among other things, was attributed to the use of tobacco.

Composition of Cigarette Smoke. Cigarette smoke is a heterogeneous mixture of gases, uncondensed vapors, and liquid particulate matter.[29] In the investigation of chemical composition and biological properties, it is necessary to deal separately with the particulate phase and the gas phase.

In the particulate phase is found the alkaloid nicotine. Nicotine is rapidly changed in the body to relatively inactive substances allegedly of low toxicity, but these substances have been implicated in the development of atherosclerosis.[29] Seven polycyclic compounds isolated from this phase of tobacco smoke have been established as being carcinogenic.[29] The particulate phase also contains many other compounds including some that may be cocarcinogens, as the carcinogenic potency of tobacco tar is many times greater than any of the substances isolated from it.[29]

The gas phase of cigarette smoke accounts for 60 per cent of the total.[29] Nitrogen makes up 73 mole per cent of the total gases, oxygen and carbon dioxide about 10 mole per cent each, carbon monoxide 4, hydrogen 1, argon and methane 0.6 mole per cent each, with the remaining 0.8 mole per cent made up of trace amounts of numerous other gases, 43 of which have been identified.[29] Components of gas phase of cigarette smoke have been shown to produce various undesirable effects, one of which is suppression of ciliary activity in the trachea and bronchi.[29]

Smoking and Morbidity. Passive smoking, exposure to smoke by nonsmokers, results in an increased incidence of respiratory ailments in children.[28] Respiratory disease continues to be not only the leading cause of absenteeism in industry, but also the major factor in disability benefit payments according to a recent report by Athenason.[31] The prevalence of respiratory disease rises distinctly in smokers as opposed to nonsmokers. In one study, 40 per cent of the smokers and only 28 per cent of the nonsmokers reported respiratory diseases as the cause of work inability lasting longer than one shift. A study of 268 Boston policemen demonstrated that only 15 per cent of the subjects who had never smoked had respiratory disease compared with 60 per cent of subjects who smoked more than 35 cigarettes daily. The relationship between smoking and respiratory disease has also been demonstrated in a survey of 418 men at the Western Electric Company in New Jersey, 1,443 New Zealand public servants, 3,395 Polish textile workers, and 340 cases of disabling bronchitis in a Sheffield, England, steelworks. All of these studies are described by Athenason.[31]

Starting in July 1964 the National Center for Health Statistics of the Public Health Service introduced questions on cigarette smoking into its National Health Survey. From this source morbidity information was included in the 1967 Public Health Service Report on Smoking.[32] The morbidity ratio of days lost from work among smokers as compared with nonsmokers was 135 per cent among men and 140 per cent among women in the 17 to 44 age group. In the 45 to 64 age group the morbidity ratio among male smokers was 150 per cent and 130 per cent among the females. Similar ratios were noted for restricted activity days and bed days among men and women cigarette smokers at the younger ages. However, in the female age group 45 to 64, the morbidity ratio for the smokers was only 110 per cent for both restricted activity days and bed days.

Smoking and Mortality. Numerous follow-up studies have been reported on large groups of men and women in relation to their habits with respect to the smoking of tobacco. Results of seven studies of a total of more than one million male smokers were carefully compiled and presented in the 1964 Public Health Service Report.[29] These results form the basis for abstract §41, while two reports by Hammond have been used in abstracts §40 and §42. The latter reports concern the very large prospective study on adults age 35 up, sponsored by the American Cancer Society, the earlier one giving results on male smokers only (§40), while the 1966 report also furnished mortality results among female smokers (§42).

Table 41b presents mortality data among males taken from the 1964 Public Health Service Report. Among the seven groups studied, the overall mortality ratios of actual to expected deaths among cigarette smokers (one pack a day or more) ranged from a low of 144 per cent to a high of 199 per cent. For those who smoked 40 or more cigarettes a day, the ratios were 250 per cent for one group and 220 per cent for three others (Table 41a). Among Canadian veterans who smoked 21 or more cigarettes a day, the mortality ratio was 184 per cent.

Table 40a gives the comparative three-year experience of male smokers versus nonsmokers from the American Cancer Society Study. The mortality ratio of deaths among smokers of cigarettes only to deaths among nonsmokers was 167 per cent, all ages combined. For those smoking 40 or more cigarettes a day, the mortality ratio was 191 per cent. The mortality ratio for men who smoked pipes or cigars, but not cigarettes, was only 107 per cent. Comment is also made in the text that mortality ratios tended to decrease and excess death rates to increase with advancing age. Table 40c gives the three-year experience of cigarette smokers against the mortality among matched controls, in an effort to eliminate extraneous risk factors. Here the overall mortality ratio among cigarette smokers as compared with nonsmokers was 210 per cent, with an excess death rate of 6.6 per 1000.

The 1967 Public Health Service report states that women who smoke cigarettes show significantly elevated death rates over those who have never smoked regularly.[32] On the other hand, death rates for women smokers are noted to be lower than for male smokers whether measured by numbers of cigarettes smoked, duration of smoking or degree of inhalation. Similar results are detailed in Tables 42b and 42c, based on the American Cancer Society Study as reported by Hammond.

Tables 40e and 40g also give information relative to cause-specific mortality. In Table 40e mortality ratios among smokers were especially high for cancer of the lung, mouth and throat, larynx and esophagus. They were also at high risk for emphysema. The text comments on the fact that excess deaths from coronary artery disease were closely correlated with smoking in the middle-aged groups. In Table 40g the cause-specific mortality ratio for lung cancer among cigarette smokers was 1,080 per cent and for bronchitis and emphysema 610 per cent. Other sites with high ratios were cancer of the larynx, 535 per cent, and buccopharyngeal cancers, 410 per cent.

In conjunction with this description of experience among smokers, in terms of mortality results and causes of death, it might be of interest to translate some of these figures into life expectancies. Hammond, who has contributed so much to our knowledge of mortality in relation to smoking, has done just this, utilizing the data of the American Cancer Society Study.[33] For men who never smoked regularly the mean length of life remaining at age 35 was 42.4 years. This was cut to 37.8 years for those who smoked 1-9 cigarettes a day, 37.1 years for those who smoked 10-19 cigarettes, 36.5 years for those who smoked 20-39 cigarettes, and 34.7 for those who smoked over 40 cigarettes a day, a reduction in life expectancy of 7.7 years for this latter group. Cigarette smokers who started smoking between the ages of 25 to 34 had a life expectancy at age 35 of 38.8 years, those starting the habit between ages 20 to 24 an expectancy of 37.7 years, those who started between the ages 15 to 19 an expectancy of 36.0 years, those who started smoking before age 15 a life expectancy of 34.6 years, a reduction of 7.8 years of life for those in the last category.

The results in abstract §42 are devoted primarily to the experience among female cigarette smokers compared with non-smoking females and male cigarette smokers. It is obvious that female smokers enjoy a more favorable mortality than their male counterparts in all age groups and all degree-of-smoking groups. The overall mortality ratio, all ages combined, for women smokers compared with women nonsmokers was 121 per cent, while male smokers compared with male nonsmokers produced a ratio of actual to expected of 182 per cent. Mortality ratios among both males and females showed pronounced increases as the number of cigarettes smoked and the degree of inhalation increased, and as age of onset of smoking decreased (Table 42c).

Excess mortality in many types of cancer, referred to previously, also extends to most other causes of death in cigarette smokers—cause of death data in the various series described are consistent on this. Mortality ratios by specific cause, smokers vs. nonsmokers, are given in Table 40e for two age groups, 40 to 69 and 70 to 89 years, in which the ratios for total deaths, all causes, are 174 and 131 per cent, respectively. These mortality ratios are relative indices, of course, and do not bring out the magnitude of the absolute and excess death rates by cause. Cancer of the lung not only shows the highest mortality ratio of all forms of cancer, but is also the most important from the public health standpoint, because of the total number of deaths involved. For smokers in the 40 to 69 year age range, following lung cancers, the highest mortality ratios (350 per cent or more) resulted from cancers of the mouth and throat, larynx and esophagus. A "middle risk" group ranging from 185 to 349 per cent included leukemia and cancers of the bladder and pancreas. The rate for all cancers among men under 70 was 198 per cent. Among the older men, the overall ratio was slightly lower (175 per cent) and more favorable results were experienced in mouth and throat cases and in leukemia. The principal cancers with mortality ratios under 100 per cent were those of the colon and rectum and prostate, and the malignant lymphomas. There were 65,168 deaths from lung cancer in the United States during 1970, about 20 per cent of all cancer deaths and 3.3 per cent of total deaths for that year. A final point of interest with respect to lung cancer is the apparent synergistic action of cigarette smoking and asbestosis in producing extremely high increases in the death rate from lung cancer.

Of the various noncancer causes of death showing increased mortality ratios in Table 40e, coronary heart disease is of particular importance because of the high rate in the nonsmoking population and the large numbers of deaths involved. A causal mechanism has not been established for this association as it has in the case of lung cancer. Nicotine absorbed from the tobacco smoke may cause an increase in the myocardial tissue demand for oxygen, and it is known that patients with clinically silent coronary heart disease may be unusually susceptible to the adverse physiological effects of smoking.[29] A minority of patients with angina pectoris are reported in whom smoking precipitates an attack, so-called "tobacco angina."[35]

Although numbers of deaths are not so large, mortality ratios are in the middle risk classification, about 200 per cent, in pneumonia and "other" lung disorders, and extremely high, second only to lung cancer, in emphysema (Table 40e). Emphysema as a cause of death here undoubtedly includes what is now called chronic obstructive pulmonary disease, described in Chapter 12. Many investigators have shown the adverse effects of smoking on pulmonary function tests, on inhibiting ciliary transport in the trachea and bronchi, and on producing small airway obstruction through spasm, mucus production, and consequent disease. Chronic cough, sputum production, and chronic bronchitis are usually found in heavy smokers rather than nonsmokers. Chronic obstructive pulmonary disease is another area in which a causal mechanism for the lethal effects of cigarette smoking has been clearly established.

Family History

Genetic disorders may occur in any of the major disease categories. With the development of methods of chromosome analysis in human cells in process of fission, knowledge in this field of medicine has greatly expanded over the past 20 years. The number of proven genetic diseases is now so large that no review can be attempted in this chapter, although a few examples will be cited. The chief emphasis here is on the influence of family longevity or family history on mortality, regardless of any genetic evidence, which has not been established in major disease categories such as cancer and coronary heart disease.

Genetic disorders may involve manifestations that are obvious at birth, or do not appear until a later age, or never appear if a trait is involved which is detectable only by special screening tests in an otherwise healthy person. The prevalance of genetic diseases as a group is hard to estimate, and the same is true of deaths attributable to them. The closest approach available is through the category "Congenital Anomalies," which accounted for 16,824 deaths in the United States during 1970. However, some congenital diseases are acquired in utero and are not genetically determined. Other genetic disorders undoubtedly appear among the other cause of death categories. Congenital anomalies do not appear in Table 4-1 because they have been allocated to the appropriate disease categories discussed in later chapters. From the epidemiological viewpoint genetic diseases are collectively not well characterized at the present time.

One example of a genetic disease that has recently attracted a great deal of interest is sickle cell anemia, transmitted as an autosomal dominant defect of hemoglobin in the black population, with an estimated prevalence of about 0.2 per cent. Sickle cell anemia is considered to be a disease serious enough to result in reduced life expectancy. However, sickle cell trait has a much higher prevalence, about 10 per cent in the black population, ordinarily involves no signs or symptoms of any disease, and apparently is not associated with any increased mortality risk (unpublished data cited in a recent government report[36]). Examples of genetic disorders affecting various body systems are the following: nervous system—mongolism or Down's Syndrome (see §215); cardiovascular system—congenital heart block; lungs and respiratory system—cystic fibrosis (see §785); digestive system—glycogen storage disease (liver); genitourinary system—polycystic disease of the kidneys; skeletal, connective tissue and muscle systems—osteogenesis imperfecta, Marfan's Syndrome and peroneal muscular atrophy; endocrine system—gonadal dysgenesis (Turner's Syndrome); metabolic—phenylketonuria and a host of other inborn errors of metabolism, also called "molecular diseases." For additional information the reader is referred to standard medical texts and to monographs on genetic disorders.[37,38]

Mortality and Family Longevity. An excellent report by Hammond and others with respect to the extent of correlation between mortality rates and longevity of parents and grandparents utilized additional data from the epidemiological study of the American Cancer Society (see §40) and forms the basis for abstract §60. This involved a six-year follow-up of approximately 780,000 men and women in the age range 40 to 79 years for whom the age at death of parents and grandparents had been established by means of a detailed questionnaire. Subjects were excluded if both parents were still living and under age 70, but not otherwise. Age distribution is given in Table 60a, and distribution of cases by longevity class and ascertainable risk factors, including smoking history, in Table 60b. The range of percentage of subjects who smoked more than one pack of cigarettes per day was very small, from 29.8 to 32.9 per cent.

The longevity classes 1-7 were determined by family history of longevity of parents and grandparents, classes 1 and 2 having the longest lived antecedents and classes 6-7 the shortest. Classes 1-2, making up 15 per cent of the total, were the norms against which the mortality was measured (57.6 per cent were in classes 3-5 and 27.4 per cent in classes 6-7). Table 60c gives the comparative mortality experience by sex, age and longevity class, with classes 1-2 as the standard. In all age groups, both male and female, the longevity classes 3-5 had only a modest increase in mortality ratios ranging from 116 to 137 per cent, but there were higher ratios among classes 6-7, 141 to 182 per cent. Mortality ratios decreased with advancing age in male subjects, both classes 3-5 and 6-7, but not in females. Excess death rates increased with advancing age in both sexes, up to a maximum of 14 per 1000 in men age 65 to 74 in classes 6-7, and 8.9 per 1000 in the corresponding female group.

Table 60d presents the experience by cause of death subdivided into coronary deaths, other cardiovascular deaths, and noncardiovascular deaths. Among all groups outside the standard, male or female, mortality ratios for coronary deaths were generally higher than in the other cause of death categories and were highest at the younger ages, decreasing in each successive older age group. However, some excess mortality was observed in all categories for other cardiovascular and noncardiovascular causes of death. Excess death rates were also highest for coronary heart disease and increased by advancing age and longevity class for both sexes. The same trends are noted in Table 60e, which gives comparative male mortality due to coronary heart disease, for four age and three longevity groups through age 79. Table 60f demonstrates the effect of selection on death rates from coronary heart disease by comparing a selected population, free of the risk factors shown in Table 60b, with the majority having one or more risk factors. The effects of this selection, by questionnaire only, are especially striking in the youngest age group, 40 to 59 years, for whom the mortality ratio of unselected to selected mortality rates was 430 per cent. Again, mortality ratios decreased and excess death rates increased with advancing age.

Mortality and Family History. Table 61a gives the experience by duration among a group of male policyholders insured by the New York Life with a family history of two or more cardiovascular-renal deaths under age 60. The mortality ratios fall slightly from 186 per cent in the earliest interval to 162 per cent in the latest, with the excess death rate rising from 2.3 per 1000 in the earliest to 6.1 in the latest. From Table 61c we find that with this family history, combining all ages, the mortality ratio is essentially the same for both sexes, about 175 per cent, with an excess death rate of 3.3 per 1000 in men and 2.5 per 1000 in women. Mortality by cause of death, from Table 61d, is highest for diseases of the heart and circulatory system with a mortality ratio of actual to expected deaths from these causes of 285 per cent.

This experience of the New York Life Insurance Company may be compared with the older intercompany results, obtained from 1935 to 1950 and reported in the *1951 Impairment Study*.[39] With a similar family history of two or more cardiovascular-renal deaths under age 60 the mortality ratio, all ages and durations combined, was 141 per cent in those issued standard insurance and 185 per cent in those issued substandard insurance only because of the family history. The corresponding mortality ratios for deaths due to heart and circulatory diseases were 175 and 256 per cent, respectively. Mortality ratios found for other causes of death were 169 per cent in vascular lesions of the central nervous system, 196 per cent in diabetes, and 252 per cent in nephritis. Additional analysis of about one-third of the experience in the *1951 Impairment Study* demonstrated even higher mortality when there was a combination of the family history with other "minor impairments" considered not sufficient of themselves to justify a rating.[40] Borderline overweight and borderline blood pressure were the most common minor impairments. When these were present in combination with the family history of cardiovascular-renal disease the mortality ratio rose to 212 per cent, all causes, 263 per cent for diseases of heart and circulatory system, 258 per cent for vascular lesions of the central nervous system, and 478 per cent for nephritis. Among females with associated minor impairments the overall mortality ratio was not far from normal, but the ratio was 192 per cent for deaths due to vascular lesions of the central nervous system and 309 per cent for nephritis.

Two additional types of family history were evaluated in the *1951 Impairment Study*. With a family history of one or more cases of diabetes there was material increase in mortality for all causes combined, or for the causes cited above, except nephritis with a slightly elevated mortality ratio of 135 per cent. However, a mortality ratio of 182 per cent was found in deaths due to diabetes. In a relatively small group with a family history of two or more cancer deaths under age 60, the mortality ratio of deaths due to cancer was 206 per cent. However, there was no material increase in the total death rate, as the overall mortality ratio was only 106 per cent. The subject of genetic predictability of certain forms of cancer has been reviewed by Lynch,[41] and the subject is also discussed by McKusick.[37]

Accidental and Other Risks

Deaths due to homicide and nonindustrial accidental causes amounted to 6.9 per cent of all deaths in the United States during 1970 (Table 4-1). Homicide accounted for 16,848 of the 131,345 deaths leaving 114,497 accidental deaths. There were an additional 5,568 deaths due to accidents of an industrial type, shown elsewhere in Table 4-1. A more detailed accounting of the bulk of the accidental deaths shows that motor vehicle accidents accounted for 54,633 deaths, almost half of all accidental deaths. Other transportation categories were rather small, with 852 deaths in railway accidents, 1,651 in water transportation and 1,612 in air and space transport. There were 16,926 deaths by falls, 6,718 from fires, 6,391 from drowning, 2,753 from choking on food, and 2,406 from accidental discharge of a firearm. By their very nature most accidental deaths are unexpected and unpredictable and therefore do not lend themselves to follow-up studies. Psychological studies have been made to ascertain the characteristics of persons who have a history of repeated nonfatal accidents of a serious nature. Accidents do constitute a major cause of death, sufficiently so in young adults to product a slight hump in the curve of male mortality rates in the general population from about age 17 to about age 29 (the mortality rate actually decreases from about age 25 to about age 29). However, further analysis of accidents in general is outside the scope of this volume. For additional information the reader is referred to a monograph dealing with this subject, one of a series sponsored by the American Public Health Association.[42]

Table 4-1 shows that 3,581 accidental deaths were related to surgical or medical therapeutic or diagnostic procedures, and this brings us to the subject of surgical mortality, which is a type of risk that is well worth examining and defining. Any operation entails a risk of death, however small, and this depends on many factors, including the skill and judgment of the surgeon, the technical difficulty of the procedure, the anesthesia, the age, physical and mental status of the patient, the nature of the condition for which operation is performed, and postoperative complications. The practice of surgery transcends mere technical skill and a distinguishing characteristic of a surgeon is his ability to judge for or against an operation.[43, 44] In certain emergencies to delay operation may result in the inevitable death of the patient. However, most operations are elective in the sense that the surgeon is in a position to weigh the risks of operation and effects of not operating against the benefits that may be anticipated as the result of a successful operation. Such cost-benefit considerations are beginning to receive careful study from many aspects: the welfare of the patient (well-being, disability, morbidity and mortality risks), economics (costs of hospitalization, surgical care, and future medical care), limitations in medical manpower, planning the best use of limited resources, and epidemiological effects. With respect to surgery, questions of this kind have been raised by Bunker and Wennberg in a recent editorial in the *New England Journal of Medicine*.[45] The authors point out that the quality of surgical care remains unmeasured, that rates of certain types of elective surgery vary widely within states (surveys in Kansas and Vermont) and that operation rates in the United States are double those in England and Wales. They emphasize that discretionary operations carry a distinct and measurable risk of death, estimated to be roughly 0.5 per cent, on the basis of an overall current mortality of about 1.4 per cent for all operations in the United States. Better data are needed to weigh the risks, and better methods are needed to arrive at recommended standards of surgical care. The authors consider that there is strong evidence that some operations "are performed with a frequency in excess of documentable cost-benefit usefulness," and they ask how general this phenomenon is, and whether more operations lead to an actual increase in overall population mortality. Postsurgical mortality will therefore be the topic under consideration for the remainder of this chapter, utilizing the great mass of data collected in the Halothane Study, published in 1969.

Postsurgical Mortality. Halothane was introduced during the 1950s in the search for a nonexplosive general anesthetic agent. Some anesthetic agents have an adverse effect on the liver, and use of the bromosulphthalein retention, a liver function test, showed no more effect with halothane than with ether or cyclopropane, agents generally considered safe to use in the presence of liver damage, as chloroform is not.[46] However, hepatic damage following the use of halothane had been reported. As a result a subcommittee was set up in 1962 under the auspices of the Anesthesia Committee of the National Academy of Sciences-National Research Council. This subcommittee conducted a retrospective study on a sample of more than 800,000 operations performed from 1959 to 1962, with particular attention to mortality, anesthesia used, other patient and operative data, and the incidence of massive hepatic necrosis. Results were published in 1969 under the title of the National Halothane Study, and these results constitute the basis for abstract §80. The report is no longer in print, but a summary is available.[47] The results are of interest here not because of the data on anesthetic agent and hepatic necrosis (the incidence for which was extremely low), but because of the detailed data on postsurgical mortality.

In all of the tables except 80i mortality rates have been presented by sex, age group (0-9, 10-49, 50-59 years and 60 years up), patient status, all anesthetic agents combined. Operations were classed as "low," "moderate," and "high" risk, and generally results are given by individual operation only with all other factors combined. For the low-risk operations the surgery was also categorized as elective or emergency in character. It is important to understand that the six-weeks mortality includes *all* deaths occurring during and after operation within this period, regardless of cause. Operative deaths and anesthetic deaths are thus included, as are those due to postoperative complications, and deaths with the patient's disease as the underlying cause. The last is involved in much of the high mortality experienced in complex, high-risk operations required for difficult disease situations (advanced cancer, brain tumor, severe forms of congenital heart disease, and the like).

Average rates of mortality for low-risk operations, all ages combined, ranged from less than 1 to 16 per 1000 (Tables 80a-80b), with a general average rate, all 37 procedures combined, of 4.1 per 1000 in males and 2.9 per 1000 in females. There was an approximate nine-fold increase in these averages to the overall rates in 18 moderate-risk operations, 33 per 1000 in males and 27 per 1000 in females (Table 80e). There was a further increase to an average of 90 per 1000 for the 19 high-risk operations, both sexes combined (Tables 80f and 80h).

Emergency operations carried a higher mortality than elective operations in the best low-risk procedures (Table 80a). In all risk categories of operation, patients classified as poor risk had a much higher mortality than those classified as good risks, the differentials amounting to more than ten to one for the low-risk operations, and less than ten to one for the moderate and high-risk operations. With respect to age, the lowest rates were usually found in the age group 10 to 49 years, and rates increased in the older age groups, especially for ages 70 up. Children under age ten generally had mortality rates somewhat higher than those in the 10 to 49 age group. Mortality rates in males were generally found to be slightly higher than in females.

If we examine the male mortality rates for the low-risk operations in Table 80c, we find that the better risk patients age 0 to 9 years have a rate of 1.4 per 1000, those age 10 to 49, a rate of 0.9 per 1000, those age 50 to 69, a rate of 5.4 per 1000, and those age 70 up a rate of 19 per 1000. This illustrates the progression of mortality rate with advancing age and highlights the magnitude of the risk in older patients even in good physical status, relative to lower rates at younger ages. The mortality for all ages of better risk male patients was 2.6 per 1000; this increased to 42 per 1000 in poor risk patients, and 252 per 1000 in those classified as extreme risk (designated moribund in the protocol). Very few operations were carried out with the patient in such desperate straits, and the reasons for the high mortality are understandable. In general, a similar type of progression is seen in females, and in the other operation groups presented in Tables 80a, 80e, 80f, and 80h. With respect to the four high-risk operations in Table 80f it should be noted that there has been a substantial reduction in early mortality in open-heart surgery since 1962, the end of the period of collection of these data.

It would be of interest to know how these deaths were divided into categories such as operative deaths, anesthesia deaths, postoperative complications, and underlying disease or physical status, but such information was not reported. However, postsurgical mortality rates such as those abstracted in these tables from the Halothane Study, periodically updated, should be of great value in cost-benefit evaluations designed to aid the surgeon.

For an overview of what is new and changing in anesthesia the reader is referred to a symposium on this topic in the August, 1975 issue of *Surgical Clinics of North America.*[48] Anesthesia deaths have recently been reviewed by Cole.[49]

References

1. World Health Organization, *Expert Committee on Mental Health, Alcoholism Subcommittee,* Second Report. Geneva: WHO Technical Reports Services, No. 48 (August 1952).

2. G.A.R. Lundquist, "Alcohol Dependence—Its Course and Complications." In *Proc. 9th Inter. Cong., Life Assur. Med.,* (Tel-Aviv). Basel/New York: Karger (1968), pp. 269-276.

3. E.T. Lisansky, "Alcoholism, The Avoided Diagnosis." *Bull. Am. Coll. Physicians,* 15:18-24 (1974).

4. M.E. Chafetz, "The Crucial Challenge: Alcoholism and Prevention." *Prev. Med.,* 3:iii-iv (1974).

5. "Alcoholism: A Growing Medical-Social Problem." *Stat. Bull. Metropol. Life Ins. Co.,* 48:7-10 (April 1967).

6. J. Lereboullet, "Alcoolisme et Assurance Vie." *Proc. 9th Inter. Cong., Life Assur. Med.,* (Tel-Aviv). Basel/New York: Karger (1968), pp. 277-293.

7. F. Lundquist, "Interference of Ethanol in Cellular Metabolism." *Ann. N.Y. Acad. Sci.,* 252:11-20 (1975).

8. C.S. Lieber, "Liver Disease and Alcohol: Fatty Liver, Alcoholic Hepatitis, Cirrhosis, and Their Interrelationships." *Ann. N.Y. Acad. Sci.,* 252:63-84 (1975).

9. W.K. Lelbach, "Cirrhosis in the Alcoholic and Its Relation to the Volume of Alchol Abuse." *Ann. N.Y. Acad. Sci.,* 252:85-105 (1975).

10. H. Sarles, "Alcohol and the Pancreas." *Ann. N.Y. Acad. Sci.,* 252:171-182 (1975).

11. W.D. Johnson, Jr., "Impaired Defense Mechanisms Asscoiated with Acute Alcoholism." *Ann. N.Y. Acad. Sci.,* 252:343-347 (1975).

12. A.B. Lowenfels, "Alcoholism and the Risk of Cancer." *Ann. N.Y. Acad. Sci.,* 252:366-373 (1975).

13. G.D. Talbott, "Primary Alcoholic Heart Disease." *Ann. N.Y. Acad. Sci.,* 252:237-242 (1975).

14. R.M. Gunnar et al., "Clinical Signs and Natural History of Alcoholic Heart Disease." *Ann. N.Y. Acad. Sci.,* 252:264-272 (1975).

15. M.J. Orloff, "Surgical Consequences of Alcoholism." *Ann. N.Y. Acad. Sci.,* 252:159-169 (1973).

16. D. Hewitt and J. Milner, "Drug Related Deaths in the United States-First Decade of an Epidemic." *Health Services Rep.,* 89:211-218 (1974).

17. A. Hamilton and H. Hardy, *Industrial Toxicology,* 3rd ed. Acton, Massachusetts: Publishing Sciences Group, Inc. (1974).

18. D. Hunter, *Diseases of Occupations,* 5th ed. Boston: Little Brown & Co. (1975).

19. H.F. Howe, "Organization and Operation of an Occupational Health Program." *J. Occup. Med.,* 16:360-400 (1974).

20. W.K.C. Morgan and A. Seaton, *Occupational Lung Diseases.* Philadelphia: W.B. Saunders Co. (1975).

21. A.J. McMichael, R. Spirtas, L.L. Kupper, "An Epidemiologic Study of Mortality within a Cohort of Rubber Workers, 1964-72." *J. Occup. Med.,* 16:458-464 (1974).

22. I.R. Tabershaw, "Medical Criteria for Work in Respiratory Hazards." *J. Occup. Med.,* 16:402-405 (1974).

23. T.F. Malone, "The Future." Lecture at seminar sponsored by The Board of Life Insurance Medicine, Hartford, Connecticut (1966).

24. R. Dubos, "The Hidden Menace of Pollution." *Prism,* 2:49-53 (1974).

25. G. Bylinsky, "Tracking Down the Chemical Culprits that Endanger Man." *Prism,* 2:50-56 (1974).

26. "Medical News." *J. Am. Med. Assoc.,* 232:1105-1106 (1975).

27. I. Shigematsu, "Water Pollution and its Health Effects in Japan." *Ann. Life Ins. Med.,* 5:9-24 (1973).

28. I. Schmeltz, D. Hoffmann, E.L. Wynder, "The Influence of Tobacco Smoke on Indoor Atmospheres," *Prev. Med.,* 4:66-82 (1975).

29. Report of the Advisory Committee to the Surgeon General of the Public Health Service, *Smoking and Health*. Washington, D.C.: Dept. Health, Education, and Welfare, P.H.S. No. 1103 (1964).

30. V. Kassel, "The Penalty for Smoking." *J. Am. Med. Assoc.,* 227:941 (1974).

31. J.A. Athenason, "Sickness Absence and Smoking Behavior and Its Consequences." *J. Occup. Med.,* 17:441-445 (1975).

32. Advisory Committee to the Surgeon General of the Public Health Service, *The Health Consequences of Smoking— A Public Health Service Review: 1967,* Dept. Health, Education, and Welfare, P.H.S. No. 1696 (Rev. 1968).

33. E.C. Hammond, "Life Expectancy of American Men in Relation to Their Smoking Habits." *J. Nat. Cancer Inst.,* 42:951-962 (1969).

34. I.J. Selikoff, J. Churg, and E.C. Hammond, "Asbestos Exposure and Neoplasia." *J. Am. Med. Assoc.,* 188: 22-26 (1968).

35. G.D. Friedman, A.B. Siegelaub, and L.G. Dales, "Cigarette Smoking and Chest Pain." *Ann. Int. Med.,* 83:1-7 (1975).

36. Ad Hoc Committee on S-hemoglobinopathies, *The S-hemoglobinopathies: An Evaluation of Their Status in the Armed Forces.* Washington, D.C.: National Academy of Sciences—National Research Council (1973).

37. V.A. McKusick, *Mendelian Inheritance in Man*, 4th ed. Baltimore: Johns Hopkins University Press (1975).

38. D.Y. Hsia, *Inborn Errors of Metabolism.* Part I and II, 2nd ed. Chicago: Year Book Publishers, Inc. (1966).

39. *1951 Impairment Study.* Chicago: Society of Actuaries (1954).

40. A.P. Morton, "Family History of Cardiovascular-Renal Disease." *Trans. Soc. Actuaries*, 7:391-396 (1955).

41. H.T. Lynch, "Genetic Predictability in Certain Forms of Cancer." *Trans. Assoc. Life Ins. Med. Dir. Am.,* 55: 172-191 (1951).

42. A.P. Iskrant and P.V. Joliet, *Accidents and Homicide.* American Public Health Association Monograph. Cambridge, Massachusetts: Harvard University Press (1968).

43. C.B. Ernst, "Surgery, The Abused Word." *Surg. Gynecol. Obstet.,* 140:608 (1975).

44. L.B. Pemberton, "Value of the Decision Not to Operate." *Surg. Gynecol. Obstet.,* 135:608-609 (1972).

45. J.P. Bunker and J.E. Wennberg, "Operation Rates, Mortality Statistics and the Quality of Life." *New Eng. J. Med.,* 289:1249-1251 (1973).

46. L.S. Goodman and A. Gilman, *The Pharmacological Basis of Therapeutics*, 4th ed. New York: The MacMillan Co. (1970).

47. Subcommittee on The National Halothane Study, "Summary of the National Halothane Study." *J. Am. Med. Assoc.,* 197:775-788 (1966).

48. H. Wollman and D.E. Greenhow, eds., "Symposium on Recent Developments in Anesthesia." *Surg. Clin. N. Am.,* 55:757-1015 (1975).

49. F. Cole, "Are Anesthesia Deaths Mistakes?" *Surg. Gynecol. Obstet.,* 140:765 (1975).

5

Cancer

Edward A. Lew, F.S.A., and Richard B. Singer, M.D.

Nature of Cancer

Cancer is the generic term for a group of diseases characterized by an uncontrolled growth of abnormal cells which invade and destroy adjacent tissues and may be carried into blood or lymph vessels to set up new foci of abnormal cells (metastases). In addition to solid tumors which originate in specific tissues or organs, there are hematological and lymphatic malignancies such as the leukemias, Hodgkin's disease, and lymphosarcomas. Cells of any tissue or organ can become cancerous and yet retain their original characteristics so that more than a hundred related but unique forms of cancer have been distinguished.

Mortality from cancer has usually been analyzed with respect to the location of the primary site, age, and sex. There are, however, also distinctive patterns in the mortality from cancer according to the type of tissue involved. Cancers of muscle, bone, cartilage, and the connective tissues are called sarcomas and are derived from the embryonic mesoderm. Sarcomas occur at any age, but often arise in young people; they are transmitted by way of the blood vessels, grow very rapidly, and are extremely destructive. Cancers of the blood-forming system (leukemia), the lymphomas, and multiple myeloma are related to the sarcomas. The most common forms of cancer—carcinomas—arise from cells which line the body's internal and external surfaces and from glandular cells, all of ectodermal origin. They occur generally past age 40, extend and metastasize preferentially in the lymph channels, and, as a rule, do not grow as rapidly as sarcomas. Their malignancy varies widely by site.

Cancer is described by Shimkin (Chapter 2 in Ackerman and del Regato[1]) as basically a disease of the cell that is transferred to the descendants of the cell, with distinguishing characteristics of autonomy and anaplasia. Autonomy is "the disregard of cancer for normal limitations of growth," and anaplasia refers to "loss of organization and of useful function, in which self-propagation of cells is carried out regardless of lack of appropriate function or damage to normal tissues and organs of the body."

Intensive research has elucidated evidence that many different causative factors are involved in the production of cancer in man and other animals. The evidence is insufficient to provide a detailed picture, but enough is known to indicate that cancers comprise a group of many different diseases with different causes, which may be genetic, external chemical, internal biochemical, hormonal, environmental, occupational, nutritional, or infectious (virus) in nature. Furthermore, immune mechanisms and host resistance are known to influence the spread of a cancer once initiated in the body.

Examples of causative factors that have been established through careful research are given by Shimkin and include the following: genetic factors observed in homogeneous strains of mice that develop a very high incidence of particular types of cancer; chemical carcinogenic agents, such as benzpyrene, other polycyclic hydrocarbons, estrogenic hormones, azo dyes, and other compounds, which, in appropriate dosage, produce cancers in experimental animals and man; substances such as asbestos and others involved in certain occupational cancers; radiation in the form of excessive sunlight. X-rays and other ionizing rays; viruses such as the one producing Rous sarcoma in chickens; parasites such as schistosoma, which may produce bladder cancer in man; and habits, such as regular cigarette smoking, which may result in lung cancer and other types of cancer in man.

Dimensions of Cancer as a Public Health Problem

More than a million persons are currently under medical care for cancer in the United States, according to the American Cancer Society.[2] During 1975 some 665,000 new cases of cancer (not including skin cancer, other then melanoma, or carcinoma in situ of the cervix) are likely to be diagnosed for the first time, and about 365,000 will die of this cause. On the average one in three cases so diagnosed is expected to be alive five years hence in 1980; about 1,500,000 Americans now living are without evidence of the disease at least five years after diagnosis and treatment.

The importance of cancer of the major sites is brought out by the figures in Table 5-1 (estimated 1975).

Cancer of the colon and rectum is the leading site for both sexes (almost 100,000 new cases), but the incidence of new cases among males is highest in lung cancer, and among females, in cancer of the breast. The largest number of deaths occurs in lung cancer (males and both sexes combined) and in cancer of the breast (females). Cancer is primarily a disease

48

TABLE 5-1

Estimated 1975 Incidence of Major Types of Cancer

Sites	Total	New Cases Male	Female	Total	Deaths Male	Female	Five-Year Survival Rate Localized	Age at Death 50% Range Whites
Colon-Rectum	99000	48000	51000	49200	24800	25400	55%	62-79 Yrs
Lung	91000	72000	19000	81100	63500	17600	24	58-73
Breast	89000	1000	88000	32600	–	32600	73	54-74
Prostate	56000	56000	–	18700	18700	–	42	70-83
Uterus	46000	–	46000	11000	–	11000	74	50-72
Bladder	28700	21000	7700	9400	6500	2900	52	67-82
Stomach	22900	14000	8900	14400	8500	5900	30	63-80
Pancreas	21500	12000	9500	19500	10900	8600	3	61-77
Ovary	17000	–	17000	10800	–	10800	67	55-73
Leukemia	21200	12000	9200	15200	8500	6700	1*	49-77
All Sites	655000	334000	331000	365000	199000	166000	67	

* All cases (no localized stage)

of older adults, with 85 per cent of new cases and 80 per cent of deaths occurring at age 55 and older. Despite this predilection for older ages cancer ranks second among leading causes of death in six out of eight broad age/sex categories at ages under 75. Among women in the age range 35 to 54 cancer ranks first as a cause of death, well ahead of heart disease. In young men within the age range 15 to 34 cancer ranks fourth, behind three major categories of death by violence (accidents, homicide, and suicide). In the oldest age group 75 and up, stroke displaces cancer from second to third place among causes of death in both men and women.

Further information about cancer statistics may be found in recent reviews and surveys from various sources.[2,3,4,5] Extensive data on the incidence of cancer have recently been published in *N.C.I. Monograph 41, Third National Cancer Survey: Incidence Data.*[6]

Mortality Trends from Cancer in the United States

Over the past forty years the age-adjusted death rate from all forms of cancer has risen by about 40 per cent among men in the United States, due mainly to a twenty fold increase in mortality from lung cancer. The corresponding death rate among women has been declining slowly but steadily reflecting chiefly a sharp reduction in mortality from cancer of the cervix.

Cancer of the colon and rectum combined is currently the site of the greatest number of new cases for both sexes. There has been little change in the incidence and mortality from this cause.

Lung cancer has recently become the leading site of cancer both in incidence and death rates among men. There has been little improvement in the life expectancy of lung cancer patients despite advances in surgical techniques and other modes of therapy.

Breast cancer is the leading cause of cancer incidence and death among women. It is the principal cause of all deaths among women 40 to 44 years of age and the second leading cause of death at other age groups. Slightly better three-year survival rates have recently been reported from this cause.

Mortality from cancer of the uterus has declined steadily to about a third of the rate forty years ago, while the incidence of this cancer has about halved over this period. Distinctly better rates of survival are reflected in these figures.

The incidence of prostate cancer has been on the increase, but death rates have not changed significantly, supporting the observation of some improvement in recent survival rates. The incidence of bladder cancer has also been on the increase, but better survival rates for cancer of this site have likewise been reported.

There has been a steady decrease in stomach cancer in both sexes, so that current death rates are only about half of those two decades ago. On the other hand mortality from cancer of the pancreas has doubled in the past forty years; this highly fatal form of cancer now exacts a higher toll than stomach cancer.

Cancer of the ovary has shown little change in incidence and mortality in recent years. There has been dramatic improvement in the survival rates from some acute leukemias, but no significant change in chronic leukemia. Over the last forty years better survival rates have been reported for cancers of the kidney, brain, buccal cavity, larynx, and thyroid, and for Hodgkin's disease. In more recent years the improvements with respect to cancer of the kidney, brain, and buccal cavity have flattened out.

Cancer in Other Countries

International comparisons of cancer mortality show wide variations.[3,5] For all forms of cancer combined, white men and women in the United States have experienced below average death rates from cancer in comparison with Western Europe. For instance, white men in the United States have recently registered cancer death rates lower by 20 per cent or more than those in Scotland, Austria, Finland, Belgium, and England and Wales; white women in the United States show up similarly compared to women in Denmark, Austria, and Germany. Particularly low mortality from all forms of cancer combined is indicated in Israel, Norway, and Sweden for men, and in the southwestern countries of Europe and Japan for women.

For cancer of the colon and rectum Norway, Sweden, and the Netherlands report distinctly lower death rates than those experienced in the United States for both sexes. Norway, Sweden, Spain, and Portugal report very much lower death rates from lung cancer for both sexes. England and Wales, Belgium and the Netherlands, and particularly Scotland have experienced very much higher death rates from lung cancer than those in the United States.

White men and women in the United States have had extremely low death rates from stomach cancer, whereas the countries of southwestern Europe, Germany, Scotland, Northern Ireland, and Belgium have recently recorded death rates three times as high.

White women in the United States have registered relatively high mortality from breast cancer. Only Denmark, the Netherlands, and England and Wales have had significantly higher death rates from this cause. White men in the United States have registered relatively high death rates from leukemia.

In many countries the reporting of cancer by site may not be comparable with that in the United States with respect to the accuracy of the diagnosis of the primary site of the cancer. This is especially true at the older ages and is related to the proportion of deaths classified as of unknown cause or due to "senility." Nevertheless, careful epidemiological investigations have confirmed striking geographical differences in age-specific mortality rates for many cancer sites, such as lung, stomach, colon, and breast. It is believed that such differences may have etiological significance.[7]

Prognosis in Cancer—Nature and Sources of Data

Medical literature dealing with follow-up of cancer patients of various sites is more voluminous than that for any other disease. Ever since anesthesia and aseptic surgical techniques were developed, surgeons have been interested in the long-term results of their efforts and more generally in the mortality associated with cancer. Five years came to be regarded as a suitable period for judging the survival of operated cancer patients. The term *five-year cure rate* was properly replaced by the more accurate term *five-year survival rate* after it became evident from longer follow-up studies that many patients died from their cancer or developed a recurrence more than five years after operation.

An article written in 1950 by Berkson and Gage[8] indicated clearly how life table methods could be used in reporting cancer follow-up data. A later article by Cutler and Ederer[9] emphasized the concept of the relative survival rate, which compared the actual survival rate for the cancer group under study with the survival rate in a standard group, matched by age and sex, subject to contemporaneous death rates in the general population.

One of the principal difficulties in tracing a series of patients with a particular type of cancer over a period longer than five years is that the numbers of such cases on the service of one surgeon or one hospital are usually too small to yield significant answers. This may be true even for the most common types of cancer in the large hospital. However, larger registries of cancer patients have been formed from data collected from many hospitals on a uniform basis, submitted to a central agency for processing and analysis. The largest agency of this kind in the United States is operated by the National Cancer Institute for the so-called End Results Group. More than 100 hospitals of various types and sizes in different parts of the country participate in this program. Some hospitals contribute directly to the agency, but most of them do so through three state Cancer Registries (Connecticut, Massachusetts, and California). The End Results Group has issued periodic reports beginning in 1960 on the survival experience of patients with cancer of more than 30 sites.[10] The latest study, *End Results in Cancer, Report No. 4,* covers the experience of more than 400,000 cancer patients traced by five-year periods from 1940 through 1964. It constitutes far and away the most comprehensive source of follow-up data on cancer.

The *End Results Report,* in addition to segregating data by sex, age, and site of cancer, has also classified the materials according to the extent to which the cancer has spread, and according to the type of treatment—surgery, radiation, chemotherapy, and combinations thereof. Cancers are classified according to stages—localized, regional, and far advanced (metastatic). Both the surgeon and the pathologist are responsible for the formalized procedure of grading the malignancy of the tumor by the TNM system.[11] Size and growth characteristics enter into the classification of the tumor (T) and may alone disqualify it from the localized category, even if there is no evidence of regional extension to lymph nodes (N) or distant metastasis (M) of the tumor.

Customarily the tumor and other tissues removed at operation are turned over to a pathologist. Expert examination leads to a tissue classification (carcinoma, sarcoma, and types thereof) and appraisal of the degree of malignancy (Broder Grades I to IV or similar classifications). Because of the difficulties in obtaining a reasonable degree of uniformity in the tissue classifications such subdivision of the data was not attempted in the End Results Group studies.

In *End Results in Cancer, Report No. 4,* information on therapy is limited to the first course of treatment, initiated within four months of diagnosis. The modes of therapy considered were surgical, radiological, hormonal, and chemotherapeutic methods, and certain combinations thereof. Exploratory operations and supportive measures not tumor-directed have been classified as "no treatment." Of the patients diagnosed as having cancer during 1955 to 1965, some 19 per cent received no tumor-directed therapy, 40 per cent were treated by surgery alone, 16 per cent by radiation alone, 28 per cent by a combination of surgery and radiation, and 18 per cent by chemotherapy alone or in combination. In *End Results in Cancer* survival results are often given for the two largest categories. These figures must be used with caution in drawing conclusions about the efficiency of the treatment because "the uniformly collected information does not provide sufficient detail about the characteristics of the patient and of the tumor to permit the classification of patients into comparable groups." For example, patients considered to be poor operative risks may represent a substantial proportion of the group treated by radiation.[12] The results presented in §120-§190 are based on the findings for all treatments combined because of the questionable comparability of particular modes of treatment. Any reader interested in the difficult task of comparing results of different forms of treatment is advised to consult controlled studies on groups of patients treated in the same institutions.

A detailed description of the material taken from *End Results in Cancer, Report No. 4* and earlier findings is given in §100. Summarized information for each of 39 sites is presented in Tables 100a-b. The data on new cancer patients diagnosed during 1955 to 1964 include the number of cases, per cent of cases under age 55, distribution of patients by stage of cancer and five-year survival ratios for all stages combined. They are arranged in Table 100a for 33 male cancer sites and in Table 100b for 36 female cancer sites, in order of prevalence.

Overall Five-Year Experience

Report No. 4 of the End Results Group includes a summary showing the observed rates of survival at the end of five and ten years, respectively, for all sites of cancer combined.[13] Corresponding figures for expected survival rates can be derived either from the summary or the appropriate U.S. Life Tables. Geometric average *annual* rates of mortality and survival have been calculated from the observed and the expected five-year survival rates in the summary tables. In the detailed tables in §120-§190 the year by year figures for exposures, observed, and expected deaths have been used to calculate average annual mortality rates and survival rates, as well as the corresponding mortality and survival ratios and excess death rates for the intervals within two years and 2-5 years after diagnosis.

Comparative experience in patients with cancer of different sites has been presented in these terms, subdivided by sex, age groups at time of diagnosis, and separately for localized, regional, and metastatic stages of cancer for virtually all sites of cancer given in Report No. 4 of the End Results Group.

The five-year survival rate for all sites of cancer in toto was reported as $P_5 = .25$ in male patients and as $P_5 = .41$ in female patients—all ages combined. The corresponding ratios of actual to expected survival were 31 per cent and 47 per cent for males and females, respectively. For males the geometric average annual mortality rate was .242, where the expected annual mortality rate was .042, producing a mortality ratio of 575 per cent and an EDR of 200 extra deaths per 1000 per year. For female patients the corresponding annual mortality rate was .163, where the expected death rate was .027, producing a mortality ratio of 605 per cent and an EDR of 136 extra deaths per 1000. Because of the lower mortality rates in women the EDR is often a more meaningful index of comparative extra mortality. For instance, when all sites of cancer are combined the EDR for female patients (136 per 1000) is only about two-thirds of the EDR for male patients (200 per 1000). A similar relationship is found for most sites of cancer, with the notable exception of localized cancers in patients under 15, where the EDR for females is generally somewhat higher than for males.

Factors other than biological resistance are responsible for much of the rather wide difference between the aggregate five-year survival ratios for males and females (31 and 47 per cent, respectively). The disparate prevalence of various cancer sites in the two sexes accounts for part of this difference. As a matter of convenience, we have classified the results by site in five broad categories ranging from the poorest to the best risks (see Tables 5-2 through 5-6).

Cancers with extremely low five-year survival accounted for 32.2 per cent of all cancers in men, but for only 13.4 per cent of all cancers in women. Cancers with above average and relatively high five-year survival accounted for 12.3 per cent of all cancers in men, but for 47.9 per cent of all cancers in women.

In most sites for which staging is feasible there appears to be some correlation between prevalence of localized cancer and a higher than average survival rate. On an overall basis the excess mortality in the first five years in patients with localized cancer is about half that in patients in all stages of cancer. In men the mortality ratio is 295 per cent in localized cancer in contrast to 575 per cent in men with cancers in all stages. In women the mortality ratio in localized cancer is 315 per cent and 605 per cent for all stages. The EDR for men with localized cancer is 95 per 1000 in contrast to 200 per 1000 in all stages of cancer; the corresponding figures for women are 56 per 1000 and 136 per 1000, respectively.

There is definite evidence that a higher proportion of the cancers found among women are localized as compared to men (Tables 100a-b).

Since the experience for all stages of cancer combined represents an average for patients with localized cancers, patients with regional extension and patients with metastatic spread, it is obvious that overall excess mortality in advanced cancer is extremely high. No separate figures on advanced cancer are included in the summary table of the *End Results in Cancer, Report No. 4.*

Five-Year Excess Mortality by Age Groups

Details of the five- and ten-year experience for all sites combined are given in Table 1 of Report No. 4 of the End Results Group, by sex, age, and stage. Specifically the table presents the five- and ten-year survival rates for males and females for ages 15, 15 to 34, 35 to 54, 55 to 64 and 65 and older at time of diagnosis, separately for cancers in all stages and for localized cancers.

Except for cancer in children and for a few rare forms of cancer, the mortality ratios of actual to expected deaths tend to decrease progressively with advance in age, while the EDR shows a consistent upward trend as age increases; this is true in both sexes and for cancers in all stages as well as for localized cancers, in most sites.

In males with localized cancers the mortality ratios for the first five years of experience are very high—3,800 per cent—in the age range 15 to 34, but drop sharply to 1,100 per cent at ages 35 to 54, 550 per cent at ages 55 to 64, and 230 per cent at ages 65 and older; the corresponding figures for women are 5,100 per cent, 1,120 per cent, 545 per cent, and 230 per cent, respectively. Among men with localized cancers, the EDR rises from 59 per 1000 at ages 25 to 34 to 80 per 1000 at ages 35 to 54, 103 per 1000 at ages 55 to 64, and 109 per 1000 at ages 65 and older; the corresponding figures for women are 29 per 1000, 41 per 1000, 58 per 1000, and 75 per 1000, respectively. The patterns of the EDRs provide a more readily understandable perspective on the trends in cancer mortality for most characteristics.

At ages under 15 highly malignant types of cancer, such as acute leukemia and lymphosarcomas, predominate. The five-year survival rate in acute leukemia is only 1 to 2 per cent. Even in localized cancers EDRs at ages under 15 average 98 per 1000 in boys and 109 per 1000 in girls, whereas for cancers in all stages EDRs at ages under 15 average in excess of 200 per 1000 in both sexes. Regardless of age, it should be emphasized that acute leukemia and multiple myeloma cannot be characterized as localized, since they are by their very nature disseminated from the earliest detectable stage of their development. Accordingly, in reporting on the experience with localized cancers we have omitted the findings on acute and chronic leukemia, lymphosarcoma, reticular cell sarcoma, and multiple myeloma, inasmuch as all of these forms of cancer are not subject to staging. The same is true of Hodgkin's disease, although staging procedures have been proposed for this form of malignant lymphoma and are still in the testing process.

Localized Cancers Within Two Years and Within Two
to Five Years After Diagnosis

From a practical viewpoint, whether that of medical practice or life insurance, it is useful to distinguish between the experience at ages under 65 at time of diagnosis—predominantly persons actively at work—and the experience at ages 65

52

TABLE 5-2

Category I. Cancers with extremely low five-year survival ratios, less than 15%, all ages and stages combined.

| | Five-Year Survival Ratio | |
	Male	Female
Acute Leukemia	1%	2%
Pancreas	1%	2%
Liver	1%	6%
Esophagus	2%	7%
Gallbladder	7%	8%
Lung	8%	11%
Multiple Myeloma	9%	9%
Stomach	11%	14%

TABLE 5-3

Category II. Cancers with very low five-year survival ratios, 15-34% among males or females, all ages and stages combined.

| | Five-Year Survival Ratio | |
	Male	Female
Reticulum Cell Sarcoma	17%	15%
Pharynx	22%	32%
Brain	24%	33%
Chronic Leukemia	25%	29%
Tongue	27%	47%
Lymphosarcoma	30%	28%
Bone	32%	38%
Ovary	—	32%

TABLE 5-4

Category III. Cancers with low five-year survival ratios, 35-54% among males or females, all ages and stages combined.

| | Five-Year Survival Ratio | |
	Male	Female
Vagina	—	36%
Kidney	35%	38%
Hodgkin's Disease	36%	44%
Rectum	38%	41%
Nose and Sinuses	39%	41%
Mouth	40%	52%
Other Lymphomas	42%	46%
Colon	43%	43%
Connective Tissue	46%	53%
Prostate	51%	—
Melanoma	53%	68%
Larynx	56%	53%

TABLE 5-5

Category IV. Cancers with above average five-year survival ratios, 55-74%, all ages and stages combined.

| | Five-Year Survival Ratio | |
	Male	Female
Bladder	56%	56%
Testis	65%	—
Penis	69%	—
Cervix	—	60%
Breast	—	62%
Vulva	—	62%
Corpus Uteri	—	72%

TABLE 5-6

Category V. Cancers with relatively high five-year survival ratios, 75% or higher, all ages and stages combined.

| | Five-Year Survival Ratio | |
	Male	Female
Thyroid	75%	85%
Eye	81%	78%
Salivary Gland	81%	93%
Lip	87%	89%

or older—predominantly persons in retirement. Accordingly the experience on localized cancers is presented here in these two broad age categores.

For the sites of cancer characterized as having extremely low five-year ratios of survival (less than 15 per cent for all ages and all stages combined) the EDRs within 2 years after diagnosis and within 2-5 years after diagnosis are shown in Tables 5-7 through 5-11. In Table 5-7 and subsequent tables of similar format EDRs represent excess death rates in localized cancer.

It will be noted that the EDRs in the experience within two years after diagnosis drop very sharply in the next interval, 2-5 years after diagnosis, and that they are generally higher for ages 65 and older than for ages under 65 at time of diagnosis. This latter is particularly pronounced for localized cancers of the gallbladder, lung, and stomach within two years after diagnosis. The EDRs for cancer of the pancreas for both age groups are higher for females than for males and also for cancer of the lung 2-5 years after diagnosis, at ages 65 and older.

For the sites of cancer characterized as having very low five-year survival ratios (15 to 34 per cent for all ages and all stages among males or females) the EDRs within two years of diagnosis and within 2-5 years after diagnosis are shown in Table 5-8.

The EDRs in the experience within two years after diagnosis decline by 40 to 85 per cent to the levels found in the period from 2-5 years after diagnosis, with the largest decreases for brain and bone cancers. EDRs for females are lower than those for males within two years of diagnosis; this is also true for patients under age 65 from 2-5 years after diagnosis, except in cancer of the pharynx.

For the sites of cancer characterized as having low five-year survival ratios (35 to 54 per cent for all ages and all stages combined among males or females) the EDRs within two years of diagnosis and within 2-5 years after diagnosis are shown in Table 5-9.

Except for cancer of the prostate and melanoma, the EDRs in the experience within two years after diagnosis drop very sharply in the period 2-5 years after diagnosis and are in general markedly higher for ages 65 and older than for ages under 65 at time of diagnosis. Excess death rates of females are generally lower than those for males in corresponding categories although there are a number of exceptions, for example, in three of the four categories of cancer of the kidney.

For the sites of cancer characterized as having above average five-year survival ratios (55 to 74) per cent for all ages and all stages combined among males or females) the EDRs within two years after diagnosis and within 2-5 years after diagnosis are shown in Table 5-10.

Except for cancer of the breast, the EDRs in the experience within two years after diagnosis decline by 30 to 85 per cent to the level found 2-5 years after diagnosis. The EDRs are generally higher for ages 65 and older at time of diagnosis than for ages under 65. Women under age 65 with breast cancer have an EDR that actually *increases* from the first to second interval (from 26 to 37 extra deaths per 1000 per year).

For the sites of cancer characterized as having relatively high ratios of survival (75 per cent or higher for all ages and all stages combined) the EDRs within two years after diagnosis and within 2-5 years after diagnosis are shown in Table 5-11.

Except for cancer of the lip and cancer of the eye in the case of females, the EDRs in the experience within two years after diagnosis drop substantially in the interval 2-5 years after diagnosis. There appears to be little residual extra mortality after two years have elapsed in cancers of the thyroid and salivary glands diagnosed at ages under 65. The EDRs are generally lower for females than for males, except possibly for cancer of the lip.

Localized Cancers Five to Ten Years After Diagnosis

Special interest attaches to the experience on localized cancers beyond the fifth year following diagnosis because the five-year survival ratio has traditionally been used as a criterion of effectiveness in the treatment of cancer.

On cancers characterized as having extremely low five-year survival ratios (less than 15 per cent for all ages and all stages combined) the experience beyond the fifth year following diagnosis is rather thin and in some instances questionable on the score of accuracy of the diagnosis. For the cancers characterized as having extremely low five-year survival ratios, the EDRs during the period 5-10 years after diagnosis were as shown in Table 5-12 for the localized stages.

There were fewer than ten deaths in the experience on localized cancers of the liver and pancreas during the period 5-10 years after diagnosis in the classifications here considered. It is clear that, for localized cancers during the period 5-10 years after diagnosis, there was substantial extra mortality in excess of 30 per 1000 at ages under 65 at time of diagnosis. By way of comparison, the experience for all ages combined in Hodgkin's disease during the period 5-10 years after diagnosis produced EDRs of about 108 per 1000 and 83 per 1000 for males and females, respectively.

For the cancers characterized as having very low five-year survival ratios (15 to 35 per cent for all ages and all stages combined among males or females) the EDRs during the period 5-10 years after diagnosis were as shown in Table 5-13 for the localized stages.

TABLE 5-7

Excess death rates* in localized cancers with extremely low survival ratios (values in parentheses based on fewer than 10 deaths).

| | Within 2 Years | | | | Within 2-5 Years | | | |
| | Male | | Female | | Male | | Female | |
	Under 65	65 up	Under 65	65 up	Under 65	65 up	Under 65	65 up
Pancreas	649	704	656	749	247	372	(189)	310
Liver	802	854	602	806	(156)	(150)	†	†
Esophagus	625	657	495	571	281	297	154	231
Gallbladder	351	521	258	433	182	141	134	155
Lung	338	491	209	399	103	114	83	153
Stomach	219	343	227	359	96	103	82	61

*EDR — number of extra deaths per 1000 exposed to risk per year.
†Negative EDR — observed mortality lower than expected.

TABLE 5-8

Excess death rates* in localized cancers with very low survival ratios (values in parentheses based on fewer than 10 deaths).

| | Within 2 Years | | | | Within 2-5 Years | | | |
| | Male | | Female | | Male | | Female | |
	Under 65	65 up	Under 65	65 up	Under 65	65 up	Under 65	65 up
Pharynx	239	287	200	221	108	147	112	41
Brain	466	666	377	519	80	26	57	39
Tongue	149	208	127	134	90	148	71	26
Bone	232	245	193	242	91	(69)	62	(105)
Ovary	—	—	91	114	—	—	40	46

*EDR — number of extra deaths per 1000 exposed to risk per year.

TABLE 5-9

Excess death rates* in localized cancers with low survival ratios.

| | Within 2 Years | | | | Within 2-5 Years | | | |
| | Male | | Female | | Male | | Female | |
	Under 65	65 up	Under 65	65 up	Under 65	65 up	Under 65	65 up
Vagina	—	—	166	223	—	—	85	151
Kidney	117	177	108	187	53	58	60	72
Rectum	86	185	71	143	57	71	55	71
Nose and Sinuses	121	273	144	196	33	102	26	165
Mouth	109	140	92	128	87	66	40	68
Colon	72	130	52	125	42	51	34	32
Connective Tissue	96	163	73	111	46	71	36	73
Prostate	55	103	—	—	60	82	—	—
Melanoma	53	88	27	81	57	80	35	68
Larynx	72	108	103	91	43	42	50	59

*EDR — number of extra deaths per 1000 exposed to risk per year.

TABLE 5-10

Excess death rates* in localized cancers with above average survival ratios (values in parentheses based on fewer than 10 deaths).

| | Within 2 Years | | | | Within 2-5 Years | | | |
| | Male | | Female | | Male | | Female | |
	Under 65	65 up	Under 65	65 up	Under 65	65 up	Under 65	65 up
Bladder	74	155	72	148	36	54	25	42
Testis†	51	125	–	–	19	(29)	–	–
Penis	54	99	–	–	34	13	–	–
Cervix	–	–	55	89	–	–	33	60
Breast	–	–	26	43	–	–	37	37
Vulva	–	–	41	117	–	–	28	53
Corpus Uteri	–	–	36	90	–	–	20	37

*EDR – number of extra deaths per 1000 exposed to risk per year.
†Age break at 55 instead of 65.

TABLE 5-11

Excess death rates* in localized cancers with relatively high survival ratios (values in parentheses based on fewer than 10 deaths).

| | Within 2 Years | | | | Within 2-5 Years | | | |
| | Male | | Female | | Male | | Female | |
	Under 65	65 up	Under 65	65 up	Under 65	65 up	Under 65	65 up
Thyroid	19	156	8	106	(4)	(8)	4	16
Eye	35	43	29	28	13	37	34	76
Salivary Gland	12	71	2	42	4	29	5	(†)
Lip	13	27	(†)	36	15	28	(21)	29

*EDR – number of extra deaths per 1000 exposed to risk per year.
†Negative EDR – observed mortality lower than expected.

TABLE 5-12

Excess death rates* in localized cancers with extremely low five-year survival ratios (values in parentheses based on fewer than 10 deaths).

| | Within 5-10 Years | | | |
| | Male | | Female | |
	Under 65	65 up	Under 65	65 up
Esophagus	177	(25)	(80)	(70)
Gallbladder	(10)	(103)	(63)	40
Lung	65	82	39	90
Stomach	33	21	36	21

*EDR – number of extra deaths per 1000 exposed to risk per year.

TABLE 5-13

Excess death rates* in localized cancers with very low five-year survival ratios (values in parentheses based on fewer than 10 deaths).

| | Within 5-10 Years | | | |
| | Male | | Female | |
	Under 65	65 up	Under 65	65 up
Pharynx	85	71	30	74
Brain	50	53	39	19
Tongue	70	80	55	34
Bone	31	(14)	27	(†)
Ovary	–	–	19	36

*EDR – number of extra deaths per 1000 exposed to risk per year.
†Negative EDR – observed mortality lower than expected.

It is clear that substantial extra mortality continues on these localized cancers during the period 5-10 years after diagnosis—in excess of 30 per 1000 for males at ages under 65 at time of diagnosis and in excess of about 20 per 1000 for females at ages under 65.

For the localized cancers characterized as having low five-year survival ratios (35 to 54 per cent for all ages and all stages combined among males or females) the EDRs during the period 5-10 years after diagnosis were as shown in Table 5-14.

For these localized cancers considerable extra mortality continues during the period 5-10 years after diagnosis, ranging in the case of men at ages under 65 at time of diagnosis from 50 per 1000 for localized cancers of the mouth and of the nose and sinuses to 13 per 1000 for localized cancers of the connective tissue. Female mortality is distinctly lower than male for localized cancers of the mouth and of the rectum, and materially higher only for localized cancers of the connective tissue.

For the localized cancers characterized as having above average five-year survival ratios (55 to 74 per cent for all ages and all stages combined among males or females) the EDRs during the period 5-10 years after diagnosis were as shown in Table 5-15.

For these localized cancers (with the possible exception of cancer of the testis at ages under 55) significant extra mortality continues during the period 5-10 years after diagnosis, the highest being 20 per 1000 for localized cancer of the bladder among men at ages under 65 at time of diagnosis and 25 per 1000 for localized cancer of the breast among women at these ages.

For the localized cancers characterized as having relatively high five-year survival ratios (75 per cent or more for all ages and all stages combined) the EDRs during the period 5-10 years after diagnosis were as shown in Table 5-16.

Significant extra mortality continues during the period 5-10 years after diagnosis on localized cancers of the eye and lip, but not in the case of localized cancers of the salivary gland and thyroid.

Localized Cancers Ten Years or Longer After Diagnosis

It is surprising to find that the experience on localized cancers ten years or longer after diagnosis discloses material extra mortality for most sites where data are available. Only for localized melanoma and localized cancers of the salivary gland and thyroid is the EDR less than 20 per 1000 as shown in Table 5-17, except in one category based on fewer than ten deaths.

Among men the highest residual EDRs are in those over 65 with cancer of the pharynx (EDR 113 per 1000), cancers of the kidney and lung, and in those of all ages with cancer of the prostate (EDR 59 to 86 per 1000). For other sites, except those mentioned in the foregoing paragraph the EDR lies in the range from 15 to 30 per 1000 for localized cancers diagnosed at ages under 65. Among women the highest residual EDR for localized cancers diagnosed at ages under 65 is on cancer of the kidney—40 per 1000; EDR for women in this age group with other types of cancer ranges from 6 to 25 per 1000, excluding sites in which fewer than ten deaths occurred. This unexpected finding is commented upon in the following section that deals with the interpretation of the data.

Interpretation of Findings

The purpose of the End Results Study was to compare the mortality of treated cancer patients with that of the general population. Treated cancer patients were defined as those who received tumor-directed therapy, either curative or palliative, and excluded those for whom no tumor-directed therapy was reported during the first period of hospitalization or within four months of diagnosis. Patients with carcinoma in situ and cancers discovered at autopsy as well as those for which the only information available was obtained from death certificates were excluded, but it is possible that in some hospitals these instructions were not followed strictly.

The extent to which the patients included in this study are representative of the general population of the United States is not known. There are grounds for believing that the patients included in the study were drawn to a greater extent from the middle and lower socioeconomic segments of the population. A number of investigations have shown that the incidence and extra mortality among patients with cancer of the stomach and digestive organs, cancer of the lung and bronchus, and cancer of the cervix and body of the uterus are distinctly higher in the lower socioeconomic segments of the population, particularly among those with little formal schooling; on the other hand, cancer of the prostate and breast show significantly increased mortality in the upper socioeconomic strata. To the extent that the distribution of cancer patients in this study is biased towards the lower portion of the socioeconomic scale, the extra mortality experienced among those with cancer of the stomach and digestive organs, cancer of the lung and bronchus, and cancer of the cervix and body or the uterus may overstate that in a more representative population, while the extra mortality among

TABLE 5-14

Excess death rates* in localized cancers with low five-year survival ratios (values in parentheses based on fewer than 10 deaths).

| | Within 5-10 Years | | | |
| | Male | | Female | |
	Under 65	65 up	Under 65	65 up
Vagina	–	–	(†)	(†)
Kidney	29	55	32	31
Rectum	26	42	18	26
Nose and Sinuses	50	85	(36)	113
Mouth	50	47	23	42
Colon	19	17	19	22
Connective Tissue	13	12	21	27
Prostate	42	71	–	–
Melanoma	22	16	19	5
Larynx	24	45	25	34

*EDR – number of extra deaths per 1000 exposed to risk per year.
†Negative EDR – observed mortality lower than expected.

TABLE 5-15

Excess death rates* for localized cancers with above average five-year survival ratios.

| | Within 5-10 Years | | | |
| | Male | | Female | |
	Under 65	65 up	Under 65	65 up
Bladder	20	48	14	25
Testis†	6	33	–	–
Penis	17	63	–	–
Cervix	–	–	14	30
Breast	–	–	25	33
Vulva	–	–	21	34
Corpus Uteri	–	–	9	16

*EDR – number of extra deaths per 1000 exposed to risk per year.
†Age break at 55 instead of 65.

TABLE 5-16

Excess death rates* for localized cancers with relatively high five-year survival ratios.

| | Within 5-10 Years | | | |
| | Male | | Female | |
	Under 65	65 up	Under 65	65 up
Thyroid	3	8	2	(†)
Eye	22	6	15	12
Salivary Gland	7	31	4	(†)
Lip	15	15	11	10

*EDR – number of deaths per 1000 exposed to risk per year.
†Negative EDR – observed mortality lower than expected.

TABLE 5-17

Excess death rates* in localized cancers 10 years or more after diagnosis (values in parentheses based on fewer than 10 deaths).

| | Male | | Female | |
	Under 65	65 up	Under 65	65 up
Lung	27	86	25	(7)
Stomach	21	(†)	6	(†)
Pharynx	32	113	(26)	(107)
Brain	26	(5)	22	(†)
Tongue	33	62	(8)	†
Kidney	29	65	40	25
Rectum	15	43	7	12
Colon	26	14	10	5
Prostate	59	63	–	–
Melanoma	13	(7)	6	19
Larynx	22	35	(34)	(18)
Bladder	17	49	19	3
Cervix	–	–	13	16
Breast	–	–	21	22
Thyroid	(†)	(44)	10	(0)
Salivary Gland	5	(†)	6	14

*EDR – number of extra deaths per 1000 exposed to risk per year.
†Negative EDR – observed mortality lower than expected.

58

those with cancer of the prostate and breast may understate that in a more representative population. Of all the agencies contributing data to the End Results Study, the Connecticut Cancer Registry gives the most complete sample of a geographically defined population, as it includes virtually all diagnosed cancer patients in that state.

The data here presented are limited to white patients. A supplementary study, confined to the 1955 to 1964 experience for 18 sites, was recently carried out by Axtell, Myers, and Shambaugh of the End Results Study Section to compare the survival patterns of black and white cancer patients.[14] The study showed that the survival rates of blacks were lower and their cancer mortality rates higher than for whites in virtually all cancer sites. The five-year survival ratio for black males—all sites combined—was 22 per cent in contrast to 32 per cent of white males. The corresponding figures for females were 39 per cent and 50 per cent, respectively.

Among males, the survival ratio for blacks diverges from that for whites with time elapsed since diagnosis. Among black females, the extra mortality is concentrated largely in the first two years following diagnosis. For white males the population of localized cancers to cancers of all grades for the 18 sites considered in the supplementary report was 38 per cent; for black males it was only 29 per cent. The corresponding figures for females were 42 per cent and 32 per cent, respectively. Cancer of the prostate was the leading site of cancer deaths among black males while cancer of the cervix was the leading site of cancer deaths among black females.

In the experience here presented on whites the major inaccuracy may lie in the proportion of cases lost to follow-up and in the characteristics of these cases. It is not possible to set any percentage of cases lost to follow-up as invalidating a study because even a small percentage of the lost to follow-up cases may bias the results materially, if the proportion of deaths among those lost to follow-up deviates materially from those followed up. The experience of certain registries with intensive field investigation of cases lost to follow-up indicates that individuals who were so lost in the first five years following diagnosis often lived several years beyond the date of last contact. The characteristics of the cases lost to follow-up beyond ten years following diagnosis are not known, and this throws some doubt on the validity of the findings on cancer patients traced for ten years or longer after diagnosis.

The high mortality among cancer patients traced for ten years or longer after diagnosis found in this study suggests the likelihood that those lost to follow-up included a relatively small proportion of deaths. This possibility seems to be indicated by the relatively favorable experience among the insured lives in a number of clinical follow-up studies, notably those of the Mayo Clinic. It is of course possible that the favorable experience among insured lives and in several clinical studies reflects merely the effects of selection and the lower mortality among highly selected lives drawn from the upper socioeconomic segments of the population.

On the other hand, the findings point strongly to a relatively high residual mortality among cancer patients after ten or more years following diagnosis. Further investigation is needed to determine the reasons for this excess mortality. The End Results Section considered the cause of death data to be insufficiently reliable to warrant analysis by cause of death. Such analyses are nevertheless likely to shed light on the persistence of the excess mortality—whether it is due to recurrence of the original cancer, to increased patient susceptibility to new primary cancer, to delayed adverse effects of treatment, or otherwise to poor health.

Whatever lessons might be drawn from past experience, the findings need to be reviewed in the light of current developments. There is evidence that new carcinogens are being introduced into the environment, but control of these and other environmental carcinogens offers promise of the prevention of some forms of cancer. Advances in the detection, diagnosis, and treatment of cancer also offer hope for progress. Chemotherapy and combination of chemotherapy with surgery have shown the way toward improved treatment of cancer of the breast, bone cancer, and several of the rarer forms of cancer. An essential part of the National Cancer Program is directed towards fundamental research to obtain knowledge about the basic mechanism in cancer such as might lead to more effective measures to prevent or control this group of diseases.

A short but informative review of the general topic of chemical carcinogenesis is that by Ryser,[15] who is of the opinion that "chemical carcinogens are the major culprit in the causation of human cancers." The reader who is interested in further statistical information on cancer patients may consult the references given at the beginning of the cancer section of the abstracts, and the monographs by Lilienfeld et al.[16] and Levin et al.[5] The Fascicles of the *Atlas of Tumor Pathology*,[17] published by the Armed Forces Institute of Pathology, provide an authoritative correlation of clinical with histological information for a wide range of cancers.

References

1. L.V. Ackerman and J.A. del Regato, *Cancer Diagnosis, Treatment and Prognosis*, 4th ed. St. Louis: C.V. Mosby Co. (1970).
2. American Cancer Society, '75 *Cancer Facts and Figures*. New York: American Cancer Society (1974).

3. E. Silverberg and A.I. Holleb, "Cancer Statistics, 1974–Worldwide Epidemiology." *CA; A Cancer Journal for Clinicians*, 24:2-7 (1974).

4. E. Silverberg and A.I. Holleb, "Major Trends in Cancer: 25 Year Survey." *CA; A Cancer Journal for Clinicians*, 25:2-21 (1975).

5. D.L. Levin, S.S. Deresa, J.D. Goodwin, II, and D.T. Silverman, *Cancer Rates and Risks,* 2nd ed. Bethesda, Md.: National Cancer Institute (1974).

6. S.J. Cutler and J.L. Young, eds., *National Cancer Institute Monograph No. 41. Third National Cancer Survey: Incidence Data.* Bethesda, Md.: Biometry Branch, Division of Cause and Prevention, National Cancer Institute (1975).

7. B. MacMahon, P. Cole, and J. Brown, "Etiology of Human Breast Cancer: A Review." *J. Nat. Cancer Inst.,* 50:21-42 (1973).

8. J. Berkson and R.P. Gage, "Calculation of Survival Rates in Cancer." *Proc. Staff Meeting Mayo Clinic*, 25:270-286 (1950).

9. S.J. Cutler and F. Ederer, "Maximum Utilization of the Life Table Method in Analyzing Survival." *J. Chronic Dis.*, 8:699-712 (1958).

10. End Results Group, *End Results in Cancer. Reports Nos. 1, 2, 3, and 4.* Bethesda, Md.: End Results Section, Biometry Branch, National Cancer Institute (1961, 1964, 1968, and 1972).

11. T.W. Botsford, ed., *Cancer–A Manual for Practitioners*, 4th ed. Boston: Massachusetts Div., American Cancer Society (1968), Chapter 25.

12. End Results Group, *End Results in Cancer. Report No. 4.* Bethesda, Md.: End Results Section, Biometry Branch, National Cancer Institute (1972), p. 1.

13. Ibid., Table 1, p. 4.

14. L.M. Axtell, M.H. Meyers, and E. Shambaugh, *Treatment and Survival Patterns for Black and White Cancer Patients 1955-1964.* Bethesda, Md.: End Results Section, Biometry Branch, National Cancer Institute (1975).

15. H.J.P. Ryser, "Special Report: Chemical Carcinogenesis." *CA; A Cancer Journal for Clinicians*, 24:351-360 (1974).

16. A.M. Lilienfeld, M.L. Levin, and I.I. Kessler, *Cancer in the United States*. Cambridge, Mass.: Harvard University Press (1972).

17. *Atlas of Tumor Pathology. Fascicles 1-40. Second Series, Fascicles 1-9*. Washington, D.C.: Armed Forces Institute of Pathology (First Series 1949-1968; Second Series 1967-1974).

Neuropsychiatric Disorders
John J. Hutchinson, M.D., and *John C. Robinson, M.D.*

In the 1970 U.S. Vital Statistics Report the category "Diseases of the Nervous System and Sense Organs" accounted for 17,130 deaths, and the category "Mental Disorders" for 7,172 deaths, together amounting to only 1.3 per cent of the total of 1,921,031 deaths reported in the United States for that year.[1] However, in this volume the number of deaths included under Neuropsychiatric Disorders embraces, besides these categories, 23,480 deaths from suicide and 207,166 deaths attributable to cerebrovascular disease, the latter placed here instead of with the cardiovascular diseases (§300-§399 and Chapters 7 to 11). Table 6-1 contains a summary of 1970 U.S. deaths attributed to the principal neuropsychiatric diseases or categories by this enlarged definition, together with the numbers of the abstracts providing mortality and survival data.

Other considerations apart from cause of death add to the importance of neuropsychiatric disorders and their natural history in the general field of epidemiology. Functional disorders, including the neuroses, have a high prevalence and must be dealt with by practicing physicians regardless of their specialty. Evolving concepts of psychiatric terminology and classification of mental disorders, and both professional and public concern over confidentiality of psychiatric medical records have added to the difficulty of evaluating the mortality risk in such patients. Neurological diseases are characterized by their number, variety, and tendency to produce chronic disability or to shorten life, even though their incidence is usually low. Strokes, the predominant manifestation of cerebrovascular disease, are of obvious public health importance because of the high disability and mortality rates associated with their occurrence.

In view of the combined effects of prevalence rates and mortality rates by cause of death it is scarcely surprising that nine of the 24 abstracts dealing with specific neuropsychiatric disorders provide follow-up data on cerebrovascular disease. Among organic brain disorders eight abstracts deal with four conditions: mental retardation, cerebral palsy, epilepsy, and multiple sclerosis. Spinal cord disorders are represented by two abstracts on paraplegia and one on a long-term study of poliomyelitis. Additional neurological diseases represented in the miscellaneous abstract §279 include head injury, migraine, Parkinson's disease, various eye or ear disorders, the finding of tremors on examination, and a residual category of "brain disorders." There are three abstracts on psychosis and neurosis, and some additional data in §279 on these psychiatric disorders, "nervousness," and suicide attempt. The descriptive matter of this chapter follows the order of the abstracts, but with brief reference to a number of neurological diseases and disease categories not covered in separate abstracts. Some additional data are mentioned for both neurological and psychiatric disorders, including risk of suicide. The most detailed discussion is focused on cerebrovascular disease.

Cerebrovascular Disease
John C. Robinson, M.D.

Definition and Background. Cerebrovascular disease as discussed in this section is limited to those vascular disorders generally referred to as stroke. A stroke is an abrupt cerebrovascular event, frequently catastrophic. A stroke may be ischemic or hemorrhagic. About 75 per cent are ischemic.[2,3,4] Ischemic strokes may be thrombotic or embolic. Only a small percentage are embolic and of those 60 per cent are associated with mitral valve disease and 20 per cent with myocardial infarction.[3]

Ischemic stroke is classified by mode of onset.[5] Transient cerebral ischemic attack (TIA) is the term used to describe an episode of cerebral dysfunction lasting minutes to not more than 24 hours.[5,6,7] An attack lasting longer than 24 hours which resolves leaving minimal residuals is called a transient cerebral ischemic attack with incomplete recovery (TIA-IR).[5,6] A completed stroke (CS) is one which leaves a marked and persistent neurological deficit.[5,6]

Hemorrhagic stroke accounts for less than 25 per cent of all strokes and 60 to 90 per cent of the time is associated with hypertension.[2,3,4] Subarachnoid hemorrhage accounts for most of the remainder, and even here hypertension is not above suspicion. Intraparenchymal brain hemorrhage results in mechanical disruption of brain tissue and increased intracranial pressure. About two-thirds of these hemorrhages arise in the thalmus and basal ganglia.[2] Postmorten studies implicate microaneurysms which are found predominately in the striate arteries, although also found elsewhere in the brain. These tend to increase with age and especially with hypertension.[2] Contrasted with these are saccular macroaneurysms often found in the circle of Willis.[2] Subarachnoid hemorrhage, usually due to rupture of one of these saccular aneurysms, accounts for about 4.5 per cent of all cerebrovascular deaths.[13]

62

TABLE 6-1

Numbers of Deaths in the U.S. — 1970
Neurologic and Psychiatric Disorders

Hazard	Deaths in U.S. Number	% in Category	Follow-up Data
Cerebrovascular Disease (Stroke)	207,166	(81.7%)	§201-§209
Cerebral Thrombosis	57,845	(22.8%)	§203, §206, §208
Cerebral Hemorrhage	41,379	(16.4)	§203, §206, §208
Transient Cerebral Ischemia	55	(0.0)	§209
Subarachnoid Hemorrhage	9,235	(3.6)	§208
Extracranial Arterial Occlusion	**	—	§202
Other	98,652	(38.9)	—
Organic Brain Disorders	12,031	(4.8%)	
Mental Retardation (Deficiency)	201	(0.1%)	§215, §216
Cerebral Palsy	672	(0.3)	§220, §221
Epilepsy	1,920	(0.8)	§225, §226
Multiple Sclerosis	1,613	(0.6)	§230, §231
Paralysis Agitans	3,254	(1.3)	—
Congenital	2,402	(0.9)	—
Other	1,969	(0.8)	—
Spinal Cord Disorders	1,342	(0.5%)	
Paraplegia, Quadriplegia	302	(0.1%)	§250, §251
Paralytic Polio	202	(0.1)	§255, §279
Congenital	290	(0.1)	—
Other	548	(0.2)	—
Other Neurological	6,824	(2.7%)	§279
Psychiatric	26,180	(10.3%)	§279
Psychoses	1,390	(0.5%)	§280
Neuroses and Personality Disorders	1,310	(0.5)	§285, §286
Suicide	23,480	(9.3)	§279
Total (all listed in Cause of Death Statistics)	253,543	(13.2% of all deaths)	

**Listed elsewhere under various separate causes

Stroke is the third leading cause of death in the United States.[8] It accounts for 11 per cent of all deaths.[8,13] The death rate per 100,000 population averaged 99.7 for the years 1973-1974.[9] Over 200,000 people die from this cause each year in this country alone.[8] The average annual incidence of cerebral occlusive disease rises sharply after the age of 55[5] (see §204, §207, §208, §209). More than four-fifths of all cerebrovascular deaths occur in persons aged 65 or older.[9,12] Among policyholders of the Metropolitan Life Insurance Company death claims from this cause alone were well in excess of $33,000,000 in each of the two years 1972 and 1973, close to 7 per cent of all claim dollars paid.[11,12]

More than 80 per cent of patients with cerebral thrombosis survive 30 days, 46 per cent of those with subarachnoid hemorrhage survive that long, and only 16 per cent of those with intracerebral hemorrhage survive 30 days (§208). In a series of 275 successive cases of acute cerebral vascular episodes, 45 per cent died while still hospitalized; 7 per cent did not improve with treatment, remaining completely helpless and in need of nursing care; despite discharge from the hospital, 19 per cent continued to suffer from severe functional disability; 19 per cent demonstrated marked functional improvement, but had sufficient residuals to impair their work capabilities; and 10 per cent recovered to the point where their working abilities became substantially unimpaired.[4]

Cerebral Circulation. Anatomically, the brain has a dual blood supply, the vertebral arteries and the internal carotids. The two vertebral arteries enter the cranial cavity and, after giving rise to the right and left posterior inferior cerebellar arteries, unite at the lower border of the pons to form the basilar artery. The basilar artery gives off several branches, the largest of which are the two superior cerebellar arteries, then divides into the two posterior cerebral arteries.

The two internal carotid arteries enter the cranial cavity and, at about the level of the medial aspect of the temporal lobes, divide into their terminal branches, the anterior and middle cerebral arteries. Before so doing, they each give off a communicating branch to the posterior cerebral artery and a second branch, the choroidal artery, which eventually reaches the choroid plexus of the lateral ventricle.

This dual cerebral circulation is interconnected at the circle of Willis, a circular arterial anastomosis at the base of the brain. The two anterior cerebral arteries are joined together by the anterior communicating artery. The internal carotids are joined to the posterior cerebrals by the posterior communicating arteries. Thus there is formed an arterial ring made up of the anterior communicating artery, the two anterior cerebrals, the internal carotids, the posterior communicating arteries and the posterior cerebrals.

It is now obvious that ischemic stroke can be classified, in addition to the mode of onset, by the territory of vascular involvement.[5] Ischemic stroke syndrome resulting from transient or persistent ischemia in the cerebral territory of the vertebrobasilar arterial system will give one set of clinical symptoms while involvement of the internal carotid system will give another. For instance, stenosis of the innominate artery on the right or subclavian artery on the left can give symptoms of vertebrobasilar involvement. Lesions at the carotid bifurcation will obviously produce symptoms of carotid system involvement.

Effects of Surgical Intervention. With the advent of safe aortocranial angiography and the feasibility of surgical reconstruction for carotid and vertebral artery lesions, it became apparent that the effectiveness of surgical intervention should be evaluated. In 1959 a cooperative study designated the Joint Study of Extracranial Arterial Occlusion came into being.[6] This study was undertaken to evaluate the efficacy of arterial reconstructive surgery in the treatment of cerebrovascular disease secondary to surgically accessible lesions in the arteries of the neck and upper thorax. Reports from this study have been published in the literature from time to time since 1968.[6,13,14,15,16,17,18] For purposes of this study, a lesion was considered operable if there was arteriographically demonstrable stenosis of 30 per cent or greater, including complete occlusion, of an artery in a surgically accessible site.[15] The findings in §202 were taken from this cooperative study. Comment is made in the text accompanying §202 that there was a high surgical mortality rate of 8.4 per cent. It has further been found that in patients with cerebral infarction, surgical repair of an occluded vessel done within hours or even days after the event is associated with a surgical mortality of 40 to 50 per cent due mainly to blow-out of necrotic vessels.[6,20] The weakened vessels just cannot stand sudden revascularization. The results of §202 indicate a mortality among the operated group about the same as in the unoperated, if the experience within six months is deleted.

It has now become apparent that surgery is not the answer to completed strokes. Some feel that the best time to treat a stroke is before it occurs. A patient presenting with a transient cerebral ischemic attack (TIA) has at the least a 37 per cent chance of developing a completed stroke.[5]

In a study of 2,772 persons aged 65 to 74 who were free from completed stroke at initial examination, 176 subsequently developed a TIA, a prevalence rate of 63 per 1000.[21] This group was made up of both blacks and whites, and males and females who were receiving financial aid through a county department and were thus from a low economic stratum. Autopsy studies seem to indicate that the prevalence of cerebral atherosclerosis is higher among the poor, as is poor health in general, but this does give some measurement of the incidence of TIA. Among the 176 persons in this group who were diagnosed as having TIA, the age-adjusted incidence rate of definite stroke within three years was 132 per 1000, as opposed to 68 per 1000 among those who did not have a prior history of TIA. More detailed incidence rates for TIA by age and sex, and data on subsequent development of stroke are given in Tables 209c and 209d.

The object of extracranial arterial surgery is to prevent further ischemia and improve the long-term outlook. As most symptomatic lesions are located at the carotid bifurcation, this is the location where most of the reconstructive arterial procedures are performed.[5] The procedure of choice is that of endarterectomy. Bypass and plastic procedures are now limited mostly to occlusive innominate, subclavian and proximal vertebral arterial disease.[5]

When should surgery be undertaken? When a bruit is heard in the region of the carotid bifurcation, there is probably a 50 per cent or greater stenosis of the internal carotid.[21] The stenosis will increase in 62 per cent of these people in the next nine years.[21] TIA will occur in 38 per cent of cases and brain infarction without a preceding TIA in 27 per cent.[21] On the other hand, while the mortality from surgical removal of asymptomatic stenotic lesions of the internal carotid is very low, there is about a 4 per cent surgical morbidity which does not justify surgery in an asymptomatic patient.[21] The patient may remain asymptomatic because of the development of adequate collateral circulation.[21] If symptoms eventually do develop, then is the time to consider surgery.

If there is stenosis of both carotids, the Joint Study Group concluded that the carotid with the greater stenosis should be operated first.[16] Within the past few years the technique of superficial temporal-middle cerebral anastomosis has been perfected and is sometimes useful in patients with internal carotid occlusion with patent external carotid and middle cerebral arterial systems.[21]

The subclavian steal syndrome is produced by the reversal of the vertebral arterial blood flow associated with stenosis of the subclavian artery on the left or the innominate on the right.[19,20,22] The patent distal portion of the subclavian or innominate supplies blood to the arm by draining it from the vertebral artery and thereby decreasing the blood flow to the brain.[19,20,22]

Brain stem infarction is rare, and surgery offers relief from symptoms.[20] Intrathoracic subclavian endarterectomy has generally been abandoned in favor of extrathoracic carotid-subclavian bypass.[19,20] This has resulted in a considerable decrease in operative mortality, as a diseased subclavian artery is apt to be very friable and attempts at intrathoracic manipulation often result in catastrophe.[19,20]

Stenosis and even occlusion at the orifice of one vertebral artery are usually well tolerated and not an indication for surgery if the blood flow in the opposite vertebral artery is normal.[20] If there are symptoms of vertebral-basilar insufficiency where there is bilateral disease, surgery might be considered.[20] Sometimes there is compression on head turning due to cervical osteophytes, in which case removal of the osteophytes might be considered.[20] Symptoms of vertebral-basilar artery insufficiency have been relieved by carotid endarterectomy, and it is now recommended that repair of carotid stenosis be undertaken rather than vertebral artery surgery when both systems are affected.[16,20]

Follow-up Experience. In the study of Bauer et al. (§202), the mortality during the first six months following surgery is more than twice that for the unoperated patients both from the standpoint of mortality ratio and the excess death rate. As is pointed out, the postoperative surgical mortality, especially during the first 30 days, accounts for much of this. From six months to 42 months, the balance of the follow-up period, the mortality is about the same for both groups. This observation was also made by Hass who has stated that the effect of extracranial arterial surgery on the natural history of transient cerebral ischemic attacks remains unclear.[5]

While the entrants in both the operated and unoperated groups described in §202 were allegedly randomized, the fact remains that the inoperable patients would have to be placed in the unoperated group. This would presumably have an adverse effect on the survival experience and would, in turn, make the experience in the operated group appear less unfavorable by comparison. On the other hand, in the group with a one-sided lesion and mild residuals, the operated patients had a significantly better survival than the unoperated patients. A similar difference was observed in the cases with bilateral disease and no residuals, but the number of cases was smaller and the difference was not statistically significant. In the other surgical/nonsurgical comparisons in Table 202d, medical treatment was associated with a significantly higher 3.5-year survival rate than surgical treatment in bilateral disease with severe residuals. Higher survival rates in medically treated patients are also found in unilateral disease with no residuals, and in bilateral disease with mild residuals, but these differences were not statistically significant.

The remaining eight abstracts of cerebrovascular disease give a comprehensive picture of the natural history in medically treated patients following a stroke or transient ischemic attack. Of the different types of patient series represented in these studies the Mayo Clinic reports on the population of Rochester, Minnesota, (§208, §209) are particularly valuable because they provide reliable data on incidence and on the *early* experience in the first few days and weeks following onset of symptoms. The incidence of first transient ischemic attack (TIA) is much lower than the incidence of initial stroke, all forms combined (compare Table 209c with incidence figures in the text of §208). The incidence of completed stroke ranges from less than 1 per 1000 per year in males under age 45 to 25 per 1000 per year in males at ages 75 and up; the incidence in females is lower. As might be anticipated, the prognosis within the first month is much better for patients with TIA than for patients with completed stroke: only 4 per cent of TIAs result in early death, but the corresponding percentages are 18 in cerebral thrombosis, 32 in cerebral embolus, 84 in intracerebral hemorrhage, and 54 in subarachnoid hemorrhage (Table 208a). The average age was much lower (54 years) in patients with subarachnoid hemorrhage than the averages in the other group of completed stroke and TIA, which ranged from 69 to 72 years. In the Danish series the mortality within three weeks of hospitalization was also very high on an overall basis, 50 per cent for male patients and 45 per cent for female patients (Table 207a). The early mortality rate in the Danish patients was lowest in those age 50 to 59, under 36 per cent; it increased with advancing age in patients at ages 60 and up, and was also higher in patients under age 50. Furthermore, early mortality was markedly influenced by the level of consciousness of the patient on admission: the three-week's rate was only 24 per cent in mentally alert patients, but increased with successive degrees of loss of alertness or consciousness to 98 per cent in fully comatose patients.

Excess mortality decreased sharply after the first few weeks, but nevertheless very high levels on a comparative basis were still observed, especially in the rest of the first year, as shown in the results of Wylie and White for patients admitted to a rehabilitation hospital (§201), Robinson et al., for hospitalized patients with cerebral thrombosis (§203), Baker et al., for Veterans Administration (VA) patients with cerebral infarction (§205), Marquardsen for Danish patients hospitalized for stroke (§207), and the studies in Rochester, Minnesota (§208, §209). Excess death rates within the first 12 to 15 months were of the order of 150 to 200 extra deaths per 1000 per year, or even higher where early mortality was not excluded (§204 and §206). In the VA study (§205) an EDR of 84 per 1000 was reported in the first two years, but patients were excluded from this series who did not survive at least three months after their stroke.

In those studies with follow-up of five years or more the EDR has sometimes been reported to fall to levels below 100 per 1000 after the first year (§204, §208, §209), but to persist close to the level of the first year or two in other series (§203, §205, §207). The results of Robinson et al. (§203) show an *increase* in EDR to about 250 per 1000 in both males and females from 10¼ to 14¼ years after onset of the stroke. Because of the increase in expected mortality rates with advancing attained age, mortality ratios generally show a decrease with duration of follow-up in most of the studies. However, the magnitude of the excess mortality is underscored by the persistence of greatly elevated EDRs and the correspondingly low survival ratios.

The long-term experience in most of the studies showed an increase in the EDR with advancing age, but a decrease in mortality ratio (related to the rise in expected mortality rates, as noted above). In the youngest age groups (under 55 or under 60 years) the EDR up to five years after the stroke was in the range of 59 to 98 per 1000 in males, and 67 to 99 per 1000 in females in three studies (§203, §204, §207). The EDR over the first five years rose progressively in the older age groups, except in female patients in the Framingham series (Table 204c), in whom 65 extra deaths per 1000 were recorded for women age 65 to 74 years, and reached a level of 203 per 1000 in men age 80 to 89 years in the series of Robinson et al. (§203), 300 per 1000 in Framingham men age 65 to 74 years (§204), and 188 per 1000 in Danish men age 70 to 79 years (§207). The only experience showing a departure from this age trend in EDR was that of Baker et al. in VA patients (§205, males only): EDR was 62 per 1000 for men under 55, 107 per 1000 for those age 55 to 64 years, and 64 per 1000 for those age 65 to 74 years; in 24 patients age 75 years and up there was no excess mortality. This Veterans Administration hospital experience was obtained over ten years of follow-up, rather than five years. Except in the first year in the Danish series, the EDR over a five-year period of follow-up was consistently lower in female than in male patients.

Excess mortality in relation to severity of the stroke and to other risk factors at the time of hospitalization is given by Marquardsen (§207). When the Danish patients were graded by severity of residual effects present three weeks after onset, those with little or no disability had the best five-year prognosis, with an EDR of 94 per 1000 and a survival ratio of 60.7 per cent. The EDR increased, and survival ratio decreased with progressively more severe initial disability. The worst cases, those totally disabled, had a three-year survival ratio of only 19.6 per cent, and a very high EDR of 428 per 1000 per year. Both male and female patients in two age groups exhibited a lower EDR if their blood pressure was under 180/100 as compared with those having more severe hypertension. It is of some interest that a material sex difference in excess mortality (higher EDR in males than in females) was noted only in the more severely hypertensive older patients. In patients with a blood pressure under 180/100 the EDR was about 90 per 1000 for those under age 70 and slightly less than 120 per 1000 for those age 70 to 79 years, regardless of sex.

As might be expected, recurrent stroke is a leading cause of death on the basis of data reported in several of these studies (Tables 205d, 207f, 208c). In the residents of Rochester, Minnesota, 37.9 per cent of the deaths were due to the initial stroke as compared with 10.4 per cent due to a subsequent stroke. Stroke occurrence rates are also given in patients with transient ischemic attack (Table 209d), and completed stroke (Table 207g).

Organic Brain Disorders
John J. Hutchinson, M.D.

Mental Retardation. Mental retardation can be defined as impairment in intelligence from birth or early life and subsequent inadequate mental development.[23] There are many possible causes which include metabolic disorders, genetic patterns, infections, traumas, toxic substances, and cerebral demyelinating diseases.[24] In addition to inadequate mental development, there may be many other complicating disorders such as motor handicaps, seizures, sensory deficiencies, congential circulatory problems, skeletal or endocrine disorders. The incidence of mental retardation varies greatly depending upon the criteria of measurement. About 0.5 per cent of preschool children are recognized as having significant mental retardation. About 1.0 per cent of adults are considered to be retarded, and in the interval between early school years and adult age from 3 to 10 per cent of the population has demonstrated some evidence of mental retardation.[23] About 95 per cent of the group with intelligence quotient (IQ) above 35 but less than 80 can be trained or educated to a degree that permits reasonable economic usefulness.[23]

Mortality patterns with regard to institutionalized patients with mental retardation are included in abstracts §215 and §216. The first was completed in the United States, predominantly among children, the latter reported in England over a lengthy period of observation, was based on adults. In general there is a definite increase in mortality in both males and females with mental deficiency, and this is most marked in ages under 30; the highest levels of mortality are in those with the greatest degree of retardation. In the U.S. experience, 86 per cent under age 18, with excess death rate was almost 20 per 1000 for those with IQ under 30, and about 5 per 1000 for those with less severe retardation, as indicated by a higher IQ. In the English institutionalized population those classed in idiots (equivalent to an IQ under 30) exhibited excess death rates of 50 or more per 1000, the minimum being in the age range of 30 to 39 years. In contrast, the EDR in nonmongoloid adults with less severe retardation was in the range of four to 12 per 1000 for those under age 50 and generally somewhat higher in older patients. Excess mortality in the California hospital was cut approximately in half from the earlier period of observation, 1948 to 1952, to the second period ten years later. If a young mentally retarded, hospitalized population is especially prone to infectious disease, as it probably is, this improvement may reflect better medical management of infection with the much wider range of antibiotics available in the later period. No follow-up data were located on the noninstitutionalized mentally retarded, but their mortality could very well be even lower than those cared for in hospitals, especially among those with an IQ of 50 or higher. More severe cases, especially those with developmental cranial anomalies and older mongoloids (Down's Syndrome) would probably have higher excess death rates.

Cerebral Palsy. This is a term applied to any of a group of disorders which demonstrate nonprogressive central motor manifestations, dating from birth or neonatal period.[23] Spasticity is a predominant feature, ranging in severity from a slight impairment of voluntary movement to total disability. Other varieties include athetoid movements, ataxia, and speech difficulty, separately or in combination depending on the areas of the brain that are involved.[24] Prematurity with associated anoxia is a frequent cause; birth injury, kernicterus, congenital malformations of brain or even cerebrovascular occlusion during fetal life can produce the brain damage which underlies this disorder. There are an estimated 300,000 to 400,000 cases in the United States.[23]

Prognosis to a large extent seems to depend upon the degree of intellectual impairment rather than upon the degree of motor deficit.[23] In the long-term studies §220 and §221 there is a materially higher increase in mortality experience in the most severe cases, with EDR 14 or more per 1000, than in the mild cases, with EDR only 1.8 per 1000 (Table 221b). Excess mortality is somewhat higher in children under five than in older children (Table 221a). In the spastic type the EDR was 5.5 per 1000 versus a range of 14 to 28 extra deaths per 1000 in other clinical types of cerebral palsy (Table 220c).

Epilepsy. Epilepsy is the result of paroxysmal excessive neuronal discharges in various parts of the brain, producing attacks of alteration of consciousness, with or without convulsive movement. It has been described since recorded history began and occurs today in about 0.5 per cent of people of all ages.[24] No specific structural or biochemical cause can be found in three-fourths of patients with convulsive seizures, thus the term idiopathic epilepsy.[24] There may be a genetic factor as evidenced by the occurrence of the disease in 3 to 5 per cent of the blood relatives of an epileptic. In the acquired cases, the causes include trauma, disease, toxic substances, or metabolic disorders.

Clinically several types are recognized.

1. Grand mal is generally characterized by an aura, loss of consciousness, generalized convulsion followed by a state of confusion, fatigue, headache, and often motor or sensory disturbances. About 90 per cent of all patients with convulsive disorders have grand mal.[24]
2. Petit mal is a transient loss of consciousness lasting five to 30 seconds without convulsive manifestations. There may be postictal confusion, but only briefly. Petit mal begins in childhood and generally lessens during adolescence and early adult life; it rarely persists beyond age 30.[24]
3. Focal seizures are often called Jacksonian epilepsy and frequently follow brain trauma. The seizure may be motor or sensory or both, but loss of consciousness need not occur. The episode is usually followed by confusion and partial amnesia.
4. Psychomotor epilepsy is a focal involvement of the temporal lobe. Seizures are generally characterized by an aura of anxiety followed by a change in consciousness frequently involving complex emotional or reasoning patterns. Aimless repetitive movements are frequent (sucking movement, swallowing, twisting of arms or legs, etc.), but there is no loss of consciousness. The patient's behavior may demonstrate destructive or aggressive conduct, or he may convey anger, depression, or fear. Fugue states or hallucinations may be present, but nearly always there is subsequent amnesia.

Modern drug therapy presents a large number of very effective substances. No single medication will be totally effective in the prevention of all seizures, but individually tailored dosages of one or more drugs can usually produce dramatic benefits.

In two life insurance studies (§226 and §279) excess mortality was less in petit mal than in grand mal epilepsy. Excess death rates were 0.8 per 1000 in petit mal and 2.7 per 1000 in grand mal, based on aggregate deaths in the three series of 24 and 88, respectively. Results of the New York Life and Prudential of England were similar, with EDRs of 1.3 and 1.5 per 1000 in petit mal and 3.1 and 3.2 per 1000 in grand mal, while the New England Life rates were lower, at 0 and 1.3 per 1000, respectively, in petit mal and grand mal. However, unlike the other studies, the New England Mutual experience included female lives. The statistical significance of the excess mortality in the three petit mal series combined is not quite at the 95 per cent level, (Poisson P=0.06) but EDR for grand mal epilepsy has very high statistical significance, as does the difference between the EDRs in grand mal and petit mal epilepsy. Further confirmation is contained in the experience of epileptic patients in four Danish neurology clinics (§225), with an overall excess death rate of 6.2 per 1000 in males alone, and 4.0 per 1000 in males and females combined. No separation of petit mal cases is made, and it can be assumed that this series either contained only grand mal cases, or all types of epilepsy with the usual preponderance of grand mal. In a smaller group of insured Swedes with "epilepsy" (type not specified, see §279) the excess death rate was also significantly elevated at 4.2 per 1000.

Unlike the overall results, patterns of excess mortality by age and sex are not consistent in the two series presented in §226 and §225. In the New York Life study (§226) the female EDR for grand mal epilepsy was higher than the male, and changes with age at policy issue were relatively small. In the Danish clinic patients (§225) both EDR and mortality ratio were considerably lower in young patients, age 10 to 29 when insurance began, than in those age 30 to 49 years. Female EDR was also considerably lower than the male rate, but, as noted in the abstract, part of this difference might be an artifact if the expected rates were based on a combined male and female table of insurance experience, which usually contains many more males than females. In the Danish experience excess mortality was found to correlate with various measures of severity of the epilepsy. Those whose attacks were classified as absent or mild at a follow-up examination had an EDR of 1.9 per 1000, while those classified as moderate to severe despite treatment had an EDR of 6.9 per 1000. The best experience, with an EDR of only 0.6 per 1000, was found in a quite small group of "mentally normal" patients with a known organic brain lesion; this presumably was Jacksonian rather than idiopathic epilepsy.

In the New York Life experience excess mortality was found in most of the categories of death reported, including malignant neoplasm, cardiovascular diseases, and accidents and homicide, as well as six out of 54 due to epilepsy. The 1,920 deaths in the United States during 1970 with epilepsy reported as the cause (Table 6-1) do not accurately reflect the excess mortality in epileptics.

Multiple Sclerosis. This is the most common of the demyelinating diseases of the central nervous system and is found only in man.[24] It is characterized by a bewildering variety of neurological signs and symptoms, including spastic muscle weakness, parasthesias, ataxia, ocular disturbance (impaired vision or double vision), and many others. Diagnosis is sometimes difficult and may depend upon careful observation over a long period of time, and studies to rule out functional or other neurological disease. In other cases the pattern may consist of a complex of multiple symptoms so that the diagnosis can be made readily. There seems to be a definite geographic pattern of incidence varying from 10 per 100,000 in Southern United States to 60 per 100,000 in the North.[25] A similar pattern exists in Europe, and the disease is rare in the tropics except among those who have moved to the tropics from the more temperate regions. This geographic distribution has led to a great deal of speculation as to possible etiology, but to date the cause is unknown. The current leading theories postulate an infectious or allergic cause.[24] Male and female incidence rates are equal; there seems to be no racial or genetic pattern, and 95 per cent of the cases develop between the ages of 10 and 50 (about two-thirds between 20 and 40).[25]

Most cases are characterized by periods of symptomatic manifestations followed by remission during which the disease may show almost no progression; in about 30 per cent of the cases there will be a steadily progressive deterioration with death due to intercurrent infections of urinary or respiratory system. It is stated that three-fourths of the people with periodic symptoms and remissions will be alive twenty years after onset of the disease, but the prognosis may be much worse in progressive cases.[25] In three autopsy-proved series the mean duration was 14 years, with a range from two months to 37 years.

Abstract §230 confirms the survival at 20 years of three-fourths of the Armed Forces multiple sclerosis patients; the 15-year cumulative survival rate was .83 and the survival ratio 87 per cent. In this predominantly young group of multiple sclerosis patients (average age 25 years) almost half had their initial symptoms between the time of entry into service and diagnosis at an Army hospital. With exposure reckoned from the date of Army diagnosis the average excess death rate for the first five years of follow-up was 4 per 1000, and from 5 to 15 years was 11 to 12 per 1000. The mortality ratio also increased from 265 to about 365 per cent. The highest excess mortality rate of 12 per 1000 was observed in patients age 30 to 34 years at diagnosis. In 93 of 121 deaths recorded the death was attributed to multiple sclerosis, although pneumonia was most frequently given as the immediate cause of death.

Somewhat higher mortality is indicated in a follow-up study of cases of multiple sclerosis residents in Israel in 1960 and diagnosed within the preceding five years (§231). Over a seven-year follow-up excess death rates were 14 per 1000 in those under age 45 at time of entry and 37 per 1000 in patients age 45 and up. Excess mortality, in addition to being higher in older patients, was also higher in males than in females, and in those with severe disability or a progressive course, as opposed to patients with mild disability or a course of remission and relapse.

Other Degenerative Diseases.   Paralysis agitans or Parkinson's disease is the result of impaired function of the basal ganglia and cerebral cortex. Some cases develop after encephalitis, others may be due to toxic substances (carbon monoxide, drugs, or heavy metals), trauma, or atherosclerosis. The syndrome is characterized by a mask-like facial expression, alternating tremor, stooped posture, slowness of movement, and cogwheel rigidity of muscles. In the United States in 1970 there were 3,254 deaths attributed to paralysis agitans. Table 279 covers a small group of insured lives both male and female with an average age of 50 years. The excess death rate was 14 per 1000 per year, with a mortality ratio of 280 per cent.

Huntington's Chorea (chronic progressive chorea) is an hereditary disease of the basal ganglia and cerebral cortex with adult onset of progressive mental deterioration and choreiform movements. The genetic pattern is that of a single dominant autosomal gene.[25] It is estimated the frequency of this disease varies from 2.3 to 6.7 cases per one hundred thousand population,[24] and in 1970 there were 225 deaths in the United States.[1] The average survival following onset of symptoms is said to be 15 years.[24]

Other degenerative brain disorders include diseases such as the cerebellar ataxias, Friedreich's ataxia, familial spastic paralysis, Tay-Sachs disease and gargoylism (both involving severe mental retardation with other lesions), progressive bulbar paralysis, and hereditary hemiplegia. All or almost all of these are generally considered clinically to have a poor prognosis. No follow-up data were found in the literature search for this volume. "Other" organic brain disorders, which probably included some of these diseases, were given in 1970 as the cause of 1,969 deaths in the United States (Table 6-1).

Developmental Defects.   Certain genetic defects are the causes of specific diseases; these are the chromosomal patterns of 13 trisomy, 18 trisomy, and the much more common 21 trisomy (Down's syndrome or Mongolism). In each of these there is limited brain development with mental retardation. There may be accompanying developmental abnormalities involving the heart, bony skeleton, musculature, palate, lips, etc. The accompanying malformations frequently lead to early death—often within the first year. Down's syndrome occurs in about 1.5 to 2.0 per 1000 births and has been reported in all races.[24] Mortality data have been described in connection with mental retardation in §215 and §216. Agenesis consists of a failure of parts of the brain to develop and may be related to genetic factors in some instances. In utero anoxemia, ionizing radiation, and infections may play a causative role. Severe forms usually result in death in infancy or childhood.

Hydrocephalus results from failure of cerebrospinal fluid to flow from the ventricles through the normal pathway, and in infants and young children produces abnormal enlargement of the head. Congenital hydrocephalus is thought to be caused most commonly by in utero infections. This is a rare disorder and although the more severe cases die within the first year or two of life, there are cases where surgical bypass of the obstruction leads to at least temporary relief of the increased intracranial pressure. Prognosis is clinically regarded as serious.[25] No data were located on the natural history of hydrocephalus or the results of operative procedures in long-term follow-up.

Infections.   Infections of the brain and meninges may be bacterial, viral, fungal, rickettsial, or spirochetal. More rarely the infecting organism is one of the higher parasite forms, i.e. echinococcus, trichina, or taenia. Among the bacterial infections meningococcus is the most common organism (30 per cent); pneumococcus, influenza bacillus and streptococcus constitute the offending microorganism in most of the remaining acute meningitis cases. Prior to antibiotic therapy these acute meningeal infections carried high acute mortality rates (about 80 per cent); current antibiotic therapy has reduced the mortality to less than 10 per cent in meningococcal or influenzal infections and to about 50 per cent in pneumococcal and other types of acute meningitis.[25]

Tuberculous meningitis has likewise been reduced as a cause of death since the advent of chemotherapeutic drugs for treatment of tuberculosis infections. Prior to isoniazid and streptomycin, tuberculous meningitis was almost universally fatal; since these drugs have become available, the early mortality rate has dropped to less than 20 per cent.[25]

Rickettsial infections such as typhus, spotted fever, and scrub typhus may show central nervous system involvement during the natural course of the disease, with cerebral edema and petechial hemorrhages. Encephalitis is a serious complication in severe cases, with delirium giving way to stupor, coma, sometimes convulsions, and other symptoms. Acute mortality formerly ranged up to 50 per cent in severe cases, but is now much lower because of the success of treatment with tetracycline or other effective antibiotics.[25] Neurological residuals are rare but may occur following severe rickettsial encephalitis.

A number of viral agents may produce various types of encephalitis, including encephalitis lethargica (von Economo's

Disease), St. Louis encephalitis, and equine encephalomyelitis (a disease of horses transmitted to humans by mosquitoes). Precise clinical diagnosis and identification of the viral agent are both very difficult to accomplish in the absence of an epidemic. Early mortality is reported to range from 20 to 30 per cent in encephalitis lethargica, from 5 to 30 per cent in St. Louis encephalitis (increasing with age), and up to 65 per cent in the equine type.[25] There is no effective treatment. Some patients who survive the acute phase of the disease may be disabled to varying degrees with prolonged or permanent neurological residuals, although this is rare in the St. Louis type. Often classified with the diseases just described is post-infectious encephalitis. Pathologically this is characterized by perivascular demyelinization. As its name implies it tends to occur as an unusual complication of an infectious disease, especially those caused by viruses such as measles, or following vaccination against smallpox or rabies. The acute mortality rate is reported as approximately 10 per cent in post measles encephalitis and 50 per cent in the post vaccinial type.[25]

Syphilis of the central nervous system no longer presents the disastrous problem it did before the introduction of penicillin. Prior to antibiotic therapy the incidence of neurosyphilis was nearly 30 per cent of those who had a luetic infection.[24] Neurosyphilis today is becoming a clinical rarity. In the prepenicillin era the most common form of neuro-syphilis was tabetic (tabes dorsalis) about 30 per cent of all neurosyphilis. Paresis (general paralysis, dementia paralytica) or a combination of paresis and tabes constituted about 15 per cent. The virtual disappearance of neurosyphilis represents a tremendous saving of useful human life and eliminates the pathetic burdensome problem of the paretic or tabetic patient of yesteryear. Untreated paresis formerly progressed to a fatal termination, usually within five years of the onset of symptoms, but the disease can be arrested with prompt penicillin therapy in 80 per cent of cases.[24]

Estivo-autumnal malaria can produce occlusion of cerebral capillaries with petechial hemorrhages and can lead to death in 30 to 40 per cent of cases with cerebral malaria.[24] Those individuals who recover do not demonstrate neurological sequelae.

Infections involving the mastoid, paranasal sinuses, orbit or upper part of the face may, by direct extension or venous drainage, produce septic thrombosis of lateral cavernous or septal sinuses or brain abscess. Lung abscess may be the source of embolic infection producing similar pathology. Penetrating wounds of the skull may lead to brain abscess although with the advent of antibiotics intracranial septic involvement is rare. All types of brain abscess still involve a high mortality rate, up to 75 per cent, despite surgery and antibiotic therapy.[24]

Trauma. Motor vehicle accidents are the cause of some 3 million head injuries in the United States annually, and 30,000 deaths annually are attributed to these head injuries.[24] The extent, location, and type of injury are exceedingly important in relation to the prognosis; simple concussion is associated with no extra mortality while cases involving extradural hemorrhage may entail a mortality rate of 55 per cent.[24] When the skull is fractured, the injury to the brain substance becomes the most important factor in survival. Compound skull fractures present the added hazard of infection and can lead to an early mortality of 30 per cent of the cases.

Table 279 presents some long-term mortality results from life insurance data on cerebral concussion and on histories of skull fracture in relation to whether or not surgical intervention was required. Simple concussion produced a standard mortality experience. Skull fracture not requiring surgery produced a standard experience in one United States company. In an English insurance company the experience was moderately less favorable with a mortality ratio of 153 per cent and did not seem to reflect any significantly higher long-term mortality for those with sequelae; applicants who had required surgery at the time of head injury showed a slightly higher mortality ratio of 175 per cent.

Spinal Cord Disorders
John J. Hutchinson, M.D.

Paraplegia. Trauma, neoplastic disease, poliomyelitis, acute myelitis, or demyelinating disease can so damage the spinal cord that paraplegia (flaccid paralysis of the lower extremities with sensory loss) results. The prognosis is largely a function of the nature of the cause, the extent of the pathology, the level of cord damage, and the effective use of rehabilitation and prevention of infections. Significant complications frequently involve emotional, respiratory, circulatory, nutritional, and excretory problems. Survival is dependent in each case on proper evaluation of the complications and appropriate management in each significant area.

Considerable excess mortality is evident in a very large series of patients in Veterans Administration hospitals for spinal cord injury (§250) and in another series of Canadian patients (§251). Mortality ratios, all durations combined, ranged from 255 to 2900 per cent in the U.S. series and from 98 to 1560 per cent in the Canadian series. The only group with a normal EDR, -0.5 per 1000, was found in Canadians 44 years of age and older with incomplete paraplegia (Table 251c), but this was not confirmed in the U.S. patients with incomplete paraplegia, among whom the EDR was 36 per

1000 in those age 45 to 59 years (Table 250c). Results were reasonably consistent in the two series, showing an increase in the excess death rate and mortality ratio with severity of the lesion, incomplete to complete, and paraplegia to quadriplegia. Excess death rates increased with age in both series, with exceptions in only three of the eight groups, and in the U.S. experience there was a less consistent downward trend of mortality ratio with advancing age. The highest EDRs, over 100 per 1000, were found in the U.S. complete quadriplegics age 35 and up. The corresponding rate in Canadian quadriplegics age 44 and up was 81 per 1000, but the average duration was longer than in the U.S. group. Kidney failure (most often secondary to urinary tract infection) was the leading cause of death (36 per cent of the total) in the Canadian patients. Cardiovascular disease ranked second as a cause of death.

Infections and Sequalae. Meningitis, referred to previously, involves the covering structures of the spinal cord as well as the brain. Epidural abscess is a rare but serious acute infectious process that produces spinal cord symptoms and formerly had a high mortality.[24] Tabes dorsalis (locomotor ataxia) is neurosyphilis involving the posterior roots and highly selective portions of sensory tracts in the spinal cord. It develops usually five years or more after the primary infection, produces disability but has only minor effect on longevity.[24] With effective penicillin treatment of early and latent syphilis the incidence of tabes has been much reduced, especially the disabling far advanced stage.[24] Another formerly important infectious disease of the spinal cord is poliomyelitis (infantile paralysis) due to a virus. Active immunization has reduced the incidence to low levels, but the disease continues endemic in the United States as immunization of children is by no means as complete as it should be. Poliomyelitis involves the anterior horn cells of the spinal cord. When these cells are destroyed a flaccid paralysis of the muscles supplied is the inevitable consequence. The paralysis may be partial or complete and may involve groups of muscles or all muscles of extremities, trunk or bladder. The degree of disability depends on the extent of the residual involvement. The acute mortality rate is estimated to be about 5 per cent, is higher in adolescents and adults than in children, and is especially high in the bulbar form, in which respiratory failure may occur.[24] There is also some excess long-term mortality in patients with moderate disability due to poliomyelitis in those age 50 up at policy issue, as is evident from the results of an intercompany study of insured policyholders (see §255). On an overall basis there was no significant excess mortality in applicants under age 50, nor at durations up to five years. By duration the mortality ratio was 275 per cent and excess death rate 5.4 per 1000 at duration 10-15 years (Table 255a). A smaller insured postpoliomyelitis group in England experienced a mortality ratio of 117 per cent. Poliomyelitis victims with severe disability are ordinarily not regarded as insurable, and it is probable that their excess mortality would be considerably higher because of respiratory or urinary tract complications.

Degenerative and Developmental Diseases. The cause of amyotrophic lateral sclerosis is not known; the pathology is one of degeneration of motor cells in the spinal cord, in the brain stem, and in the cerebral cortex. This leads to degeneration of fiber tracts in the lateral and anterior portions of the spinal cord. It is estimated that about five people per 100,000 have this disease and the distribution seems fairly uniform throughout the world.[25] This disease rarely develops under age 30 or over age 70; over 80 per cent of the cases develop during the fifth, sixth, and seventh decades. There is no effective treatment, and death is generally the result of inanition and respiratory infections secondary to paralysis of accessory muscles of inspiration. The disease is not characterized by remissions and the mean duration is about three years.[24]

Syringomyelia is a rare disease of unknown cause characterized by gliosis and cavitation of the spinal cord or medulla. Most common is involvement of the cervical cord, but lumbar or bulbar involvement may exist alone or in addition to cervical pathology. Muscular atrophy with spastic weakness and segmental loss of sensibility for pain and temperature are common manifestations. The disease generally runs a long course of several years with paralysis and sensory defects varying according to the area of the cord involved.

Developmental failure of the lower spinal column to enclose the spinal cord completely is termed spina bifida. It is frequently associated with other congenital defects involving the brain or brain stem, (such as hydrocephalus), or involving other body systems. Bony defects resulting from incomplete closure of one or more vertebral arches may occur in 25 per cent of the population, but significant spinal defects occur only once in 4,000 cases.[24] Surgical correction of the single or multiple defects is sometimes feasible. Prognosis depends on the extent of the defect, the size of the protruding mass, the spinal cord damage with its resulting disability, and the degree of success achieved with surgical intervention.

Other Neurological Disorders
John J. Hutchinson, M.D.

Neuritis is the traditional term applied to disease of the peripheral nerves, although neuropathy is more inclusive, as many diseases of peripheral nerves are degenerative rather than inflammatory in character. Neuritis may be localized or generalized, and may involve the sensory nerve roots (radiculitis). Causes of neuritis are numerous and include infections, bacteriotoxins (diphtheria and tetanus), mechanical factors (cervical rib), injury, chemical factors (lead, methyl or ethyl alcohol), metabolic (diabetes), nutritional (vitamin deficiencies), vascular (peripheral arterial disease), and degenerative disorders (hereditary, secondary systemic effects of lung cancer and other neoplasms).[24] Sometimes the specific cause is not identifiable, which makes prognosis more difficult, as prognosis is related to the underlying cause. Optic or retrobulbar neuritis is a good specific example of this, as it may be due to almost any of the causes mentioned, but frequently careful diagnostic evaluation fails to reveal the etiology. Three potentially serious conditions in which optic neuritis may be the earliest manifestation are multiple sclerosis, brain tumor, and cerebrovascular disease. All of these diseases threaten life, as shown in various abstracts in this volume. It is therefore clear that one should anticipate excess mortality in a group of patients with recent optic neuritis of unknown cause, as some of them may be expected to develop evidence of one of these serious diseases within a few months or years. The mortality associated with optic neuritis of unspecified cause will reflect this tendency.

Other neurological disorders apart from those of the brain or spinal cord accounted for 6,824 deaths in the United States in 1970 (Table 6-1). No mortality data could be located for almost all forms of neuritis, but some data are presented in Table 279 on diseases of the special sense organs, and on one neurological finding, the presence of tremor on examination for insurance, that is not specific in nature. On the basis of the limited insurance experience shown there was no increased mortality in glaucoma; cataract, unilateral and total blindness showed mortality ratios varying from 130 to 136 per cent, a minimal increase, and marked impairment of vision showed the highest mortality ratio of 255 per cent. However, this was based on only six deaths, and the aggregate mortality ratio for all five eye disorders listed is barely significant at 128 per cent (Poisson P=0.05). A normal mortality was found in Ménière's disease (involving the vestibular apparatus of the inner ear), deaf-mutism and mastoidectomy. A minimal increase in mortality ratio to 114 per cent was found in otitis media by the Prudential of London, and the New York Life experience with marked deafness (not deaf-mutism) gave a mortality ratio of 130 per cent, not a significant increase. In a small group of insureds with tremors noted at examination the mortality ratio was 190 per cent, but with only seven deaths this was not quite at the 95 per cent significance level (Poisson P=0.08). Tremors are a nonspecific neurological finding, often physiological or benign in character, but they may occur in many serious types of neurological disease such as Parkinson's disease.

Psychiatric Disorders
John J. Hutchinson, M.D.

In 1966 the World Health Organization adopted a unified international system of nomenclature in psychiatry. Those psychiatric entities for which there is no known organic basis include the neuroses, the psychophysiologic disorders, personality disorders, psychoses, and transient situational disturbances. Any classification of psychiatric disorders is largely dependent upon descriptive terminology, and lack of standard definition of terms has led to other classification systems differentiating the nonorganic disorders more simply as functional psychoses, and personality disorders and neurotic symptoms.[25]

Only 2,700 deaths due to psychoses, neuroses and personality disorders were reported in the United States in 1970 (Table 6-1). However, many elderly people develop senile dementia or various forms of organic psychosis and experience a very high excess mortality. Such patients comprise a large part of those in mental institutions. Deaths are usually reported as due to the underlying cerebrovascular disease, to other brain disorders or chronic diseases, or to intercurrent disease such as pneumonia. The 23,480 suicides, which clearly belong in this category, are a substantial addition to this psychiatric death total. Nevertheless, the magnitude of the mortality risk in mental disorders cannot be estimated from the number of deaths reported by cause. Prevalence data indicate that approximately one-third of patients admitted to general hospitals and one-half or more of patients consulting physicians have an important psychiatric aspect to their presenting complaint, usually neurotic in type.[25] A 1969-1970 survey of the noninstitutionalized population of the United States disclosed over 1,000,000 persons with chronic disability due to mental or neurological disorders. The number of patients in mental hospitals was reported as 547,000 in 1966.[26] Most of these patients have functional psychiatric disorders, but patients with mental deficiency, senile dementia and other organic psychoses are also included. With the development and extensive use of psychotherapeutic drugs in the treatment of psychoses the number of hospitalized patients has decreased over the past 20 years, despite a steady rise in new admissions. More patients have been rehabilitated or restored to a status where they can be handled as outpatients.

Psychoses. Psychoses represent disturbances in thinking and perception serious enough to distort the patient's appreciation of the real world. The two principal types are schizophrenia and manic-depressive psychosis. Schizophrenia is a psychiatric disturbance characterized by hallucinations, delusions, and altered behavior which can have its onset at any age but most commonly in adolescence or early adult life. About one per cent of the population has this disorder, and there appears to be a genetic pattern upon which environmental factors have an influence. Five to 6 per cent of the siblings of a schizophrenic patient have schizophrenia,[27] yet among distant relatives of a schizophrenic patient the incidence is no higher than in the population at large. Phenothiazine drugs have proven very effective in the treatment of this disease and have served to decrease markedly the number of chronic long-term patients confined to mental hospitals. Manic-depressive or affective psychosis is characterized by excessive mood disturbances. The mood may be one of elation and self-confidence or it may be one of depression, sadness, and self-condemnation. Not infrequently there are periodic swings in mood from one extreme to the other with intervening periods of apparent mental health. During the periods of elation and overactivity there is generally poor judgment, and the patient may become involved in grandiose schemes or poor business ventures. During the periods of depression there can be a real danger of suicide or serious bodily injury. Modern drug therapy is very effective and most patients with this form of psychosis are restored to fully effective lives.

The patients studied in a five-year follow-up in abstract §280 included *all* psychiatric referrals in a region around Aberdeen, Scotland, over a period of one year, provided the patient had not seen a psychiatrist in the previous year. The group of over 2,000 patients therefore constituted a valid cross-section of persons in the population with mental illness of different types and severity; patients seen as outpatients and as patients in general hospitals were included in addition to those admitted to mental hospitals. Only 29 per cent of the patients were classified as functional or organic psychosis (Table 280b). The experience for the entire group, all diagnoses, ages, and durations combined showed a mortality ratio of 225 per cent in males and 345 per cent in females, with corresponding excess death rates of 21 and 28 per 1000 per year, respectively. The lowest EDRs were found in patients under 45, 8.1 per 1000 in males and 4.2 per 1000 in females (Table 280a). Extremely high mortality, due to organic psychosis and other infirmities of old age, was found in patients age 75 and up, with EDRs of 297 and 246 per 1000. Excess death rates were high (over 100 per 1000) in the first three months following diagnosis and tended to decrease after that (Tables 280c and 280e). The five-year mortality rates in Table 280b are about 10 per cent in the functional psychoses, and extremely high at about 70 per cent in the organic psychoses (Table 280b). It is obvious that mortality and survival in a mixed psychiatric population will be heavily influenced by the proportion of poor-risk patients with organic psychoses. However, significant excess mortality was observed in patients under age 55, predominantly those with functional psychosis and neurosis, as few organic psychosis patients are likely to be found in this age group.

In one insured group classified as having a psychosis history the mortality ratio was 155 per cent, and in another group including all psychiatric disorders the mortality ratio was 124 per cent (Table 279). Although these ratios were not significantly elevated, additional support for excess mortality in patients with functional psychosis is found in other studies of psychiatric patients, some with and some without a history of suicide attempt. One such report is a careful epidemiological investigation of psychiatric consultations and death in a county-wide population including Rochester, New York.[27] Through a special register records were established for 39,475 persons seeking advice at virtually all of the available psychiatric facilities in the county during the period 1960 through 1966: all inpatient and outpatient at mental, general, and Veterans Administration hospitals, all special clinics (mental health, alcoholism, child guidance, court), and 56 of the 60 psychiatrists with private practices in the county. Certificates for all 42,005 deaths in the county during the seven-year observation period were examined and 3,809 of these were confirmed as occurring in the psychiatric register population. Observed deaths in any diagnostic or other category of the register patients could then be compared with expected deaths calculated from exposure-years and county population mortality rates matched by sex and quinquennial age group. Although exposure data are, unfortunately, not reported except for the population as a whole, age-specific "relative risks" are given, equivalent to mortality ratios as used in the tables of this volume, except that they are reported as a decimal number rather than a percentage. Relative risks for psychosis classified as schizophrenia were 1.6 for males and 1.9 for females; among the affective psychoses (manic-depressives) the corresponding risks were 2.1 and 1.9, respectively. Much higher relative risks, 4.3 in males and 5.4 in females, were found in chronic brain syndrome (organic psychosis). Over 58 per cent of the total, that is, 2,224 deaths occurred in the elderly hospitalized group of patients with organic psychosis. The number of deaths for the generally younger patients with functional psychoses was much smaller (914), but still amply sufficient to make the increased mortality risk highly significant in both schizophrenia and the affective psychoses in both sexes. When all psychiatric diagnoses were combined the relative risk exceeded 2.0 in all major cause of death categories except neoplasms, for which the risk was only 1.2 in males and 1.5 in females. There were 133 suicides in the register population, one-third of all suicides so reported in the county. Relative risks for death by suicide were 8.0 in males and 11.1 in females, but these ratios probably would be higher in the functional psychoses if patients with organic brain disorder had been excluded: it may reasonably be assumed that most of the patients in the latter group would be mentally or physically incapable of committing suicide.

Reference should be made to three additional articles containing studies of the suicide rate in patients who formerly had been hospitalized for psychiatric illness.[28,29,30] All of these provide evidence for a greatly increased risk of suicide among former mental hospital patients. In an analysis of 1,457 suicides in Massachusetts in 1949 to 1951 Temoche, Pugh, and MacMahon were able to identify 30 who were patients in mental hospitals at the time of suicide, 153 who were patients in the past, and 1,274 who had never been treated in mental hospitals in the state.[28] Among males the overall age-standardized suicide rate was 57 per 100,000 for former patients and 15 per 100,000 for nonpatients, a relative risk of 3.7; among females the corresponding rates were 38 and 4.4 per 100,000, respectively, with a relative risk of 8.5. The relative risk for white males and females combined was much higher, 34.4 during the first six months after discharge from the mental hospital, fell to 9.6 in the next six months and 7.1 in the second year. Among such recently discharged patients with 66 observed and 4.30 expected suicides the relative risk was 15.3 for all diagnoses, 36.1 for depressive psychoses (17 suicides), and 13.2 for schizophrenia and other functional psychoses (15 suicides). Higher suicide rates were found by Pokorny in 11,585 psychiatric admissions to the Houston Veterans Administration Hospital 1949 to 1963, with 117 suicides identified in current and former patients during a maximum of 15 years follow-up.[29] In contrast to an expected suicide rate of 23 per 100,000 for male Texas veterans (higher than the national average of 10 per 100,000) Pokorny determined a rate of 165 per 100,000 for all patients, 566 and 167 per 100,000, respectively, for psychotic patients diagnosed as depressives and schizophrenics. These indicate an excess death rate of 5.4 per 1000 per year due to suicide alone in male veterans previously or currently hospitalized for depressive psychosis. James and Levin studied 629 suicides in Western Australia in 1955 to 1961 and found that 75 of these occurred in ex-patients of the only psychiatric hospital in the state.[30] Age-standardized suicide rates were 155 per 100,000 for former male patients and 35 per 100,000 for non-patient males, with a suicide mortality ratio of 440 per cent. Among females the corresponding rates were 76 and 8.5 per 100,000, respectively, with a suicide mortality ratio of 890 per cent. These figures include other psychiatric diagnoses as well as the psychoses. The authors estimate that 3.1 per cent of all male patients and 1.5 per cent of all female patients admitted to the hospital, which opened in 1929, subsequently committed suicide. The suicide rate was more than four times as high for men and nearly nine times as high for women as in the rest of the population excluding former patients.

Neuroses. A simple exact definition of neurosis is difficult if not impossible. It has been described as a disorder in which the individual has an excessive inappropriate emotional response without obvious cause. The common symptoms may be those of anxiety, depression, or a host of psychophysiological reactions (such as the hyperventilation syndrome), or they may mimic the manifestation of physical illness (such as hysterical paralysis). Neurosis made up 44 per cent of all psychiatric referrals in the follow-up study in northeast Scotland (§280), and 23 per cent of patients in the psychiatric registry in a county of New York State, reported by Babigian and Odoroff.[27] A survey in a town in England conducted by Taylor and Chaves and quoted by Kolb[31] provided the following estimates for prevalence of neurotic symptoms in the population: 33 per cent of the people in that community had neurotic symptoms but were not seeking any medical care or advice; 8.1 per cent of the population were receiving individual physician care; 4.4 per cent were receiving care from a psychiatric outpatient clinic; and 1.9 per cent required hospital treatment. Such figures reflect severity of symptoms, and probably individual willingness to seek medical care as well as availability of psychiatric facilities.

Long-term follow-up studies of individuals with a history of neurosis demonstrate a generally small but consistent increased mortality, with average mortality ratios in the range of 124 to 215 per cent, and excess death rates about 1 to 3 per 1000 (§279, §285, §286). The highest mortality was found in the New York Life experience with males having a history of single episode of neurosis classified as moderate to severe. The EDR was 7.8 per 1000 in this group among men age 40 to 49 years, and 3.0 per 1000 among men of all ages (Table 286c). Another group in the New York Life Study consisted of men with varied number of episodes of neurosis, all severities combined; here the EDR was 1.9 per 1000, increasing slightly with advancing age at policy issue, with a mortality ratio of 174 per cent. The corresponding groups of females in the New York Life Study (Table 286c) and male insured groups followed by the Prudential of London (Table 279) all experienced an excess death rate close to 1.0 per 1000, with a mortality ratio averaging 154 per cent or less. In another carefully planned study among men with neurosis severe enough to result in a disability separation from the service in 1944 were followed by Veterans Administration records for up to 24 years (§285). The study was restricted to men age 25 to 30 years at the time of discharge. Mortality in the neurosis group, consisting of 1,140 deaths out of 9,813 cases, with well over 200,000 exposure years, were matched against mortality rates in a control group of Army men without neurosis and not prematurely separated from the service. War deaths, of course, were excluded. The mortality ratio decreased with duration of follow-up from 146 to 112 per cent, averaging 121 per cent, but EDR exhibited a slight tendency to increase, the range being 0.6 to 1.3 per 1000 and the average 0.9 per 1000. It is of interest that the control group of veterans had a mortality ratio only 87 per cent of the contemporaneous U.S. male population (Table 285c). If population rates had been used as a basis of the expected, the mortality ratio in the veterans with neurosis would have been only 105 per cent, not a significant increase with this clearly less suitable yardstick. Deaths by violence—accident, suicide and homicide—were significantly increased in the neurosis as compared with the control group (Table 285d). Significant increases were also observed in deaths attributed to mental disorders and neurological diseases.

In the follow-up study of patients in a psychiatric register, already referred to under the psychoses, Babigian and Odoroff found a relative mortality risk of 2.0 for males with neurosis as the priority diagnosis (134 observed deaths) and a relative risk of 1.8 for females (89 deaths). Suicide rates in patients with a history of hospitalization for treatment of neuroses have also been found to be markedly elevated above the suicide rates in the general population matched by age and sex. Temoche, Pugh, and MacMahon found a suicide mortality ratio of 1840 per cent,[28] and Pokorny records a suicide mortality ratio of 525 per cent,[29] over a longer follow-up. These studies have also been described previously under the psychoses.

Personality Disorders. Personality refers to traits of character that represent an individual's ability to respond in a particular way to circumstances. All degrees of variation exist in personality traits. When an individual demonstrates a degree of variation in any trait so that he or others complain of its extent, it may be said that person has a personality disorder. He may be unduly suspicious or he may demonstrate a tendency to lie or cheat or steal; he may demonstrate hypochondriasis or social antagonism. Additions are often included in this category, for which the term "character disorder" is a synonym.

In the study by Innes and Millar character disorders and addictions made up 9 per cent of all psychiatric diagnoses (§280). The five-year mortality rate was the lowest of all the diagnostic classifications, 5.6 per cent in males and 7.3 per cent in females, but these rates were based on fewer than ten deaths in each sex (Table 280b). Babigian and Odoroff reported a relative mortality risk of 2.3 in male registry patients and 2.9 in females.[27] The prevalence of character disorder in all psychiatric diagnoses was 31 per cent in males and 17 per cent in females in this registry. The suicide risk in ex-hospital patients with personality disorder and alcoholism was found by Pokorny to be almost six times that of the general population, a ratio about the same as the ratios for neurosis and schizophrenia but considerably below the ratio in depressive psychosis.[29]

Suicide Attempt. The reasons a person may attempt suicide are numerous. Personal conflict, financial or social difficulty, and illness constitute the principal motives.[32] Over half of those attempting suicide have depressive or neurotic symptoms and up to 40 per cent have histories of one or more hospitalizations for psychiatric problem. In a very small insured group with a history of suicide attempt there were four observed and 0.39 expected deaths, a mortality ratio of more than 1000 per cent. Despite the small number of deaths the ratio does have statistical significance (Poisson P less than 0.001). More extensive experience confirming a marked increase in mortality risk in persons with a history of suicide attempt is described in additional studies below.

Attempted Suicide

Udsen has reported an average four-year follow-up of 4,628 patients treated at the Intoxication Center of Bispibjerg following discharge after treatment for attempted suicide by poisoning in 1949 to 1955.[32] There were 212 deaths among 1,848 males, compared with 60 deaths expected from mortality rates in the Danish male population, giving a mortality ratio of 353 per cent. Out of the 212 deaths 73 were classified as "natural causes" (diseases of all types), 120 as suicides, and 19 as accidental or unknown cause, of which some were suspected as being due to suicide. In women attempting suicide there were 195 observed and 74 expected deaths during follow-up, with a mortality ratio of 264 per cent. As with males, suicides predominated, constituting 90 of the female deaths, leaving 86 due to natural causes and 19 due to accidents and unknown causes. About 20 per cent of the patients were readmitted following another suicide attempt by poisoning; successful suicides ensued in almost 5 per cent of the initial group of patients. Udsen estimated the average suicide rate in the male patients at 12 per 1000 per year, and in the females 8 per 1000, with corresponding expected suicide rates of 0.3 and 0.15 per 1000, respectively, in the male and female segments of the Danish population. These rates yield suicide mortality ratios of 4000 per cent in males and 5300 per cent in females. The annual EDRs due to suicide alone were 12 per 1000 among males and 7.8 per 1000 among females. Risk of suicide was highest in the first year following discharge and decreased progressively throughout the next five years. Only 10 per cent of the patients were classified as psychotic; more than half had a psychiatric diagnosis of neurosis or "affect reaction"; about one-sixth were classified as alcoholics and another one-sixth as psychopaths. Over one-third had previously been hospitalized for psychiatric treatment. It is apparent that recognized depression classified as psychotic in character was present in only a small minority of those who attempted suicide at the time of initial treatment. All types of psychiatric disorders were involved.

Another follow-up study is that reported by Pokorny on a predominantly male group of veterans seen during 1949 to 1963 in psychiatric consultation because of an unsuccessful suicide attempt, suicide threat, or ideas of suicide.[33] There were 582 males in the group, followed an average of 4.6 years, with 21 suicides, observed, about 35 times the expected number of 0.6. The average annual suicide rate was 7.9 per 1000, giving an EDR of 7.7 per 1000 when compared with the annual suicide rate found in male Texas veterans of 0.23 per 1000. Although numbers of deaths were small in individual categories, the suicide rate appeared to increase with advancing age up to 60 years, but decreased sharply with duration (nine of the 21 suicides occurred in the first year of follow-up). The risk was almost as high in patients with suicide ideas or threats as in patients who actually attempted suicide. All psychiatric diagnoses were represented in the patient group. The most numerous were 262 male patients with depression, but their annual suicide rate of 7.0 per 1000 was slightly below the average. The lowest suicide rate of 2.9 per 1000 was found in 64 men with neurosis, but this was still more than 12 times the expected rate.

It is evident that the risk of suicide contributes to significant excess mortality in all psychiatric disorders, especially in the psychoses and depressive states. The risk is greatly magnified in patients who express suicidal ideas or attempt suicide, regardless of the psychiatric diagnosis. The risk is lowest in persons with nondisabling neurotic symptoms, provided they have not contemplated or attempted suicide.

References

1. National Center for Health Statistics, *Vital Statistics of the United States 1970, Volume II—Mortality, Part A*. Rockville, Md.: U.S. Dept. of Health, Education, and Welfare (1974).

2. H.B. Locksley, "Strokes in Hypertension." *Trans. Assoc. Life Ins. Med. Dir. Am.*, 50:272-285 (1966).

3. J.P. Whisnant, M.J. Martin, and G.P. Sayre, "Atherosclerotic Stenosis of Cervical Arteries. Clinical Significance." *Arch. Neurol.*, 5:429-432 (1961).

4. A. Bernsmeier, U. Gottstein, K. Held, and W. Niedermayer, "The Stroke—Pathogenesis, Course and Prognosis." In *Annals of Life Insurance Medicine*, 3:165-184. New York: Springer-Verlag (1967).

5. K. Hass, "Occlusive Cerebrovascular Disease." *Med. Clin. North Am.*, 56:1281-1297 (1972).

6. R.H. Clauss, G.M. Sanoudos, J.F. Ray, III, and S. Moallem, "Carotid Endarterectomy for Cerebrovascular Ischemia." *Surg. Gynecol. Obstet.*, 136:993-1000 (1973).

7. W.S. Fields, R.R. North, W.K. Hass et al., "Joint Study of Extracranial Arterial Occlusion as A Cause of Stroke. I. Organization of Study and Survey of Patient Population." *J. Am. Med. Assoc.*, 203:955-960 (1968).

8. "Cancer Statistics, 1975." *Ca; A Cancer Journal for Clinicians*, 25:8-21 (1975).

9. National Center for Health Statistics, *Monthly Vital Statistics Report*, 24:1-8 (March 27, 1975).

10. "Recent Mortality from Cerebral Vascular Diseases." *Stat. Bull. Metropol. Life Ins. Co.*, 51:5-7 (Sept. 1970).

11. "Amounts Disbursed on Account of Deaths from Selected Causes Among Policyholders Covered Under Ordinary Life Insurance." *Stat. Bull. Metropol. Life Ins. Co.*, 54:11 (March 1973).

12. "Amounts Disbursed on Account of Deaths from Selected Causes Among Policyholders Covered Under Ordinary Life Insurance." *Stat. Bull. Metropol. Life Ins. Co.*, 55:11 (March 1974).

13. "Regional Variations in Mortality from Cerebrovascular Diseases." *Stat. Bull. Metropol. Life Ins. Co.*, 54:5-7 (April 1973).

14. W.K. Hass, W.S. Fields, R.R. North, I.I. Kricheff, N.E. Chase, and R.B. Bauer, "Joint Study of Extracranial Arterial Occlusion. II. Arteriography, Techniques, Sites, and Complications." *J. Am. Med. Assoc.*, 203:961-968 (1968).

15. R.B. Bauer, J.S. Meyer, W.S. Fields, R. Remington, M.C. Macdonald, and P. Callen, "Joint Study of Extracranial Arterial Occlusion. III. Progress Report of Controlled Study of Long-Term Survival in Patients With and Without Operation." *J.Am. Med. Assoc.*, 208:509-518 (1969).

16. W.F. Blaisdell, R.H. Clauss, J.G. Galbraith, A.M. Imparato, and E.J. Wylie, "Joint Study of Extracranial Arterial Occlusion. IV. A Review of Surgical Considerations." *J. Am. Med. Assoc.*, 209:1889-1895 (1969).

17. W.S. Fields, V. Maslenikow, J.S. Meyer, W.K. Hass, R.D. Remington, and M. Macdonald, "Joint Study of Extracranial Arterial Occlusion. V. Progress Report of Prognosis Following Surgery or Nonsurgical Treatment for Transient Cerebral Ischemic Attacks and Cervical Carotid Artery Lesions." *J. Am. Med. Assoc.*, 211:1993-2003 (1970).

18. A. Heyman, W.S. Fields, and R.D. Keating, "Joint Study of Extracranial Arterial Occlusion. VI. Racial Differences in Hospitalized Patients with Ischemic Stroke." *J. Am. Med. Assoc.*, 222:285-289 (1972).

19. W.S. Fields and N.A. Lemak, "Joint Study of Extracranial Arterial Occlusion. VII. Subclavian Steal—A Review of 168 Cases." *J. Am. Med. Assoc.*, 222:1139-1143 (1972).

20. A.B. Grindal and J.F. Toole, "Surgical Treatment of Carotid and Vertebral Artery Disease—An Updating to 1974." *Ann. Int. Med.*, 81:647-649 (1974).

21. A.M. Ostfeld, R.B. Shekelle, and H.L. Klawns, "Transient Ischemic Attacks and Risk of Stroke in an Elderly Poor Population." *Stroke*, 4:980-986 (1973).

22. I.S. Wright, "Strokes—Diagnosis and Modern Treatment (1)." *Mod. Concept Cardiovasc. Dis.,* 34:31-34 (1965).

23. V.C. Vaughan, III, and R.J. McKay, eds., *Nelson's Textbook of Pediatrics,* 10th ed. Philadelphia, Pa.: W.B. Saunders Co. (1975).

24. H.H. Merritt, *A Textbook of Neurology*, 5th ed. Philadelphia, Pa.: Lea and Febiger (1973).

25. P.B. Beeson and W. McDermott, eds., *Cecil-Loeb Textbook of Medicine*, 14th ed. Philadelphia, Pa.: W.B. Saunders Co. (1975).

26. M. Kramer, E.S. Pollack, R.W. Redick, and B.Z. Locke, *Mental Disorders/Suicide*. Cambridge, Mass.: Harvard University Press (1972).

27. H.M. Babigian and C.L. Odoroff, "The Mortality Experience of a Population with Psychiatric Illness." *Am. J. Psychiatry*, 126:470-480 (1969).

28. A. Temoche, T.F. Pugh, and B. MacMahon, "Suicide Rates among Current and Former Mental Institution Patients." *J. Nerv. Ment. Dis.,* 138:124-130 (1964).

29. A.D. Pokorny, "Suicide Rates in Various Psychiatric Disorders." *J. Nerv. Ment. Dis.,* 139:499-506 (1964).

30. I.P. James and S. Levin, "Suicide following Discharge from Psychiatric Hospital." *Arch. Gen. Psychiatry*, 10:67-70 (1964).

31. L.C. Kolb, *Modern Clinical Psychiatry*, 8th ed. Philadelphia, Pa.: W.B. Saunders Co. (1973).

32. P. Udsen, "Prognosis and Follow-up of Attempted Suicide." *Int. Anesthesiol. Clin.,* 4:379–388 (1966).

33. A.D. Pokorny, "A Follow-up Study of 618 Suicidal Patients." *Am. J. Psychiatry*, 122:1109-1116 (1966).

7

Coronary Heart Disease
Paul S. Entmacher, M.D.

Coronary heart disease results from a pathologic process of uncertain etiology involving the deposition of lipoid materials in the intima and subintimal portions of the involved coronary arteries. These lesions which later include fibrosis and calcification are known as atheromatous plaques. They tend to increase in size and eventually to occlude the lumina of the affected vessels. The atherosclerotic process is generally a progressive one that, in varying degrees, causes interference with the free flow of blood to the myocardium. Low grade obstruction in one or more major coronary vessels may not result in clinical expression of the disease. Further degrees of obstruction result in more severe reduction of blood flow associated with chest pain (angina pectoris), and total occlusion of a critically placed lesion in a major coronary vessel results in myocardial infarction.

Terms frequently used in describing coronary artery disease include ischemic heart disease and coronary insufficiency. Coronary thrombosis implies total occlusion of a segmental portion of a coronary vessel and results in myocardial infarction. The disease is also referred to as coronary heart disease, coronary arteriosclerosis, and coronary atherosclerosis.[1]

Angina pectoris is a clinically descriptive term which implies chest pain of relatively brief duration usually brought on by physical exertion or emotional stress and relieved by rest or by nitroglycerine.[1] Typical angina pectoris may follow the ingestion of a heavy meal or exposure to cold or wind. The discomfort is characteristically substernal in location and often radiates to the upper extremities—usually the left—or to the jaw, neck, or left interscapular area. It is usually described as aching, squeezing, pressing, or may be attributed to indigestion or heartburn.

Angina pectoris may be classified as stable or unstable. Stable angina occurs in a fairly predictable way under circumstances involving a specific degree of exertion. It is not characterized by an increase in frequency or severity. Unstable angina is that which is progressive in terms of severity, frequency, or both (crescendo angina), or which occurs at rest (angina decubitus), or angina in its initial stage (de novo angina). These latter types of angina are often grouped together under the term "preinfarction syndrome" or the "intermediate syndrome," i.e., a state between stable angina and myocardial infarction.

It should be noted that while coronary atherosclerosis is the most common cause of angina pectoris it is not the only cause, since the same type of chest pain may be produced by luetic coronary ostial disease, periarteritis, congenital anomalies of the coronary vessels, aortic valve disease, various cardiomyopathies, and by several additional less common disease states.

The diagnosis of angina pectoris is made primarily from the characteristic history of chest pain, particularly with regard to the relationship to exertion and relief with rest or nitroglycerine. Unfortunately, the classical typical history cannot always be obtained. Physical findings are meager. These may include transient cardiac murmurs or gallop sounds especially if these occur in relation to increased exertion. The electrocardiogram may show suspicious changes in terms of primary repolarization abnormalities, conduction defects, ventricular hypertrophy, etc., but it is not unusual for the patient with advanced degrees of coronary insufficiency to have an absolutely normal electrocardiogram. Stress electrocardiography, particularly submaximal stress tests performed on a treadmill or bicycle ergometer, increase the diagnostic yield significantly. Stress electrocardiography will also frequently disclose the presence of asymptomatic coronary atherosclerosis. Chest X-rays are rarely helpful in diagnosis. The most specific but not always definitive diagnostic procedure is coronary arteriography in which arterial obstructive lesions can be directly visualized.

Myocardial infarction is the ultimate expression of the coronary atherosclerotic process and is caused in most cases by coronary thrombosis.[1] This results in ischemia and eventually necrosis of that portion of myocardium supplied by the occluded coronary vessel. Myocardial infarction may be subdivided according to its anatomic location—anterior, inferior, etc.—and by the depth of involvement—transmural or subendocardial.

The diagnosis of myocardial infarction depends upon the typical clinical history of severe substernal chest pain of longer duration than angina pectoris together with a constellation of associated symptoms that may include various dysrhythmias, fever, congestive failure, and cardiovascular collapse. The electrocardiogram and the measurement of various specific enzymes in the blood often provide conclusive evidence for the diagnosis.

The specific pathophysiology of coronary artery disease is not fully understood, but it has been repeatedly shown that the disease is associated with a variety of so-called risk factors.[1,2,3,4,5,6] These include hypertension, hyperlipidemia, glucose intolerance, obesity, cigarette smoking, and especially a family history of premature myocardial infarction or angina pectoris. Certain other less well-defined factors such as the use of contraceptive medications may also be associated.

Dimensions of Coronary Heart Disease as a Public Health Problem

Coronary heart disease accounts for 90 per cent of all heart disease deaths and 35 per cent of deaths due to all causes—by far the leading cause of death. Table 7-1 gives the distribution of 666,665 deaths in the United States during 1970 attributed to the various forms of coronary heart disease as currently classified. A breakdown of the 16 abstracts containing related mortality data is also shown, with emphasis on the type of follow-up study.

Mortality from heart disease among men and women in the general population of the United States which began to diminish in the sixties, has continued on its downward course in the seventies and the decrease in death rates has become more pronounced. Recent mortality rates from heart disease in the general population of the United States are presented in Table 7-2. Death rates are shown for particular years, with per cent change computed for the periods from 1962 to 1967 and from 1969 to 1973. These periods have been used to provide a basis for comparison both before and after the introduction of the Eighth Revision of the International Classification of Diseases in 1968. The changes in classification and coding procedures resulting from the Eighth Revision led to significant breaks on the continuity of mortality statistics for certain categories, especially hypertensive heart disease and, to a lesser degree, rheumatic heart disease and ischemic heart disease.

The overall ratio of mortality rates for the later period commencing in 1969 as compared to the period prior to 1968 for all diseases of the heart indicates, however, that there was no appreciable break in the comparability of mortality data for this disease grouping as a whole;[7] changes for some of the major components of the disease category were offset by changes in the opposite direction for other components.

Between 1962 and 1967, death rates from all forms of heart disease declined for both males and females in the general population. The decrease in mortality was 2.7 per cent among white men in the general population and among white women a decline of 6.8 per cent was noted. From 1969 to 1973, heart disease mortality decreased by 4.9 per cent among white men and by 8.8 per cent among white women.

The death rates from heart disease at all ages combined have been age-adjusted to allow for changes in the age composition of the population—such as the increasing proportion of older people in recent years. As can be seen from Table 7-2, in each year the death rates for specific age groups progressed steadily upward with advance in age—ranging in 1973 from a low of 3.7 per 100,000 at ages 20 to 24 among men in the general population to 5,503.9 at ages 75 and over. The corresponding rates among women in the general population rose from 2.0 per 100,000 at the younger ages to 4,146.3 at the older ages.

The mortality from ischemic and related heart disease, which represents the preponderant portion of the deaths from heart disease is shown in Table 7-3. Between 1962 and 1967 there was a decline of less than one per cent in the

TABLE 7-1

Numbers of Deaths in the U.S. — 1970
Coronary Heart Disease

Hazard	Deaths in U.S. Number	% in Category	Follow-up Data
Acute Myocardial Infarction	357,241	(53.6%)	See below
Early Mortality	**	—	§301
Large Population Study	**	—	§302, §303, §312, §313
Hospitalized Patients	**	—	§310, §311 §317
Life Insurance Experience	**	—	§305, §306
Coronary Arteriography and Bypass	**	—	§307, §308, §309, §316
Acute and Subacute Ischemic Heart Disease	4,246	(0.6)	See above
Chronic Ischemic Heart Disease	304,962	(45.7)	§304, §307, §308, §309, §315, §316, §317
Angina Pectoris	216	(0.03)	§302, §303, §305, §306, §314, §315, §316
Total (all listed in Cause of Death Statistics)	666,665 (34.6% of all deaths)		

**Listed elsewhere under various separate causes

TABLE 7-2

Mortality from Heart Disease — All Forms

United States White Population 1962-73

	Death Rate per 100,000					Per cent Change	
Age	Male	Female	Male	Female		Male	Female
	1962		**1967**			**1962 to 1967**	
20-24	4.8	3.1	3.2	2.0		−33.3	−35.5
25-29	8.5	5.9	7.3	4.0		−14.1	−32.2
30-34	24.0	9.3	19.4	7.8		−19.2	−16.1
35-39	65.0	19.2	60.7	17.1		− 6.6	−10.9
40-44	148.1	35.4	141.4	34.4		− 4.5	− 2.8
45-49	293.6	71.0	283.2	67.9		− 3.5	− 4.4
50-54	526.5	138.0	504.1	125.3		− 4.3	− 9.2
55-59	829.8	254.6	828.4	241.3		− 0.2	− 5.2
60-64	1,276.1	482.2	1,269.8	438.6		− 0.5	− 9.0
65-69	1,954.4	892.9	1,865.3	823.0		− 4.6	− 7.8
70-74	2,719.8	1,568.9	2,801.7	1,483.1		+ 3.0	− 5.5
75 and over	5,399.7	4,390.5	5,344.5	4,271.2		− 1.0	− 2.7
All Ages*	368.7	189.1	358.9	176.2		− 2.7	− 6.8
	1969		**1973**			**1969 to 1973**	
20-24	3.5	2.4	3.7	2.0		+ 5.7	−16.7
25-29	7.0	3.6	6.6	3.5		− 5.7	− 2.8
30-34	18.5	7.2	16.5	6.7		−10.8	− 6.9
35-39	57.8	15.7	48.8	14.8		−15.6	− 5.7
40-44	136.1	32.7	123.5	30.0		− 9.3	− 8.3
45-49	272.9	62.9	254.1	58.6		− 6.9	− 6.8
50-54	482.4	121.4	436.9	110.5		− 9.4	− 9.0
55-59	796.0	228.0	754.8	217.0		− 5.2	− 4.8
60-64	1,251.2	422.6	1,161.3	392.7		− 7.2	− 7.1
65-69	1,818.3	788.8	1,714.4	684.5		− 5.7	−13.2
70-74	2,791.6	1,448.1	2,569.4	1,285.8		− 8.0	−11.2
75 and over	5,374.8	4,272.3	5,503.9	4,146.3		+ 2.4	− 2.9
All Ages*	352.4	171.9	335.0	156.8		− 4.9	− 8.8

*Adjusted on basis of age distribution of United States total population, 1940. Ages under 20 included in "All Ages."
Source of United States data: Reports of Division of Vital Statistics, National Center for Health Statistics.
Source of Table — Metropolitan Statistical Bulletin, June 1975.

death rate at all ages combined among white men, but mortality among white women decreased by 3.6 per cent. In the later period (from 1969 to 1973) there was a considerably greater decrease—5.7 per cent among men and 9.3 per cent among women.

There was a substantial sex differential in the mortality from ischemic and related heart disease, as there was in the mortality from all forms of heart disease. Age-specific death rates among women were approximately half those among men for each of the years shown and the ratio has remained at about this level for some time.

Ischemic and related heart disease accounts for nearly 88 per cent of deaths from heart disease at ages 35 to 64, considered the most productive years of life, as well as the period of heaviest family responsibilities. Mortality rates at these ages for the periods under review are shown in Table 7-4.

Between 1962 and 1967 there was virtually no change in the mortality from ischemic and related heart disease among white males aged 35 to 64 in the general population. A decrease of 8.1 per cent was registered, however, in the 1969 to

TABLE 7-3

Mortality from Ischemic and Related Heart Disease

United States White Population 1962-73

Age	Death Rate per 100,000				Per cent Change	
	Male	Female	Male	Female	Male	Female
	1962		1967		1962 to 1967	
20-24	1.6	0.6	1.3	0.5	−18.8	−16.7
25-29	4.6	1.5	4.4	1.3	− 4.3	−13.3
30-34	17.2	3.7	14.0	3.8	−18.6	+ 2.7
35-39	52.3	8.5	51.3	9.4	− 1.9	+10.6
40-44	126.6	19.9	126.3	21.1	− 0.2	+ 6.0
45-49	259.3	45.7	255.6	47.5	− 1.4	+ 3.9
50-54	468.6	97.0	458.8	93.8	− 2.1	− 3.3
55-59	742.8	194.6	753.8	188.8	+ 1.5	− 3.0
60-64	1,151.9	387.7	1,159.3	361.7	+ 0.6	− 6.7
65-69	1,765.8	737.2	1,705.2	701.4	− 3.4	− 4.9
70-74	2,447.0	1,317.6	2,555.0	1,280.2	+ 4.4	− 2.8
75 and over	4,793.1	3,698.3	4,828.4	3,708.4	+ 0.7	+ 0.3
All Ages*	327.9	153.0	324.8	147.5	− 0.9	− 3.6
	1969		1973		1969 to 1973	
20-24	1.4	0.7	1.1	0.5	−21.4	−28.6
25-29	3.6	1.2	3.2	1.2	−11.1	−
30-34	13.7	3.3	12.1	3.3	−11.7	−
35-39	49.0	9.6	41.4	9.4	−16.2	− 2.1
40-44	121.0	23.4	109.8	20.7	− 9.3	−11.5
45-49	248.3	46.7	230.3	44.8	− 7.2	− 4.1
50-54	445.0	97.2	399.7	89.2	−10.2	− 8.2
55-59	738.0	191.3	695.6	182.9	− 5.7	− 4.4
60-64	1,167.8	367.3	1,074.1	341.7	− 8.0	− 7.0
65-69	1,710.2	712.7	1,592.8	613.9	− 6.9	−13.9
70-74	2,629.4	1,337.2	2,401.3	1,175.5	− 8.7	−12.1
75 and over	5,053.2	3,978.1	5,136.5	3,841.4	+ 1.6	− 3.4
All Ages*	327.7	153.9	309.0	139.6	− 5.7	− 9.3

*Adjusted on basis of age distribution of United States total population, 1940. Ages under 20 included in "All Ages."
Source of United States data: Reports of Division of Vital Statistics, National Center for Health Statistics.
Source of Table — Metropolitan Statistical Bulletin, June 1975.

1973 period, when death rates at these ages dropped from 374.8 per 100,000 in 1969 to 344.6 in 1973. Among white women there was a 3.4 per cent decline in mortality in the earlier period and a 6.3 per cent decline in the later period. There was a much greater sex differential at these ages than at all ages combined.

The decrease in death rates from heart disease after the introduction of the Eighth Revision in 1968 has been considered to be partly an artifact of coding procedures. The persistence and size of the decline suggests, however, that there has been an actual decrease. Opinions vary as to the relative importance of the many factors that may be responsible for the decline in mortality from heart disease. Among the factors mentioned most often are the increased detection and treatment of hypertension, the change in consumption of saturated fats, and improved medical care. Some observers believe the decline may be attributed to the success of health education efforts resulting in an overall change in life style and the adoption of more prudent living habits.

TABLE 7-4

Mortality from Ischemic and
Related Heart Disease

Ages 35-64

Age-Adjusted Death Rates per 100,000

United States White Population

Year	Male	Female
1962	381.4	97.0
1967	381.2	93.7
1969	374.8	95.5
1973	344.6	89.5

International Comparisons. It has been customary to draw comparisons between the mortality rates in the United States with those in Canada and the countries of Western Europe. It is misleading, however, to compare the average death rates for the United States—a nation of the size, diversity and degree of industrialization of a continent—with the death rates of small national units such as Norway or Denmark merely because one would expect that some selected parts of the continent of Western Europe would experience lower death rates than the average for the entire continental area of the United States. Within the United States there are regional differences that are as great as differences between countries. It is more meaningful to compare the average mortality rates for the two hundred ten plus million people in the United States with the average rates for the bloc of industrialized countries of Western Europe.

Table 7-5 presents the 1972 age-adjusted death rates from coronary heart disease for persons aged 45 to 74 by sex in the United States, Canada, and selected Western European countries. The very low death rates in the southern countries such as Spain, Portugal, and France may be due to a very high proportion of deaths in those countries which are assigned to ill-defined and unknown causes; many of those deaths might have been classified as cardiac deaths in the other countries. The highest mortality among men occurred in Finland, Scotland, Northern Ireland, and the United States. Among females, the highest death rate occurred among nonwhites in the United States followed by Scotland and Northern Ireland. For both sexes combined, the highest death rate occurred in the nonwhite population of the United States followed by Scotland, Northern Ireland, the United States white population, Finland, and Ireland. The lowest rates were found in Spain, France, Portugal, and Italy. When blocs of countries are considered and the white and nonwhite populations of the United States are combined, the highest death rate occurred in the United States and the lowest in the countries of Southern Europe, the latter possibly for the previously described reason.

Additional statistical information on cardiovascular diseases in the United States may be found in a recent monograph.[8]

Early Mortality—Myocardial Infarction. The early mortality in coronary heart desease is described in §301. The populations studied included Army men during World War II, men and women enrolled in the Health Insurance Plan (HIP) of Greater New York, which is a prepaid health insurance plan, residents of Framingham who were included in the Framingham Heart Study, an employed population of men at the duPont Company and male patients hospitalized at Veterans Administration (VA) hospitals.

The study of Army men included a substantial number of young men which is unusual in most heart studies. There was a high mortality rate within 24 hours of the acute attack for men in their 20's and the mortality rate tended to decrease with age through the 40's, then increased with age with the highest mortality rate being in the 55 to 64 year age group.

Any evaluation of early mortality must take into account sudden deaths which occur before the patients can be hospitalized. In various studies it has been estimated that between 50 and 70 per cent of all deaths in acute myocardial infarction occur before the patient can be hospitalized. Some definitions of sudden death include only those that occur within one hour, and others include all that occur within 24 hours. The early mortality reported in the study of Army men, the HIP study, the Framingham Study, and the duPont study, all include sudden deaths. Studies of early death which include only hospitalized patients, such as the VA study, do not present the full picture of the early mortality associated with coronary heart disease.

TABLE 7-5

Mortality from Ischemic Heart Disease by Sex, Ages 45-74
United States, Canada, and Selected European Countries, 1972

	Annual Death Rate per 100,000*		
Country	Total	Male	Female
United States			
White	541.3	829.7	295.0
Non-White	656.2	829.3	508.8
Total	552.5	829.9	315.8
Canada	453.5	687.2	235.6
Finland	523.8	885.6	253.2
Denmark	389.8	596.6	206.8
Norway	356.0	566.9	167.7
Sweden	366.3	551.7	195.5
Netherlands	344.9	532.8	170.9
Weighted Average	361.1	555.4	184.1
United Kingdom			
England and Wales	448.8	707.2	229.8
Northern Ireland	574.9	887.6	326.8
Scotland	581.2	884.9	336.4
Ireland	477.7	681.1	281.4
Belgium	302.8	470.9	159.0
France	131.9	207.6	68.2
Germany, Federal Republic	269.5	454.2	138.4
Weighted Average	299.6	480.6	155.1
Italy	194.0	292.8	110.6
Spain	111.6	179.7	55.3
Portugal	165.4	241.7	104.8
Weighted Average	163.8	250.5	91.5

*Adjusted on basis of age distribution of the United States total population, 1940
Note: Belgium — only 1971 data available
Source of basic data: Reports of Division of Vital Statistics, National Center for
Health Statistics, and World Health Statistics Annuals, 1972

In the first month, the highest mortality was found in the first 24 hours, tapering off after that with no apparent peaks to the end of the first 30 days. Preexisting factors associated with high initial mortality were evaluated in some of the studies. In the HIP study, hypertension, angina, lack of physical activity, and other cardiovascular disease were all associated with high mortality rates, while a history of smoking was not. There was no significant difference by sex, but women did not show an adverse effect of preexisting angina on early mortality as was demonstrated in men. This was also true in the Framingham Study. On the other hand, women diabetics in the HIP study showed a high early mortality but men did not. The effect of overweight on immediate mortality was found in the duPont study not to be significant, whereas increasing age, hypertension, and certain preexisting electrocardiographic abnormalities, particularly bundle branch block, all had an adverse impact on immediate mortality.

Long-Term Mortality—Myocardial Infarction. In the VA study of hospitalized patients who survived two months and who were followed for five years (§310), mortality ratios decreased with age but mortality rates and excess death rates increased with age. The annual excess death rate averaged 47 per 1000 for patients under age 50 who survived more than two months, and 67 per 1000 for those age 50 and over. Also there was a tendency for mortality ratios to decrease with duration. This was not true for mortality rates or for excess death rates. Advanced age, history of hypertension, history of angina pectoris of more than one month's duration, shock, congestive failure, serious arrhythmias or conduction defect in the ECG, and prolonged high fever had an adverse effect on the early mortality. All of those factors except shock also adversely affected the five-year mortality.

An additional five-year follow-up was carried out at a later date (§311), and it was found that mortality measured as average annual excess death rate continued high in the second five years with the highest excess rates in the older patients. Mortality ratios continued their downward trend in the second five years. Hypertension and angina history of more than a month's duration were associated with higher mortality rates and ratios. Of interest was a favorable effect on mortality of "premonitory angina." A history of angina of less than one month's duration was associated with a lower mortality than a history of no angina.

The study of Army men admitted to Army hospitals (§303) provides a fifteen-year follow-up. Those with a confirmed diagnosis of myocardial infarction, coronary occlusion, or coronary thrombosis who did not die in the first month had an average annual excess death rate that ranged from 42 to 53 per thousand for the broad age groups studied. There was no increase in EDR with age as in the VA study, but the mortality ratios did show a decreasing trend with age and duration.

Data from the employed population at the duPont Company (§312) show results similar to the Army data. Rates of mortality and excess rates of death were highest in the first year among those who survived for one month, but there was no consistent trend in the remaining four years of the study. The highest excess death rates were in the middle-age group, 45 to 54. The average excess death rates varied from 43 per 1000 for the age group under 45, to 62 per 1000 for the age group 45 to 54. For age group 55 to 64, it was 52 per 1000, and for all ages combined it was 55 per 1000.

The cumulative five-year experience with the first month excluded showed an adverse effect of hypertension and overweight on mortality with hypertension apparently exerting more of an influence than overweight.

Two insurance studies (§305, §306) are analyzed and it is immediately apparent that the selection of risks by the underwriting process has eliminated the least favorable cases. This is manifested by much lower excess death rates in the range of 15 to 35 per 1000, rather than 45 to 65 as seen in the previous studies. Since the basis of expected deaths used to derive the mortality ratios is a standard insured population where there is also a selection of risks with lower mortality rates, the mortality ratios continue to be elevated.

The study done at the Lincoln National Life Insurance Company (§305) divided the myocardial infarction cases into those which were documented by history and those which were not. In both of these groups, the excess death rates increased with age at issuance of insurance, and the mortality ratios decreased. Mortality ratios also tended to diminish during the first ten policy years, but after ten years a reversal in direction occurred and the mortality ratios increased. The excess death rates did not display a clear pattern. An abnormal ECG at the time the policy was issued and overweight tended to affect mortality adversely.

The New England Mutual Life Insurance Company study (§306) included a high proportion of pension policies which utilized a graded death benefit in underwriting situations that would require either a very high rating or outright delination of regular nonpension applications. Although many of these cases were characterized by high risk features, all pension applicants were required to be actively at work in order to qualify for insurance. The myocardial infarction group included other manifestations of coronary heart disease, such as coronary insufficiency and myocardial ischemia. Analysis of the data was made with respect to the presence or absence of cardiovascular complications represented by elevated blood pressure or by any cardiovascular impairment other than coronary heart disease. Cases with cardiovascular complications generally had a higher relative mortality than cases without complications. However, among insureds with a history of myocardial infarction five years or more prior to application, a lower mortality ratio was found in those with cardiovascular complications. There was a pattern of decreasing mortality by duration after issuance of insurance. The trend of decreasing mortality is not as clear-cut when duration is evaluated by time of attack preceding application for insurance. Mortality by age shows that in each age group mortality ratios are highest in the initial observation interval and decrease with longer durations. The mortality ratios are somewhat higher at the older ages. A comparative mortality experience by blood pressure classification, regardless of other cardiovascular complications, shows that cases with definite hypertension have a mortality ratio and an excess death rate much greater than respective values for normotensive cases. Borderline hypertensives show intermediate results.

Two additional studies that provide detailed follow-up data of persons with a history of myocardial infarction are the Framingham Study and the study done of patients enrolled in the Health Insurance Plan (HIP) of Greater New York. The Framingham Study (§302) showed that the excess death rates were greater for females than for males and greater for those over age 65. The excess death rates were also high in the first year after the attack for both sexes. It is difficult to evaluate any trend by duration because of the small number of deaths especially in the female subjects.

The HIP study of men after a first myocardial infarction (§313) showed that mortality ratios and excess death rates are highest in the interval from one to six months and then fall to lower levels. The excess mortality is relatively constant in men age 45 to 54 after the first year of follow-up, but in the younger and older age groups, mortality dips in the interval from 3-4 years. Mortality ratios for the five-year follow-up period decrease with advancing age with a slight tendency for the excess death rates to increase.

Women also experienced the highest mortality ratio in the period of one to six months after the attack (Table 314d). There was a decrease in the second six months and then it stayed almost unchanged for the remainder of the five-year follow-up period. For the entire follow-up, the female mortality ratio was slightly higher than the male ratio but the excess death rates were lower (Table 313c).

The extensive study of the Coronary Drug Project Research Group provides five-year comparative mortality and survival data on a large number of risk factors associated with a generally good recovery following myocardial infarction (Table 315d). The text and tables of §315 deserve careful attention with respect to the results, which are too numerous to detail here.

Mortality of Angina Pectoris; Coronary Insufficiency; Myocardial Ischemia. Many of the studies evaluated separately the mortality experience associated with coronary artery disease other than myocardial infarction. The entities that were studied included angina pectoris, coronary insufficiency and myocardial ischemia. In almost all instances, the mortality was less than that resulting from myocardial infarction and the trends by age and duration were not as clearly defined.

The Army study (§303) had a small number of deaths, but it was clear that the early risk of death following hospitalization was much less than for myocardial infarction. In the period one month to one year after hospitalization, there were no deaths in the age group 50 and over. In the other age groups, the EDRs ranged from 8 to 36 per 1000. The range was 27 to 88 per 1000 in the myocardial infarction group during the same interval. The risk of death after the first year was significantly higher than that expected in the general population and on the average during the last 14 years of observation, the excess death rate was 19 per 1000 compared to 45 in the myocardial infarction group. The cumulative survival ratios at the end of 15 years varied by age from 70.7 to 80 per cent in the angina pectoris group and 43.4 to 52.5 per cent in the myocardial infarction group.

The study done by the Lincoln National Life Insurance Company (§305) also showed excess death rates that were lower in the coronary insufficiency group than in the myocardial infarction group and this was also true for the mortality ratios. There was no definite trend of mortality ratios according to duration or age, but the EDRs tended to increase with both.

The New England Mutual Life Insurance Company study (§306) did not show a large differential between the angina pectoris group and the myocardial infarction group. In some instances, the mortality ratios were higher in the angina pectoris group than in the myocardial infarction group. This may be a reflection of the fact that in the myocardial infarction group there were cases of other types of coronary heart disease including coronary insufficiency and myocardial ischemia. The mortality was highest in the early follow-up periods and there was a decrease in mortality ratios by policy duration. There was no clear-cut trend according to age; hypertension had a significant effect on mortality ratios and excess death rates. The cases with definite hypertension had mortality ratios almost four times greater than those with normal blood pressure, and the cases with borderline blood pressure had intermediate mortality ratios. A similar differential was found with respect to the excess death rates.

In the Framingham Study (§302) the average EDR of 15 and 13 extra deaths per thousand during the nine-year follow-up for males and females respectively is much less than the average EDR in the myocardial infarction group. The survival ratios are correspondingly higher in the angina patients as well. At the end of nine years, the cumulative survival ratios were 58.9 and 37.8 per cent for the males and females respectively in the myocardial infarction group and 86 and 89.2 per cent in the angina pectoris group.

In the HIP study (§314) excess mortality was the same for men with angina pectoris as with myocardial infarction: a mortality ratio of 385 per cent and an EDR of 31 per 1000. The New England Mutual Life Insurance Company study showed a similar pattern. The women in the HIP study with angina pectoris showed a lower excess mortality than men, and a lower excess mortality than women with myocardial infarction. There was a definite trend by age among women, with higher mortality ratios and higher excess death rates at the older ages. In the case of men, on the other hand, both mortality ratios and EDRs were lower at the older ages. The trends of mortality by duration for men were irregular with interval mortality ratios and excess death rates varying within fairly narrow limits. The cumulative survival ratio at the end of 4.5 years was 86.7 per cent. For women interval mortality ratios and excess death rates tended to increase with duration. The cumulative survival ratio was 91.7 per cent. This compared to cumulative survival ratios at the end of 4.5 years in myocardial infarction patients of 86.7 per cent for men and 88.0 per cent for women.

Prognostic Significance of Coronary Arteriography. In the past decade coronary arteriography has become a safe diagnostic technique and is being used extensively.[9] It permits a quantitative evaluation of the extent of coronary artery disease present by measuring the degree of arterial narrowing and the number of vessels involved. Several medical centers have conducted prospective studies based on the findings of coronary arteriography. Studies done at the Cleveland Clinic, Johns Hopkins Hospital, and the University of Alabama Medical Center have been analyzed.

Three separate reports from the Cleveland Clinic (§307) permitted a comparison among patients with normal or slightly abnormal arteriograms indicated by less than 50 per cent narrowing of the lumen, those with moderate abnormalities manifested by 50 per cent or more obstruction in at least one major artery, and those with severe disease shown by 80 to 100 per cent obstruction in any of the major coronary arteries. As would be expected, the excess mortality increased as the severity of the disease increased. The patients with normal arteriograms or with less than 30 per cent narrowing had mortality and survival rates very close to those expected in the general population. The patients with 30 to 49 per cent narrowing had a mortality ratio at seven years of 235 per cent and EDR of 13 per 1000.

The group of patients with single vessel narrowing of 50 per cent or more had a mortality ratio of 465 per cent with 35 extra deaths per 1000 at the end of one year after arteriography. The excess mortality for patients with 50 per cent or more narrowing in two-vessel or three-vessel disease was much greater: mortality ratios 1260 and 2270 per cent, and EDRs 112 and 210 per 1000, respectively. Among patients with single vessel disease, the five-year excess mortality was greatest among those with obstruction of the left anterior descending artery. The three combinations of double vessel disease ranged from a low mortality ratio of 750 per cent to a high of 930 per cent found in the combination of left anterior descending and circumflex arteries. The five-year experience with triple vessel disease showed a mortality ratio of 1370 per cent and 147 excess deaths per 1000 per year.

For patients with severe coronary narrowing of 80 per cent or more, the mortality was exceedingly high. For patients with triple vessel disease the excess death rate was 254 per 1000 in the first year and decreased during the remainder of the five-year period, though at the end of five years it was still higher than the other groups. There was a progressive increase in mortality ratio with increase in number of vessels diseased. Excess mortality did not depend greatly on which vessel was involved but patients with only the right coronary artery involved had the lowest mortality. Higher mortality was experienced by patients with two-vessel disease, especially in combinations which included the left anterior descending artery. Three-vessel disease caused the highest mortality.

The studies done at the Johns Hopkins Hospital and University of Alabama (§308) showed the same general results that were found at the Cleveland Clinic in patients with 50 per cent or more narrowing. The mortality ratios increased progressively with the number of vessels involved and there was no excess mortality if the arteriogram was normal.

Prognostic Significance of Electrocardiograph Abnormalities. In abstract §317, two studies, the VA study (also discussed in §310), and the Coronary Drug Project (also discussed in §315) are analyzed to evaluate the impact of ECG abnormalities on prognosis.

In the VA study, patients hospitalized with transmural infarct manifested by abnormal Q waves, experienced about the same early mortality within the first two months as those with nontransmural or subendocardial infarcts manifested by T and ST changes without Q waves. Patients with bundle branch block had the highest early mortality. In the time interval two months to five years, excess mortality was about the same in the older age groups for both transmural and nontransmural infarction patients, but at the younger ages nontransmural infarction appears to be associated with a lower mortality than transmural infarction. This is also true for all ages combined. The small series with bundle branch block developed at the time of myocardial infarction had the most unfavorable experience of all. The average age of the bundle branch block group was somewhat older and these patients had a higher incidence of stroke, congestive failure and serious arrhythmias.

Coronary patients in the Coronary Drug Project were classified in detail as to their ECG findings at the time of their baseline examination. In all of the ECG abnormality classes, the excess death rates were higher than the average of 29 per 1000 for the entire group, ranging from 35 per 1000 for serious arrhythmias and QRS axis deviation, to 60 per 1000 or more for the categories of ST depression, more than one extra beat per 10 QRS complexes and tall R waves. The EDRs for transmural infarcts (abnormal Q waves) were lower than in the VA study probably because all patients in the Coronary Drug Project had made a good functional recovery after their acute infarct. Abnormal T waves occurred in almost 50 per cent of the tracings and were associated with an EDR of 44 per 1000 compared to 16 per 1000 with normal T waves. In the small portion of cases with normal ECG at the time of entry a remarkably low mortality was observed—11 excess deaths per 1000 per year. A similar favorable prognostic effect of "ECG recovery" following documented myocardial infarction was noted in the men insured by the Lincoln National Life Insurance Company (Table 305i).

Impact of Coronary Artery Bypass on Prognosis. Three studies of the impact of coronary artery bypass surgery have been analyzed (§309, §316): one from the Texas Heart Institute, one from the Cleveland Clinic, and one from the University of Oregon.

The early mortality after surgery has been improving from year to year falling to 3.2 per cent in 1972 at the Texas Heart Institute and to 1.2 per cent in 1971 at the Cleveland Clinic. It is higher if additional procedures such as endarterectomy and internal mammary implant are done at the same time. The number of vessels involved did not affect early mortality in the Texas Heart Institute study. In the Cleveland Clinic series the excess mortality was lower for the operated group than for the unoperated in each time interval after the first month with correspondingly higher cumulative survival rates. The average follow-up in the surgical patients in the Cleveland Clinic series was 30 months with a range of 22-60 months. The nonsurgical patients were followed for at least six years. It is important to note, however, that these were not matched series. The surgical series was comprised of 1000 patients operated on from 1967 to 1970, whereas the nonsurgical series was comprised of 469 patients selected from a consecutive series of 3,527 patients who underwent coronary angiographic evaluation during the years 1960 to 1965. The nonsurgical patients had coronary lesions similar to the surgical group and would have been suitable for surgery by criteria prevalent in 1970 to 1971. They did not have surgery, however, because they did not fulfill criteria for selection for the surgical procedures being done at the time, such as internal mammary implants and patchgraft reconstructions. In view of these important differences between the surgical and nonsurgical patients, the apparently superior survival of the operated group must be interpreted with caution.

The University of Oregon study showed increased excess mortality after the first month according to the number of vessels involved. For the total series, the excess mortality after one month was quite small; the mortality ratio was 168 per cent and EDR 7.6 per 1000. The survival ratio at four years was 96.4 per cent. These very favorable results must be interpreted with caution, however, because the total number of deaths in the series was very small and no results could be reported beyond four years.

Dunkman et al.[9] have emphasized the need for caution in interpreting currently available information on the results of coronary bypass surgery.

References

1. J.W. Hurst and R.B. Logue, *The Heart*, 3rd ed. New York: McGraw-Hill (1974).

2. W.B. Kannel, "Some Lessons in Cardiovascular Epidemiology from Framingham." *Am. J. Card.*, 37:269-282 (1976).

3. J.T. Doyle and W.B. Kannel, "Coronary Risk Factors. Ten Year Findings in 7446 Americans," Pooling Project, American Heart Association Council on Epidemilogy. In *Proc. VI World Congress Cardiology* (1970).

4. L.M. Hagerup, "Coronary Heart Disease Risk Factors in Men and Women." *Acta Med. Scand.*, 195 (Suppl. 557): 1-116 (1974).

5. J. Stamler, *Lectures on Preventive Cardiology*. New York: Grune and Stratton, Inc. (1967).

6. Report of Inter-Society Commission for Heart Disease Resources, "Primary Prevention of the Atherosclerotic Diseases." *Circulation*, 42:A5-A95 (1970).

7. Dept. of Health, Education and Welfare, *Mortality Trends for Leading Causes of Death, United States 1950-69*. Vital and Health Statistics, Series 20, No. 16. Rockville, Md.: National Center for Health Statistics (1974)..

8. I.M. Moriyama, D.E. Krueger, and J. Stamler, *Cardiovascular Diseases in the United States*. Cambridge, Massachusetts: Harvard University Press (1971).

9. W.B. Dunkman, J.K. Perloff, J.A. Kastor, and J.C. Shelburne, "Medical Perspectives in Coronary Artery Surgery— A Caveat." *Ann. Int. Med.*, 81:817-837 (1974).

8

Hypertension

Edward A. Lew, F.S.A., and
Richard B. Singer, M.D.

Nature of Hypertension

The discussion of hyerptension in this chapter is focused on elevated blood pressure. This represents an epidemiological approach, stemming from the well-documented rise in morbidity and mortality with increase in blood pressure. Such a viewpoint gives primary consideration to blood pressure and secondary consideration to other criteria which are of importance in clinical medicine in evaluation of patients with hypertension. These additional criteria—abnormalities of the eye fundus, heart size or electrocardiogram, or evidence of abnormal function in other target organs, such as the kidneys, or the results of sophisticated physiological tests—affect the significance of elevated blood pressure materially.

Blood pressure may be considered "elevated" only in terms of some normal standard. The definition proposed by the New York Heart Association[1] has been widely accepted and will be used here, despite the fact that significant differences in mortality with blood pressure level are observed in the "normal" or normotensive range. Any blood pressure combination up to and including 139/89 (139 mm Hg systolic and 89 mm Hg diastolic) is regarded as normotensive in the definition. Any combination including a systolic pressure of 160 and up, or a diastolic pressure of 95 and up, or both, is classified as definitely hypertensive. Any combination below 160/95 is classified as borderline hypertensive, provided it is not within the normotensive limit. Although physicians have long thought that diastolic pressure is a better prognostic indicator than systolic pressure, a series of extensive investigations of insured lives (reviewed by Lew[2]), as well as some prospective studies of samples from the general population[3] show that mortality increases with elevation of either systolic or diastolic pressure, and even more sharply with elevation of both. The blood pressure taken with the subject seated and at rest, but without other special precautions, is termed a "casual" reading. Any single, elevated casual reading should be confirmed by additional readings in both arms, and by further readings on subsequent days. Although averages from multiple observations are to be preferred in consideration of the individual patient, the single casual reading is a good prognostic indicator statistically.[4] Recommended technical details for the taking and recording of blood pressure may be found in various manuals.[5]

From the clinical standpoint hypertension may be classified by its rate of progression and by its severity, usually determined by a combination of degree of blood pressure elevation and presence of complications such as hypertensive heart disease, renal damage, eyeground changes, and evidence of cerebrovascular disease. Hypertension which progresses rapidly to very high blood pressure levels, eyeground changes, and critical events or death, all in a period of months, is called malignant. The typical course, however, is a much more benign one, with insidious onset, a long asymptomatic period, and gradual development of progressively higher levels of blood pressure with one or more attendant complications, a course that may last as much as 20 years or even longer. It should be realized that "benign" hypertension, in the traditional clinical sense, stands in contrast to a highly lethal disease, malignant hypertension. It is benign only in relative terms because even mild degrees of borderline hypertension, with readings in the vicinity of 140/90, entail a significantly increased mortality risk compared with normotensive subjects of the same age and sex. The importance of all degrees of blood pressure elevation above 140/90 as a mortality and morbidity risk factor is stressed in the epidemiological viewpoint of hypertension, which is now receiving even wider clinical recognition in the United States, due in part to the efforts of the National High Blood Pressure Education Program.[6]

In the present state of medical knowledge cases of hypertension can be classified as "essential" (primary), constituting the vast majority, or secondary to one of a long list of diseases: many types of chronic renal disease (glomerulonephritis, pyelonephritis, diabetic nephropathy, polycystic disease, nephrosclerosis, some cases of major renal arterial disease), some adrenal tumors, pheochromocytoma, and others. Secondary hypertension is amenable to treatment to the extent that the primary disease can be successfully treated, which is seldom the case with chronic renal disease. From the standpoint of numbers of cases, control of hypertension depends on success in the prevention and treatment of essential hypertension, the etiology of which is still unclear despite all of the knowledge that has accumulated as the result of many years of intensive medical research. Current concepts emphasize the interaction of numerous distinctive control mechanisms in the pathogenesis of essential hypertension, a viewpoint that has been developed in great detail by Guyton and others.[7] As described by Dustan, Tarazi and Bravo,[8] "Arterial pressure is a hemodynamic variable reflecting the interplay of a number of other hemodynamic variables, and it becomes elevated because of a failure of one or more of these variables to be controlled within the normal range. When considering any type of hypertension it is helpful to view the circulation as a whole, since the elevated arterial pressure is only one aspect of a highly integrated system." The following list has been suggested as inclusive of major and well-documented mechanisms in the control of arterial pressure and production of essential hypertension, but by no means all such mechanisms:[7]

(1) Baroreceptor
(2) Chemoreceptor
(3) Central Nervous System Ischemic
(4) Renin-Angiotensin Vasoconstrictor
(5) Stress Relaxation
(6) Capillary Fluid Shift
(7) Renal-Body Fluid
(8) Aldosterone

Guyton et al.[7] describe these mechanisms in some detail, comparing the blood pressure range at which they operate, their speed of response, and differences in "feed back gain," the ratio of relative return of displaced blood pressure toward normal to the remaining degree of abnormality. The central role of the kidney in long-term regulation of the blood is emphasized. The renal output of water and salt is the only one of these mechanisms that has the capacity to return arterial pressure all the way to normal, given sufficient time, and hence may be regarded as having an "infinite gain" control characteristic.

The reader who is interested in the etiology of essential hypertension will have to consult the abundant medical literature on this subject as only a few additional points will be mentioned here. The recent *Hypertension Manual,* edited by J.H. Laragh,[9] should prove to be a convenient source. The articles are authoritative and cover a wide range of research work into causative mechanisms in addition to other material on hypertension. Contributions are included on some of the extensive work of Laragh and his colleagues on the renin-angiotensin mechanism and its relation to the aldosterone mechanism. On the basis of this work Laragh believes that a group of hypertensives can be defined on the basis of a low plasma renin level (in relation to their renal salt output). Laragh adduces evidence to indicate that this group, which comprises about 15 per cent of patients with essential hypertension, is at a much lower risk for vascular complications, such as stroke, than are hypertensives with a normal or elevated plasma renin. If confirmed this work might lead to a method of evaluating persons with hypertension that would have therapeutic and prognostic importance. Unfortunately, technical difficulties in the plasma renin assay preclude the widespread routine use of this method at the present time, and follow-up evidence has not yet been published to prove the existence of a reduced mortality and morbidity in the patients with a low plasma renin level. Another important aspect of the etiology of hypertension is the extent to which genetic factors play a determining role. Epidemiological evidence on an inherited tendency to hypertension in man has been ably developed and summarized by Pickering.[10] A possible relations of habitual level of salt intake to hypertension in man has been proposed by Dahl, and he and his colleagues have bred two different strains of rats, one of which is very susceptible to development of hypertension on a high salt diet, while the other strain is very resistant.[11]

One outstanding characteristic of blood pressure is its physiological variability in response to stimuli such as change in posture, activity, sleep, and action of drugs such as caffein in coffee or tea and nicotine in cigarette smoking. Both normotensive and hypertensive individuals differ widely in their blood pressure response to normal or test stimuli. When the blood pressure response is an increase, those who show a marked increase to a test stimulus are called hyperreactors. Some investigators feel that excess lability of blood pressure in a normotensive individual is a predictor of future hypertension. Borderline hypertensives usually hyperreact more than normotensives. All normal persons manifest marked elevation of blood pressure following heavy exercise, but this is a transient phenomenon. As stated previously, despite the pronounced variability of blood pressure, single casual blood readings provide a reliable prognostic indicator of the longevity of large groups. The entire subject of borderline hypertension, including lability of blood pressure, has been thoroughly reviewed by Julius and Schork.[12]

Dimensions of the Hypertension Problem

The 1960-1962 National Health Survey[13] was conducted by the Division of Health Examination Status on a small but carefully stratified sample of the U.S. population age 18 to 79 years. Blood pressure readings on 6672 male and female subjects yielded a prevalence of borderline hypertension (under 160/95, but not under 140/90, as previously defined) of about 15 per cent in the adult U.S. population in this age range. An additional 15 per cent of the population had definite hypertension, that is, a systolic blood pressure of 160 mm Hg or higher, or a diastolic of 95 or higher.

In the 1960-1962 survey the prevalence of systolic hypertension increased markedly with advance in age up to at least age 75 in men and 65 in women, but the prevalence of diastolic hypertension leveled off or decreased about age 45 in men and age 55 in women.[13] Under age 35 the prevalence of borderline hypertension is much higher in males than females, but this differential disappears at the older ages. The prevalence of definite hypertension is smaller in females than in males under age 55, but the reverse is true at ages 55 and up. The prevalence of hypertension among blacks is substantially higher than among whites in every age-sex category. These trends by age, sex and race from the 1960-1962 survey are generally confirmed by the first report of the blood pressure results of the 1971-1972 survey.[14] The prevalence of hypertension, borderline and definite combined, is shown in Table 8-1 based on data in this report.

TABLE 8-1

Prevalence of Borderline or Definite Hypertension, U.S. Adults Age 18-74 Years, National Health Survey 1971-72, Series 11, No. 150. (Hypertension defined solely by elevated blood pressure, single systolic reading 140 mm Hg or greater, or single diastolic reading 90 mm Hg or greater, or both.)

Sex/Age		Prevalence Rate per 100				Hypertensive	Total
		White	Negro	Other	Total	Population (1000s)	Population (1000s)
Male	18-44 yrs	21.1	30.6	11.1	21.9	7,500	35,546
	45-59 yrs	45.0	46.2	6.0	45.0	7,391	16,424
	60-74 yrs	38.6	54.9	18.8	40.1	3,607	8,995
	18-74 yrs	–	–	–	30.3	18,498	60,965
Female	18-44 yrs	10.6	20.5	16.6	11.8	4,367	37,009
	45-59 yrs	28.8	55.8	33.6	31.5	5,581	17,717
	60-74 yrs	35.7	55.0	33.0	37.3	4,291	11,504
	18-74 yrs	–	–	–	21.5	14,239	66,230

These prevalence figures have been confirmed in other surveys, and they imply very large numbers of hypertensives in the adult U.S. population. The figure of 23,000,000 frequently quoted in the extensive literature of the National High Blood Pressure Education Program actually corresponds to the number of definite hypertensives only, as estimated from the 1960 to 1962 survey. The number of borderline hypertensives is almost as large—a number exceeding 20,000,000. It is now generally acknowledged that a great many hypertensives are unaware of any elevation of their blood pressure and that most physicians have not treated patients with blood pressure elevation in the borderline hypertensive range or in the lower part of the definite hypertensive range. The National High Blood Pressure Education Program was organized as a co-operative effort of federal and state health agencies, professional and research organizations, and voluntary health agencies to increase public and professional awareness of hypertension as a major chronic disease problem, and to increase detection and control efforts.[6] A comprehensive review by Stamler[15] was presented at the January 1973 conference at which the program was formally launched; the review summarizes the evidence justifying a public health effort of this sort. Stamler has reduced the problem to these simple terms: about one-half of all hypertensives are unaware of their hypertension; about one-half of those who are aware are not under treatment; and one-half of those who are under treatment are not under effective treatment—their blood pressure still exceeds 150/95. Thus, only one-eighth of all definite hypertensives are under effective treatment. The ultimate goal of the National High Blood Pressure Education Program is to reduce mortality and morbidity in essential hypertension by better detection, more widespread use of treatment, and better treatment methods. The impact of mortality and prevalence in forecasting ten-year deaths among hypertensives and normotensives has been explored.[16]

Mortality Trends in Hypertension

During 1970 there were 23,264 deaths attributed to the various forms of hypertension as a cause of death (Table 8-2). These amounted to only 1.2 per cent of total deaths in 1970, but hypertension was mentioned as a contributory cause in 57,124 additional cardiovascular or cerebrovascular deaths. There is little doubt that these figures underestimate the major role of hypertension as at least a contributory cause in cardiovascular deaths, especially deaths attributed to ischemic (coronary) heart disease. Although no accurate estimates are available on numbers of deaths attributed to hypertension from cause of death statistics, some indication of trends in hypertension mortality is given by the past course of mortality from hypertensive heart disease and cerebrovascular diseases. Also shown in Table 8-2 are the seven abstracts dealing specifically with mortality and survival in hypertension; one of these, §399, contains data on various cardiovascular diseases, including hypertension.

TABLE 8-2

Numbers of Deaths in the U.S. — 1970
Hypertension

Hazard	Deaths in U.S.		Follow-up Data
	Number	% in Category	
Malignant Hypertension	1,370	(5.9%)	§323, §324
Benign Essential Hypertension	1,142	(4.9)	§320-§326, §399
Hypertensive Heart Disease	8,413	(36.1)	§324
Hypertensive Renal Disease	5,761	(24.8)	§324
Hypertensive Heart and Renal Disease Combined	6,578	(28.3)	—
Total Hypertension	23,264	(1.2% of all deaths)	
All Other Cardiovascular and Cerebrovascular Diseases with Mention of Hypertension	57,124	(3.0% of all deaths)	

The term hypertensive heart disease as a cause of death has been used to characterize cardiac abnormalities, such as X-ray and electrocardiographic evidence of hypertrophy, when found in combination with and attributed to hypertension. It is, therefore, primarily an ante mortem diagnosis and is not likely to appear on the death certificate in connection with sudden death or catastrophic illness. Physicians frequently cite hypertensive heart disease as a contributory rather than as the underlying cause of death, and in such circumstances the death is coded to the underlying cause and not to hypertensive heart disease. Published statistics on mortality from hypertensive heart disease thus understate the importance of this cause of death. Furthermore the hypertensive heart disease category was formally introduced in the Sixth Revision of the International Classification of Diseases in 1949, and estimates of death rates from this cause have been extrapolated back only to 1940. Insofar as these estimates go, they indicate a steady and pronounced downward trend through the 1960s for white men and white women, but a much less marked decline beginning in the mid 1950s for black men and women. White females have recorded the largest decreases in hypertensive heart disease. Current mortality rates from hypertensive heart disease among nonwhites for all ages combined are nearly four times as high as those for whites; at ages under 55 the nonwhite death rates are more than ten times those for whites.

Cerebrovascular diseases include atherosclerotic and hypertensive pathological processes. Cerebrovascular disease and hypertensive heart disease may both appear on a death certificate, in which case the classification of the particular death would depend on the sequence reported. Similar problems arise in other listings of multiple causes. While it is very difficult to appraise the degree of association between hypertension and cerebrovascular disease, it is highly noteworthy that in the *Build and Blood Pressure Study 1959* the mortality from cerebrovascular disease rose progressively with increases in blood pressure.[4]

Mortality from cerebrovascular disease has been declining since 1940 among both whites and blacks; but the decreases have been much greater for whites than for blacks, and for women than for men. The most clear-cut downward trends were recorded among whites, men and women in the age range 35 to 74, for black men in the age range 25 to 54 and for black women in the age range 35 to 64. Only among whites at ages 85 and over and blacks at ages 75 and over have the death rates from cerebrovascular disease increased.

Current mortality from cerebrovascular disease among blacks for all ages combined is somewhat less than twice that of whites; however, in the age range 25 to 54 the death rates for blacks are more than four times those for whites. The marked trends in death rates from both hypertensive heart disease and cerebrovascular disease, in both of which hypertension plays a major role, suggest that total mortality due to hypertension has been on the decrease. The long-term decline in mortality from chronic nephritis, which has hypertension as a finding in common with the diseases just mentioned, supports this view. Whether declining mortality in hypertension is part of a secular trend reflecting changing modes of life or whether other influences, such as the lesser impact of infections, have also been implicated is not clear. Antihypertensive drugs probably began to have a beneficial effect on hypertensive mortality in the late 1950s, but their effect in earlier years was probably negligible for the population as a whole.

Prognosis in Hypertension Prior to Wide Scale Use of Chemotherapy

Mortality studies completed before the mid 1950s reflect experience prior to extensive use of modern antihypertensive drugs, as reports of clinical studies concerning them first appeared in the medical literature about 1950.[17],[18] Medical treatment during this "prechemotherapy" period was largely symptomatic. Two surgical procedures were in use about 1950 for the treatment of hypertension—sympathectomy and adrenalectomy—but troublesome side effects limited their usefulness.

The most extensive information about mortality in hypertension during the prechemotherapy period is derived from the experience among insured lives. Mortality studies of insured lives indicate the long-range effects on longevity associated primarily with borderline hypertension in persons free of other abnormalities or disorders. The principal features of six of these studies of insured lives are summarized in Table 8–3.

TABLE 8-3

Investigations of Blood Pressure Among Insured Lives

Study, Number of Individuals and Period Covered	Principal Findings and Their Credibility		
	Blood Pressure*	Mort. Ratio & Std. Dev. as Per Cent of Standard	No. of Deaths
	Standard Risks		
Blood Pressure Study. New York: Acturial Soc. Am. and Assoc. Life Ins. Med. Dir. (1925).	S5-15mm△	114 ± 2	3,023
	D5-15mm△	116 ± 2	3,152
About 560,000 men issued as standard risks and about 4000	Substandard Risks		
men issued as substandard risks, observed from about 1915 to 1924; maximum duration of follow-up 10 years.	S16+mm△	207 ± 22	91
Medical Impairment Study, 1929. New York: Actuarial Soc. Am. and Assoc. Life Ins. Med. Dir. (1931).	S16-24mm△	181 ± 9	382
	S25-34mm△	205 ± 10	412
About 25,000 men insured as substandard risks from 1909 to	S35-44mm△	265 ± 23	138
1928; maximum duration of follow-up 20 years.	S45+mm△	384 ± 66	34
	S16+mm△	202 ± 6	966
	New York Life		
A. Hunter, "Supplementary Note on Blood Pressure," Trans., Actuarial Soc. Am., Vol. 32 (1931).	S5-15mm△	114 ± 5	481
	S16-24mm△	128 ± 17	59
About 35,000 men insured as standard risks, observed from	Metropolitan		
1916 to 1930; maximum duration of follow-up 15 years.	S5-15mm△	112 ± 4	991
	S16-24mm△	148 ± 13	133
Blood Pressure Study, 1939. New York: Actuarial Soc. Am. and Assoc. Life Ins. Med. Dir. (1940).	S138-142mm	120 ± 1.1	10,986
	S143-147mm	139 ± 2.4	3,460
About 1,300,000 men insured as standard or substandard	S148-157mm	175 ± 2.7	4,199
risks, observed from 1925 to 1938; maximum duration of	S158-167mm	238 ± 7.6	987
follow-up 13 years.	D94-98mm	152 ± 2.2	4,957
	D99-103mm	186 ± 4.9	1,441
	D104-108mm	246 ± 16.2	230
	S138-142mm		
	D84-93mm	121 ± 1.5	6,447
	D94-98mm	148 ± 3.8	1,494

Table 8-3 (Continued)

Study, Number of Individuals and Period Covered	Blood Pressure*	Principal Findings and Their Credibility Mort. Ratio & Std. Dev. as Per Cent of Standard	No. of Deaths
	S143-147mm		
	D84-93mm	132 ± 3.1	1,864
	D94-98mm	165 ± 5.7	834
	S148-157mm		
	D84-93mm	160 ± 3.7	1,899
	D94-98mm	190 ± 5.7	1,132
W. Bolt et al., "A Study of Mortality in Moderate and Severe Hypertension," Trans., Assoc. Life Ins. Med. Dir., Vol. 41 (1957). About 2500 male applicants for insurance with systolic pressures in excess of 162 mm or diastolic pressures in excess of 102 mm, observed from 1946 through 1956; maximum duration of follow-up 11 years.	S158-177mm	282 ± 21	185
	178-197mm	364 ± 35	108
	198 & over	559 ± 76	54
	D 98-107mm	332 ± 28	137
	108-117mm	441 ± 43	103
	118 & over	708 ± 91	61
Build & Blood Pressure Study, 1959. Chicago: Society of Actuaries (1959). About 3,900,000 men and women insured as standard or substandard risks, observed from 1935 to 1954; maximum duration of follow-up 19 years.	S128-137mm	118 ± 0.7	29,355
	138-147mm	155 ± 1.2	17,252
	148-157mm	194 ± 3.3	3,512
	158-167mm	244 ± 8.8	774
	D 83-87mm	129 ± 1.0	15,901
	88-92mm	150 ± 1.4	12,253
	93-97mm	188 ± 3.6	2,767
	98-102mm	234 ± 8.0	856

*S-systolic; D-diastolic; Δ-above average pressure

Studies of the experience among insured policyholders provide only limited data about mortality in definite hypertension, and almost none when the systolic pressure exceeded 167 mm or the diastolic exceeded 102 mm. It has been necessary for insurance companies to supplement them with additional observations of the experience among persons rejected for life insurance on account of high blood pressure and with the findings of clinical investigations. For the most part, clinical studies of hypertension have dealt with patients who, in addition to the finding of high blood pressure, also manifested symptoms or other signs of hypertensive cardiovascular disease. Their disease had more often than not progressed beyond the stage of asymptomatic hypertension without complications generally seen in life insurance applicants. However, a few investigators have assessed the significance of transient elevation of the blood pressure in otherwise healthy persons. Thus Hines[19] reviewed the records of some 1,500 patients who returned to the Mayo Clinic 10 and 20 years after their first examination and concluded that transient elevations of systolic or diastolic pressures into the borderline range were prognostic of later definite hypertension in a large proportion of cases. In the mid 1940s Levy et al.[20] analyzed the records of 22,700 U.S. Army officers and reported that transient hypertension increased the chances of subsequent development of definite hypertension. As indicated previously, the subject of borderline hypertension has been reviewed by Julius and Schork.[12]

By far, the most comprehensive body of data bearing on the mortality in untreated hypertension is that assembled in the *Build and Blood Pressure Study 1959*, which covered the experience of 26 large life insurance companies under some 4,000,000 policies issued to men and women from 1935 through 1953, traced to policy anniversaries in 1954. It included the experience on approximately 200,000 persons whose systolic blood pressures at the time the insurance was issued ranged from 138 to 167 mm Hg or whose diastolic pressure ranged similarly from 88 to 102 mm Hg. There were a few cases with higher pressures than these. The investigation was carried out separately for the following: applicants with elevated blood pressure unaccompanied by any minor impairments; applicants with minor impairments such as overweight, albuminuria, and rapid pulse; and applicants who were markedly overweight.

Among the significant findings of the *Build and Blood Pressure Study 1959* was the observation that mortality was lowest among persons with systolic pressures 98-127 and diastolic 48-67. It is not surprising, therefore, that the *Build and Blood Pressure Study* demonstrates that even slight elevations in blood pressure (above average) are associated with mortality distinctly higher than that among risks with average blood pressures, and that progressive elevations in blood pressure are associated with progressively higher mortality. This is brought out clearly in Table 8-4.

The relatively high mortality ratio found in the *Build and Blood Pressure Study 1959* among those with slight and moderate elevations in blood pressure raised questions about the accuracy of the blood pressure readings on life insurance examinations. Tests indicated, however, that although blood pressures on life insurance examinations were occasionally understated, the overall effect was not material. More recently, essentially the same distribution of prevalence of blood pressure readings in insurance applicants has been found with automatic equipment.[21]

Mortality among insured hypertensives exhibits characteristic features by cause of death. The excess mortality associated with definite hypertensives is seen in Table 8-4 to be chiefly due to heart and other circulatory diseases, cerebral hemorrhage, and nephritis.

TABLE 8-4

Variations in Mortality among Men and Women According to Systolic and Diastolic Pressures. Ratios of Actual to Expected Mortality: Standard Male or Female Risks, 100 Per Cent. Build and Blood Pressure Study 1959.

Blood Pressure (mm Hg)		Mortality Ratio* (Men)			Mortality Ratio* (Women)		
Systolic	Diastolic	15-39 yrs†	40-69 yrs†	All Ages	15-39 yrs†	40-69 yrs†	All Ages
128-137	<83	111%	108%	109%	137%	93%	101%
	83-87	133	125	127	147	100	107
	88-92	157	134	140	179	113	123
	93-97	221	156	168	209	92	110
	98-102	(127)	213	197	—	—	—
138-147	<83	130	142	141	161	116	118
	83-87	171	150	153	162	120	122
	88-92	213	166	170	150	119	120
	93-97	238	195	199	(398)	186	195
	98-102	288	215	224	—	171	220
148-157	<88	186	179	180	—	117	120
	88-92	196	191	191	(301)	157	160
	93-97	258	221	224	—	159	163
	98-102	499	243	269	—	214	232
158-167	<88	(167)	219	215	—	209	214
	88-92	(235)	240	240	—	202	208
	93-97	(441)	260	268	—	296	287
	98-102	(350)	286	289	—	(325)	(362)

*Where the number of policies terminated by death is 10 to 34, the mortality ratio is enclosed in parentheses.

The most extensive information about mortality in definite hypertension was developed in a study by Bolt, Bell and Harnes of almost 3300 life insurance applicants with blood pressures high enough to result in their being charged very high extra premiums or being declined for life insurance altogether (systolic exceeding 162 mm or diastolic exceeding 102 mm). The study involved 2497 men and 786 women who applied for insurance during 1946-1950, with almost complete follow-up through 1956. The detailed findings of this investigation are presented in abstract §326. The men in this study with systolic pressures of 178 mm or higher accompanied by diastolic pressures of 108 mm or higher experienced a mortality ratio approaching 600 per cent. Men with systolic pressures of 198 mm or higher registered approximately the same mortality, while those with diastolic pressures of 118 mm or higher showed a mortality ratio of 710 per cent.

To obtain more information about mortality in definite hypertension, it is necessary to have recourse to various clinical studies of hypertensive patients. Classification of patients in such studies emphasizes findings other than blood pressure level, findings such as eyeground changes and cardiovascular or renal complications, all of which greatly influence the prognosis. In the Mayo Clinic series (§323) the Keith-Wagener classification of eyeground changes was used; in the studies by Palmer and Muench[22] and Smithwick et al.[23] severity was graded according to the evidence of cardiac, cerebrovascular, or renal damage, or a combination of these with papilledema or very high levels of diastolic pressure. In all series Grade 1 signified the most "benign" cases, Grades 2 and 3 progressively more severe degrees of disease or functional impairment, and Grade 4, the most severe category, generally termed malignant hypertension.

Excess mortality of varying degrees were found in the Grade 1 patients of all these series, often higher than in the Bolt, Bell and Harnes study of insurance applicants (§326). Although the methods of grading severity were different in each of these series, the cross-correlation of the indices used was such that identically numbered grades showed generally comparable levels of excess death rates. This is evident from the results by grade of severity in Table 8-5, which demonstrate a progressive increase in EDR with increasing severity in each series. There was no overlap in the range of EDRs from one grade to another: 14 to 49 per 1000 in males and 1.3 to 20 per 1000 in females in Grade 1; 70 to 110 per 1000 in Grade 2 males, and 29 to 51 per 1000 in females; 191 to 248 per 1000 in males and 135 to 141 per 1000 in females in Grade 3; and in Grade 4 (malignant hypertension) 418 to 880 per 1000 in males and 209 to 540 per 1000 in females. Even higher excess death rates would have been found in the Mayo Clinic series (M) and the unoperated patients of Smithwick et al. (S) if more weight had been given to mortality in the first two years. Mortality rates were so high in the patients with malignant hypertension that most of the deaths and exposures were concentrated in the first year of follow-up. The extremely wide range of excess mortality from Grade 1 to Grade 4 attests to the prognostic significance of the severity indices used in classifying the severity of the hypertensive cardiovascular disease in these patients who did not have the benefit of modern antihypertensive chemotherapy.

TABLE 8-5

Excess Mortality in Hypertensive Cardiovascular Disease
Prior to Use of Antihypertensive Drugs

	Male						Female					
Series	No. of Pts.	(Ave. Age)	Follow-up	Observed Rate	Mortality Rate Ave. Ann.	Excess	No. of Pts.	(Ave. Age)	Follow-up	Observed Rate	Mortality Rate Ave. Ann.	Excess
	ℓ	$\bar{x}$		P or d/E	1000 q	1000(q-q')	ℓ	$\bar{x}$		P or d/E	1000 q	1000(q-q')
Grade 1 — Least Severe Hypertension —												
M	52	(45)	5 Yr P	.894	22	14	74	(52)	5 Yr P	.955	9.2	1.3
P	40	(44)	8.7 Yr d/E	.060	60	40	70	(47)	9.7 Yr d/E	.028	28	6.8
S	42	(39)	5 Yr P	.760	53	49	36	(42)	5 Yr P	.890	23	20
Grade 2 — Moderately Severe Hypertension —												
M	134	(57)	5 Yr P	.617	92	70	145	(57)	5 Yr P	.808	42	29
P	29	(54)	6.5 Yr d/E	.095	95	70	59	(53)	8.0 Yr d/E	.070	70	44
S	136	(47)	5 Yr P	.530	119	110	126	(47)	5 Yr P	.750	56	51
Grade 3 — Severe Hypertension —												
M	105	(52)	5 Yr P	.316	206	191	46	(52)	5 Yr P	.462	143	135
P	99	(53)	3.5 Yr d/E	.278	278	248	102	(55)	5.0 Yr d/E	.167	167	137
S	103	(51)	5 Yr P	.250	242	229	47	(51)	5 Yr P	.450	148	141
Grade 4 — Malignant Hypertension —												
M	53	(48)	5 Yr P	.061	428	418	22	(44)	5 Yr P	.190	283	279
P	32	(39)	1.1 Yr d/E	.889	889	880	22	(38)	1.7 Yr d/E	.544	544	540
S	88	(47)	5 Yr P	.030	504	495	41	(47)	5 Yr P	.300	214	209

*M — Mayo Clinic patients, diagnosed 1940, followed to 1960. Classified by ophthalmoscopic criteria of Keith, Wagener and Barker. See §323.

P — Palmer and Muench,[22] series of private patients, first seen for hypertension 1935-1941, followed to 1952.

S — Smithwick et al.[23] hospital evaluated and medically treated patients 1939-1955 (patients treated surgically, by sympathectomy, not reported in this table).

Additional results of the study of Mayo Clinic patients may be found in §323. This study extended to 20 years of follow-up. Excess death rates tended to increase with duration after the first five years in Grade 1 and 2 males and Grade 1 females, but decreased with duration in Grade 3 males and Grade 2 and 3 females (Table 232a). There were so few five-year survivors in Grade 4 that no mortality data were presented beyond that duration. The grading of severity in this series was by ophthalmoscopic observation of the retinal arteries and eyegrounds. As a consequence the patients could be further categorized by the presence or absence of cardiovascular complications in Grades 1 and 2, and excess mortality was increased when complications were present (Table 323b) as much as 70 extra deaths per 1000 per year. The patients in Grades 1, 2, and 3 were also classified by diastolic blood pressure, with results that could be anticipated: in each severity grade excess mortality was highest with a diastolic pressure of 120-139 mm and lowest when the pressure was below 100 mm (Table 323b). Mortality differences due to blood pressure, however, tended to be smaller than those associated with the severity grading. As shown in the description of "Subjects Studied" in §323, average diastolic pressure increased progressively from Grade 1 (about 102 mm) to Grade 3 (about 125 mm).

Hypertension and Associated Impairments

Hypertension is commonly found with a number of other impairments, notably overweight. The prevalence and incidence of hypertension are highly correlated with overweight, as has been demonstrated in various studies, both among insured lives and in the general population. The nature of this association is not well understood. However, most physicians handling overweight patients with mild hypertension anticipate correctly that the blood pressure will be reduced in many of them if weight is successfully reduced. Weight control is considered to be an integral part of blood pressure control.

The *Build and Blood Pressure Study 1959* documents the higher mortality experienced among insured lives who in addition to hypertension were mildly overweight, or had albuminuria, or a family history of cardiovascular disease, as indicated in Table 8-6. These were included with "minor impairments," which were defined as those considered in the underwriting analysis as entailing a mortality ratio not in excess of 120 per cent. The mortality data in the volume are presented throughout for insured individuals with and without minor impairments, or both together. The data in Table 8-6 have been taken from tables in which the effects of individual minor impairments have been evaluated.

TABLE 8-6

Mortality Ratios among Hypertensive Men with Minor Impairments
Build and Blood Pressure Study 1959[4]

Blood Pressure Group		Mortality Ratios (Standard Expected = 100%)			
Systolic	Diastolic	Without any Known Minor Impairment	With Mild Overweight as Minor Impairment	With Albumin-uria as Minor Impairment	With Early Cardiovascular-Renal Family History
<138	<83	85%	100%	105%	105%
138-147	<83	135	165	165	165
<138	83-92	120	135	150	180
138-147	83-92	155	180	175	180
148-177	48-92	180	225	270	—
98-147	93-102	175	210	—	—
148-177	93-102	250	250	—	—

The *Build and Blood Pressure Study* also included the experience among insured lives who were markedly overweight in addition to being hypertensive. The death rates at ages under 55 among these obese hypertensive subjects were significantly higher than would have been expected from the combination of the extra mortality associated with pronounced overweight and several levels of high blood pressure; this excess mortality was due primarily to heart disease, cerebrovascular disease, nephritis, and diabetes. Diabetes is another disease associated with a higher prevalence of hypertension, entirely apart from overweight.

The Framingham Study indicates that elevated blood pressure, accompanied by several impairments with which it is commonly found, is the most serious risk factor in coronary heart disease.[25] In a high proportion of hypertensive Framingham subjects their elevated blood pressure was associated with cardiovascular complications. It should be emphasized that Framingham experience according to blood pressure reflects the composite effect of high mortality and morbidity in hypertensive cardiovascular disease with the more favorable prognosis found in asymptomatic, uncomplicated, Grade 1 benign hypertension.

In the *Build and Blood Pressure Study 1959*, the mortality rates among hypertensives with normal electrocardiograms and with normal chest X-rays were found to be distinctly lower than among those who had not been so screened. This was true not only of borderline and mild hypertension covered in the *Build and Blood Pressure Study 1959,* but also of moderate and severe hypertensives investigated in the Bolt, Bell and Harnes study previously mentioned (§326).

In addition to evidence of heart enlargement in the chest X-ray and left ventricular hypertrophy or strain patterns in the electrocardiogram, other findings on clinical evaluation are of great importance as prognostic indicators in hypertension. These include ophthalmoscopic findings, abnormalities of the urine (protein, red cells, or casts suggesting associated nephritis or nephrosclerosis), and evidence of functional renal damage, through special tests, or elevation of blood urea nitrogen and serum creatinine in advanced states (azotemia and ultimately uremia, reflecting chronic renal failure). They are some of the important factors used to grade the severity of hypertensive cardiovascular disease. Their effect on mortality is presented in Table 8-5, previously discussed, in abstracts §323, §324, and in other cardiovascular abstracts §315, §317 and §371.

The mounting impact on mortality of several associated impairments or risk factors is perhaps the most important point to be kept in mind with regard to hypertension and other cardiovascular diseases. This was brought out dramatically in The National Cooperative Pooling Project, which showed that the likelihood of a first coronary event multiplied as the number of risk factors, including hypertension, increased.[24] The annual rate of first coronary event in men age 30 to 59 years was correlated with the number of risk factors present as follows: with no risk factor, 20 per 1000; with a single risk factor, 48 per 1000; with two risk factors, 90 per 1000; and with three factors, 171 per 1000. Similar findings based on various overall risk severity functions have been described by Kannel.[25]

Prognosis in Hypertension Since 1955

As indicated previously, 1955 is a convenient year to separate mortality experience collected prior to general use of modern antihypertensive drugs from the more recent experience which reflects the increasing use of such drugs in the treatment of hypertensive patients. Several clinical trials of antihypertensive drugs in relatively small samples of patients have indicated reductions in mortality by at least 30 per cent in the short run in benign hypertension, and considerably greater reductions in severe hypertension with complications. The current prognosis in hypertension under treatment is, therefore, significantly better than in untreated hypertension as recorded in earlier studies (Table 8-5). Before the results of such clinical trials are discussed, mortality experience will be presented on various groups with hypertension observed since 1955 when antihypertensive therapy was not a subject under investigation.

Valuable information as to the extra mortality in borderline and definite hypertension has been developed in a number of follow-up studies of special sample populations. The findings of the Framingham Study deserve special attention because they include elaborate analyses of a 16-year follow-up that covered blood pressures reviewed on biennial examinations (§320). Observations on the Framingham cohort of more than 5000 adult residents of the Town of Framingham, Massachusetts, initial age 30 to 59 commenced about 1950, and details of this noted epidemiological study are given in §380. Based on the blood pressures recorded in the first, second and third examinations combined, excess death rates over an average follow-up of 14 years, in six age/sex categories, ranged from 1.4 to 7.7 per 1000 per year among borderline hypertensives, and from 4.6 to 31 per 1000 per year among definite hypertensives (Table 320a). Standard mortality rates were those experienced by Framingham subjects who were normotensive at the first three examinations. Excess death rates tended to increase with age group (35 to 44, 45 to 54, and 55 to 64 years), and were higher in male than female subjects with the same age and blood pressure classification. Definitions of borderline and definite hypertension were those of the New York Heart Association.[1] Mortality ratios for the borderline hypertensives were in the range from 132 to 188 per cent and for the definite hypertensives from 205 to 310 per cent. As noted previously, this experience reflects the higher mortality of various cardiovascular complications as risk factors associated with the elevated blood pressure in many of the hypertensive subjects. Nevertheless, mortality rates in the entire Framingham cohort, estimated on a biennial basis and including hypertensives and all other subjects with risk factors such as known coronary heart disease, were below those in the U.S. white population and about the same as those found in recent ultimate insurance tables. These rates, along with rates by hypertensive status, are given in Tables 320f and 320g.

The Framingham experience has also been presented in terms of systolic pressure, all diastolics combined, and independently by diastolic pressure, all systolics combined. The long-range mortality over an average follow-up of 14 years is given in Tables 320a and 320b, and similar data between biennial examinations (internal follow-up only two years) are contained in Tables 320c and 320d. Mortality rates for the systolic class 110-129 mm (under 140 mm in the youngest age group) have been used as a standard for comparison with all other systolic pressure categories, and 75-84 mm as the diastolic standard class (under 90 mm in the youngest group). It is of interest that mortality rates were higher when the diastolic pressure was under 75 than when it was in the standard class 75-84 mm, in both male and female subjects in a majority of the groups over 44 years of age. At diastolic pressures 85 mm and up and systolic pressures 130 mm and up mortality rates increased with pressure in all age groups and both sexes, with an occasional irregularity probably due to a random variation.

Four single-company studies of applicants insured despite evidence of hypertension are reported in the abstracts, but all of these are of somewhat limited value as no blood pressure classification is given. The Life Insurance Company of Virginia study actually goes back to 1946-1955 issues, followed to 1962, and therefore straddles the two therapeutic eras. The mortality ratio for all substandard cases was 168 per cent (Table 322a). Another study was limited to cases of standard insurance issued by The Northwestern Mutual Life Insurance Company in 1953-1954 despite borderline hypertension. In this group the mortality ratio was 220 per cent, while the ratio in a normotensive control group was well below 100 per cent (Table 321). The experience in this study and the one made by the New York Life Insurance Company in 1954 to 1970 was accumulated in the era of antihypertensive chemotherapy. The overall results of the New York Life Study showed mortality ratios of 124 and 110, respectively, among male and female standard issues, and a male ratio of 194 per cent and a female ratio of 152 per cent for substandard issues (Table 325c). Most of the excess mortality was in diseases of the heart and circulatory system (Table 325d). Hypertensive applicants in Europe insured by The Sverige Reinsurance Company showed a mortality ratio of 177 per cent (Table 399).

The mortality experience of the Prudential of London does provide a breakdown of three blood pressure categories for male applicants age 40 to 59 years, but no breakdown for females or males of other ages (Table 399). The seemingly low mortality ratios reported cannot be directly compared with the experience of United States companies, as standard mortality rates were higher than those of the various 15-year select tables used in North America. Furthermore, the experience was accumulated in 1947 to 1963, and therefore part of it was in the prechemotherapy era.

Three additional life insurance studies, recent in date, also deserve mention. One report was made on Connecticut General Life Insurance Company policies issued on a rated basis because of elevated blood pressure, 1960 to 1971, followed to the 1972 policy anniversary.[26] The experience showed only 65 per cent of the mortality expected on the basis of underwriting rating multiples of standard mortality rates in the 1955-1960 Basic Select Tables. Another study of rated hypertensive applicants insured 1960-1972 was made by the Aetna Life and Casualty, with the experience divided into treated and untreated categories.[27] The mortality ratio of 127 per cent found in those under treatment for hypertension at the time of application was significantly lower (at better than the 99 per cent confidence level) than the ratio of 183 per cent in those without any history of treatment.

No data were reported in relation to blood pressure categories in either of the above studies. However, a 1976 report by the New England Mutual Life Insurance Company[28] does contain a detailed comparison of mortality in men insured 1950 to 1971 by categories of elevated blood pressure that correspond exactly with those of the *Build and Blood Pressure Study 1959*. It was determined that aggregate expected mortality rates, all durations combined, were very nearly the same in the two studies because the longer average duration of the New England Life experience compensated for the decrease in standard select mortality from the 1935-1954 tables to the 1955-1960 tables. As a consequence, it was thought that observed mortality rates and mortality ratios could be directly compared. In 22 of 24 categories of elevated blood pressure in the two age groups reported (men 40 to 49 and 50 to 59 years), the mortality ratios were lower in the New England Life experience than in the *Build and Blood Pressure Study 1959*. In nine of the sixteen subtotals with larger numbers of deaths the differences were statistically significant at the 95 per cent level or better. Although other factors were considered and could not be ruled out, it was believed that more effective treatment of hypertensives with modern drugs was at least partly responsible for this improvement in mortality among life insurance applicants with elevated blood pressure.

The most striking benefit of antihypertensive drugs is seen in malignant hypertension, which, when untreated, is characterized by first-year mortality up to 900 per 1000 or higher, and correspondingly low five-year survival rates of .05 or less.[23, 29, 30] Although the small numbers of patients in many of these series impose a limitation on the number of deaths, the very high early mortality to some extent compensates for this. With mortality of this magnitude the excess death rate becomes nearly equal to the annual mortality rate because it is so much larger than the mortality rate of less than 10 per 1000 expected in the white male population about age 50 (most groups of patients with malignant hypertension cited in this chapter had an average age below 50 years). Similarly, the five-year survival rate can be interpreted as being nearly equivalent to the survival ratio for all practical purposes. As a first approximation, published rates of first-year mortality and five-year survival in treated malignant hypertension may be evaluated in comparison with corresponding rates experienced among patients who did not have the benefit of antihypertensive drug therapy, even in the absence of detailed age data.

Mortality and survival rates of this type have been collected in Table 8-7 from representative studies of patients specifically treated for malignant hypertension. These clinical trials started about 1950 at the earliest and generally utilized various combinations of antihypertensive drugs rather than a single agent. They include the investigations of Dustan et al.,[31] Sokolow et al.[32] (data not given in Table 8-7 because of the small size of the group), Breckenridge et al.,[33] Hood et al.,[34] Perry et al. (§324), and Harington et al.[30] These results for malignant hypertensives treated with antihypertensive drugs can be compared with results for other groups not receiving such treatments, most of which have been previously mentioned. The data shown are number and sex of the patients in each group, first-year mortality rate, average annual mortality rate over five years (as a geometric mean), and five-year survival rate.

TABLE 8-7

**Malignant and Moderate to Severe Hypertension—Treated and "Untreated"
Series of Patients (With and Without Antihypertensive Drugs)**

Series		Antihyper-tensive Drug Treatment	No. of Patients (Sex) ℓ(M or F)	Annual Mort. Rate		Cumulative 5-Yr Surv. Rate P_s
				1st Year 1000 q_i	Ave. 5 Yrs 1000q	
Malignant (Grade 4) Hypertension						
Breslin et al. (§323)		None	53 (M)	—	430	.061
		None	22 (F)	—	280	.190
Palmer et al.[22]		None	54 (MF)	500	410	.074
Smithwick et al.[23]		None	88 (M)	620	500	.03
		None	41 (F)	500	210	.30
Simpson et al.[29]		None	70 (MF)	960	>650	.00
Harington et al.[30]		None	105 (MF)	900	600	.01
Dustan et al.[31]		Yes	84 (MF)	300	180	.36
Perry et al. (§324)	MN*	Yes	97 (MF)	150	93	.615
	MA*	Yes	68 (MF)	420	250	.245
Breckenridge et al[33]		Yes	104 (MF)	480	250	.240
		Yes	58 (F)	400	190	.345
Hood et al.[34]		Yes	128 (MF)	250	130	.50
Harington et al.[30]		Yes	82 (MF)	300	180	.36
Severe (Grade 3) and Moderate (Grade 2) Hypertension						
Breslin et al. (§323)		None	95 (M)	—	210	.316
		None	38 (F)	—	140	.462
Palmer et al.[22]		None	202 (MF)	124	190	.352
Smithwick et al.[23]		None	103 (M)	280	240	.25
		None	47 (F)	100	150	.45
Simpson et al.[29]		None	54 (MF)	(700)	(430)	(.06)
(Grade 2)		None	84 (MF)	220	150	.43
Perry et al. (§324)		Yes	51 (MF)	120	96	.605
Hood et al.[34]		Yes	177 (MF)	90	90	.61
Breckenridge et al.[33]		Yes	142 (M)	90	80	.662
(Grade 3)		Yes	84 (F)	70	44	.798
Breckenridge et al.[33]		Yes	402 (M)	20	38	.826
(Grade 2)		Yes	504 (F)	14	16	.921

See Chapter references and abstracts §323 and §324 for additional details.
*MN — malignant non-azotemic hypertension
MA — malignant azotemic hypertension

Among malignant hypertensive patients five-year survival rates averaged about .36 for the seven groups treated with antihypertensive drugs, as opposed to much lower rates in patients not so treated: average of .035 in five groups composed of both sexes or males exclusively, and one of .24 in two female groups. These five-year survival rates can be converted into average annual mortality rates of 180 per 1000 for the treated patients and 490 per 1000 for the untreated, excluding the two female groups. A similar mortality differential of more than two untreated patient deaths for every treated patient death is seen in the extremely high first-year mortality rates. Comparisons of different series of patients such as these always present difficulties and dangers in attempting to interpret their significance. However, the mortality differentials are both large in magnitude and consistent. Setting aside the lighter mortality in untreated females with malignant hypertension, the lowest mortality rate in the untreated patients still exceeds the highest mortality in the treated groups: there is no overlap in the mortality rates, nor in the five-year survival rates. There were 623 patients in the combined series of malignant hypertensives treated with antihypertensive drugs and 433 in those not so treated. Aggregate numbers of deaths were therefore substantial in view of the high mortality rates observed.

In the medical community today there appears to be universal acceptance of the efficacy of antihypertensive drugs in substantially reducing mortality in patients with malignant hypertension. Despite the lack of randomized controls and the difficulties inherent in comparing different series of patients, the evidence in Table 8-7 does appear to support this conclusion. Two groups, one treated and the other untreated, were drawn from the same patient population at the Hammersmith Clinic,[30] thus reducing the possibility of extraneous factors other than malignant hypertension accounting for some of the mortality difference.

In the lower part of Table 8-7 a similar comparison is presented between various series of patients treated with antihypertensive drugs for lesser degrees of hypertensive cardiovascular disease, and other series not so treated. Most of the series consisted of Grade 3 hypertensives, those with severe disease and complications, but not in Grade 4 or malignant hypertension. However, there were some Grade 2 patients as well. In general, mortality rates were substantially lower in the patients of a particular grade if they were treated with antihypertensive drugs. There was a total of 454 Grade 3 patients who received antihypertensive drugs and 906 Grade 2 patients, the latter all from one clinic.[33] Average annual mortality rates in the Grade 2 patients were down to 38 per 1000 in the males and 16 per 1000 in the females who received treatment, and these rates were reported by the authors as lower in the second half of the study period than in the first half.[33] Rates of this relatively small magnitude would be materially reduced by substraction of the expected mortality in order to obtain the excess death rates generally used in this volume.

Of the various series of patients treated with antihypertensive drugs cited in Table 8-7 that of Perry et al. has been abstracted in detail in §324. Over 12 years of observation on 316 patients, with 2310 person-years of exposure and 190 deaths, the excess death rate was lowest, 17 per 1000, in cases with benign uncomplicated hypertension and highest, 276 per 1000, in those with malignant hypertension and azotemia. Many patients with malignant hypertension show evidence of azotemia and renal damage at the time of diagnostic evaluation. Absence of azotemia greatly improves the prognosis, as shown by an excess death rate of 78 per 1000 for such patients in Table 324a, a rate that was actually lower than the level of 105 per 1000 shown by patients with "benign" (nonmalignant) hypertension who had complications.

Hypertension, in addition to increasing mortality, imposes an increased risk of serious morbidity, such as nonfatal stroke or myocardial infarction. The most convincing evidence of the beneficial effects of antihypertensive therapy comes from the Veterans Administration Cooperative Group on Antihypertensive Agents. Their first report dealt with 143 male hypertensive patients whose initial diastolic pressure ranged from 115 to 129 mm Hg, followed an average period of 24 months.[36] The second report related to 380 male hypertensive veterans with initial diastolic pressures in the range from 90 to 114 mm Hg followed for an average of 40 months.[37] The treated patients showed significant decreases in blood pressures, whereas the veterans receiving a placebo did not. Among those in the treated group with the higher initial diastolic pressures, 115 to 129 mm, there were no deaths and only two nonfatal morbid events, whereas in the untreated controls there were four deaths and 23 cases of major cardiovascular or renal complications. Among those with initial diastolic pressures of 90 to 114 mm Hg there were eight cardiovascular deaths during follow-up of 186 treated patients and 19 cardiovascular deaths among the 194 untreated controls.[38]

Treatment and control groups were carefully randomized in this series of studies. Nonfatal terminating events were congestive heart failure, stroke, progression of hypertension to a more severe stage, etc. all of which resulted in termination of placebo in the control group and substitution of antihypertensive agents. With life table analysis the five-year cumulative rate of terminating morbid events, including cardiovascular deaths, was found to be .048 in the treatment group and .180 in the control group. When other cardiovascular events, not a cause for termination, were added, the corresponding rates were .118 in the treatment group and .392 in the control group, a difference that was highly significant statistically. Twenty of the patients in the control group were started on antihypertensive medication simply because diastolic pressures rose to a sustained level of 125 mm Hg or higher. The life table analysis permitted withdrawal of these patients and the ones experiencing a nonfatal terminating event from exposure to risk in the control group at the appropriate duration, without sacrifice of the prior exposure.

These findings indicate that antihypertensive therapy is effective at least in the short run. Such therapy appears to have decreased the incidence of stroke by about three-fourths and has been preventive of accelerated hypertension and renal deterioration. Freis, who carried out and directed the Veterans Administration study, indicated that in his judgment antihypertensive therapy was of great value in controlling both morbidity and mortality in hypertension, except perhaps for coronary heart disease.[37] The higher the initial diastolic pressure, the greater was the benefit observed.

Hypertension: A Prospective View

Some aspects of hypertension as a chronic disease and public health problem were discussed earlier in this chapter (Dimensions of the Hypertension Problem), and mention was made of the National High Blood Pressure Education Program. In view of this current interest and the mortality data here reviewed what is the prospect for the future?

100

From the available evidence antihypertensive therapy holds out the promise of material decreases in morbidity and mortality associated with hypertension, at least during a minimum period of five years of treatment that is effective in reducing blood pressure to or close to normal levels. Continuing lower mortality from cardiovascular disease, hypertensive heart disease, and renal complications is anticipated among those treated for hypertension, but the effect of current antihypertensive therapy on coronary heart disease remains doubtful. Most of the limited mortality data currently available suggest that even adequately treated hypertensives may continue to experience death rates higher than those among healthy normotensive persons, although Mathisen reported a mortality similar to that of the general population in hypertensive patients classified as Grade 1 or 2 and adequately treated (only 10 deaths were observed).[35] However, most of the data on treatment have dealt with severe hypertension. In mild and moderate hypertension it will be necessary to follow large numbers of subjects for long periods in order to assess the effectiveness of antihypertensive therapy, especially to answer the question as to whether it is possible to eliminate excess mortality completely.

An important issue arises from the observations that average blood pressure levels among persons with slight or moderate hypertension remain relatively stable for considerable periods of time in a high proportion of cases. The higher the blood pressure, the greater is the probability of further elevation of pressure and of development of complications with the passage of time. One of the major challenges in medicine is to identify those hypertensives in whom the underlying pathological process is most acutely progressive. Laragh[9] has suggested that low-renin hypertension is much less likely to produce cardiovascular complications and increased risk of death than other types of hypertension identifiable by his testing methods. However, the analytical techniques are difficult and much additional investigation is needed for assessment of the significance of these concepts.

The prospects for further reduction in the mortality associated with hypertension are good. The long-term trends in hypertensive heart disease and cerebrovascular disease have been downward. The intensive efforts now being mounted to detect and treat hypertension are likely to accelerate this trend. Under the aegis of the National High Blood Pressure Education Program, broadbased efforts are under way to inform the public at large, to establish facilities in addition to the physician's office for blood pressure screening—community and industry programs, and the use of nonphysician allied medical personnel, such as dentists, pharmacists, nurses and technicians—to increase physician awareness of all aspects of hypertension problem, and to encourage early and effective treatment. With such increasing publicity and education more and more persons with hypertension should avail themselves of treatment opportunities and facilities and continue such treatment as long as it is needed. Hypertension is a life-long disease requiring life-long observation, even if the blood pressure level is brought to normal and appears to remain there after treatment is discontinued.

References

1. New York Heart Association: *Nomenclature and Criteria for Diagnosis of Diseases of the Heart and Blood Vessels.* New York Heart Association (1955).

2. E.A. Lew, "Blood Pressure and Mortality—Life Insurance Experience." In *Epidemiology of Hypertension,* edited by J. Stamler, R. Stamler and T.N. Pullman. New York: Grune and Stratton (1967), pp. 392-397.

3. O. Paul, "Risks of Mild Hypertension: A Ten-Year Report." *Brit. Heart J.,* 33 (Suppl.):116-121 (1971).

4. *Build and Blood Pressure Study 1959.* Chicago: Society of Actuaries (1960), Volume I, pp. 36-42.

5. G.A. Rose and H. Blackburn, *Cardiovascular Survey Methods.* Geneva: World Health Organization, Monograph Series 56 (1968), pp. 90-93.

6. *National Conference on High Blood Pressure Education, 15 January 1973.* Washington, D.C.: U.S. Government Printing Office, DHEW Publication No. (NIH) 73-486 (1973).

7. A.C. Guyton, T.G. Coleman, A.W. Cowley, Jr., K.W. Scheel, R.D. Manning, Jr., and R.A. Norman, Jr., "Arterial Pressure Regulation. Overriding Dominance of the Kidneys in Long-Term Regulation and in Hypertension." In *Hypertension Manual. Mechanisms, Methods, Management,* edited by J.H. Laragh. New York: Dun-Donnelley (1974), pp. 111-134.

8. H.P. Dustan, R.C. Tarazi, and E.L. Bravo, "Physiologic Characteristics of Hypertension." In *Hypertension Manual* ibid., pp. 227-256.

9. J.H. Laragh, ed., *Hypertension Manual. Mechanisms, Methods, Management.* New York: Dun-Donnelley (1974).

10. G. Pickering, *High Blood Pressure,* 2nd ed. New York: Grune and Stratton (1968).

11. L.K. Dahl, "Salt and Hypertension." *Am. J. Clin. Nutr.,* 25:231-244 (1974).

12. S. Julius and M.A. Schork, "Borderline Hypertension—a Critical Review." *J. Chron. Dis.,* 23:723-754 (1971).

13. Dept. of Health, Education, and Welfare, *Blood Pressure of Adults by Age and Sex, U.S., 1960-62.* Vital and Health Statistics, Series 11, No. 4. Rockville, Md.: National Center for Health Statistics (1964).

14. Dept. of Health, Education, and Welfare, *Blood Pressure of Persons 18-74 Years, U.S., 1971-72.* Vital and Health Statistics, Series 11, No. 150. Rockville, Md.: National Center for Health Statistics (1975).

15. J. Stamler, "High Blood Pressure in the U.S.—An Overview of the Problem and the Challenge." In *National Conference on High Blood Pressure Education, 15 January 1973.* Washington, D.C.: U.S. Government Printing Office. DHEW Publication No. (NIH) 73-486 (1973).

16. R.B. Singer, "To Treat or Not to Treat." *J. Chron. Dis.,* 28:125-134 (1975).

17. H.A. Schroeder, "Effect of 1-Hyrazinophthalazine and Hexamethonium on Hypertension." *J. Lab. Clin. Med.,* 38:949 (1951).

18. F.H. Smirk, "Practical Details of Methonium Treatment of High Blood Pressure." *New Zealand Med. J.,* 49:637-643 (1950).

19. E.A. Hines, Jr., "Range of Normal Blood Pressure and Subsequent Development of Hypertension: A Follow-up Study of 1522 Patients." *J. Am. Med. Assoc.,* 115:271-274 (1940).

20. R.I. Levy, C.C. Hillman, W.D. Stroud, "Transient Hypertension: Its Significance in Terms of Later Development of Sustained Hypertension and Cardiovascular-Renal Diseases." *J. Am. Med. Assoc.,* 126:829-833 (1944).

21. E.A. Lew, personal communication (1976).

22. R.S. Palmer and H. Muench, "Course and Prognosis of Essential Hypertension." *J. Am. Med. Assoc.,* 153:1-4 (1953).

23. R.H. Smithwick, R.D. Bush, D. Kinsey, and G.P. Whitelaw, "Hypertension and Associated Cardiovascular Disease—Comparison of Male and Female Mortality Rates and Their Influence on Selection of Therapy." *J. Am. Med. Assoc.,* 160:1023-1026 (1956).

24. E.A. Lew, "High Blood Pressure, Other Risk Factors and Longevity: The Insurance Viewpoint." In *Hypertension Manual,* edited by J.H. Laragh. New York: Dun-Donnelley (1974), pp. 43-70.

25. W.B. Kannel, "Role of Blood Pressure in Cardiovascular Disease: The Framingham Study." *Angiology,* 26:1-14 (1975).

26. G.L. Corliss, "Recent Intracompany Mortality Experience on Treated Hypertensives." *Trans. Assoc. Life Ins. Med. Dir. Am.,* 58:90-105 (1974).

27. J.W. Pilgrim, "1973 Connecticut General Blood Pressure Study." *Trans. Assoc. Life Ins. Med. Dir. Am.,* 58:81-89 (1974).

28. A.E. Brown and R.B. Singer, "Hypertension: Trend of Excess Mortality Since the 1959 Build and Blood Pressure Study." 12th International Congress of Life Assurance Medicine, Munich, Germany (May 30-June 3, 1976).

29. F.O. Simpson and A.R. Gilchrist, "Prognosis in Untreated Hypertensive Vascular Disease," *Scot. Med. J.,* 3:1-14 (1958).

30. M. Harington, P. Kincaid-Smith, and J. McMichael, "Results of Treatment in Malignant Hypertension. A Seven-Year Experience in 94 Cases." *Brit. Med. J.,* 4:969-980 (1959).

31. H.P. Dustan, R.E. Schneckloth, A.C. Corcoran, and I.H. Page, "The Effectiveness of Long-Term Treatment of Malignant Hypertension," *Circulation,* 18:644-651 (1958).

32. M. Sokolow and D. Perloff, "Five Year Survival of Consecutive Patients with Malignant Hypertention Treated with Antihypertensive Agents." *Am. J. Card.,* 6:858-863 (1960).

33. A. Breckenridge, C.T. Dollery, and E.H.O. Parry, "Prognosis of Treated Hypertension. Changes in Life Expectancy and Causes of Death between 1952 and 1967." *Quart. J. Med.,* 39:411-429 (1970).

34. B. Hood, G. Örndahl, and S. Björk, "Survival and Mortality in Malignant (Grade IV) and Grade III Hypertension." *Acta Med. Scand.,* 187:291-302 (1970).

35. H.S. Mathisen, H. Löken, D. Brox, and Ö. Stenbaek, "The Prognosis in Long Term Treated and 'Untreated' Essential Hypertension." *Acta Med. Scand.,* 185:253-258 (1969).

36. Veterans Administration Cooperative Study Group on Antihypertensive Agents, "Effects of Treatment on Morbidity in Hypertension. Results in Patients with Diastolic Blood Pressures Averaging 115 through 129 mm Hg." *J. Am. Med. Assoc.,* 202:1028-1034 (1967).

37. Veterans Administration Cooperative Study Group on Antihypertensive Agents, "Effect of Treatment on Morbidity in Hypertension. II. Results in Patients with Diastolic Blood Pressure Averaging 90 through 114 mm Hg." *J. Am. Med. Assoc.,* 213:1143-1152 (1970).

Congenital and Valvular Heart
Disease

Philip G. Sullivan, M.D., and
Richard B. Singer, M.D.

Statistics on numbers of deaths in the United States by cause during 1970 show 8,137 deaths due to congenital cardio-vascular diseases (all but 580 due to congenital heart disease), and 15,719 due to valvular heart disease, the two categories of cardiovascular disease covered in this chapter. Most of the valvular disease deaths are in the category of chronic rheumatic heart disease. Together these constitute only 2.3 per cent of deaths from diseases of the circulatory system and 1.2 per cent of almost two million total deaths in the United States during 1970. The distribution of deaths among various types of congenital and valvular heart disease is given in Table 9-1, together with the numbers of the abstracts containing mortality and survival data concerning them. Congenital heart disease will be considered first, then various types of valvular heart disease, including heart murmurs without particular identification of the valvular disease producing the murmur.

Congenital Heart Disease—Incidence and Etiology

This segment deals with structural defects of the heart and great vessels. Estimates of the incidence of these structural defects vary, depending on the methods of data collection.[1] Determination of the true incidence is hampered by difficulties in early and accurate diagnosis and incomplete reporting of cases. In 1953 MacMahon et al. presented estimates of the incidence and life expectation at birth based on all identifiable cases of congenital malformations of the circulatory system detected at birth or later in a population of 199,418 total births in Birmingham, England, between 1940 and 1949 (abstract §334). In this study, the incidence was 3.17 per 1000 births. Other estimates are 5 per 1000 births[2] and 8 per 1000 births.[3] The highest estimate (8 per 1000 births) is from the 1973 Report of the Heart and Blood Vessel Diseases Panel for the Department of Health, Education and Welfare.

Perhaps the best estimate of the frequency distribution of different types of congenital heart disease is found in MacMahon's study (Table 334d), in which septal defects are the most frequent, followed by patent ductus arteriosus and transposition of the great vessels. Whereas MacMahon investigated a cohort of total births from 1940 to 1949, studies of the prevalence of congenital malformations of the circulatory system in school children have ranged from 1.4 per 1000 children in Chicago[4] to 5.5 per 1000 children in Durango, Colorado.[5] It is clear that frequencies of the various types of congenital cardiac and circulatory defects may change, and that the overall prevalence decreases as children grow older. One-half of the children born with congenital malformations of the heart and great vessels die during the first year of life—most of these in the first six months. Such early mortality occurs despite a recent estimate that 90 per cent of congenital cardio-vascular malformations can be corrected or palliated. The distribution of defects shown in Table 9-2 is taken from Morton and Huhn,[6] and compared with the results of consultant examination in MacMahon's study.

The etiology of congenital malformations of the heart and great vessels is unknown in most cases. Viral infections, drugs, genetic aberrations, high altitude, ionizing radiation and maternal illness—such as diabetes—have been implicated as causative factors. The only viral disease definitely associated with congenital heart disease is rubella, which during early gestation may be followed by cardiovascular anomalies—commonly patent ductus arteriosus and interventricular septal defects. Genetic aberrations, such as Down's Syndrome and other trisomies, are associated with congenital cardiovascular defects. Although other specific factors have been implicated in some series, no etiological agent can be identified in the majority of children with congenital structural malformations of the heart and great vessels.

Congenital Heart Disease—Mortality

The prognosis of congenital malformations of the heart and great vessels, taken as a whole, is poor, although technical advances in diagnosis and treatment have occurred since MacMahon's study in 1953 when only 198 children of 628 born with some sort of congenital cardiovascular defect were alive at one year of age (Table 334c). After this period of very high mortality the annual excess death rate was found to be 11 per 1000 from the first to the fifth year of attained age, and 25 per 1000 from the fifth to the tenth year (Table 334a). As has been noted, it is estimated today that one-half of infants diagnosed in the first year of life will survive to one year of age.[3] Those children with the severe forms of heart disease, showing cyanosis or heart failure, have the greatest mortality and come to medical attention early. Others, with less severe

TABLE 9-1

Numbers of Deaths in the U.S. — 1970

Congenital and Valvular Heart Disease

Hazard	Deaths in U.S. Number	(% in Category)	Follow-up Data
Congenital Heart Disease	8,137	(34.1%)	
Tetralogy of Fallot	414	(1.7%)	§330
Stenosis or Atresia of Pulmonary Artery	192	(0.8)	§334
Coarctation of Aorta	224	(0.9)	§332, §334
Other Anomalies of Aorta	75	(0.3)	§331
Patent Ductus Arteriosus	210	(0.9)	§333, §334
Transposition of Great Vessels	488	(2.0)	§334
Ventricular Septal Defect	641	(2.7)	§335
Atrial Septal Defect	420	(1.8)	—
Common Truncus	151	(0.6)	§334
Ostium Atrioventriculare Commune	93	(0.4)	—
Anomalies of Heart Valves	813	(3.4)	—
Fibroelastosis Cordis	226	(0.9)	—
Other Specified Anomalies of the Heart	539	(2.3)	—
Subtotal Specified	(4,486)	(18.8)	—
Other Unspecified Anomalies of the Heart	3,071	(12.9)	—
Other Congenital Cardiovascular Diseases	580	(2.4)	—
Chronic "Rheumatic" Heart Disease*	14,549	(61.0%)	
Diseases of the Mitral Valves	3,821	(16.0%)	§349, §353, §354
Mitral Stenosis	**	—	§353
Diseases of the Aortic Valve	3,910	(16.4%)	§355, §356, §358
Diseases of Mitral & Aortic	1,287	(5.4)	—
Diseases of Tricuspid	37	(0.2)	—
Diseases of Other Endocardial Structures	683	(2.9)	—
Other Chronic R.H.D.	4,811	(20.2)	
Non Rheumatic Chronic Diseases of Endocardium	1,170	(4.9%)	
Mitral Valve	60	(0.3%)	(see above)
Aortic Valve	221	(0.9)	(see above)
Other Endocardial Structure	889	(3.7)	—
Heart Murmurs	**	—	
Apical Systolic	**	—	§349, §351, §352
Apical Diastolic	**	—	§349
Aortic Systolic	**	—	§349
Aortic Diastolic	**	—	§349
Pulmonic Systolic	**	—	§349
Other Murmurs	**	—	§350
Total (all listed in Cause of Death Statistics)	23,856	(1.2% of all deaths)	

*Pericarditis excluded

**Listed elsewhere under various separate causes

defects, are more likely to be diagnosed during school ages or in adulthood. Current surgical treatment has resulted in the salvage of numbers of children with severe congenital heart defects, such as transposition of the great vessels, tetralogy of Fallot, and large septal defects, but these defects still contribute heavily to the excess early mortality from congenital heart disease.

TABLE 9-2

Relative Frequency of Various Types of Congenital Heart Disease

	Morton and Huhn[6]	MacMahon (§334)
Atrial and Septal Defects	32.5%	44%
Pulmonic Stenosis	20.2	18
Aortic Stenosis	17.5	—
Patent Ductus Arteriosus	11.3	15
Coarctation of the Aorta	7.5	4
Tetralogy of Fallot	3.5	8
Others	7.5	11

Transposition of the Great Vessels. In one series of infants, investigated during the first week of life because of severe congenital cardiovascular disease, transposition of the great vessels accounted for 38 per cent of all infants catheterized and for about 50 per cent of all infants with severe cyanosis.[8] Although transposition of the great vessels is amenable to palliation and potentially correctible, Miller found that only 60 per cent of these children were alive at one year of age. The one-year survival rate for the total group of infants studied from 1970 to 1973 was only 40 per cent.[8]

Tetralogy of Fallot. Taussig et al. studied a consecutive series of 780 cases of tetralogy of Fallot submitted to the Blalock-Taussig operation between 1946 and 1950 with a 15-year follow-up (§330). Of those operated upon, 88 per cent survived the initial operation and, of the survivors, 41 per cent underwent a subsequent operation. Among survivors of the initial operation, the excess death rate during the first year was 34 per 1000 per year if reoperation mortality was excluded and 38 per 1000 if reoperation mortality was included. After the first year following initial operation excess death rates were variable, with the highest rates 10 to 15 years after operation. The overall excess death rates for the 15-year follow-up period were 11 per 1000 if reoperation mortality was excluded and 16 per 1000 if reoperation mortality was included (Table 330a). Those children operated upon under one year of age, perhaps the sickest, have the highest mortality rate—47 per cent (Table 330c).

Palliative procedures carried a lower surgical mortality rate than "totally corrective" procedures—13 per cent vs. 29.8 per cent (Table 330d). However, most centers now have immediate surgical mortality rates (0–30 days) between five per cent and ten per cent for definitive intracardiac repair of tetralogy of Fallot—the procedure of choice today. "Late" deaths generally occur during the first year, but long-term results have not been reported. In Olley's study, 27 per cent of the survivors had some pulmonary outflow obstruction, 15 per cent had a persistent ventricular septal defect, 52 per cent had trivial, and 18 per cent severe pulmonary incompetence.[9] In addition, of the 149 survivors, 144 had complete right bundle branch block. The statement is made that when this group reaches the age of ischemic heart disease, one might anticipate a high prevalence of complete heart block.[9] In general those children with severe pulmonic stenosis, as a component of the tetralogy, who require patch-grafting, do less well than those who require only infundibular resection.

Ventricular Septal Defect. Severity of isolated defect of this type, excluding associated structural anomalies of the heart and great vessels, depends on the size of the defect and the extent of pulmonary and systemic vascular resistance. Small ventricular septal defects, with minimal left to right flow, are usually associated with normal pulmonary artery pressures and are well tolerated. A large ventricular septal defect, in the presence of low pulmonary vascular resistance, will result in substantial left to right flow with resultant overload of the pulmonary circulation and left ventricular failure. On the other hand, if pulmonary vascular resistance is high, for whatever reason, one may see a progressive reduction in left to right flow, a "balanced shunt," or even right to left flow. There is a tendency in infancy for smaller ventricular septal defects to close and for the larger defects to become smaller.

The hemodynamic classification of Kidd et al. (Table 335a) is widely used as an index of prognosis and therapy of those with ventricular septal defect. Several points are of interest in the follow-up study of Keith et al. (§335). Those infants in Group I (low pulmonary flow; low pulmonary vascular resistance) showed no excess mortality. Those infants in Group V (low pulmonary flow; high pulmonary vascular resistance) had the next lowest excess death rate (Table 335c), but this finding was based on very small numbers and the significance is questionable. However, follow-up studies did demonstrate that 7 of the 11 children initially in Group V became reclassified in Group I in time, due probably to the gradual resolution of the fetal pattern of thick-walled, muscular pulmonary vasculature. Thus is is reasonable to consider initial classification in Group V in infancy as relatively benign prognostically. Children classified in Groups II, III, IV, and VI, those with high pulmonary blood flow or right to left shunting (Eisenmenger syndrome) were found to have a poor prognosis. Among the adults studied (Table 335b) 80 per cent were in Group I. This is not surprising since early deaths and spontaneous closures had been eliminated. The major hazard in this group is bacterial endocarditis; only 9.5 per cent of the adults were in Group VI with high pulmonary vascular resistance and reversal of flow. The outlook for adults in Group VI is, of course, limited.

Atrial Septal Defect. The various types of this defect, primum, secundum, and complete artrioventricular (A-V) canal, may vary in size and significance. The trend today is to operate on children or young adults with atrial septal defects usually between ages one and 20 years. Those individuals with primum defects, or complete A-V canal, tend to be symptomatic early—congestive heart failure, atrial arrhythmias—and are operated upon early. Those with secundum type defects are usually seen in adulthood since symptoms tend to develop late. The average age of death for those with unoperated atrial septal defect of the secundum type is 40 years, and most of those who live beyond 50 years are incapacitated.

In a study by Parisi and Nadas[10] of a group of catheterized but unoperated individuals 80 per cent of those with secumdum defect and 45 per cent of those with A-V canal were alive after ten years. The group with a primum defect was extremely small, but all eight patients were alive after ten years.

Surgical repair of atrial septal defect is being done now at earlier ages, reducing the pool of adult cases. The major risk factors in surgical repair are pulmonary hypertension and congestive heart failure. Closure of the septal defect will not reverse established pulmonary hypertension, and those with preoperative pulmonary hypertension do badly despite surgery.[11] Other difficulties following surgery are embolic episodes, particularly if a patch graft is used, and atrial arrhythmias of all types. After six years of follow-up, 7 per cent of those operated upon have embolic complications and 12 per cent have atrial arrhythmias. Operative mortality was 9 per cent in those without pulmonary hypertension and 50 per cent in those with pulmonary hypertension.[11]

Congenital Aortic Stenosis. The various types of congenital aortic stenosis comprise about 5 per cent of all cases of congenital structural defects of the heart and great vessels. About 80 per cent of the stenoses are valvular or subvalvular—fibrous ring—with the remainder being idiopathic hypertrophic subaortic stenosis, supravalvular stenosis, and left ventricular outflow obstruction due to abnormal mitral valve attachments.[12] Congenital aortic stenosis is more common in males, the male to female ratio ranging from two to one to five to one (Table 331a).

It is clear from several studies, including that of Lambert et al.[12] and the ones reported in §331, that unoperated congenital aortic stenosis tends to progress in severity at a variable rate, and children with mild stenosis freqently become worse during the first two decades. Excess mortality is seen at all ages with an EDR of the order of 10 to 20 per 1000 in chlidren and adults under age 40, and considerably higher rates in older adults (Table 330c). Deaths are often due to heart failure and bacterial endocarditis, and sudden death is not uncommon. Syncope and angina are frequent symptoms. Valvulotomy of a severely malformed aortic valve early in life may not be definitive, and restenosis, insufficiency, or calcification may require valve replacement in subsequent years. Idiopathic hypertrophic subaortic stenosis, described by Brock in 1957, is discussed in Chapter 11.

Coarctation of the Aorta. Coarctation of the aorta is a relatively uncommon defect, more prevalent in males, and variable in its severity. The mean age of death in several series of autopsied cases is about 34 years.[13] The severity of the effects of aortic coarctation depends upon the degree of aortic narrowing and the length and location of the narrowed segment. Commonly seen is systolic and, less often, diastolic hypertension, which is labile in response to exercise. Left heart failure may be early or late, depending upon the degree of aortic narrowing. Dyspnea, claudication, headache, and fatigue are frequent.

Although not large, the series reported by Campbell is of interest in providing data on the natural history of the disease in unoperated patients from age one year to over 50 years (§332). Excluding the very high mortality in the first year of life, excess death rates ranged from 15 per 1000 per year in the first two decades to more than 50 per 1000 in patients age 40 and up (Table 332a).

J.A. Key's report of long-term follow-up in 79 operated patients showed an operative mortality of 5 per cent, a subsequent aggregate mortality rate of 7 per 1000 per year (maximum follow-up 15 years, average 8.1 years), and a satisfactory decrease in blood pressure in 94 per cent.[13] Surgical correction early in childhood may require reoperation later due to scarring. Even with surgical repair there is a high percentage of early cardiovascular disease in postoperative cases. In a retrospective analysis of 248 operated cases, Maron et al. found that 12 per cent had died within 11 to 25 years of surgery.[14] Of the 23 deaths recorded all but one were due to cardiovascular causes. Mean age at surgery was 20 years. Of these patients, 59 were reexamined in-hospital and 78 per cent had evidence of cardiovascular disease; 40 per cent had hypertension. Premature mortality appeared to be related to the degree of preoperative hypertension.[14] It must be noted that a significant number of patients with coarctation of the aorta will have bicuspid aortic valves.

Patent Ductus Arteriosus. The persistence of this fetal vessel, connecting the aortic arch with the pulmonary artery, is an unusual anomaly, in that the majority of victims are female. The male to female ratio is 1 to 2.5 (§333). Patency of the ductus arteriosus after three months of age is considered abnormal. The dangers of patent ductus arteriosus are those of left to right shunting of blood—pulmonary hypertension and eventual pulmonary vascular obstruction. In the preantibiotic era, bacterial endocarditis was a major threat to life. Unoperated patent ductus arteriosus is found to have an excess death rate in patients under 20 averaging about 4 per 1000 per year, based on several series (Table 333b). In a small group of unoperated older patients followed by Campbell himself, the EDR was 25 or more per 1000 per year.

The etiology of patent ductus arteriosus is multifactorial and has been associated with maternal rubella, hypoxia, and genetic or familial factors. Nearly all patients with persistent patent ductus arteriosus are operated upon now, with ligation and division of the ductus. In Mustard's series of about 1000 cases, average age at operation about eight years, there were nine deaths, five under the age of six months and three associated with the Eisenmenger complex.[15] Those with established pulmonary hypertension benefit little from surgery. However, when the complicated cases are removed from consideration, the mortality of surgical correction is low, and the prognosis appears excellent in the great majority of cases.

Congenital Pulmonic Stenosis. Congenital pulmonic stenosis is relatively common, comprising about 20 per cent of all congenital structural defects of the heart and great vessels. The severity of this anomaly will depend upon the degree of stenosis, the age of the patient, and the adequacy of the right ventricle. Those infants with severe stenosis, particularly if this is associated with a hypoplastic right ventricle, have a very high mortality. Patients with mild pulmonic stenosis may survive to old age with little or no evidence of clinical disease. Moderate to severe valvular stenosis, if of long duration, may result in muscular or fibrotic infundibular hypertrophy. In a series of 83 patients operated upon from 1953 to 1969, Dobell et al. had only one postoperative death.[16] Operation for the majority was open valvulotomy. Symptomatic and hemodynamic results were reported as good. Only those with severe disease (resting systolic right ventricular pressure of over 100 mm Hg) or moderate disease (resting systolic right ventricular pressure of 75 to 100 mm Hg) were operated upon. Any pulmonary valvular insufficiency resulting from valvulotomy does not appear to be clinically significant at least for a number of years.[17] No doubt this benign course is related to the low pressure prevailing in the normal pulmonary vascular tree.

Transposition of the Great Vessels. Until recently those individuals with transposition of the aorta and pulmonary artery died in infancy, had simple repairs or palliative procedures, or reached maturity with hemodynamically mild abnormalities. Gersony and Krongrad state:[18] "In the past ten years, however, technical advances and remarkable surgical accomplishments have led to physiologic correction of a large number of patients who hitherto would not have reached maturity. Thus, among the present generation of children who have been operated upon for congenital heart disease, many will emerge into adulthood with 'repaired' complex lesions, and some will present to the adult cardiologist and internist with a number of new diagnostic and therapeutic challenges."

Much additional follow-up study is needed to assess the long-term results and effectiveness of the newer surgical procedures in the treatment of congenital structural defects of the heart and great vessels. The short-term results among survivors of surgery are encouraging. Operative mortality in many types of open-heart surgery has been reduced well below 5 per cent in good-risk patients. Whatever its magnitude, the risk of the operation must be balanced against any long-term benefits in reduction of future mortality and functional improvement.

Valvular Heart Disease—Incidence and Classification

Diesease of the heart valves, a result of acute or chronic endocarditis, was the cause given for almost 16,000 deaths in the United States during 1970, about 7,800 more than the number of deaths attributed to congenital heart disease (Table 9-1). Over 90 per cent of these were classified as rheumatic heart disease, but the further classification in the Vital Statistics list is somewhat confusing, as 35 per cent of the deaths due to mitral valve disease were "not specified as rheumatic," and the same was true of 71 per cent of the deaths due to aortic valve disease. The term "not specified as rheumatic" apparently has a different significance from "nonrheumatic chronic diseases of the endocardium," which accounted for only 60 additional deaths involving the mitral valve and 221 deaths involving the aortic valve. It is apparent that the valve or valves involved were not specified on the death certificate in a large fraction of the cases of valvular heart disease.

Most valvular heart diesease is rheumatic in origin, especially in the mitral valve. Congenital aortic stenosis is fairly common, but congenital mitral stenosis is rare. Mitral insufficiency of a "functional" nature is observed in many cases of congestive heart failure when the heart is dilated. Aortic insufficiency that is nonrheumatic may be due to disease of the aorta with dilation of the ring. Bacterial rather than rheumatic endocarditis may produce chronic valvular disease if the patient survives the acute episode. Less common causes are idiopathic hypertrophic subaortic stenosis (see cardiomyopathies in Chapter 11), fibroelastosis, and a variety of other diseases of the endocardium, which may involve other parts of the lining of the heart rather than the valves themselves. Among adults the prevalence of chronic rheumatic heart disease has been decreasing, while that of congenital heart disease has been increasing as more children with severe disease survive to reach adult life. The 1960 to 1962 National Health Survey indicated about 1,300,000 adults age 18 to 79 in the United States with definite chronic rheumatic heart disease or 1.2 per cent of the adult noninstitutionalized population.[19] The death rate from rheumatic fever and chronic rheumatic heart disease decreased from 20.3 per 100,000 in 1940 to 8.3 per 100,000 in 1970. The incidence of first attacks of rheumatic fever has apparently not decreased as much as the incidence of new cases of rheumatic heart disease.

The diagnosis of valvular heart disease depends primarily on the location, timing, intensity, and other characteristics of a heart murmur heard on auscultation. However, auscultatory evidence should be supported by the medical history, other findings on examination, and special studies such as chest X-rays. A more precise diagnosis of the anatomical and functional nature of the valvular lesion may be obtained with the help of more elaborate diagnostic procedures, such as echocardiography and cardiac catheterization studies. Not all heart murmurs are produced by a damaged valve: some, such as a soft systolic murmur in the pulmonic area, are innocent and may not indicate any valvular or other disease of the heart; others may be due to such relatively common forms of congenital heart disease as the septal defects, in the absence of any valvular abnormality. The precision of the diagnosis of a particular type of valvular disease thus varies greatly, depending on the collateral evidence as well as the examiner's skill in detecting and describing the murmur. For additional information on the clinical aspects of valvular heart disease the reader is referred to standard texts, such as that of Hurst.[20]

Mortality Associated with Heart Murmurs

In a general way apical heart murmurs are considered evidence for the existence or suspicion of disease of the mitral valve, and basal murmurs, of the aortic valve. A diastolic murmur near the apex of the heart suggests mitral stenosis, and a systolic murmur suggests mitral regurgitation or insufficiency of the valve. The timing relationship is reversed for the aortic valve with the basal or aortic systolic murmur indicating stenosis and the diastolic, insufficiency of the aortic valve. Disease of the pulmonic valve, usually congenital stenosis, is relatively uncommon, and disease of the tricuspid valve, usually rheumatic, is rare. There are other locations of maximum intensity for heart murmurs and many variations in other characteristics. One common type is a systolic murmur heard to the left of the sternum over the mid-portion of the heart; this is often found in congenital septal defects.

Despite the diagnostic uncertainities involved, insurance studies have confirmed the value of a well-described heart murmur found on the insurance examination in predicting mortality and hence in aiding risk classification. Recent mortality investigations by three different companies are abstracted in §349, §350 and §351, with one additional line of data in §399. As these results are described by type of murmur, two aspects deserve a word of caution. Applicants with heart murmurs who are issued life insurance are apt to represent a better than average sample of the valvular heart disease producing a particular type of murmur. As a result of the selction process persons with heart enlargement or other evidence of advanced disease either do not apply, or are refused insurance, or often do not accept an offer of insurance with a high rating. The other word of caution concerns the small numbers of deaths in many of the categories reported. Nevertheless, if results from different sources are consistent, a mortality pattern by type of murmur can be discerned. Individual abstracts should be consulted for the results by age and duration.

Apical Heart Murmur. Experience with apical systolic heart murmurs has been reported by the New England Mutual Life Insurance Company (§349), by the New York Life Insurance Company (§349, §351), and the Prudential Assurance Company of America (§352). Localized murmurs, soft in intensity, often variable in character have been distinguished from louder murmurs, with transmission of the sound to other parts of the precordial area, which are considered to represent definite valvular heart disease, usually mitral insufficiency.

There were over 61,000 exposure years and 213 death claims in the combined experience for localized or "functional" apical systolic murmur. A near-normal mortality was observed in the 88 per cent of cases that were issued standard insurance, the mortality ratio being 113 per cent. In the remaining 12 per cent there was sufficient doubt regarding the character of the murmur to result in substandard insurance. The underwriting distinction appeared to be a valid one, as the mortality ratio in this group was 198 per cent, with an excess death rate of 5.3 per 1000 per year. Statistically, the difference was highly significant. However, the mortality ratio was almost the same in the rated cases with localized apical systolic murmur as it was in the larger group with transmitted apical systolic murmur, also classified as "organic." The mortality ratio was 215 per cent in the combined experience of the latter murmur, based on 308 death claims. The lower excess death rate of 3.5 per 1000 despite a higher mortality ratio reflects a younger average age. These results have been obtained by adding exposure and observed and expected deaths in the appropriate categories of Tables 349, 351c, and 352a.

The experience for apical diastolic murmur was much more limited, and the bulk of it was reported by New England Life (Table 349). With 28 death claims the mortality ratio was 245 per cent and the excess death rate 4.9 per 1000. The difference in mortality between organic systolic and diastolic apical murmurs was relatively small and not statistically significant. Mitral stenosis has generally been considered in life insurance medicine to involve a greater mortality risk than mitral insufficiency, but these results do not confirm such a differential.

Aortic Heart Murmurs. As was the case with the apical systolic murmurs, aortic systolic murmurs have been divided into faint and localized ones ("functional") and louder ones with transmission ("organic"). With the experience in Table 349 from the New England Life and the New York Life combined, under the "functional" cases a mortality ratio of 176 per cent was obtained, and an excess death rate of 3.8 per 1000. All of the New York Life cases were rated, but this was true in only about one-half of the New England Life experience with localized aortic systolic murmur. The combined experience for aortic systolic murmurs classified as "organic" was considerably worse: the mortality ratio was 400 per cent and the excess death rate 11 per 1000.

Aortic diastolic murmurs were a relatively small group, almost all from the New England Life, with a mortality ratio of 285 per cent and excess death rate of 6.0 per 1000. This type of murmur is considered to represent aortic insufficiency and a potentially more serious prognosis than aortic stenosis (aortic systolic murmur). However, excess mortality was actually greater in the applicants insured despite an aortic systolic murmur.

Other Heart Murmurs. The benign character of a pulmonic systolic murmur was confirmed by a normal mortality in all of the categories shown in Table 349, the overall mortality ratio being 94 per cent, based on 50 death claims. Even the rated cases showed a mortality ratio of 102 per cent. These murmurs in the rated cases presumably differed in character from the typical soft, localized pulmonic systolic murmur which is generally felt to be a physiological murmur and not a sign of valvular disease. This mortality experience supports such a view.

The residual category of "other murmurs" is a rather extensive one, with the substandard experience of the New York Life presented in a separate abstract §350. The combined substandard experience in both abstracts produces a mortality ratio of 202 per cent and an excess death rate of 3.6 per 1000. This is naturally worse than the mortality in the standard cases, a smaller group with a mortality ratio of 138 per cent. There were 161 substandard death claims and 44 among the standard cases. The selection was not quite as successful in this heterogeneous group of murmurs as it was with the apical systolic murmurs. Many of these cases with "other" heart murmurs may have had a congenital septal defect rather than valvular heart disease.

A large group classified simply as "valvular heart disease" was found by the Sverige Reinsurance Company of Sweden to have a mortality ratio of 235 per cent and an excess death rate of 5.3 per 1000 (Table 399). If select mortality rates instead of population rates had been used to calculate expected deaths, the mortality ratio would have been considerably higher. There were 171 death claims in this experience.

Mortality in Valvular Heart Disease

Mitral Disease. The operation of closed mitral valvuloplasty was extensively used to alleviate mitral stenosis in the 1950s. Since restenosis was frequent, the operation has largely been supplanted by open-heart replacement of the mitral valve. The experience of a large series of patients with mitral valvuloplasty performed in the period 1950 to 1956 is reported in abstract §353. These patients had severe mitral stenosis, 25 per cent being in functional Class IV and all but 21 of the remainder in Class III. Evidence of considerable functional disability was therefore present in all cases, and 80 per cent had one or more additional risk factors, such as atrial fibrillation (Table 353b). Females outnumbered males by three to one (Table 353a), and their excess death rates were approximately one-half those of the male patients (Table 353d). Excess mortality increased with number of additional risk factors: mortality ratio just under 400 per cent and excess death rate about 10 per 1000 for patients with only one additional risk factor or none at all; an excess death rate of 31 per 1000 in cases with two additional risk factors, and 46 per 1000 with three or more additional risk factors (Table 353e). Excess mortality in the best cases was about twice that experienced by life insurance policyholders with apical diastolic murmur.

In another series of patients with mitral valvular disease and functional impairment, Class III or IV, Starr reported excess death rates ranging from 7 to 57 per 1000 more than one year after replacement of the mitral valve with a ball-valve prosthesis (Tables 354a–354b). Four types of prosthetic valves were used during the ten-year period 1960 to 1970, each successive modification designed to decrease thromboembolism and increase valve durability. There was a resultant decrease in the incidence rate of thromboembolic events from 172 per 1000 per year with the earliest model to 19 per 1000 per year with the last one used (Table 354d). Numbers of deaths were very small in the follow-up period beyond the first month, which extended only four to five years: 19 deaths in the group receiving the earliest model valve, and only six deaths with the next model, among patients who experienced replacement of the mitral valve alone. Over 40 per cent of the patients had sufficient disease of one or more additional valves to justify multiple valve replacements. Excess death rates were roughly two to three times as high in these patients as in those with mitral valve replacement alone.

In a later paper,[21] Bonchek and Starr analyze their results and document the lower incidence of thromboembolic phenomena with the newer cloth-covered prostheses. The cloth-covered prostheses had 1.9 emboli per 100 patient-years versus 6 emboli per 100 patient-years with the earlier noncloth-covered prostheses. The safety of the cloth-covered prostheses was enhanced by anticoagulant therapy. Operative mortality—deaths within the first month after surgery—decreased from 10 per cent to 3 to 5 per cent due to advancements and refinements in technique rather than to the use of different prostheses or a change in patient selection. Most of the late deaths were not directly related to the prosthesis, and were due mainly to congestive heart failure and arrhythmias. The duration of preoperative symptoms and the response to medical treatment were found to be better prognostic indices of postoperative functional result than the preoperative functional classification. Those patients with a favorable response to medical treatment and a short duration of symptoms, regardless of severity, will usually have a favorable postoperative functional result.

In a comparison of five different mitral valve prostheses, Brawley, Donahoo, and Gott[22] reached the conclusion that "early and late mortality following mitral valve replacement appears to be largely influenced by factors other than current design of the prosthesis." No one valve appeared to have significant hemodynamic advantage over the others. Most available data were interpreted as indicating that patients should remain on anticoagulant treatment after mitral valve replacement.

Spagnuolo et al. in 1971 presented a study of rheumatic aortic regurgitation in a population of 174 young people admitted to the Irvington House Clinic and Bellevue Hospital Pediatric and Adolescent Cardiac Clinic from 1952 to 1966 (§355). The aim was to find criteria predictive of death, congestive heart failure, and angina. The patients were divided into three groups: high risk, with moderate to marked cardiomegaly, two or more electrocardiographic abnormalities, or abnormal blood pressure (greater than 140 mm systolic or less than 40 mm diastolic); low risk, with normal blood pressure, no electrocardiographic abnormalities, and no cardiomegaly; and intermediate risk, with slight cardiomegaly, one electrocardiographic abnormality and normal blood pressure. Table 355c suggests a gradation in excess mortality with each risk criterion, the highest risk criteria having the greatest excess mortality. However, numbers of deaths were very small. In this study, the best predictor of excess mortality appeared to be the presence of electrocardiographic abnormalities. Overall, those in the high risk group had 51 excess deaths per 1000 while those in the low risk group had less than one excess death per 1000. Risk classification was repeated on an annual basis; the criteria for high risk were therefore useful in determining the need for operation in the hope of averting very high mortality. The excess death rate for the entire group of 174 patients was 6.6 per 1000.

When surgical correction of aortic valvular disease is contemplated, it is useful to develop prognostic indicators for postoperative survival. Hirshfeld et al.[23] in 1974 correlated long-term survival after aortic valve replacement with Starr-Edwards prostheses with preoperative variables found in 88 patients with isolated aortic regurgitation and 103 patients with isolated aortic stenosis. All patients were operated upon at the National Heart and Lung Institute between 1963 and 1971. Early, or operative, mortality was very high (17 per cent) in those with aortic regurgitation and 10 per cent in those with aortic stenosis.

Analysis of late deaths, produced some useful predictive information, the elements of which were different for the two groups. In the group with aortic regurgitation, those with ECG abnormalities suggesting left atrial enlargement or left ventricular hypertrophy had only a 25 per cent six-year survival rate; those with normal or only slightly abnormal ECG's (Estes score 6) had a six-year survival rate of 55 percent. The left ventricular end-diastolic pressure was a useful predictor in ortic regurgitation. Those with left ventricular end-diastolic pressures of 10 mm Hg or less had a 74 per cent six-year survival; those with pressures of 11 to 20 mm Hg had 41 per cent survival, and those with greater than 20 mm Hg had only 30 per cent survival. When patients had other abnormalities, such as ECG abnormalities, in conjunction with left ventricular end-diastolic pressure measurements, the end-diastolic pressure was the determining factor. For example, if the end-diastolic pressure was less than 10 mm Hg, survival was good regardless of the severity of the ECG pattern. Women, after one year following operation, had no further mortality, while men had continued attrition. It is interesting that preoperative symptoms, functional classification, and heart size were not predictive of long-term survival in aortic regurgitation. However if the heart size, as measured by X-ray, decreased postoperatively, 85 per cent survived six years. The six-year survival rate when heart size did not diminish was only 43 per cent.

The predictive factors were quite different in patients with aortic stenosis. The better the functional classification, the greater the long-term survival with aortic stenosis, although the presence of individual symptoms (angina, syncope, dyspnea, or orthopnea) was not predictive of survival. Several other factors predictive of long-term survival in patients with aortic regurgitation were not useful in aortic stenosis. However, left ventricular size, measured by X-ray, was predictive in an unexpected way. Survival was lowest in those with normal-sized heart. The survival curves were not significantly different statistically except in the cause of death category. Those with normal-sized hearts had a significantly greater incidence of sudden, unexplained deaths, presumably due to arrhythmias. When one examines the causes of late mortality in both groups—those with aortic stenosis and those with aortic regurgitation—over one-half of all late postoperative deaths are sudden or unexplained or are the result of progressive heart failure. These late deaths—34 per cent in aortic regurgitation and 37 per cent in aortic stenosis—often occur despite successful mechanical correction of the hemodynamic abnormality.

Shean et al., in a report of 507 patients undergoing Starr-Edwards aortic valve replacement between 1963 and 1969, noted (Table 358b) an overall excess death rate of 40 per 1000 per year. When analyzed by type of aortic valve lesion, the excess death rate was about 50 per 1000 in those with aortic stenosis or regurgitation, and only 23 per 1000 in those with mixed aortic lesions. Operative mortality (Table 358c) was highest, 16.4 per cent, in those with rheumatic aortic stenosis, and lowest, 8.1 per cent, in those with mixed stenosis and regurgitation. Sudden death, myocardial infarction, and congestive failure were prominent among causes of late deaths.

In their analysis of the current status of various prosthetic heart valves, Brawley, Donahoo, and Gott[22] devote a section to aortic valve prostheses. Four prosthetic values, Bjork-Shiley, Braunwald-Cutter, Lillehei-Kaster and Smeloff-Cutter, were evaluated, and it appeared that hospital mortality and late mortality were related to patient selection rather than valve design. Evidence suggested that patients should be given anticoagulant therapy, if possible, after aortic valve replacement.

Aortic valves have been replaced by homografts and heterografts as well as artificial prostheses. Barratt-Boyes and Roche have reported a review and follow-up of 564 aortic homograft replacements in New Zealand from 1962 to 1968. Operative mortality (within three months of surgery) averaged 8.9 per cent overall, with no trend by year of entry (Table 356a). The annual excess death rate tended to decline, from 44 per 1000 in 1962-63 to 16 per 1000 in 1968. The overall excess death rate was 26 per 1000 per year. Causes of death among the 76 late deaths are noted in Table 356d: cardiac disorders (coronary heart disease, sudden death, myocardial infarction) accounted for 47.3 per cent of late deaths. Valve failure (cusp rupture, valve leak, misplacement, endocarditis) accounted for 34.2 per cent of late deaths and 18.4 per cent of late deaths were of uncertain etiology or noncardiovascular. It is noteworthy that thromboembolism is not mentioned as a cause of late death.

"Despite continuing advances in surgical techniques and postoperative care and improvements in prosthetic heart valve design, complications after valve replacement remain a substantial source of morbidity and mortality."[24] Kloster's excellent review, with an extensive bibliography, summarizes the major life-threatening complications of heart valve replacement in these words.

Infectious endocarditis has an overall incidence between 1 and 10 per cent, is a very dangerous complication (mortality 36 to 87 per cent), and not infrequently necessitates reoperation. Thromboembolic complications have continued to be a problem with prosthetic heart valves despite anticoagulant therapy. Reoperation may be mandatory with significant valve dysfunction due to thrombus formation. Adequate anticoagulation is recommended for prophylaxis in all valve recipients.

Lesser problems include significant hemolytic anemia in 5 to 15 per cent of valve recipients; the postpericardiotomy syndrome (fever, pericardial and pleuritic chest pain, fatigue, myalgia, arthralgia) in 6 to 30 per cent; and the postperfusion syndrome (fever, splenomegaly, atypical lymphocytosis) in 3 to 10 per cent of recipients. Although not specifically mentioned by Kloster, sudden death (presumably from arrhythmias) myocardial infarct, and heart failure are well known as major causes of late death after heart valve replacement.

With improved surgical technology it is reasonable to anticipate that both early and late mortality associated with reconstructive valvular surgery will decrease. Remaining will be the difficult decision of when surgery should be offered.

References

1. J. Warkany and H. Kalter, "Congential Malformations," *New Eng. J. Med.,* 265: 993-1001 (1961).

2. J. Stamler, "Cardiovascular Diseases in the United States." *Am. J. Card.*, 10:319–340 (1962).

3. Dept. Health, Education, and Welfare, *National Heart, Blood Vessel, Lung and Blood Program, Panel Reports,* Volume IV, Part I. Washington, D.C.: National Institutes of Health (April 6, 1973), p. 2-49.

4. J.M. Smith, J. Stamler, R.A. Miller, et al., "The Detection of Heart Disease in Children." *Circulation,* 32:966–976 (1965).

5. W.E. Morton, "Heart Disease Prevalence in School Children in Two Colorado Communities." *Am. J. Pub. Health,* 52:991–1001 (1962).

6. W.E. Morton and L.A. Huhn, "Epidemiology of Congenital Heart Disease. Observations in 17,366 Denver School Children." *J. Am. Med. Assoc.,* 195:1107–1110 (1966).

7. I.T.T. Higgins, "The Epidemiology of Congenital Heart Disease." *J. Chron. Dis.,* 18:699–721 (1965).

8. G.A.H. Miller, "Congenital Heart Disease in the First Week of Life." *Brit. Heart J.,* 36:1160–1166 (1974).

9. P.M. Olley, "Follow-up of Children Treated with Intracardiac Repair for Tetralogy of Fallot." In *Congenital Heart Defects,* edited by B.S.L. Kidd and J.D. Keith. Springfield, Ill.: Charles C. Thomas (1971), pp. 105-110.

10. L.F. Parisi and A.S. Nadas, "Natural History of Atrial Septal Defects." Ibid., pp. 183-196.

11. H.B. Burchell, "Atrial Septal Defect. Prognosis in Adult Life–Risks and Benefits of Surgery." Ibid., pp. 197-202.

12. E.C. Lambert, M. Colombi, H.R. Wagner, and P. Vlad, "The Clinical Outlook of Congenital Aortic Stenosis (Valvar and Discrete Subvalvar) Prior to Surgery." Ibid., pp. 205-213.

13. J.A. Key, "Coarctation of the Aorta. Long-term Follow-up of Surgical Correction." Ibid., pp. 275-279.

14. B.J. Maron, J.D. Humphries, R.D. Rowe, et al., "Prognosis of Surgically Corrected Coarctation of the Aorta. A 20-Year Postoperative Appraisal." *Circulation,* 47:119-126 (1973).

15. W.T. Mustard, "Surgery for Patent Ductus Arteriosus." In *Congenital Heart Defects,* edited by B.S.L. Kidd and J.D. Keith. Springfield, Ill.: Charles C. Thomas (1971), pp. 57-58.

16. A.R.C. Dobell, J.E. Fagan, M. Sheverini, et al., "Results of Pulmonary Valvotomy–Early and Late." Ibid., pp. 68-77.

17. S.G. Blount, Jr., "Follow-up of Five Patients with Pulmonic Valve Insufficiency as Result of Pulmonic Valvuloplasty in 1953." Ibid., pp. 78-80.

18. W.M. Gersony and E. Krongrad, "Evaluation and Management of Patients after Surgical Repair of Congenital Heart Diseases." *Prog. Cardiovasc. Dis.,* 18:39-56 (1975).

19. Dept. Health, Education, and Welfare, *Heart Disease in Adults, U.S., 1960-62.* Vital and Health Statistics, Series 11, No. 6. Washington, D.C.: National Center for Health Statistics (1964).

20. J.W. Hurst and R.B. Logue, eds., *The Heart: Arteries and Veins,* 3rd ed. New York: McGraw-Hill Book Company, (1974).

21. L.I. Bonchek and A. Starr, "Ball Valve Prostheses: Current Appraisal of Late Results." *Am. J. Card.,* 35:843–854 (1975).

22. R.K. Brawley, J.S. Donahoo, and V.L. Gott, "Current Status of the Beall, Bjork-Shiley, Braunwald-Cutter, Lillehei-Kaster and Smeloff-Cutter Cardiac Valve Prostheses." *Am. J. Card.,* 35:855-865 (1975).

23. J.W. Hirshfeld, Jr., S.E. Epstein, A.J. Roberts, et al., "Indicies Predicting Long-term Survival after Valve Replacement in Patients with Aortic Regurgitation and Patients with Aortic Stenosis." *Circulation,* 50:1190-1199 (1974).

24. F.E. Kloster, "Diagnosis and Management of Complications of Prosthetic Heart Valves." *Am. J. Card.,* 35: 872-885 (1975).

10 Arrhythmias and ECG Abnormalities

C. Perry Norton, M.D., and *Richard B. Singer, M.D.*

Two closely associated groups of conditions are the subject matter of this chapter: arrhythmias (disorders of the normal rate or rhythm of cardiac activity) and electrocardiographic (ECG) abnormalities. Considering them together is appropriate, since the electrocardiogram is a most important means for the diagnosis of disturbances of cardiac rhythm. These conditions, furthermore, differ from the disease states considered in other chapters of this volume in that they comprise a collection of findings or "signs" rather than a group of definite disease entities.

To illllustrate this distinction, any one of the arrhythmias or ECG abnormalities may be associated with more than one cause, some of which may be a type of heart disease and some of which may exist in the absence of any cardiac pathology whatsoever. In the latter group causative factors can be distinguished which are either functional or part of a noncardiac pathological process, in that no organic disease state exists. Tachycardia, for example, may be due to aortic regurgitation (cardiac disease), to thyrotoxicosis (noncardiac disease), or to exertion (physiological or functional effect). Similarly, T wave lowering may be due to myocardial ischemia (cardiac disease), to generalized potassium cation deficiency (noncardiac disease), or to factors not presently understood and presumed to be physiological in origin.

Most ECG abnormalities are "nonspecific" in that they neither lead to nor exclude the diagnosis of a single disease state, either cardiac or noncardiac. As such, they are of interest as isolated findings. They may, however, have prognostic significance for an understanding of the course of a particular cardiac condition which has produced them, if this condition can be inferred from other diagnostic data. On the other hand, some ECG abnormalities tend to be more specific: prominent Q waves, elevated ST segments, and inverted T waves in combination typically characterize an acute myocardial infarction.

Electrocardiogram—A Brief Description

Central to an understanding of what constitute ECG abnormalities is a concept of what the ECG consists of, and some idea as to what range of "normal" variation may be anticipated. As with most biological determinations, any one measurement or group of measurements accepted at a normal state runs the double-edged risk of including as normal some individuals with disease (loss of diagnostic sensitivity) and of excluding as abnormal some individuals without disease (loss of diagnostic specificity). The generally accepted approach to this dilemma is to recognize a continuum along which the findings lie, from "free of abnormality," "within normal limits" to distinctly "abnormal," with some rough gradation of likelihood of abnormality between (such as "probably within normal limits," "borderline," etc.).

The electrocardiogram (ECG) is a graphic record of the variations of electrical potential produced during cardiac activity and reflected on the surface of the body, and of the time relationships of these variations. Thus, the vertical displacement of a recording needle reflects changing electrical potential at 10 mm for each mv, and the horizontal movement of the record is usually set to measure 25 mm per second. The standard ECG consists of 12 leads, or different combinations of vantage points on the body surface from which the potential is measured by means of metal electrodes. The electric potential, or signal, is processed by the electronic circuitry of the electrocardiograph, or ECG machine, amplified, and recorded on graph paper specially prepared to record deflections of the writing arm, or stylus. A portion of the finished record of one lead might look like Figure 10-1.

The cardiac cycle, usually initiated in a specialized group of cells near the junction of the superior vena cava and the right atrium (the sinoatrial node), consists of several processes. First there is propagation of a sudden reversal of the normal resting voltage gradient across myocardial cell walls, first in the atria then the ventricles, called "depolarization." Then there is restoration, through metabolic work, of this gradient, first in the atria, then the ventricles, called "repolarization." Finally electrical activity remains quiescent until the cycle is repeated.

In the ECG, depolarization of the atria is reflected as the P wave, and depolarization of the ventricles as the more jagged QRS complex, the R wave being the upright or positive deflection, the Q wave any preceding negative and the S wave any following negative deflections, all reflecting chiefly electrical activity of the much more massive left ventricle. Repolarization of the ventricles is seen as the T wave, while atrial repolarization, involving much less muscle mass, is usually obscured within the QRS complex. The origin of the barely perceptible U wave is not well understood. The resting portion of the cycle is represented by the flat or "isoelectric" portion between the end of the T wave and the next P wave,

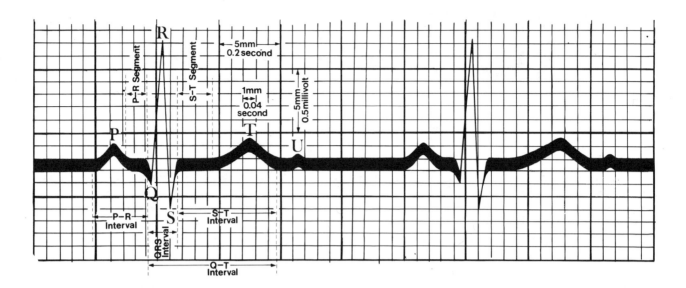

Figure 10-1. Stylized tracing of one lead from an electrocardiogram, showing amplitudes and intervals in relation to complexes used in interpretation (P wave, QRS complex, T and U waves)

even though the repolarized atrial and ventricular muscles maintain a potential gradient across their myocardial cell membranes, readied for the next triggering of their abrupt depolarization, much like a bow with its bowstring pulled taut. During each cardiac cycle, it is the depolarization which initiates the actual muscular contraction of the myocardial muscle fibers. Synchronous left ventricular contraction results in measurable pulse and blood pressure.

Several time intervals are of importance in the ECG. These, as shown in the diagram, include the PR interval, the QRS interval, and the QT interval. The ST segment starts at the J (junctional) point, where the QRS interval terminates, but in the normal ECG this segment curves gradually into the T wave with no perfectly horizontal component, so it has no clearly definable duration. The interval between cycles corresponds to the interval between heart beats, and several can thus be used for accurate determination of the heart rate if the rhythm is regular. For a more detailed description of the electrocardiogram and its interpretation, the reader may refer to any one of several standard references on the subject, such as Marriott[1] or on the broader subject of cardiology.[2]

Organization of Abstracts

Interpretation of the ECG reveals a number of variations from normal, an analysis and understanding of which are of importance in the diagnosis and follow-up of disease states, both cardiac and noncardiac. The organization of the subject matter of the abstracts in this chapter depends on the fact that such variations can generally be categorized on the basis of which portion of the normal ECG cycle is primarily altered.

First, disturbances in the interrelationship of successive cardiac cycles constitute the arrhythmias. Such arrhythmias may consist of altered heart rate (tachycardia and bradycardia) or of altered heart beat regularity (premature beats, bigeminy, the totally irregular pulse, atrial fibrillation, etc.). While an ECG is always helpful and sometimes essential in the study of arrhythmias, useful clinical and mortality studies of some arrhythmias may serve adequately in its absence. For example, simple sinus tachycardia or bradycardia may be usually diagnosed correctly by measurement of the pulse, and atrial as opposed to ventricular premature beats may be inferred by the lack of a "compensatory pause" in the pulse. Population studies of arrhythmias diagnosed clinically may reveal significant experience, but the pitfalls in individual case diagnosis without an ECG are of questionable validity; a pulse of 150 may be atrial flutter with two to one block rather than sinus tachycardia, for example. The arrhythmias are reported in abstracts §360, §361, §363, and §364.

Second, disturbances in the intracyclical components of the ECG constitute uniquely electrocardiographic abnormalities and are not susceptible of study in the absence of this test. Variations in the several components of a single cycle form a general organizational scheme for this study:

(1) P wave – clinically important, but in the absence of population studies not a subject of these abstracts.
(2) PR interval – AV conduction defects.

(3) QRS complex — bundle branch block and other QRS abnormalities (§368, §369, and §370). Also part of the ECG pattern of LVH (§371).

(4) ST junction and segment — abnormalities of ST segment at rest (§375) and in relationship to exercise (§376).

(5) T wave — T wave abnormalities (§374).

(6) QT interval — no abstracts.

(7) U wave — no abstracts.

In addition, abstract §379 presents a picture of the combined mortality experience in a group of insurance applicants with abnormal ECGs, not differentiated by type of abnormality.

Finally, it is important to keep in mind that other abstracts in this monograph contain useful information related to electrocardiography. §317 under "Coronary Heart Disease" ("CHD — ECG abnormalities") is one such study. Diagnosis, prognosis, and follow-up study of a wide variety of the disease entities in this entire chapter, and in abstracts §301 through §399, often depend on the useful noninvasive technique of the ECG.

Epidemiology

The incidence or the prevalence of arrhythmias and ECG abnormalities are not figures readily derived from large population studies as a whole, partly because of the fact previously alluded to that they do not form a single disease complex like tuberculosis or cancer. For example, the *Vital Statistics of the U.S. — 1970*,[3] a compilation of deaths by cause, reported a total in the United States for that year of about two million. It categorizes under "Symptomatic Heart Disease" the diagnoses shown in Table 10-1.

TABLE 10-1

Numbers of Deaths in the U.S. — 1970
Arrhythmias and ECG Disorders

Hazard	Deaths in U.S. Number	% in Category	Follow-up Data
Paroxysmal Tachycardia (Atrial)	53	(0.6%)	§360
Cardiac Arrest not Otherwise Specified	5,261	(60.6)	—
Other Heart Block	507	(5.8)	—
Atrial Fibrillation or Flutter	1,114	(12.8)	—
Ventricular Fibrillation or Flutter	582	(6.7)	—
Other & Unspecified Disorders of Heart Rhythm	823	(9.5)	§363, §364
Cardiac Enlargement and Hypertrophy	341	(3.9)	§371
Cardiac Arrhythmias	**	—	§361
Premature Contractions	**	—	§363, §364
Atrioventricular Block	**	—	§367
Bundle Branch Block	**	—	§368, §369
ECG Abnormality	**	—	§379
Total (all listed in Cause of Death Statistics)	8,681 (0.5% of all deaths)		

**Listed elsewhere under various separate causes

These are included with other types of symptomatic heart disease, including categories such as "congestive heart failure" and "left ventricular failure" with 20,136 deaths attributed to all of these categories combined. The fallacy of considering these figures as meaningful in a review of the incidence of death as related to ECG abnormalities is readily apparent. In the first place, a condition such as atrial fibrillation or heart block is not a disease itself, but generally a result of some other identifiable disease. In the second place, even if this were not so, the likelihood of obtaining a terminal ECG which indicates a direct relationship between such a finding and death is not great. Indeed, ECGs taken on patients dying of other causes frequently show an agonal rhythm disturbance such as ventricular fibrillation, not as the underlying cause but as a stage of dying; in purely semantic terms, cardiac arrest is a universal cause of death if one relies on purposeful cardiac activity as a sign of life.

The reverse is also true: ECG abnormalities are frequently found as an integral part of diseases listed elsewhere in population statistics, such as those shown above. For instance, ischemic heart disease, divided into acute (with or without hypertensive heart disease) or chronic and including such important entities as myocardial infarction, was listed as responsible for 666,665 deaths, none of which appear in the much less numerous category of symptomatic heart disease, even though ECG changes are a usual hallmark of and integral diagnostic component of such diseases.

On the other hand, though prevalence as a cause of death is relatively meaningless as an indicator of the importance of arrhythmias and ECG abnormalities, it is useful to examine the relative incidence of certain ECG abnormalities derived from various population studies. One such study by Lamb's group consisted of a review of ECGs from 67,375 healthy Air Force personnel, in whom 2,499 subjects (3.7 per cent) presented a total of 2,527 instances of 20 different electrocardiographic abnormalities.[4] The data were further broken down by age and race. This is a most interesting study, if one recognizes the obvious limitations imposed by the fact that service personnel do not constitute a random sample of the total population. The age distribution is very different, with a preponderance of younger subjects and virtual absence of any over age 60. Other differences include lack of data on females, prior selection which excluded recognized cases of heart disease, and differences in many socioeconomic and educational factors. Some of the data from this study are shown in Table 10-2.

TABLE 10-2

Occurrence of Various Electrocardiographic Abnormalities in 67,375 Normal Subjects (Air Force Personnel Studies by Averill and Lamb[4])

	Atrial Rhythm	Wandering Pacemaker	Premature Beats Supravent.*	Premature Beats Ventr.†	1° AV Block	RBBB□	WPW Syndrome	Possible MI△	T/ST▲
Number	328	152	329	419	350	106	106	66	581
% Total Abnormalities	13.0	6.0	13.0	16.6	13.8	4.2	4.2	2.6	23.0
Incidence per 1000 Total	4.9	2.3	4.9	6.2	5.2	1.6	1.6	1.0	8.6
By Age:									
16-20	21.9	7.9	4.0	4.7	5.5	—	3.2	—	11.1
20-24	9.0	5.0	5.3	5.4	6.0	1.2	1.8	0.3	5.2
25-29	4.6	1.9	5.7	4.4	5.1	1.1	1.6	0.6	8.9
30-34	2.0	1.2	4.0	7.7	4.6	2.1	1.8	1.3	7.2
35-39	1.7	0.7	4.6	6.4	4.7	1.8	1.3	1.5	11.4
40-44	3.5	—	4.0	10.7	6.2	2.7	1.0	1.5	12.0
45 +	1.4	—	4.4	16.1	3.0	4.4	2.9	4.4	19.0

* Supraventricular
† Ventricular
• First degree atrioventricular block
□ Right bundle branch block
■ Wolff-Parkinson-White Snydrome
△ Possible Myocardial Infarction
▲ Non-specific T wave and S-T segment changes

Significant incidence trends with age in this generally healthy group of males may be summarized in the following manner.

The incidence of nonspecific T wave and ST segment changes, ventricular ectopic beats, right bundle branch block and evidence of possible MI tended to increase with advancing age.

The incidence of atrial rhythm, wandering pacemaker, and AV dissociation tended to decrease with advancing age. First degree atrioventricular block, supraventricular premature contractions, and Wolff-Parkinson-White syndrome showed no definite age trend with respect to their incidence rates. Subsequent articles from the same group provide a more detailed analysis of eight of these twenty conditions and a reevaluation of a number of "normal limit" ranges previously used in electrocardiographic interpretation.

Another study showing some indication of the relative incidence of various ECG abnormalities is that by Brandon et al., who reported data from a collection of the ECGs used in life insurance underwriting at the Aetna Life Insurance Company from 1924 through 1949.[5] In all, 6,387 tracings were reviewed, of which 50 per cent were considered to show at least one type of abnormality, but only about 20 per cent of which adversely influenced the rating offered to the applicant. As in the previous study, certain population characteristics peculiar to the formation of the series must be kept in mind. In Brandon's series are found applicants for life insurance who are generally in good health and might be considered likely to show fewer major ECG abnormalities than are seen in clinical medicine; the reasons for analyzing an ECG on an insurance applicant are frequently for routine screening rather than for diagnostic amplification of an actual or suspected cardiovascular abnormality. Some of the results of this study may be summarized as in Table 10-3.

TABLE 10-3

Occurrence of Selected Electrocardiographic Abnormalities in Insurance Applicants (Brandon et al[5])

Abnormality	Prevalence	
	No. of Cases	No. per 1000
Premature contractions	961	150.5
Auricular Fibrillation	35	5.5
Abnormal P waves	37	5.8
PR interval > 0.20 sec.	225	35.2
Complete AV Block	10	1.6
Bundle Branch Block	29	4.5
QRS 0.10 to 0.12 sec.	475	74.3
Left axis deviation	414	64.8
Low QRS voltage	276	43.2
Deep Q3 (both "favorable" & "adverse")	326	51.0
Low or inverted T1 and/or T2	712	111.5
Abnormal ST interval	110	17.2

Mortality and Survival Experience

Tachycardia and Irregular Pulse. Abstracts §360 and §361 relate to the mortality experience in insurance policyholders who exhibited tachycardia and pulse irregularities (not including tachycardia, bradycardia, or atrial fibrillation), as found on examination. All were issued substandard policies because the arrhythmias were considered to be a significant extra mortality risk factor. No ECG findings were reported. In each of the two groups, all ages combined, the mortality ratios and excess death rates showed a sharp increase in the first two years, followed by a distinct decrease with the passage of time. The mortality ratio exceeded 400 per cent in both groups within the first two years and subsequently fell to about 150 per cent in the period from five to 17 years after policy issue. The corresponding change in EDR was from more than six extra deaths per 1000 per year to about three to four per 1000. It is further noted in each group that not only the mortality *rates,* as expected, but also the mortality *ratios* increased somewhat at ages over 50. When analyzed by cause of death, it is noted that in both the tachycardia and the irregular pulse groups the leading cause of death was diseases of the heart and circulatory system, with mortality ratios of 280 per cent and 310 per cent, respectively. Malignant neoplasms were next in importance, having somewhat lower mortality ratios as well as frequencies.

These statistics indicate that the presence of either a regular tachycardia or a pulse irregularity other than tachycardia or atrial fibrillation is associated with an adverse effect on mortality which diminishes with the passage of time, which is somewhat more pronounced in older subjects, and which is characterized by an increased likelihood of death from cardiovascular disease.

Premature Beats. Abstracts §363 and §364 relate to the mortality experience in three different groups exhibiting premature beats: insurance applicants with supraventricular or ventricular premature beats, insurance company employees with either, and clinical outpatients with ventricular premature beats alone. Delineation of each group depended on electrocardiographic diagnosis. The following conclusions appear reasonable in the light of these results.

First, the morality ratio in subjects with either supraventricular or ventricular premature beats, otherwise issued standard insurance, tends to be little increased above normal, except for a modest increase at age 45 and up when ten or more per minute are present (148 per cent, Table 363a). Mortality ratios of 200 per cent for multifocal premature beats and 185 per cent in older applicants with premature beats increasing after exercise are not statistically significant, as they are based on four and five deaths respectively.

Second, in the case of males, the mortality ratio in subjects with ventricular premature beats who are rated for hypertension or other cardiovascular condition (but with ratings not exceeding 200 per cent of standard) is somewhat more ominous (225 per cent, Table 363a). Those rated for noncardiovascular conditions in the same range do not show the same results. As shown in Table 363b, the greater the degree of hypertension, the greater is the impact on mortality. Thus, "simple" premature beats, either supraventricular or ventricular, show an increasing mortality ratio, between 235 per cent for "slight" to 635 per cent for "very marked" hypertension, while the corresponding increase with degrees of hypertension in the absence of ectopic beats (pairs or runs, bigeminy, bundle branch block after atrial premature beats, or T wave change in the sinus complex following the ectopic beat) is a change in mortality ratio from 300 to 715 per cent, between the "slight" and "very marked" groups of hypertension.

Third, ventricular premature beats in an otherwise normal ECG imply little effect on mortality when compared with a carefully selected control·group (mortality ratio of 122 per cent with EDR of 4 per 1000), but in the presence of other ECG abnormalities the risk is increased (mortality ratio of 132 per cent but EDR of 22 per 1000 in Table 364c).

Finally, ventricular premature beats in patients without clinical heart disease as a group, whether the ECG was other-wise normal or not, showed a mortality ratio of 200 per cent with an EDR of 8 per 1000, but in the presence of clinical heart disease these figures were 180 per cent and 43 per 1000, respectively. The latter figure is the more meaningful, the minor difference in mortality ratios reflecting the difference in average age in the groups with or without heart disease.

Atrioventricular Block. Abstract §367 relates to the experience associated with atrioventricular block using three different groups: insurance applicants with first degree or third degree block; Canadian Air Force personnel with the same conditions; and an English series of patients receiving electrical pacing, most of them for third degree atrioventricular. block, compared with a control group exhibiting this condition but without the pacing.

As shown in the tabulated data, the experience with first degree block in the absence of other cardiovascular abnormalities suggests that there is no adverse effect on mortality, the mortality ratio being close to 100 per cent in each of the first two groups. The presence of other cardiovascular abnormalities, however, presents an increased risk, with a mortality ratio of 172 per cent and an excess death rate of 8.2 per 1000. Two observations associated with the Canadian Air Force group are of interest: the PR interval was found to vary markedly in individual subjects at different times, sometimes from a normal or less than 0.20 sec. to 0.25 sec. or more; the prognostic significance of the measured PR interval was considered less important than the age of onset of the first degree block and its tendency to progress.

Third degree or complete AV block, on the other hand, appears to have a definite adverse effect on survival. In the insurance group a mortality ratio of 275 per cent and an EDR of 18 were based on only three deaths in 10 cases, a very small sample. However, the English series' control group of 113 patients showed a four-year mortality ratio of 280 per cent and EDR of 113 per 1000. Of incidental note in this latter study is that this unfavorable experience is particularly noticeable in the first year of observation, with a mortality ratio of 390 per cent and EDR of 175 per 1000; in the fourth year the equivalent figures have fallen to 230 per cent and 83 excess deaths per 1000 respectively. Clinicians who treat older patients with complete heart block generally find evidence of coronary artery or other serious heart disease. The excess mortality in this series of patients doubtless should be regarded as reflecting that of the underlying heart disease, often with other complications as well as complete heart block. These high mortality levels should not be ascribed to younger patients without evidence of heart disease (and sometimes no symptoms), in whom the prognosis can be reasonably presumed to be much better. It was a central purpose of the English study to determine survival experience in their patients with complete heart block after surgical implantation of an artificial pacemaker, with the previous nonrandomized group serving as a basis for comparison. The results are noteworthy: the group with artificial pacing exhibited a lower first year risk, with a mortality ratio of 205 per cent and EDR of 64 per 1000. This risk fell toward or below normal with a resulting aggregate six-year experience approaching that of the population at large, the mortality ratio being 122 per cent and the EDR 14 per 1000. The very high average age of the group, and the probable presence of underlying heart disease in most of the patients should again be emphasized. With insurance select mortality rates as a basis for comparison there would be a considerable degree of excess mortality in this experience. Nevertheless, from the clinical viewpoint pacemakers seem to have been remarkably successful in improving the prognosis of patients with complete heart block.

Bundle Branch Block. Abstracts §368 and §369 relate to the experience associated with intraventricular blocks of various types, complete right and left bundle branch block, incomplete right bundle branch block, and cases of prolonged intraventricular conduction which are not identified as characteristic of interruption of either right or left bundle branches. There is some difficulty comparing the results of these various series, because of several factors, including differences in series, different ways of classifying characteristics, the bundle branch block, and ECG or cardiovascular abnormalities. With these limitations in mind, however, a number of conclusions can be proposed from the results summarized in these two abstracts.

In the absence of associated cardiovascular abnormalities, incomplete right bundle branch block and indeterminate intraventricular conduction delay (QRS interval 0.10 sec. or longer without the characteristic pattern of either right or left bundle branch block) show no observable increase in mortality risk. In the presence of other cardiovascular abnormalities (BP of 140/90 or greater, or other ratable cardiovascular abnormality except for coronary heart disease), the mortality of these two conditions is about the same as that for complete bundle branch block (Table 368a).

In the absence of associated cardiovascular abnormalities, complete bundle branch block, either of the right or left bundle pattern, the increase of both mortality ratio and EDR is based on samples so small (7 and 2 deaths, respectively) as not to be statistically significant in the New England Life study which used these categories (Table 368a). In a U.S. Air Force study, composed of generally younger subjects in whom a much smaller percentage had known cardiovascular disease, right bundle branch block showed a mortality ratio of only 55 per cent with a negative EDR, based on 14 deaths, while left bundle branch block showed a mortality ratio of 129 per cent and an EDR of 2.2 per 1000, based on 9 deaths. There was only one death in the first five years of exposure, with a corresponding mortality ratio of less than 100 per cent and a negative EDR (Table 369b). In the Equitable experience, in the absence of other cardiovascular abnormalities and with right and left bundle branch block patterns considered together, a mortality ratio of 126 per cent with an EDR of two per 1000 was observed.

The presence of cardiovascular abnormalities in addition to intraventricular conduction delays of one of the four types described poses an increase in mortality risk. The highest mortality ratio, 430 per cent, is seen in coronary heart disease with an EDR of 26 per 1000. Other cardiovascular conditions, ratable blood pressure, and noncoronary heart disease, show corresponding mortality ratios between 200 and 270 per cent, and EDRs of 8.7 to 11 per 1000 (Table 368a). The Equitable experience showed a corresponding mortality ratio of 194 per cent, with both right and left bundle branch block considered together (Table 369a). The two Aetna studies considered cases with and without cardiovascular abnormalities together, and in the presence of both right and left bundle branch block the mortality ratio exceeded 200 per cent (Table 369a). One cannot conclusively demonstrate from these studies that in the presence of other cardiovascular defects, bundle branch block of either complete type increases the mortality risk more than in their absence.

In the presence of cardiovascular defects other than coronary heart disease, a study of the effect of age on the New England Life subjects shows a tendency for the mortality ratio to diminish as age of entry increases from 30 to 59 with a fairly constant EDR, with a lower EDR below age 30 and a higher EDR age 60 and up (Table 368a).

A study of the effect of duration of observation in the Air Force experience suggests little conclusive difference between complete right and complete left bundle branch block in the first five years of follow-up. From 5-15 years, however, the complete left bundle branch block pattern appears to have a more pronounced effect than the right, with higher mortality ratios and with EDRs of 8 to 10 per 1000 in the former, while in the latter the EDRs are negative (Table 369b). This finding is felt to correlate with the known higher proportion of cardiovascular abnormalities in subjects with left than in those with right bundle branch defects.

Other QRS Abnormalities. Abstract §370 presents data concerning three other types of QRS abnormalities, left axis deviation (LAD), Q waves in lead III, and low QRS amplitude in the standard leads. Comparison of the several studies of subjects with LAD poses the same types of difficulties as experienced in those relating to bundle branch block. In general, however, the following conclusions appear reasonable.

The prevalence of LAD increases with age and is greater at each age among males than among females (Table 370a). These data from the Tecumseh, Michigan, survey show that substantial numbers of subjects with LAD, somewhat over half, exhibit evidence of other cardiovascular abnormalities.

In the absence of such evidence of coexisting cardiovascular defects, the finding of LAD poses no particular increased risk of mortality in three independent studies (Table 370b). The series of Army men reported by Eliot et al. had a negative cardiovascular history, but 39 per cent were found to have other abnormal findings after the isolated LAD was discovered. In this group the mortality ratio was 385 per cent and the EDR 13 per 1000, but this was based on only six deaths (Table 370b). More confidence can be placed in the close to normal mortality of the two series of insureds, especially the extensive experience of the Massachusetts Mutual.

In the Prudential employees with left anterior hemiblock, characterized in part by left axis deviation −45° and beyond, Schaaf reported a normal mortality ratio below age 60, but this figure rose to 198 per cent with an EDR of 30 per 1000 at 60 and older (based on 18 deaths in the older employees). The group consisted of 110 men and women with isolated left anterior hemiblock (no associated cardiovascular or ECG abnormality), drawn from a larger group, all 273 cases of left anterior hemiblock in the Home Office medical files. The excess mortality in the older, apparently healthy employees cannot be attributed to heart disease detectable by the usual careful screening methods.

The papers of Brandon et al. and Bolt et al. relate to the experience in populations with Q waves in lead III (Table 370b). Again, comparison between the two studies is hampered by variation in criteria used. The former study defines an "adverse" Q3 as being one-fourth or greater with respect to the amplitude of the maximum QRS deflection in any standard lead; the latter subdivides Q3 on the basis of its being $\geqslant 0.04$ seconds in duration and on the basis of QRS findings in leads I and II. The former study notes a normal mortality experience with the finding of a "small" Q3 less than one-fourth of the maximum QRS deflection, but a mortality ratio of 169 per cent and an EDR of 7.7 per 1000 with the finding of an "adverse" Q3. The latter study shows a normal mortality experience in 198 subjects with no associated cardiovascular abnormalities, whether Q3 was of short or long duration, and an adverse experience if such abnormalities were present regardless of whether the QRS duration was less than 0.04 sec. (mortality ratio 200 per cent) or 0.04 sec. or greater (mortality ratio 176 per cent).

The experience with low QRS voltage suggests that there is no discernible increase in mortality risk with this finding, as seen by the normal mortality ratios in the last portion of Table 370b, despite the fact that most of the cases had other cardiovascular abnormalities that were not defined.

Left Ventricular Hypertrophy. Abstract §371 relates to the mortality experience in subjects with the electrocardiographic diagnosis of definite or possible left ventricular hypertrophy (LVH). These cases were found during a long period of observation of the Framingham Study group (§380). Strictly speaking, hypertrophy of the left ventricle is an anatomical not an ECG diagnosis. However, the term is frequently used to characterize a constellation of abnormalities frequently seen in the ECG of patients with heart disease including left ventricular hypertrophy (hypertensive, coronary and rheumatic heart disease are common causes). Definite LVH was defined in this study as increased R associated with a prolonged ventricular activation time of 0.05 sec. or more, depressed ST segment, and flattened or inverted T waves in the left chest leads. The results of the Framingham Study indicate that the ECG diagnosis of definite LVH presents a markedly adverse effect on mortality, with an overall EDR of 47 per 1000 in men and 37 per 1000 in women, and that possible LVH (some but not all of the characteristic features present) produces a less marked but still definite effect. As might be expected, the presence of possible LVH produced a greater predisposition to the subsequent development of definite LVH than its absence. The figures suggest that the mortality experience is more ominous for men than for women. In men the mortality ratio tended to decline with the passage of time, from 440 per cent to 173 per cent, although the EDR was not so predictable; among women the mortality ratio was lowest in the first two years, and the EDR rose with duration. In both sexes, the mortality ratio decreased somewhat with advancing age, while the EDR tended to increase. As the authors point out in the article itself, the pattern of LVH in the ECG has two prognostic meanings: in a patient with heart disease already apparent, it provides a measure of the seriousness of the disease, the prognosis being worse than in the absence of this finding; in the absence of known heart disease, the ECG diagnosis of LVH presents the increased likelihood of its development, and is itself a predictor of increased mortality.

Abnormal T Waves. Abstract §374 presents data from five studies concerning the effect of T wave changes on mortality. The distinction is generally made between "minor" T wave changes (lowering, flattening, or notching of T waves in leads normally presenting an upright wave) and "major" T wave changes (diphasic or inverted T waves in similar leads). From a comparison of these reports it is possible to summarize the significance of T wave abnormalities as follows.

Minor T waves, in the absence of other ECG abnormalities, clinical evidence of heart disease, or hypertension, were found to have mortality ratios of 166 and 143 per cent, respectively, in two long studies of Prudential employees, 1933 to 1960 (Table 374a) and 1933 to 1964 (Table 374b); an overall mortality ratio of 177 per cent was reported in a 1924 to 1949 series of Aetna insureds (Table 374c, low T waves in leads I and II), and one of 120 per cent in a 1946 to 1962 series of Equitable insurance applicants (Table 374d). Although numbers of entrants were not large, prolonged observation resulted in exposure sufficient to produce from 33 to 71 deaths in the four study groups, with a total of 222 deaths and aggregate mortality ratio of 154 per cent. With 222 deaths this is a highly significant increase in mortality, as the 95 per cent confidence limits are 133 to 175 per cent.

Excess mortality was affected by the ECG lead in which the T wave abnormality occurred, as shown in three of the studies. A normal mortality was found with minor T wave abnormality of lead aVf only, and a mortality ratio of 140 per cent for similar changes in lead aVl only (Table 374a). In this same Prudential employee group a higher mortality ratio of 196 per cent developed out of the experience with minor T wave changes in other leads, presumably leads I and II and the left chest leads. In the Aetna series the mortality ratio for low T waves was 148 per cent in lead II, 191 per cent in lead I, and 194 per cent in both leads (Table 374a). In the New England Life series with a younger average age a normal mortality with respect to minor T wave changes in the chest leads was observed if the applicants were normotensive

(Table 374e). Thus, in the various insurance groups with isolated minor T wave abnormality the mortality ratios varied from normal levels if it occurred in the chest leads or lead aVf alone to slightly under 200 per cent in lead I, with intermediate ratios for lead II and lead aVl alone.

Such minor T wave abnormalities are accompanied by a higher mortality ratio, 138 per cent in applicants age 50 up as opposed to 97 per cent in younger applicants (Table 374d), and a higher mortality ratio in the first five years of follow-up, 332 per cent when in leads other than aVl and aVf (Table 374a). Minor changes later reverting to normal in the Prudential employees still presented an increased risk, with a mortality ratio of 196 per cent (Table 374b).

Although major T wave changes in the absence of other ECG abnormalities, clinical heart disease, or hypertension are uncommon, the evidence is clear that mortality ratios are considerably elevated: 220 per cent in leads I and II (Table 374c); 280 per cent in the chest leads (Table 374e); and 158 per cent in various leads combined (Table 374b).

The presence of heart disease in conjunction with either minor or major T wave changes is correlated with a mortality risk greater than in the absence of such changes. This was especially true in the case of manifest coronary heart disease among Prudential employees: mortality ratios of 405 per cent with current minor T wave changes (375 per cent after return to normal), and 645 per cent with EDR of 45 per 1000 in cases with major T wave abnormalities (Table 374b).

Another example is provided by a mortality ratio of 150 per cent in insurance applicants with elevated blood pressure and minor T waves in the chest leads (Table 374e). Expected mortality was based not on standard mortality rates, but on rates increased by an amount corresponding to the results of the 1959 Blood Pressure Study. The EDR of nearly 5 per 1000 therefore represents an excess mortality above that anticipated for the blood pressure elevation alone. There was no excess mortality in a small group with major T wave changes (only three deaths), but the results in cases exhibiting LVH pattern in their ECG (§371) suggest the need for concern in evaluating inverted or diphasic T waves in any individuals with hypertension.

Post exercise ECG (Master's Test). Abstracts §375 and §376 are concerned with the results from three studies in which comparison was made between clinical subjects or insurance applicants exhibiting a positive ECG response to exercise stress ("Master's Test") and those with a negative response. The studies are not strictly comparable because of differences in the composition of the groups and in the stress test procedures and interpretation. Despite these limitations, however, there seems to be no doubt that the diagnosis of a positive Master's Test result in each study separated out a group of subjects whose risk of death from coronary artery disease was greatly enhanced.

The first study, of clinical patients studied by Master et al. for possible coronary artery disease, showed a negative response group with unusually low mortality, well below the rate expected in the general population; in the corresponding group with positive response the mortality ratio was 205 per cent and EDR 13 per 1000 (Table 375a). The second study, involving railroad employees, differentiated a negative response group with mortality ratio of 166 per cent and EDR of 16 per 1000 from a positive response group with corresponding values of 335 per cent and 58 per 1000 (Table 375b). The above-normal mortality in the negative response group appears to be related to the high prevalence of hypertension and valvular or coronary heart disease even in those subjects with negative Master's Tests; the average age was 59 years. A three-fold increase in the incidence of subsequent myocardial infarction in those with a positive as compared with a negative test result was noted.

The third study was of a large group of more than 3,000 applicants to the Metropolitan Life Insurance Company who underwent exercise tolerance testing for various reasons, about one-half for nonspecific chest pain and one-quarter for abnormalities in the resting ECG. The same overall conclusion may be drawn, namely that differentiation between an ischemic and a nonischemic response in the postexercise tracings permits the definition of a group at substantially increased risk of death, particularly from coronary disease. A carefully standardized double Master's Test was used, with only minor modifications of the procedure used by Master. Furthermore, this study of insurance applicants is sufficiently extensive to permit classification of positive and negative test results into subgroups, which permit more specific and detailed conclusions regarding interpretation of the test.

It appears valid to consider as nonischemic those responses in which the only ST segment depression is junctional, as the mortality ratio was 109 per cent, almost identical to the ratio among those with no ST depression and negative response (Table 376a). Isolated T wave changes consisting of T wave inversion with no ST junctional depression were classified as a nonischemic response, but a mortality ratio of 166 per cent suggests the need for caution in doing so. When cases of coronary artery disease were removed from the negative response group the mortality ratio fell from 110 to 97 per cent (Table 376a).

Within the ischemic response group, three factors enhance the adverse effect of the positive test: downsloping of the depressed ST segment, EDR 22 as opposed to 2.1 per 1000 with a horizontal depression of the ST segment (Table 376a); a higher grade of ischemic ST depression, with EDR 85 per 1000 in grade 3, the most severe depression of 2 mm or more,

22 per 1000 in grade 2, and 7.3 per 1000 in grade 1 (Table 376b); the presence of a definite diagnosis of coronary artery disease, EDR 38 per 1000 in contrast to 8.3 per 1000 in noncoronary applicants (Table 376a).

In the first ten years of follow-up mortality ratios remained about the same in a given severity classification and EDRs increased (Table 376c). Similar trends were observed in grade 2 cases from 10-20 years after testing, but in grade 1 (six deaths) and grade 3 (no deaths) excess mortality appeared to lessen.

Abnormal ECG. The experience of the New York Life Insurance Company (§379) is of interest in reflecting mortality among all those issued insurance with a rating because of the ECG alone, regardless of the type of ECG abnormality. As with life insurance policyholders in general these constituted a group generally in good health: cases with hypertension, known cardiovascular, and all other significant risk factors were excluded. Under these circumstances it is not surprising that the overall experience was relatively favorable, with a mortality ratio of 167 per cent and an EDR of 3.6 per 1000. Excess death rates were low in applicants under age 40, 1.4 per 1000, reached a peak of 6.1 per 1000 in those 40 to 49 years, and fell between 3 to 4 per 1000 in the two older age groups (Table 379c). Most of the excess mortality was confined to the first ten years of follow-up (Table 379a), and appeared in the cause of death category of diseases of the heart and circulatory system (Table 379d). These results confirm the experience previously cited for many individual ECG abnormalities, indicating a moderate but significant increased mortality even in the absence of other evidence of heart disease.

Attention should be called to other abstracts in the coronary heart disease section, some of which contain data in relation to ECG abnormalities. The two studies reported in §317 are devoted exclusively to this topic.

The incidence of and mortality experience associated with various ECG abnormalities is the subject of a comprehensive analysis by Mihara of applicants insured by the Meiji Mutual Life Insurance Company of Tokyo.[6] Although a comprehensive and detailed investigation of intrinsic interest, this follow-up study has not been abstracted because of the marked epidemiological differences in the prevalence of cardiovascular diseases that exist in the Japanese population as compared with the United States population. Japanese adults in general have a much higher prevalence of hypertension and a lower prevalence of coronary heart disease than adults in the United States of similar age and sex. It would be very difficult to interpret the results of such an ECG study in the Japanese population without a great deal of attention to these differences and to differences in normal standards.

References

1. H.J.L. Marriott, *Practical Electrocardiography,* 5th ed. Baltimore, Md.: Williams and Wilkins Co. (1972).

2. C.K. Friedberg, *Diseases of the Heart,* 3rd ed. Philadelphia: W.B. Saunders Co. (1966).

3. Dept. of Health, Education, and Welfare, *Vital Statistics in the United States, 1970, Volume II-Mortality, Part A.* Bethesda, Md.: National Center for Health Statistics (1974).

4. K.H. Averill and L.E. Lamb, "Electrocardiographic Findings in 67,375 Asymptomatic Subjects. I. Incidence of Abnormalities." *Am. J. Card.,* 6:76-83 (1960).

5. K.F. Brandon, M.H. Neill, and G.C. Streeter, "The Use of the Electrocardiogram in Twenty-Five Years of Insurance Selection." *Trans. Assoc. Life Ins. Med. Dir. Am.,* 34:143-155 (1950).

6. T. Mihara, "Distribution of ECG Findings in an Insured Population and their Prognostic Significance." *J. Life Insurance Med.,* 67:16-79 (1968). Copies of an English translation from Japanese are on file with the Association of Life Insurance Medical Directors of America.

11

Other Cardiovascular Diseases
John C. Robinson, M.D.

In the four preceding chapters consideration has been given to Coronary Artery Disease, Hypertension, Congenital and Valvular Heart Disease, Arrhythmias and Electrocardiographic Abnormalities. Cerebrovascular Disease was reviewed with the Neuropsychiatric Diseases in Chapter 6. There is still a residue of "Other Cardiovascular Diseases," and these constitute the subject matter of this chapter, the separate abstracts remaining in the cardiovascular disease area, including §399 dealing with miscellaneous data. Table 11-1 contains a list of some of these remaining cardiovascular diseases, related abstracts, and the numbers of deaths attributed to these diseases in the United States during 1970.

TABLE 11-1

Numbers of Deaths in the U.S. — 1970
Other Cardiovascular Diseases

	Deaths in U.S.		
Hazard	Number	% in Category	Follow-up Data
Framingham Study (General)	**	—	§380
Acute Rheumatic Fever	256	(0.3%)	—
Acute Pericarditis, Nonrheumatic	55	(0.07)	—
Chronic Disease of Pericardium, Nonrheumatic	523	(0.7)	—
Acute, Subacute Endocarditis	673	(0.9)	—
Acute Myocarditis	488	(0.6)	—
Cardiomyopathy	1,351	(1.8)	§383
Congestive Heart Failure*	17,331	(22.7)	§381, §399
Pulmonary Heart Disease	1,228	(1.6)	—
Cardiac Transplant	**	—	§390
Aortic Aneurysms	13,511	(17.7)	—
Other Aneurysms	1,349	(1.8)	—
Arteriosclerosis of Aorta	83	(0.1)	—
Arteriosclerosis Other Specified Arteries	20	(0.03)	—
Peripheral Atherosclerosis	121	(0.2)	§382, §399
Renal Artery Atherosclerosis	30	(0.04)	§385
Arteriosclerosis Generalized and Unspecified	31,428	(41.2)	—
Other Cardiovascular Disease	7,838	(10.3)	§399

Total (all listed in Cause of Death Statistics)   76,285   (4.0% of all deaths)

*Includes 5,535 deaths due to "Other Myocardial Insufficiency"
**Listed elsewhere under separate causes

The miscellaneous cardiovascular diseases in Table 11-1 accounted for 76,285 deaths during 1970, 4.0 per cent of the total deaths in the United States. The principal individual diseases were congestive heart failure, with 23 per cent of the subtotal, aortic aneurysms, with 18 per cent, and generalized and unspecified arteriosclerosis, 41 per cent. It is of interest that so few deaths were attributed to specific sites of arteriosclerosis. Most of the aortic aneurysm deaths were probably due to arteriosclerosis, and a more precise cause of death procedure undoubtedly would have assigned most of the unspecified arteriosclerotic deaths to one of the sites given here, or to ischemic (coronary) heart disease or to cerebrovascular disease, both of which have been listed previously. Congestive heart failure and pulmonary heart disease are functional disorders rather than specific diseases, and undoubtedly deaths that might have been so classified were assigned to other causes. The numbers of deaths in Table 11-1 therefore provide an imperfect and distorted picture of the relative epidemiological importance of these cardiovascular diseases. Another feature of interest in the table is the small numbers of deaths attributed to rheumatic fever, pericarditis, endocarditis, and acute myocarditis. Mortality in acute rheumatic fever is much reduced now in comparison with 30 or 40 years ago. Cardiomyopathy is a relatively new entity (first described in 1957), and it is likely that cardiomyopathy deaths will increase in coming years as more cases are diagnosed.

The Framingham Study

As is stated in the text accompanying abstract §380, the Framingham Study was designed as a long-term prospective investigation to characterize the development of and mortality from cardiovascular diseases. An epidemiological approach to the study of a disease often aids in its prevention long before an essential etiological factor is identified. It may enable the detection of highly susceptible individuals and early asymptomatic disease many years before the onset of symptoms.[1]

Prospective studies of this type have demonstrated that certain host factors and personal habits are associated with a substantial increase in susceptibility to coronary heart disease. Also identified are a number of host factors particularly related to fatal outcome in persons sustaining an attack. Interestingly, factors precipitating heart attacks and those adversely affecting survival are not necessarily the same as those related to the development of the underlying disease.[2]

The text of §380 describes in detail the methods used to form the Framingham Study Group and Table 380a gives the prevalence of certain cardiovascular disorders by sex at the time of entry into the study. Table 380b gives the age and sex distribution of the cohort at entry into the study and the deaths by cause and number over the ensuing 14 years.

Table 380c presents annual mortality rates for the study population by sex and attained age compared with U.S. rates. It is noteworthy that except for the females aged 50 to 54 years and those in the 29 to 39 age group, where there were only 9 deaths, the rates were consistently lower than for the U.S. population as a whole. This can be explained in part by the fact that residents of Framingham who were institutionalized, very ill, and incapacitated never did get into the study. In some respects the Framingham Study Group was a select group, although not to the extent that persons issued standard insurance constitute a cohort with select mortality rates (note that subjects with the conditions listed in Table 380a were not excluded from the study). Other factors that might have produced a more favorable mortality than in the general population were the relatively high average socioeconomic class of Framingham residents and the potentially beneficial effects of the biennial examinations themselves in early detection of serious disease.

Table 380d gives the annual incidence rate for a number of cardiovascular disorders by sex and attained age while Table 380e presents the status of the cohort by sex at each of the eight biennial examinations, with some supplemental data including numbers of individuals not examined or lost to examination. The Framingham Study has been a landmark in the long-term investigation of chronic disease. A recent review by Kannel describes some of the "lessons in cardiovascular epidemiology" that have been learned.[2]

Congestive Heart Failure

Cardiac failure is a condition in which the heart becomes unable to maintain an adequate cardiac output and circulation. This results in vascular stasis in various parts of the body. The clinical syndrome thus produced is known as congestive heart failure, and is characterized by dyspnea, orthopnea, paroxysmal nocturnal dyspnea, congestive hepatomegaly, dependent edema, basilar pulmonary rales and cardiac enlargement. Pleural effusion and ascites may develop, with additional signs and symptoms. The commonest causes of heart failure include hypertension, coronary artery disease, and valvular defects, or combinations of hypertension with the other two. Less common causes include rheumatic carditis, thyrotoxicosis, pulmonary fibrosis, congenital defects, cardiomyopathy, anemia and thiamine deficiency.

Heart failure may be acute or chronic, may produce minimal or total disability, is sometimes readily reversed by treatment, and at other times is intractable. For an in-depth discussion the reader is referred to standard medical texts of medicine or cardiology.[3, 4, 5, 6]

Incidence and mortality data are presented in abstract §381 on the basis of development of 142 cases in the course of follow-up of 5,192 subjects of the Framingham Study followed from 1950 to the ninth biennial examination in 1966. The annual incidence varied from considerably less than 1 per 1000 in subjects under age 45 to 6.1 per 1000 in men age 65 to 74 years and 3.9 per 1000 in women in this age group. Preexisting hypertensive cardiovascular disease was present in two-thirds of the cases, more often than not complicated by coronary or valvular heart disease. Strict criteria were defined for the diagnosis of definite, probable and questionable congestive heart failure.

The data in Table 381c reflect the very high mortality observed. The excess death rate averaged 155 per 1000 in men, with little age variation, 76 per 1000 in women under age 65 and 140 per 1000 in women age 65 to 74 years. The five-year survival ratio was only 42 per cent in male patients and 60 per cent in female (Table 381c). Excess mortality persisted at high levels throughout the nine years of follow-up for which data have been reported in Table 381a. These high mortality rates attest to the lack of success in controlling congestive heart failure despite modern therapeutic methods available. As a manifestation of the common forms of heart disease, especially hypertensive cardiovascular disease, congestive heart failure implies a poor prognosis. The published article from which some of the data in §381 were drawn should be consulted for further details.

Some evidence is available in Table 399 on applicants who were issued life insurance despite symptoms or signs suggestive of congestive heart failure, including dyspnea, and peripheral edema. A mortality ratio of 255 per cent was reported by the New England Life for a (suspected) congestive heart failure code and a ratio of 460 per cent by the New York Life in a smaller group with the edema code. Insurance companies, of course, do not accept applicants with current evidence or recent history of congestive heart failure. Dyspnea, or shortness of breath, is always a difficult symptom to evaluate, and ankle edema may be caused by other conditions much less serious than congestive heart failure. Excess death rates were only a small fraction of those found in the Framingham subjects with definite congestive heart failure complicating other serious heart disease, but they were considerably elevated by life insurance standards for applicants with average age under 45.

Peripheral Arterial Occlusive Disease

The occurrence of severe cramping pain in the calf muscles while walking which subsides with rest is called intermittent claudication.[4,5,6] It represents in the calf muscles the same changes which take place in the heart muscle during a bout of angina pectoris.[4] The blood supply to the muscle is adequate at rest but inadequate during exercise. Intermittent claudication is secondary to arterial occlusive disease in the extremities and develops before signs of complete occlusion develop.[5] Atherosclerosis is the commonest cause of arterial disease in the extremities; it is rare before the age of 55 except in individuals with diabetes mellitus in whom it may appear in early life.[5] Intermittent claudication is also a symptom of thromboangiitis obliterans (Buerger's disease) which is an inflammatory type of occlusive vascular disease affecting the peripheral arteries and veins.[5] This is a disease chiefly affecting males in early adult life.[5]

Abstract §382 presents data gathered on 107 subjects in the Framingham Study who developed intermittent claudication subsequent to the first biennial examination. The incidence increased with advancing age and was higher in males than in females. The mortality ratio of actual to expected deaths for the entire nine-year interval was approximately 200 per cent among the males and 300 per cent among the females, but excess death rates were not very different, 20 and 24 per 1000 per year (Table 382a). Although numbers of deaths were small in individual duration and age categories there did appear to be a trend for both mortality ratios and EDRs to increase with duration. The author also comments in the text that in almost half of the subjects there was preexisting or coexisting coronary heart disease, cerebrovascular disease or congestive heart failure. Most of the excess mortality was found in these individuals, giving the impression that the high mortality is related to the generalized and not the localized arterial occlusive disease. Additional discussion may be found in a published article by Kannel and Shurtleff on the natural history of the disease.[7]

Two small groups of applicants insured by the New England Life and New York Life showed a rather modest level of increased mortality, with ratios of 170 and 149 per cent, respectively (Table 399). These applicants were rated for their peripheral vascular disorder, some of which were presumably arterial occlusive disease with intermittent claudication. However, those issued insurance undoubtedly had milder symptoms and far fewer complications than the Framingham subjects of §382. A somewhat larger group with "arteriosclerosis" insured by The Prudential of London was found to have a normal mortality when the finding was classified as mild, and a mortality ratio of only 124 per cent with "moderate to severe" arteriosclerosis.

Cardiomyopathy

Cardiomyopathy is a disease entity or group of diseases in which the presenting signs and symptoms result entirely or predominately from dysfunction of the myocardium.[4] The term simply means disease of the heart muscle; it was introduced in the medical literature only in 1957, and its use has generally been restricted to heart disease of unknown etiology in which the dominant features are cardiomegaly and congestive heart failure.[8] The diagnosis is usually one of exclusion, as is evident from the descriptive text of §383. Cardiomyopathies may be classified as primary or secondary.[4] The primary types include idiopathic, familial, alcoholic, postpartum, endocardial fibroelastosis, and endomyocardial fibrosis. Secondary types include those secondary to a variety of systemic diseases such as amyloidosis, hemochromatosis, sarcoidosis, collagen vascular diseases, and others.[4]

126

Cardiomyopathy can also be classified from a functional standpoint.[8] The first type, congestive cardiomyopathy, is characterized by congestive heart failure, arrhythmias, embolic phenomenon and murmurs of mitral or tricuspid insufficiency. The second most common type is obstructive cardiomyopathy, usually known in the United States as idiopathic hypertrophic subaortic stenosis (IHSS). Other types, which are less common, include obliterative and restrictive cardiomyopathies.

Follow-up studies of patients with cardiomyopathy are very limited in numbers. Data from six different series of patients with different types of cardiomyopathy as reviewed by Reynolds and VanderArk[8] have been collected in abstract §383. There were 399 entrants in all groups combined, with a total of 106 deaths where 9.37 were expected. The resulting overall mortality ratio was 1,130 per cent and the excess death rate 49 per 1000.

There was a wide range of mortality variation among the various types of cardiomyopathy reported in Table 383a. For all ages, durations and classes combined excess death rates averaged 29 per 1000 in the two series with IHSS (5 and 6 in Table 383a), 56 per 1000 in women with peripartum cardiomyopathy, 72 per 1000 in patients classified simply as primary cardiomyopathy (Series 1), and 101 per 1000 in alcoholic cardiomyopathy (Series 3 and 4). A very strong prognostic factor in the peripartum group was the persistence of heart enlargement more than six months postpartum: 11 of 13 deaths and most of the extra mortality were concentrated in the women with such prolonged cardiomegaly. In the Series 6 patients with IHSS excess death rates increased markedly according to degree of disability by the New York Heart Association Functional Class, which was also correlated with the age of the patients (footnote, Table 383a).

Other Heart Diseases

Rheumatic Fever. Deaths attributed to acute rheumatic fever (Table 11-1) are due to acute rheumatic heart disease, which involves endocardium, myocardium, and pericardium. Congestive heart failure resulting from severe rheumatic myocarditis is the usual manner of death during the attack; this is reported to occur in about 5 per cent of all patients with acute rheumatic fever, but in 75 per cent of those with congestive failure.[5] Rheumatic fever has dwindled to a very small fraction of its former dimensions as a public health problem, because of the success of antibiotics in reducing the incidence of primary and recurrent attacks of streptococcal pharyngitis which appear to be the chief causative factor of the rheumatic fever.[9] Follow-up studies of children and young adults with rheumatic fever have been carried out in the preantibiotic era prior to World War II. These studies indicated that 65 per cent of patients surviving the acute attack had evidence of heart disease, mostly valvular, and ten years later 32 per cent showed no signs of cardiac disability, 48 per cent had chronic rheumatic heart disease and 20 per cent had died.[10] Rheumatic valvular disease is discussed in Chapter 9.

Pericarditis. Acute pericarditis may be caused by a virus, by bacterial agents such as the pneumococcus or the tubercle bacillus, by rheumatic fever, and by various collagen vascular diseases.[5] It can also occur in acute myocardial infarction, uremia, and rarely in other conditions. When pericarditis is a secondary manifestation of other disease the prognosis naturally reflects the gravity of that disease, as in myocardial infarction, uremia, and scleroderma (see §850). Purulent and tuberculous pericarditis were almost always fatal in the past, but acute mortality has been greatly reduced with the many antibiotics now available. Chronic pericarditis, with adhesions, scarring, even calcification, sometimes results from the above causes, but many patients with this condition give no history of prior acute pericarditis.[5] Chronic constrictive pericarditis is a life-threatening disorder. Surgical removal of a sufficient part of the constricting scarred pericardium is the only method of cure; operative mortality is high because congestive failure is often present when the patient must be operated on, and results are not uniformly successful.[5] About ten times as many deaths were attributed to chronic as to acute pericarditis in 1970 (Table 11-1). No follow-up data on pericarditis were located in the medical or insurance literature suitable for including in this volume.

Myocarditis. Inflammatory changes in the myocardium apparently may accompany a great many infectious diseases, on the basis of autopsy material accumulated during World War II at the Army Institute of Pathology.[5] However, apart from rheumatic fever and diphtheria, in both of which myocarditis is a conspicuous feature, such acute involvement of the heart has generally gone unrecognized in the past, except by the pathologist. Chronic myocarditis, apart from the cardiomyopathies, discussed previously, probably does exist as a pathological entity, but it has been misused in the past to indicate the presence of myocardial fibrosis secondary to generalized coronary artery disease or involutional changes of old age. There were 488 deaths attributed to acute myocarditis in 1970, but no follow-up data could be found.

Endocarditis. Acute inflammatory reaction of the endocardium may occur as a result of acute rheumatic fever, septicemia, or thrombus formation. When bacterial organisms are involved, the infection is difficult to treat with antibiotics because of the self-perpetuating nature of the infection as infected material breaks off and is carried by the arterial circulation to other parts of the body in the form of septic emboli. Subacute bacterial endocarditis, although much less fulminating than the acute form, has always been a serious hazard in chronic rheumatic and many forms of congenital heart disease. The incidence is relatively low, but the mortality is said to be still "less than 15 per cent," despite intensive antibiotic therapy.[5] Before antibiotics were available, the mortality in subacute bacterial endocarditis was nearly 100 per cent. In the United States 673 deaths were reported during 1970 as due to acute or subacute endocarditis (Table 11–1). Chronic endocarditis is of great importance as a sequela of rheumatic fever.[10] Valvular heart disease as a manifestation of chronic endocarditis has been discussed in Chapter 9.

Other Cardiac Abnormality. Sometimes routine chest X-rays reveal evidence of abnormality of the heart and aorta. Such findings may be difficult to interpret in the absence of other evidence of cardiovascular disease. Limited data bearing on this question are to be found in Table 399 under "Chest X-Ray." This experience is from applicants issued insurance by the New York Life rated because of one of four different abnormalities: heart enlargement (transverse diameter more than 10 per cent above the predicted value in the Clark-Ungerleider Table), abnormal heart contour without transverse enlargement, tortuosity of the aorta (overall width more than 10 per cent above the Sheridan index), and more than minimal aortic calcification. Only a slight increase in mortality was found in tortuosity of the aorta, but excess mortality was significant in all of the other categories at 97 per cent confidence level or better, despite the small numbers of deaths. Collectively these abnormalities of the heart and aorta produced a mortality ratio of 225 per cent and an excess death rate of 11 per 1000. All of these applicants may be presumed to have had normal cardiovascular findings on examination, and nothing of significance in their X-ray. Many of them undoubtedly had an electrocardiogram that was regarded as within normal limits. It is evident that these abnormalities easily detectable on the chest X-ray do have prognostic significance even as isolated findings.

Renal Artery Atherosclerosis

Incomplete occlusion of the renal artery as a result of atherosclerotic narrowing may result in secondary hypertension which is often of the rapidly progressive type though reversible by nephrectomy.[4] Intravenous pyelograms may appear normal but more often the affected kidney is found to be contracted. In a surprising number of cases there is no albuminuria and the urinary sediment is completely normal.[4] The diagnosis is made by analysis of urine obtained on bilateral ureteral catheterization, renal venous renin measurement, by aortography, renal arteriograms and isotope studies.

The subjects reported in abstract §385 had atherosclerosis of one or both kidneys diagnosed on the basis of aorticorenal arteriograms. In this series 41 per cent of the patients had coexisting atherosclerotic disease in other parts of the body. The widespread nature of atherosclerotic disease was also noted in the Framingham Study, as close to half of the subjects with intermittent claudication had coexisting coronary artery disease, congestive heart failure or cerebrovascular disease (§382). Atherosclerosis is a generalized disease process and is not limited to any one area, even when its manifestations are localized.

As previously stated, hypertension is a consequence of incomplete occlusion of the renal artery. In the Mayo Clinic series 88 per cent of the entrants had a diastolic blood pressure above 90 millimeters of mercury. With good control, where follow-up pressures were held at 90 millimeters or less, the mortality ratio of actual to expected deaths over a five-year interval was 210 per cent (Table 385a). With poor control, where diastolic pressures remained higher than 90 millimeters, the mortality ratio for the five-year interval was 560 per cent. Satisfactory control of hypertension was achieved in about half of the patients, regardless of whether they were treated by medical or surgical procedures or a combination. Annual mortality remained at high levels throughout the five-year interval, with a total of 26 deaths, 23 of which were definitely due to cardiovascular or renal causes and two to unknown causes. The average annual incidence rate for the development of new symptoms of cardiovascular disease was 115 per 1000 (Table 385c). From the causes of death listed in §385 and the figures in Table 11–1 it is evident that very few deaths in these patients are reported as specifically due to renal artery atherosclerosis.

Cardiac Transplant

During the past decade whole-organ transplantation, particularly of the kidney, has become increasingly established as a mode of treatment.[11] In the United States most of the major medical centers have at least the capability of doing renal transplants, but heart transplant still remains a highly experimental procedure.

Complications following whole-organ transplantation stem from one or more of the following factors: preexisting organ failure; technical imperfections in the performance of the procedure; inability to control rejection of the transplant; side effects of the immunosuppressive agents given to prevent rejection; and other coincidental diseases not related either to organ failure or to immunosuppression.[11]

Patients referred as possible cardiac transplant recipients are generally those considered by their physicians to have end-stage heart disease that cannot respond further to conventional medical or surgical therapy.[11] Patients from this group whose more comprehensive cardiologic evaluation suggests a poor prognosis for more than a short-term survival are then studied further to detect diseases of other organs or psychiatric illness that would preclude a successful postoperative recovery.[12]

From a sample of 20 patients who underwent heart transplantation, the average age was 49.1 years, the average length of the known disease was 6.15 years, and the average length of severe disease was 7.89 months.[12] The bulk of these patients had coronary artery disease, while the remainder had cardiomyopathy.[12]

The experience with 52 patients who underwent heart transplant at the Stanford University Hospital is presented in abstract §390. Extremely high excess death rates were observed, 140 to 360 per 1000 per year after the first three months. Only 57 per cent survived the first three months, 41 per cent the first year and 35 per cent the second year. However, the more recently reported experience at Stanford, which is the largest of any center performing cardiac transplantation, shows those who survive the first three months have cumulative survival rates of 77, 60 and 42 per cent at one, two, and three years, respectively.[13] A total of 82 patients had undergone cardiac transplantation at this center from 1968 to March 1975, the date of this report.

Miscellaneous Cardiovascular Disorders

Table 399 is a compilation of mortality and survival data taken from four series of insured individuals with various cardiovascular disorders. As is pointed out in the text, the experience among insured lives, even those accepted at substandard rates, would be expected to be more favorable than the experience with patient groups drawn from the population as a whole.

Most of the data in Table 399 have been referred to in Chapters 7 to 10, or in the preceding portions of this chapter. A relatively small group of "Other Cardiovascular Diseases" followed by the New York Life Insurance Company showed a mortality ratio of 210 per cent. The average age in this group was approximately 40 years, and the excess death rate 3.7 per 1000 per year. In a considerably larger and older group similarly designated by the Sverige Reinsurance Company excess mortality appeared to be lower, with a ratio of 141 per cent and EDR of 2.4. The real difference in mortality between the two groups may be smaller than indicated, because population tables of Western Europe, rather than select insurance tables, were used to calculate expected rates.

Both men and women with varicose veins insured by the Prudential of London showed a normal mortality. The New York Life reported a mortality ratio of 147 in a smaller group of insured with varicose veins, but this was not statistically significant. Neither was the mortality ratio of 167 per cent found by the New York Life among insureds with a history of phlebitis, although this ratio would have been significant if it resulted from only a few more deaths.

No mortality data were located on aortic aneurysms, which accounted for more than 13,000 deaths in the United States during 1970 (Table 11-1). Atherosclerosis is the most common cause for aortic aneurysms, which may also involve the iliac arteries below the bifurcation of the aorta. The prevalence of aortic or iliac calcificiation exceeds 12 per cent in screening X-rays of the abdomen in male employees age 40 to 64, and the prevalence of aneurysms, generally asymptomatic, increases from 0.4 per cent at ages 45 to 49 to 3.8 per cent at ages 60 to 64.[14] Vascular surgery can be used to treat successfully many patients with such aneurysms, especially if the renal arteries are not involved. Removal of an aneurysm and its replacement with a graft is more difficult in the thoracic aorta. On the basis of clinical experience the prognosis is regarded as a serious one for patients with aortic aneurysm.

No attempt has been made in this volume to give a unified picture of atherosclerosis, its pathology, and natural history as it may involve all parts of the vascular system. Cause of death reports give only a partial and incomplete picture of deaths in which atherosclerosis has a contributory role (Tables 6-1, 7-1, 8-2, and 11-1). Mortality data, much of which can be related to atherosclerotic disease, will be found under cerebrovascular disease in Chapter 6, coronary artery disease in Chapter 7, and hypertensive cardiovascular disease in Chapter 8, in addition to the fragmentary results in this chapter. Some data on serum cholesterol and triglyceride as risk factors in the development of atherosclerosis are given under Metabolic Disorders (Chapter 16 and abstracts §950 to §952).

References

1. T. Gordon, F.E. Moore, D. Shurtleff, and T.R. Dawber, "Some Methodologic Problems in the Long-Term Study of Cardiovascular Disease: Observations in the Framingham Study." *J. Chron. Dis.,* 10:186–206 (1959).

2. W.B. Kannel, "Some Lessons in Cardiovascular Epidemiology from Framingham." *Am. J. Card.,* 37:269–282 (1976).

3. H.I. Russek, ed., *Cardiovascular Disease, New Concepts in Diagnosis and Therapy.* Baltimore, Maryland: University Park Press (1974).

4. *Harrison's Principles of Internal Medicine,* 7th ed. New York: McGraw-Hill Book Company (1974).

5. P.B. Beeson and W. McDermott, *Cecil-Loeb Textbook of Medicine,* 14th ed. Philadelphia: W.B. Saunders Company (1975).

6. William A. Sodeman, Jr. and William A. Sodeman, *Pathologic Physiology. Mechanisms of Disease,* 5th ed. Philadelphia: W. B. Saunders Company (1974).

7. W.B. Kannel and D. Shurtleff, "The Natural History of Arteriosclerosis Obliterans." In *Peripheral Vascular Disease,* Cardiovascular Clinics Series, Vol. 3, No. 1, edited by A.N. Brest. Philadelphia: F.W. Davis Co. (1971).

8. E.W. Reynolds and C.R. VanderArk, "Primary Cardiomyopathies: A Review of Clinical Features, Pathology and Mortality." *Trans. Assoc. Life Ins. Med. Dir. Am.,* 58:146-164 (1974).

9. E.F. Bland, "Declining Severity of Rheumatic Fever." *New Eng. J. Med.,* 262:597-599 (1960).

10. E.F. Bland and T.D. Jones, "Rheumatic Fever and Rheumatic Heart Disease: 20-Year Report on 1000 Patients Followed Since Childhood." *Circulation,* 4:836-843 (1951).

11. C.P. Artz and J.D. Hardy, *Management of Surgical Complications,* 3rd ed. Philadelphia: W.B. Saunders Co. (1975).

12. D.A. Clark, E.B. Stinson, R.B. Griepp, J.S. Schroeder, N.E. Shumway, and D.C. Harrison, "Cardiac Transplantation in Man. VI. Prognosis of Patients Selected for Cardiac Transplantation." *Ann. Int. Med.,* 75:15-21 (1971).

13. A.K. Rider et al., "The Status of Cardiac Transplantation, 1975." *Circulation,* 52:531-539 (1975).

14. F.J. Schilling, G. Christakis, H.H. Hempel, and A. Orbach, "The Natural History of Abdominal Aortic and Iliac Atherosclerosis as Detected by Lateral Abdominal Roentgenograms in 2663 Males." *J. Chron. Dis.,* 27:37-45 (1974).

12

Respiratory Diseases

Harold S. Kost, M.D., W.E. Huckabee, M.D.,
and J.W. Richhart, F.S.A.

The principal chronic respiratory diseases today, other than cancer, are emphysema, bronchitis, and asthma, collectively ranking ninth among causes of death, and even more prominently in causes of disability—10 per cent of Social Security awards.[1] The death rate from these impairments is 12 to 13 per 100,000 in the United States, and has apparently risen significantly in the last 20 years,[2] especially the rate for bronchitis. This period has been one of increased interest in pulmonary function and physiology, and it is possible that more careful diagnosis generated by such interest and more accurate reporting account for a large part of the increases reported for these causes of death.

Table 12-1 gives data on numbers of deaths due to various respiratory diseases in the United States in 1970 with the diagnostic terms most used by doctors, together with the numbers of abstracts containing follow-up data. Pneumonia, all forms, accounted for 59,032 deaths, about 50 per cent of all respiratory deaths. However, pneumonia is an acute process, occurring now principally as a terminal event in the aged and in patients weakened by cancer or other serious disease. It is not a suitable disease for follow-up study, except possibly in relation to its complications. No mortality data are available for pneumonia, influenza, or upper respiratory tract diseases on a long-term basis. The latter account for more temporary disability than any other acute diseases.[3] Mortality and survival data have been abstracted for some chronic respiratory diseases, however, as shown in Table 12-1. The total number of deaths reported as being due to respiratory diseases in 1970 was 117,125, or 6.1 per cent of all deaths in the United States.

Tuberculosis, which was the chief cause of death at the turn of the century, has shown a remarkable decrease in the population mortality rate, from 194 per 100,000 in 1900 to less than 3 per 100,000 in 1970.[4] As shown in Table 12-1, in

TABLE 12-1

Numbers of Deaths in the U.S. — 1970
Respiratory Diseases

Hazard	Deaths in U.S.			Follow-up Data
	Number	% in Category		
Lung and Bronchus		114,571	(97.8%)	
Asthma	2,322	(2.0%)		§401
Pulmonary Tuberculosis	3,630	(3.1)		§410, §411
Other Respiratory Tuberculosis	368	(0.3)		—
Pneumonia	59,032	(50.4)		—
Influenza	3,707	(3.2)		—
Emphysema	22,721	(19.4)		§423
Chronic Obstructive Lung Disease	4,444	(3.8)		§421, §422
Chronic Bronchitis	5,014	(4.3)		§420
Other Bronchitis	2,142	(1.8)		—
Bronchiectasis	1,036	(0.9)		§499
Other Lung Disorder	10,155	(8.8)		§480
Other Respiratory		2,554	(2.2%)	
Upper Respiratory Tract	1,052	(0.9%)		—
Pleurisy and Empyema	730	(0.6)		§499
Spontaneous Pneumothorax	221	(0.2)		§499
Congenital Respiratory Tract	551	(0.5)		—
Other Respiratory	**			§499
Total (all listed in Cause of Death Statistics)	117,125 (6.1% of all deaths)			

**Listed elsewhere under various separate causes

the entire United States during 1970 there were only 3,630 deaths reported as due to pulmonary tuberculosis. Although public health measures did result in a steady decline of tuberculosis death rates from 1900 to World War II, the drop in mortality was especially sharp between 1945 and 1960, the first 15 years of the era of modern chemotherapy for tuberculosis.[5] The decline has continued since 1960, and mortality rates in the middle age group have now fallen to a level of 5 to 7 per 100,000.

Industrial or occupational lung diseases, especially pneumoconiosis of coal miners, silicosis, and asbestosis are important causes of disability and undoubtedly contribute to deaths due to chronic lung disease. There were 1,794 deaths attributed to these specific causes in 1970; they comprise part of the "Other Lung Disorders" in Table 12-1. There are no separate abstracts on occupational lung diseases, although some limited data are available in §20.

Emphysema and Chronic Obstructive Pulmonary Disease

Emphysema clinically, is overexpansion of the lung. There are several forms of this hyperinflation: they differ in associated symptoms and are also believed to differ in effects on mortality. Only one of the causes of emphysema, *chronic obstructive pulmonary disease* (COPD or COLD), is considered important by chest physicians, and consequently the term emphysema is now used much less often than in the past. The term is used by pathologists and radiologists, but the emphysema recognized under the microscope cannot be accurately diagnosed in life, and its significance to mortality depends on the cause. The signs of emphysema in the chest X-ray are of doubtful significance to health, in themselves, although COPD may be kept in mind in comparing mortality statistics, especially as the concept of COPD is a recent development, and older papers may use the term emphysema in a way different from recent ones. Similarly, if the diagnosis is made from history and physical examination only, rather than from pulmonary function tests, confusion may occur. The barrel chest, hyperresonant percussion note, and dark lung fields on the X-ray film indicate hyperinflation but not necessarily significant disease. If one adds audible prolongation of the expiratory phase of breathing or expiratory wheezes on auscultation of the chest, COPD becomes more likely, and a history of dyspnea adds further likelihood. However, pulmonary function tests are essential to confirm the diagnosis and determine stages of the disease necessary for comparing groups of patients. For a clinical description of emphysema and COPD the reader is referred to the monograph by Hinshaw.[6]

COPD is characterized by (1) the slow development of permanent bronchiolar obstruction, and (2) patchiness or irregularity of expansion with breakdown of septa between alveoli, the small air sacs in the lung (inhomogeneity of ventilation and perfusion). The first abnormality causes shortness of breath and early changes in pulmonary function tests of the completeness of air exchange (ventilation); the second causes, at an advanced stage, impaired diffusion of gases between alveolar air and the blood, with falling arterial blood O_2 and ultimately rising CO_2. The two types of abnormality do not necessarily develop in predictable relationship to each other, but are believed by some investigators to have differing mortality significance. If airways obstruction is predominant with little reduction in blood O_2 saturation ("pink puffers"), heart failure is said to be less likely despite the dyspnea. If blood O_2 saturation is reduced ("blue bloaters"), heart failure, edema, and a greater risk of early death are anticipated, whether or not dyspnea is mild. Heart failure secondary to pulmonary disease is called "cor pulmonale," is difficult to reverse, and is an ominous development when it does occur in COPD.

Pulmonary Function. Measurements of lung function[7, 8] for evaluation and prognostication involve estimates of airways obstruction (reduced velocity of air flow); gas exchange between alveolar air and pulmonary capillary blood; or inhomogeneity of ventilation in different lung "compartments" due to the emphysema itself. Some of these measurements will be described, since they are crucial to an understanding of the severity of COPD in its various stages.

Maximal velocity of airflow is reached during the first second of a forced expiration, and consequently the volume of air that can be forcefully exhaled in this time (FEV_1, forced expiratory volume at one second) is a sensitive measure of early COPD. It is a relatively simple test requiring relatively simple equipment. The total vital capacity (maximum volume that can be blown out after a maximum inspiration), or forced vital capacity (FVC) is not much altered until late in the disease. FVC has a predictive value for mortality, however, both cardiovascular and total mortality for reasons not entirely clear.[8] Because FEV_1 is related to body size or lung size, it must be adjusted for this variable by comparing the observed with a predicted value or expressing it as a fraction of the forced vital capacity, which is similarly related to body size and is known as timed vital capacity (TVC). The level of TVC in normal people is 70 per cent of vital capacity or more.[7, 8]

Maximum breathing capacity (MBC) or maximum voluntary ventilation (MVV) is measured over a period of a few seconds, with the subject continuously breathing as rapidly and deeply as possible to the limit of physical capacity. The result is that this test measures much the same abnormality as FEV_1 or TVC, namely, airways obstruction, but is such hard work to perform that it tends to be reduced by nonspecific illness and is less useful than the one-second forced expiratory volume.

Aeration of blood in the lung is effectively estimated by measuring O_2 or CO_2 tensions (partial pressure, designated PaO_2 and $PaCO_2$, respectively) in the blood leaving the lung, i.e., arterial blood. Resting PaO_2 is normally over 95 mm Hg, $PaCO_2$ under 45 mm Hg. PaO_2 is affected earlier and consequently is a more sensitive test than $PaCO_2$. Even more sensitive is the PaO_2 during exercise. An important function of PaO_2 is sometimes given, SaO_2 (saturation of arterial blood hemoglobin with O_2); it normally exceeds 95 per cent. Some function of $PaCO_2$ may be given, rather than CO_2 itself. One of these is serum bicarbonate or blood total CO_2 content; another approximation of arterial blood CO_2 tension is CO_2 tension of alveolar air ($PACO_2$), which can be measured in the last portion of an expired air sample; it is normally equal to $PaCO_2$. In COPD, however, $PACO_2$ cannot be used to estimate $PaCO_2$ because of differences that develop among the many alveolar air "compartments" in the lungs. For this reason $PVCO_2$ (CO_2 tension of mixed venous blood) is sometimes determined as part of the complete evaluation of a patient with advanced COPD. Mixed venous blood CO_2 is assumed to have a constant relationship to arterial blood CO_2, about 5 mm higher. Arterial blood O_2 tension is found reduced (hypoxemia) in fairly early obstructive disease, CO_2 tension, increased (respiratory acidosis) in more advanced disease.

Overexpansion of the lung may be estimated from total lung capacity (TLC) determined by inert gas dilution methods. The increased volume of the lung as a whole is less significant than the increase of that volume which is never breathed in and out, the residual volume (RV), or the volume that is not normally breathed in and out, the functional residual capacity (FRC). RV or FRC is most meaningful when expressed as a fraction of TLC. The FRC is normally about 50 per cent of TLC, residual volume less than 30 per cent,[7, 8] but in advanced obstructive disease both are markedly increased.

Pulmonary Function and Mortality in COPD

The relationship between pulmonary function studies, clinical signs and symptoms, and the progression of COPD are too complex to review in this volume. The reader is referred to the volume by Hinshaw[6] and other texts of respiratory diseases. Mortality relationships to some of these tests are presented in two abstracts, which are discussed below, and additional information about prognostic indications in COPD may be found in a study by Vandenbergh et al.[10]

The normal volume of FVC is highly correlated with body height (FVC in liters is approximately equal to the cube of the height in meters, falling off only 7 per cent from this prediction after age 65). Thus the normal value will average about 4.5 liters. A typical severely reduced FEV_1 might be 35 per cent of FVC or 1.5 liters. When values are more abnormal than this, it is no longer appropriate to derive TVC as the ratio of FEV_1 to FVC (correction for FVC is not made). When disease is severe, the total vital capacity is reduced also, usually an impairment called "restrictive disease," something additional to purely obstructive disease. Thus, for male veterans with severe COPD, Tables 421a and 421b give FEV_1 in liters, since all the values are below 1.5 liters and go as low as 10 per cent of normal FVC. This notation serves very well to delineate the increasing excess death rate with fall of FEV_1.

Detailed follow-up data were found for two different series of patients, correlating pulmonary function studies with mortality observed over periods ranging from four to a maximum of ten years. A cooperative study of 487 male veterans, average age 58 years, at entry and followed four years is described in abstract §421. Patients were classified according to their FEV_1. The least severe cases with an FEV_1 of 1.5 L or more showed a high mortality, with an excess death rate of 67 per 1000 per year, but better than the other groups (Table 421a). The middle group, with FEV_1 in the range of 0.5 to 1.49 L, experienced an EDR of 148 per 1000, and the group with most severe COPD, as shown by an FEV_1 less than 0.5 L, experienced an EDR of 368 per 1000. A markedly reduced FEV_1 is therefore associated with a very poor prognosis: a mortality ratio of 1640 per cent and a survival ratio of only 12.1 per cent. Of the 64 patients in the most severely impaired group, 56 died during follow-up, in contrast to only 3.42 deaths expected in the U.S. population, impressive witness to the lethality of COPD at this advanced stage. There was no discernible trend in excess mortality with duration over the four years of follow-up.

The other series consisted of 200 ambulant patients attending a pulmonary function clinic at the University of Chicago, selected because of an FEV_1 less than 60 per cent of both observed and predicted FVC for at least one year prior to entry. Average age was under 60 years, as in the veterans group, but 11 per cent of these patients were female. The descriptive information on the history and condition of the patients of this series was unusually complete (Tables 422a–422b). The long duration of symptoms, the frequent past history of pneumonia or other unusual respiratory infection, the fact that half the patients were still working full-time despite their symptoms, and the presence of a normal chest X-ray in one-third of the patients are among the findings of particular interest. Almost all patients had a history of cigarette smoking; 59 per cent were currently smokers.

Mortality experience is given in Table 422c for combinations of three age groups and various severity factors, of which the principal one is the FEV_1, a volume of 1.2 L or higher constituting the best category, provided the cardiac functional status was no worse than class 2 (New York Heart Association classification), arterial O_2 saturation was at least 90 per cent after moderate exercise, and there was minimal or no restrictive disease as shown by an FVC 75 per cent or more of predicted. The worst category, Grade 4, included cases with FEV_1 under 0.8 L and the intermediate ones are defined in the footnote to Table 422c. It should be noted that the severity criteria used in Tables 422c to 422e differ from those in the published articles and were developed in the preparation of the abstract, as a result of computer reprocessing of the detailed data supplied by Dr. Burrows. By these criteria the least impaired patients (Grade 1) showed the best prognosis, with an excess death rate of 23 per 1000 and a mortality ratio of 174 per cent, all ages and durations combined. The intermediate severity group (Grades 2a, 2b and 3) had an aggregate EDR of 114 per 1000, and the worst cases (Grade 4), an EDR of 210 per 1000. There was little change in excess mortality with advancing age (Table 422c). However, excess death rates increased with duration of observation in the Grade 1 and combined Grades 2 and 3 patients, as shown in Tables 422d–422e. This trend with duration was reversed in the most severe (Grade 4) patients, as EDR was at a maximum, 226 per 1000 within two years of entry into the series, and decreased to 156 per 1000 from five to ten years after entry.

Table 422c also illustrates the quantitative usefulness of FEV_1 expressed as a per cent of FVC in mild disease (Grade 1 cases with an FVC 75 per cent or more of normal). The value of 46 per cent for FEV_1/FVC is much reduced below the expected 70 per cent. However, in the more severe categories FVC itself falls to 73 per cent of normal in the Grade 2 and 3 cases and 57 per cent in the Grade 4 cases. The increase in severity of the COPD would be underestimated by the change in FEV_1/FVC, a decrease from 46 per cent in Grade 1 only to 33 per cent in Grade 4. Clearly, therefore, in very severe COPD, when FVC is diminished, FEV_1 is better given in absolute units and compared with the predicted FEV_1, rather than given as a per cent of the observed FVC.

The systematic increase of excess death rate with fall in FEV_1 is well shown in Table 422c. The further analysis of mortality prediction by levels of arterial blood O_2 saturation is of no help in differentiating Grade 1 cases but gives added refinement for the more severe categories. One interesting combination of findings, however, is seen in line 22 of Table 422c, the combination of severe reduction of FEV_1 (group 4) with high O_2 saturation maintained after exercise ("pink puffers"), giving a substantially lower mortality than in patients with reduced O_2 saturation appropriate to the advanced stage of their COPD (excess death rate 168 versus 283 per 1000).

Mortality in "Emphysema." As explained previously, it is extremely difficult to appraise the severity of chronic lung disease in the absence of pulmonary function studies. With respect to emphysema, follow-up experience on life insurance applicants is presented in abstracts §423 and §499, when the diagnosis was made clinically. In terms of pulmonary function, for which no data were reported, it is probable that the insurance applicants were, on the average, much less severely impaired than the best patients in the clinical series. This presumption is supported by the generally favorable experience of the New York Life with an EDR of 6.2 per 1000 for male applicants with emphysema (Table 423c), and a corresponding EDR of 4.3 per 1000 in men age 50 up insured by the Prudential of London (Table 499). The latter company also reported an excess death rate of 9.5 per 1000 in men with a history of chronic bronchitis and emphysema combined, including all ages 30 and up (Table 499). Most of the excess mortality in the New York Life series was concentrated in applicants under age 50, in whom the EDR was 11 per 1000 (with mortality ratio of 510 per cent), as opposed to a very low EDR, only 2.1 per 1000 in those age 50 up. A similar excess mortality was noted in the men under age 50 with both bronchitis and emphysema (Prudential of London, Table 499). From these results it would appear reasonable to conclude that a clinical diagnosis of emphysema, without supporting evidence of pulmonary function tests, is much more likely to reflect a significant proportion of cases with early COPD in men under age 50 than it does in older men, age 50 up. Relatively few patients with definite COPD develop symptoms sufficient to result in a diagnosis under age 50.

Asthma

Bronchial asthma is a chronic disease characterized by attacks of wheezing, dyspnea, and expectoration of thick, tenacious sputum, with symptom-free intervals, often quite prolonged (weeks or months).[6] It is an allergic disorder with attacks brought on by inhalation of pollen, dusts, or other substances to which the patient is sensitive, or occasionally by ingestion of such substances. About half of all asthmatics have no demonstrable sensitivity to an external agent; in most of these a bacterial sensitivity is thought to exist, but this may not be demonstrable, either. It is a common disorder, disabling when severe, and may require hospitalization. Only 2,322 deaths were attributed to asthma during 1970 (Table 12-1).

Smooth muscle spasm and excessive mucus secretion produce obstruction in the small bronchial airways during an asthmatic attack. Such acute obstruction, when present, is indistinguishable from COPD in all the functional features mentioned, but is reversible, the patient being normal between attacks. Between attacks all pulmonary function test results are normal as well. After years of asthmatic attacks, emphysema and some degree of COPD begin to be superimposed so that the patient does not return to normal after an attack, but returns to his usual state of health and subnormal level of lung function.

During attacks, administration of certain drugs by inhalation (e.g., isoproterenol) gives immediate relief and also immediate return of FEV_1 and other pulmonary function test results toward normal. Since these drugs have no effect on COPD in the absence of asthma, FEV_1 measured before and after administering isoproterenol is considered to give an estimate of the "asthmatic" and "COPD" components, respectively, of the patient's obstructive disease.

While pulmonary function tests will indicate severity of a given attack, the severity of the disease is usually described in terms of frequency of attacks and the type of medication required to control symptoms (antihistamines and oral aminophyllin versus potent sympathomimetics, oral or intravenous, versus prednisone). There appear to be no adequate data to indicate that severity in this sense is correlated with excess death rate, though it seems to be a reasonable hypothesis.

Evidence from three series of insured persons with asthma indicates an overall excess mortality of modest degree: excess death rates of 1.7 per 1000 in males insured by the New York Life and 2.6 per 1000 in females (Table 401c); an EDR of 1.6 per 1000 in men, mostly resident in Great Britain, insured by the Prudential of London (Table 499); and an EDR of 3.0 per 1000 in men and women resident in Western Europe and insured by the Sverige Reinsurance Company (Table 499). The English experience is relatively large, as it is based on more than 27,000 policy years of exposure and 83 deaths. Although the excess death rates are small the mortality ratios were moderately elevated, 172 to 280 per cent in the three series, all ages combined, because of the predominance of young policyholders. Excess death rates tended to increase with advancing age, especially among the New York Life men, who showed a rate of 18 per 1000 for all ages 50 and up.

Clinically, it is often observed that asthma of childhood disappears in early years of adulthood. One would expect that mortality for the youngest age group would be low because of this tendency in young asthmatics. As indicated above, the lowest EDRs were found in the youngest age groups in both the New York Life male policyholders and in the Prudential of London series. This was not true for a small group of New York Life female policyholders.

Limited information from the New York Life experience indicates that the major part of the excess mortality was concentrated in deaths due to "allergic disorders" (presumably asthma) and respiratory disorders (Table 401d).

Chronic Bronchitis

Chronic bronchitis is chronic bacterial infection of the bronchi of the lung, manifested by more or less continuous cough and some sputum production with periods of exacerbation.[6] In prolonged and severe disease, permanent X-ray changes may be seen, but these are nonspecific. The diagnosis is not altogether exact or objective, and criteria vary from one doctor to another. This has historically been most prominent between British and American chest physicians. A chronic infectious disease associated with, or leading to COPD of the most severe type ("blue bloater") has been commonly recognized in Great Britain. This has been much less frequently diagnosed in the United States and Canada, where it may actually be of lower prevalence, although a retrospective infectious history seems to be found in the COPD cases with hypoxemia in the United States. These differences should be kept in mind in comparing published statistics on prevalence.[6]

It is difficult to say what a large heterogeneous group of doctors might mean by the diagnosis of "chronic bronchitis," but the evidence in abstract §420 suggests that such a diagnosis in connection with insurance applicants is associated with a significant increase in death rate. The numbers of deaths are small in the New York Life series (Table 420c), but excess death rates were higher for women than for men (11 versus 6.5 per 1000), and much higher for policyholders age 50 up than for those under age 50, both sexes combined (23 versus 2.0 per 1000). Male applicants under age 50 with bronchitis alone, insured by the Prudential of London had an excess death rate of only 2.2 per 1000, but when there was also a diagnosis of emphysema the rate was 10 per 1000 (Table 499). The EDR for men age 50 up was 12 per 1000, on the average, and the associated diagnosis of emphysema actually resulted in a somewhat lower rather than a higher rate, contrary to what might be expected. In the New York Life experience excess mortality occurred in deaths due to cardiovascular diseases, cancer of the repiratory tract and respiratory diseases (Table 420d). There are no data to suggest what proportion of these bronchitis cases might have developed COPD.

Pulmonary Tuberculosis

Pulmonary tuberculosis is a term applicable to an infection of the lung by the causative organism, Mycobacterium tuberculosis.[6] Organisms must be identified in sputum, concentrated gastric washings (swallowed sputum), or some other lung specimen; and, in addition, characteristic lesions of the disease must be found, usually by X-ray of the chest. In actual practice, the diagnosis may be made from characteristic X-ray lesions despite failure of repeated efforts to obtain typical organisms which take the acid-fast stain (acid-fast bacilli, or AFB). Such diagnoses are always in some doubt in the absence of bacteriological confirmation. However, recent conversion of tuberculin skin tests from negative to positive adds evidence for a tuberculous cause of the lesions, as this indicates recently acquired presence of the tubercle bacillus somewhere in the body.

Mortality studies in pulmonary tuberculosis are affected by the severity or stage of development of disease in the population being studied. For this determination the traditional nomenclature of the extent of disease, as seen on chest X-rays, usually has been employed: (1) minimal, (2) moderately advanced, and (3), far advanced.[6] These are defined as follows:

(1) Minimal: No cavities, total area of disease is less than the equivalent of one lung apex (above second rib);
(2) Moderately Advanced: Cavitation, if present, is of aggregate diameter less than 4 cm.; total area of small lesions is less than one lung area, and area of dense confluent lesions is less than one-third lung area;
(3) Far Advanced: More than moderately advanced.

Criteria recently adopted by the American Lung Association for the classification of patients with suspected or actual pulmonary tuberculosis place much more emphasis on clinical activity, bacteriological status and adequacy of medical treatment than they do on the findings in the chest X-ray alone, which were formerly of paramount importance.[11] Rates of incidence, prevalence, and mortality have been so drastically reduced during the past 30 years by modern chemotherapeutic agents that all medical aspects of pulmonary tuberculosis have undergone a radical change. In direct antithesis to previous views, pulmonary tuberculosis is now regarded as a disease of low prevalence, no longer a major public health problem, with infectivity readily controlled, and generally treatable on an ambulatory outpatient basis, with or without a generally short initial period of hospitalization. This new viewpoint of experts assumes that the patient has been evaluated as free of unusual complications and follows a supervised long-term course of treatment with a recommended combination of drugs. Isoniazid, PAS, ethambutol, streptomycin, rifampin are the principal drugs in current use.[12, 13] Prescribed courses of chemotherapy cure the disease in a high percentage of cases.[14] Treatment failures, relapses, and reinfections are rare, and it is often not necessary to restrict a patient with a reduced positive sputum from his immediate contacts except under unusual circumstances.[12] Surgical intervention is now seldom indicated. Most tuberculosis deaths occur today in neglected cases or in patients with unusual and severe complications. No other major infectious disease has undergone such a complete transformation as a result of the introduction of effective chemotherapy.

Mitchell's follow-up study on advanced pulmonary tuberculosis (§410) was conducted on patients admitted to the Trudeau Sanatorium from 1930 through 1939 and followed to 1953 and 1954. All initial treatment and the major portion of treatment for all survivors were therefore carried out without benefit of modern chemotherapy. Although the mortality experience is now chiefly of historical interest, the natural history of pulmonary tuberculosis prior to the late 1940s was considered to be of sufficient importance to include among the abstracts.

For the group of about 1,200 patients with moderately advanced TB the 20-year excess death rates were in the range of 8.6 to 14 per 1000 per year (Tables 410a and 410c). Rates for females were slightly higher than for males, and there was little variation by age, except that in men the highest level was found in the oldest group of patients, age 34 up. Although rates were lower during the second ten years of follow-up, excess mortality persisted in all age groups to the end of the study. At the end of follow-up 16 per cent of the patients had died of TB, less than 6 per cent from other causes, two-thirds were living and well, and contact had been lost with the remainder, the majority of whom were well at the time of latest contact. Excess death rates were considerably higher for the 298 patients with far advanced TB, in the range of 22 to 56 per 1000 in male patients, and 21 to 51 in female patients, the rates increasing with advancing age in both sexes. Mortality rates generally decreased with duration but remained considerably above rates in the general population to the end of the study. Over 40 per cent of the patients had died of TB by 1953-54 and only 47 per cent were living and well. The overall mortality ratio in terms of observed and expected cases was 340 per cent for the moderately advanced and 825 per cent for the far advanced.

The high mortality characteristic of pulmonary TB in these patient groups 25 or more years ago is no longer evident in the experience of three different series of applicants issued life insurance despite a history of pulmonary TB. The experience of New York Life policyholders from 1954 to the 1971 policy anniversary produced a normal mortality for those without operation, but a mortality ratio of 220 per cent and an EDR of 4.9 per 1000 in those who gave a history of operation for their disease. Excess death rates in a large group of applicants with TB history and insurance issued by the Prudential of London were quite low, 0.7 per 1000 for "mild cases," 1.0 per 1000 for "moderate or severe," and only 1.2 per 1000 for those with a history of therapeutic pneumothorax or major surgery. An undifferentiated large group insured by the Sverige Reinsurance Company experienced a mortality almost the same as that of the general population used for a standard. These results are not conclusive, but they do tend to support the contention of physicians currently handling TB patients that the extra mortality risk under adequate chemotherapy must be extremely small. No clinical follow-up studies were found to document this contention.

Other Respiratory Diseases

Diseases of the upper respiratory tract, larynx, and pleura and congenital diseases have been placed under this heading. Together they account for only 2.2 per cent of all repiratory deaths (Table 12-1). However, for convenience, bronchiectasis and other lung disorders have been carried over from the discussion of Diseases of the Lung and Bronchus to this section.

Bronchiectasis, strictly speaking, is a saccular or fusiform widening of major intermediate bronchi, usually in the lower lobes; but practically speaking, it is a chronic infectious process with cough, heavy sputum production and hemoptysis. Moreover, in high proportion these patients have widespread bronchitis, and the symptoms and test findings of obstructive lung disease.[14] The diagnosis may be suspected from clinical history or incidental findings in a plain chest X-ray film, but is made definitively only by special X-ray studies, with the help of the bronchoscope. The limited New York Life experience in Table 499 shows a near-normal mortality, with a ratio of 120 per cent. This would seem to confirm the clinical impression that bronchiectasis is now much more amenable to medical treatment than it was in the preantibiotic era.

Data are also reported in Table 499 on applicants with other respiratory disorders, insured by the Prudential of London. This experience was favorable, with mortality ratios of 102 per cent reported in spontaneous pneumothorax, only 81 per cent in pleurisy with effusion, and 117 per cent in other pleurisy. Many different respiratory diseases may produce pleurisy—infections, tumors, collagen vascular diseases, and others—but manifest or occult pulmonary tuberculosis has always been a leading cause. The essentially normal mortality found in this series may reflect the greatly improved mortality in pulmonary tuberculosis, as previously discussed. The English experience on pleurisy was a relatively large one, with 145 deaths in the two classes.

The final bit of information in Table 499 is in a miscellaneous category of "Lung Disorders" reported by the New York Life. With 9 observed and 2.99 expected deaths the apparent increase in mortality does possess statistical significance at the 99 per cent confidence level. However, in the absence of information on cause of death, the ratio of policies to lives, and the nature of the diseases covered (a history of penumonia was included), it is impossible to interpret this observation. One fairly rare disease of unknown cause that often involves the lung is sarcoidosis; mortality data on this disease are given in §780. No mortality data were located on diseases of the upper respiratory tract, which produce few deaths. Cancers of the entire respiratory tract were reviewed in Chapter 5. The final part of this section on Other Respiratory Diseases will be devoted to a topic of current importance, the occupational lung diseases.

Occupational Lung Diseases

While there are many conditions involving the respiratory system which are influenced by occupation, those of major concern are the impairments which are, or were thought to be, peculiar to specific occupations. Occupational lung diseases of special interest are asbestosis, silicosis, and coal worker's pneumoconiosis.

The deleterious effects of dusts generated in the production of asbestos have been known for the greater part of this century. After a period of increasing incidence of asbestosis it now seems that workers in the production phase of the industry are better protected than formerly.[16] The problem in the future is more likely to be that of the lightly exposed workers. The synergistic relationship between smoking and exposure to asbestos to development of lung cancer is striking. There is nearly a hundred-fold increase in risk of death from lung cancer among asbestos workers who smoke as compared to those who neither smoke nor work with the material.[17] Long-term studies of men and women involved in the production of asbestos products show increasing excess deaths from cancer of the lung and from other respiratory diseases with increasing intensity and duration of exposure. Workers with over two years moderate to heavy exposure, regardless of age at first exposure, experience mortality ratios from 120 per cent to 233 per cent.[17, 18, 19, 20] The basis for expected mortality was not identical in all studies, and the number of workers in some categories were small, which calls for caution in interpretation. Nonetheless, there is excessive mortality accompanying this occupation which is associated with diseases affecting the respiratory system.

Silicosis, caused by the inhalation of silicon dioxide dust is one of the most ancient and ubiquitous of the occupational diseases. Much shorter periods of exposure than in the case of asbestos may lead to serious consequences. While many case reports and pathological descriptions have been published, the survival pattern from a risk analysis viewpoint must be inferred rather than derived. The expected survival would be that of progressive chronic fibrosis often complicated by other respiratory disease.[16, 19, 21] Life insurance studies do not identify silicosis as a specific entity.

Coal workers' pneumoconiosis (CWP), while a later arrival than silicosis on the scene of occupational lung disease, has generated considerable interest and study.[6, 22] Perhaps the concentration of workers in more easily identifiable groups and increasing social concern for the welfare of miners have contributed to the intensive recent study of CWP. Coal mining has long been recognized as a dangerous occupation. The death rate of coal workers is approximately twice that of other types of workers[23] (see also §20). When accidental deaths are included, the increased mortality varies little by age. The exclusion of violent deaths from the comparison reveals a modest increase in mortality at the younger ages with an increase to over 200 per cent mortality at the advanced ages. This pattern suggests an environmental factor.[23, 24, 25] Analysis by specific causes of death indicates increased mortality from most causes with special concentration in disease of the respiratory system.

The finding of radiologic abnormalities of the lungs of workers with these occupational diseases is related to age and exposure. The correlation between these abnormalities and pulmonary impairment is poor except for the most severe categories of X-ray abnormalities. Mortality can be more closely related to pulmonary function and symptomatology than to radiologic changes. Any consideration of reduced survival in coal miners due to respiratory impairments must include the full spectrum of respiratory disease and not be limited to CWP.[24, 25, 26] Also of importance is the disability hazard in coal workers with advanced disease. Studies including ex-miners as well as those still active in this occupation shed more light on the natural history of their occupational lung disease.[23]

References

1. I.T.T. Higgins, "The Epidemiology of Chronic Respiratory Disease." *Prev. Med.*, 2:14-33 (1973).

2. Dept. of Health, Education, and Welfare, *Mortality Trends of Leading Causes of Death, U.S. 1950-69.* Vital and Health Statistics, Series 20, No. 16. Rockville, Md.: National Center for Health Statistics (1974).

3. Dept. of Health, Education, and Welfare, *Facts of Life and Death.* Rockville, Md.: National Center for Health Statistics (1974).

4. A.M. Lowell, L.B. Edwards, and C.E. Palmer, *Tuberculosis.* Cambridge, Mass.: Harvard University Press (1969).

5. T.G. Doege, "Tuberculosis Mortality in the U.S., 1900 to 1960." *J. Am. Med. Assoc.*, 192:1045-1048 (1965).

6. H.C. Hinshaw, *Diseases of the Chest,* 3rd ed. Philadelphia: W.B. Saunders Co. (1969).

7. W.O. Fenn and H. Rahn, eds., *Handbook of Physiology, Respiration,* Vol. II. Washington, D.C.: American Physiologic Society (1965).

8. J.H. Comroe, R.E. Forster, A.B. Dubois, W.A. Briscoe, and E. Carlsen, *The Lung,* 2nd ed. Chicago: Year Book Medical Publishers (1962).

9. T. Gordon and W.B. Kannel, eds., *The Framingham Study—An Epidemiologic Investigation of Cardiovascular Disease.* Washington, D.C.: U.S. Government Printing Office (1974).

10. E. Vandenbergh, J. Clement, and K.P. van de Woestijne, "Course and Prognosis of Patients with Advanced Chronic Obstructive Pulmonary Disease." *Am. J. Med.*, 55:736-746 (1973).

11. Ad Hoc Committee, American Thoracic Society, *Diagnostic Standards and Classification of Tuberculosis and Other Mycobacterial Diseases.* New York: American Lung Association (1974).

12. American Thoracic Society, *Guidelines for Work for Patients with Tuberculosis.* New York: American Lung Association (1973).

13. J.J. Gunnels, J.H. Bates, and H. Swindoll, "Infectivity of Sputum Positive Tuberculosis Patients on Chemotherapy." *Am. Rev. Resp. Dis.*, 109:323-330 (1974).

14. J.A. Sbarbaro, "Tuberculosis: The New Challenge to the Practicing Clinician." *Chest,* 68(Suppl.):436-443 (1975).

15. N.S. Cherniak and R.W. Carton, "Factors Associated with Respiratory Insufficiency in Bronchiectasis." *Am. J. Med.*, 41:562-571 (1966).

16. W.K.C. Morgan and A. Seaton, *Occupational Lung Diseases.* Philadelphia: W.B. Saunders Co. (1975).

17. I.J. Selikoff, E.C. Hammond, and J. Churg, "Asbestos Exposure, Smoking, and Neoplasia." *J. Am. Med. Assoc.,* 204:106-112 (1968).

18. M.L. Newhouse, "A Study of the Mortality of Workers in an Asbestos Factory." *Brit. J. Ind. Med.,* 26:294-301 (1969).

19. M.L. Newhouse, G. Berry, J.C. Wagner, and M.E. Turok, "A Study of the Mortality of Female Asbestos Workers." *Brit. J. Ind. Med.,* 29:134-141 (1972).

20. J.C. McDonald, A.D. McDonald, G.W. Gibbs, J. Siemiatycki, and C.E. Rossiter, "Mortality in the Chrysotile Asbestos Mines and Mills of Quebec." *Arch. Environ. Health,* 22:677-686 (1971).

21. I.J. Selikoff, "Widening Perspectives of Occupational Lung Disease." *Prev. Med.,* 2:412-437 (1973).

22. P.E. Enterline, "Mortality Rates Among Coal Miners." *Am. J. Pub. Health,* 54:758-768 (1964).

23. C.E. Ortmeyer, J. Costello, W.K.C. Morgan, S. Sweeker, and M. Peterson, "The Mortality of Appalachian Coal Miners, 1963 to 1971." *Arch. Environ. Health,* 29:67-72 (1974).

24. A.L. Cochrane, "Relation between Radiographic Categories of Coal Workers' Pneumoconiosis and Expectation of Life." *Brit. Med. J.,* 2:532-534 (1973).

25. D.L. Rasmussen, "Patterns of Physiological Impairment in Coal Workers' Pneumoconiosis." *Ann. N.Y. Acad. Sci.,* 200:455-462 (1972).

26. A. Seaton, N.L.R. Lapp, and W.K.C. Morgan, "Relationship of Pulmonary Impairment in Simple Coal Workers' Pneumoconiosis to Type of Radiographic Opacity." *Brit. J. Ind. Med.,* 29:50-55 (1972).

13

Diseases of the Digestive System
John C. Robinson, M.D.

Deaths attributed to digestive system diseases numbered 75,395 in the United States during 1970, constituting 3.9 per cent of all deaths (Table 13-1). Over one-half of the deaths were due to diseases of the liver, gallbladder and pancreas, cirrhosis of the liver accounting for about 42 per cent of the digestive system total, the largest number for a single disease entity. Diseases of the small intestine, colon, and rectum account for 18 per cent, peptic ulcer and other diseases of the stomach, duodenum and esophagus, for 15 per cent, and all other digestive system diseases for 9 per cent. Table 13-1 also shows the distribution of the abstracts with respect to the categories and individual diseases.

Ten of the 20 abstracts dealing with specific digestive system disorders are in the peptic ulcer category. Most of these studies have been made on insured groups and reflect the high prevalence of a history of peptic ulcer in the healthier segment of the general population who qualify for individual life insurance. Mortality data in the other abstracts, including §599, are scattered among the remaining diseases of the fairly long list in Table 13-1, with many gaps. Conspicuous by their absence are acute infectious disorders of the gastrointestinal tract, which produce considerable temporary disability but seldom cause death. The digestive system diseases will be discussed in the order of the major categories as shown.

Peptic Ulcer Disease

Nature of the Disease. Peptic ulcer can be described as a sharply circumscribed loss of tissue usually in the stomach or first part of the duodenum, occurring almost always in the presence of acid gastric juice.[1, 2] Anatomically, 80 per cent of peptic ulcers are duodenal, usually located within 3-4 cm of the pylorus, and 20 per cent are gastric, most frequently on the lesser curvature of the stomach or in the prepyloric area.[2] Exact diagnosis, including the site of the ulcer, usually by X-ray study, is important in the management of patients with peptic ulcer disease, because of the cancer risk in gastric ulcer. Duodenal ulcer rarely develops into cancer. Typical symptoms consist of epigastric pain, usually relieved by intake of food or antacid, but atypical histories are common, and tarry stools from bleeding may be a presenting symptom. Complications include intractable pain, perforation into the peritoneal cavity or penetration into an adjacent organ, hemorrhage, pyloric obstruction, as well as the risk of developing cancer noted previously. Not more than 2 per cent of ulcers perforate, but this is a most dangerous complication, accounting for 65 to 85 per cent of all ulcer deaths.[3]

The cause of peptic ulcer is generally considered to be the action of highly acid gastric juice on mucosa that has somehow lost the normal defense mechanisms which resist the very potent digestive action exerted by gastric juice on all types of living tissue.[1, 3] Normal gastric juice contains hydrochloric acid in concentrations up to 0.1N, or about one million times the acidity of both extracellular and intracellular fluid. Hypersecretion of acid gastric juice, and presence of the hormone gastrin undoubtedly play a part in both gastric and duodenal ulcer.[2, 4] Contributory factors include psychosomatic, genetic and endocrine ones, association with certain chronic diseases such as rheumatoid arthritis, cirrhosis of the liver, chronic pancreatitis, the use of drugs such as salicylates and steroids, and acute stress, as from surgical operations, burns, severe sepsis or myocardial infarction. Stress-induced ulcers were found to have an acute mortality of 57 per cent in a Mayo Clinic series.[5] Another type of ulcer with a high mortality occurs in association with certain islet cell tumors of the pancreas (Zollinger-Ellison syndrome).[2]

Epidemiology of Peptic Ulcer Disease. Peptic ulcers are found throughout the world, in all races and at all ages. Although rare in young children they have been diagnosed even in the newborn.[1] The peak incidence of duodenal ulcer is in the 35 to 45 year age group, while gastric ulcers occur most frequently in those age 45 to 55 years.[2] A study of Metropolitan Life Insurance Company employees demonstrated an average annual incidence of disability due to ulcers and other diseases of the stomach to be 5.3 per 1000 for men and 3.5 per 1000 for women.[6] It is estimated that approximately 10 to 15 per cent of the population is afflicted with a peptic ulcer during the course of a lifetime.[1, 2, 3]

Advances in surgical technique have undoubtedly had an impact on the overall mortality and morbidity in peptic ulcer disease in recent years. The generally preferred type of operation today is a combination of one of several types of vagotomy with pyloroplasty or distal gastric resection. This type of operation appears to be more effective than the previous subtotal gastrectomy in reducing gastric secretion, improving gastric emptying, and preventing recurrence and undesirable postoperative consequences.[8, 9] Surgery is ordinarily reserved for the more severe peptic ulcer case, with

TABLE 13-1

Numbers of Deaths in the U.S. — 1970
Digestive System

Hazard	Deaths in U.S. Number	% in Category		Follow-up Data
Peptic Ulcer Disease	9,346		(12.4%)	
Gastric Ulcer	3,502	(4.6%)		§504-§507, §599
Duodenal Ulcer	3,916	(5.2)		§510-§512, §599
Other Peptic Ulcer	1,928	(2.6)		§501-§503, §599
Esophagus, Stomach and Duodenum	2,349		(3.1%)	
Disorders of Esophagus	1,082	(1.4%)		—
Gastritis and Duodenitis	568	(0.8)		§520
Other Stomach and Duodenal	699	(0.9)		—
Intestines, Colon and Rectum	13,796		(18.3%)	
Ulcerative Colitis	786	(1.0%)		§530-§534
Chronic Enteritis, Gastroenteritis	424	(0.6)		—
Intestinal Obstructions	4,322	(5.7)		—
Appendicitis	1,397	(1.9)		—
Peritonitis	1,038	(1.4)		—
Congenital-Intestines, Colon, Rectum	411	(0.5)		—
Diseases of the Rectum	309	(0.4)		§599
Other Intestinal Diseases	5,109	(6.8)		§599
Liver, Gallbladder and Pancreas	43,163		(57.2%)	
Cirrhosis of the Liver	31,399	(41.6%)		§550
Other Liver	2,918	(3.9)		—
Cholelithiasis	2,313	(3.1)		§551
Cholecystitis and Cholangitis	1,660	(2.2)		§599
Cholecystectomy	**	—		§551
Other Gallbladder Diseases	1,446	(1.9)		—
Diseases of the Pancreas	3,179	(4.2)		—
Congenital—Liver, Gallbladder, Pancreas	248	(0.3)		—
Other Gastro-intestinal	6,741		(9.0%)	
Hernia	2,913	(3.9%)		§570, §599
Diverticula of Intestine and Meckel's	3,452	(4.6)		§571, §599
Other Congenital Anomalies	246	(0.3)		—
Dis. of Oral Cavity, Salivary Glands & Jaws	130	(0.2)		—
Total (all listed in Cause of Death Statistics)	75,395 (3.9% of all deaths)			

**Listed elsewhere under separate causes

intractability, obstruction, repeated hemorrhage, and threatened or actual perforation. Most of the mortality is concentrated in those with perforation or severe hemorrhage. Age-adjusted death rates for peptic ulcer increased slightly, from 5.0 in 1950 to 5.4 per 100,000 in 1962.[10] The rate then decreased to 3.6 per 100,000 in 1969. Although part of this downturn is attributable to a change in coding procedures,[10] it is apparent that improved results of the newer surgical procedures are also a factor. Medical management of the less severe cases of peptic ulcer is usually effective on the basis of antacids, anticholinergic drugs, and sedation. Dietary measures are much less emphasized now than formerly. Failure of a gastric ulcer to respond to intensive medical management within a few weeks is an indication for surgery because of the cancer risk. Deaths due to cancer of the stomach arising in a gastric ulcer are exluded from all of the mortality statistics cited above.

Mortality in Peptic Ulcer Disease. Almost all of the experience with peptic ulcer disease reported in this volume has been obtained from studies of life insurance policyholders. These cover a long span of observation: 1935 to 1950 in the *1951*

Impairment Study (§504, §505, §510); 1953 to 1963 in the Prudential Insurance Company of America study (§501, §506); 1947 to 1963 in the data of the Prudential of London (§502); and 1954 to 1971 in the New York Life Single Impairment Study (§507, §512). Overall mortality data in the various categories of peptic ulcer disease, all ages and policy durations combined, have been summarized in Table 13-2. Relatively very little excess mortality was found in unoperated duodenal ulcer, with mortality ratios of 130 and 114 per cent in the two earlier series and a normal mortality in the most recent study by the New York Life Insurance Company. There were 243, 465, and 246 deaths in the respective series, sufficiently large numbers to make the mortality ratios in both of the earlier studies significant at better than the 95 per cent confidence level, even though the ratios are only slightly above the standard expected level of 100 per cent. Somewhat higher mortality ratios, 187 and 160 per cent, were found in the same two earlier series among applicants with a history of duodenal ulcer treated by operation, but again the 1954 to 1970 experience of the New York Life Insurance Company was more favorable with a mortality ratio of only 91 per cent. There did not appear to be any consistent trend in excess death rates by age at issue or policy duration in the individual series of insureds with duodenal ulcer history (§504 to §507). However, the secular trend in mortality has been downward, if results in the three insurance studies can be regarded as comparable.

The reported experience with gastric ulcer is less extensive and somewhat less favorable than the experience with duodenal ulcer just cited: a mortality ratio of 126 per cent among unoperated cases in the *1951 Impairment Study,* and one of 156 per cent in the much more recent New York Life Study of unoperated gastric ulcer. When there was a

TABLE 13-2

Mortality in Peptic Ulcer Disease, Life Insurance Experience Summarized (All Ages and Durations Combined)

Abstract	Type of Ulcer/Period Observed	Ave. Age (Yrs)	Sex	Follow-up (Yrs)	Total No. of Deaths	Mortality Ratio	Excess Death Rate
		$\bar{x}$	%M/%F	Δt	d	100 d/d'	1000(d-d')/E
	Duodenal, No Operation						
§504	1951 Imp. Study 1935-50	38	96/ 4	Ave. 5.0	243	130%	0.9
§506	Prudential Am. 1952-65	36	100/ 0	1-13	465	114	0.3
§507	N.Y. Life 1954-71	38	92/ 8	1-17	246	101	0.0
	Duodenal, With Operation						
§505	1951 Imp. Study 1935-50	40	96/ 4	Ave. 6.0	261	187	3.5
§506	Prudential Am. 1952-65	40	100/ 0	1-13	186	160	2.0
§507	N.Y. Life 1954-71	42	100/ 0	1-17	60	91	−0.4
	Gastric, No Operation						
§510	1951 Imp. Study 1935-50	37	94/ 6	Ave. 3.7	79	126	0.8
§512	N.Y. Life 1954-71	38	85/15	1-17	45	156	2.2
	Gastric, With Operation						
§511	1951 Imp. Study 1935-50	39	96/ 4	Ave. 6.2	174	201	4.1
§512	N.Y. Life 1954-71	43	87/13	1-17	38	205	6.9
	Peptic Ulcer, No Operation						
§501	Prudential Am. 1952-65	36	100/ 0	1-13	99	156	1.2
§502	Prudential London 1947-63	43	100/ 0	1-16	229	121	0.8
	Peptic Ulcer, With Operation						
§502	Prudential London 1947-63	45	100/ 0	1-16	231	140	1.9

For additional details of the various series, consult the abstracts.

history of operation for gastric ulcer the mortality ratios were almost identical, 200 and 205 per cent, respectively. Un-operated cases in the *1951 Impairment Study* showed the highest mortality ratio, 230 per cent, in the first two years of policy duration (Table 510a); the highest mortality ratio (215 per cent) was also experienced in this interval among New York Life insureds (Table 512a). There was no consistent age trend in the unoperated cases in either series, but in those with operation EDRs were highest, over 6 per 1000, among applicants age 40 and up in the *1951 Impairment Study* (Table 511c), and were higher in the older New York Life applicants: almost 10 per 1000 for those age 50 to 59 years, and 32 per 1000 for those age 60 up, although the latter rate was based on only eight deaths (Table 512c). The New York Life applicants, with all ages combined, showed an excess death rate from cancer of 2.3 per 1000 among the operated cases of gastric ulcer, in contrast to a rate of only 0.8 per 1000 among the unoperated. However, in both groups more excess deaths were attributed to diseases of the heart and circulatory system than to any other cause of death, including cancer.

Additional data from life insurance sources are given in abstracts §501 and §502 on peptic ulcer. It may reasonably be assumed that this experience represents a mixture of duodenal and gastric ulcer, weighted in favor of the former type. Again, the mortality experience was relatively favorable, with mortality ratio of 156 per cent, among male applicants with no history of operation insured by the Prudential Insurance Company of America (Table 13-2). Mortality ratios were slightly higher, at or close to 175 per cent, when the last episode of activity of the ulcer was less than five years prior to application, and lower, 122 per cent, when the interval was five to ten years (Table 501b), with no real trend by age or duration. The applicants insured by the Prudential Assurance Company of London, England were classified according to duration of history (short or long), history of operation and history of complications. A normal mortality was experienced by those with a short history and no operation (Table 502), thus resembling the unoperated duodenal ulcer cases previously described. A definitely increased mortality was observed in two operated groups, those with a short history (mortality ratio 165 per cent) and those with a long history and complications (mortality ratio 162 per cent). Intermediate ratios, 123 to 138 per cent, were found in the other groups. All of this experience in peptic ulcer is closer to the duodenal ulcer results described above than it is to gastric ulcer, a result that could have been anticipated, given a preponderance of duodenal ulcer cases. Additional confirmation is suggested by the normal mortality experienced by the Sverige Reinsurance Company on residents of Western Europe with a history of gastric or duodenal ulcer (Table 599). If a select standard insured mortality had been used instead of population tables, the mortality ratio in this experience might well have been of the order of 150 per cent or more, similar to the results cited above.

The only data of a different type are those reported by Sultz et al. from a follow-up of 106 children with peptic ulcer disease, in 90 of whom the ulcer was duodenal in location. Comparative mortality was extremely high, with a ratio of 3,100 per cent and excess death rate of 15 per 1000, excluding both entrants and exposures beyond age 15 (Table 503). All of the five deaths occurred within one year of diagnosis. These figures reflect both the severity of peptic ulcer disease in childhood and the extremely low mortality levels in the general population under age 16.

Esophagus, Stomach and Duodenum

Diseases of the duodenum are grouped with diseases of the stomach in this chapter because they are more closely related to them than to diseases of the distal part of the intestinal tract (peptic ulcer disease, previously discussed, is a noteworthy example of this relationship). Diseases of these organs, the upper portion of the gastrointestinal tract, produce a variety of functional disturbances and interrelated symptoms such as dysphagia (difficulty in swallowing), flatulence, belching, heartburn, dyspepsia (epigastric discomfort following meals), hunger pains, other types of retrosternal or epigastric pain, nausea, and vomiting. Mild degrees of many of these symptoms are extremely common. Treatment by the physician or self-treatment by the patient is more often than not carried out for symptomatic relief, on an empirical basis, without benefit of X-rays or other special tests directed to a specific diagnosis. Among the disorders likely to be encountered are esophagitis, spasm, and ulceration in the esophagus; hiatus or diaphragmatic hernia (X-ray evidence of this displacement of the upper end of the stomach is a common finding, and the evaluation of its significance may be difficult); acute gastritis, various forms of chronic gastritis, and functional dyspepsia in the stomach; peptic ulcer in the stomach or duodenum, pylorospasm, and duodenitis. The various diseases of the esophagus, stomach, and duodenum are described in standard textbooks.[1, 2, 3] Two recent reviews of the physiology of the upper gastrointestinal tract are those of Hansky[4] on the stomach and Pope[11] on the esophagus.

The generally limited mortality data on diseases or symptoms in this category are all from life insurance sources (§520, §599). The New York Life experience on applicants having a medical history coded as dyspepsia, indigestion, or gastritis showed a mortality ratio of 86 per cent among male applicants issued standard insurance, and a ratio of 135 per cent for substandard issues (Table 520c). With males and females combined the excess mortality in the standard issue cases was entirely concentrated in the first five years of policy issue, whereas very little excess mortality was encountered during this period in the substandard issues (Table 520a). Mortality experience of this type, in which the chief presenting symptom is epigastric pain, may be compared with the mortality ratios in nonspecific chest pain, which were found in applicants insured by The Lincoln National Life Insurance Company to lie in the range from 110 to 198 per cent (Table 305b). Undoubtedly some adults, especially males age 40 and up, "diagnosed" as gastritis or dyspepsia, may have atypical angina pectoris as their true diagnosis, but thorough clinical evaluation is often not feasible. The New York Life five-year mortality ratio of 157 per cent among applicants issued standard insurance despite a history of indigestion (Table 520a), suggests this possibility, but unfortunately no details were reported on the distribution of causes in the 20 deaths. There was no excess cardiovascular mortality in the substandard issues (Table 520d).

In Table 599 mortality ratios of 245 per cent were reported by the New York Life in applicants with a diagnostic code for pylorospasm, and 121 per cent in those with duodenitis. Although there were only seven death claims in the pylorospasm group, the excess mortality was significant at a 94 per cent confidence level, not quite attaining the 95 per cent level. Two rather large groups of insureds with dyspepsia, reported by the Prudential of London, showed a mortality ratio of 142 per cent in those classified as "chronic, (peptic ulcer suspected)," but a virtually normal ratio of 108 per cent in all others. These results were on male applicants. The mortality ratio for a small group of females with dyspepsia was 152 per cent. Finally, a normal mortality, with a ratio of 97 per cent, was experienced among New York Life applicants with a history of diaphragmatic hernia. There is no information as to the proportion of cases diagnosed by X-ray or the severity of the symptoms. Although clinicians are impressed with the hazards of complications and operation in severe cases of diaphragmatic hernia, significantly increased mortality is not found among applicants who are actually issued insurance.

Intestines, Colon, and Rectum

The reader will find a number of diseases of the "Intestines, Colon and Rectum" listed in Table 13-1, but apart from ulcerative colitis, for which there are five separate abstracts (§530-§534), only a few of these have limited mortality data in §599. Numbers of deaths for the categories shown range from 309 (diseases of the rectum) to 4,322 for intestinal obstruction, which may have a variety of causes, including peritonitis and appendicitis (over 1000 deaths apiece on their direct account). The total number of deaths during 1970 was about 14,000, 18 per cent of the total for all gastrointestinal diseases, and somewhat greater than the deaths attributed to diseases of the esophagus, stomach and duodenum, including peptic ulcer disease. Most of the discussion in this part of the chapter will focus on ulcerative colitis.

Ulcerative Colitis. Chronic nonspecific ulcerative colitis may be defined as a disorder characterized by an inflammatory reaction involving the mucosa and submucosa of the colon or rectum, not ascribable to invasion of these tissues by identifiable pathogenic organisms.[2] It has some similarities to Crohn's disease, or regional enteritis (regional ileitis), which is a granulomatous response of the sumucosa of the small intestine to an unknown agent or agents.[2] Prior to 1950 it was believed that chronic ulcerative colitis was limited to the colon and regional enteritis to the small intestine. It is now known that regional enteritis can involve the colon, in which case it is called granulomatous colitis or Crohn's disease of the colon.[2, 12] Ileocolitis is the term used to designate the extension of regional ileitis into the proximal colon, while "backwash ileitis," a poor term, describes the uncommon backward extension of chronic ulcerative colitis into the terminal ileum.[12]

Ulcerative colitis is a disease characterized by multiple attacks with serious local and systemic manifestations, including bleeding, diarrhea, abdominal pain, anorexia, weakness, fever, and profound debility. Both symptoms and findings are highly variable. The rectum is usually involved, and the disease seems to run a milder course when it is confined to the rectum and sigmoid colon. Complications include severe anemia, rectal abscess, perforation of the colon with abscess formation or peritonitis, stricture and fistula (more common in granulomatous colitis), intractability, occasionally rheumatoid arthritis and other systemic manifestations, and a strong tendency to develop cancer of the colon. Medical treatment, with steroids, azosulfidine, and supportive measures is rarely curative but may produce partial or complete remission in many patients.[12] When surgery is necessary, the procedure of choice is total colectomy with a permanent ileostomy.

Ulcerative colitis is found throughout the world. It affects both sexes about equally and occurs at all ages, although the Mayo Clinic patients were mostly under age 50 (§530). The mortality rate of all types of enteritis and diarrhea is 1.1 per 100,000, according to recent data for the United States,[7] and this includes the rate for ulcerative colitis of 0.5 per 100,000. The average annual incidence of disability due to diarrhea and enteritis among Metropolitan Life Insurance Company employees was found to be 1.8 per 1000 for men and 6.3 per 1000 for women. A major fraction of long-term disability may be presumed to consist of ulcerative colitis and regional ileitis, which occur in the ratio of about five to one in the United States.[2, 12]

Prognosis in Ulcerative Colitis. From the foregoing description of the disease it is evident that ulcerative colitis is a very serious affliction with considerable morbidity, and it is not surprising that it is also associated with a greatly increased mortality. Several reports from the Mayo Clinic present a detailed analysis of hospitalized patients with ulcerative colitis confirmed by X-rays or proctoscopic examination, including admissions as far back as 1918 and as recently as 1959. The overall experience on admissions from 1918 through 1937 is presented in abstract §530 with follow-up data for a minimum of 10 years and a maximum of 20 years. A special study was made of 178 patients with ulcerative colitis, followed between 1918 and 1958, who subsequently developed cancer of the colon (§531). Another study of 427 children with ulcerative colitis under age 15 included follow-up through 1960 (§533). Edwards and Truelove have described results with their series of 624 patients seen in Oxford, England, from 1938 to 1962, with a minimum of one year of follow-up (§532). This series includes outpatients as well as those hospitalized, and entry started some 20 years later than in the Mayo Clinic material. A still more recent series of a different type consists of applicants with a history of ulcerative colitis issued insurance by the New York Life Insurance Company 1954 to 1970 (§534).

As might be anticipated, excess death rates were highest in the first year or two after hospital diagnosis or insurance application: 85 per 1000 in the total Mayo Clinic series of 2,000 patients, during the first year (Table 530a); a smaller first-year rate of 33 per 1000 in patients under age 50 (Table 530c); a rate of 62 per 1000 in the English patients (Table 532a); rates of 59 per 1000 in the Mayo Clinic children (Table 533a) and 109 per 1000 in Mayo Clinic patients who developed cancer of the colon after diagnosis of ulcerative colitis (Table 531a); and a rate of only 4.2 per 1000 during the first two policy years of the New York Life Study (Table 534a). In the study of Edwards and Truelove deaths among relapse cases during hospitalization (intraattack mortality) were analyzed and annual rates of mortality were found to range between 9 and 258 per 1000, increasing with clinical severity, extent of involvement of the colon and age of the patient (Table 532c). The single exception occurred in ulcerative colitis localized in the rectum or sigmoid, with no deaths in 61 attacks. When the ulcerative colitis was confined to the rectum and sigmoid no short-term deaths occurred in 55 patients. Average intraattack mortality decreased from 106 per 1000 in 1938-1952, to 47 per 1000 in 1952-1962, when cortisone and better supportive therapy were available.

Excess death rates fell considerably after the first year in the clinical series. The five-year experience of the total Mayo Clinic group produced an EDR of 38 per 1000 and mortality ratio of 625 per cent, and the ten-year experience an EDR of 26 per 1000 and mortality ratio of 415 per cent. Excluding the first-year mortality, the Mayo Clinic patients were found to have excess death rates of 16 per 1000 in the total group (Table 530a), 14 per 1000 in patients under age 50 (Table 530c), 20 per 1000 in children (Table 533a), and 37 per 1000 in those with complicating colonic cancer (Table 531a). In the English series EDR from 1-20 years was 12 per 1000, slightly lower than in the Mayo Clinic patients of all ages followed for the same length of time (Table 532a). There was not much decrease in EDR with duration in the New York Life Study (Table 534a). The low average EDR of 3.9 per 1000, all ages and durations combined, reflects the less severe disease in those issued insurance, as applicants with complications, active or severe disease, would probably have been declined.

Table 530b presents ten-year comparative experience by age at first examination of the 2000 patients in the Mayo Clinic series. Excess death rates were highest, 30 to 34 per 1000, in the young patients under age 20 and in the oldest patients age 60 and up. In the patients with decennial age groups from 20 to 59 years the EDRs averaged 23 to 29 per 1000, except in one group (40 to 49 years), in which the lowest EDR of 16 per 1000 occurred. As indicated previously, the excess death rate for all ages combined was lower with a follow-up of ten years than with a shorter follow-up of five years. Mortality experience by age was not given in the English patients except for the intraattack mortality. In the New York Life series applicants age 40 up had an EDR of 6.7 per 1000 and those under age 40 a lower rate, 2.9 per 1000 (Table 534c). The 20-year follow-up of the children under 15 years of age in the Mayo Clinic patients yielded an average EDR of 24 per 1000; the mortality ratio of 2600 per cent is what might be expected in a juvenile group with such an excess death rate.

The distribution of cases and deaths in the Mayo Clinic patients who developed cancer of the colon is of interest (§531). Cancer deaths occurred in 25 of 225 patients diagnosed as having ulcerative colitis under age 20, whereas less than 0.1 of a cancer death was expected (Table 531d). Since cancer of the colon has a very low incidence in the general population under age 30, these figures underscore the cancer risk for young patients with ulcerative colitis. With respect to onset of symptoms less than 5 per cent of the cases developed cancer within five years, but the incidence rose to more than 37 per cent if the five-year interval was measured from the date of diagnosis (Table 531c). Further evidence on the risk of cancer in juvenile ulcerative colitis is given in Table 533c, which shows that 40 of 112 deaths among these children were due to cancer of the colon. Seven of the cancer deaths occurred within 5 to 10 years of diagnosis, and the others at various later intervals up to 35 years. Slightly over half the deaths were due to causes directly related to ulcerative colitis, other than cancer. Only six of the 112 deaths were due to unrelated causes, and in nine the cause of death was not known.

It should be pointed out that most of the extensive experience in the Mayo Clinic series was accumulated prior to 1950. Somwhat lower mortality levels undoubtedly prevail today. There is evidence of such improvement in the short-term mortality reported by Edwards and Truelove (Table 532c, later vs. earlier entry period).

Other Diseases of the Intestines, Colon and Rectum. No mortality data were found for regional enteritis, which was mentioned in connection with ulcerative colitis. In Table 599 one group of applicants with a history of amebic dysentery, insured by the Prudential of London, showed a normal mortality (ratio 107 per cent), and another group with fistula in ano, a mortality ratio of 143 per cent. Gastrointestinal bleeding without specific diagnosis was found to have a mortality ratio of 210 per cent among those insured by the New York Life, and a residual category of "other diseases of the intestine" showed a mortality ratio of 255 per cent, based on only seven deaths. The numbers of deaths in the other above-mentioned diseases ranged from 11 to 30.

Liver, Gallbladder, and Pancreas

As shown in Table 13-1, deaths due to diseases in this category constituted over 57 per cent of all digestive system deaths in the United States during 1970. Cirrhosis of the liver alone accounted for 31,399 deaths, or almost 42 per cent of all digestive system deaths. Four per cent were attributed to other diseases of the liver, 7 per cent to gallbladder diseases and 4 per cent to pancreatic disorders, with a very small fraction to congenital diseases of these organs.

Because of its epidemiological importance, some background description will be given for cirrhosis of the liver. With a death rate of 16 per 100,000 population cirrhosis ranks eighth among the leading causes of death in the United States.[7] Evidence of cirrhosis is found in the liver in approximately 2 to 3 per cent of routine autopsies in the United States and in 2 to 10 per cent of autopsies in the Orient, Near East, and South Africa.[1] It occurs most often in the age group 45 to 65 years, and is more frequent in men than in women.[1]

The predominant pathological type of cirrhosis is known as Laennec's cirrhosis and is characterized by a fine, diffuse fibrosis of the liver with degeneration of functioning hepatic cells.[2] Alcoholism appears to be the principal causative factor in cirrhosis of the liver, as there is a history of chronic alcoholism in over 50 per cent. Another potential factor is a history of prior hepatitis which is recorded in about 10 per cent of cases of cirrhosis.[1] Fatty liver is found in about 90 per cent of liver biopsies made in chronic alcoholics,[13] whereas cirrhosis is found in only 30 per cent.[14] However, it appears that fatty liver progresses to a state of chronic hepatitis and ultimately to Laennec's cirrhosis in a high proportion of alcoholics. These relationships are extensively discussed in the medical literature, including some recent reviews.[13, 14, 15] The high incidence of cirrhosis as a cause of death is given in some of the abstracts dealing with alcoholism (§1-§6). Serious complications of cirrhosis of the liver in its advanced form include ascites (collection of fluid in the abdomen), esophageal varices which may lead to fatal hemorrhage, jaundice, and hepatic failure, which is inevitably fatal. Low grade cirrhosis, however, may remain nonprogressive for many years in some patients, with very little in the way of signs or symptoms.

Mortality in Cirrhosis of the Liver. There is no experience available from insured groups with a history of cirrhosis of the liver. An applicant with a definite diagnosis of this chronic disorder is generally considered uninsurable. However, Powell and Klatskin have reported on a group of 283 patients followed at the Liver Study Unit of the Yale-New Haven Hospital 1951 to 1963 (§550). Patients were divided into follow-up groups according to their resumption of alcohol or abstention from alcohol after initial diagnostic evaluation, and according to the presence or history of jaundice, ascites or hematemesis (vomiting blood from esophageal varices). In all of these patients the diagnosis of Laennec's cirrhosis was documented histologically by liver biopsy.

In the six months after the first visit to the clinic, mortality was extremely high, 350 to 375 extra deaths per 1000 per year in the two main follow-up groups (Table 550a). However, mortality fell substantially at 6-12 months, and again in the period from 1-5 years after first clinic visit. The excess death rate in the latter period averaged 127 per 1000 among those who continued to use alcohol, with a mortality ratio of 1,400 per cent. The prognosis was relatively much improved in those who stopped the use of alcohol with EDR only 24 per 1000 and a mortality ratio of 275 per cent. From the initial point of entry, the cumulative five-year survival ratio was 67.6 per cent in those who refrained from alcohol and 42.6 per cent in those who did not (Table 550c).

Mortality was also lower and survival better in the absence of jaundice, ascites, or hematemesis as compared to the situation in which one or more of these conditions was present. Even in patients continuing their alchoholic intake, those who were free of these complications had an aggregate EDR of 57 per 1000 per year and a mortality ratio of 680

148

per cent (Table 550c) after the first year. Excess death rates from 1-5 years averaged 150 per 1000 in those with jaundice, 155 per 1000 in those with ascites, 227 per 1000 in those with hematemesis, and 151 per 1000 in those with any one or a combination of these findings. There were only nine patients free of these findings among the patients who discontinued the use of alcohol, and no deaths occurred from 1-5 years after entry, with 0.41 deaths expected. However, the prognosis was better in the patients with any of these findings than it was in patients without them who nevertheless continued to use alcohol: the aggregate EDR was only 31 per 1000 per year and the mortality ratio 315 per cent (Table 550e). In the group of patients who discontinued alcohol the highest mortality was found in those with hematemesis, with EDR of 84 per 1000 and mortality ratio 680 per cent (Table 550e).

The wide variation in mortality in cirrhosis is thus seen to depend on whether or not the patient discontinues use of alcohol, on severity as judged by signs of certain complications, and on duration of follow-up after diagnosis.

Mortality in Other Diseases of the Liver, Gallbladder, and Pancreas. In Table 599 there is a limited experience reported by the New York Life Insurance Company for applicants insured despite a history of past jaundice or "other diseases" of the liver. The mortality ratio of 265 per cent is based on 13 deaths. The codes used for this group exclude gallbladder disease not listed elsewhere, cholelithiasis, cholecystectomy, cholecystotomy, and cholecystitis. A history of infectious hepatitis was specifically included.

Some additional experience of the New York Life Insurance Company in gallbladder disease is shown in §551. Most cases of acute cholecystitis are associated with a stone in the cystic duct and therefore with gallbladder colic.[2] Gallstones (cholelithiasis) constitute a major health problem in the United States, with an estimated prevalence of 20 million cases.[16] The incidence increases with age and is especially high in women over age 45.[16] The average annual incidence of disability due to all forms of gallbladder disease has been reported to be 1.9 per 1000 for men and 2.7 per 1000 for women.[6] Despite the prevalence of gallbladder disease in the general population, the New York Life experience is of modest proportions, as there were only 30 deaths among those with a history of gallbladder colic and 19 deaths among those with a history of cholecystectomy. The mortality was normal, with a ratio under 100 per cent in both men and women with a history of previous cholecystectomy (Table 551a). In those with gallbladder colic but no operation the mortality ratio was 129 per cent among female insureds and 159 per cent among males (Table 551a). Excess death rates averaged 4.1 per 1000 in men, showed no change with policy duration, and an apparent marked increase from 2.0 to 41 per 1000 for men under age 60 against those age 60 and up. Although there were only six deaths in the men age 60 up, the mortality ratio of 325 per cent was significantly increased above the expected normal 100 per cent, at the 95 per cent confidence level. Excess mortality in the gallbladder colic series, male and female combined, was concentrated in deaths due to cancer and cardiovascular diseases (Table 551d). It is possible that atypical pain due to coronary heart disease may have received a clinical diagnosis of gallbladder colic in some of these cases.

Some additional experience of the New York Life Insurance Company is shown in Table 599 for a group classified as cholecystitis rather than gallbladder colic. The mortality ratio of 220 per cent, based on 13 deaths, was significantly elevated at the 98 per cent confidence level. The experience of the Prudential Assurance Company of London on men insured with a history of cholecystitis and operation showed a mortality ratio of 139 per cent (Table 599). The mortality experienced among women with cholecystitis was normal.

The only mortality data available on pancreatic diseases are those of the New York Life Insurance Company, with a significantly elevated mortality ratio of 320 per cent (98 per cent confidence level despite only nine deaths). Chronic or recurrent pancreatitis is a serious disease that entails considerable morbidity and mortality risk.[1] The proportion of such cases in the life insurance series is not known.

Other Gastrointestinal Diseases

Hernia. The most frequent type of abdominal hernia is inguinal, in which an intraabdominal structure such as omentum or small intestine protrudes through a weakened portion of the abdominal wall into the inguinal canal. Femoral hernias and ventral hernias (the latter usually the result of a surgical scar or injury) are less frequent types. Diaphragmatic or hiatus hernias have been discussed under "Diseases of the Esophagus and Stomach," and are excluded from consideration here. Slightly under 3,000 deaths were attributed to hernias in the United States during 1970 (Table 13-1), but many intestinal obstruction deaths (classified elsewhere in Table 13-1) were undoubtedly caused by strangulated hernias. The disorder is a very common one, especially in males, and operative repair of an inguinal or femoral hernia (herniorrhaphy) is also a common operation. Disability due to hernia is reported with an incidence of 4.6 per 1000 for men and 0.9 per 1000 for women.[6] The benefit of surgical repair consists in elimination of the risk of complications (strangulation or intestinal obstruction, requiring potentially high risk emergency surgical procedures), as well as elimination of discomfort and restricted activity. However, hernias sometimes recur following operation.

The experience of the New York Life Insurance Company includes all types of hernia except diaphragmatic. Undoubtedly most of these were cases of inguinal hernia. For men issued standard insurance a normal mortality was experienced, and among those issued substandard insurance the mortality ratio of 142 per cent, based on 17 deaths, was not significantly elevated (Table 570c). With these overall results, numbers of deaths are too small to justify comment with respect to duration, age, or cause of death in the substandard cases. An even smaller but more recent experience with nondiaphragmatic hernia was reported by the New York Life to show a normal mortality ratio, under 100 per cent (Table 599). Another small group with hernia issued insurance by the Prudential Life Assurance Company of London showed a slightly but not significantly elevated mortality ratio of 128 per cent. On an overall basis it is fair to say that any extra mortality risk associated with existence of an inguinal hernia must be very slight, at least among those accepted for life insurance.

Diverticulum of the Intestinal Tract. Saccular outpouchings of the colon are very common and are reported to occur in 10 per cent of persons over age 50.[1, 2] Diverticula may also occur in the small intestine or even the stomach, but are much less common than in the colon. Intestinal diverticulosis is usually asymptomatic. However, sometimes infections can occur (diverticulitis), possible complications of which are obstruction, perforation, abscess or fistula formation, and peritonitis.

A group of men with intestinal diverticulum and issued substandard insurance is reported in §571 by the New York Life Insurance Company. The mortality ratio of 179 per cent, all ages combined, in Table 571c is highly significant at the 99 per cent confidence level. Although the highest excess death rates were found in the oldest and longest duration groups, the numbers of deaths in subdivided categories were too small to establish a significant trend. Most of the excess mortality was attributed to deaths due to cancer and cardiovascular disease. This same experience with male insureds is combined with female cases and divided into two groups for displaying in Table 599. There was more exposure in cases classified as "Other" than in those classified as diverticulum of the colon. The mortality ratio for diverticulum of the colon was 148 per cent, not a significant elevation. However, the mortality ratio of 179 per cent for other intestinal diverticula was significantly elevated at the 95 per cent confidence level even though based on only 19 deaths. It would appear likely that excess mortality might develop at significant levels also for diverticula of the colon with larger exposures and numbers of deaths.

Other Diseases. Table 599 contains limited mortality data on a number of digestive tract diseases, most of which have been presented in the foregoing sections. The only group remaining is a miscellaneous one categorized as "Other Diseases of the Digestive Organs." These data were also collected by the New York Life Insurance Company and include only substandard issues. On the basis of 13 observed deaths the mortality ratio of 340 per cent was significantly elevated at better than the 99 per cent confidence level. This was the highest level of excess mortality recorded in Table 599. There is no information available as to the diagnoses included in this heterogeneous group.

References

1. P.B. Beeson and W. McDermott, eds., *Cecil and Loeb Textbook of Medicine,* 14th ed. Philadelphia: W.B. Saunders Company (1975).

2. *Harrison's Principles of Internal Medicine,* 7th ed. New York: McGraw-Hill Book Company (1974).

3. W.A. Sodeman, Jr. and W.A. Sodeman, eds., *Pathologic Physiology. Mechanisms of Disease,* 5th ed. Philadelphia: W.B. Saunders Company (1974).

4. J. Hansky, "Clinical Aspects of Gastrin Physiology." *Med. Clin. North Am.,* 58:1217-1230 (1974).

5. E. David, D.C. McIlrath, and J.A. Higgins, "Clinical Experience with Acute Peptic Gastrointestinal Ulcers." *Mayo Clin. Proc.,* 46:15-24 (1971).

6. "Disability from Diseases of the Digestive System." *Stat. Bull. Metropol. Life Ins. Co.,* 48:10-12 (April 1967).

7. National Center for Health Statistics, *Monthly Vital Statistics Report,* Vol. 24, No. 1 (March 27, 1975).

8. T. Kennedy, "The Vagus and the Consequences of Vagotomy." *Med. Clin. North Am.,* 58:1231-1246 (1974).

9. W. Silen, "Consequences of Gastric Resection and Vagotomy." *Mayo Clin. Proc.,* 48:653-655 (1973).

10. Dept. of Health, Education, and Welfare, *Mortality Trends of Leading Causes of Death, U.S. 1950–69.* Vital and Health Statistics, Series 20, No. 16. Rockville, Md.: National Center for Health Statistics (1974).

11. C.E. Pope, II, "Esophageal Physiology." *Med. Clin. North Am.,* 58:1181-1199 (1974).

12. R.A. Albacete, "Nonspecific Inflammatory Diseases of the Intestines." *Med. Clin. North Am.,* 52:1387-1396 (1968).

150

13. C.S. Lieber, "Liver Disease and Alcohol: Fatty Liver, Alcoholic Hepatitis, Cirrhosis, and their Interrelationships." *Ann. N.Y. Acad. Sci.*, 252:63-84 (1975).

14. C.M. Leevy, "Cirrhosis in Alcoholics." *Med. Clin. North Am.*, 52:1445-1455 (1968).

15. W.K. Lelbach, "Cirrhosis in the Alcoholic and Its Relation to the Volume of Alcohol Abuse." *Ann. N.Y. Acad. Sci.*, 252:85-105 (1975).

16. L. Swell, and D.H. Gregory, and Z.R. Vlahcevic, "Current Concepts of the Pathogenesis of Cholesterol Gallstones." *Med. Clin. North Am.*, 58:1449-1471 (1974).

14 Genitourinary Diseases

Jerzy Gajewski, M.D., Ph.D., Cesar I. Gonzales, M.D., and Michael Rich, F.S.A.

Prior to a discussion of the epidemiology of genitourinary diseases and their importance in clinical medicine and public health, it may be well to review very briefly the structure and function of the kidneys in order to show how these are affected by different diseases of the urinary tract.

The two kidneys are relatively small organs, located one on each side of the lower part of the back, and weighing only about 250 grams apiece. Despite their small size, the kidneys are remarkable for the magnitude of their blood flow. The normal individual at rest passes over 20 per cent of the total cardiac output through the renal arteries to the kidneys, the main function of which is to eliminate water and waste from the blood as well as to retain some valuable components. The kidney also serves as a regulator in maintaining the normal chemical pattern of blood plasma and other body fluids. Urine is produced by the process of filtration from the relatively large amount of blood passing through the kidneys, and then by selective reabsorption and some secretion as the glomerular filtrate travels down. The volume and composition of urine may vary widely according to changes in the intake of water, and of salt, acidic, and basic substances in the body. Normally, the urine contains very little, if any, glucose or proteins, and only a very small number of red cells and white cells. Urinalysis tests for these cells and formed elements as well as certain chemical substances. Abnormalities of these tests provide valuable clues to the presence of urinary tract diseases. For more accurate diagnosis, however, urinalysis must be supplemented by a variety of other tests.

Many of the pathological processes producing kidney disease are inflammatory or degenerative in nature, described in the general term "nephritis." Such processes commonly impair renal function and cause marked changes in the urine as it leaves the kidney, usually in the form of hematuria (red blood cells in the urine), proteinuria (protein in the urine), casts (formed elements from the kidney tubules), or a combination of these. Infections of the kidney are another major type of kidney disease usually called pyelonephritis, and they can often be recognized by the presence of pyuria (white blood cells in abnormal numbers in the urine).

Another important group of urinary tract diseases is characterized by the formation of a stone (calculus) at various levels of the urinary tract. Although the exact cause is not well understood, such stones often represent a combination of systemic abnormalities, such as increased calcium in the blood plasma or uric acid disturbance together with local factors. Urinary stones, when sufficiently large, can cause obstruction preventing urine from being freely excreted, in some instances leading to hydronephrosis (dilated and obstructed kidney) and renal damage.

Congenital abnormalities also contribute significantly to pathology of the genitourinary system. Some abnormalities are benign and compatible with relatively normal life (for example, horseshoe kidney), while others can cause abnormal urine drainage and lead to serious disorder and ultimately to death. When such impaired drainage is complicated by an infection of the kidney, the prognosis is grave. Polycystic kidney disease represents yet another form of congenital abnormality; its significance depends on the extent of the kidney involvement, the tendency to progress, and the presence of hypertension. Generally, this condition carries a poor prognosis leading in more advanced cases to death from renal failure.

Kidneys are also at times a target organ in pathological processes originating elsewhere. Good examples of these are nephrosclerosis in the course of hypertension and renal damage secondary to diabetes. In both instances, proteinuria and appearance of kidney involvement in other tests are poor prognostic signs.

Epidemiology of Genitourinary Diseases

Death caused primarily by genitourinary tract pathology represents a relatively minor part of general mortality. Analysis of major causes of death in 1969[1] indicates that nephritis and nephrosis, the two most significant pathological processes of the kidney, ranked fourteenth among the leading causes of death (4.7 per 100,000). As shown in Table 14-1 genitourinary diseases accounted for over 30,000 deaths in the United States in 1970, approximately 1.5 per cent of all deaths. Most of the kidney disease deaths were due to various forms of nephritis or to pyelonephritis and other types of infection in the kidneys. Hypertrophy and other disorders of the prostate were by far the predominant category of death under "Male Genital Disorders." Complications of pregnancy and childbirth were responsible for more than half of the deaths classified under "Female Genital Disorders." Despite the relatively small number of abstracts dealing with genitourinary diseases, results are available in three major categories, including urinary abnormalities without a diagnosis of specific renal

152

disease, kidney stone, and chronic renal failure, treated by kidney transplant or hemodialysis. The deceptively high proportion of other diseases with follow-up results noted in Table 14-1 is related almost entirely to meager data on a variety of genitourinary disorders in a single abstract, §699.

TABLE 14-1

Numbers of Deaths in the U.S. — 1970
Genitourinary Diseases

Hazard	Deaths in U.S.		Follow-up Data
	Number	% in Category	
Urinary Abnormality	**		
Albuminuria	**		§601-§604, §699
Abnormal Sediment	**		§699
Diseases of Kidney and Ureters	24,052	(79.3%)	
Chronic Nephritis	6,399	(21.1%)	§699
All Other Nephritis and Nephrosis	2,478	(8.2)	§699
Chronic Pyelonephritis	4,864	(16.0)	§699
Other Pyelonephritis, Pyelitis	3,052	(10.1)	§699
Urinary Tract Infection Not Listed Elsewhere	1,865	(6.1)	—
Kidney Stone	790	(2.6)	§620, §699
Nephrectomy	**		§699
Kidney Failure	**		—
Kidney Transplant	**		§625
Dialysis	**		§626
Congenital Diseases of Kidneys and Ureters	1,200	(4.0)	—
Other Diseases of the Kidney and Ureters	3,404	(11.2)	§699
Diseases of the Bladder and Urethra (including congenital)	997	(3.3%)	—
Male Genital Disorders	2,876	(9.5%)	
Hypertrophy and Other Disorders of the Prostate	2,679	(8.8%)	§699
Prostatectomy	**		§670
Congenital Anomalies	4	(0.0)	—
Other Male Genital	193	(0.7)	—
Female Genital Disorders	1,511	(4.9%)	—
Diseases of Breast, Ovary and Parametrium	288	(0.9%)	—
Diseases of Uterus and Other Female Genital Organs	405	(1.3)	—
Complications of Pregnancy, Childbirth and the Puerperium	803	(2.7)	—
Caesarean Section	**		§699
Hysterectomy	**		§699
Congenital Anomalies	15	(0.0)	
Other Genitourinary	880	(2.9%)	
Total (all listed in Cause of Death Statistics)	30,316 (1.6% of all deaths)		

**Listed elsewhere under various separate causes

Statistics published by cause of death, which were based on death certificates,[2] provide only a partial picture of genitourinary diseases because of the complexity of human pathology and frequent coexistence of renal abnormalities with other diseases. The contribution of the genitourinary system to total mortality can be illustrated by the fact that in 1967 there were about 20,000 deaths in the United States attributed to nephritis, nephrosis, and kidney infection. When nephritis and nephrosis were combined and specifically analyzed, these conditions caused 11,000 deaths within the United States, which indicated a mortality rate of 5.5 per 100,000 population.[3] A review published in the Metroplitan Statistical Bulletin indicates that the death rate for nephritis and nephrosis declined between 1962 and 1967 among white males and females in the U.S. population; a similar trend prevailed among policyholders of the Metropolitan Life Insurance Company. The mortality rates were consistently higher for males than for females and were higher in the general population than among insured persons. Similarly, the Metropolitan Life Insurance data indicate that there were about 9,000 deaths from infection of the kidney in the general population of the United States in 1967, associated with a mortality rate of 4.6 per 100,000. Again, the death rates were consistently higher for males than females, similar to the experience from nephritis and nephrosis.[3] It has also been estimated that approximately 10,000 new cases of chronic renal failure occur each year in the United States.[4]

Urinary Abnormalities

Urinalysis is a simple procedure and the most valuable method of detecting evidence of urinary tract disease. It consists of an analysis of chemical and microscopic components. The most important tests indicative of abnormal function are as follows:

1. *Proteinuria (albuminuria).* Protein in urine in amounts greater than 10 mg per 100 ml, is usually suggestive of involvement of kidney tissue. When marked, it is indicative of the nephrotic syndrome, frequently associated with a poor prognosis.

2. *Hematuria.* Up to five red cells per high power field are usually considered a normal finding in the urine sediment. Hematuria may be caused by abnormalities at any level of the urinary tract, although sporadically it is seen without any demonstrable pathology. The wide variety of causes makes this particular finding difficult to interpret in terms of prognosis without more extensive studies.

3. *Casts.* These are cylindrical formed elements, extremely infrequent in normal urine. Their significance depends on their contents (proteins, lipids, red cells or white cells).

4. *Pyuria.* White cells up to five per high power field are seen in the urinary sediment of totally healthy subjects. Pyuria, with 20 or more white cells, indicates infection at any level of the urinary tract (or possibly contamination if the specimen is not properly collected in females). Chronic pyelonephritis is an important potential cause that should be evaluated.

5. *Glycosuria.* Glucose, a form of sugar, in amounts in excess of 0.05 gm per 100 ml of urine usually indicates an abnormality of carbohydrate metabolism. Its significance is discussed in connection with diabetes in Chapter 16.

Other methods of evaluating the genitourinary tract include radiological studies (e.g., intravenous and retrograde pyelography), direct examination through the cystoscope, chemical tests in the blood (serum creatinine, blood urea nitrogen—BUN), and many special tests of function. Consistent abnormality in creatinine, BUN or renal function tests indicative of renal failure is associated with a very unfavorable prognosis.

Albuminuria. If the results in abstracts §601–§603 are compared, it will be seen that young insureds under age 30 with small amounts of proteinuria (defined as 10-50 mg per 100 ml) exhibit very little excess mortality, less than 0.2 extra deaths per 1000 per year. This is true for persons issued standard insurance and those issued substandard for whom the amount of proteinuria presumably averaged somewhat higher. The mortality ratio for standard issues was 136 per cent for all ages combined and 159 per cent for those issued substandard. As is evident from Table 603b, excess mortality showed a definite increasing pattern with an increase in the amount of albumin. Coexistence of slight degrees of overweight or blood pressure elevation was associated with an increase in the degrees of excess mortality, as shown by the results in Table 603a for overweight and Table 602a for blood pressure elevation. It should be kept in mind that the degrees of blood pressure elevation as defined in Table 602 are very slight, and start well within the conventional normotensive range.

The finding of proteinuria in apparently healthy young adults without other evidence of renal disease may be diagnosed as orthostatic proteinuria if it totally disappears at night when the subject is recumbent. In cases where no other signs of renal involvement can be detected, orthostatic proteinuria is commonly regarded as a benign condition. In an intensive ten-year follow-up study of 43 young men in whom the diagnosis of orthostatic proteinuria was initially established, no clinical or laboratory evidence of progressive renal disease developed in even a single patient.

From the available insurance studies, it would appear that the risk of extra mortality is minimal in young adults under the age of 30 when the proteinuria does not exceed 50 mg per 100 ml. However, with amounts in excess of 50 mg per 100 ml the risk increases, especially in those over age 30. Even slight amounts of associated overweight or blood pressure elevation are correlated with an increased mortality risk in insurance applicants with proteinuria and no other evidence of renal disease. Excess mortality was also experienced in the recent New York Life Study of insured policyholders with proteinuria but no other ratable urinary or renal impairment found on examination (§604). Excess death rates averaged 2.1 per 1000 in standard issues and 3.5 per 1000 in substandard issues; EDR also tended to increase with age at issue and at the later policy durations. Additional groups with albuminuria reported by the New York Life (Table 699) showed EDRs that increased substantially with the amount of albumin found or in the presence of a history of albuminuria. Persons with albuminuria insured by the Prudential of London were found to have a relatively small increase in mortality (Table 699). This table also contains limited data from the New York Life on abnormalities of the urinary sediment as isolated findings, unaccompanied by proteinuria. Insureds with casts in their sediment showed substantial excess mortality, those with pyuria a modest excess, and those with hematuria, none of significance (Table 699).

Kidney Diseases

Genitourinary Stones. The results presented in Table 620c indicate that the overall excess mortality for unoperated cases is truly minimal with the mortality ratio being 111 per cent. Similar to the situation in the general population, the major cause of death for both operated and unoperated cases was cardiovascular disease; the overall mortality ratio in operated cases was 151 per cent (Table 620d). Additional evidence as to the benign character of renal calculus as a mortality risk in an insured population is contained in the experience of the Prudential of London, with a normal mortality ratio of 88 per cent (Table 699).

Renal Transplantation. Renal transplantation using either cadaver or living related donors has become a widely used method of treatment of chronic renal failure. The data from the Renal Transplant Registry (§625) revealed that 57 per cent of the transplants were performed in patients suffering from chronic glomerulonephritis.[4] Other conditions frequently requiring renal transplantation included chronic pyelonephritis, polycystic disease of the kidney, and nephrosclerosis. The major cause of graft failure, often leading to death, is rejection of the transplant or complications of drug therapy.[6] In case of graft failure a patient's survival following a second graft is less favorable than that following the first graft. The 12th Report of The Human Renal Transplant Registry shows slow but steady improvement with time in the patient survival from a first transplant.[4]

The mortality during the early period after the transplant is clearly a function of the donor source, with transplant from a sibling producing the most favorable mortality and the cadaver source giving the poorest results. Mortality rates were extremely high in the first 90 days after the transplant, ranging from 42 to 315 per 1000 for the quarter (Table 625a). Annual excess death rates decreased but still remained very high in the rest of the first year, with the lowest rate of 51 per 1000 per year found in the youngest age group of patients receiving a transplant from a sibling, and the highest rate of 347 per 1000 found in the oldest patients receiving a cadaver kidney. Excess mortality rates were generally at intermediate levels among patients with transplant from a parent donor, and tended to increase with advancing age, starting with age 20, in all donor classes. Excess death rates of this magnitude were naturally associated with extremely high mortality ratios, up to 32,000 per cent, and survival ratios were as low as 77.3 per cent, extremely low for an interval of only nine months. After this initial period of great risk mortality improved somewhat during the intervals 1-3 and 3-5 years, but excess death rates for patients age 11 and up still did not fall below 22 per 1000, at best. In these intervals young children with kidney donated by a parent showed the lowests EDRs, under 20 per 1000, but based on only 3 deaths, while those receiving cadaver transplants had the worst experience, with an EDR of 171 per 1000 and mortality ratio of 38,000 per cent. One note of encouragement is the observation that excess mortality has shown a steady improvement since 1951, but mortality ratios still exceeded 2,000 per cent during the latest period 1970-71. Recent analysis of long-term results of transplantation indicates that the three most common late complications include accelerated atherosclerosis, malignancy, and nephrotic syndrome.[4,7,8]

Hemodialysis. During the 1960s a new treatment became available providing substitution for kidney function by various specially constructed machines. While originally designed to provide short-term support in acute renal failure the procedure can also be utilized on a more permanent basis for chronic renal disease. Data supplied by the National Dialysis Registry in the United States indicate that excess mortality among those on long-term hemodialysis is very high for both sexes in all age groups, and decreases as the age and duration of treatment increase (§626). Extensive experience reported for a total follow-up of four years shows an increase in excess death rates with advancing age, from a minimum average of 83 to a maximum of 169 per 1000, a decrease with length of time on dialysis, and little difference between males and females (Tables 626a and 626b). Results on a combination of age and duration for dialysis patients in Table 626c may be compared with the corresponding results after renal transplant in Table 625c. In general excess death rates are lower for patients with transplants from a living donor than they are in dialysis patients. In patients with cadaver transplants the first year is a period of great risk, and excess death rates are higher than in the dialysis patients; after the first year the transplant patients tend to have a lower excess mortality than the dialysis patients, although there are a few exceptions. Relatively high percentages of deaths were attributed to renal diseases (7 per cent), and endocrine or metabolic diseases (5 per cent), in comparison with the percentages that would be expected in the general population.

One of the major consequences of long-term hemodialysis is accelerated atherosclerosis. Coronary death rates among dialysis patients are similar to those with familial type II hyperlipoproteinemia, and many times higher than those experienced by patients with hypertension.[9] Lindner et al. emphasize that the probability of death from cardiovascular disease essentially parallels the cumulative probability of death from all causes combined, and that deaths from coronary heart disease increase sharply after six years of hemodialysis.[9] Although of limited effect on mortality, the social and psychologic problems experienced by dialysis patients are just as important as the medical ones and probably represent the leading cause of morbidity.

Other Kidney Diseases. Limited experience on a number of other renal diseases is abstracted from insurance studies in Table 699. Among cases coded for pyelitis or pyelonephritis the New York Life found a mortality ratio of 220 per cent (only six deaths), but a much lower ratio of 60 per cent was found in insureds coded for "pyelitis or cystitis" by the Prudential of London (12 deaths). The New York Life and the Sverige Reinsurance Company reported mortality ratios exceeding 200 per cent for insureds with a nephritis history, but the ratio experienced by the Prudential of London was only 125 per cent. Some excess mortality was also found by two of the companies among insureds with a history of nephrectomy: mortality ratios of 240 and 210 per cent. Presumably cases were excluded from both studies if the nephrectomy had been performed for cancer of the kidney. A small group of "other" kidney diseases was found to have a normal mortality by the New York Life.

Male Genital Disorders

Prostate Disease. The only known large compilation of mortality experience related to diseases of the prostate comes from New York Life Insurance Company. Once again it has to be stressed that the whole spectrum of prostate abnormalities is so wide that it is difficult to interpret the significance of an "average" mortality experience. This may be clearly illustrated by the fact that prostatectomy is commonly performed for a totally benign hypertrophy as well as for a malignant growth. Although cases of known prostatic cancer were excluded from the New York Life series, the overall experience for prostatectomy produced a mortality ratio of 177 per cent and an EDR of 12 per 1000, as almost half of the exposure was in applicants age 60 and up (Table 670c). As expected, other diseases of the prostate in general did not show any excess mortality (Table 670c).

Female Genital Disorders

As was evident in Table 14-1, only 1,511 deaths were reported in the entire United States under this category during 1970. It is scarcely surprising that mortality data are extremely limited. A normal mortality was experienced by the New York Life Insurance Company among females with a history of hysterectomy and among those with a history of caesarean section. A normal mortality was also found in somewhat more extensive experience in the *1951 Impairment Study* not only for these conditions but also for women with a history of oöphorectomy, salpingectomy, and uterine fibroma with hysterectomy.[10]

References

1. Dept. of Health, Education, and Welfare, *Mortality Trends of Leading Causes of Death, U.S. 1950–69.* Vital and Health Statistics, Series 20, No. 16. Rockville, Md.: National Center for Health Statistics (1974).

2. Dept. of Health, Education, and Welfare, *Vital Statistics of the United States 1970, Volume II–Mortality, Part A.* Rockville, Md.: National Center for Health Statistics (1974).

3. "Mortality from Kidney Diseases." *Stat. Bull. Metropol. Life Ins. Co.,* 52:3-5 (July 1971).

4. Advisory Committee to the Renal Transplant Registry, "The Twelfth Report of the Human Renal Transplant Registry." *J. Am. Med. Assoc.,* 233:787-796 (1975).

5. A.L. Thompson, R.R. Durrett, and R.R. Robinson, "Fixed and Reproducible Orthostatic Proteinuria." *Ann. Int. Med.,* 73:235-244 (1970).

6. Second Report by a Subcommittee, "Australian National Renal Transplantation Survey." *Med. J. Austr.,* 2:605-608 (1971).

7. J.S. Cheigh, K.H. Stenzel, M. Susin et al., "Kidney Transplant Nephrotic Syndrome." *Am. J. Med.,* 57;730-740 (1974).

8. T.E. Starzl, K.A. Porter, G. Andres et al., "Long-Term Survival after Renal Transplantation in Humans." *Ann. Surg.,* 172:437-472 (1970).

9. A. Lindner and K. Curtis, "Morbidity and Mortality Associated with Long-Term Hemodialysis." *Hosp. Practice,* 9:143-150 (1974).

10. *1951 Impairment Study.* Chicago: Society of Actuaries (1954).

15

Systemic Disorders
John J. Hutchinson, M.D.

Systemic diseases include diseases of supporting tissue (bone and joints, muscle, skin, and connective tissue); included additionally are diseases which tend to be disseminated rather than localized: infections, allergic and immune disorders, diseases of blood and lymphatic system and certain diseases of unknown cause. Chronic respiratory infections are considered with the respiratory diseases in Chapter 12.

About two-thirds of the clinically significant infections in the United States are acute respiratory infections. Influenza, upper respiratory infection, pneumonia, and bronchitis are acute disabling infections which average (1972) 17 days of restricted activity and 6.5 days bed confinement per case.[1] Among the chronic conditions producing limitation of activities, arthritis and rheumatism are exceeded only by cardiovascular diseases as causes of disability in the United States. Combined with other musculoskeletal disorders these cause disability in 4.5 million people[1] or 2.2 percent of the population of this country. These same disorders, however, account for less than 0.2 per cent of the total deaths in the United States.

Despite the prevalence of some of these diseases and despite their numbers in both acute and chronic forms, follow-up data are relatively limited. Only eight separate abstracts and one abstract including multiple impairments provide data, often very limited, on 17 different diseases. Table 15-1 provides a list of the diseases covered in this chapter, and a summary of numbers of deaths in the United States during 1970 attributed to the corresponding categories of diseases.[2] Bone and joint diseases were listed in 2,913 deaths, muscle disorders for only 504, diseases of skin and connective tissue for 2,202, and blood diseases for 5,288. It should be noted that leukemia deaths, numbering 14,492 in 1970, are classified with deaths due to cancer in Chapter 5 and have therefore been excluded from blood diseases as defined here. The 54,448 deaths for all of the categories in this Chapter amounted to 2.8 per cent of total deaths in the United States in 1970.[2]

Infectious Diseases

There has been a marked change in the clinical pattern of many infectious diseases since the advent of sulfonamide drugs in 1935 and since the introduction of antibiotics during and subsequent to World War II. This is particularly true of many of the coccal infections (pneumonia, meningitis, and streptococcal infections), tuberculosis, syphilis and malaria. There has been a marked decrease in the acute mortality from infectious diseases and in the specific mortality rates in the general population.[3,4] There are no data on mortality in acute infectious diseases in the abstracts of this volume. The limited data available in follow-up studies are for chronic infectious diseases or in relation to complications or sequelae of acute infections.

In 1970 the largest number of deaths attributed to infection was due to pneumonia (59,032); tuberculosis (all forms) accounted for 5,217 deaths; septicemia, 3,535; viral diseases, 3,530 (including 1,014 deaths due to infectious hepatitis); enteric infections, 2,762; coccal and bacterial diseases, 1,202 and 966, respectively; syphilis, 461; parasitic disease, 115; rickettsial infections, 31; and malaria, only six deaths.[2]

Table 899 indicates a normal mortality experience in nonpulmonary tuberculosis in English males. Mortality experience is also presented for two other types of infection in small groups of persons insured by the New York Life Insurance Company. A mortality ratio of 142 per cent was found in osteomyelitis and a ratio of only 59 per cent in syphilis (all types). Since there were only 6 and 5 deaths, respectively, in the latter groups, all that can be said is that there was no evidence of significant excess mortality among insureds with these infectious diseases.

Mortality ratios for these diseases among insured persons in the *1951 Impairment Study* were reported according to history and severity of the disorders: on an overall basis 183 per cent in nonpulmonary tuberculosis (28 deaths), 201 per cent in osteomyelitis (23 deaths) and 117 per cent in syphilis (51 deaths), all in substandard issues.[5] This experience was accumulated during 1935 to 1950, almost entirely before the era of modern chemotherapy.

Allergic and Immune Disorders

Immunology is today a rapidly expanding field of medicine. This is particularly true with respect to knowledge of immune reactions at the cellular level and knowledge of immunoglobulins and antibodies. Asthma, which is a disease characterized

TABLE 15-1

Numbers of Deaths in the U.S. — 1970
Systemic Disorders

Hazard	Deaths in U.S.			Follow-up Data
	Number	% in Category		
Infectious Diseases*		16,649	(30.6%)	
Nonpulmonary Tuberculosis	1,055		(1.9%)	§899
Syphilis	461		(0.8)	§899
Other Infections and Parasitic Dis.*	15,133		(27.8)	—
Allergic and Immune Disorders		8	(0.01%)	
Hay Fever	2		(0.00%)	§899
Ur'ticaria	6		(0.01)	—
All Other†	—			—
Diseases of Blood		5,288	(9.7%)	
Polycythemia Vera	541		(1.0%)	§740
Anemias	3,427		(6.3)	§899
All Other	1,320		(2.4)	§899
Diseases of Lymphatic System		294	(0.5%)	—
Diseases of Unknown Cause		26,590	(48.9%)	
Sarcoidosis	232		(0.4%)	§780
Cystic Fibrosis	577		(1.1)	§785
Other Ill-defined and Unknown	25,781		(47.3)	—
Bone and Joint Disorders		2,913	(5.4%)	
Rheumatoid Arthritis	1,296		(2.4%)	§801, §802
Arthritis, Osteo- and Other	647		(1.2)	§899
Osteomyelitis	160		(0.3)	§899
Spinal Curvature	125		(0.2)	§899
Other Spinal Disorders	65		(0.1)	§899
Poliomyelitis with deformity	121		(0.2)	§899
Other Bone and Joint Disorders	499		(0.9)	§899
Muscle Disorders		504	(0.9%)	
Myasthenia Gravis	259		(0.5%)	§830
All Other	245		(0.4)	—
Skin and Connective Tissue		2,202	(4.0%)	
Scleroderma	524		(1.0%)	§850
Systemic Lupus	755		(1.4)	—
Chronic Ulcer	788		(1.4)	—
Other	135		(0.2)	—
Total* (all listed in Cause of Death Statistics)		54,448	(2.8% of all deaths)	

*Does not include pulmonary TB, pneumonia and other respiratory infections, and other infections of nervous system, kidneys, and other organs and tissues

†Classified with other categories, e.g. hypogammaglobulinemia with metabolic disorders

by an allergic reversible bronchoconstriction and consequent air way obstruction, in 1970 was the cause of death in 2,322 cases in the United States.[2] Mortality and other data in asthma are considered with the respiratory diseases in Chapter 8. There are a dozen or more primary immunodeficiency diseases listed today and undoubtedly more will be delineated as further knowledge is developed in this field of medicine; these diseases are rare, however, and their frequency or prevalence uncertain.

Hay fever, allergic rhinitis, is a very common form of allergic disorders which, in a 1969 to 1970 health survey, was indicated as the cause of limitation of activity of some 149,000 individuals in the United States.[1] Hay fever studied in a group of insured lives in England produced a mortality experience of 118 per cent of expected, an essentially normal result (§899).

Blood and Lymphatic System Disorders

Polycythemia vera accounted for 541 deaths in the United States in 1970,[2] the anemias for 3,427 deaths, and all other blood disorders for 1,320 deaths. There figures exclude the leukemias, which are considered with Cancer in Chapter 5. In a miscellaneous category of the New York Life experience—"Disorders of the Blood"—there was an overall mortality ratio of 385 per cent of expected among a small group (§899), and an EDR of 7 per 1000. This group excluded the anemias and hemorrhagic diseases, but may well have included some cases of polycythemia vera or other uncommon but potentially serious disorders of the blood. There were only 9 observed and 2.33 expected deaths in this experience. Collectively the anemias, exclusive of primary anemia, produced a fairly good experience in a small group of insured lives with a mortality ratio of 139 per cent, based on 7 deaths (§899).

Polycythemia Vera. Polycythemia vera is a disease in which there is increased production of all cellular elements in the blood; there is an increase in blood volume. Red blood cells usually number between 7 and 10 million per cubic millimeter; white cells are generally increased to the range 10 to 25 thousand per cubic millimeter and platelet count may range as high as 3 to 6 million per cubic millimeter. Unless the total red cell volume exceeds 38 ml per kilogram of body weight for males and 36 ml per kilogram for females, the diagnosis of polycythemia vera cannot be considered established.[6] The cause of polycythemia vera is unknown; there is a certain parallel between this disease and chronic granulocytic leukemia even in those cases untreated by radioactive therapy. This disease is not to be confused with stress polycythemia, with the physiologic response to living at high altitudes, nor with secondary polycythemia.

The increased viscosity and slowing of blood flow along with the thrombocytosis lead to intravascular thrombosis as a very common complication. Stroke, coronary thrombosis, pulmonary embolism, and other thromboembolic phenomena all contribute to the higher mortality associated with polycythemia vera.

Results of four separate follow-up studies of polycythemia vera are given in §740. Two patient groups were managed without any radiation therapy, and three patient groups received radiation therapy in the form of X-ray or intravenous phosphate solution containing P[32], the average age in all groups being about 55 years. Excess death rates in these predominantly older patients ranged from 20 to 139 per 1000 in all age, duration, and treatment categories, except for Series 1 patients receiving P[32] in the first two years of follow-up, during which time the lowest EDR of all was observed, only 3.5 per 1000. Mortality ratios generally decreased but excess death rates tended to increase with advancing age regardless of treatment. However, the pattern of variation of EDR by duration was not consistent. In two of the three groups of patients treated with P[32] the excess death rates increased with duration, but in the English patients (Series 4), no increase was found in the 10 years of follow-up. There was a similar lack of consistency in the relation of EDR to duration in the patients not receiving any radiation therapy; EDR remained almost constant in the U.S. patients of Series 1, but EDR increased at 5-10 years after entry in the English patients (Series 4). On an overall basis, all ages and durations combined, excess death rates of 33, 62 and 42 per 1000 were observed in the three groups receiving P[32] therapy, and 60 per 1000 in the patients of Series 1 not treated by radiation. The Series 2 patients of Perkins et al., also not treated with radiation, had an EDR of 50 per 1000, calculated as an aggregate mean on the basis of exposure data and expected deaths (Table 740c). Halnan and Russell used 117 of these 127 patients as a basis of comparison with their Series 4 patients treated with P[32]. From the 10-year survival rates reported in their article, the excess death rate obtained as a geometric mean is 81 per 1000 (Table 740d).

In Series 1 (Table 740a) patients receiving P[32] clearly fared better than those not receiving radiation in the first 10 years of follow-up, but experienced a higher EDR from 10 to 15 years after entry. With the different groups of Series 4 patients little difference is apparent between those receiving and those not receiving P[32] in the first five years of follow-up (Table 740d), but in the next five years, the EDR was estimated at 116 per 1000 in those not receiving P[32] and 40 per 1000 in those treated with P[32]. Evidence on the value of P[32] is therefore conflicting, although the groups of patients in Series 4 are probably less qualified for valid comparison than the groups in Series 1. If P[32] does prolong life it probably does so by reducing mortality within the first ten years, at the expense of higher mortality after ten years (Table 740a). Many of the excess deaths in those Series 1 patients receiving P[32], especially after ten years, were due to leukemia. There were very few leukemia deaths in patients not treated by radiation, and the difference was statistically significant. A similar increase in leukemia deaths was observed in Series 3 patients treated with P[32], but not in Series 4 patients. The extent to which the radiation from P[32] may result in leukemia on a delayed basis is a major consideration of several of these articles in §740, and the articles themselves should be consulted for further details.

Secondary Anemia. Prognosis related to secondary anemia should be predicated upon the cause of anemia. When that cause is one easily eliminated or corrected, the anemia will disappear; when the anemia is secondary to a serious underlying problem, the prognosis must reflect the gravity of the problem. In the small life insurance group designated "Anemia" (Table 899) the degree of anemia is probably that represented by 10 to 12 grams of hemoglobin per 100 ml, and it is likely the insurance applicant had not been adequately studied to determine the underlying cause of the anemia. Based on seven deaths the mortality ratio was 139 per cent; it seems apparent the group did not include many cases where the anemia was secondary to serious underlying disease.

Bone and Joint Disorders

Rheumatoid arthritis is a systemic disease of unknown cause. While there are often many extraarticular manifestations, the most common pathology and basis for clinical manifestation is in the synovial membranes. Rheumatoid arthritis has its onset most commonly in the fourth and fifth decades but may begin at any age; it is two or three times as frequent in women as in men, and in Europe and North America the disease affects about 2 per cent of the population.

Osteoarthritis is a degenerative joint disease that probably begins in all people by the end of the second decade: about 90 per cent of the population present at least minimal roentgenological evidence of joint degenerative changes by age 40.[6] Certainly minimal X-ray evidence of osteoarthritis does not constitute clinically significant disease, but marked degrees of osteoarthritis constitute one of the most common causes of chronic disability.

Abstracts §801 and §802 provide data on long-term follow-up in rheumatoid arthritis and arthritis, "type unspecified" (by reason of only substandard insured lives being included, §802 probably includes largely rheumatoid arthritis). Both studies demonstrate a considerable degree of increased mortality. Excess death rates were well under 10 per 1000 in younger patients, but higher in older patients, especially in men age 60 up, with EDRs of 54 and 95 per 1000 in the two studies. With all ages and durations combined the excess death rate was 34 per 1000 in male patients and 19 per 1000 in female patients in the arthritis clinic series of §801. Lower values of EDR were observed in §802, with rates of 7.7 and 7.3 per 1000 for males and females, respectively. Although one might postulate a lesser degree of severity of the arthritis in the insured group, a great deal of this difference can be explained by the much higher proportion of patients age 50 and up in the patients under active clinic treatment (§801). In both series mortality ratios failed to show the usual tendency to decrease with duration, and EDRs increased with duration except in the males in Table 801c. Infectious diseases were the most important cause of death in terms of EDR in the clinic patients, and cardiovascular diseases were increased as a cause of death in both series.

Abstract §899 includes a small group of insured lives both standard and substandard with the catch-all designation of bone or joint disorder; based upon only 5 deaths this experience was almost exactly what had been expected (mortality ratio of 97 per cent). Table 899 includes data on a number of other miscellaneous disorders of bones or joints; the groups were small for the most part. Spinal curvature evaluated as being standard for life insurance produced an almost normal mortality ratio of 133 per cent, while the substandard group demonstrated a mortality ratio of 225 per cent (23 deaths). Abstract §810 includes only applicants rated substandard because of spinal curvature and shows an adverse mortality experience with a mortality ratio of 285 per cent for the first five years and a ratio of 182 per cent for years 5-17. In terms of EDR excess mortality was highest for insureds age 50 and up. Most of the excess mortality was manifested in diseases of the heart and circulatory system.

A group of spinal disorders other than spinal curvature produced a mortality ratio of 217 per cent for the standard group and one of 275 per cent for the substandard group (§899). Osteomyelitis (both standard and substandard) demonstrated a mortality ratio of 142 per cent as mentioned previously. Marked deformity secondary to poliomyelitis (marked enough to be considered substandard) produced in the New York Life group a mortality ratio of 215 per cent; the British group, which included both standard and substandard lives, produced a more favorable experience of 117 per cent. In a group where multiple amputations constituted the basis for substandard classification, the experienced based on 7 deaths was 260 per cent. The somewhat limited evidence available for these various bone and joint disorders in Table 899, therefore does suggest a tendency to increased mortality.

Muscle Disorders

Muscular Dystrophy. Muscular dystrophies are inherited myopathies involving skeletal muscles and characterized by marked progressive weakness. Three distinct types are recognized by a combination of clinical and genetic analysis; these are termed Duchenne, facioscapulohumeral, and myotonic. A fourth type is probably not a separate entity but it includes cases not clearly one of the other three; this fourth is called limb-girdle type.[6] There is no effective treatment of muscular dystrophy and prevention of respiratory infections becomes the objective of temporizing therapy. The Duchenne type occurs only in males, has its onset in early childhood, and progresses relatively rapidly with death in the second or third decade.[7] The facioscapulohumeral type occurs in both sexes, with onset from early childhood to late adult life. There is a wide range.in severity of symptoms, and rate of progression is slower, especially when onset is delayed. The limb-girdle type also occurs in both sexes, with onset usually under age 30; rate of progression is, on the average, intermediate between the rates in the other two types. Sometimes patients with milder forms of the disease may live to old age, retaining the ability to walk despite presence of symptoms for several decades, but this is rare in the Duchenne type.[7]

Myasthenia Gravis. This is a disease of unknown cause characterized by muscular weakness, particularly the ocular and other cranial muscles. There is no evidence of a neural lesion; the weakness may show fluctuation within short periods and there is partial reversibility of the weakness by use of cholinergic drugs. The clinical picture closely resembles that of curare poisoning and effective treatment involves the use of cholinesterase inhibitors. The disease occurs in about 30 to 35 cases per million population and is three times more common in females than in males.[6] Thymomas are present in 15 per cent of the cases and thyrotoxicosis complicates about 5 per cent of the cases. In 1970 in the United States four-fifths of all deaths attributed to muscle disease were caused by myasthenia gravis.[2]

Abstract §830 deals with a 20-year follow-up of 1,355 cases of myasthenia gravis treated in Boston and New York by medical methods, and in some cases by thymectomy. Patients with thymoma had a poor prognosis, with mortality ratios in the range of 765 to 350 per cent, excess death rates about 80 per 1000 at 0-5 and 15-20 years and about 50 per 1000 5-15 years, and a 20-year survival ratio of only 25 per cent. Patients without thymoma fared better, especially in the later stages of follow-up when EDR was 4 per 1000 or less after 10 years in all groups except a small series of males who had been subjected to thymectomy. Females subjected to thymectomy had lower EDRs than unoperated patients following the first five years, but this was not true for males. During the first five years the excess death rate was in a very narrow range from 17 to 23 per 1000, regardless of sex or thymectomy. In addition to producing an apparent reduction in mortality in females beyond five years, thymectomy also brought about clinical improvement (reduction in extent and severity of the weakness) in a high proportion of those surviving to 1965 (Table 830c).

Disorders of Skin and Connective Tissues

Although disorders of skin and subcutaneous tissue are extremely common, most are superficial, and of more significance to appearance than to longevity. Skin is subject to infections by a multiplicity of microorganisms, but in general these are transient, superficial and self-limited. Chronic infections can be troublesome, but most of the microoorganisms causing chronic skin infections respond to antibiotic or steroid therapy. In the United States in 1970 there were 2,202 deaths reported as due to disease of the skin and connective tissue.[2]

Pemphigus. This is a serious disease involving a generalized bullous eruption of skin and subcutaneous tissue. It was responsible for 123 deaths in the United States in 1970.[2] The cause is unknown. Modern therapy has decreased the mortality rate to half of what it had been before the advent of steroid therapy;[6] not only can the disease be reasonably well controlled on modern therapy but the patients can lead nearly normal lives while in remission.

Systemic Lupus Erythematosus. This disease (SLE) is a chronic inflammatory process involving joints, nervous system, serous membranes, kidneys, and other organs of the body. The cause is unknown, but genetic factors may play a part in the development of systemic lupus in susceptible individuals, and virus etiology has been suggested. About five persons per 100,000 have SLE;[6] it is five to ten times more common in females than males; it appears to be more frequent in blacks than whites, but it is rare among Asians. Autoimmune phenomena are common in this disease and autoantibodies of widely varying types have been demonstrated. The so-called LE cell (an in vitro formed leucocyte of unusual but characteristic appearance) is present in about 80 per cent of cases and antinuclear antibodies can be found in over 99 per cent of patients with SLE. Modern therapy can be very effective in the control of this disease, but clinically it is still regarded as having a serious prognosis.[6] In 1970 there were 755 deaths from SLE in the United States.[2]

Scleroderma. This is a rare disease of unknown cause involving blood vessels, skin and connective tissue. Arterioles and capillaries become obliterated by progressive fibrosis in multiple organs. Subcutaneous tissue is replaced by collagen bundles which bind the dermis to the underlying structures, producing a characteristic stiffening of the skin which gives the disease its name. Similar changes take place in other organs with fibrosis being the result. The principal symptomatology relates to this fibrosis process involving the lungs, esophagus, bowel, kidney, and heart. There is currently no effective form of therapy. Once the disease is recognized and the diagnosis confirmed usually through biopsy, the usual prognosis is an extremely poor one. This is evident from the two series of patients reported in abstract §850, one a combined series from two special clinics in which women outnumbered men, and the other a series of male patients discharged from several Veterans Administration hospitals. Excess mortality was extremely high in the first year with an EDR of 205 to 284 per 1000; it then tapered off but still remained at a level of 32 to 84 per 1000 from five to seven years after clinic or hospital diagnosis. Seven-year survival ratios were less than 40 per cent in male patients and 57 per cent in females. Analysis of the data in Tables 850b-c indicates a poorer prognosis for patients with the following clinical characteristics: male sex, nonwhite race, (neither of these is a very strong factor), age over 45-50 years, and involvement of kidney, heart, or lung. Patients without evidence of involvement of any of these organs had the best prognosis, with a mortality ratio close to 600 per cent in both series after the first year, and respective excess death rates of 42 and 89 per 1000. All 33 patients with kidney involvement died less than one year after entry into these series; this group had by far the worst prognosis.

Systemic Diseases of Unknown Cause

Sarcoidosis. This is a multisystemic granulomatous disorder of unknown cause. It is most frequently found in the age group 20 to 50, but the young and elderly are susceptible. Intrathoracic involvement is most common and in those communities where mass chest X-rays are used, there is more apt to be discovery of sarcoid. In many of these patients the disease is clinically asymptomatic. Varying frequencies have been reported:[6] 20 per 100,000 in England, 64 per 100,000 in Sweden, and 120 per 100,000 in Ireland. U.S. Armed Forces studies have shown the rate among negroes to be 10 to 20 times as frequent as among whites, yet African negroes do not seem to be particularly affected. Ninety per cent of the people with sarcoidosis have intrathoracic involvement; 25 per cent have eye or skin manifestations. Prompt effective treatment is important to prevent the complications of pulmonary fibrosis, blindness, and renal calcinosis. In 1970 there were 232 deaths in the United States due to sarcoidosis.[2]

In the three series of patients covered in §780 there appears to be a rather consistent pattern in the EDRs. In the Mayo Clinic series the excess death rate varies from 7 to 15 per 1000; in the Danish series the variation is from 10 to 15 per 1000 with no trend by duration in either group. In the Veterans Administration series the rate is 9 to 14 per 1000 in patients under age 55, but it rises to 57 per 1000 in those age 55 and up (Table 780d). About one-half the deaths were attributed directly to sarcoidosis in the VA patients.

Cystic Fibrosis (CF). This is a generalized inherited disease associated with overactivity of all exocrine glands including those that are mucus producing. The cause is unknown but the disease expresses itself in an autosomal recessive pattern. The large and small pancreatic ducts in the individual with CF become obstructed with amorphous concretions; dilation of the acini with degeneration of the parenchyma and subsequent fibrosis occurs. The islets of Langerhans remain intact, but diabetes mellitus is nevertheless frequent. Generalized bronchial obstruction with secondary infection is the principal pulmonary manifestation; this frequently results in chronic bronchitis, patchy atelectasis, bronchiectasis, and cor pulmonale. Very early diagnosis and prompt treatment are most important. The extensive data collected and analyzed by the Cystic Fibrosis Foundation (Table 785a) reveal a significant decline in the mortality pattern, as the average annual mortality rate for all patients exposed to risk by calendar year has decreased from 53 per 1000 in 1967 to 39 per 1000 in 1972. Cystic fibrosis is one of the relatively few diseases in which prognosis is worse in females than in males (Table 785f). On an attained age basis (Table 785d) the overall excess death rate is high in the first year of life, 57 per 1000, then drops to a minimum of 24 per 1000 in the second year, and then rises gradually to 50 per 1000 at ages 12 to 15 years. Excess mortality continues to increase, with an EDR of 61 per 1000 at ages 15 to 20 years, 84 per 1000 from 20 to 25 years, and 120 per 1000 from 25 to 30 years. The pattern of variation of mortality ratio with attained age is complicated by the *decrease* of the expected mortality rate with age in young children, especially infants (Table 785e). The increase in mortality ratio, 420 to 2,300 per cent from the first to the second year of life occurs because of the very high expected rate in the first year, and despite a decrease in the observed mortality rate from .072 to .025. Among infants and young children, EDR is a more reliable index than the mortality ratio in assessing year to year variation in excess mortality.

Although the material from the Cystic Fibrosis Registry has not been analyzed by severity of disease, some indication of the nature of the experience may be inferred from the data in Tables 788b-c, where the presentation is based on a combination of age at diagnosis and follow-up duration. One might postulate that a diagnosis of cystic fibrosis made in the first year of life would represent, on the average, a more severe degree of the disease than in cases diagnosed at older ages. Such a speculation receives some support from the EDR averaging about 35 per 1000 in patients diagnosed under age one year, for the first two years of follow-up, in contrast to 22 per 1000 among those diagnosed at age one to five years, and 20 per 1000 when the diagnosis was made at ages five to ten years. However, at follow-up durations of two to ten years the EDRs show little difference according to age at diagnosis. The apparently inexorable tendency of the disease to progress is evident in the increasing excess death rates with duration of follow-up in Table 785b as it is with advancing attained age in Table 785d. The cumulative survival ratios in Table 785d are 92.2 per cent at age 2, 83.9 per cent at age 5, 68.4 per cent at age 10, 39.1 per cent at age 20, and a discouraging 12.9 per cent at attained age 30 years.

References

1. Dept. of Health, Education, and Welfare, *Facts of Life and Death.* Rockville, Md.: National Center for Health Statistics (1974).

2. Dept. of Health, Education, and Welfare, *Vital Statistics in the United States, 1970. Volume II–Mortality, Part A.* Bethesda, Md.: National Center for Health Statistics (1974).

3. C.C. Dauer, R.F. Korns, and L.M. Schuman, *Infectious Diseases.* Cambridge, Massachusetts: Harvard University Press (1968).

4. W.J. Brown, J.F. Donohue, N.W. Axnick, J.H. Blount, N.H. Ewen, and O.G. Jones, *Syphilis and Other Venereal Diseases.* Cambridge, Massachusetts: Harvard University Press (1973).

5. Society of Actuaries, *1951 Impairment Study.* Chicago: Society of Actuaries (1954).

6. P.B. Beeson and W. McDermott, *Cecil-Loeb Textbook of Medicine,* 14th ed. Philadelphia: W.B. Saunders Co. (1975).

7. H.H. Merritt, *A Textbook of Neurology,* 5th ed. Philadelphia: Lea and Febiger (1973).

16

Endocrine and Metabolic Diseases
Paul S. Entmacher, M.D.

Although the diseases of the endocrine system and the metabolic diseases occur frequently, they are not a major cause of death. In the disease categories considered in this chapter, diabetes mellitus is predominant, and several long-term prospective studies have been carried out. These include insurance studies, as well as clinical studies. As shown in Table 16-1, there were 38,324 deaths in the United States from diabetes in 1970. This compares to a total of 2,085 deaths from other endocrine diseases and 5,273 from metabolic disorders.

TABLE 16-1

Numbers of Deaths in the U.S. — 1970
Endocrine and Metabolic

Hazard	Deaths in U.S.			
	Number	% in Category		Follow-up Data
Diabetes Mellitus		38,324	(83.9%)	
Diabetes Mellitus	34,559		(90.2%)	§901-§910, §999
Diabetes with Mention of Acidosis or Coma	3,765		(9.8)	§910
Abnormal Glucose Tolerance	**		—	§919
Glycosuria	**		—	§999
Other Endocrine		2,085	(4.6%)	
Thyroid	812		(38.9%)	§999
Adrenal	457		(21.9)	—
Pituitary	238		(11.4)	—
Other	578		(27.7)	—
Metabolic Disorders		5,273	(11.5%)	
Hyperlipidemia (Cholesterol, Triglyceride, etc.)	**		—	§950-§952
Congenital Disorders of Lipid, Carbohydrate and Protein Metabolism	162		(3.1%)	—
Obesity (Overweight)	1,174		(22.3)	§999
Gout	285		(5.4)	—
Nutritional Deficiencies	2,470		(46.8)	—
Other Metabolic Diseases	1,182		(22.4)	—
Total (all listed in Cause of Death Statistics)	45,682 (2.4% of all deaths)			

**Listed elsewhere under various separate causes

The mortality data relating to various endocrine and metabolic diseases are derived from insurance studies in the United States, Sweden and England. All of these were studies of multiple medical impairments, including metabolic and endocrine disorders. The hyperlipidemias were studied and analyzed separately.

Diabetes Mellitus

Diabetes mellitus is a chronic disease, genetically determined, in which there is a relative or absolute lack of insulin leading to elevated levels of sugar in the blood and excretion of sugar in the urine. The metabolic disorders present in diabetes are complex and involve protein and fat, as well as carbohydrate.

In its fully developed clinical state, the disease is characterized by fasting hyperglycemia, atherosclerotic and micro-angiopathic vascular disease, and neuropathy. There is controversy, however, about whether the vascular and neurological abnormalities are integral components of the inherited disorder. Hyperglycemia may become manifest years before vascular disease or neuropathy is recognized clinically, but the reverse sequence of events may also occur. The typical vascular and neurological abnormalities may occur in persons who do not have fasting hyperglycemia and who have mild, if any, abnormality of glucose tolerance.

Since diabetes is generally accepted as a disease in which heredity plays an important role, the implication is that diabetes has its origin at conception and exists for prolonged but varying periods before there is any recognized abnormality of carbohydrate metabolism. Thus, the different stages of diabetes must begin with one that includes the period of time before overt manifestations of the disease occur. The four stages of the disease with the terminology proposed by the American Diabetes Association are shown in Table 16-2.

TABLE 16-2

Natural History of Diabetes

	Prediabetes	Suspected Diabetes	Chemical or Latent Diabetes	Overt Diabetes
Fasting Blood Sugar	Normal	Normal	Normal or ↑	↑
Glucose Tolerance Test	Normal	Abnormal during Pregnancy or Stress	Abnormal	Abnormal (not necessary)
Cortisone-GTT	Normal	Abnormal	Abnormal (not necessary)	—

The earliest stage of the disorder is prediabetes. It identifies the period of time between conception and some demonstrable impairment of glucose tolerance. This stage can be suspected in the nondiabetic identical twin of a diabetic patient and in the offspring of two diabetic parents.

In the next stage of the disease, suspected diabetes, abnormality of glucose tolerance is only manifested under conditions of stress, such as pregnancy. This state is followed by the chemical or latent stage in which there are no clinical indications of the disease, but the glucose tolerance test is abnormal, and the fasting blood sugar may or may not be elevated. Finally, there is the overt stage of the disease at which time the classical symptoms of the disease are present.

It has come to be realized that the course of diabetes is not one of steady progression. There may never be progression from one stage to the next. When progression does occur, it may be very slow, or it may be extremely rapid. On the other hand, regression from a more advanced stage to an earlier stage also occurs, and, in fact, the regression may bridge two stages of the disease. Sometimes the reversal is brief; at other times it may be prolonged. The latter is especially true when an adult obese person develops overt diabetes and then loses weight. The reversal to the latent or suspected states may be for prolonged periods of time if the weight loss is maintained.

The overt stage of diabetes is generally considered to have two broad classifications. One is the juvenile-onset type which usually starts at a young age and is characterized by a lack of insulin and a proneness to develop ketosis. The other broad classification is the maturity-onset or adult-onset type which usually starts later in life, has a relative deficiency of insulin, and has a milder carbohydrate abnormality with a resistance to ketosis. The juvenile type of disease may occur in adulthood, and conversely the maturity-onset type may develop among children. To avoid this contradiction in terminology, some classifications refer to insulin-dependent, ketosis-prone diabetics versus noninsulin-dependent, ketosis-resistant diabetics.

Epidemiology. Diabetes is a universal disease that is encountered most frequently in urban and industrialized countries, among older populations, and generally in more affluent societies. The recent report of the National Commission on Diabetes[1] highlighted the following features of the disease in the United States:

Between 1965 and 1973 the prevalence of diabetes increased by more than 50% in the United States. Diabetes now affects 5% of the population.

In 1974 more than 600,000 new cases of diabetes were diagnosed, and the incidence of diabetes appears to be increasing by 6% per year. At this rate, the number of people with diabetes will double every fifteen years. The average American born today has a better than one in five chance of developing diabetes, unless a method of prevention is found.

Women are 50% more likely than men to have diabetes, nonwhites are one-fifth more likely than whites to have diabetes, and poor people (incomes less than $5,000 per year) are three times as likely as middle-income and wealthy people to have diabetes.

The chance of being diabetic more than doubles for every 20% of excess weight and doubles for every decade of life.

Despite important advances in the treatment of the disease and its complications, diabetes mellitus has accounted for about 38,000 deaths in the United States yearly since 1965. The full impact of mortality resulting from diabetes, however, is difficult, if not impossible, to measure. The causal relationship between diabetes and vascular disease, particularly large-vessel disease, has not been fully delineated. As a result, in a significant number of instances diabetes is not recorded as the underlying cause of death when the immediate cause is vascular disease. An indication of the magnitude of this problem can be gained from a study of multiple causes of death done by the National Center for Health Statistics.[2] In 1968 the ratio of the number of times that diabetes was mentioned on death certificates to the number of times it was listed as the underlying cause of death was 3.5 to 1. This was an increase from a ratio of 2.5 to 1 reported in 1955.[3] Furthermore, a study in Pennsylvania[4] showed that diagnosed diabetes is not even recorded on death certificates in approximately 10 per cent of deaths among diabetics.

In 1950 when 1.6 per cent of all deaths were attributed to diabetes, the disease ranked as the tenth leading cause of death. Since 1972 the disease has been the sixth leading cause of death accounting for 1.9 per cent of all deaths in the United States. If accidents as a cause of death are excluded, diabetes is the fifth leading cause of death by disease, and the recent National Diabetes Commission estimates that, if deaths from complications of the disease could be measured, diabetes would be the third leading cause of death.

Diabetes has been characterized by consistently higher prevalence and mortality among females than among males. In the United States, however, the sex differential in mortality from diabetes at all ages combined has been narrowing for a number of years. A review of the age-adjusted death rates from diabetes among white men and women in the general population for the period 1964 to 1973, indicates that lower mortality rates are now found among white women than among white men.

Recent mortality rates from diabetes mellitus among white men and women in the general population of the United States are presented in Table 16–3. Death rates are shown in five-year age groups for each year from 1964 to 1973 with the per cent change computed for the ten-year period. Where rates are based on fewer than 20 deaths, the per cent change has not been computed. Although the Eighth Revision of the International Classification of Diseases (used for classifying causes of death) was introduced in 1968, there was little or no break in the continuity of mortality statistics for diabetes mellitus.

On the whole, death rates from diabetes among white men in the general population of the United States increased from 1950 to 1969 while the rates among white women were decreasing. Since 1969, however, there has been some decrease in the death rates for both men and women. In 1973 the crude death rate from diabetes among white males in the general population of the United States was 14.9 per 100,000, and that for white women was 19.9 per 100,000.

While the crude death rate among women has remained higher than that among men, adjustment of the death rates to allow for changes in the age distribution of the population produced age-adjusted death rates from diabetes of 11.9 per 100,000 for white males and 11.4 for white females at all ages combined in 1973 (Table 16–3). The use of such standardized death rates permits a more meaningful evaluation of mortality trends and more precise comparisons between the sexes over a period of years.

Over the ten-year period the age-adjusted death rates from diabetes fluctuated within a narrow range among both men and women in the white population. Death rates among men rose from 11.8 per 100,000 in 1964 to a peak of 13.1 in 1968 and then declined to 11.9 in 1973, one per cent above the 1964 figure. Among women a decrease of 10 per cent was registered from 12.7 per 100,000 in 1964 to 11.4 in 1973; as was the case for men, death rates among women had peaked in 1968 before turning downward. Diabetes death rates had been higher among women than among men, but the sex difference has been diminishing for a number of years. By 1970 the age-adjusted death rate from diabetes for white females at all ages combined was the same as that for white males, and since 1971 it has been less than the age-adjusted death rate for white males.

In 1973 the death rates for nearly all age groups were somewhat higher among white males than among white females. At ages 70 and over, however, diabetes mortality continued at a higher level for females than for males. During the ten-year period under review, death rates for each age group generally declined. There were a few increased rates, but in only two instances—at ages 75 and over for males and ages 45 to 49 for females—did the increase exceed ten per cent.

168

Table 16-3
Mortality from Diabetes, 1964–1973
United States White Population

Death Rate per 100,000

MALE

Age	1964	1965	1966	1967	1968	1969	1970	1971	1972	1973	Percent Change 1964 to 1973
All Ages*	11.8	11.8	12.2	12.3	13.1	12.8	12.7	12.3	12.2	11.9	+ 1
Under 5	0.3	0.3	0.3	0.2†	0.2†	0.2†	0.2†	0.3	0.2†	0.2†	†
5-9	0.2†	0.1†	0.2	0.1†	0.1†	0.2†	0.2†	0.2†	0.1†	0.1†	†
10-14	0.2†	0.3	0.4	0.3	0.2†	0.3	0.3	0.1†	0.3	0.2†	†
15-19	0.4	0.2†	0.3	0.3	0.3	0.3	0.3	0.3	0.4	0.3	—25
20-24	0.9	0.9	0.9	0.7	1.0	0.8	1.0	0.8	0.6	0.7	—22
25-29	2.3	2.1	2.1	1.8	1.7	1.8	1.5	1.7	1.4	1.6	—30
30-34	3.7	3.7	3.5	3.5	3.5	3.2	2.9	3.2	3.3	2.1	—43
35-39	4.6	4.2	4.3	4.0	5.1	4.4	4.5	3.7	3.4	3.9	—15
40-44	5.3	5.3	5.5	6.2	5.7	5.4	6.5	6.0	5.6	4.9	—8
45-49	7.9	8.5	8.5	8.3	8.7	9.6	8.7	7.7	8.8	7.8	—1
50-54	14.2	13.8	13.9	14.1	16.0	14.5	14.7	14.3	12.8	13.4	—6
55-59	23.7	22.9	23.1	24.6	27.0	24.8	23.5	24.1	22.8	23.8	—
60-64	40.2	38.7	38.5	42.3	44.2	40.8	42.4	40.5	35.9	37.5	—7
65-69	61.2	62.6	65.9	62.5	68.7	69.4	65.3	62.8	63.1	62.7	+2
70-74	92.2	96.6	101.6	102.6	109.7	102.0	103.3	102.7	104.4	96.1	+4
75 and over	153.0	158.5	165.2	164.9	175.3	181.5	179.9	180.4	185.2	179.6	+17

FEMALE

Age	1964	1965	1966	1967	1968	1969	1970	1971	1972	1973	Percent Change 1964 to 1973
All Ages*	12.7	12.8	12.8	12.7	13.3	13.2	12.7	12.2	11.9	11.4	—10
Under 5	0.3	0.2†	0.2†	0.3	0.3	0.2†	0.2†	0.2†	0.2†	0.1†	†
5-9	0.2†	0.2†	0.2†	0.3	0.2†	0.2†	0.2†	0.2†	0.2†	0.2†	†
10-14	0.5	0.5	0.4	0.4	0.4	0.4	0.4	0.4	0.2†	0.3	—40
15-19	0.6	0.4	0.5	0.5	0.4	0.4	0.5	0.4	0.4	0.3	—50
20-24	0.9	1.0	0.9	1.0	0.9	1.1	0.9	0.7	1.0	0.6	—33
25-29	1.5	1.8	1.4	1.4	2.1	1.7	1.6	1.5	1.3	1.2	—20
30-34	2.3	2.3	2.5	2.4	2.0	2.7	2.2	2.1	2.6	2.0	—13
35-39	2.5	2.6	2.3	2.6	2.8	3.2	3.0	2.7	2.4	2.5	—
40-44	3.8	3.7	4.0	3.2	4.2	4.1	3.4	3.9	4.0	3.5	—8
45-49	5.4	5.4	5.6	6.8	6.6	6.8	7.0	6.1	5.9	6.0	+11
50-54	11.5	11.5	11.1	11.8	11.6	12.4	11.7	11.3	10.5	10.3	—10
55-59	23.9	23.2	22.8	22.1	22.5	21.5	22.6	20.3	20.1	20.9	—13
60-64	42.7	42.9	41.8	39.8	42.9	40.6	39.8	37.5	37.5	34.8	—19
65-69	75.8	74.9	74.6	73.1	74.2	70.5	69.3	67.4	63.3	59.3	—22
70-74	122.5	119.4	121.8	119.8	121.8	121.1	111.8	110.2	107.3	101.4	—17
75 and over	181.9	190.2	196.2	194.2	211.5	213.1	205.2	202.0	199.9	197.8	+9

*Adjusted on basis of age distribution of the United States total population, 1940.
†Fewer than 20 deaths.
Source of basic data: Reports of Division of Vital Statistics, National Center for Health Statistics.

Mortality and Survival Data in Diabetes. There are four insurance studies analyzed (§901-§904), one each from the Equitable Life Assurance Society of the United States, the Lincoln National Life Insurance Company, the Metropolitan Life Insurance Company, and the New York Life Insurance Company. The insurance studies are of special value because they permitted study of the mortality of diabetes as an isolated impairment; and when complications of the disease or other impairments were present, their impact was studied. The study done at Equitable (§901) was unique because it included not only those diabetic applicants who were accepted for insurance, but those who were rejected as well. A 20-year follow-up was reported in 1974.

The Lincoln National study (§902) was also an extensive one with a 19-year follow-up period. This study was limited to policyholders. Several trends are apparent in both of these studies. Excess mortality tends to increase with duration following insurance issue with a leveling off or decrease at the longest durations. For all durations the mortality ratios are lowest for the older age groups. The highest mortality ratios are found among juvenile-onset diabetics. The Equitable study showed a distinctly more unfavorable experience among those diabetics who were declined than those who were accepted for insurance. Both studies demonstrated an extremely unfavorable impact of proteinuria on mortality with mortality ratios of 935 to 1,290 per cent. Other cardiovascular impairments also adversely affected mortality but not to the same extent as proteinuria. Overweight had only a modest effect. The Equitable study also showed that diabetes under poor control at time of application had an excess mortality two and a half times that found in patients under satisfactory control.

The Metropolitan Life study (§903) showed a trend toward lower mortality ratios with increasing issue age, but the excess deaths per thousand increased. There was no clear trend by duration although after ten years there was some indication of a decrease in mortality ratios. The New York Life Study (§904) also failed to show a clear trend by duration from commencement of coverage. In the latter study the effect of the amount of insulin was measured, and those taking 25 units or more tended to have a higher mortality than those taking less than 25 units. The Equitable study showed about the same mortality ratio for all subjects taking up to 50 units but a materially higher ratio for those taking 50 units or more. The experience of the Lincoln National according to insulin dose was quite uneven although there was a trend to increased comparative ratios with higher amounts of insulin.

Female mortality was evaluated separately in the New York Life report. Although the experience was much smaller, the mortality ratio among females for all treatments combined tended to be higher after five years with EDR highest at 10 to 17 years.

Causes of death were also studied. The usual excess of deaths from cardiovascular-renal disease was found. In the Metropolitan series 68 per cent of the deaths were due to these causes and in the Equitable series, 62 per cent. Large vessel disease accounted for the preponderance of deaths at the older ages and small vessel disease, especially renal disease, at the younger ages.

There were three separate studies of the patients treated at the Joslin Clinic (§905-§907). Two of the studies (§905 and §906) were limited to residents of Massachusetts. There was a trend in all of the studies for mortality ratios to decrease with increasing age at commencement of treatment, but the EDRs tended to increase. Mortality ratios and EDRs were higher for females than for males in almost all age groups and duration categories. All three of the studies divided the patients into cohorts based on the date first seen at the Clinic. In two of the studies (§905 and §907) patients seen more recently had a better survival than those seen in earlier years, possibly representing improved treatment in the later periods. There was no significant improvement, however, after the early 1940s. The third study (§906) did not demonstrate any improvement at all in the later time periods.

Abstract §907 compared the Clinic patients both to the general population and to a standard insured group. The mortality ratios were much higher for diabetics when compared to an insured population as compared to the general population because the mortality among standard insured policyholders is lower due to the selection process at the time of application for insurance.

Causes of death were analyzed extensively in two of the studies. The great excess of deaths due to vascular diseases was shown in Table 907d, the excess being greater for females than for males. For all vascular disease the mortality of males is about two and one-half times and in females, three and one-half times that in the general population. An especially detailed analysis of deaths from cancer has been abstracted in Table 906c. The mortality ratio of deaths due to all types of cancer for males was only 85 per cent of that found in the general population. For females it was 103 per cent.

The duPont Company has analyzed the mortality experience of its employed diabetics (§908) and as a control group used a matched population of nondiabetic employees. No trend in mortality was discernible by duration, but higher mortality ratios were found among the younger employees. An unfavorable mortality was also found among diabetics with significant glycosuria and those with more than one positive test for albuminuria. In this study an examination was made of the effect on mortality of certain conditions to which diabetics are especially prone: hypertension, overweight, and coronary heart disease. Diabetics with these conditions showed an increase in mortality well above the rates of diabetics who did not exhibit these conditions, but the increment in mortality was not any greater than the increment shown by the controls with these conditions. Thus, the increasing risk of deaths incurred by hypertension, overweight, and coronary artery disease does not appear to be further aggravated by the diabetic state.

The final two studies analyzed were carried out in Scandinavian countries—one in Norway (§909) and one in Sweden (§910). Both of these studies involved patients first seen in the hospital. In the Norwegian study patients were followed after discharge from the first hospitalization. In the Swedish study both inpatients and outpatients were included. Both studies tended to show higher mortality ratios at the younger ages but increases in EDRs with advancing age. The Norwegian study showed higher mortality ratios for males than for females at all ages combined, but the female mortality ratios tended to be higher than those for males at the younger ages. In the Swedish study there was no significant sex difference for all ages combined, but under age 55 the female mortality ratios were higher. In the Norwegian studies the EDRs were higher among males commencing at age 50, but in the Swedish study there was no clear-cut difference in EDRs by sex until age 75 when the male EDR was 23 extra deaths per 1000 compared to 1.5 for females.

In the Norwegian study successive time periods from 1925 to 1955 with follow-up to 1961 were compared. Of note was a significant decrease in mortality ratios during the war years, 1941 to 1945, with a sharp postwar increase. This was true for both sexes. In Sweden the effect of duration on mortality ratios was found to be negligible for the first 15 years, and then there was a significant increase. The prevalence of complications was also studied in Sweden. The lowest prevalence was found in the earliest period of observation (0-5 years). Retinopathy had the lowest prevalence in this interval at all ages and nephropathy, the highest prevalence at the younger ages. Neuropathy had the highest prevalence among diabetics 40 years and older during the first five years of observation.

In a study done by the New York Life Insurance Company, hyperglycemia was evaluated as a single impairment in the absence of a definite diagnosis of diabetes. This study is discussed in abstract §919. The subjects in the study were policyholders in the New York Life Insurance Company issued insurance during the period 1949 to 1965 who had an elevated fasting or postprandial blood sugar or an abnormal glucose tolerance test. Among those issued standard insurance, the mortality ratio showed an upward trend with duration. Among those issued substandard insurance, there was no definite trend by duration; but the highest mortality ratio was found after ten years. Among the standard cases the mortality ratio ranged from 88 to 143 per cent with an EDR of 3.7 per 1000 after ten years. Among substandard cases the mortality ratio after ten years was 158 per cent with an EDR of 7.6 per 1000. When analyzed by age at issue in the standard group, the highest mortality ratios were found under age 50 and in the substandard group at ages 40 to 49. The highest EDRs in both groups occurred at ages 40 to 49. Comparative mortality by major causes of death showed an excess of deaths from heart and circulatory diseases.

A high mortality was also observed for diabetes in the Prudential Assurance and in the Swedish Reinsurance studies abstracted in Table 999. In the Prudential experience the extra deaths per 1000 per year increased with advancing age from 5.0 at ages under 30 to 8.7 at ages over 50. However, mortality ratios decreased with age from 835 per cent for ages under 30 to 174 per cent for ages 50 and over. These results are in general agreement with those reported in abstracts §901 through §904. The Swedish Reinsurance study combined all ages with an approximate average of 37 years and produced an overall mortality ratio of 415 per cent and EDR of 11 per 1000. The presence of glycosuria at examination was accompanied by a slight extra mortality in the Prudential experience.

Metabolic Disorders—Lipids

Cholesterol has been implicated as one of the risk factors predisposing to coronary heart disease.[5, 6, 7] Two of the abstracts (§950 and §952) deal with prospective studies to measure the impact of elevated cholesterol on mortality, while the study in abstract §951 attempts to measure the effect on mortality of lowering the serum cholesterol.

Abstract §950 analyzes a study done in Norway in which 3,751 men age 40 to 49 who were actively at work were followed for ten years, and their mortality and morbidity were related to their level of serum cholesterol. The men entered the study during the period April 1958 to June 1960. The comparative mortality and survival data are derived by using men with cholesterol levels under 275 mgs per cent to determine the expected number of deaths instead of using appropriate population life tables. The study showed that the mortality increased steadily with higher levels of cholesterol. The lowest cholesterol levels (under 200 mg per 100 ml) were associated with a mortality ratio of 59 per cent, while men whose cholesterol was 375 and up had a mortality ratio of 520 per cent. The corresponding range in EDR was -1.3 to 13 extra deaths per 1000 and in ten-year survival ratio, 101.3 to 87.4 per cent.

This study also measured the effect of elevated serum cholesterol, elevated systolic and diastolic blood pressure, and overweight on mortality, due to coronary heart disease, as well as due to all causes. All of these risk factors were associated with increased mortality rates for both coronary heart disease deaths and deaths due to all causes. The highest mortality rates for deaths from all causes were found with elevated blood pressure and the lowest, with overweight. For deaths from coronary heart disease, a cholesterol of 375 mg per 100 ml and up was associated with the highest mortality rates and overweight was the lowest.

In abstract §952 a pooled study carried out in the United States and a study of insured policyholders done in Finland are analyzed. The United States study combined six separate prospective studies with a total of 7,594 white males, age 30 to 59, who were free of definite coronary heart disease at the time of entry into the studies and who were followed for ten years. The subjects were classified in accordance with serum cholesterol level, as well as other risk factors evaluated at the time of the initial examination. In the United States study, as well as in the Finnish study, the three classes having the lowest serum cholesterol concentration were used to derive indices of comparative mortality and survival. This is similar to the technique used in the Norwegian study (abstract §950). In the range of cholesterol levels under 250 mg per 100 ml, there was no increase in mortality ratios. The average annual mortality ratio showed a minimum of 84 per cent and a maximum of 103 per cent. Some excess mortality was evident in the three categories with serum cholesterol 250 mg per 100 ml or above. The mortality ratios were 140, 124 and 140 per cent with corresponding EDRs of 2.7, 1.6 and 2.7 extra deaths per 1000.

In the Finnish study, 1,661 men age 50 to 53 years, who were insured policyholders, were followed for a period of seven yars. Both cholesterol and triglyceride were measured, and again the highest mortality was observed in the quintiles with the highest lipid levels. A mortality ratio of 178 per cent was found in men with cholesterol 331 or above and 191 per cent in men with triglycerides exceeding 167 mg per 100 ml. The corresponding excess death rates were 8.0 and 8.7 per 1000. Other coronary heart disease factors were also evaluated in this study. For the risk factor, hypertension, the mortality ratio was 165 per cent and EDR, 6.6 per 1000. For smokers the mortality ratio was 250 per cent and EDR, 11 per 1000. Men with a general category of other cardiovascular diseases experienced a mortality ratio of 131 per cent and EDR of 3.0 per 1000 as compared to men without cardiovascular disease at entry.

The study analyzed in abstract §951 was carried out in Finland. An attempt was made to determine the effect of cholesterol-lowering diet on mortality from coronary heart disease and other causes. All male and female patients over 15 years of age in two mental institutions were included in the study. The indices of comparative mortality and survival are based on a comparison of the age-adjusted death rates observed during the period of special diet with the corresponding rates found in the period of normal or control diet. It was found that during the period that the patients were on the special cholesterol-lowering diet their mean serum cholesterol levels decreased from a control of 272 mg per 100 ml to 236 mg per 100 ml. Analysis of the mortality data shows that mortality ratios of deaths from coronary heart disease among patients on cholesterol-lowering diets were lower than those of patients who were not on special diets. This was true in both hospitals and for both sexes. None of the other causes of death recorded—and these included deaths from cerebrovascular disease, malignant neoplasms, and a general category of other causes—indicated any regular significant difference in mortality ratios. Although differences in the coronary heart disease mortality were significant, the differences in mortality from all causes were not significant because of the relatively large number of deaths unaffected by diet and a slight tendency for mortality rates of deaths due to cancer to increase during the special diet periods.

Other Metabolic Disorders

Three insurance studies measured the mortality of multiple medical impairments, among them some miscellaneous endocrine and metabolic disorders (§999). The first study was comprised of policyholders of the Prudential Assurance Company of England issued insurance in the years 1947 to 1963. The second was of insured lives reinsured with Sverige Reinsurance Company of Sweden placed in force prior to 1955. The third study was of policyholders of the New York Life Insurance Company issued insurance in the period of 1954 to 1970. The Prudential Assurance and New York Life expected deaths were based on the experience of standard insured lives. The Swedish study used general population mortality.

Thyroid enlargement was studied by the New York Life, but the experience was quite limited. Nontoxic cases with operation produced a mortality ratio of 186 per cent based on four death claims and in cases with toxicity unspecified but no operation, a ratio of 205 per cent based on only five death claims. The Prudential Assurance mortality experience with a history of either toxic or nontoxic goiter was only slightly above the expected with mortality ratios of 104 and 118 per cent, respectively.

Underweight cases were studied by Prudential Assurance separately for males and females. The mortality was very slightly elevated with mortality ratios being 109 per cent for males and 112 per cent for females. The EDR was 0.4 per 1000 for both sexes.

For mortality experience on overweights, the primary source of information was the Prudential Assurance study. Females experienced a mortality close to standard, but for males the mortality was somewhat elevated. Mortality ratios were highest for entry ages 30 to 50 and increased with increasing degrees of overweight. At ages 30 to 50 the mortality ratio was 153 per cent for overweights 20 to 30 per cent above the standard weight, and 192 per cent for those who were more than 30 per cent overweight. The corresponding EDRs were 1.1 and 1.9 per 1000. For ages over 50 the mortality ratios were lower, but the EDR was 1.2 per 1000 for 20 to 30 per cent overweight and 3.0 per 1000 for heavier overweights. The Swedish Reinsurance study reported the experience of overweights on an over-all basis with all ages, both sexes, and all degrees of overweight combined. The mortality ratio was 134 per cent and the EDR, 2.3 per 1000.

References

1. Dept. Health, Education, and Welfare, *Report of the National Commission on Diabetes to the Congress of the United States. Volume I. The Long-Range Plan to Combat Diabetes.* DHEW Publication No. (NIH) 76-1018. Bethesda, Md.: National Institutes of Health (1976).

2. R.A. Israel and R. Armstrong, "An Alternative Procedure for Classifying and Analyzing Mortality Data." International Union for the Scientific Study of Population, International Population Conference, Liège, Belgium (1973).

3. *Vital Statistics of the United States, 1955 Supplement: Mortality Data, Multiple Causes of Death.* Washington, D.C.: National Center for Health Statistics (1965).

4. G.K. Tokuhata, W. Miller, E. Digon, and T. Hartman, "Diabetes Mellitus: An Underestimated Public Health Problem." *J. Chron. Dis.,* 28:23-35 (1975).

5. D.S. Fredrickson and R.S. Lees, "System for Phenotyping Hyperlipoproteinemia." *Circulation,* 31:321-327 (1965).

6. W.B. Kannel, "Some Lessons in Cardiovascular Epidemiology from Framingham." *Am. J. Card.,* 37:269-282 (1976).

7. L.M. Hagerup, "Coronary Heart Disease Risk Factors in Men and Women." *Acta Med. Scand.,* 195 (Suppl. 557):1-116 (1974).

PART II
TABULAR ABSTRACTS

Physical, Toxic and Other Risk Factors

See Also

1. *1951 Impairment Study*. Chicago: Society of Actuaries (1954).
   A76 Family history of cardiovascular-renal disease (pp. 62-63)
   B30 Family history of insanity (pp. 80-81)
   G17 Family history of cancer (pp. 220-221)
   H41 Family history of diabetes (pp. 242-243)
2. W.K.C. Morgan and A. Seaton, *Occupational Lung Disease*. Philadelphia: W.B. Saunders Co. (1975).
3. A.P. Iskrant and P.V. Joliet, *Accidents and Homicide*. Cambridge, Mass.: Harvard University Press (1968).
4. E.M. Kitagawa and P.M. Hauser, *Differential Mortality in the United States: A Study in Socio-Economic Epidemiology*. Cambridge, Mass.: Harvard University Press (1973).
5. C.L. Erhardt and J.E. Berlin, *Mortality and Morbidity in the United States*. Cambridge, Mass.: Harvard University Press (1974).

ADDICTIONS AND INTOXICATIONS

§1–ALCOHOLISM IN AN INDUSTRIAL POPULATION

Reference: S. Pell and C. A. D'Alonzo, "A Five Year Mortality Study of Alcoholics," J. Occup. Med., 15:120-125 (1973).

Subjects Studied: 922 Du Pont employees identified in 1964 as being either known alcoholics, suspected alcoholics, or recovered alcoholics. A control group was established by pairing each alcoholic with another Du Pont employee who was not known to be an alcoholic but otherwise had similar characteristics by age, sex, payroll class, and geographic location. Age distribution of the 899 alcoholics or ex-alcoholics still employed on January 1, 1965 was as follows:

Drinking Category	20-29	30-34	35-39	40-44	45-49	50-54	55-59	60-64	Total	Median Age
Known	1	6	15	21	47	53	46	27	216	51.7
Suspected	9	9	45	59	68	95	71	27	383	50.1
Recovered	0	6	21	38	54	78	61	42	300	52.0
Total	10	21	81	118	169	226	178	96	899	51.1

Follow-up: The follow-up period extended from January 1, 1965 through December 31, 1969. Deaths were reported routinely through the company-sponsored group insurance plan for active and retired employees but no attempt was made to track the 51 alcoholics and the 14 controls whose employment terminated prior to retirement. In addition, 23 identified alcoholics and 1 control whose employment terminated prior to January 1, 1965 were excluded from the study.

Results: During the follow-up period 102 alcoholics and 34 controls died, representing a mortality ratio of 300 per cent, a survival ratio of 91.5 per cent, and an average annual excess death rate of 18 per 1000.

Rates and ratios by characteristic are shown in Tables 1a-b which compare the experience of the subjects with that of the control group. The average annual mortality ratio of 380 per cent for known alcoholics is somewhat greater than for the other two categories but even the ratio of 300 per cent for the recovered category is well above normal, indicating, possibly, that certain disease processes initiated by alcohol may be irreversible or that some employees in this group may not really have recovered. By sex, there was only one death in the female control group as opposed to six deaths in the female alcoholics. By occupation, the mortality ratio of 410 per cent for salaried employees is considerably higher than the ratio of 265 per cent for hourly employees. One possible explanation is the much higher termination rate for hourly employees with possible higher mortality among those terminated (who were not followed-up).

Distribution by cause of death is presented in Table 1c. In the alcoholics there were 26 deaths from cancer and 11 from cirrhosis of the liver compared with 7 deaths from cancer and none from cirrhosis in the control group. There were 49 deaths from cardiovascular causes in the alcoholics compared with 23 control deaths but it is known that hypertension among the alcoholics was 2.3 times as great as among the controls. Excluding excess deaths due to hypertension, the authors estimated that there were 13 excess deaths from coronary heart disease due to other factors.

ALCOHOLISM IN AN INDUSTRIAL POPULATION

Table 1a Observed Data and Comparative Experience (5-Year Follow-up)

Group	No. of Entrants		No. of Deaths		Mortality Ratio		5-Year Surv. Ratio	Excess Death Rate
	Subjects	Controls*	Subjects	Controls*	Ave. Ann.	5-Yr Cum.		
	L	L'	d	d'	100 q̆/q̆'	100 Q/Q'	100 P/P'	1000(q̆-q̆')
Drinking Category								
Known	216	226	32	10	380%	360%	88.0%	25
Suspected	383	390	33	11	315	310	93.7	13
Recovered	300	305	37	13	300	290	91.4	18
Sex								
Male	842	862	96	33	320	310	91.7	17
Female	57	59	6	1	700	665	90.2	20
Occupation†								
Production	595	612	54	22	265	255	94.0	12
Salaried	247	250	42	11	410	390	86.6	28
Age as of 1/1/65†								
Under 45 yrs	215	225	6	1	630	620	97.4	5.3
45-54	369	383	30	12	270	265	94.6	11
55-64	258	254	60	20	320	295	83.2	36
All Subjects	899	921	102	34	335%	320%	91.5%	18

Table 1b Derived Mortality and Survival Data

Group	Subjects				Controls*			
	Cumulative Rates		Average Annual		Cumulative Rates		Average Annual	
	Survival	Mortality	Survival	Mortality	Survival	Mortality	Survival	Mortality
	P	Q	p̆	q̆	P'	Q'	p̆'	q̆'
Drinking Category								
Known	.841	.159	.9660	.0340	.956	.044	.9910	.0090
Suspected	.910	.090	.9813	.0187	.971	.029	.9941	.0059
Recovered	.875	.125	.9736	.0264	.957	.043	.9912	.0088
Sex								
Male	.882	.118	.9752	.0248	.962	.038	.9923	.0077
Female	.887	.113	.9763	.0237	.983	.017	.9966	.0034
Occupation†								
Production	.905	.095	.9802	.0198	.963	.037	.9925	.0075
Salaried	.828	.172	.9630	.0370	.956	.044	.9910	.0090
Age as of 1/1/65†								
Under 45 yrs	.969	.031	.9937	.0063	.995	.005	.9990	.0010
45-54	.916	.084	.9826	.0174	.968	.032	.9935	.0065
55-64	.766	.234	.9481	.0519	.921	.079	.9837	.0163
All Subjects	.881	.119	.9750	.0250	.963	.037	.9925	.0075

Table 1c Number and Distribution of Deaths by Cause (According to Drinking Category)

Cause of Death	Known		Suspected		Recovered		Total	
	Alcoh.	Control	Alcoh.	Control	Alcoh.	Control	Alcoh.	Control
Coronary Heart Dis.	9	4	16	7	12	8	37	19
Cerebrovascular Dis.	3	1	3	1	1	—	7	2
Other CV Disease	1	1	—	—	4	1	5	2
Total CV Disease	13	6	19	8	17	9	49	23
Cancer	9	2	5	2	12	3	26	7
Cirrhosis of Liver	4	—	5	—	2	—	11	—
Accidents	1	1	1	—	—	—	2	1
Suicide	—	—	—	—	2	—	2	—
Alcoholism	1	—	1	—	1	—	3	—
Emphysema	—	1	2	—	1	—	3	1
Other Causes	4	—	—	1	2	1	6	2
Total Deaths	32	10	33	11	37	13	102	34

* Controls not known to be alcoholic, matched by age, sex, payroll class and location
† Males only

ADDICTIONS AND INTOXICATIONS

§2–INSURED ALCOHOLICS

Reference: K. M. Davies, "The Influence of Alcohol on Mortality," Proc. Home Office Life Underwriters Assoc., 46:159-178 (1965).

Subjects Studied: Substandard medically examined lives, insured by the Equitable Life Assurance Society and issued policies from 1940 to 1961. The only major impairment was alcoholic habits, because of which all cases were issued rated insurance. There were 2582 policies, with a total exposure of "over 12,000"; female experience was not separated as the number of female deaths was "minimal." Additional exposure data are not available from the article or retained records of the study, but have been estimated from standard mortality rates and the expected deaths in the article. The over-all experience (all ages and durations combined) was presented as follows:

No treatment noted	Actual Claims	Expected Claims	Mortality Ratio	Estimated Exposure and Age Distribution for Cases within 2 Years		
Last intoxication						
within 2 years of issue	109	39.19	278%	Age 10-39	5508	60.1%
within 3, 4 or 5 years of issue	18	8.07	223%	40-49	2916	31.8%
more than 5 years prior	5	1.92	260%	50 up	743	8.1%
				All	9167	100.0%
Treatment more than						
2 years prior to issue	8	2.70	296%			
All Cases	140	51.88	270%			

Only the group having last intoxication reported within 2 years of issue (109 observed deaths) is reported in detail in the article and in Tables 2a and 2b. Age distribution and exposure have been estimated as shown above.

Follow-up: Data with respect to deaths and withdrawals were obtained from policy records, up to the 1962 policy anniversary. Exposure was terminated when a policy rating was removed. Expected claims were calculated on the basis of Equitable's contemporaneous standard medically examined experience for the same issue ages and durations.

Results: Mortality ratios for the younger issue ages are somewhat higher than those obtained for the older, the over-all ratio coming to 340 per cent for age group 10-39 years, 240 per cent for age group 40-49 years, and 295 per cent for ages over 50 (Tables 2a-b). The average annual number of excess deaths per 1000, however, increased with age: 4.1 at the youngest issue age group, 7.7 at the intermediate ages (40-49 years), and 29 at the oldest (50 years and older). By policy year, the mortality ratio was almost twice as great during the first two policy years as in subsequent intervals when it tended to stay quite level. The withdrawal from exposure of cases qualifying for a reduction of rating to the standard class is thought to be partly responsible for the maintenance of mortality ratios with duration. For the smaller classes with last intoxication or treatment more than 2 years prior to issue mortality ratios were quite similar to the 280 per cent for the large group with history within 2 years of issue (Tables 2a-b). The numbers of deaths in the individual age-duration cells are small — experience can be judged only from the standpoint of broad duration or age groupings.

Mortality ratios by cause of death were high for all causes, whether or not related to drinking. Of the 109 deaths among the subjects studied, 41 were attributed to arteriosclerotic and degenerative heart disease (against 15.6 expected for standard lives, a ratio of 263 per cent), 22, to malignant neoplasms (against 9.5, a ratio of 232 per cent), and 10 to other cardiovascular-renal diseases (against 4.6, a ratio of 217 per cent). The heaviest relative extra mortality arose in three other categories — diseases of the digestive system, motor vehicle accidents, and other accidents and homicide, accounting respectively for 7 (1.5 expected — ratio of 467 per cent), 9 (1.8 expected — ratio, 500 per cent) and 7 (1.6 expected — ratio, 438 per cent) deaths. Four of the seven claims due to diseases of the digestive system were attributed to cirrhosis of the liver. Incidentally, two of the nine claims classified under "all other causes" were related to alcoholism.

INSURED ALCOHOLICS

Table 2a Observed and Estimated Data and Comparative Experience by Age Group and Duration from Insurance

| Age Group | Interval | | Exposure Person-Yrs* | Deaths in Interval | | Mortality Ratio | | Survival Ratio | | Excess Death Rate |
| | No. | Start-End | | Obs. | Exp.* | Interval | Cumulative | Interval | Cumulative | |
Years	i	t to t + Δt	E	d	d'	100 d/d'	100 Σd/Σd'	100 p_i/p_i'	100 P/P'	1000(d-d')/E
10-39	1	0- 2 yrs	1629	7	1.14	615%	615%	99.3%	99.3%	3.6
	2	2- 5 yrs	1600	6	1.92	315	425	99.2	98.5	2.6
	3	5-10 yrs	1411	8	2.54	315	375	98.1	96.7	3.9
	4	10-15 yrs	654	6	2.29	260	340	97.2	93.9	5.7
	5	15-22 yrs	214	5	1.50	335	340	89.0	83.6	16
		0-22 yrs	5508	32	9.39	340	340		83.6	4.1
40-49	1	0- 2 yrs	933	10	2.24	445	445	98.3	98.3	8.3
	2	2- 5 yrs	842	9	3.79	235	315	98.1	96.5	6.2
	3	5-10 yrs	677	10	5.01	200	265	96.3	93.0	7.4
	4	10-15 yrs	350	9	4.52	200	245	93.7	87.1	13
	5	15-22 yrs	114	6	2.96	205	240	82.3	71.7	27
		0-22 yrs	2916	44	18.52	240	240		71.7	8.7
50 up	1	0- 2 yrs	245	7	1.37	510	510	95.4	95.4	23
	2	2- 5 yrs	209	6	2.30	260	355	94.7	90.4	18
	3	5-10 yrs	173	8	3.05	260	315	86.3	78.0	29
	4	10-15 yrs	88	7	2.75	255	295	77.4	60.4	48
	5	15-22 yrs	28	5	1.81	275	295	40.3	24.3	114
		0-22 yrs	743	33	11.28	295	295		24.3	29
All Ages	1	0- 2 yrs	2807	24	4.75	505	505	98.6	98.6	6.9
	2	2- 5 yrs	2651	21	8.01	260	355	98.5	97.2	4.9
	3	5-10 yrs	2261	26	10.60	245	305	96.6	93.9	6.8
	4	10-15 yrs	1092	22	9.56	230	285	94.4	88.6	11
	5	15-22 yrs	356	16	6.27	255	280	82.1	72.8	27
		0-22 yrs	9167	109	39.19	280	280		72.8	7.6

Table 2b Derived Mortality and Survival Data

Age Group	Interval		Observed Rates				Expected Rates†			
			Annual		Cumulative		Annual		Cumulative	
	No.	Start-End	Mortality	Survival	Survival	Mortality	Mortality	Survival	Survival	Mortality
Years	i	t to t + Δt	$\bar{q}_i$	$\bar{p}_i$	P	Q	$\bar{q}_i'$	$\bar{p}_i'$	P'	Q'
10-39	1	0- 2 yrs	.004	.996	.991	.009	.0007	.9993	.9986	.0014
	2	2- 5 yrs	.004	.996	.980	.020	.0012	.9988	.9950	.0050
	3	5-10 yrs	.006	.994	.953	.047	.0018	.9982	.9860	.0140
	4	10-15 yrs	.009	.991	.910	.090	.0035	.9965	.9687	.0313
	5	15-22 yrs	.023	.977	.771	.229	.0070	.9930	.9221	.0779
40-49	1	0- 2 yrs	.011	.989	.979	.021	.0024	.9976	.9952	.0048
	2	2- 5 yrs	.011	.989	.948	.052	.0045	.9955	.9818	.0182
	3	5-10 yrs	.015	.985	.880	.120	.0074	.9926	.9461	.0539
	4	10-15 yrs	.026	.974	.772	.228	.0129	.9871	.8867	.1133
	5	15-22 yrs	.053	.947	.529	.471	.0260	.9740	.7374	.2626
50 up	1	0- 2 yrs	.029	.971	.944	.056	.0056	.9944	.9888	.0112
	2	2- 5 yrs	.029	.971	.865	.135	.0110	.9890	.9565	.0435
	3	5-10 yrs	.046	.954	.683	.317	.0176	.9824	.8752	.1248
	4	10-15 yrs	.080	.920	.451	.549	.0312	.9688	.7469	.2531
	5	15-22 yrs	.179	.821	.114	.886	.0646	.9354	.4680	.5320
All Ages	1	0- 2 yrs	.009	.991	.983	.017	.0017	.9983	.9966	.0034
	2	2- 5 yrs	.008	.992	.960	.040	.0030	.9970	.9877	.0123
	3	5-10 yrs	.011	.989	.906	.094	.0047	.9953	.9647	.0353
	4	10-15 yrs	.020	.980	.818	.182	.0088	.9912	.9230	.0770
	5	15-22 yrs	.045	.955	.593	.407	.0176	.9824	.8151	.1849

*Values of E are estimated. Distribution of d and d' by duration for age subgroups is also estimated.

†Basis of expected mortality: Equitable Life contemporaneous experience on standard medically examined lives

ADDICTIONS AND INTOXICATIONS

§3—ALCOHOLISM IN INSUREDS

Reference: "New York Life Single Medical Impairment Study—1972," unpublished report made available by J.J. Hutchinson and J.C. Sibigtroth (1973).

Subjects Studied: Policyholders of New York Life Insurance Company issued insurance in 1954-1970, followed to the 1971 policy anniversary. The experience reported is for cases issued substandard due to excessive or prolonged use of alcohol. All cases with more than one ratable impairment were excluded.

Follow-up: Insurance policy records formed the basis of entry, of counting policies, exposure and death claims, and of follow-up information.

Results: Tables 3a-b present the comparative experience among males by duration, all ages combined. Mortality ratios appear to decrease with duration, ranging from 340 per cent at 0-2 years to 140 per cent at 10-17 years, with EDR highest (9.1 extra deaths per 1000) at 5-10 years. The cumulative survival ratio at 17 years was 90.0 per cent.

In Table 3c, the mortality ratio was highest at entry ages under 30, being 730 per cent. For ages above 30, the greatest excess mortality was observed in the age group 60 and up, with a mortality ratio of 395 per cent and EDR of 46 per 1000. For all ages combined, the overall mortality ratio for the male substandard experience was 245 per cent. The estimated 8-year survival index ranged from 96.8 per cent at ages 30-39 to a minimum of 68.1 per cent at ages 60 and up.

For male and female substandard cases combined, Table 3d shows that the excess mortality among alcoholics can be due to a number of causes, notably accidents and homicides, the mortality ratio being 385 per cent and EDR 1.5 per 1000. The mortality for suicides was high at 390 per cent, but for a smaller increase in EDR of 0.5 per 1000. In all the remaining causes listed, an EDR of at least 1.0 per 1000 was experienced. For "all other causes and unknown," the 14 deaths included 5 due to cirrhosis of liver.

ALCOHOLISM IN INSURED MEN

Table 3a Observed Data and Comparative Experience by Duration — Male Substandard Cases

Interval		Exposure	No. of Death Claims		Mortality Ratio		Survival Ratio		Excess
No.	Start-End	Policy-Yrs	Observed	Expected*	Interval	Cumulative	Interval	Cumulative	Death Rate
i	t to $t+\Delta t$	E	d	d'	$100\,d/d'$	$100\,\Sigma d/\Sigma d'$	$100\,p_i/p_i'$	$100\,P/P'$	$1000(d-d')/E$
1	0- 2 yrs	3357	20	5.89	340%	340%	99.2%	99.2%	4.2
2	2- 5	2327	19	7.62	250	290	98.5	97.7	4.9
3	5-10	1617	24	9.28	260	275	95.5	93.3	9.1
4	10-17	565	10	7.14	140	245	96.5	90.0	5.1

Table 3b Derived Mortality and Survival Data

Interval		Observed Rates				Expected Rates*			
		Average Annual		Cumulative		Average Annual		Cumulative	
No.	Start-End	Mortality	Survival	Survival	Mortality	Mortality	Survival	Survival	Mortality
i	t to $t+\Delta t$	$\bar{q}=d/E$	$\bar{p}$	P	Q	$\bar{q}'=d'/E$	$\bar{p}'$	P'	Q'
1	0- 2 yrs	.0060	.9940	.9881	.0119	.0018	.9982	.9965	.0035
2	2- 5	.0082	.9918	.9641	.0359	.0033	.9967	.9868	.0132
3	5-10	.0148	.9852	.8946	.1054	.0057	.9943	.9588	.0412
4	10-17	.0177	.9823	.7895	.2105	.0126	.9874	.8771	.1229

Table 3c Comparative Experience by Age Group — Male Substandard Cases, All Durations Combined

Age Group	Exposure Policy-Yrs	No. of Death Claims		Mortality Ratio	Ave. Ann. Mort. Rate	Est. 8-Yr Surv. Rate	Est. 8-Yr Surv. Index	Excess Death Rate
		Observed	Expected*					
	E	d	d'	$100\,d/d'$	$\bar{q}=d/E$	$P=(1-\bar{q})^8$	$100\,P/P'$	$1000(d-d')/E$
15-29	1202	7	.96	730%	.0058	.9544	96.1%	5.0
30-39	2502	14	3.90	360	.0056	.9561	96.8	4.0
40-49	2898	25	12.55	199	.0086	.9330	96.6	4.3
50-59	1183	22	11.26	195	.0186	.8605	92.9	9.1
60 up	81	5	1.26	395	.0617	.6007	68.1	46
All Ages	7866	73	29.93	245	.0093	.9281	95.7	5.5

Table 3d Mortality by Cause of Death — Male and Female Combined

Cause	No. of Death Claims		Mortality Ratio	Excess Death Rate
	Observed†	Expected●		
Malignant Neoplasms	17	7.25	235%	1.2
Diseases of the Heart & Circulatory System	23	11.95	192	1.4
Accidents and Homicides	16	4.18	385	1.5
Suicide	5	1.29	390	0.5
All Other Causes & Unknown	14□	5.73	245	1.0
Total	75	30.40	245	5.5

* Basis of expected mortality: 1955-60 Select Basic Table
† Includes 2 females (from 234 policy-years of exposure)
● Distribution of total expected deaths by Intercompany Medically Examined
   Standard Issues 1965-70
□ Includes 5 cirrhosis of liver and 3 cerebrovascular accidents

ADDICTIONS AND INTOXICATIONS

§4–ALCOHOLIC PATIENTS IN ONTARIO

Reference: W. Schmidt and J. de Lint, "Mortality Experience of Male and Female Alcoholic Patients," Quart. J. Stud. Alcohol, 30:112-118 (1969).

Subjects Studied: Total of 5395 male and 1119 female patients admitted to the Toronto Clinic of the Addiction Research Foundation between 1951 and 1963, and diagnosed as alcoholics. The principal purpose of the investigation was to compare the effects of alcoholism on men and women. Exposure data by age and sex are indicated in the following table; distribution of the entrants is not given.

Age	15-29	30-34	35-39	40-44	45-49	50-54	55-59	60-64	65-69	70 up
Male %	4.8	9.7	15.1	17.1	17.1	15.2	10.8	5.9	2.7	1.6
Female %	6.0	11.0	15.4	18.5	18.5	14.2	9.4	4.3	1.7	1.0

Follow-up: Search was made of deaths of Ontario residents reported in all Canadian provinces for years 1951-1964. These records showed that of the patients included in the study 639 men and 99 women had died. Other patients were assumed to be living at the end of the follow-up.

Results: Mortality ratios on the average are about 200 per cent for males and about 300 per cent for females. Ratios are highest at the younger ages and diminish with age (Table 4a). Male mortality at attained ages under 50 is more than 300 per cent; at ages 60 up, however, it is only about 130 per cent. In the case of females, mortality ratios are much higher (over 700 per cent at ages under 40) and remain higher than male ratios (extra mortality seems to disappear at ages 60 and over, on the basis of a small number of deaths). EDR for both males and females runs about 12 per 1000 per year except at ages under 40 when it is less for both sexes, and at female ages over 60 where no excess mortality is indicated.

Causes of death among the subjects studied (as shown in death certificates) revealed very high mortality ratios in both sexes for alcoholism, cirrhosis of the liver, and violent deaths (Table 4b). Less marked but substantial increases were found in pneumonia and heart disease. Deaths from cancer of the upper G.I. and respiratory tracts were in excess of expected, but other cancer deaths were fewer than expected, especially in male subjects. In terms of EDR, however, the largest fraction (one-third of the total) was in deaths due to heart disease.

Comment: The method employed in follow-up tends to underestimate the number of deaths by reason of loss of contact with subjects because of patients leaving the country, changing their names, etc. Deaths in such cases might easily be missed. Generally, excess mortality in men and women alcoholics is attributable to the same causes. The authors suggest that the higher mortality ratios of females may be due to the fact that expected for females is lower than for males, and that if the same mortality standard were used for both sexes death rates among female alcoholics would actually be lower than that among males.

ALCOHOLIC PATIENTS IN ONTARIO

Table 4a Observed Data and Comparative Experience by Age (Number of Entrants — Male 5395, Female 1119)

Attained Age and Sex	Exposure Person-Yrs	Deaths during Interval	Expected Deaths*	Mortality Ratio	Ave. Ann. Mort. Rate	Est. 5-Yr Surv. Rate	Est. 5-Yr Surv. Index	Excess Death Rate
	E	d	d'	100d/d'	$\bar{q} = d/E$	$P = (1-\bar{q})^5$	100 P/P'	1000(d-d')/E
Male								
15-39	10225	60	19.3	310%	.006	.971	98.0%	4.0
40-49	11782	187	56.0	335	.016	.923	94.5	11
50-59	8953	224	114.8	195	.025	.881	94.0	12
60 up	3485	168	125.1	134	.048	.781	93.8	12
Total	34445	639	315.2	205	.019	.910	95.3	9.4
Female								
15-39	2170	17	2.43	710	.008	.962	96.7	6.7
40-49	2484	41	7.30	560	.017	.920	93.4	14
50-59	1582	31	10.8	285	.020	.906	93.7	13
60 up	468	10	10.5	95	.021	.898	100.5	−1.1
Total	6704	99	31.0	320	.015	.928	95.0	10

Table 4b Comparative Experience by Cause of Death

	5395 Male Patients Exposure 34445 Person-Yrs				1119 Female Patients Exposure 6704 Person-Yrs			
Cause of Death	Observed Deaths	Expected Deaths*	Mortality Ratio	Excess Death Rate	Observed Deaths	Expected Deaths	Mortality Ratio	Excess Death Rate
	d	d'	100 d/d'	1000(d-d')/E	d	d'	100 d/d'	1000(d-d')/E
Cancer (Upper GI tract and Respiratory)	49	17.6	280%	0.9	1	0.53	188%	0.1
Cancer (All other)	28	40.6	69	−0.4	9	9.5	95	−0.1
Alcoholism	29	1.03	2800	0.8	3	0.06	5000	0.4
Cerebrovascular	27	23.7	114	0.1	9	3.7	245	0.8
Heart Disease	247	142.1	174	3.0	30	9.0	335	3.1
Pneumonia	22	7.15	310	0.4	5	0.71	705	0.6
Cirrhosis of the liver	56	4.87	1150	1.5	12	0.48	2500	1.7
All Violent Causes	114	34.2	335	2.3	22	1.92	1150	3.0
Other	67	44.1	153	0.7	8	5.1	156	0.4
All Causes	639	315.2	205	9.4	99	31.0	320	10

*Basis of expected mortality: Ontario Reports of Vital Statistics 1951-1964

ADDICTIONS AND INTOXICATIONS

§5—TREATED CHRONIC ALCOHOLICS - SOUTH AFRICA

Reference: L. S. Gillis, "The Mortality Rate and Causes of Death of Treated Chronic Alcoholics," South Afr. Med. J., 43:230-232 (1969).

Subjects Studied: A consecutive series of 802 white patients admitted between 1959 and 1963 to the William Slater Hospital (a special psychiatric unit of the Groote Schuur Hospital, Cape Town, South Africa), for treatment of alcoholism. Distribution by age group of the patient-subjects (707 male, 95 female) was approximated from data in the report as follows:

Age Group	20-29	30-39	40-49	50-59	60-74	Total
Male	6.2%	37.2%	39.7%	15.2%	1.7%	100%
Female	3.5%	32.5%	41.8%	20.2%	2.0%	100%

All subjects were chronic addictive alcoholics of many years standing. Treatment consisted of short-term intensive psychiatric care, chemotherapy and intensive social work. Average hospital stay, 18 days: 83 per cent of patients remained for less than 35 days. Many patients evidenced associated physical sequelae such as withdrawal symptoms, enlarged livers, ataxia, etc. If such illnesses necessitated treatment in their own right the patients were dealt with in a different hospital. There were 97 cases of associated psychiatric condition, chiefly personality disorders.

Follow-up: No information given on methods, or completeness of follow-up apart from indication that death certificates were examined. No exposure reported for any duration exceeding seven years.

Results: Males were represented more heavily than females at the younger ages, as shown in the distribution table above. The overall mortality ratio for females, 475 per cent (shown in Tables 5a and 5c), is somewhat higher than the 390 per cent for males - due basically to the lighter expected rates among women. The observed rate of death among men (all ages combined - all durations, Table 5b) did exceed the female rate: 26 per 1000 against 23.

Comparative experience by duration, all ages combined, presented in Table 5a shows distinctly higher relative risks of death in the four-year period following hospital admission than subsequently. This differentiation by duration appears with respect to mortality ratios and EDR's, and in both sexes. (The number of deaths among female subjects, 9, may be too small to permit drawing any conclusions; however, 8 of the 9 deaths among females occurred in the four-year period.)

Comparative experience by age at admission, all durations combined, Table 5c, shows for males a well-marked decline in mortality ratios with increase in age. This condition does not appear to hold for females, although 4 of the 9 deaths in the seven-year follow-up period arose in the youngest age group, 20-29 years, which embraced only 3.5 per cent of the female subjects.

Causes of Death: Cardiac diseases accounted for the largest number of deaths (26), but the proportion was not greater than that experienced in the general population. Accidents accounted for 15 per cent of the total number of deaths against the 3.5 per cent in comparable age groups generally. Death by suicide was 60 to 70 times that in the general population. Significantly higher rates of death were experienced from cirrhosis of the liver and from hepatic failure.

TREATED CHRONIC ALCOHOLICS — SOUTH AFRICA

Table 5 a Observed Data and Comparative Experience by Duration (All Ages Combined)

Sex	Interval Start-End	Exposure Person-Yrs	Deaths in Interval Observed	Deaths in Interval Expected*	Mortality Ratio Interval	Mortality Ratio Cumulative	Survival Ratio Interval	Survival Ratio Cumulative	Excess Death Rate
	t to $t+\Delta t$	E	d	d'	100 d/d'	100 $\sum$d/$\sum$d'	100 p_i/p_i'	100 P/P'	1000(d-d')/E
Male	0-1 yr	707	23	3.95	580%	580%	97.3%	97.3%	27
	1-2 yrs	675	27	4.04	670	625	96.6	94.0	34
	2-3	613	13	4.02	325	525	98.5	92.6	15
	3-4	458	13	3.36	385	495	97.9	90.6	21
	4-5	321	3	2.57	117	440	99.9	90.5	1.3
	5-6	214	1	1.88	53	405	100.4	90.9	−4.1
	6-7	92	1	0.89	112	390	99.9	90.8	1.2
	0-7 yrs	3080	81	20.71	390	390	98.0	90.8	20
Female	0-1 yr	95	2	0.38	525	525	98.3	98.3	17
	1-2 yrs	92	2	0.40	500	515	98.3	96.6	17
	2-3	84	3	0.41	730	590	96.9	93.6	31
	3-4	61	1	0.32	315	530	98.9	92.5	11
	4-5	36	0	0.20	0	470	100.6	93.0	−5.6
	5-6	23	1	0.14	715	485	96.2	89.6	37
	6-7	8	0	0.05	0	475	100.6	90.1	−6.2
	0-7 yrs	399	9	1.90	475	475	98.2	90.1	18

Table 5b Derived Mortality and Survival Data by Duration (All Ages Combined)

Sex	Interval Start-End	Observed Rates Average Annual Mortality	Observed Rates Average Annual Survival	Observed Rates Cumulative Survival	Observed Rates Cumulative Mortality	Expected Rates* Average Annual Mortality	Expected Rates* Average Annual Survival	Expected Rates* Cumulative Survival	Expected Rates* Cumulative Mortality
	t to $t+\Delta t$	$\bar{q}=d/E$	$\bar{p}$	P	Q	$\bar{q}'=d'/E$	$\bar{p}'$	P'	Q'
Male	0-1 yr	.033	.967	.967	.033	.0056	.9944	.9944	.0056
	1-2 yrs	.040	.960	.929	.071	.0060	.9940	.9884	.0116
	2-3	.021	.979	.909	.091	.0066	.9934	.9819	.0181
	3-4	.028	.972	.883	.117	.0073	.9927	.9747	.0253
	4-5	.009	.991	.875	.125	.0080	.9920	.9669	.0331
	5-6	.005	.995	.871	.129	.0088	.9912	.9584	.0416
	6-7	.011	.989	.862	.138	.0097	.9903	.9491	.0509
	0-7 yrs	.026	.974	.862	.138	.0067	.9933	.9491	.0509
Female	0-1 yr	.021	.979	.979	.021	.0040	.9960	.9960	.0040
	1-2 yrs	.022	.978	.958	.042	.0043	.9957	.9917	.0083
	2-3	.036	.964	.924	.076	.0049	.9951	.9869	.0131
	3-4	.016	.984	.908	.092	.0052	.9948	.9817	.0183
	4-5	.000	1.000	.908	.092	.0056	.9944	.9762	.0238
	5-6	.043	.957	.869	.131	.0061	.9939	.9703	.0297
	6-7	.000	1.000	.869	.131	.0063	.9937	.9642	.0358
	0-7 yrs	.023	.977	.869	.131	.0048	.9952	.9642	.0358

Table 5c Comparative Experience by Age at Admission (All Durations Combined)

Sex and Age Group	Exposure Person-Yrs	Deaths Observed	Deaths Expected*	Mortality Ratio	Ave. Ann. Mort. Rate	Est. 5-Yr Surv. Rate	Est. 5-Yr Surv. Index	Excess Death Rate
	E	d	d'	100 d/d'	$\bar{q}=d/E$	$P=(1-\bar{q})^5$	100 P/P'	1000(d-d')/E
Male								
20-39	1351	28	4.1	685%	.0207	.9007	91.4%	18
40-49	1236	34	8.0	425	.0275	.8699	89.9	21
50-59	475	17	7.0	245	.0358	.8334	89.8	21
60 up	52	2	1.6	125	.0385	.8218	96.1	7.7
All Ages	3114	81	20.7	390	.0260	.8766	90.6	19
Female								
20-39	143	4	0.2	2000	.0280	.8676	87.4	27
40-49	166	2	0.8	250	.0120	.9414	96.4	7.2
50 up	88	3	0.9	335	.0341	.8407	88.5	24
All Ages	397	9	1.9	475	.0227	.8915	91.3	18

* Basis of expected mortality: 1960 South Africa White Males and Females

ADDICTIONS AND INTOXICATIONS

§6—ALCOHOLISM AND MORTALITY

Reference: P. Sundby, *Alcoholism and Mortality*, Universitetsforlaget (Norway 1967).

Subjects Studied: All male patients, residents of Oslo, discharged from the Psychiatric Department of Ullevål Hospital in Oslo in the years 1925-1939 who had been diagnosed alchoholics. Consonant with the classification of drinkers given in the 1952 report of the World Health Organization, alcoholics were considered to be habitual symptomatic excessive drinkers and addictive drinkers in need of treatment. The distribution of the 1722 subjects by age at discharge was as follows:

Age Group (years)	Under 30	30-39	40-49	50-59	60-69	70 Up	Total
Number	193	593	554	286	82	14	1722
Per Cent	11.2%	34.4%	32.2%	16.6%	4.8%	0.8%	100%

There were 159 female alcoholics but they were not included in the study.

Follow-up: Patients were kept under observation until December 31, 1962 or earlier death. During the period of the study, 1061 (61.6 per cent) subjects died, 29 (1.7 per cent) were lost to follow-up, and 632 (36.7 per cent) survived. The average period of exposure was 20.3 years. Data with regard to time, place and cause of death were obtained for 1028 deaths from death certificates. In a further 28 cases information on the cause of death was available from other sources. Five deaths required investigation by a residual case group.

Results: Overall mortality, indicated in Tables 6a and 6c, is 169 per cent of the general male population of Oslo for the years 1925-1962. Analysis of the experience according to the number of years from discharge, reflecting advancing age as well as the passage of time is presented in Table 6a. A declining trend in mortality ratio is indicated in the 25 year post-discharge interval and then an increase: 190 per cent in the first five years, 182 per cent over the succeeding ten years, 149 per cent for the following decade, but 168 per cent for 25 years and over. Excess deaths, stable for the first 25 years after discharge (between 9.7 and 11 per 1000 per year) increase to 27 per 1000 after 25 years. Interval survival ratios, 95.2 per cent in the first five years, remain practically stationary (close to 90 per cent) in the two subsequent decades of follow-up.

The upper portion of Table 6c presents data with regard to experience according to attained age. The mortality ratios shown diminish steadily with increase in attained age, declining from 385 per cent for subjects under 30 years of age to 120 per cent for those 80 years and over. Survival indexes based on five-year survival rates for all ages combined average 93.8 per cent. This index declines with increase in age for age groups over 29 years — from 97.1 per cent for age group 30-39 years to 81.5 per cent for ages 80 years and over. Extra deaths per 1000 for ages 30 years and older increase with age, rising from an annual average of 5.8 at ages 30-39 years to 34 per 1000 at ages 80 and over.

By calendar years of observation the trend in mortality ratios for all ages combined, shown in the lower part of Table 6c, is generally downward with a marked dip during World War II years. The dip is attributable to the diminished accessibility of alcohol. EDR's follow a similar course from 1925 until 1945, thereafter appearing to reach a plateau.

The Oslo cause of death code was not sufficiently comprehensive to permit comparisons of actual experience with that expected for all cause categories. Table 6d which details causes of death compares experience among the alcoholic subjects with the male population of all Norway in 1926-1935. Mortality ratios are high for all cause categories. Comparison with experience of Oslo males would also have been high but not generally as high since mortality for the mixed urban-rural population of the country as a whole is generally lower than that of urban Oslo (mortality ratio about 79 per cent). Causes with very high ratios were alcoholism, cancer of the larynx and upper digestive tract, cirrhosis of the liver, suicide, and syphilis.

ALCOHOLISM AND MORTALITY

Table 6a Observed Data and Comparative Experience by Duration (All Ages Combined)

Interval		Exposure	No. of Deaths		Mortality Ratio		Survival Ratio		Excess
No.	Start-End	Person-Yrs	Observed	Expected*	Interval	Cumulative	Interval	Cumulative	Death Rate
i	t to $t+\Delta t$	E	d	d'	100 d/d'	$100\Sigma d/\Sigma d'$	100 p_i/p_i'	100 P/P'	1000(d-d')/E
1	0- 5 yrs	8044	165	86.7	190%	190%	95.2%	95.2%	9.7
2	5-15	13520	344	188.9	182	185	89.0	84.7	11
3	15-25	9928	322	216.8	149	169	89.7	75.9	11
4	25 up	3458	230	136.6	168	169	—	—	27

Table 6b Derived Mortality and Survival Data

Interval		Observed Rates				Expected Rates*			
		Average Annual		Interval	Cumulative	Average Annual		Interval	Cumulative
No.	Start-End	Mortality	Survival	Survival	Survival	Mortality	Survival	Survival	Survival
i	t to $t+\Delta t$	$\bar{q}=d/E$	$\bar{p}$	p_i	P	$\bar{q}'=d'/E$	$\bar{p}'$	p_i'	P'
1	0- 5 yrs	.0205	.9795	.902	.902	.0108	.9892	.9472	.9472
2	5-15	.0254	.9746	.773	.697	.0140	.9860	.8685	.8226
3	15-25	.0324	.9676	.719	.501	.0218	.9782	.8022	.6599
4	25 up	.0665	.9335	—	—	.0395	.9605	—	—

Table 6c Comparative Experience by Attained Age and by Calendar Years

Category	Exposure Person-Yrs	No. of Deaths		Mortality Ratio	Ave. Ann. Mort. Rate	Est. 5-Yr Surv. Rate	Est. 5-Yr Surv. Index	Excess Death Rate
		Observed	Expected*					
	E	d	d'	100 d/d'	$\bar{q}=d/E$	$P=(1-\bar{q})^5$	100 P/P'	1000(d-d')/E
Attained Age								
Under 30 yrs	758	10	2.6	385%	.013	.935	95.1%	9.9
30-39	4700	48	20.7	230	.010	.950	97.1	5.8
40-49	9630	158	70.0	225	.016	.921	95.5	9.1
50-59	10770	269	141.4	190	.025	.881	94.1	12
60-69	6572	320	196.6	163	.049	.779	90.7	19
70-79	2226	197	148.5	133	.088	.629	88.9	22
80 up	295	59	49.1	120	.200	.328	81.5	34
Calendar Yrs of Observation								
1925-1930	1962	58	24.2	240	.030	.860	91.5	17
1931-1935	4099	110	49.7	220	.027	.873	92.8	15
1936-1940	6294	141	86.6	163	.022	.893	95.7	8.6
1941-1945	6624	146	96.6	151	.022	.895	96.3	7.5
1946-1950	5775	173	94.7	183	.030	.859	93.3	14
1951-1955	4870	183	106.0	173	.038	.826	92.1	16
1956-1962	5327	250	171.0	146	.047*	.787	92.6	15
All Subjects	34951	1061	629.0	169	.030	.857	93.8	12

Table 6d Comparative Mortality by Cause of Death among Alcoholics

Cause of Death	No. of Deaths	Mortality Ratio†	Excess Death Rate	Cause of Death	No. of Deaths	Mortality Ratio†	Excess Death Rate
	d	100 d/d'	1000(d-d')/E		d	100 d/d'	1000(d-d')/E
Tuberculosis	68	210%	1.0	Other cardiovasclar dis.	66	136%	0.5
Syphilis	19	455	0.4	Other diseases of resp. org.	102	285	1.9
Cancer of larynx and upper digestive tract	67	1170	1.8	Diseases of digestive organs except cirrhosis	28	154	0.3
Cancer of other digest. organs	77	144	0.7	Cirrhosis of liver	22	990	0.6
Cancer of lung	19	355	0.4	Diseases of genitourinary org.	31	131	0.2
All other malign. tumors	41	129	0.3	Suicide	54	800	1.3
Diabetes mellitus	14	320	0.3	Accidents, homicides, intoxications	95	270	1.7
Chronic alcoholism	19	4600	0.5	All other causes	116	196	1.6
Apoplexy	103	186	1.4				
Coronary Heart Disease	120	161	1.3	Total	1061	215	16

* Basis of expected mortality: Oslo male population 1925-1962

† Basis of expected mortality: Norwegian males 1926-1935

OCCUPATIONAL HAZARDS

§20–MORTALITY BY OCCUPATIONAL GROUP

Reference: *1967 Occupation Study,* compiled and published by the Society of Actuaries, Chicago (1967).

Subjects Studied: A large group of men age 20-59 issued insurance by 17 major life insurance companies in the United States and Canada during the period 1949-1963. The occupational categories were based on the Occupation Code published in 1926 by the Joint Medico-Actuarial Committee on Mortality. This study focused primarily on occupations that were considered substandard by most insurance companies for the purpose of issuing life insurance, although some other occupations possibly subject to an increased mortality risk but issued standard insurance were also included. The companies submitted data covering 3,252,262 policy years of exposure and 9418 policies terminated by death of which 1,524,740 and 5999, respectively, were on substandard risks. All the policies were individual insurance policies with the standard and substandard risks being studied separately. The substandard ratings were based solely on occupation, policies with other significant risks being excluded.

Follow-up: The policy record over the ten-year period between the 1954 and 1964 policy anniversaries was used for follow-up information and was the basis for calculating exposure and counting the number of death claims.

Results: As evident in Table 20a, many occupational groups experienced more than 1.5 extra deaths per 1000 per year, including lumbermen, miners, explosives workers, construction crane and hoist operators, ship construction workers, structural iron workers, many railroad workers, taxi drivers, substandard truck drivers, substandard marine officers and crew, several types of guards, marshals and detectives, and persons selling, delivering or serving liquor. Several groups had little or no excess mortality (EDR less than 0.5): chemical industry workers, semi-skilled metal workers, power plant and telecommunication workers, standard guards, hotel and restaurant workers who do not handle liquor, military personnel, and standard manufacturing laborers. The remaining occupations had excess death rates ranging from 0.5 to 1.5. The mortality ratio was 147 per cent for the total substandard experience with 1.25 excess deaths per 1000 per year, while the mortality ratio was 108 per cent with 0.15 extra deaths for the total standard experience.

Accidents accounted for a large portion of the extra deaths among lumbermen, miners, structural iron workers and marine crew (Table 20b). In addition, the excess accidental death rate was high (greater than 1.0) for oil and gas field workers, while their overall excess death rate was moderately high. A few occupational groups, quarrymen, explosives workers, substandard sawmill operators, electric linemen, some railroad and marine workers, and penal guards, had moderate excess accidental death rates (0.5-0.9). For the remaining occupations, accidental deaths were low. The excess death rate due to motor vehicle accidents alone and to all accidents was lower for taxi drivers and truck drivers than for some other occupational groups. Accidental death rates were also low for firemen, policemen and military personnel.

Cardiovascular disease was, for almost all occupational groups, the leading category of cause of death. The excess death rate due to cardiovascular disease was high (greater than 1.0 per 1000) for crane and hoistmen in the construction industry, ship construction workers, railroad conductors and engineers, substandard marine officers, some guards, marshals and detectives. However, among a few of the more strenuous occupations, such as lumbermen, oil and gas field workers, several groups of metal workers, structural iron workers, marine crew, longshoremen, and non-manufacturing laborers, the incidence of cardiovascular disease as a cause of death was less than expected.

Cancer was the second major cause of death with high mortality ratios for many types of railroad workers, officers, construction crane and hoist operators, structural iron workers, some guards, chemical industry operators, taxi drivers, and persons who sell and serve liquor. In most of these categories, the excess death rate due to cancer fell into the lower or intermediate range (less than 1.0 per 1000).

The mortality ratio due to acute respiratory diseases (pneumonia and influenza) was very high for coal miners (1100 per cent). Persons who sell and serve liquor experienced a high mortality ratio due to cirrhosis of the liver (670 per cent). Because the numbers of deaths were still small relative to total deaths and exposures, the excess death rates remained low (0.3 per 1000 or less) for these causes and some others where the mortality ratio was also significantly elevated.

MORTALITY BY OCCUPATIONAL GROUP

Table 20a   Mortality Experience of Insured Men by Major Occupational Group

Occupational Class		Insurance Action	Average Issue Age	Exposure Policy-Yrs	No. of Death Claims		Mortality Ratio	Excess Death Rate
					Observed	Expected†		
		S or SS*	x	E	d	d'	100 d/d'	1000(d-d')/E
A5-A7	Lumbermen	SS	32.4	16052	76	30.8	245%	2.8
B8-B10	Underground Miners - Coal	SS	35.1	43045	215	125.1	172	2.1
B11-B12	Underground Miners - Other	SS	31.3	34332	124	58.7	210	1.9
B13-B14	Open Pit Miners, Quarrymen	SS	32.5	12278	53	30.8	172	1.8
B15	Oil & Gas Field	S & SS	32.1	18975	56	39.1	143	0.9
C1-C2	Chemical Industry Operators	S & SS	34.0	50346	133	126.6	105	0.1
C3-C6	Explosives	SS	33.1	10033	41	22.8	180	1.8
D6	Metals-Coremakers & Sandmolders	SS	33.8	13667	47	41.2	114	0.4
D7-D8	Metals-Buffers, Polishers & Grinders	SS	33.3	17153	64	48.9	131	0.9
D9	Metals-Welders	S & SS	33.5	98560	338	252.3	134	0.9
D11-D12	Metals-Furnacemen	SS	33.9	15584	60	42.4	142	1.1
D13-D14	Metals-Molders & Semi-Skilled	S & SS	34.1	53241	116	138.7	84	−0.4
D15-D16	Saw Mill	S	34.2	17476	54	42.7	126	0.7
		SS	26.3	14497	49	33.4	147	1.1
E1-E2	Construction & Linemen-Climbing	SS	27.3	56940	155	105.6	147	0.9
E3-E4	Linemen & Electricians-Non-Climb	SS	33.6	16868	66	46.4	142	1.2
E5	Power Plant-Other	S & SS	34.0	21331	61	59.8	102	0.1
E6-E7	Telecommunications-Linemen	S & SS	28.4	129442	171	167.8	102	0.0
F4	Construction-crane, hoist	SS	34.6	14678	82	47.5	173	2.4
F5	Ship Construction	SS	35.4	10070	50	30.6	164	1.9
F9	Structural Iron	SS	32.7	25752	103	49.0	210	2.1
G1-G4	Railroad	S	36.5	15320	66	37.9	174	1.8
G1	RR-Brakemen	SS	33.0	25371	75	58.3	129	0.7
G2	RR-Conductors	SS	39.5	13186	94	62.6	150	2.4
G3	RR-Engineers	SS	41.3	15544	147	92.7	159	3.5
G4	RR-Firemen	SS	32.7	25433	107	63.8	168	1.7
G6	RR-Switchmen & Flagmen	SS	33.3	20444	79	47.3	167	1.6
G9	Taxi Drivers	S & SS	36.0	16222	85	55.4	153	1.8
G10	Truck Drivers	S	32.4	144132	394	268.3	147	0.9
		SS	32.4	9520	49	25.4	193	2.5
G11	Marine-Capt., Mates, Engrs.	S	34.7	14944	50	37.6	133	0.8
		SS	35.8	12992	77	46.1	167	2.4
G12	Marine-Sailors, Deck, Oilers, Stokers	SS	32.1	30024	107	56.4	190	1.7
G13	Marine-Mechanics, Stewards, Cooks	SS	36.2	11852	45	34.6	130	0.9
G14	Marine-Longshoremen	SS	35.2	24694	91	63.3	144	1.1
I1	Guards-Penal	SS	35.3	6855	39	21.2	184	2.6
I2	Guards-Other	S	42.0	10756	49	45.8	107	0.3
		SS	39.7	13702	138	76.5	180	4.5
J1	Firemen	SS	33.9	71874	199	163.8	122	0.5
J2-J3	Marshals & Detectives	SS	36.8	8684	49	31.1	158	2.1
J5	Policemen	S	31.6	17459	36	25.0	144	0.6
		SS	33.0	69871	216	177.6	122	0.6
L3-L6	Liquor-Retail & Delivery	S & SS	35.8	37847	196	113.8	172	2.2
M1-M4	Hotel, Restaurant-Not Liquor	S & SS	37.0	152168	533	484.2	110	0.3
M5-M8	Hotel, Restaurant, Bar-Liquor	SS	37.5	157696	798	481.7	166	2.0
N1-N4	Military-Officers	S	29.2	415788	461	560.3	82	−0.2
N5	Military-Enlisted	S	28.1	340866	463	351.7	132	0.3
O1-O8	Laborers-Manufacturing	S	35.2	30067	89	84.7	105	0.1
		SS	31.6	83251	272	189.1	144	1.0
O9-O13	Laborers-Non-Manufacturing	S	32.1	31643	79	64.4	123	0.5
O9-O11	Laborers-Construction	SS	32.9	58302	164	136.3	120	0.5

* S-Standard issue. SS-Substandard (rate) issue.
† Basis of expected mortality: 1955-60 Select Basic Table (Male)

OCCUPATIONAL HAZARDS

§20–MORTALITY BY OCCUPATIONAL GROUP (continued)

Comment: The original study contains, for most occupational groups, a detailed breakdown of the mortality experience by age and policy duration. The excess death rate tended to increase with age and policy duration, but the rate of increase was less marked for occupations in which accidents were a major cause of death. Mortality ratio showed a tendency to decrease with age and duration in many substandard occupation categories, although there were some exceptions. The mortality ratios were found to have decreased in a large number of occupations since the 1928 and 1937 Occupation Studies. Even in the few categories where the mortality ratio was higher in the 1967 Study, excess death rates were generally lower, because of the improvement in the level of standard mortality in the past 40 years. The 1967 Study also summarizes mortality data by occupational category from other sources: U.S. Bureau of Labor (1963), U.S. Public Health Service (1950), and Group Life Insurance experience (1956-1964).

Footnotes for Table 20b, "Mortality By Occupational Group".

* Basis of expected mortality: 1955-60 Select Basic Table (Male)

† CAN	Malignant neoplasm	OCV	Other cardiovascular disease	RESP	Respiratory disease	LIV	Cirrhosis
CHD	Coronary heart disease	CV	All cardiovascular disease	MVA	Motor vehicle accidents	DIS	Other disease

● Excludes Motor Vehicle Accidents

MORTALITY BY OCCUPATIONAL GROUP

Table 20b Cause-Specific Mortality Experience of Insured Men by Major Occupational Group

Code	Category	Exposure E	No. of Accidental Deaths Observed d_a	No. of Accidental Deaths Expected* d_a'	Excess Death Rate $1000(d_a-d_a')/E$	Cause†	d_c	Excess Death Rate $1000(d_c-d_c')/E$	Cause†	d_c	Excess Death Rate $1000(d_c-d_c')/E$
A5-A7	Lumbermen	16052	32●	3.2	1.8	MVA	16	0.8	CV	10	-0.2
B8-B10	Miners-Coal	43045	61●	9.8	1.2	DIS	23	0.3	RESP	14	0.3
B11-B12	Miners-Other	34332	49●	6.7	1.2	DIS	11	0.2	OCV	11	0.2
B13-B14	Quarrymen	12278	11●	2.7	0.7	CHD	18	0.6	CAN	7	0.1
B15	Oil and Gas Fields	18975	28	7.0	1.1	CHD	10	-0.2	CAN	8	0.0
C1-C2	Chemical Industry	50346	19	19.9	0.0	CHD	41	-0.1	CAN	33	0.1
C3-C6	Explosives	10033	12	3.7	0.8	CHD	13	0.5	CAN	7	0.2
D6	Metals-Core & Sandmold	13667	5	5.5	0.0	CAN	11	0.2	DIS	10	0.4
D7-D8	Metals-Buff, Polish & Grind	17153	10	6.9	0.2	CAN	18	0.5	CHD	15	-0.1
D9	Metals-Welders	98560	41●	21.9	0.2	OCV	35	0.1	RESP	8	0.1
D11-D12	Metals-Furnacemen	15584	6	6.2	0.0	CHD	23	0.5	CAN	10	0.1
D13-D14	Metals-Semi-skill	53241	8●	11.6	-0.1	CV	48	-0.3	MVA	13	0.1
D15-D16	Saw Mill-S	17476	11●	3.7	0.4	CV	22	0.2	—		—
	-SS	14497	14●	3.0	0.8	—		—	—		—
E1-E2	Construct. & Linemen-Climb	56940	48●	11.3	0.6	CV	45	0.0	MVA	17	0.1
E3-E4	Linemen-Elect.-Non-Climb	16868	16	6.7	0.6	CHD	20	0.2	OCV	11	0.4
E5	Power Plant-Other	21331	7●	4.7	0.1	CV	30	0.1	CAN	10	-0.1
E6-E7	Telecomm.-Linemen	129442	17●	23.8	-0.1	CHD	48	0.1	CAN	35	0.0
F4	Construction-Hoist & Crane	14678	6●	3.5	0.2	CV	38	1.1	CAN	16	0.4
F5	Ship Construction	10070	6●	2.4	0.4	CV	26	1.1	—		—
F9	Structural Iron	25752	40●	5.2	1.4	CV	16	-0.2	CAN	26	0.6
G1-G4	Railroad-S	15320	11●	3.3	0.5	CHD	22	0.5	CAN	16	0.5
G1	RR-Brakemen-SS	25371	18●	5.3	0.5	CV	25	0.0	CAN	16	0.2
G2	RR-Conductors-SS	13186	7●	3.5	0.3	CV	52	1.6	RESP	5	0.3
G3	RR-Engineers-SS	15544	5●	4.4	0.0	CV	86	2.5	CAN	33	0.8
G4	RR-Firemen-SS	25433	13●	5.6	0.3	CV	43	0.6	CAN	29	0.6
G6	RR-Switch & Flagmen-SS	20444	11●	4.3	0.3	CV	27	0.3	CAN	14	0.2
G9	Taxi drivers	16222	4	3.8	0.0	CV	39	0.8	CAN	19	0.4
G10	Truck drivers-S	144132	60●	28.9	0.2	CV	139	0.2	MVA	66	0.3
	-SS	9520	4	2.1	0.2	CV	18	0.7	CAN	11	0.6
G11	Marine-Capt, Mate, Engr.-S	14944	8●	3.2	0.3	MVA	8	0.4	CHD	10	-0.2
	-SS	12992	14●	3.1	0.8	CV	36	1.1			
G12	Marine-Sailors	30024	29●	5.9	0.8	CHD	13	-0.2	DIS	20	0.5
G13	Marine-Mech, Stew, Cook	11852	10	4.6	0.5	CHD	10	-0.2	CAN	10	0.2
G14	Marine-Longshoremen	24694	27	9.6	0.7	CHD	20	-0.1	CAN	13	0.0
I1	Guards-Penal	6855	7	2.8	0.6	CV	16	0.9	—		—
I2	Guards-Other-S	10756	6	4.6	0.1	CHD	24	0.5	CAN	11	0.1
	-SS	13702	5	6.6	-0.1	CHD	61	2.2	CAN	30	0.9
J1	Firemen	71874	25●	15.2	0.1	CV	94	0.3	DIS	26	0.1
J2-J3	Marshals & Detectives	8684	7	3.6	0.4	CV	26	1.3	—		—
J5	Policemen-S	17459	5	6.2	-0.1	CV	16	0.4	—		—
	-SS	69871	30	27.3	0.0	CHD	73	0.2	CAN	45	0.1
L3-L6	Liquor-Retail & Delivery	37847	4●	8.7	-0.1	LIV	11	0.2	CV	83	0.8
M1-M4	Hotel, Rest Not Liquor	152168	61●	61.9	0.0	CAN	127	0.1	CHD	184	0.0
M5-M8	Hotel, Rest, Bar-Liquor	157696	35●	36.4	0.0	LIV	45	0.2	CV	311	0.5
N1-N4	Military-Officers	415788	97●	77.4	0.0	CV	154	-0.1	MVA	45	-0.1
N5	Military-Enlisted	340866	86●	61.7	0.1	MVA	135	0.2	—		—
O1-O8	Laborers-Manuf-S	30067	5	11.5	-0.2	CHD	41	0.3	CAN	22	0.1
	-SS	83251	42	31.3	0.1	CV	119	0.5	CAN	53	0.2
O9-O13	Laborers-Non-manufacturing	31643	16	11.8	0.1	CHD	18	-0.1	OCV	10	0.1
O9-O11	Laborers-Construction	58302	20●	12.2	0.1	DIS	23	0.2	CAN	36	0.1

ENVIRONMENTAL RISKS

§40—RELATION OF SMOKING TO MORTALITY

Reference: E. C. Hammond, "Smoking in Relation to Mortality and Morbidity. Findings in First Thirty-Four Months of Follow-up in a Prospective Study Started in 1959," J. Nat. Cancer Inst., 32:1161-1188 (1964).

Subjects Studied: 442,094 men age 40-89 drawn from a larger group of 1,078,894 adults residing in 1121 U.S. counties of all sizes. Volunteer workers of the American Cancer Society enrolled these subjects as part of a prospective study, between October 1, 1959 and February 15, 1960. Counties were of all sizes, in urban and rural areas, and distributed in 25 different states of the U.S. Enrollment was by family units (households), based on at least one person over age 45, in which case all persons over age 30 were included. All eligible family members were requested to fill out detailed questionnaires on their smoking habits and many other factors, such as occupation, family history, past diseases, current medical symptoms, etc. The only age-eligible subjects excluded from the study were illiterates, persons too ill to answer a questionnaire, and those who could not be traced.

Follow-up: Subjects were traced annually and once every two years were asked to fill out a brief questionnaire. Whenever a death was reported, a copy of the death certificate was obtained. When cancer was mentioned in the death certificate, the doctor was asked for information on the diagnosis and the type of neoplasm. Of all persons enrolled, 99.0 per cent were successfully traced. Follow-up continued to September 30, 1962.

Results: Mortality and survival experience for three categories of smokers (cigarettes only; cigarettes and other forms of tobacco; pipes or cigars) is compared with that of non-smokers in Table 40a. Ex-smokers are included in each category. Results among men with a history of smoking only cigarettes are the most unfavorable. The overall mortality ratio is 167 per cent of that among non-smokers, and the annual average excess death rate for all ages combined is 8.3 per 1000. In this category there is a steady decline in the mortality ratios with advancing age at enrollment — from 240 per cent at ages 40-49 years to 118 per cent at ages 80-89. The EDR, however, tends to increase, advancing from 3.5 at ages 40-49 to over 20 per 1000 at ages 70 years and older. Subjects smoking pipes or cigars as well as cigarettes experience a lower, parallel, level of comparative mortality: for all ages combined, the mortality ratio is 141 per cent and the EDR, 5.1 per 1000. Pipe and cigar smokers have mortality experience only slightly higher than non-smokers: the overall mortality ratio is 107 per cent and the EDR, 0.9 per 1000.

Table 40b deals with current smokers of cigarettes only over the full age range 40-89 years and analyzes their experience according to (1) the number of cigarettes smoked per day, (2) the degree of smoke inhalation, and (3) the age at which the subject started to smoke. Experience is compared with that of non-smokers. Both mortality ratios and excess death rates increase with the number of cigarettes smoked per day. For the successive categories of the number of cigarettes smoked (1-9, 10-19, 20-39, 40 and over), the respective mortality ratios are 149, 177, 179 and 191 per cent, and EDR's, 6.0, 9.4, 9.6 and 11 per 1000. Details in the reference with respect to age in conjunction with the daily comsumption of cigarettes reveal that the general level of mortality ratios and their upward trend with the amount of smoking are most pronounced in the younger age groups. With respect to inhalation, a definite advance in extra mortality is indicated as the degree of inhalation increases. Non-inhalers, slight inhalers, moderate inhalers and deep inhalers reveal mortality ratios, respectively, of 145, 167, 178 and 215 per cent, and excess death rates of 5.5, 8.3, 9.6 and 14 per 1000. When categorized by age at which the smoking habit was started, excess mortality was at a maximum for those who started smoking at the earliest age, with a mortality ratio of 210 per cent for those commencing under age 15. The mortality ratio diminished in successively older age groups to 135 per cent for men who did not start to smoke until age 25 or later.

EFFECTS OF SMOKING ON MORTALITY

Table 40a   Comparative 3-Year Experience by Age and Smoking Category*

Smoking Category	Age at Enrollment	No. of Men	No. Deaths Observed	Ave. Ann. Mort. Rate†	Est. 3-Yr Surv. Rate	Mortality Ratio	Est. 3-Yr Surv. Index	Excess Death Rate
	x	ℓ	d	q̄	P	100 q̄/q̄'	100 P/P'	1000(q̄-q̄')
Non-Smokers	40-49 yrs	24,556	177	.0025	.9925	—	—	—
(Basis of Expected	50-59	33,514	625	.0065	.9806	—	—	—
Deaths, Mortality	60-69	21,899	1172	.0190	.9441	—	—	—
and Survival Rates)	70-79	10,273	1293	.0462	.8677	—	—	—
	80-89	2,222	648	.1186	.6847	—	—	—
	40-89	92,464	3915	.0123	.9639	(100%)	(100.0%)	(0.0)
Cigarettes Only	40-49	67,328	1144	.0060	.9821	240%	99.0%	3.5
	50-59	80,107	2912	.0131	.9612	200	98.0	6.6
	60-69	32,213	2722	.0314	.9087	165	96.2	12
	70-79	7,159	1256	.0691	.8067	150	93.0	23
	80-89	651	213	.1396	.6369	118	93.0	21
	40-89	187,558	8247	.0206	.9395	167	97.5	8.3
Cigarettes and Other	40-49	26,592	359	.0048	.9857	192	99.3	2.3
	50-59	37,775	1171	.0110	.9674	169	98.7	4.5
	60-69	21,522	1570	.0265	.9226	139	97.7	7.5
	70-79	6,206	964	.0600	.8306	130	95.7	14
	80-89	684	201	.1247	.6706	105	97.9	6.1
	40-89	92,779	4265	.0174	.9487	141	98.4	5.1
Pipe, Cigars or Both	40-49	8,965	76	.0030	.9910	120	99.8	0.5
	50-59	15,997	339	.0073	.9782	112	99.8	0.8
	60-69	14,145	840	.0210	.9383	111	99.4	2.0
	70-79	7,494	979	.0478	.8633	103	99.5	1.6
	80-89	1,723	492	.1151	.6929	97	101.2	−3.5
	40-89	48,324	2726	.0132	.9609	107	99.7	0.9

Table 40b   Comparative 3-Year Experience by Smoking Characteristic, Current Smokers, Cigarettes Only (All Ages Combined)

Smoking Characteristic	Ave. Ann. Mort. Rate	Est. 3-Yr Surv. Rate	Mortality Ratio	Est. 3-Yr Surv. Index	Excess Death Rate
	q̄	P	100 q̄/q̄'	100 P/P'	1000(q̄-q̄')
Non-Smokers (Basis of Expected Rates)	.0123	.9636	(100%)	(100.0%)	(0.0)
Number of Cigarettes per Day					
1- 9	.0183	.9461	149%	98.2%	6.0
10-19	.0217	.9363	177	97.2	9.4
20-39	.0219	.9357	179	97.1	9.6
40 and over	.0235	.9311	191	96.6	11
Degree of Inhalation					
None	.0178	.9475	145	98.3	5.5
Slight	.0205	.9398	167	97.5	8.3
Moderate	.0218	.9360	178	97.1	9.6
Deep	.0262	.9234	215	95.8	14
Age at Start of Smoking					
25 yrs and up	.0166	.9510	135	98.7	4.3
20-24	.0192	.9435	157	97.9	6.9
15-19	.0236	.9308	192	96.6	11
Under 15	.0258	.9246	210	95.9	14

*   Non-smokers are those who have never smoked.   Other categories include current and ex-smokers.
†   q̄ = Σd/ΣE by quinquennial age group, age-adjusted to total age distribution

ENVIRONMENTAL RISKS

§40—RELATION OF SMOKING TO MORTALITY

Results (continued): Analyses of combinations of the three variables dealt with in Table 40b indicate that to some extent the variables are interrelated. Thus, deep inhalation accompanies a larger number of cigarettes smoked. Those starting at a younger age tend to smoke more cigarettes and to inhale more deeply than those starting at an older age.

To throw light on the question whether the association between cigarette smoking and death rates might result from an incidental conjunction of cigarette smoking and some other factor or factors that could influence the death rate, a "matched pair" analysis was undertaken in which men who never smoked and men who currently smoked 20 or more cigarettes a day were matched as to age, race, height, nativity, residence (rural or urban), urban occupational exposure to health hazards, religion, education, marital status, drinking habits, hours slept, exercise taken, presence of severe nervous tension, use of tranquilizers, whether sick at present, history of cancer other than skin cancer, and history of heart disease, stroke, or high blood pressure. A computer process found 36975 matched pairs, i.e., pairs of men who were alike in the specifications listed differing only in their smoking habits. The results are set forth in Table 40c. In every 5-year age group, many more deaths occurred among the cigarette smokers than among the non-smokers. The mortality ratio for ages 40-79 years combined (the age range studied) was 210 per cent. For ages 40-59 the ratio was 245 per cent and for ages 60-79 it was 175 per cent. EDR increased with age, ranging from 2.5 to 35 extra deaths per 1000 per year, the average being 6.6.

Table 40d presents findings for ex-cigarette smokers and current smokers compared with men who had never smoked regularly. The analysis is arranged according to the number of years since a cigarette was last smoked, and according to the extent of smoking (1-19 and 20 or more cigarettes per day). A pronounced improvement in mortality is indicated with the passage of time after discontinuance of the habit. For those who smoked less than 20 cigarettes daily, all categories of interval since smoking was given up exhibited an excess mortality lower than the 6.5 extra deaths per 1000 per year of current smokers. The age-standardized death rate for men who discontinued smoking more than 10 years previously was actually lower than the rate for men who had never smoked, an exception to the finding of excess mortality in virtually all smoking categories. Men who had recently stopped smoking at the level of one pack (20 cigarettes) per day or more had a mortality ratio of 275 per cent, significantly greater than the 205 per cent ratio of current smokers. The explanation given for the heavier mortality is that illness often leads to cessation of smoking so that recent ex-smokers include a high proportion of men in poor health. The mortality ratio decreased to 124 per cent in ex-smokers who stopped 10 years or more prior to enrollment.

Presented in Table 40e are mortality ratio groupings according to cause of death among cigarette-smoking subjects (whether or not they also smoked cigars and pipes) relative to rates of death among non-smokers, adjusted for distribution by age. Death rates from the following diseases are much higher in cigarette smokers than in non-smokers: cancer of the lung, mouth and throat, larynx, esophagus, bladder and pancreas; gastric ulcer; emphysema; and aortic aneurysm. Coronary artery disease (CHD) death rates are closely correlated with cigarette smoking among men in the middle-aged groups, but less so among older men. In age group 40-69 the CHD mortality ratio was 182 per cent and in the men age 70-89 only 125 per cent. For cancer as a whole (i.e., for all sites combined), the death rate of cigarette smokers was considerably higher than the death rate of non-smokers, the mortality ratio being 198 per cent in age range 40-69 but somewhat less (175 per cent) in age range 70-89. The relationship between cigarette smoking and death rates from lung cancer appears to increase with advancing age: in age group 40-69 the lung cancer mortality ratio of all men with a history of cigarette smoking is 785 per cent, while in age group 70-89 the ratio rises to 1900 per cent. Additional causes of death are classified as "middle risk" and "low risk" (mortality ratio under 185 per cent) in Table 40e. In the younger men lymphomas and cancers of the colon and rectum, and prostate showed no excess mortality attributable to smoking as mortality ratios were slightly under 100 per cent; there were no such ratios in the older men. The mortality ratio for all causes combined was 174 per cent in men age 40-69 and 131 per cent in men 70-89.

RELATION OF SMOKING TO MORTALITY

Table 40c Comparative 3-Year Experience, Matched Pairs of Cigarette Smokers (20 or more per Day) vs. Men who Never Smoked

Age Group	Matched Pairs	Cigarette Smokers Estim. Total Exposure	No. of Deaths	Non-Smokers Estim. Total Exposure	No. of Deaths	Mortality Ratio	Est. 3-Yr Surv. Index	Excess Death Rate
x	$\ell=\ell'$	E 3ℓ-d	d	E' $3\ell'$-d'	d'	100 d/d'	100 P/P'	1000($\bar{q}$-$\bar{q}'$)
40-44 yrs	3410	10190	40	10215	15	265%	99.2%	2.5
45-49	10468	31212	192	31345	59	325	98.7	4.3
50-54	9583	28497	252	28626	123	205	98.6	4.6
55-59	6534	19279	323	19467	135	240	97.1	9.8
60-64	3990	11716	254	11820	150	169	97.4	9.0
65-69	2083	6056	193	6151	98	197	95.2	16
70-74	747	2143	98	2177	64	153	95.0	16
75-79	160	447	33	462	18	183	89.5	35
Total	36975	109540	1385	110263	662	210	98.0	6.6

Table 40d Comparative 3-Year Experience, Ex-Smokers Age 40-69 by Time Since Stopped Smoking

No. Cigarettes per Day	Stopped Smoking	No. of Men	No. of Deaths	Ave. Ann. Mort. Rate	Est. 3-Yr Surv. Rate	Mortality Ratio	Est. 3-Yr Surv. Index	Excess Death Rate
	Yrs	ℓ	d	$\bar{q}$	P	100 $\bar{q}/\bar{q}'$	100 P/P'	1000($\bar{q}$-$\bar{q}'$)
None (Basis of Expected Rates	—	—	—	.0081	.9759	100%	100.0%	0.0
1-19/day Ex-Smokers	<1 yr	1118	40	.0133	.9606	163%	98.5%	5.2
	1-4 yrs	2755	99	.0125	.9630	156	98.7	4.4
	5-9 yrs	2552	79	.0108	.9679	133	99.2	2.6
	10 yrs up	5852	129	.0070	.9791	86	100.3	−1.1
	All	12277	347	.0095	.9718	117	99.6	1.4
1-19/day Current Smokers		34543	1366	.0146	.9568	180	98.0	6.5
20 up/day Ex-Smokers	<1 yr	3628	190	.0222	.9349	275	95.8	14
	1-4 yrs	8050	366	.0172	.9493	210	97.3	9.0
	5-9 yrs	8588	282	.0123	.9636	151	98.7	4.2
	10 yrs up	10788	334	.0101	.9700	124	99.4	2.0
	All	31054	1172	.0136	.9598	168	98.3	5.5
20 up/day Current Smokers		97776	3703	.0167	.9507	205	97.4	8.6

Table 40e Severity Classification of Mortality Ratios by Cause of Death - Male Cigarette Smokers*

Mortality Risk Group	Age 40-69 Cancer Deaths	Other Deaths	Age 70-89 Cancer Deaths	Other Deaths
High Risk (350% up)	Lung (790) Mouth & Throat (555)† Larynx (360)† Esophagus (365†)	Emphysema (885)† Gastric Ulcer (540)†	Lung (1910)† Esophagus (830)† Larynx (>600)†	Emphysema (1550)† Aortic Aneurysm (425)
Middle Risk (185-349%)	Bladder (330)† Pancreas (295) Leukemia (187) All Cancers (198)	Aortic Aneurysm (295) Duodenal Ulcer (197)† Pneumonia, Other Lung (192)	Bladder (315)† Mouth & Throat (235) Pancreas (190)	Gastric Ulcer (295)† Other Lung Dis. (210)
Low Risk (<185%)	Liver (184)† Kidney (143) Stomach (139) Colon, Rectum (98) Prostate (97) Lymphomas (91)	Cor. Heart Dis. (182) Other Heart Dis. (139) Cerebrovascular (128) Other Circulatory (151) Cirrhosis of Liver (170) Diabetes (121) Kidney Dis. (114)	All Cancers (175) Leukemia (158) Kidney (149)† Stomach (138) Lymphomas (129) Colon, Rectum (114) Prostate (111)	Cor. Heart Dis. (125) Other Heart Dis. (138) Cerebrovascular (94)† Other Circulatory (113) Pnemonia (154) Duodenal Ulcer (147) Diabetes, Kidney Dis. (88)
Average	All Causes (174)		All Causes (131)	

* Basis of expected mortality rates: men who never smoked regularly
† Mortality ratio based on fewer than 10 deaths in men who never smoked regularly

ENVIRONMENTAL RISKS

§41–RELATION OF CIGARETTE SMOKING TO MORTALITY

Reference: "Smoking and Health - Report of the Advisory Committee to the Surgeon General of the Public Health Service," U.S. Department of Health, Education and Welfare Publication No. 1103 (1964). See Chapter 8, "Mortality."

Subjects Studied: 1,123,000 male smokers reported on in seven large prospective studies conducted over several periods between 1951 and 1963. The seven groups of male subjects were:

(1) *British Doctors* (based on questionnaires sent to all members of the medical profession in the United Kingdom). See R. Doll and A. B. Hill, "Lung Cancer and Other Causes of Death in Relation to Smoking," Brit. Med. J., 2:1071-1081 (1956).

(2) *Nine States* (based on questionnaires filled in by white American men between ages 50 and 69 in nine states). See E. C. Hammond and D. Horn, "Smoking and Death Rates - Report on Forty-Four Months of Follow-up on 187,783 Men. Part I. Total Mortality. Part II. Death Rates by Cause," J. Am. Med. Assoc., 166:1159-1172, 1294-1308 (1958).

(3) *U.S. Veterans* (data on men who served in the armed forces between 1917 and 1940 and were holders of U.S. Government life insurance policies). See H. F. Dorn, "The Mortality of Smokers and Non-Smokers," Proc. Soc. Stat. Sec. Am. Stat. Assoc., 34-71 (1958).

(4) *Nine Occupations* (data with regard to men aged 35-64 in nine occupations in California suspected of being subject to a higher than usual occupational risk of developing lung cancer). See J. E. Dunn, Jr., G. Linden, L. Breslow, "Lung Cancer Mortality Experience of Men in Certain Occupations in California," Am. J. Pub. Health, 50:1475-1487 (1960).

(5) *American Legion* (California members of the American Legion and their wives). See J. E. Dunn, Jr., P. Buell, L. Breslow, "California State Department of Public Health, Special Report to the Surgeon General's Advisory Committee on Smoking and Health."

(6) *Canadian Veterans* (data on pensioned Canadian veterans of World Wars I and II and the Korean War). See E. W. R. Best, G. H. Josie, C. B. Walker, "A Canadian Study of Mortality in Relation to Smoking Habits, A Preliminary Report," Can. J. Pub. Health, 52:99-106 (1961).

(7) *25 States* (compilation by American Cancer Society of American men in 25 states, members of families with at least one person over 45). See E. C. Hammond, "Special Report to the Surgeon General's Advisory Committee on Smoking and Health." (Details of this study in §40.)

Details of the populations studied are exhibited in the following table:

Subjects	British Doctors	Nine States	U.S. Veterans	Nine Occupations	American Legion	Canadian Veterans	25 States	Total
Usable Replies	34,000	188,000	248,000	67,000	60,000	78,000	448,000	1,123,000
Enrollment	10/1951	1-3/1952	1/54-1/57	11/53-5/57	5-11/57	9/55-7/56	10/59-2/60	(1951-1960)
Age Range (yrs)	35-75+	50-69	30-75+	35-69	35-75+	35-75+	35-89	35-89
Months Followed	120	44	78	About 48	About 24	72	About 22	40.6
Number of Deaths	4,534	11,870	24,519	1,714	1,704	9,070	11,612	65,023
Exposure (Per.-yrs)	269,000	668,000	1,312,000	222,000	119,000	383,000	820,000	3,793,000

Follow-up: Provision was made in the several studies to obtain death certificates for all members of the group who died during the period of observation. Data with regard to the numbers dying and their ages and the underlying causes of death were abstracted from the death certificates. Careful estimates indicate it unlikely that more than about 5 per cent of the deaths had been missed.

Results: Mortality ratios for various types of smokers relative to non-smokers are given in Table 41a for observations summarized from five of the studies. In current cigarette smokers there was a consistent progressive increase in mortality ratio with number of cigarettes smoked. For all current cigarette smokers combined mortality ratios ranged from 144 to 183 per cent, and in each group the mortality ratio exceeded the corresponding ratio for ex-cigarette smokers and for those who also smoked tobacco in other forms. Subjects who smoked only a pipe or cigars had mortality ratios that were slightly elevated (maximum 111 per cent), or actually below 100 per cent in two of the studies.

SMOKING AND MORTALITY

Table 41a   Mortality Ratios, Current and Ex-Cigarette Smokers, Current Pipe and Cigar Smokers (5 Studies)

Smoking Category	Mortality Ratios by Study*				
	British Doctors	Men in 9 States	U.S. Veterans	Men in 25 States	Canadian Veterans
Current Cigarette Smokers Only					
Under 10 per day	106%	133%	135%	145%	155%
10 to 20 per day	131	166	176	175	168
21 to 39 per day	162†	193	199	190	184
40 and over per day	250●	220	220	220	184
All amounts	144	170	179	183	165
Ex-Cigarette Smokers	104	140	141	150	142
Current Cigarette and Other	105	145	146	154	123
Ex-Cigarette and Other	121	129	121	151	118
Current Cigar Smokers (Only)	95	110	107	97	111
Current Pipe Smokers (Only)	95	105	106	86	110

Table 41b   Comparative Age-Adjusted Mortality for Current Smokers of Cigarettes Only by Amount of Cigarette Smoking (7 Studies)

Study	Non-Smoker Ave. Ann. Mort. Rate	Under One Pack per Day			One Pack per Day or More		
		Ave. Ann. Mort. Rate	Mortality Ratio	Excess Death Rate	Ave. Ann. Mort. Rate	Mortality Ratio	Excess Death Rate
	$\bar{q}'$	$\bar{q}$	$100\,\bar{q}/\bar{q}'$	$1000(\bar{q}-\bar{q}')$	$\bar{q}$	$100\,\bar{q}/\bar{q}'$	$1000(\bar{q}-\bar{q}')$
British Doctors	.0158	.0192	122%	3.4	.0232	147%	7.4
Men in 9 States□	.0144	.0224	156	8.0	.0271	188	13
U.S. Veterans	.0120	.0181	151	6.1	.0239	199	12
California Occupations□	.0105	.0142	135	3.7	.0180	171	7.5
American Legion in Calif.	.0113	.0164	145	5.1	.0163	144	5.0
Canadian Veterans	.0141	.0221	157	8.0	.0242	172	10
Men in 25 States■	.0128	.0185	145	5.7	.0192	150	6.4

Table 41c   Mortality Ratios, Current Smokers of Cigarettes Only by Age and Amount Smoked (Men in 25 States)

Cigarettes per Day	Mortality Ratio by Age at Start of Study*				
	40-49 yrs	50-59 yrs	60-69 yrs	70-79 yrs	80-89 yrs
Under 10	225%	144%	140%	140%	108%
10-19	210	194	169	150	165
20-39	220	205	178	148	116
40 and up	305	235	168	128	58
All Amounts	235	205	170	147	122

Table 41d   Comparative Mortality, Current Smokers of Cigarettes Only by Age (U.S. Veterans)

Age	Ave. Ann. Mort. Rate		Mortality Ratio	Excess Death Rate	Age	Ave. Ann. Mort. Rate		Mortality Ratio	Excess Death Rate
	Smoker	Non-Smoker				Smoker	Non-Smoker		
(years)	$\bar{q}$	$\bar{q}'$	$100\,\bar{q}/\bar{q}'$	$1000(\bar{q}-\bar{q}')$	(years)	$\bar{q}$	$\bar{q}'$	$100\,\bar{q}/\bar{q}'$	$1000(\bar{q}-\bar{q}')$
40-44	.0033	—	—	—	60-64	.0244	.0132	185%	11
45-49	.0058	.0028	205%	3.0	65-69	.0352	.0200	176	15
50-54	.0103	.0044	235	5.9	70-74	.0507	.0298	170	21
55-59	.0159	.0085	187	7.4	75-79	.0968	.0730	133	24

* Age-adjusted mortality rates of smokers vs. non-smokers observed in each study

† 20-34 cigarettes per day

● 35 cigarettes per day and up

□ Men age 50-69 yrs

■ Rates may be underestimated by about 1.7 per cent because of over estimate of exposure

ENVIRONMENTAL RISKS

§41–RELATION OF CIGARETTE SMOKING TO MORTALITY

Results (continued):

Age-adjusted mortality rates from all seven studies are given in Table 41b for subjects smoking less than one pack daily, and those smoking one pack or more per day, in comparison with rates for non-smokers. Mortality ratios range from 122 to 157 per cent in the lighter smokers, and from 144 to 199 per cent in the heavier smokers, with an overall range of 3.4 to 13 extra deaths per 1000 per year.

Both number of cigarettes smoked and age are analyzed by mortality ratios from the study of men in 25 states and presented in Table 41c. Mortality ratios tend to increase with amount smoked and advancing age up to age 70. However, for the two oldest age groups the heaviest smokers had the lowest mortality ratios, well under 100 per cent for men age 80 to 89, a curious reversal of the usual trend. Additional comparative mortality experience by age alone for cigarette smokers in the U.S. Veterans Study is given in Table 41d. There is a downward trend in mortality ratio with advancing age, but EDR increases progressively from 3.0 extra deaths per 1000 per year in veterans age 45-49 to 24 per 1000 in those age 75-79.

Men who began smoking at younger ages experienced higher levels of mortality than those beginning at ages 25 and older. Presented in Table 41e for all amounts of cigarette smoking are mortality ratios among U.S. veterans according to initial smoking age: 198 per cent when smoking began at ages under 20, 172 per cent for starting ages 20-24 years and 139 per cent for initial ages 25 and over. A similar pattern obtained in the 25 States study, the ratios declining from 215 per cent for starting ages under 15 to 134 per cent for ages 25 and older. Table 41e also presents mortality ratios in two studies with respect to the degree of inhalation of cigarette smoke and the daily amount smoked. The study of men in 25 states indicated, that for all of the amount smoked categories together, mortality ratios increase from 149 per cent for smokers who do not inhale to 168 for those classed as "slight" inhalers, to 183 for "moderate" and 220 per cent for "deep" inhalers. Within each classification mortality ratios tend to increase with the number of cigarettes smoked per day. Results in this regard among Canadian veterans are different. This study divides cigarette smokers into two categories: those who do not inhale and those who do. The non-inhalers show very little mortality in excess of those who do not smoke — the overall ratio is only 108 per cent. The men who did inhale exhibited increasing mortality ratios with the number of cigarettes per day, but these ratios were generally lower than the mortality ratios of inhalers in the 25 States study, in comparable categories of cigarettes smoked daily. Ex-smokers revealed a progressively declining series of mortality ratios with time elapsed since discontinuance (Table 41f). Thus, in the Nine States study, men who had smoked fewer than 20 cigarettes daily and had stopped smoking less than a year showed a mortality ratio of 204 per cent that of non-smokers; those who had smoked 20 or more per day, 269 per cent. These ratios diminished for men who had stopped smoking 10 years or more prior to entry, dropping to 108 and 150 per cent, respectively, for these two classes. Results developed in the 25 States study were similar: the smokers of fewer than 20 cigarettes per day dropped from 160 per cent for the shorter term discontinuance to 81 per cent for men who had stopped smoking for ten years or longer; the heavier smokers (20 or more daily) in the same span dropped from 280 to 122 per cent. It is interesting to note that, in the Nine States study, for both light and heavy smokers, and in the 25 States study, for heavy smokers, lower mortality ratios are shown for current smokers than for those who had stopped smoking within a year. One explanation for the anomaly is that among smokers who stopped a significant proportion may have done so because of medical advice in connection with a serious condition such as coronary heart disease.

Comparative results by cause of death in the seven studies are presented in Table 41g. Cancers of all sites together were associated with a cause-specific mortality ratio of 200 per cent in current cigarette smokers versus non-smokers. In addition to individual cancer sites such as lung cancer, with a mortality ratio of 1080 per cent, other causes with higher mortality ratios were bronchitis and emphysema, gastric and duodenal ulcer, cirrhosis and some circulatory diseases. Coronary artery disease, with a somewhat lower ratio of 174 per cent, nevertheless accounted for almost half of the extra deaths. Every cause of death tabulated in Table 41h showed mortality in smokers to be in excess of that of non-smokers, except cancer of the intestines, for which the mortality ratio was 93 per cent.

SMOKING AND MORTALITY

Table 41e Mortality Ratios, Current Smokers of Cigarettes Only by Amount of
Smoking, Age at Start of Smoking, and Amount Inhaled (3 Studies)

Study and Category	Age at Start of Smoking	Mortality Ratios* by No. Cigarettes per Day				
		Under 10	10-19	20-39	40 up	All Amounts
U.S. Veterans	Under 20	160%	189%	215%	245%	198%
	20-24	140	172	187	225	172
	25 up	115	150	147	111	139
Men in 25 States	Under 15	179	225	220	215	215
	15-19	175	183	200	240	199
	20-24	125	152	162	193	158
	25 up	103	136	145	156	134
Canadian Veterans						
No smoke inhaled	All	105	111†	103●	—	108
Some smoke inhaled	All	135	150†	171●	—	152
Men in 25 States						
No smoke inhaled	All	129	146	156	205	149
Slight amount	All	129	168	184	197	168
Moderate amount	All	161	182	184	200	183
Large amount	All	188	176	220	250	220

Table 41f Mortality Ratios, Ex-Smokers of Cigarettes Only by Amount Smoked and
Years Since Smoking Stopped (2 Studies)

Study	Cigarettes per Day	Years Since Smoking Stopped					Current Smokers
		10 yrs up	1-9 yrs	5-9 yrs	1-4 yrs	Under 1 yr	
Men in 9 States	Under 20	108%	130%	—	—	204%	161%
	20 up	150	182	—	—	269	200
Men in 25 States	Under 20	81	—	146%	162%	160	173
	20 up	122	—	151	201	280	200

Table 41g Comparative Mortality by Cause of Death, Smokers of Cigarettes Only (7 Studies)

Non-Cancer Deaths				Cancer Deaths and Totals			
Cause of Death	No. of Deaths		Mortality Ratio	Cause of Death	No. of Deaths		Mortality Ratio
	Observed	Expected			Observed	Expected	
	d	d'	100 d/d'		d	d'	100 d/d'
Bronchitis & Emphysema	546	89.5	610%	Cancer of Lung	1833	170.3	1080%
Gastric & Duodenal Ulcer	294	105.1	280	Larynx	75	14.0	535
Other Circulatory Dis.	649	254.0	255	Mouth & Throat	152	37.0	410
Cirrhosis of Liver	379	169.2	225	Esophagus	113	33.7	335
Coronary Artery Disease	11177	6430.7	174	Bladder	216	111.6	194
Other Heart Disease	868	526.0	165	Kidney	120	79.0	152
Hypertensive Heart Dis.	631	409.2	154	Stomach	413	285.2	145
Arteriosclerosis	310	210.7	147	Prostate	318	253.0	126
Influenza & Pneumonia	415	303.2	137	Rectum	213	207.8	103
Cerebrovascular Disease	1844	1461.8	126	Intestine	395	422.6	93
Accident, Suicide, Homicide	1310	1063.2	123	All Other Cancers	1524	1061.4	144
Nephritis	173	156.4	111	All Cancers	5372	2675.6	200
Rheumatic Heart Dis.	309	290.6	106	All Non-Cancer	20851	12978.3	161
All Other Non-Cancer	1946	1508.7	129	Total-All Causes	26223	15653.9	168

* Relative to Non-Smokers
† 10 to 20 cigarettes per day
● Over 20 cigarettes per day

WOMEN CIGARETTE SMOKERS

§42–WOMEN CIGARETTE SMOKERS

Reference: E.C. Hammond, "Smoking in Relation to. the Death Rates of One Million Men and Women," in *Epidemiological Approaches to the Study of Cancer and Other Chronic Diseases*, W. Haenszel, ed. Bethesda, Md.: National Cancer Institute Monograph No. 19 (1966), pp. 127-204.

Subjects Studied: The reference is a sequel to the report used in §40 giving results on men smokers after three years of follow-up. The same procedures employed in the earlier study were followed in the present one. Included in the present series were 440,558 men and 562,671 women. Subjects enrolled between October 1, 1959 and February 15, 1960 were between ages 35 and 84 and were resident in 25 states. Experience reported is related to age groups formed at time of enrollment. Since experience of male subjects is similar to that reported in §40, in the present abstract emphasis is placed on results developed among women subjects.

Follow-up: Subjects were traced annually to September 30, 1963, with follow-up 97.4 per cent complete on that date, and 99.6 per cent complete on September 30, 1962. Each successive follow-up yielded some deaths which should have been reported in an earlier follow-up. On this basis the author estimates that deaths in the fourth 12-month period may have been understated, possibly by as much as 4 to 5 per cent, but with very little deaths reported.

Results: In Table 42a basic data are given for women smokers and non-smokers by age at entry, in five decennial groups starting with age 35-44. The distribution of entrants, exposures, deaths, and mortality rates are given for non-smokers (women who never smoked regularly). (These are used as "expected rates," against which the rates for smokers are compared.) Smokers were a predominantly younger group: 77 per cent were age 35-54, against 50 per cent for the women who were non-smokers. Non-smokers outnumbered smokers by about two to one. Comparative experience by age group is given in Table 42b over the follow-up period, which averaged 46 months. Mortality ratios among women smokers between 45 and 74 years at enrollment ranged from 122 to 127 per cent. At younger ages the ratio was 112 per cent, at older ages, 105 per cent. Excess death rates, averaging 0.9 per 1000 for all ages together, increased to age group 65-74 years — from 0.2 per 1000 in age group 35-44 years to 4.6 per 1000 at ages 65-74 years. This function decreased to 3.1 per 1000 among the oldest enrollees. When the aggregate experience was compared with that of non-smokers, age-adjusted to the age distribution of the smokers, the mortality ratio was found to be 121 per cent and EDR 0.9 per 1000. The corresponding figures in men smokers were 182 per cent and 6.8 per 1000, respectively. These measures of comparative mortality in males are given in the two right-hand columns of Tables 42b-d, and they all indicate a greater risk from cigarette smoking in men than in women.

Four-year experience of female smokers (all ages combined) compared with non-smokers is shown in Table 42c according to three criteria: the number of cigarettes smoked daily, the degree of inhalation, and the age at commencement of smoking. Overall mortality ratios increased progressively with the number of cigarettes smoked — from 116 per cent for 10-19 per day to 159 per cent for 40 or more. No extra mortality was indicated for fewer than 10 a day. Excess death rates also increased from 0.7 to 2.6 per 1000. Mortality varied with the degree of inhalation. The experience of women not inhaling smoke was about the same as for non-smokers; those inhaling deeply showed a mortality ratio of 150 per cent and excess deaths of 2.2 per 1000. About the same results developed for moderate as for slight inhalation: a mortality ratio of about 120 per cent and an EDR of 0.8 or 0.9 per 1000. The mortality of smokers commencing the habit at young ages was less favorable than for those starting at older ages. Thus, women who started to smoke before age 15 developed a mortality ratio of 175 per cent and an EDR of 3.3 per 1000. Ratios and EDR's declined as the starting age increased; women beginning to smoke at 30 years of age and older showed practically no extra mortality. Intervening ages graded between these extremes.

ENVIRONMENTAL RISKS

§42–WOMEN CIGARETTE SMOKERS

Results (continued):

Table 42d summarizes deaths among cigarette smokers by underlying cause of subjects between 45 and 64 years at enrollment. Experience among women is presented under two classifications — the entire group of smokers, on one hand, and those among them classed as "heavier" smokers, on the other. The latter is comprised of women smoking 20 or more cigarettes per day, or 10 per day if smoking began before age 25 years. All mortality rates shown in the table have been age-adjusted. Low rates in both groups were experienced in cancers of the colon and of the breast, uterus and ovary. The leading cause of death in both categories was coronary heart disease with cancers of breast, uterus and ovary second, and cerebrovascular lesions third. The greatest mortality ratio in both classes was attributed to emphysema: 490 and 740 per cent, respectively. Although emphysema was relatively infrequent as the underlying cause, accounting for only 3 and 5 per 100,000 of all deaths in the case of women, its effect was exerted additionally as contributing to death ascribed to other causes. Besides emphysema, in both groups causes displaying ratios exceeding 170 per cent were indicated for lung cancer, coronary heart disease, cerebrovascular lesions, and cirrhosis of the liver.

Salient comparable results among males adjusted for differences in age distribution are shown in columns on the right-hand side of the respective tables. With few exceptions (all in Table 42d) extra mortality, expressed either as a percentage or as deaths per 1000, was greater for men than for women. Apart from deaths caused by coronary heart disease, cerebrovascular lesions, cirrhosis of the liver and those attributable to accidents, violence and suicide, male experience for common sites was higher than among even the heavier category of women smokers.

Table 42a   Distribution of Women Non-Smokers* by Age, and Distribution of Women Smokers, Exposures and Deaths, Average Follow-up 46 Months

Category	Variable	35-44	45-54	55-64	65-74	75-84	All Ages
Non-Smokers	Entrants (ℓ)	57601	133577	109153	61865	19173	381369
	Per cent	15.1%	35.1%	28.6%	16.2%	5.0%	100.0%
	Exposure (E)	219746	509744	413914	229798	66424	1439626
	Deaths (d)	362	1548	2889	4395	3928	13122
	Mort. Rate (q̄)	.0016	.0030	.0070	.0191	.0591	.0091
Smokers	Entrants (ℓ)	52124	87655	32013	8293	1217	181302
	Per cent	28.7%	48.3%	17.7%	4.6%	0.7%	100.0%

*Women who never smoked regularly

WOMEN CIGARETTE SMOKERS

Table 42b   Comparative Experience, Women Cigarette Smokers vs. Non-Smokers, Average Follow-up 46 Months, and Comparative Mortality, Men Smokers

Age at Entry	Exposure Person-Yrs	No. of Deaths	Ave. Ann. Mort. Rate	Est. 3-Yr Surv. Rate	Est. 3-Yr Surv. Index*	Mortality Ratio*	Excess Death Rate*	Male Mort. Ratio*	Male Excess Death Rate*
Yrs	E	d	$\bar{q} = d/E$	$P = (1-\bar{q})^3$	100 P/P'	100 $\bar{q}/\bar{q}'$	1000($\bar{q}-\bar{q}'$)	100 $\bar{q}_m/\bar{q}_m'$	1000($\bar{q}_m-\bar{q}_m'$)
35-44	197849	365	.0018	.994	99.9%	112%	0.2	180%	1.7
45-54	332682	1280	.0038	.989	99.8	127	0.8	220	4.8
55-64	120646	1026	.0085	.975	99.5	122	1.5	180	9.6
65-74	30377	720	.0237	.931	98.6	124	4.6	151	16
75-84	4180	260	.0622	.825	99.0	105	3.1	130	23
All†	685734	3651	.0053	.984	99.7	121	0.9	182	6.8

Table 42c   Comparative Experience, Women by Smoking Characteristics, Average Follow-up 46 Months, and Comparative Mortality in Men Smokers

Smoking Characteristic		Ave. Ann. Mort. Rate†	Est. 3-Yr Surv. Rate	Est. 3-Yr Surv. Index*	Mortality Ratio*	Excess Death Rate	Male Mort. Ratio	Male Excess Death Rate
		$\bar{q}$	$P = (1-\bar{q})^3$	100 P/P'	100 $\bar{q}/\bar{q}'$	1000($\bar{q}-\bar{q}'$)	100 $\bar{q}_m/\bar{q}_m'$	1000($\bar{q}_m-\bar{q}_m'$)
Non-Smokers (Basis of Expected)		.0044	.9869	—	(100%)	(0.0)	(100%)	(0.0)
No. cigarettes/day	1- 9	.0042	.9874	100.1%	95	-0.2	160	3.9
	10-19	.0051	.9849	99.8	116	0.7	185	5.6
	20-39	.0060	.9823	99.5	136	1.6	195	6.2
	40+	.0070	.9791	99.2	159	2.6	220	7.8
Inhalation (Smokers)	None	.0046	.9863	99.9	105	0.2	167	4.4
	Slight	.0052	.9845	99.8	118	0.8	187	5.7
	Moderate	.0053	.9841	99.7	120	0.9	192	6.0
	Deep	.0066	.9803	99.3	150	2.2	215	7.6
Age at Start of Smoking	30 yrs up	.0047	.9860	99.9	107	0.3	134	2.2
	25-29	.0049	.9854	99.9	111	0.5	153	3.5
	20-24	.0057	.9829	99.6	130	1.3	169	4.5
	15-19	.0069	.9796	99.3	157	2.5	205	6.9
	Under 15	.0077	.9771	99.0	175	3.3	230	8.6

Table 42d   Comparative Mortality by Cause of Death, Women Smokers vs. Non-Smokers; Comparative Mortality in Men Smokers (Rates per 1000)

Cause of Death		All Regular Smokers		Heavier Smokers		Male Mort. Rate	Male Mort. Ratio
		Mort. Rate	Mort. Ratio	Mort. Rate	Mort. Ratio		
		$\bar{q}$	100 $\bar{q}/\bar{q}'$	100 $\bar{q}$	100 $\bar{q}/\bar{q}'$	$\bar{q}_m$	100 $\bar{q}_m/\bar{q}_m'$
Cancer — Lung		.15	215%	.25	365%	.87	785%
	Colon & Rectum	.21	78	.18	66	.33	101
	Breast	.56	83	.52	78	—	—
	Uterus & Ovary	.39	108	.41	116	—	—
	Other	.70	162	.84	140	1.47	179
	Total	2.01	102	2.20	112	2.67	215
Cardiovascular — Cor. Ht. Dis.		1.48	177	1.75	210	6.15	205
	Cerebrovascular	.57	174	.69	210	.74	138
	Other	.51	113	.48	107	1.13	174
	Total	2.56	158	2.92	180	8.02	190
Other Diseases — Emphysema		.03	490	.05	740	.24	655
	Cirrhosis Liver	.10	215	.15	325	.19	205
	Other	.65	123	.68	128	1.16	149
	Total	.78	134	.88	150	1.59	176
Accidents, Violence, Suicide		.32	141	.38	163	.72	120
All Certified Causes		5.68	129	6.38	145	13.00	186

*Basis of expected mortality: age- and sex-specific rates in non-smokers
†Rates adjusted to age distribution of the smokers

FAMILY HISTORY

§60—MORTALITY RATES IN RELATION TO LONGEVITY OF PARENTS AND GRANDPARENTS

Reference: E. C. Hammond, L. Garfinkel, and H. Seidman, "Longevity of Parents and Grandparents in Relation to Coronary Heart Disease and Associated Variables," Circulation, 43:31-44 (1971).

Subjects Studied: A large group of men and women age 40-79 enrolled during 1959-60 in an epidemiological study conducted by The American Cancer Society. Extensive information was obtained from the subjects by completion of a questionnaire on medical history, current medical status and health habits, and age of parents and grandparents either at death, or at the time of the questionnaire, if living. Subjects were excluded if both parents were still living but under age 70, or if information on age of parents was incomplete. The remaining subjects were divided into seven classes according to the longevity of parents and grandparents. Class 1, the longest-lived, included subjects both of whose parents either died after the age of 80, or were still living and over 70; at least one grandparent survived to 80. In Class 7, the shortest lived, both parents died before age 70. Distribution of subjects by sex, age group and longevity class is given in Table 60a. The prevalence in men of other risk factors is given in Table 60b, divided according to longevity class.

Follow-up: Subjects were traced annually from 1959 to 1965. Every two years they were asked for information concerning illness, hospitalization, etc. Copies of death certificates were obtained on decedents. Nearly 99 per cent follow-up was obtained.

Results: Table 60c indicates a distinct correlation between mortality rates and longevity of parents and grandparents for both men and women. If experience among subjects in Classes 1 and 2 are to be employed as a standard of reference, mortality ratios among men in Class 3-5 decline from 137 per cent in age group 45-54 years, to 126 per cent in age group 55-64, to 116 per cent in age group 65-74. Among women in Class 3-5 these ratios vary little by age — between 125 and 122 per cent over the whole age range. Similar differentiation by sex but at higher levels of comparative mortality applies to individuals in Classes 6 and 7: ratios among men diminish from 182 to 141 per cent with advance in age group; among women, percentages lie between 165 to 156.

Annual excess deaths by sex show similar advantages for women. This function increases by age and longevity class. Against the standard represented by Classes 1 and 2, EDR's for men in Classes 3-5 increase from 2.0 to 5.5 excess deaths per 1000. For Classes 6-7 the rates are more than doubled. Among women, EDR's range from 0.7 to 8.9 per 1000 per year, also increasing with age and longevity class.

Mortality rates and ratios by cause of death are shown in Table 60d. Among men, deaths from coronary heart disease are approximately equal to those from all other causes for almost all age groups and longevity classes; among women, on the other hand, this cause of death almost consistently is substantially exceeded by non-cardiovascular causes. For both sexes, in all age groups and in all three cause of death categories, mortality ratios increase with longevity class. Ratios in the CHD category are markedly higher for women than for men, particularly at the younger ages, but EDR values are lower. Somewhat more detailed results for excess CHD mortality in men are given in Table 60e, with four age groups ranging from 40-49 to 70-79 years. The trends by longevity class and age group are similar to those described previously.

Table 60f provides an interesting illustration of the effect of *selection* in reducing mortality over the six-year period of observation. No examination was carried out at entry; the select group consisted of men who denied a history of high blood pressure or diabetes, who were non-smokers and not obese, and who asserted that they exercised regularly and slept less than ten hours per night. Only one subject in six met all of these selection criteria. Mortality rates due to CHD were substantially higher in the unselected total group than among the selected subjects. Mortality ratios decreased with age from 430 to 129 per cent, but EDR increased from 2.0 to 5.7 excess deaths per 1000 per year. These results are for all longevity classes combined. However, as indicated in Table 60e, CHD mortality ratios increased with longevity class in the selected subjects as they did among the aggregate groups.

LONGEVITY OF PARENTS AND GRANDPARENTS

Table 60a Distribution of Subjects by Sex, Age and Longevity Class
(Omitting Subjects Not Classified for Longevity)

	All Longevity Classes by Age				Longevity Class	All Ages by Longevity Class			
	Men		Women			Men		Women	
Age	No.	%	No.	%		No.	%	No.	%
40-44	19636	5.6	45563	10.6	1	29964	8.5	35373	8.2
45-49	78044	22.2	94759	22.0	2	24702	7.0	29288	6.8
50-54	85174	24.3	95240	22.0	3	82292	23.4	104819	24.3
55-59	65173	18.5	73185	17.0	4	83734	23.9	100090	23.2
60-64	46536	13.2	52438	12.2	5	35271	10.0	43530	10.1
65-69	31619	9.0	36815	8.5	6	45022	12.8	53817	12.5
70-74	17335	4.9	21772	5.1	7	50644	14.4	64002	14.9
75-79	8112	2.3	11147	2.6	Total	351629	100.0	430919	100.0
Total	351629	100.0	430919	100.0					

Table 60b Age-Adjusted Prevalence in Men of Risk Factors from Questionnaire History
(Omitting Subjects Not Classified for Longevity)

Risk Factor		Prevalence by Longevity Class					Total
		1	2	3-5	6	7	
History of high blood pressure	No.	2247	1964	20210	5430	6650	36501
	%	7.50	7.95	10.04	12.06	13.13	10.38
History of diabetes	No.	533	459	4449	1135	1388	7964
	%	1.78	1.86	2.21	2.52	2.74	2.26
No exercise	No.	626	635	5012	1369	1545	9187
	%	2.09	2.57	2.49	3.04	3.05	2.61
Relative weight over 120*	No.	1390	1126	10327	2413	2927	18183
	%	4.64	4.56	5.13	5.36	5.78	5.17
Sleep 10+ hrs. a night	No.	521	509	3865	1008	1089	6992
	%	1.74	2.06	1.92	2.24	2.15	1.99
More than 20 cigarettes a day	No.	8935	7487	63026	14267	16682	110397
	%	29.82	30.31	31.31	31.69	32.94	31.40
History of heart disease	No.	1699	1487	14856	3849	4548	26439
	%	5.67	6.02	7.38	8.55	8.98	7.52
History of stroke	No.	273	311	2516	707	841	4648
	%	0.91	1.26	1.25	1.57	1.66	1.32
Mean age of men		55	54	55	58	56	55

* Weight more than 120 per cent of average weight for subjects with same age, sex, and height

FAMILY HISTORY

Table 60c   Comparative Experience (Developed from Data) by Sex, Age, and Longevity Class

Sex and Age Group	Longevity Classes	Exposure Person-Yrs	Deaths Observed	Deaths Expected*	Mortality Ratio	Ave. Ann. Mort. Rate	Est. 3-Yr Surv. Rate	Est. 3-Yr Surv. Index	Excess Death Rate
		E	d	d'	100 d/d'	$\bar{q} = d/E$	$P = (1-\bar{q})^3$	100 P/P'	1000(d-d')/E
Male									
45-54	1-2	165400	865	865	†	.0052	98.4%	†	†
	3-5	540800	3885	2829	137	.0072	97.9	99.4	2.0
	6-7	226000	2148	1182	182	.0095	97.2	98.7	4.3
55-64	1-2	85500	1214	1214	†	.0142	95.8	†	†
	3-5	353800	6338	5021	126	.0179	94.7	98.9	3.7
	6-7	180900	4070	2567	159	.0225	93.4	97.5	8.3
65-74	1-2	33400	1119	1119	†	.0335	90.3	†	†
	3-5	141900	5500	4749	116	.0390	88.8	98.4	5.5
	6-7	81100	3828	2715	141	.0472	86.5	95.8	14
Female									
45-54	1-2	190500	521	521	†	.0028	99.2	†	†
	3-5	646500	2158	1768	122	.0033	99.0	99.8	0.7
	6-7	267700	1149	732	157	.0043	98.7	99.5	1.7
55-64	1-2	94000	536	536	†	.0057	98.3	†	†
	3-5	411700	2934	2349	125	.0071	97.9	99.6	1.4
	6-7	214000	2010	1221	165	.0094	97.2	98.9	3.7
65-74	1-2	38400	607	607	†	.0158	95.3	†	†
	3-5	178700	3460	2826	122	.0194	94.3	98.9	3.5
	6-7	107100	2645	1694	156	.0247	92.8	97.3	8.9

Table 60d   Relative Mortality Experience by Category of Cause of Death

Sex and Age Group	Longevity Classes	Coronary Deaths Ave. Ann. Mort. Rate	Coronary Deaths Mortality Ratio	Coronary Deaths Excess Death Rate	Other CV Deaths Ave. Ann. Mort. Rate	Other CV Deaths Mortality Ratio	Other CV Deaths Excess Death Rate	Non-CV Deaths Ave. Ann. Mort. Rate	Non-CV Deaths Mortality Ratio	Non-CV Deaths Excess Death Rate
		$\bar{q} = d/E$	100 $\bar{q}/\bar{q}'$	1000($\bar{q}-\bar{q}'$)	$\bar{q} = d/E$	100 $\bar{q}/\bar{q}'$	1000($\bar{q}-\bar{q}'$)	$\bar{q} = d/E$	100 $\bar{q}/\bar{q}'$	1000($\bar{q}-\bar{q}'$)
Male										
45-54	1-2	.0023	†	†	.0007	†	†	.0022	†	†
	3-5	.0036	157	1.3	.0010	133	0.3	.0026	119	0.4
	6-7	.0054	235	3.1	.0013	184	0.6	.0028	127	0.6
55-64	1-2	.0060	†	†	.0021	†	†	.0061	†	†
	3-5	.0086	144	2.6	.0030	145	0.9	.0062	101	0.1
	6-7	.0115	191	5.5	.0035	166	1.4	.0075	123	1.4
65-74	1-2	.0142	†	†	.0079	†	†	.0114	†	†
	3-5	.0174	123	3.2	.0084	106	0.5	.0132	116	1.8
	6-7	.0216	152	7.4	.0107	136	2.8	.0148	130	3.4
Female										
45-54	1-2	.0002	†	†	.0004	†	†	.0020	†	†
	3-5	.0005	245	0.3	.0006	153	0.2	.0022	111	0.2
	6-7	.0009	430	0.7	.0008	225	0.4	.0026	127	0.6
55-64	1-2	.0010	†	†	.0012	†	†	.0035	†	†
	3-5	.0019	182	0.9	.0015	119	0.3	.0038	110	0.3
	6-7	.0032	315	2.2	.0018	149	0.6	.0044	126	0.9
65-74	1-2	.0051	†	†	.0038	†	†	.0070	†	†
	3-5	.0066	130	1.5	.0054	142	1.6	.0074	106	0.4
	6-7	.0094	184	4.3	.0071	186	3.3	.0082	119	1.2

* Basis of expected mortality: Experience in longevity classes 1 and 2
† Standard Mortality Ratio = Standard Survival Ratio = 100%. Standard EDR = 0.

LONGEVITY OF PARENTS AND GRANDPARENTS

Table 60e   Comparative Male Mortality due to CHD by Age and Longevity Class

Age	Longevity Class	Exposure Person-Yrs	Deaths Observed	Deaths Expected*	Ave. Ann. Mort. Rate	Mortality Ratio	Excess Death Rate
		E	d	d'	$\bar{q} = d/E$	100 d/d'	1000(d-d')/E
40-49	1-2	102641	148	148	.0014	†	†
	3-5	328619	793	475	.0024	167	1.0
	6-7	129042	522	186	.0040	280	2.6
50-59	1-2	133826	524	524	.0039	†	†
	3-5	489657	2772	1917	.0057	145	1.7
	6-7	226419	1798	887	.0079	205	4.0
60-69	1-2	55582	489	489	.0088	†	†
	3-5	237356	2880	2088	.0121	138	3.3
	6-7	130350	2081	1147	.0160	181	7.2
70-79	1-2	16944	365	365	.0215	†	†
	3-5	69817	1762	1504	.0252	117	3.7
	6-7	40237	1126	867	.0280	130	6.4

Table 60f   Comparative Male Mortality due to CHD by Age and Selection●

Age	Unselected Exposure Person-Yrs	Unselected Deaths Observed	Unselected Ave. Ann. Mort. Rate	Selected Exposure Person-Yrs	Selected Deaths Observed	Selected Ave. Ann. Mort. Rate	Mortality Ratio	Excess Death Rate
	E_u	d_u	$\bar{q}_u = d_u/E_u$	E_s	d_s	$\bar{q}_s = d_s/E_s$	100 $\bar{q}_u/\bar{q}_s$	1000($\bar{q}_u-\bar{q}_s$)
40-59	560302	1463	.0026	91960	58	.0006	430	2.0
50-59	849902	5094	.0060	141057	364	.0026	230	3.4
60-69	423288	5450	.0129	80898	593	.0073	177	5.6
70-79	126998	3253	.0256	30752	611	.0199	129	5.7

* Basis of expected deaths: mortality rates of classes 1-2 as standard
† Standard Mortality Ratio = 100% and Standard EDR = 0
● Selected males without a history of high blood pressure or diabetes, whose relative weight was less than 120, who took exercise, who slept less than 10 hrs. per night, and who never smoked regularly

FAMILY HISTORY

§61–CARDIOVASCULAR–RENAL DISEASE IN INSUREDS

Reference: "New York Life Single Medical Impairment Study–1972," unpublished report made available by J.J. Hutchinson and J.C. Sibigtroth (1973).

Subjects Studied: Policyholders of New York Life Insurance Company issued insurance in 1954-1970, followed to the 1971 policy anniversary. These were cases in which a family history of diseases pertaining to the heart, blood vessels, and kidneys was recorded in two or more members under age 60. The experience reported is for standard issues.

Follow-up: Insurance policy records formed the basis of entry, of counting policies, exposure and death claims, and of follow-up information.

Results: Comparative experience is given in Tables 61a-b for standard male issues by duration, all ages combined. The mortality ratio showed a slight decline with duration, ranging from 186 per cent at 0-5 years to 162 per cent at 10-17 years. The EDR was highest at 10-17 years (6.1 extra deaths per 1000). The cumulative survival ratio at 17 years was 92.8 per cent.

Table 61c presents comparative experience by sex and entry age group. The overall mortality ratio for females was slightly higher than for males, 177 per cent and 173 per cent, respectively. The greatest excess mortality for standard male policyholders was observed in the age group 50 up, with a mortality ratio of 210 per cent and EDR of 13 per 1000. The estimated 8-year survival index ranged from 98.5 per cent for males aged 40-49 to a minimum of 89.9 per cent for males aged 50 up.

Comparative mortality by major causes of death is given in Table 61d for male and female standard cases combined. The major cause of death is found in diseases of the heart and circulation, the mortality ratio being 285 per cent and EDR 3.2 per 1000.

CARDIOVASCULAR—RENAL DISEASE FAMILY HISTORY

Table 61a   Observed Data and Comparative Experience by Duration — Male Standard Insured with
Family History of Two or More CVR Deaths Under Age 60

Interval		Exposure Policy-Yrs	No. of Death Claims		Mortality Ratio		Survival Ratio		Excess Death Rate
No.	Start-End		Observed	Expected*	Interval	Cumulative	Interval	Cumulative	
i	t to t + Δ t	E	d	d'	100 d/d'	100 Σd/Σd'	100 p_i/p_i'	100 P/P'	1000(d-d')/E
1	0- 5 yrs	2030	10	5.38	186%	186%	98.7%	98.7%	2.3
2	5-10	1246	11	6.41	172	178	98.2	96.9	3.7
3	10-17	629	10	6.18	162	173	95.8	92.8	6.1

Table 61b   Derived Mortality and Survival Data

Interval		Observed Rates				Expected Rates*			
		Average Annual		Cumulative		Average Annual		Cumulative	
No.	Start-End	Mortality	Survival	Survival	Mortality	Mortality	Survival	Survival	Mortality
i	t to t + Δ t	$\bar{q}$=d/E	$\bar{p}$	P	Q	$\bar{q}'$=d'/E	$\bar{p}'$	P'	Q'
1	0- 5 yrs	.0049	.9951	.9740	.0260	.0027	.9973	.9864	.0136
2	5-10	.0088	.9912	.9318	.0682	.0051	.9949	.9613	.0387
3	10-17	.0159	.9841	.8329	.1671	.0098	.9902	.8970	.1030

Table 61c   Comparative Experience by Sex and Age Group — Standard Cases, All Durations Combined

Sex	Age Group	Exposure Policy-Yrs	No. of Death Claims		Mortality Ratio	Ave. Ann. Mort. Rate	Est. 8-Yr Surv. Rate	Est. 8-Yr Surv. Index	Excess Death Rate
			Observed	Expected*					
		E	d	d'	100 d/d'	$\bar{q}$=d/E	P=(1-$\bar{q}$)^8	100 P/P'	1000(d-d')/E
Male	0-39	1795	7	3.41	205%	.0039	.9692	98.4%	2.0
	40-49	1626	12	8.86	135	.0074	.9425	98.5	1.9
	50 up	484	12	5.70	210	.0248	.8181	89.9	13
	All Ages	3905	31	17.97	173	.0079	.9382	97.3	3.3
Female	15 up	1052	6	3.39	177%	.0057	.9553	98.0%	2.5

Table 61d   Mortality by Cause of Death — Male and Female Combined

Cause	No. of Death Claims		Mortality Ratio	Excess Death Rate
	Observed	Expected†		
Malignant Neoplasms	9	5.09	177%	0.8
Diseases of the Heart & Circulatory System	24	8.39	285	3.2
Accidents and Homicides	1	2.94	34	−0.4
Suicide	2	0.91	220	0.2
All Other Causes & Unknown	1	4.03	25	−0.6
Total	37	21.36	173%	3.2

* Basis of expected mortality: 1955-60 Select Basic Table
† Distribution of total expected deaths by Intercompany Medically
Examined Standard Issues 1965-70

OTHER RISKS

§80–POST-SURGICAL MORTALITY (HALOTHANE STUDY)

References: (1) J.P. Bunker, W.H. Forrest, Jr., F. Mosteller, and L.D. Vandam, eds., *The National Halothane Study.* Bethesda, Md.: National Institute of General Medical Sciences (1969).
(2) Y. Bishop, additional data in personal communication (1974).

Subjects Studied: A Subcommittee on the National Halothane Study was set up in 1962 under the Anesthesia Committee of the National Academy of Sciences-National Research Council. The purpose of this study was a pathologic and statistical investigation of the possible association between halothane anesthesia and post-operative hepatic necrosis, and an examination of the effect of general anesthetic agents, including halothane, and of other factors on post-operative mortality. Partly because of the low incidence of hepatic difficulty the National Halothane Study was conducted as a retrospective study of patient records in 34 cooperating hospitals. During the four years 1959-1962 records were abstracted on 16,840 deaths that occurred within 6 weeks of operation (defined as early post-surgical mortality) and on an approximate 4 per cent sample of 856,515 operations in which a general anesthetic agent was used. Data were collected on age, sex and physical status of the patient, type of operation, anesthetic agent used (halothane, nitrous oxide with intravenous barbiturate, cyclopropane, ether, and all other agents or combinations of the foregoing), and additional information, especially if there was any evidence suggestive of liver damage. The numbers of patients in each category exposed to risk of operation and anesthesia had to be estimated from the sample count and were thus subject to random error, especially when the number counted was small. In some categories in which the frequency of operation was very low this resulted in the estimate of exposed to risk being smaller than the number of deaths. For major groups where this is true, the exposed to risk has been approximated as the sum of E+d (in accordance with the statistical procedures used in the study), and such estimates are enclosed in parentheses in the tables. In most of the major groups of patients, where the mortality risk is not excessive, the unadjusted estimate of E has been retained.

Follow-up: The hospitals reporting the patient and operation data also reported survival status at six weeks, with details of death, when this occurred, and all autopsy information.

Results: The observed data and post-surgical mortality rates in deaths per 1000 patients exposed to operation are given in Tables 80a-h with all anesthetic agents combined. The reader should consult the original report for detailed information as to separate anesthetic classes and for mortality rates standardized with respect to nine variables. No tabular data are given here on hepatic necrosis. Results can be summarized briefly as being negative in character: overall rates for death by hepatic necrosis were extremely low (0.10 per 1000), and were about the same for the different anesthetic agents. The highest rate, 0.17 per 1000 was found with cyclopropane; the other mortality rates per 1000 were 0.10 for halothane, 0.08 for "other agents," 0.07 for nitrous oxide and intravenous barbiturate, and 0.05 for ether. Only 82 of the total 16,840 deaths were associated with massive hepatic necrosis at autopsy, although 140 additional cases with minimal or intermediate degrees of hepatic necrosis were noted.

In organizing the huge amount of data the authors of the report arranged the operations in order or rank for the total mortality rate, all ages, both sexes, all classifications of physical status and anesthetic agent combined. Of the 100 operations for which codes were provided data have been reported on only 75 (no deaths or too few deaths in the others). Seven common "low-risk" procedures were grouped together, and data for this group are given in Table 80a. Another group of four selected operations (large bowel, exploratory laparotomy, craniotomy and open-heart surgery) were designated "high-risk," and these results are given by individual operation in Table 80f; in all other tables mortality rates by sex, age and patient status are given by groups of operations. After separating out these two limited groups of low-risk and high-risk operative procedures the authors designated the remaining operations as "middle risk," although there was a very wide range of mortality rates, overlapping the low and the high rates found in the other two groups. The large number of operations in the middle-risk group was separated into five subgroups, and we have designated two of these in combination as "other low-risk operations" in Tables 80b-c, another two combined as "moderate-risk operations," in Tables 80d-e, and the last subgroup as "other high-risk operations" in Tables 80g-h. For low-risk operations the overall mortality rate varies from a minimum below 1 per 1000 (operations on the eye and oral cavity, and "D and C" – dilation and curettage) to 11.7 per 1000 for simple cholecystectomy, 12.2 for an air encephalogram, and 15.8 for neck operations. In addition to the seven selected ones there are 30 additional operations in the low-risk category, including hernia repair, appendectomy, mastectomy, reduction of fractures except the femur, etc. In the 18 moderate-risk operations the range of overall mortality rate is from 17.5 per 1000 for prostate operations

POST-SURGICAL MORTALITY (HALOTHANE STUDY)

Table 80a   Early Mortality Rate (6 Weeks) in Patients Subjected to Common Low-Risk Surgical Procedures, 1959-62

Patient and Operation Status*	Age	Operation†	No. of Operations•	No. of Deaths	Mortality Rate	Operation†	No. of Operations•	No. of Deaths	Mortality Rate
			E	d	1000q		E	d	1000q
All	All	1 Oral	80218	53	0.66	73 Cystoscopy	43854	169	3.8
		3 Eye	30596	22	0.72	55 Hernia	30607	118	3.9
		60 D&C	99743	90	0.90	90 Plastic	40343	280	6.9
		65 Hysterect.	40991	112	2.73				
			Male				Female		
Good Risk, Elective	0-9 yrs	All	38586	9	0.23	All	29913	20	0.67
	10-49		35486	14	0.39		115017	56	0.49
	50-69		21579	40	1.8		32050	67	2.1
	70 up		4722	30	6.4		5054	33	6.5
	All		100373	93	0.93		182034	176	0.97
Poor Risk, Elective	0-9 yrs	All	772	12	16	All	627	18	29
	10-49		854	18	21		2872	47	16
	50-69		1700	47	28		2613	53	20
	70 up		1215	42	35		1348	32	24
	All		4541	119	26		7460	150	20
Good Risk, Emergency	0-9 yrs	All	524	1	1.9	All	821	1	1.2
	10-49		1462	1	0.7		9613	3	0.3
	50-69		151	5	33		448	5	11
	70 up		34	5	147		71	3	42
	All		2171	12	5.5		10953	12	1.1
Poor Risk, Emergency	0-9 yrs	All	97	10	103	All	90	5	56
	10-49		411	14	34		1620	14	9
	50-69		105	16	152		187	7	37
	70 up		116	24	207		146	6	41
	All		729	64	87		2043	32	16
All□	0-9 yrs	All	48906	41	0.84	All	38111	56	1.5
	10-49		44880	57	1.3		150127	144	0.96
	50-69		27755	129	4.7		41378	153	3.7
	70 up		7230	130	18		7803	93	12
	All		128771	357	2.8		237419	446	1.9

* Classification of patient status: "good risk" included (1) no complicating systemic disturbance and (2) moderate complicating systemic disturbance, both as non-emergency operations, or (5) same degrees as emergency operation; "poor risk" included (3) severe and (4) extreme complicating systemic disturbance, and (6) same degrees as emergency operations. "Elective" operation is a non-emergency operation.

† 1 Includes mouth, dental, tongue, T&A, lymph node biopsy (head and neck) and myringotomy. 60 Includes dilation and curettage, cervical biopsy, culpotomy, bartholincystectomy, insertion radium. 65 Includes all types of hysterectomy, with or without salpingo-oophorectomy. 73 Retrograde cystoscopy, or fulguration bladder tumor. 55 All types of hernia repair (inguinal, femoral, ventral, umbilical, incisional), except diaphragmatic. 90 Plastic surgery, biopsy, excision small lesions, skin only.

• Estimated from an approximate 4% sample count at each hospital.

□ Includes 20,957 operations on males and 34,929 operations on females in which patient status was unknown (not reported).

OTHER RISKS

§80—POST-SURGICAL MORTALITY (HALOTHANE STUDY)

Results (continued):

to 46 per 1000 for an extensive surgical procedure, abdomino-perineal resection. Among the 19 operations classified as high-risk the better rates, about 50 per 1000, are found in operations on the lung or large bowel and in gastric resection, with the worst rates in closure of an evisceration, always an emergency procedure, at 159 per 1000 and open-heart surgery, at 191 per 1000 (there is abundant evidence that the post-surgical mortality risk in open-heart surgery has been greatly reduced since 1959-1962).

Evaluation of mortality rates by other risk factors can be made in the lower part of Table 80a and in Tables 80c, 80e-f, and 80h-i. The physical status of the patient at the time of operation is a factor of obvious importance. If the patient has a pulmonary, cardiovascular or other systemic complication that justifies a classification of "poor risk," the mortality rate is seen to be roughly 20 times as high as it is in good-risk patients who are subjected to the operations in Tables 80a-c, about 3 to 8 times as high in patients undergoing moderate-risk operations (Tables 80d-e) or high-risk operations (Tables 80f-h). Patients who are "moribund" and classified as extreme-risk naturally have the highest mortality rates, ranging from 118 to 732 per 1000 in the various age, sex, and operation categories. In Table 80a, which contains the data for seven selected low-risk operations, post-surgical mortality rates are seen to be less than 1 per 1000 for good-risk patients with elective operation, but over 20 per 1000 for poor-risk patients. However, the risk is increased when the operation is classified as emergency: mortality about 2 per 1000 for good-risk patients (both sexes combined, with a total of only 24 deaths), and 87 and 16 per 1000, respectively, in male and female poor-risk patients. With respect to age, post-surgical mortality is generally at a minimum in the range of 10 to 49 years, slightly higher in children under 10 years, definitely higher at age 50-69 years, and markedly higher for the oldest patients. This relationship holds true in all tables except for males with the elective operations in Table 80a, where the young children have the lowest mortality rates. Although mortality rates for males generally exceed those for females by an average of 15 to 20 per cent, Table 80a also reveals an exception to this sex difference: consistently lower rates in good-risk male patients with elective operations. However, one cannot attach too much significance to such an anomaly, because, in this as in the other tables, a sex difference in operative procedures (hysterectomy on females only, as an example) may bias the mortality rates for a group of operations. Table 80a does show that post-surgical mortality rates are extremely low in good-risk patients under age 50 subjected to elective surgery, being 0.5 per 1000 or less. The entire gamut of mortality risk according to patient status, age, and sex is set forth in detail for the various operation groups in these tables.

The last table (80i) contains a summary of mortality rates by anesthetic agent in selected operation/patient categories. In these categories there is an *apparent* tendency for the mortality rates with ether as the anesthetic agent to fall at the low end of the range of mortality risk, for the rates with cyclopropane and "all other agents" to fall at the upper end, with halothane and nitrous oxide/barbiturate in between. However, other variables and uneven patterns of usage are not accounted for in this display of crude mortality rates by anesthetic agents, and the reader should consult the discussion and tables of adjusted mortality rates in pages 192-198 of the Halothane Study before attempting any judgment on the results. The anesthesiologists and statisticians interpreted the aggregate of differences between anesthetic agents as being relatively small and of uncertain significance. One major conclusion was that halothane had a record as good as or better than the other agents or combinations.

POST-SURGICAL MORTALITY (HALOTHANE STUDY)

Table 80b Early Mortality Rate (6 Weeks) in Patients Subjected to Other Low-Risk Surgical Procedures, 1959-62

Operation*	No. of Operations†	No. of Deaths	Mortality Rate	Operation*	No. of Operations†	No. of Deaths	Mortality Rate
	E	d	1000q		E	d	1000q
89 Strip or Ligate Saph. Vein	8214	8	1.0	7 Exocrine Gland	2364	10	4.2
30 Biopsy or Simple Mastect.	22741	23	1.0	85 Open Reduction (not Femur)	10370	49	4.7
81 Repair Muscle, Tendon, Nerve	16883	24	1.4	87 Minor Amputation	2574	13	5.0
4 Ear operations	9097	13	1.4	50 Appendectomy	15203	83	5.4
8 Excise Embryonic Tissue	1107	2	1.8	92 Misc. minor operations	19694	120	6.1
2 Nose operations	5782	13	2.2	66 Ovary, Tube, Pelvic Lap.	11777	76	6.4
63 Ectopic Pregnancy	805	2	2.5	21 Excise (Endo) Larynx-Bronchus	5268	36	6.8
54 Hemorrhoid & Sigmoidoscopy	7585	20	2.6	99 Thoraco-lumbar Laminectomy	17665	125	7.1
68 Colporrhaphy	3727	10	2.7	80 Closed Reduction, Fract.	9510	88	9.2
6 Jaw operations	5471	15	2.7	95 I&D Abscess or Pilonidal Sinus	8890	86	9.7
32 Radical Mastectomy	6517	18	2.8	23 Laryngectomy	1851	19	10
71 Circumcision, Hydrocele, Testis	10455	33	3.2	20 Endoscopy Larynx-Bronchus	10427	120	12
10 Thyroid operations	12914	42	3.3	40 Simple Cholecystectomy	13782	161	12
84 Open Joint operations	20398	81	4.0	15 Air Encephelogram	3110	38	12
62 Caesarean Section	2477	10	4.0	9 Cervical (Neck) operations	1265	20	16

Table 80c Early Mortality Rate (6 Weeks) by Patient-Status, Sex and Age, All Other Low-Risk Surgical Procedures Combined, 1959-62

Patient Status●	Age	Male			Female		
		No. of Operations†	No. of Deaths	Mortality Rate	No. of Operations†	No. of Deaths	Mortality Rate
		E	d	1000q	E	d	1000q
Better Risk	0-9 yrs	12705	18	1.4	7512	16	2.1
	10-49	53769	51	0.9	78130	78	1.0
	50-69	20729	111	5.4	29100	87	3.0
	70 up	3079	59	19	4746	82	17
	All	90282	239	2.6	119488	263	2.2
Poor Risk	0-9 yrs	812	25	31	492	30	61
	10-49	2051	34	17	3012	63	21
	50-69	2897	126	44	2741	88	32
	70 up	1099	106	96	1604	111	69
	All	6859	291	42	7849	292	37
Extreme Risk□	0-49 yrs	(32)	8	250	(103)□	13	126
	50-69	(55)	12	218	(36)	11	306
	70 up	(52)	15	288	(56)	16	286
	All	(139)	35	252	(195)	40	205
All■	0-9 yrs	16255	52	3.2	10228	56	5.5
	10-49	66135	110	1.7	94160	179	1.9
	50-69	28636	283	9.9	39009	214	5.5
	70 up	5599	214	38.2	7903	250	32
	All	116625	659	5.7	151300	699	4.6

* See Reference (1) for detailed description of each numerical operation code

† Estimated from an approximate 4% sample count at each hospital

● "Better risk" - no or moderate systemic disturbance; "poor risk" - severe or extreme systemic disturbance; "extreme risk" - patient moribund

□ Exposed to operative risk estimated as E+d

■ Includes operations in which patient status was unknown (not reported)

OTHER RISKS

Table 80d   Early Mortality Rate (6 Weeks) in Patients Subjected to Various Moderate-Risk Surgical Procedures, 1959-62

Operation*	No. of Operations†	No. of Deaths	Mortality Rate	Operation*	No. of Operations†	No. of Deaths	Mortality Rate
	E	d	1000q		E	d	1000q
70 Prostate operations	12387	217	18	5 Radical Neck Diss.	3027	95	31
56 Retroperitoneal, all	371	7	19	58 Sympathectomy, Adren.	3156	101	32
76 Operations on Ureter	5129	104	20	41 Gallbladder & Duct. Explor.	6263	221	35
16 Arteriogram, Heart Cathet.	10875	235	22	26 Lung Biopsy	2700	101	37
39 Hiatus Hernia (Abdom.)	1122	28	25	93 Misc. Major Surgery	5238	197	38
77 Bladder operations	4761	126	26	28 Hiatus Hernia (Thoracic)	1359	57	42
75 Kidney operations	9858	263	27	88 Major Amputation	6443	283	44
98 Cervical Laminectomy	3320	96	29	42 Gallbladder & Other Abd.	7631	342	45
25 No Surgery	853	25	29	51 Abd.-Perineal Resection	2594	119	46

Table 80e   Early Mortality Rate (6 Weeks) by Patient Status, Sex and Age, All Moderate-Risk Surgical Procedures Combined, 1959-62

Patient Status●	Age	Male No. of Operations	No. of Deaths	Mortality Rate	Female No. of Operations	No. of Deaths	Mortality Rate
		E	d	1000q	E	d	1000q
Better Risk	0-9 yrs	2935	28	9.5	2305	11	4.8
	10-49	11417	69	6.0	11198	60	5.4
	50-69	14654	273	19	9419	145	15
	70 up	4676	191	41	2253	92	41
	All	33682	561	17	25175	308	12
Poor Risk	0-9 yrs	877	55	63	435	22	51
	10-49	886	99	112	1044	105	101
	50-69	2929	274	94	2343	179	76
	70 up	2499	311	124	888	153	172
	All	7191	739	103	4710	459	98
Extreme Risk□	0-49 yrs	(51)	24	471	(161)	19	118
	50-69	(110)	31	282	(72)	13	181
	70 up	(93)	46	495	(40)	25	625
	All	(254)	101	398	(273)	57	209
All ■	0-9 yrs	4770	104	22	3451	44	13
	10-49	14965	209	14	15202	216	14
	50-69	21538	684	32	14254	394	28
	70 up	9108	648	71	3798	318	84
	All	50381	1645	33	36705	972	27

* See Reference (1) for detailed description of each numerical operation code
† Estimated from an approximate 4% sample count at each hospital
● "Better risk" - no or moderate systemic disturbance; "poor risk" - severe or extreme systemic disturbance; "extreme risk" - patient moribund
□ Exposed to operative risk estimated as E+d
■ Includes operations in which patient status was unknown (not reported)

POST-SURGICAL MORTALITY (HALOTHANE STUDY)

Table 80f   Early Mortality Rate (6 Weeks) in Patients Subjected to 4 High-Risk Surgical Procedures 1959-62, by Operation*, Patient Status and Age

Patient Status†	Age	No. of Operations●	No. of Deaths	Mortality Rate	No. of Operations●	No. of Deaths	Mortality Rate
		E	d	1000q	E	d	1000q
		48 Large Bowel Operations			44 Exploratory Laporotomy		
Better Risk	0-9 yrs	637	16	25	611	26	43
	10-49	3372	44	13	4476	83	19
	50-69	5237	138	26	3770	175	46
	70 up	2441	108	44	1285	86	67
	All	11687	306	26	10142	370	37
Poor Risk	0-9 yrs	120	19	158	206	51	248
	10-49	646	57	88	1533	166	108
	50-69	1406	194	138	1809	384	212
	70 up	1439	262	182	1354	325	240
	All	3611	532	147	4902	926	189
Extreme Risk□	0-49 yrs	(32)	18	562	(212)	75	354
	50 up	(152)	80	526	(511)	181	354
	All	(184)	98	533	(723)	256	354
All ■	0-9 yrs	967	47	49	1103	111	101
	10-49	4525	134	30	7057	360	51
	50-69	7912	423	54	6997	760	109
	70 up	4487	468	104	3215	552	172
	All	17891	1072	60	18372	1783	97
		12 Craniotomy			33 Open Heart Surgery		
Better Risk	0-9 yrs	1702	69	41	816	102	125
	10-49	5724	265	46	1698	177	104
	50 up	3447	290	84	214	53	248
	All	10873	624	57	2728	332	122
Poor Risk	0-9 yrs	483	70	145	1103	268	243
	10-49	1650	283	172	2332	484	208
	50 up	1545	359	232	412	160	388
	All	3678	712	194	3847	912	237
Extreme Risk□	0-49 yrs	(279)	146	523	(64)	22	344
	50 up	(242)	111	459	(11)	4	364
	All	(521)	257	493	(75)	26	347
All ■	0-9 yrs	2692	196	73	2896	510	176
	10-49	8237	776	94	4969	874	176
	50 up	5843	871	149	817	272	333
	All	16772	1843	110	8682	1656	191

* See Reference (1) for detailed description of each numerical operation code
† "Better risk" - no or moderate systemic disturbance; "poor risk" - severe or extreme systemic disturbance; "extreme risk" - patient moribund
● Estimated from an approximate 4% sample count in each hospital
□ Exposed to operative risk estimated as E+d
■ Includes operations in which patient status was unknown (not reported)

OTHER RISKS

Table 80g   Early Mortality Rate (6 Weeks) in Patients Subjected to Other High-Risk Surgical Procedures, 1959-62

Operation*	No. of Operations†	No. of Deaths	Mortality Rate	Operation*	No. of Operations†	No. of Deaths	Mortality Rate
	E	d	1000q		E	d	1000q
86 Open Reduction, Femur	9526	460	48	34 Closed Heart Surgery	7934	805	101
27 Lung operations (Excl. Biopsy)	10026	493	49	67 Pelvic Exenteration	259	27	104
45 Gastric Resection	16042	816	51	57 Large Endarterectomy, Graft	7192	780	108
13 Ventriculogram, Burr Holes	2736	219	80	59 Spleen & Liver operations	3111	341	110
46 Close Perforated Ulcer	1218	111	91	22 Tracheotomy	1179	161	137
36 Mediastinal operations	4195	395	94	47 Small Intestine	5395	743	138
17 Carotid Endarterectomy, Graft	775	73	94	52 Close Evisceration	1239	197	159
43 Subhepatic Abscess	196	19	97				

Table 80h   Early Mortality Rate (6 Weeks) by Patient Status, Sex and Age, All Other High-Risk Surgical Procedures Combined, 1959-62

Patient Status●	Age	Male No. of Operations	No. of Deaths	Mortality Rate	Female No. of Operations	No. of Deaths	Mortality Rate
		E	d	1000q	E	d	1000q
Better Risk	0-9 yrs	2231	72	32	1679	61	36
	10-49	11539	163	14	7996	103	13
	50-69	10222	413	40	4632	153	33
	70 up	2169	186	86	1805	117	65
	All	26161	834	32	16112	434	27
Poor Risk	0-9 yrs	1410	227	161	989	187	189
	10-49	2422	313	129	2201	246	112
	50-69	4473	731	163	2488	345	139
	70 up	1595	450	282	1729	332	192
	All	9900	1721	174	7407	1110	150
Extreme Risk□	0-9 yrs	(71)	52	732	(160)	36	225
	10-49	(387)	111	287	(268)	63	235
	50-69	(568)	172	303	(239)	81	339
	70 up	(264)	120	455	(235)	92	391
	All	(1290)	455	353	(902)	272	302
All■	0-9 yrs	4585	421	92	3308	337	102
	10-49	15847	662	42	12096	469	39
	50-69	17570	1544	88	8627	672	78
	70 up	4488	900	201	4503	635	141
	All	42490	3527	83	28534	2113	74

* See Reference (1) for detailed description of each numerical operation code
† Estimated from an approximate 4% sample count at each hospital
● "Better risk" - no or moderate systemic disturbance; "poor risk" - severe or extreme systemic disturbance; "extreme risk" - patient moribund
□ Exposed to operative risk estimated as E+d
■ Includes operations in which patient status was unknown (not reported)

POST-SURGICAL MORTALITY (HALOTHANE STUDY)

Table 80i Early Mortality Risk (6 Weeks) by Anesthetic Agent*, Selected Physical Status† and Age Groups, for Low, Moderate and High Risk Surgical Procedures, 1959-62

Age	Anesthetic Agent*	Better Physical Status†			Poor Physical Status†		
		No. of Operations	No. of Deaths	Mortality Rate	No. of Operations	No. of Deaths	Mortality Rate
		E	d	1000q	E	d	1000q
Low Risk Surgical Procedures (Table 80b)							
10-49 yrs	Halothane	46510	44	0.95	1436	24	17
	IV Barbiturate & N$_2$O	35232	25	0.71	1123	21	19
	Cyclopropane	22686	31	1.4	1195	29	24
	Ether	11565	7	0.61	283	6	21
	Other Agents	15906	22	1.4	1027	17	17
	All Agents	131899	129	0.98	5064	97	19
50-69	Halothane	18030	74	4.1	1877	59	31
	IV Barbiturate & N$_2$O	13115	44	3.4	1618	49	30
	Cyclopropane	7256	33	4.6	753	35	46
	Ether	4269	9	2.1	665	17	26
	Other	7159	38	5.3	725	54	75
	All Agents	49829	198	4.0	5638	214	38
Moderate Risk Surgical Procedures (Table 80d)							
10-49 yrs	Halothane	7983	41	5.1	530	62	117
	IV Barbiturate & N$_2$O	5295	33	6.2	543	47	86
	Cyclopropane	3062	20	6.5	501	44	88
	Ether	2730	5	1.8	72	8	111
	Other Agents	3546	30	8.5	284	43	151
	All Agents	22616	129	5.7	1930	204	106
50-69	Halothane	8136	121	15	1731	134	77
	IV Barbiturate & N$_2$O	6232	93	15	1204	88	73
	Cyclopropane	3761	86	23	862	107	124
	Ether	2530	47	19	332	38	114
	Other Agents	3415	71	21	1143	86	75
	All Agents	24074	418	17	5272	453	86
High Risk Surgical Procedures (Table 80g)							
10-49 yrs	Halothane	6667	81	12	1598	167	104
	IV Barbiturate & N$_2$O	4386	54	12	781	119	152
	Cyclopropane	3530	63	18	971	152	157
	Ether	2532	18	7.1	384	27	70
	Other Agents	2421	50	21	888	94	106
	All Agents	19536	266	14	4622	559	121
50-69	Halothane	4840	154	32	1833	252	137
	IV Barbiturate & N$_2$O	2874	103	36	1313	216	165
	Cyclopropane	2852	140	49	1642	331	202
	Ether	2118	58	27	900	78	87
	Other Agents	2170	111	51	1273	199	156
	All Agents	14854	566	38	6961	1076	155
All Above Surgical Procedures							
10-69 yrs	Halothane	92166	515	5.6	9005	698	77
	IV Barbiturate & N$_2$O	67134	352	5.2	6582	540	82
	Cyclopropane	43147	373	8.6	5924	698	118
	Ether	25744	144	5.6	2636	174	66
	Other Agents	34617	322	9.3	5340	493	92
	All Agents	262808	1706	6.5	29487	2603	88

* Each agent not in combination with other agents listed. Combinations of these additional agents included under "other agents."

† See footnotes to preceding tables. Male and female patients combined in this table.

Cancer

See Also

1. End Results Section, National Cancer Institute,
   *End Results and Mortality Trends in Cancer. Part I. End Results in Cancer.
   Part II. Cancer Mortality Trends in the United States, 1930–1955, Report No. 1,*
   NCI Monograph No. 6, U.S. Government Printing Office, Washington, D.C. (1961).
   End Results in Cancer, Report No. 2, U.S. Government Printing Office, Washington, D.C. (1964).
   End Results in Cancer, Report No. 3, U.S. Government Printing Office, Washington, D.C. (1968).
   End Results in Cancer, Report No. 4, U.S. Government Printing Office, Washington, D.C. (1972).

2. M.H. Griswold et al., *Cancer in Connecticut 1935–1951,* Conn. State Dept. of Health, Hartford, Conn. (1955).

3. H. Eisenberg et al., *Cancer in Connecticut. Incidence Characteristics, 1935–1962,* Conn. State Dept. of Health, Hartford (1967).

4. California Tumor Registry Staff, *Cancer Registration and Survival in California,* State of Calif. Dept. of Public Health, Calif. (1963).

5. *1951 Impairment Study.* Chicago: Society of Actuaries (1954).

G1-G6	Carcinoma or sarcoma, with operation (pp. 211-213)
G7-G8	Adenoma, once, within 10 years of application (p. 214)
G9-G10	Papilloma (pp. 214-216)
G11-G12	Fibroma, without known hysterectomy (pp. 216-218)
G13-G16	Epithelioma (pp. 218-220)
G17	Family history of cancer, two or more cases under age 60 (pp. 220-221)

6. A.M. Lilienfeld, M.L. Levin, and I.I. Kessler, *Cancer in the United States.* Cambridge, Mass.: Harvard University Press (1972).

CANCER

§100-190–CANCER PATIENT FOLLOW-UP DATA OF END RESULTS GROUP

References: (1) L. M. Axtell, S. J. Cutler, and M. H. Myers, ed., "End Results in Cancer. Report No. 4," End Results Section, Biometry Branch, National Cancer Institute, Bethesda, Md. (1972). DHEW Pub. No. (NIH) 73-272.
(2) E. A. Lew, Life table computer output for End Results Group, Report No. 3. Personal communication (1972). [See E. A. Lew, S. J. Cutler, and L. M. Axtell, "Long Term Survival in Cancer," Trans. Assoc. Life Ins. Med. Dir. Amer., 53:163-226 (1969).]
(3) M. H. Myers, Life table computer output for Reference (1). Personal communication (1972).

Introductory Note: The mortality and survival data contained in these tables are derived from the "End Results Study," an ongoing cooperative program, nation-wide in scope, organized in 1956 to compile statistics with respect to the status of survival in cancer patients and to evaluate the end results of cancer therapy. The program is sponsored and supported, in part, by the National Cancer Institute, U.S. Department of Health, Education and Welfare, and encompasses the experience of three state registries (California, Connecticut, and Massachusetts) and six medical centers treating large numbers of cancer patients. Altogether, more than 100 hospitals of various types and sizes in different parts of the United States gather and report data in accordance with a uniform plan. Also participating in the program are several other medical organizations and health agencies, both voluntary and governmental. The statistics from these sources are collected, compiled, processed by computer, and periodically reported by the End Results Section, Biometry Branch of the National Cancer Institute.

Medical literature for more than 50 years has contained an increasing number of articles reporting survival among patients with various types of cancer. The most common method of presenting results has been the five-year survival rate by the ad hoc method (ratio of survivors at five years from entry to patients traced for a period of five years or longer). Despite some notable exceptions such articles generally did not give complete information with respect to age and sex of the reported series, the absence of which made it impossible to describe experience meaningfully. However, in 1958 Cutler and Ederer stressed the usefulness of the life table method for the presentation of follow-up data on cancer patients and the importance of adjusting for age differences by means of the "relative survival rate," which is the same index as the survival ratio used in this monograph. In the cancer literature and in the reports of the End Results Group survival rates and the survival ratio have been extensively used to present the results of follow-up studies. In Report No. 4 absolute and relative survival rates are used, both in graphs and tables, and another factor, the "median survival time," which is the duration of follow-up at which 50 per cent of the sample has died. The published data do not lend themselves readily to the calculation of mortality experience on a comparative basis. In order to present the results of this important, extensive study in the format of this monograph, the Mortality Monograph Committee solicited and obtained the cooperation of the End Results Group in supplying the voluminous computer-produced life table data from which the recent reports have been prepared. Dr. Max H. Myers, Head of the End Results Section, generously provided two complete sets of the 1955-1964 entrant data, representing the latest experience with cancer patients treated in the recent past. Dr. Myers, and Mr. Lew, of the Mortality Monograph Committee, also made available similar computer output of 1940-49 and 1950-64 experience, used in Report No. 3 and in the article by Lew, Cutler and Axtell (see Reference 2). The Committee is most grateful to these individuals and to the End Results Group for making the extensive life table data available. The Committee alone is responsible for the methodology used to calculate mortality rates, mortality ratios, and EDR in the format used in this Monograph, and for any errors that may have gone undetected as a result of these calculations.

CANCER — FOLLOW-UP DATA OF END RESULTS GROUP

Subjects Studied: Because of the state registries, the nine sources of data used by the End Results Group provide information on the experience of more than 100 hospitals in which cancer patients receive treatment. The Connecticut Registry is the only one reporting cancer data on virtually all included types of cancer within a defined population (residents of the State of Connecticut). Therefore, although this cancer experience is a broad one, it is not known to what extent it is representative of all hospitals and clinics and all cancer patients in the United States.

Information on magnetic tape is provided on each cancer patient in the following categories: age, sex, and race; the primary cancer site, histological type and clinical stage (localized, with regional extension or with metastasis); date and method of diagnosis; method of treatment; date of last contact, follow-up status, and survival time. Classification of tumor therapy distinguishes between surgical, radiological, hormonal and chemotherapeutic procedures. It is restricted to the tumor-directed first course of treatment (initiated within four months after diagnosis). The experience in Report No. 4 comprises 111,046 male and 108,087 female cancer patients.

Patients with skin cancer other than melanoma and patients with carcinoma in situ have been excluded from this experience. The data in Report No. 4 of the End Results Group and utilized in these tables are limited to white patients. Other cases excluded were the following: (1) cancers first discovered at autopsy; (2) cases lacking a report on site or origin; (3) cases for which the only information available was in the death certificates; (4) classes of cancer with numbers too limited to permit meaningful analysis (about 6 per cent of the total).

Follow-up: In Report No. 4 follow-up data have been collected from the participating hospitals and registries on patients initially registered in the period 1955-64 inclusive, with follow-up to 1970 or 1971. Collection of follow-up information was the responsibility of specially trained personnel in each participating hospital or registry. There was only a small loss to follow-up (less than 6 per cent of entrants at five years), as was also true of entrants prior to 1955, some of which experience is included in the *Mortality Monograph*, but not in Report No. 4 of the End Results Group. Follow-up information is reported on a periodic basis to the End Results Section of the Biometry Branch, National Cancer Institute, where all life table calculations have been made and data prepared for publication. The unpublished detailed life tables were made available to the Mortality Monograph Committee so that results could be compiled in the format desired by the Committee.

Organization of Results: Data have been presented in Report No. 4 for 48 specific primary sites and types of cancer, as defined by the 1955 International Classification of Diseases, and accounting for 94 per cent of all invasive cancers, excluding non-melanotic skin cancer. From the detailed tables made available a selection was made of sites and types for the construction of 30 sets of tables reproduced herewith and each consisting of two or four pages of tables. An effort was made to preserve as much of the data as possible, but in a condensed form; more than one site or subsite was used in some of the table sets. Condensation was achieved by using four age groups rather than the five presented in the data made available for the *Monograph*, by combining male and female cases where experience was limited and sex differences were not too great, and by other types of combination. Duration intervals used in our tables were the same as in Report No. 4 for the localized cases: 0-2 years and 5-10 for the 1955-64 entrants, and 10-15 and 15-20 years for the earlier entrants. In the majority of our tables the experience has been presented for cases with regional extension and for those with metastasis on the basis of all ages and both sexes combined, and for intervals up to 10 years only. Concurrent U.S. White Population mortality rates were used to calculate expected deaths.

CANCER

§100-190–CANCER PATIENT FOLLOW-UP DATA OF END RESULTS GROUP

Organization of Results (continued): For some sites in Report No. 4 no data were available from earlier reports. For other sites, such as cancer of the uterus and cancer of the prostate, only one sex is involved. The Committee has omitted from its tables any data on all stages combined, except in the leukemias and lymphomas, where staging of the cancer has no real meaning because of the disseminated nature of the tissue involved. It is therefore apparent that our tables may differ somewhat in their arrangement, depending on the characteristics of each site and data available for it. During 1955-64 treatment data on the reported cancer patients revealed that 40 per cent were treated by surgery alone, 16 per cent by radiation alone, 28 per cent by a combination of radiation and surgery, 18 per cent by chemotherapy alone or in combination, and 19 per cent received no tumor-directed therapy. In the Committee's tables all treatment methods have been combined.

The organization of data in Report No. 4 involves three pages of basic data for each cancer site as follows:

A. Relative survival rates (survival ratio) for four calendar periods: 1940-49, 1950-59, 1960-64 and 1965-69. Data are given for each stage and for all stages combined.

B. Observed and relative 5-year and 10-year survival rates are shown for patients diagnosed in the period 1955-64, by stage, all treatments, and the most frequent treatment modality. Relative frequency is also given.

C. Additional data for the 1955-64 patients, including median survival time, and observed and relative survival rates for specific age groups.

For further information, Report No. 4 of the End Results Group should be consulted.

The organization of results in the Committee's tables follows the usual pattern by duration, with full data given in a pair of tables, one presenting "Observed Data and Comparative Experience," and the other, "Derived Data" (observed and expected mortality and survival rates for each interval). Results are given in greatest detail for cases of localized cancer, with separate data by sex, age, and duration, as previously described. For the earlier experience (1955-1964 entrants), detailed results with regard to localized cancers are presented for intervals within the first 10 years after diagnosis in the upper part of the table pages; combined results for cases with regional extension and with metastasis appear below the localized cancer data. The later experience, duration 10-15 and 15-20 years, is located at the bottom portion of each table. This latter experience is for localized cancer patients only, but is separated from the earlier experience on localized cancer because it relates to a different group of patients – those entering the study in the periods 1940-49 and 1950-59 combined. For this reason the *cumulative* survival rates and ratios have been omitted from the durations over ten years, in order to avoid any implication that the experience of the two separate groups is linked together in a single cohort, which is not the case. Generally the localized cases are divided into four age groups, which vary according to the age incidence of the cancer under consideration, and results for males and females are given separately. However, there are a number of instances in which arrangement of data departs from the usual format (for example cancers confined to one sex), and there are tables where it was considered preferable to combine male and female data in order to display a larger number of age groups.

In summary, results presented in these tables are as comprehensive as possible for recent data on cancer patients, all types of treatment combined. The format of the tables differs from that used in Report No. 4: in this *Monograph* emphasis is given to mortality ratios and EDR's; Report No. 4 presents survival rates and ratios exclusively. The methods of calculating survival functions in the *Monograph* are consistent with those employed in the tables developed for other diseases. The reader who is interested in additional details should refer not only to Report No. 4, but also to the previous three reports published by the End Results Group, and the review by Lew, Cutler and Axtell (cited in Reference 2). This is particularly true for details of comparative survival by type of treatment and trends in survival rates since the 1940-49 entry period.

CANCER—FOLLOW-UP DATA OF END RESULTS GROUP

Summary of Prevalence and Patient Data: Summarized information is given in Table 100a for the male patients and Table 100b for the female patients. All cancer sites for which tables have been prepared are included in these summary tables, ranked for each sex in accordance with the prevalence. The prevalence data include the number of cases reported in the 10-year interval from 1955 through 1964, and the percentage of the total. Approximately six per cent of the total cases were excluded from the End Results Report No. 4 because of the limited experience for some sites or lack of information on site of origin.

In addition to prevalence, data are given in these tables for the percentage of cases under age 55 at diagnosis, and the precentage distribution by stage of the cancer at the time of diagnosis — localized, regional, or metastatic — and the five-year survival ratio for all stages combined. The dividing line of age 55 was chosen because cancer tends to be a disease of older patients, and those sites characterized by a higher proportion of patients at the younger ages are easily distinguished from the more common type of age distribution by such a division. For each cancer site a more detailed age distribution is given through the number of cases at entry shown in the individual tables. The five-year survival ratio reflects in a single index, comparative experience for all age groups and stages of the cancer combined.

Staging data are given in terms of percentage of cases where the staging has been definitely established (the percentage figures do not add up to 100 in most cases). The leukemias and multiple myeloma, by their very nature, can never be regarded as "localized." These and certain other forms of cancer are not characterized according to stage, because of the difficulty or impossibility of establishing criteria with present diagnostic methods. Such forms of cancer are indicated by an asterisk in the columns for distribution by stage.

Ranking of prevalence data has been based on the total cases for a given site, when a breakdown has been given by "subsite," as in the case of cancer of the colon. Prevalance data for the subsites are enclosed in parentheses as these represent duplication of the total prevalence. A reference to the table number is given with each cancer site.

Among males the six most common sites for cancer are, in order, cancer of the lung, prostate, colon, bladder, stomach, and rectum. There were 19,208 cases of lung cancer reported in men, or 17.2 per cent of the total. Cancer of the stomach and cancer of the rectum each comprised about 5.7 per cent of the total. Among females, cancer of the breast was by far the most important site, with 25,698 cases or 23.8 per cent of the total. Other leading sites with more than 5 per cent of the total were, in order, total colon, and cancer of the cervix and cancer of the body of the uterus. Cancer of the lung ranked No. 8 among females during the period 1955-1964.

An inspection of Tables 100a-b provides useful comparative information regarding prevalence, and distribution by stage, and overall five-year survival ratio. The malignant character of lung cancer is evident in the fact that only 18 per cent of cases in men are classified as localized, and the five-year survival ratio for all stages is only 8 per cent. These figures for lung cancer in women are almost as bad as they are for men. The most prevalent cancer for women, cancer of the breast, shows 45 per cent of the cases to be localized, and a relatively favorable overall five-year survival ratio of 62 per cent. On an overall basis and for many individual sites the survival ratio is more favorable for female than for male cancer patients.

The data in these tables need not be described in detail, as the statistics speak for themselves. Sex differences in prevalence and five-year survival ratio are easily determined by inspection as well as those types of cancer which have a high proportion of localized cases at diagnosis, and those which do not. The subsequent tables provide comparative experience for each type in a much more detailed fashion.

CANCER

Table 100a   Summary of Cancer Data 1955-64 - 111406 Male Patients

Rank	Site	Prevalence		% Under Age 55	Distribution by Stage			All Stages 5-Year Surv. Ratio
		No. Cases	% Total		Localized	Regional	Metastatic	
1	Lung and Bronchus (§142)	19208	17.2%	22%	18%	31%	40%	8%
2	Prostate (§162)	13790	12.4	4	57	14	20	51
3	Total Colon (§157)	8722	7.8	16	41	31	24	43
	Ascending Colon (§157)	(2375)	(2.1)	19	37	35	23	43
	Transverse Colon (§157)	(1319)	(1.2)	17	38	30	28	38
	Descending Colon (§157)	(634)	(0.6)	13	46	30	20	44
	Sigmoid Colon (§157)	(3556)	(3.2)	14	44	29	23	45
4	Bladder (§161)	7499	6.7	15	76	13	6	56
5	Stomach (§155)	6337	5.7	16	17	32	45	11
6	Rectum (§158)	6298	5.7	17	46	28	21	38
7	Larynx (§141)	3982	3.6	25	60	32	4	56
8	Pancreas (§154)	3163	2.8	19	14	19	59	1
9	Brain & Meninges (§121)	3021	2.7	64	79	12	1	24
10	Total Pharynx (§152)	2656	2.4	29	26	57	12	22
	Mesopharynx (§152)	(1136)	(1.0)	27	29	55	11	27
	Nasopharynx (§140)	(444)	(0.4)	46	23	51	20	26
	Hypopharynx (§152)	(815)	(0.7)	23	22	62	10	16
11	Esophagus (§154)	2585	2.3	16	34	32	24	2
12	Kidney (§160)	2462	2.2	32	43	18	35	35
13	Mouth (§151)	2426	2.2	24	45	46	5	41
	Mouth (Floor)	(1162)	(1.0)	27	41	50	6	40
	Mouth (Other)	(1264)	(1.1)	21	49	42	5	41
14	Lip (§150)	2398	2.2	29	91	7	0.5	87
15	Total Chronic Leukemia (§171)	2357	2.1	27	0	*	*	25
	Chronic lymphocytic leukemia	(1426)	(1.3)	19	0	*	*	34
	Chronic myelocytic leukemia	(823)	(0.7)	38	0	*	*	11
16	Total Acute Leukemia (§170)	2153	1.9	64	0	*	*	1
	Acute lymphocytic leukemia	(645)	(0.6)	83	0	*	*	2
	Acute myelocytic leukemia	(625)	(0.6)	49	0	*	*	1
	Monocytic leukemia	(428)	(0.4)	44	0	*	*	2
17	Tongue (§150)	1917	1.7	25	40	49	7	27
18	Hodgkin's Disease (§173)	1394	1.3	70	*	*	*	36
19	Melanoma of Skin (§182)	1393	1.2	60	62	16	17	53
20	Lymphosarcoma (§172)	1098	1.0	43	*	*	*	30
21	Salivary Gland (§153)	1085	1.0	54	78	17	3	81
22	Connective Tissue (§181)	1069	1.0	51	57	15	19	46
23	Testis (§163)	1013	0.9	89	60	16	20	65
24	Multiple Myeloma (§180)	1003	0.9	22	0	*	*	9
25	Gallbladder (§156)	858	0.8	12	25	35	35	7
26	Thyroid Gland (§190)	746	0.7	60	39	42	16	75
27	Eye (§120)	627	0.6	56	82	10	2	81
28	Reticulum cell sarcoma (§173)	616	0.6	47	*	*	*	17
29	Liver (§156)	585	0.5	21	31	12	43	1
30	Nose, sinuses (§140)	580	0.5	29	38	48	10	39
31	Bone (§180)	563	0.5	69	52	22	19	32
32	Penis (§163)	377	0.3	23	72	22	4	69
33	Other Lymphoma (§172)	369	0.3	52	*	*	*	42

* No staging distribution given because of disseminated character of malignancy when first diagnosed, or difficulty of attempting to determine stage.

CANCER—END RESULTS GROUP

Table 100b   Summary of Cancer Data 1955-64 - 108087 Female Patients

Rank	Site	Prevalence		% Under Age 55	Distribution by Stage			All Stages 5-Year Surv. Ratio
		No. Cases	% Total		Localized	Regional	Metastatic	
1	Breast (§167)	25698	23.8%	42%	45%	42%	10%	62%
2	Total Colon (§157)	10739	9.9	19	41	32	23	43
	Ascending Colon (§157)	(3551)	(3.3)	18	41	34	21	51
	Transverse Colon (§157)	(1625)	(1.5)	18	38	33	25	43
	Descending Colon (§157)	(839)	(0.8)	24	42	32	21	47
	Sigmoid Colon (§157)	(3743)	(3.5)	21	44	30	23	48
3	Cervix (§164)	10557	9.8	56	52	34	11	60
4	Corpus Uteri (§165)	7614	7.0	31	74	12	9	72
5	Ovary (§165)	5240	4.8	41	28	17	50	32
6	Rectum (§158)	5217	4.8	19	45	30	19	41
7	Stomach (§155)	3646	3.4	16	20	30	43	14
8	Lung & Bronchus (§142)	3377	3.1	34	19	28	43	11
9	Brain & Meninges (§121)	2741	2.5	66	81	11	0.7	33
10	Bladder (§161)	2678	2.5	16	72	16	7	56
11	Pancreas (§154)	2211	2.0	16	15	21	56	2
12	Thyroid Gland (§190)	2006	1.9	68	54	34	9	85
13	Total Acute Leukemia (§170)	1755	1.6	62	0	*	*	2
	Acute lymphocytic leukemia	(465)	(0.4)	81	0	*	*	3
	Acute myelocytic leukemia	(559)	(0.5)	49	0	*	*	1
	Monocytic leukemia	(393)	(0.4)	44	0	*	*	1
14	Total Chronic Leukemia (§171)	1534	1.4	28	0	*	*	29
	Chronic lymphocytic leukemia	(822)	(0.8)	20	0	*	*	43
	Chronic myelocytic leukemia	(624)	(0.6)	39	0	*	*	14
15	Gallbladder (§156)	1531	1.4	11	21	31	42	8
16	Kidney (§160)	1480	1.4	30	48	18	29	38
17	Melanoma of Skin (§182)	1469	1.3	61	74	11	11	68
18	Salivary Gland (§153)	1452	1.3	62	87	8	2	93
19	Hodgkin's Disease (§173)	1020	0.9	68	*	*	*	44
20	Vulva (§166)	968	0.9	23	66	25	6	62
21	Connective Tissue (§181)	945	0.9	52	60	15	17	53
22	Mouth (§151)	911	0.8	36	54	40	4	52
	Mouth (Floor)	(322)	(0.3)	43	52	43	3	52
	Mouth (Other)	(589)	(0.5)	31	55	39	4	52
23	Lymphosarcoma (§172)	864	0.8	35	*	*	*	28
24	Multiple Myeloma (§180)	858	0.8	18	0	*	*	9
25	Esophagus (§154)	761	0.7	20	37	32	21	7
26	Total Pharynx (§152)	731	0.7	41	31	56	9	32
	Mesopharynx (§152)	(360)	(0.3)	38	32	58	6	37
	Nasopharynx (§140)	(166)	(0.2)	49	33	48	15	34
	Hypopharynx (§152)	(141)	(0.1)	36	27	63	9	23
27	Tongue (§150)	638	0.6	34	51	41	4	47
28	Eye (§120)	571	0.5	57	82	9	3	78
29	Reticulum cell sarcoma (§173)	554	0.5	34	*	*	*	15
30	Bone (§180)	483	0.4	65	55	20	18	38
31	Larynx (§141)	423	0.4	41	56	35	5	53
32	Nose, sinuses (§140)	369	0.3	37	39	49	8	41
33	Vagina (§166)	333	0.3	27	46	37	11	36
34	Liver (§156)	328	0.3	27	32	18	37	6
35	Other Lymphoma (§172)	305	0.3	49	*	*	*	46
36	Lip (§150)	182	0.2	25	90	7	—	89

* No staging distribution given because of disseminated character of malignancy when first diagnosed, or difficulty of attempting to determine stage.

CANCER – NERVOUS SYSTEM AND SENSE ORGANS

§120–CANCER OF THE EYE

This is a rare form of cancer, ranking 27 in males, and 28 in females among the types contained in End Results Group Report No. 4 and listed in Tables 100a-b. It is characterized by unusually high proportions of localized cases, 82 per cent in each sex, and of young patients (31 per cent under age 15).

For localized cases cumulative survival ratios exceeded 90 per cent at 2 years in almost all categories, ranging from 72 to 95 per cent at 5 years, and 66 to 90 per cent at 10 years (Table 120a). Mortality ratios were at a maximum in the second interval, from two to five years, in all of the female age categories and in the youngest male patients. Numbers of deaths are small, but this pattern differs from that of a pronounced maximum for mortality ratio during the first two years in almost all other types of cancer. Values of EDR, ranging from 16 to 51 per 1000 per year in the first two years after diagnosis, were lower than those observed in most other types of localized cancer in this period. Derived data are in Table 120b (the relatively high expected mortality for the first interval at ages under 15 reflects the normal increased mortality in the first year of life, as a large fraction of cases of retinoblastoma would be diagnosed in infancy–almost all are diagnosed under age six). Mortality was much heavier in cases with regional extension and metastasis, EDR in the first two years exceeding 100 and 500 extra deaths per 1000 per year, respectively. Five-year survival ratios were correspondingly reduced, to about 50-65 per cent for patients with regional extension and 8 per cent for those with distant metastasis.

§121–CANCER OF THE BRAIN

Cancer of the brain and meninges ranked ninth in both males (Table 100a) and females (Table 100b), with a nearly equal sex distribution. About two-thirds of the cases were under age 55, an unusually high proportion in comparison with most types of cancer.

Results for experience with localized brain cancer are given in Table 121a for cases age 55 up and three younger age groups, male and female separately. The 10-year cumulative survival ratio is of the order of 30 per cent and tends to decrease with increasing age in males. The age trend for females with localized cancer is irregular, but survival ratios are generally a little higher than those for males. Extremely high mortality ratios are observed in all localized categories within two years of diagnosis (2200 to 35000 per cent) and these remain high even though they decrease for the subsequent intervals. Female ratios generally exceed male, especially in children. In terms of extra deaths per 1000, rates within two years tend to be lower (about 290 per year for males and 360-234 for females) among patients under age 35 than they are age 35 up. Lower rates, 33 to 87 per year, are found in the intervals 2-5 and 5-10 years, with no clear age trend, but these rates still reflect a very considerable degree of excess mortality.

Experience for an earlier group of localized cases at 10-15 and 15-20 years from entry is given at the bottom of Tables 121a-b. Despite limited exposure and numbers of deaths it seems evident that excess mortality, whether measured as mortality ratio or extra deaths per 1000, persists at significant levels from 10 to 20 years after diagnosis and treatment.

Cases of brain cancer classified as having regional extension or metastasis showed extremely high excess mortality in the first two years, well over 500 extra deaths per 1000 per year. Subsequent values of EDR appear to be more comparable to those observed in localized cases, but the experience is very limited. In general, the experience is so unfavorable with the so-called "localized" cases as to cast doubt on the validity of the staging criteria for brain cancer.

CANCER—EYE

Table 120a   Cancer of the Eye - Observed Data and Comparative Experience by Stage, Sex, Age and Duration

Stage & Sex	Interval		Exposure	Deaths		Mortality Ratio		Survival Ratio		Excess
Age Group	No.	Start-End	Person-Yrs	Observed	Expected*	Interval	Cumulative	Interval	Cumulative	Death Rate
(Yrs)	i	t to $t+\Delta t$	E	d	d'	100d/d'	100Q/Q'	100p_i/p_i'	100P/P'	1000(d-d')/E
Localized										
Male										
<15	1	0- 2 yrs	301.0	13	1.49	875%	885%	92.3%	92.3%	38
	2	2- 5	405.5	4	0.26	1560	965	97.2	89.8	9.0
	3	5-10	454.0	2	0.24	835	950	97.8	87.8	4.0
15-34	1	0- 2	56.5	2	0.093	2200	2100	93.3	93.3	34
	2	2- 5	76.0	1	0.144	695	1200	96.5	90.1	11
	3	5-10	83.5	2	0.20	985	940	91.3	82.2	22
35-54	1	0- 2	203.5	5	1.68	300	295	96.8	96.8	16
	2	2- 5	285.5	5	2.94	170	210	97.8	94.6	7.0
	3	5-10	316.0	14	4.58	305	230	87.9	83.2	30
55-64	1	0- 2	187.5	14	4.43	315	315	89.5	89.5	51
	2	2- 5	223.0	13	6.59	197	225	91.4	81.8	29
	3	5-10	213.0	19	8.47	225	184	80.7	66.0	49
65 up	1	0- 2	255.0	29	18.0	161	161	90.4	90.4	43
	2	2- 5	274.0	32	22.0	146	141	88.4	80.0	37
	3	5-10	215.0	21	19.8	106	111	104.0	83.3	6.0
Female										
<15	1	0- 2 yrs	286.0	10	1.30	770	780	94.0	94.0	30
	2	2- 5	398.5	4	0.20	2000	940	97.1	91.3	10
	3	5-10	459.5	2	0.151	1320	935	98.5	90.0	4.0
15-34	1	0- 2	39.0	1	0.033	3000	2900	95.2	95.2	25
	2	2- 5	55.5	2	0.057	3500	3200	89.6	85.3	35
	3	5-10	66.0	1	0.096	1040	1910	92.3	78.7	14
35-54	1	0- 2	215.0	6	0.88	680	680	95.3	95.3	24
	2	2- 5	289.0	14	1.41	995	815	87.6	83.4	44
	3	5-10	310.5	11	2.04	540	570	86.7	72.3	29
55-64	1	0- 2	159.0	7	1.75	400	395	93.4	93.4	33
	2	2- 5	205.5	17	2.83	600	480	80.2	74.9	69
	3	5-10	209.5	8	4.07	197	280	91.1	68.3	19
65 up	1	0- 2	211.0	17	11.1	153	151	94.2	94.2	28
	2	2- 5	242.0	34	15.6	220	183	76.2	71.8	76
	3	5-10	203.0	19	16.6	114	135	91.3	65.6	12
Regional										
Male										
All	1	0- 2 yrs	111.0	23	4.21	545	535	67.0	67.0	169
	2	2- 5	91.5	13	2.53	515	375	71.9	48.2	114
	3	5-10	88.0	3	1.55	194	235	100.7	48.5	16
Female										
All	1	0- 2 yrs	97.5	14	2.80	500	455	78.5	78.5	115
	2	2- 5	102.0	10	2.70	370	330	81.2	63.7	72
	3	5-10	108.0	3	1.00	300	210	100.6	64.1	19
Metastatic										
Male										
All	1	0- 2 yrs	18.0	11	0.32	3500	2000	22.3	22.3	594
	2	2- 5	7.0	2	0.056	3600	945	35.5	7.9	278
	3	5-10	—	—	—	—	—	—	—	—
Female										
All	1	0- 2 yrs	18.0	14	0.68	2000	1290	7.2	7.2	740
	2	2- 5	3.0	0	0.002	0	530	112.5	8.1	−1.0
	3	5-10	—	—	—	—	—	—	—	—

*Basis of expected mortality: Concurrent U.S. White Population Rates

CANCER—EYE

Table 120b   Cancer of the Eye - Derived Mortality and Survival Data

Stage & Sex Age Group	Interval		Observed				Expected*			
			Survival Rate			Ave. Ann.	Survival Rate			Ave. Ann.
	No.	Start-End	Cumulative	Interval	Ave. Ann.	Mort. Rate	Cumulative	Interval	Ave. Ann.	Mort. Rate
(Yrs)	i	t to t + Δt	P	p_i	$\check{p}$	$\check{q}$	P'	p_i'	$\check{p}'$	$\check{q}'$
Localized										
Male										
< 15	1	0- 2 yrs	.9143	.9143	.9562	.0438	.9903	.9903	.9951	.0049
	2	2- 5	.8872	.9704	.9900	.0100	.9883	.9980	.9993	.0007
	3	5-10	.8653	.9753	.9950	.0050	.9858	.9975	.9995	.0005
15-34	1	0- 2	.9304	.9304	.9646	.0354	.9967	.9967	.9983	.0017
	2	2- 5	.8924	.9592	.9862	.0138	.9910	.9943	.9981	.0019
	3	5-10	.8054	.9025	.9797	.0203	.9793	.9882	.9976	.0024
35-54	1	0- 2	.9516	.9516	.9755	.0245	.9835	.9835	.9917	.0083
	2	2- 5	.9017	.9476	.9822	.0178	.9531	.9691	.9896	.0104
	3	5-10	.7357	.8159	.9601	.0399	.8844	.9279	.9851	.0149
55-64	1	0- 2	.8536	.8536	.9239	.0761	.9535	.9535	.9765	.0235
	2	2- 5	.7144	.8369	.9424	.0576	.8730	.9156	.9710	.0290
	3	5-10	.4705	.6586	.9199	.0801	.7129	.8166	.9603	.0397
65 up	1	0- 2	.7820	.7820	.8843	.1157	.8647	.8647	.9299	.0701
	2	2- 5	.5389	.6891	.8833	.1167	.6738	.7792	.9202	.0798
	3	5-10	.3356	.6228	.9096	.0904	.4031	.5982	.9023	.0977
Female										
< 15	1	0- 2 yrs	.9313	.9313	.9650	.0350	.9912	.9912	.9956	.0044
	2	2- 5	.9034	.9700	.9899	.0101	.9897	.9985	.9995	.0005
	3	5-10	.8888	.9838	.9967	.0033	.9881	.9984	.9997	.0003
15-34	1	0- 2	.9500	.9500	.9747	.0253	.9983	.9983	.9991	.0009
	2	2- 5	.8486	.8933	.9631	.0369	.9953	.9970	.9990	.0010
	3	5-10	.7779	.9167	.9828	.0172	.9884	.9931	.9986	.0014
35-54	1	0- 2	.9450	.9450	.9721	.0279	.9919	.9919	.9959	.0041
	2	2- 5	.8154	.8629	.9520	.0480	.9773	.9853	.9951	.0049
	3	5-10	.6828	.8374	.9651	.0349	.9443	.9662	.9931	.0069
55-64	1	0- 2	.9136	.9136	.9558	.0442	.9780	.9780	.9889	.0111
	2	2- 5	.7032	.7697	.9164	.0836	.9383	.9594	.9863	.0137
	3	5-10	.5797	.8244	.9621	.0379	.8490	.9048	.9802	.0198
65 up	1	0- 2	.8455	.8455	.9195	.0805	.8976	.8976	.9474	.0526
	2	2- 5	.5364	.6344	.8593	.1407	.7472	.8324	.9407	.0593
	3	5-10	.3323	.6195	.9087	.0913	.5069	.6784	.9253	.0747
Regional										
Male										
All	1	0- 2 yrs	.6230	.6230	.7893	.2107	.9297	.9297	.9642	.0358
	2	2- 5	.4056	.6510	.8667	.1333	.8412	.9048	.9672	.0328
	3	5-10	.3513	.8661	.9717	.0283	.7236	.8602	.9703	.0297
Female										
All	1	0- 2 yrs	.7399	.7399	.8602	.1398	.9426	.9426	.9709	.0291
	2	2- 5	.5502	.7436	.9060	.0940	.8637	.9163	.9713	.0287
	3	5-10	.4839	.8795	.9746	.0254	.7550	.8741	.9734	.0266
Metastatic										
Male										
All	1	0- 2 yrs	.2143	.2143	.4629	.5371	.9616	.9616	.9806	.0194
	2	2- 5	.0714	.3332	.6933	.3067	.9015	.9375	.9787	.0213
	3	5-10	—	—	—	—	—	—	—	—
Female										
All	1	0- 2 yrs	.0667	.0667	.2583	.7417	.9276	.9276	.9631	.0369
	2	2- 5	.0667	1.0000	1.0000	.0000	.8242	.8885	.9614	.0386
	3	5-10	—	—	—	—	—	—	—	—

*Basis of expected mortality: Concurrent U.S. White Population Rates

CANCER—BRAIN

Table 121a   Cancer of the Brain - Observed Data and Comparative Experience by Stage, Sex, and Duration

Stage & Sex Age Group	No.	Interval Start-End	Exposure Person-Yrs	Deaths Observed	Expected*	Mortality Ratio Interval	Cumulative	Survival Ratio Interval	Cumulative	Excess Death Rate
(Yrs)	i	t to t + Δt	E	d	d'	100d/d'	100Q/Q'	100p$_i$/p$_i$'	100P/P'	1000(d-d')/E
Localized Male < 15	1	0- 2 yrs	542.0	161	0.98	16400%	15000%	52.2%	52.2%	295
	2	2- 5	470.5	36	0.30	12100	11500	79.6	41.6	76
	3	5-10	480.0	18	0.40	4500	7100	83.1	34.6	37
15-34	1	0- 2	520.5	147	0.83	17600	14600	53.4	53.4	281
	2	2- 5	452.0	40	0.81	4900	6900	76.1	40.6	87
	3	5-10	413.5	20	0.89	2200	3500	79.0	32.1	46
35-54	1	0- 2	1205.5	617	8.70	7100	4600	29.9	29.9	505
	2	2- 5	687.0	64	5.87	1090	1790	77.0	23.0	85
	3	5-10	595.5	42	7.37	570	780	76.9	17.7	58
55 up	1	0- 2	1025.5	726	32.7	2200	1350	16.2	16.2	676
	2	2- 5	352.5	31	13.48	230	530	85.6	13.9	50
	3	5-10	285.0	30	13.20	225	270	72.8	10.1	59
Female < 15	1	0- 2 yrs	503.5	182	0.53	35000	30000	43.8	43.8	360
	2	2- 5	377.0	31	0.151	21000	22000	78.0	34.2	82
	3	5-10	361.5	9	0.145	6200	14300	87.5	29.9	24
15-34	1	0- 2	455.0	107	0.36	29000	25000	60.2	60.2	234
	2	2- 5	433.5	33	0.40	8200	11900	79.7	47.9	75
	3	5-10	421.5	21	0.51	4100	5700	80.3	38.5	49
35-54	1	0- 2	1341.0	488	4.87	10000	7400	45.1	45.1	360
	2	2- 5	1101.0	57	4.68	1220	2900	86.6	39.0	48
	3	5-10	1137.5	52	6.60	790	1350	81.2	31.7	40
55 up	1	0- 2	986.5	535	17.78	3000	2000	28.7	28.7	524
	2	2- 5	548.0	32	10.85	295	835	89.2	25.6	39
	3	5-10	526.5	32	14.62	220	380	87.4	22.3	33
Regional M&F All	1	0- 2 yrs	882.0	504	8.71	5800	3500	25.2	25.2	562
	2	2- 5	438.0	44	3.59	1230	1430	75.9	19.2	92
	3	5-10	426.0	24	3.80	630	665	82.4	15.8	47
Metastatic M&F All	1	0- 2 yrs	63.0	43	0.76	5700	3400	19.3	19.3	670
	2	2- 5	23.5	2	0.42	480	1390	82.1	15.9	67
	3	5- 9	14.5	4	0.31	1250	780	0	0	254
Site: Brain and Cranial Meninges Localized Male < 45	4	10-15 yrs	877.0	24	3.57	670%		88.6%		23
	5	15-20	369.0	5	2.32	215		96.3		7.3
45-54	4	10-15	184.0	13	4.46	290		79.0		46
	5	15-20	39.5	4	1.50	265		63.6		63
55-64	4	10-15	68.5	9	3.41	265		64.0		82
	5	15-20	14.5	2	1.17	171		60.3		57
65 up	4	10-15	17.5	2	1.62	124		88.7		22
	5	15-18	2.5	0	0.28	0		143.1		−111
Female < 45	4	10-15 yrs	784.5	21	1.88	1110		88.5		24
	5	15-20	299.0	8	1.02	785		90.1		23
45-54	4	10-15	263.5	8	3.43	235		92.2		17
	5	15-20	119.5	7	2.46	285		83.1		38
55-64	4	10-15	142.0	5	4.33	115		96.7		4.7
	5	15-20	58.0	3	2.47	122		99.9		9.2
65 up	4	10-15	39.5	1	3.18	31		139.5		−55
	5	15-20	11.5	2	1.34	149		95.1		57

*Basis of expected mortality: Concurrent U.S. White Population Rates

CANCER—BRAIN

Table 121b   Cancer of the Brain - Derived Mortality and Survival Data

Stage & Sex Age Group	Interval		Observed				Expected*			
			Survival Rate			Ave. Ann.	Survival Rate			Ave. Ann.
	No.	Start-End	Cumulative	Interval	Ave. Ann.	Mort. Rate	Cumulative	Interval	Ave. Ann.	Mort. Rate
(Yrs)	i	t to t + Δt	P	p_i	$\breve{p}$	$\breve{q}$	P'	p_i'	$\breve{p}'$	$\breve{q}'$
Localized										
Male										
<15	1	0- 2 yrs	.5208	.5208	.7217	.2783	.9968	.9968	.9984	.0016
	2	2- 5	.4137	.7944	.9261	.0739	.9949	.9981	.9994	.0006
	3	5-10	.3425	.8279	.9629	.0371	.9908	.9959	.9992	.0008
15-34	1	0- 2	.5324	.5324	.7297	.2703	.9968	.9968	.9984	.0016
	2	2- 5	.4028	.7566	.9112	.0888	.9914	.9946	.9982	.0018
	3	5-10	.3148	.7815	.9519	.0481	.9804	.9889	.9978	.0022
35-54	1	0- 2	.2946	.2946	.5428	.4572	.9847	.9847	.9923	.0077
	2	2- 5	.2203	.7478	.9077	.0923	.9565	.9714	.9904	.0096
	3	5-10	.1580	.7172	.9357	.0643	.8923	.9329	.9862	.0138
55 up	1	0- 2	.1522	.1522	.3901	.6099	.9371	.9371	.9680	.0320
	2	2- 5	.1159	.7615	.9132	.0868	.8332	.8891	.9616	.0384
	3	5-10	.0661	.5703	.8938	.1062	.6528	.7835	.9524	.0476
Female										
<15	1	0- 2 yrs	.4371	.4371	.6611	.3389	.9981	.9981	.9990	.0010
	2	2- 5	.3405	.7790	.9201	.0799	.9970	.9989	.9996	.0004
	3	5-10	.2974	.8734	.9733	.0267	.9951	.9981	.9996	.0004
15-34	1	0- 2	.6007	.6007	.7750	.2250	.9984	.9984	.9992	.0008
	2	2- 5	.4772	.7944	.9261	.0739	.9956	.9972	.9991	.0009
	3	5-10	.3807	.7978	.9558	.0442	.9892	.9936	.9987	.0013
35-54	1	0- 2	.4473	.4473	.6688	.3312	.9925	.9925	.9962	.0038
	2	2- 5	.3819	.8538	.9487	.0513	.9789	.9863	.9954	.0046
	3	5-10	.3003	.7863	.9531	.0469	.9480	.9684	.9936	.0064
55 up	1	0- 2	.2764	.2764	.5257	.4743	.9646	.9646	.9821	.0178
	2	2- 5	.2322	.8401	.9436	.0564	.9083	.9416	.9801	.0199
	3	5-10	.1749	.7532	.9449	.0551	.7830	.8620	.9707	.0293
Regional										
M&F										
All	1	0- 2 yrs	.2469	.2469	.4969	.5031	.9785	.9785	.9892	.0108
	2	2- 5	.1806	.7315	.9010	.0990	.9425	.9632	.9876	.0124
	3	5-10	.1374	.7608	.9468	.0532	.8703	.9234	.9842	.0158
Metastatic										
M&F										
All	1	0- 2 yrs	.1887	.1887	.4344	.5656	.9761	.9761	.9880	.0120
	2	2- 5	.1490	.7896	.9243	.0757	.9386	.9616	.9870	.0130
	3	5- 9	.0000	.0000	.0000	1.0000	.8717	.9287	.9817	.0183
Site: Brain and Cranial Meninges										
Localized										
Male										
<45	4	10-15 yrs		.8677	.9720	.0280		.9794	.9958	.0042
	5	15-20		.9318	.9860	.0140		.9678	.9935	.0065
45-54	4	10-15		.6954	.9299	.0701		.8808	.9749	.0251
	5	15-20		.5173	.8765	.1235		.8132	.9595	.0405
55-64	4	10-15		.4915	.8676	.1324		.7684	.9487	.0513
	5	15-20		.3750	.8219	.1781		.6223	.9095	.0905
65 up	4	10-15		.5455	.8858	.1142		.6150	.9074	.0926
	5	15-18		1.0000	1.0000	.0000		.6989	.8874	.1126
Female										
<45	4	10-15 yrs		.8745	.9735	.0265		.9878	.9975	.0025
	5	15-20		.8857	.9760	.0240		.9828	.9965	.0035
45-54	4	10-15		.8614	.9706	.0294		.9343	.9865	.0135
	5	15-20		.7474	.9434	.0566		.8994	.9790	.0210
55-64	4	10-15		.8250	.9623	.0377		.8535	.9688	.0312
	5	15-20		.7952	.9552	.0488		.7957	.9553	.0447
65 up	4	10-15		.9130	.9820	.0180		.6545	.9187	.0813
	5	15-20		.5000	.8706	.1294		.5260	.8794	.1206

*Basis of expected mortality: Concurrent U.S. White Population Rates

1-16

CANCER–RESPIRATORY TRACT

§140–CANCER OF NOSE OR SINUSES, CANCER OF NASOPHARYNX

Data for both sexes have been combined in the several categories under both sites: the experience for cancer of the nose and sinuses is shown in the upper part of Tables 140a-b, that for the nasopharynx, in the lower part. With respect to incidence these two cancer sites in the upper respiratory tract rank near the bottom of the list of cancers in Tables 100a-b, the incidence falling between 0.2 and 0.5 per cent of all cancers.

In cancer of the nose or sinuses, classified as localized, mortality ratios over the ten-year period following diagnosis tended to decrease with age at diagnosis, while the excess death rate increased except for Intervals 1 and 2 in age group 55-64 years. From two to five years after diagnosis EDR ranged from 31 extra deaths per 1000 in the youngest age group to 127 per 1000 in the oldest. Five-year cumulative survival ratios ranged from 71.9 per cent under age 35 to 34.8 per cent in those age 65 and up. For patients with regional extension, all ages and both sexes combined, the cumulative five-year survival ratio was 31.6 per cent, and for those with metastasis only 11.7 per cent. Correspondingly high values for mortality ratio and EDR were found in these patients.

In localized cancer of the nasopharynx survival ratios and excess mortality were comparable in magnitude with those of patients with cancer of the nose or sinuses. Exposures and numbers of deaths were somewhat smaller, and differences appear to be random in character. In the interval from two to five years after diagnosis the mortality ratio ranged from 2800 to 255 per cent, decreasing from the youngest to the oldest age group, and the successive values of EDR for the groups in order of increasing age were 76, 123, 181, and 111 extra deaths per 1000, respectively. The five-year cumulative survival ratios again decreased with age from 66.2 per cent in patients under age 45 to 38.8 per cent in the oldest age group. For patients with cancer of the nasopharynx classified as regional extension or metastatic, mortality ratios and values of EDR were even higher than for their counterparts in cancer of the nose or sinuses. The five-year survival ratio for patients with metastatic cancer was 5.9 per cent.

§141–CANCER OF THE LARYNX

Incidence of cancer of the larynx shows a marked sex difference. This malignancy ranks 7th among men by virtue of 3.6 per cent incidence of cases reported in the 1955-1964 experience, but the rank is 31 in female patients, the incidence being only 0.4 per cent (Tables 100a-b). There were 3982 men and 423 women with all stages of cancer of this site.

In localized cancer of the larynx (Tables 141a-b), interval mortality ratios within two years of diagnosis ranged from 920 per cent for males, age under 45 years, to a minimum of 210 per cent for ages 75 and up. Mortality ratios for subsequent intervals tend to decrease with duration. Values of EDR for males ranged from 15 to 118 per 1000. Mortality ratios for females were higher than for males. In Interval 1 these ratios ranged from 2100 per cent at ages under 55 to 290 per cent for ages 65 and up, but they declined in later intervals. Female EDR's fell between 20 and 132 per 1000. Five-year cumulative survival ratios decreased with age at entry–from 87.4 to 59.0 per cent over the age range shown for males and from 73.4 to 67.4 per cent for females. The five-year cumulative survival ratio for all patients with cancer of the larynx manifesting regional extension was 31.1 per cent, and for those with metastasis, 7.8 per cent. These ratios are materially lower than those indicated in the localized stage.

CANCER—RESPIRATORY TRACT

§142—CANCER OF THE LUNG AND BRONCHUS

In the 1955-64 End Results Group Data, lung cancer was the leading site of cancer in men: 19,208 cases and a relative frequency of 17.2 per cent (Table 100a). Among women, lung cancer ranked eighth in incidence, with 3.1 per cent of the total reported cases (Table 100b). Less than 20 per cent of cases of lung cancer were classified as localized at time of diagnosis; this obtained for both men and women.

Excess mortality in localized cancer of the lung was extremely heavy in the first two years after diagnosis. In this interval, mortality ratios declined as age at diagnosis increased, the mortality ratio for male patients decreasing from 8400 per cent under age 45 to 915 per cent for those aged 65 years and up, and for females, from 7700 per cent to 1000 per cent. In contrast to the slope of mortality ratios, excess deaths increased with age: from 294 in the youngest age group to 491 extra deaths per 1000 in the oldest, for male patients, and from 117 to 399, for females. Two-year survival ratios decreased with advancing age, from 52.2 to 27.1 per cent in men, and from 77.9 to 36.9 per cent in women. All of these indices in Table 142a are reflected in the very high early mortality rates and correspondingly low survival rates in Table 142b.

Although excess mortality fell considerably from the first to the second interval (2-5 years after diagnosis), mortality ratios remained high, ranging from 2100 to 275 per cent for men and from 3300 to 470 per cent for women. EDR for both sexes ranged from 54 to 153 extra deaths per 1000 per year. For experience subsequent to the second interval, the course of mortality and survival may be examined in Intervals 3, 4 and 5. Experience from 5 to 10 years after diagnosis (Interval 3) was based on cases diagnosed in the period from 1955 to 1964, but experience for the next two intervals (10-15 years and 15-20 years) was based on groups of entrants going back to 1940. The most favorable experience for Intervals 4 and 5 was found for patients under 45 years of age at diagnosis. Since exposure was limited and the numbers of deaths were small, results should be interpreted with caution for these younger patients. The combined male experience from 5 to 20 years after diagnosis showed a mortality ratio of 210 per cent and an EDR of 8.5 per 1000 — based on only 5 deaths, however. In females, the corresponding ratio was 445 per cent and the EDR 11 — again with only 5 deaths. Such relatively favorable experience did not develop in patients age 45 and up. At these latter ages, substantial excess mortality in men continued, although numbers of deaths were small in intervals between 10 and 20 years after diagnosis. Cumulative survival ratios, at the end of five years, ranged from 40.5 to 18.7 per cent for males and from 66.3 to 21.9 per cent for females. At ten years, for both sexes, the extreme range of cumulative survival ratios ran from 67.2 to 12.7 per cent.

Where extension of the cancer into the region surrounding the original site had occurred, the mortality ratio in the first interval for all patients was 2300 per cent with 635 extra deaths per 1000 per year. In all patients with evidence of metastasis, the mortality ratio was 3000 per cent within two years after diagnosis, the associated EDR being 881 extra deaths per 1000 (all ages and both sexes combined). The survival ratio at the end of two years was 15.1 per cent in cases of regional extension and only 2 per cent where metastasis had occurred. A decrease in excess mortality from the very high levels of the first two years appeared in Intervals 2 and 3 among patients with regional extension of lung cancer: mortality ratios of 850 and 315 per cent, respectively, in these two intervals, and EDR's of 212 and 73 per 1000. Mortality ratios in these intervals among patients with metastasis were higher but still under those of the first interval (viz., 1210 and 360 per cent); corresponding values of EDR were 352 and 100 per 1000. Cumulative survival ratios were 7.7 per cent at five years and 5.5 per cent at ten years in patients with regional extension, and under one per cent in metastatic lung cancer.

CANCER—NOSE AND SINUSES
CANCER—NASOPHARYNX

Table 140a Cancer of the Nose, Sinuses, and Nasopharynx - Observed Data and Comparative Experience by Stage, Sex, Age and Duration

Stage & Sex Age Group	Interval No.	Start-End	Exposure Person-Yrs	Deaths Observed	Deaths Expected*	Mortality Ratio Interval	Mortality Ratio Cumulative	Survival Ratio Interval	Survival Ratio Cumulative	Excess Death Rate
(Yrs)	i	t to t+Δt	E	d	d'	100 d/d'	100 Q/Q'	100 p$_i$/p$_i$'	100 P/P'	1000(d-d')/E
Site: Nose and Sinuses										
Localized M & F										
< 35	1	0- 2 yrs	51.0	6	0.075	8000%	7400%	78.8%	78.8%	116
	2	2- 5	62.5	2	0.083	2400	4500	91.2	71.9	31
	3	5-10	55.5	1	0.098	1020	2400	94.0	67.6	16
35-54	1	0- 2	156.5	23	0.94	2400	2200	73.8	73.8	141
	2	2- 5	175.0	7	1.33	530	1040	90.6	66.8	32
	3	5-10	204.5	10	2.12	475	630	77.3	51.6	39
55-64	1	0- 2	159.0	23	3.10	740	685	76.5	76.5	125
	2	2- 5	173.5	9	4.14	220	350	92.2	70.6	28
	3	5-10	155.5	14	4.76	295	240	76.9	54.3	59
65 up	1	0- 2	277.5	87	18.86	460	400	54.6	54.6	246
	2	2- 5	194.0	38	13.37	285	250	63.7	34.8	127
	3	5-10	120.0	21	10.54	199	159	61.1	21.2	87
Regional M & F										
All	1	0- 2 yrs	737.5	257	24.0	1070	840	47.0	47.0	316
	2	2- 5	487.5	80	15.76	505	440	67.2	31.6	132
	3	5-10	405.0	37	15.65	235	250	78.9	24.9	53
Metastatic M & F										
All	1	0- 2 yrs	112.5	68	3.88	1750	1120	21.8	21.8	570
	2	2- 5	33.0	8	1.08	740	530	53.9	11.7	210
	3	5-10	22.5	3	1.32	230	305	30.6	3.6	75
Site: Nasopharynx										
Localized M & F										
< 45	1	0- 2 yrs	44.5	4	0.098	4100%	3800%	83.2%	83.2%	88
	2	2- 5	51.0	4	0.144	2800	2700	79.6	66.2	76
	3	5-10	61.5	1	0.24	410	1190	95.3	63.1	12
45-54	1	0- 2	53.0	9	0.42	2100	1960	70.1	70.1	162
	2	2- 5	53.0	7	0.49	1430	1230	67.0	46.9	123
	3	5-10	41.0	2	0.49	410	585	86.3	40.5	37
55-64	1	0- 2	86.0	21	1.70	1240	1080	60.3	60.3	224
	2	2- 5	68.0	14	1.70	825	655	55.6	33.6	181
	3	5-10	52.0	6	1.86	325	340	65.6	22.0	80
65 up	1	0- 2	89.0	26	5.34	485	420	55.7	55.7	232
	2	2- 5	60.5	11	4.28	255	245	69.6	38.8	111
	3	5-10	45.0	8	3.46	230	162	53.8	20.9	101
Regional M & F										
All	1	0- 2 yrs	496.5	167	10.66	1570	1190	47.6	47.6	315
	2	2- 5	331.0	62	6.94	895	640	59.5	28.3	166
	3	5-10	256.0	20	5.53	360	350	77.1	21.8	57
Metastatic M & F										
All	1	0- 2 yrs	154.0	97	3.12	3100	2000	15.6	15.6	610
	2	2- 5	37.0	11	0.76	1440	870	37.9	5.9	277
	3	5-10	11.5	3	0.180	1670	495	28.0	1.7	245

*Basis of expected mortality: Concurrent U.S. White Population Rates

1-18

CANCER—NOSE AND SINUSES
CANCER—NASOPHARYNX

Table 140b   Cancer of the Nose, Sinuses, and Nasopharynx - Derived Mortality and Survival Data

Stage & Sex Age Group	Interval No.	Start-End	Observed Cumulative P	Interval p_i	Ave. Ann. $\check{p}$	Ave. Ann. Mort. Rate $\check{q}$	Expected* Cumulative P'	Interval p_i'	Ave. Ann. $\check{p}'$	Ave. Ann. Mort. Rate $\check{q}'$
(Yrs)	i	t to t + Δ t								
Site: Nose and Sinuses										
Localized M & F										
< 35	1	0- 2 yrs	.7857	.7857	.8864	.1136	.9971	.9971	.9985	.0015
	2	2- 5	.7143	.9091	.9687	.0313	.9936	.9965	.9988	.0012
	3	5-10	.6667	.9334	.9863	.0137	.9862	.9926	.9985	.0015
35-54	1	0- 2	.7286	.7286	.8536	.1464	.9879	.9879	.9939	.0061
	2	2- 5	.6450	.8853	.9602	.0398	.9658	.9776	.9925	.0075
	3	5-10	.4730	.7333	.9398	.0602	.9161	.9485	.9895	.0105
55-64	1	0- 2	.7356	.7356	.8577	.1423	.9614	.9614	.9805	.0195
	2	2- 5	.6309	.8577	.9501	.0499	.8941	.9300	.9761	.0239
	3	5-10,	.4104	.6505	.9176	.0824	.7564	.8460	.9671	.0329
65 up	1	0- 2	.4750	.4750	.6892	.3108	.8694	.8694	.9324	.0676
	2	2- 5	.2436	.5128	.8004	.1996	.7003	.8055	.9304	.0696
	3	5-10	.0913	.3748	.8218	.1782	.4297	.6136	.9069	.0931
Regional M & F										
All	1	0- 2 yrs	.4386	.4386	.6623	.3377	.9333	.9333	.9661	.0339
	2	2- 5	.2628	.5992	.8431	.1569	.8328	.8923	.9627	.0373
	3	5-10	.1665	.6336	.9128	.0872	.6686	.8028	.9570	.0430
Metastatic M & F										
All	1	0- 2 yrs	.2025	.2025	.4500	.5500	.9286	.9286	.9636	.0364
	2	2- 5	.0975	.4815	.7838	.2162	.8302	.8940	.9633	.0367
	3	5-10	.0244	.2503	.7580	.2420	.6794	.8184	.9607	.0393
Site: Nasopharynx										
Localized M & F										
< 45	1	0- 2 yrs	.8278	.8278	.9098	.0902	.9955	.9955	.9977	.0023
	2	2- 5	.6535	.7894	.9242	.0758	.9870	.9915	.9972	.0028
	3	5-10	.6099	.9333	.9863	.0137	.9671	.9798	.9959	.0041
45-54	1	0- 2	.6897	.6897	.8305	.1695	.9842	.9842	.9921	.0079
	2	2- 5	.4483	.6500	.8662	.1338	.9553	.9706	.9901	.0099
	3	5-10	.3609	.8050	.9575	.0425	.8907	.9324	.9861	.0139
55-64	1	0- 2	.5800	.5800	.7616	.2384	.9612	.9612	.9804	.0196
	2	2- 5	.3000	.5172	.8027	.1973	.8935	.9296	.9760	.0240
	3	5-10	.1662	.5540	.8886	.1114	.7546	.8445	.9668	.0332
65 up	1	0- 2	.4902	.4902	.7001	.2999	.8793	.8793	.9377	.0623
	2	2- 5	.2727	.5563	.8224	.1776	.7033	.7998	.9282	.0718
	3	5-10	.0915	.3355	.8038	.1962	.4387	.6238	.9099	.0901
Regional M & F										
All	1	0- 2 yrs	.4538	.4538	.6736	.3264	.9542	.9542	.9768	.0232
	2	2- 5	.2499	.5507	.8197	.1803	.8831	.9255	.9745	.0255
	3	5-10	.1659	.6639	.9213	.0787	.7607	.8614	.9706	.0294
Metastatic M & F										
All	1	0- 2 yrs	.1491	.1491	.3861	.6139	.9576	.9576	.9786	.0214
	2	2- 5	.0526	.3528	.7066	.2934	.8912	.9307	.9763	.0237
	3	5-10	.0132	.2510	.7078	.2922	.8000	.8977	.9734	.0266

*Basis of expected mortality: Concurrent U.S. White Population Rates

CANCER—LARYNX

Table 141a Cancer of the Larynx - Observed Data and Comparative Experience by Stage, Sex, Age and Duration

Stage & Sex Age Group	Interval No.	Interval Start-End	Exposure Person-Yrs	Deaths Observed	Deaths Expected*	Mortality Ratio Interval	Mortality Ratio Cumulative	Survival Ratio Interval	Survival Ratio Cumulative	Excess Death Rate
(Yrs)	i	t to t + Δt	E	d	d'	100 d/d'	100 Q/Q'	100 p_i/p_i'	100 P/P'	1000(d-d')/E
Localized										
Male										
<45	1	0- 2 yrs	211.5	7	0.76	920%	920%	94.1%	94.1%	29
	2	2- 5	277.5	8	1.25	640	690	92.9	87.4	24
	3	5-10	279.5	6	1.81	330	450	91.7	80.1	15
45-54	1	0- 2	928.0	80	9.68	825	790	85.3	85.3	76
	2	2- 5	1138.0	57	14.90	385	480	89.3	76.1	37
	3	5-10	1221.0	44	21.9	200	280	91.3	69.5	18
55-64	1	0- 2	1594.5	158	37.2	425	405	85.2	85.2	76
	2	2- 5	1861.0	144	52.9	270	285	85.8	73.1	49
	3	5-10	1767.0	120	67.0	179	192	86.3	63.1	30
65-74	1	0- 2	1273.5	195	61.4	320	300	79.1	79.1	105
	2	2- 5	1334.0	119	76.6	155	188	90.5	71.6	32
	3	5-10	1137.5	138	84.4	164	144	79.6	57.0	47
75 up	1	0- 2	467.0	106	51.1	210	190	76.1	76.1	118
	2	2- 5	384.0	77	47.1	164	145	77.5	59.0	78
	3	5-10	233.5	44	36.5	121	114	82.2	48.5	32
Female										
<55	1	0- 2 yrs	177.0	15	0.71	2100	2000	84.5	84.5	81
	2	2- 5	221.5	11	1.06	1040	1270	86.9	73.4	45
	3	5-10	234.0	8	1.47	545	715	89.1	65.4	28
55-64	1	0- 2	133.0	19	1.47	1290	1220	75.2	75.2	132
	2	2- 5	140.5	10	1.96	510	665	84.2	63.3	57
	3	5-10	127.0	5	2.44	205	335	92.7	58.7	20
65 up	1	0- 2	128.5	18	6.24	290	270	82.0	82.0	91
	2	2- 5	135.0	16	8.10	197	198	82.2	67.4	59
	3	5-10	92.0	10	6.86	146	141	87.6	59.1	34
Regional										
M & F										
All	1	0- 2 yrs	2293.0	786	73.1	1080	865	47.2	47.2	311
	2	2- 5	1503.0	254	50.8	500	450	65.9	31.1	135
	3	5-10	1191.0	106	46.0	230	250	79.5	24.8	50
Metastatic										
M & F										
All	1	0- 2 yrs	258.0	158	10.00	1580	1030	19.7	19.7	574
	2	2- 5	66.0	23	2.00	1150	475	39.4	7.8	318
	3	5-10	28.5	4	1.04	385	255	54.4	4.2	104
Localized										
Male										
<45	4	10-15 yrs	231.5	5	2.60	192		92.2		10
	5	15-20	91.0	1	1.53	66		104.1		-5.8
45-54	4	10-15	620.5	36	17.10	210		85.2		30
	5	15-20	213.0	8	8.62	93		103.2		-2.9
55-64	4	10-15	697.5	58	37.6	154		82.6		29
	5	15-20	146.5	14	11.30	124		85.4		19
65-74	4	10-15	291.5	41	31.5	130		86.3		33
	5	15-20	57.5	10	8.97	111		91.3		18
75 up	4	10-15	38.0	11	7.99	138		63.3		79
Female										
<45	4	10-15 yrs	47.0	1	0.21	475		95.5		17
	5	15-20	22.0	1	0.145	690		80.4		39
45-54	4	10-15	39.0	3	0.46	655		83.7		65
	5	15-20	4.5	0	0.068	0		104.8		-15
55 up	4	10-15	68.0	5	4.22	119		100.6		12
	5	15-20	14.5	2	1.05	190		72.5		65

* Basis of expected mortality: Concurrent U.S. White Population Rates

CANCER—LARYNX

Table 141b Cancer of the Larynx - Derived Mortality and Survival Data

Stage & Sex Age Group (Yrs)	No. i	Interval Start-End t to $t + \Delta t$	Observed Survival Rate Cumulative P	Observed Survival Rate Interval p_i	Observed Survival Rate Ave. Ann. $\check{p}$	Observed Ave. Ann. Mort. Rate $\check{q}$	Expected* Survival Rate Cumulative P'	Expected* Survival Rate Interval p_i'	Expected* Survival Rate Ave. Ann. $\check{p}'$	Expected* Ave. Ann. Mort. Rate $\check{q}'$
Localized										
Male										
<45	1	0- 2 yrs	.9338	.9338	.9663	.0337	.9928	.9928	.9964	.0036
	2	2- 5	.8560	.9167	.9714	.0286	.9792	.9863	.9954	.0046
	3	5-10	.7581	.8856	.9760	.0240	.9460	.9661	.9931	.0069
45-54	1	0- 2	.8347	.8347	.9136	.0864	.9791	.9791	.9895	.0105
	2	2- 5	.7162	.8580	.9502	.0498	.9408	.9609	.9868	.0132
	3	5-10	.5949	.8306	.9636	.0364	.8559	.9098	.9813	.0187
55-64	1	0- 2	.8127	.8127	.9015	.0985	.9537	.9537	.9766	.0234
	2	2- 5	.6390	.7863	.9230	.0770	.8737	.9161	.9712	.0288
	3	5-10	.4510	.7058	.9327	.0673	.7142	.8174	.9605	.0395
65-74	1	0- 2	.7162	.7162	.8463	.1537	.9054	.9054	.9515	.0485
	2	2- 5	.5418	.7565	.9112	.0888	.7568	.8359	.9420	.0580
	3	5-10	.2888	.5330	.8817	.1183	.5067	.6695	.9229	.0771
75 up	1	0- 2	.6015	.6015	.7756	.2244	.7907	.7907	.8892	.1108
	2	2- 5	.3094	.5144	.8012	.1988	.5247	.6636	.8722	.1278
	3	5-10	.1035	.3345	.8033	.1967	.2135	.4069	.8354	.1646
Female										
<55	1	0- 2 yrs	.8379	.8379	.9154	.0846	.9920	.9920	.9960	.0040
	2	2- 5	.7178	.8567	.9498	.0502	.9778	.9857	.9952	.0048
	3	5-10	.6191	.8625	.9708	.0292	.9466	.9681	.9935	.0065
55-64	1	0- 2	.7361	.7361	.8580	.1420	.9783	.9783	.9891	.0109
	2	2- 5	.5948	.8080	.9314	.0686	.9390	.9598	.9864	.0136
	3	5-10	.4989	.8388	.9655	.0345	.8500	.9052	.9803	.0197
65 up	1	0- 2	.7420	.7420	.8614	.1386	.9051	.9051	.9514	.0486
	2	2- 5	.5060	.6819	.8802	.1198	.7506	.8293	.9395	.0605
	3	5-10	.2974	.5877	.8991	.1009	.5034	.6707	.9232	.0768
Regional										
M & F										
All	1	0- 2 yrs	.4415	.4415	.6645	.3355	.9353	.9353	.9671	.0329
	2	2- 5	.2597	.5882	.8379	.1621	.8346	.8923	.9627	.0373
	3	5-10	.1640	.6315	.9122	.0878	.6626	.7939	.9549	.0451
Metastatic										
M & F										
All	1	0- 2 yrs	.1813	.1813	.4258	.5742	.9204	.9204	.9594	.0406
	2	2- 5	.0622	.3431	.7001	.2999	.8025	.8719	.9553	.0447
	3	5-10	.0260	.4180	.8399	.1601	.6169	.7687	.9487	.0513
Localized										
Male										
<45	4	10-15 yrs		.8706	.9727	.0273		.9438	.9885	.0115
	5	15-20		.9545	.9907	.0093		.9170	.9828	.0172
45-54	4	10-15		.7377	.9410	.0590		.8659	.9716	.0284
	5	15-20		.8334	.9642	.0358		.8075	.9581	.0419
55-64	4	10-15		.6207	.9090	.0910		.7516	.9445	.0555
	5	15-20		.5616	.8910	.1090		.6574	.9195	.0805
65-74	4	10-15		.4702	.8599	.1401		.5451	.8857	.1143
	5	15-20		.3807	.8244	.1756		.4170	.8395	.1605
75 up	4	10-15		.1857	.7141	.2859		.2933	.7825	.2175
Female										
<45	4	10-15 yrs		.9333	.9863	.0137		.9771	.9954	.0046
	5	15-20		.7778	.9510	.0490		.9669	.9933	.0067
45-54	4	10-15		.7857	.9529	.0471		.9391	.9875	.0125
	5	15-20		1.0000	1.0000	.0000		.9544	.9907	.0093
55 up	4	10-15		.7199	.9364	.0636		.7158	.9353	.0647
	5	15-20		.5186	.8769	.1231		.7150	.9351	.0649

* Basis of expected mortality: Concurrent U.S. White Population Rates

CANCER—LUNG AND BRONCHUS

Table 142a   Cancer of the Lung and Bronchus - Observed Data and Comparative Experience by Stage, Sex, Age and Duration

Stage & Sex Age Group	Interval No.	Interval Start-End	Exposure Person-Yrs	Deaths Observed	Deaths Expected*	Mortality Ratio Interval	Mortality Ratio Cumulative	Survival Ratio Interval	Survival Ratio Cumulative	Excess Death Rate
(Yrs)	i	t to t + Δt	E	d	d'	100 d/d'	100 Q/Q'	100 p$_i$/p$_i$'	100 P/P'	1000(d-d')/E
Localized										
Male										
<45	1	0- 2 yrs	175.0	52	0.62	8400%	6800%	52.2%	52.2%	294
	2	2- 5	147.5	13	0.63	2100	2900	77.6	40.5	84
	3	5-10	146.0	3	0.89	335	1200	94.2	38.1	14
45-54	1	0- 2	853.0	265	9.21	2900	2400	49.7	49.7	300
	2	2- 5	647.5	66	8.70	760	1060	76.1	37.8	88
	3	5-10	615.5	41	11.20	365	510	76.1	28.8	48
55-64	1	0- 2	2051.0	781	48.9	1600	1250	42.3	42.3	357
	2	2- 5	1306.0	185	38.0	485	570	70.5	29.8	113
	3	5-10	1007.5	121	38.5	315	295	63.0	18.8	82
65 up	1	0- 2	2214.0	1220	133.0	915	655	27.1	27.1	491
	2	2- 5	926.5	166	60.0	275	310	68.9	18.7	114
	3	5-10	617.0	100	49.6	200	176	68.1	12.7	82
Female										
<45	1	0- 2 yrs	143.0	17	0.22	7700	7200	77.9	77.9	117
	2	2- 5	162.5	9	0.27	3300	3900	85.2	66.3	54
	3	5-10	170.0	0	0.34	0	1530	101.4	67.2	−2.0
45-54	1	0- 2	227.5	60	1.14	5300	4400	55.9	55.9	259
	2	2- 5	197.0	16	1.21	1300	2000	79.8	44.6	75
	3	5-10	166.0	10	1.38	725	990	77.7	34.6	52
55-64	1	0- 2	318.0	72	3.59	2000	1720	62.7	62.7	215
	2	2- 5	297.0	35	4.20	835	915	71.7	45.0	104
	3	5-10	257.0	20	5.08	395	465	74.2	33.4	58
65 up	1	0- 2	370.0	164	16.30	1000	795	36.9	36.9	399
	2	2- 5	205.0	40	8.55	470	425	59.3	21.9	153
	3	5-10	120.5	17	6.18	275	235	58.6	12.8	90
Regional										
M & F										
All	1	0- 2 yrs	8864.5	5885	252.0	2300	1460	15.1	15.1	635
	2	2- 5	2156.0	517	60.9	850	610	51.4	7.7	212
	3	5-10	1388.0	149	47.3	315	300	71.4	5.5	73
Metastatic										
M & F										
All	1	0- 2 yrs	9819.0	8951	300.0	3000	1580	2.0	2.0	881
	2	2- 5	307.5	118	9.75	1210	620	32.7	0.7	352
	3	5-10	130.5	18	4.97	360	305	61.5	0.4	100
Localized										
Male										
<45	4	10-15 yrs	118.5	1	0.99	101		100.0		0.1
	5	15-20	45.0	1	0.48	210		93.1		12
45-54	4	10-15	150.0	10	3.87	260		82.0		41
	5	15-20	34.0	3	1.24	240		87.6		52
55-64	4	10-15	180.5	11	9.05	122		92.4		11
	5	15-20	22.5	6	1.38	435		29.1		206
65 up	4	10-15	58.5	10	5.60	178		51.2		75
	5	15-17	2.0	1	0.22	460		0.0		392
Female										
<45	4	10-15 yrs	120.5	5	0.44	1110		81.3		38
	5	15-20	60.0	0	0.35	0		103.0		−6.0
45-54	4	10-15	60.5	1	0.66	151		95.8		6.0
	5	15-20	14.5	1	0.23	435		81.6		53
55-64	4	10-15	48.5	4	1.53	260		89.4		51
	5	15-18	2.5	0	0.109	0		114.7		−44
65 up	4	10-15	30.5	3	2.62	115		93.1		13
	5	15-20	10.5	1	1.16	87		119.7		−15

* Basis of expected mortality: Concurrent U.S. White Population Rates

CANCER—LUNG AND BRONCHUS

Table 142b   Cancer of the Lung and Bronchus - Derived Mortality and Survival Data

Stage & Sex Age Group (Yrs)	No. i	Start-End t to t+Δt	Observed Cumulative P	Observed Interval p_i	Observed Ave. Ann. p̌	Ave. Ann. Mort. Rate q̌	Expected* Cumulative P'	Expected* Interval p_i'	Expected* Ave. Ann. p̌'	Ave. Ann. Mort. Rate q̌'
Localized										
Male										
<45	1	0- 2 yrs	.5185	.5185	.7201	.2799	.9929	.9929	.9964	.0036
	2	2- 5	.3967	.7651	.9146	.0854	.9795	.9865	.9955	.0045
	3	5-10	.3611	.9103	.9814	.0186	.9466	.9664	.9932	.0068
45-54	1	0- 2	.4859	.4859	.6971	.3029	.9784	.9784	.9891	.0109
	2	2- 5	.3547	.7300	.9004	.0996	.9389	.9596	.9863	.0137
	3	5-10	.2449	.6904	.9286	.0714	.8517	.9071	.9807	.0193
55-64	1	0- 2	.4032	.4032	.6350	.3650	.9523	.9523	.9759	.0241
	2	2- 5	.2597	.6441	.8636	.1364	.8701	.9137	.9704	.0296
	3	5-10	.1330	.5121	.8747	.1253	.7073	.8129	.9594	.0406
65 up	1	0- 2	.2396	.2396	.4895	.5105	.8840	.8840	.9402	.0598
	2	2- 5	.1347	.5622	.8253	.1747	.7218	.8165	.9347	.0653
	3	5-10	.0592	.4395	.8484	.1516	.4661	.6457	.9162	.0838
Female										
<45	1	0- 2 yrs	.7763	.7763	.8811	.1189	.9969	.9969	.9984	.0016
	2	2- 5	.6572	.8466	.9460	.0540	.9911	.9942	.9981	.0019
	3	5-10	.6572	1.0000	1.0000	.0000	.9776	.9864	.9973	.0027
45-54	1	0- 2	.5531	.5531	.7437	.2563	.9899	.9899	.9949	.0051
	2	2- 5	.4335	.7838	.9220	.0780	.9718	.9817	.9939	.0061
	3	5-10	.3227	.7444	.9427	.0573	.9315	.9585	.9916	.0084
55-64	1	0- 2	.6132	.6132	.7831	.2169	.9775	.9775	.9887	.0113
	2	2- 5	.4215	.6874	.8825	.1175	.9369	.9585	.9860	.0140
	3	5-10	.2822	.6695	.9229	.0771	.8457	.9027	.9797	.0203
65 up	1	0- 2	.3387	.3387	.5820	.4180	.9170	.9170	.9576	.0424
	2	2- 5	.1766	.5214	.8049	.1951	.8062	.8792	.9580	.0420
	3	5-10	.0785	.4445	.8503	.1497	.6113	.7582	.9461	.0539
Regional										
M & F										
All	1	0- 2 yrs	.1419	.1419	.3767	.6233	.9411	.9411	.9701	.0299
	2	2- 5	.0656	.4623	.7732	.2268	.8468	.8998	.9654	.0346
	3	5-10	.0376	.5732	.8947	.1053	.6797	.8027	.9570	.0430
Metastatic										
M & F										
All	1	0- 2 yrs	.0188	.0188	.1371	.8629	.9378	.9378	.9684	.0316
	2	2- 5	.0055	.2926	.6639	.3361	.8401	.8958	.9640	.0360
	3	5-10	.0027	.4909	.8674	.1326	.6710	.7987	.9560	.0440
Localized										
Male										
<45	4	10-15 yrs		.9574	.9913	.0087		.9578	.9914	.0086
	5	15-20		.8824	.9753	.0247		.9476	.9893	.0107
45-54	4	10-15		.7165	.9355	.0645		.8733	.9733	..0267
	5	15-20		.7228	.9371	.0629		.8247	.9622	.0378
55-64	4	10-15		.7069	.9330	.0670		.7652	.9479	.0521
	5	15-20		.2116	.7330	.2670		.7269	.9382	.0618
65 up	4	10-15		.3036	.7879	.2121		.5928	.9007	.0993
	5	15-17		.0000	.0000	1.0000		.7945	.8913	.1087
Female										
<45	4	10-15 yrs		.7974	.9557	.0443		.9812	.9962	.0038
	5	15-20		1.0000	1.0000	.0000		.9697	.9939	.0061
45-54	4	10-15		.9048	.9802	.0198		.9447	.9887	.0113
	5	15-20		.7500	.9441	.0559		.9190	.9832	.0168
55-64	4	10-15		.7545	.9452	.0548		.8438	.9666	.0334
	5	15-18		1.0000	1.0000	.0000		.8717	.9553	.0447
65 up	4	10-15		.5851	.8984	.1016		.6285	.9113	.0887
	5	15-20		.6667	.9221	.0779		.5571	.8896	.1104

*Basis of expected mortality: Concurrent U.S. White Population Rates

CANCER–DIGESTIVE TRACT

§150–CANCER OF THE TONGUE, CANCER OF THE LIP

Cancer of the tongue is more prevalent in males, comprising 1.7 per cent of all cancers and ranking 17th (Table 100a), in comparison with a cancer prevalence of 0.6 per cent and a rank of 27 in females (Table 100b). Experience for both sexes has been combined in the various age categories for localized cases in Tables 150a-b. Mortality ratios for each of the three intervals within the ten years of observation decreased with age among patients with localized cancer of the tongue, while the excess death rate increased. From 2-5 years after diagnosis EDR ranged from 42 extra deaths per 1000 in the youngest age group to 101 in patients age 65 and up. Cumulative survival ratios at five years ranged from 73.2 per cent for localized cases under age 45 to 45.5 per cent in the oldest age group. For patients in the regional and metastatic stages at time of diagnosis, the cumulative five-year survival ratios for all ages and both sexes combined were 18.6 and 5.2 per cent, respectively, with very high values for interval mortality ratios and EDR's.

Experience for cancer of the lip is shown in the lower part of Tables 150a-b. As in cancer of the tongue, it is found principally in patients over age 55. It ranks 14th in prevalence for males, with a relative frequency of 2.2 per cent, but is 36th and last for females with a relative frequency of 0.2 per cent. In both sexes there was a near 90 per cent five-year survival ratio for all stages combined (Tables 100a-b). In the localized stage, experience is shown in the various age categories for males, but all ages are combined in the female data (Tables 150a-b). In the localized stage the cumulative five-year survival ratio for males ranged from 96.2 per cent in the youngest group to 85.8 per cent in those age 65 and up. The EDR's ranged from 7.9 to 28 extra deaths per 1000, respectively. The cumulative five-year survival ratio for females, all ages combined, was 91.3 per cent and the EDR was 25. No experience is shown in the metastatic stage because, since 1950, almost all cancers of the lip have been diagnosed in the localized stage. The cumulative five-year survival ratio dropped to 52.1 per cent in males, all ages combined, diagnosed in the regional stage. The EDR for the same group was 60 extra deaths per 1000. Substantial excess mortality persisted after ten years from diagnosis, even in the localized cases.

§151–CANCER OF THE FLOOR OF MOUTH, OTHER CANCER OF MOUTH

These combined cancer sites are more prevalent in males than in females: a rank of 13 for males (Table 100a) and a rank of 22 for females (Table 100b). The combined cancer sites comprise 2.2 per cent of all cancers for males as compared to a female cancer prevalence of 0.8 per cent. Experience for both sexes has been combined in the various age categories for localized cases, and for regional cases, by male and female with all ages combined (Tables 151a-b). Experience for cancer of the floor of mouth is shown in the upper half of Tables 151a-b, with cancer of other areas of the mouth, in the lower portion of Tables 151a-b. Mortality ratios for each of the three intervals within the ten years of observation decreased with age among patients with localized cancer of the floor of mouth. The excess death rate was high in each age group during the first interval, 75, 126, and 123 per 1000, respectively; it then decreased sharply at the older ages during the second interval; the lowest excess death rates were seen for those under age 55. Cumulative survival ratios for localized cases at five years were 67.7 per cent for those under age 55 and were 58.1 and 59.1 per cent at the two older ages. For patients with regional extension, all ages and both sexes combined, the cumulative five-year survival ratio was only 28.5 per cent, decreasing to 17.0 per cent at ten years.

There were more exposures and deaths for most categories of cancer of other areas of the mouth than for cancers of the floor of the mouth. After the initial two-year interval excess mortality tended to be somewhat lower in cancer of other areas of the mouth. The highest EDR's were found in the first interval – 134 extra deaths per 1000 for males and 106 per 1000 for females, all ages combined. From 2-5 years after diagnosis interval mortality ratios for localized cancer ranged from 1010 per cent to 178 per cent, decreasing from the youngest to the oldest age group; corresponding EDR's in the same interval were 27, 72, and 60 per 1000 per year. The five-year cumulative survival ratio again decreased with age from 82.5 per cent in patients under age 45 to 57.9 per cent for the oldest age group. In cases with regional extension mortality ratios were somewhat lower than those for cancer of the floor of mouth, but EDR's were about the same. Cumulative survival ratios at five and ten years were also comparable to those of cancer of the floor of the mouth.

CANCER–DIGESTIVE TRACT

§152–CANCER OF THE PHARYNX, CANCER OF THE MESOPHARYNX AND HYPOPHARYNX

Cancer of the pharynx is more prevalent in males, comprising 2.4 per cent of all cancers and ranking 10th (Table 100a), in comparison with a prevalence of 0.7 per cent and a rank of 26 in females (Table 100b). Experience for localized cancer of the pharynx (Tables 152a-b) for both sexes combined is shown in the various age categories; for regional and metastatic cases, data are presented by sex and duration, all ages combined. The lower portion of the table extends the localized data to 10-15 and 15-20 years duration at four age groups, both sexes combined. In the experience for localized cases excess death rates generally increased with advancing age, and were especially high within the first interval, ranging from 146 to 278 per 1000. Correspondingly high interval mortality ratios were observed, ranging from 5600 per cent to 355 per cent. These ratios decreased with advancing ages. When localized cancer is compared by sex, all ages combined, a preponderance of male cases is evident, associated with generally lower interval mortality ratios but somewhat higher excess death rates. Survivors of ten years or more among patients with localized cancer experienced lower mortality ratios in the age group 45-54 years than at younger or older ages. Male experience was less favorable than female in the regional stage of cancer of the pharynx in terms of EDR, despite lower mortality ratios; in metastatic cancer female experience was definitely worse than male. In regional cancer in the first two years the mortality ratio in males was 1310 per cent, with an excess death rate of 428 per 1000; these indices were 1750 per cent and 351, respectively, in females. Nearly all deaths due to metastatic cancer were concentrated in the first two years, and a very high mortality ratio and EDR were observed during this interval. Cumulative survival ratios for localized cancer at five years ranged from 63.1 per cent at the lowest age to 29.5 per cent at ages 75 and up. Ratios for females were better than for males at five years (47.7 per cent versus 36.6 per cent). Even lower cumulative five-year survival ratios were seen in advanced cancer: 18.9 per cent in male patients and 29.0 per cent in females with regional extension of their cancer, and 7.2 and 3.4 per cent, respectively, in male and female patients with metastatic cancer.

Data for mesopharynx and hypopharynx, as oral and laryngeal subsites of the pharynx, are presented in Tables 152c-d, mesopharynx in the upper part, and hypopharynx in the lower part of the tables. (Data for cancer of the nasopharynx are shown separately in Tables 140a-b.) Cancers of the mesopharynx comprise nearly half of all cancers of the pharynx in both males and females. Cumulative survival ratios at five years for localized cancer of the mesopharynx were about the same as seen for the pharynx, with values of 47.9 per cent for males and 48.4 per cent for females, but in the localized hypopharyngeal cases ratios were lower, with values of 21.1 and 31.8 per cent, respectively, all ages combined. Five-year cumulative survival ratios of patients with regional extension of cancers of the mesopharynx and the pharynx were about the same in the case of males, but for females the ratio for the former was somewhat more favorable, 37.2 vs. 29.0 per cent. Regional hypopharyngeal cases experienced even lower five-year cumulative survival ratios of 16.8 and 22.6 per cent, respectively, in male and female cases. Metastatic cancers for the three pharyngeal categories cannot be compared because no data are available for metastatic cancer of the hypopharynx. Metastatic mesopharyngeal cancer showed an extremely low five-year cumulative survival ratio of 6.8 per cent, all cases combined.

§153–CANCER OF THE SALIVARY GLAND

Prevalence of cancer of the salivary gland is similar for the sexes, ranking 21st for males (Table 100a) and 18th for females (Table 100b), with a relative frequency of 1.0 and 1.3 per cent, respectively. Combined male and female data are given for two younger age groups in localized cases, and male and female experience is presented separately in three groups starting at age 45, (Tables 153a-b); the lower portion of the table shows separate male and female experience for localized cases at durations 10-15 years and 15-20 years for four age groups. In many instances only small numbers of deaths were observed in the various duration intervals. Excess mortality was low in patients with localized cancer of the salivary gland under age 45, the excess death rate being under 4 per 1000 in all duration categories to 20 years except for men at durations 15-20 years, with an EDR of 14 per 1000 (based on only 6 deaths). This relatively benign character of salivary gland cancer in younger patients was especially remarkable in the first two years of follow-up, with EDR less than two per 1000 and a mortality not exceeding 265 per cent. Excess mortality was less favorable with advancing age, especially in male patients having localized cancer, the highest interval EDR after the first two years being 31 per 1000 in men age 65 and up. With regional extension or metastasis of the cancer much higher excess mortality was observed, especially in the first two years. However, relatively few patients with salivary gland cancer were classified in an advanced stage.

CANCER–DIGESTIVE TRACT

§154–CANCER OF THE ESOPHAGUS, CANCER OF THE PANCREAS

As may be shown from the entries in Tables 100a-b, cancer of the esophagus accounts for 1.5 per cent of all cancer cases and ranks 11th in males and 25th in females with a relative frequency of 2.3 and 0.7 per cent, respectively. Experience for both sexes has been combined in the various age categories for localized cases in Tables 154a-b (top part of the page). Mortality ratios for each of the three intervals within the ten years of observation decreased with age among patients with localized cancer of the esophagus, ranging from 6800 per cent in the first interval (0-2 years) for the youngest age group to 1020 per cent for patients age 65 and up. The majority of cases were diagnosed in patients over age 55, but regardless of age prognosis was poor. Mortality was heaviest in the first two years: EDR was 543 extra deaths per 1000 for those under age 55, 627 per 1000 for those age 55-64, and 634 per 1000 for patients age 65 and up. The cumulative five-year survival ratios for the same age groups were 10.8, 16.6, and 4.8 per cent, respectively. Experience for both sexes and all age groups has been combined for cases with regional and metastatic extension. For those patients with regional extension the cumulative survival ratio was only 7.7 per cent at two years, 2.4 per cent at five years, and 1.4 per cent at ten years, and the EDR's were 748, 347, and 100 extra deaths per 1000, respectively, over the intervals preceding these points of time. Patients with metastatic extension at time of diagnosis had an extremely low two-year cumulative survival ratio of 2.1 per cent with a corresponding EDR of 873 extra deaths per 1000. Results after the first interval must be interpreted with caution because the experience becomes scanty.

Cancer of the pancreas is more common than cancer of the esophagus ranking 8th in males and 11th in females (Tables 100a-b). It accounts for 2.4 per cent of cancer cases studied by the End Results Group. Experience for both sexes has been combined in the various age categories for localized cases in Tables 154a-b (bottom half). Mortality ratios for each of the three intervals within the ten years of observation decreased with age among patients with localized cancer of the pancreas, while the excess death rate generally increased with age. The numbers of cases in many of the age and interval categories were small, therefore the results must be interpreted with caution. For those patients age 45-64, the two-year survival ratio was 12.0 per cent with a corresponding EDR of 691 extra deaths per 1000. In the oldest age group which had the largest number of exposures and deaths, the two-year survival ratio was 7.1 per cent and the corresponding EDR, 724 extra deaths per 1000. Over 80 per cent of cases of cancer of the pancreas were diagnosed in an advanced stage, giving this disease a five-year survival ratio for all stages combined of one per cent for males and two per cent for females (Tables 100a-b). This extremely poor prognosis is further emphasized by the results in Tables 154a-b, where the two-year cumulative survival ratio for cases with regional extension, all ages and both sexes combined, is seen to be 4.5 per cent with an EDR of 797 extra deaths per 1000. For metastatic cases in the first interval, the mortality ratio was 2400 per cent, the survival ratio was an extremely low 1.6 per cent and the EDR, 907 extra deaths per 1000.

CANCER–DIGESTIVE TRACT

§155–CANCER OF THE STOMACH

The stomach is a common site of cancer, ranking fifth in males and seventh in females with relative frequencies of 5.7 and 3.4 per cent, respectively (Tables 100a-b). Almost twice as many males as females in the series had cancer of the stomach and prognosis measured by cumulative survival ratios was generally more favorable for women. The five-year cumulative survival ratio for males held at about 75 per cent between ages 55 and 74 at diagnosis and dropped to 64.1 per cent for ages 75 years and over. Such ratios for females improved from 72.9 per cent for age group 55-64 to between 80 and 85 per cent among ages 65 years and older. These survival ratios and comparative mortality experience are presented in Tables 155a-b for cases diagnosed at the localized stage for both sexes combined for ages under 45 years and for age group 45-54. Experience for older age groups is shown separately by sex. Mortality ratios diminished consistently by age and by duration for both males and females. Excess deaths per 1000 decreased by duration from diagnosis, but tended to increase in the first two-year interval by age grouping, ranging from 190 per cent for male and female experience combined at ages under 55 to 429 per 1000 for males and to 402 per 1000 for females at the older ages. Beyond the first interval an irregular trend by duration was indicated.

Data for cases with regional and metastatic extension at diagnosis were combined for both sexes and for all age groups. Approximately 70 per cent of cancers of the stomach were diagnosed in these advanced stages. The outlook was poor for these subjects. The cumulative survival ratios for cases with regional extension were low, with survival of 24.6 per cent at two years, 13.4 per cent at five years, and 10.6 per cent at ten years; the corresponding EDR's in the intervals ending at these points were, respectively, 506, 192, and 51 per 1000. In patients with metastatic spread, the survival ratios were even lower: 4.4, 1.9, and 1.3 per cent and the respective EDR's, 827, 268, and 82 per 1000.

Between 10-15 years following diagnosis of localized cancer of the stomach among males in the 55-64 year age group, the EDR was 12 per 1000 – a relatively modest level of excess mortality. A higher level, about 25 per 1000 appeared in the aggregate of both sexes at younger ages, but little or no excess deaths developed among either males or females in this interval at ages 65 years and over. Beyond the 15th post-diagnosis year extra deaths were extremely irregular, ranging from –95 to 68 per 1000 per year, but the numbers of exposures and deaths were small, limiting the significance of the results.

CANCER–DIGESTIVE TRACT

§156–CANCER OF THE LIVER, CANCER OF THE GALLBLADDER

The liver is not among the more common cancer sites, accounting for only 0.4 per cent of all cancer cases and ranking 29th in males and 34th in females (Tables 100a-b). About 75 per cent of all cancer cases were 55 years and older. A summary of experience in cancer of the liver is presented in the upper portion of Tables 156a-b: so-called localized cases (about one-third of the total) are shown by sex and by age at diagnosis relative to age 65 years. Prognosis is poor for both sexes and at all ages. The two-year survival ratio for diagnosis made before age 65 was 7.4 per cent for males and 20.7 per cent for females; when diagnosis was made at 65 years of age or older, the respective ratios were 2.5 and 5.4 per cent. EDR's in this first interval for ages under 65 years were 802 per 1000 for males and 602 for females; for ages 65 years and up the corresponding rates were 854 and 806 per 1000. Exposures and deaths after two years were so small that the derived rates and indices have little meaning.

In cancer of the liver with regional extension or metastasis, there were extremely few survivors after the first two years. The End Results Report No. 4 indicates most patients, regardless of age or stage of disease, died within five months. Therefore the EDR and mortality ratio do not fully reflect the magnitude of excess mortality. The survival ratio at two years was 1.7 per cent for patients with regional extension and 0.6 per cent for patients with metastasis.

Cancer of the gallbladder was much more common than cancer of the liver and occurred comparatively more frequently in women than in men, ranking, respectively, 15th and 25th. The relative frequency (to all cancers) was 1.4 per cent in females and 0.8 per cent in males (Tables 100a-b). The majority of cases occurred in persons over 55 years. Prognosis is only slightly better for younger subjects — the overall prospect of survival is very poor: five-year cumulative ratios, all ages and stages combined, were 8 per cent for females, 7 per cent for males.

Presented in the lower portion of Tables 156a-b is experience for both sexes combined for localized cases in three categories according to age at diagnosis. Mortality ratios for each of the three intervals within the ten-year period following diagnosis decreased with advancing age while excess death rates increased with age in all interval categories with one exception (subjects 75 years and up, 5-10 years, in which interval only two deaths were reported). Five-year cumulative survival ratios were 37.9 per cent for patients under 55 years, 26.5 per cent for those in age group 55-74, and 8.7 per cent for the oldest age group. The prognosis for patients with cancer in the localized stage was more favorable than for those with disease in the advanced stages. Unfortunately, almost 75 per cent of the cases were diagnosed with regional or metastatic extension. Experience in the advanced stages has been combined for all ages and both sexes. The two-year survival ratio for regional cases was 9.9 per cent and for metastatic cases an extremely low 1.5 per cent. The respective EDR's were 723 and 901 per 1000. After the first two years, there were so few survivors that no significant conclusion can be drawn as to excess mortality or reduced survival.

CANCER—DIGESTIVE TRACT

§157—CANCER OF THE COLON

The colon is one of the most common cancer sites. Cancer of the colon ranks second in females and third in males with respective relative frequencies of 9.9 and 7.8 per cent. Most patients with colonic cancer were over age 55 years and were diagnosed with cancer beyond the localized stage (Tables 100a-b).

Experience for localized cases of cancer of the colon has been separated by sex in the various age categories and five intervals in Tables 157a-b. Mortality ratios for each of the three intervals within the first ten years of observation decreased with age in males. The excess death rate increased with advancing age for males in all age groups, in each of the first two intervals, with one exception (75 and up, 2-5 years). In the third interval, the EDR remained fairly constant in the range of 14-22 extra deaths per 1000 per year. The two-year survival ratios ranged from 90.2 per cent for the youngest age group to 67.7 per cent in the oldest age group. At five years the range for cumulative survival ratio was 86.3 to 58.4 per cent, and at ten years it was 78.5 to 46.0 per cent. Excess mortality among males persisted to varying degrees in the fourth and fifth intervals, 10-20 years from diagnosis, in all age groups. The extreme range for EDR was from 2.3 to 50 extra deaths per 1000 per year. The mortality ratio was 120 per cent or less for men age 65 up, but exceeded 165 per cent in all age and late duration categories under age 65, except one. Some of the results must be interpreted with caution, as they are based on fewer than ten deaths.

Results for female patients are presented in the same manner as those for male patients. In Table 157a, the mortality ratios for each of the three intervals within the first ten years of observation are seen to decrease with advancing age in females with cancer of the colon. EDR generally increased with age in all duration categories within ten years, as it did in males. The five-year cumulative survival ratios ranged from 88.2 per cent in the youngest to 65.1 per cent in the oldest group. The survival ratios with one exception were higher for the females than for the males. Very little excess mortality was seen in the fourth and fifth intervals, the greatest EDR being 23 extra deaths per 1000 for those patients over age 65 at 15-20 years' duration. Persistence of substantial excess mortality beyond ten years was therefore less evident in females than in males.

In Tables 157c-d, experience for males (localized cases, all ages combined) has been divided according to specific site and all sites combined. In all sites within the colon excess mortality was greatest in the first two years and declined in the next two intervals. Cancer of the transverse colon had the highest EDR, 130 extra deaths per 1000 (compared to 106 for all sites combined in the first interval), and 35 per 1000 in the third interval (compared to 19 per 1000). Experience was most favorable for male patients with localized cancer of the ascending colon.

In Tables 157c-d, experience for females is categorized in the same manner as for males. Although results were slightly better for females than for males, the same general mortality characteristics were observed, with cancer of the ascending colon showing the most favorable experience in the first three intervals (EDR's of 89, 14, and 18 extra deaths per 1000) and cancer of the transverse colon showing the least favorable (EDR ranging from 110 to 22 extra deaths per 1000). For all areas combined the EDR ranged from 91 to 93 extra deaths per 1000 in the first two intervals to a low of about 9 per 1000 after ten years.

In Tables 157c-d, all ages and both sexes were combined to present experience for patients with regional extension, and those with metastases. In the regional category, results were given for the four specific sites of cancer of the colon and for all areas combined. The least favorable experience from 5-10 years was seen in patients with cancer of the sigmoid colon, with an EDR of 54 extra deaths per 1000 per year. The other sites of colonic cancer showed higher excess mortality than sigmoid cancer within two years; results were variable from one site to another from 2-5 years.

Results are shown for all ages, sites, and both sexes combined for patients with metastatic spread. Excess mortality was extremely high as shown by an EDR of 673 extra deaths per 1000 within two years and a corresponding survival ratio of 12.1 per cent. The cumulative survival ratio was 5.3 per cent at five years and 3.8 per cent at ten years.

CANCER–DIGESTIVE TRACT

§158–CANCER OF THE RECTUM

This cancer site is an important one, as it ranks sixth in frequency for both sexes (Tables 100a-b) with a ratio to total cases of 5.7 per cent for males and 4.8 per cent for females. Distribution of localized cases by age shows the heaviest male prevalence at ages 55 and up, and for females, at ages 65 and up. Localized cases predominated, with 46 per cent of total males and 45 per cent of total females classified in this stage of development at diagnosis.

The rectal cancer experience is presented in Tables 158a-b: separate male and female data are given for four age groups over five intervals; regional and metastatic data are given separately for male and female with all ages combined up to ten years' duration. Excess deaths per 1000 for localized cancer in males under age 55 ranged from 63 in the first two years down to 23 within the 5-10 year interval and somewhat lower but comparable values were experienced for females under age 55 — a range of 72 within the first two years to a low of 9.2 excess deaths at 5-10 years. At the upper age level the highest excess death rate was seen for males at ages 65 and up, a rate of 185 per 1000 within the first two years; among females at the same age and duration, EDR was 143 per 1000 per year. Correspondingly low cumulative survival ratios were observed at ages 65 and up: the two-year ratio in males was 65.5 per cent and the ten-year ratio, 41.7 per cent; in females these ratios were 73.1 per cent and 51.3 per cent, respectively. Interval mortality ratios for both sexes were highest for those under age 45 and remained high for females at age 45-54. These ratios ranged from 1890 per cent within the first two years down to 500 per cent at 5-10 years for males. For the youngest females the ratios decreased from 4000 per cent in the first interval to 395 per cent in the third. High interval mortality ratios, exceeding 1000 per cent, were also observed within the first five years in females age 45 to 54. However, there was a consistent downward trend in mortality ratio by age and duration in both sexes to a minimum close to 140 per cent in the third interval of the oldest age group, 65 and up.

Experience on regional extension of rectal cancer is shown by sex, all ages combined. Excess mortality was highest within the first two years of diagnosis, with an EDR of 283 per 1000 per year in males, and 260 per 1000 per year in females. Even in the third interval, from 5-10 years, EDR's remained at high levels, 86 and 59 per 1000, respectively, in males and females. Five-year cumulative survival ratios were much lower than in localized rectal cancer, 29.9 per cent in males and 31.2 per cent in females. Interval mortality ratios were higher for females. These ranged from a maximum of 930 per cent in females in the first two years to a minimum of 265 per cent in males during the third interval, from 5-10 years after diagnosis.

Metastatic cancer of the rectum was associated with an extremely poor prognosis within the first two years: EDR, 682 per 1000, all ages and both sexes combined, with an interval mortality ratio of 1700 per cent. The cumulative survival ratio at two years was only 10.4 per cent. The five- and ten-year ratios were 3.5 and 2.6 per cent, respectively.

Experience has been reported beyond ten years following diagnosis for patients with localized cancer (bottom portion of Tables 158a-b), but this is quite limited in numbers of deaths at the younger ages. Over Intervals 4 and 5, EDR's of 39 and 65 per 1000, respectively, were observed in males age 65 and up, and 12 and 15 per 1000 in the oldest females. Relatively little excess mortality was observed in patients under 65, especially in the fifth interval, from 15-20 years after diagnosis.

CANCER—TONGUE
CANCER—LIP

Table 150a Cancer of the Tongue and Lip - Observed Data and Comparative Experience by Stage, Sex, Age and Duration

Stage & Sex Age Group	No.	Interval Start-End	Exposure Person-Yrs	Deaths Observed	Deaths Expected*	Mortality Ratio Interval	Mortality Ratio Cumulative	Survival Ratio Interval	Survival Ratio Cumulative	Excess Death Rate
(Yrs)	i	t to t + Δ t	E	d	d'	100 d/d'	100 Q/Q'	100 p_i/p_i'	100 P/P'	1000 (d-d')/E
Site: Tongue										
Localized										
M & F										
<45	1	0- 2 yrs	165.5	15	0.48	3100%	3000%	83.1%	83.1%	88
	2	2- 5	199.5	9	0.71	1270	1690	88.1	73.2	42
	3	5-10	212.5	8	1.04	765	900	87.3	63.9	33
45-64	1	0- 2	919.5	154	14.13	1090	1010	71.3	71.3	152
	2	2- 5	899.5	100	16.80	595	605	74.8	53.3	92
	3	5-10	777.0	76	18.82	405	365	68.2	36.3	74
65 up	1	0- 2	891.0	227	61.2	370	335	64.0	64.0	186
	2	2- 5	693.0	123	52.8	235	215	71.1	45.5	101
	3	5-10	484.0	71	43.5	163	150	67.6	30.8	57
Regional										
M & F										
All	1	0- 2 yrs	1794.5	857	66.9	1280	950	30.8	30.8	440
	2	2- 5	786.0	158	28.9	545	455	60.4	18.6	164
	3	5-10	557.0	75	25.6	295	255	62.1	11.5	89
Metastatic										
M & F										
All	1	0- 2 yrs	216.5	139	7.34	1890	1220	15.4	15.4	608
	2	2- 5	46.5	16	1.49	1070	535	33.7	5.2	312
	3	5-10	12.0	3	0.37	815	275	54.4	2.8	219
Localized										
Male										
All	4	10-15 yrs	460.0	47	26.6	176		80.3		44
	5	15-20	134.5	12	8.93	134		88.4		23
Female										
All	4	10-15 yrs	254.5	16	15.23	105		99.9		3.0
	5	15-20	97.0	3	6.76	44		120.2		−39
Regional										
M & F										
All	4	10-15 yrs	193.5	24	10.75	225		72.4		68
	5	15-20	36.0	3	2.24	134		100.7		21
Site: Lip										
Localized										
Male										
<55	1	0- 2 yrs	1235.5	18	9.40	192%	190%	98.6%	98.6%	7.0
	2	2- 5	1718.0	30	16.43	183	183	97.6	96.2	7.9
	3	5-10	2027.0	57	27.2	210	193	92.2	88.8	15
55-64	1	0- 2	1056.0	45	24.6	183	182	96.0	96.0	19
	2	2- 5	1364.0	70	38.8	181	173	93.2	89.5	23
	3	5-10	1479.0	79	55.8	142	146	91.1	81.5	16
65 up	1	0- 2	1894.0	200	149.8	134	132	94.2	94.2	27
	2	2- 5	2088.0	241	182.4	132	126	91.1	85.8	28
	3	5-10	1776.0	212	186.1	114	112	92.6	79.4	15
Female										
All	1	0- 2 yrs	308.0	15	10.11	148	138	97.2	97.2	16
	2	2- 5	395.0	23	13.31	173	142	93.9	91.3	25
	3	5-10	401.5	20	15.60	128	127	94.7	86.5	11
Regional										
Male										
All	1	0- 2 yrs	285.5	74	16.43	450	400	62.0	62.0	202
	2	2- 5	228.0	27	13.22	205	230	84.1	52.1	60
	3	5-10	198.0	17	13.32	128	155	92.1	48.0	19
Localized										
Male										
All	4	10-15 yrs	5408.5	420	324.7	129		90.8		18
	5	15-20	1804.0	161	120.5	134		90.0		22
Female										
All	4	10-15 yrs	318.5	24	14.17	169		82.8		31
	5	15-20	74.0	4	3.37	119		96.2		9.0
Regional										
Male										
All	4	10-15 yrs	342.0	38	21.8	174		76.2		47
	5	15-20	115.5	9	7.97	113		94.4		8.9

*Basis of expected mortality: Concurrent U.S. White Population Rates

CANCER—TONGUE
CANCER—LIP

Table 150b   Cancer of the Tongue and Lip - Derived Mortality and Survival Data

Stage & Sex Age Group		Interval		Observed				Expected*			
				Survival Rate			Ave. Ann.	Survival Rate			Ave. Ann.
	No.	Start-End		Cumulative	Interval	Ave. Ann.	Mort. Rate	Cumulative	Interval	Ave. Ann.	Mort. Rate
(Yrs)	i	t to t + Δ t		P	p_i	$\stackrel{\smile}{p}$	$\stackrel{\smile}{q}$	P'	p_i'	$\stackrel{\smile}{p}'$	$\stackrel{\smile}{q}'$
Site: Tongue											
Localized											
M & F											
<45	1	0- 2 yrs		.8258	.8258	.9087	.0913	.9942	.9942	.9971	.0029
	2	2- 5		.7195	.8713	.9551	.0449	.9834	.9891	.9964	.0036
	3	5-10		.6113	.8496	.9679	.0321	.9569	.9731	.9946	.0054
45-64	1	0- 2		.6909	.6909	.8312	.1688	.9693	.9693	.9845	.0155
	2	2- 5		.4882	.7066	.8907	.1093	.9157	.9447	.9812	.0188
	3	5-10		.2930	.6002	.9029	.0971	.8064	.8806	.9749	.0251
65 up	1	0- 2		.5548	.5548	.7448	.2552	.8673	.8673	.9313	.0687
	2	2- 5		.3107	.5600	.8243	.1757	.6830	.7875	.9235	.0765
	3	5-10		.1291	.4155	.8389	.1611	.4197	.6145	.9072	.0928
Regional											
M & F											
All	1	0- 2 yrs		.2847	.2847	.5336	.4664	.9248	.9248	.9617	.0383
	2	2- 5		.1513	.5314	.8100	.1900	.8142	.8804	.9584	.0416
	3	5-10		.0738	.4878	.8663	.1337	.6396	.7856	.9529	.0471
Metastatic											
M & F											
All	1	0- 2 yrs		.1428	.1428	.3779	.6221	.9299	.9299	.9643	.0357
	2	2- 5		.0425	.2976	.6676	.3324	.8218	.8838	.9597	.0403
	3	5-10		.0180	.4235	.8421	.1579	.6403	.7791	.9513	.0487
Localized											
Male											
All	4	10-15 yrs			.5966	.9019	.0981		.7428	.9423	.0577
	5	15-20			.6256	.9105	.0895		.7080	.9333	.0667
Female											
All	4	10-15 yrs			.7323	.9396	.0604		.7332	.9398	.0602
	5	15-20			.8422	.9662	.0338		.7005	.9313	.0687
Regional											
M & F											
All	4	10-15 yrs			.5368	.8830	.1170		.7418	.9420	.0580
	5	15-20			.7220	.9369	.0631		.7167	.9356	.0644
Site: Lip											
Localized											
Male											
<55	1	0- 2 yrs		.9711	.9711	.9854	.0146	.9848	.9848	.9924	.0076
	2	2- 5		.9206	.9480	.9824	.0176	.9567	.9715	.9904	.0096
	3	5-10		.7923	.8606	.9704	.0296	.8926	.9330	.9862	.0138
55-64	1	0- 2		.9158	.9158	.9570	.0430	.9538	.9538	.9766	.0234
	2	2- 5		.7823	.8542	.9488	.0512	.8740	.9163	.9713	.0287
	3	5-10		.5827	.7449	.9428	.0572	.7149	.8180	.9606	.0394
65 up	1	0- 2		.7991	.7991	.8939	.1061	.8479	.8479	.9208	.0792
	2	2- 5		.5525	.6914	.8843	.1157	.6438	.7593	.9123	.0877
	3	5-10		.2903	.5254	.8792	.1208	.3654	.5676	.8929	.1071
Female											
All	1	0- 2 yrs		.9060	.9060	.9518	.0482	.9319	.9319	.9653	.0347
	2	2- 5		.7570	.8355	.9419	.0581	.8294	.8900	.9619	.0381
	3	5-10		.5748	.7593	.9464	.0536	.6648	.8015	.9567	.0433
Regional											
Male											
All	1	0- 2 yrs		.5506	.5506	.7420	.2580	.8877	.8877	.9422	.0578
	2	2- 5		.3818	.6934	.8851	.1149	.7322	.8248	.9378	.0622
	3	5-10		.2465	.6456	.9162	.0838	.5134	.7012	.9315	.0685
Localized											
Male											
All	4	10-15 yrs			.6648	.9216	.0784		.7321	.9395	.0605
	5	15-20			.6322	.9124	.0876		.7028	.9319	.0681
Female											
All	4	10-15 yrs			.6594	.9201	.0799		.7961	.9554	.0446
	5	15-20			.7571	.9459	.0541		.7872	.9533	.0467
Regional											
Male											
All	4	10-15 yrs			.5483	.8868	.1132		.7196	.9363	.0637
	5	15-20			.6559	.9191	.0809		.6946	.9297	.0703

* Basis of expected mortality: Concurrent U.S. White Population Rates

CANCER—MOUTH

Table 151a   Cancer of the Mouth - Observed Data and Comparative Experience by Stage, Sex, Age and Duration

Stage & Sex Age Group	No.	Interval Start-End	Exposure Person-Yrs	Deaths Observed	Deaths Expected*	Mortality Ratio Interval	Mortality Ratio Cumulative	Survival Ratio Interval	Survival Ratio Cumulative	Excess Death Rate
(Yrs)	i	t to t + Δt	E	d	d'	100 d/d'	100 Q/Q'	100 p_i/p_i'	100 P/P'	1000(d-d')/E
Site: Floor of Mouth										
Localized M & F										
<55	1	0- 2 yrs	401.0	33	3.12	1060%	1020%	85.5%	85.5%	75
	2	2- 5	476.0	40	4.48	895	815	79.2	67.7	75
	3	5-10	449.0	27	5.71	475	500	78.3	53.0	47
55-64	1	0- 2	354.5	52	7.43	700	660	75.8	75.8	126
	2	2- 5	360.0	39	9.17	425	430	76.7	58.1	83
	3	5-10	322.0	29	10.65	270	255	78.3	45.5	57
65 up	1	0- 2	440.0	84	30.0	280	260	76.0	76.0	123
	2	2- 5	413.0	63	31.1	200	189	77.7	59.1	77
	3	5-10	300.0	48	28.5	168	141	67.8	40.1	65
Male All	1	0- 2 yrs	888.5	132	34.8	380	350	78.7	78.7	109
	2	2- 5	896.0	113	37.3	305	265	76.8	60.4	84
	3	5-10	737.0	85	36.8	230	192	71.8	43.4	65
Female All	1	0- 2 yrs	307.0	37	5.81	635	580	80.8	80.8	102
	2	2- 5	353.0	29	7.36	395	405	82.4	66.6	61
	3	5-10	334.0	19	7.83	245	265	85.6	57.0	33
Regional M & F All	1	0- 2 yrs	1155.0	432	40.9	1060	825	42.8	42.8	339
	2	2- 5	678.5	116	24.2	480	425	66.6	28.5	135
	3	5-10	519.0	70	23.4	300	250	59.5	17.0	90
Site: Other Area of Mouth										
Localized M & F										
<45	1	0- 2 yrs	176.5	10	0.44	2300%	2200%	89.5%	89.5%	54
	2	2- 5	229.5	7	0.70	1010	1290	92.2	82.5	27
	3	5-10	282.5	6	1.29	465	760	90.0	74.2	17
45-64	1	0- 2	741.0	99	10.76	920	860	77.3	77.3	119
	2	2- 5	797.5	71	13.70	520	550	80.0	61.8	72
	3	5-10	766.0	43	16.83	255	320	84.7	52.4	34
65 up	1	0- 2	819.0	177	58.2	305	285	70.6	70.6	145
	2	2- 5	700.5	97	54.6	178	188	82.0	57.9	60
	3	5-10	560.5	71	51.1	139	136	84.0	48.6	35
Male All	1	0- 2 yrs	1134.0	206	53.5	385	355	73.6	73.6	134
	2	2- 5	1067.0	131	51.5	255	240	79.5	58.5	74
	3	5-10	905.0	81	47.9	169	167	85.9	50.3	37
Female All	1	0- 2 yrs	602.5	80	15.92	505	475	79.3	79.3	106
	2	2- 5	660.5	44	17.47	250	290	89.1	70.7	40
	3	5-10	704.0	39	20.9	186	200	88.3	62.4	26
Regional M & F All	1	0- 2 yrs	1210.0	468	52.6	890	685	42.5	42.5	343
	2	2- 5	717.5	136	31.2	435	370	62.4	26.5	146
	3	5-10	467.0	58	23.7	245	220	71.0	18.8	73

*Basis of expected mortality: Concurrent U.S. White Population Rates

CANCER—MOUTH

Table 151b   Cancer of the Mouth - Derived Mortality and Survival Data

Stage & Sex Age Group			Observed				Expected*			
	Interval		Survival Rate			Ave. Ann.	Survival Rate			Ave. Ann.
	No.	Start-End	Cumulative	Interval	Ave. Ann.	Mort. Rate	Cumulative	Interval	Ave. Ann.	Mort. Rate
(Yrs)	i	t to t + Δt	P	p_i	$\breve{p}$	$\breve{q}$	P'	p_i'	$\breve{p}'$	$\breve{q}'$
Site: Floor of Mouth										
Localized										
M & F										
<55	1	0- 2 yrs	.8422	.8422	.9177	.0823	.9845	.9845	.9922	.0078
	2	2- 5	.6481	.7695	.9164	.0836	.9568	.9719	.9905	.0095
	3	5-10	.4747	.7324	.9396	.0604	.8950	.9354	.9867	.0133
55-64	1	0- 2	.7265	.7265	.8523	.1477	.9587	.9587	.9791	.0209
	2	2- 5	.5155	.7096	.8919	.1081	.8868	.9250	.9743	.0257
	3	5-10	.3374	.6545	.9187	.0813	.7415	.8362	.9649	.0351
65 up	1	0- 2	.6600	.6600	.8124	.1876	.8680	.8680	.9317	.0683
	2	2- 5	.4049	.6135	.8497	.1503	.6851	.7893	.9242	.0758
	3	5-10	.1640	.4050	.8346	.1654	.4091	.5971	.9020	.0980
Male										
All	1	0- 2 yrs	.7251	.7251	.8515	.1485	.9214	.9214	.9599	.0401
	2	2- 5	.4865	.6709	.8754	.1246	.8052	.8739	.9561	.0439
	3	5-10	.2691	.5531	.8883	.1117	.6201	.7701	.9491	.0509
Female										
All	1	0- 2 yrs	.7771	.7771	.8815	.1185	.9615	.9615	.9806	.0194
	2	2- 5	.6004	.7726	.9176	.0824	.9016	.9377	.9788	.0212
	3	5 -10	.4516	.7522	.9446	.0554	.7921	.8785	.9744	.0256
Regional										
M & F										
All	1	0- 2 yrs	.3970	.3970	.6301	.3699	.9267	.9267	.9627	.0373
	2	2- 5	.2337	.5887	.8381	.1619	.8187	.8835	.9596	.0404
	3	5-10	.1098	.4698	.8598	.1402	.6466	.7898	.9539	.0461
Site: Other Area of Mouth										
Localized										
M & F										
<45	1	0- 2 yrs	.8905	.8905	.9437	.0563	.9950	.9950	.9975	.0025
	2	2- 5	.8133	.9133	.9702	.0298	.9855	.9905	.9968	.0032
	3	5-10	.7146	.8786	.9744	.0256	.9625	.9767	.9953	.0047
45-64	1	0- 2 yrs	.7506	.7506	.8664	.1336	.9710	.9710	.9854	.0146
	2	2- 5	.5698	.7591	.9122	.0878	.9217	.9492	.9828	.0172
	3	5-10	.4303	.7552	.9454	.0546	.8219	.8917	.9773	.0227
65 up	1	0- 2 yrs	.6088	.6088	.7803	.2197	.8628	.8628	.9289	.0711
	2	2- 5	.3907	.6418	.8626	.1374	.6752	.7826	.9215	.0785
	3	5-10	.2014	.5155	.8759	.1241	.4142	.6134	.9069	.0931
Male										
All	1	0- 2 yrs	.6672	.6672	.8168	.1832	.9064	.9064	.9521	.0479
	2	2- 5	.4524	.6781	.8785	.1215	.7731	.8529	.9483	.0517
	3	5-10	.2887	.6382	.9141	.0859	.5744	.7430	.9423	.0577
Female										
All	1	0- 2 yrs	.7513	.7513	.8668	.1332	.9476	.9476	.9734	.0266
	2	2- 5	.6128	.8157	.9344	.0656	.8672	.9152	.9709	.0291
	3	5-10	.4554	.7431	.9423	.0577	.7296	.8413	.9660	.0340
Regional										
M & F										
All	1	0- 2 yrs	.3870	.3870	.6221	.3779	.9103	.9103	.9541	.0459
	2	2- 5	.2083	.5382	.8134	.1866	.7849	.8622	.9518	.0482
	3	5-10	.1128	.5415	.8845	.1155	.5987	.7628	.9473	.0527

* Basis of expected mortality: Concurrent U.S. White Population Rates

CANCER—PHARYNX

Table 152a   Cancer of the Pharynx - Observed Data and Comparative Experience by Stage, Sex, Age and Duration

Stage & Sex Age Group	Interval No.	Interval Start-End	Exposure Person-Yrs	Deaths Observed	Deaths Expected*	Mortality Ratio Interval	Mortality Ratio Cumulative	Survival Ratio Interval	Survival Ratio Cumulative	Excess Death Rate
(Yrs)	i	t to t + Δt	E	d	d'	100 d/d'	100 Q/Q'	100 p_i/p_i'	100 P/P'	1000(d-d')/E
Localized										
M & F										
<45	1	0- 2 yrs	134.5	20	0.35	5600%	5200%	73.5%	73.5%	146
	2	2- 5	147.5	8	0.51	1570	2500	85.8	63.1	51
	3	5-10	163.0	7	0.75	930	1270	84.3	53.1	38
45-54	1	0- 2	341.5	76	2.96	2600	2400	60.1	60.1	214
	2	2- 5	288.0	32	3.03	1060	1190	72.8	43.8	101
	3	5-10	244.5	20	3.30	605	605	72.1	31.5	68
55-64	1	0- 2	542.0	151	10.93	1380	1210	53.6	53.6	258
	2	2- 5	393.5	64	9.61	665	630	64.7	34.7	138
	3	5-10	309.5	36	10.19	355	330	65.7	22.8	83
65-74	1	0- 2	371.0	117	16.78	695	585	52.1	52.1	270
	2	2- 5	258.0	42	13.75	305	310	70.5	36.7	110
	3	5-10	174.0	23	11.78	195	179	76.1	28.0	65
75 up	1	0- 2	176.0	68	19.10	355	305	46.6	46.6	278
	2	2- 5	89.0	23	10.65	215	180	63.4	29.5	139
	3	5-10	49.0	11	6.82	161	123	66.2	19.5	85
Male										
All	1	0- 2 yrs	1171.5	344	43.0	800	690	53.1	53.1	257
	2	2- 5	829.5	130	30.5	425	380	68.9	36.6	120
	3	5-10	629.5	76	24.7	310	230	70.7	25.9	81
Female										
All	1	0- 2 yrs	393.5	88	7.03	1250	1050	63.0	63.0	206
	2	2- 5	346.5	39	7.02	555	580	75.7	47.7	92
	3	5-10	310.5	21	8.22	255	330	80.6	38.5	41
Regional										
Male										
All	1	0- 2 yrs	2266.0	1049	80.0	1310	970	32.6	32.6	428
	2	2- 5	1062.0	221	37.0	595	470	57.9	18.9	173
	3	5-10	715.0	89	27.1	330	260	64.9	12.3	87
Female										
All	1	0- 2 yrs	652.0	243	13.93	1750	1300	42.5	42.5	351
	2	2- 5	408.5	61	9.84	620	645	68.2	29.0	125
	3	5-10	302.0	32	7.88	405	360	70.9	20.6	80
Metastatic										
Male										
All	1	0- 2 yrs	422.0	266	14.30	1860	1200	17.6	17.6	596
	2	2- 5	109.5	33	3.89	850	545	40.9	7.2	266
	3	5-10	49.5	9	1.94	465	290	50.2	3.6	143
Female										
All	1	0- 2 yrs	88.0	57	1.64	3500	2200	14.2	14.2	629
	2	2- 5	17.0	7	0.43	1620	970	23.7	3.4	386
	3	5-10	5.5	1	0.074	1350	540	55.3	1.9	168
Localized										
M & F										
<45	4	10-15 yrs	91.5	2	0.58	345		91.1		16
	5	15-20	37.0	0	0.38	0		105.5		−10
45-54	4	10-15	114.5	4	2.68	150		94.6		12
	5	15-20	43.5	3	1.55	194		79.3		33
55-64	4	10-15	84.0	10	4.08	245		75.2		70
	5	15-20	16.5	3	1.19	255		71.2		110
65 up	4	10-15	68.0	15	7.86	191		57.9		105
	5	15-20	10.0	3	1.48	203		63.2		152

*Basis of expected mortality: Concurrent U.S. White Population Rates

CANCER—PHARYNX

Table 152b   Cancer of the Pharynx - Derived Mortality and Survival Data

Stage & Sex Age Group	Interval		Observed				Expected*			
	No.	Start-End	Survival Rate		Ave. Ann. Mort. Rate		Survival Rate			Ave. Ann. Mort. Rate
			Cumulative	Interval	Ave. Ann.		Cumulative	Interval	Ave. Ann.	
(Yrs)	i	t to t + Δt	P	p_i	$\check{p}$	$\check{q}$	P'	p_i'	$\check{p}'$	$\check{q}'$
Localized M & F										
<45	1	0- 2 yrs	.7309	.7309	.8549	.1451	.9948	.9948	.9974	.0026
	2	2- 5	.6212	.8499	.9472	.0528	.9850	.9901	.9967	.0033
	3	5-10	.5109	.8224	.9616	.0384	.9614	.9760	.9952	.0048
45-54	1	0- 2	.5906	.5906	.7685	.2315	.9827	.9827	.9913	.0087
	2	2- 5	.4162	.7047	.8899	.1101	.9510	.9677	.9891	.0109
	3	5-10	.2777	.6672	.9223	.0777	.8804	.9258	.9847	.0153
55-64	1	0- 2	.5145	.5145	.7173	.2827	.9600	.9600	.9798	.0202
	2	2- 5	.3085	.5996	.8432	.1568	.8903	.9274	.9752	.0248
	3	5-10	.1704	.5524	.8881	.1119	.7486	.8408	.9659	.0341
65-74	1	0- 2	.4740	.4740	.6885	.3115	.9102	.9102	.9540	.0460
	2	2- 5	.2820	.5949	.8410	.1590	.7679	.8437	.9449	.0551
	3	5-10	.1464	.5191	.8771	.1229	.5236	.6819	.9263	.0737
75 up	1	0- 2	.3704	.3704	.6086	.3914	.7948	.7948	.8915	.1085
	2	2- 5	.1574	.4249	.7518	.2482	.5330	.6706	.8753	.1247
	3	5-10	.0432	.2745	.7722	.2278	.2210	.4146	.8385	.1615
Male All	1	0- 2 yrs	.4923	.4923	.7016	.2984	.9265	.9265	.9625	.0375
	2	2- 5	.2991	.6076	.8470	.1530	.8166	.8814	.9588	.0412
	3	5-10	.1651	.5520	.8879	.1121	.6375	.7807	.9517	.0483
Female All	1	0- 2 yrs	.6067	.6067	.7789	.2211	.9626	.9626	.9811	.0189
	2	2- 5	.4302	.7091	.8917	.1083	.9016	.9366	.9784	.0216
	3	5-10	.3029	.7041	.9322	.0678	.7876	.8736	.9733	.0267
Regional Male All	1	0- 2 yrs	.3028	.3028	.5503	.4497	.9282	.9282	.9634	.0366
	2	2- 5	.1549	.5116	.7998	.2002	.8206	.8841	.9598	.0402
	3	5-10	.0791	.5107	.8742	.1258	.6455	.7866	.9531	.0469
Female All	1	0- 2 yrs	.4059	.4059	.6371	.3629	.9543	.9543	.9769	.0231
	2	2- 5	.2567	.6324	.8583	.1417	.8848	.9272	.9751	.0249
	3	5-10	.1574	.6132	.9068	.0932	.7652	.8648	.9714	.0286
Metastatic Male All	1	0- 2 yrs	.1635	.1635	.4044	.5956	.9304	.9304	.9646	.0354
	2	2- 5	.0594	.3633	.7135	.2865	.8273	.8892	.9616	.0384
	3	5-10	.0239	.4024	.8336	.1664	.6630	.8014	.9567	.0433
Female All	1	0- 2 yrs	.1364	.1364	.3693	.6307	.9603	.9603	.9799	.0201
	2	2- 5	.0303	.2221	.6056	.3944	.9001	.9373	.9786	.0214
	3	5-10	.0152	.5017	.8711	.1289	.8172	.9079	.9809	.0191
Localized M & F										
<45	4	10-15 yrs		.8824	.9753	.0247		.9682	.9936	.0064
	5	15-20		1.0000	1.0000	.0000		.9478	.9893	.0107
45-54	4	10-15		.8379	.9652	.0348		.8855	.9760	.0240
	5	15-20		.6587	.9199	.0801		.8309	.9636	.0364
55-64	4	10-15		.5793	.8966	.1034		.7699	.9490	.0510
	5	15-20		.4701	.8599	.1401		.6607	.9205	.0795
65 up	4	10-15		.3068	.7895	.2105		.5296	.8806	.1194
	5	15-20		.3429	.7652	.2348		.5422	.8581	.1419

*Basis of expected mortality: Concurrent U.S. White Population Rates

CANCER—PHARYNX

Table 152c Cancer of the Mesopharynx and Hypopharynx - Observed Data and Comparative Experience by Stage, Sex, Age and Duration

Stage & Sex Age Group	Interval No.	Interval Start-End	Exposure Person-Yrs	Deaths Observed	Deaths Expected*	Mortality Ratio Interval	Mortality Ratio Cumulative	Survival Ratio Interval	Survival Ratio Cumulative	Excess Death Rate
(Yrs)	i	t to t + Δt	E	d	d'	100 d/d'	100 Q/Q'	100 p_i/p_i'	100 P/P'	1000(d-d')/E
Site: Mesopharynx										
Localized M & F										
<55	1	0- 2 yrs	277.0	48	2.01	2400%	2300%	68.3%	68.3%	166
	2	2- 5	269.5	19	2.36	805	1140	82.7	56.5	62
	3	5-10	255.5	17	2.86	595	645	77.5	43.8	55
55-64	1	0- 2	272.0	57	5.37	1060	975	64.0	64.0	190
	2	2- 5	225.5	36	5.22	690	580	65.0	41.6	137
	3	5-10	174.5	18	5.45	330	315	69.1	28.8	72
65 up	1	0- 2	250.0	74	16.94	435	375	58.0	58.0	228
	2	2- 5	188.5	29	13.19	220	230	76.2	44.2	84
	3	5-10	120.5	19	10.28	185	148	84.1	37.2	72
Male All	1	0- 2 yrs	594.0	138	21.4	645	580	62.7	62.7	196
	2	2- 5	502.5	62	17.81	350	340	76.4	47.9	88
	3	5-10	394.5	47	15.28	310	220	70.5	33.8	80
Female All	1	0- 2 yrs	205.0	41	2.94	1400	1230	66.0	66.0	186
	2	2- 5	181.0	22	2.94	745	695	73.4	48.4	105
	3	5-10	156.0	7	3.42	205	340	93.8	45.4	23
Regional Male All	1	0- 2 yrs	952.0	425	36.8	1160	870	34.3	34.3	408
	2	2- 5	441.5	104	17.52	595	440	53.2	18.3	196
	3	5-10	263.0	42	12.39	340	250	53.0	9.7	113
Female All	1	0- 2 yrs	343.0	109	8.39	1300	1010	50.0	50.0	293
	2	2- 5	252.5	31	7.33	425	525	74.4	37.2	94
	3	5-10	187.0	21	5.62	375	315	68.5	25.5	82
Metastatic M & F All	1	0- 2 yrs	190.0	119	7.23	1650	1050	18.2	18.2	588
	2	2- 5	48.5	16	1.76	910	490	37.5	6.8	294
	3	5-10	21.5	3	0.95	315	265	69.3	4.7	96
Site: Hypopharynx										
Localized Male All	1	0- 2 yrs	293.5	112	12.35	905%	750%	41.4%	41.4%	340
	2	2- 5	152.0	38	7.23	525	405	50.9	21.1	202
	3	5-10	107.5	12	5.64	215	225	72.7	15.3	59
Female All	1	0- 2 yrs	60.5	25	1.31	1910	1460	35.2	35.2	392
	2	2- 5	32.0	2	0.88	225	600	90.3	31.8	35
	3	5-10	24.5	4	0.99	405	350	44.7	14.2	123
Regional Male All	1	0- 2 yrs	742.5	376	26.7	1410	1040	27.3	27.3	470
	2	2- 5	304.5	58	10.66	545	475	61.5	16.8	155
	3	5-10	209.5	25	8.07	310	255	67.0	11.2	81
Female All	1	0- 2 yrs	134.0	62	2.55	2400	1740	31.6	31.6	444
	2	2- 5	67.0	9	1.29	695	765	71.4	22.6	115
	3	5-10	50.0	8	1.04	770	405	54.8	12.4	139

*Basis of expected mortality: Concurrent U.S. White Population Rates

CANCER—PHARYNX

Table 152d   Cancer of the Mesopharynx and Hypopharynx - Derived Mortality and Survival Data

Stage & Sex Age Group	Interval			Observed				Expected*			
			Survival Rate			Ave. Ann.	Survival Rate			Ave. Ann.
	No.	Start-End	Cumulative	Interval	Ave. Ann.	Mort. Rate	Cumulative	Interval	Ave. Ann.	Mort. Rate
(Yrs)	i	t to t + Δ t	P	p_i	$\stackrel{\vee}{p}$	$\stackrel{\vee}{q}$	P'	p_i'	$\stackrel{\vee}{p}'$	$\stackrel{\vee}{q}'$
Site: Mesopharynx										
Localized M & F										
<55	1	0- 2 yrs	.6735	.6735	.8207	.1793	.9855	.9855	.9927	.0073
	2	2- 5	.5424	.8053	.9304	.0696	.9597	.9738	.9912	.0088
	3	5-10	.3970	.7319	.9395	.0605	.9063	.9444	.9886	.0114
55-64	1	0- 2	.6149	.6149	.7842	.2158	.9606	.9606	.9801	.0199
	2	2- 5	.3713	.6038	.8452	.1548	.8919	.9285	.9756	.0244
	3	5-10	.2162	.5823	.8975	.1025	.7519	.8430	.9664	.0336
65 up	1	0- 2	.5034	.5034	.7095	.2905	.8680	.8680	.9317	.0683
	2	2- 5	.3084	.6126	.8493	.1507	.6974	.8035	.9297	.0703
	3	5-10	.1618	.5246	.8790	.1210	.4348	.6235	.9098	.0902
Male All	1	0- 2 yrs	.5818	.5818	.7628	.2372	.9277	.9277	.9632	.0368
	2	2- 5	.3931	.6757	.8775	.1225	.8206	.8846	.9600	.0400
	3	5-10	.2190	.5571	.8896	.1104	.6481	.7898	.9539	.0461
Female All	1	0- 2 yrs	.6404	.6404	.8002	.1998	.9708	.9708	.9853	.0147
	2	2- 5	.4453	.6953	.8859	.1141	.9201	.9478	.9823	.0177
	3	5-10	.3706	.8322	.9639	.0361	.8160	.8869	.9763	.0237
Regional Male All	1	0- 2 yrs	.3160	.3160	.5621	.4379	.9214	.9214	.9599	.0401
	2	2- 5	.1470	.4652	.7748	.2252	.8054	.8741	.9561	.0439
	3	5-10	.0600	.4082	.8359	.1641	.6204	.7703	.9491	.0509
Female All	1	0- 2 yrs	.4734	.4734	.6880	.3120	.9477	.9477	.9735	.0265
	2	2- 5	.3235	.6834	.8808	.1192	.8706	.9186	.9721	.0279
	3	5-10	.1887	.5833	.8978	.1022	.7414	.8516	.9684	.0316
Metastatic M & F All	1	0- 2 yrs	.1678	.1678	.4096	.5904	.9210	.9210	.9597	.0403
	2	2- 5	.0552	.3290	.6903	.3097	.8079	.8772	.9573	.0427
	3	5-10	.0301	.5453	.8858	.1142	.6360	.7872	.9533	.0467
Site: Hypopharynx										
Localized Male All	1	0- 2 yrs	.3801	.3801	.6165	.3835	.9176	.9176	.9579	.0421
	2	2- 5	.1677	.4412	.7613	.2387	.7953	.8667	.9534	.0466
	3	5-10	.0917	.5468	.8863	.1137	.5978	.7517	.9445	.0555
Female All	1	0- 2 yrs	.3363	.3363	.5799	.4201	.9544	.9544	.9769	.0231
	2	2- 5	.2802	.8332	.9410	.0590	.8805	.9226	.9735	.0265
	3	5-10	.1062	.3790	.8236	.1764	.7463	.8476	.9675	.0325
Regional Male All	1	0- 2 yrs	.2533	.2533	.5033	.4967	.9280	.9280	.9633	.0367
	2	2- 5	.1375	.5428	.8157	.1843	.8191	.8827	.9593	.0407
	3	5-10	.0719	.5229	.8784	.1216	.6394	.7806	.9517	.0483
Female All	1	0- 2 yrs	.3034	.3034	.5508	.4492	.9599	.9599	.9797	.0203
	2	2- 5	.2022	.6664	.8735	.1265	.8956	.9330	.9771	.0229
	3	5-10	.0962	.4758	.8620	.1380	.7782	.8689	.9723	.0277

*Basis of expected mortality: Concurrent U.S. White Population Rates

CANCER—SALIVARY GLAND

Table 153a   Cancer of the Salivary Gland - Observed Data and Comparative Experience by Stage, Sex, Age and Duration

Stage & Sex Age Group	No.	Start-End	Exposure Person-Yrs	Deaths Observed	Deaths Expected*	Mortality Ratio Interval	Mortality Ratio Cumulative	Survival Ratio Interval	Survival Ratio Cumulative	Excess Death Rate
(Yrs)	i	t to t + Δt	E	d	d'	100 d/d'	100 Q/Q'	100 p_i/p_i'	100 P/P'	1000(d-d')/E
Localized M & F										
<35	1	0- 2 yrs	1021.5	3	1.12	265%	255%	99.6%	99.6%	1.8
	2	2- 5	1480.5	2	1.88	107	162	100.0	99.6	0.1
	3	5-10	1713.5	9	2.73	330	255	98.2	97.8	3.7
35-44	1	0- 2	742.5	3	1.89	159	159	99.7	99.7	1.5
	2	2- 5	1064.0	6	3.47	173	169	99.3	99.0	2.4
	3	5-10	1185.5	10	5.33	188	182	97.8	96.8	3.9
Male										
45-54	1	0- 2 yrs	330.0	6	3.18	189	188	98.3	98.3	8.5
	2	2- 5	457.0	4	5.56	72	112	101.0	99.3	-3.4
	3	5-10	494.0	15	8.36	180	155	92.2	91.5	13
55-64	1	0- 2	315.5	17	7.29	235	230	93.8	93.8	31
	2	2- 5	404.5	19	11.42	166	179	94.5	88.7	19
	3	5-10	395.0	20	14.87	134	144	93.4	82.8	13
65 up	1	0- 2	291.0	43	22.3	193	177	86.1	86.1	71
	2	2- 5	307.0	34	25.0	136	137	92.3	79.5	29
	3	5-10	252.0	32	24.2	132	116	91.6	72.9	31
Female										
45-54	1	0- 2 yrs	544.0	1	2.56	39	39	100.6	100.6	-2.9
	2	2- 5	792.0	5	4.56	110	85	99.8	100.4	0.6
	3	5-10	887.5	12	6.90	174	130	97.5	97.9	5.7
55-64	1	0- 2	385.0	11	4.25	260	255	96.5	96.5	18
	2	2- 5	541.5	12	7.37	163	190	97.5	94.1	8.5
	3	5-10	631.0	13	12.10	108	136	99.5	93.7	1.5
65 up	1	0- 2	482.5	43	22.8	189	179	91.7	91.7	42
	2	2- 5	590.5	31	31.4	99	123	101.1	92.8	-0.7
	3	5-10	586.0	37	40.6	91	103	105.3	97.7	-6.1
Regional Male										
All	1	0- 2 yrs	299.0	95	13.10	730	580	52.2	52.2	274
	2	2- 5	212.5	38	8.07	470	335	64.9	33.9	141
	3	5-10	159.0	13	6.05	215	200	86.2	29.2	44
Female										
All	1	0- 2 yrs	221.0	44	5.20	845	690	67.5	67.5	176
	2	2- 5	205.0	22	3.63	605	420	78.1	52.7	90
	3	5-10	177.5	9	3.34	270	255	90.8	47.9	32
Metastatic M & F										
All	1	0- 2 yrs	82.0	48	3.80	1260	855	23.5	23.5	539
	2	2- 5	37.0	3	1.16	260	395	88.7	20.8	50
	3	5-10	27.5	4	0.91	440	235	75.0	15.6	112
Localized Male										
<45	4	10-15 yrs	628.0	4	4.06	99		100.2		-0.1
	5	15-20	255.0	6	2.56	235		93.9		14
45-54	4	10-15	244.0	6	6.47	93		100.1		-1.9
	5	15-20	61.5	3	2.38	126		104.1		10
55-64	4	10-15	148.5	13	8.04	162		82.6		33
	5	15-20	38.0	1	2.80	36		134.5		-47
65 up	4	10-15	125.5	14	16.20	86		115.9		-18
	5	15-20	30.0	4	5.11	78		150.3		-37
Female										
<45	4	10-15 yrs	1177.5	9	3.74	240		98.1		4.5
	5	15-20	459.0	3	1.93	156		99.1		2.3
45-54	4	10-15	556.0	13	7.26	179		94.3		10
	5	15-20	195.5	6	4.07	147		96.3		9.9
55-64	4	10-15	392.0	19	12.70	149		92.1		16
	5	15-20	112.0	3	5.55	54		116.9		-23
65 up	4	10-15	161.5	16	15.70	102		105.3		2.1
	5	15-20	26.0	6	3.78	159		76.5		85

*Basis of expected mortality: Concurrent U.S. White Population Rates

CANCER—SALIVARY GLAND

Table 153b   Cancer of the Salivary Gland - Derived Mortality and Survival Data

Stage & Sex Age Group	Interval		Observed				Expected*			
			Survival Rate			Ave. Ann.	Survival Rate			Ave. Ann.
	No.	Start-End	Cumulative	Interval	Ave. Ann.	Mort. Rate	Cumulative	Interval	Ave. Ann.	Mort. Rate
(Yrs)	i	t to $t+\Delta t$	P	p_i	$\breve{p}$	$\breve{q}$	P'	p_i'	$\breve{p}'$	$\breve{q}'$
Localized										
M & F										
<35	1	0- 2 yrs	.9941	.9941	.9970	.0030	.9977	.9977	.9988	.0012
	2	2- 5	.9901	.9960	.9987	.0013	.9939	.9962	.9987	.0013
	3	5-10	.9638	.9734	.9946	.0054	.9857	.9917	.9983	.0017
35-44	1	0- 2	.9919	.9919	.9959	.0041	.9949	.9949	.9974	.0026
	2	2- 5	.9752	.9832	.9944	.0056	.9853	.9904	.9968	.0032
	3	5-10	.9309	.9546	.9908	.0092	.9620	.9764	.9952	.0048
Male										
45-54	1	0- 2 yrs	.9640	.9640	.9818	.0182	.9808	.9808	.9904	.0096
	2	2- 5	.9390	.9741	.9913	.0087	.9455	.9640	.9879	.0121
	3	5-10	.7929	.8444	.9667	.0333	.8662	.9161	.9826	.0174
55-64	1	0- 2	.8952	.8952	.9462	.0538	.9542	.9542	.9768	.0232
	2	2- 5	.7759	.8667	.9534	.0466	.8751	.9171	.9716	.0284
	3	5-10	.5937	.7652	.9479	.0521	.7170	.8193	.9609	.0391
65 up	1	0- 2	.7297	.7297	.8542	.1458	.8472	.8472	.9204	.0796
	2	2- 5	.5121	.7018	.8887	.1113.	.6439	.7600	.9126	.0874
	3	5-10	.2699	.5270	.8798	.1202	.3704	.5752	.8953	.1047
Female										
45-54	1	0- 2 yrs	.9963	.9963	.9981	.0019	.9906	.9906	.9953	.0047
	2	2- 5	.9775	.9811	.9937	.0063	.9735	.9827	.9942	.0058
	3	5-10	.9161	.9372	.9871	.0129	.9354	.9609	.9921	.0079
55-64	1	0- 2	.9442	.9442	.9717	.0283	.9780	.9780	.9889	.0111
	2	2- 5	.8830	.9352	.9779	.0221	.9385	.9596	.9863	.0137
	3	5-10	.7958	.9012	.9794	.0206	.8497	.9054	.9803	.0197
65 up	1	0- 2	.8302	.8302	.9112	.0888	.9050	.9050	.9513	.0487
	2	2- 5	.7051	.8493	.9470	.0530	.7601	.8399	.9435	.0565
	3	5-10	.5096	.7227	.9371	.0629	.5218	.6865	.9275	.0725
Regional										
Male										
All	1	0- 2 yrs	.4751	.4751	.6893	.3107	.9098	.9098	.9538	.0462
	2	2- 5	.2648	.5574	.8230	.1770	.7816	.8591	.9506	.0494
	3	5-10	.1726	.6518	.9180	.0820	.5911	.7563	.9457	.0543
Female										
All	1	0- 2 yrs	.6393	.6393	.7996	.2004	.9478	.9478	.9736	.0264
	2	2- 5	.4585	.7172	.8951	.1049	.8703	.9182	.9720	.0280
	3	5-10	.3575	.7797	.9514	.0486	.7470	.8583	.9699	.0301
Metastatic										
M & F										
All	1	0- 2 yrs	.2131	.2131	.4616	.5384	.9082	.9082	.9530	.0470
	2	2- 5	.1639	.7691	.9162	.0838	.7879	.8675	.9537	.0463
	3	5-10	.0962	.5869	.8989	.1011	.6167	.7827	.9522	.0478
Localized										
Male										
<45	4	10-15 yrs		.9695	.9938	.0062		.9673	.9934	.0066
	5	15-20		.8916	.9773	.0227		.9494	.9897	.0103
45-54	4	10-15		.8717	.9729	.0271		.8706	.9727	.0273
	5	15-20		.8465	.9672	.0328		.8133	.9595	.0405
55-64	4	10-15		.6191	.9086	.0914		.7492	.9439	.0561
	5	15-20		.9048	.9802	.0198		.6727	.9238	.0762
65 up	4	10-15		.5665	.8926	.1074		.4889	.8667	.1333
	5	15-20		.5617	.8910	.1090		.3737	.8213	.1787
Female										
<45	4	10-15		.9654	.9930	.0070		.9840	.9968	.0032
	5	15-20		.9702	.9940	.0060		.9790	.9958	.0042
45-54	4	10-15		.8811	.9750	.0250		.9346	.9866	.0134
	5	15-20		.8608	.9705	.0295		.8940	.9778	.0222
55-64	4	10-15		.7762	.9506	.0494		.8432	.9665	.0335
	5	15-20		.8945	.9779	.0221		.7649	.9478	.0522
65 up	4	10-15		.6145	.9072	.0928		.5837	.8979	.1021
	5	15-20		.3355	.8038	.1962		.4387	.8481	.1519

*Basis of expected mortality: Concurrent U.S. White Population Rates

CANCER—ESOPHAGUS
CANCER—PANCREAS

Table 154a Cancer of the Esophagus and Pancreas - Observed Data and Comparative Experience by Stage, Sex, Age and Duration

Stage & Sex Age Group	No.	Start-End	Exposure Person-Yrs	Observed	Expected*	Interval (Mortality)	Cumulative (Mortality)	Interval (Survival)	Cumulative (Survival)	Excess Death Rate
(Yrs)	i	t to t + Δt	E	d	d'	100 d/d'	100 Q/Q'	100 pᵢ/pᵢ'	100 P/P'	1000(d-d')/E
Site: Esophagus										
Localized M & F										
<55	1	0- 2 yrs	256.0	141	2.08	6800%	4700%	23.8%	23.8%	543
	2	2- 5	94.0	24	0.92	2600	1970	45.6	10.8	246
	3	5-10	56.0	7	0.78	895	830	58.3	6.3	111
55-64	1	0- 2	372.0	241	7.79	3100	2000	13.3	13.3	627
	2	2- 5	77.0	19	1.82	1050	800	49.6	6.6	223
	3	5-10	40.5	8	1.22	655	365	37.2	2.4	167
65 up	1	0- 2	867.0	610	60.0	1020	665	13.7	13.7	634
	2	2- 5	167.5	59	12.97	455	300	34.7	4.8	275
	3	5-10	69.0	10	6.61	151	165	74.8	3.6	49
All	1	0- 2	1495.0	992	69.8	1420	900	15.4	15.4	617
	2	2- 5	338.5	102	15.71	650	405	42.5	6.5	255
	3	5-10	165.5	25	8.40	300	220	60.5	4.0	100
Regional M & F										
All	1	0- 2 yrs	1258.5	987	46.2	2100	1240	7.7	7.7	748
	2	2- 5	140.0	54	5.46	990	520	30.8	2.4	347
	3	5-10	58.5	9	3.17	285	265	60.0	1.4	100
Metastatic M & F										
All	1	0- 2 yrs	853.5	776	31.0	2500	1350	2.1	2.1	873
	2	2- 5	28.5	10	1.08	925	540	32.9	0.7	313
	3	5-10	13.0	0	0.31	0	270	129.6	0.9	−24
Site: Pancreas										
Localized M & F										
<45	1	0- 2 yrs	46.5	19	0.118	16100%	11600%	38.5%	38.5%	406
	2	2- 5	29.0	3	0.065	4700	4700	73.5	28.3	101
	3	5-10	25.0	1	0.079	1260	2000	76.9	21.7	37
45-64	1	0- 2	285.5	202	4.67	4300	2600	12.0	12.0	691
	2	2- 5	56.0	17	1.06	1610	1090	36.7	4.4	285
	3	5-10	32.0	1	0.646	155	545	97.6	4.3	11
65 up	1	0- 2	604.0	480	42.7	1120	715	7.1	7.1	724
	2	2- 5	50.5	21	3.59	585	320	31.5	2.3	345
	3	5-10	13.5	3	1.28	235	177	56.8	1.3	127
All	1	0- 2	936.0	701	47.4	1480	875	10.1	10.1	698
	2	2- 5	135.5	41	4.83	850	385	44.3	4.5	267
	3	5-10	70.5	5	1.96	255	210	101.0	4.5	43
Regional M & F										
All	1	0- 2 yrs	1236.0	1036	50.4	2100	1160	4.5	4.5	797
	2	2- 5	90.0	26	2.98	875	485	47.1	2.1	256
	3	5-10	72.0	5	2.04	245	250	84.2	1.8	41
Metastatic M & F										
All	1	0- 2 yrs	3220.0	3047	126.0	2400	1250	1.6	1.6	907
	2	2- 5	73.0	34	2.58	1320	505	23.4	0.4	430
	3	5-10	24.5	5	0.93	540	260	17.5	0.1	166

*Basis of expected mortality: Concurrent U.S. White Population Rates

CANCER—ESOPHAGUS
CANCER—PANCREAS

Table 154b   Cancer of the Esophagus and Pancreas - Derived Mortality and Survival Data

Stage & Sex Age Group	Interval		Observed				Expected*			
	No.	Start-End	Survival Rate			Ave. Ann. Mort. Rate	Survival Rate			Ave. Ann. Mort. Rate
			Cumulative	Interval	Ave. Ann.		Cumulative	Interval	Ave. Ann.	
(Yrs)	i	t to t + Δt	P	p_i	$\breve{p}$	$\breve{q}$	P'	p_i'	$\breve{p}$'	$\breve{q}$'
Site: Esophagus										
Localized										
M & F										
<55	1	0- 2 yrs	.234	.234	.483	.517	.9836	.9836	.9918	.0082
	2	2- 5	.103	.442	.762	.238	.9544	.9703	.9900	.0100
	3	5-10	.056	.541	.884	.116	.8862	.9285	.9853	.0147
55-64	1	0- 2	.127	.127	.356	.644	.9567	.9567	.9781	.0219
	2	2- 5	.058	.457	.771	.229	.8819	.9218	.9732	.0268
	3	5-10	.018	.309	.791	.209	.7318	.8298	.9634	.0366
65 up	1	0- 2	.119	.119	.345	.655	.8675	.8675	.9314	.0686
	2	2- 5	.032	.272	.648	.352	.6801	.7840	.9221	.0779
	3	5-10	.014	.441	.849	.151	.4011	.5898	.8998	.1002
All	1	0- 2	.139	.139	.373	.627	.9041	.9041	.9508	.0492
	2	2- 5,	.050	.359	.711	.289	.7648	.8459	.9457	.0543
	3	5-10	.022	.438	.848	.152	.5538	.7241	.9375	.0625
Regional										
M & F										
All	1	0- 2 yrs	.071	.071	.266	.734	.9250	.9250	.9618	.0382
	2	2- 5	.019	.270	.646	.354	.8111	.8769	.9572	.0428
	3	5-10	.009	.461	.856	.144	.6231	.7682	.9486	.0514
Metastatic										
M & F										
All	1	0- 2 yrs	.020	.020	.140	.860	.9275	.9275	.9631	.0369
	2	2- 5	.006	.289	.661	.339	.8160	.8798	.9582	.0418
	3	5-10	.006	1.000	1.000	.000	.6296	.7716	.9495	.0505
Site: Pancreas										
Localized										
M & F										
<45	1	0- 2 yrs	.383	.383	.619	.381	.9947	.9947	.9973	.0027
	2	2- 5	.279	.727	.899	.101	.9847	.9899	.9966	.0034
	3	5-10	.209	.750	.944	.056	.9609	.9758	.9951	.0049
45-64	1	0- 2	.116	.116	.341	.659	.9665	.9665	.9831	.0169
	2	2- 5	.040	.347	.702	.298	.9119	.9435	.9808	.0192
	3	5-10	.036	.881	.975	.025	.8227	.9022	.9796	.0204
65 up	1	0- 2	.062	.062	.249	.751	.8690	.8690	.9322	.0678
	2	2- 5	.016	.251	.631	.369	.6924	.7968	.9271	.0729
	3	5-10	.006	.359	.815	.185	.4379	.6324	.9124	.0876
All	1	0- 2	.091	.091	.302	.699	.8963	.8963	.9467	.0533
	2	2- 5	.034	.371	.718	.282	.7496	.8363	.9459	.0541
	3	5-10	.024	.718	.936	.064	.5328	.7108	.9340	.0660
Regional										
M & F										
All	1	0- 2 yrs	.042	.042	.204	.796	.9174	.9174	.9578	.0422
	2	2- 5	.017	.409	.742	.258	.7965	.8682	.9540	.0460
	3	5-10	.011	.641	.915	.085	.6064	.7613	.9469	.0531
Metastatic										
M & F										
All	1	0- 2 yrs	.015	.015	.121	.879	.9212	.9212	.9598	.0402
	2	2- 5	.003	.204	.589	.411	.8033	.8720	.9554	.0446
	3	5-10	.000	.133	.668	.332	.6136	.7638	.9475	.0525

*Basis of expected mortality: Concurrent U.S. White Population Rates

CANCER—STOMACH

Table 155a   Cancer of the Stomach - Observed Data and Comparative Experience by Stage, Sex, Age and Duration

Stage & Sex Age Group	Interval		Exposure Person-Yrs	Deaths		Mortality Ratio		Survival Ratio		Excess Death Rate
	No.	Start-End		Observed	Expected*	Interval	Cumulative	Interval	Cumulative	
(Yrs)	i	t to t + Δt	E	d	d'	100 d/d'	100 Q/Q'	100 p_i/p_i'	100 P/P'	1000(d-d')/E
Localized M & F										
< 45	1	0- 2 yrs	131.5	27	0.35	7700%	7100%	62.9%	62.9%	203
	2	2- 5	117.0	11	0.38	2900	3400	76.3	48.0	91
	3	5-10	115.0	7	0.50	1400	1610	79.3	38.1	57
45-54	1	0- 2	302.5	60	2.52	2400	2100	66.1	66.1	190
	2	2- 5	298.0	27	3.11	870	1080	78.0	51.5	80
	3	5-10	284.5	13	4.01	325	535	83.6	43.1	32
Male										
55-64	1	0- 2 yrs	396.0	108	9.40	1150	975	56.5	56.5	249
	2	2- 5	327.5	39	9.49	410	490	75.2	42.5	90
	3	5-10	285.5	21	11.15	188	250	88.3	37.5	35
65-74	1	0- 2	609.0	203	31.0	655	530	51.9	51.9	282
	2	2- 5	442.0	66	26.7	245	275	75.6	39.2	89
	3	5-10	394.5	37	31.3	118	162	87.6	34.4	14
75 up	1	0- 2	424.0	230	48.1	480	340	31.8	31.8	429
	2	2- 5	165.0	44	20.6	215	180	64.1	20.4	142
	3	5-10	84.0	18	13.5	133	120	80.7	16.4	54
Female										
55-64	1	0- 2 yrs	244.5	59	2.93	2000	1720	60.1	60.1	229
	2	2- 5	212.0	25	3.15	795	885	72.9	43.8	103
	3	5-10	212.5	10	4.30	235	415	88.5	38.8	27
65-74	1	0- 2	362.5	126	10.19	1240	965	47.5	47.5	319
	2	2- 5	270.0	24	8.83	270	425	85.2	40.5	56
	3	5-10	291.0	21	13.54	155	219	85.5	34.6	26
75 up	1	0- 2	334.5	166	31.4	530	375	37.0	37.0	402
	2	2- 5	177.5	31	18.90	164	189	81.4	30.1	68
	3	5-10	115.5	18	17.03	106	123	97.7	29.4	8.4
Regional M & F										
All	1	0- 2 yrs	4451.0	2446	193.0	1270	870	24.6	24.6	506
	2	2- 5	1585.0	374	69.1	540	405	54.4	13.4	192
	3	5-10	1097.5	117	61.0	192	220	79.4	10.6	51
Metastatic M & F										
All	1	0- 2 yrs	4845.5	4220	214.0	1970	1080	4.4	4.4	827
	2	2- 5	345.0	107	14.57	735	450	44.0	1.9	268
	3	5-10	200.0	27	10.6	255	235	70.1	1.3	82
Localized M & F										
< 45	4	10-15 yrs	112.5	4	1.01	395		90.0		27
	5	15-20	51.5	2	0.72	275		86.0		25
45-54	4	10-15	319.0	15	7.45	200		88.5		24
	5	15-20	136.5	11	4.74	230		82.6		46
Male										
55-64	4	10-15 yrs	364.0	24	19.7	122		96.5		12
	5	15-20	113.5	9	8.42	107		76.1		5.1
65-74	4	10-15	183.5	18	20.5	88		105.6		−14
	5	15-20	48.0	10	7.78	129		47.1		46
75 up	4	10-15	38.5	6	8.00	75		145.2		−52
	5	15-20	9.0	3	2.39	126		122.0		68
Female										
55-64	4	10-15 yrs	134.0	4	4.71	85		102.5		−5.3
	5	15-20	57.5	2	2.94	68		113.0		−16
65-74	4	10-15	173.0	15	14.7	102		91.4		1.7
	5	15-20	40.0	2	5.57	36		163.8		−89
75 up	4	10-15	51.5	6	10.9	55		193.0		−95
	5	15-20	11.5	4	3.62	110		0.0		33

*Basis of expected mortality: Concurrent U.S. White Population Rates

CANCER—STOMACH

Table 155b   Cancer of the Stomach - Derived Mortality and Survival Data

Stage & Sex Age Group	Interval No.	Interval Start-End	Observed Survival Rate Cumulative	Observed Survival Rate Interval	Observed Survival Rate Ave. Ann.	Observed Ave. Ann. Mort. Rate	Expected* Survival Rate Cumulative	Expected* Survival Rate Interval	Expected* Survival Rate Ave. Ann.	Expected* Ave. Ann. Mort. Rate
(Yrs)	i	t to t + Δt	P	p_i	$\breve{p}$	$\breve{q}$	P'	$p_i{}'$	$\breve{p}{}'$	$\breve{q}{}'$
Localized M & F										
< 45	1	0- 2 yrs	.6259	.6259	.7911	.2089	.9947	.9947	.9973	.0027
	2	2- 5	.4729	.7556	.9108	.0892	.9847	.9899	.9966	.0034
	3	5-10	.3659	.7737	.9500	.0500	.9606	.9755	.9951	.0049
45-54	1	0- 2	.6497	.6497	.8060	.1940	.9833	.9833	.9916	.0084
	2	2- 5	.4908	.7554	.9107	.0893	.9527	.9689	.9895	.0105
	3	5-10	.3811	.7765	.9507	.0493	.8847	.9286	.9853	.0147
Male										
55-64	1	0- 2 yrs	.5385	.5385	.7338	.2662	.9526	.9526	.9760	.0240
	2	2- 5	.3703	.6877	.8827	.1173	.8710	.9143	.9706	.0294
	3	5-10	.2660	.7183	.9360	.0640	.7088	.8138	.9596	.0404
65-74	1	0- 2	.4673	.4673	.6836	.3164	.8998	.8998	.9486	.0514
	2	2- 5	.2918	.6244	.8547	.1453	.7436	.8264	.9384	.0616
	3	5-10	.1665	.5706	.8939	.1061	.4846	.6517	.9179	.0821
75 up	1	0- 2	.2472	.2472	.4972	.5028	.7779	.7779	.8820	.1180
	2	2- 5	.1022	.4134	.7449	.2551	.5015	.6447	.8639	.1361
	3	5-10	.0319	.3121	.7922	.2078	.1940	.3868	.8270	.1730
Female										
55-64	1	0- 2 yrs	.5868	.5868	.7660	.2340	.9760	.9760	.9879	.0121
	2	2- 5	.4089	.6968	.8865	.1135	.9331	.9560	.9851	.0149
	3	5-10	.3249	.7946	.9551	.0449	.8379	.8980	.9787	.0213
65-74	1	0- 2	.4481	.4481	.6694	.3306	.9427	.9427	.9709	.0291
	2	2- 5	.3419	.7630	.9138	.0862	.8443	.8956	.9639	.0361
	3	5-10	.2236	.6540	.9186	.0814	.6455	.7645	.9477	.0523
75 up	1	0- 2	.3005	.3005	.5482	.4518	.8125	.8125	.9014	.0986
	2	2- 5	.1689	.5621	.8253	.1747	.5610	.6905	.8839	.1161
	3	5-10	.0714	.4227	.8418	.1582	.2427	.4326	.8457	.1543
Regional M & F										
All	1	0- 2 yrs	.2239	.2239	.4732	.5268	.9109	.9109	.9544	.0456
	2	2- 5	.1043	.4658	.7752	.2248	.7794	.8556	.9493	.0507
	3	5-10	.0610	.5849	.8983	.1017	.5740	.7365	.9407	.0593
Metastatic M & F										
All	1	0- 2 yrs	.0398	.0398	.1995	.8005	.9109	.9109	.9544	.0456
	2	2- 5	.0150	.3769	.7223	.2777	.7804	.8567	.9498	.0502
	3	5-10	.0078	.5200	.8774	.1226	.5790	.7419	.9420	.0580
Localized M & F										
< 45	4	10-15 yrs		.8589	.9700	.0300		.9545	.9907	.0093
	5	15-20		.8000	.9564	.0436		.9298	.9855	.0145
45-54	4	10-15		.7847	.9527	.0473		.8863	.9761	.0239
	5	15-20		.6871	.9277	.0723		.8323	.9640	.0360
Male										
55-64	4	10-15 yrs		.7255	.9378	.0622		.7521	.9446	.0554
	5	15-20		.5100	.8740	.1260		.6699	.9230	.0770
65-74	4	10-15		.5728	.8945	.1055		.5426	.8849	.1151
	5	15-20		.1870	.7151	.2849		.3971	.8313	.1687
75 up	4	10-15		.4344	.8464	.1536		.2991	.7855	.2145
	5	15-20		.3334	.8028	.1972		.2733	.7715	.2285
Female										
55-64	4	10-15 yrs		.8540	.9689	.0311		.8328	.9641	.0359
	5	15-20		.8636	.9711	.0289		.7640	.9476	.0524
65-74	4	10-15		.5759	.8955	.1045		.6299	.9117	.0883
	5	15-20		.7467	.9433	.0567		.4559	.8546	.1454
75 up	4	10-15		.5793	.8966	.1034		.3002	.7861	.2139
	5	15-20		.0000	.0000	1.0000		.1909	.7181	.2814

*Basis of expected mortality: Concurrent U.S. White Population Rates

CANCER—LIVER
CANCER—GALLBLADDER

Table 156a   Cancer of the Liver and Gallbladder - Observed Data and Comparative Experience by Stage, Sex, Age and Duration

Stage & Sex Age Group	No.	Interval Start-End	Exposure Person-Yrs	Deaths Observed	Deaths Expected*	Mortality Ratio Interval	Mortality Ratio Cumulative	Survival Ratio Interval	Survival Ratio Cumulative	Excess Death Rate
(Yrs)	i	t to t + Δt	E	d	d'	100 d/d'	100 Q/Q'	100 p_i/p_i'	100 P/P'	1000(d-d')/E
Site: Liver										
Localized										
Male										
< 65	1	0- 2 yrs	94.0	77	1.59	4800%	5300%	7.4%	7.4%	802
	2	2- 5	17.0	3	0.34	870	1260	53.1	3.9	156
	3	5-10	7.0	1	0.042	2400	1060	67.9	2.7	137
65 up	1	0- 2	100.5	93	7.18	1290	1320	2.5	2.5	854
	2	2- 5	5.0	1	0.25	395	470	58.6	1.5	150
	3	5-10	1.5	0	0.106	0	305	117.0	1.7	−71
All	1	0- 2	194.5	170	8.77	1940	1030	5.1	5.1	829
	2	2- 5	22.0	4	0.60	670	435	58.6	3.0	155
	3	5-10	8.5	1	0.149	670	230	101.8	3.0	100
Female										
< 65	1	0- 2 yrs	62.5	38	0.38	10100	7900	20.7	20.7	602
	2	2- 5	27.0	0	0.044	0	5400	100.5	20.8	−1.6
	3	5-10	34.0	1	0.071	1410	3200	89.8	18.7	27
65 up	1	0- 2	63.0	54	3.23	1670	2700	5.4	5.4	806
	2	2- 5	9.0	0	0.36	0	650	113.0	6.2	−40
	3	5-10	8.5	2	0.40	495	315	0.0	0.0	188
All	1	0- 2	125.5	92	3.60	2600	1370	13.0	13.0	704
	2	2- 5	36.0	0	0.40	0	535	112.0	14.6	−11
	3	5-10	42.5	3	0.47	635	275	86.2	12.6	59
Regional										
M & F										
All	1	0- 2 yrs	141.0	129	5.74	2200	1210	1.7	1.7	874
	2	2- 5	6.0	1	0.164	610	495	57.1	1.0	139
	3	5-10	1.5	0	0.007	0	100	0.0	0.0	−0.5
Metastatic										
M & F										
All	1	0- 2 yrs	386.0	370	14.40	2600	1320	0.6	0.6	921
	2	2- 5	4.5	0	0.43	0	535	113.6	0.7	−96
	3	5-10	1.5	0	0.044	0	100	—	—	−30
Site: Gallbladder										
Localized										
M & F										
< 55	1	0- 2 yrs	113.5	31	0.68	4500%	3900%	53.1%	53.1%	267
	2	2- 5	87.5	10	0.60	1670	1950	71.4	37.9	107
	3	5-10	78.0	4	0.74	540	950	70.1	26.6	42
55-74	1	0- 2	463.0	180	13.70	1320	1030	42.7	42.7	359
	2	2- 5	297.0	53	9.72	545	520	62.0	26.5	146
	3	5-10	221.5	25	9.90	255	265	71.5	18.9	68
75 up	1	0- 2	210.0	141	21.2	665	410	21.4	21.4	571
	2	2- 5	61.0	21	6.31	335	205	40.8	8.7	241
	3	5-10	25.5	2	3.84	52	125	172.9	15.1	−72
Regional										
M & F										
All	1	0- 2 yrs	961.5	737	42.2	1750	1010	9.9	9.9	723
	2	2- 5	149.0	43	5.51	780	435	48.0	4.8	252
	3	5-10	99.5	12	4.72	255	230	73.8	3.5	73
Metastatic										
M & F										
All	1	0- 2 yrs	983.5	931	45.3	2050	1050	1.5	1.5	901
	2	2- 5	22.5	8	0.58	1390	430	44.9	0.7	330
	3	5-10	16.0	1	0.36	280	225	101.4	0.7	40

*Basis of expected mortality: Concurrent U.S. White Population Rates

CANCER—LIVER
CANCER—GALLBLADDER

Table 156b   Cancer of the Liver and Gallbladder - Derived Mortality and Survival Data

Stage & Sex	Interval		Observed				Expected*			
			Survival Rate			Ave. Ann.	Survival Rate			Ave. Ann.
	No.	Start-End	Cumulative	Interval	Ave. Ann.	Mort. Rate	Cumulative	Interval	Ave. Ann.	Mort. Rate
(Yrs)	i	t to t + Δ t	P	p_i	$\breve{p}$	$\breve{q}$	P′	$p_i′$	$\breve{p}′$	$\breve{q}′$
Site: Liver										
Localized										
Male										
< 65	1	0- 2 yrs	.0723	.0723	.2689	.7311	.9824	.9824	.9912	.0088
	2	2- 5	.0361	.4993	.7933	.2067	.9237	.9402	.9797	.0203
	3	5-10	.0241	.6676	.9224	.0776	.9079	.9829	.9966	.0034
65 up	1	0- 2	.0230	.0230	.1517	.8483	.9260	.9260	.9623	.0377
	2	2- 5	.0115	.5000	.7937	.2063	.7897	.8528	.9483	.0517
	3	5-10	.0115	1.0000	1.0000	.0000	.6750	.8548	.9246	.0754
All	1	0- 2	.0462	.0462	.2149	.7851	.9076	.9076	.9527	.0473
	2	2- 5	.0231	.5000	.7937	.2063	.7747	.8536	.9486	.0514
	3	5-10	.0173	.7489	.9438	.0562	.5760	.7358	.9405	.0595
Female										
< 65	1	0- 2 yrs	.2048	.2048	.4525	.5475	.9899	.9899	.9949	.0051
	2	2- 5	.2048	1.0000	1.0000	.0000	.9852	.9953	.9984	.0016
	3	5-10	.1820	.8887	.9767	.0233	.9748	.9894	.9979	.0021
65 up	1	0- 2	.0526	.0526	.2293	.7707	.9654	.9654	.9825	.0175
	2	2- 5	.0526	1.0000	1.0000	.0000	.8542	.8848	.9600	.0400
	3	5-10	.0000	.0000	.0000	1.0000	.6834	.8000	.9564	.0436
All	1	0- 2	.1220	.1220	.3493	.6507	.9187	.9187	.9585	.0415
	2	2- 5	.1220	1.0000	1.0000	.0000	.7998	.8706	.9549	.0451
	3	5-10	.0838	.6869	.9276	.0724	.0000	.0000	.0000	1.0000
Regional										
M & F										
All	1	0- 2 yrs	.0153	.0153	.1237	.8763	.9187	.9187	.9585	.0415
	2	2- 5	.0076	.4967	.7920	.2080	.7998	.8706	.9549	.0451
	3	5-10	.0000	.0000	.0000	1.0000	.0000	.0000	.0000	1.0000
Metastatic										
M & F										
All	1	0- 2 yrs	.0054	.0054	.0735	.9265	.9247	.9247	.9616	.0384
	2	2- 5	.0054	1.0000	1.0000	.0000	.8143	.8806	.9585	.0415
	3	5-10	.0000	.0000	.0000	1.0000	.0000	.0000	.0000	1.0000
Site: Gallbladder										
Localized										
M & F										
< 55	1	0- 2 yrs	.5245	.5245	.7242	.2758	.9879	.9879	.9939	.0061
	2	2- 5	.3667	.6991	.8875	.1125	.9676	.9795	.9931	.0069
	3	5-10	.2446	.6670	.9222	.0778	.9204	.9512	.9900	.0100
55-74	1	0- 2	.4020	.4020	.6340	.3660	.9421	.9421	.9706	.0294
	2	2- 5	.2254	.5607	.8246	.1754	.8515	.9038	.9668	.0332
	3	5-10	.1271	.5639	.8917	.1083	.6719	.7891	.9537	.0463
75 up	1	0- 2	.1706	.1706	.4130	.5870	.7987	.7987	.8937	.1063
	2	2- 5	.0471	.2761	.6512	.3488	.5403	.6765	.8779	.1221
	3	5-10	.0345	.7325	.9396	.0604	.2289	.4237	.8422	.1578
Regional										
M & F										
All	1	0- 2 yrs	.0904	.0904	.3007	.6993	.9097	.9097	.9538	.0462
	2	2- 5	.0371	.4104	.7431	.2569	.7774	.8546	.9490	.0510
	3	5-10	.0201	.5418	.8846	.1154	.5704	.7337	.9399	.0601
Metastatic										
M & F										
All	1	0- 2 yrs	.0139	.0139	.1179	.8821	.9062	.9062	.9519	.0481
	2	2- 5	.0053	.3813	.7251	.2749	.7688	.8484	.9467	.0533
	3	5-10	.0039	.7358	.9405	.0595	.5577	.7254	.9378	.0622

*Basis of expected mortality: Concurrent U.S. White Population Rates

1-48

CANCER—COLON

Table 157a   Cancer of the Colon - Observed Data and Comparative Experience by Stage, Sex, Age and Duration

Stage & Sex Age Group	Interval No.	Interval Start-End	Exposure Person-Yrs	Deaths Observed	Deaths Expected*	Mortality Ratio Interval	Mortality Ratio Cumulative	Survival Ratio Interval	Survival Ratio Cumulative	Excess Death Rate
(Yrs)	i	t to t + Δt	E	d	d'	100 d/d'	100 Q/Q'	100 p_i/p_i'	100 P/P'	1000(d-d')/E
Localized										
Male										
< 45	1	0- 2 yrs	373.0	20	1.08	1850%	1760%	90.2%	90.2%	51
	2	2- 5	503.0	9	1.83	490	900	95.7	86.3	14
	3	5-10	551.5	14	3.05	460	580	90.9	78.5	20
45-54	1	0- 2	687.5	54	7.24	745	710	86.9	86.9	68
	2	2- 5	848.5	48	11.15	430	480	87.5	76.0	43
	3	5-10	914.5	30	16.78	179	270	93.8	71.4	14
55-64	1	0- 2	1613.0	165	38.8	425	405	84.9	84.9	78
	2	2- 5	1897.0	149	55.7	265	285	85.6	72.6	49
	3	5-10	1810.0	111	71.4	156	184	89.9	65.3	22
65-74	1	0- 2	2196.5	333	111.2	300	275	80.7	80.7	101
	2	2- 5	2332.5	262	140.5	187	194	84.5	68.2	52
	3	5-10	2015.5	195	157.5	124	136	91.8	62.6	19
75 up	1	0- 2	1509.0	428	168.1	255	220	67.7	67.7	172
	2	2- 5	1196.5	209	151.9	138	144	86.2	58.4	48
	3	5-10	792.5	141	129.5	109	114	78.9	46.0	15
Female										
< 45	1	0- 2 yrs	789.0	22	1.18	1860	1830	94.8	94.8	26
	2	2- 5	1060.5	27	1.94	1390	1470	93.1	88.2	24
	3	5-10	1097.0	22	2.79	790	940	92.5	81.6	18
45-54	1	0- 2	1097.0	49	5.48	895	865	92.2	92.2	40
	2	2- 5	1445.5	53	8.79	605	650	91.1	84.0	31
	3	5-10	1592.0	49	12.94	380	435	89.5	75.2	23
55-64	1	0- 2	1824.0	151	21.5	705	670	86.2	86.2	71
	2	2- 5	2222.0	125	32.4	385	440	88.1	76.0	42
	3	5-10	2331.0	87	47.5	183	255	92.3	70.1	17
65-74	1	0- 2	2551.5	332	75.6	440	410	80.8	80.8	100
	2	2- 5	2903.0	215	106.8	200	250	88.9	71.8	37
	3	5-10	2799.5	220	144.9	152	167	86.2	61.9	27
75 up	1	0- 2	1796.5	452	165.2	275	240	70.1	70.1	160
	2	2- 5	1584.0	211	174.9	121	148	92.9	65.1	23
	3	5-10	1157.0	183	169.7	108	114	91.1	59.3	12
Male										
< 45	4	10-15 yrs	439.5	7	3.69	190		96.5		7.5
	5	15-20	165.0	5	1.98	255		91.4		18
45-54	4	10-15	633.0	33	17.19	192		86.6		25
	5	15-20	174.5	7	6.59	106		94.2		2.3
55-64	4	10-15	936.0	85	50.7	168		84.2		37
	5	15-20	225.0	28	16.73	167		77.9		50
65 up	4	10-15	922.5	129	118.1	109		89.3		12
	5	15-20	133.5	26	21.70	120		65.2		32
Female										
< 45	4	10-15 yrs	903.0	6	3.59	167		98.6		2.7
	5	15-20	355.0	1	2.23	45		102.3		−3.5
45-54	4	10-15	1109.5	26	14.45	180		95.3		10
	5	15-20	356.5	12	7.09	169		94.3		14
55-64	4	10-15	1537.0	74	50.9	145		91.9		15
	5	15-20	423.5	27	21.94	123		94.9		12
65 up	4	10-15	1237.0	135	132.2	102		96.5		2.3
	5	15-20	197.5	35	30.5	115		91.2		23

* Basis of expected mortality: Concurrent U.S. White Population Rates

CANCER—COLON

Table 157b   Cancer of the Colon - Derived Mortality and Survival Data

Stage & Sex Age Group	Interval No.	Interval Start-End	Observed Survival Rate Cumulative	Observed Survival Rate Interval	Observed Survival Rate Ave. Ann.	Observed Ave. Ann. Mort. Rate	Expected* Survival Rate Cumulative	Expected* Survival Rate Interval	Expected* Survival Rate Ave. Ann.	Expected* Ave. Ann. Mort. Rate
(Yrs)	i	t to $t+\Delta t$	P	p_i	$\breve{p}$	$\breve{q}$	P'	p_i'	$\breve{p}'$	$\breve{q}'$
Localized Male										
< 45	1	0- 2 yrs	.8964	.8964	.9468	.0532	.9941	.9941	.9970	.0030
	2	2- 5	.8488	.9469	.9820	.0180	.9832	.9890	.9963	.0037
	3	5-10	.7511	.8849	.9758	.0242	.9571	.9735	.9946	.0054
45-54	1	0- 2	.8511	.8511	.9226	.0774	.9790	.9790	.9894	.0106
	2	2- 5	.7154	.8406	.9438	.0562	.9407	.9609	.9868	.0132
	3	5-10	.6105	.8534	.9688	.0312	.8556	.9095	.9812	.0188
55-64	1	0- 2	.8085	.8085	.8992	.1008	.9525	.9525	.9760	.0240
	2	2- 5	.6323	.7821	.9213	.0787	.8705	.9139	.9704	.0296
	3	5-10	.4621	.7308	.9392	.0608	.7080	.8133	.9595	.0405
65-74	1	0- 2	.7266	.7266	.8524	.1476	.9009	.9009	.9492	.0508
	2	2- 5	.5089	.7004	.8881	.1119	.7463	.8284	.9392	.0608
	3	5-10	.3064	.6021	.9035	.0965	.4893	.6556	.9190	.0810
75 up	1	0- 2	.5318	.5318	.7292	.2708	.7859	.7859	.8865	.1135
	2	2- 5	.3007	.5654	.8269	.1731	.5152	.6556	.8687	.1313
	3	5-10	.0943	.3136	.7930	.2070	.2048	.3975	.8315	.1685
Female < 45	1	0- 2 yrs	.9450	.9450	.9721	.0279	.9970	.9970	.9985	.0015
	2	2- 5	.8748	.9257	.9746	.0254	.9915	.9945	.9982	.0018
	3	5-10	.7989	.9132	.9820	.0180	.9786	.9870	.9974	.0026
45-54	1	0- 2	.9126	.9126	.9553	.0447	.9899	.9899	.9949	.0051
	2	2- 5	.8164	.8946	.9636	.0364	.9718	.9817	.9939	.0061
	3	5-10	.6999	.8573	.9697	.0303	.9313	.9583	.9915	.0085
55-64	1	0- 2	.8421	.8421	.9177	.0823	.9765	.9765	.9882	.0118
	2	2- 5	.7097	.8428	.9446	.0554	.9342	.9567	.9854	.0146
	3	5-10	.5888	.8296	.9633	.0367	.8399	.8991	.9790	.0210
65-74	1	0- 2	.7606	.7606	.8721	.1279	.9413	.9413	.9702	.0298
	2	2- 5	.6036	.7936	.9258	.0742	.8406	.8930	.9630	.0370
	3	5-10	.3946	.6537	.9185	.0815	.6373	.7581	.9461	.0539
75 up	1	0- 2	.5769	.5769	.7595	.2405	.8224	.8224	.9069	.0931
	2	2- 5	.3769	.6533	.8677	.1323	.5786	.7036	.8894	.1106
	3	5-10	.1538	.4081	.8359	.1641	.2593	.4482	.8517	.1483
Male < 45	4	10-15 yrs		.9240	.9843	.0157		.9576	.9914	.0086
	5	15-20		.8596	.9702	.0298		.9405	.9878	.0122
45-54	4	10-15		.7516	.9445	.0555		.8677	.9720	.0280
	5	15-20		.7714	.9494	.0506		.8192	.9609	.0391
55-64	4	10-15		.6317	.9122	.0878		.7498	.9440	.0560
	5	15-20		.5215	.8779	.1221		.6697	.9229	.0771
65 up	4	10-15		.4393	.8483	.1517		.4919	.8677	.1323
	5	15-20		.2483	.7568	.2432		.3806	.8243	.1757
Female < 45	4	10-15 yrs		.9665	.9932	.0068		.9798	.9959	.0041
	5	15-20		.9899	.9980	.0020		.9679	.9935	.0065
45-54	4	10-15		.8905	.9771	.0229		.9344	.9865	.0135
	5	15-20		.8498	.9680	.0320		.9011	.9794	.0206
55-64	4	10-15		.7721	.9496	.0504		.8397	.9657	.0343
	5	15-20		.7172	.9357	.0643		.7561	.9456	.0544
65 up	4	10-15		.5362	.8828	.1172		.5558	.8892	.1108
	5	15-20		.3698	.8196	.1804		.4053	.8347	.1653

* Basis of expected mortality: Concurrent U.S. White Population Rates

CANCER—COLON

Table 157c   Cancer of the Colon - Observed Data and Comparative Experience by Area, Stage, Sex, and Duration

Stage & Sex Area	Interval No.	Interval Start-End	Exposure Person-Yrs	Deaths Observed	Deaths Expected*	Mortality Ratio Interval	Mortality Ratio Cumulative	Survival Ratio Interval	Survival Ratio Cumulative	Excess Death Rate
	i	t to t + Δt	E	d	d'	100 d/d'	100 Q/Q'	100 p$_i$/p$_i$'	100 P/P'	1000(d-d')/E
Localized										
Male										
All Areas	1	0- 2 yrs	6379.0	1000	326.0	305%	275%	80.1%	80.1%	106
	2	2- 5	6777.5	677	360.9	188	190	87.3	69.9	47
	3	5-10	6084.0	491	377.5	130	140	92.3	64.6	19
	4	10-15	2931.0	254	189.4	134	—	88.4	—	22
	5	15-20	698.0	66	47.3	139	—	84.9	—	27
Ascending	1	0- 2	1580.5	244	80.9	300	270	80.5	80.5	103
	2	2- 5	1702.5	144	89.9	160	180	91.6	73.7	32
	3	5-10	1508.0	106	91.2	116	135	95.7	70.5	9.8
Transverse	1	0- 2	889.5	165	49.0	335	300	75.4	75.4	130
	2	2- 5	887.0	96	49.2	195	200	85.7	64.7	53
	3	5-10	778.0	76	49.1	155	147	87.4	56.5	35
Descending	1	0- 2	525.0	83	26.0	320	285	79.7	79.7	109
	2	2- 5	564.0	64	30.4	210	205	82.7	65.9	60
	3	5-10	441.0	41	27.3	150	148	86.5	57.0	31
Sigmoid	1	0- 2	2842.0	425	144.3	295	265	81.3	81.3	99
	2	2- 5	3029.0	311	163.0	191	188	86.8	70.6	49
	3	5-10	2747.5	222	175.3	127	139	92.8	65.5	17
Female										
All Areas	1	0- 2 yrs	8058.0	1006	269.0	375	335	82.7	82.7	91
	2	2- 5	9215.0	631	324.4	195	220	91.1	75.3	33
	3	5-10	8976.5	561	376.9	149	161	91.1	68.6	21
	4	10-15	4796.5	244	204.2	120	—	95.2	—	8.3
	5	15-20	1332.5	75	62.0	121	—	96.4	—	9.8
Ascending	1	0- 2	2675.0	333	94.8	350	315	83.1	83.1	89
	2	2- 5	3096.0	162	117.7	138	191	96.3	80.0	14
	3	5-10	2917.0	187	133.4	140	152	89.6	71.7	18
Transverse	1	0- 2	1128.5	167	43.1	385	345	79.3	79.3	110
	2	2- 5	1210.5	111	47.2	235	230	86.1	68.3	53
	3	5-10	1114.5	75	50.3	149	161	91.3	62.3	22
Descending	1	0- 2	640.5	82	18.4	445	390	81.4	81.4	99
	2	2- 5	733.0	52	22.5	230	250	89.0	72.5	40
	3	5-10	794.5	42	31.1	135	173	93.2	67.5	14
Sigmoid	1	0- 2	3021.0	342	92.0	370	335	84.2	84.2	83
	2	2- 5	3501.0	262	112.4	235	235	88.5	74.6	43
	3	5-10	3377.0	210	128.4	164	168	90.7	67.6	24
Regional										
M & F										
All Areas	1	0- 2 yrs	10266.5	2844	426.7	665	550	58.1	58.1	235
	2	2- 5	8058.0	1181	352.5	335	315	72.9	42.4	103
	3	5-10	6606.0	551	340.7	162	192	87.1	36.9	32
Ascending	1	0- 2	3424.5	1017	151.8	670	540	55.6	55.6	253
	2	2- 5	2638.5	348	120.8	290	295	77.2	42.9	86
	3	5-10	2196.0	159	118.8	134	178	95.1	40.8	18
Transverse	1	0- 2	1491.5	472	62.7	755	595	53.4	53.4	274
	2	2- 5	1136.5	140	50.4	280	315	79.4	42.4	79
	3	5-10	1001.0	74	51.6	143	188	91.6	38.8	22
Descending	1	0- 2	803.0	204	28.2	725	610	60.3	60.3	219
	2	2- ,5	643.5	102	23.5	435	365	68.2	41.2	122
	3	5-10	524.5	31	24.7	126	210	94.9	39.1	12
Sigmoid	1	0- 2	3695.5	906	146.2	620	530	62.5	62,5	206
	2	2- 5	3005.0	490	129.0	380	330	68.5	42.8	120
	3	5-10	2310.5	240	116.0	205	205	76.6	32.8	54
Metastatic										
M & F										
All Areas	1	0- 2 yrs	5616.0	4015	234.0	1720	1030	12.1	12.1	673
	2	2- 5	1015.0	307	38.4	800	450	43.6	5.3	265
	3	5-10	600.0	71	28.7	245	240	72.6	3.8	71

* Basis of expected mortality: Concurrent U.S. White Population Rates

CANCER—COLON

Table 157d   Cancer of the Colon - Derived Mortality and Survival Data

Stage & Sex Area	Interval No.	Start-End t to t+Δt	Observed Survival Rate Cumulative P	Interval p_i	Ave. Ann. $\breve{p}$	Ave. Ann. Mort. Rate $\breve{q}$	Expected Survival Rate Cumulative P'	Interval p_i'	Ave. Ann. $\breve{p}'$	Ave. Ann. Mort. Rate $\breve{q}'$
Localized Male All Areas	1	0- 2 yrs	.7183	.7183	.8475	.1525	.8970	.8970	.9471	.0529
	2	2- 5	.5246	.7303	.9005	.0995	.7500	.8361	.9421	.0579
	3	5-10	.3439	.6555	.9190	.0810	.5324	.7099	.9388	.0662
	4	10-15	—	.6304	.9118	.0882	—	.7129	.9346	.0654
	5	15-20	—	.5991	.9026	.0974	—	.7056	.9326	.0674
Ascending	1	0- 2	.7214	.7214	.8494	.1506	.8967	.8967	.9469	.0531
	2	2- 5	.5537	.7675	.9156	.0844	.7517	.8383	.9429	.0571
	3	5-10	.3830	.6917	.9289	.0711	.5434	.7229	.9372	.0628
Transverse	1	0- 2	.6723	.6723	.8199	.1801	.8911	.8911	.9440	.0560
	2	2- 5	.4777	.7105	.8923	.1077	.7384	.8286	.9393	.0607
	3	5-10	.2924	.6121	.9065	.0935	.5172	.7004	.9313	.0687
Descending	1	0- 2	.7167	.7167	.8466	.1534	.8998	.8998	.9486	.0514
	2	2- 5	.4958	.6918	.8844	.1156	.7523	.8361	.9421	.0579
	3	5-10	.3001	.6053	.9045	.0955	.5267	.7001	.9312	.0688
Sigmoid	1	0- 2	.7299	.7299	.8543	.1457	.8977	.8977	.9475	.0525
	2	2- 5	.5296	.7256	.8986	.1014	.7504	.8359	.9420	.0580
	3	5-10	.3464	.6541	.9186	.0814	.5290	.7050	.9325	.0675
Female All Areas	1	0- 2 yrs	.7700	.7700	.8775	.1225	.9313	.9313	.9650	.0350
	2	2- 5	.6232	.8094	.9319	.0681	.8278	.8889	.9615	.0385
	3	5-10	.4514	.7243	.9375	.0625	.6584	.7954	.9552	.0448
	4	10-15	—	.7644	.9477	.0523	—	.8026	.9570	.0430
	5	15-20	—	.7605	.9467	.0533	—	.7893	.9538	.0462
Ascending	1	0- 2	.7706	.7706	.8778	.1222	.9274	.9274	.9630	.0370
	2	2- 5	.6557	.8509	.9476	.0524	.8197	.8839	.9597	.0403
	3	5-10	.4639	.7075	.9331	.0669	.6471	.7894	.9538	.0462
Transverse	1	0- 2	.7313	.7313	.8552	.1448	.9217	.9217	.9601	.0399
	2	2- 5	.5497	.7517	.9092	.0908	.8048	.8732	.9558	.0442
	3	5-10	.3862	.7026	.9318	.0682	.6196	.7699	.9490	.0510
Descending	1	0- 2	.7644	.7644	.8743	.1257	.9392	.9392	.9601	.0309
	2	2- 5	.6135	.8026	.9293	.0707	.8467	.9015	.9660	.0340
	3	5-10	.4672	.7615	.9470	.0530	.6918	.8171	.9604	.0396
Sigmoid	1	0- 2	.7898	.7898	.8887	.1113	.9375	.9375	.9682	.0318
	2	2- 5	.6273	.7943	.9261	.0739	.8412	.8973	.9645	.0355
	3	5-10	.4586	.7311	.9393	.0607	.6783	.8063	.9579	.0421
Regional M & F All Areas	1	0- 2 yrs	.5316	.5316	.7291	.2709	.9147	.9147	.9564	.0436
	2	2- 5	.3344	.6290	.8568	.1432	.7894	.8630	.9521	.0479
	3	5-10	.2192	.6555	.9190	.0810	.5940	.7525	.9447	.0553
Ascending	1	0- 2	.5047	.5047	.7104	.2896	.9083	.9083	.9530	.0470
	2	2- 5	.3323	.6584	.8700	.1300	.7745	.8527	.9483	.0517
	3	5-10	.2321	.6985	.9308	.0692	.5691	.7348	.9402	.0598
Transverse	1	0- 2	.4878	.4878	.6984	.3016	.9138	.9138	.9559	.0441
	2	2- 5	.3334	.6835	.8809	.1191	.7871	.8613	.9514	.0486
	3	5-10	.2288	.6863	.9275	.0725	.5898	.7493	.9439	.0561
Descending	1	0- 2	.5598	.5598	.7482	.2518	.9278	.9278	.9632	.0368
	2	2- 5	.3372	.6024	.8446	.1554	.8192	.8829	.9593	.0407
	3	5-10	.2505	.7429	.9423	.0577	.6413	.7828	.9522	.0478
Sigmoid	1	0- 2	.5749	.5749	.7582	.2418	.9196	.9196	.9590	.0410
	2	2- 5	.3425	.5958	.8415	.1585	.8002	.8702	.9547	.0453
	3	5-10	.2003	.5848	.8983	.1017	.6108	.7633	.9474	.0526
Metastatic M & F All Areas	1	0- 2 yrs	.1103	.1103	.3321	.6679	.9135	.9135	.9558	.0442
	2	2- 5	.0414	.3753	.7213	.2787	.7871	.8616	.9516	.0484
	3	5-10	.0226	.5459	.8860	.1140	.5917	.7517	.9445	.0555

*Basis of expected mortality: Concurrent U.S. White Population Rates

CANCER—RECTUM

Table 158a Cancer of the Rectum - Observed Data and Comparative Experience by Stage, Sex, Age and Duration

Stage & Sex Age Group	Interval No.	Interval Start-End	Exposure Person-Yrs	Deaths Observed	Deaths Expected.*	Mortality Ratio Interval	Mortality Ratio Cumulative	Survival Ratio Interval	Survival Ratio Cumulative	Excess Death Rate
(Yrs)	i	t to t + Δt	E	d	d′	100d/d′	100Q/Q′	100p$_i$/p$_i$′	100P/P′	1000(d-d′)/E
Localized										
Male										
< 45	1	0- 2 yrs	276.5	18	0.95	1890%	1810%	87.9%	87.9%	62
	2	2- 5	336.5	17	1.46	1160	1250	87.0	76.5	46
	3	5-10	383.0	12	2.41	500	670	89.6	68.5	25
45-54	1	0- 2	628.5	46	6.52	705	680	87.8	87.8	63
	2	2- 5	763.5	57	9.93	575	540	82.8	72.7	62
	3	5-10	830.0	34	14.70	230	310	89.7	65.2	23
55-64	1	0- 2	1355.5	171	32.7	525	490	80.4	80.4	102
	2	2- 5	1501.0	129	44.5	290	320	83.7	67.3	56
	3	5-10	1478.0	100	59.0	169	200	86.3	58.1	28
65 up	1	0- 2	2792.0	728	210.5	345	305	65.5	65.5	185
	2	2- 5	2330.0	353	188.4	187	195	79.2	51.8	71
	3	5-10	1726.0	241	169.3	142	137	80.5	41.7	42
Female										
< 45	1	0- 2 yrs	269.5	20	0.50	4000	3870	86.0	86.0	72
	2	2- 5	333.5	13	0.77	1690	2270	89.5	76.9	37
	3	5-10	403.5	5	1.27	395	1060	96.0	73.9	9.2
45-54	1	0- 2	590.0	39	3.07	1270	1240	88.1	88.1	61
	2	2- 5	723.0	48	4.55	1050	1000	83.1	73.2	60
	3	5-10	794.5	18	6.74	265	525	92.6	67.8	14
55-64	1	0- 2	1118.5	99	13.00	760	720	85.2	85.2	77
	2	2- 5	1346.0	96	19.10	500	515	83.7	71.3	57
	3	5-10	1369.5	57	26.9	210	285	91.2	65.0	22
65 up	1	0- 2	2312.0	459	129.4	355	320	73.1	73.1	143
	2	2- 5	2177.0	285	131.3	215	220	79.7	58.2	71
	3	5-10	1783.0	187	140.2	133	145	88.0	51.3	26
Regional										
Male										
All	1	0- 2 yrs	2925.5	959	132.2	725	585	50.9	50.9	283
	2	2- 5	1930.5	408	86.8	470	340	58.8	29.9	166
	3	5-10	1239.0	171	64.1	265	205	68.1	20.4	86
Female										
All	1	0- 2 yrs	2674.0	779	83.7	930	765	53.9	53.9	260
	2	2- 5	1864.5	379	57.2	665	455	57.8	31.2	173
	3	5-10	1357.5	125	45.0	280	255	80.9	25.2	59
Metastatic										
M & F										
All	1	0- 2 yrs	2880.0	2088	122.9	1700	1020	10.4	10.4	682
	2	2- 5	414.5	153	14.60	1050	450	34.2	3.5	334
	3	5-10	210.0	25	8.69	290	240	73.9	2.6	78
Localized										
Male										
< 45	4	10-15 yrs	389.5	10	4.30	235		92.4		15
	5	15-20	139.5	2	2.35	85		101.0		−2.5
45-54	4	10-15	691.0	16	18.10	89		101.5		−3.0
	5	15-20	201.5	14	7.96	176		88.2		30
55-64	4	10-15	1114.0	92	61.0	151		83.7		28
	5	15-20	301.0	24	23.1	104		101.3		3.0
65 up	4	10-15	633.5	101	76.0	133		84.3		39
	5	15-20	104.0	25	18.3	137		68.5		65
Female										
< 45	4	10-15 yrs	510.5	7	2.51	280		96.8		8.8
	5	15-20	231.5	2	1.66	120		98.7		1.5
45-54	4	10-15	824.5	20	11.3	177		94.4		11
	5	15-20	330.0	8	7.2	111		100.7		2.4
55-64	4	10-15	1046.5	44	34.3	128		93.9		9.3
	5	15-20	301.0	13	14.4	90		104.0		−4.8
65 up	4	10-15	782.0	88	79.0	111		92.5		12
	5	15-20	156.5	26	23.7	110		92.4		15

*Basis of expected mortality: Concurrent U.S. White Population Rates

CANCER—RECTUM

Table 158b   Cancer of the Rectum - Derived Mortality and Survival Data

Stage & Sex Age Group	Interval No.	Interval Start-End	Observed Survival Rate Cumulative	Observed Survival Rate Interval	Observed Survival Rate Ave. Ann.	Observed Ave. Ann. Mort. Rate	Expected* Survival Rate Cumulative	Expected* Survival Rate Interval	Expected* Survival Rate Ave. Ann.	Expected* Ave. Ann. Mort. Rate
(Yrs)	i	t to t + Δt	P	p_i	$\check{p}$	$\check{q}$	P'	p_i'	$\check{p}'$	$\check{q}'$
Localized										
Male										
< 45	1	0- 2 yrs	.8733	.8733	.9345	.0655	.9930	.9930	.9965	.0035
	2	2- 5	.7496	.8584	.9504	.0496	.9799	.9868	.9956	.0044
	3	5-10	.6497	.8667	.9718	.0282	.9479	.9673	.9934	.0066
45-54	1	0- 2	.8604	.8604	.9276	.0724	.9794	.9794	.9896	.0104
	2	2- 5	.6847	.7958	.9267	.0733	.9417	.9615	.9870	.0130
	3	5-10	.5594	.8170	.9604	.0396	.8578	.9109	.9815	.0185
55-64	1	0- 2	.7654	.7654	.8749	.1251	.9520	.9520	.9757	.0243
	2	2- 5	.5851	.7644	.9143	.0857	.8694	.9132	.9702	.0298
	3	5-10	.4097	.7002	.9312	.0688	.7057	.8117	.9591	.0409
65 up	1	0- 2	.5597	.5597	.7481	.2519	.8548	.8548	.9246	.0754
	2	2- 5	.3436	.6139	.8499	.1501	.6628	.7754	.9187	.0813
	3	5-10	.1624	.4726	.8608	.1392	.3892	.5872	.8990	.1010
Female										
< 45	1	0- 2 yrs	.8568	.8568	.9256	.0744	.9963	.9963	.9981	.0019
	2	2- 5	.7614	.8887	.9614	.0386	.9895	.9932	.9977	.0023
	3	5-10	.7192	.9446	.9887	.0113	.9734	.9837	.9967	.0033
45-54	1	0- 2	.8719	.8719	.9338	.0662	.9897	.9897	.9948	.0052
	2	2- 5	.7112	.8157	.9344	.0656	.9711	.9812	.9937	.0063
	3	5-10	.6305	.8865	.9762	.0238	.9296	.9573	.9913	.0087
55-64	1	0- 2	.8317	.8317	.9120	.0880	.9767	.9767	.9883	.0117
	2	2- 5	.6664	.8013	.9288	.0712	.9350	.9573	.9856	.0144
	3	5-10	.5472	.8211	.9613	.0387	.8415	.9000	.9791	.0209
65 up	1	0- 2	.6513	.6513	.8070	.1930	.8912	.8912	.9440	.0560
	2	2- 5	.4301	.6604	.8708	.1292	.7388	.8290	.9394	.0606
	3	5-10	.2475	.5754	.8954	.1046	.4828	.6535	.9184	.0816
Regional										
Male										
All	1	0- 2 yrs	.4616	.4616	.6794	.3206	.9076	.9076	.9527	.0473
	2	2- 5	.2308	.5000	.7937	.2063	.7724	.8510	.9476	.0524
	3	5-10	.1149	.4978	.8698	.1302	.5645	.7308	.9392	.0608
Female										
All	1	0- 2 yrs	.5042	.5042	.7101	.2899	.9353	.9353	.9671	.0329
	2	2- 5	.2608	.5173	.8028	.1972	.8371	.8950	.9637	.0363
	3	5-10	.1696	.6503	.9175	.0825	.6729	.8038	.9573	.0427
Metastatic										
M & F										
All	1	0- 2 yrs	.0944	.0944	.3072	.6928	.9116	.9116	.9548	.0452
	2	2- 5	.0277	.2934	.6645	.3355	.7830	.8589	.9506	.0494
	3	5-10	.0153	.5523	.8880	.1120	.5855	.7478	.9435	.0565
Localized										
Male										
< 45	4	10-15 yrs		.8726	.9731	.0269		.9447	.9887	.0113
	5	15-20		.9259	.9847	.0153		.9171	.9828	.0172
45-54	4	10-15		.8864	.9762	.0238		.8729	.9732	.0268
	5	15-20		.7162	.9354	.0646		.8119	.9592	.0408
55-64	4	10-15		.6264	.9107	.0893		.7482	.9436	.0564
	5	15-20		.6711	.9233	.0767		.6626	.9210	.0790
65 up	4	10-15		.4290	.8443	.1557		.5086	.8735	.1265
	5	15-20		.2478	.7565	.2435		.3616	.8159	.1841
Female										
< 45	4	10-15 yrs		.9440	.9885	.0115		.9752	.9950	.0050
	5	15-20		.9513	.9901	.0099		.9636	.9926	.0074
45-54	4	10-15		.8794	.9746	.0254		.9315	.9859	.0141
	5	15-20		.8991	.9790	.0210		.8925	.9775	.0225
55-64	4	10-15		.7904	.9540	.0460		.8416	.9661	.0339
	5	15-20		.8042	.9574	.0426		.7735	.9499	.0501
65 up	4	10-15		.5309	.8811	.1189		.5739	.8949	.1051
	5	15-20		.3854	.8264	.1736		.4172	.8396	.1604

*Basis of expected mortality: Concurrent U.S. White Population Rates

CANCER—GENITOURINARY TRACT

§160—CANCER OF THE KIDNEY

Cancer of the kidney ranks 12th among cancer sites in males, 16th in females, and has a relative frequency of 2.2 and 1.4 per cent, respectively (Tables 100a-b). Over two-thirds of the cases diagnosed were over age 55 in both sexes; the cancers of 43 per cent of male and 48 per cent of female cases were classified in the localized stage.

Ten-year experience for patients diagnosed as having cancer of the kidney is presented in three stages in the upper portion of Tables 160a-b. In the localized stage, data are presented for males and females combined in the two youngest age groups and for the two sexes separately in three older age groups. Mortality ratios decreased with both age and duration, from 7900 per cent in children under age 15 within two years of diagnosis to 155 and 144 per cent, respectively, in the oldest males and females at durations 5-10 years. The very high early excess mortality in patients under age 15 was also evident in the EDR of 227 extra deaths per 1000 within two years of diagnosis. In the same interval, the EDR dropped to 45 per 1000 in patients age 15-34, but then increased steadily with advancing age. The cumulative five-year survival ratio was only 53.1 per cent in children, increased to 82.3 per cent in young adults, then decreased with advancing age to 55.3 per cent in male patients and 50.8 per cent in females in the oldest age group.

Following the usual trend, prognosis worsened with extension of the cancer. Within two years the mortality ratio in the regional stage was 1140 per cent, and in the metastatic stage, 2300 per cent, all ages and both sexes combined. The corresponding ratio for the localized stage was 565 per cent. EDR's in the first interval were 326 and 741 extra deaths per 1000 among those with regional and metastatic cancer, respectively, compared with 139 for the localized stage. After the first interval, mortality ratios and EDR's both decreased significantly with the passage of time. Cumulative five-year survival ratios were 31.6 per cent in patients with regional extension and 4.1 per cent in those with metastasis.

Long-term results from 10-20 years are presented for patients with localized cancer of the kidney in the lower portion of Tables 160a-b, males and females separately. Numbers of deaths were small, with fewer than ten deaths in 11 out of 16 age-duration categories. With some irregularities due to the small numbers, the general trend was for the mortality ratios to decrease with advancing age and to be somewhat higher at 15-20 years than at 10-15 years. The highest ratios were in the under age 45, 15-20 years category, with 720 per cent for males and 970 per cent for females; the lowest ratios (excluding two categories with only two deaths each) were in the 10-15 interval at the high ages, with 121 per cent for males age 55-64 and 140 per cent and 147 per cent, respectively, for males and females age 65 and over. The EDR's showed no regular trend by age but were generally higher for the 15-20 year interval. When all ages are combined, the aggregate experience clearly indicates persistence of excess mortality in both intervals: for males the EDR was 23 per 1000 at 10-15 years, and 68 per 1000 at 15-20 years, while the corresponding rates for females were 34 and 51, respectively. Mortality ratios also increased from the earlier to the later interval, in males from 157 to 280 per cent, and in females from 235 to 245 per cent.

CANCER—GENITOURINARY TRACT

§161—CANCER OF THE BLADDER

Cancer of the bladder ranks fourth among all male cancers and tenth among all female cancers, with relative frequencies of 6.7 and 2.5 per cent, respectively (Tables 100a-b). About 85 per cent of both male and female patients diagnosed were over age 55 and about three-quarters were classified in the localized stage.

Ten-year results for patients diagnosed as having cancer of the bladder are presented in three stages in the upper portion of Tables 161a-b. In the localized stage, data are presented for the two sexes separately in three age groups (under 45, 45-54 and 55-64), and for males and females combined in two high age groups (65-74 and 75 and over). In the three younger age groups female patients with localized bladder cancer were generally found to have experienced mortality ratios substantially higher than males. This was not the case for the EDR's except for the two youngest age groups within two years of diagnosis. For the three younger age groups the mortality ratios within two years of diagnosis were 2700, 1530, and 795 per cent, respectively, in female patients versus 790, 625, and 490 in the matching age groups of male patients. The comparable number of extra deaths per 1000 were 44, 73, and 81 for females and 22, 55, and 94 for males. The general trend over the whole range of ages was for the mortality ratios to decrease with both advancing age and duration. The number of extra deaths per 1000 increased with age, although to a moderate degreee after the first interval, but was lower at the longer durations. The lowest mortality ratios were experienced in the age group 75 and over, where for both sexes combined they were 265, 140, and 125 per cent, respectively, for the three duration intervals within ten years of diagnosis. The corresponding EDR's of 184, 50, and 39 for that age group were at a high level relative to the other age groups.

In accordance with the usual trend found in other types of cancer, the experience worsened with extension of the cancer. Within two years, the mortality ratio in the regional stage was 945 per cent and in the metastatic stage, 1420 per cent. The comparable ratio for the localized stage was 345 per cent. EDR's in the first interval were 456 and 753 per 1000 among those with regional and metastatic cancer, respectively, compared with 121 for the localized stage. After the first interval, mortality ratios and EDR's both decreased significantly with the passage of time. Nevertheless, the five-year survival ratio dropped sharply to 21.3 per cent in patients with regional spread and to 3.9 per cent in those with metastasis.

Long-term results from 10-20 years are presented for patients with localized cancer of the bladder in the lower portion of Tables 161a-b, males and females separately. The number of deaths is quite small in several of the categories, particularly for females, and this may be the reason why an overall pattern is not clearly discernible. The experience for the 10-15 year interval tends to be worse than for 15-20 years up through age 64, while the reverse appears to be the case after age 65. The level of mortality ratios and EDR's is generally well below the experience in the first ten years. Among male patients, no mortality ratio exceeds 166 per cent; among females in the 10-15 year interval, the under 45 age group had a mortality ratio of 251 per cent but with only four deaths, and the 45-54 group, a ratio of 290 per cent with 16 deaths.

CANCER–GENITOURINARY TRACT

§162–CANCER OF THE PROSTATE

The prostate is a common site of cancer among men, ranking second in the list of 33 sites with a relative frequency of 12.4 per cent of all cancers in men. Most cases occur over age 65 years; diagnosis is made chiefly at the localized stage.

Presented in Table 162a is experience for localized cancer by age group at time of diagnosis for three intervals within the succeeding ten years and for two intervals between 10 and 20 years after diagnosis. Mortality ratios decreased with duration for all age groups with almost complete consistency over the 20 years shown. They tended to diminish, also, with age at diagnosis. Thus, from Intervals 1 to 3 (years 0-2 and 5-10), where diagnosis was made prior to age 55 years, mortality ratios declined from 680 to 235 per cent; between ages 55 and 64 they decreased from 305 to 205 per cent, between ages 65 and 74, from 255 to 182 per cent, and over 75 years of age, from 205 to 153 per cent. Over the 4th and 5th intervals (10-15 years and 15-20 years), for diagnoses made prior to age 55 years, these ratios were 345 and 315 per cent; they diminished respectively to 141 and 95 per cent for ages 75 years and older.

Excess deaths per 1000 also tended to diminish with the lapse of time after diagnosis. By age at diagnosis, however, they generally increased. Thus, at ages under 55 years during the first three intervals, EDR's ranged from 65 to 26 per 1000; in age group 55-64 years, from 53 to 45 per 1000; in age group 65 to 74, from 81 to 64 per 1000; for ages 75 and over, from 125 to 86 per 1000. Over Intervals 4 and 5, EDR's were irregular ranging between 56 and 86 per 1000 for post-diagnosis years 10-15 and from −15 to 91 per 1000 for years 15-20. Except for age groups 55-64 and 64-74 where EDR's were virtually constant, about 60 per 1000, the numbers of deaths in Interval 5 in younger and older age groups were too small to develop reliable results. Five-year cumulative survival ratios within ten years of diagnosis decreased from 74.4 per cent for ages under 55 to 54.9 per cent for cases diagnosed at ages 75 and up.

Results are also presented in Table 162a for the same age groups and intervals, up to ten years following diagnosis, of regional extension of cancer of the prostate. Mortality ratios were substantially greater than for the localized cases and almost without exception diminished by age at diagnosis and by interval. As observed for the localized stage, EDR's tended to decrease with lapse of time after diagnosis but to increase with age. The downward progression by interval, however, was reversed in the 2-5 year interval among men diagnosed prior to age 55 years and a dip developed in the upward gradation of excess rates by age among men in the 55-64 year age group. Five-year cumulative survival ratios decreased from 65.2 per cent in men 55-64 years of age to 38.2 per cent in men 75 and up. A relatively low ratio of 46.2 per cent was associated with high excess deaths in men under 55 years of age during the first five years after diagnosis. Even higher mortality ratios and extra death rates were observed in patients with metastatic cancer of the prostate, EDR in the first two years attaining a level of 289 per 1000 in men under 65 at diagnosis and 363 per 1000 in men 65 years and older. Five-year cumulative survival ratios were 20.8 and 15.1 per cent respectively for the younger and older age groups.

The persistence of a moderate degree of excess mortality appears to be a significant phenomenon ten years and longer beyond diagnosis of localized cancer of the prostate. It should be kept in mind that attained ages at these durations are from 10 to 20 years older than the entry ages shown. Many of these patients were in their eighties when this experience was collected. The single category which did not show an excess mortality included only eight observed deaths.

§163—CANCER OF THE PENIS, CANCER OF THE TESTIS

Cancer of the penis is very rare ranking next to last in the 33 cancer sites in men (Table 100a). Over three-quarters of the cases occur in males over 55 years and most of them are diagnosed in the localized stage. Experience for all ages combined (upper part of Tables 163a-b) in localized cases showed an EDR of 76 extra deaths per 1000 per year, within the first two years after diagnosis, and rates of 26 and 32 per 1000 in the subsequent two intervals. These results were heavily weighted by the proportion of deaths in the patients age 75 and up. Variations of excess mortality with age in localized cases were irregular, owing to the small numbers of deaths (fewer than 15 in half of the categories). The five-year cumulative survival ratio was 79.8 per cent in the localized stage, 46.1 per cent in those with regional extension, and 9.6 per cent in patients with metastasis, reflecting the usual progression of excess mortality with extension of the cancer, seen in most types of malignant tumor.

Cancer of the testis ranks 23rd and has a relative frequency of 0.9 per cent. Over three-quarters of the cases are diagnosed in men under 55, an unusually high proportion in younger patients, and over half are in the localized stage (Table 100a). Levels of EDR were relatively moderate in localized testicular cancer (lower part of Tables 163a-b): 58 extra deaths per 1000 per year within two years of diagnosis, 20 per 1000 in the next interval from two to five years, and only 7.9 per 1000 from five to ten years, all ages combined. The most favorable excess death rate in the first interval, 40 per 1000, was experienced in age group 35-54 years. The oldest and youngest age groups fared the worst with respective EDR's of 125 and 64 extra deaths per 1000 during the first two years. Excess mortality decreased markedly in all age groups in the succeeding intervals. In patients showing evidence of dissemination of testicular cancer, excess mortality progressed to a very high level within the first two years, with an EDR of 189 per 1000 in men with regional extension and 631 per 1000 in those with metastasis. Excess mortality appeared to drop to relatively low levels after two years, in comparison with most other types of cancer with extension, but numbers of deaths were very small in these categories. Cumulative five-year survival ratios were 84.0 per cent in men with localized cancer of the testis, 62.5 per cent in those with regional extension, and 13.4 per cent in those with metastasis.

CANCER–GENITOURINARY TRACT

§164–CANCER OF THE CERVIX OF THE UTERUS

Cancer of the cervix ranks third of all cancer sites among women, with a relative frequency of 9.8 per cent (Table 100b). Fifty-six per cent of the patients were under age 55, and 52 per cent were diagnosed when their cancer was still in the localized stage (Table 100b).

The upper portion of Tables 164a-b presents the experience within ten years of diagnosis of the cancer. This is done in three stages: the localized stage in five age groups, the regional stage in four age groups, and the metastatic stage for all ages combined. When the data for each of the localized and regional stages are combined so as to produce all-age ratios for comparison with the metastatic stage, the usual trend of a worsening experience with the extension of the cancer is found. The all-age mortality ratios for the three stages, respectively, are 655, 1370, and 2700 per cent for the first two-year period, 420, 610, and 985 per cent for the second interval of 2-5 years, and 215, 260, and 400 per cent for the 5-10 year interval. The corresponding extra deaths per 1000 are 61, 210, and 583 for the first interval, 37, 91, and 175 for the second, and 16, 33, and 62 for the third.

The improvement in the experience with duration that is evident in the above figures is also reflected in the individual age-groups of the localized and regional stages. In these stages there is also a marked improvement in the mortality ratios as the age advances. For example, from the lowest to the highest age groups, localized cancer of the cervix shows a drop from 5700 to 305 per cent in the first interval, from 2300 to 225 per cent in the second interval, and from 520 to 150 per cent in the third. Regional cancer cases display similar decreases in the mortality ratios with advancing age, but at higher levels. The trend in the EDR's is in the opposite direction for the localized stage, increasing with advancing age. In the first interval, for example, average annual excess deaths increase from 53 to 89 per 1000 from the lowest to the highest age groups. For the regional stage, the EDR's are fairly constant for the various age groups within each interval.

The five-year cumulative survival ratio for the localized stage was 83.2 per cent for the under 35 age group and decreased steadily for each higher age group to 68.9 per cent at ages 65 and over. The comparable ratios for the regional stage were 49.6 per cent for the under 45 age group and between 43.1 and 45.6 per cent for older age groups. For the metastatic stage, where there is no age differentiation in the data, the five-year survival ratio was only 12.0 per cent.

Ten- to twenty-year experience is presented for the localized and regional stages in the lower portion of Tables 164a-b, the data being subdivided in each instance in four age groups. In each stage the general trend is for the mortality ratios to decrease with advancing age, the only exception being the age group 65 and over where there is a moderate increase over the 55-64 age group for localized cancer cases in the 15-20 year interval, and for regional cancer in both the 10-15 and 15-20 year intervals. The trend by duration is not as clear; both increases and decreases appear in proceeding from the 10-15 to 15-20 year intervals. The mortality ratios are at a lower level than for the earlier intervals, and not much different for regional cancer cases than for localized cancer. Broadly speaking, the mortality ratios are at the 300 per cent level for the age group under 45 and at the 200 per cent level for ages 45-54. Beyond age 54, the ratios were generally below 150 per cent. The EDR's were relatively low, being generally in the range of 10 to 20 per 1000 with no significant pattern of variation by age or duration. An exception was age 65 and over, where the EDR was 47 per 1000 in localized cases, 15-20 years, and 41 and 64 per 1000 in regional cases, 10-15 and 15-20 years, respectively.

CANCER–GENITOURINARY TRACT

§165–CANCER OF THE CORPUS UTERI, CANCER OF THE OVARY

Cancer of the corpus uteri ranks fourth of all cancer sites in women with a relative frequency of 7.0 per cent (Table 100b). Over two-thirds of the patients were age 55 years or over and nearly three-fourths were diagnosed in the localized stage. Cancer of the ovary ranks fifth and has a relative frequency of 4.8 per cent, with about 40 per cent of the cases diagnosed under age 55 years and 50 per cent in the metastatic stage.

The upper half of Tables 165a-b is devoted to the experience of females with cancer of the corpus uteri. The localized stage is divided into five age groups which show that mortality ratios decreased markedly with both advancing age and duration after diagnosis. For the first two-year interval, the ratio dropped from 865 per cent for ages under 45 years to 240 per cent for ages 75 and over. In the third interval (5-10 years after diagnosis), these respective ratios were 250 and 102 per cent. Excess deaths also decreased with duration within each age group. For the three successive intervals reported, EDR's for the under 45 age group were 15, 11, and 5 per 1000, while in the highest age group (75 years and older), the corresponding extra deaths were 117, 40, and 2.1 per 1000. Within each interval the extra deaths increased with advancing age. For the first interval, for example, EDR's for the five successive age groups were 15, 27, 49, 80, and 117 per 1000. In the localized stage, five-year cumulative survival ratios decreased from 94.1 per cent in the youngest age group to 66.8 in the oldest.

The more advanced stages of cancer of the corpus uteri showed considerably higher mortality. For localized, regional, and metastatic cancer (all ages combined), the mortality ratios in the first two-year period were 375, 920, and 2400 per cent and the extra deaths, 54, 212, and 606 per 1000, respectively. Succeeding intervals showed the same relationship but with a steep drop in both mortality ratios and EDR's. The cumulative five-year survival ratio was 50.4 per cent in patients with regional extension and 14.3 per cent in those with metastatic cancer.

The lower portion of Tables 165a-b contains a similar analysis for females with cancer of the ovary. Mortality levels were much higher than for cancer of the corpus uteri, but the general trends were parallel except for the absence in the localized stage of a steady progression of EDR's with advancing age over the first two intervals. The initial two-year interval showed a drop in the mortality ratio from 4800 per cent in the under 45 age group to 255 per cent for ages 75 and over; in the 5-10 year interval the respective ratios were 535 and 120 per cent. The extra deaths per 1000 for groups extending from ages 45 to 74 years were about 100 in the first interval, at the 50 level in the 2-5 year interval, and rose from 21 to 39 per 1000 in the 5-10 year interval.

The advanced stages of cancer of the ovary were subject to a sharpened worsening of mortality. In the first two-year interval, the mortality ratio for regional cancer was 1980 per cent and for metastatic cancer it increased to 3200 per cent, all ages combined, whereas for localized cases, the comparable ratio was 755 per cent (also a high ratio but well below the others). The corresponding EDR's in this interval were 298 per 1000 for regional extension, 623 for metastasized cases, and 96 per 1000 for localized.

Cumulative five-year survival ratios were about 70 per cent for women with localized cancer of the ovary diagnosed over the 45 to 74 year age span, about 35 per cent for cases with regional extension, and less than 10 per cent for patients with metastatic cancer.

CANCER–GENITOURINARY TRACT

§166–CANCER OF THE VAGINA, CANCER OF THE VULVA

The vagina is a rare site in female cancers, ranking 33rd, and has a relative frequency of only 0.3 per cent (Table 100b). Almost three-fourths of the patients were age 55 years or older and nearly half were diagnosed in the localized stage. Cancer of the vulva ranks 20th and accounted for 0.9 per cent of all cancers in women. Over three-fourths of the patients were age 55 years or over and two-thirds were in the localized stage.

Data for cancer of the vagina are presented in the upper portion of Tables 166a-b. The small numbers of deaths in the several age-duration cells of the localized stage and in the 2-10 year intervals of the regional and metastatic stages make it difficult to draw any reliable conclusions. In the localized stage, mortality ratios tended to decrease with advancing age and duration after diagnosis while EDR's dropped with the passage of time within each age group and tended to increase with age over the first two intervals. Thus, mortality ratios in the first interval were 4400 per cent in the youngest age group (only four deaths) and 390 per cent in the oldest. In the 2-5 year interval these ratios fell to 1520 per cent (only two deaths) and 300 per cent (nine deaths), respectively. There were only three deaths altogether in the third interval. The extra deaths in the initial two-year interval were 91, 139, 260, 176, and 297 per 1000 in the five successive age groups reported, proceeding from the youngest to the oldest. The five-year cumulative survival ratio decreased with age from 73.6 per cent for cases diagnosed before age 45 to 18.2 per cent in the oldest age group.

The usual increasingly unfavorable experience with the spread of cancer obtained for this site. With all ages combined for the localized stage, mortality ratios within two years of diagnosis were 720, 855, and 2300 per cent for the localized, regional, and metastatic stages, respectively. The corresponding EDR's were 193, 291, and 739 per 1000. The five-year cumulative survival ratio was 34.5 per cent in the regional cases; there were no five-year survivors among the metastatic cases.

The experience for cancer of the vulva is shown in the lower portion of Tables 166a-b. In the localized cases, the small numbers of deaths at ages under 55 may account for irregularities in the progression of results with advancing duration. In the first interval, mortality ratios for localized cancer of the vulva ranged from 910 per cent in the under 45 year age group down to 240 per cent among those 75 and older. In the 5-10 year interval these ratios dropped to 635 (only four deaths) and 92 per cent, respectively. The extra deaths in the first interval rose from 13 per 1000 in the youngest age group to 139 per 1000 in the oldest. There was no consistent progression in the 5-10 year interval. The five-year cumulative survival ratio for patients with localized cancer of the vulva dropped from 94.8 per cent in the youngest age group to 56.6 per cent in the oldest.

Patients diagnosed in the regional and metastatic stages had a much poorer prognosis than those in the localized stage. In the first interval, with all ages combined among localized cases, mortality ratios for the localized, regional, and metastatic stages were 325, 800, and 1190 per cent, and EDR's, 83, 281, and 681 per 1000, respectively. The later intervals had a similar progression at a lower level. The exposure was very small in the 5-10 year interval among patients in the metastatic stage and there were no deaths. The five-year cumulative survival ratio was 43.5 per cent for regional cancer patients and only 4.9 per cent for metastatic cases.

CANCER–GENITOURINARY TRACT

§167–CANCER OF THE BREAST

The breast is the most common site for cancer in women and breast cancer comprises a substantial 23.8 per cent of all female cancers (Table 100b). Forty-two per cent of breast cancer patients were diagnosed under the age of 55. Forty-five per cent of the cases were diagnosed in the localized stage, 42 per cent in the regional, and 10 per cent in the metastatic stage.

The ten-year experience for patients diagnosed in the localized stage is presented in five age groups in Tables 167a-b. Mortality ratios decreased with age by observation interval. However, within the age groups under 65, the mortality ratios were greatest in the 2-5 year observation interval, ranging from 1650 per cent under age 45 to 375 per cent in the 55 to 64 year category. In the older age groups, 65 to 74 and 75 years and up, the mortality ratios steadily decreased. Except in the oldest age group, the EDR's were highest in the second observation interval, remaining between 34 and 40 extra deaths per 1000. In the first interval, EDR's ranged from 24 extra deaths per 1000 in the 45-54 age group to 52 per 1000 in the 75 up age group. These are low levels of early excess mortality in comparison with most other cancer sites. Cumulative five-year survival ratios decreased with advancing age, but over a relatively narrow range from 85.8 to 80.7 per cent.

Less favorable ten-year results for women diagnosed in the regional stage are presented next, also divided into five age categories. The mortality ratios decreased with advancing age and duration, the maximum being 5500 per cent, the minimum, 161 per cent. The EDR's generally increased with advancing age and were quite high, ranging from 108 to 140 per 1000 in the first two-year interval, and from 63 to 84 per 1000 in the third interval. The five-year survival ratios were also less favorable, ranging from 55.5 per cent in the under 45 age group to 45.9 in the 75 up age group.

Ten-year experience for women diagnosed as having metastatic breast cancer, all ages combined, is shown next in Tables 167a-b. Following the usual trend, the prognosis worsened considerably. The mortality ratio decreased with duration from 1950 per cent to 535 per cent. The EDR's were very high ranging from 501 extra deaths per 1000 in the first interval to 125 per 1000 in the third interval. The cumulative five-year survival ratio was only 10.0 per cent.

Data for females obtained 10-20 years after diagnosis in the localized and regional stages are presented in the lower portion of Tables 167a-b. In the localized stage, at durations 10-15 years, the mortality ratio decreased from 425 per cent in the under 45 age group to 103 per cent in the 75 up age group. Persistence of excess mortality in localized breast cancer from 10-20 years after diagnosis was also evident in the EDR's, which were in the range of 16 to 31 per 1000 in patients under age 75, and at 5.6 and 47 per 1000 in the two intervals in women age 75 and up. This experience is based on numbers of observed deaths from 44 to 295, with only one lower figure, 23 deaths in women age 75 up at duration 15-20 years.

Patients with regional extension of their cancer observed 10-20 years after diagnosis had somewhat higher mortality ratios and EDR's. The mortality ratios decreased with age and duration having a maximum of 525 per cent and a minimum of 116 per cent. The EDR's were variable by age, but continued to decrease with duration. Excess deaths fell in the range between 21 and 54 extra deaths per 1000.

CANCER—KIDNEY

Table 160a   Cancer of the Kidney - Observed Data and Comparative Experience by Stage, Sex, Age and Duration

Stage & Sex Age Group	Interval No.	Interval Start-End	Exposure Person-Yrs	Deaths Observed	Deaths Expected*	Mortality Ratio Interval	Mortality Ratio Cumulative	Survival Ratio Interval	Survival Ratio Cumulative	Excess Death Rate
(Yrs)	i	t to t + Δt	E	d	d'	100d/d'	100Q/Q'	100 p_i/p_i'	100 P/P'	1000(d-d')/E
Localized										
M & F										
< 15	1	0- 2 yrs	226.5	52	0.66	7900%	7700%	60.1%	60.1%	227
	2	2- 5	218.0	9	0.117	7700	6900	88.5	53.1	41
	3	5-10	266.0	2	0.096	2100	5700	96.7	51.4	7.2
15-34	1	0- 2	65.0	3	0.101	3000	3000	91.2	91.2	45
	2	2- 5	82.5	3	0.145	2100	2200	90.2	82.3	35
	3	5-10	90.5	3	0.22	1400	1410	88.3	72.7	31
Male										
35-54	1	0- 2 yrs	547.5	56	4.56	1230	1160	82.1	82.1	94
	2	2- 5	636.0	33	6.52	505	650	88.3	72.5	42
	3	5-10	671.5	33	9.37	350	405	81.9	59.4	35
55-64	1	0- 2	536.0	83	12.58	660	615	74.8	74.8	131
	2	2- 5	544.5	53	15.64	340	370	80.6	60.3	69
	3	5-10	511.0	35	19.69	178	225	83.3	50.2	30
65 up	1	0- 2	681.5	168	47.2	355	315	66.8	66.8	177
	2	2- 5	584.0	80	46.3	173	192	82.8	55.3	58
	3	5-10	455.5	70	45.0	155	142	65.3	36.1	55
Female										
35-54	1	0- 2 yrs	329.5	27	1.41	1910	1860	84.9	84.9	78
	2	2- 5	395.0	27	2.01	1350	1340	81.9	69.5	63
	3	5-10	392.5	8	2.64	305	660	93.7	65.1	14
55-64	1	0- 2	300.5	29	3.48	835	795	83.6	83.6	85
	2	2- 5	349.0	28	4.98	560	560	81.6	68.2	66
	3	5-10	348.0	27	6.89	390	370	72.3	49.3	58
65 up	1	0- 2	533.0	126	26.3	480	425	64.8	64.8	187
	2	2- 5	457.0	60	26.9	225	250	78.4	50.8	72
	3	5-10	370.0	38	26.4	144	158	85.2	43.2	31
Regional										
M & F										
All	1	0- 2 yrs	1099.0	393	34.5	1140	880	46.4	46.4	326
	2	2- 5	753.0	117	22.8	515	455	68.0	31.6	125
	3	5-10	576.0	57	19.6	290	255	76.6	24.2	65
Metastatic										
M & F										
All	1	0- 2 yrs	1517.0	1174	50.3	2300	1350	8.8	8.8	741
	2	2- 5	227.5	61	6.61	925	565	46.1	4.1	239
	3	5-10	108.0	21	3.35	630	290	56.6	2.3	163
Localized										
Male										
< 45	4	10-15 yrs	253.0	7	1.44	490		89.3		22
	5	15-20	88.5	4	0.56	720		88.4		39
45-54	4	10-15	216.5	11	5.85	188		85.9		24
	5	15-20	56.0	8	2.10	380		63.4		105
55-64	4	10-15	225.5	15	12.40	121		89.3		12
	5	15-20	69.5	9	5.27	171		71.4		54
65 up	4	10-15	94.0	16	11.43	140		62.8		49
	5	15-20	2.0	2	0.30	665		0.0		850
Female										
< 45	4	10-15 yrs	226.5	3	0.64	465		95.5		10
	5	15-20	95.5	4	0.41	970		85.3		38
45-54	4	10-15	123.0	10	1.81	555		67.7		67
	5	15-20	29.5	5	0.71	700		43.8		145
55-64	4	10-15	198.0	14	6.60	210		84.8		37
	5	15-20	67.5	7	3.55	197		74.4		51
65 up	4	10-15	72.0	9	6.13	147		94.8		40
	5	15-20	18.5	2	2.61	77		111.4		-33

*Basis of expected mortality: Concurrent U.S. White Population Rates

CANCER—KIDNEY

Table 160b   Cancer of the Kidney - Derived Mortality and Survival Data

Stage & Sex Age Group	Interval		Observed				Expected*			
	No.	Start-End	Survival Rate			Ave. Ann. Mort. Rate	Survival Rate			Ave. Ann. Mort. Rate
			Cumulative	Interval	Ave. Ann.		Cumulative	Interval	Ave. Ann.	
(Yrs)	i	t to t + Δ t	P	p_i	$\check{p}$	$\check{q}$	P'	p_i'	$\check{p}'$	$\check{q}'$
Localized M & F										
< 15	1	0- 2 yrs	.5977	.5977	.7731	.2269	.9948	.9948	.9974	.0026
	2	2- 5	.5278	.8831	.9594	.0406	.9932	.9984	.9995	.00053
	3	5-10	.5096	.9655	.9930	.0070	.9914	.9982	.9996	.00036
15-34	1	0- 2	.9091	.9091	.9535	.0465	.9970	.9970	.9985	.00150
	2	2- 5	.8161	.8977	.9647	.0353	.9917	.9947	.9982	.00177
	3	5-10	.7119	.8723	.9730	.0270	.9796	.9878	.9975	.0025
Male 35-54	1	0- 2 yrs	.8074	.8074	.8986	.1014	.9834	.9834	.9917	.0083
	2	2- 5	.6910	.8558	.9494	.0506	.9526	.9687	.9895	.0105
	3	5-10	.5245	.7590	.9463	.0537	.8829	.9268	.9849	.0151
55-64	1	0- 2	.7132	.7132	.8445	.1555	.9533	.9533	.9764	.0236
	2	2- 5	.5263	.7379	.9036	.0964	.8727	.9155	.9710	.0290
	3	5-10	.3577	.6797	.9257	.0743	.7122	.8161	.9602	.0398
65 up	1	0- 2	.5777	.5777	.7601	.2399	.8651	.8651	.9301	.0699
	2	2- 5	.3721	.6441	.8636	.1364	.6731	.7781	.9198	.0802
	3	5-10	.1429	.3840	.8258	.1742	.3956	.5877	.8991	.1009
Female 35-54	1	0- 2 yrs	.8417	.8417	.9174	.0826	.9915	.9915	.9957	.0043
	2	2- 5	.6782	.8058	.9306	.0694	.9760	.9844	.9948	.0052
	3	5-10	.6129	.9037	.9800	.0200	.9412	.9643	.9928	.0072
55-64	1	0- 2	.8167	.8167	.9037	.0963	.9769	.9769	.9884	.0116
	2	2- 5	.6382	.7814	.9211	.0789	.9355	.9576	.9857	.0143
	3	5-10	.4159	.6517	.9179	.0821	.8430	.9011	.9794	.0206
65 up	1	0- 2	.5840	.5840	.7642	.2358	.9019	.9019	.9497	.0503
	2	2- 5	.3820	.6541	.8681	.1319	.7522	.8340	.9413	.0587
	3	5-10	.2191	.5736	.8948	.1052	.5067	.6736	.9240	.0760
Regional M & F All	1	0- 2 yrs	.4345	.4345	.6592	.3408	.9358	.9358	.9674	.0326
	2	2- 5	.2645	.6087	.8475	.1525	.8376	.8951	.9637	.0363
	3	5-10	.1630	.6163	.9077	.0923	.6739	.8046	.9574	.0426
Metastatic M & F All	1	0- 2 yrs	.0819	.0819	.2862	.7138	.9322	.9322	.9655	.0345
	2	2- 5	.0336	.4103	.7431	.2569	.8290	.8893	.9616	.0384
	3	5-10	.0151	.4494	.8522	.1478	.6584	.7942	.9550	.0450
Localized Male < 45	4	10-15 yrs		.8669	.9718	.0282		.9712	.9942	.0058
	5	15-20		.8571	.9696	.0304		.9691	.9937	.0063
45-54	4	10-15		.7459	.9431	.0569		.8687	.9722	.0278
	5	15-20		.5179	.8767	.1233		.8168	.9603	.0397
55-64	4	10-15		.6676	.9224	.0776		.7474	.9434	.0566
	5	15-20		.4729	.8609	.1391		.6624	.9209	.0791
65 up	4	10-15		.3207	.7966	.2034		.5103	.8741	.1259
	5	15-20		.0000	.0000	1.0000		.8500	.9680	.0320
Female < 45	4	10-15 yrs		.9414	.9880	.0120		.9855	.9971	.0029
	5	15-20		.8339	.9643	.0357		.9779	.9955	.0045
45-54	4	10-15		.6262	.9106	.0894		.9247	.9845	.0155
	5	15-20		.3839	.8257	.1743		.8759	.9738	.0262
55-64	4	10-15		.7090	.9335	.0665		.8361	.9648	.0352
	5	15-20		.5630	.8915	.1085		.7568	.9458	.0542
65 up	4	10-15		.5926	.9006	.0994		.6254	.9104	.0896
	5	15-20		.5186	.8769	.1231		.4656	.8582	.1418

*Basis of expected mortality: Concurrent U.S. White Population Rates

CANCER—BLADDER

Table 161a Cancer of the Bladder - Observed Data and Comparative Experience by Stage, Sex, Age and Duration

Stage & Sex Age Group	Interval No.	Interval Start-End	Exposure Person-Yrs	Deaths Observed	Deaths Expected*	Mortality Ratio Interval	Mortality Ratio Cumulative	Survival Ratio Interval	Survival Ratio Cumulative	Excess Death Rate
(Yrs)	i	t to t + Δt	E	d	d'	100 d/d'	100 Q/Q'	100 p_i/p_i'	100 P/P'	1000(d-d')/E
Localized										
Male										
<45	1	0- 2 yrs	593.0	15	1.90	790%	770%	95.6%	95.6%	22
	2	2- 5	805.0	16	3.19	500	575	95.3	91.1	16
	3	5-10	887.0	16	4.92	325	375	94.7	86.3	12
45-54	1	0- 2	1130.5	74	11.80	625	605	89.2	89.2	55
	2	2- 5	1432.5	64	18.90	340	405	90.8	81.0	31
	3	5-10	1579.5	48	28.8	167	240	94.6	76.7	12
55-64	1	0- 2	2569.0	304	62.1	490	465	81.7	81.7	94
	2	2- 5	2847.5	207	83.8	245	290	87.7	71.7	43
	3	5-10	2804.0	187	110.0	170	189	87.8	62.9	27
Female										
<45	1	0- 2 yrs	242.0	11	0.41	2700	2600	91.4	91.4	44
	2	2- 5	316.0	1	0.61	164	1060	99.6	91.1	1.2
	3	5-10	372.0	2	1.04	193	555	98.1	89.4	2.6
45-54	1	0- 2	399.0	31	2.03	1530	1460	86.1	86.1	73
	2	2- 5	501.5	16	3.10	515	800	92.5	79.7	26
	3	5-10	555.5	7	4.62	152	390	98.6	78.6	4.3
55-64	1	0- 2	670.0	62	7.82	795	755	84.4	84.4	81
	2	2- 5	803.0	39	11.50	340	440	90.3	76.2	34
	3	5-10	869.0	40	17.40	230	285	85.4	65.1	26
M & F										
65-74	1	0- 2 yrs	4741.5	836	215.0	390	355	74.9	74.9	131
	2	2- 5	4721.5	495	253.0	196	220	85.2	63.8	51
	3	5-10	3902.0	435	271.0	160	154	80.2	51.2	42
75 up	1	0- 2	3381.0	998	375.0	265	230	64.8	64.8	184
	2	2- 5	2556.0	450	322.0	140	148	85.0	55.1	50
	3	5-10	1587.0	311	248.0	125	115	82.0	45.2	39
Regional										
M & F										
All	1	0- 2 yrs	2053.0	1048	111.0	945	675	29.7	29.7	456
	2	2- 5	899.0	151	46.8	325	325	71.6	21.3	116
	3	5-10	746.5	74	40.6	182	189	86.6	18.4	45
Metastatic										
M & F										
All	1	0- 2 yrs	734.0	595	42.0	1420	805	8.4	8.4	753
	2	2- 5	106.0	30	6.09	490	355	45.6	3.9	226
	3	5-10	58.0	7	3.42	205	197	84.0	3.2	62
Localized										
Male										
<45	4	10-15 yrs	636.5	7	5.82	120		99.0		1.8
	5	15-20	219.0	1	3.05	33		103.7		-9.4
45-54	4	10-15	1033.5	46	27.8	166		91.3		18
	5	15-20	353.5	16	13.70	117		96.5		6.5
55-64	4	10-15	1495.5	122	80.7	151		86.8		28
	5	15-20	387.0	37	28.9	128		87.3		21
65 up	4	10-15	1056.0	177	133.0	133		78.1		42
	5	15-20	148.5	40	24.7	162		50.4		103
Female										
<45	4	10-15 yrs	359.5	4	1.59	251		97.1		6.7
	5	15-20	127.0	0	0.84	0		103.5		-6.6
45-54	4	10-15	408.5	16	5.49	290		88.1		26
	5	15-20	171.0	5	3.65	137		94.3		7.9
55-64	4	10-15	553.0	35	18.90	185		86.0		29
	5	15-20	128.0	11	6.86	160		81.3		32
65 up	4	10-15	497.5	58	58.7	99		102.9		-1.4
	5	15-20	110.0	20	17.50	114		66.2		23

* Basis of expected mortality: Concurrent U.S. White Population Rates

CANCER—BLADDER

Table 161b   Cancer of the Bladder - Derived Mortality and Survival Data

Stage & Sex Age Group	Interval No.	Interval Start-End	Observed Survival Rate Cumulative	Observed Survival Rate Interval	Observed Survival Rate Ave. Ann.	Observed Ave. Ann. Mort. Rate	Expected* Survival Rate Cumulative	Expected* Survival Rate Interval	Expected* Survival Rate Ave. Ann.	Expected* Ave. Ann. Mort. Rate
(Yrs)	i	t to t + Δ t	P	p_i	$\check{p}$	$\check{q}$	P'	p_i'	$\check{p}'$	$\check{q}'$
Localized Male										
<45	1	0- 2 yrs	.9500	.9500	.9747	.0253	.9935	.9935	.9967	.0033
	2	2- 5	.8945	.9416	.9801	.0199	.9816	.9880	.9960	.0040
	3	5-10	.8224	.9194	.9833	.0167	.9527	.9706	.9940	.0060
45-54	1	0- 2	.8736	.8736	.9347	.0653	.9791	.9791	.9895	.0105
	2	2- 5	.7623	.8726	.9556	.0444	.9410	.9611	.9869	.0131
	3	5-10	.6563	.8609	.9705	.0295	.8561	.9098	.9813	.0187
55-64	1	0- 2	.7780	.7780	.8820	.1180	.9520	.9520	.9757	.0243
	2	2- 5	.6230	.8008	.9286	.0714	.8694	.9132	.9702	.0298
	3	5-10	.4440	.7127	.9345	.0655	.7059	.8119	.9592	.0408
Female										
<45	1	0- 2 yrs	.9113	.9113	.9546	.0454	.9966	.9966	.9983	.0017
	2	2- 5	.9024	.9902	.9967	.0033	.9908	.9942	.9981	.0019
	3	5-10	.8732	.9676	.9934	.0066	.9771	.9862	.9972	.0028
45-54	1	0- 2	.8525	.8525	.9233	.0767	.9899	.9899	.9949	.0051
	2	2- 5	.7741	.9080	.9683	.0317	.9717	.9816	.9938	.0062
	3	5-10	.7314	.9448	.9887	.0113	.9310	.9581	.9915	.0085
55-64	1	0- 2	.8244	.8244	.9080	.0920	.9767	.9767	.9883	.0117
	2	2- 5	.7124	.8641	.9525	.0475	.9347	.9570	.9855	.0145
	3	5-10	.5471	.7680	.9486	.0514	.8408	.8995	.9790	.0210
M & F										
65-74	1	0- 2 yrs	.6822	.6822	.8260	.1740	.9109	.9109	.9544	.0456
	2	2- 5	.4910	.7197	.8962	.1038	.7696	.8449	.9454	.0546
	3	5-10	.2690	.5479	.8866	.1134	:5258	.6832	.9266	.0734
75 up	1	0- 2	.5100	.5100	.7141	.2859	.7865	.7865	.8868	.1132
	2	2- 5	.2856	.5600	.8243	.1757	.5181	.6587	.8701	.1299
	3	5-10	.0949	.3323	.8022	.1978	.2099	.4051	.8347	.1653
Regional M & F										
All	1	0- 2 yrs	.2650	.2650	.5148	.4852	.8908	.8908	.9438	.0562
	2	2- 5	.1574	.5940	.8406	.1594	.7390	.8296	.9396	.0604
	3	5-10	.0961	.6105	.9060	.0940	.5209	.7049	.9325	.0675
Metastatic M & F										
All	1	0- 2 yrs	.0747	.0747	.2733	.7267	.8854	.8854	.9410	.0590
	2	2- 5	.0280	.3748	.7210	.2790	.7272	.8213	.9365	.0635
	3	5-10	.0162	.5786	.8963	.1037	.5012	.6892	.9283	.0717
Localized Male										
<45	4	10-15 yrs		.9446	.9887	.0113		.9537	.9906	.0094
	5	15-20		.9643	.9928	.0072		.9301	.9856	.0144
45-54	4	10-15		.7935	.9548	.0452		.8694	.9724	.0276
	5	15-20		.7876	.9534	.0466		.8159	.9601	.0399
55-64	4	10-15		.6523	.9181	.0819		.7512	.9444	.0556
	5	15-20		.5811	.8971	.1029		.6658	.9219	.0781
65 up	4	10-15		.3879	.8275	.1725		.4966	.8694	.1306
	5	15-20		.1925	.7193	.2807		.3823	.8251	.1749
Female										
<45	4	10-15 yrs		.9496	.9897	.0103		.9776	.9955	.0045
	5	15-20		1.0000	1.0000	.0000		.9661	.9931	.0069
45-54	4	10-15		.8215	.9614	.0386		.9328	.9862	.0138
	5	15-20		.8426	.9663	.0337		.8933	.9777	.0223
55-64	4	10-15		.7171	.9357	.0643		.8342	.9644	.0356
	5	15-20		.6065	.9048	.0952		.7457	.9430	.0570
65 up	4	10-15		.5307	.8810	.1190		.5156	.8759	.1241
	5	15-20		.2749	.7724	.2276		.4154	.8389	.1611

* Basis of expected mortality: Concurrent U.S. White Population Rates

CANCER—PROSTATE

Table 162a   Cancer of the Prostate - Observed Data and Comparative Experience by Stage, Age and Duration

Stage Age Group	Interval No.	Interval Start-End	Exposure Person-Yrs	Deaths Observed	Deaths Expected*	Mortality Ratio Interval	Mortality Ratio Cumulative	Survival Ratio Interval	Survival Ratio Cumulative	Excess Death Rate
(Yrs)	i	t to t + Δ t	E	d	d′	100 d/d′	100 Q/Q′	100 p_i/p_i′	100 P/P′	1000(d-d′)/E
Localized Male										
< 55	1	0- 2 yrs	379.5	29	4.27	680%	655%	87.3%	87.3%	65
	2	2- 5	459.0	30	6.44	465	480	85.3	74.4	51
	3	5-10	443.5	20	8.54	235	295	87.0	64.7	26
55-64	1	0- 2	2374.5	187	60.9	305	295	89.5	89.5	53
	2	2- 5	2830.0	261	88.7	295	265	82.4	73.8	61
	3	5-10	2557.5	222	107.1	205	193	79.4	58.6	45
65-74	1	0- 2	5729.0	763	297.0	255	245	83.8	83.8	81
	2	2- 5	6023.5	828	371.0	225	200	77.5	64.9	76
	3	5-10	4405.5	626	344.8	182	150	71.5	46.4	64
75 up	1	0- 2	5702.0	1401	689.0	205	184	74.9	74.9	125
	2	2- 5	4475.5	1006	607.0	166	143	73.3	54.9	89
	3	5-10	2173.5	542	355.0	153	115	59.1	32.5	86
Regional Male										
< 55	1	0- 2 yrs	228.5	27	2.41	1120	1060	79.3	79.3	108
	2	2- 5	221.0	41	2.97	1380	930	58.3	46.2	172
	3	5-10	172.0	16	3.29	485	485	68.3	31.6	74
55-64	1	0- 2	766.5	89	18.73	475	450	82.2	82.2	92
	2	2- 5	853.5	88	25.6	345	330	84.7	65.2	73
	3	5-10	702.5	88	27.6	320	235	65.5	42.7	86
65-74	1	0- 2	1345.0	239	68.1	350	325	75.1	75.1	127
	2	2- 5	1247.5	218	74.5	295	245	67.7	50.8	115
	3	5-10	841.5	130	63.7	205	164	65.4	33.2	79
75 up	1	0- 2	1111.0	369	131.7	280	240	59.1	59.1	214
	2	2- 5	704.0	181	92.2	196	159	64.6	38.2	126
	3	5-10	313.0	88	49.5	178	119	47.9	18.3	123
Metastatic Male										
< 65	1	0- 2 yrs	930.0	289	20.6	1410	1200	49.6	49.6	289
	2	2- 5	562.0	159	15.37	1030	670	41.8	20.8	256
	3	5-10	275.0	54	10.15	530	335	38.7	8.0	159
65 up	1	0- 2	3415.0	1522	283.7	535	425	38.3	38.3	363
	2	2- 5	1491.5	506	135.3	375	245	39.5	15.1	249
	3	5-10	550.0	150	60.9	245	149	39.6	6.0	162
Localized Male										
< 55	4	10-15 yrs	135.0	13	3.79	345		64.6		68
	5	15-20	22.5	3	0.96	315		69.7		91
55-64	4	10-15	840.5	97	48.5	200		74.5		58
	5	15-20	187.0	26	15.43	169		66.0		57
65-74	4	10-15	1163.5	205	134.2	153		74.9		61
	5	15-20	179.0	40	30.0	133		79.9		56
75 up	4	10-15	286.0	85	60.5	141		71.6		86
	5	15-20	30.0	8	8.46	95		76.1		-15

*Basis of expected mortality: Concurrent U.S. White Population Rates

CANCER—PROSTATE

Table 162b   Cancer of the Prostate - Derived Mortality and Survival Data

Stage Age Group	Interval		Observed				Expected*			
			Survival Rate			Ave. Ann.	Survival Rate			Ave. Ann.
	No.	Start-End	Cumulative	Interval	Ave. Ann.	Mort. Rate	Cumulative	Interval	Ave. Ann.	Mort. Rate
(Yrs)	i	t to t + Δt	P	p_i	$\check{p}$	$\check{q}$	P'	p_i'	$\check{p}'$	$\check{q}'$
Localized Male										
< 55	1	0- 2 yrs	.8534	.8534	.9238	.0762	.9776	.9776	.9887	.0113
	2	2- 5	.6973	.8171	.9349	.0651	.9368	.9583	.9859	.0141
	3	5-10	.5484	.7865	.9531	.0469	.8471	.9042	.9801	.0199
55-64	1	0- 2	.8498	.8498	.9218	.0782	.9493	.9493	.9743	.0257
	2	2- 5	.6363	.7488	.9081	.0919	.8623	.9084	.9685	.0315
	3	5-10	.4053	.6370	.9138	.0862	.6919	.8024	.9569	.0431
65-74	1	0- 2	.7528	.7528	.8676	.1324	.8988	.8988	.9481	.0519
	2	2- 5	.4813	.6393	.8615	.1385	.7413	.8248	.9378	.0622
	3	5-10	.2233	.4640	.8576	.1424	.4810	.6489	.9171	.0829
75 up	1	0- 2	.5764	.5764	.7592	.2408	.7699	.7699	.8774	.1226
	2	2- 5	.2686	.4660	.7753	.2247	.4892	.6354	.8597	.1403
	3	5-10	.0601	.2238	.7413	.2587	.1851	.3784	.8234	.1766
Regional Male										
< 55	1	0- 2 yrs	.7764	.7764	.8811	.1189	.9790	.9790	.9894	.0106
	2	2- 5	.4341	.5591	.8238	.1762	.9393	.9594	.9863	.0137
	3	5-10	.2684	.6183	.9083	.0917	.8498	.9047	.9802	.0198
55-64	1	0- 2	.7820	.7820	.8843	.1157	.9513	.9513	.9753	.0247
	2	2- 5	5653	.7729	.9177	.0823	.8676	.9120	.9698	.0302
	3	5-10	.2996	.5300	.8808	.1192	.7023	.8095	.9586	.0414
65-74	1	0- 2	.6761	.6761	.8223	.1777	.9007	.9007	.9491	.0509
	2	2- 5	.3789	.5604	.8245	.1755	.7458	.8280	.9390	.0610
	3	5-10	.1623	.4283	.8440	.1560	.4883	.6547	.9188	.0812
75 up	1	0- 2	.4557	.4557	.6751	.3249	.7716	.7716	.8784	.1216
	2	2- 5	.1872	.4108	.7434	.2566	.4904	.6356	.8598	.1402
	3	5-10	.0339	.1811	.7105	.2895	.1853	.3779	.8231	.1769
Metastatic Male										
< 65	1	0- 2 yrs	.4742	.4742	.6886	.3114	.9560	.9560	.9778	.0222
	2	2- 5	.1823	.3844	.7271	.2729	.8782	.9186	.9721	.0279
	3	5-10	.0579	.3176	.7950	.2050	.7205	.8204	.9612	.0388
65 up	1	0- 2	.3218	.3218	.5673	.4327	.8413	.8413	.9172	.0828
	2	2- 5	.0951	.2955	.6661	.3339	.6288	.7474	.9075	.0925
	3	5-10	.0205	.2156	.7357	.2643	.3424	.5445	.8855	.1145
Localized Male										
< 55	4	10-15 yrs		.5570	.8896	.1104		.8621	.9708	.0292
	5	15-20		.5555	.8891	.1109		.7966	.9555	.0445
55-64	4	10-15		.5460	.8860	.1140		.7332	.9398	.0602
	5	15-20		.4219	.8415	.1585		.6390	.9143	.0857
65-74	4	10-15		.3918	.8291	.1709		.5234	.8786	.1214
	5	15-20		.3011	.7866	.2134		.3767	.8226	.1774
75 up	4	10-15		.2024	.7265	.2735		.2825	.7766	.2234
	5	15-20		.1349	.6699	.3301		.1773	.7075	.2925

*Basis of expected mortality: Concurrent U.S. White Population Rates

CANCER—PENIS
CANCER—TESTIS

Table 163a   Cancer of the Penis and Testis - Observed Data and Comparative Experience by Stage, Age and Duration

Stage	Interval		Exposure	Deaths		Mortality Ratio		Survival Ratio		Excess
Age Group	No.	Start-End	Person-Yrs	Observed	Expected*	Interval	Cumulative	Interval	Cumulative	Death Rate
(Yrs)	i	t to t + Δ t	E	d	d'	100 d/d'	100 Q/Q'	100 p_i/p_i'	100 P/P'	1000(d-d')/E
Site: Penis										
Localized										
Male										
<45	1	0- 2 yrs	34.5	0	0.119	0%	0%	100.7%	100.7%	‾3.4
	2	2- 5	41.5	1	0.171	585	360	94.1	94.7	20
	3	5-10	54.5	1	0.34	295	285	95.0	90.0	12
45-64	1	0- 2	230.5	19	4.46	425	410	87.7	87.7	63
	2	2- 5	282.0	17	6.68	255	285	89.2	78.2	37
	3	5-10	298.5	15	9.64	156	193	89.2	69.8	18
65-74	1	0- 2	125.5	12	6.32	190	182	91.0	91.0	45
	2	2- 5	151.5	8	9.15	87	120	102.6	93.4	−7.6
	3	5-10	131.5	19	10.12	188	135	68.6	64.1	68
75 up	1	0- 2	112.5	32	14.13	225	205	67.2	67.2	159
	2	2- 5	80.5	15	10.80	139	140	84.8	57.0	52
	3	5-10	43.0	9	6.97	129	108	113.9	64.9	47
All	1	0- 2	503.0	63	25.0	250	235	85.2	85.2	76
	2	2- 5	555.5	41	26.8	153	165	93.7	79.8	26
	3	5-10	527.5	44	27.2	162	139	87.7	70.1	32
Regional										
Male										
All	1	0- 2 yrs	139.0	38	5.90	645	510	60.1	60.1	231
	2	2- 5	110.0	15	4.45	335	300	76.7	46.1	96
	3	5-10	93.5	7	4.59	153	189	93.3	43.0	26
Metastatic										
Male										
All	1	0- 2 yrs	17.0	12	0.94	1270	795	16.0	16.0	651
	2	2- 5	5.0	1	0.38	260	365	59.7	9.6	123
	3	5-10	2.0	1	0.25	395	295	0.0	0.0	373
Site: Testis										
Localized										
Male										
<25	1	0- 2 yrs	166.5	11	0.40	2700%	2700%	87.4%	87.4%	64
	2	2- 5	205.0	4	0.27	1460	2000	94.8	82.9	18
	3	5-10	217.5	1	0.27	375	1310	98.3	81.4	3.4
25-34	1	0- 2	328.5	21	0.56	3800	3700	87.9	87.9	62
	2	2- 5	410.0	9	0.80	1120	1920	94.3	82.9	20
	3	5-10	489.5	0	1.34	0	790	101.4	84.0	−2.7
35-54	1	0- 2	553.5	25	2.86	875	860	92.1	92.1	40
	2	2- 5	725.0	18	4.77	375	520	94.7	87.2	18
	3	5-10	855.5	17	7.92	215	315	94.9	82.8	11
55 up	1	0- 2	121.0	20	4.83	415	350	77.4	77.4	125
	2	2- 5	130.5	9	5.27	171	200	94.4	73.1	29
	3	5-10	145.5	12	7.20	167	148	89.2	65.2	33
All	1	0- 2	1169.5	77	8.62	895	810	88.7	88.7	58
	2	2- 5	1470.5	40	11.07	360	470	94.7	84.0	20
	3	5-10	1708.0	30	16.54	181	290	96.6	81.1	7.9
Regional										
Male										
All	1	0- 2 yrs	278.5	55	2.30	2400	1830	66.6	66.6	189
	2	2- 5	289.5	9	1.82	495	840	93.9	62.5	25
	3	5-10	315.5	5	2.25	225	460	97.2	60.7	8.7
Metastatic										
Male										
All	1	0- 2 yrs	268.5	171	1.64	10400	6100	16.1	16.1	631
	2	2- 5	85.5	6	0.38	1560	2400	83.1	13.4	66
	3	5-10	75.5	2	0.51	390	1140	95.2	12.7	20

* Basis of expected mortality: Concurrent U.S. White Population Rates

CANCER—PENIS
CANCER—TESTIS

Table 163b   Cancer of the Penis and Testis - Derived Mortality and Survival Data

			Observed				Expected*			
Stage	Interval		Survival Rate			Ave. Ann.	Survival Rate			Ave. Ann.
Age Group	No.	Start-End	Cumulative	Interval	Ave. Ann.	Mort. Rate	Cumulative	Interval	Ave. Ann.	Mort. Rate
(Yrs)	i	t to t + Δt	P	p_i	$\check{p}$	$\check{q}$	P'	p_i'	$\check{p}'$	$\check{q}'$
Site: Penis										
Localized										
Male										
<45	1	0- 2 yrs	1.0000	1.0000	1.0000	.0000	.9932	.9932	.9966	.0034
	2	2- 5	.9286	.9286	.9756	.0244	.9803	.9870	.9956	.0044
	3	5-10	.8543	.9200	.9835	.0165	.9489	.9680	.9935	.0065
45-64	1	0- 2	.8433	.8433	.9183	.0817	.9617	.9617	.9807	.0193
	2	2- 5	.6999	.8300	.9398	.0602	.8946	.9302	.9762	.0238
	3	5-10	.5275	.7537	.9450	.0550	.7555	.8445	.9668	.0332
65-74	1	0- 2	.8204	.8204	.9058	.0942	.9015	.9015	.9495	.0505
	2	2- 5	.6983	.8512	.9477	.0523	.7478	.8295	.9396	.0604
	3	5-10	.3147	.4507	.8527	.1473	.4912	.6569	.9194	.0806
75 up	1	0- 2	.5130	.5130	.7162	.2838	.7631	.7631	.8736	.1264
	2	2- 5	.2757	.5374	.8130	.1870	.4838	.6340	.8591	.1409
	3	5-10	.1230	.4461	.8509	.1491	.1895	.3917	.8291	.1709
All	1	0- 2	.7677	.7677	.8762	.1238	.9008	.9008	.9491	.0509
	2	2- 5	.6105	.7952	.9265	.0735	.7646	.8488	.9468	.0532
	3	5-10	.3975	.6511	.9178	.0822	.5674	.7421	.9421	.0579
Regional										
Male										
All	1	0- 2 yrs	.5476	.5476	.7400	.2600	.9112	.9112	.9546	.0454
	2	2- 5	.3636	.6640	.8724	.1276	.7888	.8657	.9531	.0469
	3	5-10	.2620	.7206	.9366	.0634	.6093	.7724	.9497	.0503
Metastatic										
Male										
All	1	0- 2 yrs	.1429	.1429	.3780	.6220	.8921	.8921	.9445	.0555
	2	2- 5	.0714	.4997	.7935	.2065	.7468	.8371	.9425	.0575
	3	5-10	.0000	.0000	.0000	1.0000	.6598	.8835	.9399	.0601
Site: Testis										
Localized										
Male										
<25	1	0- 2 yrs	.8700	.8700	.9327	.0673	.9952	.9952	.9976	.0024
	2	2- 5	.8214	.9441	.9810	.0190	.9912	.9960	.9987	.0013
	3	5-10	.8019	.9763	.9952	.0048	.9849	.9936	.9987	.0013
25-34	1	0- 2	.8758	.8758	.9358	.0642	.9966	.9966	.9983	.0017
	2	2- 5	.8212	.9377	.9788	.0212	.9907	.9941	.9980	.0020
	3	5-10	.8212	1.0000	1.0000	.0000	.9773	.9865	.9973	.0027
35-54	1	0- 2	.9112	.9112	.9546	.0454	.9897	.9897	.9948	.0052
	2	2- 5	.8461	.9286	.9756	.0244	.9703	.9804	.9934	.0066
	3	5-10	.7655	.9047	.9802	.0198	.9250	.9533	.9905	.0095
55 up	1	0- 2	.7101	.7101	.8427	.1573	.9177	.9177	.9580	.0420
	2	2- 5	.5778	.8137	.9336	.0664	.7907	.8616	.9516	.0484
	3	5-10	.3768	.6521	.9180	.0820	.5783	.7314	.9394	.0606
All	1	0- 2	.8727	.8727	.9342	.0658	.9843	.9843	.9921	.0079
	2	2- 5	.8050	.9224	.9734	.0266	.9587	.9740	.9913	.0087
	3	5-10	.7371	.9157	.9825	.0175	.9089	.9481	.9894	.0106
Regional										
Male										
All	1	0- 2 yrs	.6529	.6529	.8080	.1920	.9810	.9810	.9905	.0095
	2	2- 5	.5947	.9109	.9694	.0306	.9518	.9702	.9900	.0100
	3	5-10	.5476	.9208	.9836	.0164	.9014	.9470	.9892	.0108
Metastatic										
Male										
All	1	0- 2 yrs	.1585	.1585	.3981	.6019	.9863	.9863	.9931	.0069
	2	2- 5	.1287	.8120	.9329	.0671	.9640	.9774	.9924	.0076
	3	5-10	.1172	.9106	.9814	.0186	.9225	.9570	.9912	.0088

* Basis of expected mortality: Concurrent U.S. White Population Rates

CANCER—CERVIX UTERI

Table 164a   Cancer of the Cervix Uteri - Observed Data and Comparative Experience by Stage, Age and Duration

Stage Age Group	No.	Interval Start-End	Exposure Person-Yrs	Deaths Observed	Expected*	Mortality Ratio Interval	Cumulative	Survival Ratio Interval	Cumulative	Excess Death Rate
(Yrs)	i	t to t + Δt	E	d	d'	100d/d'	100Q/Q'	100p_i/p_i'	100P/P'	1000(d-d')/E
Localized Female										
< 35	1	0- 2 yrs	1324.0	71	1.26	5700%	5500%	89.7%	89.7%	53
	2	2- 5	1693.5	44	1.92	2300	3300	92.8	83.2	25
	3	5-10	2057.0	17	3.26	520	1550	96.5	80.3	6.7
35-44	1	0- 2	2934.0	153	5.86	2600	2500	90.1	90.1	50
	2	2- 5	3804.0	115	9.61	1200	1540	92.0	82.9	28
	3	5-10	4473.5	69	15.86	435	800	94.8	78.6	12
45-54	1	0- 2	2532.5	155	12.02	1290	1260	88.9	88.9	56
	2	2- 5	3177.5	140	18.36	765	865	89.1	79.2	38
	3	5-10	3637.0	80	28.6	280	475	93.5	74.0	14
55-64	1	0- 2	1980.0	147	21.5	685	665	87.5	87.5	63
	2	2- 5	2410.5	131	32.3	405	455	88.2	77.2	41
	3	5-10	2627.0	107	49.4	215	275	89.8	69.3	22
65 up	1	0- 2	1725.5	227	74.1	305	285	82.7	82.7	89
	2	2- 5	1861.5	200	88.6	225	210	83.4	68.9	60
	3	5-10	1636.0	146	97.6	150	150	87.0	59.9	30
Regional Female										
< 45	1	0- 2 yrs	1622.0	349	2.88	12100	11000	61.6	61.6	213
	2	2- 5	1457.5	108	3.19	3400	5000	80.6	49.6	72
	3	5-10	1584.5	38	4.78	795	2200	90.3	44.8	21
45-54	1	0- 2	1546.5	352	7.39	4800	4300	59.8	59.8	223
	2	2- 5	1332.5	141	7.94	1780	2100	73.3	43.8	100
	3	5-10	1282.0	61	10.30	590	1010	82.4	36.1	40
55-64	1	0- 2	1481.0	320	16.50	1940	1730	62.7	62.7	205
	2	2- 5	1314.5	152	18.25	835	920	72.7	45.6	102
	3	5-10	1260.0	74	24.6	300	445	83.0	37.8	39
65 up	1	0- 2	1650.0	468	81.9	570	480	57.4	57.4	234
	2	2- 5	1263.0	186	66.7	280	270	75.0	43.1	94
	3	5-10	1010.5	107	68.8	156	167	84.1	36.2	38
Metastatic Female										
All	1	0- 2 yrs	1608.0	973	36.3	2700	1680	20.4	20.4	583
	2	2- 5	539.5	105	10.67	985	740	59.0	12.0	175
	3	5-10	445.0	37	9.30	400	380	76.5	9.2	62
Localized Female										
< 45	4	10-15 yrs	5119.0	79	23.8	330		94.9		11
	5	15-20	2014.0	38	13.9	275		93.4		12
45-54	4	10-15	3504.5	89	44.7	199		94.1		13
	5	15-20	1513.0	51	29.9	170		93.9		14
55-64	4	10-15	2068.5	112	65.6	171		88.4		22
	5	15-20	719.0	46	35.9	128		87.5		14
65 up	4	10-15	851.5	84	76.0	111		96.6		9.4
	5	15-20	180.0	32	23.5	136		64.8		47
Regional Female										
< 45	4	10-15 yrs	1795.0	24	8.45	285		95.6		8.7
	5	15-20	771.5	17	5.33	320		91.2		15
45-54	4	10-15	1375.0	47	17.69	265		89.6		21
	5	15-20	563.0	22	11.02	200		91.3		20
55-64	4	10-15	1006.0	42	33.0	127		95.4		8.9
	5	15-20	356.0	23	18.75	123		88.4		12
65 up	4	10-15	435.0	59	41.2	143		79.9		41
	5	15-20	93.0	19	13.07	145		62.1		64

*Basis of expected mortality: Concurrent U.S. White Population Rates

CANCER—CERVIX UTERI

Table 164b Cancer of the Cervix Uteri - Derived Mortality and Survival Data

Stage Age Group	Interval		Observed				Expected*			
	No.	Start-End	Survival Rate			Ave. Ann. Mort. Rate	Survival Rate			Ave. Ann. Mort. Rate
			Cumulative	Interval	Ave. Ann.		Cumulative	Interval	Ave. Ann.	
(Yrs)	i	t to $t + \Delta t$	P	p_i	$\breve{p}$	$\breve{q}$	P'	p_i'	$\breve{p}'$	$\breve{q}'$
Localized Female										
< 35	1	0- 2 yrs	.8949	.8949	.9460	.0540	.9981	.9981	.9990	.00095
	2	2- 5	.8276	.9248	.9743	.0257	.9947	.9966	.9989	.00111
	3	5-10	.7923	.9573	.9913	.0087	.9866	.9919	.9984	.00163
35-44	1	0- 2	.8978	.8978	.9475	.0525	.9959	.9959	.9979	.0021
	2	2- 5	.8195	.9128	.9700	.0300	.9883	.9924	.9975	.0025
	3	5-10	.7632	.9313	.9859	.0141	.9704	.9819	.9964	.0036
45-54	1	0- 2	.8805	.8805	.9383	.0617	.9905	.9905	.9952	.0048
	2	2- 5	.7705	.8751	.9565	.0435	.9734	.9827	.9942	.0058
	3	5-10	.6922	.8984	.9788	.0212	.9352	.9608	.9920	.0080
55-64	1	0- 2	.8557	.8557	.9250	.0750	.9783	.9783	.9891	.0109
	2	2- 5	.7249	.8471	.9462	.0538	.9394	.9602	.9866	.0134
	3	5-10	.5907	.8149	.9599	.0401	.8520	.9070	.9807	.0193
65 up	1	0- 2	.7556	.7556	.8693	.1307	.9142	.9142	.9561	.0439
	2	2- 5	.5384	.7125	.8932	.1068	.7815	.8548	.9490	.0510
	3	5-10	.3319	.6165	.9078	.0922	.5539	.7088	.9335	.0665
Regional Female										
< 45	1	0- 2 yrs	.6136	.6136	.7833	.2167	.9965	.9965	.9982	.00175
	2	2- 5	.4912	.8005	.9285	.0715	.9899	.9934	.9978	.0022
	3	5-10	.4369	.8895	.9769	.0231	.9747	.9846	.9969	.0031
45-54	1	0- 2	.5918	.5918	.7693	.2307	.9904	.9904	.9952	.0048
	2	2- 5	.4265	.7207	.8966	.1034	.9732	.9826	.9942	.0058
	3	5-10	.3376	.7916	.9543	.0457	.9346	.9603	.9919	.0081
55-64	1	0- 2	.6132	.6132	.7831	.2169	.9777	.9777	.9888	.0112
	2	2- 5	.4274	.6970	.8866	.1134	.9377	.9591	.9862	.0138
	3	5-10	.3208	.7506	.9442	.0558	.8481	.9044	.9801	.0199
65 up	1	0- 2	.5165	.5165	.7187	.2813	.8995	.8995	.9484	.0516
	2	2- 5	.3232	.6258	.8554	.1446	.7504	.8342	.9414	.0586
	3	5-10	.1850	.5724	.8944	.1056	.5107	.6806	.9259	.0741
Metastatic Female										
All	1	0- 2 yrs	.1938	.1938	.4402	.5598	.9521	.9521	.9758	.0242
	2	2- 5	.1056	.5449	.8168	.1832	.8789	.9231	.9737	.0263
	3	5-10	.0693	.6563	.9192	.0808	.7536	.8574	.9697	.0303
Localized Female										
< 45	4	10-15 yrs		.9262	.9848	.0152		.9764	.9952	.0048
	5	15-20		.9011	.9794	.0206		.9648	.9929	.0071
45-54	4	10-15		.8815	.9751	.0249		.9363	.9869	.0131
	5	15-20		.8469	.9673	.0327		.9017	.9795	.0205
55-64	4	10-15		.7484	.9437	.0563		.8470	.9673	.0327
	5	15-20		.6684	.9226	.0774		.7640	.9476	.0524
65 up	4	10-15		.5933	.9009	.0991		.6145	.9072	.0928
	5	15-20		.3143	.7934	.2066		.4852	.8653	.1347
Regional Female										
< 45	4	10-15 yrs		.9327	.9862	.0138		.9761	.9952	.0048
	5	15-20		.8801	.9748	.0252		.9648	.9929	.0071
45-54	4	10-15		.8386	.9654	.0346		.9356	.9868	.0132
	5	15-20		.8233	.9619	.0381		.9022	.9796	.0204
55-64	4	10-15		.8029	.9570	.0430		.8417	.9661	.0339
	5	15-20		.6655	.9218	.0782		.7527	.9448	.0552
65 up	4	10-15		.4753	.8618	.1382		.5948	.9013	.0987
	5	15-20		.2861	.7786	.2214		.4605	.8563	.1437

*Basis of expected mortality: Concurrent U.S. White Population Rates

CANCER—CORPUS UTERI
CANCER—OVARY

Table 165a   Cancer of the Corpus Uteri and Ovary - Observed Data and Comparative Experience by Stage, Age and Duration

Stage Age Group	No.	Start-End	Exposure Person-Yrs	Observed	Expected*	Mortality Ratio Interval	Mortality Ratio Cumulative	Survival Ratio Interval	Survival Ratio Cumulative	Excess Death Rate
(Yrs)	i	t to t + Δt	E	d	d'	100d/d'	100Q/Q'	100p$_i$/p$_i$'	100P/P'	1000(d-d')/E
Site: Corpus Uteri										
Localized										
Female										
< 45	1	0- 2 yrs	1094.5	18	2.08	865%	860%	97.1%	97.1%	15
	2	2- 5	1529.5	20	3.66	545	635	96.9	94.1	11
	3	5-10	1799.0	15	5.99	250	385	97.6	91.8	5.0
45-54	1	0- 2	2613.5	84	13.06	645	635	94.6	94.6	27
	2	2- 5	3546.5	79	21.6	365	440	95.3	90.1	16
	3	5-10	4219.0	55	35.0	157	265	97.6	88.0	4.7
55-64	1	0- 2	3492.5	209	39.4	530	515	90.4	90.4	49
	2	2- 5	4468.0	181	61.9	290	345	92.2	83.4	27
	3	5-10	4860.0	164	93.8	175	225	92.9	77.4	14
65-74	1	0- 2	2623.5	283	72.9	390	370	84.1	84.1	80
	2	2- 5	3001.0	210	101.7	205	240	89.7	75.5	36
	3	5-10	2872.5	192	136.5	141	157	92.8	70.1	19
75 up	1	0- 2	993.0	200	84.2	240	220	76.7	76.7	117
	2	2- 5	916.0	131	93.9	139	151	87.1	66.8	40
	3	5-10	655.0	92	90.6	102	114	95.9	64.1	2.1
Regional										
Female										
All	1	0- 2 yrs	1619.5	385	41.7	920	785	61.6	61.6	212
	2	2- 5	1420.5	135	35.2	385	420	81.7	50.4	70
	3	5-10	1471.5	75	40.9	183	240	92.8	46.7	23
Metastatic										
Female										
All	1	0- 2 yrs	898.5	568	23.9	2400	1440	19.9	19.9	606
	2	2- 5	327.0	45	5.83	775	620	71.7	14.3	120
	3	5-10	252.5	24	4.54	530	320	71.2	10.2	77
Site: Ovary										
Localized										
Female										
< 45	1	0- 2 yrs	717.5	53	1.11	4800%	4700%	86.2%	86.2%	72
	2	2- 5	905.5	23	1.66	1390	2400	93.2	80.3	24
	3	5-10	1046.0	14	2.63	535	1190	94.3	75.8	11
45-54	1	0- 2	771.0	83	3.77	2200	2100	80.3	80.3	103
	2	2- 5	899.0	48	5.32	905	1190	86.5	69.5	47
	3	5-10	899.5	26	7.18	360	625	90.3	62.7	21
55-64	1	0- 2	697.0	76	7.61	1000	945	81.1	81.1	98
	2	2- 5	979.5	52	10.69	485	575	85.3	69.2	42
	3	5-10	817.0	37	15.49	240	325	87.8	60.8	26
65-74	1	0- 2	398.5	51	10.94	465	430	80.9	80.9	101
	2	2- 5	447.5	36	15.08	240	270	86.6	70.1	47
	3	5-10	417.0	36	19.90	181	181	83.0	58.2	39
75 up	1	0- 2	189.5	44	17.17	255	230	72.5	72.5	142
	2	2- 5	159.0	24	16.75	143	151	88.6	64.3	46
	3	5-10	111.0	18	15.05	120	115	95.2	61.2	27
Regional										
Female										
All	1	0- 2 yrs	1498.0	470	23.8	1980	1590	49.5	49.5	298
	2	2- 5	1091.5	136	16.32	835	780	72.1	35.7	110
	3	5-10	976.5	62	18.88	330	405	81.2	28.9	44
Metastatic										
Female										
< 65	1	0- 2 yrs	2252.5	1318	15.20	8700	6100	19.1	19.1	578
	2	2- 5	691.5	156	4.45	3500	2800	49.8	9.5	219
	3	5-10	461.0	39	3.70	1050	1300	66.3	6.3	77
65 up	1	0- 2	1226.0	920	55.3	1660	1050	9.9	9.9	705
	2	2- 5	194.0	54	10.00	540	435	48.3	4.8	227
	3	5-10	93.5	13	6.30	205	215	69.5	3.3	72

*Basis of expected mortality: Concurrent U.S. White Population Rates

CANCER—CORPUS UTERI
CANCER—OVARY

Table 165b   Cancer of the Corpus Uteri and Ovary - Derived Mortality and Survival Data

Stage Age Group (Yrs)	No. i	Start-End t to t+Δt	Observed Survival Rate Cumulative P	Observed Survival Rate Interval p_i	Observed Survival Rate Ave. Ann. $\breve{p}$	Observed Ave. Ann. Mort. Rate $\breve{q}$	Expected Survival Rate Cumulative P'	Expected Survival Rate Interval p_i'	Expected Survival Rate Ave. Ann. $\breve{p}'$	Expected Ave. Ann. Mort. Rate $\breve{q}'$
Site: Corpus Uteri										
Localized Female										
< 45	1	0- 2 yrs	.9674	.9674	.9836	.0164	.9962	.9962	.9981	.0019
	2	2- 5	.9303	.9616	.9870	.0130	.9890	.9928	.9976	.0024
	3	5-10	.8922	.9590	.9917	.0083	.9721	.9829	.9966	.0034
45-54	1	0- 2	.9367	.9367	.9678	.0322	.9900	.9900	.9950	.0050
	2	2- 5	.8760	.9352	.9779	.0221	.9719	.9817	.9939	.0061
	3	5-10	.8194	.9354	.9867	.0133	.9315	.9584	.9915	.0085
55-64	1	0- 2	.8838	.8838	.9401	.0599	.9775	.9775	.9887	.0113
	2	2- 5	.7814	.8841	.9598	.0402	.9370	.9586	.9860	.0140
	3	5-10	.6553	.8386	.9654	.0346	.8461	.9030	.9798	.0202
65-74	1	0- 2	.7949	.7949	.8916	.1084	.9448	.9448	.9720	.0280
	2	2- 5	.6414	.8069	.9310	.0690	.8498	.8994	.9653	.0347
	3	5-10	.4596	.7166	.9355	.0645	.6560	.7719	.9495	.0505
75 up	1	0- 2	.6419	.6419	.8012	.1988	.8368	.8368	.9148	.0852
	2	2- 5	.4047	.6305	.8575	.1425	.6055	.7236	.8978	.1022
	3	5-10	.1820	.4497	.8523	.1477	.2839	.4689	.8594	.1406
Regional Female										
All	1	0- 2 yrs	.5836	.5836	.7639	.2361	.9468	.9468	.9730	.0270
	2	2- 5	.4356	.7464	.9071	.0929	.8649	.9135	.9703	.0297
	3	5-10	.3379	.7757	.9505	.0495	.7230	.8359	.9648	.0352
Metastatic Female										
All	1	0- 2 yrs	.1877	.1877	.4332	.5668	.9437	.9437	.9714	.0286
	2	2- 5	.1223	.6516	.8669	.1331	.8580	.9092	.9688	.0312
	3	5-10	.0722	.5904	.9000	.1000	.7112	.8289	.9632	.0368
Site: Ovary										
Localized Female										
< 45	1	0- 2 yrs	.8591	.8591	.9269	.0731	.9970	.9970	.9985	.00150
	2	2- 5	.7962	.9268	.9750	.0250	.9914	.9944	.9981	.00187
	3	5-10	.7411	.9308	.9858	.0142	.9783	.9868	.9973	.0027
45-54	1	0- 2	.7955	.7955	.8919	.1081	.9903	.9903	.9951	.0049
	2	2- 5	.6756	.8493	.9470	.0530	.9727	.9822	.9940	.0060
	3	5-10	.5854	.8665	.9717	.0283	.9335	.9597	.9918	.0082
55-64	1	0- 2	.7937	.7937	.8909	.1091	.9782	.9782	.9890	.0110
	2	2- 5	.6500	.8189	.9356	.0644	.9391	.9600	.9865	.0135
	3	5-10	.5173	.7958	.9553	.0447	.8513	.9065	.9806	.0194
65-74	1	0- 2	.7653	.7653	.8748	.1252	.9454	.9454	.9723	.0277
	2	2- 5	.5974	.7806	.9208	.0792	.8519	.9011	.9659	.0341
	3	5-10	.3848	.6441	.9158	.0842	.6610	.7759	.9505	.0495
75 up	1	0- 2	.5992	.5992	.7741	.2259	.8261	.8261	.9089	.0911
	2	2- 5	.3780	.6308	.8576	.1424	.5882	.7120	.8929	.1071
	3	5-10	.1670	.4418	.8493	.1507	.2730	.4641	.8577	.1423
Regional Female										
All	1	0- 2 yrs	.4783	.4783	.6916	.3084	.9672	.9672	.9835	.0165
	2	2- 5	.3257	.6810	.8798	.1202	.9133	.9443	.9811	.0189
	3	5-10	.2345	.7200	.9364	.0636	.8102	.8871	.9763	.0237
Metastatic Female										
< 65	1	0- 2 yrs	.1889	.1889	.4346	.5654	.9866	.9866	.9933	.0067
	2	2- 5	.0922	.4881	.7874	.2126	.9674	.9805	.9935	.0065
	3	5-10	.0586	.6356	.9133	.0867	.9278	.9591	.9917	.0083
65 up	1	0- 2	.0909	.0909	.3015	.6985	.9137	.9137	.9559	.0441
	2	2- 5	.0374	.4114	.7437	.2563	.7778	.8513	.9478	.0522
	3	5-10	.0181	.4840	.8649	.1351	.5419	.6967	.9303	.0697

*Basis of expected mortality: Concurrent U.S. White Population Rates

CANCER—VAGINA
CANCER—VULVA

Table 166a   Cancer of the Vagina and Vulva - Observed Data and Comparative Experience by Stage, Age and Duration

Stage Age Group	Interval No.	Interval Start-End	Exposure Person-Yrs	Deaths Observed	Deaths Expected*	Mortality Ratio Interval	Mortality Ratio Cumulative	Survival Ratio Interval	Survival Ratio Cumulative	Excess Death Rate
(Yrs)	i	t to t + Δt	E	d	d'	100d/d'	100Q/Q'	100p$_i$/p$_i$'	100P/P'	1000(d-d')/E
Site: Vagina										
Localized										
Female										
< 45	1	0- 2 yrs	43.0	4	0.090	4400%	4400%	82.2%	82.2%	91
	2	2- 5	48.5	2	0.132	1520	2300	89.6	73.6	39
	3	5-10	57.5	0	0.23	0	915	101.9	75.0	−4.1
45-54	1	0- 2	48.5	7	0.26	2700	2500	74.7	74.7	139
	2	2- 5	49.0	4	0.31	1280	1410	81.3	60.1	75
	3	5-10	41.5	0	0.36	0	580	107.7	62.9	−8.7
55-64	1	0- 2	48.0	13	0.53	2400	2200	53.0	53.0	260
	2	2- 5	33.0	6	0.45	1340	1140	59.6	31.6	168
	3	5-10	32.5	0	0.55	0	470	110.4	34.9	−17
65-74	1	0- 2	78.0	16	2.29	700	580	69.4	69.4	176
	2	2- 5	72.0	11	2.50	440	360	71.1	49.3	118
	3	5-10	70.5	1	3.55	28	165	125.3	61.8	−36
75 up	1	0- 2	50.0	20	5.15	390	300	47.4	47.4	297
	2	2- 5	24.0	9	3.01	300	187	38.3	18.2	250
	3	5-10	10.5	2	2.03	98	124	0	0	−2.9
Regional										
Female										
All	1	0- 2 yrs	200.0	66	7.71	855	670	49.9	49.9	291
	2	2- 5	147.5	22	5.02	440	370	69.2	34.5	115
	3	5-10	103.5	11	2.70	405	225	75.2	26.0	80
Metastatic										
Female										
All	1	0- 2 yrs	44.0	34	1.49	2300	1410	8.7	8.7	739
	2	2- 5	6.0	3	0.31	975	595	0	0	449
Site: Vulva										
Localized										
Female										
< 45	1	0- 2 yrs	133.5	2	0.22	910%	875%	97.4%	97.4%	13
	2	2- 5	181.5	2	0.38	525	640	97.3	94.8	8.9
	3	5-10	210.5	4	0.63	635	595	92.6	87.8	16
45-54	1	0- 2	181.5	4	0.88	455	450	96.6	96.6	17
	2	2- 5	253.0	7	1.48	470	445	93.6	90.4	22
	3	5-10	298.5	10	2.34	430	395	87.5	79.1	26
55-64	1	0- 2	211.5	19	2.48	765	725	85.1	85.1	78
	2	2- 5	262.0	16	3.90	410	480	86.4	73.5	46
	3	5-10	280.0	11	5.80	190	275	90.6	66.5	19
65-74	1	0- 2	352.5	45	10.66	420	405	80.5	80.5	97
	2	2- 5	372.5	28	13.88	200	245	89.5	72.1	38
	3	5-10	338.5	36	17.24	210	179	74.5	53.7	55
75 up	1	0- 2	299.0	71	29.4	240	215	73.0	73.0	139
	2	2- 5	242.0	47	28.8	163	154	77.5	56.6	75
	3	5-10	156.5	22	23.9	92	112	106.2	60.1	−12
Regional										
Female										
All	1	0- 2 yrs	395.0	127	15.80	800	615	52.2	52.2	281
	2	2- 5	311.5	32	10.96	290	315	83.3	43.5	68
	3	5-10	281.5	21	9.38	225	197	87.0	37.8	41
Metastatic										
Female										
All	1	0- 2 yrs	70.0	52	4.36	1190	715	11.8	11.8	681
	2	2- 5	15.0	4	0.74	535	330	41.3	4.9	217
	3	5-10	2.0	0	0.074	0	265	111.3	5.4	−37

*Basis of expected mortality: Concurrent U.S. White Population Rates

CANCER—VAGINA
CANCER—VULVA

Table 166b   Cancer of the Vagina and Vulva - Derived Mortality and Survival Data

Stage Age Group	Interval No.	Interval Start-End	Observed Survival Rate Cumulative	Observed Survival Rate Interval	Observed Survival Rate Ave. Ann.	Observed Ave. Ann. Mort. Rate	Expected* Survival Rate Cumulative	Expected* Survival Rate Interval	Expected* Survival Rate Ave. Ann.	Expected* Ave. Ann. Mort. Rate
(Yrs)	i	t to t + Δ t	P	p_i	$\check{p}$	$\check{q}$	P'	p_i'	$\check{p}'$	$\check{q}'$
Site: Vagina										
Localized										
Female										
< 45	1	0- 2 yrs	.8182	.8182	.9045	.0955	.9959	.9959	.9979	.0021
	2	2- 5	.7273	.8889	.9615	.0385	.9882	.9923	.9974	.0026
	3	5-10	.7273	1.0000	1.0000	.0000	.9702	.9818	.9963	.0037
45-54	1	0- 2	.7390	.7390	.8597	.1403	.9894	.9894	.9947	.0053
	2	2- 5	.5834	.7894	.9242	.0758	.9704	.9808	.9936	.0064
	3	5-10	.5834	1.0000	1.0000	.0000	.9281	.9564	.9911	.0089
55-64	1	0- 2	.5185	.5185	.7201	.2799	.9779	.9779	.9889	.0111
	2	2- 5	.2963	.5715	.8299	.1701	.9382	.9594	.9863	.0137
	3	5-10	.2963	1.0000	1.0000	.0000	.8496	.9056	.9804	.0196
65-74	1	0- 2	.6522	.6522	.8076	.1924	.9399	.9399	.9695	.0305
	2	2- 5	.4130	.6332	.8587	.1413	.8375	.8911	.9623	.0377
	3	5-10	.3901	.9446	.9887	.0113	.6313	.7538	.9450	.0550
75 up	1	0- 2	.3750	.3750	.6124	.3876	.7908	.7908	.8893	.1107
	2	2- 5	.0938	.2501	.6300	.3700	.5163	.6529	.8675	.1325
	3	5-10	.0000	.0000	.0000	1.0000	.1912	.3703	.8198	.1802
Regional										
Female										
All	1	0- 2 yrs	.4590	.4590	.6775	.3225	.9195	.9195	.9589	.0411
	2	2- 5	.2779	.6054	.8460	.1540	.8049	.8754	.9566	.0434
	3	5-10	.1636	.5887	.8995	.1005	.6300	.7827	.9522	.0478
Metastatic										
Female										
All	1	0- 2 yrs	.0811	.0811	.2848	.7152	.9350	.9350	.9670	.0330
	2	2- 5	.0000	.0000	.0000	1.0000	.8323	.8902	.9620	.0380
Site: Vulva										
Localized										
Female										
< 45	1	0- 2 yrs	.9712	.9712	.9855	.0145	.9967	.9967	.9983	.00165
	2	2- 5	.9390	.9668	.9888	.0112	.9905	.9938	.9979	.0021
	3	5-10	.8565	.9121	.9818	.0182	.9759	.9853	.9970	.0030
45-54	1	0- 2	.9564	.9564	.9780	.0220	.9903	.9903	.9951	.0049
	2	2- 5	.8794	.9195	.9724	.0276	.9729	.9824	.9941	.0059
	3	5-10	.7383	.8395	.9656	.0344	.9338	.9598	.9918	.0082
55-64	1	0- 2	.8308	.8308	.9115	.0885	.9767	.9767	.9883	.0117
	2	2- 5	.6867	.8266	.9385	.0615	.9345	.9568	.9854	.0146
	3	5-10	.5590	.8140	.9597	.0403	.8400	.8989	.9789	.0211
65-74	1	0- 2	.7570	.7570	.8701	.1299	.9401	.9401	.9696	.0304
	2	2- 5	.6035	.7972	.9272	.0728	.8373	.8906	.9621	.0379
	3	5-10	.3390	.5617	.8910	.1090	.6314	.7541	.9451	.0549
75 up	1	0- 2	.5897	.5897	.7679	.2321	.8082	.8082	.8990	.1010
	2	2- 5	.3125	.5299	.8092	.1908	.5524	.6835	.8809	.1191
	3	5-10	.1418	.4538	.8538	.1462	.2360	.4272	.8436	.1564
Regional										
Female										
All	1	0- 2 yrs	.4774	.4774	.6909	.3091	.9147	.9147	.9564	.0436
	2	2- 5	.3451	.7229	.8975	.1025	.7935	.8675	.9537	.0463
	3	5-10	.2305	.6679	.9224	.0776	.6090	.7675	.9485	.0515
Metastatic										
Female										
All	1	0- 2 yrs	.1034	.1034	.3216	.6784	.8745	.8745	.9351	.0649
	2	2- 5	.0345	.3337	.6936	.3064	.7068	.8082	.9315	.0685
	3	5-10	.0345	1.0000	1.0000	.0000	.6353	.8988	.9481	.0519

*Basis of expected mortality: Concurrent U.S. White Population Rates

CANCER—BREAST

Table 167a   Cancer of the Breast - Observed Data and Comparative Experience by Stage, Age and Duration

Stage Age Group	No.	Interval Start-End	Exposure Person-Yrs	Observed	Expected*	Mortality Ratio Interval	Cumulative	Survival Ratio Interval	Cumulative	Excess Death Rate
(Yrs)	i	t to t + Δt	E	d	d'	100d/d'	100Q/Q'	100p_i/p_i'	100P/P'	1000(d-d')/E
Localized Female										
< 45	1	0- 2 yrs	4180.0	120	8.36	1440%	1430%	94.7%	94.7%	27
	2	2- 5	5604.0	233	14.15	1650	1480	88.7	84.0	39
	3	5-10	6256.5	159	22.0	720	920	89.7	75.4	22
45-54	1	0- 2	5206.5	149	24.7	605	595	95.2	95.2	24
	2	2- 5	7016.0	279	40.4	690	620	90.1	85.8	34
	3	5-10	7628.5	237	59.1	400	440	89.2	76.5	23
55-64	1	0- 2	4617.0	177	52.3	340	335	94.6	94.6	27
	2	2- 5	6063.0	320	85.0	375	340	88.7	83.9	39
	3	5-10	6257.5	313	123.0	255	255	85.7	71.9	30
65-74	1	0- 2	4669.5	304	137.1	220	215	92.8	92.8	36
	2	2- 5	5798.0	439	209.8	210	197	88.2	81.9	40
	3	5-10	5338.0	466	269.9	173	158	82.6	67.6	37
75 up	1	0- 2	3540.0	522	337.0	155	147	89.4	89.4	52
	2	2- 5	3600.0	515	394.0	131	126	90.2	80.7	34
	3	5-10	2471.5	409	345.8	118	109	90.1	72.7	26
Regional Female										
< 45	1	0- 2 yrs	3853.0	423	7.69	5500	5400	79.2	79.2	108
	2	2- 5	4113.0	473	10.20	4600	4000	70.2	55.5	113
	3	5-10	3638.5	248	12.70	1950	2100	72.7	40.4	65
45-54	1	0- 2	5296.0	649	25.6	2500	2400	77.3	77.3	118
	2	2- 5	5514.5	655	32.1	2000	1740	70.0	54.1	113
	3	5-10	4801.5	338	37.4	905	945	73.6	39.8	63
55-64	1	0- 2	4818.5	634	53.4	1190	1130	76.8	76.8	120
	2	2- 5	4900.0	671	67.1	1000	835	67.3	51.7	123
	3	5-10	3895.0	382	74.3	515	465	67.4	34.8	79
65-74	1	0- 2	4049.5	579	114.9	505	475	77.6	77.6	115
	2	2- 5	3968.0	620	138.2	450	365	67.2	52.2	121
	3	5-10	2977.0	369	144.8	255	220	67.6	35.3	75
75 up	1	0- 2	2360.0	548	218.1	250	230	71.8	71.8	140
	2	2- 5	1830.0	429	196.8	220	174	64.0	45.9	127
	3	5-10	961.5	213	132.1	161	126	58.1	26.7	84
Metastatic Female										
All	1	0- 2 yrs	3704.5	1958	100.6	1950	1320	26.3	26.3	501
	2	2- 5	1374.5	421	36.7	1150	645	37.9	10.0	280
	3	5-10	677.0	104	19.5	535	340	57.0	5.7	125
Localized Female										
< 45	4	10-15 yrs	4935.5	108	25.6	425		92.3		17
	5	15-20	1835.0	44	14.09	310		91.8		16
45-54	4	10-15	4949.5	148	61.0	240		91.3		18
	5	15-20	1796.0	63	33.7	187		91.9		16
55-64	4	10-15	4339.5	280	145.1	193		86.2		31
	5	15-20	1334.5	102	71.24	143		90.0		23
65-74	4	10-15	2647.5	295	227.3	130		85.3		26
	5	15-20	557.0	84	72.79	115		98.1		20
75 up	4	10-15	608.5	123	119.6	103		101.6		5.6
	5	15-20	70.0	23	19.68	117		29.4		47
Regional Female										
< 55	4	10-15 yrs	4773.0	233	44.5	525		81.7		39
	5	15-20	1727.0	79	24.5	320		84.1		32
55-64	4	10-15	2056.5	179	67.6	265		75.4		54
	5	15-20	619.0	58	32.2	180		82.6		42
65 up	4	10-15	1400.0	206	139.9	147		75.3		47
	5	15-20	269.0	41	35.2	116		87.4		21

*Basis of expected mortality: Concurrent U.S. White Population Rates

CANCER—BREAST

Table 167b Cancer of the Breast - Derived Mortality and Survival Data

Stage Age Group	Interval No.	Interval Start-End	Observed Survival Rate Cumulative	Observed Survival Rate Interval	Observed Survival Rate Ave. Ann.	Observed Ave. Ann. Mort. Rate	Expected* Survival Rate Cumulative	Expected* Survival Rate Interval	Expected* Survival Rate Ave. Ann.	Expected* Ave. Ann. Mort. Rate
(Yrs)	i	t to $t+\Delta t$	P	p_i	$\breve{p}$	$\breve{q}$	P'	p_i'	$\breve{p}'$	$\breve{q}'$
Localized Female										
< 45	1	0- 2 yrs	.9429	.9429	.9710	.0290	.9960	.9960	.9980	.0020
	2	2- 5	.8303	.8806	.9585	.0415	.9885	.9925	.9975	.0025
	3	5-10	.7317	.8812	.9750	.0250	.9709	.9822	.9964	.0036
45-54	1	0- 2	.9433	.9433	.9712	.0288	.9905	.9905	.9952	.0048
	2	2- 5	.8352	.8854	.9602	.0398	.9734	.9827	.9942	.0058
	3	5-10	.7155	.8567	.9695	.0305	.9352	.9608	.9920	.0080
55-64	1	0- 2	.9245	.9245	.9615	.0385	.9774	.9774	.9886	.0114
	2	2- 5	.7857	.8499	.9472	.0528	.9369	.9586	.9860	.0140
	3	5-10	.6079	.7737	.9500	.0500	.8459	.9029	.9798	.0202
65-74	1	0- 2	.8743	.8743	.9350	.0650	.9420	.9420	.9706	.0294
	2	2- 5	.6900	.7892	.9241	.0759	.8425	.8944	.9635	.0365
	3	5-10	.4335	.6283	.9112	.0888	.6412	.7611	.9469	.0531
75 up	1	0- 2	.7296	.7296	.8542	.1458	.8158	.8158	.9032	.0968
	2	2- 5	.4589	.6290	.8568	.1432	.5690	.6975	.8868	.1132
	3	5-10	.1840	.4010	.8330	.1670	.2532	.4450	.8505	.1495
Regional Female										
< 45	1	0- 2 yrs	.7886	.7886	.8880	.1120	.9961	.9961	.9980	.0020
	2	2- 5	.5492	.6964	.8864	.1136	.9887	.9926	.9975	.0025
	3	5-10	.3922	.7141	.9349	.0651	.9713	.9824	.9965	.0035
45-54	1	0- 2	.7653	.7653	.8748	.1252	.9903	.9903	.9951	.0049
	2	2- 5	.5265	.6880	.8828	.1172	.9728	.9823	.9941	.0059
	3	5-10	.3719	.7064	.9328	.0672	.9336	.9597	.9918	.0082
55-64	1	0- 2	.7506	.7506	.8664	.1336	.9779	.9779	.9889	.0111
	2	2- 5	.4847	.6458	.8644	.1356	.9383	.9595	.9863	.0137
	3	5-10	.2956	.6099	.9058	.0942	.8493	.9051	.9803	.0197
65-74	1	0- 2	.7322	.7322	.8557	.1443	.9438	.9438	.9715	.0285
	2	2- 5	.4420	.6037	.8452	.1548	.8473	.8978	.9647	.0353
	3	5-10	.2298	.5199	.8774	.1226	.6513	.7687	.9487	.0513
75 up	1	0- 2	.5896	.5896	.7679	.2321	.8214	.8214	.9063	.0937
	2	2- 5	.2656	.4505	.7666	.2334	.5784	.7042	.8897	.1103
	3	5-10	.0696	.2620	.7650	.2350	.2609	.4511	.8528	.1472
Metastatic Female										
All	1	0- 2 yrs	.2484	.2484	.4984	.5016	.9429	.9429	.9710	.0290
	2	2- 5	.0856	.3446	.7011	.2989	.8582	.9102	.9691	.0309
	3	5-10	.0409	.4778	.8627	.1373	.7198	.8387	.9654	.0346
Localized Female										
< 45	4	10-15 yrs		.8985	.9788	.0212		.9737	.9947	.0053
	5	15-20		.8822	.9752	.0248		.9608	.9920	.0080
45-54	4	10-15		.8562	.9694	.0306		.9382	.9873	.0127
	5	15-20		.8335	.9642	.0358		.9068	.9806	.0194
55-64	4	10-15		.7225	.9371	.0629		.8382	.9653	.0347
	5	15-20		.6739	.9241	.0759		.7491	.9439	.0561
65-74	4	10-15		.5336	.8819	.1181		.6252	.9103	.0897
	5	15-20		.4625	.8571	.1429		.4714	.8604	.1396
75 up	4	10-15		.3173	.7949	.2051		.3122	.7923	.2077
	5	15-20		.0535	.5568	.4432		.1820	.7112	.2888
Regional Female										
< 55	4	10-15 yrs		.7787	.9512	.0488		.9527	.9904	.0096
	5	15-20		.7808	.9517	.0483		.9288	.9853	.0147
55-64	4	10-15		.6341	.9129	.0871		.8405	.9658	.0342
	5	15-20		.6239	.9100	.0900		.7556	.9455	.0545
65 up	4	10-15		.4359	.8470	.1530		.5788	.8964	.1036
	5	15-20		.4220	.8415	.1585		.4830	.8645	.1355

*Basis of expected mortality: Concurrent U.S. White Population Rates

CANCER–BLOOD AND LYMPHATIC SYSTEM

§170–ACUTE LEUKEMIA

Total acute leukemia, comprised of acute lymphocytic, myelocytic and monocytic leukemias, ranks 16th among cancer sites in males (Table 100a) and 13th in females (Table 100b). The prevalence of this disorder differs little between the sexes; acute leukemia accounting for 1.9 per cent of all cancers for males and 1.6 per cent for females. Experience for total acute leukemia, male and female combined, is shown in the upper portion of Table 170a-b, while a breakdown into the three types of acute leukemia, male and female separately, is displayed in the lower portion of Table 170a-b. A substantial percentage of the cases, 64 per cent of male and 62 per cent of female, were diagnosed under age 55. The mortality ratios were extremely high within each age group over the ten-year observation interval, and they decreased with age. The similarly high excess death rates in all age groups ranged from 653 extra deaths per 1000 in the youngest age group to 893 per 1000 in the 35-54 year age group in the first two-year observation interval. Five-year cumulative .survival ratios were correspondingly low in all age groups, with a range between a minimum of 0.8 per cent (age 35-54) and a maximum of 2.1 per cent in patients under age 15. There were few survivors more than five years after diagnosis. Sex differences in mortality and survival in acute leukemia were relatively small. Within two years of diagnosis the mortality ratio for patients with acute lymphocytic leukemia was considerably higher than the ratio in patients with acute myelocytic or monocytic leukemia, but the EDR was somewhat lower, indicating a younger average age.

§171–CHRONIC LEUKEMIA

Total chronic leukemia, including lymphocytic and myelocytic types, ranks 15th for males (Table 100a) and 14th for females (Table 100b). It comprises 2.1 per cent of all cancers in males and 1.4 per cent in females. Experience for total chronic leukemia is shown in the upper portion of Table 171a-b, by age group, both sexes combined, and by sex, all ages combined. Results for chronic lymphatic and chronic myeloid leukemia are given in the lower portion of Table 171a-b, each sex separately. Mortality ratios for total chronic leukemia were extremely high, reaching 34000 per cent under age 35 in the first two-year observation interval, and decreasing with advancing age to 485 per cent in the 75 up age group. Overall excess death rates during the first two years ranged from 222 extra deaths per 1000 in the 55-64 age group to 436 extra deaths per 1000 in the under 35 age group. The survival ratio in the first observation interval followed a bell-type shape starting at 33.7 per cent in the under 35 age group, peaking at 61.6 per cent in the 55-64 age group, and declining back to 33.0 per cent in the 75 up age group. The data in the lower portion of Table 171a indicate that those patients diagnosed as chronic myeloid leukemia fared less well with regard to mortality ratio, survival ratio, and EDR than those in the chronic lymphatic category. Sex differences were relatively small.

CANCER—BLOOD AND LYMPHATIC SYSTEM

§172—LYMPHOSARCOMA AND OTHER LYMPHOMAS

Lymphosarcoma ranks 20th among cancer sites in males and 23rd in females, with relative frequencies of 1.0 per cent and 0.8 per cent, respectively (Tables 100a-b). Ten-year experience in five age categories for males and females combined, and for males and females separately, all ages combined, are presented in the upper half of Tables 172a-b. The two-year mortality ratio was an extremely high 36000 per cent in patients under age 35 and decreased with age to 560 per cent at ages 75 and up. EDR's were similarly very high, ranging between 220 and 449 per 1000 in the first two-year observation interval, with the highest rate in the youngest patients. Five-year survival ratios were quite low: those in the 35-54 year age group fared the best with a ratio of 42.6 per cent; those in the 75 up age group fared the worst with a ratio of only 14.8 per cent. Females had a somewhat higher mortality ratio but sex differences were slight with respect to survival ratios and EDR's.

Other lymphomas, as a group, rank 33rd and last in prevalence among cancer sites in males, 35th out of 36 cancer sites in females, and have a relative frequency of 0.3 per cent in both sexes (Tables 100a-b). Data for other lymphomas are presented in a similar manner to lymphosarcoma in the lower half of Tables 172a-b, but with different age groups. Two-year mortality ratios were quite high starting at 9500 per cent in patients under age 15 and decreasing with age to 645 per cent at ages 65 and up. EDR in the two-year observation interval was highest for patients under 15, 483 extra deaths per 1000, and dropped to a minimum level, still 117 per 1000, in the next age group, those aged 15 to 34. Five-year survival ratios ranged from 26.9 per cent under age 15 to 65.2 per cent, age 15-34. Again, mortality ratios were somewhat higher for females, but sex differences were slight with regard to survival ratios and EDR's.

§173—HODGKIN'S DISEASE AND RETICULUM CELL SARCOMA

Hodgkin's Disease ranks 18th among all male cancers and 19th among all female cancers with a relative frequency of 1.3 and 0.9 per cent, respectively (Tables 100a-b). Seventy per cent of male and 86 per cent of female cases are diagnosed before age 55. Results for male and female patients are presented separately in five age categories in the upper portion of Tables 173a-b. Mortality ratios in the first observation interval were extremely high, 11100 per cent in male patients under age 25 and 19400 per cent in females. There was a consistent decrease in mortality ratio with advancing age, to 830 per cent in males age 65 and up, and 1070 per cent in females. In both sexes, EDR's were high, increasing with age, generally, but decreasing with duration. Within two years of diagnosis, among patients 45 years and older, EDR's were of the order of 300 to 500 per 1000. A different pattern was observed in young patients under age 25 and those age 25 to 44 years. EDR in females showed relatively little variation from an average of about 100 per 1000. In males the EDR's were in a range from 109 to 127 per 1000 from two to ten years after diagnosis with somewhat higher values in the earliest observation interval. Excess death rates were usually somewhat higher in men than in women. Five-year survival ratios decreased with advancing age, from 48.4 to 10.5 per cent in male patients and from 58.0 to 14.3 per cent in females.

Reticulum cell sarcoma ranks 28th among all male cancers and 29th among all female cancers, and has a relative frequency of 0.6 per cent and 0.5 per cent, respectively (Tables 100a-b). Data for male and female patients combined are presented in five age categories in the lower portion of Tables 173a-b. The prognosis was very poor: within two years of diagnosis mortality ratios ranged from 31000 per cent in patients under age 25 down to 750 per cent age 75 and up. EDR's were similarly very high, ranging from 454 to 636 extra deaths per 1000 in the first observation interval. Subsequent to the first interval, EDR was considerably lower in patients under age 25 than it was in those aged 25 to 64 years. Excess mortality decreased after two years, but substantial levels of mortality ratio and EDR were still observed. Some of these results should be viewed with caution, as fewer than 15 deaths were recorded in several categories.

1-80

ACUTE LEUKEMIA

Table 170a   Acute Leukemia - Observed Data and Comparative Experience by Sex, Age and Duration

Sex Age Group	No.	Interval Start-End	Exposure Person-Yrs	Deaths Observed	Deaths Expected*	Mortality Ratio Interval	Mortality Ratio Cumulative	Survival Ratio Interval	Survival Ratio Cumulative	Excess Death Rate
(Yrs)	i	t to t + Δt	E	d	d'	100d/d'	100Q/Q'	100p$_i$/p$_i$'	100P/P'	1000(d-d')/E
Total Acute Leukemia										
M&F										
< 15	1	0- 2 yrs	1868.5	1222	2.77	44000%	37000%	11.2%	11.2%	653
	2	2- 5	261.5	123	0.131	94000	25000	19.1	2.1	470
	3	5-10	62.0	10	0.026	38000	15000	59.0	1.3	161
15-34	1	0- 2	602.5	511	0.72	71000	40000	3.6	3.6	847
	2	2- 5	33.0	14	0.047	30000	15500	26.4	1.0	423
	3	5-10	13.0	2	0.022	9000	6900	38.2	0.4	152
35-54	1	0- 2	632.0	568	3.32	17000	9000	2.8	2.8	893
	2	2- 5	31.5	10	0.183	5500	3200	26.7	0.8	312
	3	5-10	14.5	0	0.096	0	1310	104.9	0.8	−6.6
55-64	1	0- 2	502.0	441	8.62	5100	2700	4.1	4.1	861
	2	2- 5	35.0	14	0.71	1990	1020	23.7	1.0	380
	3	5-10	11.5	2	0.30	675	445	41.5	0.4	148
65 up	1	0- 2	1024.5	928	65.6	1420	760	3.1	3.1	842
	2	2- 5	46.0	18	2.36	760	320	38.7	1.2	340
	3	5-10	18.0	5	1.17	425	174	46.2	0.6	213
Male										
All	1	0- 2 yrs	2573.0	2023	49.4	4100	2200	6.1	6.1	767
	2	2- 5	219.0	98	1.96	5000	965	21.6	1.3	439
	3	5-10	72.0	10	1.11	900	505	57.2	0.8	123
Female										
All	1	0- 2 yrs	2056.5	1647	31.4	5300	2800	6.3	6.3	786
	2	2- 5	188.0	81	1.47	5500	1190	25.2	1.6	423
	3	5-10	47.0	9	0.46	1970	605	55.6	0.9	182
Acute Lymphatic Leukemia										
Male										
All	1	0- 2 yrs	827.5	586	7.40	7900%	4400%	9.2%	9.2%	699
	2	2- 5	101.0	45	0.71	6400	1970	18.2	1.7	439
	3	5-10	21.5	5	0.185	2700	1030	41.0	0.7	224
Female										
All	1	0- 2 yrs	598.0	421	4.59	9200	5200	9.6	9.6	696
	2	2- 5	78.5	32	0.58	5600	2300	27.2	2.6	400
	3	5-10	26.0	5	0.21	2400	1160	48.3	1.3	184
Acute Myelocytic Leukemia										
Male										
All	1	0- 2 yrs	674.0	607	19.60	3100%	1650%	2.8%	2.8%	872
	2	2- 5	25.0	13	0.41	3200	685	20.6	0.6	504
	3	5-10	8.5	1	0.013	7500	360	70.1	0.4	116
Female										
All	1	0- 2 yrs	599.5	545	13.20	4100	2100	2.5	2.5	887
	2	2- 5	22.0	10	0.22	4500	870	24.6	0.6	444
	3	5-10	7.0	0	0.089	0	440	114.4	0.7	−13
Monocytic Leukemia										
Male										
All	1	0- 2 yrs	481.0	411	16.3	2500%	1400%	4.3%	4.3%	821
	2	2- 5	34.0	11	0.79	1390	590	39.4	1.7	300
	3	5-10	26.5	2	0.94	215	315	79.2	1.3	40
Female										
All	1	0- 2 yrs	431.0	380	10.00	3800	2100	3.5	3.5	858
	2	2- 5	28.0	9	0.56	1600	845	33.3	1.2	301
	3	5-10	5.5	3	0.143	2100	555	26.4	0.3	520

*Basis of expected mortality: Concurrent U.S. White Population Rates

1-81

ACUTE LEUKEMIA

Table 170b Acute Leukemia - Derived Mortality and Survival Data

Sex Age Group	No.	Start-End	Observed Survival Rate Cumulative	Interval	Ave. Ann.	Ave. Ann. Mort. Rate	Expected* Survival Rate Cumulative	Interval	Ave. Ann.	Ave. Ann. Mort. Rate
(Yrs)	i	t to $t+\Delta t$	P	p_i	$\check{p}$	$\check{q}$	P'	p_i'	$\check{p}'$	$\check{q}'$
Total Acute Leukemia										
M&F										
< 15	1	0- 2 yrs	.1120	.1120	.3347	.6653	.9976	.9976	.9988	.0012
	2	2- 5	.0214	.1911	.5760	.4240	.9961	.9985	.9995	.0005
	3	5-10	.0126	.5888	.8995	.1005	.9934	.9973	.9995	.0005
15-34	1	0- 2	.0361	.0361	.1900	.8100	.9976	.9976	.9988	.0012
	2	2- 5	.0095	.2632	.6409	.3591	.9936	.9960	.9987	.0013
	3	5-10	.0036	.3789	.8236	.1764	.9856	.9919	.9984	.0016
35-54	1	0- 2	.0279	.0279	.1670	.8330	.9892	.9892	.9946	.0054
	2	2- 5	.0073	.2016	.6396	.3604	.9694	.9800	.9933	.0067
	3	5-10	.0073	1.0000	1.0000	.0000	.9241	.9533	.9905	.0095
55-64	1	0- 2	.0392	.0392	.1980	.8020	.9647	.9647	.9822	.0178
	2	2- 5	.0087	.2219	.6054	.3946	.9030	.9360	.9782	.0218
	3	5-10	.0031	.3563	.8135	.1865	.7753	.8586	.9700	.0300
65 up	1	0- 2	.0274	.0274	.1655	.8345	.8720	.8720	.9338	.0662
	2	2- 5	.0084	.3066	.6743	.3257	.6908	.7922	.9253	.0747
	3	5-10	.0024	.2857	.7784	.2216	.4268	.6178	.9082	.0918
Male										
All	1	0- 2 yrs	.0589	.0589	.2427	.7573	.9580	.9580	.9788	.0212
	2	2- 5	.0119	.2020	.5867	.4133	.8974	.9367	.9784	.0216
	3	5-10	.0061	.5126	.8749	.1251	.8035	.8954	.9781	.0219
Female										
All	1	0- 2 yrs	.0611	.0611	.2472	.7528	.9665	.9665	.9831	.0169
	2	2- 5	.0146	.2389	.6205	.3795	.9169	.9487	.9826	.0174
	3	5-10	.0074	.5068	.8729	.1271	.8354	.9111	.9816	.0184
Acute Lymphatic Leukemia										
Male										
All	1	0- 2 yrs	.0902	.0902	.3003	.6997	.9794	.9794	.9896	.0104
	2	2- 5	.0159	.1763	.5607	.4393	.9500	.9700	.9899	.0101
	3	5-10	.0062	.3899	.8283	.1717	.9037	.9513	.9901	.0099
Female										
All	1	0- 2 yrs	.0946	.0946	.3076	.6924	.9826	.9826	.9913	.0087
	2	2- 5	.0251	.2653	.6426	.3574	.9570	.9739	.9912	.0088
	3	5-10	.0116	.4622	.8570	.1430	.9150	.9561	.9911	.0089
Acute Myelocytic Leukemia										
Male										
All	1	0- 2 yrs	.0262	.0262	.1619	.8381	.9409	.9409	.9700	.0300
	2	2- 5	.0049	.1870	.5718	.4282	.8551	.9088	.9686	.0314
	3	5-10	.0029	.5918	.9004	.0996	.7217	.8440	.9666	.0334
Female										
All	1	0- 2 yrs	.0236	.0236	.1536	.8464	.9543	.9543	.9769	.0231
	2	2- 5	.0054	.2288	.6116	.3884	.8860	.9284	.9755	.0245
	3	5-10	.0054	1.0000	1.0000	.0000	.7745	.8742	.9735	.0265
Monocytic Leukemia										
Male										
All	1	0- 2 yrs	.0397	.0397	.1992	.8008	.9315	.9315	.9651	.0349
	2	2- 5	.0140	.3526	.7065	.2935	.8330	.8943	.9634	.0366
	3	5-10	.0091	.6500	.9175	.0825	.6836	.8206	.9612	.0388
Female										
All	1	0- 2 yrs	.0331	.0331	.1819	.8181	.9529	.9529	.9762	.0238
	2	2- 5	.0102	.3082	.6755	.3245	.8829	.9265	.9749	.0251
	3	5-10	.0025	.2451	.7549	.2451	.8200	.9288	.9853	.0147

*Basis of expected mortality: Concurrent U.S. White Population Rates

CHRONIC LEUKEMIA

Table 171a   Chronic Leukemia - Observed Data and Comparative Experience by Sex, Age and Duration

Sex Age Group	No.	Start-End	Exposure Person-Yrs	Observed	Expected*	Interval 100d/d'	Cumulative 100Q/Q'	Interval 100p_i/p_i'	Cumulative 100P/P'	Excess Death Rate 1000(d-d')/E
(Yrs)	i	t to t + Δt	E	d	d'	100d/d'	100Q/Q'	100p_i/p_i'	100P/P'	1000(d-d')/E
Total Chronic M&F										
< 35	1	0- 2 yrs	466.5	204	0.61	34000%	27000%	33.7%	33.7%	436
	2	2- 5	240.0	58	0.31	18800	15300	42.6	14.4	240
	3	5-10	127.5	21	0.20	10400	7800	46.8	6.7	163
35-54	1	0- 2	1238.5	344	8.45	4100	3400	53.9	53.9	271
	2	2- 5	953.0	173	8.22	2100	1830	56.3	30.3	173
	3	5-10	633.5	109	7.48	1460	930	43.2	13.1	160
55-64	1	0- 2	1327.5	320	25.2	1270	1070	61.6	61.6	222
	2	2- 5	1118.0	221	25.4	870	670	55.2	34.0	175
	3	5-10	698.0	115	21.3	540	365	49.1	16.7	134
65-74	1	0- 2	1824.0	646	76.6	845	670	48.1	48.1	312
	2	2- 5	1190.5	266	58.9	450	365	55.3	26.6	174
	3	5-10	658.0	138	41.2	335	205	48.2	12.8	147
75 up	1	0- 2	1246.5	660	135.7	485	350	33.0	33.0	421
	2	2- 5	491.5	149	60.7	245	191	52.5	17.3	180
	3	5-10	216.5	59	35.3	167	125	50.6	8.8	109
Male All	1	0- 2 yrs	3685.0	1352	170.0	795	610	46.8	46.8	321
	2	2- 5	2293.0	537	104.0	515	355	52.9	24.8	189
	3	5-10	1266.0	242	65.6	370	220	48.8	12.1	139
Female All	1	0- 2 yrs	2418.0	822	76.4	1080	805	49.4	49.4	308
	2	2- 5	1700.0	330	49.5	665	460	58.6	29.0	165
	3	5-10	1067.5	200	39.5	505	280	46.5	13.5	150
Chronic Lymphatic										
Male All	1	0- 2 yrs	2341.0	676	118.3	570%	465%	58.4%	58.4%	238
	2	2- 5	1754.0	369	86.8	425	300	58.7	34.3	161
	3	5-10	1065.5	185	58.9	315	197	55.2	18.9	118
Female All	1	0- 2 yrs	1361.5	345	49.6	695	555%	62.4	62.4	217
	2	2- 5	1183.5	183	40.9	450	350	68.7	42.9	120
	3	5-10	857.0	140	35.9	390	235	54.5	23.4	122
Chronic Myeloid										
Male All	1	0- 2 yrs	1203.0	586	44.7	1310%	900%	31.0	31.0%	450
	2	2- 5	501.0	157	15.88	990	470	36.9	11.5	282
	3	5-10	181.5	52	6.34	820	270	26.9	3.1	252
Female All	1	0- 2 yrs	946.5	405	22.8	1780	1210	37.0	37.0	404
	2	2- 5	485.0	139	7.79	1780	650	38.8	14.4	271
	3	5-10	190.5	57	2.97	1920	360	22.6	3.2	284

*Basis of expected mortality: Concurrent U.S. White Population Rates

CHRONIC LEUKEMIA

Table 171b   Chronic Leukemia - Derived Mortality and Survival Data

Sex Age Group	Interval No.	Interval Start-End	Observed Survival Rate Cumulative	Observed Survival Rate Interval	Observed Survival Rate Ave. Ann.	Observed Ave. Ann. Mort. Rate	Expected* Survival Rate Cumulative	Expected* Survival Rate Interval	Expected* Survival Rate Ave. Ann.	Expected* Ave. Ann. Mort. Rate
(Yrs)	i	t to $t + \Delta t$	P	p_i	$\check{p}$	$\check{q}$	P'	p_i'	$\check{p}'$	$\check{q}'$
Total Chronic M&F										
< 35	1	0- 2 yrs	.3359	.3359	.5796	.4204	.9975	.9975	.9987	.00125
	2	2- 5	.1427	.4248	.7517	.2483	.9944	.9969	.9990	.00103
	3	5-10	.0663	.4646	.8579	.1421	.9880	.9936	.9987	.00128
35-54	1	0- 2	.5312	.5312	.7288	.2712	.9864	.9864	.9932	.0068
	2	2- 5	.2916	.5489	.8188	.1812	.9613	.9746	.9915	.0085
	3	5-10	.1187	.4071	.8355	.1645	.9050	.9414	.9880	.0120
55-64	1	0- 2	.5924	.5924	.7697	.2303	.9620	.9620	.9808	.0192
	2	2- 5	.3043	.5137	.8009	.1991	.8958	.9312	.9765	.0235
	3	5-10	.1268	.4167	.8394	.1606	.7604	.8489	.9678	.0322
65-74	1	0- 2	.4405	.4405	.6637	.3363	.9166	.9166	.9574	.0426
	2	2- 5	.2080	.4722	.7787	.2213	.7829	.8541	.9488	.0512
	3	5-10	.0700	.3365	.8043	.1957	.5469	.6986	.9308	.0692
75 up	1	0- 2	.2604	.2604	.5103	.4897	.7898	.7898	.8887	.1113
	2	2- 5	.0905	.3475	.7030	.2970	.5232	.6624	.8717	.1283
	3	5-10	.0187	.2066	.7295	.2705	.2135	.4081	.8359	.1641
Male All	1	0- 2	.4240	.4240	.6512	.3488	.9052	.9052	.9514	.0486
	2	2- 5	.1912	.4509	.7668	.2332	.7720	.8529	.9483	.0517
	3	5-10	.0698	.3651	.8175	.1825	.5772	.7477	.9435	.0565
Female All	1	0- 2	.4614	.4614	.6793	.3207	.9332	.9332	.9660	.0340
	2	2- 5	.2417	.5238	.8061	.1939	.8343	.8940	.9633	.0367
	3	5-10	.0911	.3769	.8227	.1773	.6765	.8109	.9589	.0411
Chronic Lymphatic Male All	1	0- 2 yrs	.5235	.5235	.7235	.2765	.8970	.8970	.9471	.0529
	2	2- 5	.2581	.4930	.7900	.2100	.7529	.8394	.9433	.0567
	3	5-10	.1028	.3983	.8318	.1682	.5437	.7221	.9370	.0630
Female All	1	0- 2 yrs	.5768	.5768	.7595	.2405	.9239	.9239	.9612	.0388
	2	2- 5	.3486	.6044	.8455	.1545	.8126	.8795	.9581	.0419
	3	5-10	.1489	.4271	.8435	.1565	.6371	.7840	.9525	.0475
Chronic Myeloid Male All	1	0- 2 yrs	.2857	.2857	.5345	.4655	.9205	.9205	.9594	.0406
	2	2- 5	.0925	.3238	.6867	.3133	.8067	.8764	.9570	.0430
	3	5-10	.0196	.2119	.7332	.2668	.6354	.7877	.9534	.0466
Female All	1	0- 2 yrs	.3502	.3502	.5918	.4082	.9463	.9463	.9728	.0272
	2	2- 5	.1241	.3544	.7077	.2923	.8648	.9139	.9704	.0296
	3	5-10	.0237	.1910	.7181	.2819	.7306	.8448	.9668	.0332

*Basis of expected mortality: Concurrent U.S. White Population Rates

LYMPHOSARCOMA
OTHER LYMPHOMAS

Table 172a   Lymphosarcoma and Other Lymphomas - Observed Data and Comparative Experience
by Sex, Age and Duration

Sex	Interval		Exposure	Deaths		Mortality Ratio		Survival Ratio		Excess
Age Group	No.	Start-End	Person-Yrs	Observed	Expected*	Interval	Cumulative	Interval	Cumulative	Death Rate
(Yrs)	i	t to t + Δ t	E	d	d'	100d/d'	100Q/Q'	100p$_i$/p$_i$'	100P/P'	1000(d-d')/E
Lymphosarcoma										
Male										
< 35	1	0- 2 yrs	340.0	153	0.42	36000%	28000%	34.9%	34.9%	449
	2	2- 5	210.0	22	0.27	8100	13600	72.7	25.3	103
	3	5-10	216.0	9	0.34	2600	6500	80.5	20.4	40
35-54	1	0- 2	907.0	205	5.45	3800	3200	62.1	62.1	220
	2	2- 5	850.0	106	6.21	1710	1710	68.6	42.6	117
	3	5-10	683.0	83	6.45	1290	915	57.6	24.5	112
55-64	1	0- 2	692.0	251	12.79	1960	1550	44.6	44.6	344
	2	2- 5	461.0	93	10.12	920	770	54.3	24.2	180
	3	5-10	299.5	37	8.68	425	380	62.3	15.1	95
65-74	1	0- 2	730.5	278	28.5	975	755	45.1	45.1	342
	2	2- 5	449.0	104	21.3	490	400	54.2	24.4	184
	3	5-10	243.5	53	14.95	355	220	40.7	10.0	156
75 up	1	0- 2	384.0	204	36.6	560	395	32.1	32.1	436
	2	2- 5	161.0	49	17.01	290	210	46.1	14.8	199
	3	5-10	62.5	16	8.13	197	131	39.2	5.8	126
Male										
All	1	0- 2 yrs	1721.5	612	52.8	1160	900	47.1	47.1	325
	2	2- 5	1202.0	206	36.3	570	485	63.4	29.9	141
	3	5-10	805.0	123	24.0	510	290	57.5	17.2	123
Female										
All	1	0- 2 yrs	1332.0	479	30.9	1550	1110	46.6	46.6	336
	2	2- 5	929.0	168	18.52	905	590	60.4	28.2	161
	3	5-10	699.5	75	14.60	515	325	65.6	18.5	86
Other Lymphomas										
M&F										
< 15	1	0- 2 yrs	86.0	42	0.44	9500%	8900%	30.2%	30.2%	483
	2	2- 5	50.0	2	0.033	6000	7500	89.1	26.9	39
	3	5-10	67.0	0	0.035	0	6100	100.2	27.0	−0.5
15-34	1	0- 2	110.0	13	0.154	8400	8000	77.7	77.7	117
	2	2- 5	122.5	7	0.196	3600	4600	83.9	65.2	56
	3	5-10	129.5	5	0.25	1980	2500	85.3	55.6	37
35-54	1	0- 2	408.0	54	2.30	2300	2100	76.4	76.4	127
	2	2- 5	442.5	49	2.99	1640	1430	71.7	54.8	104
	3	5-10	344.0	41	3.26	1260	865	59.0	32.3	110
55-64	1	0- 2	241.0	53	4.08	1300	1140	63.7	63.7	203
	2	2- 5	209.0	37	4.19	880	700	60.2	38.4	157
	3	5-10	152.5	21	4.29	490	380	58.5	22.4	110
65 up	1	0- 2	320.0	112	17.30	645	540	47.0	47.0	296
	2	2- 5	193.0	38	12.03	315	290	64.8	30.5	135
	3	5-10	108.5	22	8.49	260	175	57.2	17.4	125
Male										
All	1	0- 2 yrs	634.0	158	15.40	1030	875	59.8	59.8	225
	2	2- 5	535.0	74	11.59	640	510	69.5	41.6	117
	3	5-10	445.0	43	9.40	460	305	73.0	30.4	76
Female										
All	1	0- 2 yrs	531.0	116	8.85	1310	1120	63.9	63.9	202
	2	2- 5	482.0	59	7.84	755	655	72.2	46.1	106
	3	5-10	356.5	46	7.05	655	405	62.4	28.8	109

*Basis of expected mortality: Concurrent U.S. White Population Rates

LYMPHOSARCOMA
OTHER LYMPHOMAS

Table 172b   Lymphosarcoma and Other Lymphomas - Derived Mortality and Survival Data

Sex Age Group	Interval No.	Interval Start-End	Observed Survival Rate Cumulative	Observed Survival Rate Interval	Observed Survival Rate Ave. Ann.	Observed Ave. Ann. Mort. Rate	Expected* Survival Rate Cumulative	Expected* Survival Rate Interval	Expected* Survival Rate Ave. Ann.	Expected* Ave. Ann. Mort. Rate
(Yrs)	i	t to t + Δ t	P	p_i	$\check{p}$	$\check{q}$	P'	p_i'	$\check{p}'$	$\check{q}'$
Lymphosarcoma										
M&F										
< 35	1	0- 2 yrs	.3480	.3480	.5899	.4101	.9977	.9977	.9988	.00115
	2	2- 5	.2521	.7244	.8981	.1019	.9945	.9968	.9989	.00107
	3	5-10	.2016	.7997	.9563	.0437	.9877	.9932	.9986	.00136
35-54	1	0- 2	.6134	.6134	.7832	.2168	.9879	.9879	.9939	.0061
	2	2- 5	.4111	.6702	.8751	.1249	.9656	.9774	.9924	.0076
	3	5-10	.2243	.5456	.8859	.1141	.9152	.9478	.9893	.0107
55-64	1	0- 2	.4295	.4295	.6554	.3446	.9631	.9631	.9814	.0186
	2	2- 5	.2177	.5069	.7973	.2027	.8987	.9331	.9772	.0228
	3	5-10	.1157	.5315	.8813	.1187	.7663	.8527	.9686	.0314
65-74	1	0- 2	.4163	.4163	.6452	.3548	.9229	.9229	.9607	.0393
	2	2- 5	.1951	.4687	.7768	.2232	.7982	.8649	.9528	.0472
	3	5-10	.0570	.2922	.7819	.2181	.5726	.7174	.9357	.0643
75 up	1	0- 2	.2609	.2609	.5108	.4892	.8140	.8140	.9022	.0978
	2	2- 5	.0833	.3193	.6835	.3165	.5642	.6931	.8850	.1150
	3	5-10	.0143	.1717	.7030	.2970	.2473	.4383	.8479	.1521
Male										
All	1	0- 2 yrs	.4423	.4423	.6651	.3349	.9381	.9381	.9686	.0314
	2	2- 5	.2526	.5711	.8297	.1703	.8454	.9012	.9659	.0341
	3	5-10	.1195	.4731	.8610	.1390	.6953	.8225	.9617	.0383
Female										
All	1	0- 2 yrs	.4430	.4430	.6656	.3344	.9498	.9498	.9746	.0254
	2	2- 5	.2455	.5542	.8214	.1786	.8716	.9177	.9718	.0282
	3	5-10	.1361	.5544	.8887	.1113	.7361	.8445	.9668	.0332
Other Lymphomas										
M&F										
< 15	1	0- 2 yrs	.3000	.3000	.5477	.4523	.9921	.9921	.9960	.0040
	2	2- 5	.2667	.8890	.9615	.0385	.9902	.9981	.9994	.00063
	3	5-10	.2667	1.0000	1.0000	.0000	.9879	.9977	.9995	.00046
15-34	1	0- 2	.7750	.7750	.8803	.1197	.9972	.9972	.9986	.00140
	2	2- 5	.6468	.8346	.9415	.0585	.9924	.9952	.9984	.00160
	3	5-10	.5457	.8437	.9666	.0334	.9821	.9896	.9979	.0021
35-54	1	0- 2	.7552	.7552	.8690	.1310	.9884	.9884	.9942	.0058
	2	2- 5	.5297	.7014	.8885	.1115	.9671	.9785	.9928	.0072
	3	5-10	.2971	.5609	.8908	.1092	.9188	.9501	.9898	.0102
55-64	1	0- 2	.6159	.6159	.7848	.2152	.9662	.9662	.9830	.0170
	2	2- 5	.3478	.5647	.8266	.1734	.9069	.9386	.9791	.0209
	3	5-10	.1756	.5049	.8723	.1277	.7830	.8634	.9711	.0289
65 up	1	0- 2	.4197	.4197	.6478	.3522	.8925	.8925	.9447	.0553
	2	2- 5	.2228	.5309	.8097	.1903	.7315	.8196	.9358	.0642
	3	5-10	.0830	.3725	.8208	.1792	.4765	.6514	.9178	.0822
Male										
All	1	0- 2 yrs	.5689	.5689	.7543	.2457	.9507	.9507	.9750	.0250
	2	2- 5	.3641	.6400	.8618	.1382	.8754	.9208	.9729	.0271
	3	5-10	.2271	.6237	.9099	.0901	.7481	.8546	.9691	.0309
Female										
All	1	0- 2 yrs	.6172	.6172	.7856	.2144	.9658	.9658	.9828	.0172
	2	2- 5	.4204	.6811	.8798	.1202	.9112	.9435	.9808	.0192
	3	5-10	.2333	.5549	.8889	.1111	.8100	.8889	.9767	.0233

*Basis of expected mortality: Concurrent U.S. White Population Rates

HODGKIN'S DISEASE
RETICULUM CELL SARCOMA

Table 173a   Hodgkin's Disease and Reticulum Cell Sarcoma - Observed Data and
Comparative Experience by Sex, Age and Duration

Sex Age Group	Interval No.	Interval Start-End	Exposure Person-Yrs	Deaths Observed	Deaths Expected*	Mortality Ratio Interval	Mortality Ratio Cumulative	Survival Ratio Interval	Survival Ratio Cumulative	Excess Death Rate
(Yrs)	i	t to t + Δt	E	d	d'	100d/d'	100Q/Q'	100p$_i$/p$_i$'	100P/P'	1000(d-d')/E
Hodgkin's Disease										
Male										
< 25	1	0- 2 yrs	630.5	94	0.85	11100%	10700%	72.2%	72.2%	148
	2	2- 5	625.0	80	0.89	9000	7500	67.0	48.4	127
	3	5-10	467.5	58	0.71	8100	5100	54.7	26.5	123
25-44	1	0- 2	807.5	156	1.97	7900	7000	65.4	65.4	191
	2	2- 5	751.5	91	2.11	4300	4000	68.9	45.0	118
	3	5-10	603.5	68	2.33	2900	2100	58.7	26.4	109
45-54	1	0- 2	311.5	99	2.97	3300	2700	49.3	49.3	308
	2	2- 5	218.5	44	2.62	1680	1360	54.1	26.7	189
	3	5-10	131.5	13	2.19	595	630	67.0	17.9	82
55-64	1	0- 2	301.0	141	6.66	2100	1570	31.6	31.6	446
	2	2- 5	138.0	32	3.72	860	705	51.7	16.3	205
	3	5-10	88.0	8	3.42	235	325	82.1	13.4	52
65 up	1	0- 2	280.5	164	19.80	830	550	25.4	25.4	514
	2	2- 5	85.0	30	6.30	475	275	41.3	10.5	279
	3	5-10	32.0	7	2.88	245	160	58.9	6.2	129
Female										
< 25	1	0- 2 yrs	505.0	49	0.25	19400	16800	81.6	81.6	97
	2	2- 5	557.0	62	0.33	18600	15100	71.0	58.0	111
	3	5-10	437.0	38	0.29	13000	10100	63.1	36.6	86
25-44	1	0- 2	576.5	69	0.75	9200	8200	78.0	78.0	118
	2	2- 5	625.5	71	0.97	7300	6100	70.2	54.8	112
	3	5-10	516.0	44	1.15	3800	3300	68.1	37.3	83
45-54	1	0- 2	194.0	55	0.94	5900	4900	53.1	53.1	279
	2	2- 5	161.0	23	0.94	2400	2500	63.4	33.7	137
	3	5-10	131.5	12	1.07	1120	1200	65.1	21.9	83
55-64	1	0- 2	182.0	63	2.06	3100	2300	47.7	47.7	335
	2	2- 5	135.0	22	1.81	1220	1110	62.7	29.9	150
	3	5-10	109.5	11	2.04	540	520	70.9	21.2	82
65 up	1	0- 2	289.0	148	13.88	1070	740	31.0	31.0	464
	2	2- 5	125.0	35	6.11	575	365	46.1	14.3	231
	3	5-10	78.0	11	5.39	205	196	61.8	8.8	72
Reticulum Cell Sarcoma										
M&F										
< 25	1	0- 2 yrs	123.0	75	0.24	31000%	25000%	21.1%	21.1%	608
	2	2- 5	53.5	3	0.062	4800	14200	85.2	18.0	55
	3	5-10	63.0	2	0.079	2500	7900	85.5	15.4	30
25-54	1	0- 2	548.0	252	3.04	8300	6000	33.8	33.8	454
	2	2- 5	323.0	44	2.26	1950	2500	66.1	22.3	129
	3	5-10	246.5	19	2.38	800	1080	75.9	16.9	67
55-64	1	0- 2	404.5	233	6.87	3400	2300	21.3	21.3	559
	2	2- 5	149.0	21	2.86	735	910	68.8	14.6	122
	3	5-10	107.0	16	2.58	620	420	55.9	8.2	125
65-74	1	0- 2	299.0	201	10.85	1850	1160	16.4	16.4	636
	2	2- 5	85.0	17	3.66	465	475	60.6	9.9	157
	3	5-10	55.0	9	2.99	300	235	56.1	5.6	109
75 up	1	0- 2	197.0	144	19.20	750	465	15.1	15.1	634
	2	2- 5	41.0	14	4.65	300	220	43.4	6.5	228
	3	5-10	15.5	5	2.78	180	129	40.9	2.7	143

*Basis of expected mortality: Concurrent U.S. White Population Rates

HODGKIN'S DISEASE
RETICULUM CELL SARCOMA

Table 173b   Hodgkin's Disease and Reticulum Cell Sarcoma - Derived Mortality and Survival Data

Sex Age Group	No.	Start-End	Observed Survival Rate Cumulative	Interval	Ave. Ann.	Observed Ave. Ann. Mort. Rate	Expected* Survival Rate Cumulative	Interval	Ave. Ann.	Expected Ave. Ann. Mort. Rate
(Yrs)	i	t to t + Δt	P	p_i	$\check{p}$	$\check{q}$	P'	p_i'	$\check{p}'$	$\check{q}'$
Hodgkin's Disease										
Male										
< 25	1	0- 2 yrs	.7206	.7206	.8489	.1511	.9974	.9974	.9987	.00130
	2	2- 5	.4811	.6676	.8740	.1260	.9931	.9957	.9986	.00144
	3	5-10	.2613	.5431	.8851	.1149	.9855	.9923	.9985	.00154
25-44	1	0- 2	.6503	.6503	.8065	.1935	.9950	.9950	.9975	.0025
	2	2- 5	.4441	.6829	.8806	.1194	.9860	.9910	.9970	.0030
	3	5-10	.2549	.5740	.8949	.1051	.9646	.9783	.9956	.0044
45-54	1	0- 2	.4839	.4839	.6956	.3044	.9808	.9808	.9904	.0096
	2	2- 5	.2521	.5210	.8047	.1953	.9452	.9637	.9878	.0122
	3	5-10	.1546	.6132	.9068	.0932	.8656	.9158	.9826	.0174
55-64	1	0- 2	.3020	.3020	.5495	.4505	.9556	.9556	.9775	.0225
	2	2- 5	.1436	.4755	.7805	.2195	.8786	.9194	.9724	.0276
	3	5-10	.0971	.6762	.9247	.0753	.7237	.8237	.9620	.0380
65 up	1	0- 2	.2182	.2182	.4671	.5329	.8576	.8576	.9261	.0739
	2	2- 5	.0696	.3190	.6833	.3167	.6619	.7718	.9173	.0827
	3	5-10	.0242	.3477	.8095	.1905	.3906	.5901	.8999	.1001
Female										
< 25	1	0- 2 yrs	.8151	.8151	.9028	.0972	.9989	.9989	.9994	.00055
	2	2- 5	.5780	.7091	.8917	.1083	.9972	.9983	.9994	.00057
	3	5-10	.3637	.6292	.9115	.0885	.9937	.9965	.9993	.00070
25-44	1	0- 2	.7777	.7777	.8819	.1181	.9973	.9973	.9986	.00135
	2	2- 5	.5436	.6990	.8875	.1125	.9925	.9952	.9984	.00160
	3	5-10	.3657	.6727	.9238	.0762	.9810	.9884	.9977	.0023
45-54	1	0- 2	.5259	.5259	.7252	.2748	.9903	.9903	.9951	.0049
	2	2- 5	.3276	.6229	.8540	.1460	.9728	.9823	.9941	.0059
	3	5-10	.2046	.6245	.9101	.0899	.9336	.9597	.9918	.0082
55-64	1	0- 2	.4661	.4661	.6827	.3173	.9768	.9768	.9883	.0117
	2	2- 5	.2797	.6001	.8435	.1565	.9351	.9573	.9856	.0144
	3	5-10	.1786	.6385	.9142	.0858	.8422	.9007	.9793	.0207
65 up	1	0- 2	.2800	.2800	.5292	.4708	.9030	.9030	.9503	.0497
	2	2- 5	.1081	.3861	.7282	.2718	.7560	.8372	.9425	.0575
	3	5-10	.0454	.4200	.8407	.1593	.5138	.6796	.9257	.0743
Reticulum Cell Sarcoma										
M&F										
< 25	1	0- 2 yrs	.2105	.2105	.4588	.5412	.9969	.9969	.9984	.00155
	2	2- 5	.1789	.8499	.9472	.0528	.9942	.9973	.9991	.00090
	3	5-10	.1522	.8508	.9682	.0318	.9893	.9951	.9990	.00098
25-54	1	0- 2	.3344	.3344	.5783	.4217	.9889	.9889	.9944	.0056
	2	2- 5	.2164	.6471	.8649	.1351	.9685	.9794	.9931	.0069
	3	5-10	.1563	.7223	.9370	.0630	.9222	.9522	.9903	.0097
55-64	1	0- 2	.2054	.2054	.4532	.5468	.9653	.9653	.9825	.0175
	2	2- 5	.1324	.6446	.8638	.1362	.9045	.9370	.9785	.0215
	3	5-10	.0637	.4811	.8639	.1361	.7782	.8604	.9704	.0296
65-74	1	0- 2	.1519	.1519	.3897	.6103	.9268	.9268	.9627	.0373
	2	2- 5	.0802	.5280	.8082	.1918	.8069	.8706	.9549	.0451
	3	5-10	.0327	.4077	.8357	.1643	.5862	.7265	.9381	.0619
75 up	1	0- 2	.1220	.1220	.3493	.6507	.8106	.8106	.9003	.0997
	2	2- 5	.0366	.3000	.6694	.3306	.5609	.6920	.8845	.1155
	3	5-10	.0061	.1667	.6989	.3011	.2288	.4079	.8358	.1642

*Basis of expected mortality: Concurrent U.S. White Population Rates

CANCER—BONE AND SOFT TISSUES

§180–MULTIPLE MYELOMA, CANCER OF THE BONE

Multiple myeloma ranks 24th among cancer sites in both males and females and has a relative frequency of 0.9 per cent and 0.8 per cent, respectively (Tables 100a-b). Experience for multiple myeloma for male and female patients combined is presented in five age categories in the upper part of Tables 180a-b, with about 60 per cent of the exposure in the age range 55 to 74 years. Mortality ratios in the first interval were extremely high, decreasing from 11900 per cent in patients under age 45 to 645 per cent in the oldest group, age 75 up. EDR's within two years of diagnosis ranged from 344 to 549 per 1000. Decreasing but high levels of excess mortality persisted in the two subsequent intervals; exposures were limited from 5-10 years after diagnosis. Cumulative five-year survival ratios ranged between a maximum of 21.9 per cent for patients under age 45 to about 7 per cent in those age 55 and up.

Bone cancer ranks 31st among male cancers and 30th among female cancers and has a relative frequency of 0.5 per cent and 0.4 per cent, respectively (Tables 100a-b). Comparative experience is presented in the lower portion of Tables 180a-b. Mortality ratios in the first observation interval, starting at 32000 per cent in males and females under age 25, decreased with age to 545 per cent, age 65 and up. EDR's observed within two years of diagnosis ranged from 71 to 274 extra deaths per 1000, the minimum occurring in younger adults age 25 to 44 years. Within the first five years EDR's were highest and survival ratios lowest in the youngest age group, children and adults under age 25, who comprised an unusually high fraction of the total experience. There was not much change in EDR with advancing age in the oldest age groups, but EDR's, like the mortality ratios, did decrease from one interval to the next. The best cumulative five-year survival ratio, 75.9 per cent, was found in patients age 25-44, and the worst, 37.2 per cent, in patients under age 25. When all ages were combined in patients with localized bone cancer males tended to have higher EDR's and lower survival ratios than the females. Sex differences in patients with regional extension of bone cancer followed a similar pattern, but EDR's were higher than in the localized cases, and worst of all in patients in the metastatic stage, the EDR in the first observation interval being 737 per 1000, and the cumulative five-year survival ratio only 3.4 per cent, males and females combined.

§181–CANCER OF THE CONNECTIVE TISSUE

Cancer of the connective tissue ranks 22nd among cancer sites in males and 21st in females (Tables 100a-b); it accounts for 1.0 per cent of all male and 0.9 per cent of all female cancer cases. Ten-year results for localized cases are presented for males and females combined, in five age groups, and for males and females separately, all ages combined, in the upper portion of Tables 181a-b. Mortality ratios within two years of diagnosis were greatest under age 25 and steadily decreased with age, while the highest EDR's, 124 and 136 extra deaths per 1000, were observed in the youngest and oldest age group, respectively. Five-year survival ratios were highest, 78.5 per cent in the 45-54 age group and lowest, 58.8 per cent, in patients at ages 65 and up. Both mortality ratios and survival ratios were higher in female patients than in males, but this was not true for excess death rates in the first five years. Data for patients with regional extension reveal higher EDR's for males, decreasing by interval from 374 to 68 per 1000, compared with a corresponding range of 244 to 35 per 1000 in females. Very high levels of excess mortality were observed in patients with metastatic cancer of the connective tissue: a mortality ratio of 2900 per cent and a rate of 679 extra deaths per 1000 per year during the first observation interval. As EDR's increased, cumulative five-year survival ratios decreased with stage of cancer extension, from about 70 per cent in localized cancer, to roughly 35 per cent in patients with regional extension, to 6.5 per cent in those with evidence of metastasis at diagnosis. Survival ratios were better in female than in male patients. Limited data for the 10-20 year experience for patients diagnosed as having cancer of the connective tissue in the localized stage (shown at the bottom of Tables 181a-b) suggest that excess mortality persisted in most of the age and duration categories. However, care must be taken in interpreting these figures because of the small exposures and numbers of deaths.

CANCER—BONE AND SOFT TISSUES

§182—MELANOMA OF THE SKIN

Melanoma of skin ranks 19th among all male cancers and 17th among all female cancers and accounts for 1.2 and 1.3 per cent of the total cases, respectively (Tables 100a-b). Sixty per cent of cases were diagnosed under age 55 and about 70 per cent were classified in the localized stage.

Ten-year experience for three stages of this type of cancer is presented in the upper portion of Tables 182a-b. In the localized stage, results are presented for males and females combined, under age 25, and for males and females separately in four older age categories. The mortality ratio for patients under 25 was 2300 per cent in the first interval, rose to 3700 per cent in the second, and dropped back to 1820 per cent in the third interval. The EDR's followed a similar pattern in the three intervals with 20, 32, and 18 extra deaths per 1000, respectively. The cumulative five-year survival ratio was 87.1 per cent, also reflecting a relatively good prognosis in children and young adults. Among the older patients, the interval mortality ratios decreased with advancing age from 1530 to 113 per cent in males, and from 1910 to 106 per cent in females. There was no consistent pattern of sex differences in mortality ratios. Excess death rates in the two intervals within five years of diagnosis increased with advancing age in all but two of the age and duration categories. Contrary to what is observed in most other types of cancer, EDR's were not always higher in the first than in the second interval; there was, however, a consistent decrease in EDR in the third interval, 5-10 years after diagnosis. Cumulative five-year survival ratios tended to decrease from 80.9 per cent in males age 25-44 to about 62 per cent in the age groups 55-64 and 65 up, and from 87.0 per cent in females age 25-44 to 65.2 per cent in the oldest age group.

Ten-year results for patients of all ages diagnosed in the regional stage, males and females separately, and for patients diagnosed in the metastatic stage, both sexes combined, are presented next. In the regional stage, males had somewhat higher mortality ratios and EDR's, and lower interval survival ratios in the first two intervals, with the pattern reversing in the third interval. Mortality ratios and EDR's decreased with duration in both sexes. Within two years of diagnosis, the mortality ratio in males was 1250 per cent and the EDR 290 per 1000, while the corresponding female figures were 1120 per cent and 189 per 1000. Cumulative five-year survival ratios were 33.1 per cent for males and 47.2 per cent for females. For patients with metastasis, the mortality ratio decreased with duration from 2800 to 82 per cent. The EDR within two years of diagnosis was an extremely high 643 extra deaths per 1000 and the cumulative five-year survival ratio was only 9.9 per cent.

In the 10-20 year observation period, data for patients in the localized stage are presented in the lower portion of Tables 182a-b. The data should be interpreted with caution because there were fewer than ten deaths in all categories except one. When all data by age and sex are combined, a mortality ratio of 142 per cent and EDR of 11 per 1000 reflect some continued excess mortality in the fourth interval, 10-15 years after diagnosis. However, there was no significant excess mortality 15-20 years after diagnosis, based on 12 observed and 11.54 expected deaths.

Tables 182c-d present data for melanoma of skin, all sites combined, and separately for four regional body sites: face, head and neck, trunk, upper extremities and lower extremities. Results have been combined for patients of all ages, but in the localized stage, male and female data are given separately.

In patients with localized malignant melanoma of the face, head or neck, the excess death rate in the first interval was the highest of the four body surface areas (sites). In the first interval the EDR in male patients was 75 per 1000 for this site, 60 per 1000 in melanoma of the trunk, 51 per 1000, arm and hand, and 35 per 1000, leg and foot. Corresponding EDR's by site in female patients were 44, 55, 38, and 30 per 1000, respectively. Excess mortality decreased from the first to the second interval in patients with melanoma of the arm and hand, but in all other areas of the body a consistent and unusual increase was observed for both EDR and mortality ratio. In the third interval, 5-10 years after diagnosis, mortality ratios and EDR's were lower. For all sites combined EDR was close to 60 per 1000 in males and 40 per 1000 in females within five years of diagnosis; from 5-10 years EDR's were 19 and 17 per 1000, respectively, in males and females. The cumulative five-year survival ratios in the localized stage were 73.1 per cent in men and 81.5 per cent in women, all sites combined.

In the regional stage for all sites, males and females combined, the EDR's decreased with duration from 246 to 39 per 1000. The overall cumulative five-year survival ratio dropped to only 39.3 per cent. All of the melanoma subsites followed a similar pattern of decreasing EDR's with duration. EDR's in the first interval were very high, ranging from 304 per 1000 in patients with melanoma of the trunk to 193 per 1000 in those with melanoma of the leg and foot. Cumulative five-year survival ratios by site were: 29.0 per cent for melanoma of the face, head or neck; 32.3 per cent for the trunk; 46.0 per cent for the arm and hand; and 47.7 per cent for the leg and foot.

MULTIPLE MYELOMA
CANCER—BONE

Table 180a   Multiple Myeloma and Cancer of the Bone - Observed Data and Comparative Experience by Stage, Sex, Age and Duration

Stage & Sex Age Group	Interval No.	Interval Start-End	Exposure Person-Yrs	Deaths Observed	Deaths Expected*	Mortality Ratio Interval	Mortality Ratio Cumulative	Survival Ratio Interval	Survival Ratio Cumulative	Excess Death Rate
(Yrs)	i	t to t + Δt	E	d	d'	100d/d'	100Q/Q'	100p$_i$/p$_i$'	100P/P'	1000(d-d')/E
Multiple Myeloma										
All Cases										
M&F										
< 45	1	0- 2 yrs	164.5	57	0.48	11900%	9500%	45.1%	45.1%	344
	2	2- 5	99.5	23	0.38	6000	4700	48.5	21.9	227
	3	5-10	65.0	6	0.38	1600	2000	62.9	13.8	87
45-54	1	0- 2	403.0	189	3.29	5700	4300	30.6	30.6	461
	2	2- 5	186.0	43	1.84	2300	1850	48.4	14.8	221
	3	5-10	104.5	19	1.29	1480	835	44.4	6.6	170
55-64	1	0- 2	817.0	426	14.51	2900	2100	26.0	26.0	504
	2	2- 5	276.0	106	5.97	1770	955	26.1	6.8	362
	3	5-10	72.5	23	1.78	1290	435	22.5	1.5	293
65-74	1	0- 2	785.5	457	30.0	1520	1030	21.9	21.9	544
	2	2- 5	217.5	86	9.59	895	470	28.3	6.2	351
	3	5-10	61.5	17	3.57	475	230	42.4	2.6	218
75 up	1	0- 2	429.5	279	43.3	645	425	21.6	21.6	549
	2	2- 5	110.5	43	13.48	320	215	34.0	7.4	267
	3	5-10	26.0	7	4.55	154	130	47.0	3.5	94
Bone										
Localized										
M&F										
< 25	1	0- 2 yrs	433.5	119	0.37	32000%	31000%	51.1%	51.1%	274
	2	2- 5	317.0	34	0.26	12900	15000	72.7	37.2	106
	3	5-10	298.0	9	0.29	3100	7200	88.0	32.7	29
25-44	1	0- 2	192.5	14	0.40	3500	3200	86.4	86.4	71
	2	2- 5	243.5	11	0.57	1940	2100	87.9	75.9	43
	3	5-10	289.0	9	0.90	1000	1180	86.8	65.9	28
45-54	1	0- 2	113.0	22	0.82	2700	2500	64.9	64.9	187
	2	2- 5	101.5	8	0.89	900	1190	81.1	52.6	70
	3	5-10	101.0	3	1.25	240	560	90.4	47.5	17
55-64	1	0- 2	130.0	35	2.24	1560	1360	55.2	55.2	252
	2	2- 5	107.5	10	2.20	455	635	79.9	44.1	73
	3	5-10	98.0	7	2.65	265	330	78.9	34.8	44
65 up	1	0- 2	124.0	37	6.82	545	470	56.0	56.0	243
	2	2- 5	94.0	14	5.37	260	260	75.4	42.2	92
	3	5-10	84.0	3	4.80	62	147	122.3	51.6	−21
Male										
All	1	0- 2 yrs	513.0	126	6.20	2000	1770	58.0	58.0	234
	2	2- 5	424.0	43	5.19	830	935	76.7	44.4	89
	3	5-10	411.5	18	5.68	315	515	87.4	38.8	30
Female										
All	1	0- 2 yrs	480.0	101	4.45	2300	2000	62.9	62.9	201
	2	2- 5	439.5	34	4.07	835	1030	81.4	51.2	68
	3	5-10	458.5	13	4.27	305	540	91.3	46.7	19
Regional										
Male										
All	1	0- 2 yrs	195.5	73	4.70	1550	1230	41.8	41.8	349
	2	2- 5	119.5	18	3.29	545	635	67.1	28.0	123
	3	5-10	105.0	10	3.18	315	380	66.9	18.8	65
Female										
All	1	0- 2 yrs	160.0	54	2.09	2600	1920	45.7	45.7	324
	2	2- 5	115.0	11	1.54	715	885	77.7	35.5	82
	3	5-10	107.5	5	1.73	290	460	84.0	29.8	30
Metastatic										
M&F										
All	1	0- 2 yrs	238.0	180	4.50	4000	2300	7.5	7.5	737
	2	2- 5	28.0	8	0.53	1520	965	45.7	3.4	267
	3	5-10	21.5	2	0.49	405	490	60.0	2.1	70

*Basis of expected mortality: Concurrent U.S. White Population Rates

MULTIPLE MYELOMA
CANCER—BONE

Table 180b   Multiple Myeloma and Cancer of the Bone - Derived Mortality and Survival Data

Stage & Sex Age Group	No.	Start-End	Cumulative P	Interval p_i	Ave. Ann. $\breve{p}$	Ave. Ann. Mort. Rate $\breve{q}$	Cumulative P'	Interval p_i'	Ave. Ann. $\breve{p}'$	Ave. Ann. Mort. Rate $\breve{q}'$
(Yrs)	i	t to t+Δt								
Multiple Myeloma										
All Cases M&F										
< 45	1	0- 2 yrs	.4483	.4483	.6696	.3304	.9942	.9942	.9971	.0029
	2	2- 5	.2149	.4794	.7826	.2174	.9832	.9889	.9963	.0037
	3	5-10	.1316	.6124	.9066	.0934	.9566	.9729	.9945	.0055
45-54	1	0- 2	.3012	.3012	.5488	.4512	.9836	.9836	.9918	.0082
	2	2- 5	.1413	.4691	.7770	.2230	.9536	.9695	.9897	.0103
	3	5-10	.0583	.4126	.8377	.1623	.8869	.9301	.9856	.0144
55-64	1	0- 2	.2511	.2511	.5011	.4989	.9643	.9643	.9820	.0180
	2	2- 5	.0613	.2441	.6250	.3750	.9018	.9352	.9779	.0221
	3	5-10	.0118	.1925	.7193	.2807	.7725	.8566	.9695	.0305
65-74	1	0- 2	.2019	.2019	.4493	.5507	.9226	.9226	.9605	.0395
	2	2- 5	.0494	.2447	.6255	.3745	.7973	.8642	.9525	.0475
	3	5-10	.0150	.3036	.7879	.2121	.5709	.7160	.9354	.0646
75 up	1	0- 2	.1740	.1740	.4171	.5829	.8050	.8050	.8972	.1028
	2	2- 5	.0405	.2328	.6152	.3848	.5505	.6839	.8810	.1190
	3	5-10	.0082	.2025	.7266	.2734	.2371	.4307	.8450	.1550
Bone Localized M&F										
< 25	1	0- 2 yrs	.5106	.5106	.7146	.2854	.9984	.9984	.9992	.00080
	2	2- 5	.3703	.7252	.8984	.1016	.9958	.9974	.9991	.00087
	3	5-10	.3240	.8750	.9736	.0264	.9906	.9948	.9990	.00104
25-44	1	0- 2	.8604	.8604	.9276	.0724	.9957	.9957	.9978	.0022
	2	2- 5	.7501	.8718	.9553	.0447	.9879	.9922	.9974	.0026
	3	5-10	.6388	.8516	.9684	.0316	.9695	.9814	.9963	.0037
45-54	1	0- 2	.6393	.6393	.7996	.2004	.9853	.9853	.9926	.0074
	2	2- 5	.5041	.7885	.9238	.0762	.9584	.9727	.9908	.0092
	3	5-10	.4266	.8463	.9672	.0328	.8976	.9366	.9870	.0130
55-64	1	0- 2	.5333	.5333	.7303	.2697	.9656	.9656	.9826	.0174
	2	2- 5	.3996	.7493	.9083	.0917	.9052	.9374	.9787	.0213
	3	5-10	.2716	.6797	.9257	.0743	.7794	.8610	.9705	.0295
65 up	1	0- 2	.5000	.5000	.7071	.2929	.8932	.8932	.9451	.0549
	2	2- 5	.3108	.6216	.8534	.1466	.7368	.8249	.9379	.0621
	3	5-10	.2532	.8147	.9598	.0402	.4908	.6661	.9220	.0780
Male All										
	1	0- 2 yrs	.5655	.5655	.7520	.2480	.9754	.9754	.9876	.0124
	2	2- 5	.4166	.7367	.9032	.0968	.9375	.9611	.9869	.0131
	3	5-10	.3385	.8125	.9593	.0407	.8713	.9294	.9855	.0145
Female All										
	1	0- 2 yrs	.6165	.6165	.7852	.2148	.9809	.9809	.9904	.0096
	2	2- 5	.4863	.7888	.9240	.0760	.9500	.9685	.9894	.0106
	3	5-10	.4170	.8575	.9697	.0303	.8923	.9393	.9876	.0124
Regional Male All										
	1	0- 2 yrs	.3977	.3977	.6306	.3694	.9509	.9509	.9751	.0249
	2	2- 5	.2471	.6213	.8533	.1467	.8810	.9265	.9749	.0251
	3	5-10	.1453	.5880	.8992	.1008	.7742	.8788	.9745	.0255
Female All										
	1	0- 2 yrs	.4433	.4433	.6658	.3342	.9710	.9710	.9854	.0146
	2	2- 5	.3279	.7397	.9044	.0956	.9239	.9515	.9836	.0164
	3	5-10	.2496	.7612	.9469	.0531	.8376	.9066	.9806	.0194
Metastatic M&F All										
	1	0- 2 yrs	.0722	.0722	.2687	.7313	.9601	.9601	.9798	.0202
	2	2- 5	.0309	.4280	.7536	.2464	.8997	.9371	.9786	.0214
	3	5-10	.0165	.5340	.8821	.1179	.8003	.8895	.9769	.0231

*Basis of expected mortality: Concurrent U.S. White Population Rates

CANCER—CONNECTIVE TISSUE

Table 181a   Cancer of the Connective Tissue - Observed Data and Comparative Experience by Stage, Sex, Age and Duration

Stage & Sex Age Group	No.	Start-End	Exposure Person-Yrs	Observed	Expected*	Interval	Cumulative	Interval	Cumulative	Excess Death Rate
(Yrs)	i	t to t + Δt	E	d	d'	100d/d'	100Q/Q'	100p_i/p_i'	100P/P'	1000(d-d')/E
Localized										
M&F										
< 25	1	0- 2 yrs	350.0	44	0.71	6200%	6000%	76.9%	76.9%	124
	2	2- 5	389.5	19	0.31	6100	5400	86.6	66.6	48
	3	5-10	469.0	5	0.38	1310	3500	94.8	63.2	9.8
25-44	1	0- 2	506.0	31	1.11	2800	2700	88.4	88.4	59
	2	2- 5	624.0	31	1.70	1820	1920	86.8	76.8	47
	3	5-10	730.5	12	2.83	425	945	93.8	72.0	13
45-54	1	0- 2	361.5	28	2.56	1090	1050	86.3	86.3	70
	2	2- 5	455.0	18	3.98	450	615	91.0	78.5	31
	3	5-10	503.5	15	6.07	245	360	91.2	71.6	18
55-64	1	0- 2	369.0	43	6.19	695	650	80.9	80.9	100
	2	2- 5	424.0	24	8.61	280	370	89.7	72.5	36
	3	5-10	433.0	26	12.20	215	240	85.6	62.1	32
65 up	1	0- 2	605.0	122	40.0	305	285	72.9	72.9	136
	2	2- 5	534.0	75	36.4	205	195	80.7	58.8	72
	3	5-10	440.5	45	35.5	127	136	92.9	54.6	22
Male										
All	1	0- 2 yrs	1128.5	159	31.3	510	485	77.9	77.9	113
	2	2- 5	1195.5	90	29.9	300	315	86.4	67.4	50
	3	5-10	1259.0	47	30.5	154	210	95.9	64.6	13
Female										
All	1	0- 2 yrs	1063.0	109	19.20	570	525	83.7	83.7	85
	2	2- 5	1231.0	77	21.2	365	360	87.8	73.5	45
	3	5-10	1317.5	56	26.5	210	240	90.4	66.4	22
Regional										
Male										
All	1	0- 2 yrs	247.0	99	6.51	1520	1100	40.8	40.8	374
	2	2- 5	158.0	25	4.26	585	550	65.5	26.7	131
	3	5-10	128.0	12	3.32	360	310	75.5	20.2	68
Female										
All	1	0- 2 yrs	245.0	64	4.18	1530	1200	57.7	57.7	244
	2	2- 5	206.5	23	2.72	845	655	75.1	43.3	98
	3	5-10	181.0	9	2.69	335	370	88.8	38.5	35
Metastatic										
M&F										
All	1	0- 2 yrs	456.5	321	11.00	2900	1780	13.5	13.5	679
	2	2- 5	107.0	26	2.86	910	780	48.3	6.5	216
	3	5-10	54.0	7	1.71	410	405	63.5	4.1	98
Localized										
M&F										
< 45	4	10-15 yrs	1016.0	8	4.14	193		98.4		3.8
	5	15-20	409.0	2	2.13	94		99.9		−0.3
45-54	4	10-15	306.5	11	6.00	183		91.4		16
	5	15-20	131.5	4	3.88	103		97.7		0.9
55-64	4	10-15	283.5	21	12.60	167		85.7		30
	5	15-20	87.5	9	5.80	155		86.5		37
65-74	4	10-15	118.5	15	12.00	125		89.3		25
	5	15-20	29.0	7	3.99	176		45.8		104
75 up	4	10-15	23.0	7	4.49	156		116.8		109
	5	15-20	5.0	0	1.41	0		528.8		−283

*Basis of expected mortality: Concurrent U.S. White Population Rates

CANCER—CONNECTIVE TISSUE

Table 181b   Cancer of the Connective Tissue - Derived Mortality and Survival Data

Stage & Sex Age Group	Interval			Observed				Expected*			
	No.	Start-End	Survival Rate			Ave. Ann. Mort. Rate	Survival Rate			Ave. Ann. Mort. Rate
			Cumulative	Interval	Ave. Ann.		Cumulative	Interval	Ave. Ann.	
(Yrs)	i	t to $t + \Delta t$	P	p_i	$\breve{p}$	$\breve{q}$	P'	p_i'	$\breve{p}'$	$\breve{q}'$
Localized										
M&F										
< 25	1	0- 2 yrs	.7660	.7660	.8752	.1248	.9961	.9961	.9980	.0020
	2	2- 5	.6620	.8642	.9525	.0475	.9937	.9976	.9992	.0008
	3	5-10	.6249	.9440	.9885	.0115	.9892	.9955	.9991	.0009
25-44	1	0- 2	.8803	.8803	.9382	.0618	.9956	.9956	.9978	.0022
	2	2- 5	.7581	.8612	.9514	.0486	.9874	.9918	.9973	.0027
	3	5-10	.6971	.9195	.9834	.0166	.9679	.9803	.9960	.0040
45-54	1	0- 2	.8504	.8504	.9222	.0778	.9858	.9858	.9929	.0071
	2	2- 5	.7536	.8862	.9605	.0395	.9598	.9736	.9911	.0089
	3	5-10	.6456	.8567	.9695	.0305	.9017	.9395	.9876	.0124
55-64	1	0- 2	.7817	.7817	.8841	.1159	.9663	.9663	.9830	.0170
	2	2- 5	.6580	.8418	.9442	.0558	.9073	.9389	.9792	.0208
	3	5-10	.4869	.7400	.9416	.0584	.7843	.8644	.9713	.0287
65 up	1	0- 2	.6358	.6358	.7974	.2026	.8721	.8721	.9339	.0661
	2	2- 5	.4097	.6444	.8637	.1363	.6968	.7990	.9279	.0721
	3	5-10	.2409	.5880	.8992	.1008	.4412	.6332	.9127	.0873
Male										
All	1	0- 2 yrs	.7370	.7370	.8585	.1415	.9455	.9455	.9724	.0276
	2	2- 5	.5858	.7948	.9263	.0737	.8694	.9195	.9724	.0276
	3	5-10	.4861	.8298	.9634	.0366	.7526	.8657	.9716	.0284
Female										
All	1	0- 2 yrs	.8061	.8061	.8978	.1022	.9631	.9631	.9814	.0186
	2	2- 5	.6666	.8269	.9386	.0614	.9072	.9420	.9803	.0197
	3	5-10	.5369	.8054	.9576	.0424	.8086	.8913	.9772	.0228
Regional										
Male										
All	1	0- 2 yrs	.3851	.3851	.6206	.3794	.9440	.9440	.9716	.0284
	2	2- 5	.2298	.5967	.8419	.1581	.8601	.9111	.9694	.0306
	3	5-10	.1458	.6345	.9130	.0870	.7229	.8405	.9658	.0342
Female										
All	1	0- 2 yrs	.5556	.5556	.7454	.2546	.9630	.9630	.9813	.0187
	2	2- 5	.3930	.7073	.8910	.1090	.9074	.9423	.9804	.0196
	3	5-10	.3127	.7957	.9553	.0447	.8132	.8962	.9783	.0217
Metastatic										
M&F										
All	1	0- 2 yrs	.1283	.1283	.3582	.6418	.9511	.9511	.9752	.0248
	2	2- 5	.0573	.4466	.7644	.2356	.8791	.9243	.9741	.0259
	3	5-10	.0315	.5497	.8872	.1128	.7612	.8659	.9716	.0284
Localized										
M&F										
< 45	4	10-15 yrs		.9635	.9926	.0074		.9796	.9959	.0041
	5	15-20		.9728	.9945	.0055		.9740	.9947	.0053
45-54	4	10-15		.8251	.9623	.0377		.9029	.9798	.0202
	5	15-20		.8358	.9648	.0352		.8559	.9694	.0306
55-64	4	10-15		.6780	.9252	.0748		.7915	.9543	.0457
	5	15-20		.6075	.9051	.0949		.7027	.9319	.0681
65-74	4	10-15		.5126	.8749	.1251		.5740	.8949	.1051
	5	15-20		.2143	.7349	.2651		.4674	.8589	.1411
75 up	4	10-15		.3714	.8203	.1797		.3180	.7952	.2048
	5	15-20		1.0000	1.0000	.0000		.1891	.7167	.2833

*Basis of expected mortality: Concurrent U.S. White Population Rates

MELANOMA

Table 182a   Melanoma-Observed Data and Comparative Experience by Stage, Sex, Age and Duration

Stage & Sex Age Group	No.	Start-End	Exposure Person-Yrs	Observed	Expected*	Mortality Ratio Interval	Mortality Ratio Cumulative	Survival Ratio Interval	Survival Ratio Cumulative	Excess Death Rate
(Yrs)	i	t to $t + \Delta t$	E	d	d'	100 d/d'	100 Q/Q'	100 p_i/p_i'	100 P/P'	1000(d-d')/E
Localized M & F										
< 25	1	0- 2 yrs	245.0	5	0.22	2300%	2400%	96.1%	96.1%	20
	2	2- 5	333.0	11	0.30	3700	3000	90.7	87.1	32
	3	5-10	369.0	7	0.38	1820	2100	92.1	80.2	18
Male										
25-44	1	0- 2 yrs	600.5	20	1.65	1210	1200	93.9	93.9	31
	2	2- 5	790.5	41	2.68	1530	1300	86.1	80.9	48
	3	5-10	795.5	25	3.82	655	790	87.9	71.0	27
45-54	1	0- 2	361.0	31	3.52	880	870	84.9	84.9	76
	2	2- 5	421.0	29	5.17	560	590	84.1	71.4	57
	3	5-10	410.0	10	6.89	145	300	96.4	68.8	7.6
55-64	1	0- 2	255.5	28	5.74	490	470	82.6	82.6	87
	2	2- 5	269.5	32	7.40	430	375	74.7	61.7	91
	3	5-10	220.5	9	7.96	113	205	98.1	60.5	4.7
65 up	1	0- 2	358.0	62	30.5	205	197	80.9	80.9	88
	2	2- 5	314.5	54	29.0	186	161	77.7	62.9	80
	3	5-10	242.5	28	24.2	116	122	94.4	59.4	16
Female										
25-44	1	0- 2 yrs	810.5	24	1.26	1910	1910	94.4	94.4	28
	2	2- 5	1075.5	31	2.07	1490	1550	92.2	87.0	27
	3	5-10	1149.5	21	3.06	685	930	93.0	80.9	16
45-54	1	0- 2	416.5	16	2.00	800	800	93.2	93.2	34
	2	2- 5	547.5	25	3.19	785	740	88.4	82.4	40
	3	5-10	529.5	16	4.09	390	450	91.8	75.6	22
55-64	1	0- 2	281.0	7	3.11	225	225	97.2	97.2	14
	2	2- 5	364.0	26	4.99	520	380	83.9	81.6	58
	3	5-10	344.5	17	6.58	260	275	84.7	69.1	30
65 up	1	0- 2	464.0	70	32.3	215	215	82.4	82.4	81
	2	2- 5	456.5	64	33.0	194	177	79.2	65.2	68
	3	5-10	351.5	29	27.4	106	126	102.1	66.6	4.5
Regional Male All										
	1	0- 2 yrs	368.0	116	9.31	1250	940	49.8	49.8	290
	2	2- 5	243.0	40	3.82	1050	520	66.4	33.1	149
	3	5-10	225.5	10	3.99	250	295	95.4	31.6	27
Female All										
	1	0- 2 yrs	288.5	60	5.34	1120	920	65.8	65.8	189
	2	2- 5	254.0	33	4.08	810	585	71.7	47.2	114
	3	5-10	221.0	15	3.67	410	350	81.8	38.6	51
Metastatic M & F All										
	1	0- 2 yrs	496.0	331	11.87	2800	1740	15.9	15.9	643
	2	2- 5	137.5	25	3.53	710	755	62.1	9.9	156
	3	5-10	130.0	4	4.86	82	390	97.0	9.6	−6.6
Localized Male										
< 45	4	10-15 yrs	264.5	5	1.45	345		90.9		13
	5	15-20	46.5	0	0.38	0		104.2		−8.1
45-54	4	10-15	75.5	2	1.86	108		98.1		1.9
	5	15-20	24.0	2	0.87	230		92.3		47
55-64	4	10-15	78.0	7	4.24	165		77.7		35
	5	15-20	19.0	1	1.57	64		128.7		−30
65 up	4	10-15	46.0	5	5.26	95		127.3		−5.7
	5	15-20	8.5	2	1.38	145		0		73
Female										
< 45	4	10-15 yrs	459.0	4	1.26	315		97.2		6.0
	5	15-20	104.5	1	0.34	290		98.4		6.3
45-54	4	10-15	131.5	4	1.66	240		92.3		18
	5	15-20	40.0	1	0.87	115		91.7		3.3
55-64	4	10-15	151.0	3	4.83	62		106.6		−12
	5	15-20	35.5	3	1.80	167		101.9		34
65 up	4	10-15	150.0	21	15.30	137		73.4		38
	5	15-20	31.0	2	4.33	46		139.3		−75

*Basis of expected mortality: Concurrent U.S. White Population Rates

MELANOMA

Table 182b   Melanoma - Derived Mortality and Survival Data

Stage & Sex Age Group	Interval No.	Interval Start-End	Observed Survival Rate Cumulative	Observed Survival Rate Interval	Observed Ave. Ann.	Observed Ave. Ann. Mort. Rate	Expected* Survival Rate Cumulative	Expected* Survival Rate Interval	Expected* Ave. Ann.	Expected* Ave. Ann. Mort. Rate
(Yrs)	i	t to t + Δt	P	p_i	$\breve{p}$	$\breve{q}$	P'	p_i'	$\breve{p}'$	$\breve{q}'$
Localized										
M & F										
< 25	1	0- 2 yrs	.9591	.9591	.9793	.0207	.9983	.9983	.9991	.00085
	2	2- 5	.8670	.9040	.9669	.0331	.9955	.9972	.9991	.00093
	3	5-10	.7945	.9164	.9827	.0173	.9904	.9949	.9990	.00102
Male										
25-44	1	0- 2 yrs	.9340	.9340	.9664	.0336	.9945	.9945	.9972	.0028
	2	2- 5	.7959	.8521	.9480	.0520	.9843	.9897	.9966	.0034
	3	5-10	.6818	.8566	.9695	.0305	.9597	.9750	.9949	.0051
45-54	1	0- 2	.8322	.8322	.9122	.0878	.9807	.9807	.9903	.0097
	2	2- 5	.6743	.8103	.9323	.0677	.9450	.9636	.9877	.0123
	3	5-10	.5952	.8827	.9754	.0246	.8651	.9154	.9825	.0175
55-64	1	0- 2	.7889	.7889	.8882	.1118	.9552	.9552	.9773	.0227
	2	2- 5	.5411	.6859	.8819	.1181	.8776	.9188	.9722	.0278
	3	5-10	.4365	.8067	.9579	.0421	.7218	.8225	.9617	.0383
65 up	1	0- 2	.6771	.6771	.8229	.1771	.8365	.8365	.9146	.0854
	2	2- 5	.3919	.5788	.8334	.1666	.6234	.7452	.9066	.0934
	3	5-10	.2082	.5313	.8812	.1188	.3508	.5627	.8914	.1086
Female										
25-44	1	0- 2 yrs	.9409	.9409	.9700	.0300	.9969	.9969	.9984	.0016
	2	2- 5	.8624	.9166	.9714	.0286	.9911	.9942	.9981	.0019
	3	5-10	.7909	.9171	.9828	.0172	.9775	.9863	.9972	.0028
45-54	1	0- 2	.9234	.9234	.9609	.0391	.9904	.9904	.9952	.0048
	2	2- 5	.8019	.8684	.9541	.0459	.9732	.9826	.9942	.0052
	3	5-10	.7069	.8815	.9751	.0249	.9346	.9603	.9919	.0081
55-64	1	0- 2	.9504	.9504	.9749	.0251	.9780	.9780	.9889	.0111
	2	2- 5	.7653	.8052	.9303	.0697	.9382	.9593	.9862	.0138
	3	5-10	.5865	.7664	.9482	.0518	.8489	.9048	.9802	.0198
65 up	1	0- 2	.7143	.7143	.8452	.1548	.8668	.8668	.9310	.0690
	2	2- 5	.4497	.6296	.8571	.1429	.6892	.7951	.9264	.0736
	3	5-10	.2939	.6535	.9184	.0816	.4413	.6403	.9147	.0853
Regional										
Male										
All	1	0- 2 yrs	.4703	.4703	.6858	.3142	.9435	.9435	.9713	.0287
	2	2- 5	.2858	.6077	.8470	.1530	.8631	.9148	.9708	.0292
	3	5-10	.2335	.8170	.9604	.0396	.7389	.8561	.9694	.0306
Female										
All	1	0- 2 yrs	.6313	.6313	.7945	.2055	.9600	.9600	.9798	.0202
	2	2- 5	.4254	.6738	.8767	.1233	.9015	.9391	.9793	.0207
	3	5-10	.3103	.7294	.9388	.0612	.8034	.8912	.9772	.0228
Metastatic										
M & F										
All	1	0- 2 yrs	.1513	.1513	.3890	.6110	.9511	.9511	.9752	.0248
	2	2- 5	.0868	.5737	.8309	.1691	.8788	.9240	.9740	.0260
	3	5-10	.0731	.8422	.9662	.0338	.7632	.8685	.9722	.0278
Localized										
Male										
< 45	4	10-15 yrs		.8829	.9754	.0246		.9716	.9943	.0057
	5	15-20		1.0000	1.0000	.0000		.9596	.9918	.0082
45-54	4	10-15		.8622	.9708	.0292		.8788	.9745	.0255
	5	15-20		.7563	.9457	.0543		.8197	.9610	.0390
55-64	4	10-15		.5830	.8977	.1023		.7507	.9443	.0557
	5	15-20		.8182	.9607	.0393		.6355	.9133	.0867
65 up	4	10-15		.6875	.9278	.0722		.5402	.8841	.1159
	5	15-20		.0000	.0000	1.0000		.4797	.8322	.1678
Female										
< 45	4	10-15 yrs		.9586	.9916	.0084		.9860	.9972	.0028
	5	15-20		.9677	.9935	.0065		.9831	.9966	.0034
45-54	4	10-15		.8640	.9712	.0288		.9359	.9868	.0132
	5	15-20		.8182	.9607	.0393		.8921	.9774	.0226
55-64	4	10-15		.9006	.9793	.0207		.8448	.9668	.0332
	5	15-20		.7668	.9483	.0517		.7524	.9447	.0553
65 up	4	10-15		.4180	.8399	.1601		.5695	.8935	.1065
	5	15-20		.6303	.9118	.0882		.4524	.8533	.1467

*Basis of expected mortality: Concurrent U.S. White Population Rates

MELANOMA

Table 182c Melanoma Subsites - Observed Data and Comparative Experience by Stage, Sex, Age and Duration

Stage & Sex / Age Group (Yrs)	No. i	Start-End t to t + Δt	Exposure Person-Yrs E	Deaths Observed d	Deaths Expected* d'	Mortality Ratio Interval 100 d/d'	Mortality Ratio Cumulative 100 Q/Q'	Survival Ratio Interval 100 p_i/p_i'	Survival Ratio Cumulative 100 P/P'	Excess Death Rate 1000(d-d')/E
All Sites										
Localized										
Male										
All	1	0- 2 yrs	1664.5	142	41.5	345%	335%	87.8%	87.8%	60
	2	2- 5	1918.5	161	44.5	360	295	83.3	73.1	61
	3	5-10	1799.5	77	42.9	180	210	92.2	67.4	19
Female										
All	1	0- 2 yrs	2127.5	121	38.6	315	310	92.1	92.1	39
	2	2- 5	2653.5	152	43.5	350	295	88.5	81.5	41
	3	5-10	2613.0	85	41.1	205	215	93.8	76.4	17
Regional										
M & F										
All	1	0- 2 yrs	656.5	176	14.67	1200	935	56.7	56.7	246
	2	2- 5	497.0	73	7.92	920	545	69.2	39.3	131
	3	5-10	446.5	25	7.67	325	315	88.9	34.9	39
Face, Head, Neck										
Localized										
Male										
All	1	0- 2 yrs	488.5	56	19.40	290%	285%	84.5%	84.5%	75
	2	2- 5	517.0	61	20.14	305	255	77.5	65.5	79
	3	5-10	439.0	28	16.50	170	184	89.1	58.4	26
Female										
All	1	0- 2 yrs	424.0	37	18.49	200	196	90.9	90.9	44
	2	2- 5	492.5	45	20.19	225	188	85.8	78.0	50
	3	5-10	457.0	22	16.13	136	144	97.2	75.8	13
Regional										
M & F										
All	1	0- 2 yrs	161.0	45	4.85	930	725	55.8	55.8	249
	2	2- 5	111.0	26	1.92	1360	480	52.0	29.0	217
	3	5-10	90.0	3	1.65	181	270	103.2	30.0	15
Trunk										
Localized										
Male										
All	1	0- 2 yrs	567.5	42	7.86	535%	520%	88.0%	88.0%	60
	2	2- 5	659.0	55	7.40	745	475	81.0	71.2	72
	3	5-10	612.0	22	8.16	270	305	90.5	64.4	23
Female										
All	1	0- 2 yrs	363.5	23	3.09	745	720	89.0	89.0	55
	2	2- 5	433.5	30	3.20	935	625	83.5	74.4	62
	3	5-10	432.5	21	3.77	555	420	84.4	62.8	40
Regional										
M & F										
All	1	0- 2 yrs	144.0	46	2.17	2100	1460	47.6	47.6	304
	2	2- 5	95.0	14	0.90	1560	755	67.8	32.3	138
	3	5-10	77.0	4	0.68	590	405	91.1	29.4	43
Arm & Hand										
Localized										
Male										
All	1	0- 2 yrs	300.5	22	6.64	330%	320%	89.7%	89.7%	51
	2	2- 5	370.0	16	7.50	215	225	94.0	84.3	23
	3	5-10	382.5	13	7.68	169	171	95.6	80.6	14
Female										
All	1	0- 2 yrs	485.5	27	8.37	325	345	91.9	91.9	38
	2	2- 5	613.5	27	8.71	310	305	91.1	83.8	30
	3	5-10	596.0	14	6.49	215	225	95.5	80.1	13
Regional										
M & F										
All	1	0- 2 yrs	129.5	38	3.37	1130	980	52.5	52.5	267
	2	2- 5	92.5	7	2.01	350	475	87.7	46.0	54
	3	5-10	89.0	7	2.29	305	295	78.0	35.9	53
Leg & Foot										
Localized										
Male										
All	1	0- 2 yrs	288.0	17	6.87	245%	235%	93.1%	93.1%	35
	2	2- 5	357.5	27	9.09	295	250	85.7	79.8	50
	3	5-10	353.0	13	10.16	128	178	95.1	75.8	8.1
Female										
All	1	0- 2 yrs	840.5	34	8.66	395	380	94.0	94.0	30
	2	2- 5	1094.5	49	11.23	435	360	90.3	84.8	35
	3	5-10	1109.5	28	14.72	190	245	95.5	81.0	12
Regional										
M & F										
All	1	0- 2 yrs	194.0	41	3.62	1130	875	65.5	65.5	193
	2	2- 5	169.5	22	2.65	830	540	72.8	47.7	114
	3	5-10	160.0	10	2.48	405	320	86.1	41.1	47

*Basis of expected mortality: Concurrent U.S. White Population Rates

MELANOMA

Table 182d Melanoma Subsites - Derived Mortality and Survival Data

Stage & Sex Age Group	No.	Start-End	Observed Cumulative P	Observed Interval p_i	Observed Ave. Ann. $\check{p}$	Observed Ave. Ann. Mort. Rate $\check{q}$	Expected* Cumulative P'	Expected* Interval p_i'	Expected* Ave. Ann. $\check{p}'$	Expected* Ave. Ann. Mort. Rate $\check{q}'$
(Yrs)	i	t to t + Δ t	P	p_i	$\check{p}$	$\check{q}$	P'	p_i'	$\check{p}'$	$\check{q}'$
All Sites										
Localized										
Male										
All	1	0- 2 yrs	.8343	.8343	.9134	.0866	.9503	.9503	.9748	.0252
	2	2- 5	.6432	.7709	.9169	.0831	.8793	.9253	.9745	.0255
	3	5-10	.5177	.8049	.9575	.0425	.7680	.8734	.9733	.0267
Female										
All	1	0- 2 yrs	.8879	.8879	.9423	.0577	.9640	.9640	.9818	.0182
	2	2- 5	.7443	.8383	.9429	.0571	.9132	.9473	.9821	.0179
	3	5-10	.6367	.8554	.9692	.0308	.8329	.9121	.9818	.0182
Regional										
M & F										
All	1	0- 2 yrs	.5389	.5389	.7341	.2659	.9506	.9506	.9750	.0250
	2	2- 5	.3453	.6407	.8621	.1379	.8795	.9252	.9744	.0256
	3	5-10	.2675	.7747	.9502	.0498	.7664	.8714	.9728	.0272
Face, Head, Neck										
Localized										
Male										
All	1	0- 2 yrs	.7795	.7795	.8829	.1171	.9229	.9229	.9607	.0393
	2	2- 5	.5360	.6876	.8826	.1174	.8184	.8868	.9607	.0393
	3	5-10	.3905	.7285	.9386	.0614	.6691	.8176	.9605	.0395
Female										
All	1	0- 2 yrs	.8311	.8311	.9116	.0884	.9140	.9140	.9560	.0440
	2	2- 5	.6242	.7511	.9090	.0910	.7999	.8752	.9565	.0435
	3	5-10	.4883	.7823	.9521	.0479	.6441	.8052	.9576	.0424
Regional										
M & F										
All	1	0- 2 yrs	.5213	.5213	.7220	.2780	.9340	.9340	.9664	.0336
	2	2- 5	.2447	.4694	.7772	.2228	.8428	.9024	.9663	.0337
	3	5-10	.2118	.8655	.9715	.0285	.7067	.8385	.9654	.0346
Trunk										
Localized										
Male										
All	1	0- 2 yrs	.8550	.8550	.9247	.0753	.9720	.9720	.9859	.0141
	2	2- 5	.6614	.7736	.9180	.0820	.9286	.9553	.9849	.0151
	3	5-10	.5846	.8295	.9633	.0367	.8514	.9169	.9828	.0172
Female										
All	1	0- 2 yrs	.8747	.8747	.9353	.0647	.9826	.9826	.9913	.0087
	2	2- 5	.7089	.8104	.9323	.0677	.9534	.9703	.9900	.0100
	3	5-10	.5620	.7928	.9546	.0454	.8956	.9394	.9876	.0124
Regional										
M & F										
All	1	0- 2 yrs	.4588	.4588	.6773	.3227	.9630	.9630	.9813	.0187
	2	2- 5	.2927	.6380	.8609	.1391	.9066	.9414	.9801	.0199
	3	5-10	.2387	.8155	.9600	.0400	.8116	.8952	.9781	.0219
Arm & Hand										
Localized										
Male										
All	1	0- 2 yrs	.8566	.8566	.9255	.0745	.9553	.9553	.9774	.0226
	2	2- 5	.7504	.8760	.9568	.0432	.8902	.9319	.9768	.0232
	3	5-10	.6337	.8445	.9668	.0332	.7862	.8832	.9755	.0245
Female										
All	1	0- 2 yrs	.8901	.8901	.9435	.0565	.9681	.9681	.9839	.0161
	2	2- 5	.7764	.8723	.9555	.0445	.9266	.9571	.9855	.0145
	3	5-10	.6915	.8906	.9771	.0229	.8637	.9321	.9860	.0140
Regional										
M & F										
All	1	0- 2 yrs	.4980	.4980	.7057	.2943	.9489	.9489	.9741	.0259
	2	2- 5	.4025	.8082	.9315	.0685	.8741	.9212	.9730	.0270
	3	5-10	.2699	.6706	.9232	.0768	.7511	.8593	.9701	.0299
Leg & Foot										
Localized										
Male										
All	1	0- 2 yrs	.8859	.8859	.9412	.0588	.9516	.9516	.9755	.0245
	2	2- 5	.7019	.7923	.9253	.0747	.8800	.9248	.9743	.0257
	3	5-10	.5793	.8253	.9623	.0377	.7640	.8682	.9721	.0279
Female										
All	1	0- 2 yrs	.9199	.9199	.9591	.0409	.9788	.9788	.9893	.0107
	2	2- 5	.8019	.8717	.9553	.0447	.9451	.9656	.9884	.0116
	3	5-10	.7155	.8923	.9775	.0225	.8829	.9342	.9865	.0135
Regional										
M & F										
All	1	0- 2 yrs	.6273	.6273	.7920	.2080	.9573	.9573	.9784	.0216
	2	2- 5	.4266	.6801	.8794	.1206	.8937	.9336	.9774	.0226
	3	5-10	.3246	.7609	.9468	.0532	.7901	.8841	.9757	.0243

*Basis of expected mortality: Concurrent U.S. White Population Rates

CANCER–ENDOCRINE SYSTEM

§190–CANCER OF THE THYROID GLAND

Cancer of the thyroid gland ranks 26th among male cancers and has a relative frequency of 0.7 per cent (Table 100a). This type of cancer is much more prevalent among females, ranking 12th and having a relative frequency of 1.9 per cent (Table 100b). Most cases in the End Results' experience, 60 per cent of males and 68 per cent of females, were diagnosed before age 55, and about 40 per cent of male and over 50 per cent of female cases were classified as localized.

Ten-year results for patients in the localized stage are presented in Tables 190a-b in two younger age categories for males and females combined and in three older age categories for males and females separately. Patients under age 45 had the best prognosis, with an average EDR of only 2.7 per 1000 and a cumulative survival ratio close to 98.7 per cent within the first five years after diagnosis. The aggregate EDR was even lower, less than one per 1000 in the third interval, 5-10 years after diagnosis. Despite the very small numbers of deaths, only two deaths in patients under age 25, and 23 in those aged 25-44, the pattern of unusually small excess mortality is consistent for these younger patients with thyroid cancer. Within the first two years after diagnosis EDR increased steeply with advancing age, from 21 to 156 per 1000 in males and from 11 to 106 per 1000 in females, in the older patients age 45 and up. The mortality risk then diminished in the second interval, 2-5 years after diagnosis, with EDR's ranging from 0.4 to 16 per 1000, and still further in the third interval, 5-10 years after diagnosis, with EDR's ranging from −8.0 to 7.4 per 1000, except in men at ages 55-64, in whom the EDR was 27 per 1000. Except in the oldest female patients there were fewer than ten deaths in most age-duration categories, and all rates and ratios for localized thyroid cancer must be interpreted with this limitation in mind. Cumulative five-year survival ratios decreased with advancing age and were somewhat higher in females.

Ten-year experience for thyroid cancer beyond the localized stage is next presented, for males and females separately, in cancer showing regional extension and for males and females, all ages combined, in patients with evidence of metastasis. Although prognosis worsened with each successive stage, excess mortality dropped sharply in patients with regional extension after the first two years. In terms of EDR excess mortality was somewhat greater in males than in females: 96 versus 79 extra deaths per 1000 in the first interval, 27 versus 9.0 per 1000 in the second, and 10 versus 6.4 per 1000 in the third, 5-10 years after diagnosis. These EDR's in the third interval and mortality ratios close to 175 per cent reflect a remarkable drop in excess mortality in patients with regional cancer of the thyroid who survive at least five years. The cumulative survival ratios at five years were 77.1 per cent in men and 85.0 per cent in women. Prognosis was considerably worse in patients having metastatic thyroid cancer: the mortality ratio was 1710 per cent and EDR 474 per 1000 within two years of diagnosis. The mortality ratio decreased to 535 per cent in the third interval and the EDR to 53 per 1000. The five-year survival ratio of 26.2 per cent, although low, was still better than in most other types of metastatic cancer.

Experience for male and female patients, separately, in four age categories, 10-20 years after diagnosis is presented at the bottom of Tables 190a-b. Because of the very small numbers of deaths in most categories, especially in the male patients, not much can be said about these results beyond the general impression that overall mortality is close to normal in men and in most of the female age categories. The one apparent exception is found in female patients in the 55-64 age range. In this group the aggregate mortality ratio was 250 per cent and the EDR 50 per 1000, based on a total of 26 observed deaths. Otherwise, the very limited evidence suggests a normal level of mortality for patients with localized thyroid cancer who have survived at least ten years.

CANCER—THYROID GLAND

Table 190a Cancer of the Thyroid Gland - Observed Data and Comparative Experience by Stage, Sex, Age and Duration

Stage & Sex Age Group	Interval No.	Interval Start-End	Exposure Person-Yrs	Deaths Observed	Deaths Expected*	Mortality Ratio Interval	Mortality Ratio Cumulative	Survival Ratio Interval	Survival Ratio Cumulative	Excess Death Rate
(Yrs)	i	t to t + Δt	E	d	d'	100 d/d'	100 Q/Q'	100 p_i/p_i'	100 P/P'	1000(d-d')/E
Localized M & F < 25	1	0- 2 yrs	253.0	1	0.177	565%	535%	99.3%	99.3%	3.3
	2	2- 5	363.5	1	0.29	345	425	99.4	98.8	2.0
	3	5-10	485.0	0	0.44	0	194	100.5	99.2	−0.9
25-44	1	0- 2	1176.0	5	2.12	235	235	99.5	99.5	2.5
	2	2- 5	1706.0	9	3.75	240	235	99.1	98.6	3.1
	3	5-10	2084.5	9	6.46	139	165	99.7	98.3	1.2
Male 45-54	1	0- 2 yrs	129.0	4	1.29	310	305	95.8	95.8	21
	2	2- 5	184.0	3	2.33	129	189	98.8	94.7	3.6
	3	5-10	207.0	2	3.66	55	106	104.6	99.0	−8.0
55-64	1	0- 2	85.0	6	1.84	325	310	90.6	90.6	49
	2	2- 5	107.0	4	2.91	137	192	96.8	87.8	10
	3	5-10	113.0	7	4.00	175	170	84.8	74.4	27
65 up	1	0- 2	86.0	19	5.57	340	290	70.6	70.6	156
	2	2- 5	85.0	6	5.33	113	161	101.5	71.7	7.9
	3	5-10	80.5	7	6.40	109	121	99.7	71.5	7.4
Female 45-54	1	0- 2 yrs	457.5	7	2.13	330	325	97.9	97.9	11
	2	2- 5	661.0	4	3.77	106	184	99.9	97.8	0.4
	3	5-10	831.5	10	6.45	155	163	97.9	95.7	4.3
55-64	1	0- 2	238.0	11	2.63	420	405	93.1	93.1	35
	2	2- 5	328.5	9	4.46	200	265	95.8	89.2	14
	3	5-10	380.0	8	7.17	112	161	99.9	89.1	2.2
65 up	1	0- 2	265.5	40	11.86	335	295	80.4	80.4	106
	2	2- 5	304.0	19	14.23	134	173	97.1	78.1	16
	3	5-10	332.0	19	20.2	94	124	102.2	79.8	−3.5
Regional Male All	1	0- 2 yrs	574.0	64	9.12	700	590	82.2	82.2	96
	2	2- 5	697.5	28	9.10	310	335	93.8	77.1	27
	3	5-10	768.0	19	11.08	172	210	98.3	75.8	10
Female All	1	0- 2 yrs	1272.0	113	12.83	880	640	85.7	85.7	79
	2	2- 5	1662.0	27	12.01	225	315	99.2	85.0	9.0
	3	5-10	2026.0	30	16.96	177	200	99.8	84.8	6.4
Metastatic M & F All	1	0- 2 yrs	421.5	212	12.40	1710	1090	32.9	32.9	474
	2	2- 5	250.0	27	4.45	605	485	79.5	26.2	90
	3	5-10	230.0	15	2.81	535	260	92.2	24.1	53
Localized Male < 45	4	10-15 yrs	232.5	2	1.65	121		99.6		1.5
	5	15-20	87.5	1	1.06	95		102.1		−0.7
45-54	4	10-15	71.5	1	1.77	57		108.7		−11
	5	15-20	26.5	0	0.88	0		118.5		−33
55-64	4	10-15	30.5	3	1.40	215		76.9		53
	5	15-20	10.0	0	0.66	0		140.9		−66
65 up	4	10-15	32.0	6	4.18	143		78.4		57
	5	15-20	6.0	1	1.13	88		145.5		−22
Female < 45	4	10-15 yrs	1185.0	8	4.10	195		98.3		3.3
	5	15-20	390.0	2	2.05	98		100.5		−0.1
45-54	4	10-15	379.0	9	4.61	195		95.3		12
	5	15-20	94.0	1	1.87	53		106.8		−9.3
55-64	4	10-15	263.5	23	8.19	280		73.1		56
	5	15-20	47.0	3	2.18	138		72.6		18
65 up	4	10-15	72.0	6	5.64	106		105.3		5.0
	5	15-20	13.0	1	1.37	73		139.9		−28

*Basis of expected mortality: Concurrent U.S. White Population Rates

CANCER—THYROID GLAND

Table 190b Cancer of the Thyroid Gland - Derived Mortality and Survival Data

Stage & Sex Age Group	Interval No.	Interval Start-End	Observed Survival Rate Cumulative	Observed Survival Rate Interval	Observed Survival Rate Ave. Ann.	Observed Ave. Ann. Mort. Rate	Expected Survival Rate Cumulative	Expected Survival Rate Interval	Expected Survival Rate Ave. Ann.	Expected Ave. Ann. Mort. Rate
(Yrs)	i	t to t+Δt	P	p_i	$\breve{p}$	$\breve{q}$	P'	p_i'	$\breve{p}'$	$\breve{q}'$
Localized M & F										
< 25	1	0- 2 yrs	.9920	.9920	.9960	.0040	.9985	.9985	.9992	.00075
	2	2- 5	.9839	.9918	.9973	.0027	.9962	.9977	.9992	.00077
	3	5-10	.9839	1.0000	1.0000	.0000	.9917	.9955	.9991	.00090
25-44	1	0- 2	.9915	.9915	.9957	.0043	.9964	.9964	.9982	.00180
	2	2- 5	.9759	.9843	.9947	.0053	.9898	.9934	.9978	.0022
	3	5-10	.9573	.9809	.9962	.0038	.9741	.9841	.9968	.0032
Male										
45-54	1	0- 2 yrs	.9394	.9394	.9692	.0308	.9801	.9801	.9900	.0100
	2	2- 5	.8934	.9510	.9834	.0166	.9436	.9628	.9874	.0126
	3	5-10	.8535	.9553	.9909	.0091	.8620	.9135	.9821	.0179
55-64	1	0- 2	.8676	.8676	.9315	.0685	.9572	.9572	.9784	.0216
	2	2- 5	.7749	.8932	.9631	.0369	.8828	.9223	.9734	.0266
	3	5-10	.5454	.7038	.9322	.0678	.7330	.8303	.9635	.0365
65 up	1	0- 2	.6122	.6122	.7824	.2176	.8671	.8671	.9312	.0688
	2	2- 5	.4898	.8001	.9284	.0716	.6834	.7881	.9237	.0763
	3	5-10	.2997	.6119	.9064	.0936	.4193	.6135	.9069	.0931
Female										
45-54	1	0- 2 yrs	.9698	.9698	.9848	.0152	.9907	.9907	.9953	.0047
	2	2- 5	.9521	.9817	.9939	.0061	.9739	.9830	.9943	.0057
	3	5-10	.8964	.9415	.9880	.0120	.9363	.9614	.9922	.0078
55-64	1	0- 2	.9106	.9106	.9543	.0457	.9780	.9780	.9889	.0111
	2	2- 5	.8373	.9195	.9724	.0276	.9385	.9596	.9863	.0137
	3	5-10	.7576	.9048	.9802	.0198	.8499	.9056	.9804	.0196
65 up	1	0- 2	.7313	.7313	.8552	.1448	.9091	.9091	.9535	.0465
	2	2- 5	.6013	.8222	.9368	.0632	.7697	.8467	.9460	.0540
	3	5-10	.4294	.7141	.9349	.0651	.5380	.6990	.9309	.0691
Regional Male All										
	1	0- 2 yrs	.7935	.7935	.8908	.1092	.9650	.9650	.9823	.0177
	2	2- 5	.7027	.8856	.9603	.0397	.9111	.9441	.9810	.0190
	3	5-10	.6207	.8833	.9755	.0245	.8184	.8983	.9788	.0212
Female All										
	1	0- 2 yrs	.8353	.8353	.9139	.0861	.9743	.9743	.9871	.0129
	2	2- 5	.7952	.9520	.9837	.0163	.9353	.9600	.9865	.0135
	3	5-10	.7375	.9274	.9850	.0150	.8695	.9296	.9855	.0145
Metastatic M & F All										
	1	0- 2 yrs	.3080	.3080	.5550	.4450	.9364	.9364	.9677	.0323
	2	2- 5	.2195	.7127	.8932	.1068	.8390	.8960	.9641	.0359
	3	5-10	.1631	.7431	.9423	.0577	.6759	.8056	.9577	.0423
Localized Male										
< 45	4	10-15 yrs		.9602	.9919	.0081		.9639	.9927	.0073
	5	15-20		.9583	.9915	.0085		.9386	.9874	.0126
45-54	4	10-15		.9545	.9907	.0093		.8784	.9744	.0256
	5	15-20		1.0000	1.0000	.0000		.8438	.9666	.0334
55-64	4	10-15		.6038	.9040	.0960		.7847	.9527	.0473
	5	15-20		1.0000	1.0000	.0000		.7099	.9338	.0662
65 up	4	10-15		.3750	.8219	.1781		.4784	.8629	.1371
	5	15-20		.5000	.8706	.1294		.3436	.8076	.1924
Female										
< 45	4	10-15 yrs		.9659	.9931	.0069		.9824	.9965	.0035
	5	15-20		.9780	.9956	.0044		.9731	.9946	.0054
45-54	4	10-15		.8939	.9778	.0222		.9376	.9872	.0128
	5	15-20		.9615	.9922	.0078		.9007	.9793	.0207
55-64	4	10-15		.6189	.9085	.0915		.8472	.9674	.0326
	5	15-20		.5657	.8923	.1077		.7789	.9513	.0487
65 up	4	10-15		.6926	.9292	.0708		.6580	.9197	.0803
	5	15-20		.8000	.9564	.0436		.5717	.8942	.1058

*Basis of expected mortality: Concurrent U.S. White Population Rates

CANCER AND BENIGN TUMORS

§199–CANCER AND BENIGN TUMORS (MISCELLANEOUS)

References: (1) T. W. Preston and R. D. Clarke, "An Investigation into the Mortality of Impaired Lives During the Period 1947-63," J. Inst. Act., 92:27-74 (1966).
(2) "New York Life Single Medical Impairment Study - 1972," unpublished report made available by J. J. Hutchinson and J. C. Sibigtroth (1973).

Subjects Studied: (1) Policyholders of Prudential Assurance Co., London, England, issued insurance 1947-1963 followed to 12/31/63. Both standard and substandard issues were included. Applicants with two or more ratable impairments were generally excluded.
(2) Policyholders of New York Life Insurance Co., issued insurance 1954-1970 followed to 1971 policy anniversary. Both standard and substandard issues were included. Applicants with more than one ratable impairment were excluded.

Follow-up: Insurance policy records formed the basis of entry, counting policies, exposures and death claims, and of follow-up information.

Results: Experience from the New York Life and Prudential of London studies with respect to persons with a history of malignant tumor granted insurance is presented in the A section of Table 199. The New York Life data based on substandard issues showed an overall mortality ratio for all durations and ages and including both sexes of 225 per cent and an annual average excess death rate of 4.7 per 1000. Experience on lives insured within five years of the history of treatment for cancer was relatively favorable: the mortality ratio, 163 per cent of that expected among standard lives, and the excess death rate, 2.2 per 1000. The mortality ratio of applicants insured from 6 to 10 years after diagnosis and treatment increased to 270 per cent and the EDR to 6.7 per 1000. Those with a history more than 10 years prior to application showed a moderate decline in both these indexes — the mortality ratio, 220 per cent, the EDR, 5.0 per 1000. Under the English experience representing males granted coverage on both standard and extra premium basis, mortality indexes were more adverse: for all durations together, the mortality ratio was 340 per cent and the excess death rate, 11 per 1000 per year. New York Life experience on males and females with a history of epithelioma is also shown in the A section. Policies issued in these cases were substandard. Mortality on this class of cancer, both basal cell and others was comparable with standard issues, both classes together revealing a mortality ratio of 104 per cent and excess deaths of 0.3 per 1000 (basal cell mortality ratio 88 per cent, others, 116 per cent).

Presented in the B section of Table 199 is the experience of the same two companies under policies issued to males and females with history of benign tumors. The New York Life cases, all substandard, disclosed for both sexes combined, insured within five years of diagnosis, a mortality ratio of 127 per cent and excess deaths of 1.0 per 1000 per year. The experience on those applying more than five years after diagnosis showed higher rates (mortality ratio 192 per cent, EDR, 4.5 per 1000) but there were only 3 deaths at those durations. Standard and substandard issues to applicants with histories of benign tumors of the female organs indicated mortality almost three times the expected and excess deaths of 4.7 per year. The Prudential of London non-malignant cases consisting of standard and substandard policies issued to men and women exhibited mortality practically that experienced by standard lives.

Also shown in Table 199 are results under New York Life insurance (standard basis) to males and females where information as to the character of the tumor is not given. The overall mortality ratio was 152 per cent and the EDR, 1.5 per 1000.

Comment: It is the customary in underwriting applicants with a history of internal cancer to decline insurance if there is a history of cancer extension beyond the localized stage, recurrence, diagnosis within three years, or evidence of recurrence on examination. It is evident that such a waiting period and selection criteria are sufficient to result in a much more favorable experience than that of localized cancer patients in general, at equivalent intervals after diagnosis without such selection (Tables 100a-b). Most companies require no waiting period to adequately treated patients with a history of epithelioma.

CANCER AND BENIGN TUMORS

Table 199   Comparative Experience, Two Series of Insureds

History of Tumor Category (Ref.)	Sex/Age	Policies in Force at Start ℓ	Exposure Policy-Yrs E	No. of Death Claims Observed d	No. of Death Claims Expected* d'	Ave. Ann. Mort. Rate Observed $\bar{q}=d/E$	Ave. Ann. Mort. Rate Expected* $\bar{q}'=d'/E$	Mortality Ratio 100 d/d'	Est. 5-Yr Surv. Rate $P=(1-\bar{q})^5$	Est. 5-Yr Surv. Index 100 P/P'	Excess Death Rate $1000(\bar{q}-\bar{q}')$
A. Malignant Tumors											
SS† Within 5 Years (2)	M&F 40	—	3113	17	10.41	.0055	.0033	163%	.9730	98.9%	2.2
6-10 Years Ago	M&F 42	—	3826	41	15.13	.0107	.0040	270	.9476	96.7	6.7
11 Years Ago & Up	M&F 42	—	1320	12	5.41	.0091	.0041	220	.9554	97.5	5.0
Total	M&F 41	—	8259	70	30.95	.0085	.0037	225	.9583	97.6	4.7
S†SS (1)	M&F 49	186	695	11	3.23	.0158	.0046	340	.9233	94.5	11
SS Epithelioma (2)	M&F 53	—	5259	34	32.61	.0065	.0062	104	.9681	99.9	0.3
Basal Cell	M&F 52	—	2317	12	13.64	.0052	.0059	88	.9744	100.4	-0.7
Not Basal	M&F 53	—	2942	22	18.97	.0075	.0064	116	.9632	99.5	1.1
B. Benign Tumors (2)	M&F 50	—	7425	35	26.72	.0047	.0036	131	.9767	99.4	1.1
SS Within 5 Years (2)	M&F 50	—	7102	32	25.16	.0045	.0035	127	.9777	99.5	1.0
6 Years Ago & Up (2)	M&F 49	—	323	3	1.56	.0093	.0048	192	.9544	97.8	4.5
S&SS Female Organs (2)	F 47	—	1558	11	3.81	.0071	.0024	290	.9652	97.7	4.7
S&SS Non-malignant (1)	M&F 46	1525	6600	19	19.93	.0029	.0030	95	.9857	100.1	-0.1
C. Other Tumors											
S Not detailed (2)	M&F 45	—	5515	24	15.84	.0044	.0029	152	.9784	99.3	1.5

* Basis of expected mortality: (Ref. 1) Prudential Assurance Co. (England) standard lives mortality 1957-1958;
  (Ref. 2) N. Y. Life, Basic Select Tables (1955-60).
† "S" - Standard, "SS" - Substandard.

Neurological Diseases

See Also

1. *1951 Impairment Study.* Chicago: Society of Actuaries (1954).
   B1-B4   Epilepsy (pp. 65–66)
   B5-B6   Insanity (pp. 66–68)
   B7-B9   Neurasthenia or nervous prostration (pp. 68–71)
   B10-B12   Psychasthenia or psychoneurosis (pp. 72–73)
   B13-B14   Migraine (pp. 73–74)
   B15-B16   Vertigo or syncope (p. 74)
   B17-B18   Cerebral concussion (pp. 74–76)
   B19-B26   Fractured skull (pp. 76–79)
   B27-B29   Sunstroke or heat prostration (p. 80)
2. L.T. Kurland, J.F. Kurtzke, and I.D. Goldberg, *Epidemiology of Neurologic and Sense Organ Disorders.*
   Cambridge, Mass.: Harvard University Press (1973).
3. M. Kramer, E.S. Pollack, R.W. Redick, and B.Z. Locke, *Mental Disorders/Suicide.*
   Cambridge, Mass.: Harvard University Press (1972).
4. E.C. Hutchinson and E.J. Acheson, eds., *Strokes. Natural History, Pathology and Surgical Treatment.* Philadelphia: W.B. Saunders Co. Ltd. (1975).

CEREBROVASCULAR DISEASE

§201–CEREBROVASCULAR ACCIDENTS

Reference: C. M. Wylie and B. K. White, "Mortality in Cerebrovascular Accident Applicants to A Rehabilitation Center," J. Chron. Dis., 17:713-719 (1964).

Subjects Studied: A group of 1193 patients with cerebrovascular accidents (CVA's) who applied for admission to the Montebello State Hospital (Maryland) during 1956-61. This hospital provides a well-organized program for the treatment and rehabilitation of patients of all income levels in the metropolitan Baltimore area. All subjects in the present series had survived at least 3 days following the onset of their CVA's and 50 per cent had survived 8 or more weeks. The ages of 29 applicants were unknown, the series being confined to 1164 persons of known age distributed as follows:

Age Group (years)	Under 55	55-64	65-74	75 up	Total
Number (per cent)	225 (19%)	329 (28%)	371 (32%)	239 (21%)	1164 (100%)

White persons represented about 70 per cent of the applicants; the proportions of males and females for both whites and non-whites were about equal.

Follow-up: Follow-up continued through December 1962, so that all patients were traced for at least one year. Average period of follow-up was 2.4 years. Information on deaths was obtained by search of the death certificate files of 1956-62 for Baltimore and for the State of Maryland.

Results: Mortality and survival statistics during the first 50 weeks after application for admission to Montebello are presented in Tables 201a and b. Comparative mortality experienced (relative to that of the general population) was very high for all durations shown. The first four-week period was particularly critical; the number of deaths represented 114 times (11400 per cent) the expected for ages under 55 years, 98 times, for ages between 55 and 64 years, 61, for ages 65-74 years, and 38, for ages 75 and over. Mortality ratios descended consistently with duration, and, as may be noted, with advancing age. Mortality ratios over the concluding 30-week observation interval were, for the four age groups, respectively, 1670 per cent, 805 per cent, 665 per cent, and 360 per cent – still extremely high relative to the general population.

The very high mortality in the first four-week period is dramatized by the number of excess deaths per 1000 over this interval. For subjects under age 55 this EDR comes to 79 per 1000; for the highest age group, the EDR of 257 per 1000 per four-week period, if maintained, would leave relatively few survivors at the end of the year. However, improvement of mortality with duration is reflected in the EDR. Over the 50-week term following hospital admission the average EDR per 1000 for all ages combined comes to 30 per 4 weeks, or 362 per 50 weeks (almost one year). These are very high death losses but relatively light compared with the rate for the first four-week period. Survival rates for the 50-week period are further evidence of the severity of CVA's. They range from 75 per cent for the youngest age group to 44 per cent for ages 75 and over. Normally, the range would run approximately from 99 per cent to 92 per cent.

Most deaths were attributable to multiple causes. CVA's were listed as the underlying cause in 44 per cent of the deaths. In 24 per cent of the deaths, CVA was indicated as a contributing cause; no mention of CVA as a cause was made in 32 per cent. In these latter categories, 62 per cent of the deaths were attributed to cardiovascular disease other than CVA.

Comment: The special nature of this hospital as a rehabilitation center has undoubtedly served to develop a series with a high average severity of CVA. Patients experiencing transient symptoms without hospitalization, and those hospitalized elsewhere who made a rapid recovery would be automatically excluded, because they would not need nor qualify for admission to a rehabilitation center. Only cases with disability remaining an average of 8 weeks after the attack were included. The high mortality in this series of severe CVA cases with disability should not be considered as characteristic of less severe and minimally disabled cases.

CEREBROVASCULAR ACCIDENTS

Table 201a Observed Data and Comparative Experience by Age and Duration
(Duration from Application for Admission to Rehabilitation Center)

Age Group	Interval No.	Interval Start-End	No. Alive at Start of Interval	Deaths Obs.	Deaths Exp.*	Mortality Ratio Interval	Mortality Ratio Cumulative	Survival Ratio Interval	Survival Ratio Cumulative	EDR per 4 wk unit
	i	t to t + Δt	ℓ	d	d'	100 d/d'	100 $\Sigma d/\Sigma d'$	100 (p_i/p_i')	100 P/P'	$\dfrac{4000(d-d')/\ell}{\Delta t}$
Under 55	1	0- 4 wks	225	18	.158	11400%	11400%	92.1%	92.1%	79
	2	4- 8 wks	207	12	.145	8300	9900	94.3	86.8	57
	3	8-20 wks	195	10	.41	2400	5600	95.2	82.5	16
	4	20-50 wks	185	16	.96	1670	3300	91.8	75.9	11
55-64	1	0- 4 wks	329	48	.49	9800	9800	85.5	85.5	144
	2	4- 8 wks	281	12	.42	2900	6600	95.8	81.9	41
	3	8-20 wks	269	22	1.24	1770	3800	92.2	75.6	26
	4	20-50 wks	247	23	2.86	805	2100	91.8	69.3	11
65-74	1	0- 4 wks	371	73	1.19	6100	6100	80.6	80.6	194
	2	4- 8 wks	298	17	.95	1790	4200	94.6	76.2	54
	3	8-20 wks	281	36	2.70	1330	2600	88.0	67.1	40
	4	20-50 wks	245	39	5.88	665	1540	86.1	57.8	18
75 up	1	0- 4 wks	239	63	1.65	3800	3800	74.1	74.1	257
	2	4- 8 wks	176	29	1.21	2400	3200	84.1	62.4	158
	3	8-20 wks	147	19	3.06	620	1880	88.9	55.4	36
	4	20-50 wks	128	24	6.66	360	1070	85.7	47.5	18

Table 201b Derived Mortality and Survival Data

Age Group	Interval No.	Interval Start-End	Observed Rates Survival Interval	Observed Rates Survival Ave/4 wk†	Observed Rates Survival Cumulative	Observed Rates Ave. Mort. Rate/4 wk	Expected Rates* Survival Interval	Expected Rates* Survival Ave/4 wk†	Expected Rates* Survival Cumulative	Expected Rates* Ave. Mort. Rate/4 wk
	i	t to t + Δt	p_i	$\breve{p}$	P	$\breve{q}$	p_i'	$\breve{p}'$	P'	$\breve{q}'$
Under 55	1	0- 4 wks	.920	.920	.920	.080	.9993	.9993	.9993	.0007
	2	4- 8 wks	.942	.942	.867	.058	.9993	.9993	.9986	.0007
	3	8-20 wks	.949	.983	.822	.017	.9979	.9993	.9965	.0007
	4	20-50 wks	.914	.988	.751	.012	.9948	.9993	.9913	.0007
55-64	1	0- 4 wks	.854	.854	.854	.146	.9985	.9985	.9985	.0015
	2	4- 8 wks	.957	.957	.818	.043	.9985	.9985	.9970	.0015
	3	8-20 wks	.918	.972	.751	.028	.9954	.9985	.9924	.0015
	4	20-50 wks	.907	.987	.681	.013	.9884	.9985	.9809	.0015
65-74	1	0- 4 wks	.803	.803	.803	.197	.9968	.9968	.9968	.0032
	2	4- 8 wks	.943	.943	.757	.057	.9968	.9968	.9936	.0032
	3	8-20 wks	.872	.955	.660	.045	.9904	.9968	.9841	.0032
	4	20-50 wks	.841	.977	.555	.023	.9760	.9968	.9605	.0032
75-84	1	0- 4 wks	.736	.736	.736	.264	.9931	.9931	.9931	.0069
	2	4- 8 wks	.835	.835	.615	.165	.9931	.9931	.9862	.0069
	3	8-20 wks	.871	.955	.536	.045	.9792	.9931	.9657	.0069
	4	20-50 wks	.812	.973	.435	.027	.9480	.9931	.9155	.0069

* Basis of expected mortality: 1959-61 U.S. Population Rates

† $\breve{p} = \sqrt[\Delta]{p_i}$: $\breve{p}' = \sqrt[\Delta]{p_i'}$, Δ = number of 4-week units t to t + Δ t

CEREBROVASCULAR DISEASE

§202–EXTRACRANIAL ARTERIAL OCCLUSION

Reference: R. B. Bauer, J. S. Meyer, W. S. Fields, R. Remington, M. C. Macdonald, and P. Callen, "Joint Study of Extracranial Arterial Occlusion. III: Progress Report of Controlled Study of Long-Term Survival in Patients With and Without Operation," J. Am. Med. Assoc., 208:509-518 (1969).

Subjects Studied: In order to appraise the relative advantages of treating symptomatic cerebral arterial occlusive disease by surgical means and by medical treatment alone, survival results experienced among 1225 patients admitted to 13 cooperating institutions between March 1962 and August 1968 were analyzed over a 42-month survival period. Only patients who had undergone four-vessel arteriography and who demonstrated the existence of surgically accessible lesions or a single lesion were admitted to the study. The presence of potentially fatal medical disease (e.g., cardiovascular, metabolic, infectious, malignant or degenerative disorder) and an estimate of a mortality risk from proposed operative procedure of ten per cent or more due to concurrent medical disease were also considered contraindicative for inclusion in the study. Subjects in the series were analyzed at time of hospitalization under three classifications: (a) pattern of arterial lesion; (b) neurological status, viz. level of consciousness, and status of gait, motor power and speech (characteristics of six such classes, data with respect to numbers and the distribution of patients in them and three and one-half year cumulative survival rates are set out in Table 202e); and (c) mode of onset of neurological deficit, i.e., transient attack or completed stroke with sequelae (the respective numbers in these categories and measures of survival and mortality are given in the lower portion of Table 202d).

Two groups of the subjects were formed by random selection: 621 patients treated by surgical reconstruction of the arteries in the neck, and 604, by nonsurgical medical treatment. The distribution was on a random basis, with similar composition in the two groups by age, sex, and race, as the following distributions show:

Number (Percentage) of Surgical and Nonsurgical Patients by Age, Sex and Race

Cases	\multicolumn{6}{c}{Age (years)}
	21-44	45-54	55-64	65-74	75 up	Total
Surgical	25 (4.0%)	141 (22.7%)	238 (38.3%)	189 (30.5%)	28 (4.5%)	621 (100%)
Non-Surgical	30 (4.9%)	114 (18.9%)	240 (39.7%)	190 (31.5%)	30 (5.0%)	604 (100%)

	Male	Female	White	Non-White
Surgical	444 (71.5%)	177 (28.5%)	519 (83.6%)	102 (16.4%)
Non-Surgical	447 (74.0%)	157 (26.0%)	496 (82.1%)	108 (17.9%)

Further comparability was achieved with respect to history of concomitant disease (Table 202f), clinical course of the cerebrovascular events and clinical features of the attacks (202e).

Follow-up: At hospital discharge each patient was asked to return within two months and every six months thereafter; if possible, the patient was to have postoperative arteriographic visualization of the vessels on which operation was performed. There were 78 surgical and 96 nonsurgical entrants lost to follow-up. Included in these losses were patients not seen for 12 months or more after a follow-up visit. Source documents of the 1225 cases were submitted to, and maintained at, a central registry so that record treatment was uniform.

EXTRACRANIAL ARTERIAL OCCLUSION

Table 202a Observed Data and Comparative Experience by Duration — All Ages Combined

Group	Interval No.	Start-End	No. Alive at Start of Interval	Exposure Person-Yrs	Deaths Obs.	Deaths Exp.*	Mortality Ratio Interval	Mortality Ratio Cumulative	Survival Ratio Interval	Survival Ratio Cumulative	Excess Death Rate
	i	t to t + Δt	ℓ	E	d	d'	100d/d'	100Σd/Σd'	100p_i/p_i'	100 P/P'	1000(d-d')/E
Surgery	1	0- 6 mos.	621	283	92	7.53	1220%	1220%	84.9%	84.9%	298
	2	6-18 mos.	419	367.5	30	10.22	295	685	94.5	80.2	54
	3	18-30 mos.	286	247.5	29	7.52	385	600	91.0	73.0	87
	4	30-42 mos.	180	150	13	4.98	260	540	94.5	69.0	53
No Surgery	1	0- 6 mos.	604	272.5	45	7.60	590	590	93.0	93.0	137
	2	6-18 mos.	441	392	36	11.41	315	425	93.5	87.0	63
	3	18-30 mos.	307	269.5	28	8.57	325	395	92.6	80.5	72
	4	30-42 mos.	204	167	15	5.81	260	370	94.3	76.0	55
Total	1	0- 6 mos.	1225	555.5	137	15.13	905	905	88.9	88.9	219
	2	6-18 mos.	860	759.5	66	21.63	305	550	94.0	83.5	58
	3	18-30 mos.	593	517	57	16.09	355	490	91.8	76.7	79
	4	30-42 mos.	384	317	28	10.79	260	455	94.4	72.4	54

Table 202b Derived Mortality and Survival Data

Treatment	Interval No.	Start-End	Observed Rates Interval Mortality	Observed Rates Interval Survival	Observed Rates Cumulative Survival	Observed Rates Cumulative Mortality	Expected Rates* Interval Mortality	Expected Rates* Interval Survival	Expected Rates* Cumulative Survival	Expected Rates* Cumulative Mortality
	i	t to t + Δt	q_i	p_i	P	Q	q_i'	p_i'	P'	Q'
Surgery	1	0- 6 mos.	.163	.837	.837	.163	.0133	.9867	.9867	.0133
	2	6-18 mos.	.082	.918	.769	.231	.0278	.9722	.9593	.0407
	3	18-30 mos.	.117	.883	.679	.321	.0304	.9696	.9301	.0699
	4	30-42 mos.	.087	.913	.620	.380	.0332	.9668	.8992	.1008
No Surgery	1	0- 6 mos.	.083	.917	.917	.083	.0140	.9860	.9860	.0140
	2	6-18 mos.	.092	.908	.833	.167	.0291	.9709	.9574	.0426
	3	18-30 mos.	.104	.896	.747	.253	.0318	.9682	.9270	.0730
	4	30-42 mos.	.090	.910	.680	.320	.0348	.9652	.8947	.1053
Total	1	0- 6 mos.	.123	.877	.877	.123	.0136	.9864	.9864	.0136
	2	6-18 mos.	.087	.913	.801	.199	.0285	.9715	.9583	.0417
	3	18-30 mos.	.110	.890	.712	.288	.0311	.9689	.9285	.0715
	4	30-42 mos.	.088	.912	.649	.351	.0340	.9660	.8969	.1031

Table 202c Comparative Survival Experience by Age Group — All Durations Combined (Total 3½ Years)

Treatment	Age Group	No. Alive at Start of Interval	Cumulative Survival Rate Observed	Cumulative Survival Rate Expected*	Cumulative Surv. Ratio	Estim. Ave. Ann. Mort. Rate Observed	Estim. Ave. Ann. Mort. Rate Expected	Mortality Ratio	Excess Death Rate
		ℓ	P	P'	100 P/P'	$\breve{q}$	$\breve{q}$'	100 $\breve{q}$/$\breve{q}$'	1000($\breve{q}$-$\breve{q}$')
Surgery	21-44	22	.803	.9926	80.9%	.061	.0021	2900%	59
	45-54	122	.674	.9658	69.8	.107	.0099	1080	97
	55-64	214	.578	.9242	62.5	.145	.0223	650	123
	65-74	177	.569	.8454	67.3	.149	.0468	320	102
	75 up	26	.459	.7279	63.1	.199	.0867	230	112
No Surgery	21-44	24	.883	.9924	89.0	.035	.0022	1590	33
	45-54	101	.819	.9651	84.9	.055	.0101	545	45
	55-64	198	.669	.9227	72.5	.108	.0227	475	85
	65-74	170	.578	.8434	68.5	.145	.0475	305	97
	75 up	26	.240	.7268	33.0	.335	.0871	385	248
Total	21-44	46	.845	.9925	85.1	.047	.0022	2100	45
	45-54	223	.740	.9655	76.6	.082	.0100	820	72
	55-64	412	.622	.9234	67.4	.127	.0225	565	104
	65-74	347	.573	.8445	67.9	.147	.0471	310	100
	75 up	52	.350	.7274	48.1	.259	.0869	300	172

* Basis of expected mortality: U.S. 1964 Population Rates

CEREBROVASCULAR DISEASE

§202–EXTRACRANIAL ARTERIAL OCCLUSION (continued)

Results: At the end of six months after attack, as indicated in Table 202b, 83.7 per cent of the subjects in the surgical group survived; in the nonsurgical group, 91.7 per cent. Post-operative surgical mortality (8.4 per cent dying within 30 days of surgery) is responsible for the less favorable experience of that class. The advantage at the six-month point was maintained in cumulative survival rates throughout the three and one-half year period. However, survival rates in the three individual 12-month intervals subsequent to the first six-month period were extremely close to one another. The initial advantage is reflected in the cumulative survival rate at the end of 42 months: among surgical subjects this rate was 62 per cent, in the nonsurgical group, 68 per cent.

Mortality ratios in the initial six-month interval presented in Table 202a are 1220 per cent among the surgical subjects and 590 per cent among the nonsurgical controls. This differential, as in the case with survival rates, is attributable to the 8.4 per cent surgical mortality rate. In intervals subsequent to the initial six months, mortality ratios among both surgical and nonsurgical groups diminished and tended to flatten at a level of about 300 per cent of expected, with ratios running between 260 and 385 per cent. Excess deaths per 1000 display a similar pattern, both groups showing like rates of a substantial magnitude (from 53 to 87 per 1000 per year) following six months after attack. In the initial six-month period, however, for the reason already mentioned, surgical cases exhibited an EDR of 298 against 137 per 1000 per year for nonsurgical.

In general, over the full three and one-half year period, the older the age group the poorer the rate of survival and the higher the EDR — both in those treated with surgery and those treated by medical management alone (Table 202c). Mortality ratios averaged on an annual basis decreased with age.

Experience with respect to patients who had, respectively, unilateral stenosis of the carotid arteries, and unilateral carotid artery occlusion and contralateral carotid artery stenosis is presented in Table 202d. Among patients with one side stenosis, those with minor residual effects (falling within Class 2, Table 202e) who were treated surgically experienced a statistically significant advantage at the 5 per cent level in the 42-month cumulative survival rate (83, against 50 per cent) over the patients subject to medical treatment alone. Patients with neurological abnormalities either more or less severe developed small differences between surgical and nonsurgical cases in the survival function, but without statistical significance.

Cases with one side occluded and the opposite side stenotic, unexpectedly showed that surgical and nonsurgical patients with the least abnormality on neurological examination had almost the least favorable three and one-half year cumulative survival rate. Among patients with most adverse neurological effects, medical treatment showed a statistically significant advantage over surgical treatment at the one per cent level.

Results according to clinical course are also presented in Table 202d. The survival function for nontransient cases (completed strokes) is significantly more favorable for nonsurgical management of patients, but no material difference in result according to method of treatment appears in transient cases.

Comment: The authors conclude that surgical treatment is indicated in patients with less severe and transient neurological deficits who are found to have unilateral carotid artery stenosis. However, surgery is contraindicated in patients with more severe and persistent neurological deficits, particularly if one carotid artery occluded and the other stenosed.

EXTRACRANIAL ARTERIAL OCCLUSION

Table 202d Comparative Experience by Type and Severity of Lesion and by Mode of Onset

Group		Number of Patients	Cumulative Survival Rate		Cumulative Surv. Ratio	Estim. Ave. Ann. Mort. Rate		Mortality Ratio	Excess Death Rate
			Observed	Expected*		Observed	Expected		
		ℓ	P	P'	100 P/P'	$\breve{q}$	$\breve{q}'$	100 $\breve{q}/\breve{q}'$	1000($\breve{q}$-$\breve{q}'$)
Type of Lesion									
One Side Stenotic									
No Residual	Surg.	59	.77	.9019	85.4%	.072	.0291	250%	43
	Nonsurg.	52	.83	.8878	93.5	.052	.0334	156	19
Mild	Surg.	36	.83†	.9019	92.0	.052	.0291	179	23
	Nonsurg.	33	.50†	.8878	56.3	.180	.0334	540	147
Severe	Surg.	56	.59	.9019	65.4	.140	.0291	480	111
	Nonsurg.	59	.63	.8878	71.0	.124	.0334	370	91
One Side Occluded									
Opp. Side Stenotic									
No Residual	Surg.	29	.46	.9000	51.1	.199	.0297	670	169
	Nonsurg.	25	.17	.9026	18.8	.397	.0289	1370	368
Mild	Surg.	24	.54	.9000	60.0	.161	.0297	540	131
	Nonsurg.	21	.63	.9026	69.8	.124	.0289	430	95
Severe	Surg.	55	.39†	.9000	43.3	.236	.0297	795	206
	Nonsurg.	57	.80†	.9026	88.6	.062	.0289	215	33
Mode of Onset									
Transient	Surg.	435	.67	.90	74.0	.11	.030	370	80
	Nonsurg.	401	.66	.90	73.0	.11	.030	370	80
Nontransient	Surg.	186	.48	.90	53.0	.19	.030	630	160
	Nonsurg.	203	.71	.90	79.0	.09	.030	300	60

Table 202e Distribution by Neurological Status and 3½ Year Cumulative Survival

Class	Consciousness	Paresis	Disturbance of Gait	Speech	Surgical No.	(%)	C.S. Rate	Nonsurgical No.	(%)	C.S. Rate
1	Normal	No	No	No	203	32.7	.66	182	30.1	.68
2	Normal	Monoparesis	With or Without		160	25.8	.62	136	22.5	.63
3	Normal	Hemiparesis	With or Without		197	31.7	.58	216	35.8	.72
4	Disturbed	Monoparesis	With or Without		19	3.1	.51	16	2.7	.78
5	Disturbed	Hemiparesis	With or Without		38	6.1	.55	50	8.3	.61
6	Comatose — With or Without Other Neurological Deficit				4	0.6		4	0.6	

Table 202f History of Concomitant Disease●

	Surgical (%)	Nonsurgical (%)
Hypertension	38.7	42.4
Diabetes	15.0	17.1
Peripheral Vascular Disease	20.3	20.9
Heart Disease	19.2	19.8
Renal Disease	3.8	3.5

* Basis of expected mortality: U.S. 1964 Population rates (Estimated for Mode of Onset)
† Difference between surgical and nonsurgical significant (at least 5 per cent level)
● 28 per cent of surgical patients and 29 per cent of nonsurgical patients had more than one of the indicated diseases.

2-8

CEREBROVASCULAR DISEASE

§203–CEREBRAL THROMBOSIS

Reference: R. W. Robinson, M. Demirel, and R. J. LeBeau, "Natural History of Cerebral Thrombosis. Nine to Nineteen Year Follow-up," J. Chron. Dis., 21:221-230 (1968).

Subjects Studied: Patients with a diagnosis of cerebral thrombosis admitted to the three major hospitals in Worcester, Mass. during the period from 1947 through 1956. The following cases were excluded from the study: (1) patients with possible intracranial hemorrhage, cerebral embolism or tumor; (2) cases with a likely source of embolism in the heart; (3) any case in which the diagnosis was in doubt, and (4) cases where the first attack occurred prior to 1947 or was of unknown date.

There were 195 deaths within three months among the 843 patients comprising the series, distributed as shown below. Mortality increased with age; the higher mortality for females was associated with a higher average age — 68.3 for female vs. 65.7 years for male survivors, 74.1 years for deaths in females vs. 69.6 years for deaths in males.

Age Distribution and Early Mortality (Within 3 Months)

Age/Sex	Cases No.	Per cent	No. of Deaths	No. of Survivors (at 3 months)	Mortality Rate (for 3 months)
30-39	8	1%	0	8	.00
40-49	34	4%	3	31	.09
50-59	123	15%	16	107	.13
60-69	279	33%	51	228	.18
70-79	283	33%	82	201	.29
80-89	108	13%	38	70	.35
90-99	8	1%	5	3	.63
Male	402	48%	74	328	.18
Female	441	52%	121	320	.27
Total	843	100%	195	648	.23

Follow-up: The observation period ranged from 9 to 19 years. Data for follow-up were obtained from the patients, their families, hospital records, attending physicians and death certificates. Lost to observation were 37 subjects after an average period of five and one-third years.

Results: As shown in the tables above, a high percentage of the cases died within three months after onset, particularly at the higher ages and among females. Among those who survived the initial three months, Table 203a shows that mortality ratios continued to be high. Such ratios for females were substantially higher than for males in the first three years but declined steadily during the first ten years — after the third year they fell below the male ratios. Mortality ratios for males did not display a consistent decline during the first five years but did drop sharply in the 5-10 year period. Both male and female ratios rose considerably in the 10-14 year period. Recurrent cerebrovascular disease accounted for 41 per cent of the deaths; heart disease, 30 per cent. In a general way by duration from attack, excess deaths per 1000 per cent per year ran parallel to the mortality ratios. By age, mortality ratios decreased, but extra deaths per 1000 increased (Table 203c).

Hypertension was found in about 70 per cent of all patients but was not associated with any adverse effect, either on initial or late mortality. Cases with complete functional recovery from a relatively minor temporary neurological deficit had a better 4-year survival rate (73 per cent) than groups with more severe neurological deficit or disability (48 and 41 per cent). However, at 10 years, the differences in survival rate had become minimal. Recurrent cerebrovascular disease (thrombosis or hemorrhage) was the principal cause of death.

CEREBRAL THROMBOSIS

Table 203a Observed Data and Comparative Experience by Duration

Group	Interval No.	Start-End	No. Alive at Start of Interval	Deaths Obs.	Deaths Exp.*	Mortality Ratio Interval	Mortality Ratio Cumulative	Survival Ratio Interval	Survival Ratio Cumulative	Excess Death Rate
	i	t to t + Δt	ℓ	d	d'	100d/d'	100$\sum$d/$\sum$d'	100p_i/p_i'	100 P/P'	1000($\breve{q}$-$\breve{q}$')
Male	1	¼ yr - 1¼	328	59	11.97	495%	495%	85.1%	85.1%	144
	2	1¼ - 2¼	269	39	10.33	380	440	88.9	75.7	107
	3	2¼ - 3¼	230	33	9.27	355	415	89.3	67.6	103
	4	3¼ - 4¼	197	40	8.29	485	430	83.2	56.2	161
	5	4¼ - 5¼	157	28	6.92	405	425	85.8	48.3	136
	6	5¼ - 10¼	129	77	29.24	265	365	52.5	25.3	114
	7	10¼ - 14¼	52	39	11.65	335	360	32.5	8.2	230
Female	1	¼ - 1¼	320	64	9.44	680	680	82.4	82.4	170
	2	1¼ - 2¼	256	48	8.04	600	640	83.8	69.1	157
	3	2¼ - 3¼	208	35	6.91	505	605	86.1	59.5	135
	4	3¼ - 4¼	173	23	6.06	380	560	89.8	53.5	98
	5	4¼ - 5¼	150	19	5.60	340	525	90.6	48.4	91
	6	5¼ - 10¼	131	65	26.42	245	405	63.1	30.6	84
	7	10¼ - 14¼	66	53	13.50	395	405	24.9	7.6	277

Table 203b Derived Mortality and Survival Data by Duration — All Ages Combined

Sex	Interval No.	Start-End	Observed Rates Cumulative Survival	Observed Rates Interval Survival	Observed Rates Geom. Mean Ann. Surv.	Observed Rates Geom. Mean Ann. Mort.	Expected Rates* Cumulative Survival	Expected Rates* Interval Survival	Expected Rates* Geom. Mean Ann. Surv.	Expected Rates* Geom. Mean Ann. Mort.
	i	t to t + Δt	P	p_i	$\breve{p}_i$	$\breve{q}_i$	P'	p_i'	$\breve{p}_i$'	$\breve{q}_i$'
Male	1	¼ yr - 1¼	.820	.820	.820	.180	.9635	.9635	.9635	.0365
	2	1¼ - 2¼	.701	.855	.855	.145	.9265	.9616	.9616	.0384
	3	2¼ - 3¼	.601	.857	.857	.143	.8892	.9597	.9597	.0403
	4	3¼ - 4¼	.479	.797	.797	.203	.8518	.9579	.9579	.0421
	5	4¼ - 5¼	.393	.820	.820	.180	.8142	.9559	.9559	.0441
	6	5¼ - 10¼	.159	.405	.835	.165	.6280	.7713	.9494	.0506
	7	10¼ - 14¼	.040	.252	.709	.291	.4873	.7760	.9386	.0614
Female	1	¼ - 1¼	.800	.800	.800	.200	.9705	.9705	.9705	.0295
	2	1¼ - 2¼	.650	.812	.812	.188	.9400	.9686	.9686	.0314
	3	2¼ - 3¼	.541	.832	.832	.168	.9088	.9668	.9668	.0332
	4	3¼ - 4¼	.469	.867	.867	.133	.8770	.9650	.9650	.0350
	5	4¼ - 5¼	.409	.872	.872	.128	.8443	.9627	.9627	.0373
	6	5¼ - 10¼	.206	.504	.872	.128	.6740	.7983	.9559	.0441
	7	10¼ - 14¼	.041	.199	.668	.332	.5382	.7985	.9453	.0547

Table 203c Comparative Survival Experience by Age Group

Interval Start-End	Age Group	No. Alive at Start of Interval	Cumulative Survival Rate Observed	Cumulative Survival Rate Expected*	Cumulative Surv. Ratio	Estim. Ave. Ann. Mort. Rate Observed	Estim. Ave. Ann. Mort. Rate Expected	Mortality Ratio	Excess Death Rate
		ℓ	P	P'	100 P/P'	$\breve{q}$	$\breve{q}$'	100 $\breve{q}$/$\breve{q}$'	1000($\breve{q}$-$\breve{q}$')
3 mos. - 5¼ yrs.	50-59 yrs	107	.620	.953	.651	.091	.0096	950%	81
	60-69	228	.450	.895	.503	.148	.0219	675	126
	70-79	201	.270	.775	.348	.230	.0497	465	180
	80-89	70	.140	.522	.268	.325	.1219	265	203
5¼ - 10¼ yrs.	50-59	66	.570	.930	.613	.106	.0144	735	92
	60-69	103	.450	.847	.531	.148	.0327	455	115
	70-79	54	.300	.669	.448	.214	.0772	275	137
	80-89	10	.100	.342	.292	.369	.1931	191	176

* Basis of expected mortality: U.S. White Males and Females 1959-1961

CEREBROVASCULAR DISEASE

§204–CEREBROVASCULAR ACCIDENT

Reference: (1) J. Schiffman, "The Framingham Study. Section 25. Survival Following Certain Cardiovascular Events," Govt. Printing Office, Washington, D. C. (September 1970).

Subjects Studied: Examinee-participants in the Framingham Study (see §380) with a diagnosis of overt vascular disease of the brain based on the occurrence of apoplexy (CVA) during the 14-year interval from the initial examination about 1950 through the eighth biennial examination about 1964. There were 132 subjects (out of 5209) diagnosed as having suffered CVA; of these 97 survived the first acute episode. Distribution of subjects and incidence rates by sex and by age at diagnosis were as follows: (Section 7, Table 7-9):

Age at Diagnosis (Years)	29-44	45-54	55-64	65-74	Total
Males-Exposure (person-years)	10340	10888	7742	1906	30876
Incidence*	0.4 (4)	1.9 (21)	3.7 (29)	5.8 (11)	2.1 (65)
Females-Exposure (person-years)	12654	13762	10030	2590	39036
Incidence*	0.3 (4)	1.2 (16)	2.7 (27)	8.9 (23)	1.8 (70)

*Cases/1000/year.   (Number of cases in parentheses.)

Follow-up: Experience of subjects with CVA episodes after the first examination about 1950, followed to the ninth examination about 1966 has been used to develop age-specific life tables for males and females, recalculated in the format of this Mortality Monograph. Because the regularly scheduled biennial examinations constituted the time-frame for follow-up in the Framingham Study, Interval 1 of follow-up can vary in length from less than one to 23 months, but with an average duration of one year. For further details consult §380 or Reference 1.

Results: Tables 204a-b show the high mortality in subjects with CVA, with 68 deaths out of 132 entrants. Mortality in the first interval after diagnosis is about 4 times what it is in succeeding intervals, for both men and women. Mortality is higher for males than for females, with correspondingly lower survival rates and ratios. For males there appears to be a tendency for excess mortality to increase with age, EDR over the first five years ranging from 59 excess deaths per 1000 per year at ages under 55 to 300 for ages over 65 (Table 204c). There is no significant difference in the EDR's of the two female age groups.

CEREBROVASCULAR ACCIDENT — FRAMINGHAM STUDY

Table 204a Observed Data and Comparative Experience by Duration - All Ages Combined

Sex and Interval* No.	Start-End	No. Alive at Start of Interval	Deaths in Interval	Interval Mortality Rate	Mortality Ratio		Survival Ratio		Excess Death Rate
					Interval	Cumulative	Interval	Cumulative	
i	t to $t + \Delta t$	ℓ	d	$q_i = d/\ell$	$100\, q_i/q_i{}'$	$100\, Q/Q'$	$100\, p_i/p_i{}'$	$100\, P/P'$	$1000(\breve{q}-\breve{q}')$
	Male								
1	0-1 yr	66	22	.333	1990%	1990%	67.8%	67.8%	316
2	1-3	44	8	.182	520	890	84.8	57.4	77
3	3-5	28	5	.179	500	645	85.2	49.0	76
4	5-7	16	1	.062	165	485	97.4	47.7	13
5	7-9	12	3	.250	595	435	78.3	37.3	113
	0-9	66	39	.591	435	435	37.3	37.3	132
	Female								
1	0-1 yr	66	13	.197	2300%	2300%	81.0%	81.0%	188
2	1-3	53	7	.132	555	945	88.9	72.0	56
3	3-5	37	2	.054	220	610	97.0	69.8	15
4	5-7	28	6	.214	890	610	80.5	56.2	102
5	7-9	15	1	.067	240	495	96.0	53.9	20
	0-9	66	29	.439	495	495	53.9	53.9	78

Table 204b Derived Mortality and Survival Data

Sex and Interval* No.	Start-End	Observed				Expected†			
		Survival Rate			Ave. Ann. Mort. Rate	Survival Rate			Ave. Ann. Mort. Rate
		Cumulative	Interval	Ave. Ann.		Cumulative	Interval	Ave. Ann.	
i	t to $t + \Delta t$	P	p_i	$\breve{p}$	$\breve{q}$	P'	$p_i{}'$	$\breve{p}'$	$\breve{q}'$
	Male								
1	0-1 yr	.667	.667	.667	.333	.9833	.9833	.9833	.0167
2	1-3	.545	.818	.905	.095	.9488	.9649	.9823	.0177
3	3-5	.448	.821	.906	.094	.9147	.9641	.9819	.0181
4	5-7	.420	.938	.968	.032	.8804	.9625	.9811	.0189
5	7-9	.315	.750	.866	.134	.8434	.9579	.9787	.0213
	Female								
1	0-1 yr	.803	.803	.803	.197	.9914	.9914	.9914	.0086
2	1-3	.697	.868	.932	.068	.9679	.9763	.9881	.0119
3	3-5	.659	.946	.973	.027	.9439	.9752	.9875	.0125
4	5-7	.518	.786	.886	.114	.9212	.9760	.9879	.0121
5	7-9	.483	.933	.966	.034	.8956	.9722	.9860	.0140

Table 204c Comparative Survival Experience by Age Group - First 5 Years Combined

Sex and Age Group	No. Alive at Start of Interval	Deaths during Interval	Survival Rate		Cumulative Survival Ratio	Estimated Average Ann. Mort. Rate		Mortality Ratio	Excess Death Rate
			Observed	Expected†		Observed	Expected		
	ℓ	d	P	P'	$100\, P/P'$	$\breve{q}$	$\breve{q}'$	$100\, \breve{q}/\breve{q}'$	$1000(\breve{q}-\breve{q}')$
Male									
Under 55	20	6	.700	.9531	73.4%	.069	.0096	720%	59
55-64	28	16	.402	.9152	43.9	.167	.0176	950	149
65-74	18	13	.130	.8360	15.6	.335	.0352	950	300
All Ages	66	35	.448	.9147	49.0	.148	.0177	835	130
Female									
Under 65	38	12	.680	.9652	70.5%	.074	.0071	1040%	67
65-74	28	10	.643	.9071	70.9	.084	.0193	435	65
All Ages	66	22	.659	.9439	69.8	.080	.0115	695	68

* Interval No. 1 ends with biennial exam next after first cerebrovascular accident

† Basis of expected mortality: Framingham subjects free from cerebrovascular accident

CEREBROVASCULAR DISEASE

§205–ISCHEMIC STROKE

Reference: R. N. Baker, W. S. Schwartz, and J. C. Ramseyer, "Prognosis Among Survivors of Ischemic Stroke," Neurology, 18:933-941 (1968).

Subjects Studied: Patients surviving a stroke of the ischemic cerebral infarction type admitted to Wadsworth Veterans Administration Hospital (Los Angeles) during the period 1955-1966. Patients with suspected cerebral embolism were excluded. All 430 subjects in the study had survived the stroke by at least 3 months. The patients were all male veterans: 342 Caucasians; 77 Negro; 11 Orientals. Ages were distributed as follows:

Age Group (years)	Under 55	55-64	65-74	75 Up	Total
Number	96	137	173	24	430
Per Cent	22%	32%	40%	6%	100%

Follow-up: Patients after discharge returned to the clinic for periodic evaluation and treatment at one to four-month intervals. In the case of subjects unable to return, follow-up information was obtained by telephone or letter from the patient, his family, or his physician. There was a 7 per cent follow-up loss. The average exposure was 44.5 months. The period of observation terminated in 1966.

Results: Mortality among subjects surviving the stroke remained high during the period of observation. Table 205a indicates an overall mortality ratio of 290 per cent, a 10-year cumulative survival ratio of 47.6 per cent, and an average annual excess death rate over the follow-up period of 74 per 1000. Mortality ratios were somewhat lower in the intervals after the first (215 to 270 per cent versus 370 per cent), but there was no clear trend in the excess death rate.

Experience according to age at stroke, all durations combined, is presented in Table 205c (based on estimated exposure data). Mortality ratios here display a marked diminution with age at time of stroke: at ages under 55 years, the mortality ratio is 960 per cent; between 55 and 64, 500 per cent; and between 65 and 74, 215 per cent. Subjects aged 75 years and older appear to have a slightly more favorable survival rate than men in the general population but the significance of this is limited by reason of the small number of deaths (9).

Of the 172 deaths reported, Table 205d shows that 40, almost one-quarter, were due to recurrent stroke. Congestive heart failure and pneumonia occurred in relatively high proportions, 13 and 17 per cent respectively. Only 5 deaths were due to malignancy, a remarkably low proportion.

The toll taken by death, as the figures in Table 205e indicate, increases with the severity of the disability brought on by the stroke. No deaths were reported among patients in Disability Class 2 (subjects able to carry on normal activity). In Class 3 (able to care for personal needs but unable to work) 30 per cent deaths were recorded; in Class 4 (requiring frequent medical care and help for personal needs), 41 per cent; and Class 5 (requiring nearly complete care), 50 per cent.

Comment: The authors report that a substantial proportion of disablements sustained at the entry stroke manifest some functional improvement. For example, almost two-thirds of those with initial severe disability (Classes 4 and 5) reverted to moderate or mild disability at the time of maximum recovery. Other data reported by the authors include the influence of prior cerebrovascular disease on survival, new cerebral events and disability, relationships of follow-up status to vascular localization and to hypertension, occurrence of myocardial infarction and frequency of associated diseases.

ISCHEMIC STROKE

Table 205a Observed and Estimated Data and Comparative Experience by Duration

No.	Interval Start-End	No. Alive at Start of Interval	Exposure Person-Yrs	Deaths in Interval Observed	Deaths in Interval Expected*	Mortality Ratio Interval	Mortality Ratio Cumulative	Survival Ratio Interval	Survival Ratio Cumulative	Excess Death Rate
i	t to t + Δt	ℓ	E	d	d'	100 d/d'	100 Σd/Σd'	100 p_i/p_i'	100 P/P'	1000(d-d')/E
1	3 mos- 2 yrs	430	667	77	20.7	370%	370%	85.3%	85.3%	84
2	2- 4 yrs	278	446	43	18.1	240	310	88.7	75.7	56
3	4- 6 yrs	161	267	34	12.7	270	300	83.9	63.5	80
4	6-10 yrs	95	146	18	8.3	215	290	74.8	47.6	66
	3 mos-10 yrs	430	1526	172	59.8	290%	290%	—	47.6	74

Table 205b Derived Mortality and Survival Data

No.	Interval Start-End	Observed Rates Average Annual Mortality	Observed Rates Average Annual Survival	Observed Rates Interval Survival	Observed Rates Cumulative Survival	Expected Rates* Average Annual Mortality	Expected Rates* Average Annual Survival	Expected Rates* Interval Survival	Expected Rates* Cumulative Survival
i	t to t + Δt	$\bar{q}$ = d/E	$\bar{p}$	p_i	P	$\bar{q}'$ = d'/E	$\bar{p}'$	p_i'	P'
1	3 mos- 2 yrs	.115	.885	.8087	.8087	.0310	.9690	.9464	.9464
2	2- 4 yrs	.096	.904	.8172	.6608	.0406	.9594	.9204	.8711
3	4- 6 yrs	.127	.873	.7621	.5035	.0476	.9524	.9071	.7902
4	6-10 yrs	.123	.877	.5916	.2979	.0568	.9432	.7914	.6254

Table 205c Comparative Experience by Age at Stroke

Age Group	No. Alive at Start	Estimated Exposure Person-Yrs	Deaths Observed	Deaths Expected*	Mortality Ratio	Ave. Ann. Mort. Rate	Est. 4-Yr Surv. Rate	Est. 4-Yr Surv. Index	Excess Death Rate
(Years)	ℓ	E	d	d'	100 d/d'	$\bar{q}$ = d/E	P = $(1-\bar{q})^4$	100 P/P'	1000(d-d')/E
Under 55	96	333	23	2.4	960%	.069	.752	77.4%	62
55-64	137	492	66	13.2	500	.134	.562	62.7	107
65-74	173	616	74	34.7	215	.120	.599	75.6	64
75 Up	24	85	9	9.5	95	.106	.639	102.7	−5.9
All Ages	430	1526	172	59.8	290%	.113	.620	72.7	74

Table 205d Causes of Death

Cause	Number	Per Cent
Recurrent cerebral infarction	40	23%
Myocardial infarction	42	24
Congestive heart failure	22	13
Sudden death	8	5
Pneumonia	30	17
Acute GI disease	10	6
Malignancy	5	3
Renal failure	5	3
Unknown	10	6
Total	172	100%

Table 205e Status after Follow-up according to Initial Disability

Class	Disability Status	Alive	Dead	Lost	Total
1	No Disability	—	—	—	—
2	Mild-Normal activity	5	0	1	6
3	Moderate-partially independent	66	31	8	105
4	Moderately severe - dependent	110	87	14	211
5	Very severe - complete care	46	54	8	108
	Total	227	172	31	430

* Basis of expected mortality: U.S. White Males 1959-61

CEREBROVASCULAR DISEASE

§206–SURVIVAL AFTER STROKE

Reference: J. C. Goldner, G. H. Payne, F. R. Watson, and H. M. Parrish, "Prognosis for Survival after Stroke," Am. J. Med. Sci., 253:129-133 (1967).

Subjects Studied: All of the major cerebrovascular attacks reported in Boone, Cooper and Howard counties in Central Missouri from July 1, 1963 through June 30, 1964. The study was a cooperative undertaking of the University of Missouri School of Medicine and agencies of the State of Missouri health departments. All information from sources other than attending physician was verified. Etiology of the stroke, (thrombus, embolus, hemorrhage, unknown), any hypertension, any previous major cerebrovascular attacks and the date of onset of first attack were indicated in the reporting of cases. Of the 221 subjects, 95 were under 75 years of age and 126, 75 years or older. Data with respect to sex, race or county of residence were not presented in the reference but the authors assert that no significant differences in incidence or case-fatality rates were noted in these respects.

Follow-up: Observation was continued until April 1, 1965. The range of the follow-up interval was 9 to 21 months, averaging 15 months. Reporting was conducted by employment of physician's reports, hospital records, death certificates, nursing home records and cases reported by public health nurses and University of Missouri extension agents assigned to the counties covered in the study.

Results: Comparative experience over the period of observation by age at time of stroke is presented in Table 206a. Mortality ratios based on deaths from all causes following stroke are very high, averaging for all ages together about six times the general population experience. For ages at onset under 55, this function reaches 4200 per cent; it diminishes with increase in age, falling to 1800 per cent for age group 55-64 years, to 1110 per cent for ages 65-74 years, to 590 for ages 75-84, and to 320 for ages over 85 years. Survival rates over the 15-month average period of observation decline from .700 at the youngest age group shown to .114 in the case of subjects 85 years and older.

Fifteen-month ratios comparing survival with that expected in the general population are comparable in magnitude with the survival rates, tending to become worse with increase in age. These ratios range from 70.5 per cent for age group 35-54 years to 15.7 per cent at the oldest ages. Excess deaths increase with age at onset of stroke growing from 242 per 1000 per year for the youngest age group to 595 for the oldest ages.

The incidence of stroke is indicated in Table 206b. The overall average is 7.1 per 1000 but the incidence increases sharply with age. At ages under 55 years, .65 strokes per year per 1000 persons occur. In the next age bracket (55-64 years), the incidence rises to 4.12; in the ensuing 10-year group, to 10.7; for ages 75-84 years, to 27.2; and for ages 85 years and older, to 58.2 per 1000.

Comment: The authors reported over 90 per cent of deaths in the series as due to cerebrovascular disease. The difference in mortality rates for hypertensive (160/95 mm Hg or higher, any systolic reading over 179 mm, or any diastolic reading over 99 mm Hg) and nonhypertensive stroke patients was not statistically significant. For any given age hypertension did not appear to affect prognosis for survival. No statistical significance was indicated in mortality rate differences between patients who had experienced an earlier stroke and subjects having a first one. Attempts were made by the authors to differentiate subjects on the basis of thrombus, embolus, and hemorrhage. No differences were found in the tested variables.

CEREBROVASCULAR DISEASE

Table 206a Comparative Experience by Age, All Major Cerebrovascular Attacks

Age Group	No. Stroke Patients	No. Deaths (Ave. 15 mos.)		Mortality Ratio	Ave. Ann. Mort. Rate†	Surv. Rate (15 months)	15-Month Surv. Ratio	Excess Death Rate
		Observed	Expected*					
	ℓ	d	d'	100 d/d'	$\check{q}$	P = 1-d/ℓ	100 P/P'	1000($\check{q}$-$\check{q}$')
35-54	10	3	.072	4200%	.248	.700	70.5%	242
55-64	27	11	.61	1800	.342	.593	60.7	324
65-74	58	33	2.96	1110	.490	.431	45.4	449
75-84	82	65	9.42	690	.716	.207	23.4	623
85 up	44	39	12.2	320	.825	.114	15.7	595
All Ages	221	151	25.3	590	.601	.317	35.8	518

Table 206b Incidence of Stroke (per year)

Age Group	Exposure Person-Yrs	No. of Strokes	Strokes per 1000
(Years)	E		
35-54	15466	10	0.65
55-64	6561	27	4.12
65-74	5408	58	10.7
75-84	3019	82	27.2
85 up	756	44	58.2
All Ages	31210	221	7.1

* Basis of expected mortality: U.S. White Population 1959-61
† Average annual mortality rate for 15 months $\check{q} = 1-(1-d/\ell)^{0.8}$

CEREBROVASCULAR DISEASE

§207–ACUTE CEREBROVASCULAR DISEASE IN DENMARK

Reference: J. Marquardsen, "The Natural History of Acute Cerebrovascular Disease," Acta Neurol. Scand., 45 (Suppl. 38) :1-192 (1969).

Subjects Studied: Patients admitted between April 1, 1940 and December 31, 1952 to the Frederiksberg Hospital, Denmark, with diagnosis and evidence of recent acute cerebrovascular accident. The series selected for study consisted of 769 out of 1084 such patients. Of the 279 patients excluded 90 were excluded because of onset of stroke more than 2 weeks previously, 16 because all neurological signs had disappeared, 112 because sequelae from a previous stroke were still present, and the remainder for various other reasons. The sex and age distribution of the 769 patients making up the series is given in Table 207a. Mean age of the males was 67.3 years, of the females, 69.9 years; only 7 patients were under age 40.

Follow-up: Follow-up continued until January 1963 at which time only 29 of the original 769 patients were still alive. Information with regard to the survival and condition of subjects was derived from the patients themselves, hospital records, the Public Record Office, the Central Register of the Board of Health, physicians, health insurance companies, or relatives of patients. Causes of death were obtained from death certificates or autopsy records. Only one patient could not be traced - she was removed from the study.

Results: The number of stroke cases reported, incidence and early deaths (within three weeks of attack) are presented in Table 207a. Early mortality is high: 50.5 per cent of men stricken died within the three weeks; 44.8 per cent of women; it advances with age at the time of attack, although mortality for the youngest patients was higher than it was in patients age 50-59. Early mortality also increased markedly with degree of coma observed on admission (Table 207b). Only one-quarter of patients mentally alert died within three weeks, but 109 out of 111 completely comatose patients were dead at the end of this period. Initial level of consciousness is therefore a most important prognostic sign for the early outcome of stroke patients.

Later mortality and survival experience during follow-up from three weeks to five years is shown for the stroke patients, by various factors in Table 207c, and by age, sex and duration in Tables 207d-e. Residual disability, graded at the end of the early period, was found to have a high correlation with excess mortality. Patients with negligible disability or none at all (Grade I-II) exhibited a mortality ratio of 510 per cent and an EDR of 94 extra deaths per 1000 per year. Patients with total disability (Grade V) had the highest EDR, at 428 extra deaths per 1000. These patients were older than the other groups with an average age of 76.5 years, and they had the lowest survival ratio, only 19.6 per cent, measured of necessity at three years instead of five years in the less disabled patients. In the lower part of Table 207c the effect of degree of blood pressure elevation on comparative experience is seen in two age categories for each sex. Excess mortality was higher and survival ratios were lower in patients with severe blood pressure elevation (180/100 or more).

Comparative mortality is also seen to be higher than that of the general population throughout all of the intervals from three weeks to five years, as shown in Tables 207d-e. Mortality ratios tend to diminish with increasing age and duration, from a maximum of 2300 per cent in females under age 60 during the remainder of first post-stroke year to ratios under 300 per cent in patients age 70-79 of both sexes in the interval from three to five years. Differences in excess death rates are irregular with no consistent trend by age, sex or duration, except for a decrease with duration in the youngest patients. All of these rates are high, ranging from 54 to 241 extra deaths per 1000 per year. Five-year cumulative survival ratios do tend to decrease with advancing age, from a maximum value of 59.6 per cent (men under 60) to a low of 32.2 per cent (men age 70-79).

Table 207f gives the distribution of deaths by cause. The leading category, with 30.1 per cent of the deaths included both congestive heart failure and pneumonia, and the second highest cause was recurrent stroke, at 22.7 per cent. Because of its importance with respect to morbidity as well as mortality extensive data with respect to recurrence rates of stroke were collected by the author. As shown in Table 207g recurrence rates cluster in the range of 8 to 12 per cent of patients exposed to risk per year, in the various age and duration categories. The risk of recurrence is increased in patients with two or more strokes, with auricular fibrillation or abnormal electrocardiogram, and in those with diastolic blood pressure 100 mm. and up. On the other hand, risk of recurrence is *reduced* in patients with, as compared to those without, hemiplegia resulting from the initial stroke.

ACUTE CEREBROVASCULAR DISEASE IN DENMARK

Table 207a   Early Mortality (Within 3 Weeks) by Sex and Age

	Males				Females			
Age	Incidence over 12.7 Yrs	No. of Patients	No. Deaths in 3 Weeks	Mortality Rate	Incidence over 12.7 Yrs	No. of Patients	No. Deaths in 3 Weeks	Mortality Rate
	No./1000	ℓ_o	d_o	q_o	No./1000	ℓ_o	d_o	q_o
Under 50 yrs	1.6	25	12	.480	1.0	21	8	.381
50-59	8.0	51	16	.314	6.8	59	21	.356
60-69	20.5	92	39	.424	19.4	133	56	.421
70-79	48.5	106	64	.604	48.7	179	79	.441
80 up	62.8	29	22	.759	63.9	74	45	.608
Total	—	303	153	.505	—	466	209	.448

Table 207b   Early Mortality (Within 3 Weeks) by Duration and Level of Consciousness

Interval No.	Start-End	No. of Pts. Start of Int.	No. of Deaths During Interval	Cumulative Surv. Rate	Daily Excess Death Rate	No. of Pts. Start of Int.	No. of Deaths During Interval	Cumulative Surv. Rate	Daily Excess Death Rate
i	t to t + Δt	ℓ	d	P	*	ℓ	d	P	*
			Alert				Somnolent		
1	0- 3 days	477	29	.939	21	111	26	.766	85
2	3- 7	448	38	.860	22	85	21	.577	68
3	7-21	410	47	.761	8.7	64	32	.288	48
			Semi-Comatose				Comatose		
1	0- 3 days	70	37	.471	222	111	100	.099	537
2	3- 7	33	11	.314	96	11	9	.018	347
3	7-21	22	13	.129	62	2	0	.018	0

Table 207c   Comparative 5-Year Experience by Various Factors (Exclude 1st 3 Weeks)

Factor (Age)		No. of Patients	5-Year Survival Rate Observed	5-Year Survival Rate Expected†	Survival Ratio	Geom. Mean Ann. Mort. Rate Observed	Geom. Mean Ann. Mort. Rate Expected†	Mortality Ratio	Excess Death Rate
		ℓ	P	P′	100 P/P′	$\breve{q}$	$\breve{q}'$	100 $\breve{q}/\breve{q}'$	1000($\breve{q}$-$\breve{q}'$)
Disability●									
Grade I-II	(63.4 yrs)	210	.541	.892	60.7%	.117	.023	510%	94
Grade III	(68.5)	63	.408	.822	49.6	.166	.039	425	127
Grade IV	(67.8)	62	.222	.834	26.6	.263	.036	730	227
Grade V	(76.5)	47	.123□	.780□	15.8	.509□	.081□	630	428
Blood Pressure									
S≥180 or D≥100	M <70	40	.375	.918	40.8%	.180	.017	1060%	163
	F <70	60	.378	.930	40.6	.179	.015	1190	164
	M 70-79	16	.115□	.732□	15.7	.422	.076	555	346
	F 70-79	48	.280	.677	41.4	.227	.076	300	151
Under 180/100	M <70	61	.578	.918	63.0	.105	.017	620	88
	F < 70	68	.574	.930	61.7	.106	.015	705	91
	M 70-79	26	.333	.662	50.3	.199	.080	250	119
	F 70-79	52	.344	.677	50.8	.194	.076	255	118

*Daily excess death rate = $1000(1 - \sqrt[\Delta t]{p_i})$

†Basis of expected mortality: 1955 Danish population mortality rates, 1966 U.N. Demographic Yearbook
●Disability: Grades I & II - independent; Grade III - requires help, but walks without help; Grade IV - dependent but walks with help; Grade V - bedfast or chairfast
□3 - Year Survival rate
■4 - Year Survival rate

2-18

CEREBROVASCULAR DISEASE

Table 207d   Observed Data and Comparative Experience in Early Survivors by Age, Sex and Duration

Sex and Age		Interval	No. Alive at Start of Int.	No. of Deaths		Mortality Ratio		Survival Ratio		Excess Death Rate
	No.	Start-End		Observed	Expected*	Interval	Cumulative	Interval	Cumulative	
	i	t to $t+\Delta t$	ℓ	d	d'	$100\ d/d'$	$100\ \Sigma d/\Sigma d'$	$100\ p_i/p_i'$	$100\ P/P'$	$1000(\check{q}-\check{q}')$
Males										
Under 60 yrs	1	3 wks-1 yr	48	7	0.45	1560%	1560%	86.2%	86.2%	144
	2	1-3 yrs	41	10	0.92	1090	1240	77.3	66.7	119
	3	3-5	31	4	0.82	490	960	89.4	59.6	54
60-69	1	3 wks-1 yr	53	8	1.23	650	650	86.9	86.9	134
	2	1-3 yrs	45	12	2.51	480	535	77.7	67.5	115
	3	3-5	33	9	2.19	410	490	77.9	52.6	113
70-79	1	3 wks-1 yr	42	9	2.57	350	350	83.7	83.7	161
	2	1-3 yrs	33	17	4.77	355	355	56.7	47.4	229
	3	3-5	16	7	2.78	250	325	68.0	32.2	159
Females										
Under 60 yrs	1	3 wks-1 yr	51	8	0.35	2300%	2300%	84.9%	84.9%	159
	2	1-3 yrs	43	8	0.72	1110	1500	82.8	70.3	90
	3	3-5	35	6	0.69	870	1250	84.6	59.4	79
60-69	1	3 wks-1 yr	77	19	1.41	1350	1350	76.7	76.7	241
	2	1-3 yrs	58	12	2.60	460	775	83.0	63.7	87
	3	3-5	46	12	2.51	480	660	78.3	49.9	112
70-79	1	3 wks-1 yr	100	19	5.65	335	335	85.9	85.9	140
	2	1-3 yrs	81	25	11.04	225	265	80.0	68.7	98
	3	3-5	56	24	9.32	260	260	68.5	47.1	157

Table 207e   Derived Mortality and Survival Data

Sex and Age		Interval	Observed Rates				Expected Rates*			
			Survival			Mortality	Survival			Mortality
	No.	Start-End	Cumulative	Interval	Mean Ann.	Mean Ann.	Cumulative	Interval	Mean Ann.	Mean Ann.
	i	t to $t+\Delta t$	P	p_i	$\check{p}$	$\check{q}$	P'	p_i'	$\check{p}'$	$\check{q}'$
Males										
Under 60 yrs	1	3 wks-1 yr	.854	.854	.846	.154	.9907	.9907	.9901	.0099
	2	1-3 yrs	.646	.756	.870	.130	.9685	.9776	.9887	.0113
	3	3-5	.562	.870	.933	.067	.9428	.9735	.9867	.0133
60-69	1	3 wks-1 yr	.849	.849	.841	.159	.9768	.9768	.9754	.0246
	2	1-3 yrs	.623	.734	.857	.143	.9224	.9443	.9718	.0282
	3	3-5	.453	.727	.853	.147	.8612	.9337	.9663	.0337
70-79	1	3 wks-1 yr	.786	.786	.774	.226	.9388	.9388	.9352	.0648
	2	1-3 yrs	.381	.485	.696	.304	.8032	.8556	.9250	.0750
	3	3-5	.214	.562	.750	.250	.6638	.8264	.9091	.0909
Females										
Under 60 yrs	1	3 wks-1 yr	.843	.843	.834	.166	.9931	.9931	.9927	.0073
	2	1-3 yrs	.686	.814	.902	.098	.9765	.9833	.9916	.0084
	3	3-5	.569	.829	.911	.089	.9572	.9802	.9901	.0099
60-69	1	3 wks-1 yr	.753	.753	.740	.260	.9817	.9817	.9806	.0194
	2	1-3 yrs	.597	.793	.890	.110	.9376	.9551	.9773	.0227
	3	3-5	.442	.740	.860	.140	.8864	.9454	.9723	.0277
70-79	1	3 wks-1 yr	.810	.810	.800	.200	.9435	.9435	.9401	.0599
	2	1-3 yrs	.560	.691	.831	.169	.8149	.8637	.9294	.0706
	3	3-5	.320	.571	.756	.244	.6793	.8336	.9130	.0870

* Basis of expected mortality: Danish Population Mortality 1951-55

ACUTE CEREBROVASCULAR DISEASE IN DENMARK

Table 207f   Mortality by Cause of Death, Age and Sex

Cause of Death	Under 60	60-69	70-79	80 up	All Male	All Female	Total Deaths Number	Total Deaths Per Cent
Recurrent Stroke	28	32	25	1	35	51	86	22.7
Myocardial Infarction	11	12	11	4	18	20	38	10.0
Heart Fail. or Pneumonia	18	38	47	11	41	73	114	30.1
Pulmonary Infarction	2	4	10	5	5	16	21	5.6
Uremia	4	5	3	1	4	9	13	3.4
Cancer	3	4	3	0	6	4	10	2.6
Miscellaneous Causes	5	6	8	3	6	16	22	5.8
Cause Uncertain	10	21	33	11	23	52	75	19.8
Total	81	122	140	36	138	241	379	100.0%

Table 207g   Stroke Recurrence Rate by Sex, Duration, Age and Other Factors

Category		Male Exposure Person-Yrs	Male No. of Recurrences	Male Recurrence Rate	Female Exposure Person-Yrs	Female No. of Recurrences	Female Recurrence Rate
		E^*	u	$r=100\ u/E$	E^*	u	$r=100\ u/E$
Duration	0- 2 yrs	252.0	26	10.3%	400.0	42	10.5%
	2- 5	210.5	16	7.6	338.0	29	8.6
	5-10	176.5	10	5.7	245.0	20	8.2
Age	Under 60 yrs	376.0	20	5.3%	431.5	52	12.1%
	60-69	303.5	37	12.1	369.5	37	10.0
	70-79	136.0	15	11.0	436.0	41	9.4
	80 up	14.5	2	(13.8)	33.5	5	(15.0)
Prior Stroke None		779.5	68	8.7%	1142.0	108	9.5%
Yes		50.5	6	11.9	128.5	27	21.0
Heart Failure None		419.5	22	5.2%	380.5	39	10.0%
Yes		169.5	27	15.9	426.0	45	10.5
Grade of Hemiplegia							
None or partial		104.5	16	15.2%	244.0	40	16.4%
Mild to Moderate		310.5	26	8.4	239.0	44	18.4
Severe or Complete		415.0	32	7.7	657.5	51	7.8
Auricular Fibrillation None		773.0	66	8.5%	1120.0	111	9.0%
Yes		57.0	8	14.0	150.5	24	15.9
Electrocardiogram Normal		280.0	19	6.8%	356.5	34	9.5%
Abnormal		294.5	39	13.2	571.0	71	12.4
Diastolic Pressure Under 100		628.5	39	6.2%	901.0	79	8.8%
100-119		167.5	25	14.9	295.5	42	14.2
120 up		34.0	10	29.4	74.0	14	18.9

*Adjusted for terminations by death. $E = \sum_{1}^{i} (\ell_i - \tfrac{1}{2}d_i)$

CEREBROVASCULAR DISEASE

§208–NATURAL HISTORY OF STROKE

Reference: N. Matsumoto, J. P. Whisnant, L. T. Kurland, and H. Okazaki, "Natural History of Stroke in Rochester, Minnesota, 1955 through 1969: An Extension of a Previous Study, 1945 through 1954," Stroke, 4:20-29 (1973).

Subjects Studied: All patients in Rochester, Minnesota (population 32,600 in 1955, 51,269 in 1969) who were known to have had a stroke during the period 1955 through 1969. Strokes were studied in four categories: cerebral thrombosis; cerebral embolus; intracerebral hemorrhage; and subarachnoid hemorrhage. All medical records for residents of Rochester were reviewed for the 15-year period 1955-1969, as contained in the Mayo Clinic, the Olmsted Medical Group and hospitals in Rochester and southeastern Minnesota. All of these medical facilities have a medical record indexing and retrieval system similar to that used at the Mayo Clinic for several decades. A review was also made of autopsy protocols and all death certificates listing stroke as cause of death, during 1955 through 1969. Some undocumented deaths attributed to stroke were excluded, also 261 autopsy cases of old stroke with no known clinical event. Cases with transient cerebral ischemic attack were studied separately (§209), but cases with mild stroke, not hospitalized, but seen in the home, in the office or a nursing home, were included. Out of 1245 patients accepted on the basis of diagnosis and residence, 993 had their initial stroke while resident in Rochester during the study period. Of these 53 had a stroke of unknown type, while the others were divided into the four diagnostic categories as shown in Table 208a, the predominant type being cerebral thrombosis with 71 per cent of the total. Distribution of cases and incidence rates for all 993 causes of stroke by age and sex were as follows:

Age Group (Years)	Under 35	35-44	45-54	55-64	65-74	75 and up	Total
Male - No. of Cases	6	15	43	104	147	163	478
Annual Incidence per 1000	0.03	0.43	1.58	5.1	10.8	25.0	1.65
Female - No. of Cases	10	10	24	75	127	269	515
Annual Incidence per 1000	0.05	0.27	0.71	2.6	6.0	19.9	1.46

Follow-up: Follow-up was carried to January 1, 1970 on all 993 patients, through medical and hospital records, death certificates and autopsy protocols, as described above.

Results: Early experience (within 30 days) is given in Table 208a for the four diagnostic categories of stroke, all ages and both sexes combined. (Data in Tables 208a-b have been derived from survival curves presented in the article, and not from tabular data.) Mortality is extremely high during the first month, and especially in the first two days, where the interval mortality rate ranges from a low of .051 for cerebral thrombosis to a high of .530 in patients with intracerebral hemorrhage. The 30-day survival rates are correspondingly low: P of .160 in intracerebral hemorrhage, .460 in subarachnoid hemorrhage, .684 in cerebral embolus, and .823 in cerebral thrombosis.

It should be noted that the average age of stroke patients in the three groups comprising most of the cases is about 70 years, but the group with subarachnoid hemorrhage is distinctly younger, by more than 15 years on the average.

Comparative experience after the first month is shown in Table 208b. Mortality ratios and EDR's continued at a very high level in the first year, with EDR in the range of 112 to 341 extra deaths per 1000 per year. After the first year patients with subarachnoid hemorrhage had the lowest excess mortality (EDR, 6 to 33 per 1000), and patients with intracerebral hemorrhage exhibited the highest EDR, 290 per 1000, in the interval from 3 to 7 years after their stroke. Comparative rates and ratios should be interpreted with some caution for these two categories because of the small numbers of one-month survivors. Patients with cerebral thrombosis, the largest group, showed an almost constant EDR between 42 and 47 per 1000 from 1 to 15 years after their stroke, with a slight decrease in mortality ratio from 161 to 149 per cent. The survival ratio at 7 years was only 13.6 per cent in intracerebral hemorrhage; 10-year survival ratios were 54.1 per cent in cerebral thrombosis, 33.5 per cent in cerebral embolus, and 73.8 per cent in subarachnoid hemorrhage.

NATURAL HISTORY OF STROKE

Table 208a   Comparative Early Mortality (Within 30 Days) by Type of Stroke

Type of Stroke	Interval No.	Interval Start-End	No. of Days Exposed	No. Alive at Start of Interval	Deaths during Interval	Interval Mort. Rate	Cumulative Surv. Rate	Daily Excess Death Rate
	i	t to t + Δt	Δt	ℓ	d	$q_i = d_i/\ell_i$	P	$1000(1-{}^{\Delta t}\!\sqrt{1-q_i})$
Cerebral Thrombosis	1	0- 2 days	2	701	36	.051	.949	26
(Ave. Age 72 Yrs)	2	2-10	8	665	50	.075	.878	10
	3	10-30	20	615	39	.063	.823	3.2
Cerebral Embolus	1	0- 2	2	76	8	.105	.895	54
(Ave. Age 69 Yrs)	2	2-10	8	68	9	.132	.777	18
	3	10-30	20	59	7	.119	.684	6.3
Intracerebral	1	0- 2	2	100	53	.530	.470	314
Hemorrhage	2	2-10	8	47	23	.489	.240	81
(Ave. Age 70 Yrs)	3	10-30	20	24	8	.333	.160	20
Subarachnoid	1	0- 2	2	63	23	.365	.635	203
Hemorrhage	2	2-10	8	40	6	.150	.540	20
(Ave. Age 54 Yrs)	3	10-30	20	34	5	.147	.460	7.9

Table 208b   Comparative Experience, Excluding First Month, by Type of Stroke and Duration

Type of Stroke (No. of Patients)	Interval No.	Interval Start-End	Cumulative Surv. Rate Observed	Cumulative Surv. Rate Expected*	Cumulative Surv. Ratio	Estim. Ave. Ann. Mort. Rate† Observed	Estim. Ave. Ann. Mort. Rate† Expected	Mortality Ratio	Excess Death Rate
	i	t to t + Δt	P	P′	100 P/P′	$\breve{q}$	$\breve{q}'$	100 $\breve{q}/\breve{q}'$	$1000(\breve{q}-\breve{q}')$
Cerebral Thrombosis	1	1 mo-1yr	.796	.943	84.4%	.223	.062	360%	161
(576)	2	1-5 yrs	.498	.708	70.3	.111	.069	161	42
	3	5-10	.255	.471	54.1	.125	.078	160	47
	4	10-15	.126	.297	42.4	.131	.088	149	43
Cerebral Embolus	1	1 mo-1yr	.627	.947	66.2	.399	.058	690	341
(52)	2	1-5 yrs	.392	.730	53.7	.111	.063	176	48
	3	5-10	.171	.510	33.5	.153	.069	220	84
Intracerebral	1	1 mo-3yrs	.500	.840	59.5	.212	.058	365	154
Hemorrhage (16)	2	3-7	.088	.648	13.6	.352	.063	560	289
Subarachnoid	1	1 mo-1 yr	.880	.983	89.5	.130	.018	720	112
Hemorrhage (29)	2	1-5 yrs	.789	.902	87.5	.027	.021	129	6.0
	3	5-10	.583	.790	73.8	.059	.026	225	33

Table 208c   Causes of Death by Type of Stroke

Type of Stroke	Initial Stroke	Subsequent Stroke	Coronary Heart Dis.	Cardiac Failure	Respiratory Diseases	Pulmonary Embolism	Cancer	Other Causes & Unknown	Total
Cerebral Thromb.	105	51	54	47	44	9	24	95	429
Cerebral Embolus	21	9	4	4	2	0	4	14	58
Intracereb. Hemor.	75	3	5	1	6	0	2	5	97
Subarach. Hemor.	33	4	1	1	1	0	0	2	42
Unknown	21	3	4	2	6	1	3	6	46
All Types - No.	255	70	68	55	59	10	33	122	672
Per Cent	37.9%	10.4%	10.1%	8.2%	8.8%	1.5%	4.9%	18.2%	100.0%

* Basis of expected survival: Minnesota Life Tables 1960

† $\breve{q} = 1 - {}^{\Delta t}\!\sqrt{p_i}$ $p_i = P_i/P_{i-1}$

CEREBROVASCULAR DISEASE

§209–TRANSIENT ISCHEMIC ATTACK

References: (1) J. P. Whisnant, N. Matsumoto, and L. R. Elveback, "Transient Cerebral Ischemic Attacks in a Community - Rochester, Minnesota, 1955 Through 1969," Mayo Clin. Proc., 48:194-198 (1973).
(2) J. P. Whisnant, "Epidemiology of Stroke: Emphasis on Transient Cerebral Ischemic Attacks and Hypertension," Stroke, 5:68-70 (1974).
(3) J. P. Whisnant, supplementary data in personal communication (1974).

Subjects Studied: Persons living in Rochester, Minnesota, who had their first transient ischemic attack (TIA) during the period from 1955 through 1969. For purposes of the study, a TIA is an episode of focal neurologic symptoms with abrupt onset and rapid resolution, lasting usually 30 minutes or less, but never over 24 hours, and due to altered circulation in a limited region of the brain. The central file of medical records compiled for the Rochester Epidemiologic Project provided the source data. This file includes records of the Mayo Clinic and the Olmsted Medical and Surgical Group as well as those of other medical institutions in and around Rochester. The authors estimate that fewer than 10 per cent of the persons with TIA were missed by the reporting and search procedures. There were 198 subjects in the study, 88 men and 110 women. The average age at first TIA was 70 years.

Follow-up: All patients were followed up at least to January 1, 1970 for determination of mortality, recurrence of TIA, or occurrence of a stroke.

Results: Mortality and survival rates and ratios over a ten-year period for the subjects in the series are presented in Tables 209a-b. Mortality ratios are high (900 per cent) in the month following attack but decrease subsequently to a low point of 129 per cent in the 3-5 year post-attack interval before beginning to increase. Excess death rates follow a similar course: EDR's of 431 per 1000 per year in the first month decline to 17 per 1000 in the 3-5 year interval but thereafter increase, reaching 81 per 1000 from 7 to 10 years after attack. Interval survival ratios are irregular, ranging from 90.7 to 97.2 per cent, in the first seven post-attack years, but drop to 73.2 per cent in the 7-10 year interval.

The incidence rates of TIA per 100,000 per year are given by sex and age in Table 209c. The overall average annual incidence rate for first attacks was 31 per 100,000. Rates were higher for men than for women at all ages except for those over 75 years. The age-adjusted incidence rates were 36 per 100,000 for men and 27 for women.

Thirty-six per cent of the patients with TIA had a subsequent stroke during follow-up. Strokes occurred in 30 per cent of those between 45 and 54 years, 29 per cent of those 55-64 years, 38 per cent of those 65-74 years, and 43 per cent of those 75 years of age and over. In all, 72 subjects with TIA had a subsequent stroke. The time intervening is shown by interval for males and females in Table 209d. Fifty-one per cent of such strokes occurred in the first year after TIA, including 21 per cent in the first month. At the end of a year after the first TIA, stroke occurred 16.5 times as frequently as in the general population, and for the full period of the study, 9.5 times as frequently. The study also included cumulative ratios of survival-free-from-stroke for the TIA patients and for the total population in Rochester. Among all persons in the population having cerebral infarction, a little less than 10 per cent had prior TIA.

Over the entire follow-up, 96 of the TIA patients died from causes indicated in Table 209a. Among the deaths, 28 per cent involved a first or a subsequent stroke and 37 per cent, cardiac disease.

TRANSIENT ISCHEMIC ATTACKS

Table 209a   Observed Data and Comparative Experience by Duration (All Ages, Male and Female Combined)

No.	Interval Start-End	No. Alive at Start of Interval	Exposure Person-Yrs	Deaths in Interval Observed	Deaths in Interval Expected*	Mortality Ratio Interval	Mortality Ratio Cumulative	Survival Ratio Interval	Survival Ratio Cumulative	Excess Death Rate
i	t to $t+\Delta t$	ℓ	E	d	d'	$100\,d/d'$	$100\sum d/\sum d'$	$100\,p_i/p_i'$	$100\,P/P'$	$1000(d-d')/E$
1	0-1 mo	198	16.5	8	0.89	900%	900%	96.4%	96.4%	431
2	1 mo - 3 mos	190	31.0	8	1.67	480	625	96.7	93.2	204
3	3 mos - 1 yr	181	130.0	12	7.02	171	290	97.3	90.6	38
4	1- 3 yrs	165	284.1	22	15.96	138	196	95.2	86.3	21
5	3- 5	110	194.1	15	11.61	129	175	96.5	83.2	17
6	5- 7	76	128.4	14	8.25	170	174	90.7	75.5	45
7	7-10	42	85.9	13	6.07	215	179	73.2	55.4	81
3-7	3 mos-10 yrs	181	822.5	76	48.91	155	—	59.3	—	33

Table 209b   Derived Mortality and Survival Data

No.	Interval Start-End	Observed Rates Cumulative Survival	Observed Rates Interval Survival	Observed Rates Geom. Mean Ann. Surv.	Observed Rates Geom. Mean Ann. Mort.	Expected Rates* Cumulative Survival	Expected Rates* Interval Survival	Expected Rates* Geom. Mean Ann. Surv.	Expected Rates* Geom. Mean Ann. Mort.
i	t to $t+\Delta t$	P	p_i	$\breve{p}$	$\breve{q}$	P'	p_i'	$\breve{p}'$	$\breve{q}'$
1	0-1 mo	.960	.960	.610	.390	.9954	.9954	.9460	.0540
2	1 mo - 3 mos	.919	.958	.772	.228	.9862	.9908	.9460	.0540
3	3 mos - 1 yr	.857	.933	.911	.089	.9460	.9592	.9460	.0540
4	1- 3 yrs	.727	.848	.921	.079	.8426	.8907	.9438	.0562
5	3- 5	.620	.853	.924	.076	.7447	.8838	.9401	.0599
6	5- 7	.492	.794	.891	.109	.6518	.8753	.9356	.0644
7	7-10	.289	.586	.837	.163	.5219	.8007	.9286	.0714

**Table 209c   Incidence of First Transient Ischemic Attack by Age and Sex
Annual Incidence Rate per 100,000 (Number of Attacks)**

Age:	Under 45	45-54	55-64	65-74	75 up	All Ages Crude Rate	All Ages Age-Adjusted
Male	2 (4)	21 (6)	96 (20)	263 (38)	267 (20)	31 (88)	36 (88)
Female	0.4 (1)	12 (4)	50 (15)	192 (42)	306 (48)	31 (110)	27 (110)
Combined	1 (5)	16 (10)	69 (35)	220 (80)	293 (68)	31 (198)	31 (198)

Table 209d   Interval from First Transient Ischemic Attack to Stroke

Interval:	0-1 mo	1 mo - 3 mos	3 mos - 1 yr	1-3 yrs	3-5 yrs	5 yrs up	Total
Male	7	1	9	3	5	6	31
Female	8	4	8	10	7	4	41
Combined No.	15	5	17	13	12	10	72
Per Cent	21%	7%	23%	18%	17%	14%	100%

Table 209e   Cause of Death after First Transient Ischemic Attack

Cause:	Initial Stroke	Subsequent Stroke	Cardiac Disease	Respiratory Disease	Cancer	Other Causes	Total Deaths
Number	18	9	35	13	5	16	96
Per Cent	19%	9%	37%	13%	5%	17%	100%

*Basis of expected mortality: Life Table for Minnesota 1960

ORGANIC BRAIN DISORDERS

§215—MENTAL RETARDATION IN CHILDREN

Reference: G. Tarjan, R. K. Eyman, and C. R. Miller, "Natural History of Mental Retardation in a State Hospital, Revisited," Am. J. Dis. Child., 117:609-620 (1969).

Subjects Studied: The study is comprised of two cohorts of mentally retarded, predominantly juvenile patients admitted to the Pacific State Hospital in Pomona, California. The first cohort consisted of patients admitted between July 1, 1948 and June 30, 1952, the second cohort, patients admitted from July 1, 1959 to June 30, 1962. Patients not mentally retarded, those admitted only for observation, and those transferred to another hospital were not included in the study. The cohorts were further subdivided into groups according to sex, age, IQ, and four diagnostic categories. Distribution by age and sex was as follows:

	Age						**Sex**	
	0-5 Yrs	**6-11 Yrs**	**12-17 Yrs**	**18 Yrs up**	**Total**		**Males**	**Females**
1948-52 Cohort	173	155	278	118	724		416	308
Per Cent	23.9%	21.4%	38.4%	16.3%	100.0%		57.5%	42.5%
1958-62 Cohort	447	433	273	172	1325		778	547
Per Cent	33.7%	32.7%	20.6%	13.0%	100.0%		58.7%	41.3%

Follow-up: Patients were followed in time blocks of six months for four years. Information on patient status and change of address was obtained from data accumulated by the Socio-Behavioral Laboratory. Exposure in "person half-years" was calculated after deducting the time following unauthorized absence or termination due to death or discharge.

Results: Mortality and survival data for both cohorts are presented by duration with all ages combined (Table 215a), and for the 1958-62 cohort by age and IQ (Table 215b), and by diagnosis (Table 215c). The 1948-52 cohort is composed of older, less severely retarded patients, and yet the mortality experience was about twice as great, on the average, as in those of the 1958-62 cohort. In both cohorts the mortality ratios were highest in the first year after admission - 7400 per cent for the 1948-52 cohort and 3400 per cent for the later cohort. The excess death rates were correspondingly high at 66 and 23 per 1000 cases per year. It is evident from the mortality ratios and average annual excess death rates in Table 215b that patients with IQ's under 30 experience very high mortality no matter what their age, while excess mortality is lower in those with IQ's of 30 and up. The excess death rate for developmental cranial anomalies (Table 215c) is at least four times that of any of the other categories. The lowest excess mortality was experienced by the functional group (those without evidence of organic brain damage); EDR was only 3.2 per 1000, but the mortality ratio was still 550 per cent. Although the four-year survival index was well over 90 per cent in all of these categories except developmental cranial anomalies, mortality was very high relative to the low levels found in normal children.

MENTAL RETARDATION IN CHILDREN

Table 215a   Observed Data and Comparative Experience by Duration — All Ages and I. Q.'s Combined

Cohort	Interval Start-End	No. Alive at Start of Interval	Exposure* Person-Yrs	Deaths Observed	Deaths Expected†	Mortality Ratio	Cumulative Surv. Rate	Cumulative Surv. Ratio	Excess Death Rate
	t to t +Δt	ℓ	E	d	d'	100 d/d'	P	100 P/P'	1000(d-d')/E
1948-52	0-1 yr	724	722.5	48	0.65	7400%	.934	93.4%	66
	1-2	672	672.0	8	0.60	1320	.922	92.4	11
	2-3	664	664.0	12	0.60	2000	.906	90.8	17
	3-4	652	651.2	9	0.59	1540	.893	89.6	13
	0-4	724	2709.7	77	2.44	3160	.893	89.6	28
1958-62	0-1 yr	1325	1319.2	31	0.92	3400%	.977	97.7%	23
	1-2	1279	1277.8	21	0.90	2300	.960	96.2	16
	2-3	1255	1254.2	8	0.88	910	.954	95.6	5.7
	3-4	1246	1246.0	9	0.87	1030	.947	95.0	6.5
	0-4	1325	5097.2	69	3.57	1930	.947	95.0	13

Table 215b   Observed Data and Comparative Experience for the 1958-62 Cohort by Age and I. Q. — All Durations Combined

Age	I. Q.	Entrants	Exposure* Person-Yrs	Deaths Observed	Deaths Expected†	Mortality Ratio	Est. 4-Yr Surv. Rate	Est. 4-Yr Surv. Index	Excess Death Rate
		ℓ	E	d	d'	100 d/d'	P = $(1-\bar{q})^4$	100 P/P'	1000(d-d')/E
Under 12 yrs	Under 30	610	2321.0	47	1.63	2900%	.921	92.4%	20
Under 12 yrs	30 up	270	1054.5	6	0.74	815	.977	98.0	5.0
12 yrs up	Under 30	218	849.7	12	0.59	2000	.945	94.7	13
12 yrs up	30 up	227	872.0	4	0.61	655	.982	98.5	3.9
Total		1325	5097.2	69	3.57	1930	.947	95.0	13

Table 215c   Observed Data and Comparative Experience for the 1958-62 Cohort by Diagnosis — All Ages and Durations Combined

Diagnosis	Entrants	Exposure* Person-Yrs	Deaths Observed	Deaths Expected†	Mortality Ratio	Est. 4-Yr Surv. Rate	Est. 4-Yr Surv. Index	Excess Death Rate
	ℓ	E	d	d'	100 d/d'	P = $(1-\bar{q})^4$	100 P/P'	1000(d-d')/E
Functional	333	1298.5	5	0.91	550%	.985	98.7%	3.2
Down's Syndrome	187	724.7	7	0.51	1380	.962	96.5	9.0
Developmental Cranial Anomalies	80	284.0	16	0.20	8000	.793	79.5	56
Other	725	2790.0	41	1.95	2100	.943	94.5	14
Total	1325	5097.2	69	3.57	1930	.947	95.0	13

* Exposure at 6-month intervals calculated after deducting from number alive at start of interval the fractional time following unauthorized absence or termination due to death or discharge.

† Basis of expected mortality: 1949-51 U. S. Life Tables for 1948-52 Cohort (q' = .0009) and 1959-61 U. S. Life Tables for 1958-62 Cohort (q' = .0007). q' does not vary significantly with duration or ages within cohorts.

ORGANIC BRAIN DISORDERS

§216–MORTALITY TREND IN A MENTAL DEFICIENCY INSTITUTION

Reference: B. W. Richards and P. E. Sylvester, "Mortality Trends in Mental Deficiency Institutions," J. Mental Defic. Dis., 13:276-292 (1969).

Subjects Studied: Mentally subnormal patients resident in St. Lawrence's Hospital, Surrey, England during the period 1936-1965, with some observations going back to 1921 and as recently as 1968. Attained age and sex distributions are given by person-years of exposure in Table 216a for 1961-65, age 10-79, and age distribution, both sexes combined, is shown in Table 216b for 1955-67, age 5-89. Patients have been classified as to severity of mental deficiency according to the traditional terms: idiot - most severe, requiring total care; imbecile - severe, but capable of some training; feeble-minded - least severe, capable of some education (equivalent to the U.S. term "moron"). Patients were further classified by the presence or absence of the congenital defects of mongolism.

Follow-up: Hospital records were used.

Results: Comparative mortality experience is given in Table 216a for males and females by decennial age group during the period 1961-65 (deaths in children under 10 were too few to include). In males the mortality ratio decreased from 1840 per cent for those age 20 to 29 to 127 per cent for patients age 60-69, then rose slightly to 133 per cent at age 70-79. The corresponding excess death rates were in the range of 18 to 6.9, with a level of 26 extra deaths per 1000 in the oldest age group. Mortality·ratios for females also decreased with age from the youngest to the oldest age group (7900 to 125 per cent), but were at a higher level than male ratios in almost every age group. However, excess death rates were similar in both sexes under age 40, and thereafter were higher for females (except for the oldest patients age 70-79). Mortality rates over the 5-year period of observation were used to estimate a 3-year survival index, which averaged 97.7 per cent for males and 96.1 per cent for females.

Table 216a also contains mortality rates for male and female patients, all ages combined, in preceding 5-year periods, going back to 1936-40. Expected mortality rates are not available for these earlier periods on a combined basis, so the usual comparative indices are not shown. To some extent, however, the mortality rates themselves can be compared from one time period to another. The adverse effect of wartime conditions is evident from the fact that the mortality rate doubled in females and more than doubled in males in the period 1941-45 as compared with 1936-40. The mortality rate for females fell promptly in 1946-50, but continued in subsequent years at a level above the male rate and above the immediate pre-war female rate. The recent higher rate among females may possibly result from an increase in average age of the female population. The male patient mortality rate remained high in 1946-50, the period immediately after World War II, but then fell to the pre-war level.

Mortality data in Table 216b provide a comparison of age-specific mortality rates by grade of severity of mental deficiency, and between patients with the trait of mongolism and the majority without this trait. Mortality was much higher at every age level in the most severely retarded group (idiots) than it was in the other two classifications (imbecile and feeble-minded). There was little difference in mortality between the less severe groups. Patients with mongolism showed slightly lower mortality than patients without this trait, at age levels under age 50. Mongols age 50-59, however, had a considerably higher mortality rate, and very few patients with mongolism were found in this hospitalized population at age 60 and up. Total mortality rates in Table 216b have not been age-adjusted, and are therefore not strictly comparable.

MORTALITY TREND IN A MENTAL DEFICIENCY INSTITUTION

Table 216a Comparative Experience by Sex, Age (1961-1965) and Period (All Ages Combined)

Period of Observation	Sex/Age	Estimated Exposure Person-Yrs	No. of Deaths Observed	Ave. Ann. Mort. Rate	Expected Mort. Rate*	Mortality Ratio	Est. 3-Yr Surv. Index	Excess Death Rate
		E	d	$\bar{q}=d/E$	$\bar{q}'$	$100\,\bar{q}/\bar{q}'$	$100\,P/P'$	$1000(\bar{q}-\bar{q}')$
1961-65	Male							
	10-19	744	9	.0121	.00075	1610%	96.6%	11
	20-29	1183	22	.0186	.00101	1840	94.8	18
	30-39	1236	11	.0089	.00147	605	97.8	7.4
	40-49	815	11	.0135	.00406	335	97.2	9.4
	50-59	721	15	.0208	.01269	164	97.6	8.1
	60-69	435	14	.0322	.02528	127	97.9	6.9
	70-79	130	14	.1076	.08118	133	91.6	26
	All†	5373	108	.0201	.01234	163	97.7	7.8
1956-60	All	5672	114	.0201				
1951-55	All	5824	99	.0170				
1946-50	All	5362	215	.0401				
1941-45	All	6252	352	.0563				
1936-40	All	6408	132	.0206				
1961-65	Female							
	10-19	680	7	.0103	.00013	7900%	97.0%	10
	20-29	775	11	.0142	.00051	2800	95.9	14
	30-39	882	9	.0102	.00105	970	97.3	9.2
	40-49	963	18	.0187	.00275	680	95.3	16
	50-59	885	27	.0305	.01206	255	94.5	18
	60-69	556	20	.0360	.01689	215	94.3	19
	70-79	315	19	.0603	.04836	125	96.3	12
	All†	5228	126	.0241	.01114	215	96.1	13
1956-60	All	5417	143	.0264				
1951-55	All	5244	118	.0225				
1946-50	All	5288	110	.0208				
1941-45	All	5571	200	.0359				
1936-40	All	5511	97	.0176				

Table 216b Mortality Rates (1955-1967) by Age and Degree of Mental Deficiency (Males and Females Combined)

Age	All Patients Except "Mongols"						"Mongol" Patients			General Population
	Idiot Mort. Rate	Imbicile Mort. Rate	Feeble-Minded Mort. Rate	All Severities			All Severities			Mort. Rate
				Exposure	No. of Deaths	Mort. Rate	Exposure	No. of Deaths	Mort. Rate	
x	$\bar{q}$	$\bar{q}$	$\bar{q}$	E	d	$\bar{q}=d/E$	E	d	$\bar{q}=d/E$	$\bar{q}'$
5- 9	.154	.011	—	639	7	.0110	118	1	.008	.00037
10-19	.058	.004	.005	3284	13	.0040	541	6	.011	.00046
20-29	.079	.007	.004	4088	30	.0073	675	3	.004	.00076
30-39	.051	.007	.005	4180	28	.0067	530	3	.006	.0012
40-49	.060	.016	.011	3280	52	.0159	260	2	.008	.0034
50-59	.105	.018	.044	2500	45	.0180	130	9	.069	.0125
60-69	.207	.033	.041	1699	56	.0330	43	0	.000	.0248
70-79	.111	.106	.050	564	60	.1064	—	—	—	.0605
80-89	—	.166	.067	175	29	.1657	—	—	—	.1327
Total	.070	.017	.022	20409	320	.0157	2297	24	.010	.0117

* Basis of expected mortality: U.K. Registrar General's Statistical Review - 1966

† Data for ages under 10 and over 79 included

ORGANIC BRAIN DISORDERS

§220–CEREBRAL PALSY

Reference: P. Cohen and P. Mustacchi, "Survival in Cerebral Palsy," J. Am. Med. Assoc., 195:130-132 (1966).

Subjects Studied: The study includes 1,416 children under the age of twenty-one referred to the Cerebral Palsy Clinic of the Department of Pediatrics, University of California, San Francisco, from 1946-1955 inclusive. All patients were referred by private physicians, schools, or health agencies. There were 809 males, or 57 per cent, and 607 females, comprising 43 per cent. The greatest number of children studied were under age ten (76 per cent). Distribution by age and diagnostic type was as follows:

Age at First Clinic Visit (Years)

Diagnostic Type	0-4	5-9	10-14	15-19	20	Total	Per Cent
Spastic	331	239	131	60	6	767	54.2%
Athetoid	189	134	63	34	4	424	29.9
Ataxic	37	19	2	1	0	59	4.2
Mixed	36	35	13	16	1	101	7.1
Nonclassifiable	36	19	7	3	0	65	4.6
Total No.	629	446	216	114	11	1416	100.0%
Per cent	44.4%	31.5%	15.3%	8.0%	0.8%	100.0%	

Follow-up: Patients were followed by the clinic until June 30, 1964, or until death or last contact *prior* to that date. Follow-up information was obtained at the time of a scheduled return visit or by correspondence with the patient's family or physician.

Results: The mortality and survival data are presented by duration in Table 220a, by sex and age in Table 220b, and by diagnosis in Table 220c. The mortality ratio tended to decrease with duration, especially after 10 years. The excess death rate fluctuated within fairly narrow limits up to 15 years after entry (between 8.2 and 14 per 1000), but fell to 4.5 per 1000 in the last interval, 15-18 years following initial clinic visit. The cumulative survival ratio was 90.2 per cent at 10 years and 84.4 per cent at 18 years. The mortality ratio for the females was higher, at 2100 per cent, than that for the males, at 1280 per cent, but the average annual excess death rate per 1000 showed no significant difference between sexes (Table 220b). In Table 220c, where the results are presented by diagnostic class after ten years, the excess mortality for the ataxic group (an EDR of 28 per 1000) was about twice that experienced by any other group, except where the type of palsy was nonclassifiable (an EDR of 24). The spastic group experienced the lowest excess mortality, with an EDR of 5.5 and an average annual mortality ratio of 885 per cent. The highest average annual mortality ratio of 4100 per cent was seen in the ataxic group.

CEREBRAL PALSY

Table 220a   Comparative Mortality and Survival by Duration - All Cases Combined (Age under 21)

No.	Start-End	Cumulative Surv. Rate Observed	Cumulative Surv. Rate Expected*	Survival Ratio	Observed Rate Int. Surv.	Observed Rate Ave. Ann. Mort.	Expected Rate* Int. Surv.	Expected Rate* Ave. Ann. Mort.	Mortality Ratio	Excess Death Rate
i	t to t + Δ t	P	P'	100 P/P'	p_i	$\check{q}$	p_i'	$\check{q}'$	100 $\check{q}/\check{q}'$	1000$(\check{q}-\check{q}')$
1	0- 2 yrs	.970	.9983	97.2%	.970	.0151	.9983	.0009	1760%	14
2	2- 5	.945	.9968	94.8	.974	.0087	.9985	.0005	1700	8.2
3	5-10	.896	.9931	90.2	.948	.0106	.9963	.0007	1430	9.9
4	10-15	.845	.9878	85.5	.943	.0117	.9947	.0011	1090	11
5	15-18	.831	.9846	84.4	.983	.0056	.9968	.0011	515	4.5

Table 220b   Observed Data and Comparative Experience by Sex - All Ages and Durations Combined

Sex	No. of Entrants	Exposure Person-Yrs	Observed Deaths	Ave. Ann. Mort. Rate Observed	Ave. Ann. Mort. Rate Expected*	Mortality Ratio	Est. 6-Yr Surv. Rate Observed	Est. 6-Yr Surv. Rate Expected*	Est. 6-Yr Surv. Index	Excess Death Rate
	ℓ	E	d	$\bar{q}=d/E$	$\bar{q}'$	100 $\bar{q}/\bar{q}'$	$P=(1-\bar{q})^6$	$P'=(1-\bar{q}')^6$	100 P/P'	1000$(\bar{q}-\bar{q}')$
Male	809	4625	54	.0117	.0009	1280%	.9318	.9946	93.7%	11
Female	607	3606	34	.0094	.0004	2100	.9449	.9973	94.7	9.0
Total	1416	8231	88	.0107	.0007	1530	.9375	.9958	94.1	10

Table 220c   Experience at 10 Years by Diagnostic Class - All Ages and Both Sexes Combined

Class	No. Alive at Start of Interval	Cumulative Surv. Rate Observed	Cumulative Surv. Rate Expected*	Survival Ratio	Ave. Ann. Mort. Rate Observed	Ave. Ann. Mort. Rate Expected*	Ave. Ann. Mort. Ratio	Excess Death Rate
	ℓ	P	P'	100 P/P'	$\check{q}$	$\check{q}'$	100 $\check{q}/\check{q}'$	1000$(\check{q}-\check{q}')$
Spastic	767	.94	.9931	94.7%	.0062	.0007	885%	5.5
All others	649	.83	.9931	83.6	.0185	.0007	2600	18
Athetoid	424	.85	.9931	85.6	.0161	.0007	2300	15
Ataxia	59	.75	.9931	75.5	.0284	.0007	4100	28
Mixed	101	.86	.9931	86.6	.0150	.0007	2100	14
Nonclassifiable	65	.78	.9931	78.5	.0245	.0007	3500	24
Total	1416	.89	.9931	89.6	.0116	.0007	1660	11

*Basis of expected mortality: U.S. White Males and Females 1959-1961

ORGANIC BRAIN DISORDERS

§221–CEREBRAL PALSY

Reference: E. R. Schlesinger, N. C. Allaway, and S. Peltin, "Survivorship in Cerebral Palsy," Am. J. Pub. Health, 49:343-349 (1959).

Subjects Studied: The study includes 3,108 children with cerebral palsy under age 18 at time of initial report. Data were supplied by the mandatory reporting system in effect in New York State (exclusive of New York City) for three years beginning January 1, 1950, with cases born after this date excluded from the study.

Age Distribution (per cent in parentheses)

Sex	0-5 yrs	5-10 yrs	10-17 yrs	Total
Male	708 (41.4%)	601 (35.2%)	399 (23.4%)	1708 (100.0%)
Female	572 (40.9%)	448 (32.0%)	380 (27.1%)	1400 (100.0%)

Follow-up: An effort was made to determine survivorship status of each child as of June 30, 1957, by means of follow-up through various health and education agencies, both at the state and local level, by mail follow-up of those moving out of the registration area, and by intensive search of New York State vital records for the deaths. Individuals for whom complete follow-up information was lacking were considered to be alive on the cutoff date.

Results: Mortality and survival data are presented by sex and age in Table 221a, and by severity of disability in Table 221b. High mortality was experienced by all age groups in Table 221a, with no consistent pattern by age. The mortality ratios for females are higher than those for males, but the average annual excess death rate per 1000 shows no significant difference between sexes (Table 221a). In Table 221b, where the results are presented by severity of disability, mortality ratios and EDR increased with severity of disability as expected, with EDR ranging from a low of 1.8 deaths per 1000 per year for the mild cases to a high of 20 deaths per 1000 per year for the severe cases, a striking difference.

CEREBRAL PALSY

Table 221a   Observed Data and Comparative Experience at 7.5 Years

Sex and Age as of 1/1/50*	No. Alive at start of Interval	Exposure Person-Yrs	Deaths in Interval		Mortality Ratio	Est. 5-Yr Surv. Rate		Est. 5-Yr Surv. Index	Excess Death Rate
			Observed	Expected†		Observed	Expected†		
	ℓ	E	d	d′	100 d/d′	P	P′	100 P/P′	1000(d-d′)/E
Males									
0- 4 yrs	708	5082	61	3.72	1640%	.941	.9963	94.4%	11
5- 9	601	4356	38	2.81	1350	.957	.9968	96.0	8.1
10-17	399	2907	20	2.57	780	.966	.9956	97.0	6.0
Total	1708	12345	119	9.10	1310	.953	.9963	95.6	8.9
Females									
0- 4 yrs	572	4093	41	2.17	1890%	.951	.9974	95.3%	9.5
5- 9	448	3285	23	1.10	2100	.965	.9983	96.7	6.7
10-17	380	2755	22	1.49	1480	.961	.9973	96.3	7.4
Total	1400	10133	86	4.76	1810	.958	.9977	96.1	8.0

Table 221b   Mortality by Severity of Physical Limitation

Sex and Degree of Disability	Ave. Ann. Mort. Rate		Mortality Ratio	Est. 5-Yr Surv. Rate		Est. 5-Yr Surv. Index	Excess Death Rate
	Observed	Expected†		Observed	Expected†		
	$\bar{q}$	$\bar{q}′$	100 $\bar{q}$/$\bar{q}′$	P	P′	100 P/P′	1000($\bar{q}$-$\bar{q}′$)
Males							
Mild	.0025	.00071	350%	.988	.9965	99.1%	1.8
Moderate	.0048	.00075	640	.976	.9963	98.0	4.0
Severe	.0212	.00078	2710	.898	.9961	90.2	20
Total	.0096	.00076	1260	.953	.9962	95.7	8.8
Females							
Mild	.0023	.00048	480%	.988	.9976	99.0%	1.8
Moderate	.0065	.00048	1340	.968	.9976	97.0	6.0
Severe	.0149	.00050	2980	.928	.9975	93.0	14
Total	.0085	.00049	1730	.958	.9976	96.0	8.0

* Data given by individual year of birth, 1933-1949. Data age 0-5 yrs. taken as sum of birth years 1945-1949, etc.

† Basis of expected mortality: 1949-51 New York State Life Tables

ORGANIC BRAIN DISORDERS

§225–EPILEPSY

Reference: B. Henriksen, P. Juul-Jensen, and M. Lund, "The Mortality of Epileptics," Proc. 10th Int. Congress of Life Assur. Med. (London, June 1970).

Subjects Studied: Adult patients discharged from four Danish neurological clinics with the diagnosis of epilepsy, excluding patients with intracranial tumor. In all 3761 patients were registered, the first one in 1950, the last in 1964. An objective of the study was the assessment of the insurability of applicants for life insurance. Accordingly, of the 3761 patients registered, patients who might not have qualified for insurance coverage because of handicaps other than epilepsy were excluded. The number included in the study was 2763 men and women, the estimated patient-years of exposure as follows:

Estimated Exposure

Attained Age Group (years)	10-29	30-49	50-69	70-89	Total
Patient-Years (Per cent)	11710 (46%)	10640 (41%)	3305 (13%)	105 (−)	25760 (100%)
(Distribution – Sample of Group)	9731 (47%)	8338 (41%)	2360 (12%)	75 (<1%)	20504 (100%)

Follow-up: Information of all deaths was obtained from the physicians' death certificates required by law and on file in the Danish State Health Department. The examinations mentioned in the study refer to an initial examination made on admission to a neurological clinic and to a subsequent one following treatment at discharge. The end of follow-up was July 1969, with an average exposure of 9.3 years.

Results: Leading features of the study are presented in Table 225 according to sex, age at examination and various features. The overall mortality ratio was 275 per cent and the average excess death rate, 4 per 1000. The ratio was 350 per cent for men against 196 per cent for women, and the EDR 6.2 and 2.1, per 1000, respectively. If expected deaths are based on a predominantly male standard insured population – as they appear to be – they are considerably higher than they would be if calculated on female standard rates. The apparent sex difference may be markedly exaggerated because of inflation of the expected rate for females. Excess mortality is less at ages under 30 and age 70 up than for adults in the range 30 to 69. However, only three deaths were observed in the small group of subjects age 70 up.

Mortality was higher for those cases graded as severe or moderately severe than for cases of slight severity or almost seizure-free. This was true for first examination (section c) and even more so for differences in severity as graded at a second examination (section d). Change in severity between examinations was also studied (section e). A mortality ratio of 169 per cent was found for cases of slight severity at both examinations, and 215 per cent for cases classified severe at first examination but slightly severe at the second. Consistently severe cases had a mortality ratio of 355 per cent, while those cases whose severity changed for the worse had the highest mortality ratio, 460 per cent. This suggests that a good response to treatment is a favorable prognostic sign.

There was no difference in mortality according to presence or absence of psychomotor fits, but cases with more than one type of seizure had a higher mortality ratio, 350 per cent, than those with only one type, 210 per cent (section f). Mortality increased according to degree of abnormality of the electroencephalogram at initial examination (section g). Mortality was also studied by combination of mental status with organic brain lesion (Jacksonian epilepsy). As shown in section h, an almost normal mortality ratio of 112 per cent was found in cases with lesion and a normal mental status. The highest mortality, a ratio of 390 per cent, was found in cases of epilepsy without lesion and with abnormal mental status, and intermediate levels of mortality were found in the other combinations of these factors.

EPILEPSY IN CLINIC PATIENTS

Table 225   Comparative Experience According to Various Features

Classification	No. Alive at Start of Interval	Exposure Person-Yrs	Deaths during Interval	Expected Deaths*	Mortality Ratio	Ave. Ann. Mort. Rate	Est. 10-Yr Surv. Rate	Est. 10-Yr Surv. Index	Excess Death Rate
	ℓ	E	d	d'	100d/d'	$\bar{q} = d/E$	$P = (1-\bar{q})^{10}$	100 P/P'	1000(d-d')/E
a. By Sex									
Male	1336	12150	105	29.9	350%	.0086	.917	94.0%	6.2
Female†	1427	13609	59	30.1	196	.0043	.957	97.9	2.1
Total	2763	25759	164	60.1	275	.0064	.938	96.0	4.0
b. By Age at Examination									
10-29		9731	23	7.1	325	.0024	.977	98.4	1.6
30-49		8338	65	11.7	555	.0078	.925	93.8	6.4
50-69		2360	32	20.9	153	.0136	.872	95.4	4.7
70-89		75	3	4.5	67	.0400	.665	123.4	−20
Total		20504	123	44.2	280	.0060	.942	96.2	3.8
c. By Severity of Epilepsy at First Examination									
Near Seizure Free	227	1906	11	3.7	295	.0058	.944	96.2	3.8
Slight Epilepsy	834	7745	43	20.9	205	.0056	.946	97.2	2.9
Moderately Severe	387	3780	33	8.8	375	.0087	.916	93.8	6.4
Severe	586	5817	49	13.6	360	.0084	.919	94.1	6.1
d. By Severity of Epilepsy at Second Examination									
None to Slight	1505	13983	60	33.8	178	.0043	.958	98.1	1.9
Mod. Severe to Severe	465	4768	45	11.9	380	.0094	.910	93.3	6.9
e. By Change of Severity between First and Second Observation									
Slight to Slight	1116	10106	43	25.5	169	.0043	.958	98.3	1.7
Severe to Slight	384	3829	17	8.0	215	.0044	.956	97.7	2.4
Severe to Severe	362	3744	34	9.6	355	.0091	.913	93.7	6.5
Slight to Severe	103	1024	11	2.4	460	.0107	.898	91.9	8.4
f. By Type of Seizure									
Psychomotor Fits	587	5552	41	14.7	280	.0074	.929	95.4	4.7
No Psychomotor Fits	2176	20207	123	45.4	270	.0061	.941	96.2	3.8
One Type Only	1452	13076	68	32.7	210	.0052	.949	97.3	2.7
More than One Type	1310	12683	96	27.4	350	.0076	.927	94.7	5.4
g. By Initial Electroencephalographic Findings									
Normal EEG	947	8770	42	23.4	179	.0048	.953	97.9	2.1
Slightly Abnormal	860	7829	48	18.6	260	.0061	.940	96.3	3.8
Mod. & Sev. Abnormal	866	7993	54	15.4	350	.0068	.934	95.3	4.8
h. By Mental Status, With and Without Organic Brain Lesion									
Mentally Normal									
With Lesion	196	1800	10	8.9	112	.0056	.946	99.4	0.6
No Lesion	1545	14124	60	24.3	245	.0042	.958	97.5	2.5
Mentally Abnormal									
With Lesion	202	1881	20	7.9	255	.0106	.899	93.7	6.4
No Lesion	811	7898	74	18.9	390	.0094	.910	93.2	7.0

* Basis of expected mortality: All Danish standard assured lives
† Presumably expected mortality is for the predominantly male total standard insured
 population. If so, comparative mortality based on female rates would be higher
 and probably similar to the male comparative mortality.

ORGANIC BRAIN DISORDERS

§226—EPILEPSY IN INSUREDS

Reference: "New York Life Single Medical Impairment Study—1972," unpublished report made available by J.J. Hutchinson and J.C. Sibigtroth (1973).

Subjects Studied: Policyholders of New York Life Insurance Company issued insurance in 1954-1970, followed to the 1971 policy anniversary. Different codes were used to distinguish cases in which the epilepsy was classified as "grand mal" from "petit mal". Only the substandard cases have been analyzed. All cases with more than one ratable impairment were excluded.

Follow-up: Insurance policy records formed the basis of entry, of counting policies, exposure and death claims, and of follow-up information.

Results: The comparative experience for grand mal epilepsy cases is given in Table 226a and Table 226b by duration, all ages combined. The mortality ratios for grand mal epilepsy showed a downward trend by duration, ranging from 400 per cent at 0-2 years to 200 per cent at 10-17 years. The EDR was highest (4.2 extra deaths per 1000) at 10-17 years. The cumulative survival ratio at 17 years was 94.2 per cent.

Table 226c shows the comparative experience for both grand mal and petit mal epilepsy, by sex and age group. The overall mortality ratio for grand mal epilepsy among female substandard issues was much greater than for males, being 825 per cent and 295 per cent, respectively. The corresponding male ratio for petit mal epilepsy is 183 per cent.

In the substandard male policyholders, the mortality ratios for grand mal epilepsy decreased with advancing age at issue of insurance. The greatest excess mortality was observed in the age group 0-29, with a mortality ratio of 465 per cent and EDR of 3.4 per 1000.

Comparative mortality by major causes of death is given in Table 226d for male and female cases combined. The major cause of death for grand mal epilepsy is accidents and homicides, the mortality being 675 per cent and EDR 1.1 per 1000. In addition, six of the 14 deaths in the "all other causes and unknown" category of the grand mal cases were due to epilepsy. The major cause of death for petit mal epilepsy is "all other causes and unknown," the mortality ratio being 660 per cent and EDR 1.5 per 1000. Of the six deaths in this cause category, two were due to epilepsy.

EPILEPSY IN INSUREDS

Table 226a   Observed Data and Comparative Experience by Duration — Male Substandard Cases

Interval		Exposure Policy-Yrs	No. of Death Claims		Mortality Ratio		Survival Ratio		Excess Death Rate
No.	Start-End		Observed	Expected*	Interval	Cumulative	Interval	Cumulative	
i	t to t + Δt	E	d	d′	100d/d′	100Σd/Σd′	100 p_i/p_i'	100 P/P′	1000(d-d′)/E
Grand Mal									
1	0- 2 yrs	3542	13	3.24	400%	400%	99.4%	99.4%	2.8
2	2- 5	2880	13	3.97	325	360	99.1	98.5	3.1
3	5-10	2125	11	4.31	255	320	98.4	97.0	3.1
4	10-17	840	7	3.49	200	295	97.1	94.2	4.2

Table 226b   Derived Mortality and Survival Data

Sex	Interval		Observed Rates				Expected Rates*			
			Average Annual		Cumulative		Average Annual		Cumulative	
	No.	Start-End	Mortality	Survival	Survival	Mortality	Mortality	Survival	Survival	Mortality
	i	t to t + Δt	q̄ = d/E	p̄	P	Q	q̄′ = d′/E	p̄′	P′	Q′
Grand Mal										
Male	1	0- 2 yrs	.0037	.9963	.9927	.0073	.0009	.9991	.9982	.0018
	2	2- 5	.0045	.9955	.9793	.0207	.0014	.9986	.9940	.0060
	3	5-10	.0052	.9948	.9542	.0458	.0020	.9980	.9840	.0160
	4	10-17	.0083	.9917	.8999	.1001	.0042	.9958	.9558	.0442

Table 226c   Comparative Experience by Sex and Age Group — Substandard Cases, All Durations Combined

Sex	Age Group	Exposure Policy-Yrs	No. of Death Claims		Mortality Ratio	Ave. Ann. Mort. Rate	Est. 8-Yr Surv. Rate	Est. 8-Yr Surv. Index	Excess Death Rate
			Observed	Expected*					
		E	d	d′	100 d/d′	q̄ = d/E	P = (1-q̄)⁸	100 P/P′	1000(d-d′)/E
Grand Mal									
Male	0-29	5852	25	5.36	465%	.0043	.9663	97.3%	3.4
	30-39	2386	9	3.93	230	.0038	.9702	98.3	2.1
	40 up	1149	10	5.72	175	.0087	.9325	97.0	3.7
	All Ages	9387	44	15.01	295	.0047	.9631	97.6	3.1
Female	All Ages	1649	10	1.21	825%	.0061	.9525	95.8%	5.3
Petit Mal									
Male	All Ages	2717	8	4.37	183%	.0029	.9767	98.9%	1.3

Table 226d   Mortality by Cause of Death — Male and Female Combined

Cause	Grand Mal				Petit Mal			
	No. of Death Claims		Mortality Ratio	Excess Death Rate	No. of Death Claims		Mortality Ratio	Excess Death Rate
	Observed	Expected●			Observed	Expected●		
Malignant Neoplasms	8	3.87	205%	0.4	0	1.15	0%	−0.3
Diseases of Heart & Circulatory Sys.	13	6.37	205	0.6	3	1.89	159	0.3
Accidents & Homicide	15	2.23	675	1.1	1	0.66	152	0.1
Suicide	4	0.69	580	0.3	1	0.20	500	0.2
All Other Causes & Unknown†	14	3.06	460	1.0	6	0.91	660	1.5
Total	54	16.22	335	3.4	11	4.81	230	1.8

* Basis of expected mortality: 1955-60 Select Basic Table
† Includes, in Grand Mal 6 Epilepsy; in Petit Mal, 2 Epilepsy, 3 Nephritis
● Distribution of total expected deaths by Intercompany Medically Examined Standard Issues 1965-70

ORGANIC BRAIN DISORDERS

§230–MULTIPLE SCLEROSIS IN YOUNG MALES

References: (1) J. F. Kurtzke, G. W. Beebe, B. Nagler, M. D. Nefzger, T. L. Auth, and L. T. Kurland, "Studies on The Natural History of Multiple Sclerosis. V. Long-Term Survival in Young Men," Arch. Neur., 22:215-225 (1970).
(2) Supplementary material furnished by authors.

Subjects Studied: Men in armed forces of the U.S. diagnosed as having multiple sclerosis (MS) in an Army hospital during 1942 to 1951. Subjects were traced to January 1, 1963. There were 762 men in the original data, but on review 235 were excluded because they did not meet the diagnostic criteria for "definite" MS of the Schumacher Committee (Ann. N.Y. Acad. Sci., 122:552-568, 1965). Of the 527 men retained in the series 476 were taken as definite, and 51 as strong possible (probable) MS cases. Over half the subjects had manifested some symptoms of the disease prior to Army diagnosis. The mean age of the subjects at onset of the disease was 25.2 years; three-fourths were under age 30. The percentage distribution of cases by age at onset:

Age at Onset

	No.	5-9	10-14	15-19	20-24	25-29	30-34	35-39	40-44	Mean Age
Onset Prior to Army Diagnosis	293 (100%)	0.7	4.8	17.4	37.5	21.8	11.6	4.8	1.4	23.8
Onset with Army Diagnosis	234 (100%)	-	0.4	9.0	27.3	29.1	25.6	7.3	1.3	26.9
Total	527 (100%)	0.4	2.9	13.7	33.0	25.0	17.8	5.9	1.3	25.2

Follow-up: Mortality facts, including date and cause, were ascertained through 1962 by means of V.A. resources which have been shown to be 98 per cent complete for World War II veterans generally. In view of the eligibility for compensation of service-connected disability it is thought that there was even greater completeness in this series.

Results: Survival rates developed in the study show that after 20 years of illness three-fourths of the patients remained alive; about two-thirds survived 25 years with little further reduction after 30 years. Survival levels of about these magnitudes applied equally to cases whose onset occurred prior to, or after, induction into the armed forces, and to the several age groups.

At the young ages of the subjects, expected rates of death are low, and comparative experience with respect to mortality shows relatively high ratios. Such comparative data are presented in Tables 230a-b. Comparisons are made on a basis used in the study reflecting the age composition of the subjects and the general mortality of the period. Mortality ratios tend to vary inversely with the age at which MS is first manifested: 15-year cumulative mortality for age group 20-24 (at onset) is 430 per cent of that expected; the ratio declines with increase in age to 196 per cent for cases in the 35-40 group. In a general way, mortality ratios tended to increase with duration of the condition. There appeared to be no correlation of EDR with age or duration of illness; on the average, over the 15-year period of comparison, subjects of all ages together experienced each year nine extra deaths per 1000 exposed. The number of deaths in individual categories is small; caution is indicated in interpreting the results.

There were 121 deaths recorded among the 476 definite MS cases, of which 93 were attributed to MS and 24 to unrelated entities; in four cases information was inadequate for judgment. Pneumonia, with and without complications, accounted for two-thirds of the deaths attributed to the MS condition. Renal and cardiac episodes and MS (with no further data) were equally represented in about one-quarter of the 93 fatal cases.

MULTIPLE SCLEROSIS EXPERIENCE — YOUNG MALES

Table 230a Observed Data and Comparative Experience by Age and Duration

Age Group	Interval No.	Interval after Diagnosis	Exposed To Risk	Deaths in Interval Obs.	Deaths in Interval Exp.*	Mortality Ratio Interval	Mortality Ratio Cumulative	Survival Ratio Interval	Survival Ratio Cumulative	Excess Death Rate
	i	t to t + Δt	E	d	d'	100 d/d'	100 Q/Q'	100 p$_i$/p$_i$'	100 P/P'	1000(d-d')/E
20-24	1	0- 5 yrs	609	4	1.28	315%	300%	97.8%	97.8%	4.5
	2	5-10 yrs	584	6	1.17	515	400	95.9	93.8	8.3
	3	10-15 yrs	552	6	1.10	545	430	95.6	89.7	8.9
		0-15 yrs	1745	16	3.55	450	430	89.7	89.7	7.2
25-29	1	0- 5 yrs	702	3	1.47	205	198	98.9	98.9	2.2
	2	5-10 yrs	667	12	1.47	815	500	92.3	91.3	16
	3	10-15 yrs	612	7	2.14	325	405	96.1	87.8	7.9
		0-15 yrs	1981	22	5.08	435	405	87.8	87.8	8.6
30-34	1	0- 5 yrs	540	4	1.51	265	270	97.7	97.7	4.6
	2	5-10 yrs	511	8	1.84	435	355	94.0	91.9	12
	3	10-15 yrs	466	13	2.52	515	400	89.0	81.7	22
		0-15 yrs	1517	25	5.87	425	400	81.7	81.7	12
35-39	1	0- 5 yrs	248	3	.99	305	300	95.9	95.9	8.1
	2	5-10 yrs	228	2	1.41	142	200	98.8	94.7	2.6
	3	10-15 yrs	214	4	1.93	205	196	95.3	90.3	9.7
		0-15 yrs	690	9	4.33	210	196	90.3	90.3	6.8
All Ages	1	0- 5 yrs	2099	14	5.25	265	265	97.9	97.9	4.2
	2	5-10 yrs	1990	28	5.89	475	365	94.6	92.6	11
	3	10-15 yrs	1844	30	7.69	390	360	94.1	87.1	12
		0-15 yrs	5933	72	18.83	380	360	87.1	87.1	9

Table 230b Derived Mortality and Survival Data

Age Group	Interval No.	Interval after Diagnosis	Observed Rates Average Annual Mortality	Observed Rates Average Annual Survival	Observed Rates Cumulative Survival	Observed Rates Cumulative Mortality	Expected Rates* Average Annual Mortality	Expected Rates* Average Annual Survival	Expected Rates* Cumulative Survival	Expected Rates* Cumulative Mortality
	i	t to t + Δt	q̄	p̄	P	Q	q̄'	p̄'	P'	Q'
20-24	1	0- 5 yrs	.007	.993	.968	.032	.0021	.9979	.9894	.0106
	2	5-10 yrs	.010	.990	.919	.081	.0020	.9980	.9797	.0203
	3	10-15 yrs	.011	.989	.870	.130	.0020	.9980	.9699	.0301
		0-15 yrs	.009	.991	.870	.130	.0020	.9980	.9699	.0301
25-29	1	0- 5 yrs	.004	.996	.979	.021	.0021	.9979	.9894	.0106
	2	5-10 yrs	.018	.982	.894	.106	.0022	.9978	.9787	.0213
	3	10-15 yrs	.011	.989	.844	.156	.0035	.9965	.9617	.0383
		0-15 yrs	.011	.989	.844	.156	.0026	.9974	.9617	.0389
30-34	1	0- 5 yrs	.007	.993	.963	.037	.0028	.9972	.9862	.0138
	2	5-10 yrs	.016	.984	.890	.110	.0036	.9964	.9688	.0312
	3	10-15 yrs	.028	.972	.771	.229	.0054	.9946	.9431	.0569
		0-15 yrs	.016	.984	.771	.229	.0039	.9961	.9431	.0569
35-39	1	0- 5 yrs	.012	.988	.940	.060	.0040	.9960	.9800	.0200
	2	5-10 yrs	.009	.991	.900	.100	.0062	.9938	.9500	.0500
	3	10-15 yrs	.019	.981	.820	.180	.0090	.9910	.9080	.0920
		0-15 yrs	.013	.987	.820	.180	.0064	.9936	.9080	.0920
All Ages	1	0- 5 yrs	.007	.993	.967	.033	.0025	.9975	.9875	.0125
	2	5-10 yrs	.014	.986	.901	.099	.0030	.9970	.9730	.0270
	3	10-15 yrs	.016	.984	.830	.170	.0041	.9958	.9530	.0470
		0-15 yrs	.012	.988	.830	.170	.0032	.9968	.9530	.0470

*Basis of expected mortality: Progressive rates, U.S. White Males 1940 and subsequent Censuses

§231—MULTIPLE SCLEROSIS IN ISRAEL

Reference: U. Leibowitz, E. Kahana, and M. Alter, "Survival and Death in Multiple Sclerosis," Brain, 92:115-130 (1969).

Subjects Studied: A country-wide survey of cases of multiple sclerosis diagnosed 1955-59 in Israel and still resident in Israel on January 1, 1960. Excluded were 16 patients with inadequate clinical data. Sex distribution and limited data on age distribution are given in Table 231a.

Follow-up: The starting point of observation for all patients was January 1, 1960, with complete follow-up to January 1967.

Results: Seven-year mortality rates are given by age in 1960, age at onset of illness, duration of illness, mild and severe disability, sex, and course of illness. High mortality was experienced in all categories with cumulative survival ratios ranging from 70.9 per cent to 93.8 per cent, mean annual mortality ratios ranging from 415 per cent to 1190 per cent, and EDR's ranging from 9.1 to 48 extra deaths per 1000 per year.

Degree of disability was the most important single determinant of multiple sclerosis death rate. The difference in EDR between mild and severe cases was 39 deaths per 1000 per year, and the mortality ratio for severe multiple sclerosis was higher by 645 per cent. Effects of age were similar whether classified by age at onset of illness or in 1960, with higher mortality ratios in the younger than in the older groups, but survival ratios were higher and EDR's lower. A less marked effect was evident from duration of illness, which was correlated to some extent with age. Males showed higher mortality ratios and EDR's than females. Cases with a progressive course had twice as high an EDR as cases with remission; this may have been due, at least in part, to the higher mean age of the cases with a progressive course.

MULTIPLE SCLEROSIS IN ISRAEL

Table 231a Observed Data and Comparative Experience at 7 Years

Group	Mean Age in 1960	No. Alive at Start	No. of Deaths	Cumulative Mort. Rate	Mortality Ratio		Cumulative Surv. Ratio	Excess Death Rate
					Ave. Ann.	Cumulative		
		ℓ	d	$Q = d/\ell$	$100\ \check{q}/\check{q}'$	$100\ Q/Q'$	$100\ P/P'$	$1000(\check{q}-\check{q}')$
Entry Age (1960)								
Under 45 yrs	33.8 yr	129	13	.101	1000%	945%	90.9%	14
45 yrs up	53.8	137	39	.285	450	405	76.9	37
Age at Onset								
Under 30 yrs	35.3	112	14	.125	1190	1090	88.5	17
30 yrs up	50.5	154	38	.247	580	520	79.0	33
Duration of M. S.								
Under 10 yrs	41.9	135	22	.163	860	805	85.4	22
10 yrs up	48.8	131	30	.229	580	540	80.5	30
Disability								
Mild	41.5	136	11	.081	415	400	93.8	9.1
Severe	46.5	130	41	.315	1060	925	70.9	48
Sex								
Male	45.0	126	28	.222	1060	965	79.6	32
Female	43.2	140	24	.171	665	640	85.2	22
Course								
Relapsing	40.8	164	23	.140	780	755	87.6	18
Progressive	49.1	98	26	.265	695	625	76.8	37

Table 231b Derived Mortality and Survival Data

Group	Observed Rates				Expected Rates*			
	Cumulative		Average Annual		Cumulative		Average Annual	
	Mortality	Survival	Survival	Mortality	Mortality	Survival	Survival	Mortality
	Q	P	$\check{p}$	$\check{q}$	Q'	P'	$\check{p}'$	$\check{q}'$
Entry Age								
Under 45 yrs	.101	.899	.985	.015	.0107	.9893	.9985	.0015
45 yrs up	.285	.715	.953	.047	.0706	.9294	.9896	.0104
Age at Onset								
Under 30 yrs	.125	.875	.981	.019	.0115	.9885	.9984	.0016
30 yrs up	.247	.753	.960	.040	.0473	.9527	.9931	.0069
Duration of M. S.								
Under 10 yrs	.163	.837	.975	.025	.0202	.9798	.9971	.0029
10 yrs up	.229	.771	.964	.036	.0425	.9575	.9938	.0062
Disability								
Mild	.081	.919	.988	.012	.0202	.9798	.9971	.0029
Severe	.315	.685	.947	.053	.0341	.9659	.9950	.0050
Sex								
Male	.222	.778	.965	.035	.0230	.9770	.9967	.0033
Female	.171	.829	.974	.026	.0268	.9732	.9961	.0039
Course								
Relapsing	.140	.860	.979	.021	.0186	.9814	.9973	.0027
Progressive	.265	.735	.957	.043	.0425	.9575	.9938	.0062

* Basis of expected mortality: 1960 Mortality Rates for Israel
(1966 United Nations Demographic Yearbook).

SPINAL CORD DISORDERS

§250–PARALYSIS DUE TO SPINAL CORD INJURY

References: (1) M. H. Burke, A. F. Hicks, M. Robins, and H. Kessler, "Survival of Patients with Injuries of the Spinal Cord," J. Am. Med. Assoc., 172:121-124 (1960).
(2) H. Kessler, unpublished additional detailed data in personal communication to Liberty Mutual Insurance Co. (1959).

Subjects Studied: 5743 patients admitted to U.S. Veterans' Hospitals between January 1, 1946 and September 30, 1955 for treatment of traumatic paraplegia or quadriplegia. Most cases received initial treatment at civilian or military hospitals, with only a minority being observed in the early period after the spinal cord injury, when the probability of death is greatest. Patients were classified in four categories by degree of paralysis, and by age and duration from onset of paralysis. Table 250a gives the distribution of the patients under 60 by age group and type of lesion.

Follow-up: The V.A. records system was employed, together with mortality data from the death certificate filed in the claim folder. End of follow-up was October 1, 1956. Previous studies have shown that follow-up with V.A. records is almost 100 per cent complete.

Results: Life table methods were utilized by the authors to calculate cumulative survival rates on an annual basis (with shorter intervals in the first year) for four different age groups and the following categories of spinal cord injury: complete and incomplete paraplegia, and complete and incomplete quadriplegia. Such rates contained in the more detailed unpublished reference material are the source of the data presented in Tables 250b-e. Early mortality (first month) has been separated out and is shown in Table 250b. During the first month higher mortality was experienced for complete than for incomplete lesions, and for quadriplegics than for paraplegics. Mortality rates for one month ranged from levels under 5 per cent for paraplegics to as high as 39 per cent in complete quadriplegics. Because most patients were admitted to the V.A. hospitals at a later time, exposure in the first month was quite limited, and no deaths were observed in three of the categories.

Long-term results over observation periods ranging from three to ten years, but excluding the first month, are given in Table 250c. Average annual mortality ratios decreased with advancing age in paraplegics and ranged from 940 to 255 per cent. Higher mortality ratios, from 475 to 2900 per cent were observed in quadriplegics, but without a clear age trend. Excess death rates, on the other hand showed a generally consistent increase with age, as well as an increase by severity of lesion. The lowest rates, about 10 extra deaths per 1000 per year were found in younger age groups of patients with incomplete lesions. The highest rate, 120 extra deaths per 1000 occurred in complete quadriplegics age 35 to 44 years.

High mortality rates usually persisted during the remainder of the first year, intervals 1 and 2 in Tables 250d-e, exceptions being attributable, in all probability, to random fluctuations with the small numbers of patients observed. During the first year the mortality ratio ranged as high as 9400 per cent and EDR as high as 234 per 1000 per year. After the first year mortality ratios were generally in the range of 800 to 1800 per cent in complete quadriplegics, with EDR 12 to 84 excess deaths per 1000 per year, despite some random fluctuations. In patients with incomplete quadriplegia and complete paraplegia under age 45 ratios fell into a lower range of about 500 to 900 per cent in most categories, and in complete paraplegics age 45 to 59, under 500 per cent. Interval mortality ratios somewhat lower than these and averaging under 500 per cent were observed in patients with incomplete paraplegia. The most consistent trends in EDR were found in the largest group-patients with complete paraplegia: EDR showed a general tendency to increase with age and duration, the range for all age categories after the first year being from 7.8 per 1000 (patients under age 25, interval 1 to 3 years), to 78 per 1000 (patients age 45 to 59, interval 5 to 9 years). In the other lesion categories with more than one interval beyond the first year fluctuations in EDR tended to be random with respect to duration of observation.

Survival ratios in those groups followed at least nine years after injury ranged from 51.5 per cent (oldest age group with complete paraplegia) to values in the youngest age groups of 91.2 per cent (incomplete quadriplegia) and 92.2 per cent (incomplete paraplegia). It is probable that quite low ten-year ratios would have been observed in older patients with complete quadriplegia, if data had been available, as three-year survival ratios were down to a level of the order of 70 per cent for those age 35 up.

PARALYSIS – SPINAL CORD INJURY

Table 250a Distribution of Cases by Age and Type of Lesion

Type of Lesion	Age at Injury				Total*
	Under 25	25-34	35-44	45-59	
Complete Paraplegia	1271	1164	313	137	2885
Incomplete Paraplegia	582	560	145	65	1352
Complete Quadriplegia	202	182	63	34	481
Incomplete Quadriplegia	405	328	91	71	895
Total No.*	2460	2234	612	307	5613
Per Cent	43.8%	39.8%	10.9%	5.5%	100%

Table 250b Early Mortality Rates (at One Month) by Age and Type of Lesion

Age Group	Paraplegia		Quadriplegia	
	Complete	Incomplete	Complete	Incomplete
(Years)	q_0	q_0	q_0	q_0
Under 25	.047	.000	.172	.000
25-34	.036	.022	.390	.099
35-44	.048	.037	.300	.087
45-59	.036	.111	.375	.000

Table 250c Comparative Terminal Experience by Age and Type of Lesion (First Month Excluded)

Age Group	Follow-up Interval	Cumulative Surv. Rate		Cumulative Surv. Ratio	Ave. Ann. Mort. Rate		Mortality Ratio	Excess Death Rate
		Observed	Expected†		Observed	Expected†		
(Years)	t to $t + \Delta t$	P	P′	100 P/P′	$\check{q}$	$\check{q}'$	100 $\check{q}/\check{q}'$	1000($\check{q}$-$\check{q}'$)
Complete Paraplegia								
Under 25	1 mo - 10 yrs	.855	.9831	87.0%	.016	.0017	940%	14
25-34	1 mo - 10 yrs	.798	.9753	81.8	.022	.0025	880	20
35-44	1 mo - 10 yrs	.678	.9389	72.2	.038	.0063	605	32
45-59	1 mo - 9 yrs	.439	.8524	51.5	.088	.0177	495	70
Incomplete Paraplegia								
Under 25	1 mo - 10 yrs	.906	.9831	92.2%	.010	.0017	590%	8.3
25-34	1 mo - 10 yrs	.881	.9753	90.3	.013	.0025	520	10
35-44	1 mo - 10 yrs	.855	.9389	91.1	.016	.0063	255	9.7
45-59	1 mo - 10 yrs	.573	.8295	69.1	.055	.0185	295	36
Complete Quadriplegia								
Under 25	1 mo - 10 yrs	.812	.9831	82.6%	.021	.0017	1240%	19
25-34	1 mo - 9 yrs	.743	.9788	75.9	.033	.0024	1370	31
35-44	1 mo - 3 yrs	.680	.9874	68.9	.124	.0043	2900	120
45-59	1 mo - 3 yrs	.691	.9615	71.9	.119	.0134	890	106
Incomplete Quadriplegia								
Under 25	1 mo - 10 yrs	.902	.9831	91.8%	.010	.0017	590%	8.3
25-34	1 mo - 10 yrs	.810	.9753	83.1	.021	.0025	840	19
35-44	1 mo - 6 yrs	.824	.9702	84.9	.032	.0051	625	27
45-59	1 mo - 5 yrs	.701	.9299	75.4	.070	.0147	475	55

*Does not include 59 cases with type of lesion unknown, nor 25 cases of paraplegia and 46 cases of quadriplegia age 60 and up.

†Basis of expected mortality and survival: U.S. Life Tables (1949-51) for white males.

SPINAL CORD DISORDERS

Table 250d Comparative Experience, V.A. Patients with Paraplegia, by Age and Duration (First Month Excluded)

Age Group	Interval No.	Interval Start-End	Cumulative Surv. Rate Observed	Cumulative Surv. Rate Expected*	Cumulative Surv. Ratio	Interval Surv. Rate	Ave. Ann. Mort. Rate Observed	Ave. Ann. Mort. Rate Expected*	Mortality Ratio	Excess Death Rate
(Years)	i	t to $t+\Delta t$	P	P'	$100\,P/P'$	p_i	$\breve{q}$	$\breve{q}'$	$100\,\breve{q}/\breve{q}'$	$1000(\breve{q}-\breve{q}')$
Under 25		Complete Paraplegia								
	1	1- 6 mos	.986	.9993	98.7%	.986	.0333	.0016	2100%	32
	2	6-12 mos	.983	.9985	98.5	.997	.0060	.0016	375	4.4
	3	1- 3 yrs	.964	.9951	96.9	.981	.0095	.0017	560	7.8
	4	3- 5 yrs	.937	.9916	94.5	.972	.0141	.0018	785	12
	5	5-10 yrs	.855	.9831	87.0	.912	.0183	.0017	1080	17
25-34										
	1	1- 6 mos	.964	.9992	96.4	.964	.0842	.0018	4700	82
	2	6-12 mos	.951	.9983	95.3	.986	.0278	.0018	1540	26
	3	1- 3 yrs	.917	.9944	92.2	.964	.0182	.0020	910	16
	4	3- 5 yrs	.884	.9900	89.3	.964	.0182	.0022	825	16
	5	5-10 yrs	.798	.9753	81.8	.903	.0202	.0030	675	17
35-44										
	1	1- 6 mos	.992	.9984	99.3	.992	.0191	.0039	490	15
	2	6-12 mos	.972	.9964	97.5	.980	.0396	.0039	1020	36
	3	1- 3 yrs	.925	.9874	93.7	.952	.0243	.0045	540	20
	4	3- 5 yrs	.867	.9764	88.8	.937	.0320	.0055	580	26
	5	5-10 yrs	.678	.9392	72.2	.782	.0480	.0078	615	40
45-59										
	1	1- 6 mos	.910	.9949	91.4	.910	.2026	.0121	1670	190
	2	6-12 mos	.889	.9888	89.9	.977	.0455	.0121	375	33
	3	1- 3 yrs	.815	.9615	84.8	.917	.0424	.0139	305	28
	4	3- 5 yrs	.743	.9299	79.9	.912	.0450	.0166	270	28
	5	5- 9 yrs	.439	.8533	51.5	.591	.0998	.0213	470	78
Under 25		Incomplete Paraplegia								
	1	1- 6 mos	.994	.9993	99.5%	.994	.0143	.0016	895%	13
	2	6-12 mos	.983	.9985	98.4	.989	.0219	.0016	1370	20
	3	1- 3 yrs	.972	.9951	97.7	.989	.0055	.0017	325	3.8
	4	3- 5 yrs	.952	.9916	96.0	.979	.0106	.0018	590	8.8
	5	5-10 yrs	.906	.9831	92.2	.952	.0098	.0017	575	8.1
25-34										
	1	1-6 mos	1.000	.9992	100.1	1.000	.0000	.0018	0	−1.8
	2	6-12 mos	.990	.9983	99.2	.990	.0199	.0018	1110	18
	3	1- 3 yrs	.972	.9944	97.7	.982	.0090	.0020	450	7.0
	4	3- 5 yrs	.945	.9900	95.5	.972	.0141	.0022	640	12
	5	5-10 yrs	.881	.9753	90.3	.932	.0140	.0030	465	11
35-44										
	1	1- 6 mos	1.000	.9984	100.2	1.000	.0000	.0039	0	−3.9
	2	6-12 mos	1.000	.9964	100.4	1.000	.0000	.0039	0	−3.9
	3	1- 3 yrs	.950	.9874	96.2	.950	.0253	.0045	560	21
	4	3- 5 yrs	.939	.9764	96.2	.988	.0060	.0055	109	0.5
	5	5-10 yrs	.855	.9389	91.1	.911	.0185	.0078	235	11
45-59										
	1	1- 6 mos	.966	.9949	97.1	.966	.0797	.0121	660	68
	2	6-12 mos	.937	.9888	94.8	.970	.0591	.0121	490	47
	3	1- 3 yrs	.863	.9615	89.8	.921	.0403	.0139	290	26
	4	3- 5 yrs	.819	.9299	88.1	.949	.0258	.0166	155	9.2
	5	5-10 yrs	.573	.8314	68.9	.700	.0688	.0221	310	47

*Basis of expected mortality and survival: U.S. Life Tables (1949-51) for white males

PARALYSIS — SPINAL CORD INJURY

Table 250e   Comparative Experience, V.A. Patients with Quadriplegia, by Age and Duration (First Month Excluded)

Age Group	Interval No.	Interval Start-End	Cumulative Surv. Rate Observed	Cumulative Surv. Rate Expected*	Cumulative Surv. Ratio	Interval Surv. Rate	Ave. Ann. Mort. Rate Observed	Ave. Ann. Mort. Rate Expected*	Mortality Ratio	Excess Death Rate
(Years)	i	t to t + Δt	P	P'	100 P/P'	p_i	q̆	q̆'	100 q̆/q̆'	1000(q̆-q̆')
Under 25		Complete Quadriplegia								
	1	1- 6 mos	.934	.9993	93.4%	.934	.1512	.0016	9400%	150
	2	6-12 mos	.934	.9985	93.5	1.000	.0000	.0016	0	−1.6
	3	1- 3 yrs	.908	.9951	91.3	.972	.0141	.0017	830	12
	4	3- 5 yrs	.872	.9916	87.9	.960	.0202	.0018	1120	18
	5	5-10 yrs	.812	.9831	82.6	.931	.0142	.0017	835	12
25-34										
	1	1- 6 mos	.977	.9992	97.8	.977	.0543	.0018	3000	52
	2	6-12 mos	.961	.9983	96.2	.984	.0318	.0018	1770	30
	3	1- 3 yrs	.920	.9944	92.5	.957	.0218	.0020	1090	20
	4	3- 5 yrs	.910	.9900	91.9	.989	.0055	.0022	250	3.3
	5	5- 9 yrs	.743	.9788	75.9	.816	.0496	.0028	1770	47
35-44										
	1	1- 6 mos	.751	.9984	75.3	.751	.4970	.0039	12700	493
	2	6-12 mos	.751	.9964	75.4	1.000	.0000	.0039	0	−4.0
	3	1- 3 yrs	.680	.9874	68.9	.905	.0487	.0045	1080	44
45-59										
	1	1- 6 mos	.850	.9949	85.4	.850	.3230	.0121	2700	311
	2	6-12 mos	.850	.9888	85.9	1.000	.0000	.0121	0	−12
	3	1- 3 yrs	.691	.9615	71.9	.813	.0983	.0139	705	84
Under 25		Incomplete Quadriplegia								
	1	1- 6 mos	1.000	.9993	100.1%	1.000	.0000	.0016	0	−1.6
	2	6-12 mos	.997	.9985	99.8	.997	.0060	.0016	375%	4.4
	3	1- 3 yrs	.982	.9951	98.7	.985	.0075	.0017	440	5.8
	4	3- 5 yrs	.955	.9916	96.3	.973	.0136	.0018	755	12
	5	5-10 yrs	.902	.9831	91.2	.945	.0113	.0017	665	9.6
25-34										
	1	1- 6 mos	.990	.9992	99.1	.990	.0238	.0018	1320	22
	2	6-12 mos	.986	.9983	98.8	.996	.0080	.0018	445	6.2
	3	1- 3 yrs	.951	.9944	95.6	.965	.0177	.0020	885	16
	4	3- 5 yrs	.928	.9900	93.7	.976	.0121	.0022	550	9.9
	5	5-10 yrs	.810	.9753	83.1	.873	.0268	.0030	895	24
35-44										
	1	1- 6 mos	.979	.9984	98.1	.979	.0497	.0039	1270	46
	2	6-12 mos	.965	.9964	96.8	.986	.0278	.0039	710	24
	3	1- 3 yrs	.938	.9874	95.0	.972	.0141	.0045	315	9.6
	4	3- 5 yrs	.852	.9764	87.3	.908	.0471	.0055	855	42
	5	5- 6 yrs	.824	.9702	84.9	.967	.0334	.0064	520	27
45-59										
	1	1- 6 mos	.889	.9949	89.4	.889	.2460	.0121	2000	234
	2	6-12 mos	.871	.9888	88.1	.980	.0396	.0121	325	28
	3	1- 3 yrs	.785	.9615	81.6	.901	.0508	.0139	365	37
	4	3- 5 yrs	.701	.9299	75.4	.893	.0550	.0166	330	38

*Basis of expected mortality and survival: U.S. Life Tables (1949-51) for white males

SPINAL CORD DISORDERS

§251—SPINAL CORD INJURY IN ONTARIO PATIENTS

References: (1) D. J. Breithaupt, A. T. Jousse, and M. Wynne-Jones, "Late Causes of Death and Life Expectancy in Paraplegia," Can. Med. Assoc. J., 85:73-77 (1961).
(2) A. T. Jousse, M. Wynne-Jones, and D. J. Breithaupt, "A Follow-up Study of Life Expectancy and Mortality in Traumatic Transverse Myelitis," Can. Med. Assoc. J., 98:770-772 (1968).
(3) D. J. Breithaupt, unpublished exposures and other data furnished (1970).

Subjects Studied: A group of 965 paraplegic and quadriplegic patients treated at Lyndhurst Lodge, Sunnybrook Veterans Hospital, and Toronto General Hospital, Toronto, Ontario, and under observation between January 1, 1945 and December 31, 1966. Cause of the paraplegia or quadriplegia was injury to the spinal cord. Excluded from the study series were 26 patients who could not be traced and 99 patients with partial paraplegia and neurological recovery of such degree that there was no residual urine and no bacteriuria. The distribution of cases by sex and type of neurological deficit was as follows:

| | Paraplegia | | Quadriplegia | |
	Partial	Complete	Partial	Complete
Male	252	335	139	116
Female	26	26	56	15
Total	278	361	195	131

Follow-up: Information was obtained first by a questionnaire addressed to all patients whose death had not been reported, and then by a special investigation of all non-responders. In this way survival status or time and place of death were ascertained for all but 26 patients in the series. Cause of death was determined through autopsy data, where available, death certificates, and hospital or physician records.

Results: The more limited experience of the 1961 report (599 patients followed to 1960, with 94 deaths) revealed overall mortality ratios that were similar to those of the 1968 article. The complete experience, based on a total of 203 deaths through 1966, is shown in Tables 251a-c. Published results have been supplemented with additional data provided by the authors. Expected deaths calculated for the 1968 article were based on the 1965 Canadian Mortality Tables.

Mortality and survival experience in the first 5½ years of observation is given in Table 251a. The indicated rates are estimates involving the assumption of a uniform rate of withdrawal but utilizing the total exposure of 4119 person-years (Table 251b) and the actual distribution of deaths reported. The resulting approximate mortality rates during this 5½-year period are fairly constant, about .020 per year — considerably above that expected. The cumulative survival rate at 5½ years is 0.889. Comparative experience by age (Table 251b), for all types of lesions combined, in the first 5½ years is characterized by a mortality ratio decreasing with age, 745 per cent to 191 per cent, but an EDR increasing from 11 to 38. For longer durations mortality ratios continue through age 61 at a somewhat lower level, but mortality is still materially higher than expected; extra mortality for durations beyond 5½ years is not evident in patients age 62 years and older at time of onset. Comparative experience by type of lesion (Table 251c) reveals an excess mortality that is much lighter when the paraplegia or quadriplegia is partial than when it is complete. In cases of partial paraplegia the mortality is normal for the older patients, as it was reported by the authors in 99 additional cases with no residual urine and no bacteriuria.

The leading cause of death was kidney failure, which accounted for 36 per cent of the deaths. Cardiovascular disease ranked second as a cause of death.

SPINAL CORD INJURY IN ONTARIO PATIENTS

Table 251a   5½-Year Mortality and Survival Experience (All Ages and Types of Lesions Combined)

No.	Interval Start-End	No. Alive at Start of Interval	Number Withdrawn*	Exposure Person-Yrs*	Deaths in Interval	Ave. Ann. Mort. Rate	Survival Rate Interval	Survival Rate Cumulative
i	t to t + Δt	ℓ	w	E	d	$\bar{q} = d/E$	p_i	P
1	0 - ½ yr	965	37	473	7	.015	.993	.993
2	½-1½ yrs	921*	72	885	18	.020	.980	.972
3	1½-2½	831*	64	799	16	.020	.980	.953
4	2½-3½	751*	58	722	18	.025	.975	.929
5	3½-4½	675*	52	649	8	.012	.988	.918
6	4½-5½	615*	48	591	14	.024	.976	.896
7	0 -5½	965	331	4119	81			.896

Table 251b   Comparative Experience by Age and Duration (All Types of Lesions Combined)

Age Group	Interval No.	Interval Start-End	Exposure Person-Yrs	Deaths in Interval Observed	Deaths in Interval Expected†	Mortality Ratio	Ave. Ann. Mort. Rate	Interval Surv. Rate	Interval Surv. Ratio	Excess Death Rate
	i	t to t + Δt	E	d	d'	100 d/d'	$\bar{q} = d/E$	p_i	100 p_i / p_i'	1000(d-d')/E
Under 44	1	0-5½ yrs	3171	42	5.64	745%	.0132	.930	93.9%	11
	2	5½-22●	3568	48	7.68	625	.0135	.941●	95.0●	11
		All	6739	90	13.32	675	.0134	.874●	89.1	11
44-62	1	0-5½ yrs	774	25	8.78	285	.0323	.835	88.9	21
	2	5½-22●	1798	47	20.35	230	.0261	.888●	93.4●	15
		All	2572	72	29.13	245	.0280	.753●	84.3●	17
62 up	1	0-5½ yrs	174	14	7.32	191	.0805	.630	79.9	38
	2	5½-22●	540	25	25.20	99	.0463	.808●	100.2●	−0.4
		All	714	39	32.52	120	.0546	.570●	90.9●	9.1

Table 251c   Comparative Experience by Age and Type of Lesion (All Durations Combined)

Category & Age Group	Exposure Person-Yrs	Deaths Observed	Deaths Expected†	Mortality Ratio	Ave. Ann. Mort. Rate	Est. 5-Yr Surv. Rate	Est. 5-Yr Surv. Index	Excess Death Rate
	E	d	d'	100 d/d'	$\bar{q} = d/E$	$P = (1-\bar{q})^5$	100 P/P'	1000(d-d')/E
Partial Paraplegia								
Ages under 44	2041	12	4.17	290%	.0059	.971	98.1%	3.8
44 up	1310	34	34.68	98	.0260	.877	100.3	−0.5
All Ages	3351	46	38.85	118	.0137	.933	98.9	2.1
Complete Paraplegia								
Ages under 44	2674	40	5.38	745	.0150	.927	93.7	13
44 up	1065	42	14.97	280	.0394	.818	87.8	25
All Ages	3739	82	20.35	405	.0219	.895	92.0	16
Partial Quadriplegia								
Ages under 44	1064	11	2.08	530	.0103	.949	.95.9	8.4
44 up	658	26	15.09	172	.0395	.818	91.8	17
All Ages	1722	37	17.17	215	.0215	.897	94.3	12
Complete Quardiplegia								
Ages under 44	855	25	1.60	1560	.0292	.862	87.0	27
44 up	142	13	1.54	845	.0915	.619	65.3	81
All Ages	997	38	3.14	1210	.0381	.823	83.7	35

* Uniform rate of withdrawal assumed

† Basis of expected mortality: 1965 Canadian Mortality Tables

● Maximum duration 22 years, assumed to average 10 years

SPINAL CORD DISORDERS

§255–POLIOMYELITIS

Reference: *1951 Impairment Study,* compiled and published by the Society of Actuaries (1954), p. 253.

Subjects Studied: The study covered the experience under ordinary insurance, issued during the years 1935 through 1949 traced to policy anniversaries in 1950, of applicants giving a history of one attack of poliomyelitis producing marked deformity at any time prior to application. The experience was compiled from contributions of 27 cooperating insurance companies which supplied data retrieved from policy records coded for poliomyelitis producing marked deformity. Cases ratable for other impairments were excluded. Some characteristics of the series were as follows:

Type of Issue	No. of Entrants	Per Cent Female	Group Mean Age	Ratio of Policy Death Claims to Lives Involved*	Average Duration
Standard (S)	5325	13%	31	1.24	6.3
Substandard (SS)	3404	17%	30	1.07	6.6

*Some applicants had more than one policy in force. The ratio of policies to lives is available in the *1951 Impairment Study* only for the policies terminating in a death claim.

Age Group	15-29	30-39	40-49	50-64
Standard:	50.7%	36.5%	11.0%	1.8%
Substandard:	58.0%	32.8%	8.0%	1.2%

Follow-up: The policy records of the 27 participating insurance companies were used for follow-up and constitute the basis for counting death claims and numbers exposed to risk.

Results: Mortality and survival data are presented for the fifteen-year study period both by interval (Tables 255a-b) and by age range (Table 255c). The mortality variations in the first five years of follow-up for the substandard issues are probably random in nature, the average mortality ratio being only 112 per cent. The mortality ratio showed an increase to 141 per cent at 5-10 years, and 275 per cent at 10-15 years, with an EDR of 5.4 per 1000 in the latter interval. The survival ratio in Table 255a is seen to be 99.5 per cent at 10 years, but drops to 96.9 per cent at 15 years.

Excess mortality, all durations combined, showed a progressive increase with advancing age (Table 255c), in both standard and substandard issues. On an overall basis the standard mortality ratio was 100 per cent, and the substandard, 149 per cent. The highest mortality appeared in the age group 50-64 years, with ratios of 144 and 255 per cent in the standard and substandard issues, respectively. The corresponding levels of EDR were 4.9 and 16 extra deaths per 1000.

PARALYSIS AND DEFORMITY DUE TO POLIOMYELITIS

Table 255a Comparative Experience by Duration — Substandard Issues

Interval Start-End	Exposure Policy-Yrs	Death Claims during Interval*	Death Claims Expected*	Mortality Ratio Interval	Mortality Ratio Cumulative	Survival Ratio Interval	Survival Ratio Cumulative	Excess Death Rate
t to t + Δ t	E	d	d'	100 d/d'	100Σd/Σd'	100 p_i/p_i'	100 P/P'	1000(d-d')/E
0- 2 yrs	6219	11 (11)	6.79	162%	162%	99.9%	99.9%	0.7
2- 5	7356	10 (10)	11.95	84	112	100.1	99.9	−0.3
5-10	6888	21 (18)	14.89	141	125	99.6	99.5	0.9
10-15	2135	18 (17)	6.57	275	149	97.4	96.9	5.4

Table 255b Derived Mortality and Survival Data — Substandard Issues

Interval Start-End	Observed Rates Average Annual Mortality	Observed Rates Average Annual Survival	Observed Rates Cumulative Survival	Observed Rates Cumulative Mortality	Expected Rates* Average Annual Mortality	Expected Rates* Average Annual Survival	Expected Rates* Cumulative Survival	Expected Rates* Cumulative Mortality
t to t + Δ t	$\bar{q}$ = d/E	$\bar{p}$	P	Q	$\bar{q}'$ = d'/E	$\bar{p}'$	P'	Q'
0- 2 yrs	.0018	.9982	.996	.004	.0011	.9989	.9978	.0022
2- 5	.0014	.9986	.992	.008	.0016	.9984	.9930	.0070
5-10	.0030	.9970	.977	.023	.0022	.9978	.9821	.0179
10-15	.0084	.9916	.937	.063	.0031	.9969	.9670	.0330

Table 255c Comparative Experience by Age and Standard or Substandard Issue

Type of Issue and Age	Exposure Policy-Yrs	Death Claims during Interval*	Death Claims Expected*	Mortality Ratio	Ave. Ann. Mort. Rate	Est. 7-Yr Surv. Rate	Est. 7-Yr Surv. Index	Excess Death Rate
	E	d	d'	100 d/d'	$\bar{q}$ = d/E	P = $(1-\bar{q})^7$	100 P/P'	1000(d-d')/E
Standard								
15-29 yrs	17118	12 (12)	19.22	62%	.0007	.995	100.3%	−0.4
30-39	12323	26 (19)	24.44	106	.0021	.985	99.9	0.1
40-49	3711	20 (18)	17.04	117	.0054	.963	99.4	0.8
50-64	618	10 (8)	6.95	144	.0162	.892	96.5	4.9
15-64	33770	68 (55)	67.65	100	.0020	.986	100.0	0.0
Substandard								
15-29 yrs	13109	17 (17)	14.66	116%	.0013	.991	99.9%	0.2
30-39	7408	20 (20)	14.32	140	.0027	.981	99.4	0.8
40-49	1808	16 (14)	8.49	188	.0088	.940	97.1	4.2
50-64	273	7 (5)	2.73	255	.0256	.834	89.5	16
15-64	22598	60 (56)	40.20	149	.0027	.981	99.4	0.9

* Death claims, with number of lives in parentheses. Basis of expected mortality:
1935-50 Intercompany Experience on Standard Issues.

§279 – NEUROLOGICAL AND PSYCHIATRIC DISEASES (MISCELLANEOUS)

References: (1) T. W. Preston and R. D. Clarke, "An Investigation into the Mortality of Impaired Lives During the Period 1947-63," J. Inst. Act., 92:27-74 (1966).
(2) A. Svensson and S. Astrand, "Substandard Risk Mortality in Sweden 1955-1965," Coopération Internationale pour les Assurances des Risques Aggravés. (See Rome Conference proceedings, 1969.)
(3) "New York Life Single Medical Impairment Study - 1972," unpublished report made available by J. J. Hutchinson and J. C. Sibigtroth (1973).
(4) R. B. Singer, New England Life unpublished mortality studies (1968 and 1974).

Subjects Studied: (1) Policyholders of Prudential Assurance Co., London, England, issued insurance 1947-1963 followed to 12/31/63. Both standard and substandard issues were included. Applicants with two or more ratable impairments were generally excluded.
(2) Lives reinsured (mostly on a substandard basis) with Sverige Reinsurance Co., Sweden, placed in force prior to 1955 and observed between anniversaries in 1955 and 1965.
(3) Policyholders of New York Life Insurance Co., issued insurance 1954-1970 followed to 1971 policy anniversary. Both standard and substandard issues were included. Applicants with more than one ratable impairment were excluded.
(4) Policyholders of New England Mutual Life Insurance Co., issued insurance 1935-1963 followed to 1968 anniversaries for epilepsy cases. Policyholders issued insurance followed to anniversaries for cerebrovascular cases.

Follow-up: Insurance policy records formed the basis of entry, of counting policies, exposures, and death claims, and of follow-up information.

Results: Mortality ratios on insured applicants with histories of several types reported on, ranged up to 290 per cent with one exception: suicide attempt (Reference 3), 1030 per cent, based on 4 deaths. (In contrast to the favorable English experience in Reference 1 migraine headache in the New York Life study indicated a mortality ratio of 179 per cent.) Coinciding with the aforementioned range limits was the experience of three companies with respect to epilepsy. Shown in the New England Life data which included standard and substandard units was the most favorable experience: the mortality ratio for petit mal was 100 per cent against the English experience of 183 per cent and, for grand mal, 141 per cent, against the English 290 per cent. The Swedish ratio of 220 per cent appears to be close to midway, but if the ratio were developed in comparison to a select insurance standard (rather than to a population standard), the ratio would be increased and probably come close to that in the English experience. Mortality ratios developed in the case of three subdivisions of skull fracture fell between 153 and 175 per cent in the Prudential experience - the New York Life ratio of 116 per cent (all types) was more favorable. Skull fracture in the New York Life experience and cerebral concussion in the English experience showed mortality ratios near normal, 116 and 118 per cent. Other neurological disorders with near normal experience were polio, mortality ratio 117 per cent, and marked deafness, mortality ratio, 130 per cent. Among disorders with more adverse experience were brain disorder and tremors (not otherwise specified), mental retardation, Parkinson's disease, and cerebrovascular disease. In these categories mortality ratios varied from 182 to 280 per cent, and EDR from 1.3 to 14 extra deaths per 1000 per year.

Psychoneurosis, as shown in three severity categories in the English study, yielded mortality ratios from 127 to 140 per cent and EDR's between 0.7 and 1.1 per 1000. The mortality ratio for nervousness (New York Life study) was in the same range, at 135 per cent. As noted above, a very high mortality ratio of 1030 per cent was found in suicide attempt, but this was based on only four deaths. Psychosis in the New York Life study yielded a mortality ratio of 155 per cent, and psychiatric disorders in the Swedish study, a ratio of 124 per cent. Again, as noted above, the mortality ratio would have been higher if a select insurance mortality had been used as a standard in the Swedish study instead of a general population mortality.

NEUROPSYCHIATRIC DISORDERS

Table 279   Comparative Experience, Four Series of Insureds

Disease/Category (Ref.)	Sex/Age	Policies in Force at Start ℓ	Exposure Policy-Yrs E	No. of Death Claims Observed d	No. of Death Claims Expected* d'	Ave. Ann. Mort. Rate Observed q̄ = d/E	Ave. Ann. Mort. Rate Expected* q̄' = d'/E	Mortality Ratio 100 d/d'	Est. 5-Yr Surv. Rate P = (1 - q̄')⁵	Est. 5-Yr Surv. Index 100 P/P'	Excess Death Rate 1000 (q̄ - q̄')
Cerebral Vascular Accident SS† (4)	M&F 43	150	1174	14	6.17	.0119	.0053	225%	.9418	96.7%	6.7
Cerebral Hemorrhage SS (3)	M&F 39	—	595	4	1.76	.0067	.0030	225	.9668	98.1	3.8
Brain Disorder S†&SS (3)	M&F 34	—	2394	8	4.39	.0033	.0018	182	.9834	99.2	1.5
Mental Retardation SS (3)	M&F 31	—	1508	4	2.03	.0027	.0013	197	.9868	99.3	1.3
Skull Fract. (no opertion) SS (3)	M&F 34	—	6076	12	10.3	.0020	.0017	116	.9902	99.9	0.3
Skull Fract. (no op: no sequelae) (1)	M 39	1607	8659	26	16.9	.0030	.0020	153	.9851	99.5	1.1
Skull Fract. (no op; no sequelae) (1)	M 41	494	2848	13	8.18	.0046	.0029	159	.9774	99.2	1.7
Skull Fract. (operated) (1)	M 39	379	2310	8	4.57	.0035	.0020	175	.9828	99.3	1.5
Cerebral Concussion (1)	M&F 39	3547	18041	44	37.3	.0024	.0021	118	.9879	99.8	0.4
Epilepsy - Petit Mal (1)	M 38	402	2065	7	3.83	.0034	.0019	183	.9832	99.2	1.5
Epilepsy - Grand Mal (1)	M 37	1076	5155	25	8.56	.0048	.0017	290	.9760	98.4	3.2
Epilepsy - All (2)	M&F 37	—	4119	32	14.6	.0078	.0035	220	.9618	97.9	4.2
Epilepsy - Petit Mal S&SS (4)	M&F 36	348	3872	9	8.96	.0023	.0023	100	.9884	100.0	0.0
Epilepsy - Grand Mal S&SS (4)	M&F 39	501	4201	19	13.4	.0045	.0032	141	.9776	99.3	1.3
Migraine, Headache S&SS (3)	M&F 38	—	2980	15	8.36	.0050	.0028	179	.9751	98.9	2.2
Migraine (1)	M 37	2127	9409	7	16.11	.0007	.0017	43	.9963	100.5	−1.0
Parkinson's Disease SS (3)	M&F 50	—	445	10	3.55	.0225	.0080	280	.8926	92.9	14
Poliomyelitis (1)	M 37	1244	6203	11	9.37	.0018	.0015	117	.9912	99.9	0.3
Blindness, one eye S (3)	M&F 41	—	3589	18	13.5	.0050	.0038	133	.9752	99.4	1.2
Total Blindness S&SS (3)	M&F 35	—	1536	4	3.07	.0026	.0020	130	.9870	99.7	0.6
Marked impaired vision SS (3)	M&F 42	—	599	6	2.35	.0100	.0039	255	.9509	97.0	6.1
Cataract S&SS (3)	M&F 45	—	1426	10	7.37	.0070	.0052	136	.9654	99.1	1.8
Glaucoma S&SS (3)	M&F 45	—	2610	14	14.2	.0054	.0055	98	.9735	100.0	−0.1
Deaf mutism S&SS (3)	M&F 38	—	3330	7	9.18	.0021	.0028	76	.9895	100.3	−0.7
Meniere's Disease SS (3)	M&F 42	—	1692	5	6.58	.0030	.0039	76	.9853	100.5	−0.9
Otitis Media, no operation (1)	M 44	9415	41076	83	73.1	.0020	.0018	114	.9899	99.9	0.2
Mastoidectomy (1)	M 43	6228	30693	51	52.0	.0017	.0017	98	.9917	100.0	0.0
Marked Deafness S&SS (3)	M&F —	—	4238	20	15.39	.0047	.0036	130	.9767	99.5	1.1
Tremors S&SS (3)	M&F 51	—	405	7	3.66	.0173	.0090	191	.9165	95.9	8.2
Psychoneurosis (1)											
- mild	M 40	4478	23493	74	58.5	.0031	.0025	127	.9843	99.7	0.7
- moderate	M 40	3653	19446	64	45.7	.0033	.0024	140	.9837	99.5	0.9
- severe	M 41	964	4157	16	11.6	.0038	.0028	138	.9809	99.5	1.1
Nervousness S&SS (3)	M&F 39	—	1542	6	4.44	.0039	.0029	135	.9807	99.5	1.0
Psychosis S&SS (3)	M&F 36	—	3345	12	7.74	.0036	.0023	155	.9822	99.4	1.3
Suicide Attempt SS (3)	M&F 34	—	216	4	0.39	.0185	.0018	1030	.9108	91.9	17
Psychiatric Disorders (2)	M&F 41	—	5064	29	23.3	.0057	.0046	124	.9716	99.4	1.1

*Basis of expected mortality: (Ref. 1) Prudential Assurance Co. (England) standard lives mortality 1957-1958;
(Ref. 2) Sverige Reins. Co., population mortality, M or F (Sweden), 1956-60 and 1961-65; (Ref. 3) N.Y. Life,
Basic Select Tables (1955-60); (Ref. 4) New England Life, Basic Tables (1955-60).

†"S" - Standard, "SS" - Substandard.

PSYCHIATRIC DISORDERS

§280–PSYCHIATRIC PATIENTS – SCOTLAND

References: (1) G. Innes and W. M. Millar, "Mortality among Psychiatric Patients," Scot. Med. J., 15:143-148 (1970). (2) G. Innes and G. A. Sharp, "A Study of Psychiatric Patients in North-East Scotland," J. Mental Sci., 108:447-456 (1962).

Subjects Studied: Psychiatric referrals of persons over 15 years of age resident within the area of the North-Eastern Regional Hospital Board (the city of Aberdeen, Scotland, and six rural counties, including the two island groups of Orkney and Shetland), during the year following March 1, 1960, who had not consulted a psychiatrist during the previous year. Included in the survey were psychiatric hospital admissions, all outpatient referrals, domiciliary and general hospital visits and patients seen in private psychiatric practice. The total series consisted of 2097 persons (861 men, 1236 women). Patients entering the experience were distributed by age and sex as follows:

Number (per cent) of Subjects

Age (years):	15-44	45-54	55-64	65-74	75 up	All Ages
Male	455 (52.9%)	144 (16.7%)	143 (16.6%)	76 (8.8%)	43 (5.0%)	861 (100%)
Female	625 (50.6%)	211 (17.1%)	176 (14.2%)	122 (9.9%)	102 (8.2%)	1236 (100%)
Total	1080 (51.5%)	355 (16.9%)	319 (15.2%)	198 (9.5%)	145 (6.9%)	2097 (100%)

Follow-up: All contacts of patients with the psychiatric services in the five-year period following initial consultation were recorded. At the close of the follow-up period, 208 subjects were in treatment and a further 1253, from hospital and general practioners' records, were found to be still living in the area. Governmental death records revealed that 343 patients had died. Lost to observation were 293 individuals, including 80 who had moved from the area. (In the absence of information with regard to age and sex of the patients lost to observation and the incidence of loss, in the accompanying tables, withdrawals have been distributed pro rata.)

Results: Mortality was substantially higher than for similar classes of persons in the general population. As shown in Table 280a mortality ratios were relatively high at the younger and the oldest age groups. The ratio for men under age 45 years was 590 per cent, for those over age 74, 320 per cent; for women under 55 years, ratios approached 500 per cent, dipped to 255 per cent in the 55-64 year age group, then increased to 365 per cent for ages over 74. The overall mortality ratio (all ages and durations) was 225 per cent for males, 345 per cent for females. Excess deaths per year for the total male experience averaged 21 per 1000, and in the case of females, 28. There was a tendency for this function to increase with age group; at the oldest ages (75 years up), average annual excess deaths were extremely high – 299 per 1000 in the case of men, 246, for women. The high mortality in the oldest age group may be due to a high proportion of organic psychosis in patients in poor physical condition (see below).

In Table 280b is shown the number of deaths during the follow-up period and their distribution into the several diagnostic categories. Neuroses represented the most common diagnostic class; 36 per cent of males and 49 per cent of females fell into this category; the overall rate of death, however, was relatively low (9.6 per cent for males; 8.1 per cent for females). Organic psychoses were a less frequent diagnosis (males, 10 per cent; females, 12 per cent) but mortality rates were very high: 70 per cent, males, and 73 per cent, females. Other diagnostic groups represented 54 per cent of the male subjects and 39 per cent of females – in both sexes the proportion of deaths among these other groups was 10 per cent.

In Tables 280c-f, comparative experience by duration (all ages combined) is presented. In the first three months after initial consultation about seven times as many men died as in the general population, ten times as many women. These ratios diminished unevenly with duration, resulting in average mortality ratios over the five-year period of 225 per cent for males and 345 per cent for females. There were differences in experience according to place of residence within the area of study, but the number of deaths was small in the sections showing the greatest departures from the overall experience and the differences are not significant.

PSYCHIATRIC PATIENTS — SCOTLAND

Table 280a   Comparative Experience by Age Group & Sex

Sex	Age Group	No. Alive at Start of Interval	Exposure Person-Yrs	Deaths during Interval	Expected Deaths*	Mortality Ratio	Ave. Ann. Mort. Rate	Est. 5-Yr Surv. Rate	Est. 5-Yr Surv. Index	Excess Death Rate
		ℓ	E	d	d'	100d/d'	$\bar{q} = d/E$	$P = (1-\bar{q})^5$	100 P/P'	1000(d-d')/E
Male	15-44	455	2052	20	3.38	590%	.0097	.9522	96.0%	8.1
	45-54	144	628	15	7.73	194	.0239	.8861	94.3	12
	55-64	143	549	39	17.50	225	.0710	.6918	81.3	39
	65-74	76	285	24	20.19	119	.0842	.6441	93.0	13
	75+	43	90	39	12.24	320	.4333	.0584	12.1	297
	All Ages	861	3604	137	61.04	225	.0380	.8239	89.7	21
Female	15-44	625	2854	15	3.05	490	.0053	.9740	97.9	4.2
	45-54	211	892	28	5.97	470	.0314	.8526	88.2	25
	55-64	176	725	31	12.09	255	.0428	.8037	87.4	26
	65-74	122	416	52	17.05	305	.1250	.5129	63.2	84
	75+	102	236	80	21.96	365	.3390	.1262	20.6	246
	All Ages	1236	5123	206	60.12	345	.0402	.8145	86.4	28

Table 280b   Mortality According to Initial Diagnosis

Diagnosis	Males			Females		
	No. Patients Recorded	5-Year Deaths No.	5-Year Deaths Per Cent	No. Patients Recorded	5-Year Deaths No.	5-Year Deaths Per Cent
Functional Psychoses	158	16	10.1	216	24	11.1
Organic Psychoses	86	60	69.8	150	109	72.7
Neuroses	313	30	9.6	607	49	8.1
Character Disorders & Addictions	144	8	5.6	41	3	7.3
Miscellaneous†	95	13	13.7	146	13	8.9
No Diagnosis ●	65	10	15.4	76	8	10.5
All Diagnoses	861	137	15.9	1236	206	16.7

* Basis of expected mortality: Register General (Scotland) Reports 1961-65

† Including mental subnormality

● Including Non-Attendees

PSYCHIATRIC DISORDERS

Table 280c   Comparative Experience by Duration for Males — All Ages Combined

Interval Start-End	No. Alive at Start of Interval	Withdrawn + Lost Cases	Exposure Person-Yrs*	Deaths in Interval Obs.	Deaths in Interval Exp.†	Mortality Ratio Interval	Mortality Ratio Cumulative	Survival Ratio Interval	Survival Ratio Cumulative	Excess Death Rate
t to t + Δt	ℓ	w + u	E	d	d′	100 d/d′	100 Q/Q′	100pᵢ/pᵢ′	100 P/P′	1000(d-d′)/E
0- 3 mo	861	8	214	27	3.83	705%	705%	97.3%	97.3%	108
3- 6 mo	826	6	206	13	3.43	380	540	98.8	96.2	46
6-12 mo	807	14	400	20	6.43	310	425	98.3	94.5	34
0- 1 yr	861	28	820	60	13.69	440	425		94.5	56
1- 2 yrs	773	24	761	24	12.75	188	300	98.5	93.1	15
2- 3 yrs	725	23	714	18	12.02	150	250	99.1	92.3	8.4
3- 4 yrs	684	22	673	15	11.51	130	215	99.5	91.8	5.2
4- 5 yrs	647	21	636	20	11.07	181	205	98.6	90.5	14
0- 5 yrs		118	3604	137	61.04	225	205		90.5	21

Table 280d   Derived Mortality and Survival Data for Males

Interval Start-End	Observed Rates Interval Mortality	Observed Rates Interval Survival	Observed Rates Cumulative Survival	Observed Rates Cumulative Mortality	Expected Rates† Interval Mortality	Expected Rates† Interval Survival	Expected Rates† Cumulative Survival	Expected Rates† Cumulative Mortality
t to t + Δt	qᵢ	pᵢ	P	Q	qᵢ′	pᵢ′	P′	Q′
0- 3 mo	.0315	.9685	.9685	.0315	.0045	.9955	.9955	.0045
3- 6 mo	.0158	.9842	.9532	.0468	.0042	.9958	.9913	.0087
6-12 mo	.0250	.9750	.9294	.0706	.0080	.9920	.9834	.0166
1- 2 yrs	.0315	.9685	.9001	.0999	.0168	.9832	.9669	.0331
2- 3 yrs	.0252	.9748	.8774	.1226	.0168	.9832	.9506	.0494
3- 4 yrs	.0223	.9777	.8578	.1422	.0171	.9829	.9344	.0656
4- 5 yrs	.0314	.9686	.8309	.1691	.0174	.9826	.9181	.0819

* Estimated
† Basis of expected mortality: Register General (Scotland) Reports 1961-1965

PSYCHIATRIC PATIENTS — SCOTLAND

Table 280e   Comparative Experience by Duration for Females — All Ages Combined

Interval	No. Alive at Start of Interval	Withdrawn + Lost Cases	Exposure Person-Yrs*	Deaths in Interval		Mortality Ratio		Survival Ratio		Excess Death Rate
Start-End				Obs.	Exp.†	Interval	Cumulative	Interval	Cumulative	
t to $t + \Delta t$	ℓ	$w + u$	E	d	d'	$100\ d/d'$	$100\ Q/Q'$	$100 p_i/p_i'$	$100\ P/P'$	$1000(d-d')/E$
0- 3 mo	1236	11	307	41	4.09	1000%	1000%	97.0%	97.0%	120
3- 6 mo	1184	10	295	12	3.60	335	675	99.3	96.3	28
6-12 mo	1162	19	576	28	6.84	410	540	98.1	94.5	37
0- 1 yr	1236	40	1178	81	14.53	555	540		94.5	56
1- 2 yrs	1115	38	1096	36	13.45	270	400	97.9	92.6	21
2- 3 yrs	1041	36	1023	47	12.39	380	385	96.6	89.4	34
3- 4 yrs	958	33	942	27	10.41	260	350	98.2	87.8	18
4- 5 yrs	898	28	884	15	9.34	161	310	99.4	87.2	6.4
0- 5 yrs		175	5123	206	60.12	345	310		87.2	28

Table 280f   Derived Mortality and Survival Data for Females

Interval	Observed Rates				Expected Rates†			
	Interval		Cumulative		Interval		Cumulative	
Start-End	Mortality	Survival	Survival	Mortality	Mortality	Survival	Survival	Mortality
t to $t + \Delta t$	q_i	p_i	P	Q	q_i'	p_i'	P'	Q'
0- 3 mo	.0333	.9667	.9667	.0333	.0033	.9967	.9967	.0033
3- 6 mo	.0102	.9898	.9568	.0432	.0031	.9969	.9936	.0064
6-12 mo	.0243	.9757	.9336	.0664	.0059	.9941	.9877	.0123
1- 2 yrs	.0328	.9672	.9030	.0970	.0123	.9877	.9756	.0244
2- 3 yrs	.0459	.9541	.8615	.1385	.0121	.9879	.9638	.0362
3- 4 yrs	.0287	.9713	.8368	.1632	.0111	.9889	.9531	.0469
4- 5 yrs	.0170	.9830	.8226	.1774	.0106	.9894	.9430	.0570

Estimated
Basis of expected mortality: Register General (Scotland) Reports 1961-1965

PSYCHIATRIC DISORDERS

§285–NEUROSIS IN ARMY VETERANS

References: (1) R. J. Keehn, I. D. Goldberg, and G. W. Beebe, "Twenty-four Year Mortality Follow-up of Army Veterans with Disability Separations for Psychoneurosis in 1944," Psychosom. Med., 36:27-46 (1974).
(2) R. J. Keehn, additional data supplied by the author (1974).

Subjects Studied: 9813 white male Army inductees given a disability separation in 1944, at age 25-30, because of psychoneurosis. Out of 13,355 Army punch cards from the 1944 disability separation file, 3542 cases were eliminated because of wrong age, or record deficiencies, or death prior to January 1, 1946. A control group of 9942 white Army enlisted personnel was selected from a 2 per cent file of National Service Life Insurance numbers, on the basis of matching the neurosis group for age, length of service, race, sex, and mode of entry into service (entry years ranged from 1940 to 1944). Only 24 per cent of the neurosis group attained an enlisted rank of corporal or sergeant and only 40 per cent had service outside the continental U.S., both percentages less than half those found in the control group. Only 9.4 per cent had any prior education beyond a high school level.

Psychoneurosis was the only diagnosis in 6616 cases and the major diagnosis responsible for admission in 2177 cases. Situational factors were considered to be more probable than pre-existing factors or a combination of the two in only 1093 cases. Type of psychoneurosis was classified as follows:

Hysteria	1125	Obsessive-compulsive	107
Anxiety	3407	Mixed type	3570
Neurasthenia	230	Reactive depression	314
Neurocirculatory asthenia	169	Other and unspecified	891

Follow-up: Mortality was determined through the VA Master Index, which has been found to be 98 per cent complete for World War II veterans with at least 90 days of service and honorably discharged. Abstracts of death certificates were received on all but 21 of the deaths in both neurosis and control groups from 1964 through 1969.

Results: Mortality experience for the neurosis group is given in Tables 285a-b, with the 24 years of follow-up divided into four quinquennial intervals and a final period of four years. Mortality was significantly greater in the neurosis group than expected from the rates in the comparable control group, especially in the first ten years. The mortality ratio of 146 per cent in the first interval decreased to 112 per cent in the last, but EDR rose slightly from 0.6 to 1.1 excess deaths per 1000 per year. The cumulative survival ratio at 24 years was 97.9 per cent.

Mortality in both neurosis and control groups is compared with that of contemporaneous U.S. white males in Table 285c. In the control group the mortality ratio of 62 per cent in the first five years of follow-up is well below the expected 100 per cent, and illustrates the effect of selection, as all veterans did, of course, pass the induction examination in 1940-1944. With the passage of time, as it would be anticipated, the mortality ratio for the control group approaches 100 per cent, with a maximum value of 96 per cent in the final period of observation. In the neurosis group the mortality ratio is only 91 per cent during the first period, but it exceeds 100 per cent in all subsequent periods. A comparison of these mortality ratios with the ones for the neurosis group in Table 285a demonstrates the importance of utilizing the best matched control group and its mortality experience as a standard for comparison.

Excess mortality for the neurosis over the control group is given in Table 285d for some major categories of cause of death (for additional details and analysis consult the article). Significantly increased mortality rates were observed in the neurosis group for deaths due to diseases of the nervous system, suicide, homicide, all violent means, and psychiatric disorders, as well as all diseases combined, and all causes. A significant increase in mortality due to mental disorders could not have been demonstrated without such a long exposure on a relatively large cohort, as the numbers of deaths are small (22 for the neurosis and 3 for the control group). When the number of deaths is small a high mortality ratio may be accompanied by a small value of EDR, as the table shows. It is noteworthy that excess mortality developed in organic disease (diseases of the nervous system and all disease), just as it did for those causes more readily linked to the diagnosis — suicide, all violent means, and mental disorders.

NEUROSIS IN ARMY VETERANS

Table 285a Observed Data and Comparative Experience by Duration — All Ages Combined (26-30 in 1944)

No.	Interval Start-End	Follow-up Years	Exposure Person-Yrs	Deaths in Interval Observed	Deaths in Interval Expected*	Mortality Ratio Interval	Mortality Ratio Cumulative	Survival Ratio Interval	Survival Ratio Cumulative	Excess Death Rate
i	t to $t+\Delta t$		E	d	d'	$100\,d/d'$	$100\sum d/\sum d'$	$100\,p_i/p_i'$	$100\,P/P'$	$1000(d-d')/E$
1	0- 5 yrs	1946-50	48855	95	65.0	146%	146%	99.7%	99.7%	0.6
2	5-10	1951-55	48282	130	89.7	145	146	99.6	99.3	0.8
3	10-15	1956-60	47482	199	164.3	121	133	99.7	99.0	0.7
4	15-20	1961-65	46198	329	269.8	122	128	99.4	98.3	1.3
5	20-24	1966-69	35468	387	346.5	112	121	99.6	97.9	1.1
	0-24 yrs	1946-69	226285	1140	934.9	121	121	97.9	97.9	0.9

Table 285b Derived Mortality and Survival Data

No.	Interval Start-End	Follow-up Years	Observed Mort. Rate Ave. Ann.	Observed Survival Rates Ave. Ann.	Observed Survival Rates Interval	Observed Survival Rates Cumulative	Control* Mort. Rate Ave. Ann.	Control* Survival Rates Ave. Ann.	Control* Survival Rates Interval	Control* Survival Rates Cumulative
i	t to $t+\Delta t$		$\bar q$	$\bar p$	p_i	P	$\bar q'$	$\bar p'$	p_i'	P'
1	0- 5 yrs	1946-50	.0019	.9981	.9905	.9905	.0013	.9987	.9935	.9935
2	5-10	1951-55	.0027	.9973	.9866	.9772	.0019	.9981	.9905	.9841
3	10-15	1956-60	.0042	.9958	.9792	.9569	.0035	.9965	.9826	.9669
4	15-20	1961-65	.0071	.9929	.9650	.9234	.0058	.9942	.9713	.9392
5	20-24	1966-69	.0109	.9891	.9571	.8838	.0098	.9902	.9614	.9029
	0-24 yrs	1946-69								

Table 285c Control Mortality Data and Comparative Experience vs. U.S. White Male

No.	Interval Start-End	Follow-up Years	Average Attained Age	Control Group Exposure Person-Yrs	Control Group No. of Deaths	Ave. Annual Mortality Rates Neurosis Group	Ave. Annual Mortality Rates Control Group	Ave. Annual Mortality Rates U.S. White Male†	Mortality Ratio vs. U.S. White Male Neurosis	Mortality Ratio vs. U.S. White Male Control
i	t to $t+\Delta t$		x	E	d	$\bar q_n$	$\bar q_c$	$\bar q_{us}$	$100\bar q_n/\bar q_{us}$	$100\bar q_c/\bar q_{us}$
1	0- 5 yrs	1946-50	32	49527	66	.00194	.00133	.00214	91%	62%
2	5-10	1951-55	37	49161	91	.00269	.00185	.00261	103	71
3	10-15	1956-60	42	48525	168	.00419	.00346	.00398	105	87
4	15-20	1961-65	47	47460	277	.00712	.00584	.00651	109	90
5	20-24	1966-69	51.5	36646	358	.01091	.00977	.01019	107	96
	0-24 yrs	1946-69	—	231319	960	.00504	.00415	.00478	105	87

Table 285d Comparative Mortality by Cause of Death — Neurosis Group vs. Control Group

Cause of Death Category	Number of Deaths Neurosis	Number of Deaths Control	Ave. Ann. Mort. Rate Neurosis	Ave. Ann. Mort. Rate Control	Mortality Ratio	Excess Death Rate
	d_n	d_c	$1000\,\bar q_n$	$1000\,\bar q_c$	$100\bar q_n/\bar q_c$	$1000(\bar q_n-\bar q_c)$
All diseases (except mental)	856	786	3.78	3.40	111%	0.37
Malignant tumors	161	174	0.71	0.75	95	−0.04
Diseases of nervous system	66	36	0.29	0.16	187	0.13
Diseases of circulatory system	419	403	1.85	1.74	106	0.11
Dis. of resp. and dig. systems	140	115	0.62	0.50	124	0.12
All Trauma	249	163	1.10	0.70	156	0.40
Accident	151	128	0.67	0.55	121	0.12
Suicide	74	24	0.33	0.10	315	0.23
Homicide	23	9	0.10	0.04	260	0.06
Mental Disorders	22	3	0.10	0.01	750	0.08
Unknown	13	8	—	—	—	—

* "Expected" deaths based on exposure of neurosis group and mortality rates of control group
† Contemporary U.S. White Male rates for attained age of neurosis and control groups

§286—NEUROSIS IN INSUREDS

Reference: "New York Life Single Medical Impairment Study—1972," unpublished report made available by J.J. Hutchinson and J.C. Sibigtroth (1973).

Subjects Studied: Policyholders of New York Life Insurance Company issued insurance in 1954-1970, followed to the 1971 policy anniversary. These were psychoneurosis or neurosis cases classified as "single episode-moderate and severe" (as distinguished from single episode-mild, and multiple episodes-mild, moderate and severe). In addition, the experience included all cases for any number of episodes - all degrees of severity. Only substandard issues were included; records with ratable impairments in addition to psychoneurosis or neurosis were excluded.

Follow-up: Insurance policy records formed the basis of entry, of counting policies, exposure and death claims, and of follow-up information.

Results: Comparative experience by sex and duration is given in Tables 286a-b, separately for cases with single episode described as moderate and severe, and for cases with any number of episodes (including single) described as mild, moderate and severe.

For males in the single episode group, mortality showed a downward trend for the first ten years, with the greatest mortality experienced at 0-2 years, the ratio being 370 per cent (3.7 extra deaths per 1000). After 10 years, the EDR was 5.5 per 1000. For cases with any number of episodes, mortality ratios also appeared to decrease with duration, ranging from 260 per cent at 0-2 years to 128 per cent at 10-17 years. The cumulative survival ratio at 17 years for males was 94.0 per cent in the single episode group and 96.7 per cent in the all episodes group. For female cases with any number of episodes, the mortality ratio was higher in the first two years than in subsequent years. The same was observed for the EDR. The cumulative survival ratio at 17 years was virtually normal.

From Table 286c, the overall male mortality ratio in the single episode group was 215 per cent, and 174 per cent where multiple episodes were also included. Corresponding overall female ratios were lower in each group, being 147 per cent and 154 per cent, respectively.

Except for females in the single episode group, the experience was shown by entry age group. For males in the single episode group, it appeared that mortality ratios tend to be higher for ages under 40 than for ages 40 up, while the EDR produced opposite results. Mortality ratios ranged from 135 per cent to 295 per cent, with EDR highest (7.8 extra deaths per 1000) for the age group 40-49. In the group with any number of episodes, there was a downward trend of mortality ratio with age among males, ranging from 225 per cent at ages 0-29 to 134 per cent at ages 50 up. The pattern was an increase in EDR, ranging from 1.1 per 1000 at ages 0-29 to 3.1 per 1000 at ages 50 up. Among females, there was no consistent pattern in the mortality ratio, but there was a tendency for the EDR to be somewhat higher for ages 50 up than for ages under 50.

Comparative experience by major causes of death is given in Table 286d for males and females combined. For the single episode group, a major cause of death is found in suicides, the mortality being 820 per cent and EDR of 0.7 per 1000. The mortality ratio was also increased for accidents and homicides, (255 per cent), and for "other causes and unknown," (245 per cent). In addition, of the 12 deaths in the "other causes and unknown" category, two were disorders of nervous system. For the group with any number of episodes, suicides were found again to be a major cause of death, the mortality ratio being 760 per cent and EDR 0.7 per 1000. The mortality ratio for "other causes and unknown" was next highest at 240 per cent, based on 24 deaths which included 5 disorders of the nervous system.

PSYCHIATRIC DISORDERS

Table 286a   Observed Data and Comparative Experience by Sex and Duration — Substandard Cases

Sex	Interval No.	Interval Start-End	Exposure Policy-Yrs	No. of Death Claims Observed	No. of Death Claims Expected*	Mortality Ratio Interval	Mortality Ratio Cumulative	Survival Ratio Interval	Survival Ratio Cumulative	Excess Death Rate
	i	t to $t + \Delta t$	E	d	d'	100 d/d'	100 Σd/Σd'	100p_i/p_i'	100 P/P'	1000(d-d')/E
Single Episode — Moderate and Severe										
Male	1	0- 2 yrs	2795	14	3.76	370%	370%	99.3%	99.3%	3.7
	2	2- 5	2226	10	5.18	193	270	99.4	98.6	2.2
	3	5-10	1673	9	5.84	154	225	99.1	97.7	1.9
	4	10-17	668	8	4.34	184	215	96.2	94.0	5.5
Any Number of Episodes — Mild, Moderate and Severe										
Male	1	0- 2 yrs	6110	22	8.44	260%	260%	99.6%	99.6%	2.2
	2	2- 5	4762	17	11.21	152	198	99.6	99.2	1.2
	3	5-10	3211	19	11.35	167	187	98.8	98.0	2.4
	4	10-17	1251	11	8.61	128	174	98.7	96.7	1.9
Female	1	0- 2 yrs	2638	8	2.48	325%	325%	99.6%	99.6%	2.1
	2	2- 5	2320	5	4.29	117	192	99.9	99.5	0.3
	3	5-17	2043	7	6.18	113	154	99.5	99.0	0.4

Table 286b   Derived Mortality and Survival Data

Sex	Interval No.	Interval Start-End	Observed Rates Average Annual Mortality	Observed Rates Average Annual Survival	Observed Rates Cumulative Survival	Observed Rates Cumulative Mortality	Expected Rates* Average Annual Mortality	Expected Rates* Average Annual Survival	Expected Rates* Cumulative Survival	Expected Rates* Cumulative Mortality
	i	t to $t + \Delta t$	$\bar{q}=d/E$	$\bar{p}$	P	Q	$\bar{q}'=d'/E$	$\bar{p}'$	P'	Q'
Single Episode — Moderate and Severe										
Male	1	0- 2 yrs	.0050	.9950	.9900	.0100	.0013	.9987	.9973	.0027
	2	2- 5	.0045	.9955	.9767	.0233	.0023	.9977	.9903	.0097
	3	5-10	.0054	.9946	.9507	.0493	.0035	.9965	.9732	.0268
	4	10-17	.0120	.9880	.8738	.1262	.0065	.9935	.9298	.0702
Any Number of Episodes — Mild, Moderate and Severe										
Male	1	0- 2 yrs	.0036	.9964	.9928	.0072	.0014	.9986	.9972	.0028
	2	2- 5	.0036	.9964	.9822	.0178	.0024	.9976	.9902	.0098
	3	5-10	.0059	.9941	.9535	.0465	.0035	.9965	.9728	.0272
	4	10-17	.0088	.9912	.8963	.1037	.0069	.9931	.9269	.0731
Female	1	0- 2 yrs	.0030	.9970	.9939	.0061	.0009	.9991	.9981	.0019
	2	2- 5	.0022	.9978	.9875	.0125	.0018	.9982	.9926	.0074
	3	5-17	.0034	.9966	.9477	.0523	.0030	.9970	.9572	.0428

* Basis of expected mortality: 1955-60 Select Basic Table

NEUROSIS IN INSUREDS

Table 286c Comparative Experience by Sex and Age Group — Substandard Cases, All Durations Combined

Sex	Age Group	Exposure Policy-Yrs	No. of Death Claims Observed	No. of Death Claims Expected*	Mortality Ratio	Ave. Ann. Mort. Rate	Est. 8-Yr Surv. Rate	Est. 8-Yr Surv. Index	Excess Death Rate
		E	d	d'	100 d/d'	q̄=d/E	P=(1-q̄)⁸	100 P/P'	1000(d-d')/E
Single Episode — Moderate and Severe									
Male	0-29	2298	6	2.02	295%	.0026	.9793	98.6%	1.7
	30-39	3017	10	5.32	188	.0033	.9738	98.8	1.6
	40-49	1423	17	5.86	290	.0119	.9083	93.9	7.8
	50 up	624	8	5.92	135	.0128	.9019	97.3	3.3
	All Ages	7362	41	19.12	215	.0056	.9563	97.6	3.0
Female	All Ages	3520	10	6.79	147%	.0028	.9775	99.3%	0.9
Any Number of Episodes — Mild, Moderate and Severe									
Male	0-29	4555	9	3.97	225%	.0020	.9843	99.1%	1.1
	30-39	6166	22	11.06	199	.0036	.9718	98.6	1.8
	40-49	3397	23	13.39	172	.0068	.9471	97.8	2.8
	50 up	1216	15	11.19	134	.0123	.9055	97.5	3.1
	All Ages	15334	69	39.61	174	.0045	.9646	98.5	1.9
Female	0-39	3579	7	3.05	230%	.0020	.9845	99.1%	1.1
	40-49	2501	6	5.81	103	.0024	.9810	99.9	0.1
	50 up	921	7	4.09	171	.0076	.9408	97.5	3.2
	All Ages	7001	20	12.95	154	.0029	.9774	99.2	1.0

Table 286d Mortality by Cause of Death — Male and Female Combined

Cause	Single Episode Moderate and Severe No. of Death Claims Observed	Single Episode Expected●	Mortality Ratio	Excess Death Rate	Any No. of Episodes All Degrees of Severity No. of Death Claims Observed	Any No. of Episodes Expected●	Mortality Ratio	Excess Death Rate
Malignant Neoplasms	7	6.18	113%	0.1	9	12.53	72%	−0.2
Diseases of Heart & Circulatory System	14	10.19	137	0.4	26	20.66	126	0.2
Accidents and Homicides	9	3.56	255	0.5	13	7.23	180	0.3
Suicide	9	1.10	820	0.7	17	2.23	760	0.7
Other Causes and Unknown†	12	4.88	245	0.7	24	9.91	240	0.6
Total	51	25.91	197	2.3	89	52.56	169	1.6

* Basis of expected mortality: 1955-60 Select Basic Table

† Includes, in Single Episode-2 disorders of nervous system, 3, of digestive system and 3, of respiratory system; in Any No. of Episodes — 5 disorders of nervous system, 7, of digestive system and 4, of respiratory system.

● Distribution of total expected deaths by Intercompany Medically Examined Standard Issues 1965-70

Cardiovascular Diseases

See Also

1. *1951 Impairment Study.* Chicago: Society of Actuaries (1954).
   A1-A6 Apex murmur, systolic, constant, not transmitted, found on examination (pp. 24-27)
   A7-A12 Apex murmur, systolic, constant, transmitted to the left, and/or mitral regurgitation, found on examination (pp. 28-31)
   A13-A18 Apex murmur, systolic, constant, and/or mitral regurgitation, found on examination, with history of rheumatism, chorea, tonsillitis, or other streptococcic infection (pp. 32-35)
   A19-A21 Apex murmur, systolic, inconstant, found on examination (pp. 36-38)
   A22-A24 Apex murmur, systolic, not clearly in (A1-A21) found on examination (pp. 38-39)
   A25-A27 Basic murmur, aortic area, systolic, constant, not transmitted, found on examination (pp. 39-42)
   A28-A30 Basic murmur, aortic area, systolic, transmitted upward, and/or aortic obstruction, found on examination (pp. 40-42)
   A31-A33 Basic murmur, pulmonic area, systolic, not transmitted, found on examination (pp. 42-44)
   A34-A36 Heart murmur, without details, or not clearly in (A1-A33), found on examination (pp. 44-46)
   A37-A39 Hypertrophy of the heart, no murmur, with X-ray or fluoroscope for diagnosis, found on examination (p. 47)
   A40-A42 Acute articular rheumatism (pp. 48-51)
   A43-A44 Chorea (pp. 52-53)
   A45-A46 Rapid pulse, found on examination (pp. 53-56)
   A47-A70 Intermittent or irregular pulse, found on examination (pp. 56-59)
   A71-A72 Paroxysmal tachycardia (p. 59)
2. I.M. Moriyama, D.E. Krueger, and J. Stamler, *Cardiovascular Diseases in the United States.* Cambridge, Mass.: Harvard University Press (1971).
3. S. Cobb, *The Frequency of the Rheumatic Diseases.* Cambridge, Mass.: Harvard University Press (1971).
4. B.S.L. Kidd and J.D. Keith, eds., *The Natural History and Progress in Treatment of Congenital Heart Defects.* Springfield, Ill.: Charles C. Thomas (1971).
5. J. Stamler, *Lectures on Preventive Cardiology.* New York: Grune and Stratton, Inc. (1967).
6. A.S. Nadas and D.C. Fyler, *Pediatric Cardiology,* 3rd ed. Philadelphia: W.B. Saunders Co. (1972).

CORONARY HEART DISEASE

§301–EARLY MORTALITY IN MYOCARDIAL INFARCTION

References: (1) W. J. Zukel, B. M. Cohen, T. W. Mattingly, and Z. Hrubec, "Survival Following First Diagnosis of Coronary Heart Disease," Am. Heart J., 78:159-170 (1969).

(2) E. Weinblatt, S. Shapiro, C. W. Frank, and R. V. Sager, "Prognosis of Men after First Myocardial Infarction: Mortality and First Recurrence in Relation to Selected Parameters," Am. J. Pub. Health, 58:1329-1347 (1968).

(3) E. Weinblatt, S. Shapiro, and C. W. Frank, "Prognosis of Women with Newly Diagnosed Coronary Heart Disease — A Comparison with Course of Disease Among Men," Am. J. Pub. Health, 63:577-593 (1973).

(4) T. Gordon and W. B. Kannel, "Premature Mortality from Coronary Heart Disease," J. Am. Med. Assoc., 215:1617-1625 (1971).

(5) S. Pell and C. A. D'Alonzo, "Immediate Mortality and Five-Year Survival of Employed Men with A First Myocardial Infarction," New Eng. J. Med., 270:915-922 (1964).

(6) G. H. Berryman, J. E. Bearman, and B. W. Brown, "Death Rate Among 795 Patients in First Year after Myocardial Infarction," J. Am. Med. Assoc., 197:906-908 (1966).

Subjects Studied: Members of five different series: (1) Army men with first MI diagnosed July 1943-December 1944, inclusive; (2,3) members covered in the Health Insurance Plan of Greater New York 1961-1968; (4) The Framingham Heart Study 1950-1964; (5) male employees of the duPont Company covered by health insurance 1956-1961; (6) male patients hospitalized in 13 cooperating V.A. hospitals 1957-1963. In the last study only deaths occurring after hospitalization were recorded. In all the other series available medical records were consulted for determination of all confirmed or probable cases of myocardial infarction (MI); in these series sudden deaths due to MI prior to hospitalization were therefore included. Additional information on subjects studied is contained in the descriptive material of (1) §303, (2) §313, (3) §314, (4) §302, and (5) §312.

Follow-up: All subjects in all studies were followed to death or beyond the arbitrary cut-off point for "early mortality," defined as 28 to 30 days following MI.

Results: Immediate mortality (within 24 hours after acute MI), shown in Table 301a, is of the order of 25 to 30 per hundred for men and 20 per hundred for women. Mortality is considerably higher for men under age 35 and age 55-64 than it is for the intermediate ages, where the minimum rate reported is below 20 per hundred. This is evident from comparison of the variation of mortality with age in the combined experience of the two series in the upper part of Table 301a. The Army Study contained an unusually high proportion of cases, 54 per cent, under age 40; the extremely large number of young men in military service during World War II counterbalanced the very low incidence of acute MI at the younger ages and provided a volume of experience not generally available. The age distribution in the New York H.I.P. Study was more typical of the general working population, with MI in men age 55-64 years constituting the largest group. Sudden death results in the Framingham Study were more detailed than in the other two studies: experience for "immediate mortality" (within one hour of the acute MI) was given, and various types of "coronary attack" were differentiated. It was possible, in the Framingham Study, to determine by ECG evidence the incidence of "silent" MI from its development in the interval between biennial examinations in subjects who had no history of a recognized attack. Such cases, by definition, involve 100 per cent survival from the acute attack to the time of the ECG at the next examination, and therefore tend to lower the overall mortality if they are detected and included in the count of attacks — this was not done in any of the other reports cited. Early mortality rates for "all coronary attacks" in the Framingham Study include cases of silent MI and attacks of coronary insufficiency (CI), recognized by symptoms and ECG evidence without evidence of infarction. Rates are also given omitting the cases of silent MI (rates for "clinical coronary attacks"). These rates are somewhat higher for men than for women, although the latter rates are based on relatively small numbers of cases with only 16 deaths.

Table 301b carries through early mortality experience in first MI cases to approximately 30 days after the attack. Extra deaths per 1000 have been estimated as a *daily* rate. Rates are by far the highest in the first day, and most of the deaths are sudden, occurring in minutes or less than one hour. Such deaths are inevitably excluded from all studies of hospitalized patients with coronary attack. Mortality tapers off rapidly after the very high initial rates, to an excess death rate between 1.5 and 3.2 per 1000 per day for all series except one. The very low EDR for Army men is only 0.3 per 1000 per day, but is based on only 4 deaths. After the first 24 hours mortality is lowest for the series with youngest average age (Army men) and highest in the series with the highest average age (V.A. Study).

EARLY MORTALITY IN CORONARY HEART ATTACK

Table 301a   Mortality within 24 Hours by Age and Type of Attack

Group*	Age	Number of Cases	No. of Early Deaths	Mortality Rate	Survival Rate
		ℓ	d	q=d/ℓ	p=1-q
U.S. Army Men, First MI 7/43—12/44	20-29	65	25	.385	.615
(All deaths, within 24 hours,	30-34	131	39	.298	.703
including 117 sudden deaths,	35-39	194	47	.242	.758
presumptive MI)	40-44	126	28	.222	.778
	45-49	105	13	.124	.876
	50 up	94	19	.202	.798
	All	715	171	.239	.761
H.I.P. of N.Y., Male Members, First MI	Under 45	99	21	.212	.788
1961-68 (All deaths within 24	45-54	334	93	.278	.722
hours, including sudden deaths)	55-64	448	157	.350	.650
	All	881	271	.308	.692
Framingham Study Sudden Deaths (Within 1 Hour), 1950-64					
Men, Clinical Coronary Attacks	35-64	175	36	.206	.794
Men, All Coronary Attacks	35-64	198	36	.182	.818
Women, Clinical Coronary Attacks	35-64	43	5	.116	.884
Women, All Coronary Attacks	35-64	49	5	.102	.898

Table 301b   Mortality by Duration within 1 Month (All Ages Combined)

Group*	Interval	No. Alive at Start of Int.	No. of Deaths	Interval Mort. Rate	Excess Death Rate per Day	Cumulative Surv. Rate
	t to t + Δ t	ℓ	d	q=d/ℓ	1000(q-q')	P†
U.S. Army Men 7/43—12/44	0-1d	715	171	.239	239	(1.000)
(First MI only)	1-2d	544	5	.009	9	.991
	2-7d	539	5	.009	1.9	.982
	7-30d	534	4	.007	0.3	.975
Framingham Men 1950-64	0-1hr	198	36	.182	(182)●	(1.000)
(First MI only)	1 hr-2d	162	15	.093	46	.907
	2-30d	147	6	.041	1.5	.869
Framingham Women 1950-64	0-1 hr	49	5	.102	(102)●	(1.000)
(First MI only)	1 hr-2d	44	3	.068	34	.932
	2-30d	41	2	.049	1.7	.886
H.I.P. of N.Y. 1961-65 (First MI)	0-1d	881	271	.308	308	(1.000)
Male Members	1-30d	610	46	.075	2.6	.925
	0-30d	881	317	.360	12	.640
Female Members	0-30d	172	64	.372	12	.628
duPont Male Employees 1956-61	0-1d	1331	336	.252	252	(1.000)
(First MI only)	1-30d	995	63	.063	2.2	.937
V.A. Hospitalized Men	Before Hosp.	—	—	—	—	(1.000)
(First MI only)	0-2d	795	53	.067	33	.933
	2-5d	742	36	.049	16	.887
	5-7d	706	13	.018	9	.871
	7-28d	693	47	.068	3.2	.812

*MI—Myocardial Infarction. CI—Coronary Insufficiency. "All Coronary Attacks"—Clinical MI and CI and Silent MI
†Excluding experience of first interval. P=1.000 at end of first interval
●Excess deaths per 1000 per hour. EDR per day not available. q' <.0005 all intervals

CORONARY HEART DISEASE

§302–CORONARY HEART DISEASE (FRAMINGHAM STUDY)

References: (1) J. Schiffman, "The Framingham Study. Section 25. Survival Following Certain Cardiovascular Events," Govt. Printing Office, Washington, D. C. (September 1970).
(2) W. B. Kannel and M. Feinleib, "Natural History of Angina Pectoris in The Framingham Study," Am. J. Card., 29:154-163 (1972).

Subjects Studied: Examinee-participants of the Framingham Heart Study (see §380) who, without prior evidence thereof, developed initial manifestations of coronary heart disease (CHD) between successive biennial examinations, in any of the following forms:
(1) *Myocardial infarction.* Recent MI was diagnosed on the basis of a record of characteristic serial ST/T changes with development of abnormal Q waves in the ECG or (beginning with Exam 4) a history of prolonged ischemic chest pain with abnormal serum enzyme levels, SGOT of 60 units or more, or LDH of 500 units or more, or autopsy evidence. An "old" MI was diagnosed when changes from the last biennial tracing showed development of abnormal Q wave or loss of R wave potential not otherwise explained, with or without a history of chest pain episode during the interval.
(2) *Angina pectoris, uncomplicated,* was defined as the occurrence of characteristic chest pain related to effort or emotion and relieved by nitroglycerine, in the biennial interval between examinations, with no other evidence of CHD in the same interval.
(3) *Coronary attack* was diagnosed on the basis of an attack of MI, or coronary insufficiency (prolonged ischemic chest pain accompanied by transient ST/T abnormalities but not by Q waves or serum enzyme changes), or sudden death (within one hour of onset of symptoms) if the cause of death could not be attributed to some potentially lethal disease other than CHD.

Follow-up: The biennial examination schedule served as the time-frame for follow-up for new CHD events and deaths occurring in the two-year interval between successive examinations, instead of the exact date or year of the occurrence (see §380). According to Reference (2), loss to follow-up amounted to less than 2 per cent of the entrants.

Results: Experience for subjects experiencing a documented myocardial infarction is shown in Tables 302a-b by duration, all ages combined, and in Table 302c by age, first five years combined. Comparative mortality by EDR was heavier for females than for males, heavier for those over 65, and in the first year after the attack for both sexes. For all males the mortality ratio was 1290 per cent in the first year, and ranged from 197 to 485 per cent in succeeding intervals; the corresponding figures for all females were 3100 per cent in the first year and 275 to 1130 per cent thereafter. It is difficult to evaluate any trend by duration because of the small numbers of deaths, especially in the female subjects. By age, EDR for females under 65 at 81 per 1000 per year exceeded the male EDR in the two age groups under 65, but for those age 65 up, the male EDR of 163 was greater than the female EDR at 131. Cumulative survival ratios for females at five years were below those of males in all categories except subjects age 65 up.

Mortality ratio and EDR were much lighter in subjects with angina pectoris, as is evident from Tables 302d-f. The average EDR of 15 to 13 extra deaths per 1000 per year, males and females separately, is well below the EDR's for Interval 2 through 5 in the myocardial infarction cases (Table 302a). Comparison is not possible for Interval No. 1 because no experience is available for the angina pectoris cases until the biennial examination at which the history was first recorded. Survival ratios are correspondingly higher in the subjects with angina.

Mortality was higher for the coronary attack experience (Tables 302g-i) than it was for the cases with myocardial infarction during the first interval, with EDR 347 versus 148 for males, and 424 versus 383 for females. This can be attributed to inclusion of sudden deaths among the coronary attack cases, but not among the MI cases, because documentation by ECG or laboratory tests was not possible for patients who succumbed in less than one hour (there was no time for hospitalization). Mortality in subsequent intervals did not differ markedly from mortality in the MI cases, but cumulative survival ratios were lower because of the high mortality in the first interval.

MYOCARDIAL INFARCTION

Table 302a Observed Data and Comparative Experience by Duration - All Ages Combined

Sex and Interval* No. Start-End	No. Alive at Start of Interval	Deaths in Interval	Interval Mortality Rate	Mortality Ratio Interval	Mortality Ratio Cumulative	Survival Ratio Interval	Survival Ratio Cumulative	Excess Death Rate
i t to $t+\Delta t$	ℓ	d	$q_i = d/\ell$	$100\, q_i/q_i'$	$100\, Q/Q'$	$100\, p_i/p_i'$	$100\, P/P'$	$1000(\check{q}-\check{q}')$
Male								
1 0-1 yr	188	30	.160	1290%	1290%	85.1%	85.1%	148
2 1-3	158	13	.082	275	545	94.6	80.5	27
3 3-5	119	19	.160	485	480	86.9	69.9	66
4 5-7.	75	11	.147	410	420	88.5	61.9	58
5 7-9	53	5	.094	197	335	95.1	58.9	24
0-9	188	78	.415	335	335	58.9	58.9	63
Female								
1 0-1 yr	48	14	.292	3100%	3100%	71.5%	71.5%	283
2 1-3	34	2	.059	275	1085	96.2	68.8	19
3 3-5	23	3	.130	515	760	89.2	61.4	54
4 5-7	16	2	.125	490	620	89.8	55.1	52
5 7-9	9	3	.333	1130	620	68.7	37.8	168
0-9	48	24	.500	620	620	37.8	37.8	104

Table 302b Derived Mortality and Survival Data

Sex and Interval* No. Start-End	Observed Survival Rate Cumulative	Observed Survival Rate Interval	Observed Survival Rate Ave. Ann.	Observed Ave. Ann. Mort. Rate	Expected† Survival Rate Cumulative	Expected† Survival Rate Interval	Expected† Survival Rate Ave. Ann.	Expected† Ave. Ann. Mort. Rate
i t to $t+\Delta t$	P	p_i	$\check{p}$	$\check{q}$	P'	p_i'	$\check{p}'$	$\check{q}'$
Male								
1 0-1 yr	.840	.840	.840	.160	.9876	.9876	.9876	.0124
2 1-3	.771	.918	.958	.042	.9581	.9701	.9849	.0151
3 3-5	.648	.840	.917	.083	.9265	.9670	.9834	.0166
4 5-7	.553	.853	.924	.076	.8933	.9642	.9819	.0181
5 7-9	.501	.906	.952	.048	.8507	.9523	.9759	.0241
Female								
1 0-1 yr	.708	.708	.708	.292	.9907	.9907	.9907	.0093
2 1-3	.667	.941	.970	.030	.9693	.9784	.9891	.0109
3 3-5	.580	.870	.933	.067	.9449	.9748	.9873	.0127
4 5-7	.507	.875	.935	.065	.9207	.9744	.9871	.0129
5 7-9	.338	.667	.817	.183	.8934	.9704	.9851	.0149

Table 302c Comparative Survival Experience by Age Group - First 5 Years Combined

Sex and Age Group	No. Alive at Start of Interval	Deaths during Interval	Survival Rate Observed	Survival Rate Expected†	Cumulative Survival Ratio	Estimated Average Ann. Mort. Rate Observed	Estimated Average Ann. Mort. Rate Expected†	Mortality Ratio	Excess Death Rate
	ℓ	d	P	P'	$100\, P/P'$	$\check{q}$	$\check{q}'$	$100\, \check{q}/\check{q}'$	$1000(\check{q}-\check{q}')$
Male									
Under 55	59	14	.739	.9673	76.4%	.059	.0066	895%	52
55-64	94	26	.708	.9211	76.8	.067	.0163	410	51
65-74	35	22	.339	.8520	39.8	.195	.0315	620	163
All Ages	188	62	.648	.9264	70.0	.083	.0152	545	68
Female									
Under 65	33	12	.628	.9595	65.5%	.089	.0082	1090%	81
65-74	15	7	.445	.9080	49.0	.150	.0191	785	131
All Ages	48	19	.580	.9449	61.4	.103	.0113	910	92

*Interval No. 1 ends with biennial exam next after first appearance of Myocardial Infarction.
 It has an average duration of 1 year (range less than 1 month to 23 months).
†Basis of expected mortality: Framingham subjects without Myocardial Infarction

ANGINA PECTORIS, WITHOUT OTHER CHD

Table 302d Observed Data and Comparative Experience by Duration - All Ages Combined

Sex and Interval* No.	Start-End	No. Alive at Start of Interval	Deaths in Interval	Interval Mortality Rate	Mortality Ratio Interval	Cumulative	Survival Ratio Interval	Cumulative	Excess Death Rate
i	t to t + Δ t	ℓ	d	$q_i = d/\ell$	100 q_i/q_i'	100 Q/Q'	100 p_i/p_i'	100 P/P'	1000($\check{q}$-$\check{q}'$)
	Male								
1	0-1 yr	—Experience Not Available—		.050	153%	153%	98.2%	98.2%	8.6
2	1-3	100	5	.050	153%	153%	98.2%	98.2%	8.6
3	3-5	81	5	.062	169	160	97.4	95.6	13
4	5-7	65	4	.062	150	153	97.9	93.7	10
5	7-9	47	6	.128	255	179	91.8	86.0	41
	1-9	100	20	.200	179	179	86.0	86.0	15
	Female								
1	0-1 yr	—Experience Not Available—							
2	1-3	104	5	.048	230%	230%	97.2%	97.2%	14
3	3-5	85	4	.047	190	205	97.7	95.0	12
4	5-7	65	2	.031	115	171	99.6	94.6	2.5
5	7-9	48	4	.083	295	200	94.3	89.2	29
	1-9	104	15	.144	200	200	89.2	89.2	13

Table 302e Derived Mortality and Survival Data

Sex and Interval* No.	Start-End	Observed Survival Rate Cumulative	Interval	Ave. Ann.	Ave. Ann. Mort. Rate	Expected† Survival Rate Cumulative	Interval	Ave. Ann.	Ave. Ann. Mort. Rate
i	t to t + Δ t	P	p_i	$\check{p}$	$\check{q}$	P'	p_i'	$\check{p}'$	$\check{q}'$
	Male								
1	0-1 yr	—Experience Not Available—							
2	1-3	.950	.950	.975	.025	.9674	.9674	.9836	.0164
3	3-5	.891	.938	.969	.031	.9319	.9633	.9815	.0185
4	5-7	.837	.938	.969	.031	.8933	.9586	.9791	.0209
5	7-9	.730	.872	.934	.066	.8488	.9502	.9748	.0252
	Female								
1	0-1 yr	—Experience Not Available—							
2	1-3	.952	.952	.976	.024	.9793	.9793	.9896	.0104
3	3-5	.907	.953	.976	.024	.9551	.9753	.9876	.0124
4	5-7	.879	.969	.984	.016	.9294	.9731	.9865	.0135
5	7-9	.806	.917	.958	.042	.9035	.9721	.9860	.0140

Table 302f Comparative Survival Experience by Age Group - First 4 Available Years Combined

Sex and Age Group	No. Alive at Start of Interval	Deaths during Interval	Survival Rate Observed	Expected†	Cumulative Survival Ratio	Estimated Average Ann. Mort. Rate Observed	Expected†	Mortality Ratio	Excess Death Rate
	ℓ	d	P	P'	100 P/P'	$\check{q}$	$\check{q}'$	100 $\check{q}/\check{q}'$	1000($\check{q}$-$\check{q}'$)
Male									
Under 55	30	3	.900	.9720	92.6%	.026	.0071	365%	19
55-74	70	7	.885	.9129	96.9	.030	.0225	133	7.5
All Ages	100	10	.891	.9319	95.6	.028	.0175	160	10
Female									
Under 65	75	4	.944	.9658	97.7%	.014	.0087	161%	5.3
65-74	29	5	.802	.9235	86.8	.054	.0197	275	34
All Ages	104	9	.907	.9551	95.0	.024	.0114	210	13

*Interval No. 1 ends with biennial examination next after first appearance of angina pectoris without other evidence of CHD. Experience is restricted to survivors at this examination (end of Interval 1 or beginning of Interval 2).

†Basis of expected mortality: Framingham subjects without angina pectoris

CORONARY ATTACK

Table 302g Observed Data and Comparative Experience by Duration - All Ages Combined

Sex and Interval*		No. Alive at Start of Interval	Deaths in Interval	Interval Mortality Rate	Mortality Ratio		Survival Ratio		Excess Death Rate
No.	Start-End				Interval	Cumulative	Interval	Cumulative	
i	t to t + Δ t	ℓ	d	$q_i=d/\ell$	$100\,q_i/q_i'$	$100\,Q/Q'$	$100\,p_i/p_i'$	$100\,P/P'$	$1000(\breve{q}-\breve{q}')$
	Male								
1	0-1 yr	284	101	.356	4100%	4100%	65.0%	65.0%	347
2	1-3	183	14	.076	260	1060	95.1	61.9	24
3	3-5	139	21	.151	455	705	87.8	54.3	62
4	5-7	92	10	.109	300	530	92.5	50.2	38
5	7-9	65	8	.123	275	420	91.8	46.2	41
	0-9	284	154	.542	420	420	46.2	46.2	110
	Female								
1	0-1 yr	95	41	.432	5400%	5400%	57.3%	57.3%	424
2	1-3	54	3	.056	250	1540	96.6	55.4	17
3	3-5	39	3	.077	320	940	94.6	52.4	27
4	5-7	27	2	.074	290	700	95.0	49.8	25
5	7-9	15	3	.200	660	600	82.5	41.0	91
	0-9	95	52	.547	600	600	41.0	41.0	132

Table 302h Derived Mortality and Survival Data

Sex and Interval*		Observed				Expected†			
		Survival Rate			Ave. Ann. Mort. Rate	Survival Rate			Ave. Ann. Mort. Rate
No.	Start-End	Cumulative	Interval	Ave. Ann.		Cumulative	Interval	Ave. Ann.	
i	t to t + Δ t	P	p_i	$\breve{p}$	$\breve{q}$	P'	p_i'	$\breve{p}'$	$\breve{q}'$
	Male								
1	0-1 yr	.644	.644	.644	.356	.9913	.9913	.9913	.0087
2	1-3	.595	.923	.961	.039	.9617	.9701	.9849	.0151
3	3-5	.505	.849	.921	.079	.9298	.9669	.9833	.0167
4	5-7	.450	.891	.944	.056	.8960	.9636	.9816	.0184
5	7-9	.395	.877	.936	.064	.8559	.9553	.9774	.0226
	Female								
1	0-1 yr	.568	.568	.568	.432	.9920	.9920	.9920	.0080
2	1-3	.537	.944	.972	.028	.9699	.9777	.9888	.0112
3	3-5	.496	.923	.961	.039	.9464	.9758	.9878	.0122
4	5-7	.459	.926	.962	.038	.9225	.9747	.9873	.0127
5	7-9	.367	.800	.894	.106	.8945	.9697	.9847	.0153

Table 302i Comparative Survival Experience by Age Group - First 5 Years Combined

Sex and Age Group	No. Alive at Start of Interval	Deaths during Interval	Survival Rate		Cumulative Survival Ratio	Estimated Average Ann. Mort. Rate		Mortality Ratio	Excess Death Rate
			Observed	Expected†		Observed	Expected†		
	ℓ	d	P	P'	$100\,P/P'$	$\breve{q}$	$\breve{q}'$	$100\,\breve{q}/\breve{q}'$	$1000(\breve{q}-\breve{q}')$
Male									
Under 55	89	31	.633	.9687	65.3%	.087	.0063	1380%	81
55-64	147	74	.485	.9258	52.4	.135	.0153	880	120
65-74	48	31	.331	.8475	39.1	.198	.0326	605	165
All Ages	284	136	.505	.9298	54.3	.128	.0145	885	114
Female									
Under 65	54	21	.608	.9594	63.4%	.095	.0083	1140%	87
65-74	41	26	.332	.9184	36.1	.198	.0169	1170	181
All Ages	95	47	.496	.9464	52.4	.131	.0110	1190	120

*Interval No. 1 ends with biennial exam next after first Coronary Attack (MI, Coronary Insufficiency or Sudden CHD death). It has an average duration of 1 year (range less than 1 month to 23 months).
†Basis of expected mortality: Framingham subjects with no Coronary Attack

CORONARY HEART DISEASE

§303–FIRST DIAGNOSIS OF CORONARY HEART DISEASE

References: (1) W. J. Zukel, B. M. Cohen, T. W. Mattingly, and Z. Hrubec, "Survival Following First Diagnosis of Coronary Heart Disease," Am. Heart J., 78:159-170 (1969).
(2) Supplementary material supplied by authors (1970).

Subjects Studied: White male Army personnel admitted to Army hospitals for coronary heart disease from July 1943 through December 1944. In order to provide uniform up-to-date classification of the material, diagnoses made at original Army hospitalization were carefully reviewed. This screening resulted in the exclusion of more than 50 per cent of the original cases from the "confirmed" cases retained in the study. The number of patients by age at date of admission to Army hospital, and their distribution, according to the indicated confirmed diagnostic class, viz. MI, CO, CT (Myocardial Infarction; Coronary Occlusion; Coronary Thrombosis), and AP, CI (Angina Pectoris; Coronary Insufficiency):

Diagnostic Class	Age Group-Number and (Per Cent)					
	to 34	35-39	40-44	45-49	50-64	Total
MI, CO, CT	151 (25.2)	160 (26.8)	107 (17.9)	95 (15.9)	85 (14.2)	598 (100.0)
AP, CI	57 (16.2)	96 (27.3)	92 (26.1)	63 (17.9)	44 (12.5)	352 (100.0)*

*excluding one of unknown age

Sudden deaths, occurring before hospitalization could be accomplished, or within 24 hours of admission, were subjected to the same careful diagnostic review and classification. The above totals include 56 such early deaths for which autopsy provided confirmation of the diagnosis of an acute coronary episode. Not included were an additional 117 sudden deaths in white males, classified as a separate group. Although an acute coronary episode appeared to be the most likely explanation in most of these, a conclusive diagnosis could not be established.

Follow-up: Studies indicate that the ascertainment of the mortality rates among World War II veterans based on records of the Veterans Administration is 98 per cent complete. Inasmuch as about one-third of the observed deaths in this investigation occurred during Army service and were completely reported, it is probable that the maximum error in this follow-up is less than 2 per cent.

Results: Two tabulations of mortality experience for the first 24 hours are shown in Table 303a: one including among the deaths the 117 cases for which diagnosis was not definite; and the other omitting these cases. Rates of death immediately following attack were extremely high, running from 124 to 385 per 1000 in the first day, with all sudden deaths included, and from 32 to 132 per 1000 when only cases with confirmed diagnoses were counted. Younger ages experienced highest levels of mortality; the level was lowest in age group 45-49, and rose again for ages 50 and over. Experience for the 30-day period following onset is shown for the 598 confirmed MI, CO, CT cases in Table 303b, by age group and for periods: first day (Interval No. 1); remainder of first week (Interval No. 2); balance of month (Interval No. 3). The excess number of deaths decreased abruptly, from an average of 90 per 1000 for the first day, all ages combined, to 3 for Interval No. 2, and to 0.3 for Interval No. 3. All age groups manifested this feature in varying degrees. These EDR values are on a per day basis; even 0.3 represents over 100 deaths per 1000 on an annual basis – a very high mortality rate. Separate data are not shown for the AP, CI group in the first 30 days as only two deaths were recorded, both of which occurred in the first day.

Mortality results for the several age groups in the indicated "confirmed" diagnostic classes are presented in Tables 303c-303f for the last eleven months of the first year and for varying intervals thereafter over the 15-year period following date of hospital admission. These results are compared with those which would have been experienced according to U. S. white male rates from 1945 to 1962.

FIRST DIAGNOSIS OF CORONARY HEART DISEASE: MI, CO, CT

Results (MI, CO, CT): Mortality rates at all ages remain high in the months following onset but drop below the rates experienced immediately following attack. On the first anniversary of the initial date, between 80 per cent and 82 per cent of those stricken survived at all ages except in the 45-49 age group in which 93 per cent remained alive. After the first year a persisting annual mortality risk of about 45 deaths per 1000 in excess of the general mortality among U. S. white males continues more or less uniformly. Among cases escaping death in the first month and age 44 or younger at time of attack the survivors at the end of 15 years represented between 43 and 50 per cent of those expected to survive, cases between 45 and 49, about 52 per cent, and individuals over age 49 at onset, about 43 per cent.

Results (AP, CI): The number of deaths developing among this class of cases was relatively small especially in the period from one month to one year (when 6 died among all exposed to risk). Due to the small number of deaths caution should be exercised in interpreting the results. However, it appears undeniable that the early risk of death following hospitalization for angina pectoris and coronary insufficiency is much lighter than for the other diagnostic classification. The risk of death after the first year is significantly higher than that expected in the general population. For this diagnostic class, on the average, during the last 14 years of observation, deaths were 19 per 1000 higher annually than indicated in corresponding general mortality rates.

Table 303a   Mortality within First 24 Hours (MI, CO, CT)

Age Group	Including 117 Sudden Deaths				Excluding 117 Sudden Deaths			
	No. Alive at Start of Interval	Deaths in Interval	Mortality per 1000*	Survival Rate	No. Alive at Start of Interval	Deaths in Interval	Mortality per 1000*	Survival Rate
	ℓ	d	1000q	p	ℓ	d	1000q	p
Under 30	65	25	385	.625	45	5	111	.889
30 - 34	131	39	297	.703	106	14	132	.868
35 - 39	194	47	242	.758	160	13	81	.919
40 - 44	126	28	222	.778	107	9	84	.916
45 - 49	105	13	124	.876	95	3	32	.968
50 up	94	19	202	.798	85	10	118	.882
All Ages	715	171	239	.761	598	54	90	.910

Table 303b   Comparative Mortality within 1 Month (MI, CO, CT by Age, Sudden Deaths Excluded)

Age Group	Interval No.	Interval Start-End	No. Alive at Start of Interval	Deaths in Interval	Interval Mortality Rate	Cumulative Survival Rate	Days/Interval Exposed to Risk	Excess Death Rate per day†
	i	t to t + Δt	ℓ	d	q_i	P	Δt	EDR
Under 35	1	0 - 1 da	151	19	.1258	.874	1	126
	2	1 - 7 da	132	3	.0227	.854	6	4
	3	7 - 30 da	129	1	.0077	.848	23	0.3
35 - 39	1	0 - 1 da	160	13	.0812	.919	1	81
	2	1 - 7 da	147	4	.0272	.894	6	5
	3	7 - 30 da	143	1	.0069	.888	23	0.3
40 - 44	1	0 - 1 da	107	9	.0841	.916	1	84
	2	1 - 7 da	98	1	.0102	.906	6	1.7
	3	7 - 30 da	97	1	.0103	.897	23	0.4
45 - 49	1	0 - 1 da	95	3	.0315	.968	1	32
	2	1 - 7 da	92	0	.0000	.968	6	0.0
	3	7 - 30 da	92	1	.0108	.958	23	0.5
50 up	1	0 - 1 da	85	10	.1176	.882	1	118
	2	1 - 7 da	75	2	.0266	.859	6	4
	3	7 - 30 da	73	0	.0000	.859	23	0.0
All Ages	1	0 - 1 da	598	54	.0903	.910	1	91
	2	1 - 7 da	544	10	.0183	.893	6	3
	3	7 - 30 da	534	4	.0074	.886	23	0.3

*1000q = EDR (excess deaths/1000/day) since q' is insignificantly small for 1 day (Σd' < 0.02 all cases)

†EDR = 1000q_i'/Δt, since q_i' is insignificantly small for 30 days (Σd' < 0.3 for all cases)

CORONARY HEART DISEASE

Table 303c   Observed Data and Comparative Experience by Age Group and Duration — MI, CO, CT (First Diagnosis of CHD)

Age Group	Interval		No. Alive at Start of Interval	Deaths in Interval		Mortality Ratio		Survival Ratio		Excess Death Rate
	No.	Start-End		Obs.	Exp.*	Interval	Cumulative	Interval	Cumulative	
	i	t to t + Δt	ℓ	d	d'	100 d/d'	100 Q/Q'	100 p/p'	100 P/P'	1000(d-d')/E
Under 35	1	1 mo - 1 yr	128	6	0.28	2100%	2100%	95.5%	95.5%	49
	2	1 - 2 yrs	122	8	0.32	2500	2300	93.6	89.5	63
	3	2 - 3 yrs	114	6	0.30	2000	2100	94.9	85.0	50
	4	3 - 5 yrs	108	2	0.58	345	1350	99.4	83.9	7
	5	5 - 7 yrs	106	6	0.61	985	1190	97.4	79.6	26
	6	7 - 10 yrs	100	18	1.01	1780	1270	93.9	66.0	61
	7	10 - 15 yrs	82	21	1.89	1110	1030	94.7	50.2	53
		1 - 15 yrs	122	61	4.71	1300				44
35 - 39	1	1 mo - 1 yr	142	12	0.48	2500	2500	91.8	91.8	88
	2	1 - 2 yrs	130	3	0.52	575	1430	98.1	90.1	19
	3	2 - 3 yrs	127	4	0.51	785	1180	97.3	87.6	27
	4	3 - 5 yrs	123	13	1.12	1160	1110	95.0	79.1	50
	5	5 - 7 yrs	110	9	1.11	810	955	96.3	73.3	37
	6	7 - 10 yrs	101	22	1.87	1180	920	92.7	58.4	72
	7	10 - 15 yrs	79	17	3.38	505	635	96.1	48.0	39
		1 - 15 yrs	130	68	8.51	800				45
40 - 44	1	1 mo - 1 yr	96	8	0.49	1630	1630	92.2	92.2	85
	2	1 - 2 yrs	88	4	0.53	755	1140	96.1	88.5	39
	3	2 - 3 yrs	84	5	0.52	960	1040	94.6	83.7	53
	4	3 - 5 yrs	79	8	1.09	735	845	95.5	76.3	45
	5	5 - 7 yrs	71	8	1.13	710	745	95.0	68.8	50
	6	7 - 10 yrs	63	10	1.86	540	600	95.3	59.6	46
	7	10 - 15 yrs	53	17	3.52	485	460	93.9	43.4	61
		1 - 15 yrs	88	52	8.65	600				51
45 - 49	1	1 mo - 1 yr	91	3	0.71	425	425	97.5	97.5	27
	2	1 - 2 yrs	88	4	0.82	490	455	96.4	93.9	36
	3	2 - 3 yrs	84	3	0.83	360	410	97.4	91.4	26
	4	3 - 5 yrs	81	7	1.85	380	380	96.7	85.5	33
	5	5 - 7 yrs	74	10	1.87	535	405	94.2	75.8	57
	6	7 - 10 yrs	64	11	2.96	370	360	95.4	65.8	45
	7	10 - 15 yrs	53	15	5.31	280	285	95.6	52.5	43
		1 - 15 yrs	88	50	13.64	365				42
50 up	1	1 mo - 1 yr	73	3	1.03	290	290	97.3	97.3	29
	2	1 - 2 yrs	70	6	1.16	515	405	92.9	90.4	69
	3	2 - 3 yrs	64	2	1.09	185	320	98.6	89.1	14
	4	3 - 5 yrs	62	7	2.41	290	295	96.1	82.2	39
	5	5 - 7 yrs	55	10	2.46	405	305	92.6	70.4	73
	6	7 - 10 yrs	45	8	3.62	220	250	96.4	63.0	36
	7	10 - 15 yrs	37	16	6.60	240	210	92.9	43.6	69
		1 - 15 yrs	70	49	17.34	285				53

*Basis of expected mortality: U.S. White Males progressive rates 1944-1962

FIRST DIAGNOSIS OF CORONARY HEART DISEASE: MI, CO, CT

Table 303d Derived Mortality and Survival Data by Age Group and Duration

Age Group	No.	Start-End	Observed Rates Average Annual† Mortality $\check{q}$	Survival $\check{p}$	Cumulative Survival P	Mortality Q	Expected Rates* Average Annual† Mortality $\check{q}'$	Survival $\check{p}'$	Cumulative Survival P'	Mortality Q'
	i	t to t + Δt								
Under 35	1	1 mo - 1 yr	.047	.953	.953	.047	.0022	.9978	.9978	.0022
	2	1 - 2 yrs	.066	.934	.891	.109	.0026	.9974	.9952	.0048
	3	2 - 3 yrs	.053	.947	.844	.156	.0026	.9974	.9926	.0074
	4	3 - 5 yrs	.009	.991	.828	.172	.0027	.9973	.9873	.0127
	5	5 - 7 yrs	.029	.971	.781	.219	.0029	.9971	.9816	.0184
	6	7 - 10 yrs	.064	.936	.641	.359	.0034	.9966	.9717	.0283
	7	10 - 15 yrs	.057	.943	.477	.523	.0046	.9954	.9493	.0507
35 - 39	1	1 mo - 1 yr	.085	.915	.915	.085	.0034	.9966	.9966	.0034
	2	1 - 2 yrs	.023	.977	.894	.106	.0040	.9960	.9926	.0074
	3	2 - 3 yrs	.031	.969	.866	.134	.0040	.9960	.9886	.0114
	4	3 - 5 yrs	.054	.946	.775	.225	.0045	.9955	.9797	.0203
	5	5 - 7 yrs	.042	.958	.711	.289	.0050	.9950	.9698	.0302
	6	7 - 10 yrs	.079	.921	.556	.444	.0062	.9938	.9518	.0482
	7	10 - 15 yrs	.047	.953	.437	.563	.0087	.9913	.9111	.0889
40 - 44	1	1 mo - 1 yr	.083	.917	.917	.083	.0051	.9949	.9949	.0051
	2	1 - 2 yrs	.045	.955	.875	.125	.0060	.9940	.9890	.0110
	3	2 - 3 yrs	.060	.940	.823	.177	.0062	.9938	.9829	.0171
	4	3 - 5 yrs	.052	.948	.740	.260	.0069	.9931	.9693	.0307
	5	5 - 7 yrs	.058	.942	.656	.344	.0080	.9920	.9538	.0462
	6	7 - 10 yrs	.056	.944	.552	.448	.0099	.9901	.9256	.0744
	7	10 - 15 yrs	.074	.926	.375	.625	.0136	.9864	.8642	.1358
45 - 49	1	1 mo - 1 yr	.033	.967	.967	.033	.0078	.9922	.9922	.0078
	2	1 - 2 yrs	.045	.955	.923	.077	.0093	.9907	.9830	.0170
	3	2 - 3 yrs	.036	.964	.890	.110	.0099	.9901	.9733	.0267
	4	3 - 5 yrs	.044	.956	.813	.187	.0115	.9885	.9511	.0489
	5	5 - 7 yrs	.070	.930	.703	.297	.0127	.9873	.9271	.0729
	6	7 - 10 yrs	.061	.939	.582	.418	.0157	.9843	.8841	.1159
	7	10 - 15 yrs	.064	.936	.418	.582	.0209	.9791	.7955	.2045
50 up	1	1 mo - 1 yr	.041	.959	.959	.041	.0141	.9859	.9859	.0141
	2	1 - 2 yrs	.086	.914	.877	.123	.0166	.9834	.9696	.0304
	3	2 - 3 yrs	.031	.969	.849	.151	.0171	.9829	.9530	.0470
	4	3 - 5 yrs	.058	.942	.753	.247	.0196	.9804	.9160	.0840
	5	5 - 7 yrs	.095	.905	.616	.384	.0226	.9774	.8750	.1250
	6	7 - 10 yrs	.063	.937	.507	.493	.0276	.9724	.8046	.1954
	7	10 - 15 yrs	.107	.893	.288	.712	.0385	.9615	.6610	.3390

*Basis of expected mortality: U.S. White Males progressive rates 1944-1962
†Rates for intervals 1 month-1 year: over interval, not annual

CORONARY HEART DISEASE

Table 303e   Observed Data and Comparative Experience by Age Group and Duration — AP, CI (First Diagnosis of CHD)

Age Group	Interval No.	Interval Start-End	No. Alive at Start of Interval	Deaths in Interval Obs.	Deaths in Interval Exp.*	Mortality Ratio Interval	Mortality Ratio Cumulative	Survival Ratio Interval	Survival Ratio Cumulative	Excess Death Rate
	i	t to t + Δt	ℓ	d	d'	100 d/d'	100 Q/Q'	100 p/p'	100 P/P'	1000(d-d')/E
Under 35	1	1 mo - 1 yr	57	2	0.126	1590%	1590%	96.7%	96.7%	36
	2	1 - 2 yrs	55	1	0.141	710	1100	98.5	95.2	15
	3	2 - 3 yrs	54	1	0.140	715	945	98.5	93.7	15
	4	3 - 5 yrs	53	1	0.28	360	695	99.4	92.4	7
	5	5 - 7 yrs	52	4	0.30	1330	860	96.4	85.8	36
	6	7 - 10 yrs	48	4	0.48	830	805	97.4	79.4	25
	7	10 - 15 yrs	44	5	1.01	495	625	98.1	72.1	19
		1 - 15 yrs	55	16	2.35	680				20
35 - 39	1	1 mo - 1 yr	96	1	0.33	305	305	99.3	99.3	8
	2	1 - 2 yrs	95	1	0.38	265	285	99.4	98.6	6
	3	2 - 3 yrs	94	1	0.38	265	270	99.3	98.0	7
	4	3 - 5 yrs	93	5	0.85	590	410	97.7	93.6	23
	5	5 - 7 yrs	88	7	0.89	785	515	96.4	87.0	36
	6	7 - 10 yrs	81	6	1.50	400	455	98.1	82.1	19
	7	10 - 15 yrs	75	5	3.21	156	305	99.5	80.0	5
		1 - 15 yrs	95	25	7.21	345				16
40 - 44	1	1 mo - 1 yr	91	2	0.46	435	435	98.3	98.3	18
	2	1 - 2 yrs	89	0	0.53	0	200	100.6	98.9	−6
	3	2 - 3 yrs	89	8	0.55	1450	645	91.6	90.5	84
	4	3 - 5 yrs	81	0	1.12	0	360	100.7	91.8	−7
	5	5 - 7 yrs	81	6	1.29	465	380	97.0	86.4	30
	6	7 - 10 yrs	75	6	2.21	270	325	98.3	81.9	17
	7	10 - 15 yrs	69	12	4.58	260	275	97.6	72.4	24
		1 - 15 yrs	89	32	10.28	310				21
45 - 49	1	1 mo - 1 yr	62	1	0.48	210	210	99.2	99.2	9
	2	1 - 2 yrs	61	1	0.57	175	188	99.3	98.5	7
	3	2 - 3 yrs	60	2	0.59	340	240	97.7	96.2	23
	4	3 - 5 yrs	58	3	1.32	225	230	98.5	93.3	15
	5	5 - 7 yrs	55	3	1.39	215	220	98.5	90.5	15
	6	7 - 10 yrs	52	5	2.41	205	210	98.2	85.7	17
	7	10 - 15 yrs	47	11	4.71	235	205	96.8	73.0	31
		1 - 15 yrs	61	25	10.99	225				21
50 up	1	1 mo - 1 yr	45	0	0.64	0	0	101.4	101.4	−16
	2	1 - 2 yrs	45	3	0.75	400	220	94.9	96.2	50
	3	2 - 3 yrs	42	1	0.72	139	189	99.3	95.6	7
	4	3 - 5 yrs	41	1	1.59	63	132	100.8	97.1	−7
	5	5 - 7 yrs	40	5	1.79	280	178	95.7	88.9	42
	6	7 - 10 yrs	35	4	2.82	142	159	98.7	85.6	12
	7	10 - 15 yrs	31	10	5.53	181	157	96.2	70.7	36
		1 - 15 yrs	45	24	13.20	182				24

*Basis of expected mortality: U.S. White Males progressive rates 1944-1962

FIRST DIAGNOSIS OF CORONARY HEART DISEASE: AP, CI

Table 303f   Derived Mortality and Survival Data by Age Group and Duration

Age Group	Interval		Observed Rates				Expected Rates*			
			Average Annual†		Cumulative		Average Annual†		Cumulative	
	No.	Start-End	Mortality	Survival	Survival	Mortality	Mortality	Survival	Survival	Mortality
	i	t to $t + \Delta t$	$\check{q}$	$\check{p}$	P	Q	$\check{q}'$	$\check{p}'$	P'	Q'
Under 35	1	1 mo - 1 yr	.035	.965	.965	.035	.0022	.9978	.9978	.0022
	2	1 - 2 yrs	.018	.982	.947	.053	.0026	.9974	.9952	.0048
	3	2 - 3 yrs	.018	.982	.930	.070	.0026	.9974	.9926	.0074
	4	3 - 5 yrs	.009	.991	.912	.088	.0027	.9973	.9873	.0127
	5	5 - 7 yrs	.039	.961	.842	.158	.0029	.9971	.9816	.0184
	6	7 - 10 yrs	.029	.971	.772	.228	.0034	.9966	.9717	.0283
	7	10 - 15 yrs	.024	.976	.684	.316	.0046	.9954	.9493	.0507
35 - 39	1	1 mo - 1 yr	.010	.990	.990	.010	.0034	.9966	.9966	.0034
	2	1 - 2 yrs	.010	.990	.979	.021	.0040	.9960	.9926	.0074
	3	2 - 3 yrs	.011	.989	.969	.031	.0040	.9960	.9886	.0114
	4	3 - 5 yrs	.027	.973	.917	.083	.0045	.9955	.9797	.0203
	5	5 - 7 yrs	.041	.959	.844	.156	.0050	.9950	.9698	.0302
	6	7 - 10 yrs	.025	.975	.781	.219	.0062	.9938	.9518	.0482
	7	10 - 15 yrs	.014	.986	.729	.271	.0087	.9913	.9111	.0889
40 - 45	1	1 mo - 1 yr	.022	.978	.978	.022	.0051	.9949	.9949	.0051
	2	1 - 2 yrs	.000	1.000	.978	.022	.0060	.9940	.9890	.0110
	3	2 - 3 yrs	.090	.910	.890	.110	.0062	.9938	.9829	.0171
	4	3 - 5 yrs	.000	1.000	.890	.110	.0069	.9931	.9693	.0307
	5	5 - 7 yrs	.038	.962	.824	.176	.0080	.9920	.9538	.0462
	6	7 - 10 yrs	.027	.973	.758	.242	.0099	.9901	.9256	.0744
	7	10 - 15 yrs	.037	.963	.626	.374	.0136	.9864	.8642	.1358
45 - 49	1	1 mo - 1 yr	.016	.984	.984	.016	.0078	.9922	.9922	.0078
	2	1 - 2 yrs	.016	.984	.968	.032	.0093	.9907	.9830	.0170
	3	2 - 3 yrs	.033	.967	.936	.064	.0099	.9901	.9733	.0267
	4	3 - 5 yrs	.026	.974	.887	.113	.0115	.9885	.9511	.0489
	5	5 - 7 yrs	.028	.972	.839	.161	.0127	.9873	.9271	.0729
	6	7 - 10 yrs	.033	.967	.758	.242	.0157	.9843	.8841	.1159
	7	10 - 15 yrs	.052	.948	.581	.419	.0209	.9791	.7955	.2045
50 up	1	1 mo - 1 yr	.000	1.000	1.000	.000	.0141	.9859	.9859	.0141
	2	1 - 2 yrs	.067	.933	.933	.067	.0166	.9834	.9696	.0304
	3	2 - 3 yrs	.024	.976	.911	.089	.0171	.9829	.9530	.0470
	4	3 - 5 yrs	.012	.988	.889	.111	.0196	.9804	.9160	.0840
	5	5 - 7 yrs	.065	.935	.778	.222	.0226	.9774	.8750	.1250
	6	7 - 10 yrs	.040	.960	.689	.311	.0276	.9724	.8046	.1954
	7	10 - 15 yrs	.075	.925	.467	.533	.0385	.9615	.6610	.3390

*Basis of expected mortality: U.S. White Males progressive rates 1944-1962
†Rates for intervals 1 month-1 year: over interval, not annual

CORONARY HEART DISEASE

§304—ARTERIOSCLEROTIC HEART DISEASE – DISABILITY INSURANCE CLAIMANTS

References: (1) G. P. Robb and H. H. Marks, "What Happens to Men Disabled by Heart Disease?", Trans. Assoc. Life Ins. Med. Dir. Amer., 37:171-198 (1953).

(2) E. A. Lew, "Survival Among Insured Men Following Disability from Coronary Heart Disease," Met. Stat. Bull., 51:5-8 (June 1970).

(3) E. A. Lew, unpublished data (1970).

Subjects Studied: White male policyholders of Metropolitan Life Insurance Company granted disability benefits by reason of arteriosclerotic heart disease considered to be totally and permanently disabled (after 1929 presumptive after complete disablement for prescribed waiting period). Two classes: (a) Recipients of benefit admitted as disabled between 1934 and 1936 traced to 1952 while disabled (540); (b) Recovered cases (resuming work or exhibiting the capacity to do so) from 1925-1949 traced to 1969 (537). The first class included 470 cases of arteriosclerotic and hypertensive heart disease cases (aside from 70 valvular heart disease claims), composed by age as follows: 4 per cent under age 40; 35 per cent between ages 40 and 49; and 61 per cent ages 50 to 64. The median age under the several categories was between 51 and 53 years of age. Distribution by age in cases recovered from the same disablements was similar with very similar median ages. Over one-third of the recovered cases had experienced acute coronary episodes, about one-sixth, renal or cerebral involvement, and about one-half were uncomplicated heart disease cases.

Follow-up: Data obtained from insurance company records. The proportion of withdrawals was small.

Results: (a) *Recipients of benefit*—Tables 304a-b present observed data and comparative experience for the three categories of claim within the arteriosclerotic-hypertensive class. Mortality rates and ratios and EDR in the coronary occlusion and uncomplicated arteriosclerotic and hypertensive heart disease categories are quite close — mortality ratios in the first five-year interval about 3½ to 4 times the expected in the contemporary general population, and diminishing with duration to about double the expected after 15 years. Extra deaths for both these categories average about 40 per 1000 per year over the 15-year follow-up period. Experience on cases with renal or cerebral involvement is much poorer; mortality rates initially are nearly triple those in the other categories (1090 per cent for interval 0-5 years against 415 per cent for coronary occlusion cases, and 355 per cent for the uncomplicated heart disease cases), averaging, over the follow-up period, about 250 per cent those of the other categories. EDR was almost 4 times as great, averaging 151 annually per 1000.

(b) *Recovered cases*—Mortality and survival experience for cases involving coronary occlusion not accompanied by hypertension is set out in Tables 304c-d; the other disease classes, in Tables 304e-f. Coronary occlusion cases with no record of hypertension constituted the largest group accounting for about two-thirds of the total entrants. In this group, individuals under age 50 at time of recovery experienced much less favorable mortality compared with expected (the general white male population as reported in U.S. Censuses 1940-1960) than for older lives. Cumulative survival ratios for the younger group ran from 80 per cent, five years after recovery, to 44 per cent, 25 years after, while of the older group 92 per cent survived five years, and 78 per cent, 25. Average annual excess deaths per 1000 over the 25-year period, similarly, were substantially greater for the younger group: 42 against 15. Mortality ratios for the older lives approached the level of the general population over the period of the study, but the younger lives, although exhibiting some lessening of extra mortality, continued to indicate mortality about double that expected after 25 years.

Men in receipt of benefit for arteriosclerotic disease with no record of coronary occlusion and hypertension (all ages combined), after recovery experienced relatively heavy mortality in the five-year period following recovery, as is indicated by a mortality ratio of 255 per cent and an EDR of 25 per 1000, but thereafter extra mortality was much lighter, disappearing after 15 years. Cases of occlusion accompanied by hypertension (all ages combined) showed a mortality ratio of 385 per cent in the first five-year post-recovery interval. This ratio diminished somewhat to 285 per cent in the 10- 15-year period and continued to decline in subsequent periods. However, only 47 per cent as many survivors remained after 25 years as was expected. Cases with a record of hypertension but no occlusion also experienced high initial relative mortality which diminished more or less regularly to virtually expected magnitude over the period of the study. The EDR for all periods averaged 29 per 1000 per year.

MEN DISABLED BY ARTERIOSCLEROTIC HEART DISEASE
According to Category of Illness and Interval after Disablement — All Ages Combined

Table 304a   Observed Data and Comparative Experience (per Interval and Cumulative to End of Interval)

Interval Start-End	Exposure Disease-Yrs	Deaths in Interval Observed	Deaths in Interval Expected*	Mortality Ratio Interval	Mortality Ratio Cumulative	Survival Ratio Interval	Survival Ratio Cumulative	Excess Death Rate
t to $t+\Delta t$	E	d	d′	100 d/d′	100 Q/Q′	100 p_i/p_i′	100 P/P′	1000(d-d′)/E
Coronary Occlusion								
0- 5 yrs	713	49	11.84	415%	375%	94.7%	76.1%	52
5-10 yrs	498	32	11.92	270	265	95.9	62.6	40
10-15 yrs	335	26	11.52	225	210	95.5	49.7	43
0-15 yrs	1546	107	35.28	305	210	95.3	49.7	46
Uncomplicated Arteriosclerotic and Hypertensive Heart Disease other than Coronary Occlusion								
0- 5 yrs	967	62	17.50	355%	320%	95.3%	78.9%	46
5-10 yrs	655	46	17.03	270	250	95.5	62.5	44
10-15 yrs	451	27	16.82	160	186	97.7	55.9	23
0-15 yrs	2073	135	51.35	265	186	96.1	55.9	40
Arteriosclerotic and Hypertensive Heart Disease with Renal or Cerebral Involvement								
0- 5 yrs	259	49	4.48	1090%	715%	82.5%	43.7%	172
5-10 yrs	119	18	2.98	605	430	87.0	21.1	126
10-15 yrs	51	7	1.83	385	280	89.5	11.9	101
0-15 yrs	429	74	9.29	795	280	85.0	11.9	151

Table 304b   Derived Mortality and Survival Data (per Interval and Cumulative to End of Interval)

Interval Start-End	Observed Rates Average Annual Mortality	Observed Rates Average Annual Survival	Observed Rates Cumulative Survival	Observed Rates Cumulative Mortality	Expected Rates* Average Annual Mortality	Expected Rates* Average Annual Survival	Expected Rates* Cumulative Survival	Expected Rates* Cumulative Mortality
t to $t+\Delta t$	$\bar{q}=d/E$	$\bar{p}$	P	Q	$\bar{q}'=d'/E$	$\bar{p}'$	P′	Q′
Coronary Occlusion								
0- 5 yrs	.069	.931	.70	.30	.0166	.9834	.9196	.0804
5-10 yrs	.064	.936	.51	.49	.0239	.9761	.8147	.1853
10-15 yrs	.078	.922	.34	.66	.0344	.9656	.6838	.3162
0-15 yrs	.069	.931	.34	.66	.0228	.9772	.6838	.3162
Uncomplicated Arteriosclerotic and Hypertensive Heart Disease other than Coronary Occlusion								
0- 5 yrs	.064	.936	.72	.28	.0181	.9819	.9128	.0872
5-10 yrs	.070	.930	.50	.50	.0260	.9740	.8003	.1997
10-15 yrs	.060	.940	.37	.63	.0373	.9627	.6619	.3381
0-15 yrs	.065	.935	.37	.63	.0248	.9752	.6619	.3381
Arteriosclerotic and Hypertensive Heart Disease with Renal or Cerebral Involvement								
0- 5 yrs	.189	.811	.40	.60	.0173	.9827	.9162	.0838
5-10 yrs	.151	.849	.17	.83	.0250	.9750	.8074	.1926
10-15 yrs	.137	.863	.08	.92	.0358	.9642	.6728	.3272
0-15 yrs	.172	.828	.08	.92	.0217	.9783	.6728	.3272

*Basis of expected mortality: Progressive rates, U.S. White Males — 1940, 1950, 1960 Censuses

CORONARY HEART DISEASE
Coronary Occlusion without Hypertension (357 cases)

Table 304c Observed Data and Comparative Experience by Age and Duration

Age Group	Interval after Recovery		Exposure	Deaths in Interval		Mortality Ratio		Survival Ratio		Excess Death Rate
	No.	Start-End	Person-Yrs	Obs.	Exp.*	Interval	Cumulative	Interval	Cumulative	
	i	t to $t+\Delta t$	E	d	d'	$100\,d/d'$	$100\,Q/Q'$	$100\,p_i/p_i'$	$100\,P/P'$	$1000(d-d')/E$
Under 50	1	0- 5	709	35	5.11	685%	640%	80.0%	80.0%	42
	2	5-10	511	37	5.44	680	545	72.5	58.0	61
	3	10-15	359	15	5.65	265	365	87.9	51.0	26
	4	15-20	255	16	5.89	270	275	82.2	41.9	40
	5	20-25	114	4	3.76	106	195	104.7	43.9	2.0
		0-25	1948	107	25.85	415	195	43.9	43.9	42
50-64	1	0- 5	920	37	21.2	175	166	91.7	91.7	17
	2	5-10	706	40	23.1	173	158	88.0	80.8	24
	3	10-15	486	30	22.7	132	137	91.7	74.1	15
	4	15-20	305	21	20.5	102	118	99.9	74.0	1.8
	5	20-25	135	10	13.0	77	107	104.8	77.6	−22
		0-25	2552	138	100.5	137	107	77.6	77.6	15
All Ages	1	0- 5	1629	72	26.3	275	260	86.3	86.3	28
	2	5-10	1217	77	28.5	270	235	80.9	69.8	40
	3	10-15	845	45	28.4	158	183	90.0	62.9	19
	4	15-20	560	37	26.4	140	151	90.9	57.2	19
	5	20-25	249	14	16.8	83	125	104.3	59.6	−12
		0-25	4500	245	126.4	194	125	59.6	59.6	26

Table 304d Derived Mortality and Survival Data

Age Group	Interval after Recovery		Observed Rates				Expected Rates*			
			Average Annual		Cumulative		Average Annual		Cumulative	
	No.	Start-End	Mortality	Survival	Survival	Mortality	Mortality	Survival	Survival	Mortality
	i	t to $t+\Delta t$	$\bar{q}=d/E$	$\bar{p}$	P	Q	$\bar{q}'=d'/E$	$\bar{p}'$	P'	Q'
Under 50	1	0- 5	.049	.951	.771	.229	.0072	.9928	.9643	.0357
	2	5-10	.072	.928	.530	.470	.0106	.9894	.9136	.0864
	3	10-15	.042	.958	.430	.570	.0157	.9843	.8432	.1568
	4	15-20	.063	.937	.314	.686	.0231	.9769	.7489	.2511
	5	20-25	.035	.965	.276	.724	.0330	.9670	.6288	.3712
		0-25	.052	.948	.276	.724	.0133	.9867	.6288	.3712
50-64	1	0- 5	.040	.960	.816	.184	.0230	.9770	.8894	.1106
	2	5-10	.057	.943	.607	.393	.0327	.9673	.7517	.2483
	3	10-15	.062	.938	.437	.563	.0467	.9533	.5901	.4099
	4	15-20	.069	.931	.307	.693	.0672	.9328	.4150	.5850
	5	20-25	.074	.926	.189	.811	.0963	.9037	.2437	.7563
		0-25	.060	.940	.189	.811	.0394	.9606	.2437	.7563
All Ages	1	0- 5	.044	.956	.796	.204	.0161	.9839	.9221	.0779
	2	5-10	.063	.937	.572	.428	.0234	.9766	.8191	.1809
	3	10-15	.053	.947	.434	.566	.0336	.9664	.6904	.3096
	4	15-20	.066	.934	.310	.690	.0471	.9529	.5424	.4576
	5	20-25	.056	.944	.228	.772	.0675	.9325	.3825	.6175
		0-25	.056	.944	.228	.772	.0281	.9719	.3825	.6175

*Basis of expected mortality: Progressive rates, U.S. White Males — 1940, 1950, 1960 Censuses

MEN DISABLED BY ARTERIOSCLEROTIC HEART DISEASE
Disabilities other than by Coronary Occlusion without Hypertension

Table 304e Observed Data and Comparative Experience by Duration (All Ages)

Type of Heart Disease	No.	Start-End	Exposure Person-Yrs	Deaths Obs.	Deaths Exp.*	Mortality Ratio Interval	Mortality Ratio Cumulative	Survival Ratio Interval	Survival Ratio Cumulative	Excess Death Rate
	i	t to t + Δt	E	d	d'	100 d/d'	100 Q/Q'	100 p_i/p_i'	100 P/P'	1000(d-d')/E
Coronary Occlusion and Hypertension	1	0-5	274	17	4.41	385%	350%	78.7%	78.7%	46
	2	5-10	173	16	4.05	395	305	69.9	55.1	69
	3	10-15	105	10	3.53	285	235	73.1	40.3	61
	4	15-20	58	5	2.73	183	179	82.9	33.4	39
	5	20-25	14	0	.95	0	133	141.8	47.3	−68
		0-25	624	48	15.67	305	133	47.3	47.3	52
Hypertension No Coronary Occlusion	1	0-5	155	7	2.50	280	275	85.3	85.3	29
	2	5-10	103	5	2.41	205	215	87.8	75.0	26
	3	10-15	72	6	2.42	250	194	76.9	57.6	49
	4	15-20	45	3	2.12	142	155	92.7	53.5	20
	5	20-25	28	2	1.89	106	129	99.3	53.1	3.5
		0-25	403	23	11.34	205	129	53.1	53.1	29
No Hypertension No Coronary Occlusion	1	0-5	369	15	5.94	255	245	87.7	87.7	25
	2	5-10	268	7	6.27	112	161	98.7	86.6	2.6
	3	10-15	205	8	6.89	116	135	97.2	84.2	5.4
	4	15-20	160	6	7.54	80	114	104.5	87.9	−9.1
	5	20-25	84	6	5.67	106	106	102.3	89.9	3.5
		0-25	1086	42	32.31	130	106	89.9	89.9	9.1

Table 304f Derived Mortality and Survival Data

Type of Heart Disease	No.	Start-End	Obs. Avg Annual Mortality	Obs. Avg Annual Survival	Obs. Cumulative Survival	Obs. Cumulative Mortality	Exp. Avg Annual Mortality	Exp. Avg Annual Survival	Exp. Cumulative Survival	Exp. Cumulative Mortality
	i	t to t + Δt	$\bar{q}$ = d/E	$\bar{p}$	P	Q	$\bar{q}'$ = d'/E	$\bar{p}'$	P'	Q'
Coronary Occlusion and Hypertension	1	0-5	.062	.938	.726	.274	.0161	.9839	.9221	.0779
	2	5-10	.092	.908	.451	.549	.0234	.9766	.8191	.1809
	3	10-15	.095	.905	.278	.722	.0336	.9664	.6904	.3096
	4	15-20	.086	.914	.181	.819	.0471	.9529	.5424	.4576
	5	20-25	.000	1.000	.181	.819	.0675	.9325	.3825	.6175
		0-25	.067	.933	.181	.819	.0281	.9719	.3825	.6175
Hypertension No Coronary Occlusion	1	0-5	.045	.955	.787	.213	.0161	.9839	.9221	.0779
	2	5-10	.049	.951	.614	.386	.0234	.9766	.8191	.1809
	3	10-15	.083	.917	.398	.602	.0336	.9664	.6904	.3096
	4	15-20	.067	.933	.290	.710	.0471	.9529	.5424	.4576
	5	20-25	.071	.929	.203	.797	.0675	.9325	.3825	.6175
		0-25	.063	.937	.203	.797	.0281	.9719	.3825	.6175
No Hypertension No Coronary Occlusion	1	0-5	.041	.959	.809	.191	.0161	.9839	.9221	.0779
	2	5-10	.026	.974	.709	.291	.0234	.9766	.8191	.1809
	3	10-15	.039	.961	.581	.419	.0336	.9664	.6904	.3096
	4	15-20	.038	.962	.477	.523	.0471	.9529	.5424	.4576
	5	20-25	.071	.929	.344	.656	.0675	.9325	.3825	.6175
		0-25	.043	.957	.344	.656	.0281	.9719	.3825	.6175

*Basis of expected mortality: Progressive rates, U.S. White Males — 1940, 1950, 1960 Censuses

CORONARY HEART DISEASE

§305–CORONARY HEART DISEASE AND CHEST PAIN IN INSUREDS

Reference: H. A. Cochran, Jr. and N. F. Buck, "Coronary Artery Disease and Other Chest Pain, A Fourth Report," Trans. Assoc. Life Ins. Med. Dir. Am., 54:63-90 (1970).

Subjects Studied: All paid-for life insurance policies issued by the Lincoln National Life Insurance Company during the period 1947-1961, to applicants age 10 to 64 years (almost all U.S. residents), for whom the principal medical coding fell into one of the categories of coronary artery disease (CHD) or chest pain as classified in the eight groups below. The final classification was made through expert re-evaluation of all application records initially coded for angina pectoris, CHD, chest pain not listed elsewhere, or disorder of the heart not listed elsewhere. The study covered 10,434 policies and 882 death claims.

Definite Coronary Artery Disease Groups

A – Myocardial infarction (MI) or coronary occlusion (CO) or coronary thrombosis (CT) when such a diagnosis was made in a report from an attending physician, hospital or clinic, or when warranted in the opinion of the medical director reviewing the case on the basis of evidence available at the time of issue.

B – Cases in which the Group A diagnosis was contained in the statements of the applicant only or in the insurance history without details ("undocumented").

C – Cases in which a variety of other diagnostic terms for CHD appeared; e.g., angina pectoris, coronary insufficiency or failure, coronary sclerosis, heart attack, or others of a like nature, whether documented as in Group A cases, or undocumented as in Group B.

Cases Classified as Chest Pain (Not Definite CHD)

Point values were assigned to "major" or "minor clues" in the description of the chest pain episode(s), the history, findings and other evidence in the case file. Examples of major clues with a value of one point are chest pain described as constricting, or radiation to the left shoulder or arm; examples of minor clues with a value of ½ point are left chest pain, ratable blood pressure and family history of CHD prior to age 65.

D – Cases with clues having a point value of 3 or more.

E – Cases with clues having a point value of 2 to 2½. Groups D/E are given the designation "Most suspicious" (for CHD) in the tables of this section.

F – Cases with clues having a point value of 1 to 1½, termed "Suspicious" in the tables.

G – Cases with a point value less than one, termed "Least suspicious" in the tables.

H – Other chest pain cases not classifiable in Groups D to G, because of being too ill-defined, or because the evidence indicated a probable cause not CHD, such as gallbladder disease, hiatus hernia, pericarditis, etc.

Follow-up: The policy record was used to follow each case to the 1969 policy anniversary or prior termination and constituted the basis for counting exposure and numbers of death claims.

Results: Tables 305a-b show results for the several groups by age at issue. The highest mortality appears among the definite coronary cases (Groups A,B,C). Observed deaths for all ages combined are 3.6 times the expected in Group A, 4.55 in Group B, and 2.25 in Group C. Overall experience in the groups characterized by undiagnosed chest pain (Groups D/E,F,G,H) is less unfavorable; mortality ratios range from 110 per cent for Group G (least suspicious) to 198 per cent for Groups D/E (most suspicious). Policies in the CHD groups issued at ages under 50 generally reveal higher mortality ratios than those issued at older ages, these ratios tending to decline with advance in age at issue of insurance. Mortality ratios in the chest pain categories (Groups D/E,F,G,H) tend to vary little by age at issue. When experience is expressed as extra deaths per 1000 policy years of exposure, however, older ages tend to produce increasing EDR's in all age groups. Average survival rates consistently decline with advance in age at issue and this is almost invariably the case with respect to survival ratios as well. In the "miscellaneous" Group H, many of whom were diagnosed as having chest pain due to conditions other than CHD, excess mortality was comparable in magnitude to that observed in Group F, those with chest pain classified as suspicious for CHD at an intermediate level.

CORONARY HEART DISEASE IN INSUREDS

Table 305a   Comparative Experience of Coronary Heart Disease by Group and Age at Issue

CHD Group	Age (Years)	Exposure Policy-Yrs	No. of Death Claims		Mortality Ratio	Ave. Ann. Mort. Rate	Est. 8-Yr Surv. Rate	Est. 8-Yr Surv. Index	Excess Death Rate
			Observed	Expected*					
		E	d	d'	100 d/d'	$\bar{q} = d/E$	$P = (1-\bar{q})^8$	100 P/P'	1000(d-d')/E
A (MI/CO/CT) Documented	10-39	1182	10	3.08	325%	.008	.934	95.4%	5.9
	40-49	3318	80	18.4	435	.024	.823	86.0	19
	50-64	2492	77	25.2	305	.031	.778	84.4	21
	Total	6992	167	46.7	360	.024	.824	87.0	17
B (MI/CO/CT) Undocumented	10-39	376	6	0.93	645	.016	.879	89.7	13
	40-49	843	25	5.12	490	.030	.786	82.5	24
	50-64	733	31	7.62	405	.042	.708	76.9	32
	Total	1952	62	13.7	455	.032	.772	81.7	25
C (AP/CI/CHD)	10-39	1362	8	3.14	255	.006	.954	97.2	3.6
	40-49	3634	49	21.2	230	.013	.897	94.0	7.6
	50-64	2503	60	27.1	220	.024	.824	89.9	13
	Total	7499	117	51.5	225	.016	.882	93.2	8.7
C (Documented)	AP	1904	32	12.7	250	.017	.873	92.1	10
	CI	1959	23	12.7	181	.012	.910	95.8	5.3
	Other	1335	21	8.96	235	.016	.881	93.0	9.0
C (Undocumented)	AP	792	7	5.88	119	.009	.931	98.9	1.4
	CI	214	2	1.43	140	.009	.928	97.9	2.7
	Other	1295	32	9.76	330	.025	.819	87.0	17

Table 305b   Comparative Experience of Chest Pain by Group and Age at Issue

Degree of Suspicion for CHD†	Age (Years)	Exposure Policy-Yrs	No. of Death Claims		Mortality Ratio	Ave. Ann. Mort. Rate	Est. 8-Yr Surv. Rate	Est. 8-Yr Surv. Index	Excess Death Rate
			Observed	Expected*					
		E	d	d'	100 d/d'	$\bar{q} = d/E$	$P = (1-\bar{q})^8$	100 P/P'	1000(d-d')/E
D/E (Most suspicious)	10-39	6339	33	14.9	220%	.005	.959	97.7%	2.9
	40-49	8982	107	49.8	215	.012	.909	95.0	6.4
	50-64	3865	72	42.5	169	.019	.860	94.0	7.6
	Total	19186	212	107.2	198	.011	.915	95.7	5.5
F (Suspicious)	10-39	6194	24	14.3	168	.004	.969	98.8	1.6
	40-49	7567	41	42.3	97	.005	.958	100.1	−0.2
	50-64	2868	53	33.1	160	.018	.861	94.5	6.9
	Total	16629	118	89.7	132	.007	.945	98.6	1.7
G (Least suspicious)	10-39	9198	20	18.9	106	.002	.983	99.9	0.1
	40-49	10519	69	60.0	115	.007	.949	99.3	0.9
	50-64	3515	43	41.3	104	.012	.906	99.6	0.5
	Total	23232	132	120.2	110	.006	.955	99.6	0.5
H (All other chest pain)†	10-39	3787	11	9.32	118	.003	.977	99.6	0.4
	40-49	3405	34	23.0	148	.010	.923	97.4	3.2
	50-64	1610	29	22.3	130	.018	.865	96.7	4.2
	Total	8802	74	54.6	136	.008	.935	98.2	2.2

* Basis of expected mortality: Contemporaneous standard insurance intercompany experience
† Graded by a point system in accordance with the description of the chest pain (see Subjects Studied).
   Group H included all other chest pain cases not classifiable in Groups D to G.

CORONARY HEART DISEASE

§305—CORONARY HEART DISEASE AND CHEST PAIN IN INSUREDS (continued)

Analysis of experience according to the number of years elapsed between the most recent attack and the application for insurance is presented in Tables 305c-d. Cases accepted within 2 years of attack or last episode of chest pain show relatively more favorable results than in the 2-5 year interval. Mortality ratios tend to peak either during the 2-5 year interval or in the following five policy years, but in the definite coronary heart disease groups and in the most suspicious chest pain category, the level of mortality remains high even 10 years after the most recent attack preceding policy issue; in Group A the mortality ratio comes to 290 per cent; in Group B, 415 per cent; in Group C, 245 per cent; and in Group D/E, 315 per cent.

Comparative experience for the several groups according to policy duration is shown in Tables 305e-h. Mortality ratios in the CHD groups and the most suspicious of the chest pain groups during the first 10 policy years tend to diminish with duration. For Groups A and B there is then a reversal in direction and mortality ratios increase. Survival ratios for Groups A and B take a particularly sharp drop after the tenth policy year because of the adverse mortality experience. EDR's do not display a clear pattern. The tendency for this function to increase with advancing age is offset in large measure by the substantial downward movement in mortality ratios during the first 10 policy years. Normal mortality and survival ratios were observed in the chest pain Groups F,G and H after 10 years, but those with the most suspicious chest pain, Group D/E, also exhibited a persistently high mortality ratio (193 per cent) and a peak EDR level (10 extra deaths per 1000 per year) during this last follow-up interval.

Results related to electrocardiographic findings are indicated in two tables according to the time the finding is made: at time of diagnosis or initial investigation (305i); or at time of issue of insurance, or within 30 days prior thereto (305k). Experience on cases having no ECG record at either time is also presented. The abnormal ECG cases are confined to what is referred to as "Major Abnormality Type I" — changes consistent with coronary heart disease, as for example, abnormal Q waves, ST and T changes, and positive exercise test. Results with respect to time of diagnosis do not show much variation by ECG classification for Groups A and C (Table 305i). Group B cases, with more limited data, show a very high mortality if there was no ECG, or if the ECG was abnormal at the time of the episode, but a much lower mortality ratio and EDR if the ECG was normal. Experience in Groups A and B with respect to ECG findings at time of application for insurance discloses that, generally, the lowest mortality is associated with a normal ECG. In other groups the relationship is not consistent. Abnormal ECG's are accompanied by a distinctly high mortality in Group A (490 per cent), and in Group C (405 per cent), but the data for the latter are quite limited as there are only 9 deaths.

In the chest pain cases (Table 305k) the relationship of mortality to ECG is less consistent. A normal ECG at the time of the episode was a favorable finding in Group D/E, but this was not true for a normal ECG at the time of application. Very little experience is available for cases with abnormal ECG in any of the groups, presumably because such abnormality may have resulted in the case being classified as probable CHD. In Group H, a normal ECG was associated with a normal mortality and survival, whether taken at the time of the episode or on application.

Results of the subdivision of the data according to three categories of build of the applicant are shown in Tables 305j and 305l. Normal build is defined to cover a range within 10 per cent above through 10 per cent below the average height on the Lincoln National Build Chart. Body weights beyond these extremes are classified in either the under or overweight groups. Overweights are not markedly overweight, underwriting criteria tending to eliminate such cases. In each group, almost invariably, experience among overweights is more unfavorable than among the normal weights. Results for underweights are inconclusive since the findings are inconsistent and based on small numbers of claims.

Comment: The pattern of results is similar to that observed in earlier studies made by the authors, and leads them to repeat observations made in a 1958 report, namely, (i) while CHD cases are hazardous risks for insurance, they can be offered insurance within acceptable substandard levels, (ii) the less known about a case (e.g., Group B cases), the more hazardous the risk, and (iii) a first essential in the underwriting is to develop a full and accurate history (the similarity of Group D and E results to those of Group C was noted in this connection.

CORONARY HEART DISEASE IN INSUREDS

Table 305c   Observed Data and Comparative Experience of Coronary Heart Disease by Interval from Attack to Application

CHD Group	Years Since Attack	Exposure Policy-Yrs	No. of Death Claims Observed	No. of Death Claims Expected*	Mortality Ratio	Ave. Ann. Mort. Rate	Est. 8-Yr Surv. Rate	Est. 8-Yr Surv. Index	Excess Death Rate
		E	d	d'	100 d/d'	$\bar{q} = d/E$	$P = (1-\bar{q})^8$	100 P/P'	1000(d-d')/E
A (MI/CO/CT)	0- 2 yrs	514	12	3.05	395%	.023	.828	86.8%	17
Documented	2- 5	1939	46	10.8	425	.024	.825	86.3	18
	5-10	3359	80	22.5	355	.024	.825	87.0	17
	10 yrs up	1145	29	10.0	290	.025	.814	87.4	17
B (MI/CO/CT)	0- 2 yrs	132	3	0.79	380	.023	.832	87.3	17
Undocumented	2- 5	398	12	2.58	465	.030	.783	82.5	24
	5-10	918	31	6.38	485	.034	.760	80.3	27
	10 yrs up	496	16	3.87	415	.032	.769	81.9	24
C (AP/CI/CHD)	0- 2 yrs	1281	12	6.82	176	.009	.928	96.8	4.0
	2- 5	2181	37	15.2	245	.017	.872	92.2	10.0
	5-10	3035	48	20.7	230	.016	.880	93.0	9.0
	10 yrs up	901	20	8.13	245	.022	.836	89.8	13

Table 305d   Observed Data and Comparative Experience of Chest Pain by Interval from Attack to Application

Degree of Suspicion for CHD†	Years Since Attack	Exposure Policy-Yrs	No. of Death Claims Observed	No. of Death Claims Expected*	Mortality Ratio	Ave. Ann. Mort. Rate	Est. 8-Yr Surv. Rate	Est. 8-Yr Surv. Index	Excess Death Rate
		E	d	d'	100 d/d'	$\bar{q} = d/E$	$P = (1-\bar{q})^8$	100 P/P'	1000(d-d')/E
D/E (Most	0-2 yrs	10198	98	50.8	193%	.010	.926	96.3%	4.6
suspicious)	2- 5	5459	61	30.5	200	.011	.914	95.6	5.6
	5-10	3011	40	21.8	183	.013	.898	95.2	6.0
	10 yrs up	518	13	4.1	315	.025	.816	87.0	17
F (Suspicious)	0- 2 yrs	11143	72	56.7	127	.006	.950	98.9	1.4
	2- 5	4262	35	25.2	139	.008	.936	98.2	2.3
	5-10	1093	10	6.62	151	.009	.929	97.5	3.1
	10 yrs up	131	1	1.18	85	.008	.940	101.1	−1.4
G (Least Susp.)	0- 2 yrs	15928	74	77.1	96	.005	.963	100.2	−0.2
	2- 5	5659	45	31.3	144	.008	.938	98.1	2.4
	5-10	1414	12	10.7	112	.008	.934	99.3	0.9
	10 yrs up	231	1	1.09	91	.004	.966	100.3	−0.4
H (All other	0- 2 yrs	4174	38	25.2	151	.009	.929	97.6	3.1
chest pain)†	2- 5	2454	17	14.5	117	.007	.946	99.2	1.0
	5-10	1230	13	7.93	164	.011	.918	96.7	4.1
	10 yrs up	944	6	6.99	86	.006	.950	100.8	−1.0

* Basis of expected mortality: Contemporaneous standard insurance intercompany experience

† Graded by a point system in accordance with the description of the chest pain (see Subjects Studied).

Group H included all other chest pain cases not classifiable in Groups D to G.

CORONARY HEART DISEASE

Table 305e Observed Data and Comparative Experience of Coronary Heart Disease by Group and Policy Duration

CHD Group	Policy Duration		Exposure Policy-Yrs	No. of Death Claims		Mortality Ratio		Survival Ratio		Excess Death Rate
	Int.	Start-End		Observed	Expected*	Interval	Cumulative	Interval	Cumulative	
	i	t to t + Δt	E	d	d'	100 d/d'	100 Σd/Σd'	100 p_i/p_i'	100 P/P'	1000(d-d')/E
A (MI/CO/CT)	1	0- 3 yrs	2450	43	8.07	535%	535%	95.8%	95.8%	14
Documented	2	3- 5	1214	30	6.54	460	500	96.1	92.1	19
	3	5-10	2199	44	17.6	250	365	94.1	86.6	12
	4	10 yrs up†	1129	50	14.4	345	360	85.1	73.7	32
B (MI/CO/CT)	1	0- 3 yrs	673	17	2.32	735	735	93.6	93.6	22
Undocumented	2	3- 5	335	12	1.91	630	685	94.0	88.0	30
	3	5-10	584	14	4.78	295	475	92.3	81.2	16
	4	10 yrs up†	360	19	4.66	410	455	81.2	65.9	40
C (AP/CI/CHD)	1	0- 3 yrs	2520	24	8.00	300	300	98.1	98.1	6.3
	2	3- 5	1291	13	6.84	190	250	99.0	97.2	4.8
	3	5-10	2342	42	17.7	235	245	94.9	92.2	10
	4	10 yrs up†	1346	38	18.9	200	225	93.1	85.8	14

Table 305f Derived Mortality and Survival Data Experience of Coronary Heart Disease by Group and Policy Duration

CHD Group	Policy Duration		Observed Rates				Expected Rates*			
			Average Annual		Survival		Average Annual		Survival	
	Int.	Start-End	Mortality	Survival	Interval	Cumulative	Mortality	Survival	Interval	Cumulative
	i	t to t + Δt	q̄ = d/E	p̄	p_i	P	q̄' = d'/E	p̄'	p_i'	P'
A (MI/CO/CT)	1	0- 3 yrs	.018	.982	.948	.948	.0033	.9967	.9901	.9901
Documented	2	3- 5	.025	.975	.951	.902	.0054	.9946	.9893	.9794
	3	5-10	.020	.980	.904	.815	.0080	.9920	.9606	.9408
	4	10-15†	.044	.956	.798	.650	.0128	.9872'	.9374	.8819
B (MI/CO/CT)	1	0- 3 yrs	.025	.975	.926	.926	.0034	.9966	.9898	.9898
Undocumented	2	3- 5	.036	.964	.930	.861	.0057	.9943	.9886	.9785
	3	5-10	.024	.976	.886	.762	.0082	.9918	.9597	.9391
	4	10-15†	.053	.947	.761	.580	.0129	.9871	.9369	.8798
C (AP/CI/CHD)	1	0- 3 yrs	.010	.990	.972	.972	.0032	.9968	.9904	.9904
	2	3- 5	.010	.990	.980	.952	.0053	.9947	.9894	.9799
	3	5-10	.018	.982	.914	.870	.0076	.9924	.9626	.9433
	4	10-15†	.028	.972	.867	.754	.0140	.9860	.9316	.8787

*Basis of expected mortality: Contemporaneous standard insurance intercompany experience

† Survival rates and ratios calculated with a 15-year cut off point. q̄, p̄, and d' calculated on basis of observed data from 10-22 years

CORONARY HEART DISEASE IN INSUREDS

Table 305g Observed Data and Comparative Experience of Chest Pain by Group and Policy Duration

Degree of Suspicion for CHD*	Policy Duration Int.	Policy Duration Start-End	Exposure Policy-Yrs	No. of Death Claims Observed	No. of Death Claims Expected†	Mortality Ratio Interval	Mortality Ratio Cumulative	Survival Ratio Interval	Survival Ratio Cumulative	Excess Death Rate
	i	t to t + Δ t	E	d	d'	100 d/d'	100Σd/Σd'	100 p_i/p_i'	100 P/P'	1000(d–d')/E
D/E (Most	1	0- 3 yrs	6261	32	16.1	199%	199%	99.2%	99.2%	2.5
Suspicious)	2	3- 5	3278	32	14.0	230	215	98.9	98.1	5.5
	3	5-10	6138	73	38.2	191	200	97.2	95.4	5.7
	4	10 yrs up	3509	75	38.9	193	198	95.1	90.7	10
F (Suspicious)	1	0- 3 yrs	5266	25	12.6	199	199	99.3	99.3	2.4
	2	3- 5	2797	7	11.1	63	135	100.3	99.6	−1.5
	3	5-10	5338	53	31.0	171	155	97.9	97.5	4.1
	4	10 yrs up	3228	33	34.7	95	132	100.4	97.9	−0.5
G (Least Susp.)	1	0- 3 yrs	7595	24	17.1	140	140	99.7	99.7	0.9
	2	3- 5	3993	16	14.8	108	125	99.9	99.7	0.3
	3	5-10	7264	44	39.6	111	117	99.7	99.4	0.6
	4	10 yrs up	4380	48	48.5	99	110	100.0	99.5	−0.1
H (All other	1	0- 3 yrs	2337	8	5.37	149	149	99.7	99.7	1.1
chest pain)*	2	3- 5	1238	9	4.66	193	169	99.3	99.0	3.5
	3	5-10	2538	27	14.5	186	179	97.5	96.5	4.9
	4	10 yrs up	2689	30	30.0	100	136	100.1	96.7	0.0

Table 305h Derived Mortality and Survival Data Experience of Chest Pain by Group and Policy Duration

Degree of Suspicion for CHD*	Policy Duration Int.	Policy Duration Start-End	Observed Rates Average Annual Mortality	Observed Rates Average Annual Survival	Observed Rates Survival Interval	Observed Rates Survival Cumulative	Expected Rates† Average Annual Mortality	Expected Rates† Average Annual Survival	Expected Rates† Survival Interval	Expected Rates† Survival Cumulative
	i	t to t + Δ t	$\bar{q} = d/E$	$\bar{p}$	p_i	P	$\bar{q}' = d'/E$	$\bar{p}'$	p_i'	P'
D/E (Most	1	0- 3 yrs	.005	.995	.985	.985	.0026	.9974	.9923	.9923
suspicious)	2	3- 5	.010	.990	.981	.966	.0043	.9957	.9915	.9838
	3	5-10	.012	.988	.942	.910	.0062	.9938	.9693	.9536
	4	10-15●	.021	.979	.899	.818	.0111	.9889	.9455	.9016
F (Suspicious)	1	0- 3 yrs	.005	.995	.986	.986	.0024	.9976	.9928	.9928
	2	3- 5	.003	.997	.995	.981	.0040	.9960	.9920	.9849
	3	5-10	.010	.990	.951	.933	.0058	.9942	.9713	.9566
	4	10-15●	.010	.990	.951	.887	.0107	.9893	.9475	.9063
G (Least Susp.)	1	0- 3 yrs	.003	.997	.991	.991	.0023	.9977	.9931	.9931
	2	3- 5	.004	.996	.992	.983	.0037	.9963	.9926	.9858
	3	5-10	.006	.994	.970	.953	.0055	.9945	.9728	.9590
	4	10-15●	.011	.989	.946	.902	.0111	.9889	.9455	.9067
H (All other	1	0- 3 yrs	.003	.997	.990	.990	.0023	.9977	.9931	.9931
chest pain)*	2	3- 5	.007	.993	.986	.975	.0038	.9962	.9925	.9857
	3	5-10	.011	.989	.948	.925	.0057	.9943	.9718	.9578
	4	10-15●	.011	.989	.946	.875	.0112	.9888	.9450	.9051

* Graded by a point system in accordance with the description of the chest pain (see Subjects Studied).
  Group H included all other chest pain not classifiable in Groups D to G
† Basis of expected mortality: Contemporaneous standard insurance intercompany experience
● Survival rates and ratios calculated with a 15-year cut off point. $\bar{q}$, $\bar{p}$, and d' calculated on basis of observed data
  from 10-22 years

CORONARY HEART DISEASE

Table 305i   Comparative Experience of Coronary Heart Disease by Group and Electrocardiographic Finding

CHD Group	ECG Reading	Exposure Policy-Yrs	No. of Death Claims		Mortality Ratio	Ave. Ann. Mort. Rate	Est. 8-Yr Surv. Rate	Est. 8-Yr Surv. Index	Excess Death Rate
			Observed	Expected*					
		E	d	d'	100 d/d'	$\bar{q} = d/E$	$P = (1-\bar{q})^8$	100 P/P'	1000(d-d')/E
— ECG at time of Episode —									
A (MI/CO/CT) Documented	No ECG	1121	28	7.25	385%	.025	.817	86.0%	19
	Normal	654	17	4.62	370	.026	.810	85.7	19
	Abnormal	4488	111	30.1	370	.025	.818	86.4	18
B (MI/CO/CT) Undocumented	No ECG	946	36	6.34	570	.038	.733	77.4	31
	Normal	401	7	3.06	230	.017	.869	92.3	9.8
	Abnormal	341	14	2.26	620	.041	.715	75.4	34
C (AP/CI/CHD)	No ECG	2139	34	15.6	220	.016	.880	93.3	8.6
	Normal	2369	40	16.7	240	.017	.873	92.3	9.8
	Abnormal	1634	24	10.7	225	.015	.888	93.6	8.1
— ECG at time of Application —									
A (MI/CO/CT) Documented	No ECG	2016	46	12.7	360	.023	.831	87.5	17
	Normal	2510	47	17.7	265	.019	.860	91.0	12
	Abnormal	1410	45	9.22	490	.032	.772	81.3	25
B (MI/CO/CT) Undocumented	No ECG	903	28	6.15	455	.031	.777	82.1	24
	Normal	821	24	5.85	410	.029	.789	83.5	22
	Abnormal	—	—	—	—	—	—	—	—
C (AP/CI/CHD)	No ECG	2692	38	18.5	205	.014	.892	94.3	7.2
	Normal	3271	47	22.6	210	.014	.891	94.1	7.5
	Abnormal	311	9	2.21	405	.029	.791	83.7	22

Table 305j   Comparative Experience of Coronary Heart Disease by Group and Build

CHD Group	Build	Exposure Policy-Yrs	No. of Death Claims		Mortality Ratio	Ave. Ann. Mort. Rate	Est. 8-Yr Surv. Rate	Est. 8-Yr Surv. Index	Excess Death Rate
			Observed	Expected*					
		E	d	d'	100 d/d'	$\bar{q} = d/E$	$P = (1-\bar{q})^8$	100 P/P'	1000(d-d')/E
A (MI/CO/CT) Documented	Underweight	379	6	2.38	250%	.016	.880	92.6%	9.6
	Normal Weight	4146	85	26.9	315	.021	.847	89.3	14
	Overweight	2434	74	17.1	435	.030	.781	82.6	23
B (MI/CO/CT) Undocumented	Underweight	133	2	0.74	270	.015	.886	92.6	9.5
	Normal Weight	1221	41	9.30	440	.034	.761	80.9	26
	Overweight	598	19	3.63	525	.032	.772	81.1	26
C (AP/CI/CHD)	Underweight	598	11	3.79	290	.018	.862	90.7	12
	Normal Weight	3860	58	27.0	215	.015	.886	93.7	8.0
	Overweight	3008	47	20.4	230	.016	.882	93.1	8.8

* Basis of expected mortality: Contemporaneous standard insurance intercompany experience

CORONARY HEART DISEASE IN INSUREDS

Table 305k   Comparative Experience of Chest Pain by Group and Electrocardiographic Finding

Degree of Suspicion for CHD*	ECG Reading	Exposure Policy-Yrs	No. of Death Claims Observed	No. of Death Claims Expected†	Mortality Ratio	Ave. Ann. Mort. Rate	Est. 8-Yr Surv. Rate	Est. 8-Yr Surv. Index	Excess Death Rate
		E	d	d'	100 d/d'	$\bar{q} = d/E$	$P = (1-\bar{q})^8$	100 P/P'	1000(d-d')/E
— ECG at time of Episode —									
D/E (Most suspicious)	No ECG	3564	58	20.9	280%	.016	.877	91.9%	10
	Normal	11049	103	62.2	166	.009	.928	97.1	3.7
	Abnormal	688	9	3.83	235	.013	.900	94.1	7.5
F (Suspicious)	No ECG	3880	27	19.3	140	.007	.946	98.4	2.0
	Normal	10262	75	58.1	129	.007	.943	98.7	1.6
	Abnormal	—	—	—	—	—	—	—	—
G (Least Susp.)	No ECG	6704	35	31.5	111	.005	.959	99.6	0.5
	Normal	14900	76	80.0	95	.005	.960	100.2	−0.3
	Abnormal	—	—	—	—	—	—	—	—
H (All other chest pain)*	No ECG	4333	40	23.5	170	.009	.928	97.0	3.8
	Normal	3030	22	20.8	106	.007	.943	99.7	0.4
	Abnormal	—	—	—	—	—	—	—	—
— ECG at time of Application —									
D/E (Most suspicious)	No ECG	9294	105	50.8	205	.011	.913	95.4	5.8
	Normal	7500	82	42.9	191	.011	.916	95.9	5.2
	Abnormal	—	—	—	—	—	—	—	—
F (Suspicious)	No ECG	10590	60	54.1	111	.006	.956	99.6	0.6
	Normal	4915	44	29.7	148	.009	.931	97.7	2.9
	Abnormal	—	—	—	—	—	—	—	—
G (Least Susp.)	No ECG	15885	88	75.2	117	.006	.956	99.4	0.8
	Normal	6633	37	40.7	91	.006	.956	100.4	−0.6
	Abnormal	—	—	—	—	—	—	—	—
H (All other chest pain)*	No ECG	5762	50	30.9	162	.009	.933	97.4	3.3
	Normal	2479	17	19.3	88	.007	.946	100.8	−0.9
	Abnormal	—	—	—	—	—	—	—	—

Table 305l   Comparative Experience of Chest Pain by Group and Build

Degree of Suspicion for CHD*	Build	Exposure Policy-Yrs	No. of Death Claims Observed	No. of Death Claims Expected†	Mortality Ratio	Ave. Ann. Mort. Rate	Est. 8-Yr Surv. Rate	Est. 8-Yr Surv. Index	Excess Death Rate
		E	d	d'	100 d/d'	$\bar{q} = d/E$	$P = (1-\bar{q})^8$	100 P/P'	1000(d-d')/E
D/E (Most suspicious)	Underweight	1700	15	9.15	164%	.009	.932	97.3%	3.4
	Normal Weight	10944	105	59.7	176	.010	.926	96.7	4.1
	Overweight	6489	90	38.2	235	.014	.894	93.8	8.0
F/G/H (All other chest pain categories)*	Underweight	6003	36	25.2	143	.006	.953	98.6	1.8
	Normal Weight	27431	164	150	109	.006	.953	99.6	0.5
	Overweight	15049	124	87.7	141	.008	.936	98.1	2.4

* Graded by a point system in accordance with the description of the chest pain (see Subjects Studied).
  Group H included all other chest pain cases not classifiable in Groups D to G
† Basis of expected mortality: Contemporaneous standard insurance intercompany experience

CORONARY HEART DISEASE

§306–CORONARY HEART DISEASE IN INSUREDS

References: (1) R. B. Singer, "Insurance Mortality Experience in Coronary Heart Disease," Proc. Medical Section, Am. Life Convention, 57:131-144 (1969)
(2) R. B. Singer, unpublished data (1971).

Subjects Studied: Lives insured by the New England Mutual Life Insurance Company from 1935 through 1965 for whom (a) a medical examination was completed, (b) there was a history of coronary heart disease, and (c) standard insurance could not be granted because of the heart history. There were 991 policies — on applicants predominantly white males resident in the U. S. Only 33 policies were issued to females.

This series is distinguished from other life insurance studies by the high proportion of pension type policies, which, since 1948, have utilized a graded death benefit in underwriting situations that would require either a rating or outright declination of a regular, non-pension application. Thus, 63 per cent of the policies were issued under pension plans, and over 90 per cent of these, or 57 per cent of the total involved this declinable type of graded death benefit action. Although many of these latter cases were characterized by high-risk features, such as very recent history, hypertension, or other cardiovascular complication, all pension applicants were required to be actively at work at their place of employment in order to qualify for insurance.

Follow-up: The follow-up period ended June 30, 1970. The company's actuarial policy record was used for counting entrants and death claims, and for computing exposures. The 991 policies generated 6867 years of exposure — an average duration of 6.9 years per policy. There were 167 death claims involving 149 individuals; 18 policyholders who died had two policies which matured by death. Other replicate policies were excluded from the present series because they had not been subject to medical examination; these had not been excluded from the data reported in 1969.

Results: The series was classified according to age, duration from inception of coverage, blood pressure level, type of coronary heart disease, the presence of other ratable cardiovascular impairments, and the interval between coronary attack and application for insurance. The study is divided into two basic categories; angina pectoris (AP), and myocardial infarction (MI) or other CHD. In the latter category MI was the most common diagnostic class; in addition to equivalent diagnoses such as coronary thrombosis or coronary occlusion, smaller numbers of other diagnostic terms were included in this category, terms such as coronary insufficiency and myocardial ischemia attack. There were 197 policies in the AP group, the average age at application, 48.7 years, and 794 policies in the MI or other CHD group, the average age, 48.2 years. Analysis of the data was made with respect to the presence or absence of "CV complication," represented by elevated blood pressure on examination (systolic, 140 or over, diastolic, 90 or over), or by any CV impairment other than CHD serious enough to justify an insurability rating on its own account (estimated mortality ratio greater than 125 per cent). Results according to age at application, CV complication, interval from attack to application, or some combination of these are presented in Tables 306a-g.

Cases with CV complication comprised about 40 per cent of the total, had a higher proportion of older subjects, and generally a higher relative mortality, than cases without complications (Table 306a). However, among insureds with a history of MI five years or more prior to application, a lower mortality ratio was found for those with CV complications. In subsequent treatment of data on this group with interval from attack to application of five or more years no differentiation is made with respect to CV complications.

Comparative mortality in Table 306a is presented by interval from attack to application and in Table 306b by age at application. In the MI group there is a consistent downward trend in MR and EDR when attack preceded application by at least a year. However, cases issued insurance within one year of attack showed comparative mortality during the follow-up period lower than that experienced where the attack had occurred more than one year but less than five years prior to issuance of insurance. (The difference between such first year deaths, age-adjusted, and the number derived by extending the EDR line backward from intervals 1-10 years to the first interval is significant at the 99 per cent level, Poisson P = .005.) Mortality ratios in AP cases do not decrease in a consistent manner by interval of attack to application but reliable conclusions cannot be drawn since the number of deaths is small in the several interval categories. The distribution by age group of subjects at time of insurance application, the exposures, and comparative mortality are presented in Table 306b. The overall mortality ratios and EDR functions for the MI and AP groups, all ages combined, are not far apart: mortality ratio, 380 per cent for the AP cases and 340 per cent for MI; EDR, 20 per

CORONARY HEART DISEASE IN INSURED MEN

Table 306a   Comparative Mortality by CHD Diagnosis, CV Complication, and Interval from Attack to Application

Category		Average Age	No. Policy Entrants	Exposure Policy-Yrs	No. of Death Claims Observed*	No. of Death Claims Expected†	Mortality Ratio	Excess Death Rate
		yrs	ℓ	E	d	d'	100 d/d'	1000(d-d')/E
Angina Pectoris								
No CV complication		48.1	122	758	16 (16)	5.62	285%	14
With CV complication		49.8	75	460	17 (16)	3.05	560	30
0- 1 yr Attack to app.		48.9	64	426	8 (8)	3.28	245	11
1- 2 yrs		48.2	27	141	6 (6)	1.04	580	35
2- 5 yrs		47.3	52	340	8 (8)	2.26	355	17
5-10 yrs		50.5	38	198	7 (7)	1.27	555	29
10 yrs up		50.6	9	68	1 (1)	0.52	195	7.1
Uncertain		46.6	7	45	3 (3)	0.30	1010	60
MI and Other CHD●								
0- 5 yrs	No. CV comp.	47.3	278	1969	42 (37)	12.40	340%	15
	With CV comp.	49.0	209	1369	53 (49)	9.71	545	32
5 yrs up	No CV comp.	46.8	184	1431	27 (23)	9.76	275	12
	With CV comp.	50.8	123	880	12 (12)	7.41	162	5.2
0- 1 yr	Attack to app.	46.7	168	1225	31 (31)	8.08	385	19
1- 2 yrs		47.7	102	645	23 (23)	4.17	550	29
2- 5 yrs		48.9	194	1326	37 (34)	8.80	420	21
5-10 yrs		48.0	223	1649	28 (25)	11.88	235	9.8
10 yrs up		49.7	84	662	11 (10)	5.29	205	8.6
Uncertain		51.7	23	142	4 (4)	1.05	380	21

Table 306b   Comparative Mortality by CHD Diagnosis and Age

Category		Average Age	No. Policy Entrants	Exposure Policy-Yrs	No. of Death Claims Observed*	No. of Death Claims Expected†	Mortality Ratio	Excess Death Rate
		yrs	ℓ	E	d	d'	100 d/d'	1000(d-d')/E
Angina Pectoris								
Age	Under 45 yrs	39.6	64	441	5 (5)	1.84	270%	7.2
	45-54 yrs	49.9	85	506	20 (19)	3.18	630	33
	55 yrs up	59.7	48	271	8 (8)	3.65	220	16
	All	48.7	197	1218	33 (32)	8.67	380	20
MI and other CHD●								
Age	Under 30 yrs	26.1	8	48	0 (0)	0.04	0%	-0.9
	30-34 yrs	32.1	35	371	0 (0)	0.85	0	-2.3
	35-39	37.1	62	493	6 (6)	1.47	410	9.2
	40-44	42.0	150	1173	17 (16)	5.39	315	9.9
	45-49	46.9	177	1309	35 (30)	8.21	425	20
	50-54	51.9	180	1297	40 (38)	11.59	345	22
	55-59	56.5	117	647	24 (22)	6.71	360	27
	60-64	61.2	47	209	8 (8)	2.78	290	25
	65 yrs up	66.4	18	102	4 (4)	2.22	180	17
	All	48.2	794	5649	134 (117)	39.26	340	17

* Number of actual deaths in parentheses
† Basis of expected mortality: 1955-60 Select Basic Table
● Myocardial infarction, coronary insufficiency and other CHD terms except angina

CORONARY HEART DISEASE

§306—CORONARY HEART DISEASE IN INSUREDS

Results (continued):

1000 for AP cases and 17 for MI. In both types of CHD, relative mortality is somewhat lighter for cases issued under age 45 years than for those in age group 45-54. In the AP group, mortality ratios and EDR's decrease materially for ages 55 up, but MI cases in age groups 55-59 and 60-64 years continue to indicate high comparative mortality, decreasing, however, for ages over 64 years. Exposure is small and deaths are few in the oldest age groups; nevertheless, there appears to be a definite tendency for comparative mortality to peak at some age under 65 years at issuance of insurance: the maximum EDR for AP cases is 33 per 1000 in age group 45-54, and for MI cases, 27 in age group 55-59 years.

Comparative mortality and survival by duration after insurance issue are shown in Tables 306c-306f for four clinical groups — all ages combined for both AP and MI groups in the first two of these tables, and by age group for MI cases within five years of attack only in Tables 306e-306f. Most of the exposure (86 per cent) is concentrated in the first 10 years of follow-up. In all groups mortality ratios are highest in the period within 2 years following issue and in most the rates generally decrease in subsequent periods. When all ages are combined, the highest comparative mortality ratio, 1140 per cent, and the highest EDR, 37 per 1000, occur in the 0-2 year interval following issue of insurance in the MI group with CV complications within five years of attack at time of application (Table 306c). The lowest initial comparative mortality in this table is in the MI group issued coverage five years or more after attack — MR, 385 per cent and EDR, 10 per 1000. Intermediate initial comparative mortality levels are found in the MI groups without complications within five years of attack, and in the AP group. Considering the small number of deaths in some follow-up intervals, the pattern of decreasing mortality by policy duration is remarkably consistent. Cumulative survival ratios at 10 years range between 71.9 and 91.3 per cent.

Experience by age and duration (Tables 306e-306f) discloses very high mortality ratios in the initial observation interval and subsequent decreasing ratios (irregularity in this respect in age group under 45 may be attributable to the small number of deaths after five years). The highest initial mortality ratio, 2100 per cent, is found in those under age 45, but the highest EDR, 40 per 1000, is found in the oldest group, viz., those 55 years up.

Comparative mortality experience by blood pressure classification, regardless of other CV complications, is presented in Table 306g. Cases with definite hypertension (systolic 160 up, or diastolic 95 up) have a mortality ratio twice as great, and an EDR three times as great as the respective values for normotensive cases (under 140/90). Borderline hypertensives show intermediate results.

Table 306h contains comparative mortality results by age group for five categories of cause of death, all MI and AP cases combined. The category "all others" includes a relatively high proportion of cases where information was lacking as to cause of death; some of these probably died of CHD. Shown at the bottom of this table is comparative CHD mortality for the five major clinical groups, all ages and durations combined.

CORONARY HEART DISEASE IN INSURED MEN

Table 306c   Observed Data and Comparative Experience by CHD Classification and Duration

Category	Interval No.	Start-End	No. Policy Entrants	Exposure Policy-Yrs	No. of Death Claims Observed*	Expected†	Mortality Ratio Interval	Cumulative	Cumulative Surv. Ratio	Excess Death Rate
	i	t to t + Δt	ℓ	E	d	d'	100 d/d'	100 Σd/Σd'	100 P/P'	1000(d-d')/E
Angina	1	0- 2 yrs	197	367	8 (8)	1.28	625%	625%	96.4%	18
	2	2- 5	150	410	14 (14)	2.58	545	570	88.5	28
	3	5-10	96	312	10 (10)	2.94	340	470	81.5	23
	4	10 yrs up	22	129	1 (1)	1.85	54	380	80.1	−6.6
		All yrs	197	1218	33	8.65	380	380	−	20
MI ≤ 5 yrs● (No CV comp.)	1	0- 2 Yrs	278	525	14 (14)	1.62	865	865	95.3	24
	2	2- 5	213	584	11 (10)	3.21	345	520	91.6	13
	3	5-10	151	562	10 (10)	4.43	225	380	86.9	9.9
	4	10 yrs up	61	298	7 (5)	3.14	225	340	78.5	13
		All yrs	278	1969	42	12.40	340	340	−	15
MI ≤ 5 yrs● (with CV comp.)	1	0- 2 yrs	209	396	16 (16)	1.41	1140	1130	92.8	37
	2	2- 5	163	441	19 (18)	2.84	670	825	82.8	37
	3	5-10	105	367	11 (10)	3.36	325	605	71.9	21
	4	10 yrs up	33	165	7 (7)	2.10	335	545	62.6	30
		All yrs	209	1369	53	9.71	545	545	−	32
MI > 5 yrs●	1	0- 2 yrs	307	584	8 (8)	2.09	385	385	98.0	10
	2	2- 5	254	700	10 (10)	4.53	220	270	95.7	7.8
	3	5-10	181	688	12 (12)	6.41	187	230	91.3	8.1
	4	10 yrs up	77	339	9 (8)	4.11	220	230	82.1	14
		All yrs	307	2311	39	17.14	225	230	−	9.5

Table 306d   Derived Mortality and Survival Data

Category	Interval No.	Start-End	Observed Rates Cumulative Survival□	Interval Survival	Geom. Mean Ann. Surv.	Geom. Mean Ann. Mort.	Expected Rates† Cumulative Survival□	Interval Survival	Geom. Mean Ann. Surv.	Geom. Mean Ann. Mort.
	i	t to t + Δt	P	p_i	p̌	q̌	P'	p_i'	p̌'	q̌'
Angina	1	0- 2 yrs	.957	.957	.978	.022	.9929	.9929	.9964	.0036
	2	2- 5	.862	.901	.966	.034	.9741	.9811	.9937	.0063
	3	5-10	.756	.878	.974	.026	.9272	.9519	.9902	.0098
	4	10-15	.698	.923	.984	.016	.8710	.9394	.9876	.0124
MI ≤ 5 yrs● (No CV comp.)	1	0- 2 yrs	.947	.947	.973	.027	.9938	.9938	.9969	.0031
	2	2- 5	.895	.945	.981	.019	.9773	.9834	.9944	.0056
	3	5-10	.816	.912	.982	.018	.9387	.9605	.9920	.0080
	4	10-15	.701	.859	.970	.030	.8930	.9513	.9901	.0099
MI ≤ 5 yrs● (with CV comp.)	1	0- 2 yrs	.921	.921	.960	.040	.9928	.9928	.9964	.0036
	2	2- 5	.806	.874	.956	.044	.9736	.9807	.9935	.0065
	3	5-10	.668	.830	.963	.037	.9285	.9537	.9906	.0094
	4	10-15	.544	.814	.960	.040	.8697	.9367	.9870	.0130
MI > 5 yrs●	1	0- 2 yrs	.973	.973	.986	.014	.9928	.9928	.9964	.0036
	2	2- 5	.932	.959	.986	.014	.9735	.9807	.9935	.0065
	3	5-10	.847	.908	.981	.019	.9280	.9533	.9905	.0095
	4	10-15	.717	.846	.967	.033	.8732	.9410	.9879	.0121

* Number of actual deaths in parentheses
† Basis of expected mortality: 1955-60 Select Basic Table
● Myocardial infarction and other CHD. Interval attack to application ≤ 5 years and uncertain, or > 5 years.
  CV complication = ratable CV abnormality other than CHD, or systolic BP ≥ 140 or diastolic ≥ 95
□ P and P' derived from life table calculations on an annual basis (also E, d, and d')

CORONARY HEART DISEASE

Table 306e   Observed Data and Comparative Experience of MI within 5 Years by Age and Duration

Age	Interval No. Start-End		No. Policy Entrants	Exposure Policy-Yrs	No. of Death Claims Observed	No. of Death Claims Expected*	Mortality Ratio Interval	Mortality Ratio Cumulative	Cumulative Surv. Ratio	Excess Death Rate
	i	t to t + Δ t	ℓ	E	d	d'	100 d/d'	100 $\sum$d/$\sum$d'	100 P/P'	1000(d-d')/E
Under 45 yrs	1	0- 2 yrs	150	283	8	0.39	2100%	2100%	94.6%	27
	2	2- 5	112	306	4	0.70	575	1100	91.4	11
	3	5-10	80	329	1	1.23	81	560	91.2	−0.7
	4	10-15	44	184	2	1.24	161	420	89.2	4.2
	5	15 yrs up	24	91	1	1.02	98	350	—	−0.2
		All yrs	150	1193	16	4.58	350	350	—	9.6
45-54 yrs	1	0- 2 yrs	232	444	13	1.43	910	910	94.8	26
	2	2- 5	189	519	15	2.99	500	635	88.4	23
	3	5-10	134	481	17	4.54	375	500	76.0	26
	4	10-15	50	166	10	2.52	395	480	60.7	45
	5	15 yrs up	8	22	1	0.47	215	470	—	24
		All yrs	232	1632	56	11.95	470	470	—	27
55 yrs up	1	0- 2 yrs	105	194	9	1.21	745	745	92.3	40
	2	2- 5	75	200	11	2.36	465	560	80.8	43
	3	5-10	42	119	3	2.02	150	410	78.9	8.2
	4	10-15	0	0	—	—	—	410	—	—
	5	15 yrs up	0	0	—	—	—	410	—	—
		All yrs	105	513	23	5.59	410	410	—	34

Table 306f   Derived Mortality and Survival Data

Age	Interval No. Start-End		Observed Rates Cumulative Survival†	Observed Rates Interval Survival	Observed Rates Geom. Mean Ann. Surv.	Observed Rates Geom. Mean Ann. Mort.	Expected Rates* Cumulative Survival†	Expected Rates* Interval Survival	Expected Rates* Geom. Mean Ann. Surv.	Expected Rates* Geom. Mean Ann. Mort.
	i	t to t + Δ t	P	p_i	$\breve{p}$	$\breve{q}$	P'	p_i'	$\breve{p}$'	$\breve{q}$'
Under 45 yrs	1	0- 2 yrs	.943	.943	.971	.029	.9972	.9972	.9986	.0014
	2	2- 5	.905	.959	.986	.014	.9904	.9931	.9977	.0023
	3	5-10	.886	.980	.996	.004	.9716	.9810	.9962	.0038
	4	10-15	.837	.944	.987	.013	.9386	.9660	.9931	.0069
45-54 yrs	1	0- 2 yrs	.942	.942	.971	.029	.9935	.9935	.9967	.0033
	2	2- 5	.863	.916	.971	.029	.9763	.9826	.9942	.0058
	3	5-10	.706	.818	.961	.039	.9294	.9519	.9902	.0098
	4	10-15	.520	.737	.941	.059	.8568	.9218	.9838	.0162
55 yrs up	1	0- 2 yrs	.911	.911	.955	.045	.9874	.9874	.9937	.0063
	2	2- 5	.769	.844	.945	.055	.9523	.9644	.9880	.0120
	3	5-10	.684	.889	.977	.023	.8667	.9101	.9813	.0187
	4	10-15	—	—	—	—	—	—	—	—

* Basis of expected mortality: 1955-60 Select Basic Table
† P and P' derived from life table calculations on an annual basis (also E, d, and d')

CORONARY HEART DISEASE IN INSURED MEN

Table 306g Comparative Mortality by Hypertensive Status and CHD Diagnosis (Interval from Attack to Application within 5 Years or Uncertain)

Category	Average Age	No. Policy Entrants	Exposure Policy-Yrs	No. of Death Claims Observed	No. of Death Claims Expected*	Mortality Ratio	Excess Death Rate
	Yrs	ℓ	E	d	d'	100 d/d'	1000(d-d')/E
Normal (Ave. BP 123/77)							
Angina Pectoris	46.8	102	679	11	4.83	230%	9.1
MI and Other CHD†	47.4	334	2346	55	15.25	360	17
Total	47.3	436	3025	66	20.08	330	15
Borderline (Ave. BP 141/80)							
Angina Pectoris	52.0	24	127	6	1.06	565	39
MI and Other CHD†	48.9	93	600	20	4.14	485	26
Total	49.5	117	727	26	5.20	500	29
Definite (Ave. BP 164/99)							
Angina Pectoris	50.1	24	146	8	0.99	810	48
MI and Other CHD†	49.8	61	397	21	2.81	750	46
Total	49.9	85	543	29	3.80	765	46

Table 306h Comparative Mortality by Age, Cause of Death and CHD Category

Age at Issue and Cause of Death	No. Policy Entrants	Exposure Policy-Yrs	No. of Death Claims Observed●	No. of Death Claims Expected*	Mortality Ratio	Excess Death Rate
	ℓ	E	d	d'	100 d/d'	1000(d-d')/E
Age under 40 yrs						
All CV Causes (including CVA)	130	1043	6 (6)	1.10	545%	4.7
Coronary Heart Disease alone	130	1043	5 (5)	0.78	640	4.0
Malignant Tumor and Leukemia	130	1043	0	0.40	0	−0.4
Accidental	130	1043	0	0.35	0	−0.3
All Other	130	1043	1 (1)	0.78	128	0.2
All Causes	130	1043	7 (7)	2.63	265	4.2
Age 40-49						
All CV Causes (including CVA)	408	3061	43 (40)	8.93	480	11
Coronary Heart Disease alone	408	3061	40 (37)	6.30	635	11
Malignant Tumor and Leukemia	408	3061	9 (6)	3.17	285	1.9
Accidental	408	3061	1 (1)	1.70	59	−0.2
All Other	408	3061	9 (9)	2.86	315	2.0
All Causes	408	3061	62 (62)	16.66	370	15
Age 50-59						
All CV Causes (including CVA)	373	2367	67 (61)	12.28	545	23
Coronary Heart Disease alone	373	2367	55 (51)	8.03	685	20
Malignant Tumor and Leukemia	373	2367	5 (5)	4.57	109	0.2
Accidental	373	2367	0 (0)	1.62	0	−0.7
All Other	373	2367	9 (8)	3.73	240	2.2
All Causes	373	2367	81 (81)	22.20	365	25
Age 60-69						
All CV Causes (including CVA)	80	396	12 (12)	3.75	320	21
Coronary Heart Disease alone	80	396	9 (9)	2.03	445	18
Malignant Tumor and Leukemia	80	396	3 (3)	1.37	220	4.1
Accidental	80	396	0 (0)	0.22	0	−0.6
All Other	80	396	2 (2)	1.30	154	1.8
All Causes	80	396	17 (17)	6.64	255	26
CHD—All Ages Combined† (Ave. Age)						
Angina, with CV complication (49.7)	75	460	8 (8)	1.96	410	13
Angina, no CV complication (48.1)	122	758	9 (9)	1.06	850	10
MI ≤ 5 yrs, with CV complication (49.1)	209	1369	37 (33)	3.39	1090	25
MI ≤ 5 yrs, no CV complication (47.3)	278	1969	26 (23)	4.34	600	11
All MI > 5 yrs (48.4)	307	2311	29 (28)	6.00	485	10
All CHD Cases (48.3)	991	6867	109 (101)	16.75	650	13

* Basis of expected mortality: 1955-60 Select Basic Table
† Myocardial Infarction and other CHD except angina. CV complication = ratable CV abnormality other than CHD, or systolic BP ≥ 140 or diastolic ≥ 95
●Number of actual deaths in parentheses

CORONARY HEART DISEASE

§307–CORONARY ARTERIOGRAM (CLEVELAND CLINIC)

References: (1) A.V.G. Bruschke, W. L. Proudfit, and F. M. Sones, Jr., "Clinical Course of Patients with Normal, and Slightly or Moderately Abnormal Coronary Arteriograms. A Follow-up Study on 500 Patients," Circulation, 47:936-945 (1973).
(2) A. V. G. Bruschke, W. L. Proudfit, and F. M. Sones, Jr., "Progress Study of 590 Consecutive Nonsurgical Cases of Coronary Disease Followed 5-9 Years. I. Arteriographic Correlations. II. Ventriculographic and Other Correlations," Circulation, 47:1147-1153, 1154-1163 (1973).
(3) J. S. Webster, C. Moberg, and G. Rincon, "Natural History of Severe Proximal Coronary Artery Disease as Documented by Coronary Cineangiography," Am. J. Card., 33:195-200 (1974).

Subjects Studied: (1) 521 consecutive patients studied by coronary arteriography at the Cleveland Clinic January 1964 through July 1965, who had normal arteriograms or less than 50 per cent narrowing of the lumen. Patients were excluded if they had other types of cardiac disease, such as valvular lesions, congenital defects, idiopathic hypertrophic subaortic stenosis, or evidence of diffuse impairment of cardiac contractility in the ventriculogram. Other abnormalities, such as hypertension, arrhythmias and electrocardiographic (ECG) changes were not a cause for exclusion. Patients were reported as to age, sex and other characteristics as follows for those followed up at least five years:

| | Male | | | Female | | | | |
Characteristic	Under 45 yrs	Age 45 up	All	Under 45 yrs	Age 45 up	All	Total M&F	
Atypical Chest Pain	134	95	229	71	109	180	409	
Angina Pectoris	15	30	45	2	5	7	52	(1)
No Chest Pain	10	20	30	6	3	9	39	
Normal Arteriogram	124	65	189	67	86	153	342	
Mildly Abnormal (30%)	24	51	75	10	16	26	101	(2)
Moderately Abnormal (30-49%)	11	29	40	2	15	17	57	(3)
Total	159	145	304	79	117	196	500	(4)

Note (1) Includes 13 cases of coronary insufficiency without angina.
Note (2) 57 cases involved more than one artery.
Note (3) 4 cases involved narrowing of 50 per cent or more in a small branch; 9 cases involved more than one artery.
Note (4) 82 patients had hypertension (systolic 150 mm. and up, or diastolic 100 mm. and up); 134 smoked cigarettes, one pack or more per day; 109 had a serum cholesterol in excess of 275 mg. per 100 ml.; 9 had previously been diagnosed as diabetic, and 19 had abnormal glucose tolerance tests (out of 48 such tests made).

(2) 590 consecutive patients with coronary disease documented by coronary arteriography at the Cleveland Clinic from January 1963 through July 1965. All had 50 per cent or more obstruction in at least one major artery. Patients with congenital or rheumatic heart disease and those who underwent coronary surgery within 5 years of arteriography were excluded. The sex and age distribution was as follows (average age 49.4 for male and 52.5 for female):

| | Male | | | Female | Both Sexes |
Under 45 yrs	45-54	Over 54	All	All	Total
149	240	138	527	63	590

(3) 469 patients with 80 to 100 per cent occlusion in any of the major coronary arteries as determined by arteriography, selected from 3,527 patients at the Cleveland Clinic Cardiac Laboratory between 1960 and 1965. Patients with congestive heart failure, severe cardiomegaly, rheumatic or other cardiac disease were excluded from the study. The patients were classified according to number of vessels involved and functional disability using the New York Heart Association criteria. There were only 45 female patients. Age distribution was as follows:

No. of Vessels	Single	Double	Triple	Total
Age 30-50	111	104	56	271
Age 51-70	67	73	58	198
All Ages	178	177	114	469

CORONARY ARTERIOGRAM (CLEVELAND CLINIC)

Table 307a Observed Data and Comparative Experience, Patients with Normal Coronary Arteriogram or Mild or Moderate Narrowing (Series 1)

Interval		No. Alive at Start of Interval	Withdrawn during Interval	Exposure Person-Yrs	No. of Deaths		Mortality Ratio		Survival Ratio		Excess Death Rate
No.	Start-End				Observed	Expected*	Interval	Cumulative	Interval	Cumulative	
i	t to t + Δ t	ℓ	w	E	d	d'	100 d/d'	100 Σd/Σd'	100 p_i/p_i'	100 P/P'	1000(d-d')/E
342 pts. normal arteriogram; 101 pts. narrowing under 30%											
1	0-3 yrs	443	0	1329	4	6.95	58%	58%	100.7%	100.7%	−2.2
2	3-5 yrs	439	0	871	9	5.82	155	102	99.2	100.0	3.6
3	5-7 yrs	430	236	728	5	5.86	85	97	100.2	100.1	−1.1
All	0-7 yrs	443	236	2928	18	18.63	97	97	100.1	100.1	−0.2
57 pts. moderate narrowing (30-49%)											
1	0-3 yrs	57	0	166	4	1.28	310%	310%	95.2%	95.2%	16
2	3-5 yrs	53	0	106	0	1.04	0	172	102.0	97.1	−9.8
3	5-7 yrs	53	30	94	4	1.08	370	235	93.0	90.3	31
All	0-7 yrs	57	30	366	8	3.40	235	235	90.3	90.3	13

Table 307b Derived Mortality and Survival Data

Interval		Observed Rates				Expected Rates*			
		Survival			Ave. Ann.	Survival			Ave. Ann.
No.	Start-End	Cumulative	Interval	Ave. Ann.	Mortality	Cumulative	Interval	Ave. Ann.	Mortality
i	t to t + Δ t	P	p_i	$\breve{p}$	$\breve{q}$	P'	p_i'	$\breve{p}$'	$\breve{q}$'
342 pts. normal arteriogram; 101 pts. narrowing <30%									
1	0-3 yrs	.991	.991	.997	.003	.9844	.9844	.9948	.0052
2	3-5 yrs	.971	.979	.990	.010	.9713	.9867	.9933	.0067
3	5-7 yrs	.957	.986	.993	.007	.9557	.9840	.9920	.0080
57 pts. moderate narrowings (30-49%)									
1	0-3 yrs	.930	.930	.976	.024	.9771	.9771	.9922	.0078
2	3-5 yrs	.930	1.000	1.000	.000	.9581	.9806	.9903	.0097
3	5-7 yrs	.845	.909	.953	.047	.9361	.9770	.9884	.0116

Table 307c Cumulative Incidence of C.H.D. Complication† in Follow-up of 5 to 7 Years, According to Various Risk Factors (Series 1)

Risk Factor	Cumulative Incidence Rate			
	Risk Factor Present		Risk Factor Absent	
	No. Entrants	Complications	No. Entrants	Complications
History of Angina	20	25.0%	480	5.0%
Hypertension (systolic ≥150 or diastolic ≥100)	82	13.4	418	4.3
Overweight (more than 15% above average)	35	16.7	465	4.9
Clinical Diabetes Mellitus	9	33.3	491	5.3
Serum Cholesterol over 275	109	11.0	357	4.3
Abnormal ECG	116	7.3	384	5.4
Smoking, 1 pack or more per day	134	6.6	366	5.5

Table 307d Cumulative Incidence of C.H.D. Complication† and Mortality in Follow-up of 5 to 7 Years by Degree of Coronary Narrowing (Series 1)

Degree of Narrowing	No. of Patients	C.H.D. Complication Incidence Rate	5-Yr C.H.D. Mort.		Mortality Ratio
			Observed	Expected●	
	ℓ	per cent	Q_c	Q_c'	100 Q/Q_c'
None	342	2.0%	.006	.011	54%
Slight (under 30%)	101	6.0	.022	.022	100
Moderate (30 to 49%)	57	28.1	.053	.021	250

* Basis of expected mortality: U.S. Life Tables 1959-61

† Including cardiac death, M.I. and angiographic development or progression of narrowing

● Basis of expected C.H.D. mortality: U.S. Vital Statistics 1967

CORONARY HEART DISEASE

§307–CORONARY ARTERIOGRAM (CLEVELAND CLINIC) (continued)

Follow-up: (1) In the total series 500 patients were successfully traced for 5 to 7 years by means of questionnaires, · telephone interviews, review of medical and other records, autopsy reports and contact with attending physicians. Since only 21 patients were not traced for the minimum possible period of five years, loss to follow-up was 4 per cent.

(2) All 590 patients were followed for a minimum of 5 years (range 5-9 years). Data were obtained primarily from physicians, patients, relatives and the Bureau of Vital Statistics using questionnaires and telephone interviews.

(3) Hospital or out-patient department records and communications with the referring physician, the patient or his family were obtained for a minimum of 6 years (range 6-11 years) after the initial arteriogram was evaluated.

Results: Cumulative survival rates and other data have been used to develop comparative mortality and survival experience in patients with and without moderate narrowing of the coronary arteries (Series 1) at 3, 5 and 7 years of follow-up, as shown in Tables 307a-b. Two groups are shown, with all ages and both sexes combined: a small group of 57 patients with moderate narrowing; and a large group of 443 patients made up of 342 patients with normal arteriogram and 101 patients with less than 30 per cent narrowing. The mortality and survival rates in the latter group were very close to those expected from 1959-61 U.S. Life Table rates, with 18 observed and 18.63 expected deaths. However, in the patients with moderate narrowing the mortality ratio at 7 years was 235 per cent, EDR was 13 excess deaths per 1000 per year, and the survival ratio 90.3 per cent, based on 8 deaths. Fluctuations in mortality ratio and EDR in successive intervals are probably random, due to the small numbers of deaths in each interval.

Rates are given in Table 307c for development of coronary heart disease complications (myocardial infarction, cardiac death, progression of coronary narrowing as revealed by later arteriogram) according to degree of coronary narrowing and other risk factors at the initial arteriogram. The cumulative complication rate over 5 to 7 years was 2.0 per cent for those with normal arteriograms, 6.0 per cent for patients with slight, and 28.1 per cent for patients with moderate narrowing. For other risk factors rates were highest for those with definite coronary heart disease (CHD) or diabetes, moderately elevated for those with overweight, hypertension or serum cholesterol over 275 mg./100 ml., and close to the series average rate of 5.8 per cent in those with smoking history and abnormal ECG. Five-year observed and expected mortality rates for CHD deaths only are also shown in Table 307d. The mortality ratio is well under 100 per cent for those with normal arteriograms, 100 per cent for those with slight narrowing and 250 per cent for patients with moderate narrowing. Among the 26 deaths, 15 were non-coronary, and 11 were attributed to CHD, including 8 sudden deaths.

During the first year following arteriography, patients in Series 2 with narrowing of 50 per cent or more in one vessel had a mortality ratio of 465 per cent with 35 extra deaths per 1000 (Table 307e). This experience, indicative of serious impairment, was yet substantially better than the excess mortality for patients with two- or three-vessel disease (mortality ratios 1260 and 2270 per cent, and EDR's, 112 and 210 per 1000, respectively). These latter rates diminished with duration after arteriography but no trend was discernible in patients with only one diseased vessel. The patients with one diseased vessel were also classified according to the presence or absence of additional narrowing in other vessels between 30 to 50 per cent (Table 307f). The mortality ratio was 215 per cent for patients without additional lesions and climbed to 465 per cent with additional lesions. The corresponding excess death rates were 13 and 42 per 1000 per year. Among patients with single-vessel disease, the particular vessel involved did not cause a large change in the mortality ratio, range 265 per cent to 390 per cent, (Table 307g). The three combinations of double-vessel disease ranged from a low mortality ratio of 750 per cent to a high of 930 per cent. However, a diseased left main artery was indicative of a very high mortality ratio of 1500 per cent with 162 excess deaths per 1000 per year. These figures exceeded the 1370 per cent with 147 excess deaths per 1000 per year for triple-vessel disease. For patients with severe coronary narrowing of 80 per cent or more (Table 307h), excess mortality was highest in the second year in those with single-vessel disease, and in the first two years in those with two-vessel disease, with significantly higher average mortality ratio (865 per cent) and EDR (80 per 1000 per year) in the latter group. For patients with triple-vessel disease, the excess death rate was extremely high (254 per 1000) in the first year and decreased during the remainder of the five-year period, though at the end of five years it was still above the average excess death rate of the other groups.

CORONARY ARTERIOGRAM (CLEVELAND CLINIC)

Table 307e Comparative Mortality and Survival Experience by Duration and Number of Vessels with 50% or More Narrowing (Series 2)

Interval	Exposure Person-Yrs	No. of Deaths	Mortality Rate Observed	Mortality Rate Expected*	Cumulative Survival Observed	Cumulative Survival Expected	Mortality Ratio	Survival Ratio	Excess Death Rate
t to $t + \Delta t$	E	d	$\bar{q}$	$\bar{q}'$	P	P'	100 $\bar{q}/\bar{q}'$	100 P/P'	1000($\bar{q}-\bar{q}'$)
One-vessel									
0-1 yr	202	9	.045	.0097	.955	.9903	465%	96.4%	35
1-2	193	1	.005	.0106	.950	.9798	47	97.0	−5.6
2-3	192	8	.042	.0116	.911	.9685	360	94.1	30
3-4	184	5	.027	.0126	.886	.9563	215	92.6	14
4-5	179	12	.067	.0138	.827	.9431	485	87.7	53
0-5	950	35	.037	.0116	.827	.9431	320	87.7	25
Two-vessels									
0-1 yr	270	33	.122	.0097	.878	.9903	1260%	88.7%	112
1-2	237	30	.127	.0106	.767	.9798	1200	78.3	116
2-3	207	18	.087	.0115	.700	.9685	755	72.3	76
3-4	189	15	.079	.0126	.644	.9563	625	67.3	66
4-5	174	14	.080	.0138	.592	.9431	580	62.8	66
0-5	1077	110	.102	.0116	.592	.9431	880	62.8	90
Three-vessels									
0-1 yr	118	26	.220	.0097	.780	.9903	2270%	78.8%	210
1-2	92	14	.152	.0106	.662	.9798	1430	67.6	141
2-3	78	13	.167	.0115	.551	.9685	1450	56.9	156
3-4	65	9	.138	.0126	.474	.9563	1100	49.6	125
4-5	56	3	.054	.0138	.449	.9431	1390	47.6	40
0-5	409	65	.159	.0116	.449	.9431	1370	47.6	147
All patients									
0-1 yr	590	68	.115	.0097	.885	.9903	1190%	89.4%	105
1-2	522	45	.086	.0106	.808	.9798	810	82.5	75
2-3	476	39	.082	.0115	.742	.9685	715	76.6	70
3-4	438	29	.066	.0126	.693	.9563	525	72.5	53
4-5	409	29	.071	.0138	.644	.9431	515	68.3	57
0-5	2435	210	.086	.0116	.644	.9431	740	68.3	74

Table 307f Comparative 5-Year Experience in Single-vessel disease (Series 2) with and without Additional Moderate Narrowing (30-50%)

	No. Alive at Start	No. of Deaths	Cumulative Survival	Ann. Mortality Observed	Ann. Mortality Expected*	Mortality Ratio	Survival Ratio	Excess Death Rate
	ℓ	d	P	$\check{q}$	$\check{q}'$	100 $\check{q}/\check{q}'$	100 P/P'	1000($\check{q}-\check{q}'$)
With Additional Lesions	91	22	.758	.054	.0116	465%	80.4%	42
Without Additional Lesions	111	13	.883	.025	.0116	215	93.6	13

Table 307g Comparative 5-Year Experience by Particular Vessel Involved (Series 2)

Vessel Involved†	No. Alive at Start	Exposure Person-Yrs	No. of Deaths	Mortality Rate Observed	Mortality Rate Expected*	Cumulative Survival	Mortality Ratio	Survival Ratio	Excess Death Rate
	ℓ	E	d	$\bar{q}$	$\bar{q}'$	P	100 $\bar{q}/\bar{q}'$	100 P/P'	1000($\bar{q}-\bar{q}'$)
RCA	98	463	15	.032	.0116	.850	275%	90.1%	20
CX	27	130	4	.031	.0116	.854	265	90.5	19
LAD	77	357	16	.045	.0116	.794	390	84.2	33
RCA + LAD	140	588	51	.087	.0116	.634	750	67.2	75
RCA + CX	53	220	22	.100	.0116	.590	860	62.5	88
LAD + CX	40	148	16	.108	.0116	.565	930	59.9	96
LMCA	37	121	21	.174	.0116	.385	1500	40.8	162
RCA, LAD, CX	118	409	65	.159	.0116	.421	1370	44.6	147

* Basis of expected mortality: 1964 U.S. Life Table

† RCA-Right coronary artery, CX-Left Circumflex Artery, LAD-Left Anterior Descending Artery, LMCA-Left Main Coronary Artery

CORONARY HEART DISEASE

§307–CORONARY ARTERIOGRAM (CLEVELAND CLINIC)

Results (continued):

Table 307i again shows a significant increase in mortality ratio from 275 per cent to 1240 per cent with progressive increase in the number of vessels diseased in Series 3 patients. Excess mortality did not depend greatly on the particular vessel involved except that patients with the right coronary artery as the only diseased vessel had a lower mortality ratio (275 per cent) and excess death rate (16 per 1000) as compared with patients with either a diseased left circumflex or left anterior descending. Higher mortality was experienced in patients with two-vessel disease, especially in the combinations which included the left anterior descending artery, and the highest of all in patients having three-vessel disease, as noted above. The presence of good collateral circulation or the absence of prior MI history was associated with lower mortality ratios in comparison to cases with poor collateral circulation (670 vs. 840 per cent) and those with a history of MI (600 vs. 880 per cent). The highest excess mortality (mortality ratio 1920 per cent and excess death rate 226 per 1000) occurred in subjects with triple-vessel disease and prior MI history.

Comments: The patients in Series 2 were also evaluated using left ventriculograms and classified as normal, with localized "scar" tissue, with aneurysms, and with diffuse "scar" tissue. The mortality was lowest in patients with normal left ventricular function (26 per cent over 5 years) and highest in cases with diffuse "scar" tissue (69 per cent over 5 years). The mortality was also correlated with the severity and duration of the chest pain, being worst in patients with angina pectoris, Class 3-4 of more than 72 months duration.

Webster, et al., (Series 3) reported data concerning the correlation between number of vessels diseased and functional class. They found that 80 per cent of Class I patients had single-vessel disease, nearly half the Class II patients had single-vessel disease. Class III patients were nearly evenly divided as to number of vessels involved, while Class IV patients consisted primarily of those with disease of two or three vessels.

CORONARY ARTERIOGRAM (CLEVELAND CLINIC)

Table 307h   Comparative 5-Year Experience by Duration and Number of Vessels in Patients with Narrowing of 80 per cent or More (Series 3)

Interval	No. Alive at Start	Exposure Person-Yrs	No. of Deaths Observed	No. of Deaths Expected*	Cumulative Surv. Observed	Cumulative Surv. Expected*	Mortality Ratio	Survival Ratio	Excess Death Rate
t to $t + \Delta t$	ℓ	E	d	d'	P	P'	100 d/d'	100 P/P'	1000(d-d')/E
Single-vessel Obstruction†									
0-1 yr	178	178	4	1.28	.978	.9928	310%	98.5%	15
1-2	174	174	9	1.38	.927	.9849	650	94.1	44
2-5	165	474	15	4.59	.843	.9566	325	88.1	22
0-5	178	826	28	7.25	.843	.9566	385	88.1	25
Double-vessel Obstruction									
0-1 yr	177	177	20	1.55	.887	.9912	1290%	89.5%	104
1-2	157	157	17	1.52	.791	.9817	1120	80.6	99
2-5	140	391	29	4.57	.627	.9475	635	66.2	62
0-5	177	725	66	7.64	.627	.9475	865	66.2	80
Triple-vessel Obstruction									
0-1 yr	114	114	30	1.10	.737	.9903	2700%	74.4%	254
1-2	84	84	11	0.89	.640	.9798	1240	65.3	120
2-5	73	194	24	2.48	.430	.9424	970	45.6	111
0-5	114	392	65	4.47	.430	.9424	1450	45.6	154

Table 307i   Comparative 6-Year Mortality Experience by Detailed Result of Arteriogram and MI History (Series 3)

Vessels Involved● and Other Findings		No. of Patients	No. of Deaths	Cumulative Survival	Average Annual Survival	Average Annual Mortality	Expected Mortality*	Mortality Ratio	Excess Death Rate
		ℓ	d	P	$\breve{p}$	$\breve{q}$	$\breve{q}'$	100 $\breve{q}/\breve{q}'$	1000($\breve{q}-\breve{q}'$)
Single-vessel	RCA	77	11	.857	.975	.025	.0093	275%	16
	LAD	69	17	.754	.954	.046	.0093	495	37
	CX	32	8	.750	.953	.047	.0093	505	38
Double-vessel	RCA + CX	48	17	.646	.930	.070	.0113	620	59
	LAD + CX	51	24	.530	.899	.101	.0113	895	90
	RCA + LAD	78	32	.590	.916	.084	.0113	745	73
Triple-vessel	RCA, LAD + CX	114	72	.368	.846	.154	.0124	1240	142
Single-vessel	Collateral	95	13	.863	.976	.024	.0093	260%	15
	No Collateral	83	23	.723	.947	.053	.0093	570	44
Double-vessel	Collateral	136	51	.625	.925	.075	.0113	665	64
	No Collateral	41	22	.463	.880	.120	.0113	1060	109
Triple-vessel	Collateral	74	47	.365	.845	.155	.0124	1250	143
	No Collateral	40	25	.375	.849	.151	.0124	1220	139
All types	Collateral	305	111	.636	.927	.073	.0109	670	62
	No Collateral	164	70	.573	.911	.089	.0106	840	78
Single-vessel	No MI	110	19	.827	.969	.031	.0093	335%	22
	MI history	68	15	.779	.959	.041	.0093	440	32
Double-vessel	No MI	111	41	.631	.926	.074	.0113	655	63
	MI history	60	28	.533	.900	.100	.0113	885	89
Triple-vessel	No MI	73	37	.493	.889	.111	.0124	895	99
	MI history	41	33	.195	.762	.238	.0124	1920	226
All types	No MI	294	97	.670	.935	.065	.0108	600	54
	MI history	169	76	.550	.905	.095	.0108	880	84

* Basis of expected mortality: 1964 U.S. Life Tables

† Narrowing of 80% or more in the affected vessel(s), with not more than 50% in other arteries

● RCA-Right coronary artery, LAD-Left anterior descending artery, CX-Left circumflex artery

CORONARY HEART DISEASE

§308–PROGNOSTIC SIGNIFICANCE OF CORONARY ARTERIOGRAPHY

References: (1) G. C. Friesinger, E. E. Page, and R. S. Ross, "Prognostic Significance of Coronary Arteriography," Trans. Assoc. Am. Physicians, 83:78-92 (1970).
(2) A. Oberman, W. B. Jones, C. P. Riley, T. J. Reeves, L. T. Sheffield, and M. E. Turner, "Natural History of Coronary Artery Disease," Bull. N.Y. Acad. Med., 48:1109-1125 (1972).

Subjects Studied: (1) 224 of 350 patients evaluated 1960-1967 by coronary arteriography at Johns Hopkins Hospital, Baltimore, because of definite or suspected coronary artery disease. Reasons for exclusion were unsatisfactory study, a diagnosis of valvular or primary myocardial disease, and subsequent coronary surgical procedures. Patients retained in the series were classified by category of chest pain and a scoring system based on degree of coronary narrowing (0-none, 1-minor, 2-localized stenosis from 50-90 per cent, 3-multiple narrowing in the same vessel from 50-90 per cent, 4-severe narrowing greater than 90 per cent, 5-total obstruction) in each artery, and number of major coronary arteries involved. "Normal" arteriograms were those with a score of 0-3 but not more than 50 per cent narrowing in any major coronary artery. Age and sex distribution were as follows:

Age Group (Years)	20-29	30-39	40-49	50-60	All Ages	Male	Female
Normal arteriogram	11	31	62	17	121	74	47
Abnormal	12	22	54	15	103	88	15

(2) 246 of 437 patients referred to the University of Alabama Medical Center 1965 to 1970 for evaluation of ischemic heart disease by coronary arteriography. Patients with associated cardiovascular disease, unsatisfactory arteriographic studies, and those who subsequently underwent corrective surgery were omitted. The remaining patients were classified by number of vessels diseased (maximal obstruction in any vessel of 50 per cent or more), presence of angina pectoris (AP) and history of myocardial infarction (MI). Age and sex distribution were as follows:

Male	<35 Yrs	35-55	>55	All	Female	<35 Yrs	35-55	>55	All	Total
Normal	13	45	3	61	Normal	3	27	7	37	98
Abnormal	8	88	37	133	Abnormal	1	8	6	15	148
Total	21	133	40	194	Total	4	35	13	52	246

Follow-up: In Series (1) information was obtained from the referring physician by letter or telephone at least one year after the arteriographic procedure with a mean follow-up period of 53 months.
In Series (2) the referring physician or the patient was contacted to obtain follow-up information and schedule a re-examination approximately 20 months after the original evaluation.

Results: The number of observed deaths for patients with normal arteriograms (Tables 308a-b) was only slightly different from the expected number of deaths (an aggregate of 5 observed and about 3.7 expected). The mortality ratio increased progressively with number of coronary arteries involved reaching over 1300 per cent for triple vessel disease (Series 2), and the excess death rate increased from 12 to 176 per 1000 per year. The mortality ratios for all patients with abnormal arteriograms were 1060 per cent in Series 1 and 975 per cent in Series 2. There was no consistent pattern during the five-year follow-up in Series 1. Most of the patients in Series 1 (Table 308c) who suffered from typical angina pectoris (AP) were rated as abnormal (arteriographic score greater than 2), with almost half suffering from severe atherosclerosis (score over 10). Cases of atypical AP, were more evenly distributed throughout the range of scores, and patients with other pain were usually found to have a normal score. Subjects who suffered AP (both typical and atypical) or exhibited severe atherosclerosis experienced a higher death rate than those without either trait. The mortality rate was very high for patients with arteriographic scores of 10 or more who suffered from typical AP (16 died out of 35) and atypical AP (5 out of 8). The number of deaths also increased as the degree of occlusion increased from 2 deaths in 121 patients with scores of 0-2 to 22 deaths in 46 with scores of 10-15.

In Series 2, a history of AP was again a potent risk factor (Table 308d). In addition, several other traits were linked to higher mortality ratios, including ECG evidence of MI, congestive heart failure, and an enlarged heart.

PROGNOSTIC SIGNIFICANCE OF CORONARY ARTERIOGRAPHY

Table 308a Comparative Experience by Arteriogram Severity Score* (Series 1)

| Interval | | No. Alive at Start | Exposure Person-Yrs | No. of Deaths | | Cumulative Surv. Rate | | Mortality Ratio | Cumulative Surv. Ratio | Excess Death Rate |
No.	Start-End			Observed	Expected†	Observed	Expected†			
i	t to t + Δt	$\cdot\ell$	E	d	d'	P	P'	100 d/d'	100 P/P'	1000(d-d')/E
	Normal Arteriogram (Score 0-3)									
	0-5 yrs	121	487	2	2.46	.975	.974	81%	100.1%	−1.0
	Abnormal Arteriogram (Score 4 and up)									
1	0-1 yr	103	103	5	0.53	.951	.9948	945	95.6	43
2	1-2	98	97.5	8	0.55	.873	.9892	1450	88.3	76
3	2-3	89	82.5	6	0.51	.810	.9830	1180	82.4	67
4	3-5	70	107	6	0.76	.729	.9690	790	75.2	49
	0-5	103	390	25	2.35	.729	.9690	1060	75.2	58

Table 308b Comparative Experience, Coronary Narrowing 50% or More (Series 2)

| No. of Major Arteries Involved | Average Follow-up | No. Alive at Start | No. of Deaths | Survival Rate | Ave. Ann. Mort. Rate | | Mortality Ratio | Survival Ratio | Excess Death Rate |
					Observed	Expected†			
	Δt	ℓ	d	P = 1 - (d/ℓ)	$\breve{q}$	$\breve{q}'$	100 $\breve{q}$/$\breve{q}'$	100 P/P'	1000 ($\breve{q}$-$\breve{q}'$)
None (Normal)	1.81 yrs	98	3	.969	.017	.0050	340%	97.8%	12
One Vessel	1.66	46	2	.957	.026	.0097	270	97.2	16
Two Vessels	1.89	50	13	.740	.147	.0132	1110	75.9	134
Three Vessels	1.61	52	15	.712	.191	.0147	1300	72.9	176
All Abnormal	1.72	148	30	.797	.124	.0127	975	81.5	111

Table 308c Distribution of Cases (Deaths in Parentheses) by Arteriogram Score and Type of Chest Pain, Average Follow-up 53 Months (Series 1)

| Classification | Normal | Abnormal | | | | | All Cases | |
	0-2	3-4.5	5-9.5	10-15	Total 3 up			
Typical Angina Pectoris	10	7	20 (3)	35 (16)	62 (19)		72	(19)
Atypical Angina Pectoris	14	3	9 (1)	8 (5)	20 (6)		34	(6)
Uncertain Pain	55 (2)	5	6	3 (1)	14 (1)		69	(3)
Not Angina Pectoris	38	1	2 (1)	0	3 (1)		41	(1)
No Pain	4	1	3	0	4 (1)		8	(1)
Total	121 (2)	17 (0)	40 (5)	46 (22)	103 (27)		224	(29)

Table 308d Distribution of Cases (Deaths in Parentheses) by Arteriogram and Other Factors (Series 2)

| No. of Vessels Abnormal | History of Angina | | ECG Evidence of MI | | Congestive Heart Failure | | Heart Size ≥396 cc/M² | |
	yes	none	yes	none	yes	none	yes	no (normal)
None (Normal)	18 (0)	80 (3)	3 (1)	95 (2)	9 (1)	89 (2)	36 (2)	47 (0)
Mortality Rate Q	.000	.038	.333	.021	.111	.022	.056	.000
Abnormal								
One Vessel	29 (2)	17 (0)	16 (2)	30 (0)	6 (1)	40 (1)	21 (1)	22 (0)
Two Vessels	35 (9)	15 (4)	19 (7)	31 (6)	14 (9)	36 (4)	27 (11)	15 (1)
Three Vessels	42 (13)	10 (2)	26 (10)	26 (5)	16 (7)	36 (8)	34 (13)	9 (2)
Total	106 (24)	42 (6)	61 (19)	87 (11)	36 (17)	112 (13)	82 (25)	46 (3)
Mortality Rate Q	.226	.143	.311	.126	.472	.116	.305	.065

* Degree of Coronary Narrowing: 0-none, 1-minor, 2-localized stenosis from 50-90 per cent,
  3-multiple narrowing in the same vessel from 50-90 per cent, 4-severe narrowing greater than 90 per cent, and
  5-total obstruction. No "normal" arteriogram had a maximum narrowing as much as 50 per cent.

† Basis of expected mortality: 1964 U.S. Life Tables

3-42

CORONARY HEART DISEASE

§309–CORONARY ARTERY BYPASS

References: (1) R. J. Hall, J. T. Dawson, D. A. Cooley, G. L. Hallman, D. C. Wukasch, and E. Garcia, "Coronary Artery Bypass," Circulation, 48 (Suppl. III):III-146 - III-150 (1973).

(2) W. C. Sheldon, G. Rincon, D. B. Effler, W. L. Proudfit, and F. M. Sones, Jr., "Vein Graft Surgery for Coronary Artery Disease," Circulation, 48 (Suppl. III):III-184 - III-189 (1973).

Subjects Studied: (1) 1105 patients who underwent coronary artery bypass surgery alone, with or without endarterectomy at the Texas Heart Institute from October 1969 through March 1972. There were 962 men and 143 women included in this study with an average age of 53 years. Almost 80 per cent of the patients showed evidence of a previous myocardial infarction, and 98.6 per cent experienced angina. The subjects were rated according to the New York Heart Association criteria, with most in classes III and IV (72 and 24 per cent, respectively); 22 per cent had symptoms of congestive heart failure.

(2) 1000 patients at the Cleveland Clinic who underwent coronary bypass surgery (560 of them had other corrective heart surgery at the same time) from May 1967 to July 1970. The group consisted of 874 men and 126 women with an average age of 52 years. These patients were compared to a group of 469 men and women, average age 49 years, with coronary atherosclerosis who did not undergo coronary bypass surgery.

Follow-up: (1) A post-operative evaluation was conducted on the patients from three to twenty-seven months after surgery to determine the degree of relief from chest pain, ability to work, and survival status.

(2) Patients, their physicians, or families were contacted in May 1972 if a post-operative arteriogram was not available. The average follow-up was 30 months (range 22 to 60 months). The nonsurgical group was followed for a minimum of six years.

Results: Early mortality, within 30 days of operation in Series 1, was higher for women (13.3 vs 5.6 per cent, Table 309a). In both sexes this mortality increased with age. Prior myocardial infarction (MI) increased the risk of early mortality with the greatest risk arising when the MI occurred less than one week before surgery. The number of vessels bypassed did not influence mortality. However, when the bypass surgery was accompanied by endarterectomy, there was an increase in the early mortality rate from approximately 5 per cent for bypass alone to 9.5 per cent for bypass plus endarterectomy. Since 1969 there has been a progressive improvement in early mortality from 9.5 per cent to 3.2 per cent in 1972. Early mortality in Series 2, with a one-month rate of 4 per cent, was similar to the more favorable results of Series 1. However, on a comparative basis, excess mortality is extremely high in this first month, with a mortality ratio of 4400 per cent and an EDR of 39 per 1000 per *month*. As is evident from Table 309b early mortality was lower for the patients with bypass operation alone than it was for the patients who also had additional surgery, generally an internal mammary artery implant. As in Series 1, the authors report improvement in early mortality from year to year, the rate for patients with vein graft only falling to 1.2 per cent in 1971.

In Series 2 the mortality ratio ranged from 174 per cent in the second year following operation to 300 per cent in the third and fourth years (Table 309c); it was 240 per cent in the first interval from 1 to 12 months. EDR after the first month had a corresponding range from a minimum of 8.5 to 28 extra deaths per 1000 per year. Excess mortality was lower for the coronary bypass than for the unoperated patients studied by angiogram in each interval after the first month, with correspondingly higher cumulative survival rates, even at the end of the first year. Limited follow-up experience in Series 1 after the first month indicated an observed annual mortality rate of .023 based on 25 late deaths and an exposure of approximately 1127 person-years.

Comments: For a majority of the operated patients in Series 1, incidence of chest pain decreased and ability to work improved. In Series 2, the 619 patients with a total of 719 grafts were reexamined in May 1972 (minimum follow-up of 22 months). The grafts were patent in over 80 per cent of the cases. Graft occlusions, as evidenced by a reappearance of symptoms, usually occurred within 6 months of surgery.

CORONARY ARTERY BYPASS

Table 309a   Acute Mortality following Coronary Bypass - Series 1. (Within 30 days after operation)

Age or Other Characteristic		No. Patients	No. Early Deaths	30-Day Mort. Rate	Age or Other Characteristic		No. Patients	No. Early Deaths	30-Day Mort. Rate
		ℓ	d	q_i			ℓ	d	q_i
Male	under 40	63	4	.063	Female				
	40-49	280	10	.036		under 50	34	3	.088
	50-59	412	24	.058		50-59	56	7	.125
	60-69	189	14	.074		60-69	49	8	.163
	70-79	18	2	.111		70-79	4	1	.250
	All Ages	962	54	.056		All Ages	143	19	.133
Prior MI	0-7 days	18	9	.500	Year of Operation				
	8-30 days	45	6	.133		1969-70	179	17	.095
	1-2 mos	32	2	.063		1971	738	50	.068
	over 2 mos	782	47	.060		1972	188	6	.032
No Prior MI		228	9	.039		Total	1105	73	.066
Bypass Alone					Bypass with Endarterectomy				
1 vessel	(6.5)*	205	9 (5)†	.044	1 vessel	(8.0)*	33	3 (0)†	.091
2 vessel	(9.3)	453	27 (14)	.060	2 vessel	(10.3)	259	24 (6)	.093
3 vessel	(11.0)	93	4 (0)	.043	3 vessel	(11.3)	62	6 (0)	.097

Table 309b   Acute Mortality (within 1 month of operation) - Series 2

Category	No. Pts. Operated	No. of Deaths	Interval Mort. Rate		Mortality Ratio	Survivors at 1 Month	Interval Surv. Rate	Excess Death Rate/Month
			Observed	Expected●				
	ℓ_o	d_o	$q_i = d_o/\ell_o$	q_i'	$100\, q_i/q_i'$	$\ell_1 = \ell_o - d_o$	$p_i = 1 - q_i$	$1000(q_i - q_i')$
Vein graft surgery alone	440	13	.0295	.0009	3300%	427	.9705	29
Graft and other surgery□	560	27	.0482	.0009	5400	533	.9518	47
All patients	1000	40	.0400	.0009	4400	960	.9600	39

Table 309c   Comparative Experience with and without Coronary Bypass - Series 2

No.	Interval Start-End	Entry to End of Interval		Cumulative Survival	Interval Survival	Interval Mortality	Expected Mortality●	Mortality Ratio	Cumulative Surv. Ratio	Excess Death Rate
		No. Followed	No. of Deaths							
i	t to t + Δ t	F	Σd	$P = 1 - (\Sigma d/F)$	p_i	q_i	q_i'	$100\, q_i/q_i'$	$100\, P/P'$	$1000(q_i - q_i')$
Coronary Bypass Patients□										
1	1 mo-1 yr	960	22	.977	.977	.023	.0096	240%	98.7%	13
2	1-2 yr	778	33	.958	.980	.020	.0115	174	97.8	8.5
3	2-3 yr	253	20	.921	.962	.038	.0127	300	95.3	25
4	3-4 yr	68	8	.882	.958	.042	.0139	300	92.6	28
Patients with Angiogram, no operations (See §308 - Series 2)										
1	0-1 yr	469	56	.881	.881	.119	.0079	1510%	88.8%	111
2	1-2 yr	469	91	.806	.915	.085	.0088	965	82.0	76
3	2-3 yr	469	117	.751	.931	.069	.0097	710	77.1	59
4	3-4 yr	469	138	.706	.940	.060	.0106	565	73.3	49

* Coronary Arteriogram Score, sum of scores 0 (no obstruction) to 5 (total obstruction) for each vessel
† Late deaths (after 1 month) in parentheses
● Basis of expected mortality: 1964 U. S. Life Tables
□ 512 patients also had internal mammary artery implant, and 62 had valvular or other defects repaired

CORONARY HEART DISEASE

§310–MYOCARDIAL INFARCTION

Reference: O. W. Beard, H. R. Hipp, M. Robins, J. S. Taylor, R. V. Ebert, and L. G. Beran, "Initial Myocardial Infarction Among 503 Veterans," Am. J. Med., 28:871-883 (1960).

Subjects Studied: Male patients with diagnosis of first transmural myocardial infarction, discharged between 1950 and 1952 from 33 large teaching Veterans Administration Hospitals. The patients were from 34 states, and all but 15 were white.

Age Distribution at Hospitalization and Two Months Later:

Age	No. Admitted	No. Surviving at 2 Months	Age	No. Admitted	No. Surviving at 2 Months
Under 30	4 (0.8%)	4 (0.9%)	50-59	208 (41.3%)	182 (42.6%)
30-39	72 (14.3%)	65 (15.3%)	60-69	87 (17.3%)	66 (15.5%)
40-49	107 (21.3%)	94 (22.0%)	70 up	25 (5.0%)	16 (3.7%)
Under 50	183 (36.4%)	163 (38.2%)	50 up	320 (63.6%)	264 (61.8%)
			All	503 (100.0%)	427 (100.0%)

Method of Selection: Clinical records of 3086 patients were reviewed: a randomly selected 50 per cent sample of all patients discharged with a diagnosis of coronary artery disease 1950-52. The sample was weighted to yield a higher proportion of young patients by review of all records of patients under age 50, with only a stratified sample of those age 50 up. Cases were excluded for any one of the following reasons: delay in admission more than 96 hours from onset of the acute myocardial infarction; a history of previous infarction; a history of prolonged chest pain more than one month prior to admission. Out of 631 patients accepted on these criteria, nine were eliminated because of other serious illness, and 119 were analyzed separately because of an ECG diagnosis of non-transmural infarction (96 cases) or permanent bundle branch block (23 cases), leaving a study group of 503 male patients hospitalized for acute, confirmed, transmural first myocardial infarction.

Follow-up: The integrated records system of the Veterans Administration was utilized for follow-up at an interval of five years after the infarction. On the basis of previous studies of the completeness of V. A. death records it was assumed that all patients not reported as dying within five years did survive, but subsequent follow-up (Tables 311a-b) showed that 136 deaths actually occurred within five years instead of the 133 given in this article. Computations with respect to this five-year period in Tables 310a-c have béen adjusted by estimate tó correct the understatement of deaths.

Results: In the article mortality and survival data for five years are presented on an annual basis (with a further breakdown in the first year) for two age groups, those under 50, and those 50 up. Comparative annualized mortality rates are given for the serial intervals, and comparative rates at two months and five years for a wide variety of clinical and ECG factors known shortly after admission. Average annual mortality rates over the five-year interval in decennial age groups are compared with expected rates for U. S. white male population, 1953. Advanced age, history of hypertension, history of angina pectoris of more than one month's duration, shock, congestive failure, serious arrhythmias or conduction defect in the ECG, and prolonged high fever had an adverse effect on the immediate (two-month) rate. All of these factors except shock also adversely affected the five-year mortality rate. Extremely high mortality ratios are reflected in the first two months' experience (Table 310c). Mortality *ratios* decrease with age, but mortality *rates* increase with age (Tables 310a-c). The annual excess death rate averaged 47 per 1000 for patients under age 50 who survived more than two months, and 67 per 1000 for those age 50 up (Table 310a).

FIRST MYOCARDIAL INFARCTION IN V. A. HOSPITAL PATIENTS

Table 310a   Observed Data and Comparative Experience by Age and Duration (Excluding First Two Months)

Age Group	Interval		No. Alive at Start of Interval	Exposure Person-Yrs	Deaths in Interval		Mortality Ratio		Survival Ratio		Excess Death Rates
	No.	Start-End			Obs.	Exp.*	Interval	Cumulative	Interval	Cumulative	
	i	t to t + Δt	ℓ	E	d	d'	100 d/d'	100 Q/Q'	100 p/p'	100 P/P'	1000(d-d')/E
Under 50	1	2 mos - 6 mos	163	54.3	4	.25	1600%	1600%	97.6%	97.6%	69
	2	6 mos - 12 mos	159	79.5	7	.37	1900	1760	95.8	93.7	83
	3	1 yr - 2 yrs	152	152.0	5	.76	660	1110	97.2	91.0	28
	4	2 yrs - 3 yrs	147	147.0	10	.82	1220	1110	93.7	85.3	62
	5	3 yrs - 4 yrs	137	137.0	5	.83	600	935	97.0	82.7	30
	6	4 yrs - 5 yrs	132	132.0	6	.88	680	840	96.1	80.1	39
	All	2 mos - 5 yrs	163		37	3.91	945	840		80.1	47
50 up	1	2 mos - 6 mos	264	88.0	12	2.03	590	590	96.2	96.2	113
	2	6 mos - 12 mos	252	126.0	12	3.05	395	460	96.4	92.7	71
	3	1 yr - 2 yrs	240	240.0	21	6.02	350	385	93.5	86.8	62
	4	2 yrs - 3 yrs	219	219.0	19	5.93	320	345	93.8	81.5	60
	5	3 yrs - 4 yrs	200	200.0	20	5.86	340	325	92.7	75.6	71
	6	4 yrs - 5 yrs	180	180.0	15	5.67	265	300	94.7	71.5	52
	All	2 mos - 5 yrs	264		99	28.56	345	300		71.5	67

Table 310b   Derived Mortality and Survival Data (Excluding First Two Months)

Age Group	Interval		Observed Rates				Expected Rates*			
			Interval		Cumulative		Interval		Cumulative	
	No.	Start-End	Mortality	Survival	Survival	Mortality	Mortality	Survival	Survival	Mortality
	i	t to t + Δt	q	p	P	Q	q'	p'	P'	Q'
Under 50	1	2 mos - 6 mos	.025	.975	.975	.025	.0015	.9985	.9985	.0015
	2	6 mos - 12 mos	.044	.956	.933	.067	.0023	.9977	.9962	.0038
	3	1 yr - 2 yrs	.033	.967	.902	.098	.0050	.9950	.9912	.0088
	4	2 yrs - 3 yrs	.068	.932	.841	.159	.0056	.9944	.9857	.0143
	5	3 yrs - 4 yrs	.036	.964	.810	.190	.0061	.9939	.9797	.0203
	6	4 yrs - 5 yrs	.045	.955	.773	.227	.0068	.9932	.9730	.0270
50 up	1	2 mos - 6 mos	.045	.955	.955	.045	.0077	.9923	.9923	.0077
	2	6 mos - 12 mos	.048	.952	.909	.091	.0121	.9879	.9803	.0197
	3	1 yr - 2 yrs	.088	.912	.830	.170	.0251	.9749	.9557	.0443
	4	2 yrs - 3 yrs	.087	.913	.758	.242	.0271	.9729	.9298	.0702
	5	3 yrs - 4 yrs	.100	.900	.682	.318	.0293	.9707	.9025	.0975
	6	4 yrs - 5 yrs	.083	.917	.625	.375	.0315	.9685	.8741	.1259

Table 310c   Comparative Experience — Two Months Following Hospitalization

Age Group	No. Alive at Start of Interval	Deaths during Interval	Deaths Expected*	Excess Death Rate	Interval Start-End	No. Alive at Start of Interval	Deaths during Interval	Deaths Expected	Excess Death Rate
(Yrs)	ℓ	d	d'	per day†	(days)	ℓ	d	d'	per day†
Under 40	76	7	.031	1.5	0- 7	503	38	.165	10.7
40 - 49	107	13	.109	2.0	8-14	465	16	.165	4.9
50 - 59	208	26	.58	2.0	15-28	449	10	.33	1.5
60 - 69	87	21	.44	3.9	29-61	439	12	.78	0.8
70 up	25	9	.28	5.7					
All Ages	503	76	1.44	2.4	0-61	503	76	1.44	2.4

*Basis of expected mortality: U.S. White Males 1953
†EDR = 1000(d-d')/(E)(Δt in days)

§310–MYOCARDIAL INFARCTION (continued)

Comment: Early mortality in this, as in any series of patients hospitalized for acute myocardial infarction, does not include sudden deaths prior to the opportunity for hospitalization. Fatality rates immediately after an attack, before hospitalization, are extremely high. Early mortality rates from a closed population, with complete record of all deaths, would therefore be considerably higher. The influence of some cardiovascular complications on five-year and ten-year comparative mortality is shown in Table 311b. Additional data are in the original article.

§311–MYOCARDIAL INFARCTION

Reference: O. W. Beard, H. R. Hipp, M. Robins and V. R. Verzolini, "Initial Myocardial Infarction Among Veterans: Ten-Year Survival," Am. Heart J., 73:317-321 (1967).

Subjects Studied: Same patients selected and described for Tables 310a-c.

Follow-up: The integrated records system of the Veterans Administration was utilized for follow-up at five years and ten years following the infarction. Three additional deaths within five years were added to the total previously reported.

Additional follow-up by questionnaire was used in February 1963 to ascertain the status of 186 ten-year survivors. Completed questionnaires giving employment and clinical status were received from 140 patients alive at that time, 10 to 13 years after the initial infarction. An additional 37 patients had died subsequent to the tenth anniversary of their initial attack; three patients known to be alive did not return the questionnaire; only six patients could not be located.

Results: Data are presented in terms of survival curves for patients under 50 and age 50 up, over the interval from two months after the attack to ten years. Five-year and ten-year cumulative mortality rates are given by age, associated hypertension, and history of angina of various prior durations. Mortality measured as average annual excess death rate continued high in the second five years, with the highest excess rates in the older patients (Table 311b). Hypertension and angina history of more than one month's duration were also associated with higher mortality rates and ratios, even after age adjustment (Table 311b). In the follow-up evaluation 49 per cent of 140 survivors responding to the questionnaire in 1963 had gone through one or more subsequent heart attacks, and 84 per cent had angina or shortness of breath or both. However, of those under age 65 on evaluation, 70 per cent were still employed.

Comment: This provides an additional five years of follow-up to the results of the earlier report (Tables 310a-c). Note that a history of angina of less than one month's duration is associated with a *lower* mortality than a history of *no angina* preceding the infarction, during the earlier follow-up period from two months to five years after onset. "Premonitory angina" therefore appears to be a favorable prognostic sign in the first five-year period (26 observed deaths significantly lower than 39 deaths expected from the cumulative mortality for cases with no angina, by the Poisson test, $P = 0.011$).

FIRST MYOCARDIAL INFARCTION IN V. A. HOSPITAL PATIENTS

Table 311a Comparative Experience During Two Successive 5-Year Intervals (First Two Months Excluded)

Age Group	Interval	No. Alive at Start of Interval	Deaths during Interval	Average Annual Mortality Rate		Mortality Ratio		Survival Ratio		Excess Death Rate
	Start-End	Interval	Interval	Obs.	Exp.	Ave. Ann.	Interval	Ave. Ann.	Interval	
Years	t to t + Δt	ℓ	d	$\check{q}$	$\check{q}'$	100 $\check{q}/\check{q}'$	100 q_i/q_i'	100 $\check{p}/\check{p}'$	100 p_i/p_i'	1000($\check{q}-\check{q}'$)
Under 40	2 mo - 5 yrs	69	13	.042	.0030	1400%	1290%	96.1%	82.4%	39
	5 - 10 yrs	56	15	.060	.0050	1200	1080	94.5	75.1	55
	2 mo - 10 yrs	69	28	.052	.0041	1270	1040	95.2	61.8	48
40 - 49	2 mo - 5 yrs	94	24	.059	.0076	775	710	94.8	77.3	51
	5 - 10 yrs	70	12	.037	.0119	310	295	97.5	88.0	25
	2 mo - 10 yrs	94	36	.048	.0098	490	415	96.1	67.9	38
50 - 59	2 mo - 5 yrs	182	65	.087	.0202	430	380	93.2	70.9	67
	5 - 10 yrs	117	55	.119	.0304	390	330	90.9	61.8	89
	2 mo - 10 yrs	182	120	.104	.0254	410	295	91.9	43.9	79
60 up	2 mo - 5 yrs	82	34	.105	.0440	240	210	93.6	72.8	61
	5 - 10 yrs	48	23	.122	.0595	205	181	93.4	70.8	62
	2 mo - 10 yrs	82	57	.114	.0519	220	170	93.5	51.5	62
All Ages	2 mo - 5 yrs	427	136	.076	.0188	405	365	94.2	74.7	57
	5 - 10 yrs	291	105	.086	.0259	330	295	93.8	72.9	60
	2 mo - 10 yrs	427	241	.081	.0224	360	280	94.0	54.5	58

Table 311b Subjects with History of Hypertension or Angina. Comparative Experience during Two Successive 5-Year Intervals (First Two Months Excluded). Observed Experience (Expected Shown at Bottom of Table).

Category and Interval	No. Alive Start Int.	Interval		Average Annual		Mortality Ratio		Survival Ratio		Excess Death Rate
		Surv. Rate	Mort. Rate	Surv. Rate	Mort. Rate*	Ave. Ann.	Interval	Ave. Ann.	Interval	
t to t + Δt	ℓ	p_i	q_i	$\check{p}$	$\check{q}$	100 $\check{q}/\check{q}'$	100 q_i/q_i'	100 $\check{p}/\check{p}'$	100 p_i/p_i'	1000($\check{q}-\check{q}'$)
All Cases										
2 mo - 5 yrs	427	.68	.32	.924	.076	405%	365%	94.2%	74.7%	57
5 - 10 yrs	291	.64	.36	.914	.086	330	295	93.8	72.9	60
2 mo - 10 yrs	427	.44	.56	.919	.081	360	280	94.0	54.5	58
No Hypertension										
2 mo - 5 yrs	305	.70	.30	.929	.071	380	340	94.7	76.7	52
5 - 10 yrs	214	.67	.33	.923	.077	295	270	94.8	76.4	51
2 mo - 10 yrs	305	.47	.53	.926	.074	330	265	94.7	58.8	52
Hypertension										
2 mo - 5 yrs	77	.58	.42	.893	.107	565	480	91.1	63.6	88
5 - 10 yrs	45	.57	.43	.894	.106	410	350	91.7	65.0	80
2 mo - 10 yrs	77	.33	.67	.893	.107	475	335	91.4	41.2	84
No Angina History										
2 mo - 5 yrs	154	.70	.30	.929	.071	380	340	94.7	76.7	52
5 - 10 yrs	108	.64	.36	.915	.085	330	295	93.9	73.0	60
2 mo - 10 yrs	154	.45	.55	.922	.078	350	275	94.3	56.2	56
Angina < 1 mo										
2 mo - 5 yrs	132	.80	.20	.955	.045	240	230	97.3	87.7	26
5 - 10 yrs	106	.66	.34	.920	.080	310	275	94.5	75.3	54
2 mo - 10 yrs	132	.53	.47	.937	.063	280	235	95.9	66.2	40
Angina ≥ 1 mo										
2 mo - 5 yrs	121	.56	.44	.887	.113	600	500	90.4	61.4	94
5 - 10 yrs	68	.59	.41	.900	.100	385	335	92.4	67.3	74
2 mo - 10 yrs	121	.33	.67	.893	.107	475	335	91.4	41.2	84
Expected Experience†		p_i'	q_i'	$\check{p}'$	$\check{q}'$					
2 mo - 5 yrs		.9122	.0878	.9812	.0188					
5 - 10 yrs		.8770	.1230	.9741	.0259					
2 mo - 10 yrs		.8000	.2000	.9776	.0224					

*Mortality Rates adjusted for age distributions
†Basis of expected mortality: U.S. White Males 1953

CORONARY HEART DISEASE

§312–MYOCARDIAL INFARCTION–EMPLOYED MEN

References: (1) S. Pell and C. A. D'Alonzo, "Acute Myocardial Infarction in A Large Industrial Population," J. Am. Med. Assoc., 185:831-838 (1963).
(2) S. Pell and C. A. D'Alonzo, "Immediate Mortality and Five-Year Survival of Employed Men with A First Myocardial Infarction," New Eng. J. Med., 270:915-922 (1964).
(3) Supplementary data supplied by the authors (1970).

Subjects Studied: Employees of E. I. duPont de Nemours and Company, January 1, 1956 through December 31, 1961. Age range was 17 to 64 and average number of employees 73,573 males and 12,997 females. Employees were located in 79 installations throughout the U. S., concentrated in Middle Atlantic and Southeastern states.

Data employed in the study were obtained from the cases of first myocardial infarction reported under company-sponsored health insurance and life insurance plans covering about 97 per cent of employees working six months or more. Sudden deaths were included unless circumstances indicated another cause. Early and total mortality therefore were *not* dependent on hospitalization as a requirement for entry into the study. Cases with a history of prior myocardial infarction were excluded. Confirmation of diagnosis was made in each case by review of company medical records. There were only 25 cases in female employees, and these have been excluded from further analysis.

Follow-up: Life insurance claims were utilized for obtaining data on all deaths. Male survivors were followed by annual medical reports from plant physicians for employees still working, and by pension payment records for employees retired or disabled. Only 49 male employees were lost to follow-up because of leaving employment prior to eligibility for retirement or disability benefits.

Results: Early mortality (deaths occurring within 30 days after attack) was high. There were 399 deaths out of 1331 men stricken, and, as indicated in Table 312a, mortality increased with age. Pre-existing hypertension and certain ECG abnormalities (especially bundle-branch blocks and premature ventricular contractions) adversely affected survival (Table 312b) directly after attack; effects of a pre-existing hypertensive condition continued during the 5-year period following attack (Table 312c); overweight at time of attack indicated no significant effect on mortality if not associated with hypertension.

Rates of mortality (q in Table 312e) and excess rates of death (EDR in Table 312d) were highest in the first year but showed no consistent change in the succeeding four years. Five-year cumulative mortality rates tended to increase with age, but the corresponding mortality ratios decreased. The highest excess death rate and the lowest survival ratio were in the middle age group, 45-54.

The incidence of myocardial infarction was lowest for executives and higher salaried employees; highest for lower salaried employees (white collar workers); and intermediate for blue collar workers. Five-year survival was 81 per cent for salaried employees, 74 per cent for wage earners.

Comment: In citing comparative rates, the authors used as a standard of reference a control group composed of duPont employees dying from causes other than myocardial infarction. For purposes of this monograph expected deaths were recalculated using U. S. White Male mortality rates (1959-1961).

FIRST MYOCARDIAL INFARCTION IN MALE INDUSTRIAL POPULATION

Table 312a   Case Incidence Rate — Early Death Experience

Age Group	Annual/Case Incidence Rate/1000	No. of Cases	Distribution of Cases	No. of Deaths in 30 Days	Mortality Rate per Month	No. Surviving 30 Days	Distribution of Survivors
25 - 34	0.12	15	1.1%	1	.067	14	1.5%
35 - 39	0.96	71	5.3	17	.239	54	5.8
40 - 44	2.45	166	12.5	43	.259	123	13.2
45 - 49	4.78	276	20.7	78	.283	198	21.2
50 - 54	7.93	340	25.6	100	.294	240	25.7
55 - 59	10.36	280	21.1	92	.329	188	20.2
60 - 64	10.80	183	13.7	68	.372	115	12.4
All Ages	3.02	1331	100.0	399	.300	932	100.0

Table 312b   Comparative Early Mortality (Within 30 Days)

Category	Age Group	Interval Start-End	No. Alive at Start of Interval	Deaths in Interval	Expected Deaths*	Mort. Rate over Interval	Survival Rate	Excess Death Rate
		t to t + Δ t	ℓ	d	d'	q	p	per day □
All Cases	All Ages	0 - 24 hrs	1331	336	.045	.252	.748	252
		1 - 30 da	995	63	.91	.063	.937	2.1
		0 - 30 da	1331	399	1.34	.300	.700	10
Normotensive	Under 45	0 - 30 da	194	46	.054	.237	.763	7.9
	45 - 54	0 - 30 da	433	123	.34	.284	.716	9.4
	55 - 64	0 - 30 da	295	87	.51	.295	.705	9.8
	All Ages	0 - 30 da	922	256	.90	.278	.722	9.2
Hypertensive†	Under 45	0 - 30 da	58	15	.016	.259	.741	8.6
	45 - 54	0 - 30 da	183	55	.142	.301	.699	10
	55 - 64	0 - 30 da	165	71	.28	.430	.570	14
	All Ages	0 - 30 da	406	141	.44	.347	.653	12
ECG History Normal	All Ages	0 - 30 da	925	269	.93	.291	.709	9.7
Abnormal●		0 - 30 da	255	94	.26	.369	.631	12
None Available		0 - 30 da	151	36	.15	.238	.762	7.9

Table 312c   Comparative 5-Year Experience by Pre-existing Hypertensive and Overweight Status (First Month Excluded)

Category	No. Alive at 1 Month	5-Year Survival Rate Observed	5-Year Survival Rate Expected	5-Year Survival Ratio	Average Annual Mortality Rate Observed	Average Annual Mortality Rate Expected	Average Mortality Ratio	Excess Death Rate
	ℓ	P	P'	100 P/P'	$\breve{q}$	$\breve{q}'$	100 $\breve{q}/\breve{q}'$	1000($\breve{q}-\breve{q}'$)
Normotensive	666	.780	.933	83.6	.0493	.0141	350%	35
Hypertensive†	265	.631	.928	68.0	.0894	.0151	590	74
Not Overweight	633	.752	.930	80.9	.0563	.0146	385	42
Overweight■	298	.705	.933	75.6	.0686	.0139	495	55

* Basis of expected mortality: U.S. White Male 1959-1961
† Two Successive Annual Readings of 150/94 or more
● Includes 148 Abnormal T-Wave; 88 ST-T Change; 48 prem. V.B.; 43 BBB
□ Expected deaths and EDR based on exposed to risk at 1 day (24 hrs) rather than 0 day. (EDR = 1000 (d-d')/(E/(Δt in days))
■ Over Ideal Weight by 20% or more

CORONARY HEART DISEASE

Table 312d Observed Data and Comparative Experience by Age Group and Duration (First Month Excluded)

Age and Interval	No. Alive at Start of Interval	Withdrawn + Lost Cases	Exposure Person-Yrs	Deaths in Interval		Mortality Ratio		Survival Ratio		Excess Death Rate
No. Start-End				Obs.	Exp.*	Interval	Cumulative	Interval	Cumulative	
i t to $t + \Delta t$	ℓ	$w + u$	E	d	d'	100 d/d'	100 Q/Q'	100p_i/p_i'	100 P/P'	1000$(d-d')/E$
Under 45 yrs										
1 1 mo - 1 yr	190	38	156.7	9	0.51	1760%	1760%	95.0%	95.0%	54
2 1 yr - 2 yrs	143	32	127.0	4	0.46	870	1240	97.3	92.4	28
3 2 yrs - 3 yrs	107	31	91.5	6	0.37	1620	1350	93.8	86.6	62
4 3 yrs - 4 yrs	70	19	60.5	2	0.27	740	1140	97.1	84.2	29
5 4 yrs - 5 yrs	49	21	38.5	1	0.19	525	970	97.9	82.3	21
1 mo - 5 yrs			474.2	22	1.80	1220	970	95.7	82.3	43
45 - 54 yrs										
1 1 mo - 1 yr	434	83	359.8	43	3.34	1290	1290	89.8	89.8	110
2 1 yr - 2 yrs	308	72	272.0	12	2.80	430	795	96.6	86.7	34
3 2 yrs - 3 yrs	224	55	196.5	9	2.24	400	630	96.5	83.7	34
4 3 yrs - 4 yrs	160	61	129.5	7	1.61	435	555	95.8	80.2	42
5 4 yrs - 5 yrs	92	45	69.5	4	0.93	430	505	95.5	76.5	44
1 mo - 5 yrs			1027.3	75	10.92	685	505	93.7	76.5	62
55 - 64 yrs										
1 1 mo - 1 yr	305	66	249.3	28	5.11	550	550	91.4	91.4	92
2 1 yr - 2 yrs	211	45	188.5	8	4.24	189	345	98.0	89.6	20
3 2 yrs - 3 yrs	158	39	138.5	10	3.41	295	315	95.1	85.2	48
4 3 yrs - 4 yrs	109	34	92.0	5	2.46	205	275	97.2	82.8	28
5 4 yrs - 5 yrs	70	37	51.5	3	1.49	200	250	97.0	80.4	29
1 mo - 5 yrs			719.8	54	16.71	325	250	94.6	80.4	52
All Ages										
1 1 mo - 1 yr	929†	187	765.8	80	8.96	895	895	91.4	91.4	93
2 1 yr - 2 yrs	662	149	587.5	24	7.50	320	570	97.1	88.8	28
3 2 yrs - 3 yrs	489	125	426.5	25	6.02	415	495	95.4	84.7	45
4 3 yrs - 4 yrs	339	114	282.0	14	4.34	325	435	96.5	81.8	34
5 4 yrs - 5 yrs	211	103	159.5	8	2.61	305	390	96.6	78.9	34
1 mo - 5 yrs			2221.3	151	29.43	515	390	94.4	78.9	55

*Basis of expected mortality: U.S. White Males 1959-1961

†The lives whose experience is traced include all but three of the total 30-day survivors given in Table 312a

FIRST MYOCARDIAL INFARCTION IN MALE INDUSTRIAL POPULATION

Table 312e   Derived Mortality and Survival Data (First Month Excluded)

Age Group	Interval		Observed Rates				Expected Rates*			
			Interval		Cumulative		Interval		Cumulative	
	No.	Start-End	Mortality	Survival	Survival	Mortality	Mortality	Survival	Survival	Mortality
	i	t to t + Δt	q	p	P	Q	q'	p'	P'	Q'
Under 45	1	1 mo - 1 yr	.053	.947	.947	.053	.0030	.9970	.9970	.0030
	2	1 yr - 2 yrs	.031	.969	.918	.082	.0036	.9964	.9934	.0060
	3	2 yrs - 3 yrs	.066	.934	.857	.143	.0040	.9960	.9894	.0106
	4	3 yrs - 4 yrs	.033	.967	.829	.171	.0045	.9955	.9850	.0150
	5	4 yrs - 5 yrs	.026	.974	.807	.193	.0050	.9950	.9801	.0199
45 - 54	1	1 mo - 1 yr	.110	.890	.890	.110	.0085	.9915	.9915	.0085
	2	1 yr - 2 yrs	.044	.956	.851	.149	.0103	.9897	.9813	.0187
	3	2 yrs - 3 yrs	.046	.954	.812	.188	.0114	.9886	.9701	.0299
	4	3 yrs - 4 yrs	.054	.946	.768	.232	.0124	.9876	.9581	.0419
	5	4 yrs - 5 yrs	.058	.942	.723	.277	.0134	.9866	.9452	.0548
55 - 64	1	1 mo - 1 yr	.103	.897	.897	.103	.0188	.9812	.9812	.0188
	2	1 yr - 2 yrs	.042	.958	.859	.141	.0225	.9775	.9591	.0409
	3	2 yrs - 3 yrs	.072	.928	.797	.203	.0246	.9754	.9355	.0645
	4	3 yrs - 4 yrs	.054	.946	.754	.246	.0267	.9733	.9105	.0895
	5	4 yrs - 5 yrs	.058	.942	.711	.289	.0289	.9711	.8842	.1158
All Ages	1	1 mo - 1 yr	.096	.904	.904	.096	.0107	.9893	.9893	.0107
	2	1 yr - 2 yrs	.041	.959	.867	.133	.0128	.9872	.9766	.0234
	3	2 yrs - 3 yrs	.059	.941	.816	.184	.0141	.9859	.9629	.0371
	4	3 yrs - 4 yrs	.050	.950	.775	.225	.0154	.9846	.9480	.0520
	5	4 yrs - 5 yrs	.050	.950	.736	.264	.0164	.9836	.9325	.0675

*Basis of expected mortality: U.S. White Males 1959-1961

CORONARY HEART DISEASE

§313–MYOCARDIAL INFARCTION AMONG MEMBERS OF HEALTH PLAN

References: (1) E. Weinblatt, S. Shapiro, C. W. Frank, and R. V. Sager, "Prognosis of Men after First Myocardial Infarction: Mortality and First Recurrence in Relation to Selected Parameters," Am. J. Pub. Health, 58:1329-1347 (1968).
(2) E. Weinblatt, S. Shapiro, and C. W. Frank, "Prognosis of Women with Newly Diagnosed Coronary Heart Disease-A Comparison with Course of Disease among Men," Am. J. Pub. Health, 63:577-593 (1973).
(3) E. Weinblatt, supplementary data in personal communication (1974).

Subjects Studied: Members of the Health Insurance Plan of Greater New York (HIP) who had a first myocardial infarction (MI) between 25 and 64 years of age. HIP is a prepaid comprehensive group practice plan with a membership of about 110,000. The subjects of the study were found by a review of the Plan's records of those members who, during the period 1961-1965, had sought medical care for symptoms suggesting the possibility of a first MI. Occurrence of a prior MI was disclosed by medical tests (ECG, physical examination, laboratory findings, etc.) and by doctors' and hospital records. There were 1054 subjects distributed by sex and age as follows:

Age Group (Years)	Under 55	55-64	All Ages	Mean Age
Male	433(41%)	449(43%)	882(84%)	55 Years
Female	50(5%)	122(11%)	172(16%)	57 Years
Male and Female	483(46%)	571(54%)	1054(100%)	55 Years

Follow-up: About 90 per cent of the subjects were examined on their entry into the study in 1961-1965 and at intervals in the succeeding 5 years. Data with regard to the others who did not accept the offered examination were obtained in the files maintained by HIP, from hospital records and physicians' reports. Subjects who died before medical care was obtainable were identified by screening all deaths among members of the Plan in the follow-up period. Additional information in such cases was acquired by next of kin interviews and from medical records. Over the course of the observation period five men were lost to follow-up for mortality and seven men for recurrence status.

Results: Early mortality results (over the first month following MI) are presented in Table 313a. The rate of mortality is extremely high in the first 24-hour period reaching 263 per 1000 in the case of men under 55 years of age and 350 per 1000 for men between 55 and 64. After the first day the rate drops sharply, falling to 44 per 1000 for men under 55 years and to 113 for men 55-64 years. Over the first month the overall mortality rate among men is .361 and among women, .372. Also exhibited in Table 313b is mortality experience within one month of attack according to selected accompanying observations. Hypertension prior to onset of the attack was associated with higher mortality in both sexes: subjects with elevated blood pressure showed a mortality rate over .420 against less than .200 where pressure was normal. Women diabetics, but not men, experienced very high early mortality. However, women reporting angina prior to the event showed no early mortality disadvantage, while men had a significantly higher early mortality rate. Both sexes who were hospitalized for first MI presented the expected early mortality disadvantage associated with congestive heart failure and clinically severe episodes.

Mortality and survival rates and ratios beyond the first month are shown in Tables 313c-d. Mortality ratios and EDR's are high in the first interval from one to six months, and then fall to lower levels. Excess mortality is relatively constant in men age 45 to 54 years after the first year of follow-up, but in younger and older age groups mortality dips in the interval from three to four years, due possibly to random variation. In men the mortality ratio for the five years decreases with advancing age, with a slight tendency for EDR to increase. The experience among females shows the highest mortality in the first interval, with irregular fluctuations thereafter (only 15 deaths as a total). For the entire follow-up, female mortality ratio was slightly higher than the male ratio, but EDR was lower, 25 vs. 33 extra deaths per 1000. Cumulative five-year survival ratios are all in the range, 84.8 to 88.6 per cent.

MYOCARDIAL INFARCTION AMONG MEMBERS OF HEALTH PLAN

Table 313a   Early Mortality (Within 1 Month) by Age and Sex

Sex and Age	Interval	Number at Risk ℓ_0	Number of Deaths d	Interval Mort. Rate q_i	Interval Surv. Rate p_i	Number Survivors ℓ_1
Male						
Under 55 yrs	0 - 1 da	433	114	.263	.737	319
	1 da - 1 mo	319	14	.044	.956	305
	0 - 1 mo	433	128	.296	.704	305
55-64 yrs	0 - 1 da	449	157	.350	.650	292
	1 da - 1 mo	292	33	.113	.887	259
	0 - 1 mo	449	190	.423	.577	259
All Ages	0 - 1 da	882	271	.307	.693	611
	1 da - 1 mo	611	47	.077	.923	564
	0 - 1 mo	882	318	.361	.639	564
Female						
Under 55 yrs	0 - 1 mo	50	18	.360	.640	32
55-64 yrs	0 - 1 mo	122	46	.377	.623	76
All Ages	0 - 1 mo	172	64	.372	.628	108
Male & Female All Ages	0 - 1 mo	1054	382	.362	.638	672

Table 313b   Early Mortality (At End of 1 Month) by Associated Medical Criteria and Sex

Category		Number at Risk ℓ_0	Number of Deaths d	Interval Mort. Rate q_i	Interval Surv. Rate p_i	Number Survivors ℓ_1
Male						
Hospitalized only		604	101	.167	.833	503
Blood Pressure*	Normal	283	59	.208	.792	224
	Borderline	270	97	.359	.641	173
	Elevated	222	94	.423	.577	128
Angina	No History	717	229	.319	.681	488
	History	157	78	.497	.503	79
Diabetes	Not present	724	231	.319	.681	493
	Present	105	36	.343	.657	69
Cong. Ht. Failure	Not present	497	54	.109	891	443
	Before or with M.I.	105	44	.419	.581	61
Severity	Less severe	412	9	.022	.978	403
	Most severe	146	52	.356	.644	94
Female						
Hospitalized only		120	22	.183	.817	98
Blood Pressure*	Normal	32	6	.188	.812	26
	Borderline	48	16	.333	.667	32
	Elevated	75	33	.440	.560	42
Angina	No History	127	48	.378	.622	79
	History	44	15	.341	.659	29
Diabetes	Not present	133	38	.286	.714	95
	Present	29	18	.621	.379	11
Cong. Ht. Failure	Not present	105	15	.143	.857	90
	Before or with M.I.	15	7	.467	.533	8
Severity	Less severe	84	1	.012	.988	83
	Most severe	27	12	.444	.556	15

* Blood pressure classified "elevated" if systolic 160 mm Hg or higher, or diastolic, 95 mm Hg or higher

CORONARY HEART DISEASE

Table 313c   Observed Data and Comparative Experience by Age, Sex and Duration (Excluding First Month after MI)

Age and Sex	Interval No.	Interval Start-End	No. Alive at start of Interval	Exposure* Person-Yrs	Deaths Obs.	Deaths Exp.†	Mortality Ratio Interval	Mortality Ratio Cumulative	Survival Ratio Interval	Survival Ratio Cumulative	Excess Death Rate
	i	t to t + Δt	ℓ	E	d	d'	100 d/d'	100 ∑d/∑d'	100 p_i/p_i'	100 P/P'	1000(d-d')/E
Male Under 45 yrs	1	1 mo-6 mos	74	30.8	2	0.13	1540%	1540%	97.4%	97.4%	61
	2	6 mos-1 yr	72	36.0	1	0.15	665	1070	98.8	96.3	24
	3	1-2 yrs	71	70.5	2	0.32	625	835	97.6	94.0	24
	4	2-3	69	67.7	3	0.34	880	850	96.1	90.3	39
	5	3-4	58	53.3	0	0.30	0	645	100.6	90.8	−5.6
	6	4-5	38	34.3	2	0.21	950	690	94.8	86.0	52
		1 mo-5 yrs	74	292.6	10	1.45	690	690		86.0	29
45-54 yrs	1	1 mo-6 mos	231	96.2	6	0.92	650	650	97.8	97.8	53
	2	6 mos-1 yr	225	112.5	4	1.07	375	505	98.7	96.4	26
	3	1-2 yrs	221	219.0	8	2.32	345	420	97.3	93.9	26
	4	2-3	213	208.0	11	2.42	455	430	95.8	90.0	41
	5	3-4	176	157.0	6	1.98	305	400	97.4	87.7	26
	6	4-5	118	101.1	4	1.38	290	385	97.3	85.3	26
		1 mo-5 yrs	231	893.8	39	10.09	385	385		85.3	32
55-64 yrs	1	1 mo-6 mos	259	107.9	13	2.45	530	530	95.7	95.7	98
	2	6 mos-1 yr	246	122.9	8	2.79	285	400	97.8	93.6	42
	3	1-2 yrs	236	232.5	9	5.76	156	275	98.5	92.3	14
	4	2-3	227	218.2	17	5.87	290	280	94.7	87.4	51
	5	3-4	181	162.8	4	4.74	84	235	100.4	87.8	−4.5
	6	4-5	123	108.8	7	3.42	205	230	96.6	84.8	33
		1 mo-5 yrs	259	953.1	58	25.03	230	230		84.8	35
All Ages	1	1 mo-6 mos	564	234.9	21	3.50	600	600	96.8	96.8	74
	2	6 mos-1 yr	543	271.4	13	4.01	325	455	98.3	95.2	33
	3	1-2 yrs	528	522.0	19	8.40	225	335	98.0	93.2	20
	4	2-3	509	493.9	31	8.63	360	340	95.4	88.9	45
	5	3-4	415	373.1	10	7.02	142	300	99.2	88.2	8.0
	6	4-5	279	244.2	13	5.01	260	295	96.7	85.2	33
		1 mo-5 yrs	564	2139.5	107	36.57	295	295		85.2	33
Female All Ages	1	1 mo-6 mos	108	45.0	4	0.39	1030%	1030%	96.5%	96.5%	80
	2	6 mos-1 yr	104	52.0	1	0.45	220	595	99.5	96.1	11
	3	1-2 yrs	103	102.5	1	1.00	100	325	100.0	96.0	0
	4	2-3	102	98.8	4	1.06	375	345	97.0	93.1	30
	5	3-4	85	75.2	4	0.91	440	365	95.9	89.3	41
	6	4-5	54	48.2	1	0.66	152	335	99.3	88.6	7.1
		1 mo-5 yrs	108	421.7	15	4.47	335	335		88.6	25

* Exposure data given in person-months for terminations, at 6-month intervals and converted to person-years

† Basis of expected mortality: U.S. White Males and Females 1959-1961

MYOCARDIAL INFARCTION AMONG MEMBERS OF HEALTH PLAN

Table 313d   Derived Mortality and Survival Data

Sex and Age	Interval No.	Interval Start-End	Observed Rates				Expected Rates*			
			Cumulative Survival	Interval Survival	Ave. Ann. Survival	Ave. Ann. Mortality	Cumulative Survival	Interval Survival	Ave. Ann. Survival	Ave. Ann. Mortality
	i	t to t + Δt	P	p_i	$\check{p}$	$\check{q}$	P'	p_i'	$\check{p}'$	$\check{q}'$
Male										
Under 45 yrs	1	1 mo-6 mos	.973	.973	.936	.064	.9983	.9983	.9958	.0042
	2	6 mos-1 yr	.960	.986	.972	.028	.9961	.9978	.9956	.0044
	3	1-2 yrs	.932	.972	.972	.028	.9917	.9955	.9955	.0045
	4	2-3	.891	.956	.956	.044	.9867	.9950	.9950	.0050
	5	3-4	.891	1.000	1.000	.000	.9812	.9944	.9944	.0056
	6	4-5	.840	.942	.942	.058	.9752	.9939	.9939	.0061
45-54 yrs	1	1 mo-6 mos	.974	.974	.939	.061	.9960	.9960	.9904	.0096
	2	6 mos-1 yr	.957	.982	.964	.036	.9912	.9952	.9904	.0096
	3	1-2 yrs	.922	.964	.964	.036	.9807	.9894	.9894	.0106
	4	2-3	.874	.948	.948	.052	.9694	.9884	.9884	.0116
	5	3-4	.841	.963	.963	.037	.9571	.9874	.9874	.0126
	6	4-5	.808	.960	.960	.040	.9441	.9864	.9864	.0136
55-64 yrs	1	1 mo-6 mos	.950	950	.884	.116	.9905	.9905	.9774	.0226
	2	6 mos-1 yr	.919	.968	.937	.063	.9792	.9886	.9773	.0227
	3	1-2 yrs	.884	.962	.962	.038	.9549	.9752	.9752	.0248
	4	2-3	.817	.924	.924	.076	.9292	.9731	.9731	.0269
	5	3-4	.797	.976	.976	.024	.9022	.9709	.9709	.0291
	6	4-5	.747	.938	.938	.062	.8738	.9686	.9686	.0314
All Ages	1	1 mo-6 mos	.963	.963	.913	.087	.9938	.9938	.9852	.0148
	2	6 mos-1 yr	.940	.976	.953	.047	.9864	.9926	.9852	.0148
	3	1-2 yrs	.906	.964	.964	.036	.9705	.9839	.9839	.0161
	4	2-3	.850	.938	.938	.062	.9535	.9825	.9825	.0175
	5	3-4	.828	.974	.974	.026	.9356	.9812	.9812	.0188
	6	4-5	.785	.948	.948	.052	.9164	.9795	.9795	.0205
Female										
All Ages	1	1 mo-6 mos	.963	.963	.913	.087	.9964	.9964	.9914	.0086
	2	6 mos-1 yr	.954	.990	.980	.020	.9920	.9956	.9912	.0088
	3	1-2 yrs	.944	.990	.990	.010	.9823	.9902	.9902	.0098
	4	2-3	.906	.959	.959	.041	.9718	.9893	.9893	.0107
	5	3-4	.856	.945	.945	.055	.9600	.9879	.9879	.0121
	6	4-5	.837	.978	.978	.022	.9469	.9863	.9863	.0137

* Basis of expected mortality: U.S. White Males and Females 1959-1961

CORONARY HEART DISEASE

§314–CORONARY HEART DISEASE IN MEN AND WOMEN

References: (1) C. W. Frank, E. Weinblatt, and S. Shapiro, "Angina Pectoris in Men: Prognostic Significance of Selected Medical Factors," Circulation, 47:509-517 (1973).
(2) E. Weinblatt, S. Shapiro, and C. W. Frank, "Prognosis of Women With Newly Diagnosed Coronary Heart Disease — A Comparison With Course of Disease Among Men," Am. J. Pub. Health, 63:577-593 (1973).

Subjects Studied: Members of the Health Insurance Plan of Greater New York (HIP), a prepaid comprehensive group practice plan with a membership of about 110,000, between 25 and 64 years of age, with diagnosis of first acute myocardial infarction (MI), or angina pectoris (AP) without previous MI, made during the years 1961-1965. There were 882 men and 172 women with first acute MI during the four years. Most of these patients who survived at least a month and most of the AP patients responded to an invitation for participation in a follow-up study, with baseline examination approximately six months after the MI or AP diagnosis. Clinical and ECG criteria were required in all hospitalized MI cases (about two-thirds of the early deaths in the MI cases took place prior to hospitalization), and the AP diagnosis was based entirely on an assessment of a structured medical history record by the study's internist at the time of the baseline examination. Patients with prior MI were excluded from both groups, and cases with aortic valvular disease and duration of angina under two months were excluded from the AP cohort. Patients comprising the series followed from the baseline examination included 470 men and 91 women in the MI cohort and 275 men and 137 women in the AP cohort. Age distribution and incidence of the MI and AP cases in a three-year entry sample are given in Table 314a.

Follow-up: Medical and hospital records, findings at baseline examination and subsequent re-examinations, and telephone interviews were used in follow-up to 4.5 years after the baseline examination. Patients dying before medical care could be obtained were identified by screening all deaths in the population during the entry period. Previous medical records and interviews with relatives were used to classify these patients with sudden death. Mortality follow-up was complete for 4.5 years.

Results: The incidence of first acute MI and AP without prior MI is much higher in men than in women under age 65 (Table 314a). The incidence is about five times as great in men as in women for first MI, and twice as great in AP. The differential is even greater for persons under age 45. Patients with MI outnumbered those with AP as the presenting form of coronary heart disease, especially in men. The authors have estimated a lag of about 15 years between men and women for incidence of MI and 7-8 years for AP.

Early mortality within one month of acute MI, is reported in Table 314b. Early mortality exceeded 35 per cent in both men and women. There was no age differential in female cases, but the older men had a less favorable immediate prognosis than those under age 55. Hypertensive patients had a considerably higher early mortality than normotensives, in whom the rate was close to 20 per cent. An even more significant early risk factor was the occurrence of congestive heart failure during the acute episode, a prior history of failure. Such patients experienced an early mortality rate close to 45 per cent, in contrast to rates of 11 per cent in men and 14 per cent in women without evidence or history of failure.

Detailed results on men following MI are given in §313, including the interval from one to six months. Comparative mortality and survival are given in Table 314c and later tables, starting with the baseline examination for a follow-up of 4.5 years, and therefore exclude the experience of the first six months. Excess mortality was the same for men with AP and MI, all ages combined: a mortality ratio of 385 per cent and an EDR of 31 per 1000. Women after MI experienced a mortality ratio of 410 per cent and an EDR of 27 per 1000, not very different from the male patients. However, women with AP had a more favorable prognosis than men, as their mortality ratio was 315 per cent and excess death rate 19 per 1000. Women showed a variable pattern of excess mortality with age: mortality ratios for MI were higher in the younger patients, under age 55, than in those age 55 and up, but the reverse was true for AP. Excess death rates, however, increased with advancing age in both types of CHD: from 17 to 28 per 1000 in female patients after MI, and from 5.6 to 26 per 1000 in those with AP. Male patients, on the other hand, showed a narrow range of variation in EDR from 28 to 34 per 1000 and no consistent trend with age, although mortality ratios were considerably higher in men under age 55 than they were in older men.

CORONARY HEART DISEASE IN MEN AND WOMEN

Table 314a   Incidence of Coronary Heart Disease, 3-Year Average, HIP Plan

Type of Cor. Ht. Dis.	Sex	Incidence, No/1000/Yr (No. Cases)			
		35-44	45-54	55-64	All Ages
First Myocardial Infarction	Male	1.4 (59)	5.5 (234)	9.4 (320)	5.2 (613)
	Female	0.1 (3)	0.7 (34)	2.7 (92)	1.0 (129)
Angina Without Prior MI	Male	0.5 (19)	2.1 (86)	3.9 (128)	2.0 (233)
	Female	0.1 (5)	0.8 (40)	2.2 (173)	0.9 (118)

Table 314b   Early Mortality (Within 1 Month) in Myocardial Infarction

Category	Men				Women			
	No. of Patients	No. of Early Deaths	1-Month Mort. Rate	No. Survivors at 1 Month	No. of Patients	No. of Early Deaths	1-Month Mort. Rate	No. Survivors at 1 Month
	ℓ_o	d_o	$q_o = d_o/\ell_o$	ℓ_1	ℓ_o	d_o	$q_o = d_o/\ell_o$	ℓ_1
Age under 55	433	128	.296	305	50	18	.360	32
Age 55 up	449	190	.423	259	122	46	.377	76
All Ages	882	318	.361	564	172	64	.372	108
Definite Hypertension	222	94	.423	128	75	33	.440	42
Borderline Hypertension	270	97	.359	173	48	16	.333	32
Normotension	283	59	.208	224	32	6	.188	26
Prior or Acute Cong. Ht. Fail.	105	44	.419	61	15	7	.467	8
No Heart Failure	497	54	.109	443	105	15	.143	90

Table 314c   Comparative Experience of Men and Women 4.5 Years after Baseline Examination Following First MI or Diagnosis of Angina

Sex	Age	No. of Patients	Cum. 4.5-Yr Surv. Rate		Survival Ratio	Ave. Ann. Mort. Rate		Mortality Ratio	Excess Death Rate
			Observed	Expected*		Observed	Expected*		
	Yrs	ℓ	P	P'	100 P/P'	$\breve{q}$	$\breve{q}'$	100 $\breve{q}/\breve{q}'$	1000($\breve{q}-\breve{q}'$)
Myocardial Infarction									
Men	Under 55	242	.853	.974	87.6%	.035	.0058	600%	29
	55 up	228	.796	.933	85.3	.049	.0153	320	34
	All	470	.825	.952	86.7	.042	.0109	385	31
Women	Under 55	23	.913	.985	92.7	.020	.0034	590	17
	55 up	68	.831	.948	87.7	.040	.0118	340	28
	All	91	.846	.961	88.0	.036	.0088	410	28
Angina Without Prior MI									
Men	Under 55	120	.831	.974	85.3%	.040	.0058	690%	34
	55 up	155	.821	.933	88.0	.043	.0153	280	28
	All	275	.825	.952	86.7	.042	.0109	385	31
Women	Under 55	50	.960	.985	97.5	.009	.0034	265	5.6
	55 up	87	.839	.948	88.5	.038	.0118	325	26
	All	137	.881	.961	91.7	.028	.0088	315	19
Total CHD — MI and Angina									
Men	All Ages	745	.825	.952	86.7%	.042	.0109	385%	31
Women	All Ages	228	.867	.961	90.2%	.031	.0088	355%	22

* Basis of expected mortality: cohorts of male and female HIP members free of CHD initially, matched by age

CORONARY HEART DISEASE

§314–CORONARY HEART DISEASE IN MEN AND WOMEN

Results (continued):

Comparative mortality and survival by duration are given in Table 314d for patients with AP, all ages combined, separately for males and females, starting at the baseline examination. In the case of men with AP, interval mortality ratios and excess death rates were irregular, but varying within relatively narrow limits — the former between 315 and 490 per cent, and the latter from 24 to 41 per 1000. The cumulative survival ratio at the close of the 4.5-year period was 86.7 per cent. Interval mortality ratios and EDR's experienced by females displayed an upward trend with duration: except for one interval, the ratios increased regularly from 189 per cent in the first interval to 495 per cent in the fifth, and the excess death rates from 6.6 to 41 per 1000. The cumulative survival ratio was 91.7 per cent.

In Table 314e the experience over 4.5 years for the MI and AP patients has been combined to present comparative mortality and survival according to various findings at the baseline examination. Elevated serum cholesterol, at or exceeding 270 mg. per 100 ml., was associated with an increased mortality in women, but not in men. Diabetic patients, on the other hand, showed a very high excess death rate, about 60 per 1000 in both sexes, and correspondingly high mortality ratios, 650 and 795 per cent, respectively, in males and females. Approximately 13 per cent of these patients had diabetes complicating their coronary heart disease, and this complication was found to have the worst prognosis of all of the risk factors evaluated. Both hypertension and specific ECG abnormalities at the time of the baseline examination were correlated with higher mortality ratios and EDR's. Men with both of these risk factors showed an aggregate mortality ratio of 865 per cent and EDR of 84 per 1000, while those without either of the risk factors experienced a much lower mortality ratio, 169 per cent, and an EDR of 7.5 per 1000. The presence of both of the risk factors in female patients was associated with a mortality ratio of 500 per cent and an EDR of 35 per 1000. Among the 47 women with normal blood pressure and nothing worse than minor changes in their ECG, only a single death occurred in the 4.5 years of follow-up, a smaller number than that expected from the cohort of HIP female members without evidence of coronary heart disease. All of the excess mortality in women developed in those with hypertension, or specific ECG abnormality, or both. This was not true in men, but excess mortality was nevertheless at a remarkably low level for males with definite coronary disease in the absence of these risk factors, as the mortality ratio was well under 200 per cent and EDR less than 10 per 1000. Patients of both sexes who had either hypertension or abnormal ECG (but not both) experienced levels of excess mortality within the limits just described. Since most of the patients had a history of MI, which more often than not leaves residual Q waves in the post-recovery ECG, it is not surprising that only a minority were in the select normotensive group without specific ECG abnormality (26 per cent of the men and 21 per cent of the women).

CORONARY HEART DISEASE IN MEN AND WOMEN

Table 314d Comparative Experience in Angina Pectoris by Sex and Duration from Baseline Examination, All Ages Combined

Interval		Observed Rates			Expected Rates*			Interval Mortality Ratio	Cumulative Survival Ratio	Excess Death Rate
No.	Start-End	Cumulative Survival	Interval Survival	Ave. Ann. Mortality	Cumulative Survival	Interval Survival	Ave. Ann. Mortality			
i	t to t + Δ t	P	p_i	$\breve{q}$	P'	p_i'	$\breve{q}'$	100 $\breve{q}/\breve{q}'$	100 P/P'	1000($\breve{q}-\breve{q}'$)
Male Patients										
1	0-0.5 yrs	.979	.979	.042	.9955	.9955	.0090	465%	98.3%	33
2	0.5-1.5	.945	.965	.035	.9857	.9902	.0098	355	95.9	25
3	1.5-2.5	.896	.948	.052	.9753	.9894	.0106	490	91.9	41
4	2.5-3.5	.864	.964	.036	.9641	.9885	.0115	315	89.6	24
5	3.5-4.5	.825	.955	.045	.9520	.9874	.0126	355	86.7	32
Female Patients										
1	0-0.5 yrs	.993	.993	.014	.9963	.9963	.0074	189%	99.7%	6.6
2	0.5-1.5	.973	.980	.020	.9886	.9923	.0077	260	98.4	12
3	1.5-2.5	.955	.982	.018	.9803	.9916	.0084	215	97.4	9.6
4	2.5-3.5	.928	.972	.028	.9712	.9907	.0093	300	95.6	19
5	3.5-4.5	.881	.949	.051	.9612	.9897	.0103	495	91.7	41

Table 314e Comparative Experience in 4.5 Years, Myocardial Infarction and Angina Patients Combined, by Sex and Various Risk Factors

Category		No. of Patients	4.5 Yr Cumulative		Ave. Ann. Mortality		Excess Death Rate
			Surv. Rate	Surv. Ratio	Rate	Ratio	
		ℓ	P	100 P/P'	$\breve{q}$	100 $\breve{q}/\breve{q}'$	1000($\breve{q}-\breve{q}'$)
Male Patients							
Cholesterol 270 up		167	.853	89.6%	.035	320%	24
Cholesterol Under 270		533	.825	86.7	.042	385	31
Diabetic		97	.719	75.5	.071	650	60
Not Diabetic		648	.841	88.3	.038	345	27
ECG	Blood Pressure†						
Abnormal	Elevated	170	.640	67.2	.094	865	84
Abnormal	Not Elevated	292	.851	89.4	.035	325	24
Normal or Minor	Elevated	86	.849	89.2	.036	330	25
Normal or Minor	Not Elevated	196	.920	96.7	.018	169	7.5
Female Patients							
Cholesterol 270 up		98	.820	85.3%	.043	490%	34
Cholesterol Under 270		114	.898	93.4	.024	270	15
Diabetic		29	.722	75.1	.070	795	61
Not Diabetic		199	.888	92.4	.026	295	17
ECG	Blood Pressure†						
Abnormal	Elevated	67	.817	85.0	.044	500	35
Abnormal	Not Elevated	45	.816	84.9	.044	500	35
Normal or Minor	Elevated	69	.875	91.1	.029	330	20
Normal or Minor	Not Elevated	47	.975	101.4	.006	64	−3.2

* Basis of expected mortality: cohorts of male and female HIP members free of CHD initially, matched by age

† Blood Pressure: Elevated — 3 or more readings or 160 mm. Hg. Systolic or 95 diastolic or more; Hypertensive — 1 or 2 readings as for elevated, accompanied by diagnosis of hypertension or left ventricular hypertrophy on ECG

CORONARY DRUG PROJECT

§315–FIVE-YEAR FOLLOW-UP OF MEN AFTER MYOCARDIAL INFARCTION

References: (1) Coronary Drug Project Research Group, "Clofibrate and Niacin in Coronary Heart Disease," J. Am. Med. Assoc., 231:360-381 (1975).
(2) Coronary Drug Project Research Group, "The Coronary Drug Project. Design, Methods and Baseline Results," Circulation, 47(Suppl. I):I-1 – I-50 (1975).

Subjects Studied: Men age 30-64 years, at least three months after documented myocardial infarction (MI) meeting selection criteria for inclusion in the Coronary Drug Project, a National Heart and Lung Institute clinical study, designed to ascertain if long-term lowering of serum lipids would have a beneficial effect on morbidity and mortality in individuals with coronary heart disease (CHD). Additional objectives were the securing of information on the natural history of CHD and development of methodology for the design and conduct of large collaborative clinical trials. After a planning and organizational phase of several years, 8341 post-MI patients were enrolled during the period from March 1966 to October 1969 in 53 project clinical centers if they met the age and other selection criteria, one being good functional capacity (New York Heart Association functional Classes III and IV were excluded). Patients were randomly assigned in a double-blind fashion to one of five treatment groups, about 1100 men each, or to a larger placebo control group of 2789 men. Three modes of treatment were omitted from the project before the close of observations and data reported on are limited to clofibrate, niacin and placebo. Presented in Table 315a is a detailed distribution synopsis of characteristics of patients at entry according to age, race, geographic area, physical characteristics (including history of prior cardiovascular events, blood pressure, ECG abnormalities; data with respect to MI – duration since attack, accompanying complications); physical activity at work, and cigarette smoking habits.

Follow-up: At entry and at annual intervals following each patient's entry date, a complete report of the patient's status was made consisting of a physical examination, assessment of drug adherence, resting electrocardiogram, chest roentgenogram, glucose tolerance test, and a battery of biochemical and hematological determinations. At four month intervals intervening, an interval medical history was completed which was less extensive. Periodic reports were submitted of deaths (noting particularly coronary mortality and sudden death) and of nonfatal cardiovascular events (recurrent MI, acute coronary insufficiency, development of angina pectoris, congestive heart failure, stroke, pulmonary embolism, and arrhythmias). Such data were reviewed for treatment group differences and possible drug side effects. Only four patients were lost to follow-up such that their vital status as of August 31, 1974 was not known. However, 7.4 per cent of clofibrate patients failed to continue clinic visits and their maintenance on medication could not be ascertained; 10.7 per cent of the niacin cases and 8.0 per cent of the placebo group dropped out.

Results: Clofibrate and niacin were included in the project because of their reported ability to lower levels of both serum cholesterol and triglyceride. In both the clofibrate and niacin groups, mean decreases in cholesterol and triglyceride levels were achieved and maintained throughout the follow-up period. On the average, over the 15 follow-up visits, in the clofibrate group, cholesterol dropped 6.5 per cent from entry level and triglyceride, 22.3 per cent. In the niacin group, the mean reductions were, for cholesterol, 9.9 per cent, and for triglyceride, 26.1 per cent.

Comparisons of the distribution of entry characteristics in the respective drug-placebo groups are presented in Table 315b. Analyses of these comparisons indicate no large statistical imbalance in the distribution of any of the variables within the treatment groups.

Five-year cumulative mortality and cardiovascular morbidity rates within the three treatment groups are shown in Table 315c. Included in the table are adjusted cumulative rates which take into account minor differences in the treatment groups in the distribution of the variables enumerated in Table 315a. As shown in Table 315c, the adjusted rates do not deviate significantly from the unadjusted conventional rates, reflecting the success with which randomization was carried out in the assignment of patients to the treatment groups.

The five-year cumulative mortality rates, deaths from all causes, for the drug and placebo groups were not far apart: .200 for clofibrate, .212 for niacin, .209 for placebo. These rates represented, respectively, about 255, 270, and 265 per cent of the rates expected in the general population. For sudden cardiovascular mortality, the five-year rates were .084 for clofibrate, .105 for niacin, and .096 for placebo. The five-year incidence rates for the combination of death due to coronary heart disease or the occurrence of definite nonfatal MI (i.e., total incidence of recurrent major coronary heart disease events, nonfatal plus fatal) were .238 in the clofibrate, .228 in the niacin, and .262 in the placebo group. None of the differences in these rates is statistically significant.

CORONARY HEART DISEASE

§315—FIVE-YEAR FOLLOW-UP OF MEN AFTER MYOCARDIAL INFARCTION

Results (continued):

Five-year overall comparative experience of 5011 patients in the three drug-placebo groups combined, according to the presence or absence of 25 variables at entry, is given in Table 315d. These variables correspond with the majority of those listed in Table 315b. Classes in the category of general characteristics (age, race, risk classification, ECG at MI, leisure activity) exhibiting substantially higher excess death rates in the presence of the variable included patients who had more than a single MI (EDM* 34 deaths per 1000), patients categorized in Class II of the New York Heart Association functional classification (EDM 25 per 1000), and subjects in Risk Group 1 (more than one MI, or a single MI with complications — EDM 22 per 1000). Relatively smaller excess margins occurred among patients who had experienced an MI within two years of entry (EDM 3 per 1000) and among nonwhites (EDM 6 per 1000). Other variables fell between.

Among patients with a history of cardiovascular disease at entry, also indicated in Table 315d, those who had had peripheral arterial occlusion (EDM 52 per 1000), congestive heart failure (EDM 38 per 1000), and intermittent claudication (EDM 38 per 1000) experienced relatively high excess margins. Those who had had intermittent cerebral ischemic attack (EDM 9 per 1000), acute coronary insufficiency (EDM 12 per 1000), stroke (EDM 13 per 1000) and angina pectoris (EDM 18 per 1000) exhibited smaller margins of excess mortality. Five-year excess margins according to medication at time of entry shown in the same table (315d) reveals that the greatest EDM's occurred among patients being treated with digitalis (EDM 48 per 1000), with diuretic agents (EDM 43 per 1000), with oral antidiabetic drugs (EDM 28 per 1000), and with antiarrhythmic agents (EDM 27 per 1000); lesser margins were experienced among patients taking nitroglycerin (EDM 17 per 1000) and antihypertensive agents (EDM 19 per 1000).

Classification by findings at entry in the bottom section of Table 315d shows the highest excess death margin on heart enlargement (EDM 43 per 1000) and the lowest on systolic blood pressures of 130 mm. Hg. or more (EDM 9 per 1000). Heart rates of 70 or more per minute and ECG abnormalities showed margins of about 20 per 1000.

*EDM is used to indicate the difference between the number of excess deaths per 1000 where the variable is present and the number where the variable is absent. $EDM=EDR_1-EDR_2$.

THE CORONARY DRUG PROJECT

Table 315a Entry Characteristics, Total Post MI Patients Selected and Randomized

Characteristic		No. Patients	% Total	No. Patients	% Total	Characteristic	No. Patients	% Total
		At Entry		At First MI				
Age	Under 30 yrs	0	0.0%	53	0.7%	Race White	7788	93.4%
	30-34	76	0.9	248	3.1	Black	407	4.9
	35-39	310	3.7	787	9.7	Other	146	1.8
	40-44	846	10.1	1472	18.2	Geographic Area		
	45-49	1571	18.8	1932	23.9	West (10 clinics)	1674	20.1%
	50-54	1923	23.1	1825	22.5	Midwest (11 clinics)	1693	20.3
	55-59	2042	24.5	1333	16.4	Mideast (11 clinics)	1700	20.4
	60-64	1573	18.9	450	5.5	New England (11 clinics)	1645	19.7
	Total	8341		8100		South (10 clinics)	1629	19.5
History of Prior CV Events		Suspected		Definite		No. of Previous MIs		
Acute Coronary Insuff.		396	4.7%	1028	12.3%	1	6743	80.8%
Angina Pectoris		973	11.7	3906	46.8	2	1316	15.8
Congestive Heart Failure		483	5.8	819	9.8	3 up	282	3.4
Int. Cerebral Ischemic Attack		228	2.7	97	1.2	Time from Last MI		
Stroke		39	0.5	136	1.6	3-6 months	1160	14.2%
Intermittent Claudication		239	2.9	453	5.4	6-12 months	1396	17.1
Periph. Arterial Occlusion		64	0.8	125	1.5	1-3 years	2730	33.5
Cardiomegaly (Baseline X-ray)		691	8.3	770	9.2	3-5 years	1262	15.5
Blood Pressure						5-10 years	1282	15.7
Systolic	Diastolic	Systolic		Diastolic		over 10 years	320	3.9
<110	<70	710	8.5%	589	7.1%	No data	191	
110-129	70-79	3373	40.4	2271	27.2	Complications with MI		
130-139	80-89	1627	19.5	3167	37.9	Arrhythmias	681	8.2%
140-159	90-94	1890	22.7	1308	15.7	Shock	427	5.1
160-179	95-104	571	6.9	754	9.0	Cong. Heart Failure	652	7.8
180 up	105 up	170	2.0	252	3.0	Extension of Infarct.	285	3.4
						Pericardial Friction	278	3.3
						Thromboembolism	111	1.3
						Any Complication(s)	1719	20.6
ECG Abnormality		ECG at Time of MI		ECG at Time of Entry		No Complications	6620	79.4
Q deep or wide (major)		4072	48.8%	1899	23.0%	Risk Group		
Q other		2807	33.7	3120	37.9	1 Single MI No Compl.	5498	65.9%
Q No Signif. Abnorm.				3227	39.1	2 Multiple MI or Compl.	2843	34.1
T Major (Inverted)				2650	32.1	N.Y.H.A. Functional Class		
T Other				1391	16.9	I (No limitation)	3834	46.0%
T No Signif. Abnorm.				4205	51.0	II (Slight limitation)	4507	54.0
ST Ischemic Depression				826	10.0	Physical Activity at Work		
ST Other Depr. or Elev.				1581	19.2	Sedentary	1650	19.8%
ST No Depr. or Elev.				5839	70.8	Light	2912	34.9
AV Conduction Abnorm.				337	4.2	Moderate	1436	17.2
Vent. Conduction Abnorm.				766	9.3	Heavy	193	2.3
Arrhythmias				671	8.1	Unemployed or Retired	2149	25.8
						Cigarette Smoking		
Any Codable Q		5800	70.4%	5019	60.9%	Former Smoker	6579	86.5%
Any Codable T/ST		1813	22.0	6448	78.1	Never Smoked	1028	13.5
Any Other Codable Abn.		485	5.9	1774	21.7	Non-smoker at entry	5225	62.6
Any Codable Abn.		8098	98.3	7674	93.1	1-20 Cigarettes/day	2185	26.3
No Codable Abn.		135	1.6	572	6.9	Over 20 Cigarettes/day	921	9.0
ECG not available		(108)	—	(95)	—			

CORONARY HEART DISEASE

Table 315b Entry Characteristics, Three Randomized Groups of Post MI Male Patients

Characteristic	Clofibrate (1103 Pts)	Niacin (1119 Pts)	Placebo (2789 Pts)	Characteristic	Clofibrate (1103 Pts)	Niacin (1119 Pts)	Placebo (2789 Pts)
	% Total	% Total	% Total		% Total	% Total	% Total
Age at entry 55 up	43.5%	45.0%	43.0%	Finding at Entry:			
Race nonwhite	6.5	7.1	6.8	Over Std. Wt. 15% up	43.6%	44.4%	46.4%
MI >1 or with Complication	33.8	34.1	34.3	Systolic BP ≥130	52.8	52.9	51.4
More than 1 MI	18.0	18.7	19.9	Diastolic BP ≥85	39.1	37.4	36.7
Interval from MI 2 Yrs up	46.9	50.3	49.4	Current Cigarette Smoker	39.0	36.6	37.9
NYHA Functional Class II	55.9	51.9	53.5	Heart Enlarged	17.8	15.7	18.2
History of:				ECG Abnorm. at Entry:			
Major Q in ECG at MI	51.5	46.6	49.1	Any Q/QS	63.6	59.4	62.1
Acute Cor. Insufficiency	16.2	18.3	16.4	Any T Abnormality	50.9	46.5	49.5
Angina Pectoris	58.9	60.1	57.8	Any ST Abnormality	25.0	24.0	25.1
Congestive Heart Failure	17.1	13.3	16.0	Frequent Prem. Beats	4.4	4.7	3.6
Medication Used at Entry:				Lab. Data at Entry:			
Digitalis	15.3	13.5	15.0	Serum Cholesterol ≥250	48.0	48.4	46.9
Antiarrhythmic Agent	3.7	4.5	3.6	Serum Triglyceride ≥ 5 mEq/L.	50.1	52.6	50.2
Diuretic	15.8	13.4	14.1	Proteinuria	16.0	16.6	16.5
Antihypertensive Agent	7.7	5.2	6.9	Glucosuria	0.9	2.9	1.5
Nitroglycerin	45.5	44.7	42.4	Fasting Plasma Glucose ≥100	43.2	41.2	42.2
				Oral Hypoglycemic Agent	5.9	5.4	5.4

Table 315c Five-Year Cumulative Mortality and Cardiovascular Morbidity

Event	Clofibrate (1103 Pts)			Niacin (1119 Pts)			Placebo (2789 Pts)		
	No. Events	Cumulative Rate		No. Events	Cumulative Rate		No. Events	Cumulative Rate	
		Crude	Adjusted*		Crude	Adjusted*		Crude	Adjusted*
	n	Q	Q_a	n	Q	Q_a	n	Q	Q_a
Deaths									
Total	221	.200	.195	237	.212	.217	583	.209	.209
All CV	191	.173	—	210	.188	—	528	.189	—
Sudden CV	93	.084	.081	118	.105	.108	269	.096	.114
All CHD	156	.141	.137	178	.159	.163	452	.162	.162
Cancer	7	.006	—	7	.006	—	16	.006	—
Other Non CV	16	.015	—	17	.015	—	26	.009	—
CV Events									
Nonfatal MI	128	.116	.114	100	.089	.089	339	.122	.122
CHD Death or MI	263	.238	.233	.255	.228	.231	731	.262	.263
Pulm. Emb.	20	.018	.018	11	.010	.010	30	.011	.011
Cerebrovas. Attack	117	.106	.103	86	.077	.077	271	.097	.117
Total Fatal or Nonfatal	929	.842	.836	875	.782	.786	2251	.807	.842

*Adjustment taking into account differences in treatment under the variables enumerated in Table 315a

THE CORONARY DRUG PROJECT

Table 315d   Five-Year Comparative Experience, Clofibrate, Niacin and Placebo Groups Combined, Paired Dichotomous Groups by Entry Characteristic

Entry Characteristic*	No. of Patients	No. of Deaths	5-Year Surv. Rate	Survival Ratio*	Ave. Ann. Mort. Rate	Mortality Ratio†	Excess Death Rate	
							vs. U.S. Men†	Group 1 vs. 2
	ℓ	d	$P=1-(d/\ell)$	$100\,P/P'$	$\breve{q}=1-\sqrt[5]{P}$	$100\,\breve{q}/\breve{q}'$	$1000(\breve{q}-\breve{q}')$	EDR_1-EDR_2
Basic Risk Factors								
1 Entry Age ≥55 yrs	2182	545	.7502	85.4%	.0559	220%	30	—
2 <55 yrs	2829	496	.8247	86.4	.0378	405	29	1
1 Race Nonwhite	340	78	.7706	83.6	.0508	315	35	—
2 White	4671	963	.7938	86.1	.0451	280	29	6
1 Higher Risk >1 MI or Compl.	1713	456	.7338	79.6	.0600	370	44	—
2 Single MI, no Compl.	3298	585	.8226	89.3	.0383	235	22	22
1 More than 1 MI	963	304	.6843	74.3	.0731	450	57	—
2 Single MI	4047	737	.8179	88.8	.0394	245	23	34
1 Interval MI to Entry <2 yrs	2493	526	.7890	85.6	.0463	285	30	—
2 2 yrs up	2401	478	.8009	86.9	.0434	270	27	3
1 NYHA Funct. Class II	2690	689	.7439	80.7	.0575	355	41	—
2 Funct. Class I	2321	352	.8483	92.1	.0324	200	16	25
1 Major Q/QS, ECG at MI	2459	589	.7605	82.5	.0533	330	37	—
2 ST/T or Minor Q	2551	452	.8228	89.3	.0383	235	22	15
1 Leisure Activity, Light	3522	805	.7714	83.7	.0506	310	34	—
2 Activity, Mod.	1488	236	.8414	91.3	.0340	210	18	16
Cardiovascular History								
1 Acute Coronary Insuff.	842	208	.7530	81.7%	.0552	340%	39	—
2 None	4169	833	.8002	86.8	.0436	270	27	12
1 Angina Pectoris	2934	701	.7611	82.6	.0531	330	37	—
2 None	2077	340	.8363	90.8	.0351	215	19	18
1 Congestive Heart Fail.	784	263	.6646	72.1	.0785	485	62	—
2 None	4227	778	.8160	88.6	.0399	245	24	38
1 Interm. Cerebral Ischemia	180	44	.7556	82.0	.0545	335	38	—
2 None	4831	997	.7936	86.1	.0452	280	29	9
1 Stroke	100	26	.7400	80.3	.0584	360	42	—
2 None	4911	1015	.7933	86.1	.0453	280	29	13
1 Intermittent Claudication	426	145	.6596	71.6	.0799	495	64	—
2 None	4585	896	.8046	87.3	.0426	265	26	38
1 Peripheral Art. Occlus.	121	48	.6033	65.5	.0961	595	80	—
2 None	4890	993	.7969	86.5	.0444	275	28	52
Entry Medication								
1 Oral Antidiabetic Agent	277	87	.6859	74.4%	.0726	450%	56	—
2 None	4734	954	.7985	86.7	.0440	270	28	28
1 Digitalis	737	269	.6350	68.9	.0868	535	71	—
2 None	4274	772	.8194	88.9	.0391	240	23	48
1 Antiarrhythmic Agent	191	59	.6911	75.0	.0712	440	55	—
2 None	4820	982	.7963	86.4	.0445	275	28	27
1 Diuretic	717	252	.6485	70.4	.0830	510	67	—
2 None	4294	789	.8163	88.6	.0398	245	24	43
1 Antihypertensive Agent	336	93	.7232	78.5	.0628	390	47	—
2 None	4675	948	.7972	86.5	.0443	275	28	19
1 Nitroglycerin	2186	538	.7539	81.8	.0549	340	39	—
2 None	2825	503	.8219	89.2	.0385	240	22	17
Entry Finding								
1 Heart Enlarged	880	305	.6534	70.9%	.0816	505%	65	—
2 Not Enlarged	4131	736	.8218	89.2	.0385	240	22	43
1 Heart Rate ≥70 (ECG)	2225	559	.7488	81.3	.0562	345	40	—
2 Rate <70	2743	473	.8276	89.8	.0371	230	21	19
1 Any Coded ECG Abn.	4647	991	.7867	85.4	.0468	290	31	—
2 Normal ECG	321	41	.8723	94.7	.0270	167	11	20
1 Systolic BP ≥130	2609	589	.7742	84.0	.0499	310	34	—
2 BP <130	2402	452	.8118	88.1	.0408	250	25	9

*Group 1 as defined or risk factor present; Group 2 as defined or risk factor absent
†Basis of expected mortality: U.S. Life Tables 1970. For combined group P' at five years = .9215 and $\breve{q}'$ = .0162. For men under 55 P' = .9542 and $\breve{q}'$ = .0093. For men age 55 up P' = .8788 and $\breve{q}'$ = .0255. For both white and nonwhite men $\breve{q}'$ = .0162 (different age distributions)

CORONARY HEART DISEASE

§316—CORONARY BYPASS IN DISABLING ANGINA

Reference: R. P. Anderson, S. H. Rahimtoola, L. I. Bonchek, and A. Starr, "The Prognosis of Patients with Coronary Artery Disease after Coronary Bypass Operations. Time-Related Progress of 532 Patients with Disabling Angina Pectoris," Circulation, 50:274-282 (1974).

Subjects Studied: 532 patients with disabling angina pectoris (New York Heart Association Functional Class III and IV) who received aorta-to-coronary artery vein bypass grafts at the University of Oregon Medical School, St. Vincent's and Portland V. A. Hospitals from December 1968 to July 1973. The following categories of patients were excluded from the series: unstable and accelerated angina; coexisting valvular heart disease; evidence of complicating congestive heart failure; and documented recent myocardial infarction. The study group consisted of 471 men (mean age 51.7 years) and 61 women (mean age 53.7 years). On the basis of pre-operative coronary arteriography patients were classified as having significant disease of one, two, or three vessels if the diameter of the lumen was reduced to 50 per cent or less, the respective numbers being 113, 216 and 203 patients. At operation 214 patients received a single vessel bypass graft, 260 double bypass grafts, and 58 triple bypass grafts.

Follow-up: Data as to functional and survival status were obtained on a yearly basis by reexamination of patients, by contact with physicians, by questionnaires and telephone interviews. Follow-up was continued to December 15, 1973 and was complete for 494 patients, or 93 per cent of the total.

Results: The experience by duration from one month to four years after operation is given in Tables 316a-b. For the total series excess mortality was greatest in the first year, with a mortality ratio of 240 per cent and 14 extra deaths per 1000 per year. Over the next three years mortality was only slightly above the expected level, with mortality ratios under 125 per cent and EDR under 3 per 1000 per year. The survival ratio at four years was 96.4 per cent. Comparative mortality tended to increase with number of vessels which showed narrowing: the overall mortality for four years was 124 per cent in single-vessel disease, 158 per cent in two-vessel, and 215 per cent in three-vessel disease. Corresponding values of EDR were 2.6, 6.5 and 13 extra deaths per 1000 per year, respectively. All of these results should be interpreted with caution, because there were only 17 deaths in the total series.

Comment: Early mortality within one month (not shown in the tables) amounted to 18 deaths in 532 patients, a rate of .034. Early mortality rates also increased with number of vessels involved, with rates of .009, .028, and .054, according to narrowing demonstrated in one, two, or three vessels.

CORONARY ARTERY BYPASS

Table 316a   Observed Data and Comparative Experience, Disabling Angina

Interval No.	Start-End	No. Alive at Start of Interval ℓ	No. Withdrawn during Interval* u + w	Exposure Person-Yrs E	Observed d	Expected† d'	Interval 100 d/d'	Cumulative 100 ∑d/∑d'	Cumulative Surv. Ratio 100 P/P'	Excess Death Rate 1000(d-d')/E
	113 Patients with Single-vessel Involvement									
1	1 mo-1 yr	112	24	91.7	2	.935	215%	215%	98.9%	12
2	1-2 yrs	86	32	70	1	.791	126	174	98.6	3.0
3	2-4 yrs	53	48	54	0	.702	0	124	101.2	−13
All	1 mo-4 yrs	112	104	215.7	3	2.43	124	124	101.2	2.6
	216 Patients with Two-vessel Involvement									
1	1 mo-1 yr	210	42	173.3	3	1.77	169	169	99.3	7.1
2	1-2 yrs	165	64	133	2	1.50	133	153	98.9	3.8
3	2-4 yrs	99	88	90	2	1.17	171	158	95.7	9.2
All	1 mo-4 yrs	210	194	396.3	7	4.44	158	158	95.7	6.5
	203 Patients with Three-vessel Involvement									
1	1 mo-1 yr	192	65	146.2	5	1.49	335	335	97.8	24
2	1-2 yrs	122	61	91.5	1	1.03	97	240	97.8	−0.3
3	2-4 yrs	60	56	57	1	.741	135	215	93.5	4.5
All	1 mo-4 yrs	192	182	294.7	7	3.26	215	215	93.5	13
	532 Patients with Angina, Total Series									
1	1 mo-1 yr	514	131	411.1	10	4.19	240	240	98.7	14
2	1-2 yrs	373	157	294.5	4	3.33	122	186	98.4	2.3
3	2-4 yrs	212	192	201	3	2.61	115	168	96.4	1.9
All	1 mo-4 yrs	514	480	906.6	17	10.13	169	168	96.4	7.6

Table 316b   Derived Mortality and Survival Data

Interval No.	Start-End	Cumulative Survival P	Interval Survival p_i	Geom. Mean Ann. Surv. $\check{p}$	Geom. Mean Ann. Mort. $\check{q}$	Cumulative Survival P'	Interval Survival p_i'	Geom. Mean Ann. Surv. $\check{p}'$	Geom. Mean Ann. Mort. $\check{q}'$
	113 Patients with Single-vessel Involvement								
1	1 mo-1 yr	.980	.980	.978	.022	.9906	.9906	.9898	.0102
2	1-2 yrs	.966	.986	.986	.014	.9794	.9887	.9887	.0113
3	2-4 yrs	.966	1.000	1.000	.000	.9540	.9741	.9870	.0130
	216 Patients with Two-vessel Involvement								
1	1 mo-1 yr	.984	.984	.983	.017	.9906	.9906	.9898	.0102
2	1-2 yrs	.969	.985	.985	.015	.9794	.9887	.9887	.0113
3	2-4 yrs	.913	.942	.971	.029	.9540	.9741	.9870	.0130
	203 Patients with Three-vessel Involvement								
1	1 mo-1 yr	.969	.969	.966	.034	.9906	.9906	.9898	.0102
2	1-2 yrs	.958	.989	.989	.011	.9794	.9887	.9887	.0113
3	2-4 yrs	.892	.931	.965	.035	.9540	.9741	.9870	.0130
	532 Patients with Angina, Total Series								
1	1 mo-1 yr	.978	.978	.976	.024	.9906	.9906	.9898	.0102
2	1-2 yrs	.964	.986	.986	.014	.9794	.9887	.9887	.0113
3	2-4 yrs	.920	.954	.977	.023	.9540	.9741	.9870	.0130

* Includes 8 patients who were subjected to re-operation and 36 partially traced

† Basis of expected mortality: 1964 U. S. White population rates. Average age for each group assumed to be the same as average for entire series.

CORONARY HEART DISEASE

§317–ECG IN CORONARY HEART DISEASE

References: (1) H. R. Hipp, O. W. Beard, J. S. Taylor, R. V. Ebert, and M. Robins, "Initial Myocardial Infarction among Veterans–Nontransmural Myocardial Infarction – Bundle Branch Block," Am. Heart J., 62:43-50 (1961).
(2) Coronary Drug Project Research Group, "Clofibrate and Niacin in Coronary Heart Disease," J. Am. Med. Assoc., 231:360-381 (1975).

Subjects Studied: (1) 631 male patients with first myocardial infarction treated in 33 large teaching Veterans Administrations Hospitals 1950-1952. Of these, 512 were classified as having a transmural infarction (abnormal Q waves in the ECG), 96 as nontransmural (T and ST changes without Q waves), and 23 with persistent bundle branch block. Further details on selection and characteristics of this series are given in §310. Age distribution of the two larger groups is shown in Table 317a. Mean age of the bundle branch block group was somewhat older, with 20 of 23 patients (87 per cent) age 50 or older.
(2) Three randomized groups of post-myocardial infarction (MI) patients (clofibrate, niacin and placebo) enrolled in the Coronary Drug Project during the period from March 1966 to October 1969. Additional details of this follow-up study are given in §315. There was no significant difference in the total mortality experience for the three groups, hence comparative mortality by ECG finding is given in this abstract for all groups combined. The ECG findings reported were not at the time of the acute infarction, but at the baseline examination for entry into the study. The baseline ECG was made three months to over ten years following the MI, the average interval being two years. There were 1103 patients in the clofibrate group, 1119 in the niacin, and 2789 in the placebo, a total of 5011 men.

Follow-up: (1) Survival status five years following the acute MI was determined through V. A. death benefit records.
(2) Through annual re-examination and other direct contact all except 4 subjects were followed to August 31, 1974, at least as to vital status. For additional details see §315.

Results: The V. A. patients hospitalized for acute MI experienced about the same early mortality rate in the transmural group with abnormal Q waves as in the patients diagnosed as nontransmural or subendocardial infarction because of serial T and ST segment changes without abnormal Q waves. The two-month mortality rate was about 15 per cent in the former and 13 per cent in the latter. Early mortality increased with age in the transmural group; in the nontransmural group the highest mortality was in the age group 50-59 years, but the numbers of patients in the other age groups were small enough to make it probable that lower rates in those over age 60 years reflect only random differences. Twelve of 23 patients with bundle branch block in their ECG died within two months, an extremely high mortality rate of 52 per cent, far above the overall mortality rate for the great majority of the patients without bundle branch block.

Comparative experience for the various ECG groups of the V. A. patients surviving two months is given in Tables 317b-c, up to five years following the acute MI. Excess mortality was comparable in the two older age groups: mortality ratio 375 per cent in patients with transmural MI age 50-59, and 320 per cent in patients of the same age with nontransmural infarction, and ratios of 230 and 250 per cent, respectively in those age 60-69. Excess death rates were in the range of 42 to 52 per 1000, and 5-year survival ratios in the vicinity of 80 per cent. In the youngest age group, 40-49 years, patients with transmural infarction had an EDR of 42 per 1000, comparable to the rates in the older patients, with a mortality ratio of 700 per cent. The patients with nontransmural infarction had a much lower EDR of only 4 per 1000 and a mortality ratio of 157 per cent. However, this was a small group, with the rates based on only a single death, and the apparently lower excess mortality may very well have been a random deviation. In contrast to the similar experience for the bulk of the patients age 50 to 69, the mortality was much lower for those with nontransmural infarction than it was for those with transmural MI, in the combined youngest and oldest groups. Data for men under age 40 and over age 69 are not shown in Table 317b, but are included in the aggregate experience, all ages combined, in Table 317c. This does show a higher EDR, 52 per 1000 in patients with transmural infarction versus 36 per 1000 in those with nontransmural MI. The corresponding mortality ratios were 365 and 265 per cent, respectively. The very small series of patients with bundle branch block developed at the time of their MI showed a highly unfavorable experience: mortality ratio 650 per cent, EDR 128 per 1000, and 5-year survival ratio of 50.9 per cent. The average age of the bundle branch block group was somewhat older and these patients had a high incidence of shock, congestive heart failure, and serious arrhythmias. Of the eight early deaths with heart examined at autopsy all had large transmural infarctions.

ECG IN CORONARY HEART DISEASE

Table 317a Early Mortality (within 2 Months), Hospitalized VA Patients with Acute Myocardial Infarction, Classified by ECG Finding

Age	Abn. Q Waves (Transmural)			ST-T Only (Nontransmural)			Bundle Branch Block		
	No. Cases	No. Deaths	Int. Mort. Rate	No. Cases	No. Deaths	Int. Mort. Rate	No. Cases	No. Deaths	Int. Mort. Rate
Years	ℓ	d	q_i	ℓ	d	q_i	ℓ	d	q_i
Under 40	76	7	.092	7	0	.000	—	—	—
40-49	107	13	.121	22	3	.136	—	—	—
50-59	208	26	.125	44	8	.182	—	—	—
60-69	87	21	.241	18	1	.056	—	—	—
70 up	25	9	.360	3	0	.000	—	—	—
All	503	76	.151	94	12	.128	23	12	.522

Table 317b Comparative Experience, 2-Month Survivors of Acute MI up to 5 Years by Initial ECG Finding, and Age Group

Age	No. of Patients	Ave. Ann. Mort. Rate		Mortality Ratio	5-Yr Surv. Rate		Survival Ratio	Excess Death Rate
		Observed	Expected*		Observed	Expected*		
Years	ℓ	$\bar{q}$	$\bar{q}'$	100 $\bar{q}/\bar{q}'$	P	P'	100 P/P'	1000($\bar{q}-\bar{q}'$)
Abnormal Q Waves (Transmural MI)								
40-49	94	.049	.007	700%	.785	.967	81.2%	42
50-59	182	.071	.019	375	.701	.912	76.9	52
60-69	66	.076	.033	230	.683	.850	80.3	43
Abnormal T/ST (Nontransmural MI)								
40-49	19	.011	.007	157%	.948	.967	98.1%	4
50-59	36	.061	.019	320	.738	.912	81.0	42
60-69	17	.082	.033	250	.662	.850	77.8	49

Table 317c Comparative Experience, 2-Month Survivors of Acute MI up to 5 Years by Initial ECG Finding, All Ages Combined

ECG Abnormality	Ave. Age	No. of Patients	No. of Deaths	5-Yr Surv. Rate		Survival Ratio	Ave. Ann. Mort. Rate		Mortality Ratio	Excess Death Rate
				Observed	Expected*		Observed	Expected*		
	$\bar{x}$	ℓ	d	P	P'	100 P/P'	$\check{q}$	$\check{q}'$	100 $\check{q}/\check{q}'$	1000($\check{q}-\check{q}'$)
Q Wave	55	427	133	.689	.911	75.6%	.074	.019	390%	55
T/ST	54	82	21	.744	.901	82.6	.059	.021	280	38
BBB†	60	11	6	.455	.881	51.6	.150	.025	600	125

* Basis of expected mortality: U.S. Life Tables, white male, 1953
† BBB — right or left bundle branch block

§317–ECG IN CORONARY HEART DISEASE

Results (continued):

Coronary patients followed in the Coronary Drug Project were classified in detail as to their ECG findings at the time of their baseline examination, a minimum of three months and an average of six years following their MI. The proportion of patients with abnormal Q waves (transmural MI) is somewhat lower in this series, as compared with V. A. patients, 62 versus 82 per cent. Such a finding is not unexpected, since the abnormal Q waves tend to disappear with passage of time in some patients who recover from a transmural MI. Excess mortality was higher in Coronary Drug Project subjects with abnormal Q waves than without: mortality ratios of 320 and 215 per cent, respectively, and corresponding excess death rates of 36 and 19 per 1000 (Table 317d). These EDR's are substantially lower than the corresponding rates in the V. A. series in Table 317c. The same is true for cases with ventricular conduction defect (bundle branch block or wide QRS), who had an EDR of 49 per 1000. All subjects in the Coronary Drug Project had made a good functional recovery as post-MI patients — New York Heart Association classifications of Grade III and Grade IV were excluded. This feature of selection probably accounts for the generally more favorable experience in this series: a mortality ratio of 280 per cent, an EDR of 29 per 1000, and a 5-year survival ratio of 86 per cent for the combined groups as a whole. Only a small proportion of the group had no codable ECG abnormalities at all, 6.5 per cent, and these subjects had the smallest excess mortality, with a mortality ratio of 165 per cent and EDR only 11 per 1000. In all of the ECG classes in Table 317d the presence of a particular coded finding was invariably associated with an EDR higher than the average of 29 per 1000, ranging from 35 per 1000 (serious arrhythmia and QRS axis deviation) to 60 per 1000 or more (ST depression, more than one premature beat per 10 QRS complexes, and tall R waves). Abnormal T waves occurred in almost 50 per cent of the tracings and was associated with an EDR of 44 per 1000, while subjects with ECG's exhibiting normal T waves had an EDR of 16 per 1000, lower than the EDR of 19 per 1000 in the absence of abnormal Q waves. One interesting finding was that subjects with a relatively slow ventricular rate in their ECG under 70 per minute had a more favorable experience, with an EDR of 21 per 1000, than subjects with a rate of 70 per minute or higher, EDR 40 per 1000.

ECG IN CORONARY HEART DISEASE

**Table 317d Comparative 5-Year Experience in Post-MI Patients by Later ECG Findings
(Average 2 Years after MI), Coronary Drug Project**

ECG Finding	No. of Patients	No. of Deaths	Cum. 5-Yr Surv. Rate	Survival Ratio*	Ave. Ann. Mort. Rate	Mortality Ratio*	Excess Death Rate*
	ℓ	d	P	100 P/P′	q̌=1-⁵√P̄	100 q̌/q̌′	1000(q̌-q̌′)
With Q/QS Abn.	3072	720	.766	83.1%	.052	320%	36
None	1896	313	.835	90.6	.035	215	19
With Abnormal T	2441	650	.734	79.7	.060	370	44
None	2527	382	.849	92.1	.032	200	16
With ST Depression	1235	411	.667	72.4	.078	480	62
None	3733	621	.834	90.5	.036	220	20
With ST Elevation	207	65	.686	74.4	.073	450	57
None	4761	966	.797	86.5	.044	270	28
With AV Cond. Defect	190	48	.747	81.1	.057	350	41
None	4778	984	.794	86.2	.045	280	29
With Vent. Cond. Defect	455	130	.714	77.5	.065	400	49
None	4513	901	.800	86.8	.044	270	28
With Prem. Beats ≥ 1/10	200	65	.675	73.3	.076	470	60
< 1/10 beats	4768	968	.797	86.5	.044	270	28
With Sinus Arrhythmia	175	40	.771	83.7	.051	315	35
None	4793	990	.793	86.1	.045	280	29
With QRS Axis Dev.	633	147	.768	83.3	.051	315	35
None	4335	884	.796	86.4	.045	280	29
With Tall R Waves	346	113	.673	73.0	.076	470	60
None	4622	920	.801	86.9	.043	265	27
With Any ECG Abn.	4647	990	.787	85.4	.047	290	31
None	321	41	.872	94.6	.027	165	11
Heart Rate by ECG ≥ 70	2225	559	.749	81.3	.056	345	40
Rate < 70/min.	2743	473	.828	89.9	.037	230	21

* Basis of expected mortality: U.S. Life Tables 1970. P′ at 5 years = .9215, q̌′ = .0162 for all groups

HYPERTENSION

§320–BLOOD PRESSURE (FRAMINGHAM STUDY)

Reference: J. Schiffman, "The Framingham Study. Section 26. Survival Following Certain Cardiovascular Events," Govt. Printing Office, Washington, D. C. (September 1970).

Subjects Studied: All examinee-participants in the Framingham Heart Study, categorized by blood pressure readings obtained at eight biennial examinations in the period 1950-1964. For further information on the subjects and design of the Framingham Study see §380. Two independent blood pressure readings were made at each examination, but data in Section 26 are based on readings made by the "first examiner." All 5,209 subjects participated in Examination 1; the blood pressure of the last available preceding examination was assumed for those who missed Examination 2 or 3 ("A" tables of Section 26, and Tables 320a-b). Subjects were not excluded if other risk factors were present, such as coronary heart disease, or history of cerebrovascular accident or diabetes mellitus, either at the initial or subsequent examinations.

Follow-up: The results in Section 26 have been carried up to the date of the ninth biennial examination, about 1966. For additional information concerning follow-up procedures see §380.

Results: Comparative experience has been reported and calculated by sex, age, and systolic pressure, disregarding diastolic pressure, and by sex, age and diastolic pressure, disregarding systolic pressure (Tables 320a-d). Combinations of systolic and diastolic pressure have been analyzed in terms of the New York Heart Association definitions of *normotension* (systolic under 140 mm. and diastolic under 90 mm.), and definite hypertension (systolic 160 mm. up or diastolic 95 mm. up). Subjects were classified as *borderline hypertension* if there was a combination of normotensive with hypertensive readings at the same examination, or if all readings were borderline (systolic 140-159 or diastolic 90-94). These results are in Tables 320e-f.

Tables 320a-b present long-range experience of subjects with blood pressures taken at Examinations 1, 2 and 3 and followed to the ninth biennial examination about 1966. For each sex, age and blood pressure category the mortality rate, q_i, over the average 14-year period of observation has been calculated from the ratio of deaths (Σd) to entrants ($\Sigma \ell$). The complementary survival rate has, in turn, been used to calculate the geometric mean annual survival and mortality rates. Comparative ratios and EDR values have been based on the rates obtained from a standard blood pressure class taken as 110 to 129 mm. systolic or 75 to 84 mm. diastolic for those age 45 up with a somewhat wider range for those age 35-44. Generally these are the blood pressure classes with the lowest mortality and highest survival rates. For the age groups under 55 comparative mortality tends to rise with increased systolic pressures above 139 mm. and diastolic pressures above 94 mm. For the oldest age group 55-64, all other blood pressure classes exhibit a mortality ratio higher than that of the standard class, *including the classes with low pressure* (under 110 mm. systolic and under 75 mm. diastolic). In the highest blood pressure classes (systolic 160 up, diastolic 105 up) the mortality ratios range from 190 to 580 per cent. The survival ratios vary from 96.3 to 45.4 per cent, and EDR from 2.7 to 54 extra deaths per 1000 per year. EDR tends to increase with age and is higher for male than for female subjects.

Mortality results shown in Tables 320c-d are based on inter-examination experience over the entire follow-up period for subjects reclassified by age attained at each successive examination. The basis for expected mortality in these combined two-year intervals is essentially the same set of standard blood pressure classes used for the long-range experience in Tables 320a-b. Comparative mortality as shown in Tables 320c-d exhibits patterns of variation with age, sex, and blood pressure class that are generally similar to those of the long-range experience. Deaths are too few in the youngest age group, 35-44, to permit more than two systolic and two diastolic classes, but the other age groups exhibit a trend for mortality ratio and EDR to increase with increasing pressure above the standard category, despite occasional irregularities. Excess mortality at systolic pressures below 110 and diastolic pressures below 75 is found in six of eight categories of older subjects, age 55 and up. Mortality in female hypertensives is again somewhat less than for males, in terms of EDR.

BLOOD PRESSURE (FRAMINGHAM STUDY)

Table 320a   Observed Data and Long-Range Experience, Male Subjects by Entry Age and Blood Pressure (Exams 1, 2 and 3 Combined) to 9th Examination 12-16 Years Later

| Entry Age | Blood Pressure | Entrants (Exams 1,2,3) | Deaths (to Exam 9) | 14-Year Interval | | Ave. Ann. Mort. Rate | Mortality Ratio* | Survival Ratio | Excess Death Rate |
				Mort. Rate	Surv. Rate				
Yrs	mm Hg.	ℓ	d	$q_i=d/\ell$	p_i	$\breve{q}$	100 $\breve{q}/\breve{q}'$	100 p_i/p_i'	1000($\breve{q}-\breve{q}'$)
	Systolic								
35-44	<110	199	8	.0402	.9598	.0029	58%	102.9%	−2.1
	110-139	1752	118	.0674	.9326	.0050	−	−	−
	140-159	527	45	.0854	.9146	.0064	128	98.1	1.4
	160 up	167	33	.1976	.8024	.0156	310	86.0	11
	All	2645	204	.0771	.9229	.0057	114	99.0	0.7
45-54	<110	125	7	.0560	.9440	.0041	46	107.1	−4.9
	110-129	825	98	.1188	.8812	.0090	−	−	−
	130-139	454	76	.1674	.8326	.0130	144	94.5	4.0
	140-159	539	117	.2171	.7829	.0173	192	88.8	8.3
	160-179	183	57	.3115	.6885	.0263	290	78.1	17
	180 up	89	47	.5281	.4719	.0522	580	53.6	43
	All	2215	402	.1815	.8185	.0142	158	92.9	5.2
55-64	<110	83	25	.3012	.6988	.0253	149	88.9	8.3
	110-129	407	87	.2138	.7862	.0170	−	−	−
	130-139	285	69	.2421	.7579	.0196	115	96.4	2.6
	140-159	366	115	.3142	.6858	.0266	156	87.2	9.6
	160-179	166	73	.4398	.5602	.0405	240	71.3	25
	180 up	129	83	.6434	.3566	.0710	420	45.4	54
	All	1436	452	.3148	.6852	.0266	157	87.2	9.7
	Diastolic								
35-44	<75	618	39	.0631	.9369	.0046	92%	100.5%	−0.4
	75-84	872	59	.0677	.9323	.0050	−	−	−
	85-89	350	31	.0886	.9114	.0066	132	97.8	1.6
	90-94	375	24	.0640	.9360	.0047	94	100.4	−0.3
	95-104	305	28	.0918	.9082	.0069	138	98.5	1.9
	105 up	125	23	.1840	.8160	.0144	290	87.5	9.4
	All	2645	204	.0771	.9229	.0057	114	99.0	0.7
45-54	<75	390	49	.1256	.8744	.0095	103	99.6	−0.3
	75-84	715	87	.1217	.8783	.0092	−	−	−
	85-89	280	52	.1857	.8143	.0146	159	92.7	5.4
	90-94	330	69	.2091	.7909	.0166	180	90.0	7.4
	95-104	339	84	.2478	.7522	.0201	220	85.6	11
	105 up	161	61	.3789	.6211	.0335	365	70.7	24
	All	2215	402	.1815	.8185	.0142	154	93.2	5.0
55-64	<75	316	92	.2911	.7089	.0243	133	91.8	6.0
	75-84	461	105	.2278	.7722	.0183	−	−	−
	85-89	150	41	.2733	.7267	.0225	123	94.1	4.2
	90-94	195	63	.3231	.6769	.0275	150	87.7	9.2
	95-104	178	70	.3933	.6067	.0351	192	78.6	17
	105 up	136	81	.5956	.4044	.0626	340	52.4	44
	All	1436	452	.3148	.6852	.0266	145	88.7	8.3

*Basis of expected mortality: Framingham male rates for systolic pressure 110-139 (age 35-44) or 110-129 (age 45-64), and diastolic pressure 75-84 (all ages)

HYPERTENSION

§320–BLOOD PRESSURE (FRAMINGHAM STUDY)

Results (continued):

The preceding tables categorize subjects in terms of systolic or diastolic blood pressure, each considered independently of the other. Tables 320e-f present another set of results on the Framingham experience with subjects divided into three classes, normotensive, borderline, and definitely hypertensive, based on the systolic/diastolic blood pressure combination (see above). Mortality and survival rates in the normotensive group provide standards for comparative experience, and these approximate the standard rates in the other tables. Excess mortality is consistently observed in all hypertensive groups, both male and female, and is more marked for the definite hypertensives (systolic pressure 160 up or diastolic 95 up or both) than for the borderline hypertensives. In Table 320e the mortality ratios range from 130 to 188 per cent for borderline hypertensives and 205 to 310 per cent for the subjects with definite hypertension. The corresponding ranges for excess death per 1000 per year are 1.4 to 7.7 for borderline and 4.6 to 31 for definite hypertensives. Survival ratios over this follow-up period averaging 14 years range from a maximum of 98.1 to a minimum of 63.3 per cent. A similar pattern of excess mortality is seen in the short-range experience in Table 320f based on the interval of two years between successive biennial examinations. Borderline hypertensives have a mortality ratio varying from 107 to 177 per cent, and an EDR from 0.4 to 6.8 excess deaths per 1000 per year. For definite hypertensives the corresponding values are 105 to 390 per cent (mortality ratio) and 0.4 to 19 excess deaths per 1000 per year. Two-year mortality rates for all male or female subjects in each age group are compared in Table 320g with the standard rates for the most favorable systolic class and the most favorable diastolic class (as given in the footnote to Tables 320c-d). The standard rates in any age group usually differ one from another depending on whether they have been obtained from experience in the normotensive class (Table 320e), or systolic or diastolic classes (Tables 320c-d). Corresponding differences therefore appear in the values of mortality ratio and EDR.

Comment: These data indicate a higher prevalence of borderline hypertension in the Framingham Study group than reported in the 1962 Health Examination Survey (National Center for Health Statistics, "Blood Pressure by Age and Sex," USPHS Publication No. 1000, Series 11, No. 4, Washington, D. C., Govt. Printing Office, June 1964). Part of this difference may be due to a difference in classification: in the National Survey an *average* was taken for three different blood pressure readings and the classification of normotensive, borderline or definite hypertensive was based on the average. In the Framingham Study subjects were classified on the basis of the reading of the "first examiner"; no average was taken although at least one additional reading was made. Total hypertensives outnumbered normotensives in both males and females age 55-74 (Table 320f). Whatever the explanation for this high prevalence, the fact remains that increasing degrees of blood pressure elevation above the normotensive or standard level are strongly correlated with increasing mortality. The results are consistent with those observed in the very large population of insured lives as reported in the 1959 Build and Blood Pressure Study. Mortality rates tend to run lower at all blood pressure levels in the insurance experience because applicants with other known risk factors such as CHD and diabetes were excluded from the follow-up material, and *no* exclusion of this sort was carried out in the Framingham Study. Because of the lower mortality rates in the standard insurance, both mortality ratios and EDR values tend to run somewhat higher in the life insurance experience than in the Framingham Study.

BLOOD PRESSURE (FRAMINGHAM STUDY)

Table 320b Observed Data and Long-Range Experience, Female Subjects by Entry Age and Blood Pressure (Exams 1, 2 and 3 Combined) to 9th Examination 12-16 Years Later

Entry Age	Blood Pressure	Entrants (Exams 1,2,3)	Deaths (to Exam 9)	14-Year Interval		Ave. Ann. Mort. Rate	Mortality Ratio*	Survival Ratio	Excess Death Rate*
				Mort. Rate	Surv. Rate				
Yrs	mm Hg.	ℓ	d	$q_i = d/\ell$	p_i	$\breve{q}$	$100\ \breve{q}/\breve{q}'$	$100\ p_i/p_i'$	$1000(\breve{q}-\breve{q}')$
	Systolic								
35-44	<110	554	23	.0415	.9585	.0030	100%	100.0%	0.0
	110-139	2198	91	.0414	.9586	.0030	—	—	—
	140-159	409	45	.1100	.8900	.0083	275	92.8	5.3
	160 up	144	11	.0764	.9236	.0057	190	96.3	2.7
	All	3305	170	.0514	.9486	.0038	127	99.0	0.8
45-54	<110	177	23	.1299	.8701	.0099	200	93.3	5.0
	110-129	834	56	.0671	.9329	.0049	—	—	—
	130-139	532	44	.0827	.9173	.0061	124	98.3	1.3
	140-159	658	56	.0851	.9149	.0063	129	98.1	1.4
	160-179	322	49	.1522	.8478	.0117	240	90.9	6.8
	180 up	217	41	.1889	.8111	.0148	300	86.9	9.9
	All	2740	269	.0982	.9018	.0074	151	96.7	2.5
55-64	<110	58	6	.1034	.8966	.0078	115	98.7	1.0
	110-129	327	30	.0917	.9083	.0068	—	—	—
	130-139	280	35	.1250	.8750	.0095	140	96.3	2.7
	140-159	496	77	.1552	.8448	.0120	176	93.0	5.2
	160-179	334	65	.1946	.8054	.0153	225	88.7	8.5
	180 up	294	97	.3299	.6701	.0282	415	73.8	21.4
	All	1789	310	.1733	.8267	.0135	198	91.0	6.7
	Diastolic								
35-44	<75	1252	53	.0423	.9577	.0031	100%	100.1%	0.0
	75-84	1181	51	.0432	.9568	.0031	—	—	—
	85-89	306	15	.0490	.9510	.0036	116	99.4	0.5
	90-94	285	26	.0912	.9088	.0068	220	95.0	3.7
	95-104	211	17	.0806	.9194	.0060	194	96.1	2.9
	105 up	70	8	.1143	.8857	.0086	275	92.6	5.5
	All	3305	170	.0514	.9486	.0038	123	99.1	0.7
45-54	<75	516	48	.0930	.9070	.0069	111	98.9	0.7
	75-84	905	75	.0829	.9171	.0062	—	—	—
	85-89	336	23	.0685	.9315	.0051	82	101.6	−1.1
	90-94	386	39	.1010	.8990	.0076	123	98.0	1.4
	95-104	355	38	.1070	.8930	.0081	131	97.4	1.9
	105 up	242	46	.1901	.8099	.0149	240	88.3	8.7
	All	2740	269	.0982	.9018	.0074	119	98.3	1.2
55-64	<75	282	42	.1489	.8511	.0115	132	96.2	2.8
	75-84	495	57	.1152	.8848	.0087	—	—	—
	85-89	231	46	.1991	.8009	.0157	180	90.5	7.0
	90-94	276	40	.1449	.8551	.0111	128	96.6	2.4
	95-104	298	65	.2181	.7819	.0174	200	88.4	8.7
	105 up	207	60	.2899	.7101	.0242	280	80.3	16
	All	1789	310	.1733	.8267	.0135	155	93.4	4.8

*Basis of expected mortality: Framingham female rates for systolic pressure 110-139 (age 35-44) or 110-129 (age 45-64), and diastolic pressure 75-84 (all ages)

3-76

HYPERTENSION

Table 320c Observed Data and Two-Year Comparative Mortality, Males by Attained Age and Blood Pressure at Last Biennial Examination (Framingham Study)

Age	Blood Pressure	Exposure Person-Yrs	Exposure Distribution	Deaths Observed	Ave. Ann. Mort. Rate	Mortality Ratio*	Excess Death Rate*
Yrs	mm Hg.	E	%	d	q̄=d/E	100 q̄/q̄'	1000(q̄-q̄')
	Systolic						
35-44	<140	6752	76%	11	.0016	—	—
	140 up	2170	24	9	.0041	255%	2.5
45-54	<110	766	6	4	.0052	85	−0.9
	110-129	4790	38	29	.0061	—	—
	130-139	2696	22	22	.0082	134	2.1
	140-159	2900	23	24	.0083	136	2.2
	160-179	940	8	16	.0170	280	11
	180 up	404	3	9	.0223	365	16
55-64	<110	528	6	9	.0170	124	3.3
	110-129	2770	30	38	.0137	—	—
	130-139	1740	19	31	.0178	130	4.1
	140-159	2350	26	34	.0145	106	0.8
	160-179	1086	12	25	.0230	168	9.3
	180 up	684	7	28	.0409	300	27
65-74	<110	142	5	7	.0493	245	29
	110-129	648	22	13	.0201	—	—
	130-139	542	19	16	.0295	147	9.4
	140-159	836	29	27	.0323	161	12
	160-179	390	14	17	.0436	215	24
	180 up	320	11	18	.0562	280	36
	Diastolic						
35-44	<90	6418	72%	10	.0016	—	—
	90 up	2504	28	10	.0040	250%	2.4
45-54	<75	2296	18	20	.0087	185	4.0
	75-84	4246	34	20	.0047	—	—
	85-89	1692	14	19	.0112	240	6.5
	90-94	1778	14	15	.0084	179	3.7
	95-104	1732	14	17	.0098	210	5.1
	105 up	752	6	13	.0173	370	13
55-64	<75	1964	22	28	.0143	94	−0.9
	75-84	2962	32	45	.0152	—	—
	85-89	1008	11	15	.0149	98	−0.3
	90-94	1294	14	29	.0224	147	7.2
	95-104	1250	14	26	.0208	137	5.6
	105 up	680	7	22	.0324	215	17
65-74	<75	820	28	36	.0439	210	23
	75-84	912	32	19	.0208	—	—
	85-89	306	11	9	.0294	141	8.6
	90-94	368	13	11	.0299	144	9.1
	95-104	304	11	13	.0428	205	22
	105 up	168	6	10	.0595	285	39

*Basis of expected mortality: Framingham male rates for systolic pressure under 140 (age 35-44) or 110-129 (age 45 up), and diastolic pressure under 90 (age 35-44) or 75-84 (age 45 up)

BLOOD PRESSURE (FRAMINGHAM STUDY)

Table 320d Observed Data and Two-Year Comparative Mortality, Females by Attained Age and Blood Pressure at Last Biennial Examination

Age	Blood Pressure	Exposure Person-Yrs	Exposure Distribution	Deaths Observed	Ave. Ann. Mort. Rate	Mortality Ratio*	Excess Death Rate*
Yrs	mm Hg.	E	%	d	$\bar{q}=d/E$	$100\,\bar{q}/\bar{q}'$	$1000(\bar{q}-\bar{q}')$
	Systolic						
35-44	<140	9244	85%	12	.0013	—	—
	140 up	1690	15	6	.0036	275%	2.3
45-54	<110	1390	9	9	.0065	215	3.5
	110-129	5734	37	17	.0030	—	—
	130-139	3042	20	12	.0039	130	0.9
	140-159	3338	21	21	.0063	210	3.3
	160-179	1322	8	6	.0045	150	1.5
	180 up	824	5	10	.0121	405	9.1
55-64	<110	444	4	6	.0135	225	7.5
	110-129	2646	22	16	.0060	—	—
	130-139	1956	16	13	.0066	110	0.6
	140-159	3334	28	20	.0060	100	0.0
	160-179	2006	17	19	.0095	158	3.5
	180 up	1552	13	18	.0116	193	5.6
65-74	<110	72	2	0	(0)	(0)	−13
	110-129	536	14	7	.0131	—	—
	130-139	540	14	9	.0167	127	3.6
	140-159	1208	30	19	.0157	120	2.6
	160-179	888	22	18	.0203	155	7.2
	180 up	734	18	25	.0341	260	21
	Diastolic						
35-44	<90	9252	85%	10	.0011	—	—
	90 up	1682	15	8	.0048	435%	3.7
45-54	<75	3848	25	20	.0052	149	1.7
	75-84	5386	34	19	.0035	—	—
	85-89	1878	12	3	.0016	46	−1.9
	90-94	1996	13	11	.0055	157	2.0
	95-104	1592	10	13	.0082	235	4.7
	105 up	950	6	9	.0095	270	6.0
55-64	<75	2182	18	19	.0087	121	1.5
	75-84	3628	30	26	.0072	—	—
	85-89	1476	12	10	.0068	94	−0.4
	90-94	1890	16	17	.0090	125	1.8
	95-104	1720	15	8	.0047	65	−2.5
	105 up	1042	9	12	.0115	160	4.3
65-74	<75	780	20	13	.0167	103	0.5
	75-84	1238	31	20	.0162	—	—
	85-89	388	10	9	.0232	143	7.0
	90-94	654	16	9	.0138	85	−2.4
	95-104	610	15	10	.0164	101	0.2
	105 up	308	8	17	.0552	340	39

*Basis of expected mortality: Framingham Female rates for systolic pressure under 140 (age 35-44) or 110-129 (age 45 up), and diastolic pressure under 90 (age 35-44) or 75-84 (age 45 up)

3-78

HYPERTENSION

Table 320e   Observed Data and Long-Range Experience by Entry Age and Hypertensive Status (Exams 1, 2 and 3 Combined) to 9th Examination (12-16 Years Later)

Sex and Entry Age	Hypertension	Entrants (Exams 1,2,3)	Deaths (to Exam 9)	14-Year Interval Mort. Rate	14-Year Interval Surv. Rate	Ave. Ann. Mort. Rate	Mortality Ratio*	Survival Ratio*	Excess Death Rate*
Yrs		ℓ	d	$q_i=d/\ell$	p_i	$\breve{q}$	100 $\breve{q}/\breve{q}'$	100 P/P'	1000($\breve{q}-\breve{q}'$)
Male 35-44	Normal	1490	90	.0604	.9396	.0044	—	—	—
	Bord.	833	65	.0780	.9220	.0058	132%	98.1%	1.4
	Definite	322	49	.1522	.8478	.0117	265	90.2	7.3
	All	2645	204	.0771	.9229	.0057	130	98.2	1.3
45-54	Normal	1062	124	.1168	.8832	.0088	—	—	—
	Bord.	734	148	.2016	.7984	.0160	182	90.4	7.2
	Definite	419	130	.3103	.6897	.0262	300	78.1	17
	All	2215	402	.1815	.8185	.0142	161	92.7	5.4
55-64	Normal	643	145	.2255	.7745	.0181	—	—	—
	Bord.	477	146	.3061	.6939	.0258	143	89.6	7.7
	Definite	316	161	.5095	.4905	.0496	275	63.3	31
	All	1436	452	.3148	.6852	.0266	147	88.5	8.5
Female 35-44	Normal	2454	104	.0424	.9576	.0031	—	—	—
	Bord.	647	45	.0696	.9304	.0051	165%	97.2%	2.0
	Definite	204	21	.1029	.8971	.0077	250	93.7	4.6
	All	3305	170	.0514	.9486	.0038	123	99.1	0.7
45-54	Normal	1243	94	.0756	.9244	.0056	—	—	—
	Bord.	931	91	.0977	.9023	.0073	130	97.6	1.7
	Definite	566	84	.1484	.8516	.0114	205	92.1	5.8
	All	2740	269	.0982	.9018	.0074	132	97.6	1.8
55-64	Normal	520	47	.0904	.9096	.0067	—	—	—
	Bord.	664	108	.1627	.8373	.0126	188	92.1	5.9
	Definite	605	155	.2562	.7438	.0209	310	81.8	14
	All	1789	310	.1733	.8267	.0135	200	90.9	6.8

*Basis of expected rates: Framingham male or female normotensive subjects

BLOOD PRESSURE (FRAMINGHAM STUDY)

Table 320f Observed Data and Two-Year Comparative Mortality by Attained Age and Hypertensive Status at Last Biennial Examination

Attained Age Hypertension Status	Male					Female				
	Exposure Person-Yrs	Deaths Observed	Ave. Ann. Mort. Rate	Mortality Ratio*	Excess Death Rate*	Exposure Person-Yrs	Deaths Observed	Ave. Ann. Mort. Rate	Mortality Ratio*	Excess Death Rate*
	E	d	$\bar{q}=d/E$	$100\,\bar{q}/\bar{q}'$	$1000(\bar{q}-\bar{q}')$	E	d	$\bar{q}=d/E$	$100\,\bar{q}/\bar{q}'$	$1000(\bar{q}-\bar{q}')$
35-44 yrs										
Normal	5280	7	.0013	—	—	8338	10	.0012	—	—
Borderline	2624	6	.0023	177%	1.0	1962	5	.0025	210%	1.3
Definite	1018	7	.0069	530	5.6	634	3	.0047	390	3.5
All	8922	20	.0022	169	0.9	10934	18	.0016	133	0.4
45-54 yrs										
Normal	6458	43	.0067	—	—	8664	35	.0040	—	—
Borderline	3838	29	.0076	113	0.9	4536	20	.0044	110	0.4
Definite	2200	32	.0145	216	7.8	2450	20	.0082	205	4.2
All	12496	104	.0083	124	1.6	15650	75	.0048	120	0.8
55-64 yrs										
Normal	4128	56	.0136	—	—	4182	31	.0074	—	—
Borderline	2962	50	.0169	124	3.3	4294	34	.0079	107	0.5
Definite	2068	59	.0285	210	15	3462	27	.0078	105	0.4
All	9158	165	.0180	132	4.4	11938	92	.0077	104	0.3
65-74 yrs										
Normal	1138	32	.0281	—	—	902	10	.0111	—	—
Borderline	1064	34	.0320	114	3.9	1560	28	.0179	161	6.8
Definite	676	32	.0473	168	19	1516	40	.0264	240	15
All	2878	98	.0341	121	6.0	3978	78	.0196	177	8.5

Table 320g Comparative Two-Year Mortality Experience by Attained Age (All Blood Pressure Classes Combined)

Sex/Age	Ave. BP	Exposure	Deaths	Mort. Rate	Mortality Ratio†		Excess Death Rate†	
		E	d	$\bar{q}=d/E$	vs. Syst. $\bar{q}'$	vs. Diast. $\bar{q}'$	vs. Syst. $\bar{q}'$	vs. Diast. $\bar{q}'$
Male								
35-44	130/83	8922	20	.0022	138%	138%	0.6	0.6
45-54	135/85	12496	104	.0083	136	177	2.2	3.6
55-64	142/85	9158	165	.0180	131	118	4.3	2.8
65-74	148/82	2878	98	.0340	170	164	14	13
Female								
35-44	123/76	10934	18	.0016	123%	145%	0.3	0.5
45-54	136/83	15650	75	.0048	160	137	1.8	1.3
55-64	151/87	11938	92	.0077	128	107	1.7	0.5
65-74	160/86	3978	78	.0196	150	121	6.5	3.4

*Basis of expected rates: Framingham male or female normotensive subjects
†Basis of expected mortality: Framingham rates for male or female subjects for "best" systolic or diastolic blood pressure class (see footnote Tables 320c or 320d)

HYPERTENSION

§321–BORDERLINE BLOOD PRESSURE

Reference: J. A. End, Northwestern Mutual Life Insurance Co., unpublished study (personal communication 1972).

Subjects Studied: The study is comprised of two age-matched groups of males who were issued standard life insurance by Northwestern Mutual Life Insurance Co. in 1953-54. The first group was made up of a random sample of 500 men whose highest blood pressure reading on examination or recorded within the prior five years was in the range of 141/91 to 160/100. The second group of 500 age-matched standard insured men was used as a control: all recorded current and previous blood pressure readings were below or no higher than 140/90.

Follow-up: Cases were followed up through policy records to the 1965 policy anniversary or prior termination. Start of follow-up was the time of earliest elevated blood pressure reading (within five years prior to application) for those with such a history. For those with elevated blood pressure on examination only, and for the control group the start of follow-up was the time of application.

Results: Table 321 shows comparative experience of the impaired subjects by age at issue, together with total experience for the control group. Mortality ratios of over 200 per cent are displayed in each age group of hypertensive subjects. Excess annual rates of death increased with age from 1.6 per 1000 for ages under 40 to 14 per 1000 for ages 50 and up. Incidence of arteriosclerotic heart disease as the cause of death increased with age, rising from 57 per cent for ages under 40 to 84 per cent for ages 50 and up. Mortality in the carefully selected control group was 33 per cent of that expected from the 1955-60 Basic Select Tables.

BORDERLINE BLOOD PRESSURE – INSURED LIVES

Table 321   Comparative Experience by Age Group

Age Group	No. Alive at Start of Interval	Exposure Person-Yrs	Deaths during Interval	Expected Deaths*	Mortality Ratio	Average Annual Mort. Rate	Estimated 6-Year Surv. Rate	6-Year Surv. Index	Excess Death Rate
	ℓ	E	d	d'	100 d/d'	$\bar{q} = d/E$	$P = (1-\bar{q})^6$	100 P/P'	1000(d-d')/E
Impaired Subjects									
14-39 yrs	244	2278	7(4)†	3.40	205%	.003	.982	99.1%	1.6
40-49	161	1335	12(8)	5.82	205	.009	.947	97.2	4.6
50-65	92	768	19(16)	8.04	235	.025	.860	91.7	14
14-65	497	4381	38(28)	17.26	220	.009	.947	97.2	4.7
Control Group									
16-65	499	3811	5(1)	15.16	33	.001	.992	101.6	−2.7

*Basis of expected mortality: 1955-1960 Select Basic Rates
  A uniform annual distribution of total deaths and estimated withdrawals has been assumed for age 16-24 and each quinquennial age group over a 10-year period, based on total exposure for each age group.
†Number of deaths from coronary artery disease in parentheses

HYPERTENSION

§322–HYPERTENSION IN RATED INSUREDS

References: (1) H. M. McCue, Jr., "Hypertension — A Single Company Study," Trans. Assoc. Life Ins. Med. Dir. Am., 49:110-119 (1965).

(2) H. M. McCue, Jr., personal communication of additional data (1972).

Subjects Studied: Policyholders of the Life Ins. Co. of Va. with insurance issued 1946-1955 inclusive. The study group consisted of 2083 males and 336 females, including 245 cases with standard insurance issued (not a part of Table 322a). The bulk of the experience was on applicants age 15 to 65, but there were a few cases over age 65. From a small sample, the average blood pressure was 147/89 and 7 per cent of the cases had another significant impairment in addition to hypertension.

Follow-up: Policy records were used to follow up to January 1, 1962 or prior termination and constituted the basis for counting exposures and deaths.

Results: Comparative experience for the 2174 rated cases is given by rating classification in Table 322a, and by age in Table 322b, all durations combined (average duration was 7.3 years). Except in the first two classes the mortality ratio increased with the rating classification. The mortality ratio of 168 per cent for the total is quite close to the value of 172 per cent provided for in the average rating. Excess death rate also tend to increase and the 5-year survival index to decrease with rating classification. The mortality ratio showed a downward trend with age (Table 322b). The lower average mortality ratio and larger number of deaths in Table 322b are a result of including the standard cases, (mortality ratio 102 per cent based on 1967 policy years of exposure and 12 death claims).

Table 322a   Comparative Experience in Insureds Rated for Hypertension (Life Insurance Company of Virginia)

Rating Class (Mort. Ratio Anticip.)		Exposure Policy-Yrs	No. of Death Claims		Mortality Ratio	Ave. Ann. Mort. Rate	Est. 5-Yr Surv. Rate	Est. 5-Yr Surv. Index	Excess Death Rate
			Observed	Expected*					
		E	d	d'	100 d/d'	q̄ = d/E	P = (1-q̄)⁵	100 P/P'	1000(d-d')/E
SS1	(137.5%)	6567	63	39.29	160%	.0096	.953	98.2%	3.6
SS2	(162.5%)	3901	28	22.96	122	.0072	.965	99.4	1.3
SS3	(200%)	2642	24	14.19	169	.0091	.956	98.1	3.7
SS4	(250%)	1493	20	8.61	230	.0134	.935	96.2	7.6
SS5	(300%)	814	10	3.92	255	.0123	.940	96.3	7.5
SS6-7	(400-500%)	236	6	1.16	515	.0254	.879	90.1	21
All SS	(172%)	15653	151	90.13	168	.0096	.953	98.1	3.9

Table 322b   Comparative Mortality by Age (Including Standard Cases)

Age	No. of Death Claims		Mortality Ratio	Age	No. of Death Claims		Mortality Ratio
	Observed	Expected*			Observed	Expected*	
Under 35	18	6.75	265%	50-54	39	21.90	178%
35-39	16	6.59	245	55-59	28	21.48	130
40-44	18	11.89	151	60 up	14	17.25	81
45-49	30	15.63	192	All	163	101.49	161

* Basis of expected deaths: 1946-1949 Basic Tables (Select and Ultimate)

HYPERTENSION

§323–ESSENTIAL HYPERTENSION

Reference: D. J. Breslin, R. W. Gifford, Jr., and J. F. Fairbairn, II, "Essential Hypertension. A Twenty-Year Follow-Up Study," Circulation, 33:87-97 (1966).

Subjects Studied: Hypertensive patients with a diastolic blood pressure over 90 mm. or a systolic pressure over 160 mm. diagnosed at the Mayo Clinic in 1940. There were 631 subjects in the series, 344 male and 287 female. The purpose of the study was to investigate the prognostic value of ophthalmoscopic findings as reflected in survival rates. Subjects were classified according to the ophthalmoscopic criteria of Keith, Wagener and Barker (Am. J. Med. Sci., 197:332, 1939). They were distributed in 1940 into four hypertensive groups as follows:

Group	Principal Ophthalmoscopic Finding	No. of Cases Male	Female	Approximate Average Age Male	Female	Approximate Ave. Dias. BP Male	Female
1	Minimum Sclerosis	52	74	45	52	101	103
2	Grade 1 or more Sclerosis	134	145	57	57	111	105
3	One or more Retinal Exudates	105	46	52	52	126	123
4	Papilledema	53	22	48	44	–	–
Total		344	287				

Follow-up: Survival rates were developed by the ad hoc method, i.e., by tracing the group of patients selected in 1940 in subsequent years. Follow-up was achieved for at least 5 years in 557 cases and for at least 20 years in 540. Attempt was made to obtain follow-up information for all cases diagnosed in 1940 in Groups 3 and 4, and for those patients in Groups 1 and 2 seen in the first half of 1940, but only every third patient in the latter groups seen in the second half of the year.

Results: Mortality and survival data over the 20 year study period for the four groups are presented in Table 323a by sex for all ages combined. Positive correlation between survival ratios and hypertensive grouping is indicated by the progressive diminution of the ratios from Group 1 to Group 3 – declining, in the case of men, from 56.6 per cent in the former to 3.8 per cent for the latter; for women, from 71.4 per cent to 18.9 per cent. Only 5 patients with Group 4 hypertension survived 10 years from diagnosis and only 3 survived 20 years. Survival ratios are less favorable for males in each group for all intervals. Mortality ratios, except for Group 1 are highest in the interval immediately following diagnosis, diminishing with the passage of time, although comparative mortality remains high throughout. The emerging availability of antihypertensive agents in the 1950's may have had favorable effects on the experience of the series; it is known that some of the patients surviving into the second decade received such treatment, but no attempt was made to separate those who received treatment from those who did not.

For broad hypertensive categories, all ages combined, ten-year survival rates, estimated average annual mortality rates over the initial ten-year period, and survival and mortality ratios, for males and females, are shown in Table 323b. The categories presented include, respectively, hypertension complicated by renal and cardiac findings; hypertension without such complications; and three classifications of diastolic blood pressure (under 100, 100-119, and 120-139 mm. Hg). Where data are adequate, comparative experience is shown for 3 of the Keith-Wagener-Barker hypertensive groups. Mortality ratios and excess death rates per 1000 are lower for uncomplicated cases than for complicated, and survival ratios are higher. The differences are marked in the case of men, especially in Group 1 where the ten-year mortality ratio is 875 per cent in complicated cases, EDR, 77 per 1000 and the Cumulative Survival Ratio, 43.3 per cent. In uncomplicated cases these functions are, respectively, 175 per cent, 7.5 per 1000, and 92.7 per cent. In Group 2, among men and women, mortality ratios in complicated cases are roughly double those in uncomplicated cases. Survival ratios within any diastolic blood pressure grouping tend to be less favorable for patients with the more severe ophthalmoscopic grading.

ESSENTIAL HYPERTENSION

Table 323a Comparative Survival Experience by Hypertensive Group
Total Experience

Sex	Hyp. Group No.	Interval		No. Alive at Start of Interval	Cumulative Survival Rate		Cumulative Surv. Ratio	Estim. Ave. Ann. Mort. Rate		Mortality Ratio	Excess Death Rate
		No.	Start-End		Observed	Expected*		Observed	Expected*		
		i	τ to $t+\Delta t$	ℓ	P	P'	100 P/P'	$\breve{q}$	$\breve{q}'$	100 $\breve{q}/\breve{q}'$	1000($\breve{q}-\breve{q}'$)
Male	1	1	0- 5 yrs	47	.894	.9618	93.0%	.0222	.0078	285%	14
		2	5-10	42	.745	.9044	82.4	.0359	.0122	295	24
		3	10-20	35	.404	.7139	56.6	.0594	.0234	255	36
	2	1	0- 5	120	.617	.8940	69.0	.0921	.0222	415	70
		2	5-10	74	.333	.7589	43.9	.1159	.0322	360	84
		3	10-20	40	.076	.4160	18.3	.1374	.0583	235	79
	3	1	0- 5	95	.316	.9290	34.0	.2058	.0146	1410	191
		2	5-10	30	.137	.8305	16.5	.1538	.0222	695	132
		3	10-20	13	.021	.5545	3.8	.1710	.0396	430	131
	4	1	0- 5	53	.061	.9500	6.4	.4284	.0102	4200	418
Female	1	1	0- 5	65	.955	.9611	99.4	.0092	.0079	116	1.3
		2	5-10	62	.862	.9033	95.4	.0202	.0123	164	7.9
		3	10-20	56	.500	.7004	71.4	.0530	.0251	210	28
	2	1	0- 5	119	.808	.9398	86.0	.0417	.0123	340	29
		2	5-10	96	.689	.8532	80.8	.0313	.0192	163	12
		3	10-20	82	.360	.5587	64.4	.0629	.0414	152	22
	3	1	0- 5	38	.462	.9611	48.1	.1431	.0079	1810	135
		2	5-10	18	.237	.9033	26.2	.1250	.0123	1020	113
		3	10-20	9	.132	.7004	18.9	.0568	.0251	225	32
	4	1	0- 5	22	.190	.9797	19.4	.2826	.0041	6900	279

Table 323b Comparative 10-Year Experience of Hypertensive Patients
by Complication and by Blood Pressure (Diastolic)

Category	Hyp. Group No.	No. Alive at Start of Interval	Cumulative Survival Rate		Cumulative Surv. Ratio	Estim. Ave. Ann. Mort. Rate		Mortality Ratio	Excess Death Rate
			Observed	Expected*		Observed	Expected*		
		ℓ	P	P'	100 P/P'	$\breve{q}$	$\breve{q}'$	100 $\breve{q}/\breve{q}'$	1000($\breve{q}-\breve{q}'$)
Complicated Male	1	10	.401	.9044	44.3%	.0873	.0100	875%	77
	2	102	.304	.7589	40.1	.1123	.0272	415	85
	3	88	.102	.8305	12.3	.2041	.0184	1110	186
Female	1	21	.812	.9033	89.9	.0206	.0101	205	11
	2	98	.653	.8532	76.5	.0417	.0158	265	26
	3	33	.243	.9033	26.9	.1319	.0101	1300	122
Uncomplicated Male	1	37	.838	.9044	92.7	.0175	.0100	175	7.5
	2	18	.500	.7589	65.9	.0670	.0272	245	40
Female	1	44	.886	.9033	98.1	.0120	.0101	119	1.9
	2	21	.857	.8532	100.4	.0153	.0158	97	−0.5
B.P. < 100 Male	1	24	.750	.9044	82.9	.0284	.0100	285	18
	2	32	.406	.7589	53.5	.0862	.0272	315	59
Female	1	32	.906	.9033	100.3	.0098	.0101	96	−0.3
	2	45	.756	.8532	88.6	.0276	.0158	175	12
B.P. 100-119 Male	1	21	.714	.9044	78.9	.0331	.0100	330	23
	2	56	.321	.7589	42.3	.1074	.0272	395	80
	3	25	.160	.8305	19.3	.1674	.0184	915	149
Female	1	26	.808	.9033	89.4	.0211	.0101	205	11
	2	59	.695	.8532	81.5	.0357	.0158	225	20
	3	14	.357	.9033	39.5	.0979	.0101	960	88
B.P. 120-139 Male	2	26	.308	.7589	40.6	.1111	.0272	410	84
	3	42	.167	.8305	20.1	.1639	.0184	895	146
Female	2	14	.500	.8532	58.6	.0670	.0158	425	51
	3	15	.200	.9033	22.1	.1487	.0101	1460	139

* Basis of expected mortality: 1949-51 U. S. White Male & Female Tables

HYPERTENSION

§324–SEVERE HYPERTENSION

Reference: H. M. Perry, Jr., H. A. Schroeder, F. J. Catanzaro, D. Moore-Jones, and G. H. Camel, "Studies on the Control of Hypertension. VIII. Mortality, Morbidity, and Remissions During Twelve Years of Intensive Therapy," Circulation, 33:958-972 (1966).

Subjects Studied: Patients with moderate to severe and complicated hypertension in St. Louis, under treatment with gangioplegic agents and hydralazine initiated in the interval from August 1951 to August 1957. All subjects had a mean diastolic pressure at rest of 110 mm Hg or more. Only 12 patients meeting the criteria for entry could not be traced and they were excluded. There were 316 fully traced patients in the series, classified into four groups according to severity of the disease, with characteristics as follows:

		Hypertensive Group (Definition)	No. Pts.	Median Age	Non-White
1.	(BU)	Benign uncomplicated (no papilledema, DBP 110-139, and no CV damage to target organs).	103	49 yrs.	5%
2.	(BC)	Benign complicated (no papilledema, DBP 140 up, or with CV damage to heart, brain or kidneys)	51	49	6%
3.	(MN)	Malignant nonazotemic (with papilledema, DBP 120 up, 15-min. PSP $\leqslant$ 15%, NPN $\leqslant$ 30 with top normal 26)	97	45	20%
4.	(MA)	Malignant azotemic (with papilledema, DBP 120 up, 15-min. PSP $\leqslant$ 15%, NPN $>$ 30 with top normal 26)	65	45	41%

The proportion of males to females was about the same in each group; in the total series there were 144 males and 172 females. There was an increase in the proportion of cases of malignant hypertension from 40 per cent of the total in 1951-52 to 80 per cent at the end of the entry period.

Follow-up: Contact was maintained with all 316 patients until death or the close of observation. For patients who died medical records and cause of death were obtained wherever possible. In August 1964, 12½ years after the midpoint of the first entry year, blood pressure, antihypertensive regimen and cardiovascular and renal status were evaluated for all surviving patients.

Results: As shown in Table 324a, excess mortality differed markedly from one severity group to another. Overall average mortality ratios ranged from 260 per cent for the benign uncomplicated group to 3600 per cent for malignant hypertensives with azotemia; the corresponding range in EDR was from 17 to 276 extra deaths per 1000 per year. Extremely high mortality rates were sustained in the most severe group even after five years. Excess mortality was lower for the other two groups, with an average mortality rate of 1180 per cent for benign hypertensives with cardiovascular complications and 1080 per cent for nonazotemic malignant hypertensives. In the first two years of observation EDR for the latter group was considerably higher than EDR for the former (149 versus 86 extra deaths per 1000 per year), but this pattern was reversed over the succeeding 10 years.

Comment: Other relationships analysed in this highly informative paper (but not presented in the tables) include cause of death, control of blood pressure, status of survivors throughout follow-up, and complications of treatment. Hypertension was uncontrolled, with diastolic pressure over 120 mm, in 38 patients who discontinued therapy against advice, (12 per cent of the entire series of 316 patients). In patients who continued chemotherapy as prescribed hypertension was partially controlled (diastolic pressure generally 100 to 110 mms) in 58 or 18 per cent of the total and "adequately" controlled (diastolic pressure under 100 mm) in 220 or 70 per cent. No patient who discontinued therapy survived as long as 12 years, but 113 or 51 per cent of adequately controlled hypertensives survived to the end of follow-up. There was an intermediate survival rate of 21 per cent for those whose blood pressure was controlled inadequately. Statistically, these were highly significant differences. Remission of hypertension persisted in 27 of 126 surviving patients after complete withdrawal of antihypertensive medication or substitution of less potent drugs (in 16 patients with full blood pressure records the mean diastolic pressure after therapy was 81 mm and the mean duration of remission was 75 months). Known causes of death were 51 per cent "hypertensive" (mainly renal failure), 24 per cent "arteriosclerotic," 7 per cent due to hexamethonium toxicity and 18 per cent to unrelated conditions. Renal failure predominated even more in malignant hypertensives and those under poor control.

TREATED SEVERE HYPERTENSION

Table 324a Observed Data and Comparative Experience by Duration

Group*	Interval No.	Interval Start-End	No. Alive at Start of Interval	Exposure Person-Yrs	Deaths Obs.	Deaths Exp.†	Mortality Ratio Interval	Mortality Ratio Cumulative	Survival Ratio Interval	Survival Ratio Cumulative	Excess Death Rate
	i	t to t+Δt	ℓ	E	d	d'	100d/d'	100$\sum$d/$\sum$d'	100p_i/p_i'	100 P/P'	1000(d-d')/E
BU	1	0- 2 yrs	103	205	2	1.42	141%	141%	99.4%	99.4%	2.8
	2	2- 5	101	295	10	2.58	390	300	92.7	92.1	25
	3	5-12	91	559.5	17	7.15	240	260	88.0	81.1	18
		0-12	103	1059.5	29	11.15	260	—	81.1	—	17
BC	1	0- 2 yrs	51	97	9	.67	1340	1340	82.6	82.6	86
	2	2- 5	42	114	11	.99	1110	1200	76.2	62.1	88
	3	5-12	31	139	20	1.72	1160	1180	36.3	22.8	132
		0-12	51	350	40	3.38	1180	—	22.8	—	105
MN	1	0- 1 yr	97	97	15	.50	3000	3000	85.4	85.5	149
	2	1- 2	82	82	11	.46	2400	2700	87.0	74.3	129
	3	2- 5	71	202	11	1.37	805	1590	85.4	63.6	48
	4	5-12	60	307	21	3.03	695	1080	64.9	41.3	61
		0-12	97	688	58	5.36	1080	—	41.2	—	78
MA	1	0- 1 yr	65	65	27	.40	6800	6800	58.4	58.4	409
	2	1- 2	38	38	11	.25	4400	5800	72.9	42.5	283
	3	2- 5	27	68	11	.53	2100	4200	59.7	25.4	154
	4	5-12	16	51	14	.57	2500	3600	0.0	0.0	263
		0-12	65	222	63	1.75	3600	—	0.0	—	276
All		0-12 yrs	316	2319.5	190	21.64	880	—	41.4	—	73

Table 324b Derived Mortality and Survival Data

Group*	Interval No.	Interval Start-End	Observed Rates Cumulative Survival	Observed Rates Interval Survival	Observed Rates Geom. Mean Ann. Surv.	Observed Rates Geom. Mean Ann. Mort.	Expected Rates† Cumulative Survival	Expected Rates† Interval Survival	Expected Rates† Geom. Mean Ann. Surv.	Expected Rates† Geom. Mean Ann. Mort.
	i	t to t+Δt	P	p_i	$\breve{p}_i$	$\breve{q}_i$	P'	p_i'	$\breve{p}_i'$	$\breve{q}_i'$
BU	1	0- 2 yrs	.980	.980	.990	.010	.9862	.9862	.9931	.0069
	2	2- 5	.885	.903	.967	.033	.9605	.9740	.9913	.0087
	3	5-12	.710	.802	.969	.031	.8754	.9114	.9868	.0132
		0-12	.710	.710	.972	.028	.8754	.8754	.9890	.0110
BC	1	0- 2 yrs	.815	.815	.903	.097	.9862	.9862	.9931	.0069
	2	2- 5	.605	.742	.905	.095	.9605	.9740	.9913	.0087
	3	5-12	.200	.331	.854	.146	.8754	.9114	.9868	.0132
		0-12	.200	.200	.874	.126	.8754	.8754	.9890	.0110
MN	1	0- 1 yr	.850	.850	.850	.150	.9949	.9949	.9949	.0051
	2	1- 2	.735	.865	.865	.135	.9893	.9944	.9944	.0056
	3	2- 5	.615	.837	.942	.058	.9693	.9798	.9932	.0068
	4	5-12	.370	.602	.930	.070	.8988	.9272	.9893	.0107
		0-12	.370	.370	.920	.080	.8988	.8988	.9911	.0089
MA	1	0- 1 yr	.580	.580	.580	.420	.9939	.9939	.9939	.0061
	2	1- 2	.420	.724	.724	.276	.9873	.9934	.9934	.0066
	3	2- 5	.245	.583	.835	.165	.9640	.9764	.9921	.0079
	4	5-12	.000	.000	.725•	.275•	.8830	.9160	.9875	.0125
		0-12	.000	.000	.716•	.284•	.8830	.8830	.9897	.0103
All		0-12 yrs	.365	.365	.920	.080	.8825	.8825	.9896	.0104

* B U - Benign Uncomplicated; BC - Benign Complicated; MN - Malignant Nonazotemic; MA - Malignant Azotemic
† Basis of expected mortality: 1959-61 U.S. Life Tables: Male 46%; BU and BC 95% White; MN 80% White; MA 59% White
• $\bar{p}$ and $\bar{q}$ substituted for $\breve{p}_i$ and $\breve{q}_i$

HYPERTENSION IN INSUREDS

§325–HYPERTENSION IN INSUREDS

Reference: "New York Life Single Medical Impairment Study—1972," unpublished report made available by J.J. Hutchinson and J.C. Sibigtroth (1973).

Subjects Studied: Policyholders of New York Life Insurance Company issued insurance in 1954-1970, followed to the 1971 policy anniversary. The experience reported is for both standard and substandard issues. Records involving ratable impairment in addition to elevated blood pressure were excluded.

Follow-up: Insurance policy records formed the basis of entry, of counting policies, exposure and death claims, and of follow-up information.

Results: Comparative experience is given in Tables 325a-b for standard and substandard cases by sex and duration, all ages combined. Among standard males, the excess mortality was greatest at 5-10 years, with a mortality ratio of 161 per cent and EDR of 4.0 per 1000. Among standard females, mortality was substantially higher after 10 years, with a mortality ratio of 205 per cent and EDR of 13 per 1000. Among substandard males, the mortality ratio ranged from 177 per cent to 210 per cent, with EDR increasing by duration from 2.2 per 1000 at 0-2 years to 10 per 1000 at 10-17 years. Among substandard females, the mortality ratio showed a downward trend, ranging from 177 per cent at 0-2 years to 141 per cent at 10-17 years; the corresponding change in EDR was an increase from 1.7 to 4.9 extra deaths per 1000.

The overall mortality ratio was 124 per cent for standard males, 110 per cent for standard females, 194 per cent for substandard males and 152 per cent for substandard females (Table 325c). Thus, it will be noted that mortality ratios were generally higher for males than for females, and more favorable among standard than for substandard cases.

From Table 325c, it will be observed that the mortality ratio among male standard cases was somewhat higher for ages 50 up than for lower entry ages. There was no excess mortality found in the younger men, under age 40, with only 14 death claims resulting from 8130 policy years of exposure. The estimated eight-year survival index ranged from a normal level for men under 40 to a minimum of 93.3 per cent at ages 60 up. Among female standard cases, the greatest excess mortality occurred for ages under 50, with a mortality ratio of 180 per cent and EDR of 1.9 per 1000. Among male substandard cases, it is noteworthy that the higher overall mortality ratio in this as compared with the standard group appears in all age groups. The trend in EDR is an increase from 0.8 per 1000 at ages under 30 to 14 per 1000 at ages 60 up. The estimated eight-year survival index ranged from an almost normal level for men under 30 to 89.4 per cent at ages 60 up. Among female substandard cases, the mortality ratios decreased with advancing age, ranging from 240 per cent at ages 15-39 to 112 per cent at ages 60 up. In most age groups a higher mortality ratio was experienced among female substandard cases than for standard cases. The EDR was highest (3.5 per 1000) at ages 50-59.

For male and female substandard cases combined, the major cause of death is found in diseases of the heart and circulation, the mortality being 255 per cent and EDR 3.5 per 1000. The mortality due to "all other causes and unknown" was next in significance, the ratio being 225 per cent and EDR 1.3 per 1000. Of the 410 deaths in the latter cause category, 135 were due to cerebrovascular accidents.

Comment: Although no blood pressure data were reported with this study, it should be noted that most insurance companies underwrite borderline or definite hypertension with an average blood pressure level at or slightly above 140/90 as a dividing line between standard and substandard, depending on age, sex, minor risk factors and company practice. The standard experience represents a 10 per cent sample, whereas the substandard includes all coded cases. It may be presumed that the average blood pressure was higher for the substandard than for the standard cases.

HYPERTENSION

Table 325a   Observed Data and Comparative Experience by Sex and Duration — All Ages Combined

Sex	No.	Start-End	Exposure Policy-Yrs	Observed	Expected*	Interval	Cumulative	Interval	Cumulative	Excess Death Rate
		Interval		No. of Death Claims		Mortality Ratio		Survival Ratio		
	i	t to $t + \Delta t$	E	d	d'	100 d/d'	100 $\sum$d/$\sum$d'	100 p_i/p_i'	100 P/P'	1000(d-d')/E
Standard Cases										
Male	1	0- 2 yrs	6038	17	15.05	113%	113%	99.9%	99.9%	0.3
	2	2- 5	6261	30	27.16	110	111	99.9	99.8	0.5
	3	5-10	5267	56	34.82	161	134	98.0	97.8	4.0
	4	10-17	2155	30	29.96	100	124	100.0	97.8	0.0
Female	1	0-10	3227	11	13.81	80%	80%	100.5%	100.5%	0.9
	2	10-17	354	9	4.34	205	110	91.0	91.5	13
Substandard Cases										
Male	1	0- 2 yrs	39749	193	103.83	186%	186%	99.5%	99.5%	2.2
	2	2- 5	38451	357	181.35	197	193	98.6	98.2	4.6
	3	5-10	35761	552	265.01	210	200	96.0	94.3	8.0
	4	10-17	15390	363	205.49	177	194	93.0	87.6	10
Female	1	0- 2 yrs	12122	47	26.61	177%	177%	99.7%	99.7%	1.7
	2	2- 5	12155	83	54.16	153	161	99.3	99.0	2.4
	3	5-10	11028	119	78.85	151	156	98.2	97.2	3.6
	4	10-17	4457	75	53.08	141	152	96.6	93.8	4.9

Table 325b   Derived Mortality and Survival Data

Sex	No.	Start-End	Mortality $\bar{q} = d/E$	Survival $\bar{p}$	Survival P	Mortality Q	Mortality $\bar{q}' = d'/E$	Survival $\bar{p}'$	Survival P'	Mortality Q'
		Interval	Observed Rates				Expected Rates*			
			Average Annual		Cumulative		Average Annual		Cumulative	
	i	t to $t + \Delta t$								
Standard Cases										
Male	1	0- 2 yrs	.0028	.9972	.9944	.0056	.0025	.9975	.9950	.0050
	2	2- 5	.0048	.9952	.9802	.0198	.0043	.9957	.9821	.0179
	3	5-10	.0106	.9894	.9292	.0708	.0066	.9934	.9501	.0499
	4	10-17	.0139	.9861	.8423	.1577	.0139	.9861	.8614	.1386
Female	1	0-10 yrs	.0034	.9966	.9536	.0464	.0043	.9957	.9491	.0509
	2	10-17	.0254	.9746	.7963	.2037	.0123	.9877	.8706	.1294
Substandard Cases										
Male	1	0- 2 yrs	.0049	.9951	.9903	.0097	.0026	.9974	.9948	.0052
	2	2- 5	.0093	.9907	.9630	.0370	.0047	.9953	.9808	.0192
	3	5-10	.0154	.9846	.8909	.1091	.0074	.9926	.9450	.0550
	4	10-17	.0236	.9764	.7538	.2462	.0134	.9866	.8601	.1399
Female	1	0- 2 yrs	.0039	.9961	.9923	.0077	.0022	.9978	.9956	.0044
	2	2- 5	.0068	.9932	.9721	.0279	.0045	.9955	.9823	.0177
	3	5-10	.0108	.9892	.9207	.0793	.0071	.9929	.9477	.0523
	4	10-17	.0168	.9832	.8176	.1824	.0119	.9881	.8715	.1285

* Basis of expected mortality: 1955-60 Select Basic Table

HYPERTENSION IN INSUREDS

Table 325c   Comparative Experience by Sex and Age Group — All Durations Combined

Sex	Age Group	Exposure Policy-Yrs	No. of Death Claims		Mortality Ratio	Ave. Ann. Mort. Rate	Est. 8-Yr Surv. Rate	Est. 8-Yr Surv. Index	Excess Death Rate
			Observed	Expected*					
		E	d	d'	100 d/d'	$\bar{q} = d/E$	$P = (1-\bar{q})^8$	100 P/P'	1000(d-d')/E
Standard Cases									
Male	0-39	8130	14	15.21	92%	.0017	.9863	100.1%	−0.1
	40-49	6890	38	34.86	109	.0055	.9567	99.6	0.5
	50-59	3619	49	34.03	144	.0135	.8967	96.7	4.1
	60 up	1082	32	22.89	140	.0296	.7865	93.3	8.4
	All Ages	19721	133	106.99	124	.0067	.9473	99.0	1.3
Female	15-49	1622	7	3.88	180%	.0043	.9660	98.5%	1.9
	50-59	1415	5	7.00	71	.0035	.9721	101.1	−1.4
	60 up	544	8	7.27	110	.0147	.8882	98.9	1.3
	All Ages	3581	20	18.15	110	.0056	.9561	99.6	0.5
Substandard Cases									
Male	0-29	15961	29	16.37	177%	.0018	.9855	99.4%	0.8
	30-39	31612	155	66.30	235	.0049	.9615	97.8	2.8
	40-49	46044	465	238.34	195	.0101	.9220	96.1	4.9
	50-59	28132	558	279.89	199	.0198	.8519	92.3	9.9
	60 up	7602	258	154.78	167	.0339	.7586	89.4	14
	All Ages	129351	1465	755.68	194	.0113	.9129	95.7	5.5
Female	15-39	2563	7	2.89	240%	.0027	.9784	98.7%	1.6
	40-49	14930	85	42.82	199	.0057	.9554	97.8	2.8
	50-59	15255	133	78.90	169	.0087	.9323	97.2	3.5
	60 up	7014	99	88.09	112	.0141	.8925	98.8	1.6
	All Ages	39762	324	212.70	152	.0081	.9366	97.8	2.8

Table 325d   Mortality by Cause of Death — Male and Female Combined, Substandard Cases

Cause	No. of Death Claims		Mortality Ratio	Excess Death Rate
	Observed	Expected●		
Malignant Neoplasms	272	230.86	118%	0.3
Diseases of the Heart & Circulatory System	970	380.77	255	3.5
Accidents and Homicides	105	133.15	79	−0.1
Suicide	32	41.06	78	−0.1
All Other Causes and Unknown†	410	182.54	225	1.3
Total	1789	968.38	185	4.9

* Basis of expected mortality: 1955-60 Basic Select Table

† Includes 135 deaths due to Cerebrovascular Accident, 47 due to Respiratory Disorders,
   34 due to Digestive Disorders, 34 due to Cirrhosis of Liver, 15 due to G.U. System Disorders, 9 due to Diabetes

● Distribution of total expected deaths by Intercompany Medically Examined Standard Issues 1965-70

HYPERTENSION

§326–MODERATE AND SEVERE HYPERTENSION

References: (1) W. Bolt, M. F. Bell, J. R. Harnes, "A Study of Mortality in Moderate and Severe Hypertension," Trans. Assoc. Life Ins. Med. Dir. Am., 41:61-100 (1957).

(2) M. F. Bell and C. A. Schwab, re-estimated exposure data in personal communication (1973).

Subjects Studied: Applicants to the New York Life Insurance Company for life insurance between January 1, 1946 and December 31, 1950 whose blood pressure readings at examination exceeded 162 mm. Hg systolic or 102 mm. Hg diastolic. Included were subjects with heart enlargement, abnormal electrocardiograms, excessive weight or tachycardia, but excluded were applicants with any other impairment. Distribution of the 3283 subjects, with exposure to risk, by age and sex is presented in the following table:

Age (years)	Under 40	40-49	50-59	60 up	All Ages
Men	722	821	753	201	2497
Women	50	272	365	99	786
Total	772	1093	1118	300	3283
	23.5%	33.3%	34.1%	9.1%	100.0%

Follow-up: Observation of subjects was maintained through 1956. Information relative to survival and death in the case of applicants accepted was obtained from the insurance company's records. For others, information was acquired from various other insurance records, from contact with the individual, his family or acquaintances, by letter or telephone, and from attending physicians. Only 48 individuals (1.5 per cent) of all subjects could not be fully traced.

Results: Results are presented in the article for all combinations of four systolic blood pressure classes (under 158, 158-177, 178-197 and 198 up) and four diastolic classes (under 98, 98-107, 108-117 and 118 up), using various averages for current readings, current and past readings, and "mean" blood pressure (estimated as diastolic plus one-third of the pulse pressure). In Table 326 the experience is shown for men in seven blood pressure categories and for women in two or four blood pressure categories. The average current blood pressures have been used. Experience is omitted for men with systolic pressures under 178 mm. and diastolic 118 mm. up, with loss of only nine deaths. Also omitted are the data for women under 40, involving only 50 cases with one death.

With but few exceptions mortality ratios and excess death rates increase with each successive combination of higher systolic/diastolic pressures, and the exceptions involve very small numbers of deaths. The mortality ratios decrease with age, from 590 per cent for men under 40, to 200 per cent for men age 60 up, all blood pressure classes combined. Excess death rates, on the other hand, increase with age from 11 to 25 extra deaths per 1000 per year for men in these age groups. A similar increase of EDR with age is seen in women, but female mortality ratios show little variation with age in the age groups 40-49, 50-59 and 60 up. Although no data are available by duration of follow-up, the estimated 5-year survival index changes in a direction opposite to change in EDR: it decreases with age and higher blood pressure category in both men and women. In Table 326 comparative indices of mortality and survival have been calculated on the basis of separate male and female mortality rates, the latter being considerably lower than the former. Mortality ratios in the table differ from those in the article, where a single intermediate set of expected mortality rates has been used, based on insurance combined male/female standard experience.

MODERATE AND SEVERE HYPERTENSION

Table 326 Comparative Experience of Life Insurance Applicants (Highly Rated or Declined) by Age and Blood Pressure Class

Sex/Age Years	Blood Pressure		Exposure Person-Yrs	No. of Deaths		Mortality Ratio	Ave. Ann. Mort. Rate	Est. 5-Yr Surv. Rate	Est. 5-Yr Surv. Index	Excess Death Rate
	Diastolic	Systolic		Observed	Expected*					
			E	d	d′	100 d/d′	$\bar{q} = d/E$	$P = (1-\bar{q})^5$	100 P/P′	1000(d-d′)/E
Male <40	<98	<178	1908	11	4.12	265%	.0058	.971	98.2%	3.6
		178 up	118	1	.23	435	.0085	.958	96.9	6.5
	98-107	<178	1359	15	2.95	510	.0110	.946	95.7	8.9
		178 up	141	3	.31	970	.0213	.898	90.8	19
	108-117	<178	603	15	1.31	1150	.0249	.882	89.2	23
		178 up	141	4	.32	1250	.0284	.866	87.6	26
	118 up	178 up	211	8	.46	1740	.0379	.824	83.3	36
	All	All†	4481	57	9.70	590	.0127	.938	94.8	11
Male 40-49	<98	<178	1314	22	8.60	255	.0167	.919	94.9	10
		178 up	174	4	1.13	355	.0230	.890	91.9	16
	98-107	<178	1512	38	9.90	385	.0251	.881	91.0	19
		178 up	334	7	2.17	325	.0210	.899	92.9	14
	108-117	<178	706	16	4.62	345	.0227	.892	92.1	16
		178 up	344	16	2.26	710	.0465	.788	81.4	40
	118 up	178 up	289	20	1.89	1060	.0692	.699	72.2	63
	All	All†	4673	123	30.57	400	.0263	.875	90.4	20
Male 50-59	<98	<178	1601	33	22.86	144	.0206	.901	96.8	6.3
		178 up	407	20	5.82	345	.0491	.777	83.5	35
	98-107	<178	1013	36	14.49	250	.0355	.835	89.7	21
		178 up	434	18	6.21	290	.0415	.809	86.9	27
	108-117	<178	343	19	4.91	385	.0554	.752	80.8	41
		178 up	444	21	6.34	330	.0473	.785	84.3	33
	118 up	178 up	215	17	3.07	555	.0791	.662	71.1	65
	All	All†	4457	164	63.70	255	.0368	.829	89.0	23
Male 60-69	<98	<178	430	18	10.63	169	.0419	.807	91.5	17
		178 up	182	4	4.51	89	.0220	.895	101.5	−2.8
	98-107	<178	165	12	4.08	295	.0727	.686	77.8	48
		178 up	179	8	4.41	181	.0447	.796	90.2	20
	108-117	<178	124	8	3.06	260	.0645	.717	81.3	40
		178 up	98	4	2.43	165	.0408	.812	92.1	16
	118 up	178 up	49	7	1.22	575	.1429	.463	52.5	118
	All	All†	1227	61	30.34	200	.0497	.775	87.9	25
All Male	All	All†	14838	405	134.31	300	.0272	.871	91.1	18
Female 40-49	<108	All	1161	10	4.40	225	.0086	.958	97.7	4.8
	108 up	All	538	7	2.04	345	.0130	.937	95.5	9.2
	All	All	1699	17	6.44	265	.0100	.951	96.9	6.2
Female 50-59	<108	<178	1073	18	7.99	225	.0168	.919	95.4	9.3
		178 up	646	10	4.63	215	.0155	.925	96.1	8.3
	108 up	<178	103	5	.79	635	.0485	.780	81.0	41
		178 up	353	6	2.80	215	.0170	.918	95.3	9.1
	All	All	2175	39	16.21	240	.0179	.914	94.9	10
Female 60-69	<108	<178	273	8	3.76	215	.0293	.862	92.4	16
		178 up	214	11	2.94	375	.0514	.768	82.3	38
	108 up	<178	23	0	.31	(0)	(.0000)	(1.000)	(107.0)	(−13)
		178 up	86	3	1.17	255	.0349	.837	89.7	21
	All	All	596	22	8.18	270	.0369	.828	88.7	23
All Female	All	All●	4470	78	30.83	255	.0175	.916	94.8	11

* Basis of expected mortality: contemporary life insurance standard select rates, males or females
† Excludes small number males with systolic under 178 and diastolic 118 up (9 deaths)
● Excludes small number females under age 40 (1 death)

CONGENITAL HEART DISEASE

§330–TETRALOGY OF FALLOT (BLALOCK-TAUSSIG OPERATION)

References: (1) H. B. Taussig, A. Crocetti, E. Eshaghpour, R. Keinonen, N. Yap, D. Bachman, N. Momberger, and H. Kirk, "Fifteen-year Follow-up on the First Six Years of the Blalock-Taussig Operation," *The Natural History and Progress in Treatment of Congenital Heart Defects*, Kidd and Keith, ed., pp 83-95, Charles C. Thomas Co., Springfield, Ill. (1971).
(2) H. B. Taussig, personal communication (1970).

Subjects Studied: A consecutive series of 780 cases of tetralogy of Fallot (a severe, cyanotic form of congenital heart disease) with palliative operation performed at the Johns Hopkins Hospital, Baltimore, 1945 through 1950. There were, initially, 729 Blalock-Taussig procedures carried out, 18 Potts and 8 Brock operations, and 25 exploratory thoracotomies. Eighty-eight per cent (685) of those operated on survived; of the survivors, 281 underwent a subsequent operation. Age distribution of patients and their mortality rates upon first operation are presented in Table 330c; mean ages at first and second operations were, respectively, 7 years, 6 months and 18 years, 5 months, an eleven year difference.

Follow-up: Contact was maintained with most patients from the initial entry point through 1966; however, detailed experience presented by the authors, for the most part, is given for 15 years. Information with regard to deaths and survivors was obtained from the Hospital's own records, from records of other hospitals, from other doctors, from autopsy reports, from death certificates and from patients or their families. There were 70 patients lost to follow-up in the first 15 years. In Tables 330a-b patients undergoing a second operation were at that point treated as having come to the end of follow-up for the first operation (upper part of each table); in the lower parts of these tables early post-surgical survival (three months) after the second operation is also taken into account in the first operation follow-up.

Results: Following the 780 initial operations, 95 patients died within 3 months, a mortality rate of 0.122. The early mortality rates in Table 330c tended to be heavier among patients operated on at ages under 6 years and over 15 than among those operated on at the intermediate ages. Data were not provided in the reference as to late mortality or survival rates according to age at second operation, but the surgical mortality rate in these second operations was heavier than in the case of the first operations — about 20 per cent against 12.2 per cent (Table 330d). Mortality was higher with total corrective procedures than with Blalock-Taussig and other palliative procedures at second and subsequent operations, in the period covered by this report.

Even with deaths at re-operation excluded, excess mortality remained at high but variable levels throughout the fifteen years of observation in this predominantly juvenile population (Tables 330a-d). The mortality ratio during the rest of the first post-operative year for the 685 patients surviving the operation three months was 3000 per cent; the ratio fell to a minimum of 765 per cent in the next four years, then increased to almost 1200 per cent in the interval from 10 to 15 years. Corresponding figures for EDR were 34 extra deaths per 1000 per year in the first post-operative year, between 6 and 8 in the next two periods, and 14 from 10 to 15 years after operation. Cumulative survival ratio was 84.8 per cent at 15 years. When the 42 deaths associated with re-operation were added, considerably higher levels of excess mortality were observed at durations from 5 to 15 years, when most of the re-operations were performed. For the entire follow-up there were 16 extra deaths per 1000 per year when mortality at re-operation was included, as compared to 11 extra deaths per 1000 when this mortality was excluded, by termination of follow-up at the second operation.

Comment: Tetralogy of Fallot is a severe form of congenital heart disease characterized by low arterial O_2 as well as a greatly increased circulatory strain on the heart. As a palliative procedure the Blalock-Taussig operation does not fully correct these functional defects or all of the anatomical ones. The authors point out that many of their patients nevertheless survived to enter successful careers as adults, and 84 of 474 patients alive at last contact had attained an age in the range 30 to 54 years. The mortality risk of re-operation was considerable (30 per cent for total corrective procedures), but no information is available as to functional and clinical status of these patients prior to re-operation. This study will provide an excellent basis with which to compare results of "total surgical correction" of Tetralogy of Fallot when these are reported in adequate numbers.

TETRALOGY OF FALLOT AFTER BLALOCK-TAUSSIG OPERATION

Table 330a   Observed Data and Comparative Experience by Duration after First Operation (All Ages Combined)

No.	Interval Start-End	No. Alive at Start of Interval	No. Withdrawn Untraced	No. Withdrawn Re-op	Exposure Person-Yrs	Deaths Observed	Deaths Expected*	Mort. Ratio Interval	Surv. Ratio Cumulative	Excess Death Rate
i	t to t + Δt	ℓ	u	w	E	d	d'	100 d/d'	100 P/P'	1000(d-d')/E
Re-operation Mortality Excluded										
1	3 mo - 1 yr	685	7	5	509.0	18	0.60	3000%	97.4%	34
2	1- 5 yrs	655	19	25	2505.0	19	2.49	765	94.9	6.6
3	5-10 yrs	592	19	69	2710.0	24	2.53	950	91.1	7.9
4	10-15 yrs	480	25	110	2028.5	32	2.68	1190	84.8	14
	3 mo-15 yrs	685	70	209	7752.5	93	8.30	1120	84.8	11
Re-operation Mortality Included										
1	3 mo - 1 yr	685	7	3	510.0	20	0.60	3300%	97.1%	38
2	1- 5 yrs	655	19	22	2506.5	22	2.49	885	94.2	7.8
3	5-10 yrs	592	19	57	2716.0	36	2.54	1420	88.4	12
4	10-15 yrs	480	25	85	2041.0	57	2.70	2100	77.1	27
	3 mo-15 yrs	685	70	167	7773.5	135	8.33	1620	77.1	16

Table 330b   Derived Mortality and Survival Data

Interval No. Start-End	Observed Rates Cumulative Survival	Observed Rates Interval Survival	Observed Rates Geom. Mean Ann. Surv.	Observed Rates Geom. Mean Ann. Mort.	Expected Rates* Cumulative Survival	Expected Rates* Interval Survival	Expected Rates* Geom. Mean Ann. Surv.	Expected Rates* Geom. Mean Ann. Mort.
i t to t + Δt	P	p_i	$\breve{p}$	$\breve{q}$	P'	p_i'	$\breve{p}'$	$\breve{q}'$
Re-operation Mortality Excluded								
1 3 mo - 1 yr	.9735	.9735	.9648	.0352	.9991	.9991	.9988	.0012
2 1- 5 yrs	.9443	.9699	.9924	.0076	.9951	.9960	.9990	.0010
3 5-10 yrs	.9027	.9559	.9910	.0090	.9905	.9954	.9991	.0009
4 10-15 yrs	.8340	.9239	.9843	.0157	.9839	.9933	.9987	.0013
Re-operation Mortality Included								
1 3 mo - 1 yr	.9706	.9706	.9608	.0392	.9991	.9991	.9988	.0012
2 1- 5 yrs	.9369	.9653	.9912	.0088	.9951	.9960	.9990	.0010
3 5-10 yrs	.8755	.9345	.9866	.0134	.9905	.9954	.9991	.0009
4 10-15 yrs	.7585	.8664	.9717	.0283	.9839	.9933	.9987	.0013

Table 330c   First Operation — Early Mortality (0-3 Months)

Age	No. of Patients 1st Operation	Post-op. Deaths	Mortality Rate	Survivors at 3 mos.
x	ℓ_0	d	q	$\ell_{1/4}$
Under 1 yr	17	8	.470	9
1 yr	45	9	.200	36
2- 5 yrs	297	39	.131	258
6- 9 yrs	200	13	.065	187
10-14 yrs	113	8	.071	105
15-19 yrs	55	10	.182	45
20-24 yrs	36	6	.167	30
25 yrs up	17	2	.118	15
Total	780	95	.122	685

Table 330d   Re-operation — Surgical Mortality (0-3 Months)

Interval after 1st Op.	No. of Patients Re-operation	No. of Deaths	Mortality Rate
t to t + Δt	ℓ_{op+}	d	q_{op+}
2nd Operations			
3 mo - 1 yr	5	2	.400
1- 5 yrs	25	3	.120
5-10 yrs	69	12	.174
10-15 yrs	110	25	.227
15 yrs up	72	13	.181
Total 2nd	281	55	.196
3rd Oper.	46	21	.457
Palliative	123	16	.130
"Total Correct"	201	60	.298

* Basis of expected mortality: contemporaneous U.S. Population Rates

CONGENITAL AORTIC STENOSIS

§331–CONGENITAL AORTIC STENOSIS

References: (1) M.Campbell, "The Natural History of Congenital Aortic Stenosis," Brit. Heart J., 30:514-526 (1968).

(2) R.M. Marquis and A. Logan, "Congenital Aortic Stenosis and its Surgical Treatment," Brit. Heart J., 17:373-390 (1955).

(3) I.B. Braverman and S. Gibson, "The Outlook for Children with Congenital Aortic Stenosis," Am. Heart J., 53:487-493 (1957).

(4) P.A. Ongley, A.S. Nadas, M.H. Paul, A.M. Rudolph, and G.W.B. Starkey, "Aortic Stenosis in Infants and Children," Pediatrics, 21:207-221 (1958).

(5) F.R. Edwards and R.S. Jones, "Congenital Aortic Stenosis," Thorax, 17:218-229 (1962).

(6) B. Landtman, I. Louhimo, and E.I. Wallgren, "Congenital Aortic Stenosis in Children. Follow-up of 103 Conservatively Treated Cases," Acta Chir. Scand., Suppl. 356B:26-34 (1966).

Subjects Studied: (1) 87 patients with a diagnosis of congenital aortic stenosis seen by the author at the Cardiac Clinic, Guy's Hospital, London, England, prior to 1958. There were 65 male and 22 female patients. In this series the murmur was recognized in 69 before the age of 20, but only 44 were first seen by the author and admitted for follow-up before age 20:

Age in Years:	Under 6	6-10	11-19	20-29	30-39	40-49	50 up	Total
Murmur First Noted	41	17	11	8	4	6	0	87
First Seen, Guy's Hospital	12	15	17	13	12	14	4	87

Only five patients had any history of rheumatic fever, and the murmur preceded the rheumatic fever in all of these. It is inferred that the murmur reflected stenosis developing with a congenital bicuspid valve in some of the patients not diagnosed until after age 20. From operative and necropsy data it is known that the aortic stenosis was valvar in 33 patients and subvalvar in 7 patients.

(2) 28 patients with congenital aortic stenosis seen and followed at the Royal Infirmary, Edinburgh, Scotland prior to about 1952. Six cases age under one year or 20 up when first seen were excluded from the data reported here, leaving 18 male and 4 female patients. In all patients the murmur was first heard under age six, generally in infancy.

(3) 85 patients with classical signs of congenital aortic stenosis seen at Children's Memorial Hospital, Chicago, 1947-1955. Of the 26 patients with symptoms, one infant who died at age four months has been excluded from the data reported here. The remaining patients included 66 males and 18 females.

(4) 67 patients with congenital aortic stenosis seen at the Congenital Heart Clinic of the Children's Medical Center, Boston, 1950-1956. Males outnumbered females in the ratio of five to one. Most of the patients were asymptomatic.

(5) 120 patients with uncomplicated congenital aortic stenosis studied at the heart clinic of the Royal Liverpool Children's Hospital, 1956-1961. Five infant deaths and one patient first seen at age 26 have been excluded from the data reported here, leaving 114 patients with a ratio of two males to one female.

(6) 103 children with congenital aortic stenosis seen at the Children's Hospital, University of Helsinki, Helsinki, Finland. There were 70 boys and 33 girls, but one infant death was excluded from the data reported here. In the total series 43 patients were asymptomatic, and the remainder reported dyspnea on exertion, fatiguability, occasional chest pain or syncopal attacks; symptoms were generally mild and non-disabling.

Follow-up: (1) Follow-up started when the patient was first seen by the author or a colleague, and continued until termination by death (22 patients), aortic valvotomy (27 cases), loss from observation (8 patients in first two years), or end of follow-up. Principal follow-up was carried out in 1958 when nearly all surviving patients were re-examined, but some supplementary experience was added in 1966.

(2) Follow-up methods are not given in the article, but the average duration of follow-up, excluding two infants, is stated as "nearly four years."

(3) Follow-up beyond January 1, 1956, was carried out by re-examination of 15 surviving patients, and by information obtained from patients or referring physicians in 58 patients. Twelve patients were lost to follow-up.

(4) Methods and completeness of follow-up are not given in the article. Follow-up was terminated in 1956.

(5) Follow-up methods are not given in the article, but follow-up about 1961 accounted for all except three of the 120 patients. In the total series 28 patients were operated on. Additional information given by the authors and quoted by

CONGENITAL AND VALVULAR HEART DISEASE

§331–CONGENITAL AORTIC STENOSIS

Follow-up (continued):

Campbell (Reference 1) cites a total of 1395 patient-years of follow-up. However, this includes retrospective follow-up prior to 1956, the start of the entry period for selection of the series. Since "most of the patients were followed from infancy" it has been assumed that average follow-up was five years, from 1956 to 1961.

(6) Follow-up was carried to 1965, and only 8 patients were lost (examined only once). Maximum follow-up was 15 years, and 48 were followed five years or more. All but one of the surviving patients were able to lead a normal life; 43 children remained asymptomatic and seven died.

Results: The series reported by Campbell (Reference 1) is the only one that provides significant follow-up observations in adults, but the other series, all referred to and analyzed by Campbell, add considerably to the exposure and deaths observed in children and young adults up to age 20. When congenital aortic stenosis is diagnosed in infancy, in the first or second year of life the lesion is apt to be a severe one, with consequent high mortality. For this reason the results in Tables 331a-b conform to the procedure followed by Campbell and exclude cases diagnosed in and resulting in death in early infancy. In several of the series it has been necessary to estimate exposure of the patients on the basis of number of entrants followed up, average duration of follow-up, and adjustments for distribution of the deaths. The estimate of exposure in the other series does not always agree with Campbell's estimate, especially in Series 5 (see under Follow-up). The summary of the juvenile cases, observed data and comparative experience in Series 2-6 in Tables 331a-b represents the best approximation it was possible to make from a careful study of all of these articles as well as Campbell's. Despite the manifest uncertainties in estimating exposure, the average annual mortality rates and comparative indices are grouped in surprisingly close proximity to the aggregate results, which give an average annual mortality rate of .016, based on 30 deaths, an average annual mortality ratio of 2200 per cent, and an EDR of 15 per 1000 per year, and a survival index at age 20 of approximately 75 per cent for patients who survive the first year of life. The aggregate experience can be viewed with considerably more confidence than the much more limited experience in any of the individual series. It is thus evident that considerable excess mortality is encountered in children with unoperated congenital aortic stenosis, despite the fact that most of them do well clinically, with relatively few cases exhibiting disabling symptoms. In all of the series the problem of sudden and unexpected death is emphasized. Campbell estimates that about half of the deaths encountered in these patients are sudden deaths, presumably associated with arrhythmias such as ventricular fibrillation or arrest.

Comparative experience reported by Campbell by attained age, between ages one to 60, is given in Tables 331c-d. Cumulative survival rates have been approximated from the average annual mortality rate in each successive range of attained age. The cumulative survival ratio diminishes steadily to an estimated level of about 8 per cent at age 60. Mortality ratios were relatively stable (845 to 1270 per cent) in the four decades between 20 and 60, and below the level of 2400 per cent seen in childhood, when expected mortality rates are at their lowest. However, a different pattern of excess mortality variation with age is evident in terms of EDR, which was 10 to 22 per 1000 up to age 40, but *increased* to 44 per 1000 in the decade 40-50, and even higher to 120 per 1000 in the decade 50-60 years. The increasing risk of death with advancing age in unoperated congenital aortic stenosis is clearly evident, despite the small number of deaths in each attained age group.

Comment: As pointed out by Campbell, it is becoming increasingly difficult to collect follow-up data on patients with congenital aortic stenosis who have not been subjected to corrective operation. Some of the patients in these series had other valvular lesions. Additional topics discussed in these articles include diagnostic information at the beginning of study, clinical condition, complications and findings in the course of follow-up, operative findings and autopsy findings. Campbell reports 33 cases of valvar and 7 cases of subvalvar stenosis in patients subjected to operation or autopsy. Campbell also estimates mortality in the first year of life to be in the range from 18 to 28 per cent, based on other reports. Campbell has shown great ingenuity in his analysis of mortality in this type of congenital heart lesion as well as in coarctation of the aorta (§332) and patent ductus arteriosus (§333). Average annual rate of sudden death was estimated to be 4 per 1000 or higher, and of subacute bacterial endocarditis, 9 per 1000.

CONGENITAL AORTIC STENOSIS

Table 331a Congenital Aortic Stenosis in Childhood (Infant Deaths Excluded)

Ref.	Series	M/F Sex Ratio	Age at Entry	Entry Period	Followed to Year	Average Follow-up
1	Cardiac clinic referrals — London	3/1	3-19	1946-57	1958	9
2	Selected cardiology referrals — Edinburgh	4.5/1	2-19	to ca 1952	ca 1954	4
3	Hospitalized patients — Chicago	3.7/1	½-16	1947-55	1956	4
4	Congenital H.D. Clinic patients — Boston	5/1	1-ca 10	1950-56	1956	3
5	Cardiac clinic referrals — Liverpool	2/1	N.A.	1956-61	1961	5
6	Cardiac clinic referrals — Helsinki	2.1/1	2-ca 18	1951-65	ca 1965	5

Table 331b Comparative Experience, Congenital Aortic Stenosis in Childhood

Reference	No. of Subjects Traced	Est. Exposure Person-Yrs	No. of Deaths	Ave. Ann. Mort. Rate	Expected Mort. Rate*	Mortality Ratio	Surv. Index at Age 20	Excess Death Rate
	ℓ	E	d	$\bar{q}=d/E$	$\bar{q}'$	$100\ \bar{q}/\bar{q}'$	$100\ P/P'$	$1000(\bar{q}-\bar{q}')$
1 — Campbell	44	306	5	.016	.0007	2300%	74.2%	16
2 — Marquis	22	88	3	.034	.0007	4900	52.4	33
3 — Braverman	72	288	5	.017	.0007	2500	72.6	17
4 — Ongley	67	201	5	.025	.0007	3600	62.7	24
5 — Edwards	114	550	6	.011	.0007	1560	82.3	10
6 — Landtman	94	504	6	.012	.0007	1700	80.7	11
Total	413	1937	30†	.016	.0007	2200	75.3	15

Table 331c Observed Data and Comparative Experience by Attained Age, Congenital Aortic Stenosis Patients Followed by Campbell (Ref. 1)

Attained Age Range	Exposure Person-Yrs	No. of Deaths Observed	No. of Deaths Expected●	Mortality Ratio Age Range	Mortality Ratio Cumulative	Survival Ratio Age Range	Survival Ratio Cumulative†	Excess Death Rate
	E	d	d'	$100\ d/d'$	$100\ \Sigma d/\Sigma d'$	$100\ p_i/p_i'$	$100\ P/P'$	$1000(d-d')/E$
1-10 yrs	93	2	0.09	2200%	2200%	82.9%	82.9%	21
10-20	213	3	0.13	2300	2300	87.1	72.4	13
20-30	182	2	0.24	845	1520	90.7	65.7	9.7
30-40	124	3	0.24	1270	1450	79.7	52.4	22
40-50	125	6	0.56	1070	1280	63.9	33.6	44
50-60	45	6	0.58	1040	1200	27.2	9.1	120

Table 331d Derived Mortality and Survival Data (Campbell — Ref. 1)

Attained Age Range	Observed Rates Average Annual Mortality	Observed Rates Average Annual Survival	Observed Rates Interval Survival	Observed Rates Cumulative Survival	Expected Rates● Average Annual Mortality	Expected Rates● Average Annual Survival	Expected Rates● Interval Survival	Expected Rates● Cumulative Survival
	$\bar{q}$	$\bar{p}$	p_i	P	$\check{q}'$	$\check{p}'$	p_i'	P'
1-10 yrs	.022	.978	.822	.822	.0010	.9990	.991	.991
10-20	.014	.986	.868	.713	.0006	.9994	.996	.985
20-30	.011	.989	.895	.639	.0013	.9987	.987	.972
30-40	.024	.976	.783	.500	.0019	.9981	.982	.954
40-50	.048	.952	.611	.306	.0045	.9955	.956	.912
50-60	.133	.867	.239	.073	.0128	.9872	.879	.802

*Basis of expected mortality: Estimated weight average rate in national populations

†From age 1 year to end of attained age group

●Basis of expected mortality: English Life Tables, P' from Table 5 of Campbell (Ref. 1)

CONGENITAL AND VALVULAR HEART DISEASE

§332–COARCTATION OF THE AORTA

Reference: M. Campbell, "Natural History of Coarctation of The Aorta," Brit. Heart J., 32:633-640 (1970).

Subjects Studied: Patients with unoperated coarctation of the aorta, diagnosed in three different British series, for which person-years of exposure and mortality rates by attained age could be calculated. Two small series involved 8 Army pensioners (Lewis 1938) and 20 Army personnel diagnosed 1939-45 and 3 Army pensioners from World War I (Newman 1948), with a total of 257 patient-years and 10 deaths. In a larger series of 130 Guy's Hospital out-patients (Campbell and Baylis 1956) there were 459 patient-years of exposure and 12 deaths, mostly at ages under 30. No patients were observed in the first year of life, when the mortality is reported to range from 45 to 84 per cent. Patients had few or no symptoms at the time of entry; about two-thirds of the experience was on male lives. The composite exposure was distributed as follows:

Attained Age	1-19	20-29	30-39	40-49	50 up	Total
Patient-Years	252	217	123	64	60	716
Per cent of Total	35.2	30.3	17.2	8.9	8.4	100.0

Follow-up: Patients were followed up to death or termination by end of follow-up, untraced status, or operation to correct the coarctation. Follow-up lasted from 1 to 25 years, with an average of 4.4 years. Patient-years of exposure and deaths were classified by attained age rather than entry age; some patients therefore appear in more than one age group. The age groups by decade constitute periods with a duration of 10 years in terms of survival, except the first decade, which includes only 9 years (ages 1 through 9).

Results: The number of deaths for the total study, 22, is small, and some caution in interpreting results is called for. However, the experience is quite consistent, producing results of a regular character by attained age group. Mortality experience is extremely high, mortality ratios averaging 2000 per cent that of the general United Kingdom population for ages under 40 years, but diminishing somewhat to 555 per cent for ages over 50 (Table 332a). Excess deaths per 1000, however, increase from an average of 15 per year for ages through 19 years, to more than 55 per year for ages 40 and over. The mean age at death is 34 years in contrast to 71 years among the general population.

Expected survival rates (P') as derived by the author from Table No. 11 of the Registrar General are given in Table 332b, together with average observed mortality rates (q̄). These have been used to derive the geometric mean expected annual mortality rate (q̂'), and the cumulative survival that might be observed in a group of patients with coarctation starting at age 1, based on the data in Table 332a and values of q̄ for each decade of attained age. Cumulative survival ratios decrease steadily from 85.8 per cent at age 10 to 12.6 per cent at age 60. Interval survival ratios (not shown) are highest in the first decade (85.8 per cent) and decrease to about 55 per cent in the last two decades.

Deaths in the author's series contained a greater proportion of cases of congestive failure than in the autopsy series collected by Abbott in 1928 (Table 332c). The author also reports six cases developing bacterial endocarditis with an exposure of 459 patient-years, an annual incidence of 13 per 1000, which appears to be somewhat higher than he has calculated for congenital aortic stenosis, pulmonic stenosis and persistent ductus arteriosus (9 to 5 per 1000 per year).

NATURAL HISTORY — COARCTATION OF THE AORTA

Table 332a   Composite Observed Data and Comparative Experience (for Cases Alive at Age 1 Year)

Age Group	No. of Patients*	Exposure Person-Yrs	Deaths		Mortality Ratio		Survival Ratio		Excess Death Rate
			Obs.	Exp.†	Age Group	Cumulative	Age Group	Cumulative●	
(Years)	ℓ	E	d	d'	100 d/d'	100∑d/∑d'	100 p_i/p_i'	100 P/P'	1000(d-d')/E
1-19	78	252	4	.20	2000%	2000%	74.7%	74.7%	15
20-29	53	217	6	.27	2200	2100	76.3	57.0	26
30-39	29	123	4	.23	1740	2000	72.5	41.4	31
40-49	12	64	4	.29	1380	1820	53.8	22.2	58
50 up	9	60	4	.72	555	1290	56.7	12.6	55
All Ages	181*	716	22	1.71	1290	1290	—	12.6	28

Table 332b   Derived Mortality and Survival Data by Attained Age (for Cases Alive at Age 1 Year)

Attained Age	Observed Rates				Expected Rates†			
	Cumulative Survival □	Interval Survival ■	Geom. Mean Ann. Surv.	Geom. Mean Ann. Mort.	Cumulative Survival	Interval Survival	Geom. Mean Ann. Surv.	Geom. Mean Ann. Mort.
(Years)	P	p_i	$\check{p}$	$\check{q}$	P'	p_i'	$\check{p}'$	$\check{q}'$
1	1.000	—	—	—	1.000	—	—	—
20	.736	.736	.984	.016	.985	.9850	.9992	.0008
30	.555	.754	.972	.028	.973	.9878	.9988	.0012
40	.395	.712	.967	.033	.955	.9815	.9981	.0019
50	.203	.514	.937	.063	.913	.9560	.9955	.0045
60	.102	.502	.933	.067	.809	.8861	.9880	.0120

Table 332c   Causes of Death (Reported Autopsies-Abbott 1928)

Cause of Death	Per Cent	Mean Age	Usual Decades
Congestive Heart Failure	25.5%	39	3rd-5th
Not Connected with Coarctation	24.0	47	4th-6th
Aortic Rupture	21.0	25	2nd & 3rd
Bacterial Endocarditis	18.0	29	1st-5th
Intracranial Hemorrhage	11.5	29	2nd & 3rd
All 304 Cases	100.0	34.4	—

* Some patients observed in more than one age group (161 actual patients)
† Basis of expected mortality: Life Table No. 11 of Registrar General (U.K.)-1957
● Cumulative to beginning of next age group, with attained age 60 for age group 50 up
□ Estimated from mortality rates within the range of successive attained ages
■ Survival rate from preceding attained age

PATENT DUCTUS ARTERIOSUS

§333–PATENT DUCTUS ARTERIOSUS

References: (1a) M. Campbell, "Patent Ductus Arteriosus. Some notes on prognosis and on Pulmonary Hypertension," Brit. Heart J., 17:511-533 (1955).

(1b) M. Campbell, "Natural History of Persistent Ductus Arteriosus," Brit. Heart J., 30:4-13 (1968).

(2) J.W. Brown, "Discussion on Patent Ductus Arteriosus and its Surgical Treatment," Brit. Heart J., 7:212 (1945).

(3) J.J. Welti and G. Koerperich, "Remarques sur le Pronostic de la Persistance Simple du Canal Artériel à propos de 54 Cas Non Opéres," Arch. Mal. Coeur, 41:428-435 (1948).

(4) J.A. Cosh, "Patent Ductus Arteriosus. A Follow-up Study of 73 Cases," Brit. Heart J., 19:13-22 (1957).

(5) M.G. Wilson and R. Lubschez, "Prognosis for Children with Congenital Anomalies of the Heart and Central Vessels. Life Expectancy in Patent Ductus Arteriosus," J. Pediat., 21:23-30 (1942).

Subjects Studied: (1a) and (1b) Patients diagnosed as having patent ductus arteriosus and seen in the cardiac department of Guy's Hospital, London, England during the period from about 1948 to about 1954. There were 160 persons, 43 males and 117 females in the series; of these, 32 males and 90 females were under 20 years of age when first seen. Patients with pulmonary hypertension from infancy with a balanced or reversed shunt and cases of morbus coeruleus and other abnormalities were excluded. Most subjects were operated on for the condition with a high degree of success — at operation they were withdrawn from observation.

(2) 63 cases ranging in age from 3 to 45 encountered in personal practice over a period of at least 11 years prior to 1945. There were 20 males and 43 females in the series. Electrocardiograms showed normal axis in 46, left axis in 9 and a right axis in 1. It appears that no operations were performed on these subjects.

(3) 54 cases seen between 1920 and 1947 in the cardiology clinic of Professor C. Lian (France). Thirteen of the patients were between 4 and 19 when first brought under observation.

(4) A series of 73 patients (53 female, 20 male) referred to the Bristol (England) Royal Infirmary in the period from about 1925 to 1955. It is estimated that 58 of the subjects were younger than 20 years of age when first observed.

(5) 38 patients observed over a 20-year period (1921-1941) in the Pediatric Cardiac Clinics of the New York Nursery and Child's Hospital and the New York Hospital. The reference cites autopsy reports compiled at the same sources which indicate that uncomplicated patent ductus arteriosus represented 10.5 per cent of 152 cases of congenital malformations of the heart.

Follow-up: (1a) and (1b) Follow-up started when the patient was first seen by the author or a colleague, and continued until termination by death (2 cases), closing of the ductus by operation (111 cases), or end of the period of observation. Due mainly to the high proportion of operations for closing the ductus, follow-up averaged only 2.7 years.

(2) The series cited by Brown represented patients in his own practice and presumably under his personal observation from first observation to death or to the end of an observation period ending in 1945. No operations were reported in this series.

(3) The period of observation covered the period from 1920 to 1947 and the experience was reviewed by Professor Lian in February 1948. Follow-up started at the initial observation and continued to 1947, to death (2 cases), or to loss from observation (13 cases). No operations were reported in this series.

(4) Follow-up of the experience under the Bristol series commenced on referral to clinics or wards of the Infirmary during the period from about 1925 to 1955 and ended upon death, termination of the observation period, closing of the ductus or loss to observation. No information with respect to follow-up procedure is furnished.

(5) Follow-up extended over the 20-year period 1921-1941, ending at death or completion of the period of observation. No patients were lost to observation. No operations were reported.

Results: Table 333a presents the salient features of the experience reported in the five references for ages under 20 but excluding the infantile ages. Shown in this table is the characteristic high ratio of females to males, ranging from 2.1 to 2.8 females to each male and averaging 2.5 to 1. Entry periods began as early as 1920 and extended to 1967. All follow-up periods were of relatively short duration, on the average.

Comparative mortality and survival experience among the children and young adults embraced in the foregoing table is presented in Table 333b. The number of deaths is very small in each study but the individual annual mortality rates (except for the Welti study) disclose small deviations from the average of the overall experience — a circumstance which promotes somewhat greater significance to the several results. Mortality ratios range from 210 per cent in the Wilson

CONGENITAL AND VALVULAR HEART DISEASE

§333–PATENT DUCTUS ARTERIOSUS

Results: (continued)

report to 860 per cent in the Campbell study. The mortality ratio shown for the Welti experience, 1550 per cent, is relatively high as is the EDR of 19 per 1000 against the range of extra deaths of from 1.4 to 5.3 per 1000 shown for the other series. Survival indices at age 20, again excepting the Welti series (with its much lower index of 70 per cent), lie between 90 and 97 per cent. A uniform death rate of .0013 has been used as the expected standard mortality in the four earlier series starting in the 1920's. This rate is an estimate of the weighted average mortality experienced in the several studies, giving effect to the period of observation and the age and sex distribution. In the Campbell series the average annual mortality rate of .0007 for those under age 20 has been derived from the expected survival rate in Table V of Reference (1b).

Comparative experience reported in the Campbell study at the younger ages, shown in Tables 333a-b, together with such data for ages over 20 years, is presented in Tables 333c and d. The mortality ratio over the first two decades of life for patients with the disorder is 860 per cent – a high figure. However, in the third decade the mortality ratio is more than tripled and the EDR reaches 30 per 1000 compared with 5.3 per 1000 in the first interval. There is some improvement for ages 30 years and over: the mortality ratio drops to 1490 per cent, and in view of the increasing age, the excess deaths of 25 per 1000 is relatively favorable. The cumulative survival ratio is 51.7 per cent, estimated at age 40.

Comment: Campbell notes the not uncommon occurrence of spontaneous closure of patent ductus and quotes Brown *(Congenital Heart Disease, 1950)*, " . . . the adult case of patent ductus is a rare visitor to the clinic and the condition appears equally rare in the routine postmortem examination. It therefore seems that . . . there must be spontaneous closure of the ductus more often than is generally realized." Campbell also calls attention to the salutary effect of penicillin dating from 1946-47 on subacute bacterial endocarditis which had been a leading cause of death in cases of patent ductus. The risk of bacterial endocarditis is estimated to be about 4.5 per 1000 exposed to risk per year from ages 10 to 40 up.

PATENT DUCTUS ARTERIOSUS

Table 333a Patent Ductus Arteriosus in Childhood (Infant Deaths Excluded)

Ref.	Series	M/F Sex Ratio	Age at Entry	Entry Period	Followed to Year	Average Follow-up
1a-b	Cardiac clinic referrals — London	1/2.8	1-19	ca 1950-66	ca 1967	2.7 yrs
2	Cardiac referrals — England	1/2.2	3-19	ca 1924-44	ca 1944	8.7
3	Cardiac referrals — France	1/2.2	4-19	ca 1920-47	1948	7.7
4	Cardiac referrals — Bristol, England	1/2.6	2-19	ca 1925-55	1955	10.3
5	Pediatric cardiac clinic — New York	Not Avail.	2-19	1921-41	1941	5.4

Table 333b Comparative Experience, Patent Ductus Arteriosus in Childhood

Reference	No. of Subjects Traced	Est. Exposure Person-Yrs	No. of Deaths	Ave. Ann. Mort. Rate	Expected Mort. Rate*	Mortality Ratio	Surv. Index at Age 20	Excess Death Rate
	ℓ	E	d	$\bar{q}=d/E$	$\bar{q}'$	100 $\bar{q}/\bar{q}'$	100 P/P'	1000$(\bar{q}-\bar{q}')$
1 — Campbell	123	332	2	.0060	.0007	860%	90.5%	5.3
2 — Brown	44	383	2	.0052	.0013	400	92.9	3.9
3 — Welti	13	99	2	.0202	.0013	1550	69.6	19
4 — Cosh	58	599	2	.0033	.0013	255	96.2	2.0
5 — Wilson	38	368	1	.0027	.0013	210	97.4	1.4
Total	276	1781	9	.0051	.0012	425	92.8	3.9

Table 333c Observed Data and Comparative Experience by Attained Age, Patent Ductus Arteriosus Followed by Campbell (Ref. 1b)

Attained Age Range	Exposure Person-Yrs	No. of Deaths		Mortality Ratio		Survival Ratio		Excess Death Rate
		Observed	Expected*	Age Range	Cumulative	Age Range	Cumulative†	
	E	d	d'	100 d/d'	100 $\Sigma d/\Sigma d'$	100 p_i/p_i'	100 P/P'	1000(d-d')/E
1-20 yrs	332	2	0.23	860%	860%	90.5%	90.5%	5.3
20-30	65	2	0.07	2800	1320	73.8	66.8	30
30 up	149	4	0.27	1490	1400	77.4	51.7	25
All Ages	546	8	0.57	1400	1400	51.7	51.7	14

Table 333d Derived Mortality and Survival Data (Campbell-Ref. 1b)

Attained Age Range	Observed Rates				Expected Rates*			
	Average Annual		Interval Survival	Cumulative Survival	Average Annual		Interval Survival	Cumulative Survival
	Mortality	Survival			Mortality†	Survival		
	$\bar{q}$	$\bar{p}$	p_i	P	$\breve{q}'$	$\breve{p}'$	p_i'	P'
1-20 yrs	.0060	.994	.892	.892	.0007	.9993	.986	.986
20-30	.0308	.969	.730	.651	.0011	.9989	.989	.975
30-40	.0268	.973	.761	.495	.0018	.9982	.983	.958

*Basis of expected rates: Campbell-English Life Tables (Table V of Ref. 1b);
weighted average contemporary life tables, Series 2-5
†Derived from cumulative survival rates in Table V of Ref. 1b (geometric mean)

CONGENITAL HEART DISEASE

§334–CONGENITAL HEART DISEASE IN CHILDREN

Reference: B. MacMahon, T. McKeown, and R. G. Record, "The Incidence and Life Expectation of Children with Congenital Heart Disease," Brit. Heart J., 15:121-129 (1953).

Subjects Studied: Among 199,418 total births reported in the years 1940-49 in the administrative boundary of Birmingham, England, there were 628 live births (53 per cent male) identified as having congenital heart disease. Sources of information were: records of postmortem examinations in maternity, pediatric, and general hospitals in the city of Birmingham; clinical records of all patients seen by consulting physicians and surgeons in these hospitals; records of all patients attending special schools or under the supervision of school medical officers in ordinary schools; Local Authority registers of stillbirths and neonatal and infant deaths. Diagnoses were based on postmortem examination (236 cases, a majority of first year deaths), observation on operation for patent ductus arteriosus (19 cases), examination by consulting physician (223) or by school medical officer (10), and Local Authority infant death registers. On the basis of evidence for a disproportionately high percentage of unconfirmed early deaths in infants born at home and attributed to congenital heart disease the authors conclude that the number of such deaths is materially overstated in the infant death registers. An adjustment on this account was made by the authors in the data on which Table 334c was constructed. The yearly incidence of the disease in Birmingham in the ten-year period 1940-49 ranged from 2.1 to 4.5 per 1000 total births, averaging 3.2 per 1000.

Follow-up: Observation was completed in January 1952. The contacts maintained for diagnosis with hospitals and physicians and with records of death appear to have been also the source of follow-up data. Numbers of patients lost sight of or coming to end of follow-up during each attained age period are given and used in life table calculations in the article, but without separate specification of the untraced patients.

Results: Mortality and survival rates and ratios are presented in Tables 334a-b. Death rates, shown from birth to 10 years of age, are high. In the first day, 86 of 1000 newly born with congenital heart disease are estimated to die, 580 per cent of the corresponding rate in the general population. Mortality ratios within the first year after birth, subsequent to the first day, range from 1850 to 3200 per cent, but excess deaths per 1000 which, in the first day represent a rate of 572 per month, and which, in the succeeding six days, reach 663 per month, in the remainder of the first year progressively decline to a monthly rate of 29 per 1000 in the latter half of the year. Both mortality ratios and EDR's progress irregularly in the succeeding nine years of age, but only eight deaths were reported in the first four of those years and nine in the following five years. Of 1000 children born with the disease 707 would survive one week, 592 one month and 324 one year. Compared with the general population, these numbers of survivors represent, respectively, 72.6, 61.2, and 34.4 per cent of all newly born remaining alive at these ages.

The decrements among the survivors of children with this congenital defect are reflected in a diminishing incidence of the disease. Table 334c shows the substantial reduction in the incidence per 1000 of population - from 3.2 in the day following birth to 1.1 at age 10. These figures have been adjusted by the authors of the article to correct for the apparent excess of unconfirmed congenital heart disease diagnoses in infants born at home, referred to above.

In Table 334d are indicated the types of cardiac malformation characteristic of congenital heart disease and their proportions by sex according to the mode of diagnosis. There are almost three males to two females overall, where definite diagnosis is made by postmortem examination or at operation. There are indications of differences by sex in type of defect: males appear to have a significantly higher percentage of transposition of the great vessels and of pulmonary stenosis, while they have an appreciably lower proportion of coarctation of the aorta and patent ductus arteriosus. The uncertainty of identifying the type of congenital heart disease may be noted in Table 334d by the marked disparities in the proportions of several types of defect confirmed, on one hand, by necropsy or operation, and diagnosed, on the other, by consultant physicians, despite the latters' thorough knowledge of the disease.

CONGENITAL HEART DISEASE (ENGLAND)

Table 334a Observed Data and Comparative Experience by Attained Age

Attained Age Period	No. Alive at Start	Withdrawn Alive	No. Exposed to Risk*	Exposure Person-Yrs	Deaths Observed	Deaths Expected†	Period Mort. Ratio	Cumulative Surv. Ratio	Excess Death Rate●
x to x + Δ x	ℓ	w	ℓ - f w	E	d	d'	100 d/d'	100 P/P'	1000($\breve{q}$-$\breve{q}$')
0- 1 day	628	0	628	1.7	54	9.29	580%	92.8%	572/mo
1- 7 days	574	0	574	9.5	130	7.03	1850	72.6	663/mo
7-30 days	444	0	444	25.6	72	2.73	2600	61.2	195/mo
1- 3 mos	372	2	371	61.8	73	2.29	3200	49.5	99/mo
3- 6 mos	297	1	296	74.0	52	3.44	1510	41.3	58/mo
6-12 mos	244	4	241	120.5	42	2.17	1940	34.4	29/mo
1- 5 yrs	198	55	171	684.0	8	1.39	575	33.1	11/yr
5-10 yrs	135	106	74	370.0	9	0.13	6900	29.0	23/yr
0-10 yrs		168		1347.1	440	28.47	1550	29.0	305/yr

Table 334b Derived Mortality and Survival Data for Constructed Life Table

Attained Age Period	Observed Rates				Expected Rates†			
	Per Period		Cumulative		Per Period		Cumulative	
	Mortality	Survival	Survival	Mortality	Mortality	Survival	Survival	Mortality
x to x + Δ x	$q_i = d/(\ell - fw)$	p_i	P	Q	q_i'	p_i'	P'	Q'
0- 1 day	.086	.914	.914	.086	.0148	.9852	.9852	.0148
1- 7 days	.226	.774	.707	.293	.0122	.9878	.9732	.0268
7-30 days	.162	.838	.592	.408	.0061	.9939	.9673	.0327
1- 3 mos	.197	.803	.476	.524	.0062	.9938	.9613	.0387
3- 6 mos	.176	.824	.392	.608	.0116	.9884	.9501	.0499
6-12 mos	.174	.826	.324	.676	.0090	.9910	.9415	.0585
1- 5 yrs	.047	.953	.309	.691	.0081	.9919	.9339	.0661
5-10 yrs	.110	.890	.275	.725	.0016	.9984	.9480	.0520

Table 334c Incidence per 1000 Population for Each Age Period
(Unconfirmed Diagnoses Adjusted)

Age Period	Incidence	Age Period	Incidence	Age Period	Incidence
0- 1 day	3.2 per 1000	1- 3 mos	2.1 per 1000	1- 5 yrs	1.3 per 1000
1- 7 days	3.0 per 1000	3- 6 mos	1.8 per 1000	5-10 yrs	1.2 per 1000
7-30 days	2.5 per 1000	6-12 mos	1.5 per 1000	10 yrs up	1.1 per 1000

Table 334d Types of Congenital Heart Disease by Diagnosis

Congenital Malformation	Autopsy (236) or Operative (19) Diagnosis						Consultant Examination	
	Male		Female		Both Sexes		Both Sexes	
	Number	Per Cent	Number	Per Cent	Number	Per Cent	Number	Per Cent
Transposition of Great Vessels	29	20%	9	8%	38	15%	9	8%
Persistent Common Arterial Trunk	8	6	8	7	16	6	1	1
Pulmonary Stenosis	15	10	6	6	21	8	21	18
Coarctation of Aorta	10	7	17	16	27	11	5	4
Septal Defects	37	25	32	29	69	27	52	44
Patent Ductus Arteriosus	18	12	27	25	45	18	17	15
Other Specified Defects	29	20	10	9	39	15	12	10
Total	146	100%	109	100%	255	100%	117	100%

* Average for the age period. f is a fraction, approximately 0.5, but adjusted to the known survival of those withdrawn alive during the age period

† Basis of expected mortality: estimated United Kingdom population rates 1946-48

● $\breve{q} = 1 - (p_i)^{\Delta t/\Delta x}$ where Δ t is unit of time used and Δ x is age period. $\breve{q}' = 1 - (p_i')^{\Delta t/\Delta x}$

CONGENITAL AND VALVULAR HEART DISEASE

§335—VENTRICULAR SEPTAL DEFECT

Reference: J. D. Keith, V. Rose, G. Collins, and B. S. L. Kidd, "Ventricular Septal Defect — Incidence, Mortality and Morbidity in Various Age Groups," Brit. Heart J. 33(Suppl.): 81-87 (1971).

Subjects Studied: Two principal groups of patients with isolated ventricular septal defect studied at the Hospital for Sick Children, Toronto, Canada: 630 infants diagnosed in the first year of life; 295 adolescents or young adults, born before 1955, but also seen initially in infancy or early childhood. Cases of ventricular septal defect with associated congenital lesions of the heart or great vessels were excluded. Clinical criteria for diagnosis were a blowing systolic murmur over the lower precordium without a thrill, coupled with repeated observations which ruled out the presence of aortic or pulmonic stenosis or patent ductus arteriosus. If there was doubt regarding the clinical diagnosis the patient was subjected to cardiac catheterization. On the basis of the catheterization studies and clinical finding patients were classified into six functional categories according to these criteria: (1) a shunt blood flow (through the septal defect) less than or greater than 50 per cent of the left ventricular output; (2) evidence of increased pulmonary vascular resistance; (3) evidence of reversal of blood flow through the septal defect, from right to left instead of left to right. The functional classification and method of evaluation used are shown for the 630 infants during their first year of life in Table 335a. A similar classification for these 630 infants and the 295 older patients is given in Table 335b to characterize the evaluation at the close of observation.

Follow-up: This was accomplished through re-examinations and personal contact. The average period of follow-up for the 630 infants was 7.5 years (average age 1/2 to 8 years). The more recent follow-up of adolescents and young adults averaged 10 years (average age 13 to 23 years); total follow-up in this group, going back to initial visit in childhood, ranged from 16 to 42 years.

Results: Only 200 of the infants were catheterized during the first year of life, but in the course of follow-up there were 312 patients catheterized (Table 335b) of whom 104 were also subjected to surgery. In the older group 137 patients were catheterized, including 38 heart operations, during the follow-up period. The most benign group was also the largest. Functional Class I consisted of patients with a shunt less than 50 per cent and normal pulmonary vascular resistance. About 50 per cent of the infants were so classified at initial diagnosis, but by the end of follow-up almost 70 per cent were classified as still Class I, and spontaneous closure of the defect had occurred in 16.5 per cent. There were no deaths recorded in 43 catheterized infants (322 exposure-years and 1.29 expected deaths), and none in the larger group of 318 infants never subjected to catheterization, 92 per cent of whom were considered to be in Class I. The latter group generated an exposure estimated at 2385 person-years and 9.54 expected deaths, assuming a start of follow-up at birth in every case. The mortality among infants catheterized during the first year of life was increased in the less benign functional groups: EDR increased from 21 per 1000 in Class II to 34 per 1000 in Class IV. There were 42 deaths in the entire 630 cases followed from infancy, and 27 of these were in the 104 patients with lesions severe enough to result in heart surgery (EDR 36 per 1000), and only 15 deaths in 208 catheterized but unoperated patients (EDR 6 per 1000). The authors report that deaths in this group occurred in the first two years of life or in connection with surgery especially in those with severe congestive heart failure. Pulmonary vascular disease associated with increased pulmonary resistance takes a considerable number of years to develop in the larger septal defects to the point where pulmonary arterial pressure rises and eventually exceeds left ventricular pressure with reversal of flow (Eisenmenger complex, Class VI). There were no deaths in Class IV in the infant group, but some of the ten deaths in the adult group were in Class VI patients who survived to their late teens and twenties. Although the authors do not so state, it may be presumed that all or almost all of the deaths in the adult group were also in the less benign functional Classes II to VI. These results give no evidence of excess mortality in patients with isolated small intraventricular septal defect in functional Class I.

VENTRICULAR SEPTAL DEFECT

Table 335a   Initial Functional Classification in Infants with Isolated Ventricular Septal Defect

Functional Classification	No. Cases Evaluated		Total Cases	
	Clinical	Catheter	No.	Per Cent
I IV Shunt <50% and normal PVR*	271	43	314	49.8%
II IV Shunt >50% and normal PVR	102	64	166	26.4
III IV Shunt >50%, slightly increased PVR	55	46	101	16.0
IV IV Shunt >50%, mod. increased PVR	2	36	38	6.0
V IV Shunt <50%, high PVR, no reversal of flow	0	11	11	1.7
VI IV Shunt <50%, high PVR, with reversal of flow†	0	0	0	0.0
Total	430	200	630	100.0%

Table 335b   Follow-up Functional Classification in Children and Young Adults to 1971

Functional Class	Children Diagnosed in Infancy					Young Adults Diagnosed before 1955				
	Clinical Evaluation	Catheter Evaluation	Catheter and Surgery	Total No.	(%)	Clinical Evaluation	Catheter Evaluation	Catheter and Surgery	Total No	(%)
Cases I	292	143	1	436	(69.2)	155	72	8	235	(79.7)
II	25	42	21	88	(14.0)	1	2	12	15	(5.1)
III	1	11	64	76	(12.1)	0	1	4	5	(1.7)
IV	0	9	15	24	(3.8)	0	1	10	11	(3.7)
V	0	2	2	4	(0.6)	0	0	1	1	(0.3)
VI	0	1	1	2	(0.3)	2	23	3	28	(9.5)
Total Cases	318	208	104	630	(100.0)	158	99	38	295	(100.0)
Spontaneous Closures	82	22	0	104	(16.5)	—	—	—	12	(4.1)
Deaths in Follow-up	0	15	27	42	(6.7)	—	—	—	10	(3.4)

Table 335c   Comparative Mortality in Infants with Average 7.5-Year Follow-up and In Adolescents and Young Adults with Average 10-Year Follow-up

Category	No. of Cases	Est. Exposure● Person-Yrs	No. of Deaths		Mortality Ratio	Excess Death Rate
			Observed	Expected□		
	ℓ	E	d	d'	100 d/d'	1000(d-d')/E
Infants catheterized under 1 yr of age						
Class I	43	322	0	1.29	0%	−4.0
Class II	64	439	11	1.76	625	21
Class III	46	311	9	1.24	725	25
Class IV	36	236	9	0.94	955	34
Class V	11	79	1	0.32	310	8.6
Total	200	1388	30	5.55	540	18
Infants catheterized later	112	795	12	3.18	375	11
Infants catheterized - Total	312	2183	42	8.73	480	15
Infants catheterized, with heart surgery	104	679	27	2.72	995	36
Infants catheterized, no heart surgery	208	1504	15	6.02	250	6.0
Infants not catheterized, (no surgery)	318	2385	0	9.54	0	−4.0
Adolescents and young adults (average 10 yrs follow-up)	295	2900	10	2.32	430	2.6

* IV — Intraventricular. PVR — Pulmonary vascular resistance

† Criteria for Eisenmenger complex

● Estimated from average duration 7.5 years for the infants and 10 years for the older group

□ Basis of expected mortality: Canadian Life Table Rates, 1963-65, Male and Female Combined, age 0 to 7.5 years and age 13 to 23 years

CONGENITAL AND VALVULAR HEART DISEASE

§349—HEART MURMURS—INSURANCE EXPERIENCE

References: (1) New England Life unpublished mortality studies made available by R.B. Singer (1974).
(2) "New York Life Single Medical Impairment Study—1972" unpublished report made available by J.J. Hutchinson and J.C. Sibigtroth (1973).

Subjects Studied: (1) Policyholders of the New England Mutual Life Insurance Company issued insurance 1952-1970 and followed to the 1971 policy anniversary. Codes were used to distinguish cases according to the characteristics of the heart murmur: apical systolic, apical diastolic, aortic systolic, aortic diastolic, pulmonic systolic and all others. Standard issues were analyzed separately from substandard issues, and the latter were divided into cases rated for the specified heart murmur alone, and cases rated for other reasons as well as the murmur.

(2) Policyholders of New York Life Insurance Company issued insurance 1954-1970 and followed to the 1971 policy anniversary. Coding practices were similar to those noted above. Records involving ratable impairment(s) other than the heart murmur under study were excluded.

Follow-up: Insurance policy records formed the basis of entry, of counting policies, exposure and death claims, and of follow-up information.

Results: For many of the male and all of the female murmur categories shown in Table 349 the experience is so limited that results must be interpreted with great caution. In part, the small number of deaths is related to the low average age, well under 40 years in most groups.

In the apical systolic murmurs the New England Life standard male cases classified as "functional" (localized or non-transmitted murmur) showed a mortality very close to the expected, based on the largest exposure in the table and 40 death claims. However, in those apical systolic murmurs classified as "organic" because of their intensity and transmitted characteristics both the New York Life and New England Life cases showed increased mortality ratios of 210 and 345 per cent respectively. Additional New York Life experience on cases rated for apical systolic heart murmurs is given in §351; the category shown here consisted of those cases where there was an associated history of rheumatic fever. Most of the organic apical systolic murmurs would be diagnosed as mitral insufficiency.

The New England Life experience for cases rated for apical diastolic murmurs (mitral stenosis) showed a moderate excess mortality, with a mortality ratio of 255 per cent and EDR of 5.8 extra deaths per 1000 per year, somewhat lower values than observed in the cases rated for organic apical systolic murmur. The experience with cases rated for aortic diastolic murmur (aortic insufficiency) is limited, with a mortality ratio of 415 per cent and 11 extra deaths per 1000 annually.

As with the apical systolic murmur, aortic systolic murmurs were also subdivided into a localized type, with many cases issued standard insurance, and those felt to be "organic" (aortic stenosis). However, both standard and rated groups of the New England Life displayed an increased mortality, with a ratio close to 180 per cent and 3 to 4 extra deaths per 1000 per year, slightly under the corresponding values of the New York Life rated cases. The worst experience in these heart murmur groups was observed in the New England Life cases rated for organic aortic systolic murmur: mortality ratio 540 per cent and EDR of 16 for all rated cases, with a mortality ratio even higher in those rated for the murmur alone (only 6 deaths).

The experience with pulmonic systolic murmur was favorable in all groups, even when a rating was imposed because the murmur was felt to be organic in nature. In contrast to this, the mortality ratio for all New England Life cases rated for other murmurs was 245 per cent, and the standard issues had a slightly elevated mortality ratio of 141 per cent. Additional New York Life experience for this miscellaneous group of murmurs is in §350.

HEART MURMURS - INSURANCE EXPERIENCE

Table 349   Comparative Experience by Heart Murmur (All Ages and Durations Combined)

Murmur Category Source, Insurance Action*	Sex/Age	No. of Policies ℓ	Exposure Policy-Yrs E	No. of Death Claims — Observed d	No. of Death Claims — Expected† d'	Mortality Ratio 100d/d'	Est. 8-Yr Surv. Index 100P/P'	Excess Death Rate 1000(d-d')/E
"Functional" Apical Systolic								
NEL Standard	M 34	1539	11696	40	37.07	108%	99.8%	0.3
NEL Rated Murmur	M 32	184	1486	7	4.12	170	98.5	1.9
NEL Standard	F 35	230	1684	2	2.63	76	100.3	−0.4
NEL Rated Murmur	F 26	45	327	1	0.20	500	98.1	2.4
NYL Standard	M&F 31	—	3649	5	9.21	54	100.9	−1.2
"Organic" Apical Systolic								
NEL Rated Murmur	M 35	374	3100	32	9.30	345	94.3	7.3
NEL Rated Murmur	F 36	86	761	5	1.06	470	95.9	5.2
NYL Rated Murmur & R.F.	M&F 30	—	7447	32	15.23	210	98.2	2.3
Apical Diastolic								
NEL Standard	M&F 32	32	326	2	1.09	183	97.8	2.8
NEL Rated Murmur	M&F 36	262	2101	20	7.87	255	95.5	5.8
NYL Rated Murmur	M&F —	—	945	6	2.42	245	97.0	3.8
Localized Aortic Systolic								
NEL Standard	M 36	202	1264	9	4.95	182	97.5	3.2
NEL All Rated	M 43	185	1167	11	6.43	171	96.9	3.9
NEL Standard & All Rated	F 42	98	655	3	2.71	111	99.6	0.4
NYL Rated Murmur	M&F 45	—	1263	15	7.44	200	95.3	6.0
"Organic" Aortic Systolic								
NEL Rated Murmur	M 33	46	332	6	0.80	750	88.1	16
NEL All Rated	M 37	252	1467	29	5.38	540	87.8	16
NEL All Rated	F 44	52	279	2	1.05	190	97.3	3.4
NYL Standard & Rated Murmur	M&F —	—	779	6	2.83	210	96.8	4.1
Aortic Diastolic								
NEL Standard	M&F 37	39	304	1	1.24	81	100.6	−0.8
NEL All Rated	M&F 37	159	1138	16	3.86	415	91.8	11
NYL Standard & Rated Murmur	M&F —	—	501	1	1.20	83	100.3	−0.4
Pulmonic Systolic								
NEL Standard	M 32	1164	9789	27	28.79	94	100.1	−0.2
NEL All Rated	M 34	285	2179	9	8.86	102	99.9	0.1
NEL Standard & All Rated	F 35	308	2208	5	4.78	105	99.9	0.1
NYL Standard & Rated Murmur	M&F —	—	3285	9	10.82	83	100.4	−0.6
All Other Murmurs								
NEL Standard	M 34	1156	9102	39	27.61	141	99.0	1.3
NEL Rated Murmur	M 30	145	1186	9	3.59	250	96.4	4.6
NEL All Rated	M 36	1091	8515	78	32.08	245	95.8	5.4
NEL Standard	F 36	147	1055	1	2.04	49	100.8	−10
NEL All Rated	F 38	164	1415	11	4.20	260	96.2	4.8
NYL Standard	M&F 30	—	953	4	2.31	173	98.6	1.8

*NEL - New England Life. NYL - New York Life

 Rated - extra premium above standard charged for murmur alone, or murmur and other reasons ("all")

†Basis of expected deaths: Intercompany 1955-60 Basic Select Table, Male or Female

CONGENITAL AND VALVULAR HEART DISEASE

§350–OTHER HEART MURMURS

Reference: "New York Life Single Medical Impairment Study—1972," unpublished report made available by J.J. Hutchinson and J.C. Sibigtroth (1973).

Subjects Studied: Policyholders of New York Life Insurance Company issued insurance in 1954-1970, followed to the 1971 policy anniversary. These were cases in which the residual category "other heart murmurs" has been assigned because the murmur could not be classified more specifically as mitral systolic or diastolic, aortic systolic or diastolic, or pulmonic systolic. Most of the experience reported is for substandard issues; all cases with ratable impairment in addition to the other heart murmur code were excluded.

Follow-up: Insurance policy records formed the basis of entry, of counting policies, exposure and death claims, and of follow-up information.

Results: Comparative experience is given in Tables 350a-b for substandard cases by duration, all ages combined. The mortality ratio showed no trend during the first three intervals, ranging between 169 and 225 per cent, with EDR highest (5.9 extra deaths per 1000) at 5-10 years. There was no excess mortality observed after 10 years, but there were only seven death claims in this interval. The cumulative survival ratio at 10 years was 96.1 per cent.

From Table 350c the very limited standard experience (only 4 death claims) is seen to produce a mortality ratio very close to the overall ratio of 176 per cent for the male substandard experience, all ages combined. The mortality ratio for substandard females was more favorable at 124 per cent, based on 11 claims (excess mortality appeared to be concentrated in older women, age 60 up). In the substandard male policyholders the greatest excess mortality was observed in the age group 50-59, with a mortality ratio of 260 per cent and EDR of 15 per 1000. There was no excess mortality found in the younger men, under age 40, with only 7 death claims resulting from 6079 policy years of exposure. The estimated 8-year survival index ranged from a normal level for men under 40 to a minimum of 88.4 per cent for the men age 50-59.

Comparative mortality by major causes of death is given in Table 350d for male and female substandard cases combined. There is some increase in cancer mortality with an EDR of 0.5 per 1000, but the major cause of death is found in diseases of the heart and circulation, the mortality being 235 per cent and EDR 1.8 per 1000.

OTHER HEART MURMURS

Table 350a Observed Data and Comparative Experience by Duration — Insured Men Rated for Murmur Alone, All Ages Combined

Interval		Exposure Policy-Yrs	Deaths in Interval		Mortality Ratio		Survival Ratio		Excess Death Rate
No.	Start-End		Observed	Expected*	Interval	Cumulative	Interval	Cumulative	
i	t to t + Δ t	E	d	d'	100 d/d'	100 Σd/Σd'	100 p_i/p_i'	100 P/P'	1000(d-d')/E
1	0- 2 yrs	2909	11	5.25	210%	210%	99.6%	99.6%	2.0
2	2- 5	2829	15	8.90	169	184	99.4	99.0	2.2
3	5-10	2628	28	12.42	225	205	97.1	96.1	5.9
4	10-17	1022	7	8.04	87	176	100.7	96.7	−1.0

Table 350b Derived Mortality and Survival Data

Interval		Observed Rates				Expected Rates*			
		Average Annual		Cumulative		Average Annual		Cumulative	
No.	Start-End	Mortality	Survival	Survival	Mortality	Mortality	Survival	Survival	Mortality
i	t to t + Δ t	$\bar{q}$ = d/E	$\bar{p}$	P	Q	$\bar{q}'$ = d'/E	$\bar{p}'$	P'	Q'
1	0- 2 yrs	.0038	.9962	.9925	.0075	.0018	.9982	.9964	.0036
2	2- 5	.0053	.9947	.9767	.0233	.0031	.9969	.9870	.0130
3	5-10	.0107	.9893	.9258	.0742	.0047	.9953	.9639	.0361
4	10-17	.0068	.9932	.8823	.1177	.0079	.9921	.9120	.0880

Table 350c Comparative Experience by Sex, Age and Insurance Action — All Durations Combined

Category†	Exposure Policy-Yrs	No. of Deaths		Mortality Ratio	Ave. Ann. Mort. Rate	Est. 8-Yr Surv. Rate	Est. 8-Yr Surv. Index	Excess Death Rate
		Observed	Expected*					
	E	d	d'	100 d/d'	$\bar{q}$ = d/E	P = $(1-\bar{q})^8$	100 P/P'	1000(d-d')/E
Standard Male and Female—All Ages	953	4	2.31	173%	.0042	.9666	98.6%	1.8
Substandard Male								
Age 0-39 yrs	6079	7	7.91	88	.0012	.9908	100.1	−0.1
40-49	1997	21	9.74	215	.0105	.9189	95.6	5.6
50-59	776	19	7.24	260	.0245	.8201	88.4	15
60-64	536	14	9.72	144	.0261	.8092	93.7	8.0
All Male	9388	61	34.61	176	.0065	.9492	.97.8	2.8
Substandard Female								
Age 0-59 yrs	2796	5	5.86	85	.0018	.9858	100.2	−0.3
60-64	260	6	3.04	197	.0231	.8296	91.1	11
All Female	3056	11	8.90	124	.0036	.9716	99.4	0.7

Table 350d Major Causes of Death — Substandard Cases†, Male and Female Combined

Cause of Death	Exposure Policy-Yrs	No. of Deaths		Mortality Ratio	Excess Death Rate
		Observed	Expected●		
	E	d_c	d_c'	100d_c/d_c'	1000(d_c-d_c')/E
Dis. Heart and Circulation	12444	40	17.10	235%	1.8
Cancer - All Types	12444	17	10.37	164	0.5
Accidents, Homicide, Suicide	12444	5	7.82	64	−0.2
All Other Causes	12444	10	8.20	122	0.1
Total - All Causes	12444	72	43.49	166	2.3

* Basis of expected mortality: 1955-60 Intercompany Select Basic Tables, Male or Female
† Substandard Issues — rated for murmur alone
● Distribution of total expected deaths by Intercompany Medically Examined Standard Issues 1965-70

CONGENITAL AND VALVULAR HEART DISEASE

§351—APICAL SYSTOLIC MURMUR

Reference: "New York Life Single Medical Impairment Study—1972," unpublished report made available by J.J. Hutchinson and J.C. Sibigtroth (1973).

Subjects Studied: Policyholders of New York Life Insurance Company issued insurance in 1954-1970, followed to the 1971 policy anniversary. Different codes were used to distinguish cases in which the murmur was regarded as "organic" (due to mitral insufficiency), from those regarded as "non-organic." Only the substandard cases have been analyzed here. Records involving more than one ratable impairment were excluded.

Follow-up: Insurance policy records formed the basis of entry, of counting policies, exposure and death claims, and of follow-up information.

Results: The experience for cases of apical systolic murmur attributed to mitral insufficiency is given in the upper parts of Tables 351a-c. The lower part of each table contains the corresponding experience for apical systolic murmurs described as localized, of low intensity, and non-organic in nature, although a low rating (average 163 per cent) was applied because of the murmur. The overall male mortality was actually higher for the non-organic than for the organic murmurs, with mortality ratios of 220 and 186 per cent respectively (EDR's 9.0 and 4.0 extra deaths per 1000 per year).

There was a tendency for the mortality ratios to be somewhat higher in the first five years of policy duration than in subsequent years, but there was no consistent trend in EDR (Table 351a). In the group with murmurs classified as mitral insufficiency, there was a slight downward trend of mortality ratio with age, from 225 per cent for men age under 40 to 164 per cent for the oldest group (Table 351c). The corresponding change in EDR from the youngest to the oldest age group was an increase from 1.8 to 12 extra deaths per 1000 per year. In the non-organic murmur experience the variation of mortality ratio with age is irregular. It is noteworthy that the higher overall mortality in this as compared with the organic murmur group appears in all age groups except in men age 50-59. There were 16 death claims, with a mortality ratio of 240 per cent and an EDR of 34 in the oldest age group, 60-64.

The experience for female insureds was much smaller than for the men, and no breakdown by age or duration could be made. In the organic murmur group the mortality ratio of 194 per cent was similar to the 186 per cent for males. However, mortality in the women with non-organic murmur was only slightly above expected (mortality ratio 112 per cent), in sharp contrast to the male experience.

For male and female insureds combined there were 2.9 extra deaths per 1000 per year due to disease of the heart and circulatory system, out of an EDR of 3.6 for all causes, in those with an organic murmur. Among insureds with a non-organic murmur the corresponding rates were 5.0 out of a total 6.5 extra deaths per 100 per year. The preponderance of excess mortality was therefore due to cardiovascular causes.

APICAL SYSTOLIC MURMUR

Table 351a Observed Data and Comparative Experience by Duration — Male Insureds with Apical Systolic Heart Murmur, Substandard Issues

Interval		Exposure	No. of Death Claims		Mortality Ratio		Survival Ratio		Excess
No.	Start-End	Policy-Yrs	Observed	Expected*	Interval	Cumulative	Interval	Cumulative	Death Rate
i	t to t + Δt	E	d	d'	100 d/d'	100$\sum$d/$\sum$d'	100 p_i/p_i'	100 P/P'	1000(d-d')/E
Murmur Classified as Organic or Mitral Insufficiency									
1	0- 2 yrs	2752	12	5.47	220%	220%	99.5%	99.5%	2.4
2	2- 5	2777	30	9.78	305	275	97.8	97.4	7.3
3	5-10	2765	22	15.37	143	210	98.8	96.2	2.4
4	10-17	1293	18	13.37	135	186	97.5	93.8	3.6
Murmur Classified as Non-Organic, Localized or Inconstant									
1	0- 2 yrs	1163	15	3.41	440%	440%	98.0%	98.0%	10
2	2- 5	1100	11	5.92	186	280	98.6	96.7	4.6
3	5-10	978	15	9.40	160	220	97.1	93.9	5.7
4	10-17	492	21	9.59	220	220	84.6	79.4	23

Table 351b Derived Mortality and Survival Data

Interval		Observed Rates				Expected Rates*			
		Ave. Annual		Cumulative		Ave. Annual		Cumulative	
No.	Start-End	Mortality	Survival	Survival	Mortality	Mortality	Survival	Survival	Mortality
i	t to t + Δt	$\bar{q}$ = d/E	$\bar{p}$	P	Q	$\bar{q}'$	$\bar{p}'$	P'	Q'
Murmur Classified as Organic or Mitral Insufficiency									
1	0- 2 yrs	.0044	.9956	.9913	.0087	.0020	.9980	.9960	.0040
2	2- 5	.0108	.9892	.9595	.0405	.0035	.9965	.9855	.0145
3	5-10	.0080	.9920	.9219	.0781	.0056	.9944	.9585	.0415
4	10-17	.0139	.9861	.8358	.1642	.0103	.9897	.8912	.1088
Murmur Classified as Non-Organic, Localized or Inconstant									
1	0- 2 yrs	.0129	.9871	.9744	.0256	.0029	.9971	.9941	.0059
2	2- 5	.0100	.9900	.9454	.0546	.0054	.9946	.9782	.0218
3	5-10	.0153	.9847	.8751	.1249	.0096	.9904	.9321	.0679
4	10-17	.0427	.9573	.6448	.3552	.0195	.9805	.8121	.1879

Table 351c Comparative Experience by Sex and Age Group — All Durations Combined

Sex/Age	Exposure	No. of Death Claims		Mortality	Ave. Ann.	Est. 8-Yr	Est. 8-Yr	Excess
	Policy-Yrs	Observed	Expected*	Ratio	Mort. Rate	Surv. Rate	Surv. Index	Death Rate
	E	d	d'	100 d/d'	$\bar{q}$ = d/E	P = (1-$\bar{q}$)[8]	100 P/P'	1000(d-d')/E
Male Murmur Classified as Organic or Mitral Insufficiency								
Under 40	5269	17	7.54	225%	.0032	.9747	98.6%	1.8
40-49	2479	24	13.71	175	.0097	.9251	96.7	4.2
50-59	1432	28	14.80	189	.0196	.8539	92.8	9.2
60-64	407	13	7.94	164	.0319	.7713	90.3	12
All Male	9587	82	43.99	186	.0086	.9336	96.9	4.0
All Female	2228	9	4.65	194	.0040	.9681	98.4	2.0
Male Murmur Classified as Non-Organic, Localized or Inconstant								
Under 40	614	2	0.76	265%	.0033	.9742	98.4%	2.0
40-49	1803	29	9.93	290	.0161	.8783	91.8	11
50-59	1039	15	10.94	137	.0144	.8902	96.9	3.9
60-64	277	16	6.69	240	.0578	.6213	75.5	34
All Male	3733	62	28.32	220	.0166	.8746	93.0	9.0
All Female	1585	7	6.24	112	.0044	.9652	99.6	0.5

* Basis of expected death: 1955-60 Select Basic Tables

CONGENITAL AND VALVULAR HEART DISEASE

§352–SYSTOLIC HEART MURMURS – INSURED LIVES

References: (1) B. S. Pauley, "Mortality Experience: Systolic Heart Murmurs and Peptic Ulcer," Trans. Soc. Actuaries, 20 (Part 1):39-43 (1968).
(2) Supplementary data supplied by the author (1974).

Subjects Studied: Males issued policies by the Prudential Insurance Company of America during 1950-1962 who were classified on examination as having a systolic heart murmur at the apex. Two categories are reported on: functional murmurs accepted at standard rates; and organic murmurs, some with related impairments, mostly hypertension and cardiac arrhythmia, accepted subject to various extra premium payments (substandard).

Follow-up: Policy records were used for follow-up to the 1966 policy anniversary or to earlier death or termination, and policy records constituted the basis for counting death claims and numbers exposed to risk.

Results: Both classes of murmur exhibit higher rates of mortality than are experienced among select unimpaired lives accepted for insurance as shown in Tables 352a-c. Overall death rates, all ages combined, presented in Table 352a, indicate a mortality ratio of 124 per cent for functional murmur cases and 215 per cent for the organic murmurs. The ratio for the former diminishes from 140 per cent in the first five policy years to 110 per cent in the eleven succeeding years of observation (Table 352b). Table 352a reveals that the extra mortality developed in the functional experience arises among applicants age 40 years and older — younger lives appear to be subject to standard mortality. Organic murmur cases on the other hand were found to have a lower mortality ratio in older policyholders than in those under 50. Excess death rate averaged only 0.5 per 1000 for all functional murmurs, and 3.3 per 1000 for the organic murmurs. EDR showed a tendency to increase with age.

Tables 352b-c contain the experience by duration for all ages combined. Comparative mortality in the category of organic murmurs tends to increase slightly with duration. The mortality ratio was 200 per cent in the first five policy years, with an EDR of 1.9 per 1000; in the remainder of the observation period the mortality ratio was 225 per cent, with an EDR of 5.6 per 1000. In the functional murmurs the mortality ratio decreased from 140 to 110 per cent after the first five policy years, and EDR from 0.6 to 0.3 per 1000.

An anomalous feature of the experience on organic murmurs was the relatively favorable mortality in cases accompanied by other impairments. The portion of the issues in which there was no other detected impairment, even minor, developed an overall mortality ratio of 280 per cent based on 73 deaths against the aggregate 215 per cent noted above. The author suggests that when other circulatory impairments are present, some murmurs are classified as organic which, in the absence of any other impairment, would be classified as functional.

APICAL SYSTOLIC MURMURS

Table 352a Comparative Experience by Age (All Durations Combined)

Age at Issue (years)	Exposure Policy-Yrs E	No. of Death Claims Observed d	No. of Death Claims Expected* d'	Mortality Ratio 100 d/d'	Ave. Ann. Mort. Rate $\bar{q} = d/E$	Est. 5-Yr Surv. Rate $P = (1-\bar{q})^5$	Est. 5-Yr Surv. Index 100 P/P'	Excess Death Rate 1000(d-d')/E
Murmur Classified as Functional								
0-39	28561	32	34.02	94%	.0011	.9945	100.0%	−0.1
40-64	8462	57	37.49	152	.0067	.9669	98.8	2.3
0-64	37023	89	71.51	124	.0024	9881	99.8	0.5
Murmur Classified as Organic								
15-39	16429	51	20.96	245%	.0031	.9846	99.1%	1.8
40-49	5435	59	23.33	255	.0109	.9467	96.7	6.6
50-64	2217	38	24.80	153	.0171	.9174	97.1	6.0
15-64	24081	148	69.09	215	.0061	.9699	98.4	3.3
15-64		73	25.89	280% (No other impairment)				
15-64		75	43.20	174% (With other CV impairment)				

Table 352b Observed Data and Comparative Experience by Duration (All Ages Combined)

Interval No.	Start-End t to t + Δt	Exposure Policy-Yrs E	Observed d	Expected* d'	Mortality Ratio Interval 100 d/d'	Mortality Ratio Cumulative 100 Σd/Σd'	Survival Ratio Interval 100 p_i/p_i'	Survival Ratio Cumulative 100 P/P'	Excess Death Rate 1000(d-d')/E
Murmur Classified as Functional									
1	0- 5 yrs	24306	49	35.10	140%	140%	99.7%	99.7%	0.6
2	5-16	12717	40	36.41	110	124	99.8	99.5	0.3
Murmur Classified as Organic									
1	0- 5 yrs	15290	59	29.37	200	200	99.0	99.0	1.9
2	5-16	8791	89	39.72	225	215	94.0	93.1	5.6

Table 352c Derived Mortality and Survival Data

Interval No.	Start-End t to t + Δt	Observed Rates Average Annual Mortality $\bar{q} = d/E$	Observed Rates Average Annual Survival $\bar{p}$	Observed Rates Interval Survival p_i	Observed Rates Cumulative Survival P	Expected Rates* Average Annual Mortality $\bar{q}'$	Expected Rates* Average Annual Survival $\bar{p}'$	Expected Rates* Interval Survival p_i'	Expected Rates* Cumulative Survival P'
Murmur Classified as Functional									
1	0- 5 yrs	.0020	.9980	.9900	.9900	.0014	.9986	.9930	.9930
2	5-16	.0031	.9969	.9664	.9568	.0029	.9971	.9686	.9618
Murmur Classified as Organic									
1	0- 5 yrs	.0039	.9961	.9807	.9807	.0019	.9981	.9905	.9905
2	5-16	.0101	.9899	.8943	.8771	.0045	.9955	.9516	.9426

* Basis of expected mortality: Intercompany 1955-60 Select Male

CONGENITAL AND VALVULAR HEART DISEASE

§353–MITRAL STENOSIS AND CLOSED VALVULOPLASTY

References: (1) L. B. Ellis, J. B. Singh, D. D. Morales, and D. E. Harken, "Fifteen- to Twenty-Year Study of One Thousand Patients Undergoing Closed Mitral Valvuloplasty," Circulation, 48:357-364 (1973).
(2) L. B. Ellis, additional data made available to the Editors (1974).

Subjects Studied: 1091 patients with mitral stenosis and operation involving closed mitral valvuloplasty in Boston, Massachusetts hospitals, from January 1, 1950 to December 31, 1956 (2). This comprises the earlier and major fraction of a larger series of 1878 such patients operated on between late 1949 and 1968 (1). The only patients excluded were those with very substantial disease of other valves, who were subjected to exploratory cardiotomy. Females outnumbered males by more than three to one, mean age being 39.7 and 41.1 years respectively. Patients were grouped according to the New York Heart Association Classification: 794 in Group III, with progressive symptoms and moderate or greater disability, to which were added 21 patients functionally Group II, but with frequent embolization or other reasons for operation; and 276 patients with chronic congestive heart failure and essentially total disability in Group IV. A detailed distribution by age, sex, and functional classification is given in Table 353a. Various associated pre-operative abnormalities, mostly cardiovascular in nature, are given in Table 353b.

Follow-up: Patients were contacted annually by questionnaires with additional information obtained from physicians, hospital records and sometimes re-examination. Date and cause of death were established, when this occurred, with available autopsy records. In all traced patients the annual information was used to evaluate functional capacity, therapy and cardiovascular complications, the subjective report of the patient being checked against medical records whenever possible. Patients were withdrawn from the valvuloplasty life table calculations at the time of any re-operation on the heart; only 5 per cent of other survivors were not followed at least 15 years (1), although the latest follow-up in 1970 made possible an observation period up to 20 years. Life table calculations reported in this abstract have been cut off at a maximum duration of 15 years.

Results: Early mortality (Table 353c) includes not only operative and immediate post-operative mortality but also all deaths while the patient was continuously hospitalized, even if three months or more after the valvuloplasty. The early mortality rate achieved with closed mitral valvuloplasty was quite low, less than 0.03 for both sexes in functional Class III, but about ten times greater in the severely impaired Class IV patients.

Long-term comparative experience (up to 15 years after operation) is presented in Table 353d for the early survivors, classified by functional status, sex and age, all durations combined. Mortality ratios were in the range of 210 to 860 per cent for Class III patients and considerably higher - 470 to 3000 per cent - for the Class IV patients. Mortality ratios decreased with age at operation in all categories. However, there was no clear age trend in the excess death rate, which averaged 30 and 16 extra deaths per 1000 per year in Class III male and female patients, respectively. In Class IV patients EDR averaged 82 for the men and 45 for the women. Excess mortality was thus about twice as great for males as it was for female patients in the same age and functional group, although there was relatively little sex difference in mortality ratio. Survival ratios at 15 years were more favorable for the female than for the male patients, ranging from 46.7 to 83.9 per cent in the former against 17.3 to 65.4 per cent in men, excluding the smallest group, of male Class IV patients under age 40, in which there were no survivors.

Comparative experience is given in Table 353e for all patients classified by number of associated risk factors. These include the hazard of a Class IV functional classification as well as the risk factors enumerated in Table 353b. By this means two large groups of patients have been defined as having a relatively favorable experience regardless of age or sex: those with only a single associated risk factor, or none at all (the latter being a selected group of the best Class III patients). These two groups, totaling 463 early survivors, exhibited experience that was quite similar over 15 years, a mortality ratio under 400 per cent, a survival ratio in excess of 80 per cent, and about 10 extra deaths per 1000 per year. Significantly higher excess mortality and poorer survival were found in the groups with two and with three or more associated risk factors. The experience for the last group was the worst; it was similar to the experience for the female Class IV patients, but not as bad as in the male Class IV patients.

MITRAL STENOSIS — VALVULOPLASTY

Observed data and comparative experience by duration are shown in Tables 353f-g by functional class and sex, all ages combined. There appears to be a tendency for EDR to increase with duration in the male patients, from 13 to 26 extra deaths per 1000 per year in Class III and from 47 to 127 in Class IV, although numbers of deaths are small in the latter group. There is no clear trend in EDR by duration in the female patients. Mortality ratios, on the other hand, show a downward trend with time elapsed after operation in the female patients and only irregular variations in the male patients. The cumulative survival ratio at 15 years ranges from 17.9 per cent in the male Class IV patients to 77.7 per cent in the best group, the female Class III patients.

Table 353a   Age Distribution by Functional Class and Sex

Functional Class* and Sex	Under 30	30-34	35-39	40-44	45-49	50-54	55 up	All Ages	Average Age
III Male	22	23	34	39	38	14	3	173	39.6
III Female	111	122	134	131	94	37	13	642	37.8
IV Male	1	9	7	21	12	12	9	71	44.6
IV Female	5	12	28	49	39	37	35	205	45.7

Table 353b   Distribution of Patients by Associated Risk Factors

Risk Factor†	1 or 2	3 or More	All Addit.	Risk Factor	1 or 2	3 or More	All Addit.
Class IV Funct. Status	57	219	276	Auricular Fibrillation	251	338	589
Borderline Hypertension	40	103	143	Coronary Heart Dis.	23	65	88
Definite Hypertension	12	51	63	Other CV Disease	46	76	122
Mitral Insufficiency	39	133	172	Non CV Disease	157	195	352
Mitral Valve Calcification	81	173	254	One or More (All Male)	111	113	224
Other Valvular Disease	26	67	93	One or More (All Female)	390	273	663

* N.Y. Heart Association Functional Class (with 21 Class II patients included in Class III)
† Minor degrees of mitral insufficiency or calcification were not classified as a significant associated risk factor

CONGENITAL AND VALVULAR HEART DISEASE

Table 353c   Early (In-Hospital) Mortality by Functional Status, Sex and Age

Category*	Males				Females			
	No. Patients Operated	In-Hospital Deaths	Mortality Rate	No. Early Survivors	No. Patients Operated	In-Hospital Deaths	Mortality Rate	No. Early Survivors
	ℓ_0	d_0	$q_0 = d_0/\ell_0$	$\ell = \ell_0 - d_0$	ℓ_0	d_0	$q_0 = d_0/\ell_0$	$\ell = \ell_0 - d_0$
III (Better)								
Under 40	79	3	.038	76	367	11	.030	356
40-49	77	2	.626	75	225	6	.027	219
50 up	17	0	.000	17	50	1	.020	49
All	173	5	.029	168	642	18	.028	624
IV (Worse)								
Under 40	17	5	.294	12	45	11	.244	34
40-49	33	8	.242	25	88	16	.182	72
50 up	21	8	.381	13	72	18	.250	54
All	71	21	.296	50	205	45	.220	160

Table 353d   Comparative 15-Year Experience by Functional Status, Sex and Age

Category*	No. Early Survivors	Exposure Person-Yrs	No. of Deaths		Mortality Ratio	15-Yr Survival Rate		15-Year Surv. Ratio	Excess Death Rate
			Observed	Expected†		Observed	Expected†		
	ℓ	E	d	d'	100 d/d'	P	P'	100 P/P'	1000(d-d')/E
Male	Better Functional Status (Class III)								
Under 40	76	803.5	24	2.79	860%	.617	.9430	65.4%	26
40-49	75	675.0	31	6.01	515	.480	.8504	56.4	37
50 up	17	168.0	7	3.37	210	.395	.7095	55.7	22
All Ages	168	1646.5	62	12.17	510	.537	.8811	60.9	30
Female									
Under 40	356	3827.5	51	7.36	695	.812	.9682	83.9	11
40-49	219	2298.5	60	11.10	540	.659	.9222	71.5	21
50 up	49	523.0	19	5.46	350	.519	.8385	61.9	26
All Ages	624	6649.0	130	23.92	545	.732	.9421	77.7	16
Male	Worse Functional Status (Class IV)								
Under 40	12	65.0	6	0.20	3000%	.000	.9469	0.0%	89
40-49	25	197.5	17	1.86	915	.200	.8363	23.9	77
50 up	13	93.0	10	1.69	590	.124	.7168	17.3	89
All Ages	50	355.5	33	3.75	880	.149	.8279	18.0	82
Female									
Under 40	34	261.5	11	0.54	2000	.568	.9606	59.1	40
40-49	72	620.5	31	2.79	1110	.432	.9251	46.7	45
50 up	54	469.0	28	5.95	470	.377	.8028	47.0	47
All Ages	160	1351.0	70	9.28	755	.426	.8832	48.2	45

Table 353e   Comparative 15-Year Experience by Number of Associated CV Risk Factors
(Both Sexes and All Ages Combined, Early Deaths Excluded)

Other CV Risk Factors	No. Early Survivors	Exposure Person-Yrs	No. of Deaths		Mortality Ratio	15-Yr Survival Rate		15-Year Surv. Ratio	Excess Death Rate
			Observed	Expected†		Observed	Expected†		
	ℓ	E	d	d'	100 d/d'	P	P'	100 P/P'	1000(d-d')/E
Best Cases	201	2297.0	25	6.60	380%	.823	.954	86.3%	8.0
1 Additional	262	2862.5	47	11.88	395	.776	.933	83.2	12
2 Additional	212	1996.0	72	10.72	670	.549	.911	60.3	31
3 or More Addit.	327	2846.5	151	21.00	720	.414	.878	47.2	46
All Cases	1002	10002.0	295	50.20	590	.623	.919	67.8	24

* N.Y. Heart Association Functional Class (with 21 Class II patients included in Class III)
† Basis of expected mortality: U.S. Life Tables 1964

MITRAL STENOSIS — VALVULOPLASTY

Table 353f   Observed Data and Comparative Experience by Duration, Functional Status* and Sex
(All Ages Combined, Early Deaths Excluded)

No.	Start-End	No. Alive at Start of Interval	Exposure Person-Yrs	Observed	Expected†	Interval	Cumulative	Interval	Cumulative	Excess Death Rate
i	t to t + Δt	ℓ	E	d	d'	100 d/d'	100 Σd/Σd'	100 p_i/p_i'	100 P/P'	1000(d-d')/E
	Males	Better Functional Status (Class III)								
1	Under 2 yrs	168	331.5	6	1.54	390%	390%	97.3%	97.3%	13
2	2- 5	161	450.5	13	2.59	500	460	93.2	90.7	23
3	5-10	135	545.5	31	4.31	720	595	77.8	70.6	49
4	10-15	85	319.0	12	3.73	320	510	86.4	60.9	26
	Females									
1	Under 2 yrs	624	1224.5	22	2.64	835	835	96.9	96.9	16
2	2- 5	591	1685.5	31	4.51	685	740	95.3	92.3	16
3	5-10	515	2274.5	38	8.67	440	575	93.7	86.4	13
4	10-15	382	1464.5	39	8.10	480	545	89.8	77.7	21
	Males	Worse Functional Status (Class IV)								
1	Under 2 yrs	50	91.5	5	0.70	715%	715%	91.2%	91.2%	47
2	2- 5	42	115.5	11	1.07	1030	905	75.4	68.7	86
3	5-10	28	106.5	11	1.29	855	880	58.8	40.4	91
4	10-15	12	42.0	6	0.69	870	870	44.4	17.9	127
	Females									
1	Under 2 yrs	160	304.5	17	1.28	1330	1330	90.0	90.0	52
2	2- 5	138	376.0	15	1.95	770	990	89.9	80.9	35
3	5-10	107	435.5	21	3.25	645	820	81.4	65.9	41
4	10-15	65	235.0	17	2.80	605	755	73.2	48.2	60

Table 353g   Derived Data by Duration, Functional Status and Sex

No.	Start-End	Cumulative Survival	Interval Survival	Geom. Mean Ann. Surv.	Geom. Mean Ann. Mort.	Cumulative Survival	Interval Survival	Geom. Mean Ann. Surv.	Geom. Mean Ann. Mort.
i	t to t + Δt	P	p_i	$\breve{p}$	$\breve{q}$	P'	p_i'	$\breve{p}'$	$\breve{q}'$
	Males	Better Functional Status (Class III)							
1	Under 2 yrs	.964	.964	.982	.018	.9907	.9907	.9953	.0047
2	2- 5	.883	.916	.972	.028	.9737	.9828	.9942	.0058
3	5-10	.660	.748	.944	.056	.9351	.9604	.9919	.0081
4	10-15	.537	.814	.959	.041	.8811	.9423	.9882	.0118
	Females								
1	Under 2 yrs	.964	.964	.982	.018	.9957	.9957	.9978	.0022
2	2- 5	.912	.945	.981	.019	.9877	.9920	.9973	.0027
3	5-10	.838	.919	.983	.017	.9689	.9809	.9961	.0039
4	10-15	.732	.874	.973	.027	.9421	.9723	.9944	.0056
	Males	Worse Functional Status (Class IV)							
1	Under 2 yrs	.898	.898	.948	.052	.9846	.9846	.9923	.0077
2	2- 5	.658	.733	.902	.098	.9574	.9724	.9907	.0093
3	5-10	.364	.553	.888	.112	.9003	.9404	.9878	.0122
4	10-15	.149	.408	.836	.164	.8279	.9195	.9834	.0166
	Females								
1	Under 2 yrs	.892	.892	.944	.056	.9916	.9916	.9958	.0042
2	2- 5	.790	.885	.960	.040	.9762	.9845	.9948	.0052
3	5-10	.619	.784	.952	.048	.9395	.9624	.9924	.0076
4	10-15	.426	.688	.928	.072	.8832	.9400	.9877	.0123

* N.Y. Heart Association Functional Class (with 21 Class II patients included in Class III)

† Basis of expected mortality: U.S. Life Tables 1964

CONGENITAL AND VALVULAR HEART DISEASE

§354–MITRAL VALVE REPLACEMENT

Reference: A. Starr, "Mitral Valve Replacement with Ball Valve Prostheses," Brit. Heart J., 33, Suppl.:47-55 (1971).

Subjects Studied: A series of 544 patients categorized in cardiac function Classes III or IV (New York Heart Association), on whom replacement of the mitral valve was performed during the period from August 1960 to June 1970 at the University of Oregon Medical School. Ages of the subjects ranged from 13 to 74 years with a mean age of 49 years. Most of the patients requiring replacement of the mitral valve alone, and all multiple valve cases, had chronic rheumatic valvulitis. While some patients with coronary artery disease were accepted for the procedure, those with advanced disease were not. The mitral valve alone was replaced in 312 subjects, the mitral and other valves, in 232.

Four prosthetic designs were employed in the series: Model 6000, from August 1960 until February 1966; Model 6120 from April 1965 until April 1969; Model 6300 from September 1967 until December 1968; and Model 6310 from December 1968 until June 1970. The successive designs were adopted to improve mechanical effectiveness, reduce the incidence of thromboembolic complications and extend the durability of the material.

Follow-up: The complete count of all patients, surviving and dead, at the end of the observation period, June 1970, indicates no losses to follow-up. In cases of death, necropsy data were obtained and the condition of the prosthetic device examined. The maximum follow-up results cited cover periods ranging from 60 months for the earlier models to 18 months for the later ones.

Results: Except for operations performed on the mitral valve alone in 1969-1970 (no deaths), operative mortality for all operations cited in Tables 354a-b was consistently 12 to 13 per cent. Experience beyond the month following operation, derived from readings of graphs in the reference (and hence approximated) is shown in these tables for Models 6000 (for 5 years) and 6120 (for 4 years). Table 354a pertains to patients operated on for replacement of the mitral valve, Table 354b to cases in which other valves together with the mitral valve were replaced. The number of deaths in all categories shown is small and caution is called for in interpreting results. However, in every classification, mortality rates and ratios are highest in the first interval (from the end of the first post-operative month to the first anniversary of the operation). The replacement of only the mitral valve by Model 6000 developed first interval mortality rate of .101 and a mortality ratio of 1710 per cent. EDR amounted to 95 per 1000. Over the four years following the first interval, annual mortality averaged .033, the mortality ratio 400 per cent, and the EDR, 25 per 1000 per year. The mortality experience where Model 6120 was used was, for the first interval, in every respect, about 40 per cent of that for Model 6000. For the three succeeding years, overall mortality (based on two deaths), was only slightly higher than that of the general population.

As presented in Table 354b, where other valves in addition to the mitral were replaced mortality tended to be higher and survival lower. Implantation of Model 6000 developed somewhat less favorable experience than for 6120. The mortality rate over the first interval was 1170 per cent for the former, 695 per cent for the latter. The average mortality ratio over the four subsequent years came to 795 per cent for Model 6000, the EDR, 57 per 1000 per year, and the cumulative survival ratio 78.9 per cent; for 6120, these functions, over the three intervals following the post–operative month, respectively, 450 per cent, 27 per 1000 per year, and 91.9 per cent.

Causes of death following the month subsequent to implantation for the entire series (all models) are given in Table 354c. Of special note is the high incidence of fatal thromboembolic complications, especially in the mitral and other valve group. The substantial diminution in thromboembolic complications brought about by the changes in design is presented in Table 354d.

MITRAL VALVE REPLACEMENT

Table 354a   Comparative Experience (Approximated) — Replacement of Mitral Valve Alone

No.	Start-End	No. Alive at Start of Interval	No. of Deaths	Survival Rate Cumulative	Survival Rate Interval	Interval Mort. Rate Observed	Interval Mort. Rate Expected*	Mortality Ratio	Survival Ratio	Excess Death Rate
i	t to t + Δt	ℓ	d	P	p_i	q_i	q_i'	100 q_i/q_i'	100 P/P'	1000(q_i-q_i')
	Starr Valve Model 6000									
1	1 mo-1 yr	89	9	.899	.899	.101	.0059	1710%	90.4%	95
2	1-2 yrs	80	3	.865	.962	.038	.0071	535	87.1	31
3	2-3	77	2	.843	.974	.026	.0078	335	84.9	18
4	3-4	75	2	.820	.973	.027	.0086	315	82.7	18
5	4-5	73	3	.787	.959	.041	.0093	440	79.4	32
	1-5 yrs	305†	10	.875	.967	.033●	.0082●	400	90.4	25
	Starr Valve Model 6120									
1	1 mo-1 yr	71	3	.958	.958	.042	.0059	710%	96.3%	36
2	1-2 yrs	68	1	.944	.985	.015	.0071	210	95.6	7.9
3	2-3	67	1	.930	.985	.015	.0078	192	94.9	7.2
4	3-4	66	1	.915	.985	.015	.0086	174	94.3	6.4
	1-4 yrs	201†	3	.956	.985	.015●	.0078●	192	97.9	7.2

Table 354b   Comparative Experience (Approximated) — Replacement of Mitral and Other Valves

No.	Start-End	No. Alive at Start of Interval	No. of Deaths	Survival Rate Cumulative	Survival Rate Interval	Interval Mort. Rate Observed	Interval Mort. Rate Expected*	Mortality Ratio	Survival Ratio	Excess Death Rate
i	t to t + Δt	ℓ	d	P	p_i	q_i	q_i'	100 q_i/q_i'	100 P/P'	1000(q_i-q_i')
	Starr Valve Model 6000									
1	1 mo-1 yr	204	14	.931	.931	.069	.0059	1170%	93.7%	63
2	1-2 yrs	190	14	.863	.926	.074	.0071	1040	87.4	67
3	2-3	176	10	.814	.943	.057	.0078	730	83.1	49
4	3-4	166	8	.775	.952	.048	.0086	560	79.8	39
5	4-5	158	13	.711	.918	.082	.0093	880	73.9	73
	1-5 yrs	690†	45	.763	.935	.065●	.0082●	795	78.9	57
	Starr Valve Model 6120									
1	1 mo-1 yr	122	5	.959	.959	.041	.0059	695%	96.5%	35
2	1-2 yrs	117	4	.926	.966	.034	.0071	480	93.8	27
3	2-3	113	5	.885	.956	.044	.0078	565	90.4	36
4	3-4	108	3	.861	.972	.028	.0086	325	88.6	19
	1-4 yrs	332†	12	.897	.965	.035●	.0078●	450	91.9	27

Table 354c   Cause of Death (after First Month) Valve Models 6000, 6120, 6300, 6310

Related to Prosthesis	Mitral Alone	Mitral & Other	Unrelated to Prosthesis	Mitral Alone	Mitral & Other
Bacterial Endocarditis	2	2	Coronary Artery Disease	4	5
Mechanical (ball, variance, leak)	0	3	Chronic Congestive failure	0	3
Thromboembolism	10	15	Myocardial Fibrosis	6	3
Reoperation	0	2	Arrhythmias, Sudden death	3	3
No necropsy or unknown	4	12	Residual valve disease	1	0
			Other disease or trauma	7	2
			Total (related and unrelated to prosthesis)	37	50

Table 354d   Incidence of Late Thromboembolic Complications Related to Valve Design in 312 Patients, August 1960 to June 1970

Valve Model	Approximate No. of Complications	Exposure Patient-Months	Exposure Patient-Years	Incidence per 1000 Patient-Months	Incidence per 1000 Patient-Years
6000	84	5855	488	14.3	172
6120	15	2837	236	5.3	64
6300	3	969	80.8	3.1	37
6310	1	629	52.4	1.6	19

* Basis of expected mortality: 1959-61 U.S. Life Tables

† Exposed to risk over indicated interval

● Mean annual rate: $\breve{q} = 1 - \sqrt[\Delta t]{P}$ (not an interval rate)

CONGENITAL AND VALVULAR HEART DISEASE

§355–RHEUMATIC AORTIC REGURGITATION

Reference: M. Spagnuolo, H. Kloth, A. Taranta, E. Doyle, and B. Pasternack, "Natural History of Rheumatic Aortic Regurgitation. Criteria Predictive of Death, Congestive Heart Failure, and Angina in Young Patients," Circulation, 44:368-380 (1971).

Subjects Studied: All of 174 young patients with a diagnosis of acute rheumatic fever and rheumatic aortic regurgitation, admitted to the Irvington House Clinic and the Bellevue Hospital Pediatric and Adolescent Cardiac Clinic, New York, in the period from 1952 through 1966. There were 124 males and 50 females aged 5 to 22 years, average age 11 years at the "index attack" of rheumatic fever (entry into the study). In 133 patients the index attack was the first attack of rheumatic fever and in 41 patients, a recurrence. Mitral regurgitation as an associated valvular lesion was present in many of the patients. Heart size by chest X-ray, ECG abnormalities and blood pressure findings at end of the index attack were used to classify the patients.

Follow-up: The study was planned to determine incidence rates of angina and congestive heart failure as well as death, utilizing life table methods. Of the initial group 107 patients continued to attend the clinic regularly (for the most part examined every two months, and hospitalized for study or treatment if the need arose); 15 patients died (three following surgical correction of their aortic disease, and one in an episode of subacute bacterial endocarditis); 36 of 52 patients who dropped out of the clinic returned for a follow-up examination; nine others were examined in other New York City clinics or by internists where they resided outside of New York City, and results of these examinations were made available. Only seven patients were lost to follow-up (4 per cent of the total). Patients who experienced angina or congestive heart failure were irreversiby removed from the group at risk for these events unless the event took place during a recurrence of acute rheumatic fever or an episode of subacute bacterial endocarditis. Year-by-year prognosis was also assessed by dividing patients annually into three risk groups: a low-risk group with no cardiomegaly, no ECG abnormality and normal blood pressure (systolic not above 140 mm., and diastolic 40 mm. or higher); a high risk group comprising patients who had moderate or marked left ventricular enlargement, two or three major ECG abnormalities, and abnormal blood pressure, with systolic above 140 mm. or diastolic under 40 mm.; and an intermediate risk group. The diastolic murmur of aortic regurgitation had disappeared in 30 per cent of the patients at one year after the index attack, but was present in over 90 per cent of those surviving to the 15th year.

Results: In the absence of complete life table data in the published article, the number and distribution of deaths have been estimated from the detailed survival curves, and exposures from the "number of patients followed," as given with each survival curve and for the total group in Table 1 of the article. The authors state that four of the 15 deaths were excluded (see Follow-up), but the most complete survival curves, in Figure 3 of the article, indicate a total of 13 deaths. These are the data shown in the comparative mortality and survival experience for the total group by duration in Tables 355a-b. In these young patients the mortality ratio decreased from 1000 to 625 per cent, and EDR increased slightly from 5.4 to 8.5 extra deaths per 1000 per year, from the first to the last five-year interval of observation. The 15-year cumulative survival ratio was 91.2 per cent.

Table 355c presents comparative experience by various medical characteristics over the 15 years of follow-up. Despite the small numbers of deaths there was a consistent increase in mortality ratio and EDR with severity in each of the risk categories investigated. The widest range of excess mortality by medical finding at the index attack was found in major ECG abnormalities: patients with two or more abnormalities had a mortality ratio of 4700 per cent, in contrast to a relatively low ratio of 465 per cent for those with a normal ECG. The mortality ratio was 2100 per cent in patients with moderate to marked left ventricular enlargement, 1000 per cent in slight enlargement and 415 per cent when heart size was normal. The difference was less marked with blood pressure as the criterion. However, the combination of these risk factors determined on an annual basis produced the widest difference: a mortality ratio of 179 per cent, based on a single death, in the low-risk category, and a ratio of 5800 per cent in the high risk category. Differences in excess death rates corresponded to the differences in mortality ratios with an extreme range of 0.7 to 51 per 1000 per year in the various categories of Table 355c.

RHEUMATIC AORTIC REGURGITATION

Table 355a   Observed Data and Comparative Experience by Duration

No.	Interval Start-End	No. Alive at Start of Interval	Est. Exposure Person-Yrs*	No. of Deaths Observed	No. of Deaths Expected†	Mortality Ratio Interval	Mortality Ratio Cumulative	Survival Ratio Interval	Survival Ratio Cumulative	Excess Death Rate
i	t to $t + \Delta t$	ℓ	E	d	d'	100 d/d'	100Σd/Σd'	100 p_i/p_i'	100 P/P'	1000(d-d')/E
1	0- 5 yrs	174	838	5	0.50	1000%	1000%	97.4%	97.4%	5.4
2	5-10	146	591	5	0.65	770	870	96.5	94.0	7.4
3	10-15	82	297	3	0.48	625	800	97.0	91.2	8.5
All	0-15	174	1726	13	1.63	800				6.6

Table 355b   Derived Mortality and Survival Data

No.	Interval Start-End	Observed Rates Survival Cumulative	Observed Rates Survival Interval	Observed Rates Survival Ave. Ann.	Observed Rates Ave. Ann. Mortality	Expected Rates† Survival Cumulative	Expected Rates† Survival Interval	Expected Rates† Survival Ave. Ann.	Expected Rates† Ave. Ann. Mortality
i	t to $t + \Delta t$	P	p_i	$\check{p}$	$\check{q}$	P'	p_i'	$\check{p}'$	$\check{q}'$
1	0- 5 yrs	.9711	.9711	.9942	.0058	.9972	.9972	.9994	.0006
2	5-10	.9321	.9598	.9918	.0082	.9917	.9945	.9989	.0011
3	10-15	.8969	.9622	.9923	.0077	.9839	.9921	.9984	.0016

Table 355c   Comparative 15-Year Experience by Medical Characteristics

Category	No. of Patients	Est. Exposure Person-Yrs*	No. of Deaths Observed	No. of Deaths Expected†	Mortality Ratio	Est. 15-Yr Surv. Rate	Est. 15-Yr Surv. Index	Excess Death Rate
	ℓ	E	d	d'	100 d/d'	P	100 P/P'	1000(d-d')/E
Left Ventric. Enlarg.								
None	83	785	3	0.72	415%	.936	95.1%	2.9
Slight	48	433	4	0.40	1000	.841	85.5	8.3
Moderate or Marked	39	304	6	0.28	2100	.794	80.7	19
Blood Pressure								
S < 140 and D > 40	118	1049	6	0.96	625	.913	92.8	4.8
S > 140 or D < 40	43	377	6	0.35	1710	.833	84.7	15
Major ECG Abnormalities								
None	96	935	4	0.86	465	.932	94.7	3.3
One	46	382	3	0.35	855	.869	88.3	6.9
Two or more	23	159	7	0.15	4700	.572	58.1	43
Continuous Risk Class								
Low	72	610	1	0.56	179	.967	98.3	0.7
High	31	134	7	0.12	5800	.738	75.0	51

* Exposure estimated from numbers of patients followed up at each interval
† Basis of expected mortality: U.S. Life Tables, 1959-61, total male and total female

VALVULAR HEART DISEASE

§356—AORTIC VALVE HOMOGRAFTS

References: (1) B. G. Barratt-Boyes and A. H. G. Roche, "A Review of Aortic Valve Homografts over a Six and One-half Year Period," Ann. Surg., 170:483-492 (1969).
(2) B. G. Barratt-Boyes, "Long-term Follow-up of Aortic Valvar Grafts," Brit. Heart J., 33 (Suppl.):60-65 (1971).

Subjects Studied: Patients having isolated aortic valve replacement with an aortic homograft valve at Green Lane Hospital, Auckland, New Zealand. The series is composed of all such operations, 564 in number, performed over a seven-year period commencing with the initial operation in August 1962. No other prosthesis was used; all variants of aortic valve disease are included. The replacements were almost exclusively chemically treated homograft valves — a technique of valve preparation abandoned in August 1968.

The distribution of subjects according to age and year of operation was approximately as follows:

Age (years)	1962-63 No.	%	1964 No.	%	1965 No.	%	1966 No.	%	1967 No.	%	1968 No.	%
Under 50	22	(43)	31	(41)	55	(46)	55	(39)	43	(35)	19	(24)
50 - 59	20	(40)	21	(28)	37	(31)	43	(31)	42	(34)	27	(34)
60 - 75	9	(17)	24	(31)	28	(23)	42	(30)	39	(31)	33	(42)
All Ages	51	(100)	76	(100)	120	(100)	140	(100)	124	(100)	79	(100)

Follow-up: Follow-up was complete to August 1969 except for one untraced patient. All subjects during the period of the study were observed by cardiologists — over 90 per cent by one cardiologist at Green Lane Hospital.

Results: Table 356a shows that of the 564 operations performed, 50 deaths occurred in hospital — a post-operative death rate of 8.9 per cent for all years' experience combined. The rate ranged from 4.4 to 12.5 per cent with no trend revealed by year of entry. Comparative experience of late deaths (occurring 3 months or more after operation) by year of entry or by duration of follow-up is presented in Tables 356b-c. There were 76 late deaths among the 514 survivors of the operation during the seven-year study, representing an average rate of death 265 per cent that of a corresponding group in the general population of New Zealand. Mortality ratios according to the year of operation declined almost consistently — from 400 per cent among the initial patients of 1962-63 to 186 per cent among those of 1968 (no extra late mortality in the short period following operations performed in 1969). Overall excess death rates averaged 26 per 1000 per year and tended to be somewhat smaller for operated patients in the later years of the study period. However, for these rates as well as for the other functions, the small numbers of deaths and the diminishing durations of experience with the year of operation warrant only qualified confidence in the significance of the results.

Causes of the 76 late deaths are noted in Table 356d. Failure of the valve was responsible for 26 of the deaths (34.2 per cent); cardiac disorders (coronary heart disease, myocardial infarction, and sudden death) accounted for 47.4 per cent. Attributable to uncertain and other than cardiovascular causes were 14 deaths (18.4 per cent).

Some differences in survival appear according to the method of preparing valves for replacement. The most important complication of homograft valves was cusp rupture, verified as a cause of late incompetence, causing death or requiring reoperation in 37 patients. While there was no statistically significant difference in the incidence of rupture according to chemical sterilization (beta propriolactone or ethylene oxide gas) or storage (freeze drying or in Hanks' solution) it is significant that no rupture was noted in any of 13 sterile untreated valves — all followed from five to seven years. The newer technique of antibiotic sterilization, although followed-up for less than two years may turn out to be superior to the earlier methods involving chemical sterilization.

AORTIC VALVE HOMOGRAFTS

Table 356a   Early (In Hospital) Mortality

Year of Operation	No. of Cases	No. of Deaths	Mortality Rate	No. of Survivors	Year of Operation	No. of Cases	No. of Deaths	Mortality Rate	No. of Survivors
	ℓ_o	d	$q=d/\ell_o$	$\ell=\ell_o-d$		ℓ_o	d	$q=d/\ell_o$	$\ell=\ell_o-d$
1962-63	45	2	.044	43	1967	104	13	.125	91
1964	68	7	.103	61	1968	67	7	.104	60
1965	109	7	.064	102	1969	40	4	.100	36
1966	131	10	.076	121	All Years	564	50	.089	514

Table 356b   Observed Data and Comparative Experience by Entry-Year Cohort (All Ages and Durations Combined)

Cohort Entry-Year	Duration of Follow-up	No. Alive 3 mos. Post-Op.	No. of Deaths	Ave. Ann. Mort. Ratio	Cumulative Surv. Ratio	Excess Death Rate
	Δt	ℓ	d	$100\ \breve{q}/\breve{q}'$	$100\ P/P'$	$1000(\breve{q}-\breve{q}')$
1969	0.5 yrs	36	0	0%	100.9%	−18
1968	1.5	60	3	186	97.7	16
1967	2.5	91	8	225	94.9	20
1966	3.5	121	19	295	89.3	32
1965	4.5	102	12	192	94.2	13
1964	5.5	61	20	390	74.2	52
1962-63	6.5	43	14	400	74.2	44

Table 356c   Survival Experience and Derived Data by Entry-Year Cohort Arranged from Shortest to Longest Duration

Duration of Follow-up	Observed Rates				Expected Rates*			
	Cumulative		Geometric Mean Ann.		Cumulative		Geometric Mean Ann.	
	Mortality	Survival	Survival	Mortality	Mortality	Survival	Survival	Mortality
Δt	$Q=d/\ell$	P	$\breve{p}$	$\breve{q}$	Q'	P'	$\breve{p}'$	$\breve{q}'$
0.5 yrs	.000	1.000	1.000	.000	.0089	.9911	.9823	.0177
1.5	.050	.950	.966	.034	.0273	.9727	.9817	.0183
2.5	.088	.912	.964	.036	.0392	.9608	.9841	.0159
3.5	.157	.843	.952	.048	.0564	.9436	.9836	.0164
4.5	.118	.882	.972	.028	.0641	.9359	.9854	.0146
5.5	.328	.672	.930	.070	.0948	.9052	.9821	.0179
6.5	.326	.674	.941	.059	.0919	.9081	.9853	.0147

Table 356d   Causes of Late Deaths (More than 3 Months Post-Operatively)

Related to Valve Failure				Other Deaths			
Cause of Death	Deaths		Cumulative Mort. Rate	Cause of Death	Deaths		Cumulative Mort. Rate
	Number	Proportion			Number	Proportion	
	d_c	%	$Q_c=d_c/\ell$		d_c	%	$Q_c=d_c/\ell$
Peripheral Leak	6	7.9	.012	Coronary Ht. Disease	13	17.1	.025
Malplacement	2	2.6	.004	Myocardial	14	18.4	.027
Cusp Rupture	10	13.2	.019	Sudden	9	11.9	.018
Endocarditis	8	10.5	.016	Total Cardiac	36	47.3	.070
Total Value Failure	26	34.2	.051	Not Cardiovascular	11	14.5	.021
Total All Deaths	76	100.0%	.148	Uncertain	3	3.9	.006

*Basis of expected mortality: 1966 New Zealand population tables

CONGENITAL AND VALVULAR HEART DISEASE

§358–STARR-EDWARDS AORTIC VALVE REPLACEMENT

Reference: F. C. Shean, W. G. Austen, M. J. Buckley, E. D. Mundth, J. G. Scannell, and W. M. Daggett, "Survival after Starr-Edwards Aortic Valve Replacement," Circulation, 44:1-8 (1971).

Subjects Studied: Patients at the Massachusetts General Hospital between 1963 and 1969 who underwent aortic valve replacement. There were 507 such operations during the period but adequate follow-up was not available on 52 patients. Of the 455 patients with adequate follow-up 310 were men and 145 women. By type of lesion, there were 192 subjects with aortic stenosis (average age 58 years), 97 with aortic regurgitation (average age 49) and 166 with mixed aortic lesions (average age 54). No double valve replacements were included (but six patients had a subsequent mitral procedure). Patients with previous aortic replacements done elsewhere were excluded.

Follow-up: Information was based on written communication with the patient, his local physician, the consulting cardiologist, the operating surgeon, or a combination thereof. The minimum period of follow-up was 12 months, the maximum 6 years 8 months, and the average, 36 months.

Results: Early mortality and follow-up data by year of operation are shown in Table 358a. Exposure has been estimated from the average duration and follow-up data (ℓ, u and d) for each group of early survivors treated as a cohort. The in-hospital mortality rate following operation was .286 in 1963 but decreased to a level below .08 from 1965 through 1967, attributed by the authors to use of more adequate anticoagulation procedures and an improved valve design, Model 1000 having been replaced by Model 1200 in 1966. The higher early mortality rate of .127 in 1968 is partially explained by the increasing proportion in that year of functional class 4 patients (New York Heart Association classification), at high risk for major surgery.

Follow-up experience for the early survivors is presented in Table 358b by type of aortic lesion. The aggregate mortality ratio is 490 per cent with 61 deaths. The ratio for mixed lesions (15 deaths) is lower - 350 per cent. The highest ratio is shown for aortic regurgitation (14 deaths) - 885 per cent. Survival indexes based on the 3-year average period of observation are about the same for aortic stenosis and aortic regurgitation (85.1 and 85.9 per cent, respectively) and again most favorable for the mixed lesions. Excess deaths per 1000 show a similar relationship, EDR's for the mixed lesions being about half those of the other two categories.

In-hospital estimated mortality experience by aortic lesion is indicated in Table 358c. The overall rate of operative mortality indicated was .108 (55 deaths). The estimated rates for aortic stenosis (.126) and for aortic regurgitation (.120) were higher, and the rate for mixed aortic disease (.081) was lower. Within the group of aortic stenosis cases, those of rheumatic origin registered the highest estimated rate.

Comment: The number of sudden deaths and deaths due to persistent congestive heart failure and myocardial infarction was relatively high among the causes of late deaths in this series. Twelve patients died suddenly and eight in unremitting congestive failure. Twenty-one patients suffered an infarction intraoperatively or immediately postoperatively, with 16 deaths. Autopsies were conducted on approximately one-third of patients who died suddenly. For the remaining two-thirds identification of cause could not be made.

Surviving the period of observation were 339 subjects of whom 239 were totally free of symptoms, 32 had angina, 58 had some congestive heart failure, and 10 had both angina and failure.

AORTIC VALVE REPLACEMENT

Table 358a Operative and Follow-up Data by Year of Operation (All Lesions Combined)

Year of Operation	No. of Patients Operated	In-hospital Deaths	Post-Op Mort. Rate	No. of Early Survivors	No. of Untraced	Est. Exposure* Person-Yrs	No. of Late Deaths	1/1/70 Known Survivors
(Δt)	ℓ_o	d_o	q_o	ℓ	u	E	d	S
1963 (6.5)	21	6	.286	15	1	82	4	10
1964 (5.5)	60	9	.150	51	6	223	12	33
1965 (4.5)	73	5	.068	68	12	245	16	40
1966 (3.5)	82	6	.073	76	6	238	11	59
1967 (2.5)	114	9	.079	105	10	239	11	84
1968 (1.5)	157	20	.127	137	17	189	7	113
All (3)	507	55	.108	452	52	1216	61	339

Table 358b Comparative Experience by Valvular Lesion (Early Deaths Excluded)

Valvular Lesion	No. of Early Survivors	Est. Exposure* Person-Yrs	No. of Deaths Observed	Expected†	Mortality Ratio	Ave. Ann. Mort. Rate	Est. 3-Yr Surv. Rate	Est. 3-Yr Surv. Index	Excess Death Rate
	ℓ	E	d	d'	100 d/d'	$\bar{q} = d/E$	P	100 P/P'	1000(d-d')/E
Stenosis	—	496.0	32	6.65	480%	.065	.817	85.1%	51
Regurgitation	—	254.5	14	1.58	885	.055	.844	85.9	49
Mixed	—	465.5	15	4.26	350	.032	.907	93.2	23
All	452	1216.0	61	12.49	490	.050	.857	88.4	40

Table 358c Operation Mortality and Follow-up Data by Type of Aortic Lesion

Valvular Lesion	No. Operations on Patients Followed-up	Est Total No. Patients Operated	No of In-hospital Deaths	Estimated Post-Op Mort. Rate	Estimated No. Early Survivors	Number Late Deaths	1/1/70 Known Survivors
	ℓ'	L_o	d_o	q_o	ℓ	d	S
Aortic Stenosis							
Rheumatic	49	55	9	.164	46	10	30
Congenital	42	47	5	.106	42	8	29
Degenerative	101	112	13	.116	99	14	74
Total Stenosis	192	214	27	.126	187	32	133
Aortic Regurgitation	97	108	13	.120	95	14	70
Mixed Aortic Dis.	166	185	15	.081	170	15	136
Total	455	507●	55	.108●	452●	61	339

* Approximate figures estimated from available follow-up data
† Basis of expected mortality: 1959-61 U.S. White Male and Female Tables
● Data and q_o for total series observed, not estimated

ARRHYTHMIAS AND ECG ABNORMALITIES

§360—TACHYCARDIA IN INSUREDS

Reference: "New York Life Single Medical Impairment Study—1972," unpublished report made available by J.J. Hutchinson and J.C. Sibigtroth (1973).

Subjects Studied: Policyholders of New York Life Insurance Company issued insurance in 1954-1970, followed to the 1971 policy anniversary. These were cases found to have a rapid resting pulse rate of 90 or more per minute. Only the substandard issues have been analyzed here. All cases with more than one ratable impairment were excluded.

Follow-up: Insurance policy records formed the basis of entry, of counting policies, exposure and death claims, and of follow-up information.

Results: Tables 360a-b present the comparative experience among males by duration, all ages combined. The mortality ratio showed a downward trend, ranging from 480 per cent at 0-2 years to 151 per cent at 5-17 years. The same trend was observed in EDR, a decrease from 6.4 to 2.8 extra deaths per 1000.

The overall mortality ratio was 240 per cent, and the cumulative survival ratio at 17 years was 93.9 per cent (Table 360a). Excess mortality was significantly higher for ages 50 up than for lower ages, with a mortality ratio of 300 per cent and EDR of 18 per 1000 being experienced at the older ages. The spread in the estimated 8-year survival index between ages under 50 and ages 50 up was 10.9 percentage points (97.4 per cent to 86.5 per cent).

The experience by cause of death for males and females combined is given in Table 360d. The leading cause of death is found in diseases of the heart and circulation, with a mortality ratio of 280 per cent and EDR of 2.1 per 1000. There is some increase in mortality due to malignant neoplasms and from "all other causes and unknown," with an EDR of 0.6 per 1000 in each case.

TACHYCARDIA IN INSUREDS

Table 360a   Observed Data and Comparative Experience by Duration — Male Substandard Cases

Interval		Exposure	No. of Death Claims		Mortality Ratio		Survival Ratio		Excess
No.	Start-End	Policy-Yrs	Observed	Expected*	Interval	Cumulative	Interval	Cumulative	Death Rate
i	t to t + Δ t	E	d	d'	100 d/d'	100 Σd/Σd'	100p_i/p_i'	100 P/P'	1000(d-d')/E
1	0- 2 yrs	1243	10	2.08	480%	480%	98.7%	98.7%	6.4
2	2- 5	1060	9	3.05	295	370	98.3	97.1	5.6
3	5-17	1349	11	7.27	151	240	96.7	93.9	2.8

Table 360b   Derived Mortality and Survival Data

Interval		Observed Rates				Expected Rates*			
		Average Annual		Cumulative		Average Annual		Cumulative	
No.	Start-End	Mortality	Survival	Survival	Mortality	Mortality	Survival	Survival	Mortality
i	t to t + Δ t	$\bar{q}$=d/E	$\bar{p}$	P	Q	$\bar{q}'$=d'/E	$\bar{p}'$	P'	Q'
1	0- 2 yrs	.0080	.9920	.9840	.0160	.0017	.9983	.9967	.0033
2	2- 5	.0085	.9915	.9591	.0409	.0029	.9971	.9881	.0119
3	5-17	.0082	.9918	.8694	.1306	.0054	.9946	.9260	.0740

Table 360c   Comparative Experience by Age Group — Male Substandard Cases, All Durations Combined

Age Group	Exposure Policy-Yrs	No. of Death Claims		Mortality Ratio	Ave. Ann. Mort. Rate	Est. 8-Yr Surv. Rate	Est. 8-Yr Surv. Index	Excess Death Rate
		Observed	Expected*					
	E	d	d'	100 d/d'	$\bar{q}$=d/E	P=(1-$\bar{q}$)^8	100 P/P'	1000(d-d')/E
0-49	3284	20	9.04	220%	.0061	.9523	97.4%	3.3
50 up	368	10	3.36	300	.0272	.8022	86.5	18
All Ages	3652	30	12.40	240	.0082	.9362	96.2	4.8

Table 360d   Mortality by Cause of Death — Male and Female Combined

Cause	No. of Death Claims		Mortality Ratio	Excess Death Rate
	Observed†	Expected●		
Malignant Neoplasms	7	3.70	190%	0.6
Diseases of the Heart & Circulatory System	17	6.10	280	2.1
Accidents and Homicides	2	2.13	94	0.0
Suicide	1	.66	152	0.1
All Other Causes and Unknown	6	2.92	205	0.6
Total	33	15.51	215	3.4

* Basis of expected mortality: 1955-60 Select Basic Table
† Includes 3 females (from 1457 policy-years of exposure)
● Distribution of total expected deaths by Intercompany Medically
   Examined Standard Issues 1967-70

ARRHYTHMIAS AND ECG ABNORMALITIES

§361–CARDIAC ARRHYTHMIAS IN INSUREDS

Reference: "New York Life Single Medical Impairment Study–1972," unpublished report made available by J.J. Hutchinson and J.C. Sibigtroth (1973).

Subjects Studied: Policyholders of New York Life Insurance Company issued insurance in 1954-1970, followed to the 1971 policy anniversary. The experience reported is for cases with irregular pulse or premature beats, which are rated substandard at issue. Cases with rapid pulse, slow pulse or atrial fibrillation were not included in this code. Cases involving more than one ratable impairment were excluded.

Follow-up: Insurance policy records formed the basis of entry, of counting policies, exposure and death claims, and of follow-up information.

Results: Comparative experience is given in Tables 361a-b by duration, all ages combined. Male mortality ratios showed a sharply decreasing trend, dropping from 420 per cent at 0-2 years to about one-third, or 144 per cent at 5-17 years. The EDR also declined rapidly with duration, from 10 extra deaths per 1000 at 0-2 years to less than half, or 4 extra deaths per 1000 at 5-17 years. The cumulative survival ratio at 17 years was 93.8 per cent.

From Table 361c, male mortality appeared to be somewhat higher for entry ages 50 up than for ages under 50, with EDR definitely increasing with advancing age from 3 per 1000 at ages 0-49 to 25 per 1000 at ages 60 up. The overall mortality ratio for males was 225 per cent, with an EDR of 7.4 per 1000. The experience for female insureds was much smaller than for males, and no breakdown by age or duration was feasible. The overall mortality ratio for females was 149 per cent, with an EDR of 2.2 per 1000, signifying a more favorable experience than for males.

Comparative experience by major causes of death is given in Table 361d for males and females combined. The major cause of death is found in diseases of the heart and circulation, with a mortality ratio of 310 per cent and EDR of 4.6 per 1000. This was followed closely by malignant neoplasms, the mortality being 270 per cent and EDR 2.3 per 1000. There was no excess mortality found among the other causes of death.

CARDIAC ARRHYTHMIAS IN INSUREDS

Table 361a   Observed Data and Comparative Experience by Duration — Male Substandard Cases

No.	Interval Start-End	Exposure Policy-Yrs	Observed	Expected*	Mortality Ratio Interval	Cumulative	Survival Ratio Interval	Cumulative	Excess Death Rate
i	t to t + Δ t	E	d	d'	100 d/d'	100 Σd/Σd'	100p_i/p_i'	100 P/P'	1000(d-d')/E
1	0- 2 yrs	1353	18	4.29	420%	420%	98.0%	98.0%	10
2	2- 5	1162	16	6.54	245	315	97.6	95.6	8.1
3	5-17	1309	17	11.78	144	225	98.1	93.8	4.0

Table 361b   Derived Mortality and Survival Data

No.	Interval Start-End	Observed Rates Avg Annual Mortality	Survival	Cumulative Survival	Mortality	Expected Rates Avg Annual Mortality	Survival	Cumulative Survival	Mortality
i	t to t + Δ t	$\bar{q}$=d/E	$\bar{p}$	P	Q	$\bar{q}'$=d'/E	$\bar{p}'$	P'	Q'
1	0- 2 yrs	.0133	.9867	.9736	.0264	.0032	.9968	.9937	.0063
2	2- 5	.0138	.9862	.9339	.0661	.0056	.9944	.9770	.0230
3	5-17	.0130	.9870	.8085	.1915	.0090	.9910	.8620	.1380

Table 361c   Comparative Experience by Sex and Age Group — Substandard Cases, All Durations Combined

Sex	Age Group	Exposure Policy-Yrs	Observed	Expected*	Mortality Ratio	Ave. Ann. Mort. Rate	Est. 8-Yr Surv. Rate	Est. 8-Yr Surv. Index	Excess Death Rate
		E	d	d'	100 d/d'	$\bar{q}$=d/E	P=(1-$\bar{q}$)^8	100 P/P'	1000(d-d')/E
Male	0-49	2619	16	8.21	195%	.0061	.9522	97.6%	3.0
	50-59	749	16	6.85	235	.0214	.8414	90.6	12
	60 up	456	19	7.55	250	.0417	.7114	81.3	25
	All Ages	3824	51	22.61	225	.0133	.8982	94.2	7.4
Female	All Ages	1200	8	5.38	149%	.0067	.9479	98.3%	2.2

Table 361d   Mortality by Cause of Death — Male and Female Combined

Cause	Observed	Expected†	Mortality Ratio	Excess Death Rate
Malignant Neoplasms	18	6.66	270%	2.3
Diseases of the Heart & Circulatory System	34	11.01	310	4.6
Accidents and Homicides	2	3.85	52	−0.4
Suicide	0	1.19	0	−0.2
All Other Causes & Unknown	5	5.28	95	−0.1
Total	59	27.99	210	6.2

* Basis of expected mortality: 1955-60 Select Basic Table

† Distribution of total expected deaths by Intercompany Medically
  Examined Standard Issues 1965-70

ARRHYTHMIAS AND ECG ABNORMALITIES

§363–ECG: PREMATURE CONTRACTIONS

References: (1) M. Rodstein, L. Wolloch, and R. S. Gubner, "Mortality Study of the Significance of Extrasystoles in An Insured Population," Circulation, 44:617-625 (1971).

(2) A. M. Lyle, "A Study of Premature Beats by Electrocardiogram," Trans. Soc. Actuaries, 14:493-508 (1962).

Subjects Studied: (1) Applicants insured by the Equitable Life Assurance Society of the U.S. between 1930 and 1956 in whom one or more extrasystoles were found in the ECG, usually made at examination or shortly thereafter. Out of a total of 712 persons (almost all male) 604 were standard insurance risks apart from any rating for extrasystoles, 77 were substandard for some other risk, and 31 were declined. Age distribution was as follows:

Age (years)	Under 25	25-34	35-44	45-54	55-65	Total
Number	25	178	258	190	61	712
Per Cent	3.5%	25.0%	36.2%	26.7%	8.6%	100%

(2) Employees of Prudential Insurance Co., Newark, with an ECG made between 1933 and 1959 which displayed premature beats. There were 1139 individuals: 968 initial ECG's showed simple, and 171 variant*, premature beats; 180 persons with simple premature beats had later ECG's showing variant beats. In the total series 429 had no clinical or ECG abnormalities except the premature beats; 710 had a variety of associated impairments.

Follow-up: (1) To policy anniversary in 1968, or prior termination, using records of policy issued at time of application, or, in declined cases, previously issued policy. Duration of follow-up averaged 18 years.

(2) To June 30, 1960, or prior termination through clinic, personnel or pension records. A control group of employees was also followed up; these had normal ECG without premature beats.

Results: (1) Experience under the Equitable Life study is presented in Table 363a. In practically all indicated categories the mortality of applicants classifiable as standard risks for insurance except for the extrasystoles is essentially normal. An intimation of extra hazard appears in the case of applicants 45 years and older with 10 or more premature beats per minute; this group shows a mortality ratio of 148 per cent (18 deaths). Mortality ratios in other categories range between 65 and 200 per cent but the ratios at both ends of this range are not statistically significant because of the small numbers of deaths. However, the association of a ratable cardiovascular abnormality with extrasystoles does seem to result in a significant mortality hazard. Thus, the category of persons with ventricular extrasystoles and a rating for hypertension or other cardiovascular condition (ratings not exceeding 195 per cent of standard) experience a mortality ratio of 225 per cent. Association of other impairments does not produce such results. The authors note that among subjects with ventricular extrasystoles there appears to be an exceptional number of sudden deaths at ages under 56 years from acute myocardial infarction.

(2) Table 363b focuses on the experience among Prudential employees according to the presence of varying degrees of hypertension and of other cardiovascular impairments: (a) without premature beats; and (b) in association with simple and variant extrasystoles. In the absence of any elevation of blood pressure, mortality ratios in groups with or without extrasystoles are confined to a narrow range (79 to 108 per cent, for males). Progressive degrees of hypertension without extrasystoles develop steady increases in mortality ratios – in the case of males, from 128 per cent for slight blood pressure elevation to 565 per cent for very marked hypertension. With simple premature beats, mortality ratios tend to increase with rising levels of hypertension varying for men from 235 per cent in cases of slight blood pressure elevation to 635 per cent for very marked elevation. Variant premature beats tend to produce even higher mortality ratios. Female mortality ratios show the same trends but at lower levels, presumably because of use of the combined male/female basic tables (heavily weighted with male policyholders) to calculate expected deaths. Very high mortality ratios were observed in employees with rheumatic heart disease, with or without premature beats.

*Pairs or brief runs of premature beats; premature beats alternating with sinus beats; failure of bundle branch to conduct auricular premature beat; depressed T wave in the first sinus beat following a premature beat; multifocal origin.

ECG—PREMATURE CONTRACTIONS

Table 363a   Comparative Mortality by Age, ECG Characteristics in an Insured Population (Equitable Life Assur.)

Age or Other Factor	Number Insured	Deaths Observed	Deaths Expected*	Mortality Ratio	Number Insured	Deaths Observed	Deaths Expected*	Mortality Ratio
	ℓ	d	d'	100 d/d'	ℓ	d	d'	100 d/d'
Type of Extrasystole			Simple				Complex†	
Supraventricular	83	15	12.69	118%	39	6	6.22	96%
Ventricular	359	56	59.79	94	123	21	17.34	121
Frequent	(0)	—	—	—	50	5	6.68	75
Multifocal, etc.	(0)	—	—	—	14	4	1.99	200
Close to T wave	(0)	—	—	—	59	12	8.68	138
Frequency			Under 10 per minute				10 and up per minute	
Ages under 45 yrs	249	25	31.55	79	151	19	17.79	107
Ages 45 yrs up	142	36	34.53	104	62	18	12.17	148
All Ages	391	61	66.08	92	213	37	29.96	123
Frequency after Exercise			Decreased or Unchanged				Increased	
Ages under 45 yrs	181	19	24.40	78	46	5	7.74	65
Ages 45 yrs up	90	29	21.43	135	16	5	2.71	185
All Ages	271	48	45.83	105	62	10	10.45	96
CV or Other Abnormality			None				Associated	
Supraventricular	122	21	18.91	111	22	4	3.33	120
Ventricular	482	77	77.14	100	86	23	12.79	180
BP or other CV					42	15	6.70	225
Non CV rating					44	8	6.10	131

Table 363b   Comparative Mortality by Type and Associated CV Abnormality (Prudential Employees)

Associated CV Abnormality	Extra Systoles	Number of Men	Deaths Observed	Deaths Expected●	Mortality Ratio	Number of Women	Deaths Observed	Deaths Expected●	Mortality Ratio
(Rating Range)		ℓ	d	d'	100 d/d'	ℓ	d	d'	100 d/d'
Hypertension									
None	None	1805	145	187	78%	902	29	103	28%
(No Rating)	Simple	267	25	26.1	96	109	6	12.5	48
	Variant	63	7	6.5	108	28	1	1.5	66
Slight	None	472	58	45.4	128	247	14	36.5	38
(+30% to +80%)	Simple	82	17	7.3	235	51	4	4.0	100
	Variant	27	9	3.0	300	9	1	0.7	139
Moderate	None	341	61	31.0	197	234	26	36.1	72
(+81% to +200%)	Simple	59	10	6.7	149	46	4	3.5	115
	Variant	23	9	3.0	300	9	1	0.6	165
Marked	None	126	32	9.3	340	71	12	10.4	115
(+201% to +400%)	Simple	27	5	1.3	390	19	4	2.2	185
	Variant	9	2	0.5	425	6	0	0.4	0
Very Marked	None	220	95	16.9	565	179	51	26.6	192
(over +400%)	Simple	61	28	4.4	635	58	16	7.4	215
	Variant	28	14	2.0	715	18	10	2.5	405
Rheumatic Heart Disease	None	39	14	4.0	350	41	13	2.7	485
(All Ratings)	Simple	15	8	1.2	655	18	8	1.1	700
	Variant	6	3	0.7	420	10	2	0.4	470
Associated CV	Simple	174	30	15.3	196	80	8	7.2	112
Minor (+30% to +200%)	Variant	62	19	6.9	275	20	4	1.8	225
Major (over +200%)	Simple	224	98	20.3	480	114	35	13.4	260
	Variant	130	57	11.4	500	48	17	4.3	400

* Basis of expected mortality: Intercompany 1955-60 Basic Tables

† Bigeminy or trigeminy; multifocal, paired, or post EST inversion; close to preceding T wave

● Basis of expected mortality: Intercompany 1946-49 Basic Tables

ARRHYTHMIAS AND ECG ABNORMALITIES

§364–VENTRICULAR PREMATURE BEATS

Reference: D. C. Desai, P. I. Hershberg, and S. Alexander, "Clinical Significance of Ventricular Premature Beats in an Outpatient Population," Chest, 64: 564-569 (1973).

Subjects Studied: Outpatients at the Lahey Clinic in Boston who had ECG's performed in 1967. Out of 12751 such persons with standard 12-lead ECG's, 539 with ventricular premature beats (VPB) were selected for the study. A control group of 494 subjects selected where possible from the same clinic outpatients was matched with the VPB group members according to chief medical diagnosis, sex, and age by decade. The only difference between the VPB and control groups was the absence of these premature contractions in the ECG's of the latter. Distribution of both groups by sex and age was as follows:

Number (Per cent) in Age Class

Sex	Group	Under 41	41-50	51-60	61-70	71-80	81 up	Total
Male	VPB	15 (4%)	40 (12%)	106 (31%)	111 (33%)	53 (16%)	12 (4%)	337 (100%)
	Control	13 (4)	38 (13)	99 (33)	99 (33)	44 (14)	8 (3)	301 (100)
Female	VPB	14 (7)	32 (16)	52 (26)	58 (30)	43 (21)	3 (1)	202 (100)
	Control	12 (6)	30 (16)	50 (26)	59 (30)	40 (21)	2 (1)	193 (100)
M & F	VPB	29 (6)	72 (13)	158 (29)	169 (31)	96 (18)	15 (3)	539 (100)
	Control	25 (5)	68 (14)	149 (30)	158 (32)	84 (17)	10 (2)	494 (100)

Follow-up: Started in October 1970 and completed by January 15, 1971, carried out through a medical questionnaire, by telegram, and by telephone. The average period of follow-up was about 3½ years with a range of three to four years. Only 3 patients in the VPB group, and 6 in the control group, were lost to follow-up; they are excluded from this abstract.

Results: Table 364a analyzes differences in experience in the VPB and control groups by primary (most important) medical diagnosis. Three broad categories of diagnosis are employed: cardiovascular diseases, cancer, and other non-cardiovascular impairments (diabetes, lung disease, gastrointestinal disease, miscellaneous). Except in the case of cancer, where mortality for the control group is higher than that of the VPB subjects, mortality of patients with VPB for both cardiovascular and non-cardiovascular diseases consistently exceeds that of patients in the control group. However, the significance of the comparison is compromised in some categories by the paucity of experience; statistical significance can be attributed only to the myocardial infarction and miscellaneous cardiovascular categories and on their account to the total cardiovascular group and to all patients combined:

Observed mortality data are presented in Table 364b according to the presence or absence of cardiovascular disease as the major diagnosis, or the presence or absence of ECG abnormality apart from the VPB's. The comparative experience and rates derived from the 3½ year cumulative mortality rates are given in Table 364c. Mortality rates were several times higher in patients with cardiovascular disease or abnormal ECG than in patients without such abnormality, and the average age was also higher. In all four groups of patients mortality in those with VPB's exceeded mortality in their control counterparts: mortality ratios of 180 and 200 per cent in those with or without cardiovascular disease and 132 and 122 per cent in those with or without the associated criterion of an abnormal ECG. Excess deaths showed substantially greater relative differences: EDR of 43 per 1000 in the cardiovascular group versus 8 per 1000 in the non-cardiovascular, and EDR of 22 versus 4 per 1000 in the groups with and without an abnormal ECG. Survival ratios were correspondingly lower in patients with cardiovascular disease or abnormal ECG.

Comment: Conclusions of the authors may be summarized: (1) the most important determinants of prognosis in ambulatory patients with or without VPB's are age and underlying cardiac status; (2) in patients with heart disease, the presence of VPB's in an otherwise normal ECG is associated with a small but statistically significant increase in mortality; (3) in the absence of clinical heart disease, the presence of VPB's in an otherwise normal ECG appears to have little effect on mortality; (4) in both matched groups, patients with clinical history of MI or angina, and ECG abnormalities (MI patterns, left ventricular hypertrophy, and bundle branch block) have a particularly high mortality.

ECG — PREMATURE BEATS

Table 364a Lahey Clinic Outpatients with Ventricular Premature Beats in ECG Compared with Matched Control Patients by Medical Diagnosis — Average Duration 3½ Years

Primary Diagnosis	Ventricular Premature Beats			Control*			Difference-Statistical Significance Prob. Level†
	No. of Patients	Deaths Observed	Mortality Rate	No. of Patients	Deaths Observed	Mortality Rate	
	ℓ	d	$Q = d/\ell$	ℓ'	d'	$Q' = d'/\ell'$	
Cardiovascular							
Myocardial Infarction	60	24	.400	52	12	.231	<0.05
Angina Pectoris	40	15	.375	38	10	.263	N.S.
Valvular Heart Dis.	19	4	.210	14	2	.143	N.S.
Hypertension	71	12	.170	67	9	.134	N.S.
Other Cardiovascular	30	11	.367	23	1	.043	<0.01
Total Cardiovascular	220	66	.300	194	34	.175	<0.01
Cancer	25	10	.400	19	11	.579	N.S.
Other Diseases	291	16	.055	279	8	.029	N.S.
Total All Patients	536	92	.171	492	53	.107	<0.01

Table 364b Observed Data by Associated Medical or ECG Factor — All Ages Combined, Average Duration 3½ Years

Category	Average Age (Yrs)	Ventricular Premature Beats			Control*		
		No. of Patients	Deaths Observed	Mortality Rate	No. of Patients	Deaths Observed	Mortality Rate
	X	ℓ	d	$Q = d/\ell$	ℓ'	d'	$Q' = d'/\ell'$
All CV Disease	64	220	66	.300	194	34	.175
Non CV Disease●	57	291	16	.055	279	8	.029
Other ECG Abnormality	—	250	70	.280	143	31	.217
No other ECG Abnormality	—	289	22	.076	355	22	.062

Table 364c Derived Data and Comparative Experience

Category	Ventricular Premature Beats			Control*			Mortality Ratio	Cumulative Surv. Ratio (3½ Years)	Excess Death Rate
	Survival Rate		Ave. Ann. Mort. Rate	Survival Rate		Ave. Ann. Mort. Rate			
	3½ Yr Cum.	Ave. Ann.		3½ Yr Cum.	Ave. Ann.				
	P	p̆	q̆	P'	p̆'	q̆'	100 q̆/q̆'	100 P/P'	1000(q̆-q̆')
All CV Dis.	.700	.903	.097	.825	.946	.054	180%	84.8%	43
Non CV Dis.●	.945	.984	.016	.971	.992	.008	200	97.3	8
Other ECG Abn.	.720	.910	.090	.783	.932	.068	132	92.0	22
No ECG Abn.	.924	.978	.022	.938	.982	.018	122	98.5	4

* Patients matched by sex, age, medical diagnosis, but without ventricular premature beats in their ECG

† Probability level of the difference Q - Q' being random. N.S. — not statistically significant, with probability level exceeding 0.05

● Excluding cancer cases

ARRHYTHMIAS AND ECG ABNORMALITIES

§367—ATRIOVENTRICULAR CONDUCTION DEFECTS

References: (1) K. F. Brandon, M. H. Neill, and G. C. Streeter, "The Use of the Electrocardiogram in Twenty-Five Years of Insurance Selection," Trans. Assoc. Life Ins. Med. Dir. Am., 34:143-155 (1950).

(2) F. A. L. Mathewson and D. C. Brereton, "Atrio-ventricular Heart Block," Trans. Assoc. Life Ins. Med. Dir. Am., 48:210-234 (1964).

(3) H. Siddons, "Deaths in Long-Term Paced Patients," Brit. Heart J., 36:1201-1209 (1974).

Subjects Studied: (1) 178 applicants with atrioventricular (AV) block (PR interval 0.20 seconds or longer) in an ECG taken in conjunction with an examination for the Aetna Life Insurance Company and drawn from a series of 6387 tracings coded and placed on file 1924-1949. Additional descriptive information on this series is given in §370.

(2) 95 men with AV block in an ECG taken on Royal Canadian Air Force personnel or pilots licensed by the Department of Transport in Canada. These were part of the University of Manitoba Follow-up Study, consisting of 3983 men with examinations 1946-1948 and known to be alive and free from clinical evidence of disease on July 1, 1948. There were 92 cases with PR interval exceeding 0.20 seconds and three cases of complete block thought to be congenital in origin. The men were distributed by age with 30 under age 25, 21 age 25-29, 19 age 30-34, 14 age 35-39, and 11 age 40 and older.

(3) 649 patients treated with an implanted pacemaker and transvenous endocardial electrode at St. George's Hospital, London, England. The reason for pacemaker implantation was complete AV block in over 96 per cent of this series of 375 men and 274 women with age distribution as follows:

Age	0-9 yrs	10-39	40-49	50-59	60-69	70-79	80-89	90 up
No. of Cases	12	9	22	74	188	243	96	5

For comparison with this series data were collected on 113 unpaced patients with complete AV block whose mean age and sex distribution were similar. These consisted of all other such patients seen in the department in the period 1960-1965 just before artificial pacing was introduced or in the early days when pacing was not very reliable.

Follow-up: (1) Aetna policy records were used to follow up 3802 of the applicants. On another 2585 applicants who were not Aetna policyholders follow-up was attempted through insurance records of cooperating companies or other means. Only two per cent of the series were untraced, with 93 per cent completely traced to January 1, 1950, and partial follow-up information obtained on the remaining 5 per cent.

(2) Annual contact was maintained with members of the Study group, and periodic examinations were also carried out, to June 30, 1963.

(3) No mention is made in the article of methods and completeness of follow-up. Survival data for the paced patients are presented for six years of follow-up, at which time there were 50 patients exposed to risk.

Results: Mortality ratios in Table 367a were very close to normal for the Aetna insurance applicants with no other significant cardiovascular abnormality and also for the Canadian pilots and Air Force men. The latter group did include three cases of complete block, and three cases of atrial fibrillation developed during follow-up, but there was no increased evidence of coronary heart disease, either clinically or as a cause of death. A very small group of the Aetna series with complete heart block developed three observed deaths as against 1.1 expected in 108 person-years of follow-up (mortality ratio 275 per cent). A larger group with incomplete block and other CV abnormality also manifested some excess mortality, with a ratio of 172 per cent and EDR of 8.2 per 1000. However, this excess may have been attributable to other cardiovascular abnormalities present and not the AV conduction defect. The authors of the Canadian report emphasize the variability of the PR interval in follow-up ECG's, from less than 0.20 to 0.25 seconds or more, which occurred as a maximum in less than one-fourth of the series.

The experience of the English patients with complete block and implanted pacemaker is shown in the upper part of Table 367b. In the first four years of follow-up the mortality ratio ranged from 114 to 205 per cent and the EDR from 9 to 64 per 1000. However, with a mortality lower than that expected during the last two years of follow-up, the aggregate excess mortality was at a low level: mortality ratio only 122 per cent and EDR 14 per 1000. The six-year survival ratio was 91.8 per cent. In view of the high average age of this series and the presumed incidence of serious heart disease the patients with pacemaker did remarkably well. The experience was much less favorable in the group of patients not treated with pacemaker implantation: the four-year survival ratio was less than 60 per cent, the mortality ratio 280 per cent, and the aggregate EDR 113 per 1000.

ATRIOVENTRICULAR CONDUCTION DEFECTS

Table 367a   Comparative Experience, Atrioventricular Block, Various Series

Ref.	Category	No. of Cases	Exposure Person-Yrs	No. of Deaths Observed	No. of Deaths Expected*	Mortality Ratio	Ave. Ann. Mort. Rate	Est. 5-Yr Surv. Index	Excess Death Rate
		ℓ	E	d	d′	100 d/d′	$\bar{q}$=d/E	100 P/P′	1000(d-d′)/E
1	Incomplete PR 0.20 up								
	All Insureds (Aetna)	168	1073	21	12.2	172%	.0196	95.9%	8.2
	No Other CV Abn.	57	339	4	4.1	98	.0118	100.2	−0.3
2	PR .021 secs. up								
	(Univ. Manitoba Series)	95	1267	6	5.6	107	.0047	99.8	0.3
1	Complete AV Block								
	All Insureds (Aetna)	10	108	3	1.1	275	.028	91.4	18

Table 367b   Comparative Experience, Patients with Complete AV Block, With and Without Pacemaker, Series 3

No	Start-End	No. of Cases at Start	Cum. Surv. Rate Observed	Cum. Surv. Rate Expected*	Cumulative Surv. Ratio	Ave. Ann. Mort. Rate Observed	Ave. Ann. Mort. Rate Expected*	Mortality Ratio	Excess Death Rate
i	t to t + Δt	ℓ	P	P′	100 P/P′	$\breve{q}$	$\breve{q}′$	100 $\breve{q}/\breve{q}′$	1000($\breve{q}-\breve{q}′$)
Patients with Pacemaker									
1	0-1 yr	649	.876	.940	93.2%	.124	.060	205%	64
2	1-2 yrs	455	.804	882	91.2	.082	.062	132	20
3	2-3	324	.746	.826	90.3	.072	.063	114	9
4	3-4	231	.683	.772	88.5	.084	.065	129	19
5	4-5	138	.648	.721	89.9	.051	.066	77	−15
6	5-6	81	.617	.672	91.8	.048	.068	71	−20
All	0-6	649	.617	.672	91.8	.078	.064	122	14
Patients Not Treated with Pacemaker									
1	0-1 yr	113	.765	.940	81.4%	.235	.060	390%	175
2	1-2 yrs	84	.634	.882	71.9	.171	.062	275	109
3	2-3	61	.541	.826	65.5	.147	.063	235	84
4	3-4	44	.461	.772	59.7	.148	.065	230	83
All	0-4	113	.461	.772	59.7	.176	.063	280	113

* Basis of expected mortality: (1) Contemporaneous experience of standard Aetna insureds with favorable ECG; (2) Contemporaneous Canadian life tables; (3) 1961 Life Tables for England and Wales

§368–LIFE INSURANCE APPLICANTS WITH BUNDLE BRANCH BLOCK OR WIDE QRS

Reference: R. B. Singer, "Mortality in 966 Life Insurance Applicants with Bundle Branch Block or Wide QRS," Trans. Assoc. Life Ins. Med. Dir. Am., 52:94-114 (1968).

Subjects Studied: 741 male life insurance applicants to New England Mutual Life Insurance Co. 1954 through 1960, whose ECG(s) revealed any of these conduction defects: complete right or left bundle branch block (QS width 0.12 second or more); incomplete right bundle branch block (QS width under 0.12 seconds), or widened QS (0.10 seconds or more) without a characteristic bundle branch block pattern. These represented 6.8 per cent of all male applicants with ECG(s) reviewed during these years (10,900 cases). An additional 230 applicants with bundle branch or intraventricular block were located by a retrospective search of the actuarial file of policy records for which any ECG code had been entered from 1935 to 1953 inclusive, giving a total of 971 cases. Coded information included ECG characteristics, blood pressure, presence of any major cardiovascular (CV) impairment other than the ECG defect or any major non-cardiovascular impairment, as well as age, year of entry and other statistical data. "Major" impairment is meant to indicate any historical factor (e.g., heart attack) or finding on examination (e.g., heart enlargement by X-ray) serious enough to entail a rating (extra premium) on the insurance offer, or a declination. A blood pressure above the New York Heart Association normotensive range (140/90 up) was classified as a "major" CV impairment even if insurance was issued on a standard basis.

Follow-up: Applicants were followed to June 30, 1965 by the original policy issued (36 per cent), by another policy of the company (17 per cent), by policy or application records of other companies (24 per cent), by individual correspondence (3 per cent), or by use of a special tracing service (20 per cent). Only 5 cases or 0.5 per cent of the total 971 could not be traced. Because of uncertainty regarding completeness of records in the retrospective series, exposure on the 230 policyholders with insurance issued prior to 1954 was limited to the period from 1950 to the end of follow-up, all prior exposure and deaths being excluded. The experience on the 966 traced applicants therefore comprised 8349 person-years of exposure and 108 deaths from 1950 to June 30, 1965. This exclusion of the early exposure on some applicants has resulted in a smaller number of cases for the early durations than for all durations, where the experience has been reported by policy duration.

Results: Applicants with no significant CV abnormality exhibited a normal experience for those with incomplete right bundle branch block (RBBB) or wide QRS, or the group as a whole (Table 368a). The increased mortality ratio for applicants with complete RBBB and LBBB is not significant even at a 10 per cent level. By contrast a mortality ratio of 430 per cent and an EDR of 26 extra deaths per 1000 were observed in applicants with associated CHD, and in those with elevated blood pressure or other ratable CV impairment the mortality ratio ranged from 200 to 270 per cent in the four types of conduction defect, with an EDR from 8.7 to 11. For the group as a whole (CHD cases included) the mortality ratio decreased with age from 610 to about 185 per cent, with a trend to increasing EDR. The five-year survival index for the group as a whole was 94.4 per cent.

Comparative experience by duration is shown in Tables 368b-c for the 81 CHD cases and the 414 cases with other major CV defect. There was a tendency for the mortality ratio to decrease and for EDR to increase with duration. Cumulative survival ratios were 74.6 per cent for the CHD cases at 10 years and 84.6 per cent for the other CV cases at 15 years.

BUNDLE BRANCH BLOCK OR WIDE QRS

Table 368a Comparative Experience in Life Insurance Applicants by Age, ECG and Other CV Factors

ECG and Other Factors	No. of Cases	Exposure Person-Yrs	No. of Deaths Observed	No. of Deaths Expected*	Mortality Ratio	Est. 5-Yr Surv. Index	Excess Death Rate
	ℓ	E	d	d'	100 d/d'	100 P/P'	1000(d-d')/E
No Major CV Complication							
All BBB and Wide QRS	471	4078	25	27.42	91%	100.3%	−0.6
Age < 40	178	1500	4	2.89	138	99.6	0.7
40-49	173	1532	9	8.77	103	99.9	0.2
50-59	87	756	7	8.48	83	101.0	−2.0
60 up	33	290	5	7.28	69	104.1	−7.9
Complete Right BBB	81	696	7	5.65	124	99.1	1.9
Complete Left BBB	15	150	2	0.89	225	96.3	7.4
Incomplete Right BBB	212	1687	7	9.73	72	100.9	−1.6
Wide QRS (.10 sec up)	163	1544	9	11.20	80	100.7	−1.4
With Major CV Complication							
All BBB and Wide QRS	495	4274	80	31.01	260	94.4	12
Age < 30	86	777	6	0.98	610	96.8	6.5
30-39	81	718	10	1.99	500	94.5	11
40-44	78	690	10	3.02	330	95.1	10
45-49	82	667	14	4.37	320	92.9	14
50-54	64	546	13	6.07	215	93.7	13
55-59	65	566	15	8.17	184	94.0	12
60 up	39	310	12	6.41	187	91.2	18
With CHD† (All BBB and Wide QRS)	81	619	21	4.89	430	87.5	26
With Other Major CV Comp.●	414	3653	59	26.14	225	95.5	9.0
Complete Right BBB	93	815	15	7.42	200	95.4	9.3
Complete Left BBB	31	249	5	2.19	230	94.4	11
Incomplete Right BBB	128	1017	14	5.18	270	95.7	8.7
Wide QRS (.10 sec up)	162	1572	25	11.35	220	95.7	8.7

Table 368b Observed Data and Comparative Experience by Duration

Interval No.	Interval Start-End	No. Alive at start of Interval	Exposure Person-Yrs	Deaths in Interval Observed	Deaths in Interval Expected*	Mortality Ratio Interval	Mortality Ratio Cumulative	Survival Ratio Interval	Survival Ratio Cumulative	Excess Death Rate
i	t to t + Δt	ℓ	E	d	d'	100 d/d'	100 Σd/Σd'	100p_i/p_i'	100 P/P'	1000(d-d')/E
All BBB and Wide QRS with Coronary Heart Disease										
1	0- 2 yrs	79	151	4	0.58	690%	690%	95.5%	95.5%	23
2	2- 5	77	222	8	1.55	515	565	91.5	87.4	29
3	5-10	63	192	8	2.07	385	475	85.3	74.6	31
All BBB and Wide QRS with Other Major CV Defect●										
1	0- 5 yrs	403	1852	25	7.74	325%	325%	95.4%	95.4%	9.3
2	5-10	338	1222	13	9.35	139	220	98.5	94.0	3.0
3	10 up	127	581	21	9.03	235	225	90.0	84.6	21

Table 368c Derived Mortality and Survival Data

Interval No.	Interval Start-End	Observed Rates Average Mortality	Observed Rates Annual Survival	Observed Rates Interval Survival	Observed Rates Cumulative Survival	Expected Rates* Average Mortality	Expected Rates* Annual Survival	Expected Rates* Interval Survival	Expected Rates* Cumulative Survival
i	t to t + Δt	$\bar{q} = d/E$	$\bar{p}$	p_i	P	$\bar{q}' = d'/E$	$\bar{p}'$	p_i'	P'
All BBB and Wide QRS with Coronary Heart Disease									
1	0- 2 yrs	.0265	.9735	.948	.948	.0038	.9962	.9924	.9924
2	2- 5	.0360	.9640	.896	.849	.0070	.9930	.9790	.9715
3	5-10	.0417	.9583	.808	.686	.0108	.9892	.9470	.9200
All BBB and Wide QRS with Other Major CV Defect●									
1	0- 5 yrs	.0135	.9865	.934	.934	.0042	.9958	.9790	.9790
2	5-10	.0106	.9894	.948	.886	.0077	.9923	.9623	.9424
3	10-15	.0361	.9639	.832	.737	.0155	.9845	.9247	.8711

* Basis of expected deaths: 1955-60 Basic Select Table, 1957-60 Ultimate Table (Male)
† Coronary Heart Disease (CHD)
● Blood Pressure 140 up or 90 up, or Other Ratable CV Abnormality (not CHD)

§369—BUNDLE BRANCH BLOCK

References: (1) K. F. Brandon, M. H. Neill, and G. C. Streeter, "The Use of the Electrocardiogram in Twenty-Five Years of Insurance Selection," Trans. Assoc. Life Ins. Med. Dir. Am., 34:143-155 (1950).
(2) M. Rodstein, R. Gubner, J. P. Mills, J. F. Lovell, and H. E. Ungerleider, "A Mortality Study in Bundle Branch Block," Arch. Int. Med., 87:663-668 (1951).
(3) F. B. Agee, Jr., (Aetna data given in discussion of a previous paper). Proc. Med. Section, Am. Life Convention, 138-144 (1962).
(4) M. Rotman and J. H. Triebwasser, "A Clinical and Follow-up Study of Right and Left Bundle Branch Block," Circulation, 51:477-484 (1975).

Subjects Studied: (1) 29 applicants with right or left bundle branch block (BBB) in an ECG taken in conjunction with an examination for the Aetna Life Insurance Company 1924-1949, and drawn from a series of 6387 tracings coded and placed on file. Additional descriptive information on this series is given in §370.
(2) 183 applicants with right or left bundle branch block in an ECG (QRS width 0.12 seconds or more) taken in conjunction with an examination made at the Diagnostic Laboratory of the Equitable Life Assurance Society, New York, 1929-1948, and drawn from a series of about 30,000 tracings coded and placed on file. There were 131 cases with complete right BBB, and 52 cases with complete left BBB. Of the total group 36 persons had isolated BBB, 35 had ratable cardiovascular impairments, 83 would have been declined for insurance because of major cardiovascular abnormalities such as hypertension and cardiac enlargement, and only partial medical information was available in 29 cases.
(3) 719 applicants with right or left bundle branch block, complete and incomplete, in an ECG taken in conjunction with an examination for the Aetna Life Insurance Company, Hartford, Connecticut, 1950-1962, drawn from a series of 14,860 tracings coded and placed on file. Of these, 177 were excluded because the application was declined, incomplete or not taken, and 39 were excluded because of policy lapse, leaving 503 cases.
(4) 394 cases with complete right BBB and 125 cases with complete left BBB drawn from a file of ECG's on about 237,000 Air Force personnel collected by the U.S. Air Force Central Electrocardiographic Laboratory, School of Aerospace Medicine, Brooks Air Force Base, Texas, 1957-1972. These tracings were made as routine initial ECG's on flight personnel under 30 years of age, and as serial ECG's on such personnel throughout their Air Force career. Although less than five per cent of the subjects had any symptoms at the time of their examination and ECG, 44 were found to have significant cardiovascular abnormalities, such as asymptomatic hypertension, a history of angina, evidence of coronary heart disease by angiogram, congenital or valvular heart disease, etc. In the series of right BBB cases 93.5 per cent had a normal cardiovascular evaluation (except for the ECG), and in the left BBB series 83.5 per cent were otherwise normal.

Follow-up: (1) Aetna policy records were used to follow up 3802 of the applicants. On another 2585 applicants who were not Aetna policyholders follow-up was attempted through insurance records of cooperating companies or other means. Only two per cent of the series were untraced, with 93 per cent completely traced to January 1, 1950, and partial follow-up information obtained on the remaining five per cent.
(2) All except 4 cases were successfully traced to July 1, 1949.
(3) Aetna policy records were used to trace the 503 cases to April 1, 1962.
(4) Follow-up to 1973 was carried out through use of Air Force health records, questionnaires and direct telephone contact. Follow-up was complete on 372 of the 394 cases with right BBB and 114 of the 125 cases of left BBB.

§369—BUNDLE BRANCH BLOCK (continued)

Results: Comparative experience for these series of insurance applicants with bundle branch block is given in Table 369a. Associated cardiovascular abnormalities were not excluded in any of these groups, except for 36 applicants to the Equitable (Series 2), who experienced a total of eight deaths, with a mortality ratio of only 126 per cent. This may be compared with a mortality ratio of 194 per cent in cases with other cardiac risk factors. In other categories of Series 2 the right BBB cases showed a lower level of excess mortality than those with left bundle branch block. Among the insurable cases the mortality ratio was 111 per cent and the EDR 1.9 per 1000 for right BBB, in contrast to 146 per cent and 10 per 1000 for left BBB. As might be anticipated, mortality was greater when the cardiovascular abnormalities were serious enough to warrant declining the application: among these cases the mortality ratio was 186 per cent in the right BBB group and 260 per cent in the left; the corresponding excess death rates were 16 and 29 per 1000, respectively. Series 1 and Series 3 were both made up of applicants to the Aetna Life Insurance Company, the former during the period 1924-1949, and the latter a much more numerous but younger group collected 1950-1962. The mortality ratio in Series 1 was 250 per cent with an EDR of 16 per 1000, based on only 4 deaths. In Series 3 the mortality of 215 per cent was slightly less than in Series 1, but the EDR of 3.7 per 1000 was much lower.

The Air Force men with complete right bundle branch block showed a remarkably low mortality ratio of 55 per cent over a long follow-up, average almost 11 years. Three of the 14 deaths were due to aircraft accident, five to other accidental causes and only three were cardiovascular. Despite the risk of accidental death, men on active duty in the Air Force and other services tend to have a materially lower mortality than the U.S. male population. Only 6.5 per cent had a known associated cardiovascular abnormality other than the right BBB, a lower percentage than in the insurance series. If select mortality rates had been used to calculate expected deaths the mortality ratio would have been close to 100 per cent in right BBB, and over 200 per cent in left BBB. The aggregate mortality ratio for the cases with left bundle branch block against U.S. population rates was actually 129 per cent with an EDR of 2.2 per 1000. This reflects a substantially higher mortality rate than that observed in right BBB, but it should be remembered that the left BBB cases included a higher percentage of recognized cardiovascular abnormalities (about one case out of six). On an overall basis the results of this study indicate an absence of increased mortality risk in a generally healthy group of service men with right BBB, but a substantial hazard of extra mortality in the case of such men with left BBB among whom a larger proportion of other cardiovascular abnormalities is likely to be found.

BUNDLE BRANCH BLOCK

Table 369a Comparative Experience, Bundle Branch Block, Insurance Series

Ref.	Category	No. of Cases	Exposure Person-Yrs	No. of Deaths Observed	No. of Deaths Expected*	Mortality Ratio	Ave. Ann. Mort. Rate	Est. 5-Yr Surv. Index	Excess Death Rate
		ℓ	E	d	d'	100 d/d'	$\bar{q}$ = d/E	100 P/P'	1000(d-d')/E
1	Aetna, All Cases								
	Right and Left BBB	29	149	4	1.6	250%	.027	92.1%	16
2	Equitable (N.Y.)								
	Rt. BBB, Insurable	77	616†	12	10.81	111	.020	99.0	1.9
	Rt. BBB, Declinable	54	432†	15	8.06	186	.035	92.1	16
	Lt. BBB, Insurable	23	184†	6	4.11	146	.033	94.9	10
	Lt. BBB, Declinable	29	232†	11	4.21	260	.047	85.9	29
	Both, No Other CV Abn.	36	288†	8	6.35	126	.028	97.1	5.7
	Both, with CV Abn.	—	—	21	10.82	194	—	—	—
3	Aetna								
	Right and Left BBB	503	2063	14	6.45	215	0068	98.2	3.7

Table 369b Comparative Experience, Right and Left Bundle Branch Block, Air Force Men

No.	Start-End	No. of Cases	Est. Exposure† Person-Yrs	No. of Deaths Observed	No. of Deaths Expected*	Mortality Ratio	Cumulative Surv. Rate Observed	Cumulative Surv. Rate Expected*	Cumulative Surv. Ratio	Excess Death Rate
i	t to t + Δt	ℓ	E	d	d'	100 d/d'	P	P'	100 P/P'	1000(d-d')/E
	Right Bundle Branch Block									
1	0- 5 yrs	372	1712	5	8.16	61%	.986	.9764	100.9%	−1.8
2	5-10	312	1310	3	9.58	31	.974	.9412	103.5	−5.0
3	10-15	212	683	6	7.54	80	.932	.8903	104.7	−2.3
All	0-15	372	3705	14	25.28	55	.932	.8903	104.7	−3.0
	Left Bundle Branch Block									
1	0- 5 yrs	114	478	1	2.68	37%	.990	.9723	101.8%	−3.5
2	5-10	77	296	5	2.60	192	.909	.9303	97.7	8.1
3	10-15	41	129	3	1.72	174	.808	.8699	92.9	9.9
All	0-15	114	903	9	7.00	129	.808	.8699	92.9	2.2

*Basis of expected mortality: (1) Contemporaneous experience of standard Aetna insureds with favorable ECG; (2) Equitable (N.Y.) 1940-45 standard ultimate table; (3) Standard intercompany experience 1950-54; (4) U.S. total male tables (1959-61)
†Exposure estimated from partially complete information in the reference article

ARRHYTHMIAS AND ECG ABNORMALITIES

§370–QRS ABNORMALITIES

References: (1) L. D. Ostrander, Jr., "Left Axis Deviation: Prevalence, Associated Conditions, and Prognosis," Ann. Int. Med., 75:23-28 (1971).

(2) K. F. Brandon, M. H. Neill, and G. C. Streeter, "The Use of The Electrocardiogram in Twenty-five Years of Insurance Selection," Trans. Assoc. Life Ins. Med. Dir. Am., 34:143-155 (1950).

(3) R. S. Eliot, W. A. Millhon, and J. Millhon, "The Clinical Significance of Uncomplicated Marked Left Axis Deviation in Men Without Known Disease," Am. J. Card., 12:767-771 (1963).

(4) P. W. Seavey and T. S. Sexton, "Left Axis Deviation. An Electrocardiographic Mortality Study," Trans. Assoc. Life Ins. Med. Dir. Am., 54:27-34 (1970).

(5) R. S. Schaaf, "Left Anterior Hemiblock: The Prudential Experience," Trans. Assoc. Life Ins. Med. Dir. Am., 58:197-215 (1974).

(6) W. Bolt and M. F. Bell, "Prognostic Import of a Large Q3 Deflection: A Mortality Study," Trans. Assoc. Life Ins. Med. Dir. Am., 34:87-98 (1950).

Subjects Studied: (1) This series was drawn from 4678 residents, about 88 per cent of the adult population of Tecumseh, Michigan, examined in 1959-60 as part of a prospective epidemiologic study of health and disease in a community. There were 2235 men and 2443 women 20 years of age or older who had a standard 12-lead ECG, chest X-ray, blood glucose and serum cholesterol in addition to a careful history and physical examination. Of the 248 adults with left axis deviation ($-30°$ or more) 103 had this as an isolated finding, with no other historical or physical evidence of cardiovascular disease.

(2) 6387 applicants to the Aetna Life Insurance Company 1924-1949, with an ECG obtained in addition to the usual screening examination. One-half of the tracings had coded abnormalities, which were classified into 23 different categories for study. At the time of selection 6.7 per cent of the applicants were under age 30, 21.2 per cent age 30-39, 36.2 per cent age 40-49, and 35.9 per cent age 50-70, with an average age of 46 years. Reasons for obtaining the tracings in a 1948-1949 sample were amount of insurance and related considerations in 23 per cent, medical history in 50 per cent, examination findings in 14 per cent, and loan with a physician's report in 13 per cent. The study included some categories with isolated ECG defect and many in which the defect was associated with other ECG or cardiovascular abnormalities.

(3) 195 U. S. Army men with isolated left axis deviation found in routine 13-lead ECG's at the U. S. Army Hospital, Fort Hood, Texas. These were screened from about 5200 examinations performed annually on active-duty personnel. Men with known *pre-existing* cardiovascular disease, renal disease, diabetes, or with current ECG abnormalities were excluded. The age range was 23 to 61 years, with an average of 41 years.

(4) 1257 male applicants to Massachusetts Mutual Life Insurance Company with isolated left axis deviation (LAD) screened from a file of 31,689 tracings made from 1930 to early 1966. All of these applicants were issued standard insurance, evidence that no other significant risk factor was discovered through the customary insurance screening procedure, which, in these cases had included an ECG as well.

(5) 273 cases with ECG criteria of left anterior hemiblock (LAH—including left axis deviation of $-45°$ or more) were found by reviewing about 40,000 tracings in a medical file of 15,000 home office employees of the Prudential Life Insurance Company, dating back to 1933. Of this total 110 cases of isolated LAH were extracted for follow-up study by excluding cases with additional ECG abnormality, other cardiovascular-renal disease, or a blood pressure exceeding 150/90. Cases with diabetes, cancer and tuberculosis were also excluded. All employees were under the age of 65 and actively at work in the initial part of follow-up; most had more than one tracing on file.

(6) 340 cases with prominent Q wave in lead 3 of ECG's on file at the New York Life Insurance Company. The tracings and related examinations were all made in the period from 1930 to 1941 in connection with an insurance application (69 per cent) or a medical disability application (31 per cent). There were 131 cases with associated cardiovascular abnormalities such as significant history, hypertension, organic murmurs, or cardiac enlargement (most of these cases were disability claimants), and 209 cases with Q3 in the ECG as the only significant "abnormality" (all insurance applicants). Only a few cases were in women, and the age distribution for the two groups was as follows:

	Age 21-30 yrs	31-40 yrs	41-50 yrs	51-60 yrs	61-70 yrs	Total
Isolated Q3	7 (3%)	54 (26%)	92 (44%)	48 (23%)	8 (4%)	209
Q3 with Other CV Abn.	0 (0%)	13 (10%)	51 (39%)	59 (45%)	8 (6%)	131

§370–QRS ABNORMALITIES (continued):

Follow-up: (1) The first series of examinations in the Tecumseh Study was conducted in 1959-1960, the second series in 1962-1965. The time between examinations varied from 20 to 72 months, with a median of 47 months. Of the 103 persons with isolated LAD at initial study 77 were re-examined, and death certificates were obtained in the nine deaths that occurred, all in subjects prior to re-examination.

(2) Follow-up was carried out on 3802 cases through records of insurance issued by the Aetna. Follow-up on cases with no Aetna insurance in force at the time of follow-up was accomplished through a search of insurance records by cooperating companies and through other measures. Of the total group of 6387 persons, 93 per cent were traced to January 1, 1950, five per cent were traced for partial follow-up, and only two per cent were completely untraced.

(3) Subjects were followed up through re-examination, and medical records at the Army Hospital, Fort Hood. There were no losses to follow-up, which lasted 22 months for 95 per cent of the study group, and shorter periods for five per cent.

(4) Policy records of the Massachusetts Mutual Life Insurance Company were used for follow-up of subjects to the policy anniversary in 1969 or the date of death or other early termination.

(5) Clinic and personnel benefit records were used to follow up employees not only during active work but also in retirement for those past age 65.

(6) Policy and claim records were used for follow-up, which was completed in 1949.

Results: Data from the Tecumseh series in Table 370a demonstrate that prevalence of left axis deviation in this adult population increased from a very low level at the youngest ages to a maximum above 200 per 1000 at the oldest. The prevalence was higher in males than in females, especially in cases of isolated LAD under age 60. Although 58 per cent of the total group with LAD did manifest other evidence of cardiovascular disease at the outset, the cases with isolated LAD showed no excess morbidity or mortality during the follow-up period above that expected in the Tecumseh population matched by age and sex.

Comparative experience for three other series of cases with LAD is given with the mortality experience in the Tecumseh population in the upper part of Table 370b. Two groups of insureds with isolated LAD had an observed mortality very close to that expected: a mortality ratio of 119 per cent and EDR of 2.3 in the Aetna series of 414 cases with 32 deaths in an average follow-up of 5.4 years. The Massachusetts Mutual cases with isolated LAD constituted an even larger series, with over 1200 entrants followed an average of 8.7 years. The QRS axis ranged from $-15°$ to $-30°$ in about one-third of this group, with a mortality ratio of 103 per cent and an EDR of 0.3 per 1000. For the larger fraction of this series, with more severe LAD, $-30°$ or more, there was still no significant excess mortality, the ratio of observed to expected being 109 per cent and the EDR 1.0 per 1000. Some of this experience was accumulated prior to 1950, when mortality rates in general showed a downward trend associated with the impact of antibiotics on infectious disease mortality. If contemporaneous mortality rates for standard insureds had been used for the earlier part of this experience instead of the 1955-60 rates, somewhat higher values of d' would have been derived, resulting in even lower mortality ratios than those reported. The much smaller Army experience (195 men followed less than two years, Series 3) did reveal a mortality ratio of 385 per cent and an EDR of 13 per 1000, based on only six deaths, however. As far as LAD is concerned this excess mortality is more apparent than real, because only 61 per cent of the men had isolated LAD. The screening procedure brought to light significant risk factors, such as a history of angina, hypertension (diastolic pressure exceeding 90 mm.), abnormal ECG response to exercise, and abnormal glucose tolerance test in the remaining 39 per cent. The authors do not indicate which of the six deaths occurred in the men with these cardiovascular complications.

Series 5, giving the experience with 110 employees with isolated left anterior hemiblock, is included in this abstract rather than in §369 on conduction defects, because the principal ECG characteristic is an LAD between $-45°$ and $-90°$. The unusually long follow-up averaging over 15 years was possible because of the retrospective identification of the tracings with LAH in a file going back to 1933, as hemiblocks are a relatively recent electrocardiographic concept. The experience with these cases having isolated LAH yielded fewer observed than expected deaths in employees under age 60, but a mortality ratio of 198 per cent and EDR of 30 per 1000 in older employees age 60 up. The excess mortality is significant at the one per cent level, based on 18 observed and 9.08 expected deaths. The excess was found in both male and female older employees, but the female exposure was very small.

ARRHYTHMIAS AND ECG ABNORMALITIES

§370–QRS ABNORMALITIES

Results (continued):

Prominent Q Waves in lead 3, suspicious or abnormal, are the subject of two insurance studies in Table 370b. In the Aetna file there were 162 cases of Q3 less than one-fourth of the maximum QRS deflection in the standard leads, with a favorable mortality experience. However, in a group of similar size but with a deeper Q3 the mortality ratio was 169 per cent and EDR 7.7 per 1000. In the New York Life Study (Series 6) the mortality observed was also close to that expected, even for cases with Q3 having a duration of 0.04 or more or associated with a Q2, in cases without other significant cardiovascular abnormality. Mortality ratios for cases with other cardiovascular abnormality were 200 per cent for those with Q3 less than 0.04 seconds in duration, and 176 per cent for those with wider (presumably "pathological") Q3. Despite this negative evidence from total mortality in the New York Life series, the authors reported an increased mortality ratio of 256 per cent for deaths due to cardiovascular causes (11 such deaths observed) in cases with isolated Q3 of 0.04 seconds or more, in contrast to a corresponding ratio of 90 per cent when the Q3 width was less than 0.04 seconds. The cardiovascular mortality ratios averaged about 2½ times the total mortality ratios in the group with other cardiovascular abnormality. The original article should be consulted for more detailed data than those given in Table 370b.

The final QRS abnormality for which data were available was low amplitude, maximum under 5 mm. in the standard leads. In such cases drawn from the Aetna series the mortality experience was favorable (ratio of 106 per cent) even in the total group, which included a preponderance of insureds with some cardiovascular abnormality other than the low QRS amplitude.

QRS ABNORMALITIES

Table 370a   Prevalence of Left Axis Deviation by Sex and Age, Tecumseh Study

Series	Category	Sex	Prevalence Rates per 1000 (No. of Cases)							
			20-29 yrs	30-39 yrs	40-49 yrs	50-59 yrs	60-69 yrs	70-79 yrs	80 yrs up	All Ages
1	All Cases LAD	M	11 (5)	35 (24)	56 (26)	85 (28)	180 (32)	257 (26)	231 (6)	66 (147)
		F	7 (4)	14 (10)	21 (10)	58 (19)	148 (29)	151 (18)	256 (11)	41 (101)
1	Isolated LAD	M	4 (2)	19 (13)	28 (13)	45 (15)	78 (14)	89 (9)	115 (3)	31 (69)
		F	2 (1)	4 (3)	13 (6)	15 (5)	61 (12)	50 (6)	23 (1)	14 (34)

Table 370b   Comparative Experience Left Axis Deviation, Hemiblock, Abnormal Q Waves and Low Amplitude, Various Series

Series	Category	No. of Cases	Exposure Person-Yrs	No. of Deaths		Mortality Ratio	Ave. Ann. Mort. Rate	Est. 5-Yr Surv. Index	Excess Death Rate
				Observed	Expected*				
		ℓ	E	d	d'	100 d/d'	$\bar{q}=d/E$	100 P/P'	1000(d-d')/E
	Left Axis Deviation								
1	Tecumseh Population								
	Isolated LAD −30° up	103	386	9	⩾9	⩽100%	.023	⩾100%	⩽0
2	Insureds (Aetna)								
	Isolated LAD	414	2256	32	26.9	119	.0142	98.8	2.3
3	Army Men								
	LAD −30° up (39% CV+)†	195	346	6	1.56	385	.0173	93.7	13
4	Insureds (Mass. Mut.)								
	Isolated LAD −15° to −30°	421	3302	29	28.04	103	.0088	99.9	0.3
	Isolated LAD −30° up	836	7691	86	78.67	109	.0112	99.5	1.0
	Isolated Left Anterior Hemiblock (Axis −45° up)								
5	Employees (Prudential)								
	M&F Age <50	—	852	7	9.16	76%	.0082	101.4%	−2.5
	50-59	—	515	9	10.51	86	.0175	101.5	−2.9
	60 up	—	300	18	9.08	198	.060	85.7	30
	Male, All Ages	84	1283	29	23.18	125	.0226	97.7	4.5
	Female, All Ages	26	384	5	5.58	90	.0130	100.8	−1.5
	Abnormal Q Wave, Lead 3								
2	Insureds (Aetna)								
	Q < ¼ max. R	162	1171	9	11.8	76%	.0077	101.2%	−2.4
	Q ⩾ ¼ max. R	164	1168	22	13.0	169	.0188	96.1	7.7
6	Insureds (N.Y. Life)								
	Q < 0.04 sec., no Q2	94	—	11	11.52	95	—	—	—
	Q 0.04 sec. up or Q2	104	—	15	14.54	103	—	—	—
6	With Other CV Abn.								
	Q < 0.04 sec., no Q2	39	—	11	5.50	200	—	—	—
	Q 0.04 sec. up or Q2	87	—	29	16.49	176	—	—	—
	Low QRS under 5 mm., Standard Leads								
2	Insureds (Aetna)								
	All Cases	212	1556	19	17.9	106%	.0122	99.6%	0.7
	Isolated Low QRS	64	452	1	4.6	22	.0022	104.1	−8.0

* Basis of expected mortality: (1) Tecumseh series mortality; (2) Contemporaneous experience of standard Aetna insureds with favorable ECG; (3) U. S. Life Tables, total male, attained age 42, (1959-61); (4) 1955-60 Basic Select and Ultimate Tables; (5) 1955-60 Basic Select and Ultimate Tables; (6) Contemporaneous N. Y. Life standard experience

† Includes 54 men with angina or hypertension, 10 with positive exercise test, and 13 with latent diabetes mellitus, developed on the screening studies

ARRHYTHMIAS AND ECG ABNORMALITIES

§371–LEFT VENTRICULAR HYPERTROPHY

References: (1) W. B. Kannel, T. Gordon and D. Offutt, "Left Ventricular Hypertrophy by Electrocardiogram Prevalence, Incidence, and Mortality in the Framingham Study," Ann. Int. Med., 71:89-105 (1971).
(2) D. Shurtleff, "The Framingham Study, Section 26. Some Characteristics Related to The Incidence of Cardiovascular Disease and Death," Govt. Printing Office, Washington, D. C. (December 1970).

Subjects Studied: Examinee-participants in the Framingham Heart Study who developed left ventricular hypertrophy (LVH) pattern in one or more routine electrocardiograms taken during the 14-year interval from the initial examination about 1950 to the eighth biennial examination, about 1964. There were 76 subjects out of 5,209 with definite LVH at the initial examination, and an additional 157 developed this pattern as a new ECG finding at Examinations 2 through 7. Definite LVH was defined as a prolonged ventricular activation time of 0.05 seconds or more associated with an increased R wave, depressed S-T segment, and flattened or inverted T waves in the left chest leads. Many of the 233 subjects with definite LVH pattern had pre-existing or associated cardiovascular abnormalities: hypertension (140/90 and up) in 192 subjects and cardiomegaly by X-ray in 49 subjects, first observed at the initial exam; and diagnosis of coronary heart disease in 43 subjects, congestive heart failure in 22 subjects, and rheumatic heart disease in 9 subjects, such diagnoses having been made at any time prior to the exam at which definite LVH was first noted. For additional information on the Framingham Study subjects see §380. Distribution of cases and prevalence rates by age at exam and sex were as follows:

Age at Examination (Years)	29-44	45-54	55-64	65-74	Total
Males - No. of Exams	5147	5477	3977	985	15586
Prevalence*	5.6(29)	14.4(79)	30.7(122)	44.7(44)	17.6(279)
Females - No. of Exams	6299	6915	5135	1348	19697
Prevalence*	3.0(19)	7.4(51)	24.9(128)	36.4(49)	12.5(247)

*Cases per 1000 Exams. (Number of cases in parentheses.)

Follow-up: Life table data have been presented in Reference 1, based on LVH first observed at Examinations 1 through 7, followed to Examination 8 about 1964. The period of follow-up was extended to the ninth examination about 1966, in Reference 2. Expected mortality rates were derived from the Framingham experience for subjects without definite LVH. For further information on follow-up methods consult the references and §380.

Results: As shown in Tables 371a-b mortality was high in subjects with LVH in the Framingham Study, with 102 deaths out of 233 entrants up to the 1964 anniversary, or 19.2 per cent of *all* deaths in this period. Interval mortality ratios exhibit a downward trend with duration in men, but are relatively constant in women. Corresponding values of EDR show an irregular fluctuation in men, and an upward trend in women over the 14-year follow-up period. Mortality ratios are higher for males than for females, and corresponding survival ratios are lower.

Table 371c presents comparative experience by age on a short-range basis, the exposure in two-year intervals between successive examinations, and Table 371d long-range experience by age from Examinations 1, 2, or 3 to the ninth examination, 12 to 16 years later. These results suggest a downward trend in mortality ratio with age, but an upward trend in EDR. However, there are very few deaths in the age group 35-44, and other irregularities, so these trends must be viewed with caution. A higher mortality and lower survival for males as compared with females is found in these tables as in Tables 371a-b.

Comment: Experience with cases of possible LVH pattern is also presented in Reference 1, together with much additional information not shown in Tables 371a-d. Of the subjects free of LVH at Exam 1, 157 developed definite LVH and 202 developed possible LVH in the 12 years to Exam 7, a total of 7.5 per cent for the cohort. The probability of developing definite LVH was much greater for those with possible LVH than for those without. Excess mortality was a less prominent feature of the possible LVH experience than it was in subjects with definite LVH.

LEFT VENTRICULAR HYPERTROPHY BY ELECTROCARDIOGRAM

Table 371a   Observed Data and Comparative Experience by Duration — All Ages Combined (Definite Cases)

Sex	Interval* No.	Interval* Start-End	No. Alive at Start of Interval	Deaths during Interval	Cumulative Mortality	Mortality Ratio Ave. Ann.	Mortality Ratio Cumulative	Survival Ratio Interval	Survival Ratio Cumulative	Excess Death Rate
	i	t to t + Δt	ℓ	d	Q	100 $\check{q}/\check{q}'$	100 Q/Q'	100 p_i/p_i'	100 P/P'	1000($\check{q}-\check{q}'$)
Male	1	0- 2 yrs	137	21	.153	440%	430%	87.8%	87.8%	62
	2	2- 4	102	13	.261	300	335	91.2	80.1	44
	3	4- 8	80	26	.511	365	295	73.8	59.1	71
	4	8-14	39	10	.668	173	199	84.5	49.9	26
Female	1	0- 2 yrs	96	4	.042	295	295	97.2	97.2	14
	2	2- 4	83	6	.111	450	365	94.3	91.7	29
	3	4- 8	72	11	.253	420	365	87.5	80.3	33
	4	8-14	44	11	.506	415	325	72.9	58.5	51

Table 371b   Derived Mortality and Survival Data (Definite Cases)

Sex	Interval No.	Interval Start-End	Observed Rates Cumulative Survival	Observed Rates Interval Survival	Observed Rates Geom. Mean Ann. Surv.	Observed Rates Geom. Mean Ann. Mort.	Expected Rates† Cumulative Survival	Expected Rates† Interval Survival	Expected Rates† Geom. Mean Ann. Surv.	Expected Rates† Geom. Mean Ann. Mort.
	i	t to t + Δt	P	p_i	$\check{p}$	$\check{q}$	P'	p_i'	$\check{p}'$	$\check{q}'$
Male	1	0- 2 yrs	.847	.847	.920	.080	.9642	.9642	.9819	.0181
	2	2- 4	.739	.873	.934	.066	.9224	.9566	.9781	.0219
	3	4- 8	.489	.662	.902	.098	.8273	.8969	.9732	.0268
	4	8-14	.332	.679	.938	.062	.6649	.8037	.9642	.0358
Female	1	0- 2 yrs	.958	.958	.979	.021	.9858	.9858	.9929	.0071
	2	2- 4	.889	.928	.963	.037	.9697	.9837	.9918	.0082
	3	4- 8	.747	.840	.957	.043	.9308	.9599	.9898	.0102
	4	8-14	.494	.661	.933	.067	.8440	.9067	.9838	.0162

Table 371c   Observed Data and Two-Year Comparative Experience by Attained Age and Definite LVH at Last Biennial Examination

Sex	Attained Age	Exposure Person-Yrs	Deaths Observed	Ave. Ann. Mort. Rate	Stand. Mort. Rate (No LVH)	Mortality Ratio	Survival Ratio	Excess Death Rate
	(Years)	E	d	$\bar{q} = d/E$	$\bar{q}'$	100 $\bar{q}/\bar{q}'$	100 P/P'	1000($\bar{q}-\bar{q}'$)
Male	35-44	68	2	.029	.0021	1400%	94.6%	27
	45-54	272	17	.062	.0068	915	89.1	55
	55-64	484	38	.079	.0134	590	87.2	66
	65-74	258	24	.093	.0265	350	86.8	66
Female	35-44	56	2	.036	.0014	2600	93.2	35
	45-54	146	5	.034	.0046	750	94.1	29
	55-64	454	13	.029	.0062	460	95.5	23
	65-74	270	23	.085	.0134	635	86.0	72

Table 371d   Observed Data and Long-Range Comparative Experience by Entry Age, Definite LVH (Exams 1, 2 and 3 combined) to 8th Examination (12-16 years later)

Sex	Entry Age	Combined Entrants (Exams 1,2,3)	Combined Deaths (to Exam 8)	Cumulative Mortality (Ave. 14 yrs)	Cumulative Survival (Ave. 14 yrs)	Ave. Ann. Mort. Rate	Standard Mort. Rate	Mortality Ratio	Survival Ratio	Excess Death Rate
	(Years)	$\Sigma\ell$	Σd	Q = $\Sigma d/\Sigma\ell$	P	$\check{q}$	$\check{q}'$	100 $\check{q}/\check{q}'$	100 P/P'	1000($\check{q}-\check{q}'$)
Male	35-44	22	9	.409	.591	.037	.0054	685%	63.7%	32
	45-54	63	42	.667	.333	.075	.0124	610	39.7	63
	55-64	90	70	.778	.222	.102	.0227	450	30.6	79
Female	35-44	11	4	.364	.636	.032	.0037	860	67.0	28
	45-54	42	23	.548	.452	.055	.0068	810	49.7	48
	55-64	75	40	.533	.467	.053	.0117	450	55.0	41

* After first appearance of LVH

† Basis of expected mortality: experience for Framingham subjects without LVH

ARRHYTHMIAS AND ECG ABNORMALITIES

§374–ABNORMAL T WAVES

References: (1) C. E. Kiessling, R. S. Schaaf, and A. M. Lyle, "A Reevaluation of the T-Wave Changes in the Electrocardiograms of Otherwise Normal Individuals," Trans. Assoc. Life Ins. Med. Dir. Am., 45:70-80 (1961). See also C. E. Kiessling, R. S. Schaaf, and A. M. Lyle, "A Study of T Wave Changes in the Electrocardiograms of Normal Individuals," Am. J. Card., 13:598-602 (1964).

(2) A. M. Lyle, "Selection of Applicants for Insurance with Isolated T-Wave Abnormalities in the Electrocardiogram," Trans. Soc. Actuaries, 17:357-366 (1965).

(3) K. F. Brandon, M. H. Neill, and G. C. Streeter, "The Use of the Electrocardiogram in Twenty-five Years of Insurance Selection," Trans. Assoc. Life Ins. Med. Dir. Am., 34:143-155 (1950).

(4) M. Rodstein, L. Wolloch, and R. S. Gubner, "The Significance of Minor Electrocardiographic T Wave Changes. A Mortality Study of 518 Applicants for Insurance," Am. J. Med. Sci., 252:21-25 (1966).

(5) F. I. Pitkin, "The Prognostic Significance of Non-specific T-Wave Changes in the Chest Leads in an Insured Population," Trans. Assoc. Life Ins. Med. Dir. Am., 48:235-249 (1964).

Subjects Studied: (1) From a file of 30,000 electrocardiograms collected at the Home Office of The Prudential Insurance Company in Newark, New Jersey from 1933-1959, ECG's on 422 male employees were selected on the basis of the following criteria: the ECG showed only minor T wave changes and was normal in all other respects; the employee was between the ages of 40 and 69, with no other evidence of ratable disease, cardiovascular or noncardiovascular, and with no history of suspicious chest pain. A control group was also selected, consisting of 1805 male employees of similar age and history, but with a normal ECG exhibiting normal T waves. Minor T wave changes were defined as low, notched or flat, even slightly inverted or diphasic in the presence of a low QRS, or as deeply inverted in the presence of a downward QRS in leads aVF and aVL. Low T waves in lead 1 with horizontal QRS axis and in lead 2 with vertical axis were considered normal, as were inverted T waves in leads 3, V1 and V2. Abnormal progression of T wave amplitude in the left chest leads was also regarded as a minor change even if of normal amplitude and upright.

(2) From the same Prudential ECG file of Home Office employees described in Series 1 data were extracted on 471 men age 40-69 with isolated minor or major T wave abnormalities. These cases entered into observation from 1933 to 1963 and were subdivided into five groups: 288 with no symptoms; 102 with symptoms considered to be noncardiac; 26 with symptoms suspicious of coronary disease (CHD); 28 with angina pectoris; and 27 with coronary occlusion at least two months prior to the first ECG. Cases with hypertension, other disease ratable for insurance, and abnormalities in their ECG other than T waves were excluded (this applies also to CHD patients with abnormal Q waves or ST segment deviations). Minor T waves were as defined in Series 1; major T waves were diphasic or inverted in the presence of a predominantly upward QRS. However, inverted T waves were not regarded as abnormal in leads 3, aVR, V1 and V2. If a minor T wave abnormality changed to a major one, or if CHD developed during the period of observation the case was entered again into the appropriate group; some cases were therefore included in two or more groups. A control group of 1952 men age 40-69 with normal ECG and no CHD or other significant disease was also observed in follow-up.

(3) 548 applicants with low T wave and 164 with diphasic or inverted T wave, in leads 1 or 2 of an ECG taken in conjunction with an examination for the Aetna Life Insurance Company, 1924-1949, and drawn from a series of 6387 tracings coded and placed on file. Additional descriptive information on this series is given in §370.

(4) 518 applicants with minor T wave abnormality in an ECG taken in conjunction with an examination made at the home office of the Equitable Life Assurance Society in New York, 1946-1953, and drawn from a file of about 20,000 cases. Minor T waves were defined as low amplitude (under 1 mm.), notched or flat in leads 1, 2, V3-V6. Cases were excluded if other significant ECG abnormality was present (including diphasic or inverted T waves in the leads mentioned), if the low T wave was confined to leads aVL, aVF, V1 or V2, or low in the presence of an R wave under 5 mm. or if tachycardia was present. Cases with major clinical abnormality were also excluded. All but 17 of the cases were men. The age distribution was as follows: 3 per cent age 20-29; 22 per cent, 30-39; 44 per cent, 40-49; 26 per cent, 50-59; 5 per cent, 60-69.

(5) 612 applicants with abnormal chest lead T waves in an ECG reviewed in connection with an insurance application to the New England Mutual Life Insurance Company, 1954-1960, and drawn from a file of 18,450 ECG's on 13,192 applicants. Cases with blood pressure elevation or chest pain classified as noncardiovascular were identified and analyzed together with asymptomatic individuals, but cases with other major impairments were excluded. Other cases excluded were those with any chest lead abnormality of rhythm, the P wave, QRS complex or ST segment. All the cases were men, and about one-third were under age 40. Minor T wave abnormalities included low amplitude ($T < 1/7$ of R), notching and tall T waves; diphasic or inverted T waves were major abnormalities.

ABNORMAL T WAVES

Table 374a   Comparative Mortality, Isolated Minor T Waves in the ECG of Otherwise Normal Male Prudential Employees, 1933-1960

Category	Interval Start-End	No. of Cases	No. of Deaths Observed*	No. of Deaths Expected†	Mortality Ratio	Later Cor. Occlusion
	t to t + Δt	ℓ	d	d'	100 d/d'	% ℓ
Normal T Waves and ECG	0-5 yrs	1805	29 (10)	34.1	85%	1%
	5 yrs up	1776	116 (42)	152.6	76	4
	All	1805	145 (52)	185.9	78	6
Minor T Waves in aVL Only	0-5 yrs	132	8 (2)	3.94	203	3
	5 yrs up	124	10 (4)	8.85	113	7
	All	132	18 (6)	12.86	140	9
Minor T Waves in aVF Only	All	63	3 (1)	3.85	78	3
Minor T Waves in Other Leads	0-5 yrs	227	18 (11)	5.42	332	8
	5 yrs up	209	26 (14)	17.11	152	9
	All	227	44 (25)	22.45	196	16
All Minor T Waves	All	422	65 (32)	39.2	166	12

Table 374b   Comparative Experience, Prudential Male Employees with Minor or Major T Waves, 1933-1964

Category	No. of Cases	Exposure Person-Yrs	No. of Deaths Observed	No. of Deaths Expected●	Mortality Ratio	Est. 5-Yr Surv. Index	Excess Death Rate
	ℓ	E	d	d'	100 d/d'	100 P/P'	1000(d-d')/E
Minor T Waves							
Noncardiac or No Symptoms	372	3832	53	37.08	143%	98.0%	4.2
Suspicious CHD Symptoms	27	238	4	2.22	180	96.3	7.5
Manifest Cor. Ht. Dis.	64	525	25	6.18	405	83.1	36
Major T Waves							
Noncardiac or No Symptoms	61	653	12	7.60	158	96.6	6.7
Suspicious CHD Symptoms	12	106	2	0.84	240	94.6	11
Manifest Cor. Ht. Dis.	40	280	15	2.33	645	79.1	45
Minor T Waves Returned to Normal							
Noncardiac or No Symptoms	142	1122	20	10.22	196	95.7	8.7
Suspicious CHD Symptoms	10	70	1	0.66	152	97.5	4.9
Manifest Cor. Ht. Dis.	18	175	6	1.60	375	87.9	25

*Deaths from coronary occlusion in parentheses
†Basis of expected mortality: 1946-49 Basic Tables, Select and Ultimate
●Basis of expected mortality: 1955-60 Basic Select Table (Male) and 1957-60 Ultimate Table, adjusted to 92.5% mortality ratio observed for normal male employee control group with normal ECG

ARRHYTHMIAS AND ECG ABNORMALITIES

§374–ABNORMAL T WAVES (continued):

Follow-up: (1) Cases were followed to June 30, 1960 through clinic, personnel and benefit records for an average duration of about 8 years.

(2) Cases were followed to June 30, 1964 as in Series 1 for an average of 12.4 years.

(3) Aetna and other policy records were used to trace the cases to July 1, 1949 (average duration 7 years).

(4) Insurance records were used to trace the cases to December 31, 1962 for an average of 9.2 years.

(5) Follow-up to January 1, 1964 was carried out through policy records of the New England Mutual and other companies where insurance was in force. Average duration was 4.0 years.

Results: Comparative experience is given in Tables 374a-b for the two studies of Prudential employees with T wave abnormalities. The authors point out the rarity of major T wave change in a carefully evaluated male population when the presence of known cardiovascular disease is excluded. Minor T wave abnormalities were more common, and showed an overall mortality ratio of 166 per cent in the first study. All mortality ratios related to T wave abnormalities in Series 1 (Table 374a) should be compared to the ratio of 78 per cent in the control group of healthy employees with normal ECG's. Low, flat or notched T waves in lead aVF only were associated with a normal mortality in a small group of 63 employees. However, when the T wave abnormality was in lead aVL alone the mortality ratio was 140 per cent, based on 18 deaths, and when in other leads, 196 per cent, based on 44 deaths. In both groups the mortality ratio was about twice as great in the first five years as afterward: most of the excess mortality was therefore concentrated in the earlier part of follow-up. In the second study major T wave changes were studied in addition to minor ones. In otherwise normal employees minor T wave changes were accompanied by an excess death rate of 4.2 per 1000 and a mortality ratio of 143 per cent. In a smaller group with major T wave changes these indices were somewhat higher; 6.7 per 1000 and 158 per cent, respectively. Larger differences and greater excess mortality were encountered in employees with CHD: a mortality ratio of 405 per cent for those with isolated minor T wave change in their ECG, and 645 per cent for those with isolated major T wave changes (in the absence of abnormal Q, ST segment or other ECG characteristic). Some excess mortality was found in employees with a previous major T wave change which returned to normal.

The Aetna Study on persons insured despite the presence of abnormal T wave in leads 1 or 2 also showed excess mortality: a mortality ratio just under 200 per cent and EDR close to 9 per 1000 for low T wave in lead 1 or both leads 1 and 2, and a mortality ratio of 148 per cent, EDR 5.1 per 1000, when lead 2 alone was involved (Table 374c). The excess death rate was substantially higher, 17 per 1000, with a mortality ratio of 220 per cent, for inverted T waves in leads 1 or 2. The Equitable experience on insureds with minor T wave abnormalities was normal for those under age 50 at time of application, but the mortality ratio was 138 per cent and EDR 3.9 per 1000 in older applicants (Table 374d). When all ages were combined the EDR of 1.1 per 1000 in the Equitable series was substantially lower than the EDR of 5 to 10 per 1000 for the categories of low T wave in leads 1 or 2 in the Aetna series. Possibly this difference may be related to the admixture of low T waves in the left chest leads of uncertain significance in the Equitable insureds (low T waves in the unipolar limb leads alone were excluded). The apparently benign character of minor T wave changes in the chest leads receives some support from the mortality ratio of 84 per cent in the New England Mutual applicants with normal blood pressure (Table 374e). This is in contrast to a mortality ratio of 280 per cent and EDR of 8.1 per 1000 for major T wave changes (diphasic or inverted T waves). In this New England Mutual study the expected deaths were adjusted upward by the amount indicated by age and blood pressure level from the results of the 1959 Build and Blood Pressure Study. In cases with elevated blood pressure there was an EDR of 4.8 per 1000 in the presence of minor T wave changes, but no excess mortality in the very small group with major T wave changes in the chest leads. In addition, there was no evidence of significant increased mortality in three small groups with notching of T waves, tall T waves, and localized variation of amplitude.

ABNORMAL T WAVES

Table 374c Comparative Experience, Aetna Insureds with Abnormal T Waves, 1924-1949

Category	No. of Cases	Exposure Person-Yrs	No. of Deaths Observed	No. of Deaths Expected*	Mortality Ratio	Est. 5-Yr Surv. Index†	Excess Death Rate
	ℓ	E	d	d'	100 d/d'	100 P/P'	1000(d-d')/E
Low T Wave Lead 1	284	1917	36	18.8	191%	95.5%	9.0
Low T Wave Lead 2	171	1346	21	14.2	148	97.4	5.1
Low T Leads 1 and 2	93	691	14	7.2	194	95.1	9.8
Inverted T, Leads 1 or 2	164	1345	42	19.0	220	91.6	17

Table 374d Comparative Experience, Equitable Insurance Applicants with Minor T Wave Abnormalities, 1946-1962

Age at Entry	No. of Cases	Exposure Person-Yrs	No. of Deaths Observed	No. of Deaths Expected●	Mortality Ratio	Est. 5-Yr Surv. Index†	Excess Death Rate
	ℓ	E	d	d'	100 d/d'	100 P/P'	1000(d-d')/E
Under 50 Yrs	357	3300□	12	12.37	97%	100.1%	−0.1
50 Yrs and up	161	1488□	21	15.20	138	98.1	3.9
All Ages	518	4788	33	27.57	120	99.5	1.1

Table 374e Comparative Experience, New England Mutual Insurance Applicants with Abnormal Chest Lead T Waves, 1954-1963

Category	No. of Cases	Exposure Person-Yrs	No. of Deaths Observed	No. of Deaths Expected■	Mortality Ratio	Est. 5-Yr Surv. Index†	Excess Death Rate
	ℓ	E	d	d'	100 d/d'	100 P/P'	1000(d-d')/E
Cases with Normal BP							
Normal T Waves	462	2651	6	7.11	84%	100.2%	−0.4
Minor T Waves	240	1401	5	6.19	81	100.4	−0.8
Major T Waves	112	634	8	2.86	280	96.0	8.1
Cases with Elevated BP							
Minor T Waves	118	690	10	6.67	150	97.6	4.8
Major T Waves	56	346	3	3.78	79	101.1	−2.3
Normal and Elevated BP							
Notched T Waves	78	441	2	3.33	60	101.5	−3.0
Tall T Waves	86	474	1	1.56	64	100.6	−1.2
Localized T Waves	68	396	4	2.65	150	98.3	3.4

*Basis of expected mortality: contemporaneous risks with normal ECG
†$P=\bar{p}^5 = (1-d/E)^5$ $P'=\bar{p}'^5 = (1-d'/E)^5$
●Basis of expected mortality: 1953-58 Equitable Select Standard Mortality Table
□Estimated from ℓ and average duration 9.24 years for entire group
■Basis of expected mortality: 1955-60 Basic Select Tables and 1957-60 Ultimate Tables. Expected deaths with elevated BP (140/90 or above and ratable for insurance) calculated by multiplying standard expected deaths by mortality ratio factor appropriate to age and blood pressure, from 1959 Build and Blood Pressure Study.

ARRHYTHMIAS AND ECG ABNORMALITIES

§375–POSTEXERCISE ECG

References: (1) A. M. Master, L. Pordy, and K. Chesky, "Two-Step Exercise Electrocardiogram. Follow-up investigation in Patients with Chest Pain and Normal Resting Electrocardiogram." J. Am. Med. Assoc., 151:458-462 (1953).
(2) G.E. Dimond, "The Exercise Test and Prognosis of Coronary Heart Disease," Circulation, 24:736-738 (1961).

Subjects Studied: (1) 300 consecutive patients examined by A.M.M. in 1946 because of definite or suspected coronary heart disease (CHD), all with a normal resting ECG. The standardized single exercise test (Master's test) was repeated as a double test if the response to the single test was negative. The criteria for a positive test were an ST depression of 0.5 mm. or more below the baseline (PR segment), or T wave inversion in leads 1, 2 or V4 or V5. The patients were characterized as follows with respect to age, sex, presenting symptoms and final diagnosis (at the end of follow-up):

Presenting Symptoms	Negative Response	Positive Response	Final Diagnosis	Negative Response	Positive Response
Chest Pain	95*	108	Normal	9	0
Hypertension	14	9	Functional	86	15†
Arrhythmias	10	16	Hypertension	41	0
Dyspnea or Fatigue	9	4	Prior Cor. Occlusion	7	17
Heart Failure	0	2	Prior Cor. Insuff.	0	45
Coronary Occlusion	5	6	Later Cor. Occlusion	1	6
Other CHD	0	2	Later Cor. Insuff.	0	18
Rheumatic Ht. Dis.	2	0	Angina	0	49
Routine exam	15	3	Rheumatic Ht. Dis.	5	0
Total	150	150	Congenital Ht. Dis.	1	0
Male (Mean Age)	120(49.6)	109(52.9)	Total	150	150
Female (Mean Age)	30(51.0)	41(51.9)			

*Associated diagnoses were arthritis (15 cases), gallbladder disease (8), and other gastro-intestinal diseases (10).
†Normal response following dihydroergocornine, no CHD or death in follow-up.

(2) 153 New York Central railway employees with known or suspected CHD and evaluated while actively at work prior to 1956. The exercise consisted of 40 trips over the Master steps carried out rapidly (60 to 90 seconds). A single 14-lead tracing, starting with lead V8 was taken immediately after exercise, and a positive response was diagnosed if there was a typical ischemic ST depression. All employees had minor ST depression or flattened T waves in their resting tracing. In addition 36 employees had returned to work following recovery from a myocardial infarction, 25 had probable angina pectoris, 83 had hypertension or valvular heart disease, and 9 were obese or diabetic. The average age was 59 years.

Follow-up: (1) Patients were followed up by periodic examinations or by direct contact with the patient or physician a maximum of six years (detailed follow-up data indicate that only 47 patients were followed longer than four years). The average was about 3.3 years.
(2) Patients were followed five years to January 1, 1961 by means of re-examination, reports from attending physicians, records of the Railroad Retirement Board and death certificates.

Results: In the first series of private patients with negative response to single and double Master test only a single death was recorded with 4.93 expected on the basis of age, sex and follow-up data, with U.S. white population mortality rates. Although the authors make no statement as to completeness of follow-up, the exposure data suggest that follow-up may have been incomplete for many of the entrants with possible under reporting of deaths. However, in the 150 patients with positive response excess mortality was observed, with a mortality ratio of 205 per cent and EDR of 13 per 1000. The authors report that 10 of the 12 deaths were due to coronary occlusion; the single death in the negative test group was attributed to stomach cancer. The occurrence of acute coronary events in the group with positive response was at an aggregate rate of 52 events per 1000 exposed to risk per year (coronary occlusions and 18 episodes of coronary insufficiency) as compared with 2 per 1000 in the group with negative response. It should be emphasized that prior acute coronary events were finally diagnosed in 62 patients with positive response as compared to only 7 patients with negative response. Nevertheless, all of these 300 patients had a normal resting ECG at the time of examination.

§375—POSTEXERCISE ECG

Results (continued):

The railroad employees constituted a group with a higher average age, 59 years, and a high prevalence of CHD, hypertension and valvular heart disease. Although 76 per cent of these employees had a negative response in their postexercise ECG the mortality ratio was 166 per cent, EDR 16 per 1000, and the five-year survival ratio 91.9 per cent. The prognosis was worse in the smaller group of employees with a positive response: mortality ratio 335 per cent, EDR 58 per 1000 and survival ratio 73.6 per cent. The incidence of myocardial infarction during the follow-up period was reported as being about three times greater in those with a positive response. The test used in this study was not a standardized Master's test.

Table 375a   Comparative Experience after Master's Test ECG (Series 1)

Response	No. of Patients	Exposure Person-Yrs	No. of Deaths		Mortality Ratio	Est. 3-Yr Surv. Index†	Excess Death Rate
			Observed	Expected*			
	ℓ	E	d	d'	100 d/d'	100 P/P'	1000(d-d')/E
Negative	150	472.5	1	4.93	20%	102.6%	−8.3
Positive	150	458.0	12	5.86	205	95.9	13

Table 375b   Comparative Experience after Master's Test, Railway Men with Actual or Suspected Cardiovascular Disease (Series 2)

Response	No. of Patients	No. of Deaths	5-Yr Surv. Rate		Survival Ratio	Ave. Ann. Mort. Rate	Mortality Ratio	Excess Death Rate
			Observed	Expected●				
	ℓ	d	P = 1-d/ℓ	P'	100 P/P'	$\check{q}$	100 $\check{q}$/$\check{q}$'	1000($\check{q}$-$\check{q}$')
Negative	116	22	.810	.8818	91.9%	.0412	166%	16
Positive	37	13	.649	.8818	73.6	.0830	335	58

* Basis of expected mortality: U.S. White Male or Female 1949-51
† P = $(1-d/\ell)^3$ P' = $(1-d'/\ell)^3$
● Basis of expected mortality: U.S. White Male, 1959-61. At age 59 5-Year P' = .8818, $\check{q}$' = .0249

POSTEXERCISE (MASTER'S TEST) ECG
IN MALE LIFE INSURANCE APPLICANTS

§376–POSTEXERCISE (MASTER'S TEST) ECG IN MALE LIFE INSURANCE APPLICANTS

References: (1) G. P. Robb and H. H. Marks, "Postexercise Electrocardiogram in Arteriosclerotic Heart Disease. Its Value in Diagnosis and Prognosis," J. Am. Med. Assoc., 200:918-926 (1967).
(2) Statistical Bulletin, Metropolitan Life Insurance Co., 53:2-9 (July 1972).
(3) P. S. Entmacher, additional data submitted in personal communication (1972).

Subjects Studied: 3,325 male applicants for life insurance to Metropolitan Life. The applications were received, and the exercise tests were done during the period 1949-1970. A small number of applicants were mildly hypertensive or overweight, but none had other major impairments that would cause them to be rejected for insurance. The test was performed because of a history of chest pain in 49 per cent of the cases, a history of healed myocardial infarction in 2 per cent, ECG abnormalities 27 per cent, family history of coronary artery disease 2 per cent, large amount of insurance applied for 14 per cent, and other miscellaneous reasons 6 per cent. A double two-step exercise test was done in all instances, and after exercise seven leads, V4, V5, V6, I, II, aVL and aVF were recorded immediately and at 2, 4, 6 and 10 minutes. The age distribution of the cases studied was as follows:

Age (years)	20-29	30-39	40-49	50-59	60 up
Non-ischemic	65	640	1264	731	176
Ischemic	6	65	160	167	51

Follow-up: Insurance policies issued to the applicants were traced to June 30, 1971. The maximum period of follow-up was 22 years and the average was 9.0 years.

Results: The non-ischemic responses to exercise were divided into a negative group in which there were no changes on the postexercise ECG other than rate increase, a group with junctional S-T segment depression, a group with T wave changes only and an "other" group with rhythm and conduction disturbances after exercise. The ischemic response cases, which comprised 13.5 per cent of the entire group, were divided into those with downsloping S-T segment depression after exercise and those with horizontal S-T segment depression. In Table 376a it is shown that the mortality ratio for the total non-ischemic group was 110 per cent and for the ischemic group 295 per cent. Although T wave changes were classified as non-ischemic, the mortality ratio was somewhat elevated, 166 per cent, and the EDR was 4.2/1000 as compared to 0.8/1000 for the entire non-ischemic group. In the ischemic response cases a downsloping S-T segment depression was associated with a much higher mortality ratio, 370 per cent, than cases with horizontal S-T segment depression, 123 per cent. The EDR's for these two categories were 22.0 and 2.1 respectively. In both the non-ischemic (normal) group and the ischemic group a history of coronary heart disease was associated with a higher mortality than the absence of a definite history.

In Table 376b the ischemic response cases are analyzed by age and by degree of response to exercise. In every age group the mortality increases with a greater depression of the S-T segment after exercise. The mortality ratio decreases with age but the EDR tends to increase. In Tables 376c and 376d the effect of duration is shown. The cumulative survival decreases by duration to a greater extent as the degree of abnormal response to exercise increases. There is no clear trend for the mortality ratios to increase or decrease with duration.

Comment: In the ischemic response group there were 91 deaths, and there were 210 in the non-ischemic group. A study of the causes of death showed that 80 per cent of the deaths in the ischemic group were due to coronary artery disease as compared to approximately 53 per cent in the non-ischemic group.

POSTEXERCISE (MASTER'S TEST) ECG
IN MALE LIFE INSURANCE APPLICANTS

Table 376c   Observed Data and Comparative Experience by Duration — All Ages Combined (Ischemic)

Grade*	Interval		Exposure Person-Yrs	Deaths		Mortality Ratio		Survival Ratio		Excess Death Rate
	No.	Start-End		Obs.	Exp.†	Interval	Cumulative	Interval	Cumulative	
	i	t to $t + \Delta t$	E	d	d'	$100d/d'$	$100\sum d/\sum d'$	$100p_i/p_i'$	$100 P/P'$	$1000(d-d')/E$
1	1	0- 5 yrs	1392	13	6.77	192%	192%	97.8%	97.8%	4.5
	2	5-10	839	19	7.62	250	220	92.5	90.4	14
	3	10-20	333	6	4.99	120	196	89.6	81.0	3.0
2	1	0- 5 yrs	425	8	2.74	290	290	93.9	93.9	12
	2	5-10	276	10	3.26	305	300	87.8	82.4	24
	3	10-20	137	9	2.69	335	310	73.3	60.4	46
3	1	0- 5 yrs	172	16	.99	1620	1620	60.5	60.5	87
	2	5-10	73	10	.80	1250	1450	51.8	31.3	127
	3	10-20	31	0	.74	0	1030	118.7	37.2	—24

Table 376d   Derived Mortality and Survival Data (Ischemic)

Grade*	Interval		Observed Rates				Expected Rates (Estimated)†			
	No.	Start-End	Cumulative Survival	Interval Survival	Geom. Mean Ann. Surv.	Geom. Mean Ann. Mort.	Cumulative Survival	Interval Survival	Geom. Mean Ann. Surv.	Geom. Mean Ann. Mort.
	i	t to $t + \Delta t$	P	p_i	$\check{p}_i$	$\check{q}_i$	P'	p_i'	$\check{p}_i$	$\check{q}_i'$
1	1	0- 5 yrs	.954	.954	.991	.009	.9759	.9759	.9951	.0049
	2	5-10	.843	.884	.976	.024	.9323	.9553	.9909	.0091
	3	10-20	.648	.769	.974	.026	.8004	.8585	.9849	.0151
2	1	0- 5 yrs	.907	.907	.981	.019	.9657	.9657	.9930	.0070
	2	5-10	.750	.827	.963	.037	.9098	.9421	.9881	.0119
	3	10-20	.450	.600	.950	.050	.7446	.8184	.9802	.0198
3	1	0- 5 yrs	.588	.588	.899	.101	.9716	.9716	.9943	.0057
	2	5-10	.288	.490	.867	.133	.9191	.9460	.9890	.0110
	3	10-20	.288	1.000	1.000	0.0	.7742	.8423	.9758	.0242

* Grade 1 - S-T depression under 1.0 mm. Grade 2 - S-T depression 1.0 to 1.9 mm.
  Grade 3 - S-T depression 2.0 mm or more
† Basis of expected mortality: 1955-60 Select Basic Tables (Male)

ARRHYTHMIAS AND ECG ABNORMALITIES

Table 376a   Comparative Experience by Type of Response and Cor. Ht. Dis. History (All Ages and Durations Combined)

Type	Number of Cases	Exposure Person-Yrs	Deaths during Interval	Expected Deaths*	Mortality Ratio	Ave. Ann. Mort. Rate	Est. 7-Yr Surv. Rate	Est. 7-Yr Surv. Index	Excess Death Rate
	ℓ	E	d	d'	100d/d'	$\bar{q}=d/E$	$P=(1-\bar{q})^7$	100 P/P'	1000(d-d')/E
Non-Ischemic									
Negative	1344	13650	106	98.33	108%	.0078	.947	99.6%	0.6
Junctional	1350	11031	90	82.62	109	.0082	.944	99.5	0.7
T Wave Change	169	1339	14	8.44	166	.0105	.929	97.1	4.2
Other †	13	109	0	0.79	0	.0000	1.000	105.2	−7.3
Total	2876	26129	210	190.18	110	.0080	.945	99.5	0.8
Normal ●									
CHD Hist. □	306	3280	49	28.81	170	.0149	.900	95.7	6.2
No CHD Hist. ■	2388	21401	147	152.14	97	.0069	.953	100.2	−0.2
Total	2694	24681	196	180.95	108	.0079	.946	99.6	0.6
Ischemic									
Horizontal	116	991	11	8.94	123	.0111	.925	98.5	2.1
Downsloping	333	2687	80	21.67	370	.0298	.809	85.7	22
Total	449	3678	91	30.61	295	.0247	.839	89.0	16
CHD Hist. □	118	1010	48	9.82	490	.0475	.711	76.2	38
No CHD Hist. ■	331	2662	43	20.93	205	.0161	.892	94.3	8.3

Table 376b   Ischemic Response — Comparative Experience by Age and Degree (All Durations Combined)

Grade and Age △	Number of Cases	Exposure Person-Yrs	Deaths during Interval	Expected Deaths*	Mortality Ratio	Ave. Ann. Mort. Rate	Est. 7-Yr Surv. Rate	Est. 7-Yr Surv. Index	Excess Death Rate
	ℓ	E	d	d'	100d/d'	$\bar{q}=d/E$	$P=(1-\bar{q})^7$	100 P/P'	1000(d-d')/E
Under 40									
All Grades	71	642	6	1.43	420%	.0092	.936	95.1%	7.0
Age 40-49									
Grade 1	117	1003	15	5.74	260	.0149	.900	93.7	9.2
Grade 2	32	312	9	1.90	475	.0288	.815	85.0	23
Grade 3	11	77	6	0.34	1770	.0779	.568	58.6	73
Total	160	1392	30	7.98	375	.0216	.859	89.4	16
Age 50-59									
Grade 1	112	875	16	9.37	171	.0183	.879	94.8	7.6
Grade 2	30	259	9	2.87	315	.0347	.781	84.4	24
Grade 3	25	137	15	1.32	1140	.1095	.444	47.5	100
Total	167	1271	40	13.56	295	.0315	.800	86.2	21
Age 60 up									
All Grades	51	373	15	7.63	197	.0402	.750	86.7	20
All Ages									
Grade 1	314	2564	38	19.38	196	.0148	.901	95.0	7.3
Grade 2	91	839	27	8.70	310	.0322	.796	85.6	22
Grade 3	44	275	26	2.53	1040	.0943	.500	53.3	85
All	449	3678	91	30.61	295	.0247	.839	89.0	16

* Basis of expected deaths: 1955-60 Select Basic Tables (Male)

† Disturbances of rhythm or conduction

● Negative and junctional depression. T wave change and other cases excluded

□ Definite or probable history of Coronary Heart Disease

■ No history of Coronary Heart Disease or equivocal chest pain history

△Grade 1 - S-T depression under 1.0 mm. Grade 2 - S-T depression 1.0 to 1.9 mm.
  Grade 3 - S-T depression 2.0 mm. or more

ARRHYTHMIAS AND ECG ABNORMALITIES

§379–ABNORMAL ECG IN INSUREDS

Reference: "New York Life Single Medical Impairment Study–1972," unpublished report made available by J.J. Hutchinson and J.C. Sibigtroth (1973).

Subjects Studied: Policyholders of New York Life Insurance Company issued insurance in 1954-1970, followed to the 1971 policy anniversary. The experience reported is for cases with abnormal electrocardiogram; only substandard issues were analyzed here. Cases with more than one ratable impairment were excluded.

Follow-up: Insurance policy records formed the basis of entry, of counting policies, exposure and death claims, and of follow-up information.

Results: Tables 379a-b present the comparative experience by duration, all ages combined. The excess mortality among males was greatest at 2-5 years, with a mortality ratio of 225 per cent and EDR of 6.9 per 1000. The cumulative survival ratio at 17 years was 95.9 per cent.

Table 379c showed that mortality was highest at entry ages 40-49, the mortality ratio being 235 per cent (6.1 extra deaths per 1000). The overall mortality ratio was 167 per cent, and EDR was 3.6 per 1000. The estimated eight-year survival index by age ranged from 95.2 per cent to 98.9 per cent.

Diseases of the heart and circulation constituted the leading cause of death, with a mortality ratio of 215 per cent and EDR of 2.3 per 1000. There is some increase in mortality due to accidents and to "all other causes and unknown," with an EDR of 0.7 per 1000 in each category. Of the 9 deaths in the latter cause category, 4 were due to cerebrovascular accident.

Comment: All types of electrocardiographic abnormalities were included in this experience: major disturbances of rhythm and conduction, very low, diphasic or inverted T waves, S-T segment abnormalities, wide Q waves and QRS abnormalities, and abnormal responses to exercise tests. Standards for "abnormal" were those utilized by the Medical Department of the New York Life Insurance Company.

ABNORMAL ELECTROCARDIOGRAM IN INSUREDS

Table 379a   Observed Data and Comparative Experience by Duration — Male Substandard Cases

Interval		Exposure	No. of Death Claims		Mortality Ratio		Survival Ratio		Excess
No.	Start-End	Policy-Yrs	Observed	Expected*	Interval	Cumulative	Interval	Cumulative	Death Rate
i	t to t + Δt	E	d	d'	100 d/d'	100 $\sum$d/$\sum$d'	100 p_i/p_i'	100 P/P'	1000(d-d')/E
1	0- 2 yrs	1864	9	4.72	191%	191%	99.5%	99.5%	2.3
2	2- 5	1569	18	7.17	250	225	97.9	97.5	6.9
3	5-10	1207	12	8.77	137	189	98.7	96.2	2.7
4	10-17	473	7	6.82	103	167	99.7	95.9	0.4

Table 379b   Derived Mortality and Survival Data

Interval		Observed Rates				Expected Rates*			
		Average Annual		Cumulative		Average Annual		Cumulative	
No.	Start-End	Mortality	Survival	Survival	Mortality	Mortality	Survival	Survival	Mortality
i	t to t + Δt	$\bar{q}$ = d/E	$\bar{p}$	P	Q	$\bar{q}'$ = d'/E	$\bar{p}'$	P'	Q'
1	0- 2 yrs	.0048	.9952	.9904	.0096	.0025	.9975	.9949	.0051
2	2- 5	.0115	.9885	.9567	.0433	.0046	.9954	.9814	.0186
3	5-10	.0099	.9901	.9101	.0899	.0073	.9927	.9462	.0538
4	10-17	.0148	.9852	.8199	.1801	.0144	.9856	.8547	.1453

Table 379c   Comparative Experience by Age Group — Male Substandard Cases, All Durations Combined

Age Group	Exposure Policy-Yrs	No. of Death Claims		Mortality Ratio	Ave. Ann. Mort. Rate	Est. 8-Yr Surv. Rate	Est. 8-Yr Surv. Index	Excess Death Rate
		Observed	Expected*					
	E	d	d'	100 d/d'	$\bar{q}$ = d/E	P = $(1-\bar{q})^8$	100 P/P'	1000(d-d')/E
0-39	1924	6	3.25	185%	.0031	.9753	98.9%	1.4
40-49	1787	19	8.01	235	.0106	.9181	95.2	6.1
50-59	1061	13	9.52	137	.0123	.9061	97.4	3.3
60 up	341	8	6.70	119	.0235	.8270	96.9	3.8
All Ages	5113	46	27.48	167	.0090	.9302	97.1	3.6

Table 379d   Mortality by Cause of Death — Male and Female Combined

Cause	No. of Death Claims		Mortality Ratio	Excess Death Rate
	Observed	Expected●		
Malignant Neoplasms	6	6.82	88%	−0.1
Diseases of the Heart & Circulatory System	24	11.24	215	2.3
Accidents and Homicides	8	3.93	205	0.7
Suicide	—	1.21	0	−0.2
All Other Causes and Unknown†	9	5.39	167	0.7
Total	47□	28.59	164	3.4

* Basis of expected mortality: 1955-60 Select Basic Table
† Includes 4 deaths due to cerebrovascular accident
● Distribution of total expected deaths by Intercompany Medically Examined Standard Issues 1965-70
□ Includes 1 female death (376 policy-years exposure)

OTHER CARDIOVASCULAR DISEASES

§380–FRAMINGHAM HEART STUDY

References: (1) T. Gordon, F. E. Moore, D. Shurtleff, and T. R. Dawber, "Some Methodologic Problems in the Long-Term Study of Cardiovascular Diseases: Observations on the Framingham Study," J. Chron. Dis., 10:186-206 (1959).

(2) T. Gordon and W. B. Kannel, "The Framingham Study. Section 1. Introduction and General Background. Section 2. Follow-up to the Eighth Examination," Govt. Printing Office, Washington, D. C. (June 1968).

(3) M. Feinleib, "The Framingham Study. Section 7. Average Two-Year Incidence Rates by Age at Exam Preceding Event and Sex, with Total Number of Events and Total Population at Risk. Section 8. Two-Year Incidence by Exam Interval by Age at Exam 1 and Sex," Govt. Printing Office, Washington, D. C. (June 1968).

(4) J. Schiffman, "The Framingham Study. Section 25. Survival Following Certain Cardiovascular Events," Govt. Printing Office, Washington, D. C. (September 1970).

(5) D. Shurtleff, "The Framingham Study. Section 26. Some Characteristics Related to The Incidence of Cardiovascular Disease and Death: Framingham Study, 16-Year Follow-up," Govt. Printing Office, Washington, D. C. (December 1970).

Subjects Studied: Examinee-participants of the Framingham Heart Study. These consisted of 5209 adult residents of Framingham, Mass., a town situated 21 miles west of Boston, having a 1950 population of 28,086. The residents agreed to enter a health surveillance program involving a long-term series of biennial medical examinations. There were 4494 persons who entered the program out of a list of 6532 residents invited to participate. The list was made up as a stratified sample of adults in the age group 30-59 years, approximately 65 per cent of the adult population of Framingham in this age group in the years 1949-1950, excluding those in institutions. The reasons for non-response on the part of 2038 invitees who did not enter the program were 72 per cent refusal, 21 per cent moved from Framingham, and 3.6 per cent each for those who died or were too ill or incapacitated. To supplement the numbers in the Study 740 persons in the same age range were added at the second biennial examination from a group of volunteers who had been examined 1948-1950, prior to the start of initial examinations for the sample responders in 1950. The age distribution at examination, is given in Table 380b for the 2336 male and 2873 female examinee-participants. The prevalence of certain cardiovascular diseases noted on initial examination is given in Table 380a (the incidence data in Table 380d are much to be preferred to the prevalence rates in Table 380a as estimates of the occurrence of cardiovascular disease in a community population). The initial entrants age 35 up also included 50 men and 43 women with diabetes mellitus.

The Framingham Study was designed as a long-term prospective investigation to characterize the development of and mortality from cardiovascular diseases. The program was designed, staffed and funded by the U.S. Public Health Service. Planning help was provided by state health authorities and medical advisory committees. The Study could not have been conducted, however, without the cooperation of all segments of the community — local health agencies, the medical profession, hospitals, civic organizations, and a major part of the adult population in the target age range. With the history, physical examination, electrocardiogram, chest X-ray and various laboratory studies obtained at biennial examinations at a clinic set up near the Framingham Union Hospital, it was planned, through follow-up observation to detect and evaluate the significance of various findings as risk factors or predictors of cardiovascular disease, and the mortality associated with its development.

Follow-up: Although the initial examinations were spread out over a longer time-span than originally intended, the scheduling of subsequent examinations adhered as closely as possible to a biennial anniversary date. The central year for Examination 1 may be taken as 1950, and for Examination 9 as 1966, 16 years later, the longest follow-up for which results have been published in detail. The biennial examination schedule therefore served as the time-frame for follow-up both for findings at each new examination and for deaths and new cardiovascular events occurring by the two-year interval between successive examinations. Follow-up data have been reported according to three general patterns:

FRAMINGHAM HEART STUDY

Table 380a Cardiovascular Diseases Noted at Examination 1 in Framingham Subjects

Sex	No. of Subjects	Total Cor. Ht. Dis.	Definite MI	Definite Angina Pect.	Cerebrovasc. Accident	Intermit. Claudic.	Congestive Heart Failure
				Number of Cases			
Male	2336	54	13	28	14	17	5
Female	2873	28	2	17	10	14	12

Table 380b Age and Sex Distribution of Framingham Subjects at Examination 1 and Distribution of Deaths to Examination 8 (Follow-up of 14 Years)

Sex/Age	No. of Subjects	Sudden CHD	Non-Sudden CHD	Cerebrovasc. Accident	Other CV Dis.	Cancer	All Other Causes	Total
Male								
29-34	392	2	2	0	1	0	7	12
35-39	443	5	1	0	1	8	5	20
40-44	422	8	10	4	1	11	8	42
45-49	357	15	9	6	4	8	12	54
50-54	374	21	17	5	13	16	16	88
55-62	348	18	23	9	7	23	28	108
All	2336	69	62	24	27	66	76	324
Female								
29-34	458	0	2	0	2	2	6	12
35-39	584	0	1	2	3	11	8	25
40-44	511	1	0	0	2	15	9	27
45-49	451	3	2	2	3	11	9	30
50-54	432	4	2	6	11	13	12	48
55-62	437	8	15	7	6	19	10	65
All	2873	16	22	17	27	71	54	207

Table 380c Annual Mortality Rates over Biennial Intervals, Framingham Subjects, Based on Age at Biennial Examination (Follow-up of 14 Years)

Attained Age Range	Ave.	Male No. Exam.	Male No. Deaths	Male Mort. Rate	Male U.S. Rate*	Female No. Exam.	Female No. Deaths	Female Mort. Rate	Female U.S. Rate*
	x	ℓ	d	$q=1000d/2\ell$	$1000\,q'$	ℓ	d	$q=1000d/2\ell$	$1000\,q'$
29-39	36.2	2273	7	1.5	2.3	2735	9	1.6	1.4
40-44	42.1	2737	17	3.1	4.2	3366	10	1.5	2.3
45-49	47.0	2794	30	5.4	6.7	3563	21	2.9	3.6
50-54	52.0	2585	55	10.6	11.7	3225	43	6.7	5.6
55-59	56.9	2215	71	16.0	17.5	2858	35	6.1	8.3
60-64	61.8	1693	76	22.4	26.8	2178	41	9.4	13.3
65-69	66.6	800	50	31.3	42.3	1105	36	16.3	23.5
70-74	71.0	177	18	50.8	56.4	239	12	25.1	34.8

*U.S. White Population Rates 1958 to nearest integral year, average age

OTHER CARDIOVASCULAR DISEASES

§380–FRAMINGHAM HEART STUDY

Follow-up (continued):

    (1) Long-range experience, over 12 to 16 years, based on the incidence of death or the occurrence of a new cardiovascular event between the first, second or third examination and the latest examination for which data have been processed, e.g., the ninth examination about 1966 for the results in Sections 25-26. The "A" tables in Section 26 give follow-up data from Examinations 1, 2 and 3 to the end of follow-up at Examination 9, or intervals of 16, 14, and 12 years respectively, an average of 14 years.

    (2) Short-range experience over two years, based on the incidence of death or new cardiovascular event between successive examinations. After being characterized at entry, persons were characterized anew at each following biennial examination and were shifted from one age group to the next as they grew older. Thus, individual subjects in most cases contributed experience to more than one age group. Annual mortality or incidence rates have been calculated from the sum of the deaths or new cardiovascular events observed over all of the two-year intervals combined, and the exposure-years counted as twice the sum of those participants examined who met appropriately defined criteria. Participants lost to follow-up, and deaths in the second year of follow-up were not deducted from the exposure thus calculated.

    (3) Follow-up studies in a life table format, which, however, utilize the biennial examination next after occurrence of the event (such as myocardial infarction) as the key point in time for reckoning duration of follow-up instead of the exact date or year of occurrence of the event. Survival experience between a precisely dated event, such as a heart attack or stroke, and the next biennial examination is presented in some of the life tables, with an assigned average duration of one-half the biennial interval that is one year. This is based on the assumption that the actual intervals are randomly distributed from less than one to 23 months, with an average of one year.

During the 14 years of follow-up to Examination 8, 324 male and 207 female participants died (Table 380b). Subsequent to the initial examination, 9.4 to 13.8 per cent of the surviving participants failed to show up at the various scheduled anniversary dates for re-examination. However, most of the participants who missed a particular examination did appear for one or more subsequent examinations. For example, of the 485 participants who failed to take Examination 2, 334 appeared at one or more subsequent examinations, and only 151 were lost to all subsequent examinations, including 47 who moved away from Framingham, and 104 continuing residents. Every effort was made to trace *all* participants who failed to take each subsequent examination, in order to ascertain survival status, state of health and biennial medical history. Additional information obtained on participants who died included a copy of the death certificate, the report of any autopsy performed, and reports from the physician, hospital, or relatives involved. Follow-up information was therefore unusually complete, and was inadequate on less than two per cent of the series, according to a 1972 published report (Kannel, et al., Am. J. Card., 29:154).

Results: Selected results from the Framingham Study are given in various tables of the cardiovascular and other sections (§204, §301, §302, §320, §371, §381, and §382). The accompanying tables present data on prevalence and incidence of various cardiovascular disorders, (380a and 380d), distribution of deaths by attained age, sex and cause of death (380b), and distribution of survivors, deaths and numbers examined by sex and examination number (380e). Mortality rates for all male and female participants are given in Table 380c, based on attained age 29-39 and quinquennial age groups to 70-74 and the experience of biennial observation periods to Examination 8. For all of the male and all except two of the female age groups, the mortality rates were smaller than the corresponding U.S. white rates for 1958 (the mid-point of the interval from Examination 1 to Examination 8). The difference was relatively greater at ages 60 and up.

FRAMINGHAM HEART STUDY

Table 380d Annual Incidence Rates for CHD, MI, AP and CVA, Based on Biennial Follow-up of Selected Subjects without CHD (14-Year Follow-up)

Sex and Attained Age	No. Exam. Free of CHD	Cor. Ht. Dis.		Myocardial Inf.		Angina Pectoris		Cerebrovasc. Accident	
		Cases	Rate*	Cases	Rate*	Cases	Rate*	Cases	Rate*
	ℓ	n	i=1000n/2ℓ	n	i=1000n/2ℓ	n	i=1000n/2ℓ	n	i=1000n/2ℓ
Male									
29-39	2355	12	2.5	8	1.7	1	0.2	2	0.4
40-44	2741	27	4.9	16	2.9	2	0.4	2	0.4
45-49	2748	39	7.1	21	3.8	10	1.8	7	1.3
50-54	2503	64	12.8	31	6.2	8	1.6	14	2.8
55-59	2067	86	20.8	39	9.4	24	5.8	13	3.1
60-64	1475	64	21.7	43	14.6	17	5.8	16	5.4
65-69	653	27	20.7	19	14.5	7	5.4	9	6.9
70-74	138	4	14.5	3	10.9	1	3.6	2	7.2
Total	14680	323	11.0	180	6.1	70	2.4	65	2.2
Female									
29-39	2892	0	0	0	0	0	0	2	0.3
40-44	3431	7	1.0	2	0.3	4	0.6	2	0.3
45-49	3600	14	1.9	6	0.8	6	0.8	7	1.0
50-54	3212	22	3.4	6	0.9	12	1.9	9	1.4
55-59	2785	38	6.8	7	1.3	27	4.8	11	2.0
60-64	2023	52	12.9	12	3.0	22	5.4	16	4.0
65-69	991	25	12.6	7	3.5	15	7.6	21	10.6
70-74	214	11	25.7	3	7.0	5	11.7	2	4.7
Total	19148	169	4.4	43	1.1	91	2.4	70	1.8

Table 380e Distribution of Subject Population by Examination and Deaths by Biennial Interval to Examination 8 (Follow-up of 14 Years)

Year (Approx.) / Examination	1950 / 1	1952 / 2	1954 / 3	1956 / 4	1958 / 5	1960 / 6	1962 / 7	1964 / 8
Males								
Survivors†	2336	2316	2275	2245	2193	2138	2083	2012
Deaths●	20	41	30	52	55	55	71	—
Females								
Survivors†	2873	2864	2854	2829	2797	2759	2721	2666
Deaths●	9	10	25	32	38	38	55	—
Total Survivors	5209	5177	5125	5073	4990	4895	4803	4678
No. Examined								
Sample	4469	4052	3935	3843	3750	3593	3551	3402
Volunteers	740	740	481□	698	671	666	640	628
Total	5209	4792	4416	4541	4421	4259	4191	4030
No. Not Examined	0	385	709	532	569	636	612	648
No. Lost to Exam■								
Moved Away	47	36	32	33	40	34	55	—
Still Resident	104	51	56	38	52	46	104	—

*Rates based on population free of each form of CHD, slightly different from data in ℓ column
†At time of indicated examination
●Deaths due to all causes within the biennial interval following examination
□Some of group not recalled for Examination 3 because of short interval from preceding examination
■Did not return for any subsequent exam within the follow-up period

OTHER CARDIOVASCULAR DISEASES

§381–CONGESTIVE HEART FAILURE (FRAMINGHAM STUDY)

References: (1) P. A. McKee, W. P. Castelli, P. M. McNamara, and W. B. Kannel, "The Natural History of Congestive Heart Failure: The Framingham Study," New Eng. J. Med., 285:1441-1446 (1971).
(2) J. Schiffman, "The Framingham Study, Section 25. Survival Following Certain Cardiovascular Events," Govt. Printing Office, Washington, D. C. (September 1970).

Subjects Studied: Examinee-participants in the Framingham Heart Study who developed congestive heart failure (CHF) during the 16-year interval from the initial examination about 1950 to the ninth biennial examination about 1966. Among 5,192 subjects free of CHF at initial examination 142 developed evidence thereof during follow-up. To establish the diagnosis two major criteria were required, or one major and two minor. Examples of major criteria were paroxysmal nocturnal dyspnea, acute pulmonary edema, rales, and cardiomegaly; examples of minor criteria were ankle edema, dyspnea on exertion, and reduction of vital capacity by one-third or more. For additional information on the Framingham Study subjects see §380. Distribution of cases and incidence rates by age at onset and sex were as follows:

Age at Onset (Years)	29-44	45-54	55-64	65-74	Total
Males - Exposure (person-years)	10352	12642	9078	2772	34844
Incidence*	0.5(5)	1.9(24)	3.9(35)	6.1(17)	2.3(81)
Females - Exposure (person-years)	12698	15814	11912	3872	44296
Incidence*	0.3(4)	0.6(10)	2.7(32)	3.9(15)	1.4(61)

*Cases/1000/year.   (Number of cases in parentheses.)

Follow-up: Because the regularly scheduled biennial examinations constituted the time-frame for life table construction in the Framingham Study, CHF would first be recorded at the examination following development of the condition, the interval representing any duration from one day to almost two years after the actual onset, with an average of one year. Life table data in Section 25 include all such experience with follow-up carried to the ninth biennial examination about 1966. Details of follow-up and biennial examination procedures are contained in §380.

Results: Tables 381a-b present mortality and survival experience over the nine-years subsequent to the first appearance of CHF during the follow-up period. Mortality indicated is high: 54 deaths in the nine-year span among the 73 male subjects and 29 deaths among the 50 females. Interval mortality ratios ranged from 1730 to 555 per cent and were generally highest in the first three years following onset of CHF. In terms of EDR excess mortality remained at very high levels, 102 or more extra deaths per 1000 per year in all intervals except one, with no clear trend by duration. There were very few deaths in some of the intervals, especially among the females. The cumulative mortality ratio of 810 per cent for females was higher than the male ratio of 530 per cent, but EDR was lower - 132 as compared with 155 extra deaths per 1000 per year. Cumulative survival ratio at 9 years was only 21.4 per cent for male patients and 33.8 per cent for females.

Comparative experience by age group for the first five years of observation (Table 381c) discloses a decrease in average annual mortality ratio by age for males, but little difference in females under age 65 versus those age 65-74. The EDR for males in all age groups was very close to the average of 155 per 1000 per year. In the case of females under age 65 EDR was about one-half that for males; for older women the rate of excess deaths was similar to that for men.

Comment: The article (Reference 1) should be consulted for additional details on the etiology of CHF and the prevalence of associated chronic diseases. Hypertensive cardiovascular disease was present in about two-thirds of male and female patients. Coronary heart disease was the second most common cause in men, and rheumatic heart disease in women. About 60 per cent of the patients also had other serious chronic disorders, such as diabetes, stroke, intermittent claudication, or chronic lung disease.

CONGESTIVE HEART FAILURE

Table 381a Observed Data and Comparative Experience by Duration - All Ages Combined

Sex	Interval* No.	Interval* Start-End	No. Alive at Start of Interval	Deaths during Interval	Mortality Ratio Ave. Ann.	Mortality Ratio Cumulative	Survival Ratio Interval	Survival Ratio Cumulative	Excess Death Rate
	i	t to t + Δt	ℓ	d	100 $\breve{q}/\breve{q}'$	100 Q/Q'	100 p_i/p_i'	100 P/P'	1000 ($\breve{q}-\breve{q}'$)
Male	1	0-1 yr	73	15	1270%	1270%	80.8%	80.8%	189
	2	1-3	58	18	925	870	71.6	57.8	151
	3	3-5	37	11	760	680	73.4	42.3	141
	4	5-7	21	5	555	560	79.8	33.5	104
	5	7-9	13	5	730	530	65.3	21.4	187
		0-9	73	54	940	530	21.4	21.4	155
Female	1	0-1 yr	50	7	1730	1730	86.7	86.7	132
	2	1-3	43	9	1190	1180	80.6	69.9	102
	3	3-5	30	5	700	920	85.4	59.5	75
	4	5-7	20	6	1230	890	71.9	42.6	150
	5	7-9	9	2	780	810	80.2	33.8	103
		0-9	50	29	1230	810	33.8	33.8	132

Table 381b Derived Mortality and Survival Data

Sex	Interval* No.	Interval* Start-End	Observed Survival Rate Cumulative	Observed Survival Rate Interval	Observed Survival Rate Ave. Ann.	Observed Ave. Ann. Mort. Rate	Expected† Survival Rate Cumulative	Expected† Survival Rate Interval	Expected† Survival Rate Ave. Ann.	Expected† Ave. Ann. Mort. Rate
	i	t to t + Δt	P	p_i	$\breve{p}$	$\breve{q}$	P'	p_i'	$\breve{p}'$	$\breve{q}'$
Male	1	0-1 yr	.795	.795	.795	.205	.9839	.9839	.9839	.0161
	2	1-3	.548	.690	.831	.169	.9481	.9637	.9817	.0183
	3	3-5	.385	.703	.838	.162	.9102	.9578	.9787	.0213
	4	5-7	.293	.762	.873	.127	.8746	.9549	.9772	.0228
	5	7-9	.181	.615	.784	.216	.8458	.9418	.9705	.0295
Female	1	0-1 yr	.860	.860	.860	.140	.9919	.9919	.9919	.0081
	2	1-3	.680	.791	.889	.111	.9728	.9814	.9907	.0093
	3	3-5	.567	.833	.913	.087	.9529	.9754	.9876	.0124
	4	5-7	.397	.700	.837	.163	.9319	.9736	.9867	.0133
	5	7-9	.309	.778	.882	.118	.9142	.9701	.9849	.0151

Table 381c Comparative Survival Experience by Age Group — 5-Year Average after Appearance of CHF

Sex	Age Group	No. Alive at Start of Interval	Deaths during Interval	Survival Rate Observed	Survival Rate Expected†	Cumulative Surv. Ratio	Estimated Average Ann. Mort. Rate Observed	Estimated Average Ann. Mort. Rate Expected†	Mortality Ratio	Excess Death Rate
	(Years)	ℓ	d	P	P'	100 P/P'	$\breve{q}$	$\breve{q}'$	100 $\breve{q}/\breve{q}'$	1000 ($\breve{q}-\breve{q}'$)
Male	Under 55	21	13	.381	.9579	39.8%	.176	.0086	2000%	167
	55-64	32	18	.412	.9251	44.5	.163	.0155	1050	147
	65-74	20	13	.350	.8283	42.3	.189	.0370	510	152
	All Ages	73	44	.385	.9068	42.5	.174	.0194	895	155
Female	Under 65	32	11	.645	.9611	67.1	.084	.0079	1060	76
	65-74	18	10	.429	.9206	46.6	.156	.0164	950	140
	All Ages	50	21	.567	.9495	59.7	.107	.0103	1040	97

*Interval No. 1 ends with biennial exam next after first appearance of CHF
†Basis of expected mortality: Framingham subjects free from CHF on examination

OTHER CARDIOVASCULAR DISEASES

§382–INTERMITTENT CLAUDICATION

Reference: J. Schiffman, "The Framingham Study. Section 25. Survival Following Certain Cardiovascular Events," Govt. Printing Office, Washington, D. C. (September 1970).

Subjects Studied: Examinee-participants in the Framingham Heart Study (see §380) who developed intermittent claudication (IC) during the 14-year interval from just after the initial examination, about 1950, to the eighth biennial examination, about 1964, thus excluding subjects with a pre-existing condition diagnosed at the first examination. Diagnosis was based on the subject's history of pain in the lower limbs when walking, and relieved within a few minutes by resting. There were 107 subjects (out of 5,209) diagnosed as developing IC prior to Examination 8.

Distribution of subjects and incidence rates, by sex and by age at diagnosis, was as follows (Section 7, Table 7-12, including cases developing prior to Examination 9, about 1966):

Age at Diagnosis (Years)	29-44	45-54	55-64	65-74	Total
Males - Exposure (person-years)	10326	10824	7638	1792	30580
Incidence*	0.7(7)	1.8(20)	5.4(41)	6.1(11)	2.6(79)
Females - Exposure (person-years)	12644	13736	10022	2600	39002
Incidence*	0.3(4)	0.7(10)	1.8(18)	5.4(14)	1.2(46)

* Cases/1000/year.   (Number of cases in parentheses.)

Follow-up: Life table data presented in the reference were based on a history of IC first reported at Examinations 2 through 8, followed up to Examination 9, about 1966. Survival data are lacking for the first interval between onset of IC and the examination when first reported. Such data, accordingly, are not recorded prior to Interval 2 in Tables 382a-b. For further information on follow-up methods consult the reference and §380.

Results: Tables 382a-b show a high mortality rate in subjects with this disease, with 23 deaths out of 107 entrants, and roughly similar excess death rates for both sexes. From the limited data presented, it appears that excess mortality tends to increase with duration for both sexes, but numbers of deaths are very small.

Comment: In 46 subjects pre-existing or co-existing coronary heart disease (CHD), cerebrovascular accident (CVA) or congestive heart failure (CHF) was diagnosed at the time of the IC diagnosis. Survival rates for those subjects without co-existing CHD, CVA, or CHF, at the third examination after IC diagnosis (about 7 years after onset), were 89.5 per cent for males, and 94.7 per cent for women, or about what were expected in the general population. This suggests "that IC appears serious because it frequently exists with other cardiovascular diseases," in the opinion of the author.

INTERMITTENT CLAUDICATION — FRAMINGHAM STUDY

Table 382a   Observed Data and Comparative Experience by Duration — All Ages Combined

| Sex and Interval* | | No. Alive at Start of Interval | Deaths in Interval | Interval Mortality Rate | Mortality Ratio | | Survival Ratio | | Excess Death Rate |
No.	Start-End				Interval	Cumulative	Interval	Cumulative	
i	t to t + Δ t	ℓ	d	$q_i = d/\ell$	100 q_i/q_i'	100 Q/Q'	100 p_i/p_i'	100 P/P'	1000 ($\breve{q}$-$\breve{q}'$)
	Male								
1	0-1 yr	— Not Available —							
2	1-3	69	4	.058	139%	139%	98.3%	98.3%	7.9
3	3-5	56	5	.089	196	167	95.4	93.8	23
4	5-7	39	3	.077	166	163	96.8	90.8	15
5	7-9	25	4	.160	330	197	88.3	80.1	58
	1-9	69	16	.232	197	197	80.1	80.1	20
	Female								
1	0-1 yr	— Not Available —							
2	1-3	38	1	.026	95%	95%	100.1%	100.1%	−0.7
3	3-5	28	2	.071	290	188	95.2	95.3	24
4	5-7	17	1	.059	220	195	96.7	92.2	17
5	7-9	13	3	.231	660	315	79.7	73.5	105
	1-9	38	7	.184	315	315	73.5	73.5	24

Table 382b   Derived Mortality and Survival Data

| Sex and Interval* | | Observed | | | | Expected† | | | |
| | | Survival Rate | | | Ave. Ann. Mort. Rate | Survival Rate | | | Ave. Ann. Mort. Rate |
No.	Start-End	Cumulative	Interval	Ave. Ann.		Cumulative	Interval	Ave. Ann.	
i	t to t + Δ t	P	p_i	$\breve{p}$	$\breve{q}$	P'	p_i'	$\breve{p}'$	$\breve{q}'$
	Male								
1	0-1 yr	— Not Available —							
2	1-3	.942	.942	.971	.029	.9583	.9583	.9789	.0211
3	3-5	.858	.911	.954	.046	.9148	.9546	.9770	.0230
4	5-7	.792	.923	.961	.039	.8723	.9536	.9765	.0235
5	7-9	.665	.840	.917	.083	.8299	.9513	.9753	.0247
	Female								
1	0-1 yr	— Not Available —							
2	1-3	.974	.974	.987	.013	.9727	.9727	.9863	.0137
3	3-5	.904	.929	.964	.036	.9488	.9754	.9876	.0124
4	5-7	.851	.941	.970	.030	.9234	.9733	.9866	.0134
5	7-9	.655	.769	.877	.123	.8912	.9651	.9824	.0176

Table 382c   Comparative Survival Experience by Age Group — First 4 Available Years Combined

| Sex and Age Group | No. Alive at Start of Interval | Deaths during Interval | Survival Rate | | Cumulative Survival Ratio | Estimated Average Ann. Mort. Rate | | Mortality Ratio | Excess Death Rate |
			Observed	Expected†		Observed	Expected		
	ℓ	d	P	P'	100 P/P'	$\breve{q}$	$\breve{q}'$	100 $\breve{q}/\breve{q}'$	1000 ($\breve{q}$-$\breve{q}'$)
Male									
Under 65	47	5	.887	.9395	94.4%	.030	.0155	194%	14
65-74	22	4	.788	.8562	92.0	.058	.0381	152	20
All Ages	69	9	.858	.9148	93.8	.038	.0220	173	16
Female									
Under 65	24	2	.889	.9623	92.4%	.029	.0096	300%	19
65-74	14	1	.929	.9253	100.4	.018	.0192	94	−1.2
All Ages	38	3	.904	.9488	95.3	.025	.0131	191	12

*Interval No. 1 ends with biennial exam next after first appearance of intermittent claudication
†Basis of expected mortality: Framingham subjects free from intermittent claudication

CARDIOMYOPATHIES

§383–CARDIOMYOPATHIES

References: (1) G.I. Shugoll, P.J. Bowen, J.P. Moore, and M.L. Lenkin, "Follow-Up Observations and Prognosis in Primary Myocardial Disease," Arch. Int. Med., 129:67-72 (1972).

(2) J.G. Demakis, S.H. Rahimtoola, G.C. Sutton, W.R. Meadows, P.B. Szanto, J.R. Tobin, and R.M. Gunnar, "Natural Course of Peripartum Cardiomyopathy," Circulation, 44:1053-1061 (1971).

(3) C.D. McDonald, G.E. Burch, and J.J. Walsh, "Alcoholic Cardiomyopathy Managed with Prolonged Bed Rest," Ann. Int. Med., 74:681-691 (1971).

(4) J.G. Demakis, A. Proskey, S. H. Rahimtoola, M. Jamil, G.C. Sutton, K.W. Rosen, R.M. Gunnar, and J.R. Tobin, Jr., "The Natural Course of Alcoholic Cardiomyopathy," Ann. Int. Med., 80:293-297 (1974).

(5) T. Hardarson, C.S. de la Calzada, R. Curiel, and J.F. Goodwin, "Prognosis and Mortality of Hypertrophic Obstructive Cardiomyopathy," Lancet, 2:1462-1467 (1973).

(6) S. Frank and E. Braunwald, "Idiopathic Hypertrophic Subaortic Stenosis. Clinical Analysis of 126 Patients with Emphasis on the Natural History," Circulation, 37:759-788 (1968).

Subjects Studied: (1) 50 in-patients with primary myocardial disease treated at the V.A. Hospital, Washington, D.C., starting in 1961. These were men age 22-50, with low output congestive heart failure in the absence of angina, other coronary heart disease (CHD), significant hypertension, organic valvular heart disease or other serious disease. In 23 older patients CHD was ruled out by coronary arteriography. There was a high preponderance of black patients, 92 per cent, compared to an expected 46 per cent, based on admissions to the medical service of this hospital.

(2) 27 patients presenting in the puerperium at Cook County Hospital, Chicago, 1947-1967, with complications of congestive heart failure, enlarged heart and abnormal ECG, diagnosed as cardiomyopathy. This was a diagnosis of exclusion after careful study to rule out prior history of heart disease and current evidence of other types of heart disease. Only two of the patients were white, 25 of them being black; 14 of the women were under 30 years of age and six had complicating toxemia of pregnancy. They were divided into two groups on the basis of whether or not the heart size had returned to normal six months after delivery.

(3) 48 patients with alcoholic cardiomyopathy treated at the Charity Hospital and Veterans Administration Hospital, New Orleans, 1959-1969. The mean age was 38 years with a range of 21 to 57 years; all patients except one were male, with 41 black and seven white. All patients had a history, symptoms and evidence of congestive heart failure. All had a history of excessive alcohol intake, heart enlargement by X-ray, and abnormal ECG, and all were negative for coronary heart disease or other forms of heart disease. All were treated with prolonged bed rest and were repeatedly evaluated in the hospital and in follow-up, either as outpatients or in subsequent hospitalization.

(4) 57 patients with alcoholic cardiomyopathy hospitalized and studied at the Cook County Hospital, Chicago, 1962-1970. Criteria for diagnosis were congestive heart failure in patients under 50 years old, lack of evidence of the usual causes thereof, and the presence of alcoholism. The mean age was 40.5 years with a range of 22 to 50; 47 of the patients were black and 10 white; males outnumbered females 49 to 8. This group was the residue of a series of 133 patients with the criteria of alcoholic cardiomyopathy; 76 never returned for follow-up study and were therefore excluded.

(5) 119 patients with hypertrophic obstructive cardiomyopathy studied at the Hammersmith Hospital, London, England, 1958-1973. The mean age was 29.2 years with 42 patients under age 21, 41 age 21-40, 35 age 41-60, and only one patient over age 60. Males outnumbered females 65 to 54. Diagnosis was made by demonstration of a left ventricular outflow tract pressure gradient exceeding 10 mm. in 69 patients, angiocardiographic evidence of asymmetric hypertrophy of the left ventricle in 38 patients, and by non-invasive methods in 12 patients. Progressive functional disability was found to accompany advancing age: average age at first visit was 19.8 years for Class I patients, 30.9 years in Class II, and 36.3 years in Class III (New York Heart Association classification).

(6) 126 patients with hemodynamically documented idiopathic hypertrophic subaortic stenosis (IHSS) studied at the National Heart Institute, Bethesda, Maryland, 1954-1966. The male to female ratio was two to one. Patients with coronary heart disease and other forms of heart disease were excluded, together with other forms of cardiomyopathy which did not exhibit evidence of obstruction of the left ventricular outflow tract. Patients in functional Class I had an average age of 23.7 years, those in Class II, 31.6 years, and those in Class III-IV, 41.4 years (New York Heart Association Functional classification).

OTHER CARDIOVASCULAR DISEASES

§383—CARDIOMYOPATHIES (continued)

Follow-up: (1) Patients were followed up an average of 2.5 years at intervals as frequent as one month in a special clinic, and efforts were made to reschedule patients who missed an appointment.

(2) Patients were followed in a special clinic, usually at three-month intervals. Average follow-up was 10.7 years for those whose heart size had returned to normal at six months, and 5.4 years in the group with heart enlargement still persisting.

(3) Patients were followed in a special cardiomyopathy clinic and many were re-hospitalized for further tests or congestive heart failure and evaluated further. Average follow-up was 4.3 years.

(4) Patients were followed in a special clinic at intervals of three months or less. Average duration of follow-up was 3.4 years.

(5) Methods of follow-up were not described. Average follow-up was 5.6 years.

(6) Of the 126 patients 14 were seen only at the initial hospitalization, 14 were operated on during hospitalization, leaving 98 for follow-up extending a maximum of 12 years and an average of 2.9 years.

Results: The experience for all types of cardiomyopathy showed a poor prognosis (Table 373a). One group with a less adverse prognosis consisted of women with peripartum cardiomyopathy whose heart size returned to normal within six months (2 observed versus 0.56 expected deaths in about 150 person-years of observation). Another group with less adverse prognosis consisted of younger patients with IHSS who were in functional Class I (a single death observed and 0.19 deaths expected in 134 person-years of observation). In all of the remaining groups shown in Table 383a excess mortality was substantially higher with mortality ratios generally above 1000 per cent and excess death rates as high as 154 per 1000. In Series 1, patients with "primary" cardiomyopathy exhibited a mortality ratio of 1060 per cent and EDR of 72 per 1000. The worst prognosis was seen in women with peripartum cardiomyopathy when the heart size remained enlarged six months after delivery. Their mortality ratio was 5200 per cent, EDR 154 per 1000 and estimated five-year survival index 43 per cent. Most of the patients in these two series as well as Series 3 and 4 were nonwhite. Both series of patients with alcoholic cardiomyopathy, in which the age distribution was similar (average ages were 38 and 40.5 years) showed very high excess death rates of 87 and 115 per 1000. Maximum follow-up extended beyond 15 years in the patients with hypertrophic obstructive cardiomyopathy, a series which included a high proportion of young patients (35 per cent under age 21) as well as patients over age 50, in contrast to a distribution almost entirely confined to the range of 20 to 50 years in Series 1-4. The aggregate mortality ratio in this series of hypertrophic obstructive cardiomyopathy was 795 per cent with an EDR 28 per 1000—the best record except for the two special groups mentioned above. The experience in this series is given in Table 383b by duration and shows a dip in mortality ratio in the 5-10 year interval and an increase in both mortality ratio and EDR in the 10-15 year interval. Cumulative survival ratios were 89.2 per cent at 5 years, 79.8 per cent at 10 years, and 56.9 per cent at 15 years. Another series with obstructive cardiomyopathy (IHSS) demonstrates increasing mortality with progressive degrees of congestive failure (Table 383a). Forty-two patients with no failure (New York Heart Association Class I) showed only one death against 0.19 expected deaths, as noted previously. Those with mild failure, Class II, had a mortality ratio of 2500 per cent and EDR of 44 per 1000, while a smaller and older group with moderate to severe failure, Class III-IV had about the same mortality ratio, but an EDR of 92 per 1000. The increase in average age with increasing severity of congestive failure suggests a steady progression of the disease from a fairly uniform asymptomatic stage to severe failure and marked increase in mortality risk.

CARDIOMYOPATHIES

Table 383a Comparative Experience, Various Types of Cardiomyopathy

Series	Category	No. of Patients	Exposure Person-Yrs	No. of Deaths Observed	No. of Deaths Expected*	Mortality Ratio	Follow-up Years†	Est. Surv. Index	Excess Death Rate
		ℓ	E	d	d'	100 d/d'	Δt	100 P/P'	1000(d-d')/E
1	Primary	50	125.0	10	0.94	1060%	2.5	82.7%	72
2	Peripartum								
	Normal Ht. Size 6 mos.	14	149.8	2	0.56	355	5	94.9	9.6
	Ht. Enlarged at 6 mos.	13	70.2	11	0.21	5200	5	43.2	154
3	Alcoholic	48	200.0	19	1.68	1130	4	69.4	87
4	Alcoholic	57	193.8	24	1.65	1450	3	69.0	115
5	Hypertrophic-Obst.	119	929.5	30	3.77	795	5	89.2	28
6	Hypertrophic (IHSS)								
	NYHA Class I	42	133.6	1●	0.192	520	3	98.2	6.0
	NYHA Class II	40	110.2	5●	0.204	2500	3	87.5	44
	NYHA Class III-IV	16	41.5	4●	0.164	2400	3	74.7	92
	All	98	285.3	10●	0.56	1790	3	90.4	33

Table 383b Comparative Experience by Duration, Hypertrophic Obstructive Cardiomyopathy

No.	Interval Start-End	Exposure Person-Yrs	No. of Deaths Observed	No. of Deaths Expected*	Mortality Ratio	Ave. Ann. Mort. Rate	Cum. Surv. Rate Observed	Cum. Surv. Rate Expected*	Survival Ratio	Excess Death Rate
i	t to t + Δt	E	d	d'	100 d/d'	$\bar{q}$	P	P'	100 P/P'	$1000(\bar{q}-\bar{q}')$
1	0- 5 yrs	504.5	13	1.50	860%	.026	.878	.9850	89.2%	23
2	5-10	295.0	8	1.33	600	.027	.769	.9630	79.8	23
3	10-15	130.0	9	0.94	955	.069	.528	.9284	56.9	62

* Basis of expected mortality:

    Series 1 — U.S. Negro male 1969-71

    Series 2 — U.S. Nonwhite female 1959-61

    Series 3 — U.S. Nonwhite and white male 1959-61

    Series 4 — U.S. 1969-71 weighted by age, race and sex

    Series 5 — English life tables 1965, weighted by age and sex

    Series 6 — U.S. Total male and Total female 1959-61, average age Group I, 24 years; Group II, 32 years;

    Group III-IV, 41 years

† Nominal duration used to estimate survival rates and survival index. Actual survival rates used for Series 5

● Includes only deaths attributed to IHSS

OTHER CARDIOVASCULAR DISEASE

§385–RENAL ARTERY ATHEROSCLEROSIS

Reference: J. Wollenweber, S. G. Sheps, and G. D. Davis, "Clinical Course of Atherosclerotic Renovascular Disease," Am. J. Card., 21:60-71 (1968).

Subjects Studied: Patients at the Mayo Clinic with atherosclerosis of one or both renal arteries, assembled in a review of all aorticorenal arteriograms made at the Clinic between January 1960 and December 1963. There were 109 such patients available for follow-up; the mean age of the 71 men was 54.5 years, of the 38 women patients, 52.3 years. There was considerable coexisting atherosclerotic disease of various regions of the body. Fifteen of 48 patients with mild or moderate narrowing of the main renal artery (31 per cent) and 30 of 61 patients with marked or severe narrowing (49 per cent) had clinical evidence of symptomatic coronary artery, cerebrovascular or peripheral vascular disease. The aforementioned 45 subjects had histories of 55 episodes of angina pectoris, myocardial infarction, transient and completed strokes, or intermittent claudication; various combinations of these diseases had occurred in ten subjects. Fifteen patients had congestive heart failure. The diastolic blood pressure of only 13 subjects (12 per cent) was 90 mm. Hg or less; for an additional 13 it was 91 to 100; it was over 100 mm. in the case of 83 (76 per cent). Sixty-four patients were initially free of symptomatic cardiovascular disease.

Follow-up: Reviews of patients' physical status were made during the follow-up period, including blood pressure reading (of 97 patients) and examination of optic fundi (42 patients). During the summer of 1966, at the close of the follow-up period, information was obtained either by follow-up letter or by reassessment of reviews made at return visits. With respect to patients whose diastolic blood pressure was initially 90 mm. Hg or more, two groups were noted: (1) those whose blood pressure at follow-up was 90 mm. or less (well controlled hypertension), and (2) those whose blood pressure at the latter points was more than 90 mm. (poorly controlled hypertension).

Results: The mortality ratio indicated in Table 385a for all durations combined was four and one-half times that of a similarly composed sex-age grouping in the general population — individual yearly intervals ranging from 275 to 640 per cent of the expected. There was no definite trend by duration. The cumulative survival ratio was 73.2 per cent. The average number of excess deaths per 1000 was 52. The mortality ratio in the case of 43 patients classed as well controlled hypertensives was 260 per cent, for the poorly controlled group (45 subjects), 590 per cent. EDR for the latter category over the five-year period averaged 74 per 1000 per year — about three times the 24 in the well controlled group.

Mortality in patients with atherosclerosis of the renal arteries is to a large extent probably determined by many associated severe cardiovascular impairments (see above). Among the causes of the 26 deaths occurring in the present series (as indicated in the following tabulation) only one death (apart from two of unknown cause) was unrelated to cardiovascular disease:

Cause of Death	No.	Cause of Death	No.
Renal failure	6	Metastatic cancer	1
Cerebrovascular accident	6	Unknown	2
Cardiac arrest	9		
Abdominal vascular catastrophe	2	Total Deaths	26

Of the 64 patients with renal atherosclerosis who were initially free of cardiovascular disease, 24 developed symptoms of such disease over five years. The rates and incidence of the development of symptoms are presented in Table 385c. It is estimated that about half of the symptom-free patients failed to develop symptoms of cardiovascular disease within the five-year period. If a patient developed a cardiovascular symptom in the course of a year, that case was included whether or not the patient died within the year.

RENAL ARTERY ATHEROSCLEROSIS

Table 385a Observed Data and Comparative Experience by Duration - All Ages Combined

Interval		No. Alive at Start of Interval	Exposure Person-Yrs	Deaths in Interval		Mortality Ratio		Survival Ratio		Excess Death Rate
No.	Start-End			Obs.	Exp.*	Interval	Cumulative	Interval	Cumulative	
i	t to t + Δt	ℓ	E	d	d'	100d/d'	100 Q/Q'	100p_i/p_i'	100 P/P'	1000(d-d')/E
All Subjects										
1	0-1 yr	109	109	6	1.26	475%	475%	95.6%	95.6%	43
2	1-2 yrs	103	103	6	1.28	470	460	95.4	91.2	46
3	2-3 yrs	97	91	4	1.46	275	380	97.2	88.6	28
4	3-4 yrs	81	60.5	8	1.25	640	440	88.6	78.5	112
5	4-5 yrs	32	22	2	.56	355	395	93.3	73.2	65
	0-5 yrs	109	385.5	26	5.81	450	395	94.7	73.2	52
Well Controlled Hypertension †										
	0-5 yrs	43	155.5	6	2.33	260	210	97.6	89.9	24
Poorly Controlled Hypertension ●										
	0-5 yrs	45	156	14	2.38	590	560	92.4	58.2	74

Table 385b   Derived Mortality and Survival Data

Interval		Observed Rates				Expected Rates*			
		Interval		Cumulative		Interval		Cumulative	
No.	Start-End	Mortality	Survival	Survival	Mortality	Mortality	Survival	Survival	Mortality
i	t to t + Δt	q_i	p_i	P	Q	q_i'	p_i'	P'	Q'
All Subjects									
1	0-1 yr	.055	.945	.945	.055	.0116	.9884	.9884	.0116
2	1-2 yrs	.058	.942	.890	.110	.0124	.9876	.9761	.0239
3	2-3 yrs	.044	.956	.851	.149	.0160	.9840	.9605	.0395
4	3-4 yrs	.132	.868	.738	.262	.0207	.9793	.9406	.0594
5	4-5 yrs	.091	.909	.671	.329	.0256	.9744	.9166	.0834
	0-5 yrs	.067	.933	.671	.329	.0151	.9849	.9166	.0834
Well Controlled Hypertention †									
	0-5 yrs	.039	.961	.824	.176	.0151	.9849	.9166	.0834
Poorly Controlled Hypertension ●									
	0-5 yrs	.090	.910	.534	.466	.0151	.9849	.9166	.0834

Table 385c   Development of Cardiovascular Disease among Symptom-free Patients

Interval		Symptom-free Patients Surviving Start of Interval	Withdrawn + Died Cases	Exposure Person-Yrs	Cases Developing Symptoms	Symptom Incidence Rate
No.	Start-End					
i	t to t + Δt	ℓ	w + d	E	c	$q^{(c)}$
1	0-1 yr	64	2	63	4	.064
2	1-2 yrs	58	1	57.5	8	.139
3	2-3 yrs	49	6	46	6	.130
4	3-4 yrs	37	14	30	5	.167
5	4-5 yrs	18	12	12	1	.083
	0-5 yrs	64	35	208.5	24	.115

* Basis of expected mortality: U.S. White Population 1959-61

† Initial diastolic blood pressure > 90 mm Hg; follow-up pressure, 90 or less

● Initial diastolic blood pressure > 90 mm Hg; follow-up pressure, > 90

OTHER CARDIOVASCULAR DISEASES

§390–CARDIAC TRANSPLANT

References: (1) D. A. Clark, E. B. Stinson, R. B. Griepp, J. S. Schroeder, N. E. Shumway, and D. C. Harrison, "Cardiac Transplantation in Man. VI. Prognosis of Patients Selected for Cardiac Transplantation," Ann. Int. Med., 75:15-21 (1971).
(2) B. W. Turnbull, B. W. Brown, Jr., and M. Hu, "Survivorship Analysis of Heart Transplant Data," J. Am. Stat. Assoc., 69:74-80 (1974).

Subjects Studied: 52 patients with end-stage heart disease who were selected for and underwent cardiac transplant at Stanford University Hospital, Palo Alto, California, July 1967 to December 1972. Average age, based on 20 patients reported in Reference (1), was 49.1 years. Most of the patients had severe coronary heart disease, but some had cardiomyopathy.

Follow-up: This was complete for all 52 patients in the series to the closing date of March 1, 1973, (Reference 2).

Results: Mortality is very high following cardiac transplant, as evident in the results in Tables 390a-b. In the first 3 months following operation 22 of 52 patients died, a rate of .431. Interval mortality rates have been calculated on the basis of exposed to risk (E_i), with deaths during the interval considered to be at risk for the full interval, in accordance with conventional life-table methods as used in this monograph. Subsequent experience after the first 3 months revealed a mortality ratio of 4500 per cent up to one year, 1620 per cent in the second and 2800 per cent in the third year. The cumulative survival ratio was 26 per cent at 3 years after operation, with values of EDR ranging from 140 to 360 per 1000 per year. The number of deaths recorded after the initial post-operative interval is small and the rates and ratios developed are of limited significance.

Comment: Survival experience of patients accepted for the program but not actually receiving a transplant was also reported, but is difficult to compare with the experience of the operated group because of the interval between acceptance and operation, and the fact that the occasional patient who does unexpectedly well on medical therapy is removed from the program acceptance group. Various evaluations (Reference 2) suggest at least a slight improvement in prognosis as a result of the heart transplant, and quality of life is improved for some patients.

Table 390a   Observed Data and Exposed to Risk, Heart Transplant

| Interval | | No. Alive at Start of Interval | Number of Deaths | No. Withdrawn Alive | Exposure Person-Day | Exposed to Risk in Interval* | Exposure Person-Yrs* |
No.	Start-End						
i	t to t + Δt	ℓ	d	w	E'	E_i	E
1	0-3 mos	52	22	2	3494	51.1	12.8
2	¼-1 yr	28	7	5	5935	25.4	19.1
3	1-2 yrs	16	2	5	4797	13.4	13.4
4	2-3 yrs	9	2	3	2289	7.2	7.2

Table 390b   Comparative Experience by Duration, Heart Transplant

| Interval | | Interval Mort. Rate | | Mortality Ratio | Cumulative Surv. Rate | | Survival Ratio | Excess Death Rate |
No.	Start-End	Observed	Expected†		Observed	Expected		
i	t to t + Δt	$q_i = d/E_i$	q_i'	100 q_i/q_i'	P	P'	100 P/P'	1000(q_i-q_i')/Δt
1	0-3 mos	.431	.0021	21000%	.569	.9979	57.0%	143/mo
2	¼-1yr	.276	.0062	4500	.412	.9917	41.5	360/yr
3	1-2 yrs	.149	.0092	1620	.351	.9826	35.7	140/yr
4	2-3 yrs	.278	.0101	2800	.253	.9727	26.0	268/yr

* Deaths considered to be at risk for the full interval, in contrast to E'
† Basis of expected mortality: 1964 U.S. White Male rates

CARDIOVASCULAR DISEASES

§399—CARDIOVASCULAR DISORDERS (MISCELLANEOUS)

References: (1) T. W. Preston and R. D. Clarke, "An Investigation into the Mortality of Impaired Lives During The Period 1947-63," J. Inst. Act., 92:27-74 (1966).
(2) A. Svensson and S. Astrand, "Substandard Risk Mortality in Sweden 1955-1965," Coopération Internationale pour les Assurances des Risques Aggravés. (See Rome Conference proceedings, 1969.)
(3) "New York Life Single Medical Impairment Study - 1972," unpublished report made available by J. J. Hutchinson and J. C. Sibigtroth (1973).
(4) R. B. Singer, New England Life unpublished mortality studies (1968 and 1974).

Subjects Studied: (1) Policyholders of Prudential Assurance Co., London, England, issued insurance 1947-1963 followed to 12/31/63. Both standard and substandard issues were included. Applicants with two or more ratable impairments were generally excluded.
(2) Lives reinsured (mostly on a substandard basis) with Sverige Reinsurance Co., Sweden, placed in force prior to 1955 and observed between anniversaries in 1955 and 1965.
(3) Policyholders of New York Life Insurance Co., issued insurance 1954-1970 followed to 1971 policy anniversary. Both standard and substandard issues were included. Applicants with more than one ratable impairment were excluded.
(4) Policyholders of New England Mutual Life Insurance Co., issued insurance 1935-1963 followed to 1968 anniversaries for congenital heart disease, peripheral vascular disease, possible congestive heart failure. Standard and substandard issues were investigated.

Follow-up: Insurance policy records formed the basis of entry, counting policies, exposures, and death claims, and of follow-up information.

Results: A miscellany of cardiovascular disorders is presented in Table 399. While among the lives insured some were classed as standard, the predominant weight of the experience in all categories was substandard. Individuals accepted for insurance coverage, it should be kept in mind, even though substandard, generally represent the best cases in any impairment category so that results are probably not typical of the average case with a particular impairment as encountered by the physician in practice.

In the relatively limited experience of the New York Life at the top of Table 399 the mortality ratio was 330 per cent for policyholders with a history of angina pectoris, and 280 per cent for those with other coronary artery disease, the excess death rate being 12 per 1000 per year in both categories. More detailed results on insured policyholders are given in abstracts §304-306.

In the table, considerable detail is shown in the Prudential of London experience with respect to hypertension. In this experience standard and substandard lives are combined, but separation is made by sex, by age at commencement of coverage, and by weight; in the case of males between 40 and 59 years of age, analysis by blood pressure categories is also reported. The highest mortality ratio developed amongst men under 40 years of age regardless of weight: in this group, mortality was 260 per cent of the expected and there were 1.9 extra deaths per 1000 per year. Men 60 years of age and over, all weights combined, showed the lowest mortality ratio, 122 per cent, with an EDR of 6.0 per 1000. In the intermediate age range (40-59 years), the highest mortality was evidenced among overweights, all blood pressures together, the mortality ratio being 197 per cent and excess deaths amounting to 6.2 per 1000 per year. For men in this age group of standard weight, the most adverse mortality appeared where systolic blood pressures were in the range of 155-170, and diastolic between 95 and 105 mm. Hg. Lower systolic readings within the same diastolic range, and lower diastolic readings within the same systolic range showed about the same mortality ratios (175 and 176 per cent, respectively). Mortality ratios of females, all weights together, were lower at ages 60 years and over than at younger ages, being respectively 112 and 137 per cent. EDR's, however, were somewhat higher in the older age groups, viz., 2.0 vs. 1.7 per 1000. Overweight did not appear to be an important factor in the mortality experience of either sex. The Swedish study did not show results as favorable as those in the Prudential report — even when compared with an expected population standard; the mortality ratio, both sexes and all ages and weights combined, was 180 per cent and EDR, 6.8 per 1000. Such a result is perhaps not surprising since the Swedish experience embraced only substandard lives. In a small group of English insureds with hypotension a normal mortality was experienced.

CARDIOVASCULAR DISORDERS (MISCELLANEOUS)

Table 399   Comparative Experience, Four Series of Insureds (continued)

Disease/Category (Ref.)	Sex/Age	Policies in Force at Start ℓ	Exposure Policy-Yrs E	No. of Death Claims Observed d	No. of Death Claims Expected* d'	Ave. Ann. Mort. Rate Observed $\bar{q} = d/E$	Ave. Ann. Mort. Rate Expected* $\bar{q}' = d'/E$	Mortality Ratio 100 d/d'	Est. 5-Yr Surv. Rate $P = (1-\bar{q})^5$	Est. 5-Yr Surv. Index 100 P/P'	Excess Death Rate $1000(\bar{q}-\bar{q}')$
Angina Pectoris SS† (3)	M&F 45	—	1095	19	5.78	.0174	.0053	330%	.9162	94.1%	12
Coronary Artery Disease (3)	M&F 47	—	882	16	5.73	.0181	.0065	280	.9125	94.3	12
Hypertension S†&SS (1)											
Under 40 yrs - S & Overweight	M 35	4634	28113	85	32.8	.0030	.0012	260	.9850	99.1	1.9
40-59 yrs - Standard Weight											
BP S: 155-170; D: <95	M 50	1550	11322	159	90.4	.0140	.0080	176	.9317	97.0	6.1
S: 155-170; D: 95-105	M 49	1404	9026	125	64.1	.0138	.0071	195	.9326	96.6	6.7
S: <155; D: 95 up	M 48	1357	9665	110	62.9	.0114	.0065	175	.9444	97.6	4.9
40-59 yrs - Overweight	M 47	1205	6888	86	43.6	.0125	.0063	197	.9391	96.9	6.2
60 yrs up - S & Overweight	M 62	1406	8693	293	241	.0337	.0277	122	.8425	96.9	6.0
40-59 yrs - Standard Weight (1)	F 52	873	6199	41	29.0	.0066	.0047	141	.9674	99.0	1.9
Overweight	F 51	263	1723	9	7.44	.0052	.0043	121	.9742	99.5	0.9
S & Overweight	F 52	1136	7922	50	36.5	.0063	.0046	137	.9688	99.1	1.7
60 yrs up - Standard Weight	F 63	330	1880	35	31.6	.0186	.0168	111	.9103	99.1	1.8
Overweight	F 62	51	296	5	4.18	.0169	.0141	120	.9183	98.6	2.8
S & Overweight	F 63	381	2176	40	35.8	.0184	.0164	112	.9114	99.0	2.0
Hypertension SS (2)	M&F 46	—	11531	177	98.5	.0153	.0085	180	.9256	96.6	6.8
Hypotension S&SS (1)	M 40	335	2457	6	6.10	.0024	.0025	98	.9878	100.0	0.0

* Basis of expected mortality: (Ref. 1) Prudential Assurance Co. (England) standard lives mortality 1957-1958;
(Ref. 2) Sverige Reins. Co., population mortality, M or F (Sweden), 1956-60 and 1961-65; (Ref. 3) N. Y. Life, Basic Select Tables (1955-60);
(Ref. 4) New England Life , Basic Tables (1955-60)
† "S" - Standard, "SS" - Substandard

CARDIOVASCULAR DISEASES

§399–CARDIOVASCULAR DISORDERS (MISCELLANEOUS)

Results (continued):

Limited experience for congenital heart disease, all types, yields a mortality ratio of 186 per cent in the New York Life study and 173 per cent in the New England Life study. It should be realized that cyanotic and other severe forms of congenital heart disease were declinable in these observation periods. Insurance would have been issued only to applicants with good functional capacity and less severe forms of congenital heart disease, such as small septal defects, successfully operated patent ductus arteriosus and coarctation of the aorta and the like. A much larger group of substandard valvular heart disease cases in the Sverige Reinsurance Co. was found to have a mortality ratio of 235 per cent and an EDR of 5.3 extra deaths per 1000.

Several categories of abnormality revealed by chest X-ray in the New York Life study (mostly substandard cases) are presented in the table. Overall results indicate that abnormal contour of the heart accounted for the most adverse mortality (ratio, 565 per cent, EDR, 22 per 1000); calcification of the aorta developed a mortality ratio of 265 per cent and an EDR of 16 per 1000; enlargement of the heart exceeding 10 per cent indicated a mortality of 230 per cent and excess deaths of 8.3 per 1000 per year; a tortuous or widened aorta showed comparative mortality of 123 per cent and excess deaths equal to 2.8 per 1000 per year. The numbers of deaths are small and caution should be exercised in interpreting the results on that account. Average age in these categories of cardiovascular abnormality in the chest X-ray ranged from 43 to 55 years, well above the average age for most of the groups in Table 399 not classified by age.

In the category of "congestive heart failure" a mortality ratio of 255 per cent and an EDR of 9.4 per 1000 were reported from the New England Life study. Excess mortality with a ratio of 460 per cent and an EDR of 14 per 1000 were also observed in a much smaller group of New York Life policyholders with edema coded on examination. It is probable that few if any of these cases were evaluated as having dyspnea, peripheral edema or other evidence attributable to definite congestive failure and definite serious heart disease, as such applicants would ordinarily be declined for insurance. Nevertheless, even doubtful evidence of this character was associated with a considerable degree of excess mortality.

Mortality comparable with that of unimpaired standard lives was reported in the English experience for both male and female insureds with varicose veins evident on examination. In the New York Life study, on the other hand, a mortality ratio of 147 per cent was found in policyholders coded for varicose veins, and a slightly higher ratio of 167 per cent in those with a history of phlebitis.

Peripheral vascular disorder, including intermittent claudication, in substandard issues was associated with a mortality ratio of 170 per cent in the New York Life study and 149 per cent in the New England Life study (only seven death claims). English insureds coded for "moderate to severe arteriosclerosis" experienced a mortality ratio of 124 per cent, but there was no excess mortality in those classified as "mild" (average entry age was estimated to be only 37 years in both groups). Finally, in a residual category of other cardiovascular diseases, a rather small New York Life group exhibited a mortality ratio of 210 per cent, while a considerably larger group was reported by the Sverige Reinsurance Co. to have a mortality ratio of 141 per cent. This latter ratio would have been high if select rather than population mortality rates had been used as the standard for comparison.

CARDIOVASCULAR DISORDERS (MISCELLANEOUS)

Table 399   Comparative Experience, Four Series of Insureds

Disease/Category (Ref.)	Sex/Age	Policies in Force at Start	Exposure Policy-Yrs	No. of Death Claims		Ave. Ann. Mort. Rate		Mortality Ratio	Est. 5-Yr Surv. Rate	Est. 5-Yr Surv. Index	Excess Death Rate
				Observed	Expected*	Observed	Expected*				
		Q	E	d	d'	$\bar{q} = d/E$	$\bar{q}' = d'/E$	$100\, d/d'$	$P = (1-\bar{q})^5$	$100\, P/P'$	$1000(\bar{q}-\bar{q}')$
Congenital Heart Dis. S†&SS† (3)	M&F 32	–	3919	10	5.38	.0026	.0014	186%	.9873	99.4%	1.2
Congenital Heart Dis. SS (4)	M&F 30	250	1981	8	4.62	.0040	.0023	173	.9800	99.1	1.7
Valvular Heart Dis. SS (2)	M&F 39	–	18310	171	73.2	.0093	.0040	235	.9542	97.3	5.3
Chest X-ray (CV Abn.) (3)											
Heart Enlarged (>10%) SS	M&F 47	–	744	11	4.80	.0148	.0065	230	.9282	95.9	8.3
Abnormal Ht. Contour SS	M&F 43	–	114	3	0.53	.0263	.0046	565	.8752	89.6	22
Tortuous Aorta S&SS	M&F 55	–	338	5	4.06	.0148	.0120	123	.9282	98.6	2.8
Aortic Calcification SS	M&F 52	–	596	15	5.65	.0252	.0095	265	.8803	92.3	16
Dyspnea, Signs of Congestive											
Heart Failure SS (4)	M&F 44	294	2523	39	15.4	.0155	.0061	255	.9247	95.4	9.4
Edema SS (3)	M&F 42	–	270	5	1.09	.0185	.0040	460	.9108	92.9	14
Varicose Veins S&SS (3)	M&F 47	–	2370	22	15.0	.0093	.0063	147	.9544	98.5	3.0
Varicose Veins SS (1)	M 43	10513	64836	236	227	.0036	.0035	104	.9819	99.9	0.1
Varicose Veins S&SS	F 49	1392	9285	31	31.5	.0033	.0034	98	.9834	100.0	−0.1
Phlebitis SS (3)	M&F 40	–	2410	14	8.37	.0058	.0035	167	.9713	98.8	2.3
Peripheral Vascular Disorder SS (3)	M&F 43	–	2033	16	9.41	.0079	.0046	170	.9613	98.4	3.2
Peripheral Vascular Disorder SS (4)	M&F 43	109	854	7	4.71	.0082	.0055	149	.9597	98.7	2.7
Arteriosclerosis S&SS (1)											
Mild	M 37	310	2408	34	36.0	.0141	.0150	94	.9314	100.4	−0.8
Moderate to Severe	M 37	167	918	17	13.7	.0185	.0150	124	.9108	98.2	3.6
Other CV Disease S&SS (3)	M&F 40	*-	1427	10	4.75	.0070	.0033	210	.9654	98.2	3.7
Other CV Disease SS (2)	M&F 51	–	13371	111	79.0	.0083	.0059	141	.9592	98.8	2.4

* Basis of expected mortality: (Ref. 1) Prudential Assurance Co. (England) standard lives mortality 1957-1958;
  (Ref. 2) Sverige Reins. Co., population mortality, M or F (Sweden), 1956-60 and 1961-65; (Ref. 3) N. Y. Life, Basic Select Tables (1955-60);
  (Ref. 4) New England Life, Basic Tables (1955-60)

† "S" - Standard, "SS" - Substandard

Respiratory Diseases

See Also

1. *1951 Impairment Study.* Chicago: Society of Actuaries (1954).
   C1-C9   Pulmonary tuberculosis (pp. 84-93)
   C10   Chronic bronchitis, found on examination, or at any time prior to application (pp. 93-95)
   C11-C18   Pleurisy, one attack (pp. 96-99)
   C19   Bronchiectasis, found on examination (p. 100)
   C20-C35   Asthma (pp. 100-106)
   C36-C44   Tuberculosis, coresidence with (pp. 107-110)
2. A.M. Lowell, L.B. Edwards, and C.E. Palmer, *Tuberculosis.* Cambridge, Mass.: Harvard University Press (1969).
3. W.K.C. Morgan and A. Seaton, *Occupational Lung Diseases.* Philadelphia: W.B. Saunders Co. (1975).
4. International Labour Office, *Encyclopaedia of Occupational Health and Safety,* Volumes I and II. New York: McGraw-Hill Book Co. (1974).

LUNG AND BRONCHUS

§401—ASTHMA IN INSUREDS

Reference: "New York Life Single Medical Impairment Study—1972," unpublished report made available by J.J. Hutchinson and J.C. Sibigtroth (1973).

Subjects Studied: Policyholders of New York Life Insurance Company issued insurance in 1954-1970, followed to the 1971 policy anniversary. These were cases found to have primary or allergic asthma, with or without history of attacks, seasonal and non-seasonal. Most of the experience reported is for substandard issues; all cases with ratable impairment in addition to asthma were excluded.

Follow-up: Insurance policy records formed the basis of entry, of counting policies, exposure and death claims, and of follow-up information.

Results: Tables 401a-b show that the mortality ratio among male substandard cases was somewhat higher during the first 10 years than in subsequent years. Extra mortality was substantial at 2-10 years, being at least 200 per cent (about 3 extra deaths per 1000). The cumulative survival ratio was 97.2 per cent at 17 years.

The comparative experience by age (Table 401c) among substandard cases indicates an increasing trend in male mortality ratios, ranging from 108 per cent at ages 0-39 to 345 per cent at ages 60 up, while female mortality ratios showed a downward trend by age, from 580 per cent at ages under 40 to 163 per cent at ages 40 up. The EDR likewise increased with age for males, being highest (47 extra deaths per 1000) at ages 60 up; EDR decreased slightly for females at the older ages. The estimated 8-year survival index among substandard males ranged from a normal level at ages under 40 to a minimum of 67.3 per cent at ages 60 up. The data for standard males was limited and no breakdown by age was made. The overall mortality ratio was 88 per cent for male standard cases, compared with the substandard mortality ratios of 180 per cent for males and 280 per cent for females, all ages combined.

Comparative mortality by major causes of death is given in Table 401d for male and female substandard cases combined. There is some increase in the mortality due to diseases of heart and circulation, with an EDR of 0.6 per 1000, but the major cause of death is found in the "all other causes and unknown" category, the mortality being 450 per cent and EDR 1.3 per 1000. Of the 21 deaths found in the latter category, there were 9 allergic disorders and 8 respiratory disorders.

ASTHMA IN INSUREDS

Table 401a Observed Data and Comparative Experience By Duration — Male Substandard Cases

Interval		Exposure Policy-Yrs	No. of Death Claims		Mortality Ratio		Survival Ratio		Excess Death Rate
No.	Start-End		Observed	Expected*	Interval	Cumulative	Interval	Cumulative	
i	t to t + Δt	E	d	d'	100 d/d'	100$\sum$d/$\sum$d'	100 p_i/p_i'	100 P/P'	1000(d-d')/E
1	0- 2 yrs	3303	5	3.89	129%	129%	99.9%	99.9%	0.3
2	2- 5	2865	13	5.43	240	193	99.2	99.1	2.6
3	5-10	2424	14	7.00	200	196	98.6	97.7	2.9
4	10-17	1024	5	4.29	117	180	99.5	97.2	0.7

Table 401b Derived Mortality and Survival Data

Interval		Observed Rates				Expected Rates*			
		Average Annual		Cumulative		Average Annual		Cumulative	
No.	Start-End	Mortality	Survival	Survival	Mortality	Mortality	Survival	Survival	Mortality
i	t to t + Δt	$\bar{q} = d/E$	$\bar{p}$	P	Q	$\bar{q}' = d'/E$	$\bar{p}'$	P'	Q'
Substandard Issues									
1	0- 2 yrs	.0015	.9985	.9970	.0030	.0012	.9988	.9976	.0024
2	2- 5	.0045	.9955	.9835	.0165	.0019	.9981	.9920	.0080
3	5-10	.0058	.9942	.9554	.0446	.0029	.9971	.9777	.0223
4	10-17	.0049	.9951	.9232	.0768	.0042	.9958	.9494	.0506

Table 401c Comparative Experience by Sex and Age Group — All Durations Combined

Sex	Age Group	Exposure Policy-Yrs	No. of Death Claims		Mortality Ratio	Ave. Ann. Mort. Rate	Est. 8-Yr Surv. Rate	Est. 8-Yr Surv. Index	Excess Death Rate
			Observed	Expected*					
		E	d	d'	100 d/d'	$\bar{q} = d/E$	P = $(1 - \bar{q})^8$	100 P/P'	1000(d-d')/E
Standard Issues									
Male	All Ages	5327	10	11.39	88%	.0019	.9851	100.2%	−0.3
Substandard Issues									
Male	0-39 yrs	7781	9	8.35	108	.0012	.9908	99.9	0.1
	40-49	1197	9	4.95	182	.0075	.9414	97.3	3.4
	50-59	503	10	4.71	210	.0199	.8516	91.8	11
	60 up	135	9	2.60	345	.0667	.5758	67.3	47
	All Ages	9616	37	20.61	180	.0038	.9696	98.6	1.7
Female	0-39	2073	7	1.21	580	.0034	.9733	97.8	2.8
	40 up	871	5	3.06	163	.0057	.9550	98.2	2.2
	All Ages	2944	12	4.27	280	.0041	.9678	97.9	2.6

Table 401d Mortality by Cause of Death — Male and Female Combined, Substandard Issues

Cause	No. of Death Claims		Mortality Ratio	Excess Death Rate
	Observed	Expected†		
Malignant Neoplasms	8	5.93	135%	0.1
Diseases of Heart & Circulatory System	17	9.79	174	0.6
Accidents and Homicides	3	3.42	88	0.0
Suicide	0	1.05	0	−0.1
All Other Causes and Unknown	21●	4.69	450	1.3
Total	49	24.88	197	1.9

* Basis of expected mortality: 1955-60 Select Basic Table
† Distribution of total expected deaths by Intercompany Medically Examined Standard Issues 1965-70
● Includes 9 allergic disorders and 8 respiratory disorders

LUNG AND BRONCHUS

§410–ADVANCED PULMONARY TUBERCULOSIS BEFORE CHEMOTHERAPY

References: (1) R. S. Mitchell, "Mortality and Relapse of Uncomplicated Advanced Pulmonary Tuberculosis before Chemotherapy: 1,504 Consecutive Admissions Followed for Fifteen to Twenty-Five Years."

"I. The Relationship of Factors Determined on Admission," Am. Rev. Tuberc. Pulm. Dis., 72:487-501 (1955).

"II. The Relationship of Type of Treatment and Status on Discharge," Am. Rev. Tuberc. Pulm. Dis., 72:502-512 (1955).

(2) R. S. Mitchell, personal communications (1959-60).

Subjects Studied: 1206 cases with moderately advanced, and 298 cases with far advanced pulmonary tuberculosis (TB), constituting all such cases admitted to Trudeau Sanatorium, New York, 1930 through 1939, for whom the diagnosis and stage of the disease were confirmed by subsequent review of the records and no exclusion was made by reason of complication. There were only 16 non-white patients. Most of the patients were young adults, with an average age of 31, and 91 per cent under age 40 (data from Reference 2 total 1193 cases in moderately advanced TB instead of 1206, as indicated in Reference 1):

	Male				Female			
	17-23	24-33	34 up	Total	17-23	24-33	34 up	Total
Mod. Adv.	158	318	145	621	166	277	129	572
Far Adv.	31	63	70	164	47	56	31	134
Total	189	381	215	785	213	333	160	706

Certain tuberculosis complications were regarded as major ones and cause for exclusion, whereas others were not. These and other major nontuberculosis complications were distributed as follows:

Cases Excluded from the Series		Tuberculosis Complications Not Excluded from the Series	
Category	No. of cases	Category	No. of cases
Inactive pulmonary TB	61	Pleurisy with effusion	199
Active minimal pulmonary TB	14	Intestinal TB	103
Pleurisy with effusion, not TB	5	Laryngeal TB	57
Major TB complications (bone and		Endobronchial TB	37
joint, genito-urinary, peritonitis,		Ischiorectal abscess	28
and miliary TB)	21	Otitis Media	16
Major non-TB complication (diabetes,		Cervical adenitis	8
silicosis, malignancy, emphysema,		Empyema	4
severe asthma, etc.)	31	Multiple non-pulm. TB	39
Non-TB pulmonary disease only	5		
Total excluded	137	Total (32.6% of all cases)	491

The socio-economic background was distinctly higher in these patients than in governmentally supported tuberculosis hospitals. Coexisting peptic ulcer (11 cases) and latent syphilis (7 cases) were not considered sufficient reason for exclusion from the series.

Follow-up: Clinical cause and status after discharge from Trudeau Sanatorium were evaluated by records of subsequent readmission, by reports and films from physicians, hospitals and health departments, by routine yearly follow-up questionnaires, and finally by special questionnaires at the end of follow-up in 1953-54. Contact was lost with 126 patients (8.4 per cent) prior to the end of follow-up, but many of these had 10 or more years of exposure before being lost to contact. Survivors' status as to activity of TB, treatment, and other details were recorded for each year of follow-up.

ADVANCED TUBERCULOSIS BEFORE CHEMOTHERAPY

Table 410a   Observed Data and Comparative Experience by Age and Duration, Men with Moderately Advanced TB

No.	Start-End	No. Alive at Start of Interval	Withdrawn + Lost Cases	Exposure Person-Yrs	Obs.	Exp.*	Interval	Cumulative	Interval	Cumulative	Excess Death Rate
i	t to t + Δt	ℓ	w+u	E	d	d'	100 d/d'	100$\sum$d/$\sum$d'	100p_i/p_i'	100 P/P'	1000(d-d')/E
	Age 17-23										
1	0- 2 yrs	158	4	311.0	2	0.84	240%	240%	99.3%	99.3%	3.7
2	2- 5	152	5	442.5	8	1.24	645	480	95.5	94.8	15
3	5-10	139	4	662.0	11	1.66	665	560	93.1	88.3	14
4	10-15	124	14	594.0	3	1.37	220	470	98.6	87.0	2.7
5	15-20	107	49	405.5	3	1.18	255	430	97.8	85.1	4.5
All	0-20 yrs	158	76	2415.0	27	6.29	430	430	85.1	85.1	8.6
	Age 24-33										
1	0- 2 yrs	318	4	630.0	9	2.21	405%	405%	97.8%	97.8%	11
2	2- 5	305	8	890.0	15	3.29	455	435	96.1	94.0	13
3	5-10	282	6	1351.0	22	4.46	495	460	93.6	88.0	13
4	10-15	254	40	1180.0	11	5.19	210	375	97.7	85.9	4.9
5	15-20	203	126	678.0	7	4.34	160	330	98.1	84.3	3.9
All	0-20 yrs	318	184	4729.0	64	19.49	330	330	84.3	84.3	9.4
	Age 34 up										
1	0- 2 yrs	145	1	286.5	4	1.83	220%	220%	98.5%	98.5%	7.6
2	2- 5	140	1	401.5	14	3.09	455	365	92.0	90.6	27
3	5-10	125	3	590.5	15	5.26	285	325	92.0	83.3	16
4	10-15	107	19	492.5	11	6.50	169	265	95.5	79.5	9.1
5	15-20	77	37	284.5	7	5.31	132	230	97.0	77.2	6.0
All	0-20 yrs	145	61	2055.5	51	21.99	230	230	77.2	77.2	14

Table 410b   Derived Mortality and Survival Data, Men with Moderately Advanced TB

No.	Start-End	Average Annual Mortality	Average Annual Survival	Cumulative Survival	Cumulative Mortality	Average Annual Mortality	Average Annual Survival	Cumulative Survival	Cumulative Mortality
i	t to t + Δt	$\bar{q}$ = d/E	$\bar{p}$	P	Q	$\bar{q}'$ = d'/E	$\bar{p}'$	P'	Q'
	Age 17-23								
1	0- 2 yrs	.006	.994	.987	.013	.0027	.9973	.9946	.0054
2	2- 5	.018	.982	.935	.065	.0028	.9972	.9863	.0137
3	5-10	.017	.983	.859	.141	.0025	.9975	.9740	.0260
4	10-15	.005	.995	.838	.162	.0023	.9977	.9629	.0371
5	15-20	.007	.993	.807	.193	.0029	.9971	.9490	.0510
	Age 24-33								
1	0- 2 yrs	.014	.986	.972	.028	.0035	.9965	.9930	.0070
2	2- 5	.017	.983	.923	.077	.0037	.9963	.9820	.0180
3	5-10	.016	.984	.850	.150	.0033	.9967	.9659	.0341
4	10-15	.009	.991	.812	.188	.0044	.9956	.9449	.0551
5	15-20	.010	.990	.771	.229	.0064	.9936	.9150	.0850
	Age 34 up								
1	0- 2 yrs	.014	.986	.972	.028	.0064	.9936	.9872	.0128
2	2- 5	.035	.965	.874	.126	.0077	.9923	.9646	.0354
3	5-10	.025	.975	.768	.232	.0089	.9911	.9224	.0776
4	10-15	.022	.978	.686	.314	.0132	.9868	.8631	.1369
5	15-20	.025	.975	.606	.394	.0187	.9813	.7854	.2146

* Basis of expected mortality: Contemporaneous U.S. Life Tables, White Male or Female

§410–ADVANCED PULMONARY TUBERCULOSIS BEFORE CHEMOTHERAPY (continued)

Results: Experience has been compared with contemporaneous U.S. Life Table white population rates for three age groups, male and female separately, in Tables 410a-d (moderately advanced TB) and in Tables 410e-g (far advanced TB). In Table 410h where results of all age groups and durations to 20 years are combined, the total exposure of 17,583 person-years for the moderately advanced cases generated 258 observed and 75.6 expected deaths. These figures may be compared with 195 deaths due to TB and 70 to other causes (upper part of table – 7 of 265 deaths occurred after 20 years). For far advanced cases the experience to 20 years involved 139 observed and 16.9 expected deaths and an exposure of 3604 person-years; out of the 139 deaths, 120 were due to TB and only 19 to other causes. It is apparent, therefore, that the excess mortality is attributable to TB; deaths recorded as being due to *other* causes were actually smaller than total expected deaths for *all* causes. The overall mortality ratio of 820 per cent for the far advanced cases is considerably higher than the 340 per cent for the moderately advanced cases. In terms of EDR the differential is even greater: 34 versus 10 excess deaths per 1000 per year.

In the moderately advanced cases (Tables 410a-d) excess mortality was at a maximum in the periods from 2 to 10 years after start of treatment. For the youngest male age group, 15-23, the mortality ratio was 240 per cent in the first two years of observation, rose above 600 per cent from 2 to 10 years, then fell again to 220-255 per cent after 10 years. Similar trends were observed in males and females age 24 up, the mortality ratios exhibiting a tendency to decrease with age and to average higher in females. The highest mortality ratio in the first two years, 985 per cent, was found in females under age 24, but even in this group the period of maximum mortality ratio was still somewhat higher (1160 per cent) at 5 to 10 years. EDR in the period of maximum excess mortality from 2 to 10 years ranged from 4.2 to 29 extra deaths per thousand per year, the highest values being found in those age 34 up for both sexes. Significant excess mortality persisted in all groups even 10 to 20 years after start of treatment, with EDR in the range of 1.1 to 10 extra deaths per thousand per year. Cumulative survival ratios at 20 years fell between 77.2 per cent as a minimum and 85.1 per cent as a maximum.

Despite higher mortality rates in the far advanced cases, the exposures and numbers of deaths were sufficiently limited to make it necessary to show mortality by duration for all ages combined, results for both sexes being given in Tables 410e-f. The peak of excess mortality occurred in the earliest period (1490 per cent for males and 2100 per cent for females), instead of after 2 years as in the moderately advanced cases. Although the mortality ratio did tend to decrease with the passage of time, the minimum value observed from 15 to 20 years after start of treatment was still 210 per cent. Correspondingly high values of EDR were noted, with an extreme range for all intervals from 7 to 63 extra deaths per 1000 per year. The 20-year cumulative survival ratio was 54.6 per cent for males and 55.8 per cent for females. Comparative experience by age for far advanced cases (all durations combined) is shown in Table 410g. There is not much tendency for the mortality ratio to decrease with advancing age, but EDR shows a substantial increase.

Table 410h gives status of survivors at end of follow-up in 1953-54 as well as mortality by cause of death (previously described). The chronic nature of pulmonary TB is illustrated by the fact that almost 3 per cent of all patients were then under active treatment for TB. Most of the known survivors, however, were reported as "well," with their TB in an arrested state.

ADVANCED TUBERCULOSIS BEFORE CHEMOTHERAPY

Table 410c   Observed Data and Comparative Experience by Age and Duration, Women with Moderately Advanced TB

Age and Interval		No. Alive at Start of Interval	Withdrawn + Lost Cases	Exposure Person-Yrs	Deaths in Interval		Mortality Ratio		Survival Ratio		Excess Death Rate
No.	Start-End				Obs.	Exp.*	Interval	Cumulative	Interval	Cumulative	
i	t to t + Δt	ℓ	w+u	E	d	d'	100 d/d'	100Σd/Σd'	100p_i/p_i'	100 P/P'	1000(d-d')/E
	Age 17-23										
1	0- 2 yrs	166	3	323.5	7	0.71	985%	985%	96.2%	96.2%	19
2	2- 5	156	3	459.5	3	1.06	285	565	98.7	94.9	4.2
3	5-10	150	6	714.0	14	1.21	1160	805	91.3	86.7	18
4	10-15	130	20	598.0	7	0.96	730	785	95.1	82.4	10
5	15-20	103	52	371.0	2	0.71	280	710	98.3	81.0	3.5
All	0-20 yrs	166	84	2466.0	33	4.65	710	710	81.0	81.0	11
	Age 24-33										
1	0- 2 yrs	277	3	548.5	3	1.65	180%	180%	99.5%	99.5%	2.5
2	2- 5	271	5	795.5	16	2.39	670	470	94.9	94.5	17
3	5-10	250	4	1196.0	22	2.99	735	585	92.3	87.2	16
4	10-15	224	31	1047.5	8	2.93	275	490	97.6	85.1	4.8
5	15-20	185	118	630.0	3	2.33	129	425	99.4	84.6	1.1
All	0-20 yrs	277	161	4217.5	52	12.29	425	425	84.6	84.6	9.4
	Age 34 up										
1	0- 2 yrs	129	3	253.5	5	1.19	420%	420%	97.0%	97.0%	15
2	2- 5	121	4	345.0	12	1.83	655	565	91.4	88.6	29
3	5-10	105	7	491.5	7	2.80	250	410	95.8	84.9	8.5
4	10-15	91	19	417.5	4	3.09	129	315	98.9	84.0	2.2
5	15-20	68	51	192.5	3	1.96	153	285	97.3	81.7	5.4
All	0-20 yrs	129	84	1700.0	31	10.87	285	285	81.7	81.7	12

Table 410d   Derived Mortality and Survival Data, Women with Moderately Advanced TB

Age and Interval		Observed Rates				Expected Rates*			
		Average Annual		Cumulative		Average Annual		Cumulative	
No.	Start-End	Mortality	Survival	Survival	Mortality	Mortality	Survival	Survival	Mortality
i	t to t + Δt	$\bar{q}$ = d/E	$\bar{p}$	P	Q	$\bar{q}'$ = d'/E	$\bar{p}'$	P'	Q'
	Age 17-23								
1	0- 2 yrs	.022	.978	.957	.043	.0022	.9978	.9956	.0044
2	2- 5	.007	.993	.939	.061	.0023	.9977	.9887	.0113
3	5-10	.020	.980	.850	.150	.0017	.9983	.9804	.0196
4	10-15	.012	.988	.802	.198	.0016	.9984	.9725	.0275
5	15-20	.005	.995	.780	.220	.0019	.9981	.9633	.0367
	Age 24-33								
1	0- 2 yrs	.006	.994	.989	.011	.0030	.9970	.9940	.0060
2	2- 5	.020	.980	.931	.069	.0030	.9970	.9851	.0149
3	5-10	.018	.982	.848	.152	.0025	.9975	.9728	.0272
4	10-15	.008	.992	.816	.184	.0028	.9972	.9593	.0407
5	15-20	.005	.995	.797	.203	.0037	.9963	.9417	.0583
	Age 34 up								
1	0- 2 yrs	.020	.980	.961	.039	.0047	.9953	.9906	.0094
2	2- 5	.035	.965	.864	.136	.0053	.9947	.9750	.0250
3	5-10	.014	.986	.805	.195	.0057	.9943	.9475	.0525
4	10-15	.010	.990	.767	.233	.0074	.9926	.9129	.0871
5	15-20	.016	.984	.709	.291	.0102	.9898	.8673	.1327

* Basis of expected mortality: Contemporaneous U.S. Life Tables, White Male or Female

LUNG AND BRONCHUS

Table 410e   Observed Data and Comparative Experience by Sex and Duration, Patients with Far Advanced Pulmonary TB

No.	Start-End	No. Alive at Start of Interval	Withdrawn + Lost Cases	Exposure Person-Yrs	Deaths in Interval Obs.	Exp.*	Mortality Ratio Interval	Cumulative	Survival Ratio Interval	Cumulative	Excess Death Rate
i	t to t + Δt	ℓ	w+u	E	d	d'	100 d/d'	100Σd/Σd'	100p_i/p_i'	100 P/P'	1000(d-d')/E
Male
1	0- 2 yrs	164	2	311.0	21	1.41	1490%	1490%	87.9%	87.9%	63
2	2- 5	141	3	395.5	20	2.00	1000	1200	87.0	76.4	46
3	5-10	118	1	539.5	19	2.78	685	970	86.3	65.9	30
4	10-15	98	12	444.0	15	3.02	495	815	86.8	57.2	27
5	15-20	71	36	257.0	5	2.40	210	690	95.4	54.6	10
All	0-20 yrs	164	54	1947.0	80	11.61	690	690	54.6	54.6	35
Female
1	0- 2 yrs	134	0	257.0	17	.80	2100%	2100%	87.8%	87.8%	63
2	2- 5	117	0	326.0	19	1.05	1810	1950	84.6	74.4	55
3	5-10	98	1	461.5	14	1.30	1080	1590	86.7	64.5	28
4	10-15	98	13	392.5	4	1.23	325	1230	96.3	62.0	7
5	15-20	66	42	220.0	5	.89	560	1120	90.0	55.8	19
All	0-20 yrs	134	56	1657.0	59	5.27	1120	1120	55.8	55.8	32

Table 410f   Derived Mortality and Survival Data

No.	Start-End	Observed Rates Average Annual Mortality	Survival	Cumulative Survival	Mortality	Expected Rates* Average Annual Mortality	Survival	Cumulative Survival	Mortality
i	t to t + Δt	$\bar{q}$ = d/E	$\bar{p}$	P	Q	$\bar{q}'$ = d'/E	$\bar{p}'$	P'	Q'
Male
1	0- 2 yrs	.068	.932	.871	.129	.0045	.9955	.9910	.0090
2	2- 5	.051	.949	.746	.254	.0051	.9949	.9759	.0241
3	5-10	.035	.965	.627	.373	.0051	.9948	.9508	.0492
4	10-15	.034	.966	.526	.474	.0068	.9932	.9189	.0811
5	15-20	.019	.981	.479	.521	.0093	.9907	.8770	.1230
Female
1	0- 2 yrs	.066	.934	.873	.127	.0031	.9969	.9938	.0062
2	2- 5	.058	.942	.732	.268	.0032	.9968	.9843	.0157
3	5-10	.030	.970	.626	.374	.0028	.9972	.9706	.0294
4	10-15	.010	.990	.593	.407	.0031	.9969	.9557	.0443
5	15-20	.023	.977	.523	.477	.0040	.9960	.9367	.0633

* Basis of expected mortality: Contemporaneous U. S. Life Tables, White Male or Female

ADVANCED TUBERCULOSIS BEFORE CHEMOTHERAPY

Table 410g   Comparative Experience by Sex and Age, Far Advanced Tuberculosis
(All Durations Combined)

Sex and Age	No. of Patients	Exposure Person-Yrs	No. of Deaths		Mortality Ratio	20-Year Surv. Rate		Cumulative Survival Ratio	Excess Death Rate
			Observed	Expected*		Observed	Expected*		
	ℓ	E	d	d'	100 d/d'	P	P'	100 P/P'	1000(d-d')/E
Male									
17-23 yrs	31	398.5	10	1.04	960%	.638	.9488	67.3%	22
24-33	63	852.5	24	3.50	685	.588	.9150	64.3	24
34 up	70	696.0	46	7.08	650	.303	.7850	38.6	56
Female									
17-23 yrs	47	655.5	15	1.24	1210%	.663	.9633	68.8%	21
24-33	56	671.0	25	1.93	1300	.535	.9417	56.8	34
34 up	31	330.5	19	2.09	910	.326	.8678	37.5	51

Table 410h   Status of Patients in 1953-1954 and Cause of Death

Category	Moderately Advanced		Far Advanced	
	Number	Per Cent	Number	Per Cent
Living and well, 1953-54	789	65.5%	140	47.0%
Living and well when contact lost	91	7.5	10	3.4
Living but under treatment for active TB	37	3.0	8	2.7
Living but sick when contact lost	24	2.0	1	0.3
Died of TB before 1953-54	195	16.3	120	40.2
Died, non-tuberculous causes before 1953-54	70	5.7	19	6.4
Total died	265	22.0	139	46.6
Total patients	1206	100.0	298	100.0
Comparative Mortality 0-20 Years				
Deaths observed, all causes (d)	258		139	
Deaths expected, all causes (d')	75.6		16.9	
Mortality Ratio (100 d/d')		340%		820%
Excess Death Rate (1000(d-d')/E)	10		34	
Exposure, person-years (E)	17583		3604	

* Basis of expected mortality: Contemporaneous U. S. Life Tables, White Male or Female

PULMONARY TUBERCULOSIS IN INSUREDS

§411—PULMONARY TUBERCULOSIS IN INSUREDS

Reference: "New York Life Single Medical Impairment Study—1972," unpublished report made available by J.J. Hutchinson and J.C. Sibigtroth (1973).

Subjects Studied: Policyholders of New York Life Insurance Company issued insurance in 1954-1970, followed to the 1971 policy anniversary. Different codes were used to distinguish issues with pulmonary (as opposed to non-pulmonary) tuberculosis who had undergone operation, from those who had not. Only cases classified as substandard have been analyzed. Cases involving more than one ratable impairment were excluded.

Follow-up: Insurance policy records formed the basis of entry, of counting policies, exposure and death claims, and of follow-up information.

Results: Comparative experience for male substandard cases, with and without operation, is given in Tables 411a-b by duration, all ages combined. The mortality ratio decreased sharply after the first 5 years for unoperated cases, while remaining at a substantially high level for 10 years among operated cases. The overall mortality ratio for unoperated cases was favorable, while that for operated cases was elevated at 220 per cent. The cumulative survival ratio at 17 years was 101.5 per cent for unoperated males and 96.0 per cent for operated males.

From Table 411c, unoperated males were observed to experience a favorable mortality ratio throughout, except at entry ages 40-49 where such ratio was 140 per cent (EDR 2.2 per 1000). There was also excess mortality found in the oldest age group, 60 and up, with an EDR of 12.2 per 1000. The mortality among operated males appeared less favorable than for unoperated males, particularly at ages under 50 where the mortality ratios for the former were about twice as high as for the latter; operated males experienced 11.6 extra deaths per 1000 at ages 40-49 and 1.4 per 1000 at ages under 40. The overall mortality among female unoperated cases (mortality ratio 119 per cent) was only slightly above expected and the corresponding unoperated male ratio.

For all categories, males and females combined, it will be seen in Table 411d that there is some increase in excess mortality due to diseases of heart and circulation, and from "all other causes and unknown," with EDR of 0.6 and 0.4 per 1000, respectively. The latter category shows the highest mortality ratio, 163 per cent, based on 18 deaths, which included four from TB and four from other respiratory diseases.

LUNG AND BRONCHUS

Table 411a Observed Data and Comparative Experience by Duration — Male Substandard Cases

No.	Interval Start-End	Exposure Policy-Yrs	Deaths in Interval Observed	Deaths in Interval Expected*	Mortality Ratio Interval	Mortality Ratio Cumulative	Survival Ratio Interval	Survival Ratio Cumulative	Excess Death Rate
i	t to t + Δ t	E	d	d'	100 d/d'	100$\sum$d/$\sum$d'	100 p_i/p_i'	100 P/P'	1000(d-d')/E
	Without Operation								
1	0- 2 yrs	2547	9	3.72	240%	240%	99.6%	99.6%	2.1
2	2- 5	2532	8	6.82	117	161	99.8	99.4	0.5
3	5-10	2528	7	12.19	57	106	101.0	100.5	−2.0
4	10-17	1406	13	15.07	86	98	101.1	101.5	−1.5
	With Operation								
1	0- 2 yrs	634	3	0.92	325%	325%	99.4%	99.4%	3.3
2	2- 5	674	7	1.81	385	365	97.7	97.1	7.7
3	5-10	708	9	3.39	265	310	96.1	93.3	7.9
4	10-17	351	2	3.36	60	220	102.8	96.0	−3.9

Table 411b Derived Mortality and Survival Data

No.	Interval Start-End	Observed Rates Average Annual Mortality	Observed Rates Average Annual Survival	Observed Rates Cumulative Survival	Observed Rates Cumulative Mortality	Expected Rates* Average Annual Mortality	Expected Rates* Average Annual Survival	Expected Rates* Cumulative Survival	Expected Rates* Cumulative Mortality
i	t to t + Δ t	$\bar{q}$ = d/E	$\bar{p}$	P	Q	$\bar{q}'$ = d'/E	$\bar{p}'$	P'	Q'
	Without Operation								
1	0- 2 yrs	.0035	.9965	.9930	.0070	.0015	.9985	.9970	.0030
2	2- 5	.0032	.9968	.9835	.0165	.0027	.9973	.9889	.0111
3	5-10	.0028	.9972	.9697	.0303	.0048	.9952	.9652	.0348
4	10-17	.0092	.9908	.9086	.0914	.0107	.9893	.8949	.1051
	With Operation								
1	0- 2 yrs	.0047	.9953	.9906	.0094	.0015	.9985	.9970	.0030
2	2- 5	.0104	.9896	.9600	.0400	.0027	.9973	.9889	.0111
3	5-10	.0127	.9873	.9006	.0994	.0048	.9952	.9652	.0348
4	10-17	.0057	.9943	.8653	.1347	.0096	.9904	.9018	.0982

* Basis of expected mortality: 1955-60 Select Basic Table

PULMONARY TUBERCULOSIS IN INSUREDS

Table 411c   Comparative Experience by Sex and Age Group — Substandard Cases, All Durations Combined

| Sex | Age Group | Exposure Policy-Yrs | Deaths | | Mortality Ratio | Ave. Ann. Mort. Rate | Est. 8-Yr Surv. Rate | Est. 8-Yr Surv. Ratio | Excess Death Rate |
			Observed	Expected*					
		E	d	d'	100 d/d'	$\bar{q} = d/E$	$P = (1 - \bar{q})^8$	100 P/P'	1000(d-d')/E
Without Operation									
Male	<40	5777	10	10.23	98%	.0017	.9864	100.1%	−0.04
	40-49	2224	17	12.15	140	.0076	.9404	98.3	2.2
	50-59	750	6	8.22	73	.0080	.9374	102.4	−3.0
	60 up	262	4	7.20	56	.0153	.8836	110.5	−12.2
	Total	9013	37	37.80	98	.0041	.9674	100.1	−0.1
Female	Total	4031	11	9.22	119	.0027	.9784	99.7	0.4
With Operation									
Male	<40	1272	4	2.28	175	.0031	.9752	98.9	1.4
	40-49	893	15	4.64	325	.0168	.8729	91.0	11.6
	50 up	202	2	2.56	78	.0099	.9229	102.3	−2.8
	Total	2367	21	9.48	220	.0089	.9306	96.1	4.9

Table 411d   Mortality by Cause of Death — All Categories, Male and Female Combined

| Cause | No. of Death Claims | | Mortality Ratio | Excess Death Rate |
	Observed	Expected●		
Malignant Neoplasms	13	13.97	93%	−0.1
Diseases of Heart and Circulatory System	32	23.05	139	0.6
Accidents and Homicides	4	8.06	50	−0.2
Suicide	3	2.49	120	0.0
All Other Causes and Unknown†	18	11.05	163	0.4
Total	70	58.62	119	0.7

* Basis of expected mortality: 1955-60 Select Basic Table

† Includes 4 deaths due to tuberculosis and 4 deaths due to other respiratory disorders

● Distribution of total expected deaths by Intercompany Medically Examined Standard Issues 1965-70

LUNG AND BRONCHUS

§420–BRONCHITIS IN INSUREDS

Reference: "New York Life Single Medical Impairment Study–1972," unpublished report made available by J.J. Hutchinson and J.C. Sibigtroth (1973).

Subjects Studied: Policyholders of New York Life Insurance Company issued insurance in 1954-1970, followed to the 1971 policy anniversary. These were cases having chronic bronchitis, classified as substandard at issue. All cases with any ratable impairment in addition to bronchitis were excluded.

Follow-up: Insurance policy records formed the basis of entry, of counting policies, exposure and death claims, and of follow-up information.

Results: Tables 420a-b present the comparative experience by duration, all ages combined. The mortality ratio showed no trend by duration, ranging between 96 and 355 per cent, with EDR highest (20 extra deaths per 1000) at 5-10 years. There was no excess mortality observed after 10 years. The cumulative survival ratio at 17 years was 89.9 per cent.

From Table 420c, there was a tendency for the male mortality ratios to be somewhat higher for ages 50 up than at the lower ages, with EDR highest (24 extra deaths per 1000) at ages 50-59. The same trend was observed for females, where the mortality at ages 50 up was 650 per cent and EDR 33 per 1000. The overall mortality ratio for males was substantial at 205 per cent, while that for females was more than twice as high, at 520 per cent. The estimated 8-year survival index ranged between 98.9 and 82.3 per cent for males, and from 97.4 to 76.6 per cent for females.

For males and females combined, comparative mortality by cause is given in Table 420d. The preponderant cause of excess deaths was in the category of diseases of the heart and circulatory system, with an EDR of 3.5 per 1000, and a mortality ratio of 280 per cent. An even higher mortality ratio of 355 per cent was found in "all other causes and unknown," including three deaths due to respiratory disorders. In the category of malignant neoplasms (mortality ratio 280 per cent and EDR 2.1 per 1000) were 4 deaths due to cancer of the bronchi, trachea and lung.

BRONCHITIS IN INSUREDS

Table 420a Observed Data and Comparative Experience by Duration — Male Substandard Cases

Interval		Exposure	Deaths in Interval		Mortality Ratio		Survival Ratio		Excess
No.	Start-End	Policy-Yrs	Observed	Expected*	Interval	Cumulative	Interval	Cumulative	Death Rate
i	t to $t + \Delta t$	E	d	d'	$100\,d/d'$	$100\sum d/\sum d'$	$100\,p_i/p_i'$	$100\,P/P'$	$1000(d-d')/E$
1	0- 5 yrs	1238	7	4.44	158%	158%	98.9%	98.9%	2.1
2	5-10	477	13	3.65	355	245	90.5	89.5	20
3	10-17	195	3	3.11	96	205	100.4	89.9	−0.6

Table 420b Derived Mortality and Survival Data

Interval		Observed Rates				Expected Rates*			
		Average Annual		Cumulative		Average Annual		Cumulative	
No.	Start-End	Mortality	Survival	Survival	Mortality	Mortality	Survival	Survival	Mortality
i	t to $t + \Delta t$	$\bar{q} = d/E$	$\bar{p}$	P	Q	$\bar{q}' = d'/E$	$\bar{p}'$	P'	Q'
1	0- 5 yrs	.0056	.9944	.9721	.0279	.0035	.9965	.9825	.0175
2	5-10	.0272	.9728	.8467	.1533	.0076	.9924	.9456	.0544
3	10-17	.0153	.9847	.7598	.2402	.0159	.9841	.8452	.1548

Table 420c Comparative Experience by Sex and Age Group — Substandard Cases, All Durations Combined

Sex	Age Group	Exposure Policy-Yrs	Deaths in Interval		Mortality Ratio	Ave. Ann. Mort. Rate	Est. 8-Yr Surv. Rate	Est. 8-Yr Surv. Index	Excess Death Rate
			Observed	Expected*					
		E	d	d'	$100\,d/d'$	$\bar{q} = d/E$	$P = (1-\bar{q})^8$	$100\,P/P'$	$1000(d-d')/E$
Male	15-39	698	2	1.00	200%	.0028	.9776	98.9%	1.4
	40-49	605	5	4.16	120	.0082	.9359	98.9	1.4
	50-59	339	11	2.92	375	.0324	.7681	82.3	24
	60 up	176	5	3.12	160	.0284	.7938	91.6	11
	Total	1818	23	11.20	205	.0126	.9032	94.9	6.5
Female	0-49	635	3	0.93	325	.0047	.9627	97.4	3.3
	50 up	234	9	1.38	650	.0384	.7307	76.6	33
	Total	869	12	2.31	520	.0138	.8944	91.3	11

Table 420d Mortality by Cause of Death — Male and Female Combined

Cause	No. of Death Claims		Mortality Ratio	Excess Death Rate
	Observed	Expected†		
Malignant Neoplasms●	9	3.22	280%	2.1
Diseases of Heart & Circulatory System	15	5.31	280	3.5
Accidents and Homicides	1	1.86	54	−0.3
Suicide	1	.57	175	0.1
All Other Causes & Unknown□	9	2.55	355	2.3
Total	35	13.51	260	7.7

* Basis of expected mortality: 1955-60 Select Basic Table

† Distribution of total expected deaths by Intercompany Medically Examined
Standard Issues 1965-70

● Includes 4 deaths due to malignant neoplasm of bronchi, trachea and
lung not specified as secondary

□ Includes 3 deaths due to respiratory disorders

LUNG AND BRONCHUS

§421—CHRONIC OBSTRUCTIVE PULMONARY DISEASE

Reference: A. D. Renzetti, Jr., J. H. McClement, and B. D. Litt, "The Veterans Administration Cooperative Study of Pulmonary Function. III. Mortality in Relation to Respiratory Function in Chronic Obstructive Pulmonary Disease," Am. J. Med., 41:115-129 (1966).

Subjects Studied: Patients of 15 Veterans Administration Hospitals located throughout the U.S. with chronic obstructive pulmonary disease (COPD) first observed between October 1957 and July 1960. The follow-up period ended December 31, 1962. Of the 487 men 94 per cent were white. The average age was 57.8 years, with a distribution as follows:

Age Group:	20-29	30-39	40-49	50-59	60-69	70-79	Total
Number	3	36	66	96	254	32	487
Percentage	0.6%	7.4%	13.5%	19.7%	52.2%	6.6%	100%

Criteria for the selection of subjects for the study at each of the 15 cooperating hospitals were the commonly accepted clinical features characteristic of COPD; inclusion in the study was limited to patients having a ratio of residual volume to total lung capacity of 35 per cent or greater, together with a total lung capacity greater than 80 per cent of predicted normal. Patients with more than borderline restrictive pulmonary disease were thus excluded. Patients were also excluded if they had cardiac disease (except cor pulmonale) or other diseases from which premature death might be anticipated. Patients were classified primarily on the basis of the forced expiratory volume at 1 second (FEV_1) — predicted normal 3.15 L. for the group — because of its good correlation with other measurements of ventilatory disturbance and because of its wide use as part of the timed vital capacity test.

Follow-up: Veterans Administration records. No patients lost to follow-up.

Results: Mortality rates were extremely high for the more severe categories of risk and increased with degree of functional impairment (diminished FEV_1). Thus, as indicated in Table 421a, the least impaired group ($FEV_1 \geqslant 1.5$ L.) showed a cumulative mortality ratio over the period of study of 440 per cent, the group in the next higher risk class (FEV_1 0.5-1.49 L.), 605 per cent, and the highest impaired group ($FEV_1 < .05$ L.), 915 per cent. EDR exhibited a progression even more marked — for the same categories, these rates averaged, respectively, 67, 146, and 368 per 1000 per year. Mortality tended to decrease with duration in the least impaired group ($FEV_1 \geqslant 1.5$ L.) but persisted at a very high level throughout follow-up in the other groups.

Comment: Mortality was related to other factors not developed in Tables 421a-b. The authors reported that cases accompanied by cor pulmonale and abnormal arterial gas tensions (O_2 saturation under 92 per cent or Pco_2 over 48 mm.) and patients residing at altitudes of 4000-9000 feet above sea level experienced higher rates of mortality than other patients. Mortality was not increased by associated chronic non-obstructive pulmonary disease or a hematocrit value over 54 per cent. Almost all patients (87.5 per cent) had a history of pulmonary disease (pneumonia, other infection, asthma, etc.), and 96.4 per cent had a history of cigarette smoking. Moderate to severe dyspnea was present in 87.9 per cent. Even the group with the best FEV_1 (1.5 L. or more) was highly impaired: 70 per cent had moderate to severe dyspnea, and 47 per cent, abnormal arterial gas tension, including cor pulmonale.

CHRONIC OBSTRUCTIVE PULMONARY DISEASE

Table 421a Observed Data and Comparative Experience by Severity and Duration.

Group	Interval No.	Interval Start-End	No. Alive at Start of Interval	Withdrawals	Exposure Person-Yrs	Deaths Obs.	Deaths Exp.†	Mortality Ratio Interval	Mortality Ratio Cumulative	Survival Ratio Interval	Survival Ratio Cumulative	Excess Death Rate
FEV$_1$ *	i	t to t + Δt	ℓ	w	E	d	d'	100 d/d'	100 Q/Q'	100 p/p'	100 P/P'	1000(d-d')/E
All	1	0-1 yr	487	0	487	82	9.06	905%	905%	84.7%	84.7%	150
Cases	2	1-2 yrs	405	0	405	69	8.26	835	805	84.7	71.8	150
	3	2-3 yrs	336	15	328.5	63	7.33	860	735	82.7	59.3	169
	4	3-4 yrs	258	75	220.5	33	5.38	615	635	87.2	51.7	125
		0-4 yrs	487	90	1441	247	30.03	825	635	51.7	51.7	151
<0.5 L.	1	0-1 yr	64	0	64	23	1.41	1630	1630	65.5	65.5	337
	2	1-2 yrs	41	0	41	15	.99	1520	1300	65.0	42.6	342
	3	2-3 yrs	26	0	26	12	.68	1760	1100	55.3	23.5	435
	4	3-4 yrs	14	4	12	6	.34	1760	915	51.5	12.1	472
		0-4 yrs	64	4	143	56	3.42	1640	915	12.1	12.1	368
0.5 - 1.49 L.	1	0-1 yr	320	0	320	53	6.24	850	850	85.1	85.1	146
	2	1-2 yrs	267	0	267	40	5.69	705	720	86.9	73.9	129
	3	2-3 yrs	227	10	222	44	5.17	850	690	82.1	60.7	175
	4	3-4 yrs	173	49	148.5	24	3.77	635	605	86.0	52.2	136
		0-4 yrs	320	59	957.5	161	20.87	770	605	52.2	52.2	146
1.50 L. Up	1	0-1 yr	98	0	98	6	1.45	415	415	95.3	95.3	46
	2	1-2 yrs	92	0	92	12	1.46	820	600	88.4	84.2	115
	3	2-3 yrs	80	5	77.5	6	1.34	450	525	93.9	79.1	60
	4	3-4 yrs	69	22	58	3	1.10	275	440	96.7	76.4	33
		0-4 yrs	98	27	325.5	27	5.35	505	440	76.4	76.4	67

Table 421b Derived Mortality and Survival Data

Group	Interval No.	Interval Start-End	Observed Rates Interval Mortality	Observed Rates Interval Survival	Observed Rates Cumulative Survival	Observed Rates Cumulative Mortality	Expected Rates† Interval Mortality	Expected Rates† Interval Survival	Expected Rates† Cumulative Survival	Expected Rates† Cumulative Mortality
FEV$_1$ *	i	t to t + Δt	q_i	p_i	P	Q	q_i'	p_i'	P'	Q'
All Cases	1	0-1 yr	.1684	.8316	.8316	.1684	.0186	.9814	.9814	.0186
	2	1-2 yrs	.1704	.8296	.6899	.3101	.0204	.9796	.9614	.0386
	3	2-3 yrs	.1918	.8082	.5576	.4424	.0223	.9777	.9399	.0601
	4	3-4 yrs	.1497	.8503	.4741	.5259	.0244	.9756	.9170	.0830
<0.5 L.	1	0-1 yr	.3594	.6406	.6406	.3594	.0221	.9779	.9779	.0221
	2	1-2 yrs	.3659	.6341	.4062	.5938	.0241	.9759	.9543	.0457
	3	2-3 yrs	.4615	.5385	.2187	.7813	.0263	.9737	.9292	.0708
	4	3-4 yrs	.5000	.5000	.1094	.8906	.0285	.9715	.9028	.0972
0.5 - 1.49 L.	1	0-1 yr	.1656	.8344	.8344	.1656	.0195	.9805	.9805	.0195
	2	1-2 yrs	.1498	.8502	.7094	.2906	.0213	.9787	.9596	.0404
	3	2-3 yrs	.1982	.8018	.5688	.4312	.0233	.9767	.9373	.0627
	4	3-4 yrs	.1616	.8384	.4769	.5231	.0254	.9746	.9135	.0865
1.50 L. Up	1	0-1 yr	.0612	.9388	.9388	.0612	.0148	.9852	.9852	.0148
	2	1-2 yrs	.1304	.8696	.8164	.1836	.0159	.9841	.9695	.0305
	3	2-3 yrs	.0774	.9226	.7532	.2468	.0173	.9827	.9528	.0472
	4	3-4 yrs	.0517	.9483	.7143	.2857	.0189	.9811	.9348	.0652

* FEV$_1$ — Forced expiratory volume at one second, Liters
† Basis of expected mortality: U.S. White Males 1959-61

LUNG AND BRONCHUS

§422–CHRONIC OBSTRUCTIVE PULMONARY DISEASE

References: (1) B. Burrows, A. H. Niden, W. R. Barclay, and J. E. Kasik, "Chronic Obstructive Lung Disease. I. Clinical and Physiologic Findings in 175 Patients and Their Relationship to Age and Sex," Am. Rev. Resp. Dis., 91:521-540 (1965).
(2) B. Burrows and R. H. Earle, "Course and Prognosis of Chronic Obstructive Lung Disease," New Eng. J. Med., 280:397-404 (1969).
(3) B. Burrows and R. H. Earle, "Prediction of Survival in Patients with Chronic Airway Obstruction," Am. Rev. Resp. Dis., 99:865-871 (1969).
(4) B. Burrows, Supplementary data supplied in personal communication (1970).

Subjects Studied: Patients selected from cooperative ambulant out-patients of a pulmonary function clinic at the University of Chicago Hospital on the basis of chronic, irreversible airway obstruction of uncertain etiology. A forced expiratory volume at one second (FEV 1) of less than 60 per cent of both observed and predicted vital capacity for at least one year of observation was the requisite for enrollment in the series. Patients were excluded if they had either a specific cause for the pulmonary insufficiency, such as advanced tuberculosis, or a complicating, progressive fatal disease. Age of the patients at entry ranged from 34 to 78 years with a mean of 59.1 years; only 27 per cent were under age 55. Males constituted 89 per cent of the series and white persons 89.5 per cent. Patients were characterized in great detail with respect to (a) respiratory history, (b) clinical and screening test findings on entry, and (c) serial pulmonary function studies. Some of these factors are summarized in tables 422a and 422b. Most of the patients were working at the time of diagnosis, 50 per cent full time and 12 per cent part time; 30 per cent had sufficient respiratory disability to prevent work, and 8 per cent were not working for other reasons, such as retirement due to age.

Follow-up: Follow-up extended over a period of five to ten years. Patients were usually admitted to the hospital for initial and yearly follow-up examinations. Regular quarterly questionnaires were mailed to the patients to assure continued contact and to evaluate acute respiratory illnesses. Few subjects were lost to follow-up: in the first seven years only four were so lost. All data were collected in a standardized manner independently of the regular patient record. Pulmonary function tests were performed over the entire period.

Results: In this analysis of the study patients were divided as evenly as possible into four groups according to initial readings for the particular variable under consideration. Such division was made with respect to ventilatory impairment: "best cases," 41 in number, with FEV 1 readings of 1.2 or more liters, whose FVC was 75 per cent or more, whose arterial oxygen saturation after exercise reached 90 per cent or more, and whose cardiac functional classification excluded severely impaired grade 3-4 cases; "moderately severe cases," 53 in number, embraced patients whose FEV 1 was 1.0 to 1.1 liters, or those with FEV 1 of 1.2 liters up who could not be included among the best cases by reason of the other criteria; "severe cases," 48 in number, patients with FEV 1 from 0.8 to 1.0 liters; "most severe cases" included 58 subjects with readings of less than 0.8 liters. In the results presented in Tables 422c-e the two middle categories are usually combined and designated "moderate to severe."

Mortality ratios in Table 422c show marked increments with degree of severity for all ages combined, increasing from 174 per cent for best cases to 440 per cent for the middle group, to 860 per cent for the most severe. Within each category ratios diminish substantially with increase in age, ages 65 years and over, on average, being only about one-third that for subjects under 55 years old. EDR indexes show similar increases according to severity, but do not display the diminution by age exhibited in mortality ratios.

Experience according to arterial oxygen saturation after exercise presented in Table 422c indicates that a reading of less than 92 per cent oxygen saturation after exercise resulted in materially higher death rates (measured either by mortality ratios or by EDR's) except in the "best" category. Table 422c also presents a breakdown of the subjects according to observed to predicted percentage of functional vital capacity (FVC) and the attendant mortality compared with that expected. The highest mortality ratio – 1460 per cent – and the highest EDR – 292 per 1000 – are associated with the lowest category of FVC as a percentage of predicted (under 50 per cent). Mortality ratios for higher predicted values decline to a level of 630 per cent for FVC readings of 50-69 per cent of predicted; for more favorable readings, mortality ratios fluctuate within the 290-325 per cent range. Values of EDR are substantially lower for predicted FVC percentages above 70 per cent.

CHRONIC OBSTRUCTIVE PULMONARY DISEASE

Tables 422d and e summarize the results of the experience for all ages combined according to duration after entry into the program. Mortality ratios and EDR values tend to increase by duration in the class of best cases, but to diminish for the most severe ones. The middle class — moderately severe to severe — shows a relatively small increase by duration.

Comment: References 2 and 3 should be consulted for results of the authors' analysis of over 200 characteristics and variables for statistical correlation with survival rates. Among 109 deaths 81 or 74 per cent were classified as cardiorespiratory (excluding acute myocardial infarction and cerebrovascular accident). Of particular interest was the finding that the combination of heart rate with FEV 1 made possible a highly correlated prediction of survival rate (Tables 5 and 6, reference 3). Patients with a heart rate under 78 per minute had the highest five-year survival rates (0.45 to 0.93), those with a heart rate of 78 to 90, intermediate survival rates, and those with a heart rate exceeding 90 per minute, the lowest survival rates (0.14 to 0.64).

Table 422a   History of Respiratory Symptoms

Factor	History and Severity						
Dyspnea (Shortness of breath)	Chief complaint	72%	Mild	14%	Ave. age at onset	50.6 ± 12.3 yrs	
	Severe	53%	None of signif.	4%	Ave. duration	8.4 ± 8.7 yrs	
	Moderate	29%			Range of duration	1-44 yrs	
Chronic Cough	Chief complaint	14%	Productive	86%	Ave. age at onset	43 ± 17 yrs	
	History of	89%	Over 10ml/day	56%	Ave. duration	16.5 ± 14 yrs	
	No history of	11%			Range of duration	1-62 yrs	
Wheezing	Chief complaint	2%	History of	77%			
Respiratory Infection	History in Childhood	18%	History of Pneumonia	57%	More than once	18%	
Cigarette Smoking	History of	94%	Regular smoker at time of exam		59%		

Table 422b   Status on Initial Examination

Factor	Classification		Factor	Classification	
Examination	Breath Sound decreased	46%	Chest X-Ray	Emphysema, definite	21%
	Rhonchi in chest	35%		Emphysema, suspect	30%
	Edema	8%		Chronic inflam. disease	34%
	Cyanosis (central)	4%		Over distention	74%
	Clubbing of fingers	4%		Bullae	13%
Blood Pressure	Normal (S<140, D<90)	52%		Normal lung fields	34%
	Borderline Hypertension	28%		Heart definitely enlarged	8%
	Definite Hypertension		ECG Findings	Normal	51%
	(S160 up or D95 up)	20%		P pulmonale only	15%
Cardiac Function (AHA Classific.)	Grade I (little or no)	18%		Rt. vent. hypertrophy, def.	7%
	Grade II (mild)	46%		Rt. vent. hypertrophy, susp.	12%
	Grade III (moderate)	29%		Other abnormality	15%
	Grade IV (severe)	7%	Associated Heart Disease	Cor pulmonale	11%
				Other	26%

LUNG AND BRONCHUS

Table 422c   Comparative Mortality by Age and Severity (All Durations Combined)

Severity*	Age Group	Ave. Age	Ave. FVC % Predicted	Ave. Vol.	FEV₁ %FVC	No. of Patients	Exposure Person-Yrs	No. of Deaths Obs.	No. of Deaths Exp.†	Mortality Ratio	Excess Death Rate
	Yrs	Yrs	%	Liters	%	ℓ	E	d	d'	100 d/d'	1000(d-d')/E
(1) Best Cases	Under 55	51.4	98%	1.59	46%	14	94.5	4	1.41	285%	27
	55-64	58.4	91	1.59	46	20	142	7	4.17	168	20
	65 up	71.1	94	1.49	47	7	45.5	4	3.04	132	21
(2+3) Moderate	Under 55	48.1	69	1.04	39	23	123.5	14	1.30	1080	103
to Severe Cases	55-64	59.5	74	1.04	39	47	233.5	32	6.87	465	108
	65 up	69.5	73	1.02	41	31	144.5	28	8.68	325	134
(4) Most Severe	Under 55	48.3	54	0.62	34	17	55	15	0.64	2360	261
Cases	55-64	59.4	58	0.62	33	28	114	22	3.19	690	165
	65 up	69.1	60	0.62	33	13	37.5	12	1.87	640	270
(1) Best	All	58.2	94	1.57	46	41	282	15	8.62	174	23
(2a) Moderate	All	67.5	79	1.42	47	20	101.5	16	3.28	490	125
(2b) Moderate	All	56.6	74	1.06	40	33	178.5	21	4.65	450	92
(3) Severe	All	61.7	68	0.85	37	48	280	37	8.92	415	100
(2+3) Mod to Sev.	All	60.0	73	1.03	40	101	501.5	74	16.85	440	114
(4) Most Severe	All	58.3	57	0.62	33	58	206.5	49	5.70	860	210
All	Under 55	49.0	72	1.05	39	54	273	33	3.35	985	109
All	55-64	59.3	73	1.03	39	95	489.5	61	14.23	430	96
All	65 up	69.6	73	0.98	40	51	227.5	44	13.59	325	134
All	All	59.1	73	1.02	39	200	990	138	31.17	445	108
Art. O₂Sat. 92% Up (After Exercise) 1	All	58.0	94	1.58	46	36	246	14	7.21	194	28
Grp. 2 + 3	All	61.5	71	1.02	41	58	295.5	39	11.09	350	95
Grp. 4	All	58.9	60	0.63	33	33	131.5	26	3.91	665	168
All FEV₁	All	59.8	75	1.07	40	127	673	79	22.21	355	84
Art. O₂ Sat. <92% Grp. 1	All	59.6	92	1.54	46	5	36	1	1.41	71	−11
Grp. 2 + 3	All	58.0	75	1.06	39	43	206	35	5.76	610	142
Grp. 4	All	57.6	54	0.61	34	25	75	23	1.79	1280	283
All FEV₁	All	58.0	69	0.94	38	73	317	59	8.96	660	158
Vital Capacity (% Predicted) 90% up	All	59.9	102	1.51	40	37	225.5	24	7.40	325	74
70-89%	All	59.2	78	1.12	40	71	413	39	13.54	290	62
50-69%	All	59.8	60	0.81	37	73	294	57	9.00	630	163
Under 50%	All	55.1	45	0.58	38	19	57.5	18	1.23	1460	292

* Group (1)   FEV₁ 1.2 L. up and FVC 75% up and Art. O₂ Sat. after moderate exercise
90% up and cardiac functional class O-2
(2a)   FEV₁ 1.2 L. up but not meeting other criteria
(2b)   FEV₁ 1.0-1.1 L.
(3)   FEV₁ 0.8-0.9 L.
(4)   FEV₁ <0.8 L.

† Basis of expected mortality: U.S. White Males 1959-61

CHRONIC OBSTRUCTIVE PULMONARY DISEASE

Table 422d   Observed Data and Comparative Experience by Severity and Duration

Severity* and Interval No. Start-End	No. Alive at Start of Interval	Withdrawals	Exposure Person-Yrs	Deaths in Interval Obs.	Deaths in Interval Exp.†	Mortality Ratio Interval	Mortality Ratio Cumulative	Survival Ratio Interval	Survival Ratio Cumulative	Excess Death Rate
i t to t + Δt	ℓ	w	E	d	d'	100 d/d'	100 Σd/Σd'	100p_i/p_i'	100 P/P'	1000(d-d')/E
Best Cases										
1 0- 2 yrs	41	1	80.5	2	1.83	109%	109%	99.6%	99.6%	2.1
2 2- 5 yrs	38	1	107.5	5	2.89	173	148	94.0	93.6	20
3 5-10 yrs	32	24	94	8	3.89	205	174	78.6	73.5	44
0-10 yrs	41	26	282	15	8.61	174	174	73.5	73.5	23
Mod-Severe Cases										
1 0- 2 yrs	101	0	189	23	5.16	445	445	81.6	81.6	94
2 2- 5 yrs	78	2	198	28	6.57	425	435	70.4	57.4	108
3 5-10 yrs	48	25	114.5	23	5.12	450	440	26.5	15.2	156
0-10 yrs	101	27	501.5	74	16.85	440	440	15.2	15.2	114
Most Severe Cases										
1 0- 2 yrs	58	0	100	25	2.36	1060	1060	59.7	59.7	226
2 2- 5 yrs	33	0	70	17	2.04	835	955	53.1	31.7	214
3 5-10 yrs	16	9	36.5	7	1.30	540	860	39.7	12.6	156
0-10 yrs	58	9	206.5	49	5.70	860	860	12.6	12.6	210

Table 422e   Derived Mortality and Survival Data

Severity*	Interval No. Start-End	Observed Rates Cumulative Survival	Observed Rates Interval Survival	Observed Rates Geom. Mean Ann. Surv.	Observed Rates Geom. Mean Ann. Mort.	Expected Rates† Cumulative Survival	Expected Rates† Interval Survival	Expected Rates† Geom. Mean Ann. Surv.	Expected Rates† Geom. Mean Ann. Mort.
	i t to t + Δt	P	p_i	$\check{p}_i$	$\check{q}_i$	P'	p_i'	$\check{p}_i$'	$\check{q}_i$'
Best Cases	1 0- 2 yrs	.951	.951	.975	.025	.9552	.9552	.9773	.0227
	2 2- 5 yrs	.824	.866	.953	.047	.8802	.9215	.9731	.0269
	3 5-10 yrs	.499	.606	.905	.095	.6786	.7710	.9493	.0507
Mod-Severe Cases	1 0- 2 yrs	.772	.772	.879	.121	.9461	.9461	.9727	.0273
	2 2- 5 yrs	.491	.636	.860	.140	.8547	.9034	.9667	.0333
	3 5-10 yrs	.103	.210	.732	.268	.6763	.7913	.9543	.0457
Most Severe Cases	1 0- 2 yrs	.569	.569	.754	.246	.9533	.9533	.9789	.0211
	2 2- 5 yrs	.276	.485	.786	.214	.8704	.9130	.9701	.0299
	3 5-10 yrs	.092	.333	.803	.197	.7306	.8394	.9656	.0344

*Best cases: FEV_1 1.2L. up and FVC 75% up and Art. O_2 Sat. after moderate exercise 90% up and cardiac functional class 0-2
  Moderate to severe cases: FEV_1 0.8 to 1.1L., or 1.2L. up but not meeting all other criteria
  Severe cases: FEV_1 less than 0.8L.

†Basis of expected mortality: U.S. White Males 1959-61

LUNG AND BRONCHUS

§423—EMPHYSEMA IN INSUREDS

Reference: "New York Life Single Medical Impairment Study—1972," unpublished report made available by J.J. Hutchinson and J.C. Sibigtroth (1973).

Subjects Studied: Policyholders of New York Life Insurance Company issued insurance in 1954-1970, followed to the 1971 policy anniversary. The experience reported is for cases found to have obstructive pulmonary emphysema, classified as substandard. Cases with more than one ratable impairment were excluded.

Follow-up: Insurance policy records formed the basis of entry, of counting policies, exposure and death claims, and of follow-up information.

Results: From Tables 423a-b, the experience by duration among male substandard cases showed a slight decline in the mortality ratio after the first 5 years, but a rise in the EDR over the same period. The cumulative survival ratio at 17 years was 86.2 per cent.

Comparative experience by sex and age is given in Table 423c. Males experienced a rapidly decreasing trend in mortality with entry age, the mortality ratio ranging from 1850 per cent (19 extra deaths per 1000) at ages under 40 to 88 per cent at ages 60 and up. The decline in EDR with advancing age was also sharp; there was no excess mortality found in males aged 60 up. The data for females were limited so that no breakdown by age or duration was made. The overall female mortality ratio was 800 per cent (only 2 death claims), as compared with 179 per cent for males.

In Table 423d, the comparative experience for males and females combined is given by major causes of death. The leading cause of death is found in the "all other causes and unknown" category, the mortality being 560 per cent and EDR 6.2 per 1000. Furthermore, 10 out of the 12 deaths found in this category were due to respiratory disorders. Excess mortality from diseases of heart and circulation was also substantial, with an EDR of 1.6 extra deaths per 1000 and a mortality ratio of 156 per cent.

EMPHYSEMA IN INSUREDS

Table 423a Observed Data and Comparative Experience by Duration — Male Substandard Cases

Interval		Exposure	Deaths in Interval		Mortality Ratio		Survival Ratio		Excess
No.	Start-End	Policy-Yrs	Observed	Expected*	Interval	Cumulative	Interval	Cumulative	Death Rate
i	t to t + Δt	E	d	d'	100 d/d'	100 Σd/Σd'	100 p_i/p_i'	100 P/P'	1000(d-d')/E
1	0- 5 yrs	1055	11	5.83	189%	187%	97.6%	97.6%	4.9
2	5-17	367	9	5.32	169	179	88.4	86.2	10

Table 423b Derived Mortality and Survival Data

Interval		Observed Rates				Expected Rates*			
		Average Annual		Cumulative		Average Annual		Cumulative	
No.	Start-End	Mortality	Survival	Survival	Mortality	Mortality	Survival	Survival	Mortality
i	t to t + Δt	$\bar{q}$ = d/E	$\bar{p}$	P	Q	$\bar{q}'$ = d'/E	$\bar{p}'$	P'	Q'
1	0- 5 yrs	.0104	.9896	.9490	.0510	.0055	.9945	.9726	.0274
2	5-17	.0245	.9755	.7043	.2957	.0144	.9856	.8169	.1831

Table 423c Comparative Experience by Sex and Age Group — Substandard Cases, All Durations Combined

Sex	Age Group	Exposure Policy-Yrs	Deaths in Interval		Mortality Ratio	Ave. Ann. Mort. Rate	Est. 8-Yr Surv. Rate	Est. 8-Yr Surv. Index	Excess Death Rate
			Observed	Expected*					
		E	d	d'	100 d/d'	$\bar{q}$ = d/E	P=$(1-\bar{q})^8$	100P/P'	1000(d-d')/E
Male	0-39 yrs	255	5	0.27	1850%	.0196	.8532	86.0%	19
	40-49	414	4	1.49	270	.0096	.9253	95.2	6.1
	50-59	521	7	4.86	144	.0134	.8974	96.7	4.1
	60 up	232	4	4.53	88	.0172	.8700	101.9	−2.3
	Total	1422	20	11.15	179	.0140	.8929	95.1	6.2
Female	Total	158	2	0.25	800	.0126	.9032	91.4	11

Table 423d Mortality by Cause of Death — Male and Female Combined

Cause	No. of Death Claims		Mortality Ratio	Excess Death Rate
	Observed	Expected●		
Malignant Neoplasms	2	2.72	74%	−0.4
Diseases of Heart & Circulatory System	7	4.48	156	1.6
Accidents and Homicides	1	1.57	64	−0.4
Suicide	0	.48	0	−0.3
All Other Causes & Unknown†	12	2.15	560	6.2
Total	22	11.40	193	6.7

* Basis of expected mortality: 1955-60 Select Basic Table
† Includes 10 respiratory disorders
● Distribution of total expected deaths by Intercompany Medically Examined Standard Issues 1965-70

RESPIRATORY DISEASES

§480–OTHER LUNG DISORDER IN INSUREDS

Reference: "New York Life Single Medical Impairment Study–1972," unpublished report made available by J.J. Hutchinson and J.C. Sibigtroth (1973).

Subjects Studied: Policyholders of New York Life Insurance Company issued insurance in 1954-1970, followed to the 1971 policy anniversary. These were cases in which the residual category has been assigned because the respiratory condition could not be classified in any of the other codes, for pulmonary tuberculosis, bronchitis, bronchiectasis or emphysema, etc. Most of the experience reported is for substandard issues; all cases with ratable impairment in addition to the other lung disorder code were excluded.

Follow-up: Insurance policy records formed the basis of entry, of counting policies, exposure and death claims, and of follow-up information.

Results: Comparative experience is given in Tables 480a-b for substandard male cases by duration, all ages combined. There was no consistent trend in the mortality ratio, ranging between 138 and 210 per cent, with the highest EDR of 6.7 per 1000 at 5-10 years. The cumulative survival ratio at 17 years was 91.7 per cent.

Table 480c gives comparative experience for standard and substandard cases by sex and entry age group. For substandard males, mortality ratios showed no clear trend, ranging between 111 and 210 per cent, with the highest EDR of 13 per 1000 observed in the age group 60 up. The estimated eight-year survival index ranged from normal at ages under 40 to a minimum of 89.9 per cent for ages 60 up. The overall mortality ratio was 170 per cent. For standard males, the overall mortality ratio was 300 per cent, with an EDR of 7.4 per 1000. Female standard and substandard cases showed a mortality ratio of 290 per cent.

Comparative mortality by major causes of death is given in Table 480d for male and female substandard cases combined. There was some increase in mortality from malignant neoplasms, but the major cause of death was found in the "all other causes and unknown" category; excess mortality was substantial with a ratio of 345 per cent and an EDR of 2.3 extra deaths per 1000, based on 12 deaths, including 3 from other respiratory diseases. An even higher mortality ratio, 515 per cent, was found for suicides, but this occurred with only 4 death claims and an EDR of 0.9 per 1000.

OTHER LUNG DISORDER*

Table 480a   Observed Data and Comparative Experience by Duration — Male Substandard Cases

Interval No.	Start-End	Exposure Policy-Yrs	Deaths in Interval Observed	Deaths in Interval Expected†	Mortality Ratio Interval	Mortality Ratio Cumulative	Survival Ratio Interval	Survival Ratio Cumulative	Excess Death Rate
i	t to t + Δt	E	d	d'	100 d/d'	100 Σd/Σd'	100p_i/p_i'	100 P/P'	1000 (d-d')/E
1	0- 2 yrs	939	4	1.92	210%	210%	99.6%	99.6%	2.2
2	2- 5	909	5	3.61	138	163	99.5	99.1	1.5
3	5-10	892	12	6.00	200	182	96.6	95.7	6.7
4	10-17	415	8	5.46	146	171	95.8	91.7	6.1

Table 480b   Derived Mortality and Survival Data

Interval No.	Start-End	Observed Rates Average Annual Mortality	Observed Rates Average Annual Survival	Observed Rates Cumulative Survival	Observed Rates Cumulative Mortality	Expected Rates† Average Annual Mortality	Expected Rates† Average Annual Survival	Expected Rates† Cumulative Survival	Expected Rates† Cumulative Mortality
i	t to t + Δt	$\bar{q}$ = d/E	$\bar{p}$	P	Q	$\bar{q}'$ = d'/E	$\bar{p}'$	P'	Q'
1	0- 2 yrs	.0042	.9958	.9916	.0084	.0020	.9980	.9960	.0040
2	2- 5	.0055	.9945	.9753	.0247	.0039	.9961	.9844	.0156
3	5-10	.0134	.9864	.9108	.0892	.0067	.9933	.9519	.0481
4	10-17	.0192	.9808	.7958	.2042	.0131	.9869	.8680	.1320

Table 480c   Comparative Experience by Sex, Insurance Action and Age Group — All Durations Combined

Sex	Age Group	Exposure Policy-Yrs	Deaths in Interval Observed	Deaths in Interval Expected†	Mortality Ratio	Ave. Ann. Mort. Rate	Est. 8-Yr Surv. Rate	Est. 8-Yr Surv. Index	Excess Death Rate
		E	d	d'	100 d/d'	$\bar{q}$ = d/E	P = $(1-\bar{q})^8$	100 P/P'	1000 (d-d')/E
Male (SStd.)	0-39	1648	3	2.70	111%	.0018	.9857	99.8%	0.2
	40-49	820	8	3.83	210	.0097	.9250	96.0	5.1
	50-59	505	11	5.85	188	.0217	.8390	92.0	10
	60 up	182	7	4.65	150	.0384	.7311	89.9	13
	Total	3155	29	17.03	170	.0091	.9295	97.0	3.8
Male (Std.)	Total	720	8	2.66	300	.0111	.9146	94.2	7.4
Female (Std. & SStd. combined)	Total	704	5	1.72	290	.0071	.9446	96.3	4.7

Table 480d   Mortality by Cause of Death — Male and Female Combined, Substandard Cases

Cause	No. of Death Claims Actual	No. of Death Claims Expected●	Mortality Ratio	Excess Death Rate
Malignant Neoplasms	7	4.38	160%	0.7
Diseases of the Heart and Circulatory System	8	7.23	111	0.2
Accidents and Homicides	2	2.53	79	−0.1
Suicide	4	0.78	515	0.9
All Other Causes and Unknown□	12	3.46	345	2.3
Total	33	18.38	180	3.9

*Including pneumonia
†Basis of expected mortality: 1955-60 Select Basic Table
●Distribution of total expected deaths by Intercompany Medically Examined Standard Issues 1965-70
□Includes 3 deaths due to other respiratory diseases

RESPIRATORY DISEASES

§499–RESPIRATORY DISORDERS (MISCELLANEOUS)

References: (1) T. W. Preston and R. D. Clarke, "An Investigation into the Mortality of Impaired Lives During The Period 1947-63," J. Inst. Act., 92:27-74 (1966).

(2) A. Svensson and S. Astrand, "Substandard Risk Mortality in Sweden 1955-1965," Coopération Internationale pour les Assurances des Risques Aggravés. (See Rome Conference proceedings, 1969.)

(3) "New York Life Single Medical Impairment Study - 1972," unpublished report made available by J. J. Hutchinson and J. C. Sibigtroth (1973).

Subjects Studied: (1) Policyholders of Prudential Assurance Co., London, England, issued insurance 1947-1963 followed to 12/31/63. Both standard and substandard issues were included. Applicants with two or more ratable impairments were generally excluded.

(2) Insured lives reinsured with Sverige Reinsurance Co., Sweden, placed in force prior to 1955 and observed between anniversaries in 1955 and 1965.

(3) Policyholders of New York Life Insurance Co., issued insurance 1954-1970 followed to 1971ʳ policy anniversary. Both standard and substandard issues were included. Applicants with more than one ratable impairment were excluded.

Follow-up: Insurance policy records formed the basis of entry of counting policies, exposures, and death claims, and of follow-up information.

Results: In the Prudential Assurance and New York Life studies, both of which compared their experience with that of standard insured lives, mortality rates close to expected were observed among policyholders with histories of pleurisy with or without effusion, or spontaneous pneumothorax, or bronchiectasis. In other categories the excess death rate ranged from about 1 to 14 extra deaths per 1000 per year. The Swedish reinsurance experience for tuberculosis cases disclosed a mortality ratio of 104 per cent and an EDR of only 0.2 per 1000 per year compared with the experience of the general population. If the lower rates associated with selected insured lives had been used as a standard, the mortality ratio and EDR might very well have been comparable with the corresponding values for tuberculosis reported in the Prudential Assurance experience (mortality ratios 140-182 per cent).

The heaviest excess mortality for these respiratory disorders was observed with the English experience in chronic bronchitis. The coexistence of emphysema with bronchitis was associated with a higher mortality ratio, 460 per cent versus the 200 per cent observed in insureds with chronic bronchitis but no emphysema, in applicants under age 50. However, this was not true for the older applicants (mortality ratios 169 and 230 per cent, respectively). In a small group of English insureds with emphysema, but no diagnosis of bronchitis the mortality ratio was only 123 per cent, but EDR was 4.3 per 1000 per year (average age about 60). The Prudential's experience with applicants with bronchial asthma showed a decrease in mortality ratio with age, from 275 per cent for those applicants under age 30 to 200 per cent, age 30 to 49, and 154 per cent for those age 50 up. The corresponding values of EDR ranged from 1.2 to 5.5 extra deaths per 1000 per year. The Sverige Reinsurance Company experience with applicants rated for asthma also showed an elevated mortality ratio (172 per cent) and an EDR of 3.0, all ages combined.

RESPIRATORY DISEASES

Table 499 Miscellaneous Respiratory Disorders

Disease/Category (Ref.)	Sex/Age	Policies in Force at Start	Exposure Policy-Yrs	Number of Death Claims		Average Annual Mortality Rate		Mortality Ratio	Est. 5-Yr Surv. Rate	Est. 5-Yr Surv. Index	Excess Death Rate
				Observed	Expected*	Observed	Expected*				
		Q	E	d	d'	$\bar{q}=d/E$	$\bar{q}'=d'/E$	$100\,d/d'$	$P=(1-\bar{q}')^5$	$100\,P/P'$	$1000(\bar{q}-\bar{q}')$
Pleurisy with Effusion (1)	M 38	1962	10767	16	19.75	.0015	.0018	81%	.9925	100.2%	−0.3
Pleurisy, Other (1)	M 42	4963	33622	129	110.39	.0038	.0033	117	.9811	99.8	0.6
Spontaneous Pneumothorax (1)	M 38	932	4430	8	7.86	.0018	.0018	102	.9910	100.0	0.0
Pulmonary Tuberculosis (1)											
Mild, negative sputum	M 38	2399	10897	27	19.33	.0025	.0018	140	.9876	99.6	0.7
Moderate or severe	M 40	5561	14007	47	33.32	.0034	.0024	141	.9831	99.5	1.0
Treated by pneumothorax	M 38	1389	7912	25	13.73	.0032	.0017	182	.9841	99.2	1.4
Treated by major surgery	M 37	1704	7876	20	12.52	.0025	.0016	160	.9876	99.6	0.9
Tuberculosis (2)	M & F 40	—	36849	170	163.1	.0046	.0044	104	.9772	99.9	0.2
Asthma (2)	M & F 39	—	4251	30	17.5	.0071	.0041	172	.9650	98.5	3.0
Bronchial Asthma (1)											
Age under 30	M 25	3797	14729	27	9.78	.0018	.0007	275	.9910	99.4	1.2
Age 30-49	M 37	2448	11651	39	19.51	.0033	.0017	200	.9836	99.2	1.7
Age 50 up	M 52	214	1093	17	11.04	.0156	.0101	154	.9244	97.2	5.5
Chronic Bronchitis (1)											
No emphysema, age 30-49	M 39	643	3223	14	6.95	.0043	.0022	200	.9787	99.0	2.2
age 50 up	M 53	211	1090	28	12.21	.0257	.0112	230	.8779	92.9	14
With emphysema, age 30-49	M 42	273	1536	20	4.37	.0130	.0028	460	.9367	95.0	10
age 50 up	M 54	166	880	18	10.63	.0205	.0121	169	.9016	95.8	8.4
Emphysema only, age 50 up (1)	M 58	68	485	11	8.91	.0227	.0183	123	.8915	97.8	4.3
Bronchiectasis, with or without operation, SS (3)	M 38	—	4213	14	11.67	.0033	.0028	120	.9836	99.7	0.6
"Lung disorders," including pneumonia Std (3)	M 39	—	825	9	2.99	.0109	.0036	300	.9467	96.4	7.3

* Basis of expected mortality: (Ref. 1) Prudential Assurance Co. (England) standard lives mortality 1957-1958;
(Ref. 2) Sverige Reins. Co., population mortality, M or F (Sweden), 1956-60 and 1961-65; (Ref. 3) N.Y. Life, Basic Select Tables (1955-60).

Digestive System

See Also

1. *1951 Impairment Study.* Chicago: Society of Actuaries (1954).
     D27-D41 Gallbladder disorder, without operation (pp. 136-138).
     D42-D44 Removal of gallbladder (pp. 140-141).
     D45-D47 Drainage of gallbladder, surgical (pp. 144-146).
     D48-D50 Fistula in ano, not known due to tuberculosis (pp. 148-149).
2. A.I. Mendeloff and J.P. Dunn, *Digestive Diseases.* Cambridge, Mass.: Harvard University
     Press (1971).

PEPTIC ULCER DISEASE

§501–PEPTIC ULCER (Unoperated)

References: (1) B. S. Pauley, "Mortality Experience: Systolic Heart Murmurs and Peptic Ulcer," Trans. Soc. Actuaries, 20(Part 1):39-43 (1968).
(2) Unpublished additional data supplied by the author.

Subjects Studied: The study covered the Prudential experiences issued during the years 1952-63 and traced to policy anniversaries in 1965, of male applicants giving a history of unoperated peptic ulcer. Classification and mortality study were carried out using data from the following groups:

Group	Years Since Last Attack	Standard or Substandard Issue
D07	0- 2	Standard
D08	2- 5	Standard
D09	5-10	Standard

Follow-up: Insurance policy records formed the basis of entry, of counting policies, exposure and death claims, and of follow-up information.

Results: Mortality and survival data are presented for the thirteen-year study period by age range and duration for the groups as shown (Table 501a). Although standard insurance was issued, a mortality ratio of about 177 per cent was experienced in groups D07 and D08 (0-2 and 2-5 years interval from last attack to application); there was persistence of excess mortality beyond five years' duration for cases with a short history of peptic ulcer and where the age at time of application was 40 and over — otherwise excess mortality was negligible after the first five years following issue. When the interval from last attack to application was 5 to 10 years (group D09) the overall mortality ratio was 122 per cent, within standard limits (Table 501b).

PEPTIC ULCER WITHOUT OPERATION IN INSURED LIVES

Table 501a Observed Data and Comparative Experience by Age and Policy Duration

Group	Age Range	Interval Start-End	Exposure Policy-Yrs	Death Claims during Interval	Death Claims Expected*	Mortality Ratio	Ave. Ann. Mort. Rate	Est. 7-Yr Surv. Rate	Est. 7-Yr Surv. Index	Excess Death Rate
		t to $t+\Delta t$	E	d	d'	100 d/d'	$\bar{q}=d/E$	$P=(1-\bar{q})^7$	100 P/P'	1000(d-d')/E
D07-D08	20-39	0- 5 yrs	10806	21	10.39	200%	.0019	.990	99.5%	1.0
		5-10	2705	7	4.86	144	.0026	.978	99.1	0.8
Interval		10-13	160	0	0.55	0	.0000	.978	100.2	−3.4
0-5 yrs		0-13	13671	28	15.80	177	.0020	—	—	0.9
	40 up	0- 5	4452	27	15.65	173	.0061	.970	98.7	2.5
		5-10	1179	14	8.46	165	.0119	.914	96.4	4.7
		10-13	66	2	0.72	280	.0303	.833	90.8	19
		0-13	5697	43	24.83	173	.0075	—	—	3.2
D09	20-39	0- 5	4377	6	4.42	136	.0014	.993	99.8	0.4
		5-10	884	2	1.64	122	.0023	.982	99.6	0.4
Interval		10-13	16	0	0.05	0	.0000	.982	100.5	−3.1
5-10 yrs		0-13	5277	8	6.11	131	.0015	—	—	0.4
	40 up	0- 5	3182	14	11.82	118	.0044	.978	99.7	0.7
		5-10	673	6	4.85	124	.0089	.935	98.8	1.7
		10-13	14	0	0.14	0	.0000	.935	101.8	−10
		0-13	3869	20	16.81	119	.0052	—	—	0.8

Table 501b Observed Data and Comparative Experience by Individual Impairment Group

Group	Age Range	Interval Start-End	Exposure Policy-Yrs	Death Claims during Interval	Death Claims Expected*	Mortality Ratio	Ave. Ann. Mort. Rate	Est. 7-Yr Surv. Rate	Est. 7-Yr Surv. Index	Excess Death Rate
		t to $t+\Delta t$	E	d	d'	100 d/d'	$\bar{q}=d/E$	$P=(1-\bar{q})^7$	100 P/P'	1000(d-d')/E
D07	20 and up	0-13	5347	17	9.84	173%	.0032	.978	99.0%	1.3
D08	20 and up	0-13	14021	54	30.79	175	.0039	.973	98.8	1.7
D09	20 and up	0-13	9146	28	22.92	122	.0031	.978	99.6	0.6

* Basis of expected mortality: 1955-60 Male Select Basic Table

PEPTIC ULCER DISEASE

§502–PEPTIC ULCER

Reference: T. W. Preston and R. D. Clarke, "An Investigation into The Mortality of Impaired Lives During The Period 1947-63," J. Inst. Actuaries, 92(Part 1):27-74 (1966).

Subjects Studied: Based on policies issued from 1947 to 1963 by the Prudential Assurance Company of London, England, the study covered the experience under ordinary insurance of applicants giving a history of peptic ulcer. Standard and substandard issues were included, but cases involving two or more major impairments were excluded from the study. The cases were divided into groups according to the following classification:

Peptic Ulcer

Group Code	Male or Female	Duration of History	History of Operation	History of Complication*	Number of Policies
200-203	M	Short	No	†	1647
204-207	M	Short	Yes	†	1262
210	M	Long	No	No	6314
211-213	M	Long	No	Yes	707
214	M	Long	Yes	No	3286
215-217	M	Long	Yes	Yes	1558
210-217	F	Long	†	†	372

*Complications – hematemesis, perforation, other. †With or without complication or operation.

Follow-up: Insurance policy records formed the basis of entry, of counting policies, exposure and death claims, and of follow-up information.

Results: Mortality and survival data are presented for the sixteen-year study period by type of history (Table 502). Normal or near-normal mortality was experienced in all groups without operation, except for those with long duration and complications. Except for the group composed of cases with a short history and no operation, there was excess mortality in all groups, with mortality ratios ranging from 123 to 165 per cent, and EDR running from .9 to 2.8 per thousand per year.

Table 502   Observed Data and Comparative Experience by History and Application

Code	Exposure Policy-Yrs	Death Claims	Death Claims Expected*	Mortality Ratio	Ave. Ann. Mort. Rate	Est. 7-Yr Surv. Rate	Est. 7-Yr Surv. Index	Excess Death Rate
	E	d	d'	100 d/d'	$\bar{q} = d/E$	$P = (1-\bar{q})^7$	100 P/P'	1000(d-d')/E
200-203	6838	22	23.88	92%	.0032	.978	100.2%	−0.3
204-207	7011	42	25.39	165	.0060	.959	98.3	2.4
210	37650	177	143.8	123	.0047	.968	99.4	0.9
211-213	4149	30	21.81	138	.0072	.950	98.6	2.0
214	18212	121	97.42	124	.0066	.954	99.1	1.3
215-217	9240	68	42.05	162	.0074	.950	98.0	2.8
210-217 (Females)	2313	11	7.94	139	.0048	.967	99.1	1.3

* Expected Death Claims from Prudential standard experience on male issues, graduated values of q'_x duration 0-4 years and duration 5 years up. Values of q'_x for female issues derived from these tables and female/male q'_x ratios in English Life Table No. 11.

PEPTIC ULCER IN CHILDREN

§503–PEPTIC ULCER IN CHILDREN

Reference: H. A. Sultz, E. R. Schlesinger, J. G. Feldman, and W. E. Mosher, "The Epidemiology of Peptic Ulcer in Childhood," Am. J. Pub. Health, 60:492-498 (1970).

Subjects Studied: All children admitted to any one of the twenty-two hospitals in or near Erie County (New York) or seen by certain physicians and diagnosed as having a peptic ulcer before the age of sixteen were included in the study. The survey of medical records from the hospitals, doctors, and birth and death certificates covered a 16-year period — 1946-1961. The male-female ratio was 1.6 to 1, with the mean age of the males 11.1 years and of the females 9.1 years. There were 90 cases of duodenal ulcer, three of gastric ulcer, and 13 described only as peptic ulcer.

Average Annual Incidence per 100,000 (No. of Cases in Parentheses)

Age	Under 1	1-4	5-9	10-14	15	All Ages
Male	1.2 (2)	0.5 (3)	1.8 (13)	5.7 (33)	13.7 (14)	2.9 (65)
Female	1.2 (2)	0.1 (1)	2.9 (20)	2.5 (14)	3.9 (4)	1.9 (41)

Follow-up: No information was given in the article as to follow-up methods used.

Results: All deaths occurred within one year of diagnosis. Table 503 discloses an excess death rate of 15 per thousand per year for the total exposure and a mortality ratio of 3100 per cent. The number of deaths is small, but at the young ages in the group, practically no deaths are normally experienced. The substantial magnitude of these indexes probably indicates that peptic ulcer is a material hazard to life at childhood ages.

Table 503   Observed Data and Comparative Experience, All Ages and Durations Combined

Years	Entrants	Cases Reaching 16 Yrs*	Exposure Patient-Yrs*	Deaths Obs.	Deaths Exp. †	Mortality Ratio	Ave. Ann. Mort. Rate	Est. 5-Yr Surv. Rate	Est. 5-Yr Surv. Index	Excess Death Rate
	ℓ	w	E	d	d'	100 d/d'	$\bar{q} = d/E$	$P = (1-\bar{q})^5$	100 P/P'	1000(d-d')/E
1947-1961	106	48	319	5	0.16	3100%	.0158	.923	92.6%	15

* Exposure was terminated at age 16
† Basis of expected mortality: U.S. Life Tables 1954

PEPTIC ULCER DISEASE

§504–DUODENAL ULCER (Uncomplicated)

Reference: *1951 Impairment Study*, compiled and published·by the Society of Actuaries (1954), pp. 122-127.

Subjects Studied: The study covered the experience under ordinary insurance, issued during the years 1935 through 1949 traced to policy anniversaries in 1950, of applicants giving a history of duodenal ulcer, without operation and not known to have had hemorrhage at the time of issue of the policy. Selected groups under study were, on the average, four per cent female with a group mean age of thirty-eight.

Age Distribution for the substandard issues with one attack within five years of application (Tables 504a-c).

Age	15-29	30-39	40-49	50-64
Distribution	22.6%	45.2%	25.9%	6.3%

Method of Selection: Experience was compiled in 1951 from contributions of 27 cooperating insurance companies. They supplied data retrieved from policy records coded for duodenal ulcer without operation, so that classification and mortality study could be carried out in accordance with a plan including these groups, designated D 19 through D 23:

Duodenal Ulcer, Without Operation, Hemorrhage Not Known

Group	No. of Attacks	Last Attack Within Yrs. of Application	Standard or Substandard Issue*	No. of Entrants	Per cent Female	Group Mean Age	Ratio of Policy Death Claims to Lives Involved†
D 19	1	0- 2	SS	6115	5	36	1.11
D 20	1	2- 5	S	3690	3	39	1.28
D 20	1	2- 5	SS	6619	4	37	1.20
D 21	1	5-10	S	5252	3	40	1.13
D 23	2 or more	2-10	SS	2150	3	39	1.04

*Group D 22 and missing S or SS groups were not reported in sufficient detail to include with the other ones in this table.

†Some applicants had more than one policy in force. The ratio of policies/lives is available in the *1951 Impairment Study* only for policies terminating in a death claim.

Follow-up: The policy records of the 27 participating companies were used for follow-up. The average duration of exposure for this study was 5.2 years, ranging from 4.6 to 6.4, compared with an average duration of exposure for the entire *1951 Impairment Study* of 6.2 years. Ratios of policies terminated by death to numbers of lives involved ranged from 1.04 (for D 23) to 1.28 (for D 20 standard) as compared with an overall range for the *1951 Impairment Study*, from 1.09 for all substandard issues to 1.19 for all standard issues.

Results: Mortality and survival data are presented for the fifteen-year study period both by age range (Table 504c) and by interval (Tables 504a and 504b) for the substandard experience in groups D 19 and D 20 combined. Table 504d shows the comparative experience by medical history of the applicant and insurance underwriting action (with all ages and durations combined) for the separate groups listed above. Generally speaking, all groups with uncomplicated duodenal ulcer show a low mortality ratio, ranging from 80 per cent to 134 per cent, correspondingly high survival ratios, and very low excess death rates, of the order of one per thousand per year. There was a tendency for mortality ratios to decrease over the fifteen-year observation period (Table 504a) and to decrease with age (Table 504c). The overall experience of groups D 21 and D 23 was highly favorable, the mortality ratio being less than one hundred per cent (Table 504d).

UNCOMPLICATED DUODENAL ULCER IN INSURED LIVES

Table 504a   Substandard Issues with History of Single Attack Within 5 Years of Application, No Operation, Not Known To Have Had Hemorrhage

Observed Data and Comparative Experience by Duration (All Ages Combined)

Interval Start-End	Exposure Policy-Yrs	Death Claims during Interval*	Death Claims Expected*	Mortality Ratio Interval	Mortality Ratio Cumulative	Survival Ratio Interval	Survival Ratio Cumulative	Excess Death Rate
t to $t + \Delta t$	E	d	d'	100 d/d'	100 Σd/Σd'	100 p_i/p_i'	100 P/P'	1000(d-d')/E
0- 2 yrs	22893	64 (53)	37.98	168%	168%	99.8%	99.8%	1.1
2- 5	22134	79 (72)	60.34	131	145	99.7	99.5	0.8
5-10	15593	82 (70)	66.43	123	137	99.5	99.0	1.0
10-15	3139	18 (16)	22.37	80	130	100.7	99.7	−1.4
0-15	63759	243 (211)	187.1	130	130	—	99.7	0.9

Table 504b   Derived Mortality and Survival Data (Same Groups)

Interval	Observed Rates Average Annual Mortality	Observed Rates Average Annual Survival	Observed Rates Cumulative Survival	Observed Rates Cumulative Mortality	Expected Rates* Average Annual Mortality	Expected Rates* Average Annual Survival	Expected Rates* Cumulative Survival	Expected Rates* Cumulative Mortality
Start-End								
t to $t + \Delta t$	$\bar{q} = d/E$	$\bar{p}$	P	Q	$\bar{q}' = d'/E$	$\bar{p}'$	P'	Q'
0- 2 yrs	.0028	.9972	.994	.006	.0017	.9983	.9966	.0034
2- 5	.0036	.9964	.984	.016	.0027	.9973	.9885	.0115
5-10	.0053	.9947	.958	.042	.0043	.9957	.9674	.0326
10-15	.0057	.9943	.931	.069	.0071	.9929	.9335	.0665
0-15	.0038	.9962	—	—	.0029	.9971	—	—

Table 504c   Comparative Experience by Age (Same Groups, All Durations Combined)

Age Range	Exposure Policy-Yrs	Death Claims*	Death Claims Expected*	Mortality Ratio	Ave. Ann. Mort. Rate	Est. 7-Yr Surv. Rate	Est. 7-Yr Surv. Index	Excess Death Rate
	E	d	d'	100 d/d'	$\bar{q} = d/E$	P = $(1-\bar{q})^7$	100 P/P'	1000(d-d')/E
15-29 yrs	14374	29 (27)	15.48	187%	.0020	.986	99.4%	0.9
30-39	28844	76 (66)	56.01	136	.0026	.982	99.5	0.7
40-49	16502	98 (79)	74.30	132	.0059	.959	99.0	1.4
50-64	4039	40 (37)	41.33	97	.0099	.933	100.2	−0.3
15-64	63759	243 (209)	187.1	130	.0038	.974	99.4	0.9

Table 504d   Comparative Experience by Individual Impairment Group (All Ages and Durations Combined)

Group† (See description)	Exposure Policy-Yrs	Death Claims*	Death Claims Expected*	Mortality Ratio	Ave. Ann. Mort. Rate	Est. 7-Yr Surv. Rate	Est 7-Yr Surv. Index	Excess Death Rate
	E	d	d'	100 d/d'	$\bar{q} = d/E$	P = $(1-\bar{q})^7$	100 P/P'	1000(d-d')/E
D 19SS	28242	97 (87)	77.48	125%	.0034	.976	99.5%	0.7
D 20S	19539	73 (57)	69.87	104	.0037	.974	99.9	0.2
D 20SS	35517	146 (122)	109.6	133	.0041	.972	99.3	1.0
D 21S	32942	121 (107)	137.6	88	.0037	.974	100.4	−0.5
D 23SS	9491	26 (25)	32.65	80	.0027	.981	100.5	−0.7

* Death claims, with number of lives in parentheses. Basis of expected mortality: 1935-50 Intercompany Experience on Standard Issues.

† "S" = Standard policy issues, "SS" = Substandard policy issues

PEPTIC ULCER DISEASE

§505—DUODENAL ULCER (With Operation)

Reference: *1951 Impairment Study,* compiled and published by the Society of Actuaries (1954), pp. 127-135.

Subjects Studied: The study covered the experience under ordinary insurance, issued during the years 1935 through 1949 traced to policy anniversaries in 1950, of applicants giving a history of duodenal ulcer with operation at the time of issue of the policy. Selected groups under study were, on the average, four per cent female with a group mean age of forty.

Age Distribution for all issues with one attack within ten years of application (Tables 505a-c).

Age	15-29	30-39	40-49	50-64
Distribution	11.9%	41.8%	33.6%	12.7%

Method of Selection: Experience was compiled in 1951 from contributions of 27 cooperating insurance companies. They supplied data retrieved from policy records coded for duodenal ulcer with operation, so that classification and mortality study could be carried out in accordance with a plan including these groups, designated D 24 through D 26:

Duodenal Ulcer, With Operation, One Attack

Group	No. of Attacks	Last Attack Within Yrs. of Application	Standard or Substandard Issue*	No. of Entrants	Per cent Female	Group Mean Age	Ratio of Policy Death Claims to Lives Involved†
D 24	1	0- 2	SS	1020	4	38	1.09
D 25	1	2- 5	S	432	2	40	1.43
D 25	1	2- 5	SS	2082	3	39	1.13
D 26	1	5-10	S	1607	5	41	1.22
D 26	1	5-10	SS'	579	4	40	1.08

*Group D24S was not reported in sufficient detail to include with the others in this table.
†Some applicants had more than one policy in force. The ratio of policies/lives is available in the *1951 Impairment Study* only for policies terminating in a death claim.

Follow-up: The policy records of the 27 participating companies were used for follow-up. The average duration of exposure for this study was 6.0 years, ranging from 4.8 to 7.3, compared with an average duration of exposure for the entire *1951 Impairment Study* of 6.2 years. Ratios of policies terminated by death to numbers of lives involved ranged from 1.08 (for D 26 substandard) to 1.43 (for D 25 standard) as compared with an overall range for the *1951 Impairment Study,* from 1.09 for all substandard issues to 1.19 for all standard issues.

Results: Mortality and survival data are presented for the fifteen-year study period both by age range (Table 505c) and by interval (Tables 505a and 505b) for all groups combined. Table 505d shows the comparative experience by medical history of the applicant and insurance underwriting action (with all ages and durations combined) for the separate groups listed above. Except for lives insured under 30 years of age, which showed a mortality ratio of 465 per cent, all groups of duodenal ulcer with operation showed moderate mortality ratios, ranging from 163 to 225 per cent, with survival indices varying between 94.6 and 99.6 per cent. Excess death rates were reasonably low, of the order of 3 to 5 per 1000 per year, with one EDR of 6.7 per 1000 in older insureds age 50-64 years. By duration mortality ratios remained at or close to 200 per cent during the first ten years of follow-up, then dropped to 133 per cent during the last interval, 10-15 years after insurance issue (Table 505a). Most of the cases insured within five years of operation were substandard issues, whereas most of those insured after a longer lapse of time were standard issues.

DUODENAL ULCER WITH OPERATION IN INSURED LIVES

Table 505a Standard and Substandard Issues, History of Single Attack of Duodenal Ulcer within 10 Years, Operated Observed Data and Comparative Experience by Duration (All Ages Combined)

Interval Start-End	Exposure Policy-Yrs	Death Claims during Interval*	Death Claims Expected*	Mortality Ratio Interval	Mortality Ratio Cumulative	Survival Ratio Interval	Survival Ratio Cumulative	Excess Death Rate
t to $t + \Delta t$	E	d	d'	100 d/d'	100 $\sum$d/$\sum$d'	100 p_i/p_i'	100 P/P'	1000(d-d')/E
0- 2 yrs	10468	45 (43)	22.28	200%	200%	99.6%	99.6%	2.2
2- 5	11141	81 (67)	40.60	200	200	98.9	98.4	3.6
5-10	9686	102 (85)	51.89	197	199	97.5	95.9	5.2
10-15	2971	33 (30)	24.76	133	187	98.6	94.6	2.8
0-15	34266	261 (225)	139.5	187	187	—	94.6	3.5

Table 505b Derived Mortality and Survival Data (Same Groups)

Interval Start-End	Observed Rates Average Annual Mortality	Observed Rates Average Annual Survival	Observed Rates Cumulative Survival	Observed Rates Cumulative Mortality	Expected Rates* Average Annual Mortality	Expected Rates* Average Annual Survival	Expected Rates* Cumulative Survival	Expected Rates* Cumulative Mortality
t to $t + \Delta t$	$\bar{q}$ = d/E	$\bar{p}$	P	Q	$\bar{q}'$ = d'/E	$\bar{p}'$	P'	Q'
0- 2 yrs	.0043	.9957	.991	.009	.0021	.9979	.9958	.0042
2- 5	.0073	.9927	.970	.030	.0036	.9964	.9851	.0149
5-10	.0105	.9895	.920	.080	.0054	.9946	.9588	.0412
10-15	.0111	.9889	.870	.130	.0083	.9917	.9197	.0803
0-15	.0076	.9924	—	—	.0041	.9959	—	—

Table 505c Comparative Experience by Age (Same Groups, All Durations Combined)

Age Range	Exposure Policy-Yrs	Death Claims*	Death Claims Expected*	Mortality Ratio	Ave. Ann. Mort. Rate	Est. 7-Yr Surv. Rate	Est. 7-Yr Surv. Index	Excess Death Rate
	E	d	d'	100 d/d'	$\bar{q}$ = d/E	P = $(1-\bar{q})^7$	100 P/P'	1000(d-d')/E
15-29 yrs	4079	21 (20)	4.53	465%	.0051	.965	97.2%	4.0
30-39	14323	63 (56)	31.90	197	.0044	.970	98.5	2.2
40-49	11525	102 (86)	56.97	179	.0089	.939	97.2	3.9
50-64	4339	75 (61)	46.13	163	.0173	.885	95.3	6.7
15-64	34266	261 (225)	139.5	187	.0076	.948	97.6	3.5

Table 505d Comparative Experience by Individual Impairment Group (All Ages and Durations Combined)

Group† (See description)	Exposure Policy-Yrs	Death Claims	Death Claims Expected*	Mortality Ratio	Ave. Ann. Mort. Rate	Est. 7-Yr Surv. Rate	Est. 7-Yr Surv. Index	Excess Death Rate
	E	d	d'	100 d/d'	$\bar{q}$ = d/E	P = $(1-\bar{q})^7$	100 P/P'	1000(d-d')/E
D24SS	4894	36 (33)	16.12	225%	.0074	.949	97.2%	4.1
D25S	2886	20 (14)	11.97	167	.0069	.953	98.0	2.8
D25SS	11580	85 (75)	42.07	200	.0073	.950	97.4	3.7
D26S	11689	93 (76)	56.77	164	.0080	.945	97.8	3.1
D26SS	3217	27 (25)	12.60	215	.0084	.943	96.9	4.5

* Death claims, with number of lives in parentheses. Basis of expected mortality: 1935-50 Intercompany Experience on Standard Issues

† "S" = standard policy issues, "SS" = substandard policy issues

PEPTIC ULCER DISEASE

§506–DUODENAL ULCER

References: (1) B. S. Pauley, "Mortality Experience: Systolic Heart Murmurs and Peptic Ulcer," Trans. Soc. Actuaries, 20(Part 1):39-43 (1968).

(2) Unpublished additional data supplied by the author.

Subjects Studied: The study covered the Prudential experience issued during the years 1952-63 and traced to policy anniversaries in 1965, of male applicants giving a history of duodenal ulcer. Classification and mortality study were carried out using data from the following groups:

Group	Operation	Yrs. Since Last Attack	Standard or Substandard Issue	Group	Operation	Yrs. Since Last Attack	Standard or Substandard Issue
D01	No	0- 2	S	D04	Yes	0- 2	S
D02	No	2- 5	S	D15	Yes	0- 2	SS
D03	No	5-10	S	D05	Yes	2- 5	S
D13	No	0- 2	SS*	D06	Yes	5-10	S
D14	No	0- 2	SS*	D16	Yes	2- 5	SS

*Temporary flat extra premium instead of tabular, graded by age.

Follow-up: Policy records were used for follow-up. The policy issued and paid for, not the individual applicant, was the unit for counting entrants, exposure and observed and expected death claims.

Results: Mortality and survival data are presented for the thirteen-year study period by age range and duration (Tables 506a-b) as well as by individual impairment group (Table 506c). The unoperated groups experienced relatively light mortality with mortality ratios ranging from a low of 108 per cent to a high of 155 per cent. Correspondingly high survival ratios and low EDR's were experienced.

The operated groups experienced higher but nevertheless moderate mortality with most mortality ratios in the vicinity of 200 per cent, high survival ratios and low EDR's. High mortality ratios, over 300 per cent, appear for groups D04 and D15 in the 20-39 age range beyond the first five years. The significance of these ratios may be limited since they develop from a small number of deaths. The results for individual impairment groups were consistent with the above findings exhibiting mortality ratios ranging from 90 per cent to 200 per cent, except for group D04, with only 321 exposure years and no observed deaths.

DUODENAL ULCER IN INSURED LIVES

Table 506a Duodenal Ulcer without Operation. Observed Data and Comparative Experience by Age and Policy Duration

Group	Age Range	Interval Start-End	Exposure Policy-Yrs	Death Claims during Interval	Death Claims Expected*	Mortality Ratio	Ave. Ann. Mort. Rate	Cumulative Surv. Rate	Cumulative Surv. Ratio	Excess Death Rate
		t to $t+\Delta t$	E	d	d'	100 d/d'	$\bar{q}=d/E$	P	100 P/P'	1000(d-d')/E
D01-D03	20-39	0- 5yrs	81742	92	81.62	113%	.0011	.994	99.9%	0.1
and D13-D14		5-10	24937	54	46.07	117	.0022	.984	99.8	0.3
S and SS		10-13	1860	8	5.81	138	.0043	.971	99.4	1.2
Interval 0-2 yrs		0-13	108539	154	133.5	115	.0014	.971	99.4	0.2
	40 up	0- 5	46647	185	169.3	109	.0040	.980	99.8	0.3
S-Interval		5-10	13588	111	96.48	115	.0082	.941	99.3	1.1
2-10 yrs		10-13	916	15	9.66	155	.0164	.895	97.6	5.8
		0-13	61151	311	275.4	113	.0051	.895	97.6	0.6

Table 506b Duodenal Ulcer with Operation. Observed Data and Comparative Experience by Age and Policy Duration

Group	Age Range	Interval Start-End	Exposure Policy-Yrs	Death Claims during Interval	Death Claims Expected*	Mortality Ratio	Ave. Ann. Mort. Rate	Cumulative Surv. Rate	Cumulative Surv. Ratio	Excess Death Rate
		t to $t+\Delta t$	E	d	d'	100 d/d'	$\bar{q}=d/E$	P	100 P/P'	1000(d-d')/E
D04 and D15	20-39	0- 5yrs	3384	8	3.54	225%	.0024	.988	99.3%	1.3
S and SS		5-10	1107	8	2.17	370	.0072	.953	96.7	5.3
Interval 0-2 yrs		10-13	101	1	0.33	305	.0099	.925	94.8	6.6
		0-13	4592	17	6.04	280	.0037	.925	94.8	2.4
	40 up	0- 5	3501	28	13.34	210	.0080	.961	97.9	4.2
		5-10	1094	10	8.35	120	.0091	.918	97.2	1.5
		10-13	73	1	0.80	125	.0137	.880	96.4	2.7
		0-13	4668	39	22.49	173	.0084	.880	96.4	3.5
D05, D06, D16	20-39	0- 5	8210	17	8.91	191	.0021	.990	99.5	1.0
S-Interval		5-10	2418	9	4.92	183	.0037	.971	98.6	1.7
2-10 yrs		10-13	149	0	0.50	0	.0000	.971	99.7	−3.4
SS-Interval		0-13	10777	26	14.33	181	.0024	.971	99.7	1.1
2-5 yrs	40 up	0- 5	11449	61	45.98	133	.0053	.974	99.3	1.3
		5-10	3299	42	25.84	163	.0127	.914	96.9	4.9
		10-13	159	1	1.83	55	.0063	.896	98.4	−5.2
		0-13	14907	104	73.65	141	.0070	.896	98.4	2.0

Table 506c Duodenal Ulcer. Observed Data and Comparative Experience by Individual Impairment Group

Group	Age Range	Interval Start-End	Exposure Policy-Yrs	Death Claims during Interval	Death Claims Expected*	Mortality Ratio	Ave. Ann. Mort. Rate	Est. 7-Yr Surv. Rate	Est. 7-Yr Surv. Index	Excess Death Rate
		t to $t+\Delta t$	E	d	d'	100 d/d'	$\bar{q}=d/E$	$P=(1-\bar{q})^7$	100 P/P'	1000(d-d')/E
D01	20 and up	0-13	25461	46	51.07	90%	.0018	.988	100.1%	−0.2
D02	(all groups)	(all groups)	56357	144	133.3	108	.0026	.982	99.9	0.2
D03			30993	90	83.51	108	.0029	.980	99.9	0.2
D04			321	0	0.77	0	.0000	1.000	101.7	−2.4
D05			4086	17	14.95	114	.0042	.971	99.6	0.5
D06			10631	60	37.55	160	.0056	.961	98.5	2.1
D13			48937	138	110.7	125	.0028	.981	99.7	0.6
D14			7942	47	30.34	155	.0059	.959	98.5	2.1
D15			8939	56	27.76	200	.0063	.957	97.8	3.2
D16			10967	53	35.48	149	.0048	.967	98.9	1.6

* Basis of expected mortality: 1955-60 Male Select Basic Table

DUODENAL ULCER IN INSUREDS

§507–DUODENAL ULCER IN INSUREDS

Reference: "New York Life Single Medical Impairment Study–1972," unpublished report made available by J.J. Hutchinson and J.C. Sibigtroth (1973),

Subjects Studied: Policyholders of New York Life Insurance Company issued insurance in 1954-1970, followed to the 1971 policy anniversary. Different codes are used to distinguish cases in which the duodenal ulcer has been operated on from those where no operation had been performed. Only the substandard issues have been analyzed here. Cases involving more than one ratable impairment were excluded.

Follow-up: Insurance policy records formed the basis of entry, of counting policies, exposure and death claims, and of follow-up information.

Results: Comparative experience for substandard cases, with and without operation, is given in Tables 507a-b by sex and duration, all ages combined. For unoperated males, the mortality ratio showed no trend by duration, ranging between 82 and 118 per cent, with EDR highest (0.5 extra deaths per 1000) at 2-5 years. For operated males, the trend in the mortality ratio was rapidly decreasing, from 143 per cent at 0-2 years to 59 per cent at 10-17 years. There was no excess mortality observed after 5 years. The mortality experience for unoperated females was about level by duration, and slightly above expected. The overall mortality ratio was favorable for operated males. Among unoperated cases, males experienced normal overall mortality, in contrast to 123 per cent for females.

From Table 507c, the mortality experience for males without operation was favorable at all age groups, except 40-49, where the mortality ratio was 115 per cent and EDR 0.7 per 1000. For males with operation, the only age group where excess mortality was observed was 50-59, the mortality ratio was 138 per cent and EDR 3.7 per 1000. In females without operation the mortality ratio did not exceed 125 per cent and was virtually uniform in the two age groups shown. The estimated 8-year survival index was 99 per cent or more in all age groups studied, except for operated males age 50-59, where it was 97 per cent.

Table 507d presents experience by cause of death, males and females combined, for both unoperated and operated cases. The leading causes by number of deaths in both categories are, respectively, diseases of the heart and circulatory system, malignant neoplasms and "all other and unknown," but mortality ratios in these categories are not unfavorable. In both the unoperated and operated classes, mortality ratios attributed to suicide are relatively high reaching 126 per cent in the former and 205 per cent in the latter. Two of the 14 deaths in operated cases due to "all other causes and unknown" were for digestive disorders.

PEPTIC ULCER DISEASE

Table 507a   Observed Data and Comparative Experience by Sex and Duration — Substandard Cases

Sex	No.	Interval Start-End	Exposure Policy-Yrs	No. of Death Claims Observed	No. of Death Claims Expected*	Mortality Ratio Interval	Mortality Ratio Cumulative	Survival Ratio Interval	Survival Ratio Cumulative	Excess Death Rate
	i	t to t + Δ t	E	d	d'	100 d/d'	100 Σd/Σd'	100 p_i/p_i'	100 P/P'	1000(d-d')/E
Without Operation										
Male	1	0- 2 yrs	17105	24	26.91	89%	89%	100.0%	100.0%	−0.2
	2	2- 5	18644	59	50.00	118	108	99.9	99.9	0.5
	3	5-10	18912	86	78.86	109	108	99.8	99.7	0.4
	4	10-17	8687	61	74.17	82	100	101.1	100.8	−1.5
Female	1	0- 5 yrs	3296	7	5.43	129	129	99.8	99.8	0.5
	2	5-17	2009	9	7.53	120	123	99.1	98.9	0.7
With Operation										
Male	1	0- 2 yrs	4027	12	8.41	143%	143%	99.8%	99.8%	0.9
	2	2- 5	3950	18	15.07	119	128	99.8	99.6	0.7
	3	5-10	3500	18	21.97	82	106	100.6	100.2	−1.1
	4	10-17	1518	12	20.23	59	91	103.9	104.1	−5.4

Table 507b   Derived Mortality and Survival Data

Sex	No.	Interval Start-End	Observed Rates Average Annual Mortality	Observed Rates Average Annual Survival	Observed Rates Cumulative Survival	Observed Rates Cumulative Mortality	Expected Rates* Average Annual Mortality	Expected Rates* Average Annual Survival	Expected Rates* Cumulative Survival	Expected Rates* Cumulative Mortality
	i	t to t + Δ t	$\bar{q}$=d/E	$\bar{p}$	P	Q	$\bar{q}'$=d'/E	$\bar{p}'$	P'	Q'
Without Operation										
Male	1	0- 2 yrs	.0014	.9986	.9972	.0028	.0016	.9984	.9969	.0031
	2	2- 5	.0032	.9968	.9878	.0122	.0027	.9973	.9889	.0111
	3	5-10	.0045	.9955	.9655	.0345	.0042	.9958	.9684	.0316
	4	10-17	.0070	.9930	.9191	.0809	.0085	.9915	.9120	.0880
Female	1	0- 5 yrs	.0021	.9979	.9894	.0106	.0016	.9984	.9918	.0082
	2	5-17	.0045	.9955	.9375	.0625	.0037	.9963	.9481	.0519
With Operation										
Male	1	0- 2 yrs	.0030	.9970	.9940	.0060	.0021	.9979	.9958	.0042
	2	2- 5	.0046	.9954	.9805	.0195	.0038	.9962	.9844	.0156
	3	5-10	.0051	.9949	.9556	.0444	.0063	.9937	.9539	.0461
	4	10-17	.0079	.9921	.9039	.0961	.0133	.9867	.8684	.1316

* Basis of expected mortality: 1955-60 Select Basic Table

DUODENAL ULCER IN INSUREDS

Table 507c Comparative Experience by Sex and Age Group — Substandard Cases, All Durations Combined

Sex	Age Group	Exposure Policy-Yrs	No. of Death Claims Observed	No. of Death Claims Expected*	Mortality Ratio	Ave. Ann. Mort. Rate	Est. 8-Yr Surv. Rate	Est. 8-Yr Surv. Index	Excess Death Rate
		E	d	d'	100 d/d'	q̄=d/E	P=(1-q̄)⁸	100 P/P'	1000(d-d')/E
Without Operation									
Male	0-29	15055	15	15.24	98%	.0010	.9920	100.0%	0.0
	30-39	25306	54	54.60	99	.0021	.9831	100.0	0.0
	40-49	16327	94	81.91	115	.0058	.9548	99.4	0.7
	50-59	5695	53	57.98	91	.0093	.9279	100.7	−0.9
	60 up	965	14	20.21	69	.0145	.8896	105.4	−6.4
	All Ages	63348	230	229.94	100	.0036	.9713	100.0	0.0
Female	0-49	4224	9	7.36	122%	.0021	.9831	99.7%	0.4
	50 up	1081	7	5.60	125	.0065	.9493	99.0	1.3
	All Ages	5305	16	12.96	123	.0030	.9761	99.5	0.6
With Operation									
Male	15-39	5927	9	10.50	86%	.0015	.9879	100.2%	−0.3
	40-49	4370	16	22.51	71	.0037	.9711	101.2	−1.5
	50-59	2138	29	21.05	138	.0136	.8965	97.0	3.7
	60 up	560	6	11.62	52	.0107	.9175	108.5	−10
	All Ages	12995	60	65.68	91	.0046	.9636	100.3	−0.4

Table 507d Mortality by Cause of Death — Male and Female Combined

Cause	Without Operation No. of Death Claims Observed	Without Operation Expected†	Without Operation Mortality Ratio	Without Operation Excess Death Rate	With Operation No. of Death Claims Observed	With Operation Expected†	With Operation Mortality Ratio	With Operation Excess Death Rate
Malignant Neoplasms	62	57.91	107%	0.1	17	16.44	103%	0.1
Diseases of Heart & Circulatory System	104	95.50	109	0.1	22	27.11	81	−0.4
Accidents and Homicides	21	33.40	63	−0.2	3	9.48	32	−0.5
Suicide	13	10.30	126	0.0	6	2.92	205	0.2
All Other Causes & Unknown	46	45.79	100	0.0	14●	13.00	108	0.1
Total	246	242.90	101	0.0	62	68.95	90	−0.5

* Basis of expected mortality: 1955-60 Select Basic Table
† Distribution of total expected deaths by Intercompany Medically Examined Standard Issues 1965-70
● Includes 3 respiratory disorders and 2 digestive disorders

PEPTIC ULCER DISEASE

§510–GASTRIC ULCER (Uncomplicated)

Reference: *1951 Impairment Study,* compiled and published by the Society of Actuaries (1954), pp. 112-116.

Subjects Studied: The study covered the experience under ordinary insurance, issued during the years 1935 through 1949 traced to policy anniversaries in 1950, of applicants having a history of gastric ulcer without operation and not known to have had hemorrhage at the time of issue of the policy. The groups reported on here had a mean age of 37 years and were, on the average, six per cent female.

Age distribution for issues with a history of one attack within five years of application (Tables 510a-c):

Age	15-29	30-39	40-49	50-64
Distribution	27.6%	42.7%	22.7%	7.0%

Method of Selection: Experience was compiled in 1951 from contributions of 27 cooperating insurance companies. They supplied data retrieved from policy records coded for gastric ulcer without operation, so that classification and mortality study could be carried out in accordance with a plan including these groups, designated D6 through D8.

Gastric Ulcer, Without Operation, Hemorrhage Not Known

Group	No. of Attacks	Last Attack Within___ Yrs. of Application	Standard or Substandard Issue*	No. of Entrants	Per cent Female	Group Mean Age	Ratio of Policy Death Claims to Lives Involved†
D6	1	0- 2	SS	1029	6	35	1.24
D7	1	2- 5	S	–	–	–	1.15
D7	1	2- 5	SS	2756	7	36	1.07
D8	1	5-10	S	1906	5	40	1.02
D8	1	5-10	SS	–	–	–	1.00

*Only limited information is given in the study with respect to D7 Standard and D8 Substandard.

†Some applicants had more than one policy in force. The ratio of policies/lives is available in the *1951 Impairment Study* only for policies terminating in a death claim.

Follow-up: The policy records of the 27 participating companies were used for follow-up. The average duration of exposure for this study was 5.9 years compared with an average for the entire *1951 Impairment Study* of 6.2 years. The ratio of policies terminated by death to numbers of lives involved ranged from 1.00 (D8S) to 1.24 (D6SS), whereas the ratio for all classes was 1.09 for all substandard issues, and 1.19 for all standard issues.

Results: Mortality and survival data are presented for the fifteen-year study period both by age range (Table 510c) and by duration (Tables 510a-b) for groups D6 (substandard) and D7 (substandard) combined. Table 510d shows comparative experience for the individual group classifications for which data are given in the study, with all ages and durations combined. Overall mortality ratios range from 86 per cent to 163 per cent, ratios which are not unfavorable. Excess death rates are relatively low as well. Mortality ratios for cases showing a single attack within 5 years prior to issuance tend to decrease by duration (Table 510a), dropping from 230 per cent in the first interval to 122 per cent in the 10 to 15-year duration bracket. There is a tendency for mortality ratios to diminish with age (Table 510c). Survival ratios vary within a narrow range - from a low of 98.3 per cent to 103.3 per cent.

GASTRIC ULCER WITHOUT COMPLICATIONS IN INSURED LIVES

Table 510a Substandard Policy Issues, History of Single Attack of Gastric Ulcer within 5 Years,
Not Operated, without Known History of Hemorrhage
Observed Data and Comparative Experience by Duration (All Ages Combined)

Interval Start-End	Exposure Policy-Yrs	Death Claims during Interval*	Death Claims Expected*	Mortality Ratio Interval	Mortality Ratio Cumulative	Survival Ratio Interval	Survival Ratio Cumulative	Excess Death Rate
t to t + Δ t	E	d	d'	100 d/d'	100$\sum$d/$\sum$d'	100 p_i/p_i	100 P/P'	1000(d-d')/E
0- 2 yrs	6736	25 (22)	10.86	230%	230%	99.6%	99.6%	2.1
2- 5	7165	19 (16)	19.18	99	146	100.0	99.6	0.0
5-10	5616	24 (23)	23.86	101	126	99.9	99.5	0.0
10-15	1269	11 (10)	9.04	122	126	99.2	98.7	1.5
0-15	20786	79 (71)	62.94	126	126	—	98.7	0.8

Table 510b Derived Mortality and Survival Data (Same Groups)

Interval Start-End	Observed Rates Average Annual Mortality	Observed Rates Average Annual Survival	Observed Rates Cumulative Survival	Observed Rates Cumulative Mortality	Expected Rates* Average Annual Mortality	Expected Rates* Average Annual Survival	Expected Rates* Cumulative Survival	Expected Rates* Cumulative Mortality
t to t + Δ t	$\bar{q}$ = d/E	$\bar{p}$	P	Q	$\bar{q}'$ = d'/E	$\bar{p}'$	P'	Q'
0- 2 yrs	.0037	.9963	.993	.007	.0016	.9984	.9968	.0032
2- 5	.0027	.9973	.985	.015	.0027	.9973	.9887	.0113
5-10	.0043	.9957	.964	.036	.0042	.9958	.9681	.0319
10-15	.0087	.9913	.922	.078	.0071	.9929	.9342	.0658
0-15	.0038	.9962	—	—	.0030	.9970	—	—

Table 510c Comparative Experience by Age (Same Groups, All Durations Combined)

Age Range	Exposure Policy-Yrs	Death Claims*	Death Claims Expected*	Mortality Ratio	Ave. Ann. Mort. Rate	Est. 7-Yr Surv. Rate	Est. 7-Yr Surv. Index	Excess Death Rate
	E	d	d'	100d/d'	$\bar{q}$ = d/E	P = (1-$\bar{q}$)^7	100 P/P'	1000(d-d')/E
15-29 yrs	5747	11 (8)	6.12	180%	.0019	.987	99.4%	0.8
30-39	8883	24 (23)	17.91	134	.0027	.981	99.5	0.7
40-49	4709	34 (31)	22.25	153	.0072	.951	98.3	2.5
50-64	1447	10 (9)	16.66	60	.0069	.953	103.3	-4.6
15-64	20786	79 (71)	62.94	126	.0038	.974	99.4	0.8

Table 510d Comparative Experience by Individual Impairment Group (All Ages and Durations Combined)

Group† (See Description)	Exposure Policy-Yrs	Death Claims*	Death Claims Expected*	Mortality Ratio	Ave. Ann. Mort. Rate	Est. 7-Yr Surv. Rate	Est. 7-Yr Surv. Index	Excess Death Rate
	E	d	d'	100d/d'	$\bar{q}$ = d/E	P = (1-$\bar{q}$)^7	100 P/P'	1000(d-d')/E
D6SS	5134	12 (17)	12.85	163%	.0041	.972	98.9%	1.6
D7S	—	15 (13)	10.42	144	—	—	—	—
D7SS	15652	58 (54)	50.09	116	.0037	.974	99.7	0.5
D8S	13303	50 (49)	57.96	86	.0038	.974	100.4	-0.6
D8SS	—	14 (14)	13.59	103	—	—	—	—

* Death claims, with number of lives in parentheses. Basis of expected mortality: 1935-50
Intercompany Experience on Standard Issues
† "S" = Standard policy issues, "SS" = Substandard policy issues

PEPTIC ULCER DISEASE

§511–GASTRIC ULCER (With Operation)

Reference: *1951 Impairment Study*, compiled and published by the Society of Actuaries (1954), pp. 116-121.

Subjects Studied: The study covered the experience under ordinary insurance, issued during the years 1935 through 1949 traced to policy anniversaries in 1950, of applicants giving a history of gastric ulcer with operation at the time of policy issue. Selected groups under study were, on the average, four per cent female with a group mean age of thirty-nine.

Age Distribution for all issues with one attack within three to ten years of application (Tables 511a-c).

Age	15-29	30-39	40-49	50-64
Distribution	16.2%	40.4%	31.2%	12.2%

Method of Selection: Experience was compiled in 1951 from contributions of 27 cooperating insurance companies. They supplied data retrieved from policy records coded for gastric ulcer with operation, so that classification and mortality study could be carried out in accordance with a predetermined plan including these groups, designated D12 through D13:

Gastric Ulcer, With Operation, One Attack

Group	Attack Within___Yrs. of Application	Standard or Substandard Issues*	No. of Entrants	Per Cent Female	Group Mean Age	Ratio of Policy Death Claims to Lives Involved†
D12	2- 5	SS	1427	4	38	1.03
D13	5-10	S	776	3	40	1.22
D13	5-10	SS	1261	4	40	1.09

*Group D11SS was not reported in sufficient detail to include with the other ones in this table.

†Some applicants had more than one policy in force. The ratio of policies/lives is available in the *1951 Impairment Study* only for the small fraction of policies terminating in a death claim.

Follow-up: The policy records of the 27 participating companies were used for follow-up. The average duration of exposure for this study was 6.2 years, ranging from 5.5 to 7.1, compared with an average duration of exposure for the entire *1951 Impairment Study* of 6.2 years. Ratios of policies terminated by death to numbers of lives involved ranged from 1.03 (for D12 substandard) to 1.22 (for D13 standard) as compared with a value of 1.09 for all substandard issues in the *1951 Impairment Study*, and 1.19 for all standard issues.

Results: Mortality and survival data are presented for the fifteen-year study period both by age range (Table 511c) and by interval (Tables 511a-b) for all groups combined. Table 511d shows the comparative experience by history and insurance action (with all ages and durations combined) for the separate groups listed above. Generally speaking, all groups of gastric ulcer with operation show *moderately high* mortality ratios varying from 147 to 240 per cent, *the higher* ratios being related to the recency of attack. Survival ratios are about 97 per cent, and excess death rates of the order of 2 to 6 per thousand per year. Mortality ratios remained fairly constant at about 200 per cent throughout the fifteen-year period, while EDR showed a tendency to increase as a function of both duration and age (Tables 511a and 511c). In group D13 the excess mortality was greater for the standard than for the substandard issues (Table 511d).

GASTRIC ULCER WITH COMPLICATIONS IN INSURED LIVES

Table 511a Standard and Substandard Policy Issues, History of Single Attack of
Gastric Ulcer within 2-10 Yrs., Operated
Observed Data and Comparative Experience by Duration (All Ages Combined)

Interval Start-End	Exposure Policy-Yrs	Death Claims during Interval*	Death Claims Expected*	Mortality Ratio Interval	Mortality Ratio Cumulative	Survival Ratio Interval	Survival Ratio Cumulative	Excess Death Rate
t to t + Δ t	E	d	d'	100 d/d'	100$\sum$d/$\sum$d'	100 p_i/p_i'	100 P/P'	1000(d-d')/E
0- 2 yrs	6168	30 (30)	12.67	235%	235%	99.4%	99.4%	2.8
2- 5	6931	47 (45)	24.55	191	205	99.0	98.4	3.2
5-10	6392	67 (58)	33.92	198	200	97.4	95.9	5.2
10-15	1832	30 (27)	15.29	196	200	96.0	92.0	8.0
0-15	21323	174 (157)	86.43	200	200	—	92.0	4.1

Table 511b Derived Mortality and Survival Data

Interval Start-End	Observed Rates Average Annual Mortality	Observed Rates Average Annual Survival	Observed Rates Cumulative Survival	Observed Rates Cumulative Mortality	Expected Rates* Average Annual Mortality	Expected Rates* Average Annual Survival	Expected Rates* Cumulative Survival	Expected Rates* Cumulative Mortality
t to t + Δ t	$\bar{q}$ = d/E	$\bar{p}$	P	Q	$\bar{q}'$ = d'/E	$\bar{p}'$	P'	Q'
0- 2 yrs	.0049	.9951	.990	.010	.0021	.9979	.9958	.0042
2- 5	.0068	.9932	.970	.030	.0035	.9965	.9854	.0146
5-10	.0105	.9895	.920	.080	.0053	.9947	.9596	.0404
10-15	.0164	.9836	.847	.153	.0083	.9917	.9204	.0796
0-15	.0082	.9918	—	—	.0041	.9959	—	—

Table 511c Comparative Experience by Age (Same Groups, All Durations Combined)

Age Range	Exposure Policy-Yrs	Death Claims*	Death Claims Expected*	Mortality Ratio	Ave. Ann. Mort. Rate	Est. 7-Yr Surv. Rate	Est. 7-Yr Surv. Index	Excess Death Rate
	E	d	d'	100 d/d'	$\bar{q}$ = d/E	P = $(1-\bar{q})^7$	100 P/P'	1000(d-d')/E
15-29 yrs	3455	8 (8)	3.88	205%	.0023	.984	99.2%	1.2
30-39	8609	42 (40)	19.06	220	.0049	.966	98.1	2.7
40-49	6647	76 (66)	34.09	225	.0114	.923	95.7	6.3
50-64	2612	48 (43)	29.40	163	.0184	.878	95.1	7.1
15-64	21323	174 (157)	86.43	200	.0082	.944	97.2	4.1

Table 511d Comparative Experience by Individual Impairment Group (All Ages and Durations Combined)

Group† (See description)	Exposure Policy-Yrs	Death Claims*	Death Claims Expected*	Mortality Ratio	Ave. Ann. Mort. Rate	Est. 7-Yr Surv. Rate	Est. 7-Yr Surv. Index	Excess Death Rate
	E	d	d'	100 d/d'	$\bar{q}$ = d/E	P = $(1-\bar{q})^7$	100 P/P'	1000(d-d')/E
D12SS	7845	63 (61)	26.27	240%	.0080	.945	96.8%	4.7
D13S	5527	62 (51)	26.79	230	.0112	.924	95.6	6.4
D13SS	7951	49 (45)	33.37	147	.0062	.957	98.6	2.0

* Death claims, with number of lives in parentheses. Basis of expected mortality: 1935-50
Intercompany Experience on Standard Issues
† "S" = Standard policy issues, "SS" = Substandard policy issues

PEPTIC ULCER DISEASE

§512–GASTRIC ULCER IN INSUREDS

Reference: "New York Life Single Medical Impairment Study–1972," unpublished report made available by J.J. Hutchinson and J.C. Sibigtroth (1973).

Subjects Studied: Policyholders of New York Life Insurance Company issued insurance in 1954-1970, followed to the 1971 policy anniversary. The experience reported is for cases with stomach ulcer, subclassified into those that had undergone surgery for it, and those that had not. Only the substandard cases were studied. Where more than one ratable impairment code appeared, such cases were excluded.

Follow-up: Insurance policy records formed the basis of entry, of counting policies, exposure and death claims, and of follow-up information.

Results: Comparative experience for male substandard cases, with and without operation, is given in Tables 512a-b, by duration, all ages combined. For unoperated males, the mortality ratio tended to be somewhat higher for the first two years than in subsequent years, with EDR highest (2.0 extra deaths per 1000) at 0-2 years. For operated males, the excess mortality was definitely greater in the first five years than in subsequent years, being 275 per cent (6.5 extra deaths per 1000). The cumulative survival ratio at 17 years was 98.9 per cent for unoperated males and only 91.5 per cent for operated males.

From Table 512c, there was no clear trend by entry age in the mortality ratio for unoperated males, ranging between 176 and 70 per cent, with EDR highest (1.4 extra deaths per 1000) at ages 50 up. The mortality trend for operated males appeared to be increasing with age, with the age group 60 up experiencing the highest mortality ratio at 250 per cent and EDR of 32 per 1000. The overall mortality ratio for males was higher among operated cases (182 per cent), than for unoperated cases (112 per cent). With or without operation, females experienced higher mortality ratios than males. The female mortality ratio was found to be higher among unoperated cases, 555 per cent, than for operated cases, 475 per cent, contrary to the male experience. The estimated 8-year survival index remained at a near normal level by age for male unoperated cases and ranged between 98.5 and 76.7 per cent for operated males.

Table 512d shows that, for all unoperated cases, malignant neoplasms and diseases of heart and circulation are the major causes of death, the mortality ratios being 190 and 168 per cent, respectively. Further, there were 1.9 extra deaths per 1000 due to these causes, out of an EDR of 2.2 for all causes. Among operated cases, the same major causes of death observed in unoperated cases were found to experience a high mortality, the ratio being 250 per cent for malignant neoplasms and 193 per cent for diseases of heart and circulation. The high mortality ratio of 260 per cent for "all other causes and unknown" was attributable to 9 deaths, 4 of which were from pneumonia and 2 from cerebrovascular accidents.

GASTRIC ULCER IN INSUREDS

Table 512a Observed Data and Comparative Experience by Duration — Male Substandard Cases

Interval		Exposure	No. of Death Claims		Mortality Ratio		Survival Ratio		Excess
No.	Start-End	Policy-Yrs	Observed	Expected*	Interval	Cumulative	Interval	Cumulative	Death Rate
i	t to $t+\Delta t$	E	d	d'	$100\,d/d'$	$100\Sigma d/\Sigma d'$	$100\,p_i/p_i'$	$100\,P/P'$	$1000(d-d')/E$
Without Operation									
1	0- 2 yrs	1833	7	3.28	215%	215%	99.6%	99.6%	2.0
2	2-10	3552	13	14.76	88	111	100.4	100.0	−0.5
3	10-17	727	9	7.87	114	112	98.9	98.9	1.6
With Operation									
1	0- 5 yrs	1374	14	5.05	275%	275%	96.8%	96.8%	6.5
2	5-17	1093	17	11.95	142	182	94.5	91.5	4.6

Table 512b Derived Mortality and Survival Data

Interval		Observed Rates				Expected Rates*			
		Average Annual		Cumulative		Average Annual		Cumulative	
No.	Start-End	Mortality	Survival	Survival	Mortality	Mortality	Survival	Survival	Mortality
i	t to $t+\Delta t$	$\bar q = d/E$	$\bar p$	P	Q	$\bar q' = d'/E$	$\bar p'$	P'	Q'
Without Operation									
1	0- 2 yrs	.0038	.9962	.9924	.0076	.0018	.9982	.9964	.0036
2	2-10	.0037	.9963	.9637	.0363	.0042	.9958	.9637	.0363
3	10-17	.0124	.9876	.8832	.1168	.0108	.9892	.8930	.1070
With Operation									
1	0- 5 yrs	.0102	.9898	.9501	.0499	.0037	.9963	.9817	.0183
2	5-17	.0156	.9844	.7872	.2128	.0109	.9891	.8604	.1396

Table 512c Comparative Experience by Sex and Age Group — Substandard Cases, All Durations Combined

Sex	Age Group	Exposure Policy-Yrs	No. of Death Claims		Mortality Ratio	Ave. Ann. Mort. Rate	Est. 8-Yr Surv. Rate	Est. 8-Yr Surv. Index	Excess Death Rate
			Observed	Expected*					
		E	d	d'	$100\,d/d'$	$\bar q = d/E$	$P = (1-\bar q)^8$	$100\,P/P'$	$1000(d-d')/E$
Without Operation									
Male	15-39	3412	10	5.69	176%	.0029	.9768	99.0%	1.3
	40-49	1732	6	8.62	70	.0035	.9727	101.2	−1.5
	50 up	968	13	11.60	112	.0134	.8975	98.8	1.4
	All Ages	6112	29	25.91	112	.0047	.9627	99.6	0.5
Female	All Ages	1103	16	2.88	555	.0145	.8896	109.9	12
With Operation									
Male	0-49	1708	10	6.80	147%	.0059	.9541	98.5%	1.9
	50-59	609	13	6.98	186	.0213	.8414	92.3	9.9
	60 up	150	8	3.22	250	.0533	.6450	76.7	32
	All Ages	2467	31	17.00	182	.0126	.9038	95.5	5.7
Female	All Ages	366	7	1.47	475	.0191	.8568	85.5	15

Table 512d Mortality by Cause of Death — Male and Female Combined

Cause	Without Operation				With Operation			
	No. of Death Claims		Mortality Ratio	Excess Death Rate	No. of Death Claims		Mortality Ratio	Excess Death Rate
	Observed	Expected†			Observed	Expected†		
Malignant Neoplasms	13	6.86	190%	0.8	11	4.40	250%	2.3
Diseases of Heart & Circulatory System	19	11.32	168	1.1	14	7.27	193	2.4
Accidents and Homicides	5	3.96	126	0.1	3	2.54	118	0.2
Suicide	0	1.22	0	−0.2	1	0.78	128	0.1
All Other Causes & Unknown	8	5.43	147	0.4	9•	3.48	260	1.9
Total	45	28.79	156	2.2	38	18.47	205	6.9

* Basis of expected mortality: 1955-60 Select Basic Table
† Distribution of total expected deaths by Intercompany Medically Examined Standard Issues 1965-70
• Includes 4 pneumonia and 2 cerebrovascular accidents

STOMACH AND ESOPHAGUS

§520–DYSPEPSIA, INDIGESTION, GASTRITIS IN INSUREDS

Reference: "New York Life Single Medical Impairment Study–1967," unpublished report made available by J.J. Hutchinson and J.C. Sibigtroth (1973).

Subjects Studied: Policyholders of New York Life Insurance Company issued insurance in 1949-1965, followed to the 1966 policy anniversary. These were cases in which no definite diagnosis was made, but because of corroborative information such as severity and frequency of attacks, were none the less classified into standard and substandard issues. The experience for both underwriting categories is reported here; excluded were cases with ratable impairment in addition to the code shown here.

Follow-up: Insurance policy records formed the basis of entry, of counting policies, exposure and death claims, and of follow-up information.

Results: Comparative experience for standard and substandard cases is given in Tables 520a-b by duration, for both sexes and all entry ages combined. Among standard cases, the mortality ratio was 196 per cent at 0-2 years, and decreased to levels below normal after five years. EDR was in the range of 1 to 2 extra deaths per 1000 in the first five years of policy duration. Among substandard cases, the mortality ratio ranged between 117 per cent at 0-5 years and 130 per cent at 5-17 years. The cumulative survival ratio at 17 years was normal for standard cases and 97.4 per cent for substandard cases.

Table 520c gives comparative experience for males by entry age group. Standard cases exhibited a normal overall mortality ratio of 86 per cent, with no trend by age. Among substandard men the overall mortality ratio was 135 per cent with an EDR of 1.5 per 1000. The highest mortality ratio, 200 per cent, occurred in the youngest group, males under 40 years of age. The very limited experience for substandard females showed a mortality ratio of 175 per cent and an EDR of 1.6 extra deaths per 1000 per year.

Comparative mortality by major causes of death is given in Table 520d, for male and female substandard cases combined. The major cause of death is found in malignant neoplasms, with a mortality ratio of 183 per cent and an EDR of 0.8 per 1000, based on seven death claims. Since there were only 20 death claims in all, the small variations in excess mortality noted in the remaining causes are probably random in character.

INDIGESTION, GASTRITIS IN INSUREDS

Table 520a Observed Data and Comparative Experience by Insurance Action and Duration — Male and Female Combined

Group	No.	Interval Start-End	Exposure Policy-Yrs	Observed	Expected*	Mortality Ratio Interval	Cumulative	Survival Ratio Interval	Cumulative	Excess Death Rate
	i	t to t + Δt	E	d	d'	100 d/d'	100 Σd/Σd'	100 p_i/p_i'	100 P/P'	1000(d-d')/E
Std	1	0- 2 yrs	2379	8	4.08	196%	196%	99.7%	99.7%	1.6
	2	2- 5	2806	12	8.63	139	157	99.6	99.3	1.2
	3	5-10	3034	11	15.12	73	111	100.7	100.0	−1.4
	4	10-17	1305	7	12.89	54	93	103.2	103.2	−5.6
SStd	1	0- 5 yrs	2553	7	5.98	117%	117%	99.8%	99.8%	0.4
	2	5-17	1474	13	10.03	130	125	97.6	97.4	2.0

Table 520b Derived Mortality and Survival Data

Group	No.	Interval Start-End	Observed Rates Average Annual Mortality	Survival	Cumulative Survival	Mortality	Expected Rates* Average Annual Mortality	Survival	Cumulative Survival	Mortality
	i	t to t + Δt	$\bar{q}$ = d/E	$\bar{p}$	P	Q	$\bar{q}'$ = d'/E	$\bar{p}'$	P'	Q'
Std	1	0- 2 yrs	.0033	.9967	.9934	.0066	.0017	.9983	.9966	.0034
	2	2- 5	.0042	.9958	.9809	.0101	.0030	.9970	.9876	.0124
	3	5-10	.0036	.9964	.9632	.0368	.0049	.9951	.9634	.0366
	4	10-17	.0053	.9947	.9278	.0722	.0098	.9902	.8988	.1012
SStd	1	0- 5 yrs	.0027	.9973	.9153	.0847	.0023	.9977	.8885	.1115
	2	5-17	.0088	.9912	.8232	.1768	.0068	.9932	.8181	.1819

Table 520c Comparative Experience by Age Group — All Durations Combined

Group	Age Group	Exposure Policy-Yrs	Observed	Expected*	Mortality Ratio	Ave. Ann. Mort. Rate	Est. 8-Yr Surv. Rate	Est. 8-Yr Surv. Index	Excess Death Rate
		E	d	d'	100 d/d'	$\bar{q}$ = d/E	P = (1 - $\bar{q}$)^8	100 P/P'	1000(d-d')/E
Male Std	<40	4763	11	9.80	112%	.0023	.9816	99.8%	0.3
	40-49	2997	6	15.51	39	.0020	.9840	102.5	−3.2
	50 up	1232	17	14.28	119	.0137	.8951	98.2	2.2
	Total	8992	34	39.59	86	.0037	.9704	100.6	−0.6
Male SStd	<40	2069	7	3.46	200%	.0033	.9736	98.6%	1.7
	40-49	858	4	4.03	99	.0046	.9635	100.0	−0.0
	50 up	593	9	7.36	122	.0151	.8851	97.8	2.8
	Total	3520	20	14.85	135	.0056	.9557	98.9	1.5
Female Std and SStd	Total	1039	4	2.29	175%	.0038	.9697	98.7%	1.6

Table 520d Mortality by Cause of Death—Substandard Cases, Male and Female Combined

Cause	Observed	Expected†	Mortality Ratio	Excess Death Rate
Malignant Neoplasms	7	3.82	183%	0.8
Diseases of the Heart and Circulatory System	5	6.29	79	−0.3
Accidents, Homicides, and Suicide	3	2.88	104	0.0
All Other Causes and Unknown	5	3.02	166	0.5
Total	20	16.01	125	1.0

*Basis of expected mortality: 1955-60 Select Basic Table
†Distribution of total expected deaths by Intercompany Medically Examined Standard Issues 1965-70

INTESTINES, COLON AND RECTUM

§530—CHRONIC ULCERATIVE COLITIS

References: (1) W. P. Sloan, Jr., J. A. Bargen, and R. P. Gage, "Life Histories of Patients with Chronic Ulcerative Colitis: A Review of 2,000 Cases," Gastroenterology, 16:25-38 (1950).

(2) J. A. Bargen, W. G. Sauer, W. P. Sloan, and R. P. Gage, "The Development of Cancer in Chronic Ulcerative Colitis," Gastroenterology, 26:32-37 (1954).

Subjects Studied: Two thousand patients given a diagnosis of chronic ulcerative colitis at the Mayo Clinic from January 1, 1918, through December 31, 1937. Cases were excluded if they had a demonstrated specific cause for the ulceration, such as tuberculosis.

Age Distribution at Onset of Symptoms of Ulcerative Colitis
(Excluding 11 men and 6 women with undetermined age at onset)

Age Group (Years)	Under 20	20-29	30-39	40-49	50 up	All Ages	Mean Age
Male	223 (20%)	392 (36%)	252 (23%)	136 (12%)	99 (9%)	1102 (100%)	30.2
Female	193 (22%)	326 (37%)	214 (24%)	89 (10%)	59 (7%)	881 (100%)	28.9
Total	416 (21%)	718 (36%)	466 (24%)	225 (11%)	158 (8%)	1983 (100%)	29.6

The second reference (1954) presents mortality from 1564 patients less than 50 years of age at the time of the diagnosis, selected from the 2000 patients in the original series. Patients who had any malignant tumors, including cancer of the colon, within a year after diagnosis were excluded; this exclusion was not exercised in the original study reported in the first reference.

Follow-up: The follow-up for the first reference was made as of January 1, 1949, with 76.6 per cent of the patients followed up for five years or longer, and 71.8 per cent followed up for ten years or longer. The second reference provided follow-up to 1952 and excluded 100 patients not heard from since their original visit to the Clinic.

Results: Survival experience is summarized in Table 530a for the entire group of 2000 patients over a period of 20 years. During the first year of follow-up the mortality rate was about 18 times that of the general population, and there were 85 extra deaths per 1000. There was a sharp decrease in extra mortality after the first year, but a significant excess was still observed 15-20 years from entry into the study. The cumulative survival ratio was 67.6 per cent at 20 years.

In Table 530b five-year and ten-year survival rates by age at diagnosis yield high mortality ratios, about 20 times those of the normal population at ages 0-9, shading off to less than twice the normal ratios at ages 60 and up, with the ratios for the ten-year experience at any age about two-thirds as high as the five-year ones. The annual extra deaths per 1000 remain fairly constant through both periods of observation, with an EDR of 38 per 1000 for the total five-year experience, and 26 for the ten-year, all ages combined. The five-year cumulative survival ratio came to 82.3 per cent, and the ten-year, 77.0 per cent.

Tables 530c and 530d, based on deaths from all causes, show observed and derived mortality and survival data by duration for the later series of cases, under age 50. The more favorable first-year experience in these tables, compared with that in Table 530a, is the result of excluding certain classes with high mortality ratios, but, after the first year, the rates are not unlike the experience previously shown. Over the entire 25 years of follow-up of this younger group the mortality ratio was 325 per cent, EDR was 16 per 1000 per year, and the survival ratio was 72.4 per cent.

Table 530a Observed Data and Comparative Experience by Duration (All Ages Combined)

Interval		Observed Rates				Exp. Ave. Ann. Mort. Rate*	Mortality Ratio	Cumulative Surv. Ratio	Excess Death Rate
No. Start-End	Cumulative Survival	Interval Survival	Geom. Mean Ann. Surv.	Geom. Mean Ann. Mort.					
i t to $t + \Delta t$	P	p_i	$\breve{p}$	$\breve{q}$	$\breve{q}'$	$100\,\breve{q}/\breve{q}'$	$100\,P/P'$	$1000(\breve{q}-\breve{q}')$
1 0- 1 yr	.910	.910	.910	.090	.0050	1800%	91.5%	85
2 1- 5	.809	.889	.971	.029	.0056	520	83.1	23
3 5-10	.739	.914	.982	.018	.0073	245	78.8	11
4 10-15	.641	.867	.972	.028	.0098	285	71.8	18
5 15-20	.563	.878	.974	.026	.0138	188	67.6	12

CHRONIC ULCERATIVE COLITIS

Table 530b Comparative Survival Experience by Age

Age Group	Number of Patients		Cumulative Survival Rate		Cumulative Surv. Ratio	Estim. Ave. Ann. Mort. Rate		Mortality Ratio	Excess Death Rate
	Admitted	Traced	Observed	Expected		Observed	Expected*		
	ℓ	ℓ tr	P	P′	100 P/P′	$\breve{q}$	$\breve{q}′$	100 $\breve{q}/\breve{q}′$	1000($\breve{q}-\breve{q}′$)
Five Year Experience									
0- 9 yrs	39	32	.812	.9908	82.0%	.041	.0018	2300%	39
10-19	213	166	.801	.9884	81.0	.043	.0023	1890	41
20-29	571	420	.817	.9805	83.3	.040	.0039	1020	36
30-39	589	457	.801	.9743	82.2	.043	.0052	835	38
40-49	335	267	.813	.9497	85.6	.041	.0103	395	30
50-59	176	133	.729	.9047	80.6	.061	.0198	310	42
60 up	77	57	.596	.7768	76.7	.098	.0493	199	49
All ages	2000	1532	.794	.9645	82.3	.045	.0072	625	38
Ten Year Experience									
0- 9 yrs	39	29	.724	.9837	73.6	.032	.0016	1990	30
10-19	213	156	.692	.9724	71.2	.036	.0028	1290	33
20-29	571	394	.739	.9600	77.0	.030	.0041	725	26
30-39	589	425	.744	.9408	79.1	.029	.0061	480	23
40-49	335	252	.754	.8900	84.7	.028	.0116	240	16
50-59	176	126	.579	.7813	74.1	.053	.0244	220	29
60 up	77	54	.370	.5343	69.3	.095	.0608	156	34
All ages	2000	1436	.710	.9219	77.0	.034	.0081	415	26

Table 530c Observed Data and Comparative Experience by Duration — Ages Under 50 Years

Interval		No. Alive at Start of Interval	Exposure Person-Yrs	Deaths		Mortality Ratio		Survival Ratio		Excess Death Rate
No.	Start-End			Obs.	Exp.†	Interval	Cumulative	Interval	Cumulative	
	t to t + Δt	ℓ	E	d	d′	100d/d′	100$\sum$d/$\sum$d′	100$p_i/p_i′$	100 P/P′	1000(d-d′)E
1	0- 1 yr	1564	1564	58	6.41	905%	905%	96.7%	96.7%	33
2	1- 2	1506	1490.5	48	6.56	730	815	97.2	94.0	28
3	2- 5	1427	3985.5	85	19.48	435	590	95.2	89.4	16
4	5-10	1219	5645.5	81	34.98	230	405	96.1	85.8	8.2
5	10-15	1037	4241.5	111	35.10	315	375	91.4	78.3	18
6	15-20	593	2184.5	54	24.21	225	345	93.2	73.1	14
7	20-25	286	878.5	15	13.33	113	325	99.1	72.4	1.9
	0-25	1564	19990	452	140.07	325	325	72.4	72.4	16

Table 530d Derived Mortality and Survival Data — Ages Under 50 Years

Interval		Observed Rates				Expected Rates†			
		Interval		Cumulative		Interval		Cumulative	
No.	Start-End	Mortality	Survival	Survival	Mortality	Mortality	Survival	Survival	Mortality
i	t to t + Δt	q_i	p_i	P	Q	$q_i′$	$p_i′$	P′	Q′
1	0- 1 yr	.037	.963	.963	.037	.0041	.9959	.9959	.0041
2	1- 2	.032	.968	.932	.068	.0044	.9956	.9915	.0085
3	2- 5	.021	.979	.874	.126	.0049	.9951	.9771	.0229
4	5-10	.014	.986	.813	.187	.0062	.9938	.9472	.0528
5	10-15	.026	.974	.712	.288	.0083	.9917	.9086	.0914
6	15-20	.025	.975	.628	.372	.0111	.9889	.8594	.1406
7	20-25	.017	.983	.576	.424	.0152	.9848	.7961	.2039
	0-25	.023	.977	.576	.424	.0070	.9930	.7691	.2039

* Basis of expected mortality: U.S. White Males and Females 1929-1931
† Basis of expected mortality: U.S. White Males and Females 1939-1941

§531–CARCINOMA AND ULCERATIVE COLITIS

References: (1) J. A. Bargen and R. P. Gage, "Carcinoma and Ulcerative Colitis: Prognosis," Gastroenterology, 39:385-392 (1960).
(2) J.A. Bargen, W. G. Sauer, W. P. Sloan, and R. P. Gage, "The Development of Cancer in Chronic Ulcerative Colitis," Gastroenterology, 26:32-37 (1954).

Subjects Studied: Patients with chronic ulcerative colitis examined or treated at the Mayo Clinic. The first reference (1960) contains experience accumulated between 1913 and 1958 on 178 patients in whom carcinoma developed. The distribution of these subjects at time of diagnosis of chronic ulcerative colitis by age-group and sex:

Number (per cent) of Subjects

Age Group (years):	Age at Diagnosis of Chronic Ulcerative Colitis						
	Under 20	20-29	30-39	40-49	50 up	All Ages	Mean Age
Male	19 (19%)	26 (26%)	32 (32%)	16 (16%)	7 (7%)	100 (100%)	31.5 yrs
Female	10 (13%)	31 (40%)	18 (23%)	11 (14%)	8 (10%)	78 (100%)	31.8 yrs
Total	29 (16%)	57 (32%)	50 (28%)	27 (15%)	15 (9%)	178 (100%)	31.6 yrs

The second reference (1954) presents mortality from carcinoma of the digestive organs and peritoneum experienced between 1918 and 1937 in a group of 1564 patients under 50 years of age at time chronic ulcerative colitis was diagnosed. Compared with this experience is the mortality indicated for members of the general population in the period with the same age-sex distribution.

Follow-up: Follow-up procedure is not described in the 1960 report — for the most part reliance is indicated on the records of the Mayo Clinic. All subjects reported on, however, are classified as having died or as living at the close of observation — patients not traced are omitted from the study. The earlier paper obtained information relative to the development of malignant neoplasms either from: (a) observation at the Clinic (43 cases); (b) letters from other physicians (33 cases); (c) letters from relatives (22 cases).

Results: Mortality in the 15-year period following diagnosis of chronic ulcerative colitis among 178 patients developing carcinoma, shown in Tables 531a and b was very high as compared with that of the general population. In the year following diagnosis of ulcerative colitis the mortality rate was 29 times that of the general population, and the EDR, 109 per 1000: the ratio and EDR both diminished subsequent to the first year but remained quite high — the mortality ratio ranged from 585 per cent to 815 per cent that of comparably aged white persons in the U.S. in the 14-year period following the first year. The EDR tended to increase with duration; in the 9-year period subsequent to the year following diagnosis it ran between 30 and 33 per 1000 per year; in the next five-year period it increased to 51 per 1000. It should be emphasized that entrants in these tables were selected retrospectively, not prospectively, by virtue of development of carcinoma of the colon in the follow-up study of the much larger group of 1564 ulcerative colitis patients under age 50.

In Table 531c are presented arrays of intervals representing the passage of time intervening between the onset of chronic ulcerative colitis or from the clinical diagnosis of that condition to the time carcinoma is diagnosed at the Clinic. In 50 per cent of the patients the carcinoma developed 5 to 19 years after the diagnosis was established.

Excess mortality due specifically to carcinoma of the colon among patients with ulcerative colitis is presented in Table 531d. Over the 30-year follow-up study of the 1564 colitis patients 178 developed such malignant lesions and 98 of these died as a result of this complication. Expected deaths are undoubtedly overestimated, as they are based on rates for cancer of all digestive organs, not of the colon alone, and the true total should be significantly less than the 9.10 expected deaths shown. Excess mortality was especially high for children and young adults. For those age 20 up EDR remained relatively constant, with corresponding diminution of mortality ratio with age. Extra deaths per 1000 due to cancer of the colon therefore constitute a significant part of total excess mortality (see EDR Tables 530a-b), and are especially high for patients under age 20.

CARCINOMA AND ULCERATIVE COLITIS

Table 531a   Observed Data and Comparative Experience among Patients in Whom Carcinoma Developed By Duration from Diagnosis of Ulcerative Colitis — All Ages Combined

Interval		No. Alive at Start of Interval	Exposure Person-Yrs	Deaths		Mortality Ratio		Survival Ratio		Excess Death Rate
No.	Start-End			Obs.	Exp.*	Interval	Cumulative	Interval	Cumulative	
i	τ to $t+\Delta t$	ℓ	E	d	d'	100d/d'	100$\sum$d/$\sum$d'	100p_i/p_i'	100 P/P'	1000(d-d')/E
1	0- 1 yr	178	177	20	.69	2900%	2900%	89.0%	89.0%	109
2	1- 5 yrs	156	566	21	2.58	815	1250	87.7	78.1	33
3	5-10 yrs	127	585.5	21	3.58	585	905	85.7	66.9	30
4	10-15 yrs	99	436.5	26	3.70	705	835	75.7	50.6	51
	0-15 yrs	178	1765	88	10.6	835	835		50.6	44

Table 531b   Derived Mortality and Survival Data

Interval		Observed Rates				Expected Rates*			
No.	Start-End	Cumulative Survival	Interval Survival	Geom. Mean Ann. Surv.	Geom. Mean Ann. Mort.	Cumulative Survival	Interval Survival	Geom. Mean Ann. Surv.	Geom. Mean Ann. Mort.
i	t to $t+\Delta t$	P	p_i	$\breve{p}$	$\breve{q}$	P'	p_i'	$\breve{p}'$	$\breve{q}'$
1	0- 1 yr	.887	.887	.887	.113	.9961	.9961	.9961	.0039
2	1- 5 yrs	.764	.861	.963	.037	.9780	.9818	.9954	.0046
3	5-10 yrs	.635	.831	.964	.036	.9483	.9696	.9938	.0062
4	10-15 yrs	.460	.725	.938	.062	.9083	.9578	.9914	.0086

Table 531c   Development of Carcinoma: Distribution by Interval Preceding Diagnosis of Carcinoma

From Onset of Chronic Ulcerative Colitis			From Clinical Diagnosis of Chronic Ulcerative Colitis		
Interval Years	Number of Patients	Per Cent	Interval Years	Number of Patients	Per Cent
Under 5	8	4.5%	Under 1	46	25.9%
5- 9	17	9.6	1- 4	21	11.8
10-14	46	25.8	5- 9	26	14.6
15-19	47	26.3	10-14	38	21.3
20-24	34	19.1	15-19	25	14.0
25-29	17	9.6	20-24	14	7.9
30-34	6	3.4	25-29	7	3.9
35 up	3	1.7	30 up	1	0.6
Total	178	100.0%	Total	178	100.0%

Table 531d   Comparative Mortality Experience — Ages Under 50 Years (All Durations Combined) Deaths from Carcinoma of Colon

Age At Diagnosis	Number Diagnosed	Exposure Person-Yrs	Deaths Observed	Deaths Expected†	Mortality Ratio	Ave. Ann. Mort. Rate	Excess Death Rate
		E	d	d'	100 d/d'	$\bar{q}$ = d/E	1000(d-d')/E
2-14 yrs	98	1300.0	13	0.020	65000%	.010	10
15-19 yrs	127	1424.5	12	0.050	24000	.008	8.4
20-24 yrs	219	2609.5	11	0.208	5300	.004	4.1
25-29 yrs	294	3945.5	17	0.767	2200	.005	4.1
30-34 yrs	301	3911.5	15	1.342	1120	.004	3.5
35-39 yrs	229	3151.5	9	1.930	465	.003	2.2
40-44 yrs	166	2144.5	15	2.107	710	.007	6.0
45-49 yrs	130	1738.5	6	2.676	225	.003	1.9
Total	1564	20225.5	98	9.100	1080	.005	4.4

* Basis of expected mortality: U.S. Life Tables 1929-31

† Basis of expected mortality from carcinoma of digestive organs and peritoneum given in 1949 U.S. Statistics of Causes of Death. See text.

INTESTINES, COLON AND RECTUM

§532–ULCERATIVE COLITIS EXPERIENCE (ENGLAND)

Reference: F. C. Edwards and S. C. Truelove, "The Course and Prognosis of Ulcerative Colitis," Gut, 4:299-315 (1963).

Subjects Studied: Patients (including out-patients) with ulcerative colitis treated at the Radcliffe Infirmary or the Churchill Hospital (Oxford, England) from 1938 to March 1962. The 624 subjects (250 "first attack" patients experiencing an initial attack, and 374 "relapse" patients undergoing recurrence of established disease) were distributed as follows:

Age at Onset	First Attacks			Relapses			Whole Series		
(Years)	Men	Women	Total	Men	Women	Total	Men	Women	Total
0-29	24	44	68	83	102	185	107	146	253
30-59	53	86	139	69	102	171	122	188	310
60 up	17	26	43	5	8	13	22	34	56
Total	94	156	250	157	217*	374*	251	373*	624*

*Includes 5 of unknown age

Follow-up: A minimum follow-up of one year was obtained. Data were obtained from questionnaires to patients, from reports by other hospitals and from family doctors and specialists. Certified causes of death and autopsy reports were obtained. No subjects were lost to follow-up.

Results: Comparative experience by duration from first examination at Churchill Hospital for all cases together is indicated in Tables 532a-b. The mortality ratio and excess deaths per 1000 were high in the year following onset — the former, 1060 per cent, the latter, 62 per 1000. Subsequent mortality ratios tended to decline with duration of the disease, dropping to less than half (450 per cent) in the succeeding two-year interval, and then ranged between 180 and 240 per cent to the end of the twentieth year. EDR's in the second interval (second and third years) dropped to 21 per 1000 and were substantially lower in succeeding durations, but this function displayed considerable irregularity by duration, varying after the third year between 6.2 and 11 per 1000. Cumulative survival ratios diminished from 93.7 per cent in the first year to 72.6 per cent at the end of 20 years.

Table 532c presents the short-term risk of death from the attack requiring hospitalization for first attacks and relapses, respectively. Fatality experience according to clinical severity (characterized by the degree of tachycardia, diarrhea, fever and anemia) is shown in the first section of this table. Mild and moderate cases indicated a relatively light risk of death. Among the most severely ill, mortality rates were high: among first attack patients 383 early deaths per 1000 were experienced, exceeding the rate among relapses (258 per 1000) by a substantial margin. Short-term mortality according to age at onset, also indicated in Table 532c, was comparable in first attacks and relapses, progressing from about 60-70 per 1000 at ages under 30 years to about 165 per 1000 for ages 60 years and older.

The extent of the disease on admission to hospital was a strong factor in the risk of death as shown in the third portion of Table 532c. Cases with minor involvement (distal type cases — rectum and rectosigmoid) made a favorable short-term showing: no death among 116 such cases. Where there was substantial involvement of the colon, the mortality rate on first attack, .073, was substantially greater than the .017 rate on relapses. Involvement of the entire colon resulted in much higher rates of death: .255 on first attacks, .178 on relapses. Early mortality decreased from about 0.10 in the early period of the study, 1938-1952, to less than half this rate in both first-attack and relapse cases, after 1952, when corticosteroids were first used in the treatment of the ulcerative colitis patients of this series. The authors reported that the shorter the history of the disease before referral to hospital the worse the immediate prognosis — the short-term death rate declined from .184 for histories of less than one month to .089 for durations of from 6 to 12 months.

Causes of early death in first referred attacks are shown in Table 532d. Of the 54 deaths, 17 occurred from uncomplicated ulcerative colitis while under medical treatment; 15 patients with severe uncomplicated ulcerative colitis died after emergency surgery; another 20 cases ended fatally because of particular complications of the disease, 5 of these having carcinoma of the colon. In two patients, death occurred from unrelated illnesses.

ULCERATIVE COLITIS (ENGLAND)

Table 532a   Observed Data and Comparative Experience by Duration — All Ages Combined

Interval		Exposure	No. of Deaths		Mortality Ratio		Survival Ratio		Excess
No.	Start-End	Person-Yrs	Observed	Expected*	Interval	Cumulative	Interval	Cumulative	Death Rate
i	t to t + Δ t	E	d	d'	100 d/d'	100 Σd/Σd'	100 p_i/p_i'	100 P/P'	1000(d-d')/E
1	0- 1 yr	624	43	4.06	1060%	1060%	93.7%	93.7%	62
2	1- 3 yrs	986	27	6.01	450	695	95.8	89.8	21
3	3- 5	749	9	4.34	205	550	98.7	88.7	6.2
4	5-10	1240	24	9.92	240	425	94.6	83.9	11
5	10-15	705	13	7.19	181	370	95.7	80.3	8.2
6	15-20	286	7	3.80	184	350	90.3	72.6	11
	0-20 yrs	4590	123	35.32	350				19

Table 532b   Derived Mortality and Survival Data

Interval		Observed Rates				Expected Rates*			
		Survival			Ave. Ann.	Survival			Ave. Ann.
No.	Start-End	Cumulative	Interval	Ave. Ann.	Mort. Rate	Cumulative	Interval	Ave. Ann.	Mort. Rate
i	t to t + Δ t	P	p_i	$\breve{p}$	$\breve{q}$	P'	p_i'	$\breve{p}$'	$\breve{q}$'
1	0- 1 yr	.931	.931	.931	.069	.9935	.9935	.9935	.0065
2	1- 3 yrs	.881	.946	.973	.027	.9814	.9878	.9939	.0061
3	3- 5	.860	.976	.988	.012	.9701	.9885	.9942	.0058
4	5-10	.782	.909	.981	.019	.9319	.9606	.9920	.0080
5	10-15	.711	.909	.981	.019	.8852	.9499	.9898	.0102
6	15-20	.601	.845	.967	.033	.8280	.9354	.9867	.0133

Table 532c   Intra-attack Mortality after First Referral ("Short-Term")

Category		First Attack Cases			Relapse Cases		
		No. of Patients	No. of Deaths	Short-Term Mort. Rate	No. of Patients	No. of Deaths	Short-Term Mort. Rate
		ℓ	d_s	q_s	ℓ	d_s	q_s
Clinical Severity	Mild	136	1	.007	225	2	.009
	Moderate	67	6	.090	82	9	.110
	Severe	47	18	.383	62	16	.258
	All	250	25	.100	369	27	.073
Age at Referral	Under 30 yrs	68	4	.059	102	7	.069
	30-59 yrs	139	14	.101	242	17	.070
	60 yrs up	43	7	.163	30	5	.167
Extent of Disease	Rectum or Sigmoid	55	0	.000	61	0	.000
	Part of Colon	96	7	.073	121	2	.017
	Entire Colon	51	13	.255	118	21	.178
Period of Entry	1938-1952	109	11	.101	170	18	.106
	1953-1962	141	6	.043	214	10	.047

Table 532d   Intra-attack Mortality after First Referral 1938-1962 by Cause of Death

Cause of Death	No. of Deaths	Per Cent	Cause of Death	No. of Deaths	Per Cent
Ulcerative Colitis	17	31%	Emergency Surgery	15	28%
Complications of Ulcer. Col.	15	28	Other Disease	2	4
Carcinoma of Colon	5	9	All Causes	54	100

* Basis of expected mortality: Contemporaneous general population (Great Britain)

INTESTINES, COLON AND RECTUM

§533–CHRONIC ULCERATIVE COLITIS IN CHILDREN

Reference: W. M. Michener, R. P. Gage, W. G. Sauer, and G. B. Stickler, "The Prognosis of Chronic Ulcerative Colitis in Children," New Eng. J. Med., 265:1075-1079 (1961).

Subjects Studied: The study related to a group of 427 children less than 15 years of age in whom a diagnosis of chronic ulcerative colitis had been established and who were observed at the Mayo Clinic in the years 1918 to 1959 inclusive. All patients had X-ray or proctoscopic evidence of the disease, or both. Twenty-six patients were lost to follow-up and were excluded from the analysis. As a result the study covers 401 patients.

Of the 427 patients, 260 (61%) were male and 167 were female. The mean age of the males was 11.2 years and of the females 11.0 years. The 401 patients included in the study were distributed by age as follows: ages 1-4 years, 26; ages 5-9 years, 88; ages 11-14 years, 287.

Follow-up: The status of the patients was determined to January 1961 by means of subsequent visits, a questionnaire to the patient or family, and sometimes from letters of inquiry to physicians. When a patient had died, the cause of death was ascertained from the death certificate, an autopsy, or both.

Results: Of the 401 patients included in the study, 112 died by the end of the observation period. This was a very high mortality experience; expected deaths according to the U.S. White Life Tables 1949-51 were estimated to be only 4.04. Tables 533a and b portray the mortality and survival experience for 20 years from the time of diagnosis of the disease. In the first year the death rate was 120 times the expected and in the second year, 45 times. The mortality ratios and excess death rates are at a minimum in the interval from 2 to 5 years, but the mortality is then still almost 12 times the expected. The survival rate of 62 per cent by the end of 20 years is very low for this age group.

Cause of death data are shown in Table 533c. Disease-related deaths account for a very high proportion of the deaths. Forty deaths were due to carcinoma of the colon or rectum — less than 1/10 of a death was expected according to a calculation based on a 1958 Special Report of the National Office of Vital Statistics, "Mortality from Selected Causes by Age, Race and Sex." It took some years for the carcinoma to develop, as is brought out in Table 533d. The mean interval from the diagnosis of chronic ulcerative colitis until the diagnosis of carcinoma of the colon or rectum was 14.8 years. In all, 46 cases of carcinoma of the colon or rectum were reported, of which 40 terminated in death.

Comment: An analysis of 85 cases according to type of operation, whether with or without carcinoma, indicated that total colectomy and ileostomy constituted a preferable method of management, although the paper advised caution in making this interpretation. There were 48 such cases, and 10 deaths had occurred. The more limited surgical procedure of a colostomy or an ileostomy was not so successful. There were 32 such cases, and 27 deaths had occurred. A subtotal colectomy and ileostomy were performed on the remaining five cases, and there were two deaths.

CHRONIC ULCERATIVE COLITIS IN CHILDREN

Table 533a Observed Data and Comparative Experience by Duration — All Ages Combined

Interval		Exposure Person-Yrs	Deaths		Mortality Ratio		Survival Ratio		Excess Death Rate
No.	Start-End		Obs.	Exp.*	Interval	Cumulative	Interval	Cumulative	
i	t to t + Δt	E	d	d'	100d/d'	100$\sum$d/$\sum$d'	100p_i/p_i'	100 P/P'	1000(d-d')/E
1	0- 1 yr	401	24	0.20	12000%	12000%	94.0%	94.0%	59
2	1- 2	366	10	0.22	4500	8100	97.3	91.5	27
3	2- 5	940	8	0.68	1180	3800	97.8	89.5	7.8
4	5-10	1172	22	1.30	1690	2700	91.1	81.5	18
5	10-20	1192	38	1.46	2600	2600	77.3	63.0	31
	0-20	4071	102	3.86	2600	2600		63.0	24

Table 533b Derived Mortality and Survival Data

Interval		Observed Rates				Expected Rates*			
No.	Start-End	Cumulative Survival	Interval Survival	Geom. Mean Ann. Surv.	Geom. Mean Ann. Mort.	Cumulative Survival	Interval Survival	Geom. Mean Ann. Surv.	Geom. Mean Ann. Mort.
i	t to t + Δt	P	p_i	$\breve{p}$	$\breve{q}$	P'	p_i'	$\breve{p}$'	$\breve{q}$'
1	0- 1 yr	.940	.940	.940	.060	.9995	.9995	.9995	.0005
2	1- 2	.914	.972	.972	.028	.9989	.9994	.9994	.0006
3	2- 5	.892	.976	.992	.008	.9967	.9978	.9993	.0007
4	5-10	.808	.906	.980	.020	.9911	.9944	.9989	.0011
5	10-20	.617	.764	.973	.027	.9790	.9878	.9988	.0012

Table 533c Distribution of Deaths by Cause

Cause of Death	Number	Percent
Chronic Ulcerative Colitis		
Progressive Disease	22	20%
Postoperative	15	13
Infection	7	7
Liver Disease	5	4
Perforation	5	4
Intestinal Hemorrhage	3	3
Total	57	51
Carcinoma of Colon and Rectum	40†	36
Unrelated Causes	6	5
Unknown	9	8
Total Observed	112●	100%

Table 533d Interval between Diagnosis of Chronic Ulcerative Colitis and Death from Carcinoma of Colon and Rectum

Interval	Number of Deaths	Percent
0- 5 yrs	0	0%
5-10	7	18
10-15	17	43
15-20	9	22
20-25	4	10
25-30	2	5
30-35	1	2
0-35 yrs	40	100%

* Basis of expected mortality: U.S. White Males and Females 1949-1951
† Expected deaths — 0.07, calculated from U.S. Special Report: Mortality from Selected Causes
● Includes 10 deaths occurring 20 years or more after diagnosis

INTESTINES, COLON AND RECTUM

§534–ULCERATIVE COLITIS IN INSUREDS

Reference: "New York Life Single Medical Impairment Study–1972," unpublished report made available by J.J. Hutchinson and J.C. Sibigtroth (1973).

Subjects Studied: Policyholders of New York Life Insurance Company issued insurance in 1954-1970, followed to the 1971 policy anniversary. These were cases with ulcerative colitis, classified as substandard at issue. Records involving more than one ratable impairment were excluded.

Follow-up: Insurance policy records formed the basis of entry, of counting policies, exposure and death claims, and of follow-up information.

Results: Comparative experience is given in Tables 534a-b for male substandard cases by duration, all ages combined. The mortality ratio decreased rapidly with duration, from 420 per cent at 0-2 years to 167 per cent at 5-17 years, with EDR highest (4.5 extra deaths per 1000) at 2-5 years. The cumulative survival ratio at 17 years was 94.7 per cent.

From Table 534c, the mortality ratio was found to decrease with advancing entry age, from 550 per cent at ages under 30 to 215 per cent at ages 40 up. The highest EDR (6.7 extra deaths per 1000 per year) was observed for the age group 40 up. For all ages combined, the overall mortality ratio was 270 per cent. The estimated 8-year survival index ranged between 97.1 and 94.8 per cent.

From Table 534d, the leading cause of death is found in malignant neoplasms; the mortality ratio was 630 per cent and the EDR, 3 per 1000. This category included 13 deaths, of which 11 were malignant neoplasm of intestine, except rectum. The mortality ratio for the "all other causes and unknown" category was also high, being 430 per cent (1.3 extra deaths per 1000).

ULCERATIVE COLITIS IN INSUREDS

Table 534a   Observed Data and Comparative Experience by Duration — Male Substandard Cases

Interval		Exposure Policy-Yrs	No. of Death Claims		Mortality Ratio		Survival Ratio		Excess Death Rate
No.	Start-End		Observed	Expected*	Interval	Cumulative	Interval	Cumulative	
i	t to t + Δ t	E	d	d'	100 d/d'	100 Σd/Σd'	100 p_i/p_i'	100 P/P'	1000(d-d')/E
1	0- 2 yrs	1284	7	1.66	420%	420%	99.2%	99.2%	4.2
2	2- 5	1067	7	2.18	320	365	98.6	97.8	4.5
3	5-17	909	6	3.59	167	270	96.9	94.7	2.7

Table 534b   Derived Mortality and Survival Data

Interval		Observed Rates				Expected Rates*			
		Average Annual		Cumulative		Average Annual		Cumulative	
No.	Start-End	Mortality	Survival	Survival	Mortality	Mortality	Survival	Survival	Mortality
i	t to t + Δ.t	$\bar{q}$=d/E	$\bar{p}$	P	Q	$\bar{q}'$ = d'/E	$\bar{p}'$	P'	Q'
1	0- 2 yrs	.0055	.9945	.9891	.0109	.0013	.9987	.9974	.0026
2	2- 5	.0066	.9934	.9698	.0302	.0020	.9980	.9913	.0087
3	5-17	.0066	.9934	.8957	.1043	.0039	.9961	.9453	.0547

Table 534c   Comparative Experience by Age Group — Male Substandard Cases All Durations Combined

Age Group	Exposure Policy-Yrs	No. of Death Claims		Mortality Ratio	Ave. Ann. Mort. Rate	Est. 8-Yr Surv. Rate	Est. 8-Yr Surv. Index	Excess Death Rate
		Observed	Expected*					
	E	d	d'	100 d/d'	$\bar{q}$ = d/E	P = $(1-\bar{q})^8$	100 P/P'	1000(d-d')/E
0-29	1333	6	1.09	550%	.0045	.9643	97.1%	3.7
30-39	1126	4	1.69	235	.0035	.9720	98.4	2.1
40 up	801	10	4.65	215	.0124	.9047	94.8	6.7
All Ages	3260	20	7.43	270	.0061	.9522	97.0	3.9

Table 534d   Mortality by Cause of Death — Male and Female Combined

Cause	No. of Death Claims		Mortality Ratio	Excess Death Rate
	Observed	Expected†		
Malignant Neoplasms	13●	1.06	630%	3.0
Diseases of the Heart and Circulatory System	2	3.41	59	−0.4
Accidents and Homicides	1	1.19	84	−0.0
Suicide	0	0.37	0	−0.1
All other Causes and Unknown	7□	1.63	430	1.3
Total	23	7.66	265	3.8

* Basis of expected mortality: 1955-60 Select Basic Table
† Distribution of total expected deaths by Intercompany Medically
   Examined Standard Issues 1965-70
● Includes 11 Malignant Neoplasm of intestine, except rectum
□ Includes 2 Pneumonia

LIVER, GALLBLADDER AND PANCREAS

§550–LAENNEC'S CIRRHOSIS

Reference: W. J. Powell, Jr. and G. Klatskin, "Duration of Survival in Patients with Laennec's Cirrhosis," Am. J. Med., 44:406-420 (1968).

Subjects Studied: Patients with histologically-documented Laennec's cirrhosis admitted to the Liver Study Unit of the Yale-New Haven Hospital in Connecticut between June 1, 1951 and July 1, 1963. Of the 283 patients studied 160 (56.5 per cent) were male and 123 (43.5 per cent), female. Twenty-seven patients were Negro. The average age at onset of the disease was 53.3 years among the men, 47.5 years among the women; in the group as a whole, 50.8 years. In each case data with respect to adequacy of dietary intake and the amount of alcohol consumed prior to onset of symptoms were noted. Patients were classified as alcoholics if daily intake exceeded one quart of wine, six glasses of beer, or four whiskey drinks. On leaving the hospital patients were urged to abstain from alcohol; about one-third did so. In the follow-up, five-year survival data for subjects who had become total abstainers and for those who continued to drink (any quantity) were studied separately; in the former category were 93 patients, in the latter, 185.

Follow-up: Many patients were followed closely throughout their illness, so that survival data could be extracted directly from their hospital and outpatient department clinical records. In the remainder, information was obtained from the patient, his family, the original referring physician, or, in the case of patients who had died, from their death certificates. Survival data were obtained for 278 of the patients investigated – (156 men, 122 women).

Results: The mortality and survival experience of subjects according to continuing intake of alcohol is given in Tables 550a and b. Experience among both continuing alcohol users and abstainers is unfavorable, more so for those continuing the use of alcohol. The mortality ratio over the five-year follow-up period among the abstainers (all ages combined) is 845 per cent and the cumulative survival ratio, 67.6 per cent, but the average mortality ratio among patients continuing alcohol intake is 2100 per cent and the cumulative survival ratio, 42.6 per cent. Deaths from hepatic failure or hemorrhage shortly after alcohol withdrawal may be attributable to previous excessive drinking. If the first year of follow-up is omitted from comparison, results in the subsequent four years reveal even greater advantages to the abstainers – average mortality ratio 275 per cent for them against 1400 per cent for continuing drinkers; cumulative survival ratio 90.5 per cent for the former, 58.5 per cent for the latter.

Subjects manifesting signs of jaundice, ascites or hematemesis represented 84 per cent of the total series. Patients exhibiting such signs showed higher mortality rates and ratios than those free of these signs (Tables 550c-f). Only 11 deaths occurred among the 45 subjects showing no signs of jaundice, ascites, or hematemesis, and only one of these was a subject who stopped alcohol intake – a first-year death (Table 550c). For patients who continued alcohol intake (Tables 550c-d) mortality indices were much higher in those with the aforementioned signs than in those without: mortality ratio of 4300 per cent vs. 1430 per cent in the first year, 1650 per cent vs. 680 per cent in the interval one to five years; EDR was 346 vs. 109 in the first year and 151 vs. 57 in the interval one to five years. Mortality was higher in patients with hematemesis than in those with jaundice or ascites. Similar comparative differences were observed among patients who stopped alcohol intake (Tables 550e-f). For each clinical category mortality declined upon cessation of drinking, with the exception of patients with hematemesis, where there was no significant difference in the first year. Survival rates and ratios were correspondingly low in all categories of patients with jaundice, ascites or hematemesis; fewer than 50 per cent of patients with hematemesis survived the first year. The leading causes of death were hepatic failure in 46 per cent of 133 deaths, gastrointestinal hemorrhage in 27 per cent, with four deaths due to infection.

LAENNEC'S CIRRHOSIS

Table 550a   Observed Data and Comparative Experience by Duration (All Ages Combined)

Group	Interval No. Start-End	No. Alive at Start of Interval	Exposure Person-Yrs	Deaths Obs.	Deaths Exp.*	Mortality Ratio Interval	Mortality Ratio Cumulative	Survival Ratio Interval	Survival Ratio Cumulative	Excess Death Rate
	i t to t + Δ t	ℓ	E	d	d'	100d/d'	100 Q/Q'	100p_i/p_i'	100 P/P'	1000(d-d')/E
Patients Continuing Alcohol Intake	1 0-½ yr	185	92.2	33	.75	4400%	4400%	82.4%	82.4%	350
	2 ½-1 yr	151	74.8	18	.61	3000	3400	88.3	72.8	233
	3 1-2 yrs	130	126.0	19	1.12	1700	2300	85.7	62.4	142
	4 2-3 yrs	103	97.5	12	.94	1280	1750	88.5	55.2	113
	5 3-4 yrs	80	75.5	12	.79	1520	1500	85.0	47.0	148
	6 4-5 yrs	59	58.5	6	.66	910	1250	90.8	42.6	91
	1-5 yrs	130	357.5	49	3.51	1400	1110	58.5	58.5	127
Patients Stopping Alcohol Intake	1 0-½ yr	93	46.5	18	.54	3300%	3300%	81.1%	81.1%	375
	2 ½-1 yr	75	37.2	7	.43	1630	2300	91.1	73.9	176
	3 1-2 yrs	67	64.0	3	.81	370	1260	96.5	71.4	34
	4 2-3 yrs	58	55.0	3	.75	400	915	95.9	68.4	41
	5 3-4 yrs	49	47.5	2	.71	280	715	97.2	66.5	27
	6 4-5 yrs	44	40.5	0	.66	0	550	101.7	67.6	−16
	1-5 yrs	67	207.0	8	2.93	275	245	91.5	91.5	24

Table 550b   Derived Mortality and Survival Data (All Ages Combined)

Group	Interval No. Start-End	Observed Rates Interval Mortality	Observed Rates Interval Survival	Observed Rates Cumulative Survival	Observed Rates Cumulative Mortality	Expected Rates* Interval Mortality	Expected Rates* Interval Survival	Expected Rates* Cumulative Survival	Expected Rates* Cumulative Mortality
	i t to t + Δ t	q_i	p_i	P	Q	q_i'	p_i'	P'	Q'
Patients Continuing Alcohol Intake	1 0-½ yr	.1789	.8211	.8211	.1789	.0041	.9959	.9959	.0041
	2 ½-1 yr	.1204	.8796	.7222	.2773	.0041	.9959	.9918	.0082
	3 1-2 yrs	.1508	.8492	.6133	.3867	.0089	.9911	.9830	.0170
	4 2-3 yrs	.1231	.8769	.5378	.4622	.0096	.9904	.9736	.0264
	5 3-4 yrs	.1589	.8411	.4524	.5476	.0104	.9896	.9634	.0366
	6 4-5 yrs	.1026	.8974	.4060	.5940	.0112	.9888	.9526	.0474
Patients Stopping Alcohol Intake	1 0-½ yr	.1935	.8065	.8065	.1935	.0058	.9942	.9942	.0058
	2 ½-1 yr	.0940	.9060	.7307	.2693	.0058	.9942	.9884	.0116
	3 1-2 yrs	.0469	.9531	.6964	.3036	.0126	.9874	.9760	.0240
	4 2-3 yrs	.0545	.9455	.6585	.3415	.0137	.9863	.9626	.0374
	5 3-4 yrs	.0421	.9579	.6307	.3693	.0150	.9850	.9482	.0518
	6 4-5 yrs	.0000	1.0000	.6307	.3693	.0163	.9837	.9327	.0673

* Basis of expected mortality: U.S. White Males and Females 1959-61

LIVER, GALLBLADDER AND PANCREAS

Table 550c   Observed Data and Comparative Experience by Clinical Signs — Patients with Laennec's Cirrhosis Continuing Alcoholic Intake

Group	Clinical Sign at Start (No. of Cases)	Interval Start-End	Exposure Person-Yrs	Deaths in Interval Observed	Deaths in Interval Expected*	Interval Mort. Ratio	Interval Surv. Ratio	Excess Death Rate
		t to t + Δt	E	d	d'	100 d/d'	100 p_i/p_i'	1000(d-d')/E
I	Free of Signs (36 Patients)	0-1 yr	34.2	4	.28	1430%	89.6%	109
		1-5 yrs	90.0	6	.88	680	78.9	57
II	Jaundice (120 Patients)	0-1 yr	105.2	42	.86	4900	65.4	391
		1-5 yrs	200.5	32	1.96	1630	51.9	150
III	Ascites (116 Patients)	0-1 yr	102.8	40	.84	4800	65.9	381
		1-5 yrs	194.5	32	1.90	1680	50.7	155
IV	Hematemesis (45 Patients)	0-1 yr	36.8	17	.30	5700	62.3	454
		1-5 yrs	63.5	15	.61	2500	35.4	227
V	Any Clinical Sign (149 Patients)	0-1 yr	132.8	47	1.09	4300	68.8	346
		1-5 yrs	267.5	43	2.61	1650	51.6	151

Table 550d   Derived Mortality and Survival Data

Group	Clinical Sign at Start	Interval Start-End	Interval Mort. Rate	Interval Surv. Rate	Cumulative Surv. Rate	Cumulative Mort. Rate
		t to t + Δt	$\bar{q}$ = d/E	$\bar{p}$	P	Q
Observed Rates						
I	Free of Signs	0-1 yr	.1168	.8832	.8832	.1168
		1-5 yrs	.0667	.9333	.7587	.2413
II	Jaundice	0-1 yr	.3990	.6010	.6010	.3990
		1-5 yrs	.1596	.8404	.4988	.5012
III	Ascites	0-1 yr	.3893	.6107	.6107	.3893
		1-5 yrs	.1645	.8355	.4873	.5127
IV	Hematemesis	0-1 yr	.4626	.5374	.5374	.4626
		1-5 yrs	.2362	.7638	.3403	.6597
V	Any Clinical Sign	0-1 yr	.3540	.6460	.6460	.3540
		1-5 yrs	.1607	.8393	.4962	.5038
Expected Rates*						
	Applicable to	0-1 yr	.0082	.9918	.9918	.0082
	All Groups	1-5 yrs	.0098	.9902	.9614	.0386

* Basis of expected mortality: U.S. White Males and Females 1959-61

LAENNEC'S CIRRHOSIS — PATIENTS STOPPING ALCOHOL INTAKE

Table 550e Observed Data and Comparative Experience By Clinical Signs

Group	Clinical Sign at Start (No. of Cases)	Interval Start-End	Exposure Person-Yrs	Deaths in Interval Observed	Deaths in Interval Expected*	Interval Mort. Ratio	Interval Surv. Ratio	Excess Death Rate
		t to t + Δt	E	d	d'	100 d/d'	100 p_i/p_i'	1000(d-d')/E
I	Free of Signs (9 Patients)	0-1 yr	9.0	1	.10	1000%	89.9%	100
		1-5 yrs	29.5	0	.41	0	106.0	−14
II	Jaundice (67 Patients)	0-1 yr	66.5	23	.77	3000	69.0	334
		1-5 yrs	134.0	6	1.93	310	88.2	30
III	Ascites (66 Patients)	0-1 yr	56.8	23	.66	3500	65.7	394
		1-5 yrs	124.5	7	1.79	390	84.1	42
IV	Hematemesis (24 Patients)	0-1 yr	19.2	12	.22	5500	49.5	612
		1-5 yrs	30.5	3	.44	680	70.0	84
V	Any Clinical Sign (84 Patients)	0-1 yr	74.8	24	.87	2800	72.2	309
		1-5 yrs	177.5	8	2.56	315	88.1	31

Table 550f Derived Mortality and Survival Data

Group	Clinical Sign at Start	Interval Start-End	Interval Mort. Rate	Interval Surv. Rate	Cumulative Surv. Rate	Cumulative Mort. Rate
		t to t + Δt	$\bar{q} = d/E$	$\bar{p}$	P	Q
Observed Rates						
I	Free of Signs	0-1 yr	.1111	.8889	.8889	.1111
		1-5 yrs	.0000	1.0000	1.0000	.0000
II	Jaundice	0-1 yr	.3459	.6541	.6541	.3459
		1-5 yrs	.0448	.9552	.8325	.1675
III	Ascites	0-1 yr	.4053	.5947	.5947	.4053
		1-5 yrs	.0562	.9438	.7935	.2065
IV	Hematemesis	0-1 yr	.6234	.3766	.3766	.6234
		1-5 yrs	.0984	.9016	.6608	.3392
V	Any Clinical Sign	0-1 yr	.3211	.6789	.6789	.3211
		1-5 yrs	.0451	.9549	.8314	.1686
Expected Rates*						
	Applicable to All Groups	0-1 yr	.0116	.9884	.9884	.0116
		1-5 yrs	.0144	.9856	.9436	.0564

*Basis of expected mortality: U.S. White Males and Females 1959-61

LIVER, GALLBLADDER AND PANCREAS

§551–GALLBLADDER DISEASE IN INSUREDS

Reference: "New York Life Single Medical Impairment Study–1972," unpublished report made available by J.J. Hutchinson and J.C. Sibigtroth (1973).

Subjects Studied: Policyholders of New York Life Insurance Company issued insurance in 1954-1970, followed to the 1971 policy anniversary. Different codes were used to distinguish cases who had cholelithiasis only (gall stones), from those who had a cholecystectomy. The experience reported is for substandard issues only. All cases with ratable impairment in addition to the gallbladder disease code were excluded.

Follow-up: Insurance policy records formed the basis of entry, of counting policies, exposure and death claims, and of follow-up information.

Results: Comparative experience is given in Tables 551a-b for substandard cases, separately for gallbladder colic (stones) and cholecystectomy, by duration, all ages combined. For males with gallbladder colic, the mortality ratio showed a downward trend with duration, from 194 per cent for the first 5 years to 137 per cent in subsequent years. The EDR remained at a high level (4.1 per 1000) throughout. For males with cholecystectomy, the mortality ratio was very favorable in all years, and there was no excess mortality observed at any time. The cumulative survival ratio at 17 years was 93.2 per cent in the former group and normal in the latter group.

Table 551c presents the comparative experience by sex and entry age group. Among male cases with gallbladder colic, the excess mortality appears to be concentrated in the oldest age group, 60 up, the mortality ratio being 325 per cent and EDR, 41 per 1000. Among males with cholecystectomy, the mortality ratio remained favorable at all ages; again, no excess mortality was found in any age group. The overall mortality ratio for males was 159 per cent among cases with gallbladder colic and 53 per cent among cases with cholecystectomy. Corresponding ratios for females were 129 and 91 per cent, respectively.

Comparative mortality by major causes of death is given in Table 551d for male and female substandard cases combined. Among cases with gallbladder colic, the two major causes of death were malignant neoplasms, the mortality ratio being 250 per cent (EDR, 2.1 extra deaths per 1000) and diseases of heart and circulation, with a mortality ratio of 200 per cent (EDR, 2.3 extra deaths per 1000). Among cases with cholecystectomy, the major cause of death is found in malignant neoplasms, with a mortality ratio of 111 per cent.

GALLBLADDER DISEASE IN INSUREDS

Table 551a Observed Data and Comparative Experience by Duration - Male Substandard Cases

No.	Interval Start-End	Exposure Policy-Yrs	Observed	Expected*	Mortality Ratio Interval	Cumulative	Survival Ratio Interval	Cumulative	Excess Death Rate
i	t to t + Δt	E	d	d'	100 d/d'	100 $\sum$d/$\sum$d'	100 p_i/p_i'	100 P/P'	1000(d-d')/E
Gallbladder Colic (Stones)								
1	0- 5 yrs	1191	10	5.16	194%	194%	98.0%	98.0%	4.1
2	5-17	714	11	8.04	137	159	95.1	93.2	4.1
Cholecystectomy								
1	0-10 yrs	2393	6	12.99	46%	46%	103.0%	103.0%	−2.9
2	10-17	642	6	9.64	62	53	104.1	107.2	−5.7

Table 551b Derived Mortality and Survival Data

No.	Interval Start-End	Observed Rates Average Annual Mortality	Survival	Cumulative Survival	Mortality	Expected Rates* Average Annual Mortality	Survival	Cumulative Survival	Mortality
i	t to t + Δt	$\bar{q}$ = d/E	$\bar{p}$	P	Q	$\bar{q}$' = d'/E	$\bar{p}$'	P'	Q'
Gallbladder Colic (Stones)								
1	0- 5 yrs	.0084	.9916	.9587	.0413	.0043	.9957	.9785	.0215
2	5-17	.0154	.9846	.7957	.2043	.0113	.9887	.8542	.1458
Cholecystectomy								
1	0-10 yrs	.0025	.9975	.9752	.0248	.0054	.9946	.9470	.0530
2	10-17	.0093	.9907	.9131	.0869	.0150	.9850	.8518	.1482

Table 551c Comparative Experience by Sex and Age Group - Substandard Cases, All Durations Combined

Sex	Age Group	Exposure Policy-Yrs	Observed	Expected*	Mortality Ratio	Ave. Ann. Mort. Rate	Est. 8-Yr Surv. Rate	Est. 8-Yr Surv. Index	Excess Death Rate
		E	d	d'	100 d/d'	$\bar{q}$ = d/E	P = (1-$\bar{q}$)^8	100 P/P'	1000(d-d')/E
Gallbladder Colic (Stones)									
Male	15-59	1804	15	11.34	132%	.0083	.9354	98.4%	2.0
	60 up	101	6	1.86	325	.0594	.6126	71.1	41
	All Ages	1905	21	13.20	159	.0110	.9152	96.8	4.1
Female	All Ages	1572	9	6.98	129	.0057	.9551	99.0	1.3
Cholecystectomy									
Male	15-49	2210	5	9.79	51%	.0023	.9821	101.8%	−2.2
	50 up	825	7	12.84	55	.0085	.9341	105.9	−7.1
	All Ages	3035	12	22.63	53	.0040	.9688	102.9	−3.5
Female	All Ages	2292	7	7.70	91	.0031	.9759	100.2	−0.3

Table 551d Mortality by Major Cause of Death - Male and Female Combined

Cause	Gallbladder Colic (Stones) Observed	Expected†	Mortality Ratio	Excess Death Rate	Cholecystectomy Observed	Expected†	Mortality Ratio	Excess Death Rate
Malignant Neoplasms	12	4.81	250%	2.1	8	7.23	111%	0.1
Diseases of the Heart and Circulatory System	16	7.94	200	2.3	8	11.92	67	−0.7
Accidents and Homicides	0	2.77	0	−0.8	1	4.17	24	−0.6
Suicide	0	0.86	0	−0.3	0	1.29	0	−0.2
All other Causes and Unknown	2	3.80	53	−0.5	2	5.72	35	−0.7
Total	30	20.18	149	2.8	19	30.33	63	−2.1

* Basis of expected mortality: 1955-60 Select Basic Table
† Distribution of total expected deaths by Intercompany Medically Examined Standard Issues 1965-70

OTHER GASTRO-INTESTINAL DISEASES

§570—HERNIAS (EXCEPT DIAPHRAGMATIC) IN INSUREDS

Reference: "New York Life Single Medical Impairment Study — 1967," unpublished report made available by J.J. Hutchinson and J.C. Sibigtroth (1973).

Subjects Studied: Policyholders of New York Life Insurance Company issued insurance in 1949-1965, followed to the 1966 policy anniversary. These were hernia cases, other than the type called hiatus or diaphragmatic. Both standard and substandard issues are analyzed here. Cases with more than one ratable impairment were excluded.

Follow-up: Insurance policy records formed the basis of entry, of counting policies, exposure and death claims, and of follow-up information.

Results: Comparative experience is given in Tables 570 a-b for standard and substandard male cases, by duration, all ages combined. Among standard cases, the excess mortality was greatest after ten years, with a mortality ratio of 136 per cent and an EDR of 4.0 per 1000. There was no excess mortality observed at 5-10 years. For substandard cases, the mortality ratio was highest at 187 per cent during the interval 5-10 years, with an EDR of 6.2 per 1000. The cumulative survival ratio after ten years was 98.2 per cent for standard cases and 96.8 per cent for substandard cases.

Table 570c gives comparative experience for standard and substandard males by entry age group. Among standard males, excess mortality was greatest at ages 40-49, with a mortality ratio of 126 per cent and EDR of 1.4 per 1000. Among substandard males, excess mortality was higher at ages 50 up than for lower ages, with a mortality ratio of 154 per cent and EDR of 7.7 per 1000. The estimated 8-year survival index was normal for standard males, while ranging between 99.2 and 93.9 per cent among substandard cases.

Comparative mortality by major causes of death is given in Table 570d for standard and substandard cases, male and female combined. Apparent differences by cause of death in the standard cases are probably not significant, because of the normal overall mortality and the small numbers of deaths in the various categories. For substandard cases the major causes were disease of the heart and circulation, with a mortality ratio of 210 per cent and EDR of 2.5 per 1000, and "all other causes and unknown." This category was next in magnitude with a mortality ratio of 175 per cent, and an EDR of 0.8 per 1000.

HERNIAS (EXCEPT DIAPHRAGMATIC) IN INSUREDS

Table 570a   Observed Data and Comparative Experience by Insurance Action and Duration — Male Cases

Group	No.	Interval Start-End	Exposure Policy-Yrs	No. of Death Claims Observed	No. of Death Claims Expected*	Mortality Ratio Interval	Mortality Ratio Cumulative	Survival Ratio Interval	Survival Ratio Cumulative	Excess Death Rate
	i	t to t + Δ t	E	d	d'	100 d/d'	100 Σd/Σd'	100p_i/p_i'	100 P/P'	1000(d-d')/E
Std	1	0- 5 yrs	2385	9	8.65	104%	104%	99.9%	99.9%	0.1
	2	5-10	1621	8	11.34	71	85	101.0	101.0	−2.1
	3	10-17	916	14	10.31	136	102	97.2	98.2	4.0
SStd	1	0- 5 yrs	973	5	3.33	150%	150%	99.1%	99.1%	1.7
	2	5-10	600	8	4.27	187	171	96.9	96.1	6.2
	3	10-17	382	4	4.37	92	142	100.7	96.8	1.0

Table 570b   Derived Mortality and Survival Data

Group	No.	Interval Start-End	Observed Rates Average Annual Mortality	Observed Rates Average Annual Survival	Observed Rates Cumulative Survival	Observed Rates Cumulative Mortality	Expected Rates* Average Annual Mortality	Expected Rates* Average Annual Survival	Expected Rates* Cumulative Survival	Expected Rates* Cumulative Mortality
	i	t to t + Δ t	$\bar{q}$=d/E	$\bar{p}$	P	Q	$\bar{q}$'=d'/E	$\bar{p}$'	P'	Q'
Std	1	0- 5 yrs	.0037	.9963	.9815	.0185	.0036	.9964	.9820	.0180
	2	5-10	.0049	.9951	.9575	.0425	.0069	.9931	.9483	.0517
	3	10-17	.0152	.9848	.8599	.1401	.0112	.9888	.8761	.1239
SStd	1	0- 5 yrs	.0051	.9949	.9746	.0254	.0034	.9966	.9830	.0170
	2	5-10	.0133	.9867	.9113	.0887	.0071	.9929	.9485	.0515
	3	10-17	.0104	.9896	.8469	.1531	.0114	.9886	.8751	.1249

Table 570c   Comparative Experience by Age Group — All Durations Combined, Male Cases

Group	Age Group	Exposure Policy-Yrs	No. of Death Claims Observed	No. of Death Claims Expected*	Mortality Ratio	Ave. Ann. Mort. Rate	Est. 8-Yr Surv. Rate	Est. 8-Yr Surv. Index	Excess Death Rate
		E	d	d'	100 d/d'	$\bar{q}$=d/E	P=(1-$\bar{q}$)^8	100 P/P'	1000(d-d')/E
Std	< 40	2108	3	4.12	73%	.0014	.9888	100.4%	−0.5
	40-49	1560	11	8.75	126	.0070	.9449	98.9	1.4
	50 up	1254	17	17.43	98	.0135	.8966	100.2	−0.3
	Total	4922	31	30.30	102	.0062	.9511	99.9	0.1
SStd	< 50	1503	7	5.46	128	.0046	.9635	99.2	1.0
	50 up	452	10	6.51	154	.0221	.8359	93.9	7.7
	Total	1955	17	11.97	142	.0086	.9329	98.0	2.6

Table 570d   Mortality by Cause of Death, Male and Female Combined, Standard and Substandard Cases

Cause	Standard No. of Death Claims Observed	Standard No. of Death Claims Expected†	Standard Mortality Ratio	Standard Excess Death Rate	Substandard No. of Death Claims Observed	Substandard No. of Death Claims Expected†	Substandard Mortality Ratio	Substandard Excess Death Rate
Malignant Neoplasms	2	7.28	27%	−1.0	3	2.89	104%	0.1
Diseases of the Heart and Circulatory System	11	12.02	92	−0.2	10	4.76	210	2.5
Accidents and Homicides	2	4.19	48	−0.4	0	1.66	0	−0.8
Suicide	3	1.29	233	0.3	0	0.51	0	−0.3
All other Causes and Unknown	13	5.76	226	1.4	4	2.28	175	0.8
Total	31	30.54	102	0.1	17	12.10	140	2.4

* Basis of expected mortality: 1955-60 Select Basic Table
† Distribution of total expected deaths by Intercompany Medically
   Examined Standard Issues 1965-70

OTHER GASTRO-INTESTINAL DISEASES

§571–DIVERTICULUM OF DIGESTIVE TRACT IN INSUREDS

Reference: "New York Life Single Medical Impairment Study–1972," unpublished report made available by J.J. Hutchinson and J.C. Sibigtroth (1973).

Subjects Studied: Policyholders of New York Life Insurance Company issued insurance in 1954-1970, followed to the 1971 policy anniversary. These were cases diagnosed to have diverticular in the gastro-intestinal tract. The experience shown is for substandard issues (chiefly multiple diverticula). Excluded were cases with more than one ratable impairment.

Follow-up: Insurance policy records formed the basis of entry, of counting policies, exposure and death claims, and of follow-up information.

Results: Comparative experience is given in Tables 571a-b for male substandard cases by duration, all ages combined. The trend in the mortality ratio was downward, ranging from 220 per cent at 0-5 years to 156 per cent at 10-17 years. The corresponding change in EDR from the earliest to the latest interval was an increase from 5.6 to 10 extra deaths per 1000. The cumulative survival ratio at 17 years was 87.3 per cent.

From Table 571c, the mortality ratio is somewhat higher for entry ages under 50 than for the older ages. The pattern in EDR appears to be an increase with advancing age, being highest (11 extra deaths per 1000) at ages 60 up. The overall mortality ratio was 179 per cent for all ages combined. The 8-year survival index ranged from 95.6 per cent at ages 0-49 to 91.1 per cent at ages 60 up.

From Table 571d, the two leading causes of death were diseases of the heart and circulation, and malignant neoplasms, with mortality ratios of 240 and 225 per cent, respectively. Corresponding EDR was 4.2 per 1000 for the former, and 2.3 for the latter. These data are based on combined male and female experience.

DIVERTICULUM OF DIGESTIVE TRACT IN INSUREDS

Table 571a   Observed Data and Comparative Experience by Duration — Male Substandard Cases

Interval		Exposure	No. of Death Claims		Mortality Ratio		Survival Ratio		Excess
No.	Start-End	Policy-Yrs	Observed	Expected*	Interval	Cumulative	Interval	Cumulative	Death Rate
i	t to t + Δt	E	d	d'	100 d/d'	100 Σd/Σd'	100p_i/p_i'	100 P/P'	1000(d-d')/E
1	0- 5 yrs	1358	14	6.37	220%	220%	96.7%	96.7%	5.6
2	5-10	687	11	6.88	160	189	97.0	93.8	6.0
3	10-17	321	9	5.76	156	179	93.0	87.3	10

Table 571b   Derived Mortality and Survival Data

Interval		Observed Rates				Expected Rates*			
		Average Annual		Cumulative		Average Annual		Cumulative	
No.	Start-End	Mortality	Survival	Survival	Mortality	Mortality	Survival	Survival	Mortality
i	t to t + Δt	$\bar{q}$=d/E	$\bar{p}$	P	Q	$\bar{q}'$=d'/E	$\bar{p}'$	P'	Q'
1	0- 5 yrs	.0103	.9897	.9437	.0563	.0047	.9953	.9755	.0245
2	5-10	.0160	.9840	.8705	.1295	.0100	.9900	.9276	.0724
3	10-17	.0280	.9720	.7134	.2866	.0179	.9821	.8172	.1828

Table 571c   Comparative Experience by Age Group — Male Substandard Cases

Age Group	Exposure Policy-Yrs	No. of Death Claims		Mortality Ratio	Ave. Ann. Mort. Rate	Est. 8-Yr Surv. Rate	Est. 8-Yr Surv. Index	Excess Death Rate
		Observed	Expected*	100 d/d'	$\bar{q}$=d/E	P=(1-$\bar{q}$)^8	100 P/P'	1000(d-d')/E
	E	d	d'					
0-49	1429	14	5.93	235%	.0098	.9242	95.6%	5.6
50-59	721	13	8.53	152	.0180	.8645	95.1	6.2
60 up	216	7	4.55	154	.0324	.7683	91.1	11
All Ages	2366	34	19.01	179	.0144	.8907	95.0	6.3

Table 571d   Mortality by Cause of Death — Male and Female Combined

Cause	No. of Death Claims		Mortality Ratio	Excess Death Rate
	Observed	Expected†		
Malignant Neoplasms	12	5.28	225%	2.3
Diseases of the Heart and Circulatory System	21	8.71	240	4.2
Accidents and Homicides	2	3.05	66	−0.4
Suicide	0	0.94	—	−0.3
All other Causes and Unknown	1	4.18	24	−1.1
Total	36●	22.16	162%	4.7

* Basis of expected mortality: 1955-60 Select Basic Table

† Distribution of total expected deaths by Intercompany Medically Examined Standard Issues 1965-70

● Includes 2 female deaths (595 policy-years exposure)

DIGESTIVE SYSTEM DISEASES

§599–DIGESTIVE DISORDERS–EXPERIENCE AMONG INSURED LIVES (MISCELLANEOUS)

References: (1) T. W. Preston and R. D. Clarke, "An Investigation into the Mortality of Impaired Lives During the Period 1947-63," J. Inst. Act., 92:27-74 (1966).
(2) A. Svensson and S. Astrand, "Substandard Risk Mortality in Sweden 1955-1965," Coopération Internationale pour les Assurances des Risques Aggravés. (See Rome Conference proceedings, 1969.)
(3) "New York Life Single Medical Impairment Study - 1972," unpublished report made available by J. J. Hutchinson and J. C. Sibigtroth (1973).

Subjects Studied: (1) Policyholders of Prudential Assurance Co., London, England, issued insurance 1947-1963 followed to 12/31/63. Both standard and substandard issues were included. Applicants with two or more ratable impairments were generally excluded.
(2) Lives reinsured (mostly on a substandard basis) with Sverige Reinsurance Co., Sweden, placed in force prior to 1955 and observed between anniversaries in 1955 and 1965.
(3) Policyholders of New York Life Insurance Co., issued insurance 1954-1970 followed to 1971 policy anniversary. Both standard and substandard issues were included. Applicants with more than one ratable impairment were excluded.

Follow-up: Insurance policy records formed the basis of entry, counting policies, exposures, and death claims, and of follow-up information.

Results: Mortality and survival results experienced by the Prudential of London, the Sverige Reinsurance Company of Sweden, and the New York Life in insuring the lives of persons with a lengthy list of digestive disorders are summarized in Table 599. Additional reports of New York Life experience in this disease category are represented in other abstracts (§507, §512, §520, §534, §551, §570, §571).

Almost half of the total policy-years of exposure recorded in Table 599 is represented by the English and Swedish experience on peptic, gastric and duodenal ulcers. Mortality ratios in these disorders given in the Prudential of London experience range from 92 per cent to 163 per cent, the level depending on the site of the ulcer, duration of the disease, the presence of complications and history of operation. The most favorable result is recorded on unoperated peptic ulcer cases with a short history, the least favorable, operated peptic ulcer cases with complication, whether of short or long duration. The Swedish data, including all types of ulcer and the experience of both males and females, showed no excess mortality, but the expected standard, the general population, represents a higher level of mortality than the select insured lives with which the English experience is compared. If a comparable basis were employed, the Sverige experience would probably be similar to that of the average of the Prudential of London.

Dyspepsia, reported in the Prudential of London study, was the most common category of digestive complaint next to stomach ulcers. Chronic dyspepsia in men with an ulcer suspected showed a mortality ratio of 142 per cent and an EDR of 1.2 per 1000. About the same indexes applied to women (not necessarily with suspected ulcer). Among men with dyspepsia, without a suspected ulcer, mortality was favorable — only 108 per cent that of standard insured lives and the excess death rate, 0.2 per 1000.

The New York Life and the Prudential studies showed a group of digestive disorders with relatively small numbers of death and person-years of exposure. These are included in Table 599. Showing low mortality ratios and EDR's, between 68 and 121 per cent, and between −2.8 and 0.6 per 1000, respectively, were the following: duodenitis; amebic dysentery; cholecystitis (Reference 1 females); diaphragmatic hernia; unclassified hernias, unoperated. Indexes of moderate extra mortality (mortality ratios ranging between 139 and 180 per cent; excess death rates from 1.6 to 5.0 per 1000) are shown for: colitis or diarrhea; fistula in ano; cholecystitis with cholecystectomy; diverticulum, colon; diverticulum, other than colon. The heaviest mortality among these various disorders (mortality ratios between 210 and 340 per cent with EDR's between 3.7 and 9.6 per 1000) was shown by: pylorospasm; disease of intestine; liver disease or jaundice; cholecystitis (Reference 3 male and female); pancreatic disorders; gastrointestinal hemorrhage; and other diseases of the digestive organs.

DIGESTIVE SYSTEM DISEASES

Table 599   Comparative Experience, Three Series of Insureds

Disease/Category (Ref.)	Sex/Age		Policies in Force at Start ℓ	Exposure Policy-Yrs E	No. of Death Claims Observed d	No. of Death Claims Expected* d'	Ave. Ann. Mort. Rate Observed q̄ = d/E	Ave. Ann. Mort. Rate Expected* q̄' = d'/E	Mortality Ratio 100 d/d'	Est. 5-Yr Surv. Rate $P = (1-\bar{q})^5$	Est. 5-Yr Surv. Index 100 P/P'	Excess Death Rate 1000(q̄-q̄')
Peptic Ulcer, Unoperated (1)												
Short history	M	43	1647	6838	22	23.9	.0032	.0035	92%	.9840	100.1%	−0.3
Long history	M	44	7021	41799	207	166	.0050	.0040	125	.9755	99.5	1.0
Peptic Ulcer, Operated (1)												
With Complications	M	44	2820	16251	110	67.4	.0068	.0041	163	.9666	98.7	2.7
No Complications†	M	46	3286	18212	121	97.4	.0066	.0053	124	.9672	99.4	1.3
Pylorospasm SS● (3)	M&F	40	—	830	7	2.87	.0084	.0035	245	.9585	97.5	4.9
Dyspepsia (1)												
Chronic, suspect ulcer	M	42	2856	14560	63	44.4	.0043	.0031	142	.9786	99.4	1.2
Other	M	41	12366	67407	188	175	.0028	.0026	108	.9861	99.9	0.2
Dyspepsia (1)	F	45	553	3750	14	9.20	.0037	.0025	152	.9815	99.4	1.2
Gastric & Duodenal Ulcer (2)	M&F	43	—	31373	171	172	.0055	.0055	100	.9730	100.0	0.0
Colitis, Diarrhea S●&SS (3)	M&F	43	—	3024	20	13.5	.0066	.0045	148	.9674	98.9	2.1
Duodenitis SS (3)	M&F	39	—	5150	19	15.7	.0037	.0031	121	.9817	99.7	0.6
Disease of Intestine S&SS (3)	M&F	40	—	818	7	2.75	.0086	.0034	255	.9579	97.4	5.2
Amebic Dysentery (1)	M	38	839	6591	13	12.2	.0020	.0018	107	.9902	99.9	0.1
Fistula in Ano (1)	M	43	871	5782	30	21.0	.0052	.0036	143	.9743	99.2	1.6
Liver Disease, Jaundice SS (3)	M&F	41	—	1326	13	4.90	.0098	.0037	265	.9519	97.0	6.1
Cholecystitis S&SS (3)	M&F	44	—	1169	13	5.85	.0111	.0050	220	.9456	97.0	6.†
Cholecystitis, Operated (1)	M	49	772	4485	47	33.8	.0105	.0075	139	.9487	98.5	3.0
Cholecystitis (1)	F	50	525	3240	13	13.0	.0040	.0040	100	.9801	100.0	0.0
Pancreatic Disorders S&SS (3)	M&F	39	—	920	9	2.82	.0098	.0031	320	.9520	96.7	6.7
Diaphragmatic Hernia SS (3)	M&F	46	—	3825	21	21.6	.0055	.0057	97	.9728	100.1	−0.2
Hernia, other S&SS (3)	M&F	50	—	2057	12	17.7	.0058	.0086	68	.9712	101.4	−2.8
Hernia, unclassified, operated (1)	F	44	598	3872	11	8.60	.0028	.0022	128	.9859	99.7	0.6
Diverticulum, Colon SS (3)	M&F	51	—	1298	17	11.5	.0131	.0089	148	.9362	97.9	4.2
Diverticulum, other SS (3)	M&F	47	—	1662	19	10.6	.0114	.0064	179	.9441	97.5	5.0
G.I. Hemorrhage S&SS (3)	M&F	40	—	1553	11	5.23	.0071	.0034	210	.9651	98.1	3.7
Other Diseases, Dig. Org. SS (3)	M&F	42	—	957	13	3.83	.0136	.0040	340	.9339	95.3	9.6

* Basis of expected mortality: (Ref. 1) Prudential Assurance Co. (England) standard lives mortality 1957-1958;
(Ref. 2) Sverige Reins. Co., population mortality, M or F (Sweden), 1956-60 and 1961-65; (Ref. 3) N. Y. Life, Basic Select Tables (1955-60)
† Cases with long history
● "S" - Standard, "SS" - Substandard

Genitourinary Diseases

See Also

1. *1951 Impairment Study.* Chicago: Society of Actuaries (1954).
    E37-E44 Albuminuria with casts, found on examination (pp. 168-170)
    E45-E52 Albuminuria with hematuria, found on examination (p. 171)
    E53-E64 Albuminuria with pyuria, found on examination (pp. 172-173)
    E65-E67 Nephritis (pp. 173-174)
    E68-E75 Casts, found on examination (pp. 174-179)
    E76-E78 Hematuria, found on examination (pp. 180-182)
    E79-E81 Pyuria, found on examination (pp. 182-186)
    E82-E86 Genitourinary stone or colic (pp. 186-192)
    E87-E90 Nephrectomy, not known due to tuberculosis or tumor (pp. 193-195)
    E91-E97 Prostate gland, enlargement of or operation on (pp. 196-198)
    F1-F2   Fibroma, with hysterectomy (p. 199)
    F3-F4   Hysterectomy, not known due to fibroma or malignant tumor (p. 200)
    F5-F6   Oophorectomy or salpingectomy, not known due to malignant tumor (pp. 202-206)
    F7-F9   Pregnancy, found on examination (pp. 206-207)
    F10-F11 Caesarean section (pp. 208-209)
2. S. Shapiro, E.R. Schlesing, and R.E.L. Nesbitt, Jr., *Infant, Perinatal, Maternal, and Childhood Mortality in The United States.* Cambridge, Mass.: Harvard University Press (1968).

URINARY ABNORMALITIES

§601–INTERMITTENT ALBUMINURIA (TRACE)

References: (1) *1951 Impairment Study,* compiled and published by the Society of Actuaries, p. 157, Chicago (1954).
(2) Supplementary details furnished by Society of Actuaries Committee on Mortality under Ordinary Insurances and Annuities (1961).

Subject Studied: The study covered the experience under ordinary insurance, issued during the years 1935 through 1949 traced to policy anniversaries in 1950, of applicants exhibiting at time of application, small amounts of albuminuria (10 to 50 mg. per 100 cc.) occurring intermittently (i.e., in about half the tests). The presence of "albumin" (protein) in the urine was detected by heat coagulation and confirmed by a semiquantitative sulfosalicylic acid method. The experience was compiled from contributions of 27 cooperating companies, which supplied data retrieved from policy records coded for trace amounts of intermittent albuminuria and for relative weight. Class E1 included records of individuals whose weight was between 30 per cent below and 10 per cent above standard weight, Class E2, those with weight from 10 to 20 per cent above. These were two of 36 different classes of insureds with albuminuria reported in the *1951 Impairment Study* (see §602 and 603 for other albuminuria results). Characteristics of Classes E1 and E2, which were also divided according to standard and substandard issue, and the age distribution of the exposed to risk under the combined group are given below:

Albuminuria, Intermittent (Trace)

Group	Standard or Substandard Issue	No. of Entrants	No. of Death Claims	Per Cent Female	Group Mean Age	Ratio of Policy Death Claims to Lives Involved*
E1	S	4306	136	19%	30	1.21
E1	SS	1420	44	18	31	1.02
E2	S	540	23	12	36	1.15
E2	SS	—	13	—	—	—

*Some applicants had more than one policy in force. The ratio of policies/lives is available in the *1951 Impairment Study* only for policies terminating in a death claim.

Age at Issue	15-29	30-39	40-49	50-64	Total
Exposure %	55.9%	18.4%	16.8%	8.9%	100.0%
No. Policy-Years	27357	8982	8219	4338	48896

Follow-up: The policy records of the 27 participating companies were used for follow-up and constituted the basis for counting deaths and numbers exposed to risk. The average duration of exposure for the four aforementioned groups was 7.6 years, compared with an average duration of exposure for the entire *1951 Impairment Study* of 6.2 years. Ratios of policies terminated by death to numbers of lives involved as shown above may be compared with overall averages for the *1951 Impairment Study,* of 1.09 for all substandard issues and 1.19 for all standard issues.

Results: Mortality and survival data are presented for the fifteen-year study period for all groups combined in Tables 601 a-b, by age group and interval. Mortality ratios and excess death rates for issue ages under 30 were very little higher than the expected. These indices tended to increase beyond that age to age 50 and then to recede. Mortality ratios averaged 138 per cent for lives insured in the thirties and 177 per cent for entrants in the forties. Excess death rate over the study period averaged less than 1 death per 1000 per year for the 30-39 year old applicants and 4.2 for the 40-49 year age group. Subjects older than 50 at issue experience a mortality ratio over the 15-year period of 136 per cent and an excess death rate of 4.8 per 1000 per year. There was a tendency for excess mortality to be more pronounced in the later periods of observation than in the first five years.

ALBUMINURIA, INTERMITTENT (TRACE)

Table 601a   Observed Data and Comparative Experience

Age	No.	Interval Start-End	Exposure Policy-Yrs	Observed	Expected*	Interval	Cumulative	Interval	Cumulative	Excess Death Rate
(Years)	i	t to t + Δ t	E	d	d'	100 d/d'	100$\sum$d/$\sum$d'	100 p/p'	100 P/P'	1000(d-d')/E
15-29	1	0- 2 yrs	6293	6	5.43	110%	110%	100.0%	100.0%	0.1
	2	2- 5	7774	6	8.29	72	87	100.0	100.1	−0.3
	3	5-10	9640	12	11.30	106	96	100.0	100.1	0.1
	4	10-15	3650	8	5.30	151	106	99.9	99.7	0.7
		0-15	27357	32	30.32	106	106		99.7	0.1
30-39	1	0- 2	2431	3	2.65	113	113	100.0	100.0	0.1
	2	2- 5	2704	6	4.65	129	123	99.9	99.8	0.5
	3	5-10	2830	14	7.65	183	154	99.8	98.7	2.2
	4	10-15	1017	4	4.58	87	138	100.1	99.0	−0.6
		0-15	8982	27	19.53	138	138		99.0	0.8
40-49	1	0- 2	2110	7	4.93	142	142	99.9	99.8	1.0
	2	2- 5	2392	12	10.00	120	127	99.9	99.6	0.8
	3	5-10	2726	33	18.32	180	156	99.5	96.9	5.4
	4	10-15	991	27	11.30	240	177	98.4	89.4	16
		0-15	8219	79	44.55	177	177		89.4	4.2
50-64	1	0- 2	1091	12	6.64	181	181	99.5	99.0	4.9
	2	2- 5	1341	8	14.74	54	94	100.5	100.5	−5.0
	3	5-10	1451	42	23.71	177	138	98.7	94.3	13
	4	10-15	455	16	12.27	130	136	99.2	90.3	8.2
		0-15	4338	78	57.36	136	136		90.3	4.8
All Ages	1	0- 2	11925	28	19.65	142	142	99.9	99.9	0.7
	2	2- 5	14211	32	37.68	85	105	100.0	100.0	−0.4
	3	5-10	16647	101	60.98	166	136	99.8	98.8	2.4
	4	10-15	6113	55	33.45	164	142	99.6	97.1	3.5
		0-15	48896	216	151.8	142	142		97.1	1.3

Table 601b   Derived Mortality and Survival Data

Age	No.	Interval Start-End	Average Annual Mortality	Average Annual Survival	Cumulative Survival	Cumulative Mortality	Average Annual Mortality	Average Annual Survival	Cumulative Survival	Cumulative Mortality
(Years)	i	t to t + Δ t	$\bar{q} = d/E$	$\bar{p}$	P	Q	$\bar{q}' = d'/E$	$\bar{p}'$	P'	Q'
15-29	1	0- 2 yrs	.0010	.9990	.998	.002	.0009	.9991	.9982	.0018
	2	2- 5	.0008	.9992	.996	.004	.0011	.9989	.9949	.0051
	3	5-10	.0012	.9988	.990	.010	.0012	.9988	.9890	.0110
	4	10-15	.0022	.9978	.979	.021	.0015	.9985	.9816	.0184
30-39	1	0- 2	.0012	.9988	.998	.002	.0011	.9989	.9978	.0022
	2	2- 5	.0022	.9978	.991	.009	.0017	.9983	.9927	.0073
	3	5-10	.0049	.9951	.967	.033	.0027	.9973	.9794	.0206
	4	10-15	.0039	.9961	.948	.052	.0045	.9955	.9575	.0425
40-49	1	0- 2	.0033	.9967	.993	.007	.0023	.9977	.9954	.0046
	2	2- 5	.0050	.9950	.979	.021	.0042	.9958	.9829	.0171
	3	5-10	.0121	.9879	.921	.079	.0067	.9933	.9504	.0496
	4	10-15	.0272	.9728	.802	.198	.0114	.9886	.8975	.1025
50-64	1	0- 2	.0110	.9890	.978	.022	.0061	.9939	.9878	.0122
	2	2- 5	.0060	.9940	.961	.039	.0110	.9890	.9556	.0444
	3	5-10	.0289	.9711	.830	.170	.0163	.9837	.8802	.1198
	4	10-15	.0352	.9648	.694	.306	.0270	.9730	.7676	.2324
All Ages	1	0- 2	.0023	.9977	.995	.005	.0016	.9984	.9968	.0032
	2	2- 5	.0023	.9977	.989	.011	.0027	.9973	.9887	.0113
	3	5-10	.0061	.9939	.959	.041	.0037	.9963	.9706	.0294
	4	10-15	.0090	.9910	.916	.084	.0055	.9945	.9442	.0558

* Basis of expected mortality: 1935-50 Basic Table (Standard Intercompany)

ALBUMINURIA AND BLOOD PRESSURE

§602–ALBUMINURIA AND BLOOD PRESSURE

Reference: *1951 Impairment Study,* compiled and published by the Society of Actuaries, pp. 161-163, Chicago (1954).

Subjects Studied: Policyholders issued life insurance between 1935 and 1950, with albuminuria noted on examination, classified according to systolic blood pressure. Material in this section is derived from the study, the main features of which are cited in §601. Most of the subjects reported on in this section revealed small or trace amounts of albumin, but for a few groups (in Table 602a) data for moderate and large amounts are also shown. Standards for systolic pressure, and for amount and persistency of albumin categories are as follows:

| | Systolic Pressure Limits (mm.) | | | | Amount of Albumin (mg. per 100 cc. by | |
Ages at Issue (years)	15-29	30-39	40-49	50-64	sulfosalicylic acid test)	
Normotensive	90-124	95-129	100-134	105-139	Small or Trace	10 to 50
Slight Hypertension	125-135	130-140	135-145	140-150	Moderate	51 to 100
Moderate Hypertension	136-144	141-149	146-154	151-159	Large	over 100

Persistency: Intermittent—once in 2 tests, twice in 3-5 tests, or three times in 6 or 7 tests. Constant—twice in 2 tests, or three times in 3-5 tests.

Follow-up: The policy records of the 27 participating insurance companies were used for follow-up and constitute the basis for counting death claims and numbers exposed to risk.

Results: Summary data for the classes reported are given in Table 602a. The bulk of the exposure is found in the classes with trace amounts of albumin, some of which constitute the data base presented in greater detail in Tables 602b-e. Higher blood pressure findings and larger amounts of albumin are each associated with increased mortality ratios. Albuminuria as a constant finding does not appear to be associated with a mortality ratio higher than in the corresponding class where this is intermittent, in most of the categories in Table 602a. For the standard normotensive group showing intermittent traces of albuminuria, a mortality ratio of 112 per cent was observed - very close to that expected. At the other extreme recorded in the study, the ratios for subjects with constant large amounts of albumin were 470 per cent in Class E34SS (normotensive), 735 per cent in Class E35SS (slight hypertension), and 1670 per cent in Class E36SS (moderate hypertension), although the last ratio is based on only two death claims.

Tables 602b-e present mortality and survival rates and ratios for two groups of subjects showing intermittent and constant traces of albumin with normotensive and slight hypertension, respectively. More detailed data than those in Table 602a, permitting calculation of all comparative indices, are given in Table 602b for eight of the categories of trace albuminuria. Subjects issued standard insurance exhibited almost no excess mortality when they were normotensive, but mortality ratios of 216 and 304 per cent when they were slightly hypertensive. All categories of substandard issue were associated with an increased mortality. Indicated in Table 602c is experience by age at issue of insurance, all durations combined. In the normotensive group, mortality ratios by age group ranged from 123 per cent to 163 per cent with an average for all ages of 146 per cent. A peak appeared in the 40-49 year age group. Subjects with slight hypertension, except at the youngest ages (15-29 years), experienced substantially higher comparative mortality, peaking at 340 per cent for ages 30-39 years and averaging 225 per cent for all ages. Excess deaths per 1000 in both of these blood pressure categories increased with age; apart from the youngest ages, excess death rates in the slight hypertension group were roughly three times the normotensive rates.

Tables 602d-e present comparative mortality and survival experience by duration, all ages combined, for the aforementioned blood pressure classes. Mortality ratios of the normotensive group rose from an initial 134 to 172 per cent in the 2-5 year duration interval and declined in subsequent durations, reaching 110 per cent in the 10-15 year interval. Excess deaths lay between 0.6 and 2.1 per 1000. In the group with slight hypertension, mortality ratios, after an initial 220 per cent in the first two years of insurance, advanced steadily from a low of 158 per cent over years 2-5 to 280 per cent in the last five years of observation. EDR's, starting at 2.1 per 1000 in the first interval climbed from 1.7 over the 2-5 year period to 9.8 per 1000 in the last five-year interval shown. The 15-year survival ratio was 97.9 per cent in the normotensives and 91.5 per cent in those with slight hypertension.

URINARY ABNORMALITIES

Table 602a   Summary of Comparative Mortality by Amount of Albumin and Blood Pressure

Amount of Albumin	Blood Pressure Class*	Intermittent Albuminuria				Constant Albuminuria			
		Category in Reference*	No. of Death Claims		Mortality Ratio	Category in Reference*	No. of Death Claims		Mortality Ratio
			Observed	Expected†			Observed	Expected†	
			d	d'	100 d/d'		d	d'	100 d/d'
Trace	Normotensive	E19S	106	94.64	112%	E28S	37	31.19	119%
		E19SS	45	27.44	164	E28SS	116	82.49	141
	Slight HT	E20S	51	23.64	215	E29S	21	6.91	305
		E20SS	24	8.63	280	E29SS	44	22.65	194
	Moderate HT	E21S	3	1.06	285	E30S	1	0.87	115
		E21SS	10	4.18	240	E30SS	12	4.32	280
Moderate	Normotension	E22S	5	3.05	164	E31S	—	—	—
		E22SS	3	5.88	51	E31SS	23	14.21	162
	Slight HT	E23SS	7	1.02	685	E32SS	7	3.72	188
	Moderate HT	E24SS	—	—	—	E33SS	2	0.46	435
Large	Normotension	E25SS	1	—	—	E34SS	17	3.60	470
	Slight HT	E26SS	—	—	—	E35SS	8	1.09	735
	Moderate HT	E27SS	—	—	—	E36SS	2	0.12	1670

Table 602b   Summary of Comparative Experience, Trace Amounts of Albumin

Category in Reference*	No. of Policies	Exposure Policy-Yrs	No. of Death Claims		Mortality Ratio	Ave. Ann. Mort. Rate	Est. 7-Yr Surv. Rate	Est. 7-Yr Surv. Index	Excess Death Rate
			Observed	Expected†					
	ℓ	E	d	d'	100 d/d'	$\bar{q} = d/E$	$P = (1-\bar{q})^7$	100 P/P'	1000(d-d')/E
Normotensive									
E19S	3999	30912	106	94.64	112%	.0034	.976	99.7%	0.4
E28S	1820	13774	37	31.19	119	.0026	.981	99.7	0.4
E19SS	1237	8538	45	27.44	164	.0053	.964	98.6	2.1
E28SS	4311	25686	116	82.49	141	.0045	.969	99.1	1.3
Slight Hypertensive									
E20S	894	7037	51	23.64	215%	.0072	.950	97.3%	3.9
E29S	437	3147	21	6.91	305	.0067	.954	96.9	4.5
E20SS	312	2047	24	8.63	280	.0117	.921	94.8	7.5
E29SS	1174	6874	44	22.65	194	.0064	.956	97.8	3.1

Table 602c   Comparative Experience by Age and Blood Pressure, Trace Amounts of Albumin

Category in Reference*	Age at Issue	Exposure Policy-Yrs	No. of Death Claims		Mortality Ratio	Ave. Ann. Mort. Rate	Est. 7-Yr Surv. Rate	Est. 7-Yr Surv. Index	Excess Death Rate
			Observed	Expected†					
	X	E	d	d'	100 d/d'	$\bar{q} = d/E$	$P = (1-\bar{q})^7$	100 P/P'	1000(d-d')/E
Normotensive									
E19,28SS	15-29	15672	21	17.1	123%	.001	.991	99.8%	0.2
	30-39	8425	28	17.9	156	.003	.977	99.2	1.2
	40-49	6519	54	33.1	163	.008	.943	97.8	3.2
	50-64	3608	58	41.8	139	.016	.893	96.9	4.5
	15-64	34224	161	109.9	146	.005	.968	99.0	1.5
Slight HT									
E20,29S+SS	15-29	9574	13	10.7	121%	.001	.990	99.8%	0.2
	30-39	4344	32	9.38	340	.007	.950	96.4	5.2
	40-49	3380	50	18.3	275	.015	.901	93.6	9.4
	50-64	1807	45	23.4	192	.025	.838	91.8	12
	15-64	19105	140	61.8	225	.007	.950	97.2	4.1

* Category identification number in reference. "S" refers to standard policy issues, "SS" to substandard or rated issues. Blood pressure categories are defined in descriptive text.

† Basis of expected mortality: 1935-50 Basic Table (Standard Intercompany)

ALBUMINURIA AND BLOOD PRESSURE

Table 602d Observed Data and Comparative Experience by Duration and Blood Pressure
(Trace Amounts of Albumin, All Ages Combined)

Interval		Exposure Policy-Yrs	No. of Death Claims		Mortality Ratio		Survival Ratio		Excess Death Rate
No.	Start-End	E	Observed	Expected*	Interval	Cumulative	Interval	Cumulative	
i	t to t + Δ t	E	d	d'	100 d/d'	100 $\sum$d/$\sum$d'	100 p_i/p_i'	100 P/P'	1000(d-d')/E
Normotensive — Categories E19,28SS†									
1	0- 2 yrs	9983	24	17.9	134%	134%	99.9%	99.9%	0.6
2	2- 5	10574	52	30.2	172	150	99.4	99.3	2.1
3	5-10	10307	62	40.9	152	155	99.0	98.2	2.0
4	10-15	3360	23	20.9	110	146	99.7	97.9	0.6
Slight Hypertension — Categories E20,29S+SS†									
1	0- 2 yrs	5134	20	8.99	220%	220%	99.6%	99.6%	2.1
2	2- 5	5725	26	16.5	158	180	99.5	99.1	1.7
3	5-10	6159	62	24.8	250	215	97.0	96.1	6.0
4	10-15	2087	32	11.5	280	225	95.2	91.5	9.8

Table 602e Derived Mortality and Survival Data

Interval		Observed Rates				Expected Rates*			
		Average Annual		Cumulative		Average Annual		Cumulative	
No.	Start-End	Mortality	Survival	Survival	Mortality	Mortality	Survival	Survival	Mortality
i	t to t + Δ t	$\bar q$ = d/E	$\bar p$	P	Q	$\bar q'$ = d'/E	$\bar p'$	P'	Q'
Normotensive — Categories E19,28SS†									
1	0- 2 yrs	.0024	.9976	.995	.005	.0018	.9982	.9964	.0036
2	2- 5	.0049	.9951	.981	.019	.0029	.9971	.9879	.0121
3	5-10	.0060	.9940	.951	.049	.0040	.9960	.9685	.0315
4	10-15	.0068	.9932	.919	.081	.0062	.9938	.9387	.0613
Slight Hypertension — Categories E20,29S+SS†									
1	0- 2 yrs	.0039	.9961	.992	.008	.0018	.9982	.9965	.0035
2	2- 5	.0045	.9955	.979	.021	.0029	.9971	.9879	.0121
3	5-10	.0101	.9899	.930	.070	.0040	.9960	,9682	.0318
4	10-15	.0153	.9847	.861	.139	.0055	.9945	.9418	.0582

* Basis of expected mortality: 1935-50 Basic Table (Standard Intercompany)
† Category identification number in reference. "S" refers to standard policy issues, "SS" to substandard or rated issues. Blood pressure categories are defined in descriptive text.

ALBUMINURIA BY AMOUNT

§603—ALBUMINURIA BY AMOUNT

Reference: *1951 Impairment Study*, compiled and published by the Society of Actuaries, pp. 157-159, Chicago (1954).

Subjects Studied: Applicants for insurance found to have albumin on examination classified according to amount of albumin and build class. Material in this section is derived from the study, the main features of which are cited in §601. Criteria for persistency and amount of albumin are given under *Subjects Studied* in §602. The build classes employed are measured by per cent deviations from standard average weights for age, sex and height parameters. The build classifications are represented by the following deviations from the standard weights:

> Normal weight: 30 per cent under standard up to 10 per cent over;
> Slightly overweight: 10 per cent up to 20 per cent over;
> Overweight: 20 per cent or more over.

Follow-up: The policy records of the 27 participating insurance companies were used for follow-up and constitute the basis for counting death claims and numbers exposed to risk.

Results: The salient features for the albumin/build classes are summarized in Table 603a. There is relatively little exposure in the overweight build categories. The more detailed experience given in Tables 603b-d was obtained on applicants less than 10 per cent above standard weight.

Table 603b presents experience by age at application for insurance under four normal weight classes. Two classes, standard and substandard, exhibited intermittent and constant traces of albumin. Mortality ratios for the standard class increased from 113 per cent for age group 15-29 years to 180 per cent for age group 40-49, and then diminished to 125 per cent over age span 50-64 years. Entrants rated substandard developed mortality ratios over the period of observation of about the same level in the 15-29 year age group; mortality ratios for older applicants (30-64 years) ranged between 161 and 184 per cent. Excess deaths for all ages and durations were 1 per 1000 for standard lives, 1.7 for substandard. The mortality ratio in policyholders with constant moderate amounts of albumin averaged 197 per cent, all ages combined, but rose to 635 per cent, with an excess death rate of 8.2 per 1000, in those with a constant large amount of albumin (over 100 mg. per 100 cc. of urine). In both amount categories the highest mortality ratio was found in the 30-39 age range, while the highest excess death rate occurred in the older policyholders, age 40 up.

Tables 603c-d present comparative experience by duration, all ages together, from commencement of rated insurance coverage for applicants of normal weight. For subjects with trace amounts of albumin, mortality ratios were virtually constant for the first ten policy years at about 170 per cent, dropping to 107 per cent over the succeeding five years. Excess death rates increased by duration from 1.1 per 1000 in the first interval to 2.5 between durations 5 to 10 years, then fell to 0.4 per 1000 in the next five-year interval. Applicants showing constant moderate amounts of albumin displayed higher mortality ratios: 290 per cent in the first two policy years, decreasing to 225 per cent in the succeeding three years, and after 5 years to 136 per cent. Excess death rates were quite uniform at a little more than 2 per 1000 for 5 years and then diminished to 0.8 per 1000. Considerably more adverse mortality occurred among normal weight applicants with constant large amounts of albumin: mortality ratios ranged from 535 to 730 per cent and excess deaths between 6.3 and 10 per 1000. Cumulative rates of survival at the end of 15 years indicated a survival ratio of less than 88 per cent in contrast to one of 98 per cent among applicants of normal weight with smaller amounts of albumin.

Table 603e gives more detailed data than available in 603a for the relation of build to various categories of trace amounts of albumin. In subjects with normal weight, mortality ratios were 136 and 159 per cent respectively, for standard and substandard issues. This ratio was only 128 per cent in slightly overweight applicants with intermittent trace albuminuria, but rose to 178 per cent when the finding was constant, and 169 per cent for those 20 per cent or more overweight.

URINARY ABNORMALITIES

Table 603a Summary of Albuminuria Classes by Amount of Albumin and Build Groups

Amount of Albumin	Build Class	Intermittent Albuminuria				Constant Albuminuria			
		Category in Reference*	No. of Death Claims		Mortality Ratio	Impairment Class	No. of Death Claims		Mortality Ratio
			Observed	Expected†			Observed	Expected†	
			d	d'	100 d/d'		d	d'	100 d/d'
Trace	Normal —	E1S	136	100.1	136%	E10S	42	30.45	138%
	(-30% to +10%)	E1SS	44	28.0	157	E10SS	125	78.45	159
	Slightly Overweight —	E2S	23	17.94	128	E11S	19	7.45	255
	(+10% to +20%)	E2SS	13	5.65	230	E11SS	33	18.46	179
	Overweight —	E3S	3	3.66	82	E12S	—	—	—
	(20% to 30%)	E3SS	8	4.79	167	E12SS	20	11.79	170
Moderate	Normal	E4S	3	3.19	94	E13S	—	—	—
	Normal	E4SS	5	5.49	91	E13SS	28	14.19	197
	Slightly Overweight	E5	3	—	—	E14SS	4	2.56	156
	Overweight	E6	1	—.	—	E15SS	4	1.21	330
Large	Normal	E7	1	—	—	E16SS	25	3.95	635
	Slightly Overweight	E8	—	—	—	E17SS	2	—	—
	Overweight	E9	—	—	—	E18SS	1	—	—

Table 603b Comparative Experience by Amount of Albumin, Age Group, All Durations Combined (Normal Weight)

Category in Reference*	Age at Issue	Exposure Policy-Yrs	No. of Death Claims		Mortality Ratio	Ave. Ann. Mort. Rate	Est. 7-Yr Surv. Rate	Est. 7-Yr Surv. Index	Excess Death Rate
			Observed	Expected†					
		E	d	d'	100 d/d'	q̄ = d/E	P = (1-q̄)⁷	100 P/P'	1000(d-d')/E
Trace (Intermittent and Constant)									
E1,10S	15-29	31173	39	34.5	113%	.001	.991	99.9%	0.1
	30-39	7608	21	16.0	131	.003	.981	99.5	0.7
	40-49	5954	59	32.8	180	.010	.933	96.9	4.4
	50-64	3524	59	47.3	125	.017	.888	97.7	3.3
	15-64	48259	178	130.6	136	.004	.974	99.3	1.0
E1,10SS	15-29	19745	25	21.5	116	.001	.991	99.9	0.2
	30-39	8931	31	19.0	163	.003	.976	99.1	1.3
	40-49	5846	55	29.9	184	.009	.936	97.0	4.3
	50-64	3107	58	36.1	161	.019	.876	95.1	7.0
	15-64	37629	169	106.5	159	.004	.969	98.8	1.7
Moderate Amount of Albumin (Constant)									
E13SS	15-29	6095	11	6.56	168%	.002	.987	99.5%	0.7
	30-39	1124	5	2.09	240	.004	.969	98.2	2.6
	40-64	994	12	5.54	215	.012	.918	95.5	6.5
	15-64	8213	28	14.2	197	.003	.976	98.8	1.7
Large Amount of Albumin (Constant)									
E16SS	15-29	1763	9	1.84	490%	.005	.965	97.2%	4.1
	30-39	561	9	1.09	825	.016	.893	90.5	14
	40-64	234	7	1.02	685	.030	.808	83.4	26
	15-64	2558	25	3.95	635	.010	.934	94.4	8.2

* Category identification number in reference. "S" refers to standard policy issues, "SS" to substandard or rated issues. Blood pressure categories are defined in descriptive text.

† Basis of expected mortality: 1935-50 Basic Table (Standard Intercompany)

ALBUMINURIA BY AMOUNT

Table 603c Observed Data and Comparative Experience by Amount of Albumin, by Duration (All Ages Combined, Normal Weight)

Interval		Exposure Policy-Yrs	No. of Death Claims		Mortality Ratio		Survival Ratio		Excess Death Rate
No.	Start-End		Observed	Expected*	Interval	Cumulative	Interval	Cumulative	
i	t to t + Δt	E	d	d'	100 d/d'	100 Σd/Σd'	100 p_i/p_i'	100 P/P'	1000(d-d')/E
	Trace (Intermittent and Constant) — E1,10SS†								
1	0- 2 yrs	10812	30	17.7	169%	169%	99.8%	99.8%	1.1
2	2- 5	11575	50	29.7	168	169	99.5	99.2	1.8
3	5-10	11539	69	40.3	171	170	98.8	98.0	2.5
4	10-15	3703	20	18.7	107	159	99.8	97.8	0.4
	Moderate Amount (Contstant) — E13SS†								
1	0- 2 yrs	2630	9	3.10	290%	290%	99.6%	99.6%	2.2
2	2- 5	2609	10	4.48	225	250	99.4	98.9	2.1
3	5-15	2974	9	6.61	136	197	99.2	98.1	0.8
	Large Amount (Constant) — E16SS†								
1	0- 2 yrs	944	7	1.09	640%	640%	98.8%	98.8%	6.3
2	2- 5	846	10	1.37	730	690	97.0	95.8	10
3	5-15	768	8	1.49	535	635	91.8	87.9	8.5

Table 603d Derived Mortality and Survival Data (Normal Weight)

Interval		Observed Rates				Expected Rates*			
		Average Annual		Cumulative		Average Annual		Cumulative	
No.	Start-End	Mortality	Survival	Survival	Mortality	Mortality	Survival	Survival	Mortality
i	t to t + Δt	$\bar{q}$ = d/E	$\bar{p}$	P	Q	$\bar{q}'$ = d'/E	$\bar{p}'$	P'	Q'
	Trace (Intermittent and Constant) — E1,10SS†								
1	0- 2 yrs	.0028	.9972	.994	.006	.0016	.9984	.9967	.0033
2	2- 5	.0043	.9957	.982	.018	.0026	.9974	.9891	.0109
3	5-10	.0060	.9940	.953	.047	.0035	.9965	.9719	.0281
4	10-15	.0054	.9946	.927	.073	.0050	.9950	.9476	.0524
	Moderate Amount (Constant) — E13SS†								
1	0- 2 yrs	.0034	.9966	.993	.007	.0012	.9988	.9976	.0024
2	2- 5	.0038	.9962	.982	.018	.0017	.9983	.9925	.0075
3	5-15	.0030	.9970	.952	.048	.0022	.9978	.9707	.0293
	Large Amount (Constant) — E16SS†								
1	0- 2 yrs	.0074	.9926	.985	.015	.0012	.9988	.9977	.0023
2	2- 5	.0118	.9882	.951	.049	.0016	.9984	.9929	.0071
3	5-15	.0104	.9896	.856	.144	.0019	.9981	.9738	.0262

Table 603e Comparative Experience by Build Class, Trace Amounts, All Ages and Durations Combined

Category in Reference†	No. of Policies	Exposure Policy-Yrs	No. of Death Claims		Mortality Ratio	Ave. Ann. Mort. Rate	Est. 7-Yr Surv. Rate	Est. 7-Yr Surv. Index	Excess Death Rate
			Observed	Expected*					
		E	d	d'	100 d/d'	$\bar{q}$ = d/E	P = $(1-\bar{q})^7$	100 P/P'	1000(d-d')/E
Trace (Intermittent and Constant) — Normal Weight									
E1,10S	6284	48259	178	131	136%	.004	.974	99.3%	1.0
E1,10SS	6013	37629	169	106	159	.004	.969	98.8	1.7
Trace (Intermittent) — Slightly Overweight									
E2S	540	4197	23	17.9	128	.005	.962	99.1	1.2
Trace (Constant) — Slightly Overweight									
E11SS	780	4459	33	18.5	178	.007	.949	97.7	3.3
Trace (Constant) — Overweight									
E12SS	146	2580	20	11.8	169	.008	.947	97.8	3.2

* Basis of expected mortality: 1935-50 Basic Table (Standard Intercompany)
† Category identification number in reference. "S" refers to standard policy issues, "SS" to substandard or rated issues. Blood pressure categories are defined in descriptive text.

URINARY ABNORMALITIES

§604–ALBUMINURIA WITHOUT CASTS, HEMATURIA, PYURIA

Reference: "New York Life Single Medical Impairment Study – 1967," unpublished report made available by J.J. Hutchinson and J.C. Sibigtroth (1973).

Subjects Studied: Policyholders of New York Life Insurance Company issued insurance in 1949-1965, followed to the 1966 policy anniversary. Cases studied were those in which the urinalysis revealed the presence of protein without abnormal numbers of red cells, white cells or casts in the urine. Most of the experience reported is for substandard issues. Cases involving ratable impairments other than the abnormal urine code were excluded.

Follow-up: Insurance policy records formed the basis of entry, of counting policies, exposure and death claims, and of follow-up information.

Results: Comparative experience by duration is given in Tables 604a-b for standard and substandard cases, both sexes, and all entry ages combined. The mortality ratio from 5-17 years was 230 per cent, only slightly higher than the ratio of 174 per cent for follow-up durations 0-5 years. The relative increase in EDR was greater (1.3 to 5.7 extra deaths per 1000), from the earlier to the later period.

In Table 604c the overall mortality ratio was 205 per cent, with the highest ratio 255 per cent observed in applicants under age 40. An upward trend with advancing age is evident in EDR: rates of 1.7, 3.7 and 10 per 1000, respectively, for the three age groups under 40, 40-49 and 50-64 years. The estimated 8-year survival index decreased with age, from 98.7 per cent in the youngest age group to 92.0 per cent in the oldest. Excess mortality was only slightly increased in applicants issued substandard as compared with those issued standard insurance, all ages combined.

Comparative mortality by major causes of death is given in Table 604d for male and female substandard cases combined. The major cause of death is found in the "all other causes and unknown" category, with a mortality ratio of 433 per cent and EDR of 1.9 per 1000. This category included nine deaths, of which three were due to nephritis and three to vascular lesions affecting the nervous system. The next leading cause of death is found in diseases of heart and circulation, the mortality ratio being 230 per cent and EDR 1.5 per 1000.

ALBUMINURIA WITHOUT CASTS, HEMATURIA, AND PYURIA IN INSUREDS

Table 604a   Observed Data and Comparative Experience by Duration — Combined Male and Female, Standard and Substandard

Interval		Exposure	No. of Death Claims		Mortality Ratio		Survival Ratio		Excess
No.	Start-End	Policy-Yrs	Observed	Expected*	Interval	Cumulative	Interval	Cumulative	Death Rate
i	t to t + Δ t	E	d	d'	100 d/d'	100 Σd/Σd'	100 p$_i$/p$_i$'	100 P/P'	1000(d-d')/E
1	0- 5 yrs	3490	11	6.34	174%	174%	99.3%	99.3%	1.3
2	5-17	2164	22	9.64	230	205	93.3	92.7	5.7

Table 604b   Derived Mortality and Survival Data

Interval		Observed Rates				Expected Rates*			
		Average Annual		Cumulative		Average Annual		Cumulative	
No.	Start-End	Mortality	Survival	Survival	Mortality	Mortality	Survival	Survival	Mortality
i	t to t + Δ t	q̄ = d/E	p̄	P	Q	q̄' = d'/E	p̄'	P'	Q'
1	0- 5 yrs	.0032	.9968	.9841	.0159	.0018	.9982	.9910	.0090
2	5-17	.0102	.9898	.8702	.1298	.0045	.9955	.9388	.0612

Table 604c   Comparative Experience by Age Group and Insurance Action, Male and Female Combined

Age Group	Exposure Policy-Yrs	No. of Death Claims		Mortality Ratio	Ave. Ann. Mort. Rate	Est. 8-Yr Surv. Rate	Est. 8-Yr Surv. Index	Excess· Death Rate
		Observed	Expected*					
	E	d	d'	100 d/d'	q̄ = d/E	P = (1 - q̄)^8	100 P/P'	1000(d-d')/E
0-39	3947	11	4.35	255%	.0028	.9779	98.7%	1.7
40-49	1095	9	4.93	183	.0082	.9361	97.1	3.7
50-64	612	13	6.70	194	.0212	.8422	92.0	10
All Ages	5954	33	15.98	205	.0058	.9543	97.6	3.0
All Std	1914	9	4.91	181	.0047	.9953	98.3	2.1
All SStd	3740	24	11.07	215	.0064	.9936	97.3	3.5

Table 604d   Mortality by Cause of Death — Substandard Cases, Male and Female Combined

Cause	No. of Death Claims		Mortality Ratio	Excess Death Rate
	Observed	Expected†		
Malignant Neoplasms	3	2.64	114%	0.1
Diseases of the Heart and Circulatory System	10	4.35	230	1.5
Accidents, Homicides, and Suicide	2	2.00	100	0.0
All Other Causes and Unknown	9●	2.08	433	1.9
Total	24	11.07	217	3.5

* Basis of expected mortality: 1955-60 Select Basic Table
† Distribution of total expected deaths by Intercompany Medically Examined Standard Issues 1965-70
● Includes 4 deaths due to Nephritis and 2 deaths due to Cirrhosis of Liver

KIDNEY AND URETERS

§620—RENAL COLIC IN INSUREDS

Reference: "New York Life Single Medical Impairment Study—1972," unpublished report made available by J.J. Hutchinson and J.C, Sibigtroth (1973).

Subjects Studied: Policyholders of New York Life Insurance Company issued insurance 1954-1970, followed to the 1971 policy anniversary. The experience reported is for cases found to have genito-urinary stones, forming in the kidney or the bladder. Only substandard cases were studied, mostly those where surgical treatment had not been performed. All cases with ratable impairment in addition to the renal colic code were excluded.

Follow-up: Insurance policy records formed the basis of entry, of counting policies, exposure and death claims, and of follow-up information.

Results: Comparative experience is given in Tables 620a-b for substandard male unoperated cases by duration, all entry ages combined. The mortality ratio showed no definite trend, ranging between 67 and 163 per cent, with EDR highest (3.0 extra deaths per 1000) at 5-10 years. The cumulative survival ratio at 17 years was normal.

From Table 620c, males under age 50 appeared to experience a higher mortality ratio than older males, with little or no excess mortality found in the latter group. The overall mortality ratio was 111 per cent for all ages combined. The estimated 8-year survival index was about normal throughout, as was the EDR.

Comparative mortality by major causes of death is given in Table 620d for males and females combined, separately for unoperated and operated cases. Among unoperated cases, diseases of the heart and circulation resulted in about 10 deaths more than expected, but cancer deaths were fewer than expected, and the net EDR for all causes was only 0.3 per 1000. The leading cause of death in operated cases was in the category "all other causes and unknown." Seven of the 10 death claims in this category were due to pneumonia, but the seven policies involved only two separate deaths.

RENAL COLIC (STONE) IN INSUREDS

Table 620a   Observed Data and Comparative Experience by Duration - Male Substandard Unoperated Cases

Interval No.	Start-End	Exposure Policy-Yrs	No. of Death Claims Observed	No. of Death Claims Expected*	Mortality Ratio Interval	Mortality Ratio Cumulative	Survival Ratio Interval	Survival Ratio Cumulative	Excess Death Rate
i	t to t + Δt	E	d	d'	100 d/d'	100 Σd/Σd'	100 p_i/p_i'	100 P/P'	1000(d-d')/E
1	0- 2 yrs	4352	8	7.61	105%	105%	100.0%	100.0%	0.1
2	2- 5	3710	11	11.60	95	99	100.1	100.0	−0.2
3	5-10	2433	19	11.63	163	123	98.5	98.5	3.0
4	10-17	881	6	8.92	67	111	102.4	100.9	−3.3

Table 620b   Derived Mortality and Survival Data

Interval No.	Start-End	Observed Rates Average Annual Mortality	Observed Rates Average Annual Survival	Observed Rates Cumulative Survival	Observed Rates Cumulative Mortality	Expected Rates* Average Annual Mortality	Expected Rates* Average Annual Survival	Expected Rates* Cumulative Survival	Expected Rates* Cumulative Mortality
i	t to t + Δt	$\bar{q}$ = d/E	$\bar{p}$	P	Q	$\bar{q}'$ = d'/E	$\bar{p}'$	P'	Q'
1	0- 2 yrs	.0018	.9982	.9963	.0037	.0017	.9983	.9965	.0035
2	2- 5	.0030	.9970	.9875	.0125	.0031	.9969	.9872	.0128
3	5-10	.0078	.9922	.9495	.0505	.0048	.9952	.9638	.0362
4	10-17	.0068	.9932	.9052	.0948	.0101	.9899	.8976	.1024

Table 620c   Comparative Experience by Age Group - Male Substandard Unoperated Cases, All Durations Combined

Age Group	Exposure Policy-Yrs	No. of Death Claims Observed	No. of Death Claims Expected*	Mortality Ratio	Ave. Ann. Mort. Rate	Est. 8-Yr Surv. Rate	Est. 8-Yr Surv. Index	Excess Death Rate
	E	d	d'	100 d/d'	$\bar{q}$ = d/E	P = (1-$\bar{q}$)^8	100 P/P'	1000(d-d')/E
0-39	6440	13	10.07	129%	.0020	.9840	99.6%	0.5
40-49	3367	19	13.94	136	.0056	.9558	98.8	1.5
50-59	1298	7	10.96	64	.0054	.9577	102.5	−3.1
60 up	271	5	4.79	104	.0185	.8616	99.4	0.8
All Ages	11376	44	39.76	111	.0039	.9695	99.7	0.4

Table 620d   Mortality by Cause of Death - Male and Female Combined

Cause	Unoperated No. of Death Claims Observed	Unoperated No. of Death Claims Expected†	Unoperated Mortality Ratio	Unoperated Excess Death Rate	Operated No. of Death Claims Observed	Operated No. of Death Claims Expected†	Operated Mortality Ratio	Operated Excess Death Rate
Malignant Neoplasm	4	10.16	39%	−0.5	3	2.99	100%	0.0
Diseases of the Heart and Circulatory System	27	16.76	161	0.8	6	4.93	122	0.4
Accidents and Homicides	8	5.86	137	0.2	0	1.73	0	−0.6
Suicide	1	1.81	55	−0.1	0	0.53	0	−0.2
All other Causes and Unknown	6	8.03	75	−0.1	10▫	2.37	420	2.5
Total	46●	42.62	108	0.3	19■	12.55	151	2.1

* Basis of expected mortality: 1955-60 Basic Select Table

† Distribution of total expected deaths by Intercompany Medically Examined Standard Issues 1965-70

● Includes 2 females (exposure 1284 policy-years)

▫ Includes pneumonia 7 policies (2 lives)

■ Includes 1 female (exposure 297 policy-years)

KIDNEY AND URETERS

§625—RENAL TRANSPLANT

References: (1) Advisory Committee to the Renal Transplant Registry, "The Eleventh Report of the Human Renal Transplant Registry," J. Am. Med. Assoc., 226:1197-1204 (1973).
(2) Additional data from the Renal Transplant Registry supplied by J. J. Bergan in personal communications (1973, 1974).

Subjects Studied: 11,264 recipients of 12,389 kidney transplants reported to the Renal Transplant Registry 1951-1972 (additional cases added in 1973 are a part of the tabulated experience, but are not included in these totals). There were 7476 transplants reported from centers in the United States with the remaining 4913 from Europe, Australia and Canada. Most cases (91 per cent) were first transplants, although some patients had multiple transplants, with a total of two to as many as five grafts. The age and sex distribution were as follows:

Age Group (yrs)	0-10	11-20	21-30	31-40	41-50	51 and up	All Ages
Male	163	1103	2169	1906	1506	524	7425
Female	196	961	1278	1080	906	286	4707
Total	359	2064	3447	2986	2412	810	12132

Of the patients receiving transplants 57 per cent had glomerulonephritis, 14 per cent had pyelonephritis, 5 per cent had polycystic disease, 4 per cent had nephrosclerosis, 4 per cent had more than one disease, and 16 per cent had other diagnoses. In the United States, there were as many living donors who gave one kidney as cadaver donors who gave two kidneys during 1972. By contrast, almost 80 per cent of the grafts in Europe and close to 98 per cent of the grafts reported from Australia were from cadavers.

Follow-up: Data from reporting agencies were submitted to the central registry in Chicago. Cooperating institutions periodically reported new transplants performed and submitted status lists with follow-up information on survival and condition of the transplant recipients. The Eleventh Report included new cases reported and follow-up information through 1972. Additional data from the Registry extended follow-up to the end of 1973. Less than one per cent of the patients reported were lost to follow-up.

Results: The mortality rate in the first three months was lowest in patients who received a sibling graft, ranging from .042 for the young recipients, age 11-20, to .143 for older patients, age 51-60 (Table 625a). Patients who received cadaver grafts experienced early mortality rates ranging from .178 to .315 in the corresponding age groups. Recipients younger than 11 years had a high rate of .281 in this same period. The early mortality rates for recipients of parental grafts fell between the rates for the above groups.

There has been a steady improvement in mortality ratios and excess death rates for 3-year survival since 1951 in each of the three donor categories (Table 625b). Patients with a sibling graft experienced a 4,000 per cent mortality ratio with 103 excess deaths per 1000 per year for transplants during the period 1951-66. The mortality ratio for three years decreased to 2200 per cent with 56 excess deaths per 1000 in 1970-71. Recipients of parental grafts had similar figures for the same interval (3 months to 3 years). The mortality was much higher for cadaver graft patients, although there has been improvement from the early period 1951-66 to 1970-71, with a decrease in mortality ratio from 8800 to 5000 per cent and a decrease in the annual excess death rate from 226 to 127 per 1000. Recipients of parental grafts again experienced slightly greater risk than patients with sibling grafts but less risk than cadaver graft recipients.

The mortality ratios of parental graft recipients in all age categories generally remained below that of cadaver transplant patients and above the risk of sibling graft recipients for the period from 3 months following transplant to 5 years (Table 625c). In most cases, the risk was greatest in the younger patients and diminished with age. The excess death rates and mortality ratios were usually highest in the period from 3 months to 1 year following surgery and decreased in the two succeeding 2-year periods. The 5-year survival ratios ranged from 54.4 per cent (cadaver age 41-50) to 84.0 per cent (sibling age 21-30).

RENAL TRANSPLANT REGISTRY EXPERIENCE

Table 625a   Early Mortality (0-90 days), First Renal Transplant Cases by Donor Source and Age, to 1972

Donor Source	Age	No. Alive at Operation	Withdrawals Alive	No. of Deaths	No. known Survivors	Cumulative Surv. Rate*	Observed Mort. Rate*	Excess Death Rate†
		ℓ	w	d	$\ell_{1/4}$	$P_{1/4}$	$Q_{1/4}$	$1000(Q_{1/4}\text{-}Q'_{1/4})$
Sibling	11-20	222	14	9	199	.958	.042	42
	21-30	720	66	55	599	.920	.080	80
	31-40	709	67	53	589	.922	.078	78
	41-50	370	38	42	290	.879	.121	120
	51-60	99	3	14	82	.857	.143	140
Parent	0-10	187	10	18	159	.902	.098	98
	11-20	914	79	117	718	.866	.134	134
	21-30	772	76	79	617	.892	.108	108
	31-40	225	15	46	164	.787	.213	213
Cadaver	0-10	164	29	42	93	.719	.281	281
	11-20	895	171	144	580	.822	.178	178
	21-30	1917	363	297	1257	.827	.173	173
	31-40	2077	337	399	1341	.789	.211	211
	41-50	2075	350	446	1279	.762	.238	237
	51-60	711	115	204	392	.685	.315	312

Table 625b   Comparative Experience by Entry Period and Type of Donor, Duration 3 Months - 3 Years (All Ages Combined)

Donor + Entry	No. Alive at Start	Exposure Person-Yrs	Deaths Observed	Deaths Expected●	Cumulative Surv. Rate	Mortality Rate	Mortality Ratio	Cumulative Surv. Ratio	Excess Death Rate
	ℓ	E	d	d'	P	$\bar{q}=d/E$	100 d/d'	100 P/P'	$1000(\bar{q}-\bar{q}')$
Sibling									
1951-66	181	418.5	44	1.09	.750	.105	4000%	75.5%	103
1967-69	494	1183.8	79	3.08	.835	.067	2600	84.1	64
1970-71	573	1117.4	65	2.91	.869	.058	2200	87.5	56
1951-71	1248	2719.6	188	7.07	.835	.069	2700	84.1	67
Parent									
1951-66	280	605.0	67	1.57	.743	.111	4300%	74.8%	108
1967-69	494	1124.2	100	2.92	.785	.089	3400	79.1	86
1970-71	497	970.2	61	2.52	.860	.063	2400	86.6	60
1951-71	1271	2699.5	228	7.02	.805	.084	3200	81.1	82
Cadaver									
1951-66	330	639.1	146	1.66	.528	.228	8800%	53.2%	226
1967-69	1237	2505.5	392	6.51	.661	.156	6000	66.6	154
1970-71	1836	3167.5	412	8.24	.730	.130	5000	73.5	127
1951-71	3403	6312.1	950	16.41	.680	.151	5800	68.5	148

* Survival rate at 3 months based on calculation for 4 intervals, 0-1, 1-2, 2-7 and 7-90 days
† EDR per quarter. Q' for 3 months ranges from .0001 to .0004 to age decade 31-40, .0010 age 41-50, and .0028 age 51-60
● Basis of expected mortality: q' = .0026 calculated from 1959-61 U.S. Life Table values, weighted mean of age and sex distribution for all entrants

KIDNEY AND URETERS

Table 625c   Observed Data and Comparative Long-Term Experience, First Renal Transplant Cases by Donor Source, Age of Recipient and Duration

Age	Interval		No. Alive at Start of Interval	Exposure Person-Yrs	Deaths during Interval		Interval Mort. Ratio	Cumulative Surv. Ratio	Excess Death Rate
	No.	Start-End			Observed	Expected*			
x	i	t to t + Δt	ℓ	E	d	d'	100 d/d'	100 P/P'	1000(d-d')/E
Sibling Donor									
11-20 yrs	1	3 mos-1 yr	199	136.5	7	0.106	6600%	96.3%	51
	2	1-3 yr	157	219.0	10	0.22	4500	87.8	45
	3	3-5 yr	65	87.5	4	0.105	3800	80.2	45
21-30	1	3 mos-1 yr	599	403.9	35	0.53	6600	93.8	85
	2	1-3 yr	473	695.5	24	0.83	2900	87.9	33
	3	3-5 yr	222	311.5	9	0.40	2200	84.0	28
31-40	1	3 mos-1 yr	589	395.6	42	0.75	5600	92.5	104
	2	1-3 yr	453	680.5	26	1.43	1820	85.9	36
	3	3-5 yr	228	330.0	18	0.82	2200	76.9	52
41-50	1	3 mos-1 yr	290	191.4	28	0.90	3100	89.8	142
	2	1-3 yr	211	290.0	25	1.60	1560	76.6	81
	3	3-5 yr	88	119.0	8	0.80	1000	68.2	61
51-60	1	3 mos-1 yr	82	56.0	8	0.69	1160	90.2	131
	2	1-3 yr	59	58.0	4	0.81	495	84.0	55
Parent Donor									
0-10 yrs	1	3 mos-1 yr	159	103.5	11	0.065	16900	91.9	106
	2	1-3 yr	109	153.5	2	0.071	2800	89.6	13
	3	3-5 yr	51	66.0	1	0.021	4800	87.0	15
11-20	1	3 mos-1 yr	718	487.5	51	0.38	13400	92.2	104
	2	1-3 yr	558	833.5	46	0.83	5500	82.4	54
	3	3-5 yr	273	390.0	9	0.47	1910	78.9	22
21-30	1	3 mos-1 yr	617	408.0	65	0.53	12300	88.7	158
	2	1-3 yr	453	682.0	43	0.82	5200	78.0	62
	3	3-5 yr	214	311.5	12	0.40	3000	72.4	37
31-40	1	3 mos-1 yr	164	108.8	21	0.21	10000	86.6	191
	2	1-3 yr	122	182.5	9	0.38	2400	77.9	47
	3	3-5 yr	62	89.0	7	0.22	3200	66.3	76
Cadaver Donor									
0-10 yrs	1	3 mos-1 yr	93	59.8	12	0.038	32000	84.5	200
	2	1-3 yr	67	87.5	15	0.040	38000	58.2	171
11-20	1	3 mos-1 yr	577	368.6	47	0.29	16200	90.5	127
	2	1-3 yr	398	539.5	36	0.53	6800	78.8	66
	3	3-5 yr	147	180.0	8	0.22	3600	72.2	43
21-30	1	3 mos-1 yr	1257	790.9	153	1.03	14900	86.6	192
	2	1-3 yr	821	1125.5	85	1.35	6300	74.5	74
	3	3-5 yr	307	380.0	14	0.49	2900	68.8	36
31-40	1	3 mos-1 yr	1335	838.9	203	1.59	12800	83.2	240
	2	1-3 yr	864	1191.5	115	2.50	4600	68.7	94
	3	3-5 yr	320	401.0	20	1.00	2000	62.8	47
41-50	1	3 mos-1 yr	1278	785.5	232	3.69	6300	80.2	291
	2	1-3 yr	796	1059.0	111	5.82	1910	64.8	99
	3	3-5 yr	255	278.5	27	1.87	1440	54.4	90
51-60	1	3 mos-1 yr	392	233.5	84	2.87	2900	77.3	347
	2	1-3 yr	222	256.5	33	3.59	920	62.3	115
	3	3-5 yr	52	54.5	4	0.90	445	55.6	57

* Basis of expected mortality: 1964 U.S. Life Tables

RENAL TRANSPLANT REGISTRY EXPERIENCE

Table 625d   Derived Data, First Renal Transplant Cases by Donor Source, Age and Duration

Age	No.	Interval Start-End	Observed Survival Rates Cumulative	Interval	Ave. Ann.	Ave. Ann. Mort. Rate	Expected* Survival Rates Cumulative	Interval	Ave. Ann.	Ave. Ann. Mort. Rate
x	i	t to t + Δ t	P	p_i	$\breve{p}$	$\breve{q}$	P'	p_i'	$\breve{p}'$	$\breve{q}'$
Sibling Donor										
11-20 yrs	1	3 mos-1 yr	.962	.962	.950	.050	.9994	.9994	.9992	.00078
	2	1-3 yr	.876	.911	.954	.046	.9974	.9980	.9990	.00099
	3	3-5 yr	.798	.911	.954	.046	.9950	.9976	.9988	.0012
21-30	1	3 mos-1 yr	.937	.937	.917	.083	.9990	.9990	.9987	.0013
	2	1-3 yr	.876	.935	.967	.033	.9966	.9976	.9988	.0012
	3	3-5 yr	.835	.953	.976	.024	.9940	.9974	.9987	.0013
31-40	1	3 mos-1 yr	.924	.924	.900	.100	.9986	.9986	.9981	.0019
	2	1-3 yr	.854	.924	.961	.039	.9944	.9958	.9979	.0021
	3	3-5 yr	.761	.891	.944	.056	.9894	.9950	.9975	.0025
41-50	1	3 mos-1 yr	.895	.895	.863	.137	.9965	.9965	.9953	.0047
	2	1-3 yr	.755	.844	.919	.081	.9855	.9890	.9945	.0055
	3	3-5 yr	.663	.878	.937	.063	.9723	.9866	.9933	.0067
51-60	1	3 mos-1 yr	.894	.894	.861	.139	.9908	.9908	.9877	.0123
	2	1-3 yr	.809	.905	.951	.049	.9633	.9722	.9860	.0140
Parent Donor										
0-10 yrs	1	3 mos-1 yr	.919	.919	.893	.107	.9995	.9995	.9994	.00063
	2	1-3 yr	.895	.974	.987	.013	.9986	.9991	.9995	.00046
	3	3-5 yr	.868	.970	.985	.015	.9980	.9994	.9997	.00032
11-20	1	3 mos-1 yr	.921	.921	.896	.104	.9994	.9994	.9992	.00078
	2	1-3 yr	.822	.893	.945	.055	.9974	.9980	.9990	.00099
	3	3-5 yr	.785	.955	.977	.023	.9950	.9976	.9988	.0012
21-30	1	3 mos-1 yr	.886	.886	.851	.149	.9990	.9990	.9987	.0013
	2	1-3 yr	.777	.877	.936	.064	.9966	.9976	.9988	.0012
	3	3-5 yr	.720	.927	.963	.037	.9940	.9974	.9987	.0013
31-40	1	3 mos-1 yr	.865	.865	.824	.176	.9986	.9986	.9981	.0019
	2	1-3 yr	.775	.896	.947	.053	.9944	.9958	.9979	.0021
	3	3-5 yr	.656	.846	.920	.080	.9894	.9950	.9975	.0025
Cadaver Donor										
0-10 yrs	1	3 mos-1 yr	.845	.845	.799	.201	.9995	.9995	.9994	.00063
	2	1-3 yr	.581	.687	.829	.171	.9986	.9991	.9995	.00046
11-20	1	3 mos-1 yr	.904	.904	.874	.126	.9994	.9994	.9992	.00078
	2	1-3 yr	.786	.870	.933	.067	.9974	.9980	.9990	.00099
	3	3-5 yr	.718	.914	.956	.044	.9950	.9976	.9988	.0012
21-30	1	3 mos-1 yr	.865	.865	.824	.176	.9990	.9990	.9987	.0013
	2	1-3 yr	.742	.858	.926	.074	.9966	.9976	.9988	.0012
	3	3-5 yr	.684	.922	.960	.040	.9940	.9974	.9987	.0013
31-40	1	3 mos-1 yr	.831	.831	.781	.219	.9986	.9986	.9981	.0019
	2	1-3 yr	.683	.822	.907	.093	.9944	.9958	.9979	.0021
	3	3-5 yr	.621	.909	.953	.047	.9894	.9950	.9975	.0025
41-50	1	3 mos-1 yr	.799	.799	.741	.259	.9965	.9965	.9953	.0047
	2	1-3 yr	.639	.800	.894	.106	.9855	.9890	.9945	.0055
	3	3-5 yr	.529	.828	.910	.090	.9723	.9866	.9933	.0067
51-60	1	3 mos-1 yr	.766	.766	.701	.299	.9908	.9908	.9877	.0123
	2	1-3 yr	.600	.783	.885	.115	.9633	.9722	.9860	.0140
	3	3-5 yr	.518	.864	.930	.070	.9318	.9673	.9835	.0165

* Basis of expected mortality: 1964 U.S. Life Tables

KIDNEY AND URETERS

§626–NATIONAL DIALYSIS REGISTRY EXPERIENCE

References: (1) B. T. Burton, K. K. Krueger, and F. A. Bryan, Jr., "National Registry of Long-Term Dialysis Patients," J. Am. Med. Assoc., 218:718-722 (1971).

(2) R. J. Wineman, F. A. Bryan, Jr., and W. K. Poole, Registry survival data by personal communications (1974-75).

Subjects Studied: Patients with irreversible kidney failure placed on long-term dialysis with treatment supervised in approximately 415 U.S. dialysis centers which regularly report follow-up data to the National Dialysis Registry, an organ of the Artificial Kidney-Chronic Uremia Program of the National Institute of Arthritis and Metabolic Diseases. The unpublished data (Reference 2) reflect experience on 17,247 patients over the period from June 1969 to October 1974. Most of the patients have been treated by one of various methods of hemodialysis, but 2.0 per cent were under peritoneal dialysis. As of December 1, 1973, 54 per cent of the patients were under treatment in dialysis units located in hospitals, 12 per cent in other dialysis centers, and 34 per cent under home dialysis programs. Age and sex distribution at the start of dialysis of patients enrolled prior to that date was as follows:

	Age under 15	15-19	20-29	30-39	40-49	50-59	60 up	Total
Male	72	205	769	971	1559	1327	717	5620
Female	82	143	456	618	830	816	388	3333
Total Number	154	348	1225	1589	2389	2143	1105	8953
Per Cent	1.7%	3.9%	13.7%	17.8%	26.7%	23.9%	12.3%	100.0%

Follow-up: Information developed in the National Dialysis Registry includes the number of patients under dialysis at home and in hospital centers, the identification of patients, their ages, sex, type of treatment (hemodialysis, peritoneal dialysis, transfer to renal transplantation and, if the transplant fails, return to dialysis), discharge from treatment and deaths. Causes of death are recorded under 18 categories.

Results: Four-year comparative experience by age and sex is given in Table 626a, and by annual durations (all ages combined) in Table 626b. More detailed data by sex, age and duration from commencement of dialysis treatment are presented in Tables 626c-d.

Excess mortality at very high levels was observed for both sexes, in all age groups, and at all durations. Mortality ratios were highest in the first year of treatment and at the youngest ages, with a range from 18400 per cent in females under age 20 to 740 per cent in males age 60 up. These extremely high mortality ratios were consistently higher in females than in males, by a factor usually exceeding two to one, a difference that is readily apparant in Tables 626a-b, but is also confirmed in the more detailed data of Tables 626c-d. The relatively high level of the female ratios is attributable largely to the lower mortality rates experienced by women and female children in the general population. When excess mortality is measured in terms of extra deaths per 1000 per year males are seen to have lower values of EDR in only three of the six categories in Table 626a. Further confirmation is provided by detailed comparison of the annual observed rates of mortality in Table 626d, which reveal relatively small differences in the rates experienced by male and female patients on dialysis.

Mortality ratios tended to decline with the passage of time after starting dialysis, in a consistent fashion for all ages combined, in Table 626b, but with evidence of leveling off in the second or third year, in some of the age categories in Table 626c. In male patients (all ages combined) the mortality ratio decreased from 1490 per cent in the first year to 860 per cent in the fourth year, and in females from 3100 to 1910 per cent. The corresponding trend in EDR was also a decrease, from 141 to 78 extra deaths per 1000 per year in men and from 139 to 85 per 1000 in women.

NATIONAL HEMODIALYSIS REGISTRY

Results (continued):

Excess mortality in terms of EDR showed a tendency to increase with age, and the four-year survival ratio, a tendency to decrease (Tables 626a and 626c). For all durations combined EDR increased from 83 per 1000 in male patients under age 20 to 157 per 1000 in those age 60 and up; the corresponding increase in female patients went from 94 to 169 per 1000. The cumulative survival ratios reflected these high EDR's, decreasing from about 74 per cent in patients under 20 to less than 60 per cent in patients of both sexes, age 60 up. The predominant category of cause of death was reported to be heart disease, with 30 per cent of all deaths. Although expected rates by cause were not given, relatively high percentages occurred in renal disease (7 per cent), cerebrovascular disease (17 per cent), infectious diseases (12 per cent), respiratory diseases (7 per cent), and endocrine and metabolic disorders (5 per cent). There is no doubt that a great many of the excess deaths were directly attributable to complications of the underlying chronic renal failure, the dialysis, or other supportive treatment.

Table 626a   Four-Year Comparative Experience by Sex and Age Group

Sex	Age Group	No. Alive at Start	Withdrawn dur. Period*	Exposure Person-Yrs	No. of Deaths Observed	No. of Deaths Expected†	Mortality Ratio	Cumulative Surv. Ratio	Excess Death Rate
	(Yrs)	ℓ	tr+u+w	E	d	d′	100 d/d′	100P/P′	1000(d-d′)/E
Male	under 20	570	433	854	72	1.45	5000%	74.3%	83
	20-29	1555	1131	2643	234	4.56	5100	72.0	87
	30-39	1786	1163	3313	388	7.88	4900	62.8	115
	40-49	2811	1770	5373	705	32.73	2200	60.2	125
	50-59	2499	1591	4461	684	70.05	975	58.8	138
	60 up	1606	1081	2413	459	79.70	575	58.8	157
Female	under 20	527	416	736	70	0.46	15200	73.4	94
	20-29	950	693	1565	148	1.09	13600	71.4	94
	30-39	1141	762	2060	238	2.71	8800	63.7	114
	40-49	1485	1017	2724	319	9.14	3500	63.7	114
	50-59	1480	1026	2577	354	19.26	1840	58.2	130
	60 up	837	578	1243	229	18.90	1210	57.1	169

Table 626b   Four-Year Comparative Experience by Sex and Interval Year (All Ages Combined)

Sex	No.	Interval Start-End	No. Alive at Start of Int.	Withdrawn dur. Int.*	Exposure Person-Yrs	No. of Deaths Observed	No. of Deaths Expected†	Mortality Ratio	Cumulative Surv. Ratio	Excess Death Rate
	i	t to t + Δt	ℓ	tr+u+w	E	d	d′	100 d/d′	100 P/P′	1000(d-d′)/E
Male	1	0-12 mos	10827	3221	9215	1397	93.86	1490%	85.7%	141
	2	12-24	6209	1961	5229	675	54.48	1240	75.4	119
	3	24-36	3573	1214	2966	325	31.15	1040	67.9	99
	4	36-48	2034	773	1647	145	16.88	860	62.5	78
Female	1	0-12	6420	2012	5414	775	24.98	3100	86.1	139
	2	12-24	3633	1269	2998	349	14.43	2400	76.4	112
	3	24-36	2015	776	1627	156	8.06	1940	69.4	91
	4	36-48	1083	435	866	78	4.09	1910	63.5	85

* tr-patients dropped because of transplant operation, u-untraced, w-alive at end of follow-up
† Basis of expected mortality: U.S. White Males and Females 1969-1971

KIDNEY AND URETERS

Table 626c   Observed Data and Comparative Experience by Sex, Age and Duration

Sex/Age	Interval No.	Interval Start-End	No. Alive at Start of Interval	Withdrawn dur. Int.*	Exposure Person-Yrs	No. of Deaths Observed	No. of Deaths Expected†	Mortality Ratio	Cumulative Surv. Ratio	Excess Death Rate
	i	t to t + Δt	ℓ	tr+u+w	E	d	d'	100 d/d'	100 P/P'	1000(d-d')/E
Male										
Under 20 yrs	1	0-12 mos	570	270	435	45	0.70	6400%	88.7%	102
	2	12-24	255	92	209	17	0.36	4700	81.1	80
	3	24-36	146	40	126	6	0.23	2600	77.8	46
	4	36-48	100	31	84	4	0.16	2500	74.3	46
20-29	1	0-12 mos	1555	581	1264	117	2.28	5100	90.6	91
	2	12-24	857	284	715	77	1.22	6300	80.9	106
	3	24-36	496	167	412	27	0.66	4100	75.7	64
	4	36-48	302	99	252	13	0.40	3200	72.0	50
30-39	1	0-12 mos	1786	515	1528	196	3.36	5800	87.2	126
	2	12-24	1075	330	910	106	2.18	4900	77.1	114
	3	24-36	639	192	543	52	1.41	3700	69.9	93
	4	36-48	395	126	332	34	0.93	3700	62.8	100
40-49	1	0-12 mos	2811	697	2462	367	13.79	2700	85.5	143
	2	12-24	1747	487	1504	174	9.17	1900	75.9	110
	3	24-36	1086	356	908	116	6.08	1910	66.4	121
	4	36-48	614	230	499	48	3.69	1300	60.2	89
50-59	1	0-12 mos	2499	655	2172	360	31.49	1140	84.6	151
	2	12-24	1484	462	1253	206	19.92	1030	71.7	149
	3	24-36	816	277	678	83	11.80	705	63.9	105
	4	36-48	456	197	358	35	6.84	510	58.8	79
60 up	1	0-12 mos	1606	503	1354	312	42.24	740	79.5	199
	2	12-24	791	306	638	95	21.63	440	69.3	115
	3	24-36	390	182	299	41	10.97	375	61.8	100
	4	36-48	167	90	122	11	4.86	225	58.8	50
Female										
Under 20 yrs	1	0-12 mos	527	249	402	46	0.25	18400	88.7	114
	2	12-24	232	94	185	18	0.12	15000	79.6	97
	3	24-36	120	50	95	5	0.06	8300	74.8	52
	4	36-48	65	23	54	1	0.03	3300	73.4	18
20-29	1	0-12 mos	950	353	774	87	0.53	16400	88.7	112
	2	12-24	510	183	418	39	0.29	13400	80.2	93
	3	24-36	288	110	233	15	0.17	8800	75.2	64
	4	36-48	163	47	140	7	0.10	7000	71.4	49
30-39	1	0-12 mos	1141	351	966	131	1.16	11300	86.4	134
	2	12-24	659	200	559	57	0.73	7800	77.6	101
	3	24-36	402	131	336	32	0.50	6400	69.9	94
	4	36-48	239	80	199	18	0.32	5600	63.7	89
40-49	1	0-12 mos	1485	397	1286	157	3.99	3900	88.2	119
	2	12-24	931	308	777	101	2.64	3800	76.5	127
	3	24-36	522	188	428	39	1.58	2500	69.7	87
	4	36-48	295	124	233	22	0.93	2400	63.7	90
50-59	1	0-12 mos	1480	398	1281	190	8.97	2100	85.8	141
	2	12-24	892	316	734	95	5.58	1700	74.9	122
	3	24-36	481	199	382	45	3.13	1440	66.3	110
	4	36-48	237	113	180	24	1.58	1520	58.2	125
60 up	1	0-12 mos	837	264	705	164	10.08	1630	78.1	218
	2	12-24	409	168	325	39	5.07	770	69.7	104
	3	24-36	202	98	153	20	2.62	765	61.7	114
	4	36-48	84	48	60	6	1.13	530	57.1	81

* tr patients dropped because of transplant operation. u-untraced. w-alive at end of follow-up

† Basis of expected mortality: U.S. White Males and Females 1969-71

NATIONAL HEMODIALYSIS REGISTRY

Table 626d   Derived Mortality and Survival Data

Sex/Age	No.	Start-End	Survival Cumulative*	Survival Annual	Mortality Annual	Mortality Cumulative	Annual Mortality	Annual Survival	Cumulative Survival	Cumulative Mortality
	i	t to t + Δt	P	p	q	Q	q'	p'	P'	Q'
Male										
Under 20 yrs	1	0-12 mos	.886	.886	.114	.114	.0016	.9984	.9984	.0016
	2	12-24	.808	.913	.087	.192	.0017	.9983	.9967	.0033
	3	24-36	.774	.957	.043	.226	.0018	.9982	.9949	.0051
	4	36-48	.738	.954	.046	.262	.0019	.9981	.9930	.0070
20-29	1	0-12 mos	.904	.904	.096	.096	.0018	.9982	.9982	.0018
	2	12-24	.806	.892	.108	.194	.0017	.9983	.9965	.0035
	3	24-36	.753	.934	.066	.247	.0016	.9984	.9949	.0051
	4	36-48	.715	.950	.050	.285	.0016	.9984	.9933	.0067
30-39	1	0-12 mos	.870	.870	.130	.130	.0022	.9978	.9978	.0022
	2	12-24	.767	.882	.118	.233	.0024	.9976	.9954	.0046
	3	24-36	.694	.904	.096	.306	.0026	.9974	.9928	.0072
	4	36-48	.622	.896	.104	.378	.0028	.9972	.9900	.0100
40-49	1	0-12 mos	.850	.850	.150	.150	.0056	.9944	.9944	.0056
	2	12-24	.750	.882	.118	.250	.0061	.9939	.9883	.0117
	3	24-36	.652	.870	.130	.348	.0067	.9933	.9817	.0183
	4	36-48	.587	.900	.100	.413	.0074	.9926	.9744	.0256
50-59	1	0-12 mos	.834	.834	.166	.166	.0145	.9855	.9855	0145
	2	12-24	.695	.833	.167	.305	.0159	.9841	.9698	.0302
	3	24-36	.609	.876	.124	.391	.0174	.9826	.9530	.0470
	4	36-48	.550	.904	.096	.450	.0191	.9809	.9348	.0652
60 up	1	0-12 mos	.770	.770	.230	.230	.0312	.9688	.9688	.0312
	2	12-24	.649	.843	.157	.351	.0339	.9661	.9360	.0640
	3	24-36	.557	.859	.141	.443	.0367	.9633	.9016	.0984
	4	36-48	.509	.913	.087	.491	.0398	.9602	.8657	.1343
Female										
Under 20 yrs	1	0-12 mos	.886	.886	.114	.114	.00061	.99939	.99939	.00061
	2	12-24	.795	.897	.103	.205	.00064	.99936	.9988	.0012
	3	24-36	.747	.940	.060	.253	.00064	.99936	.9981	.0019
	4	36-48	.732	.979	.021	.268	.00064	.99936	.9975	.0025
20-29	1	0-12 mos	.886	.886	.114	.114	.00068	.99932	.99932	.00068
	2	12-24	.801	.904	.096	.199	.00070	.99930	.9986	.0014
	3	24-36	.750	.935	.065	.250	.00072	.99928	.9979	.0021
	4	36-48	.712	.950	.050	.288	.00075	.99925	.9972	.0028
30-39	1	0-12 mos	.863	.863	.137	.137	.0012	.9988	.9988	.0012
	2	12-24	.774	.897	.103	.226	.0013	.9987	.9975	.0025
	3	24-36	.696	.900	.100	.304	.0015	.9985	.9960	.0040
	4	36-48	.633	.909	.091	.367	.0016	.9984	.9944	.0056
40-49	1	0-12 mos	.879	.879	.121	.121	.0031	.9969	.9969	.0031
	2	12-24	.760	.865	.135	.240	.0034	.9966	.9935	.0065
	3	24-36	.690	.907	.093	.310	.0037	.9963	.9898	.0102
	4	36-48	.628	.910	.090	.372	.0040	.9960	.9859	.0141
50-59	1	0-12 mos	.852	.852	.148	.148	.0070	.9930	.9930	.0070
	2	12-24	.738	.866	.134	.262	.0076	.9924	.9855	.0145
	3	24-36	.648	.878	.122	.352	.0082	.9918	.9774	.0226
	4	36-48	.564	.870	.130	.436	.0088	.9912	.9688	.0312
60 up	1	0-12 mos	.770	.770	.230	.230	.0143	.9857	.9857	.0143
	2	12-24	.676	.877	.123	.324	.0156	.9844	.9703	.0297
	3	24-36	.588	.871	.129	.412	.0171	.9829	.9537	.0463
	4	36-48	.534	.908	.092	.466	.0188	.9812	.9358	.0642

* Cumulative survival rate data on monthly basis, from which annual p and q may differ from q = d/E
† Basis of expected mortality: U.S. White Males and Females 1969-1971

MALE GENITAL

§670–PROSTATECTOMY AND DISORDERS OF THE PROSTATE IN INSUREDS

Reference: "New York Life Single Medical Impairment Study–1972," unpublished report made available by J.J. Hutchinson and J.C. Sibigtroth (1973).

Subjects Studied: Policyholders of New York Life Insurance Company issued insurance in 1954-1970, followed to the 1971 policy anniversary. Different codes were used to distinguish male applicants who had undergone a prostatectomy, from those who had either prostatitis or enlarged prostate. The experience reported is for substandard issues only. Records involving more than one ratable impairment were excluded.

Follow-up: Insurance policy records formed the basis of entry, of counting policies, exposure and death claims, and of follow-up information.

Results: Comparative experience is given in Tables 670a-b for substandard males by duration, all ages combined, separately for cases with prostatectomy and cases with disorders of the prostate. Among cases with prostatectomy the mortality ratio did not show any trend, ranging between 157 and 207 per cent, with EDR highest (40 per 1000) at 10-17 years. Cases with disorders of the prostate, experienced a favorable mortality at 0-10 years, after which the mortality ratio rose to 119 per cent and EDR 5.9 per 1000. The cumulative survival ratio at 17 years was 67.5 per cent for cases with prostatectomy, compared to normal for cases with disorders of the prostate.

From Table 670c, the mortality ratio among cases with prostatectomy decreased from 245 per cent for men under 60 to 145 per cent for men age 60 up. The corresponding change in EDR was also a decrease, from 14 to 11 per 1000. Among cases with disorders of the prostate, the mortality ratio was favorable throughout, with no excess mortality observed for any age group. The overall mortality ratio was 177 per cent for cases with prostatectomy, and 77 per cent for cases with disorders of the prostate. The estimated 8-year survival indexes were 90.3 and 102.1 per cent, respectively.

Comparative mortality by major causes of death is given in Table 670d for substandard males with prostatectomy. The major cause of death is found in the "all other causes and unknown" category, with the mortality ratio being 365 per cent and EDR 8.0 per 1000. Of the 14 deaths observed in this category, 4 were cerebrovascular accidents. Malignant neoplasms also were a significant cause of death, with a mortality ratio of 270 per cent and an EDR of 6.5 per 1000.

PROSTATECTOMY AND DISORDERS OF PROSTATE IN INSUREDS

Table 670a   Observed Data and Comparative Experience by Duration - Male Substandard Cases

Interval No.	Start-End	Exposure Policy-Yrs	No. of Death Claims Observed	Expected*	Mortality Ratio Interval	Cumulative	Survival Ratio Interval	Cumulative	Excess Death Rate
i	t to t + Δ t	E	d	d'	100 d/d'	100 $\sum$d/$\sum$d'	100 p_i/p_i'	100 P/P'	1000(d-d')/E
Prostatectomy									
1	0- 5 yrs	732	12	6.87	175%	175%	96.5%	96.5%	7.0
2	5-10	376	12	7.63	157	166	94.2	90.9	12
3	10-17	154	12	5.81	207	177	74.2	67.5	40
Disorders of Prostate									
1	0-10 yrs	1054	5	8.88	56%	56%	103.8%	103.8%	−3.7
2	10-17	138	5	4.19	119	77	95.9	99.6	5.9

Table 670b   Derived Mortality and Survival Data

Interval No.	Start-End	Observed Rates Average Annual Mortality	Survival	Cumulative Survival	Mortality	Expected Rates* Average Annual Mortality	Survival	Cumulative Survival	Mortality
i	t to t + Δ t	$\bar{q}$ = d/E	$\bar{p}$	P	Q	$\bar{q}'$ = d'/E	$\bar{p}'$	P'	Q'
Prostatectomy									
1	0- 5 yrs	.0164	.9836	.9206	.0794	.0094	.9906	.9539	.0461
2	5-10	.0319	.9681	.7829	.2171	.0203	.9797	.8609	.1391
3	10-17	.0779	.9221	.4438	.5562	.0377	.9623	.6579	.3421
Disorders of Prostate									
1	0-10 yrs	.0047	.9953	.9540	.0460	.0084	.9916	.9190	.0810
2	10-17	.0362	.9638	.7371	.2629	.0304	.9696	.7403	.2597

Table 670c   Comparative Experience by Age Group - Substandard Males, All Durations Combined

Age Group	Exposure Policy-Yrs	No. of Death Claims Observed	Expected*	Mortality Ratio	Ave. Ann. Mort. Rate	Est. 8-Yr Surv. Rate	Est. 8-Yr Surv. Index	Excess Death Rate
	E	d	d'	100 d/d'	$\bar{q}$ = d/E	P = (1-$\bar{q}$)^8	100 P/P'	1000(d-d')/E
Prostatectomy								
15-59	675	16	6.52	245%	.0237	.8255	89.2%	14
60 up	587	20	13.79	145	.0341	.7577	91.7	11
All Ages	1262	36	20.31	177	.0285	.7934	90.3	12
Disorders of Prostate								
15-59	847	4	5.32	75%	.0047	.9630	101.3%	−1.6
60 up	345	6	7.75	77	.0174	.8690	104.3	−5.1
All Ages	1192	10	13.07	77	.0084	.9347	102.1	−2.6

Table 670d   Mortality by Cause of Death - Substandard Cases (Prostatectomy)

Cause	No. of Death Claims Observed	Expected†	Mortality Ratio	Excess Death Rate
Malignant Neoplasms	13	4.84	270%	6.5
Diseases of the Heart and Circulatory System	9	7.99	113	0.8
Accidents and Homicides	0	2.79	0	−2.2
Suicide	0	0.86	0	−0.7
All other Causes and Unknown	14●	3.83	365	8.0
Total	36	20.31	177	12.4

* Basis of expected mortality: 1955-60 Select Basic Table

† Distribution of total expected deaths by Intercompany Medically Examined Std. Issues 1965-70

● Includes 4 cerebrovascular accidents

GENITOURINARY DISEASES

§699–GENITOURINARY DISORDERS–INSURED LIVES (MISCELLANEOUS)

References: (1) T. W. Preston and R. D. Clarke, "An Investigation into the Mortality of Impaired Lives During the Period 1947-63," J. Inst. Act., 92:27-74 (1966)

(2) A. Svensson and S. Astrand, "Substandard Risk Mortality in Sweden 1955-1965," Coopération Internationale pour les Assurances des Risques Aggravés. (See Rome Conference proceedings, 1969.)

(3) "New York Life Single Medical Impairment Study - 1972," unpublished report made available by J. J. Hutchinson and J. C. Sibigtroth (1973).

Subjects Studied: (1) Policyholders of Prudential Assurance Co., London, England, issued insurance 1947-1963 followed to 12/31/63. Both standard and substandard issues were included. Applicants with two or more ratable impairments were generally excluded.

(2) Lives reinsured (mostly on a substandard basis) with Sverige Reinsurance Co., Sweden, placed in force prior to 1955 and observed between anniversaries in 1955 and 1965.

(3) Policyholders of New York Life Insurance Co., issued insurance 1954-1970 followed to 1971 policy anniversary. Both standard and substandard issues were included. Applicants with more than one ratable impairment were excluded.

Follow-up: Insurance policy records formed the basis of entry, counting policies, exposures, and death claims, and of follow-up information.

Results: Table 699 contains the mortality and survival experience derived from the three insurance company studies with respect to insured subjects with histories of three disorders of the genital organs and of several disorders of the urinary system. There is considerable range in the results, mortality ratios running from 60 to 780 per cent. However, the significance of the rates and ratios in most of the categories is limited by reason of the small numbers in the experience.

Histories of benign prostate disorders, caesarian section and hysterectory show very favorable mortality results: mortality ratios were 65, 84 and 112 per cent, respectively, with comparably favorable EDR's. Results on urinary disorders show very wide variation. Experience is favorable on abnormal sediment, red cells only, (substandard males and females - 4 deaths); pyelitis and cystitis (males - 12 deaths); nephritis history (males - 10 deaths); renal calculus (males - 35 deaths); and other kidney disease, (standard and substandard males and females - 7 deaths). On this group, mortality ratios lie between 60 and 125 per cent, and excess death rates between −1.0 and 0.5 per 1000.

A moderate degree of extra mortality appeared in the case of albuminuria, trace (New York Life study, standard and substandard males and females - 16 deaths); albuminuria (Prudential of London report, males - 12 deaths); and abnormal sediment, white cells only (New York Life, males and females - 10 deaths). Mortality ratios in these groups were, respectively, 150, 147 and 166 per cent and EDR's, 1.7, 1.3, and 3.5 per 1000.

Relatively heavy mortality developed in the other disorders of the urinary system with mortality ratios ranging from 210 to 780 per cent and excess deaths, from 2.0 to 13 per 1000 per year. These included moderate and large amounts of albumin in the urine and history of albuminuria (New York Life), nephritis (New York Life and Sverige Reinsurance Co.) and nephrectomy (New York Life and Prudential of London). No details are available on the reasons for nephrectomy in these insurance applicants, but the New York Life study excluded cases coded for another ratable impairment (such as cancer of the kidney). It may also be presumed that cases with cancer of the uterus were excluded from the experience for women with a history of hysterectomy.

GENITOURINARY DISEASES

Table 699 Comparative Experience, Three Series of Insureds

Disease/Category (Ref.)	Sex/Age		Policies in Force at Start ℓ	Exposure Policy-Yrs E	No. of Death Claims Observed d	No. of Death Claims Expected* d'	Ave. Ann. Mort. Rate Observed q̄ = d/E	Ave. Ann. Mort. Rate Expected* q̄' = d'/E	Mortality Ratio 100 d/d'	Est. 5-Yr Surv. Rate P = (1 - q̄)⁵	Est. 5-Yr Surv. Index 100 P/P'	Excess Death Rate 1000(q̄-q̄')
Albuminuria (3)												
Trace S&SS†	M&F	40	—	3214	16	10.7	.0050	.0033	150%	.9754	99.2%	1.7
Moderate; Large Amt. SS	M&F	36	—	1184	11	2.49	.0093	.0021	440	.9544	96.5	7.2
History S&SS	M&F	35	—	415	6	0.77	.0145	.0019	780	.9298	93.8	13
Albuminuria (1)	M	41	609	3037	12	8.17	.0040	.0027	147	.9804	99.4	1.3
Abnormal Sediment (3)												
Casts only S&SS	M&F	46	—	528	8	3.00	.0152	.0057	265	.9265	95.3	9.5
Red Cells only S&SS	M&F	41	—	870	4	3.30	.0046	.0038	121	.9772	99.6	0.8
White Cells only SS	M&F	45	—	1142	10	6.02	.0088	.0053	166	.9570	98.3	3.5
Pyelitis & Pyelonephritis SS (3)	M&F	34	—	1621	6	2.71	.0037	.0017	220	.9816	99.0	2.0
Pyelitis & Cystitis (1)	M	40	1944	8477	12	19.9	.0014	.0024	60	.9929	100.5	-1.0
Nephritis SS (3)	M&F	33	—	1644	6	2.62	.0036	.0016	230	.9819	99.0	2.1
Nephritis, history (1)	M	39	813	3826	10	8.00	.0026	.0021	125	.9870	99.7	0.5
Nephritis, chronic (2)	M&F	41	—	3165	36	15.3	.0114	.0048	235	.9443	96.7	6.6
Nephrectomy SS (3)	M&F	39	—	3209	23	9.66	.0072	.0030	240	.9645	97.9	4.2
Nephrectomy (1)	M	40	479	2031	10	4.72	.0049	.0023	210	.9757	98.7	2.6
Renal Calculus (1)	M	42	2638	12348	35	39.7	.0028	.0032	88	.9861	100.2	-0.4
Kidney Disease, other S&SS (3)	M&F	36	—	2908	7	6.68	.0024	.0023	105	.9880	99.9	0.1
Prostate Disorders S&SS (3)	M	50	—	2989	16	24.8	.0054	.0083	65	.9735	101.5	-2.9
Caesarean Section SS (3)	F	34	—	9453	10	11.9	.0011	.0013	84	.9947	100.1	-0.2
Hysterectomy S&SS (3)	F	46	—	1577	6	5.34	.0038	.0034	112	.9811	99.8	0.4

* Basis of expected mortality: (Ref. 1) Prudential Assurance Co. (England) stardard lives mortality 1957-1958; (Ref. 2) Sverige Reins. Co., population mortality; M or F (Sweden), 1956-60 and 1961-65; (Ref. 3) N. Y. Life, Basic Select Tables (1955-60)

† "S" - Standard, "SS" - Substandard

Systemic Disorders

See Also

1. *1951 Impairment Study.* Chicago: Society of Actuaries (1954).
   H1-H2   Gout (p. 223).
   H3-H8   Arthritis (pp. 223-226).
   H9-H16 Anemia, secondary, found on examination (p. 226).
   J1-J4   Syphilis, once, thorough treatment (pp. 245-247).
   J5-J12 Tuberculosis, nonpulmonary, one attack (pp. 248-250).
   J13   Spinal Curvature, found on examination (pp. 249-252).
   J14   Poliomyelitis, with marked deformity, one attack, at any time prior to
           application (pp. 252-254).
   J15-J18 Osteomyelitis (pp. 256-258).
2. C.C. Dauer, R.F. Korns, and L.M. Schuman, *Infectious Diseases.* Cambridge, Mass.:
   Harvard University Press (1968).
3. W.J. Brown, J.F. Donohue, N.W. Axnick, J.H. Blount, N.W. Ewen, and O.C. Jones,
   Syphilis and Other Venereal Diseases, 2nd ed. Cambridge, Mass.: Harvard University
   Press (1973).
4. S. Cobb, *The Frequency of Rheumatic Diseases.* Cambridge, Mass.: Harvard University
   Press (1971).

BLOOD DISORDERS

§740–POLYCYTHEMIA VERA

References: (1) B. Modan and A. M. Lilienfeld, "Polycythemia Vera and Leukemia–The Role of Radiation Treatment," Medicine, 44:305-344 (1965).
(2) J. Perkins, M. C. G. Israëls, and J. F. Wilkinson, "Polycythaemia Vera: Clinical Studies on a Series of 127 Patients Managed without Radiation Therapy," Quart. J. Med., 33:499-518 (1964).
(3) J. H. Lawrence, H. S. Winchell, and W. G. Donald, "Leukemia in Polycythemia Vera," Ann. Int. Med., 70:763-771 (1969).
(4) K. E. Halnan and M. H. Russell, "Polycythaemia Vera," Lancet, 2:760-763 (1965).

Subjects Studied: (1) 268 white patients age 35 and up seen and treated during year of initial verified diagnosis of polycythemia vera (PV), selected from medical records rooms and hematological services of seven U.S. medical centers 1937-1955. Patients with diagnosis of leukemia and found to have PV and those referred at an advanced stage of the disease were excluded. The patients were allocated to four treatment groups: no radiation treatment, X-ray only, P^{32} only, and X-ray and P^{32}. Patients were further divided into the following three diagnostic groups for the purpose of comparison of the risk of developing leukemia: PV, polycythemia secondary to lung disease and questionable polycythemia. Sex and age distribution by diagnostic group was as follows for all patients studied (only 268 of 512 PV patients were seen and treated in the year of diagnosis):

Diagnostic Group	Male	Female	Total	Ave. Age
Polycythemia Vera	295	217	512	55.2
Questionable Polycythemia	383	93	476	54.0
Secondary Polycythemia	178	56	234	54.5
Total	856	366	1222	54.6

(2) 127 patients with polycythemia vera not treated by irradiation seen by members of the Department of Clinical Haematology of the University and Royal Infirmary at Manchester, England, 1938-June 1963. Criteria for inclusion were a red cell count persistently greater than six million per cu. mm., together with one or more of the following: splenomegaly, leucocytosis (more than 12,000 white cells per cu. mm.). There were 72 male and 55 female patients distributed by sex and age as follows:

Age Group at Onset (Years)

	21-30	31-40	41-50	51-60	61-70	71-80	81+	Total	Mean Age
Male	5	6	13	30	13	4	1	72	53.2 yrs
Female	0	4	9	15	25	2	0	55	57.8
Total	5	10	22	45	38	6	1	127	55.2

(3) 181 patients with diagnosed PV treated with P^{32} or P^{32} and X-ray, at the Donner Laboratory, Berkeley, California, starting in 1939 and all dying prior to the end of follow-up. Before 1949, the diagnosis of polycythemia vera was based on a sustained elevation of red cell count in excess of 7 million cells per cu. mm., without apparent cause and an associated elevated white cell count as splenomegaly. After 1949 diagnosis of PV was based on an increased circulating red cell volume (more than 34 ml./kg. body weight) and a normal arterial oxygen saturation.

(4) 107 patients, 64 males and 43 females, who had received radiation therapy for PV at Christie Hospital, Manchester, England, during 1944-1962. The diagnostic criteria were similar to those used by Perkins, et al., together with a raised hemaglobin concentration (over 120 per cent), unless there had been a loss of blood or iron deficiency, and at least one of splenomegaly, leucocytosis or thrombocytosis. These patients were compared to 117 of the non-irradiated patients of Reference 2 (Perkins, et al.) who were seen 1944-1962. Radiation therapy in the Series 4 patients consisted of X-ray only prior to 1949, and P^{32} in 95 patients from 1949 on, some also receiving X-ray or chemotherapy. Age and sex distributions were as follows:

Age:	Under 35 Yrs	35-44	45-54	55-64	65 up	Total
Males	1	5	18	31	9	64
Females	3	2	7	21	10	43

POLYCYTHEMIA VERA

Table 740a Observed Data and Comparative Experience by Duration and Type of Treatment (Series 1)

Interval		No. of Patients	Exposure Person-Yrs	No. of Deaths		Mortality Ratio		Survival Ratio		Excess Death Rate
No.	Start-End			Observed	Expected*	Interval	Cumulative	Interval	Cumulative	
i	t to t + Δ t	ℓ	E	d	d'	100 d/d'	100$\sum$d/$\sum$d'	100p_i/p_i'	100 P/P'	1000(d-d')/E
No Radiation Treatment										
1	0- 2 yrs	99	187.0	17	3.70	460%	460%	86.2%	86.2%	71
2	2- 5	82	221.0	17	5.24	325	380	84.9	73.2	53
3	5-10	63	261.0	23	8.04	285	335	70.4	51.4	57
4	10-15	39	87.5	9	3.61	250	320	75.2	38.8	62
	0-15	99	756.5	66	20.59	320			38.8	60
With P^{32} Radiation Treatment										
1	0- 2 yrs	102	202.0	5	4.30	116%	116%	99.3%	99.3%	3.5
2	2- 5	97	278.0	15	7.09	210	176	91.3	90.7	28
3	5-10	82	340.5	24	11.24	215	194	80.2	72.7	27
4	10-15	35	78.5	12	3.45	350	215	48.2	35.1	109
	0-15	102	899.0	56	26.08	215			35.1	33

Table 740b Derived Mortality and Survival Data (Series 1)

Interval		Observed Rates				Expected Rates*			
		Survival			Ave. Ann. Mortality	Survival			Ave. Ann. Mortality
No.	Start-End	Cumulative	Interval	Ave. Ann.		Cumulative	Interval	Ave. Ann.	
i	t to t + Δ t	P	p_i	$\breve{p}$	$\breve{q}$	P'	p_i'	$\breve{p}$'	$\breve{q}$'
No Radiation Treatment									
1	0- 2 yrs	.828	.828	.910	.090	.9608	.9608	.9802	.0198
2	2- 5	.654	.790	.924	.076	.8940	.9305	.9763	.0237
3	5-10	.393	.602	.903	.097	.7644	.8550	.9692	.0308
4	10-15	.240	.609	.906	.094	.6192	.8100	.9587	.0413
With P^{32} Radiation Treatment									
1	0- 2 yrs	.951	.951	.975	.025	.9579	.9579	.9787	.0213
2	2- 5	.804	.845	.946	.054	.8865	.9255	.9745	.0255
3	5-10	.545	.678	.925	.075	.7496	.8456	.9670	.0330
4	10-15	.210	.385	.826	.174	.5990	.7991	.9561	.0439

Table 740c Comparative Experience by Attained Age (Series 2)

Attained Age	Exposure Person-Yrs	No. of Deaths		Mortality Ratio	Ave. Ann. Mort. Rate		Est. 5-Yr Surv. Index	Excess Death Rate
		Observed	Expected*		Observed	Expected*		
(Yrs)	E	d	d'	100 d/d'	$\bar{q}$	$\bar{q}$'	100 P/P'	1000(d-d')/E
Not Irradiated								
Under 55	176.0	7	1.07	655%	.040	.0061	84.1%	34
55-64	185.5	10	3.51	285	.054	.0189	83.3	35
65 up	218.5	27	10.39	260	.124	.0476	65.8	76
All Ages	580.0	44	14.97	295	.076	.0258	76.8	50

*Bases of expected mortality: Series 1 — U.S. White Males and Females 1949-51;
Series 2 — 1960 Report of Registrar General (Great Britain)

BLOOD DISORDERS

§740–POLYCYTHEMIA VERA (continued):

Follow-up: (1) In this series 98.4 per cent of the patients were followed through December 31, 1961 by means of information from local physicians, questionnaires directly to patients reported alive, and from hospital records. Information with respect to deaths was found from autopsy records or from death certificates.

(2) All except three patients were traced until the time of death or June 30, 1963; data regarding deaths were obtained from the Registrar-General's Office.

(3) Patients were followed to death with information primarily from the referring physician and postmortem examination.

(4) All patients were followed to 1963 or until death through information from referring physicians and death certificates. Causes of deaths were critically examined if there was a long interval between last attendance at hospital and death.

Results: Comparative experience by duration is presented in Tables 740a-b for Series 1 patients with confirmed polycythemia vera seen and treated during the year of diagnosis. These patients constituted a subgroup, 268 out of a total of 512 patients with confirmed polycythemia vera. Furthermore, 67 patients receiving X-ray, alone or in combination with P^{32} were excluded, leaving 102 patients treated with P^{32} alone and 99 patients who received no radiation treatment. These are the groups reported in the tables. The average annual excess death over the 15 years of observation was 60 per 1000 for patients receiving no radiation, and 33 per 1000 for patients treated with P^{32}, a radioactive isotope (beta Emitter) with a half-life of 14.3 days, administered as a phosphate salt, with total dose from 5 to more than 60 millicuries, depending on number of treatments. In all intervals within the first 10 years the mortality ratios and EDR's were lower in the irradiated than in the non-irradiated patients. However, during the interval from 10 to 15 years after the diagnosis and beginning of treatment the reverse was true: mortality ratios of 350 and 250 per cent, respectively, in the treated and untreated groups, with corresponding EDR's of 109 and 62 per 1000 per year. The 15-year survival ratios were relatively close, at 38.8 per cent in the untreated, and 35.1 per cent in the treated group.

Comparative experience by age, all durations combined, is available in Table 740c for the patients of Series 2, and in the top part of Table 740d for Series 1. In both series the youngest patients who did not receive radiation therapy had the best prognosis: excess death rates of 34 and 30 per 1000 in Series 2 and Series 1, respectively. EDR's increased with age, although not as markedly in Series 2 as in Series 1, but mortality ratios decreased with age, from 655 to 260 per cent in Series 2 and from 505 to 280 per cent in Series 1. The increase in EDR in Series 2 was from the aforementioned 34 per 1000 to 76 per 1000 in the group age 65 and up, and in Series 1, from 30 to 139 per 1000. Cumulative survival ratios which also decreased with advancing age, are not comparable in the two groups, because the 66 per cent in Series 2 have been estimated over a much shorter average follow-up of 4.6 in Table 740d. Mortality ratios decreased sharply, from 850 per cent in patients under age 50 to 290 per cent in those age 50-64 and to 230 per cent in those age 65 years and up. The corresponding EDR's in these three age groups were 55, 48 and 101 per 1000, respectively. The excess death rate of 55 per 1000 in the youngest age group is not only higher than the 48 per 1000 in the next older age group, but also higher than the level of 30 per 1000 in the youngest patients who did not receive P^{32}; however, there were relatively few patients under age 50. For the older patients and the treatment groups as a whole EDR's were higher in those not receiving radiation than in those treated with P^{32}.

Comparative experience by duration for Series 3 patients treated with P^{32} shows an increase in mortality ratio from 210 to 355 per cent, and a fivefold increase in EDR from 20 to 105 per 1000, from the first interval (0-5 years) to the last (10-15 years). This pattern is similar to the one shown in Table 740a for patients receiving P^{32}. The final results shown in Table 740d are based on Series 4 patients treated with P^{32} over a 10-year period, with a reworking of data by duration on most of the Series 2 patients, who received no radiation. Mortality ratios in patients given P^{32} decreased from 445 to 250 per cent, and EDR's also decreased 50 to 40 per 1000. This trend is very different from the one observed in the P^{32} patients of Series 1 (Table 740a), but the highest EDR in Series 1 was encounted at 10-15 years, beyond the 10-year limit of follow-up in Series 4. The only experience differentiated by sex is from the Series 4 data. Mortality ratios for females were higher than for males in both treatment categories. In patients receiving no radiation EDR was also higher in females, 71 vs. 45 per 1000, averaged over seven years. However, the reverse was true in patients receiving P^{32}. EDR was 54 per 1000 in females and 72 per 1000 in males. When males and females were combined both mortality ratio and the excess death rate were substantially higher in the patients with no radiation than for those receiving P^{32}, a result similar to that in Series 1.

POLYCYTHEMIA VERA

§740–POLYCYTHEMIA VERA (continued):

Comment: A major question considered in some of these studies was the extent to which leukemia occurred as a cause of death, in patients treated with radiation, especially P^{32}. A highly significant proportion of the deaths was due to acute or chronic leukemia in the P^{32} cases of PV in Series 1 and Series 3, whereas leukemia deaths were infrequent in patients receiving no radiation therapy. The original articles should be consulted for a lengthy analysis of the evidence on this question. On the other hand, Halnan and Russell (Reference 4) reported no deaths due to leukemia in their Series 4 patients treated with P^{32}.

Table 740d   Comparative Experience, Different Series

Series	Treatment (Total No. Pts.)	Group	Interval Start-End	Cumulative Surv. Rate Observed	Cumulative Surv. Rate Expected*	Survival Ratio	Ave. Ann. Mort. Rate Observed	Ave. Ann. Mort. Rate Expected*	Mortality Ratio	Excess Death Rate
			Yrs t to t + Δt	P	P′	100 P/P′	$\breve{q}$	$\breve{q}'$	100 $\breve{q}$/$\breve{q}'$	1000($\breve{q}$-$\breve{q}'$)
1	No. Rad. (99 pts)	Under 50	0-13 yrs	.611	.9096	67.2%	.037	.0073	505%	30
		50-64	0-13	.271	.7143	37.9	.096	.0255	375	71
		65 up	0-13	.043	.3564	12.1	.215	.0763	280	139
1	P^{32} (102 pts)	Under 50	0-13 yrs	.434	.9096	47.7%	.062	.0073	850%	55
		50-64	0-13	.368	.7143	51.5	.074	.0255	290	48
		65 up	0-13	.080	.3564	22.4	.177	.0763	230	101
3	P^{32} (181 pts)	All Ages	0- 5 yrs	.818	.9109	89.8%	.039	.0185	210%	20
			5-10	.532	.7934	67.1	.082	.0272	300	55
			10-15	.241	.6439	37.4	.146	.0409	355	105
			0-15	.241	.6439	37.4	.091	.0289	315	62
4	No Rad. (117 pts)	All Ages	0- 2 yrs	.870	.9738	89.3%	.067	.0132	510%	54
			2- 5	.733	.9257	79.2	.056	.0167	335	39
			5-10	.344	.8189	42.0	.140	.0242	580	116
			0-10	.344	.8189	42.0	.101	.0198	510	81
		All Male	0- 7	.630	.8735	72.1	.064	.0191	335	45
		All Female	0- 7	.543	.9120	59.5	.084	.0131	640	71
4	P^{32} (107 pts)	All Ages	0- 2 yrs	.876	.9714	90.2%	.064	.0144	445%	50
			2- 5	.724	.9189	78.8	.062	.0183	340	44
			5-10	.514	.8041	63.9	.066	.0263	250	40
			0-10	.514	.8041	63.9	.064	.0216	295	42
		All Male	0- 7	.500	.8552	58.5	.094	.0221	425	72
		All Female	0- 7	.619	.9171	67.5	.066	.0123	535	54

*Bases of expected mortality: Series 1 — U.S. White Males and Females 1949-51
Series 3 — U.S. White Males and Females 1949-51
Series 4 — Great Britain Population 1958

SARCOIDOSIS

§780–SARCOIDOSIS

References: (1) D. T. Carr and R. P. Gage, "The Prognosis of Sarcoidosis," Am. Rev. Tuberculosis, 69:78-83 (1954).

(2a) K. Viskum and K. Thygesen, "Vital Prognosis in Intrathoracic Sarcoidosis," Scand. J. Respir. Dis., 53:181-186 (1972).

(2b) K. Thygesen and K. Viskum, "Manifestations and Course of the Disease in Intrathoracic Sarcoidosis," Scand. J. Repir. Dis., 53:174-180 (1972).

(3) A. Z. Keller, "Hospital, Age, Racial, Occupational, Geographical, Clinical and Survivorship Characteristics in the Epidemiology of Sarcoidosis," Am. J. Epidemiol., 94:222-230 (1971).

Subjects Studied: (1) 194 patients studied at the Mayo Clinic from 1940 through 1951 with a biopsy typical of sarcoidosis and "without any other explanation for the disease." A positive reaction was found in 19.3 per cent of 119 of the patients who had been given a tuberculin test. The mean age of 76 males was 39.7 years with a range of 9 to 70 years; the mean age of 118 females was 42.1, with a range of 12 to 78 years. Only 9 of the patients were blacks, but this is approximately 10 times the frequency of blacks in the patient population of the Mayo Clinic.

(2) 254 patients admitted to the Bispebjerg Hospital, Copenhagen in the period from 1954 through 1970, with abnormal chest X-ray diagnosed as sarcoidosis (53 per cent asymptomatic). Age and sex distribution was as follows:

Age	10-19	20-29	30-39	40-49	50-59	60 up	Total
Male	13	49	22	20	14	9	127
Female	26	54	27	12	7	1	127

(3) 420 patients with diagnosis of sarcoidosis verified by review of histological specimens, from a total of 643 patients admitted to all Veterans Administration hospitals from 1960 through 1964 with a clinical diagnosis of sarcoidosis. All patients were male, 234 blacks and 186 whites, the incidence of admissions with this diagnosis being five times as high in blacks as in whites. Blacks tended to be younger than the white patients (mean age 36.3 vs. 40.9 years), with an age distribution as follows:

	Age Under 30	30-39	40-49	50-59	60 up	Total
Black	66	108	45	7	8	234
White	29	74	49	14	20	186

Follow-up: (1) Follow-up information was obtained by subsequent examinations at the Mayo Clinic and was carried to January 1, 1953. Ninety per cent of the patients with a follow-up of five years were successfully traced.

(2) Patients were traced during 1971 through the Danish National Register. Information on deaths was compiled from death certificates and hospital records. The average observation period was 7.4 years and only 4 patients could not be traced.

(3) Follow-up through V.A. records was terminated on December 31, 1968 with a total of 56 deaths recorded. Actuarial methods were used in the computation of cumulative survival rates.

DISEASES OF UNKNOWN CAUSE

§780–SARCOIDOSIS (continued)

Results: Comparative experience of the Mayo Clinic study is presented in Table 780a. Average annual mortality rates and indices have been derived from cumulative survival rates at 3, 5, 7 and 10 years from entry, calculated by the ad hoc method on patients fully traced for these durations. Mortality ratios thus calculated were in a range from 181 to 300 per cent, and excess death rates between 7 and 15 extra deaths per 1000 per year. These must be regarded as averages on an annual basis over successively longer fractions of a ten-year period of observation. Little can be said about interval rates, because of the small numbers of deaths and the overlapping of the follow-up periods. Only 17 deaths in toto were reported.

The Danish experience on patients with intrathoracic sarcoidosis is summarized in Table 780b for three five-year duration intervals, based on actuarial calculations involving 29 deaths. Interval mortality ratios are somewhat higher than those in the Mayo Clinic study, lying in the range from 240 to 375 per cent, but values of EDR, 10 to 15 extra deaths per 1000 per year, are approximately the same. At 10 years the cumulative survival ratio was 87.8 per cent in the Danish series and 88.3 per cent in the Mayo Clinic series. Further data are given in Table 780c on the patients of the Danish series categorized by various associated findings. Somewhat higher mortality ratios were found in patients with pulmonary symptoms, abnormal spirometric tests, and longer histories (over one year), as compared with those lacking such findings, but the author states that none of the differences are statistically significant. Excess mortality was reported to be similar in male and female patients in both series.

Comparative five-year experience is developed in Table 780d from the V.A. patients, all of whom were men. The overall mortality ratio was 315 per cent and EDR 14 extra deaths per 1000 per year. The mortality ratio tended to decrease with advancing age; the excess death rate remained in a relatively narrow range between 9 and 14 extra deaths per 1000 per year in patients under age 55, but in the oldest age group was considerably higher, at 57 per 1000 per year. Excess mortality in black patients was about twice as high as in white patients, with respective mortality ratios of 390 and 220 per cent, and EDR's of 19 and 8.2 per 1000. Death certificates were available in 25 deaths, in 12 of which sarcoidosis was given as the underlying or an associated cause.

SARCOIDOSIS

Table 780a Comparative Experience, Mayo Clinic Patients (Series 1)

Duration from Entry	No. Traced Entrants	No. of Deaths	Cumulative Surv. Rate Observed*	Expected†	Cumulative Surv. Ratio	Ave. Ann. Mort. Rate Observed	Expected†	Mortality Ratio	Excess Death Rate
Δt	$\ell\text{-w}$	d	P	P'	100 P/P'	$\check{q}=1-\sqrt[\Delta t]{P}$	$\check{q}'=1-\sqrt[\Delta t]{P'}$	100 $\check{q}/\check{q}'$	1000($\check{q}-\check{q}'$)
3 yrs	134	9	.933	.977	95.5%	.023	.0077	300%	15
5 yrs	98	7	.929	.959	96.9	.015	.0083	181	6.7
7 yrs	55	6	.891	.940	94.8	.016	.0088	182	7.2
10 yrs	20	4	.800	.906	88.3	.022	.0098	225	12

Table 780b Comparative Experience, Danish Patients, by Duration (Series 2)

No.	Interval Start-End	Cumulative Surv. Rate Observed	Expected†	Cumulative Surv. Ratio	Observed Rates Int. Surv.	Ave. Ann. Mort.	Expected Rates† Int. Surv.	Ave. Ann. Mort.	Mortality Ratio	Excess Death Rate
i	t to t+Δt	P	P'	100 P/P'	p_i	$\check{q}=1-\sqrt[\Delta t]{p_i}$	p_i	$\check{q}'=1-\sqrt[\Delta t]{p_i}$,	100 $\check{q}/\check{q}'$	1000($\check{q}-\check{q}'$)
1	0- 5 yrs	.925	.979	94.5%	.925	.015	.979	.0042	355%	11
2	5-10 yrs	.838	.954	87.8	.906	.020	.974	.0053	375	15
3	10-15 yrs	.769	.921	83.5	.918	.017	.965	.0071	240	10

Table 780c Comparative Mortality, Danish Patients, by Clinical Findings (Series 2)

Characteristic	Factor Present or Positive No. of Pts. Traced	No. of Deaths Observed	Expected†	Mortality Ratio	Factor Absent or Negative No. of Pts. Traced	No. of Deaths Observed	Expected†	Mortality Ratio
	ℓ	d	d'	100 d/d'	ℓ	d	d'	100 d/d'
Positive Biopsy-Men	93	11	2.69	410%	32	4	0.94	425%
-Women	95	11	3.14	350	30	3	0.58	515
Total	188	22	5.83	375	62	7	1.52	460
Associated Symptoms	—	—	—	—	133	12	3.55	340
Erythema Nodosum	22	1	0.56	179	—	—	—	—
Pulmonary Symptoms	95	16	3.24	495	—	—	—	—
Abnormal Spirometry	46	14	2.41	580	175	12	4.31	280
Prior Duration>1 year	66	17	3.23	525	184	12	4.12	290

Table 780d Comparative 5-Year Experience, Verified Male V.A. Cases (Series 3)

Category	No. of Patients	5-Yr. Cum. Surv. Rate Observed	Expected†	Survival Ratio	Ave. Ann. Mort. Rate Observed	Expected†	Mortality Ratio	Excess Death Rate
	ℓ	P	P'	100 P/P'	$\check{q}$	$\check{q}'$	100 $\check{q}/\check{q}'$	1000($\check{q}-\check{q}'$)
White & Black								
Under Age 35 yrs	189	.9365	.9869	94.9%	.013	.0026	500%	10
Age 35-44 yrs	143	.9092	.9767	93.1	.019	.0047	405	14
Age 45-54 yrs	54	.9075	.9527	95.3	.019	.0096	198	9.4
Age 55 up	34	.6176	.8351	74.0	.092	.0354	260	57
All Ages	420	.8977	.9668	92.9	.021	.0067	315	14
White Patients	186	.9252	.9665	95.7	.015	.0068	220	8.2
Black Patients	234	.8760	.9671	90.6	.026	.0067	390	19

* Ad hoc method: Q = d/(ℓ-w) where ℓ-w = traced patients for entire duration. P = 1-Q
† Basis of expected mortality: Mayo Clinic patients (Series 1) — U.S. population rates; Danish patients (Series 2) — greater Copenhagen population rates 1961-65; V.A. patients (Series 3) — U.S. Male rates

DISEASES OF UNKNOWN CAUSE

§785–SURVIVAL OF CYSTIC FIBROSIS PATIENTS

References: (1) W. J. Warwick, R. E. Pogue, H. U. Gerber, and C. J. Nesbitt, "Survival Patterns in Cystic Fibrosis," J. Chron. Dis., 28:609-622 (1975).
(2) C. J. Nesbitt, additional data made available in personal communications (1974-75).

Subjects Studied: Children and young adults with cystic fibrosis (CF), registered through 97 clinical centers throughout the United States. These centers are supported by the Cystic Fibrosis Foundation. From these centers annual data are currently reported on a special form giving hospital or clinic code, name or initials of the patient, residence, date of birth, date of diagnosis, sex, race, single or multiple birth, complications at birth, status at the end of the year, and, in the event of death during the year, date and cause of death. An accounting of U.S. patients reported to the Registry during the years 1966-72 is given in Table 785a, including patients alive at the beginning and end of each year, deaths during the year, and various losses and additions. Of an aggregate of 15,212 patients thus reported to the Registry through 1972, 7,954 were male, 7,258 were female (sex not given in two patients); 14,734 were white; birth was reported normal in 13,196, but complicated by meconium ileus in 1,045 (6.9 per cent) and intestinal obstruction in 198 (severe early manifestations of the disease). An approximate age distribution of the cases can be made for age at diagnosis from the first interval exposure data in Table 785b, and for attained age from the exposure data in Table 785d.

Follow-up: Annual data reported by the clinical centers to the Registry were used for follow-up during the period 1966-1972. Prior exposure was excluded in patients in whom the diagnosis of CF had been made before their first clinic visit during this reporting period. In developing their life table data the authors have used the "force of mortality" concept, which involved calculating exposure as the aggregate of full or exact fractional years for all patients observed, *including those who died during the year of observation*. This results in an underestimate, by 2 to 3 per cent, of the exposure calculated by the customary actuarial method, in which subjects who die are regarded as being at risk until the end of the analysis year of death, regardless of the exact time at which death occurred during the year. Exposure data from the article have been used in Tables 785b-f without any attempt to adjust for this difference or the slight underestimate introduced in the calculation of d'. The authors' data for P calculated by the force of mortality formula (interval $p = e^{-\mu}$, where $\mu = d/E'$) have been used for the derived data in Tables 785c and 785e and for the survival ratios.

Results: Comparative experience by age at diagnosis and duration is given in Tables 785b-c. Male and female patients have been combined into three age groups: under 1 year, from 1-5 years, and from 5-10 years. Only patients with normal birth have been included. During the first two years after diagnosis the highest excess death rates were observed in infants under one year of age, about 35 per 1000 per year. There was essentially no change in rate for these infants in the interval 2-5 years, but EDR rose to 48 per 1000 at durations 5-10 years. Excess mortality in terms of EDR also increased with duration in the other age groups, reaching the very high level of 80 per 1000 at durations 10-13 years in the oldest group. Mortality ratios, in contrast to EDR, showed a maximum of 14,200 per cent at durations 2-5 years. In a reversal of the trend usually observed, mortality ratios *increased* with increasing age and duration in the two younger age groups. This trend is due to the fact that expected mortality rates decrease with age in infants and young children up to about age 11. This mortality rate in the first year of life, 18 per 1000, is far higher than in any other year of age in young or middle life, and this accounts for the extraordinarily low mortality ratio of 305 per cent in infant cystic fibrosis patients under one year of age, despite an EDR of 36 per 1000. With smaller EDR's the mortality ratio in the first two years of follow-up was 3800 per cent in patients aged 1-5 years at diagnosis, and 5200 per cent in those aged 5-10 years. The ten-year cumulative survival ratios accompanying these high levels of excess mortality were 66.1, 67.0, and 65.3 per cent, showing little variation in the three different age groups.

The committee responsible for actuarial analysis of the CF Registry data has also provided detailed results on the experience by attained age, combining all intervals since diagnosis for each year of attained age. These data and indices of comparative mortality and survival are presented in Tables 785d-e, on an annual basis under age 10, but in condensed form at ages 10-30. Cases with complications at birth (meconium ileus and intestinal obstruction) have again been excluded. Because of the pattern of expected mortality rates referred to above, changes in excess mortality are more easily evaluated in terms of EDR than mortality ratio. During the first year of life an EDR of 57 per 1000 was found,

CYSTIC FIBROSIS

Table 785a Summary of Cystic Fibrosis Registry Annual Reported Data 1966-72

Patient Category		1966	1967	1968	1969	1970	1971	1972	1967-72
No. Alive, Start of Year	ℓ_t	—	4515	5495	6362	7085	7738	8200	—
No. Alive, End of Year	ℓ_{t+1}	4515	5495	6362	7085	7738	8200	8149	8149
Deaths During Year	d	263	270	317	359	356	325	326	2216
Other Losses During Year									
Lost to Follow-up	u	169	119	172	228	202	168	191	1249
Transfers	w_1	342	319	294	323	428	332	351	2389
Unreported, Adjust.	w_2	838	13	13	159	198	334	553	2108
Total		1349	451	479	710	828	834	1095	5746
Additions During Year									
New Diagnosis	a_1	579	633	642	774	758	766	718	4870
Diagnosed Prior Yrs	a_2	5548	958	898	837	892	675	509	10317
Former Pts. Returned	a_3	0	110	123	181	187	180	143	924
Total		6127	1701	1663	1792	1837	1621	1370	16111
Exposure, Person-Years	E*	—	5140.0	6087.0	6903.0	7589.5	8131.5	8337.5	—
Ave. Ann. Mort. Rate	$\bar{q}=d/E$	—	.053	.052	.052	.047	.040	.039	—

Table 785b Observed Data and Comparative Experience by Age at Diagnosis and Duration, Male and Female, with Normal Birth

Age at Diagnosis	Interval		Exposure	No. of Deaths		Interval Mort. Ratio	Survival Ratio		Excess Death Rate
	No.	Start-End	Person-Yrs†	Observed	Expected●		Interval	Cumulative	
X	i	t to t+Δt	E'	d	d'	100 d/d'	100 p_i/p_i'	100 P/P'	1000(d-d')/E
0- 1 yr	1	0- 1 yr	1681.9	91	29.94	305%	96.4%	96.4%	36
	2	1- 2	1658.5	57	1.82	3100	96.7	93.3	33
	3	2- 5	4538.8	158	2.72	5800	90.4	84.2	34
	4	5-10	5512.0	267	2.20	12100	78.5	66.1	48
1- 5 yrs	1	0- 2 yrs	2953.9	67	1.77	3800	95.7	95.7	22
	2	2- 5	4002.4	130	1.60	8100	90.8	86.9	32
	3	5-10	4854.8	250	1.46	17100	77.0	67.0	51
5-10 yrs	1	0- 2 yrs	1152.9	24	0.46	5200	96.0	96.0	20
	2	2- 5	1592.5	68	0.48	14200	88.0	84.4	42
	3	5-10	1902.2	97	1.14	8500	77.3	65.3	50
	4	10-13	619.5	50	0.74	6800	78.6	51.3	80

Table 785c Derived Mortality and Survival Data

Age at Diagnosis	Interval		Observed Rates				Expected Rates●			
				Survival		Ave. Ann. Mort. Rate		Survival		Ave. Ann. Mort. Rate
	No.	Start-End	Cumulative	Interval	Ave. Ann.		Cumulative	Interval	Ave. Ann.	
X	i	t to t+Δt	P	p_i	$\check{p}$	$\check{q}$	P'	p_i'	$\check{p}'$	$\check{q}'$
0- 1 yrs	1	0- 1 yr	.947	.947	.947	.053	.9822	.9822	.9822	.0178
	2	1- 2	.915	.966	.966	.034	.9811	.9989	.9989	.0011
	3	2- 5	.825	.902	.966	.034	.9793	.9981	.9994	.0006
	4	5-10	.646	.783	.952	.048	.9773	.9980	.9996	.0004
1- 5 yrs	1	0- 2 yrs	.956	.956	.978	.022	.9989	.9989	.9994	.0006
	2	2- 5	.867	.907	.968	.032	.9976	.9987	.9996	.0004
	3	5-10	.667	.769	.949	.051	.9960	.9984	.9997	.0003
5-10 yrs	1	0- 2 yrs	.959	.959	.979	.021	.9992	.9992	.9996	.0004
	2	2- 5	.843	.879	.958	.042	.9984	.9991	.9997	.0003
	3	5-10	.650	.771	.949	.051	.9952	.9969	.9994	.0006
	4	10-13	.509	.783	.922	.078	.9915	.9963	.9988	.0012

* $E = \ell_t + \frac{1}{2}(a_1 + a_2 + a_3) - \frac{1}{2}(u + w_1 + w_2)$
† E' calculated from fractional years of exposure, each patient, including deaths
● Basis of expected mortality: U.S. Life Tables, White, Male and Female, 1969-71

DISEASES OF UNKNOWN CAUSE

§785—SURVIVAL OF CYSTIC FIBROSIS PATIENTS

Results (continued):

which then fell in the second year to the minimum level recorded, 24 extra deaths per 1000 per year. The generally progressive increase in excess mortality thereafter was reflected in an EDR of 30 to 35 per 1000 under age 5, about 45 per 1000 at ages 5-10, 50 per 1000 at ages 10-15, 61 per 1000 ages 15-20, 84 per 1000 ages 20-25 and 120 per 1000 ages 25-30. The mortality ratio was at a minimum, 420 per cent, in the first year after birth; rose to 2300 per cent the next year, then increased gradually to a maximum of 16,400 per cent at ages 10-12, decreased to 5700 per cent from ages 15-25, and rose again over age 25 to 8700 per cent. Slightly more than 50 per cent of children with cystic fibrosis survived to age 15, but the mortality toll exacted by the disease progressed relentlessly in young adults, as evidenced by the increasing levels of EDR to more than 100 per 1000, and a cumulative survival ratio at 30 years of 12.9 per cent.

Aggregate comparative experience by sex is given in Table 785f, where exposure and numbers of patients have been estimated from available data. Mortality was higher in females with CF, with an EDR of 56 per 1000 and mortality ratio of 21,000 per cent, as compared with an EDR of 38 per 1000 and mortality ratio of 9900 per cent in males. Three-year survival indexes were 88.9 and 84.2 per cent, respectively, for males and females.

The annual follow-up data in Table 785a have been used to estimate average annual mortality rates for all reported patients, with exposure by conventional actuarial calculations. These data appear to show a reduction in mortality during the observation period, with a mortality rate about .052 in 1967-1969, .047 in 1970, and about .040 in 1971-1972. If age distribution and other factors are comparable from year to year this trend suggests that improved medical management of the disease has resulted in a lowered mortality.

CYSTIC FIBROSIS

Table 785d Comparative Experience 1966-72 by Attained Age, Excluding
Cases with Maconium Ileus or Intestinal Obstruction at Birth

Attained Age	Exposure Person-Yrs*	No. of Deaths Observed	No. of Deaths Expected†	Mortality Ratio	Survival Ratio Interval	Survival Ratio Cumulative	Excess Death Rate
	E'	d	d'	100 d/d'	100 p_i/p_i'	100 P/P'	1000(d-d')/E
0- 1 yr	1018.6	76	18.13	420%	94.5%	94.5%	57
1- 2 yrs	2000.8	50	2.16	2300	97.6	92.2	24
2- 3	2419.6	74	1.79	4100	97.1	89.6	30
3- 4	2671.5	81	1.68	4800	97.1	87.0	30
4- 5	2739.0	96	1.42	6800	96.5	83.9	35
5- 6	2807.2	88	1.29	6800	97.0	81.4	31
6- 7	2841.5	109	1.22	8900	96.2	78.4	38
7- 8	2787.2	127	1.09	11700	95.6	74.9	45
8- 9	2643.9	130	0.95	13700	95.2	71.4	49
9-10	2459.4	107	0.79	13500	95.7	68.4	43
10-12	4303.2	212	1.29	16400	90.7	61.9	49
12-15	4964.3	249	2.48	10000	86.2	53.4	50
15-20	4816.7	301	5.30	5700	73.1	39.1	61
20-25	1633.9	139	2.45	5700	66.5	26.0	84
25-30	371.2	45	0.52	8700	49.5	12.9	120

Table 785e Derived Mortality and Survival Data

Attained Age	Observed Rates Survival Cumulative	Observed Rates Survival Interval	Observed Rates Survival Ave. Ann.	Observed Rates Ave. Ann. Mortality	Expected Rates† Survival Cumulative	Expected Rates† Survival Interval	Expected Rates† Survival Ave. Ann.	Expected Rates† Ave. Ann. Mortality
	P	p_i	$\check{p}$	$\check{q}$	P'	p_i'	$\check{p}'$	$\check{q}'$
0- 1 yr	.928	.928	.928	.072	.9822	.9822	.9822	.0178
1- 2 yrs	.905	.975	.975	.025	.9811	.9989	.9989	.0011
2- 3	.878	.970	.970	.030	.9804	.9993	.9993	.0007
3- 4	.852	.970	.970	.030	.9798	.9994	.9994	.0006
4- 5	.822	.965	.965	.035	.9793	.9995	.9995	.0005
5- 6	.797	.970	.970	.030	.9788	.9995	.9995	.0005
6- 7	.767	.962	.962	.038	.9784	.9996	.9996	.0004
7- 8	.733	.956	.956	.044	.9780	.9996	.9996	.0004
8- 9	.698	.952	.952	.048	.9776	.9996	.9996	.0004
9-10	.668	.957	.957	.043	.9773	.9997	.9997	.0003
10-12	.605	.906	.952	.048	.9768	.9994	.9997	.0003
12-15	.521	.861	.951	.049	.9755	.9986	.9995	.0005
15-20	.379	.727	.938	.062	.9701	.9945	.9989	.0011
20-25	.250	.660	.920	.080	.9630	.9927	.9985	.0015
25-30	.123	.492	.868	.132	.9564	.9932	.9986	.0014

Table 785f Comparative Experience 1966-72 by Sex, All Ages and Durations Combined,
Excluding Cases with Birth Complications

Sex	Est. No. Patients	Est. Exposure Person-Yrs*	No. of Deaths Observed	No. of Deaths Expected†	Mortality Ratio	Ave. Ann. Mort. Rate	Est. 3-Yr Surv. Rate	Est. 3-Yr Surv. Index	Excess Death Rate
	ℓ	E'	d	d'	100 d/d'	$\bar{q} = d/E'$	$P = (1-\bar{q})^3$	100 P/P'	$1000(\bar{q}-\bar{q}')$
Male	6902	22149	859	8.64	9900%	.039	.888	88.9%	38
Female	6294	18342	1025	4.95	21000	.056	.841	84.2	56
Total	13196	40491	1884	13.59	13900	.047	.867	86.8	46

* E' calculated from fractional years of exposure, each patient, including deaths
† Basis of expected mortality: U.S. Life Tables, White Male and Female, 1969-71

BONE AND JOINT DISORDERS

§801–RHEUMATOID ARTHRITIS

Reference: J. Uddin, A. S. Kraus, and H. G. Kelly, "Survivorship and Death in Rheumatoid Arthritis," Arthritis and Rheumatism, 13:125-130 (1970).

Subjects Studied: Patients with probable, definite or classic rheumatoid arthritis entered in the Queen's University (Kingston, Ontario) Rheumatic Diseases registry between 1954 and 1966. Of the 475 subjects (151 males, 324 females), approximately one third required no hospital care in this period. Life-years of exposure in this study were distributed by age and sex as follows:

	Under 50 Years	50-59 Years	60 Years Up	Total
Male	159 (28%)	138.5 (24%)	272 (48%)	569.5 (100%)
Female	389.5 (30%)	304 (23%)	622 (47%)	1315.5 (100%)
Total	548.5 (29%)	442.5 (24%)	894 (47%)	1885 (100%)

Follow-up: The number of patients, alive, dead or lost to follow-up in each successive year of the study period was determined by correspondence or interview with patients, relatives, physicians or other interested persons. Thirty-four patients (7 per cent) were lost to follow-up.

Results: As shown in Table 801b, during the entire period reported, 39 men and 55 women died, these deaths representing 198 per cent and 181 per cent of general population experience, respectively. Comparative 5-year survival indexes over the entire period of observation (1954-1966) show a decrease with age; the average index is 83.8 per cent for males and 90.7 per cent for females. Mortality ratios also tend to decrease with age at time of registration (except for males under 50 years of age, where experience was scant with only one death). Excess death rates, however, increase with age, such rates for males being roughly double those of female patients.

Results for the 10-year period by duration for all ages combined are given in Tables 801c and d. Mortality ratios among men declined somewhat over the period, while those among women showed a moderate increase. Excess deaths per 1000 revealed similar progressions for the two sexes — for men, the EDR dropped from 45 per year in the first two years to 38 in the 6-10 year interval with a dip in the intervening years to 14 per 1000 per year; for women, EDR's increased over the three intervals from 15 to 18 to 27.

The numbers of deaths observed among subjects of the study attributable to various significant causes were compared with those expected in the general population (Table 801a). Nineteen deaths from infection occurred among subjects as compared with only 1.29 expected from this cause in the general population. Relatively small numbers died from neoplastic disease, renal failure, respiratory insufficiency and gastrointestinal disease. In eight instances, the cause of death could not be determined.

Table 801a   Comparative Mortality by Cause of Death

Cause of Death	Male (569.5 person-years) No. of Deaths			Female (1315.5 person-years) No. of Deaths		
	Observed	Expected*	EDR	Observed	Expected*	EDR
	d	d′	1000(d-d′)/E	d	d′	1000(d-d′)/E
Cardiac	12	9.63	4.2	20	12.70	5.6
Infectious	9	0.52	15	10	0.77	7.0
Thromboembolic	3	2.40	1.1	14	6.27	5.9
Neoplastic	3	2.46	1.0	4	1.94	1.6
Other & Unknown	12	4.81	13	7	8.75	−1.3
Total	39	19.82	34	55	30.43	19

*Basis of expected mortality: Ontario death rates 1961

RHEUMATOID ARTHRITIS

Table 801b   Comparative Experience by Age — All Durations Combined (Entire Period of Observation)

Sex/Age	Exposure Person-Yrs	Deaths Obs.	Deaths Exp.*	Ave. Annual Mort. Rate Observed	Ave. Annual Mort. Rate Expected	Mortality Ratio	Est. 5-Yr Surv. Rate Observed	Est. 5-Yr Surv. Rate Expected*	Est. 5-Yr Surv. Index	Excess Death Rate
	E	d	d′	$\bar{q} = d/E$	$\bar{q}′ = d′/E$	$100\,d/d′$	$P = (1-\bar{q})^5$	$P′ = (1-\bar{q}′)^5$	$100\,P/P′$	$1000(d-d′)/E$
Male										
<50 yrs	159	1	0.60	.006	.0038	167%	.969	.9813	98.7%	2.5
50-59	138.5	6	1.84	.043	.0133	325	.801	.9353	85.7	30
60 up	272	32	17.3	.118	.0636	185	.535	.7199	74.3	54
All	569.5	39	19.7	.068	.0346	198	.703	.8386	83.8	34
Female										
<50 yrs	389.5	4	0.82	.010	.0021	490	.950	.9895	96.0	8.2
50-59	304	6	2.71	.020	.0089	220	.905	.9562	94.7	11
60 up	622	45	26.9	.072	.0432	167	.687	.8017	85.7	29
All	1315.5	55	30.4	.042	.0231	181	.807	.8897	90.7	19

Table 801c   Observed Data and Comparative Experience by Duration — All Ages Combined

Interval No. Start-End	Exposure Person-Yrs	Deaths in Interval Obs.	Deaths in Interval Exp.*	Mortality Ratio Interval	Mortality Ratio Cumulative	Survival Ratio Interval	Survival Ratio Cumulative	Excess Death Rate
i t to t + Δt	E	d	d′	$100\,d/d′$	$100\,Q/Q′$	$100\,p_i/p_i′$	$100\,P/P′$	$1000(d-d′)/E$
Male (151)								
1 0- 2 yrs	239	18	7.21	250%	250%	91.1%	91.1%	45
2 2- 5	213.5	11	7.99	138	191	96.4	87.7	14
3 5-10	114	9	4.62	195	192	94.9	83.2	38
Female (324)								
1 0- 2 yrs	540.5	20	11.95	167	167	97.2	97.2	15
2 2- 5	496	20	10.92	183	175	94.1	91.4	18
3 5-10	275	15	7.55	199	181	81.4	74.4	27

Table 801d   Derived Mortality and Survival Data

Sex	Interval No. Start-End	Observed Rates Cumulative Survival	Observed Rates Interval Survival	Observed Rates Geom. Mean Ann. Surv.	Observed Rates Geom. Mean Ann. Mort.	Expected Rates* Cumulative Survival	Expected Rates* Interval Survival	Expected Rates* Geom. Mean Ann. Surv.	Expected Rates* Geom. Mean Ann. Mort.
	i t to t + Δt	P	p_i	$\breve{p}_i$	$\breve{q}_i$	P′	$p_i′$	$\breve{p}_i′$	$\breve{q}_i′$
Male	1 0- 2 yrs	.857	.857	.926	.074	.9410	.9410	.9701	.0299
	2 2- 5	.735	.858	.950	.050	.8380	.8905	.9621	.0379
	3 5-10	.561	.763	.947	.053	.6740	.8043	.9574	.0426
Female	1 0- 2 yrs	.929	.929	.964	.036	.9560	.9560	.9778	.0222
	2 2- 5	.818	.881	.959	.041	.8950	.9362	.9783	.0217
	3 5-10	.584	.714	.935	.065	.7850	.8771	.9741	.0259

* Basis of expected mortality: Ontario death rates 1961

BONE AND JOINT DISORDERS

§802—ARTHRITIS IN INSUREDS

Reference: "New York Life Single Medical Impairment Study—1972," unpublished report made available by J.J. Hutchinson and J.C. Sibigtroth (1973).

Subjects Studied: Policyholders of New York Life Insurance Company issued insurance in 1954-1970, followed to the 1971 policy anniversary. The experience reported is for cases with rheumatoid, infectious, or atrophic arthritis. Only the substandard cases have been analyzed here. Cases involving more than one ratable impairment were excluded.

Follow-up: Insurance policy records formed the basis of entry, of counting policies, exposure and death claims, and of follow-up information.

Results: Comparative experience is given in Tables 802a-b for substandard cases by sex and duration, all ages combined. Among males, the mortality ratio showed no trend by duration, ranging between 355 and 194 per cent, with the EDR highest (21 per 1000) at 10-17 years. Among females, the mortality ratio was 270 per cent for the first 5 years and 370 per cent at 5-17 years, with the higher EDR of 14 per 1000 at 5-17 years. The cumulative survival ratio at 17 years was 81.3 per cent for males and 82.8 per cent for females.

From Table 802c, the overall mortality ratio was significantly high for both males and females, being 300 and 330 per cent, respectively. The excess mortality among males was greatest at ages over 60, with a mortality ratio of 680 per cent and EDR of 95 per 1000. Among females, the mortality ratio ranged from 355 per cent at ages under 50 to 320 per cent at ages 50 up, with EDR highest (17 per 1000) for ages 50 and over. The estimated 8-year survival index for males ranged from 95.8 per cent at ages under 40 to a minimum of 44.5 per cent in the oldest age group, 60 and over. The female index, on the other hand, was 96.8 per cent at ages under 50 and 87.4 per cent at ages 50 and over.

Comparative mortality by major causes of death is given in Table 802d for male and female substandard cases combined. There was some increase in mortality from each of the listed causes, but diseases of heart and circulation, and "all other causes and unknown," were found to be the two leading causes of death. The mortality ratios for these categories were 350 and 575 per cent, respectively. In addition, the latter category included 19 deaths, of which five were due to digestive disorders and four to cirrhosis of liver.

ARTHRITIS IN INSUREDS

Table 802a Observed Data and Comparative Experience by Sex and Duration - Substandard Cases

Sex	Interval No.	Interval Start-End	Exposure Policy-Yrs	No. of Death Claims Observed	No. of Death Claims Expected*	Mortality Ratio Interval	Mortality Ratio Cumulative	Survival Ratio Interval	Survival Ratio Cumulative	Excess Death Rate
	i	t to t + Δt	E	d	d'	100 d/d'	100 $\sum$d/$\sum$d'	100 p_i/p_i'	100 P/P'	1000(d-d')/E
Male	1	0- 5 yrs	2076	19	5.35	355%	355%	96.7%	96.7%	6.6
	2	5-10	882	8	4.13	194	285	97.8	94.6	4.4
	3	10-17	398	12	3.53	340	300	85.9	81.3	21
Female	1	0- 5 yrs	920	5	1.84	270%	270%	98.3%	98.3%	3.4
	2	5-17	518	10	2.69	370	330	84.3	82.8	14

Table 802b Derived Mortality and Survival Data

Sex	Interval No.	Interval Start-End	Observed Rates Average Annual Mortality	Observed Rates Average Annual Survival	Observed Rates Cumulative Survival	Observed Rates Cumulative Mortality	Expected Rates* Average Annual Mortality	Expected Rates* Average Annual Survival	Expected Rates* Cumulative Survival	Expected Rates* Cumulative Mortality
	i	t to t + Δt	$\bar{q} = d/E$	$\bar{p}$	P	Q	$\bar{q}' = d'/E$	$\bar{p}'$	P'	Q'
Male	1	0- 5 yrs	.0092	.9908	.9548	.0452	.0026	.9974	.9871	.0129
	2	5-10	.0091	.9909	.9121	.0879	.0047	.9953	.9641	.0359
	3	10-17	.0302	.9698	.7359	.2641	.0089	.9911	.9056	.0944
Female	1	0- 5 yrs	.0054	.9946	.9733	.0267	.0020	.9980	.9900	.0100
	2	5-17	.0193	.9807	.7703	.2297	.0052	.9948	.9300	.0700

Table 802c Comparative Experience by Sex and Age Group - Substandard Cases, All Durations Combined

Sex	Age Group	Exposure Policy-Yrs	No. of Death Claims Observed	No. of Death Claims Expected*	Mortality Ratio	Ave. Ann. Mort. Rate	Est. 8-Yr Surv. Rate	Est. 8-Yr Surv. Index	Excess Death Rate
		E	d	d'	100 d/d'	$\bar{q} = d/E$	$P = (1-\bar{q})^8$	100 P/P'	1000(d-d')/E
Male	0-39	1856	13	3.10	420%	.0070	.9454	95.8%	5.3
	40-49	1017	9	4.83	186	.0088	.9314	96.8	4.1
	50-59	402	8	3.76	215	.0199	.8515	91.8	11
	60 up	81	9	1.32	680	.1111	.3897	44.5	95
	All Ages	3356	39	13.01	300	.0116	.9107	93.9	7.7
Female	0-49	1066	6	1.70	355%	.0056	.9558	96.8%	4.0
	50 up	372	9	2.83	320	.0242	.8221	87.4	17
	All Ages	1438	15	4.53	330	.0104	.9195	94.3	7.3

Table 802d Mortality by Cause of Death - Male and Female Combined

Cause	No. of Death Claims Observed	No. of Death Claims Expected†	Mortality Ratio	Excess Death Rate
Malignant Neoplasms	7	4.18	167%	0.6
Diseases of the Heart and Circulatory System	24	6.90	350	3.6
Accidents and Homicides	3	2.41	124	0.1
Suicide	1	0.74	135	0.1
All other Causes and Unknown	19●	3.31	575	3.2
Total	54	17.54	310	7.6

* Basis of expected mortality: 1955-60 Select Basic Table
† Distribution of total expected deaths by Intercompany Medically Examined Standard Issues 1965-70
● Includes 5 Digestive disorders and 4 Cirrhosis of liver

BONE AND JOINT DISORDERS

§810–SPINAL CURVATURE IN INSUREDS

Reference: "New York Life Single Medical Impairment Study–1972," unpublished report made available by J.J. Hutchinson and J.C. Sibigtroth (1973).

Subjects Studied: Policyholders of New York Life Insurance Company issued insurance in 1954-1970, followed to the 1971 policy anniversary. These were cases with abnormal curvature of the spine, including kyphosis and scoliosis. Only those with substandard ratings were reported here. Cases with more than one ratable impairment were excluded.

Follow-up: Insurance policy records formed the basis of entry, of counting policies, exposure and death claims, and of follow-up information.

Results: Comparative experience for male substandard cases is given in Tables 810a-b by duration, all ages combined. The mortality ratio was higher for the first five years, 285 per cent, than for 5-17 years, 182 per cent. On the other hand, the EDR was higher in the latter interval, being 5.2 against 3.8 per 1000.

The experience by age (Table 810c) showed that the highest mortality ratio, 290 per cent, was experienced by males under age 40. The trend in EDR was an increase with advancing age, being highest (14 extra deaths per 1000) in the oldest age group, 50 and over. The overall mortality ratio was 215 per cent. The estimated 8-year survival index ranged from 97.3 per cent for males under age 40 to a minimum of 89.2 per cent for males aged 50 and over.

From Table 810d, the major cause of death was found in diseases of heart and circulation, the mortality ratio being 370 per cent and EDR 3.6 per 1000. Another significant cause of death was in the "all other causes and unknown" category, with a mortality ratio of 310 per cent and EDR 1.3 per 1000. Of the six deaths in the latter category, two were due to respiratory disorders.

SPINAL CURVATURE IN INSUREDS

Table 810a   Observed Data and Comparative Experience by Duration — Male Substandard Cases

Interval		Exposure	No. of Death Claims		Mortality Ratio		Survival Ratio		Excess
No.	Start-End	Policy-Yrs	Observed	Expected*	Interval	Cumulative	Interval	Cumulative	Death Rate
i	t to t + Δt	E	d	d'	100 d/d'	100 Σd/Σd'	100 p_i/p_i'	100 P/P'	1000(d-d')/E
1	0- 5 yrs	1351	8	2.81	285%	285%	97.9%	97.9%	3.8
2	5-17	1046	12	6.58	182	215	96.7	94.7	5.2

Table 810b   Derived Mortality and Survival Data

Interval		Observed Rates				Expected Rates*			
		Average Annual		Cumulative		Average Annual		Cumulative	
No.	Start-End	Mortality	Survival	Survival	Mortality	Mortality	Survival	Survival	Mortality
i	t to t + Δt	$\bar{q}$ = d/E	$\bar{p}$	P	Q	$\bar{q}'$ = d'/E	$\bar{p}'$	P'	Q'
1	0- 5 yrs	.0059	.9941	.9686	.0314	.0021	.9979	.9893	.0107
2	5-17	.0115	.9885	.8547	.1453	.0063	.9937	.9026	.0974

Table 810c   Comparative Experience by Age Group — Male Substandard Cases, All Durations Combined

Age Group	Exposure Policy-Yrs	No. of Death Claims		Mortality Ratio	Ave. Ann. Mort. Rate	Est. 8-Yr Surv. Rate	Est. 8-Yr Surv. Index	Excess Death Rate
		Observed	Expected*					
	E	d	d'	100 d/d'	$\bar{q}$ = d/E	P = $(1-\bar{q})^8$	100 P/P'	1000(d-d')/E
0-39	1538	8	2.75	290%	.0052	.9591	97.3%	3.4
40-49	633	6	3.81	157	.0095	.9266	97.2	3.5
50 up	226	6	2.83	210	.0265	.8063	89.2	14
All Ages	2397	20	9.39	215	.0083	.9352	96.5	4.4

Table 810d   Mortality by Cause of Death — Male and Female Combined

Cause	No. of Death Claims		Mortality Ratio	Excess Death Rate
	Observed	Expected†		
Malignant Neoplasm	2	2.45	82%	−0.2
Diseases of the Heart and Circulatory System	15	4.05	370	3.6
Accidents and Homicides	0	1.41	0	−0.5
Suicide	0	0.44	0	−0.1
All other Causes and Unknown	6●	1.94	310	1.3
Total	23□	10.29	225%	4.1

* Basis of expected mortality: 1955-60 Select Basic Table
† Distribution of total expected deaths by Intercompany Medically Examined Standard Issues 1965-70
● Includes 2 respiratory disorders
□ Includes 3 females (exposure 669 policy-years)

MUSCLE DISORDERS

§830–MYASTHENIA GRAVIS

Reference: V. P. Perlo, D. C. Poskanzer, R. S. Schwab, H. R. Viets, K. E. Osserman, and G. Genkins, "Myasthenia Gravis: Evaluation of Treatment in 1,355 Patients," Neurology, 16:431-439 (1966).

Subjects Studied: Patients admitted to the myasthenia gravis (MG) clinics of the Massachusetts General Hospital in Boston and of the Mount Sinai Hospital in New York. In both clinics eligibility for inclusion in the study called for adequate information with regard to initial diagnosis and at least one follow-up visit. The entire series consisted of 1355 patients: 553 males (41 per cent) and 802 females. Data on 723 subjects were supplied by Mount Sinai Hospital, on 632 by the Massachusetts General. The type and severity of MG were designated in accordance with Osserman's classification.* Eighty per cent of the patients were subject to drug and X-ray therapy, 14 per cent to thymectomy (without thymoma), and 6 per cent to thymectomy (with thymoma). There was a marked difference in the age at onset of the disease by sex: approximately two-thirds of the females, but only one-third of the males, experienced onset before age 40 years. Prime objectives of the study were an attempt to evaluate the relative effectiveness of medical and surgical therapy and clarification of the role of thymectomy in the treatment of myasthenia gravis.

Follow-up: Pertinent information was maintained from the establishment of the Massachusetts General Hospital Clinic in 1935 and of the Mount Sinai Clinic in 1951 for all patients from onset of disease to the evaluation of the experience in 1965. Two hundred-nineteen cases were lost to follow-up. Cumulative survival rates were calculated by the actuarial method on an annual basis.

Results: Comparative experience by duration from onset for 129 males and females in Osserman's Group 4 with thymoma is presented in Table 830a. All methods of treatment were employed. Mortality ratios, tending to decline with duration, ranged from 765 to 350 per cent, and EDR's followed a similar course with a high rate of 80, and a low rate of 45 per 1000. About one-quarter as many of the subjects survived the 20-year period as in the general population with the same age-sex composition.

The four divisions of Table 830b show results by duration and by sex, all ages combined, for patients without thymoma and with and without thymectomy. Mortality ratios for patients of both sexes subject to thymectomy were high in the first five-year interval. The ratio reached 1380 per cent in the case of females, 560 per cent for males. In subsequent intervals these ratios dropped: among female patients to levels ranging between 156 and 210 per cent, among males the decline was not as great but it was still substantial. The operation appears to have been extremely effective in reducing excess mortality among females and also, but in a lesser degree, among males (however, it is estimated there were only about 10 male deaths at all ages). In contrast, subjects not operated on showed a more moderate degree of extra mortality in the first interval (0-5 years) as measured by mortality ratios: for females, 340 per cent, for males, 179 per cent. Medical therapy was accompanied by smaller mortality ratios in the intervals beyond five years. Among males, mortality ratios for the later intervals were, in fact, very low, materially falling below those of the general population 10 years and more after onset. EDR's in all four divisions of Table 830b revealed analogous gradations in experience with duration.

Table 830c shows for surviving males and females with and without thymectomy, but excluding those with thymoma, distributions of patients in Osserman's classifications at onset of the disease and at the close of the study in 1965. Changes in distribution provide some measure of the improvement attributable to treatment, although intervening deaths and losses to follow-up exert considerable effect on these changes. Patterns of distribution changed materially, especially where thymectomy had been undergone. Of females who had had thymectomy, 93 per cent were in Groups 2B, 3 or 4 before operation, but only 35 per cent of the non-operated patients were in these groups. At the close of the study there were in these groups only 11 per cent of the former, but there were 20 per cent of the latter. The shift in distribution among males was much less marked and survival benefits were not as significantly indicated.

*Osserman's diagnostic classes – see footnote Table 830c.

MYASTHENIA GRAVIS

Table 830a Comparative Experience by Duration, Patients with Thymoma,
129 Males and Females, and All Therapies Combined

Interval		Observed Rates			Expected Rates*			Mortality Ratio	Cumulative Surv. Ratio	Excess Death Rate
No.	Start-End	Cumulative Survival	Interval Survival	Ave. Ann. Mortality	Cumulative Survival	Interval Survival	Ave. Ann. Mortality			
i	t to t + Δ t	P	p_i	$\check{q}$	P'	p_i'	$\check{q}'$	100 $\check{q}/\check{q}'$	100 P/P'	1000($\check{q}$-$\check{q}'$)
1	0- 5 yrs	.619	.619	.092	.9414	.9414	.012	765%	65.8%	80
2	5-10	.439	.709	.066	.8773	.9319	.014	470	50.0	52
3	10-15	.317	.721	.063	.8012	.9132	.018	350	39.6	45
4	15-20	.180	.568	.107	.7095	.8856	.024	445	25.4	83

Table 830b Comparative Experience by Sex, Method of Therapy, and Duration, Patients without Thymoma

Interval		Observed Rates			Expected Rates*			Mortality Ratio	Cumulative Surv. Ratio	Excess Death Rate
No.	Start-End	Cumulative Survival	Interval Survival	Ave. Ann. Mortality	Cumulative Survival	Interval Survival	Ave. Ann. Mortality			
i	t to t + Δ t	P	p_i	$\check{q}$	P'	p_i'	$\check{q}'$	100 $\check{q}/\check{q}'$	100 P/P'	1000($\check{q}$-$\check{q}'$)
478 Females — Medical Therapy										
1	0- 5 yrs	.873	.873	.027	.9606	.9606	.008	340%	90.9%	19
2	5-10	.787	.901	.020	.9181	.9558	.009	220	85.7	11
3	10-15	.732	.930	.015	.8687	.9462	.011	136	84.3	4.0
4	15-20	.670	.915	.017	.8095	.9319	.014	121	82.8	3.0
156 Females — Thymectomy										
1	0- 5 yrs	.911	.911	.018	.9935	.9935	.0013	1380%	91.7%	17
2	5-10	.896	.984	.003	.9846	.9910	.0018	167	91.0	1.2
3	10-15	.873	.974	.005	.9729	.9881	.0024	210	89.7	2.6
4	15-20	.850	.974	.005	.9574	.9841	.0032	156	88.8	1.8
346 Males — Medical Therapy										
1	0- 5 yrs	.804	.804	.043	.8856	.8856	.024	179%	90.8%	19
2	5-10	.667	.830	.037	.7683	.8676	.028	132	86.8	9.0
3	10-15	.633	.949	.010	.6496	.8455	.033	30	97.4	−23
4	15-20	.607	.959	.008	.5324	.8196	.039	21	114.0	−31
30 Males — Thymectomy										
1	0- 5 yrs	.868	.868	.028	.9752	.9752	.005	560%	89.0%	23
2	5-10	.813	.937	.013	.9463	.9704	.006	215	85.9	7.0
3	10-15	.746	.918	.017	.9090	.9606	.008	210	82.1	9.0
4	15-20	.746	1.000	.000	.8645	.9510	.010	0	86.3	−10

Table 830c Initial and Final (1965) Severity Classification by Sex and Therapy

Severity Class†	Females				Males			
	122 Pts. Initially	Operated in 1965	348 Pts. Initially	Not Operated in 1965	22 Pts. Initially	Operated in 1965	258 Pts. Initially	Not Operated in 1965
A	0%	38%	0%	14%	0%	37%	0%	11%
1	1	0	20	18	5	9	33	30
2A	6	51	45	48	0	18	32	39
2B	56	6	23	12	50	9	23	9
3	20	1	5	2	36	18	8	6
4	17	4	7	6	9	9	4	5

* Basis of expected mortality: 1949-51 U.S. White Males and Females

† Osserman's severity classes:

Class

A   Complete remission after treatment

1   Ocular involvement only (Oc. Inv.)

2A   Mild generalized MG

2B   Moderately severe generalized MG including Oc. Inv. with usually mild bulbar involvement

3   Acute severe MG developed in weeks or months with Bulb. Inv. — tracheotomy and respirator often required

4   Late, severe MG, developed gradually from 1, 2A & 2B, with Bulb. Inv.

DISEASES OF SKIN AND CONNECTIVE TISSUE

§850–SCLERODERMA

References: (1) T. A. Medsger, Jr., A. T. Masi, G. P. Rodnan, T. G. Benedek, and H. Robinson, "Survival with Systemic Sclerosis (Scleroderma). A Life-Table Analysis of Clinical and Demographic Factors in 309 Patients," Ann. Int. Med., 75:369-376 (1971).
(2) T. A. Medsger, Jr. and A. T. Masi, "Survival with Scleroderma–II: A Life-Table Analysis of Clinical and Demographic Factors in 358 Male U.S. Veteran Patients," J. Chron. Dis., 26:647-660 (1973).
(3) Detailed life table data of Reference (1) obtained from National Auxilliary Publication Service, under NAPS No. 01549, c/o Microfiche Publications, 400 Park Avenue South, New York, New York, 10016.

Subjects Studied: (1) Two series of scleroderma patients: 223 diagnosed from 1955 through 1969 in a large university and referral practice in Pittsburgh, Pennsylvania, and 86 identified in a comprehensive retrospective epidemiological survey conducted from 1947 through 1968 in Memphis, Tennessee. The initial diagnosis in Pittsburgh and Memphis was taken as the time of entry into the study, despite the fact that, in many cases, diagnosis of scleroderma by a physician had been made months to years before referral to the facilities. In both series there were almost twice as many women as men. White patients made up 85 per cent of the cases. The mean age at entry of the total group of 309 patients was 47.2 years.

(2) 358 male veterans discharged during the years 1963-1968 inclusive from U.S. Veterans Administration hospitals with an acceptable diagnosis of scleroderma. Clinical records were obtained, abstracted and reviewed; only patients satisfying defined criteria for the diagnosis of scleroderma were accepted. Patients with any *other* connective tissue disease as the primary diagnosis were excluded. Distribution of patients by age and race was as follows (79 of the 84 nonwhite patients were Negro):

Age	Under 25 yrs	25-34	35-44	45-54	55-64	65 up	Total
White	2	21	70	107	39	35	274
Nonwhite	1	5	31	30	8	9	84
Total	3	26	101	137	47	44	358

Nearly all patients had some degree of skin involvement; the interval from onset to diagnosis exceeded 36 months in only 32 per cent of the patients. Other clinical and laboratory data are given in the article.

Follow-up: Follow-up was successfully completed during 1970 on 94 per cent of the patients in Pittsburgh and 95 per cent of those in Memphis. Life table methods were used to analyze the follow-up data. However, an error occurred in the development of the intervals for the survival curves shown: each "year" was based on four intervals, which were actually four months rather than three months each. The "annual" intervals in the survival curves of Reference (1) and the life table data of Reference (3) have therefore been understated by a factor of 16/12 with respect to a twelve-month year. The authority for this correction is a footnote on page 647 of Reference (2); corrected survival curves for some of the Memphis-Pittsburgh data are given in Reference (2). All data on the Memphis-Pittsburgh series presented in Tables 850a-c are based on corrected intervals with one year equal to three four-month intervals, or twelve months.

(2) Follow-up was determined using V.A. Clinical records, V.A. Regional Office claim files, and Social Security Administration claim records. In some cases direct contact was made with patients or private physicians. Of the total series 345 patients (96 per cent) were successfully traced in 1970: 193 deaths were recorded.

SCLERODERMA

Table 850a Comparative Experience by Sex and Duration, All Ages and Severity Grades Combined, 2 Series of Scleroderma Patients

Category (No. of Patients)	Interval No.	Start-End	Cum. Surv. Rate Observed	Expected*	Cumulative Surv. Ratio	Ave. Ann. Mort. Rate Observed	Expected*	Mortality Ratio	Excess Death Rate
	i	t to $t+\Delta t$	P	P'	$100\,P/P'$	$\breve{q}$	$\breve{q}'$	$100\,\breve{q}/\breve{q}'$	$1000(\breve{q}-\breve{q}')$
Series 1 Males (117 patients)	1	0-1 yr	.759	.987	76.9%	.241	.0130	1850%	228
	2	1-3 yrs	.546	.959	56.9	.152	.0145	1050	138
	3	3-5	.408	.927	44.0	.136	.0165	825	120
	4	5-7	.356	.894	39.8	.066	.0180	365	48
Series 2 Males (358 V.A. patients)	1	0-1 yr	.701	.985	71.2%	.299	.0147	2000%	284
	2	1-3 yrs	.522	.954	54.7	.137	.0161	850	121
	3	3-5	.423	.920	46.0	.100	.0181	550	82
	4	5-7	.340	.883	38.5	.104	.0203	510	84
Series 1 Females (192 patients)	1	0-1 yr	.787	.992	79.3%	.213	.0080	2700%	205
	2	1-3 yrs	.703	.976	72.0	.055	.0081	680	47
	3	3-5	.583	.961	60.7	.090	.0077	1170	82
	4	5-7	.537	.945	56.8	.040	.0084	475	32

Table 850b Comparative First-Year Experience by Age, Race and Organ Involvement (Heart, Lung or Kidneys), 2 Series of Scleroderma Patients

Category	Series	No. of Patients	Survival Rate Observed	Expected*	Survival Ratio	Mortality Rate Observed	Expected*	Mortality Ratio	Excess Death Rate
		ℓ	P	P'	$100\,P/P'$	q	q'	$100\,q/q'$	$1000(q-q')$
Age at Entry (Sex)									
Under 45 (M&F)	1	130	.840	.998	84.2%	.160	.002	8000%	158
Under 50 (M)	2	211	.801	.994	80.6	.199	.006	3300	193
45 up (M&F)	1	179	.731	.985	74.2	.269	.015	1800	254
50 up (M)	2	147	.558	.972	57.4	.442	.028	1580	414
Race (Sex)									
White (M&F)	1	264	.790	.991	79.7%	.210	.009	2300%	201
(M)	2	274	.712	.986	72.2	.288	.014	2100	274
Nonwhite (M&F)	1	45	.701	.985	71.2	.299	.015	2000	284
(M)	2	84	.667	.983	67.9	.333	.017	1960	316
Organ Involvement									
No Heart, Lung or Kidney	1	141	.882	.992	88.9%	.118	.008	1480%	110
	2	178	.873	.985	88.6	.127	.015	845	112
Lung, No Heart or Kidney	1	98	.831	.992	83.8	.169	.008	2100	161
	2	112	.672	.985	68.2	.328	.015	2200	313
Heart, No Kidney	1	43	.612	.992	61.7	.388	.008	4800	380
	2	41	.442	.985	44.9	.558	.015	3700	543
Kidney	1	16	.000	.992	0.0	1.000	.008	12500	992
	2	17	.000	.985	0.0	1.000	.015	6700	985

*Basis of expected mortality: U.S. Life Tables 1959-61

DISEASES OF SKIN AND CONNECTIVE TISSUES

§850–SCLERODERMA (continued):

Results: Comparative experience by duration is given in Table 850a for Series 1 (Memphis-Pittsburgh) divided by sex, and Series 2 (V.A. patients, all males). Excess mortality was at a high level, extremely so in the first year, with mortality ratios of 1850 and 2000 per cent and excess death rates of 228 and 284 per 1000 in the two groups of men, and a mortality ratio of 2700 per cent and EDR of 205 per 1000 in the female patients. During the subsequent six years (three intervals each lasting two years) both mortality ratio and EDR tended to decrease with duration in all groups, although some irregularities were observed. In general, the levels of comparative mortality were highest in the Series 1 males, intermediate in the Series 2 males, and lowest in the Series 1 females. The extreme range of mortality ratio in all three groups after the first year was 365 to 1170 per cent, and range in EDR from 32 to 138 extra deaths per 1000 per year. Seven-year survival ratios were 39.8 and 38.5 per cent in the two male groups, and 56.8 per cent in the female patients.

Comparative experience by age, race and organ involvement is given for the first year of follow-up in Table 850b and at durations 1-7 years combined in Table 850c. Data in these tables are for men and women combined in Series 1, whereas Series 2 consisted of male patients only. Excess mortality during the first year is seen to be extremely high in all categories of Table 850b, the lowest mortality ratio being 845 per cent and lowest EDR 110 per 1000. Excess death rates were substantially higher in the older patients, 254 vs. 158 per 1000 in Series 1 and 414 vs. 193 per 1000 in Series 2. Mortality ratios, on the other hand, decreased with age, from 8000 per cent in the younger patients to 1800 per cent in Series 1, and from 3300 to 1580 per cent in Series 2. Prognosis was worse in nonwhite patients in terms of EDR, but the difference was small in Series 2, with EDR 316 per 1000 in nonwhite patients and 274 per 1000 in whites. Those patients without evidence of involvement of heart, lung or kidney at the time of entry into the study had the lowest mortality ratios, 1480 and 845 per cent, with excess death rates of 110 and 112 per 1000 in the two series. Excess mortality increased when the lung alone was involved, and still further when the heart was involved, but not the kidney: the respective mortality ratios were 2100 and 4800 per cent in Series 1, and 2200 and 3700 per cent in Series 2; the corresponding excess death rates were 161 and 380 per 1000 in Series 1 and 313 and 543 per 1000 in Series 2. However, kidney involvement was a highly lethal risk factor, as all 33 patients in the two series died in the first year; there was not a single survivor.

It is evident from comparison of the tables that excess mortality is considerably lower, during the interval from one to seven years after hospitalization than in the first year. The results again show a decrease in mortality ratio with advancing age from levels well above 1000 per cent to approximately 500 per cent, and an increase in EDR, from 57 to 85 per 1000 in Series 1 and from 86 to 124 per 1000 in Series 2. Excess mortality was higher in nonwhites than in whites in Series 1, but the reverse was true in the veterans group (Series 2). The trend of mortality with organ involvement was generally similar to that observed in the first year, but at a lower level. The best prognosis was found in those patients without any heart, lung or kidney involvement: mortality ratios were 615 and 590 per cent and excess death rates 42 and 89 per 1000. When only the lung was involved, the mortality ratios in the two series were 1510 and 575 per cent, and EDR's 114 and 87 per 1000, respectively. For patients with heart involvement the mortality ratios were 1630 and 1030 per cent, and the EDR's 124 and 169 per 1000. Survival ratios over the six-year interval ranged from a minimum of 32.4 per cent to a maximum of 77.4 per cent in the various categories shown in Table 850c.

Comment: Results are somewhat more reliable for Series 1, because they are based on life table data obtained from Reference (3) rather than on graphical measurements of survival curves (Series 2).

SCLERODERMA

Table 850c Comparative Experience, 1 to 7 Years, by Age, Race and Heart or Lung Involvement, 2 Series of Scleroderma Patients

Category		Series	No. of Patients	6-Yr Survival Rate		6-Yr Surv. Ratio	Ave. Ann. Mort. Rate		Mortality Ratio	Excess Death Rate
				Observed	Expected*		Observed	Expected*		
			ℓ	p_i	p_i'	$100\,p_i/p_i'$	$\breve{q}$	$\breve{q}'$	$100\,\breve{q}/\breve{q}'$	$1000(\breve{q}-\breve{q}')$
Age at Entry (Sex)										
Under 45	(M&F)	1	105	.686	.975	70.4%	.061	.0042	1450%	57
Under 50	(M)	2	169	.554	.955	58.0	.094	.0077	1220	86
45 up	(M&F)	1	131	.521	.898	58.0	.103	.0179	575	85
50 up	(M)	2	82	.355	.809	43.9	.159	.0346	460	124
Race (Sex)										
White	(M&F)	1	209	.620	.940	66.0%	.077	.0103	750%	67
	(M)	2	195	.485	.900	53.9	.114	.0175	650	97
Nonwhite	(M&F)	1	32	.427	.935	45.7	.132	.0111	1190	121
	(M)	2	56	.529	.884	59.8	.101	.0204	495	81
Organ Involvement										
No Heart, Lung or Kidney		1	124	.737	.953	77.4%	.050	.0081	615%	42
		2	155	.509	.896	56.8	.107	.0182	590	89
Lung, No Heart or Kidney		1	81	.459	.953	48.2	.122	.0081	1510	114
		2	75	.513	.896	57.3	.105	.0182	575	87
Heart, No Kidney		1	26	.427	.953	44.8	.132	.0081	1630	124
		2	18	.290	.896	32.4	.187	.0182	1030	169

*Basis of expected mortality: U.S. Life Tables 1959-61

SYSTEMIC DISORDERS

§899–SYSTEMIC DISORDERS IN INSUREDS

References: (1) T. W. Preston and R. D. Clarke, "An Investigation into the Mortality of Impaired Lives During the Period 1947-63," J. Inst. Act., 92:27-74 (1966).
(2) "New York Life Single Medical Impairment Study - 1972," unpublished report made available by J. J. Hutchinson and J. C. Sibigtroth (1973).

Subjects Studied: (1) Policyholders of Prudential Assurance Co., London, England, issued insurance 1947-1963 followed to 12/31/63. Both standard and substandard issues were included. Applicants with two or more ratable impairments were generally excluded.
(2) Policyholders of New York Life Insurance Co., issued insurance 1954-1970, followed to the 1971 policy anniversary. Both standard and substandard issues were included. Applicants with more than one ratable impairment were excluded.

Follow-up: Insurance policy records formed the basis of entry, counting policies, exposures and death claims, and of follow-up information.

Results: The only infectious diseases in this table are syphilis, non-pulmonary tuberculosis, and family history of tuberculosis, in the connotation of exposure to infection. All categories show a normal mortality and survival, including younger underweight applicants with a history of exposure. This experience demonstrates the effectiveness of modern treatment and prophylaxis. Exposures and deaths are extremely limited for syphilis, but more substantial in number for tuberculosis in the English study.

The single allergic disorder, hay fever, was characterized by a near-normal mortality ratio of 118 per cent. Substandard cases of secondary anemia in the New York Life study were found to have a mortality ratio of 139 per cent based on only seven death claims. The mortality ratio was 385 per cent (9 death claims) in the category "other disorders of the blood." This category included hematologic diagnosis not specifically codable for the anemias, polycythemia, leukemia, thrombosis and embolism.

Among the specific bone and joint disorders coded in the New York Life study mortality ratios ranged from 133 per cent for spinal curvature, standard issues, to 275 per cent for spinal disorders, other than curvature, with insurance issued on a substandard basis. Experience was limited in all categories: 23 deaths were the maximum number. Mortality ratios for osteomyelitis and injury were lower than for the other specific diagnostic codes, at 142 and 158 per cent, respectively. The mortality ratio of 117 per cent reported by Preston and Clarke for poliomyelitis was much lower than the 215 per cent observed in New York Life policyholders. However, polio was coded in the latter study only in the presence of deformity, and this may not have been a requirement in the experience of the Prudential of London. A normal mortality ratio, 97 per cent, was found in the residual New York Life category, other bone or joint disorders. The maximum EDR in all of these categories was 6.6 per 1000.

Although experience was limited, excess mortality was noted in skin disorders in the New York Life study. The mortality ratios were 250 and 385 per cent for standard and substandard issues, respectively, with EDR's of 4.7 and 7.2 per 1000.

SYSTEMIC DISORDERS

Table 899   Comparative Experience, Two Series of Insureds

Disease/Category (Ref.)	Sex/Age	Policies in Force at Start	Exposure Policy-Yrs	No. of Death Claims		Ave. Ann. Mort. Rate		Mortality Ratio	Est. 5-Yr Surv. Rate	Est. 5-Yr Surv. Index	Excess Death Rate
				Observed	Expected*	Observed	Expected*				
		ℓ	E	d	d'	$\bar{q} = d/E$	$\bar{q}' = d'/E$	100 d/d'	$P = (1 - \bar{q}')^5$	100 P/P'	$1000(\bar{q} - \bar{q}')$
Non-pulmonary Tuberculosis (1)	M 39	3037	16882	36	34.9	.0021	.0021	103%	.9894	100.0%	0.1
Tuberculosis Family History (1)											
Under age 40, Standard Weight	M 32	13669	80364	85	76.0	.0011	.0009	112	.9947	99.9	0.1
Under age 40, Underweight	M 34	2452	15648	11	16.5	.0007	.0011	67	.9965	100.2	−0.4
Ages 40 up	M 47	6494	50182	287	285	.0057	.0057	101	.9717	100.0	0.0
Syphilis S&SS† (2)	M&F 43	—	1926	5	8.47	.0026	.0044	59	.9871	100.9	−1.8
Hay Fever (1)	M 35	3051	12536	17	14.4	.0014	.0012	118	.9932	99.9	0.2
Anemia SS (2)	M&F 39	—	1611	7	5.04	.0043	.0031	139	.9785	99.4	1.2
Disorder of Blood SS (2)	M&F 37	—	947	9	2.33	.0095	.0025	385	.9534	96.5	7.0
Bone or Joint Disorder S&SS (2)	M&F 39	—	1659	5	5.18	.0030	.0031	97	.9850	100.1	−0.1
Spinal Curvature S (2)	M&F 39	—	1247	5	3.76	.0040	.0030	133	.9801	99.5	1.0
Spinal Curvature SS (2)	M&F 40	—	3066	23	10.3	.0075	.0033	225	.9631	97.9	4.2
Spinal Disorder S (2)	M&F 40	—	1261	9	4.15	.0071	.0033	217	.9648	98.1	3.8
Spinal Disorder SS (2)	M&F 41	—	1058	11	3.99	.0104	.0038	275	.9491	96.7	6.6
Osteomyelitis S&SS (2)	M&F 37	—	1801	6	4.24	.0033	.0024	142	.9835	99.5	1.0
Injury S&SS (2)	M&F 38	—	1810	8	5.07	.0044	.0028	158	.9781	99.2	1.6
Polio with Deformity SS (2)	M&F 36	—	4624	23	10.6	.0050	.0023	215	.9754	98.7	2.7
Polio (1)	M 37	1244	6203	11	9.37	.0018	.0015	117	.9912	99.9	0.3
Amputation SS (2)	M&F 39	—	880	7	2.71	.0080	.0031	260	.9609	97.6	4.9
Skin Disorders S (2)	M&F 39	—	1401	11	4.42	.0079	.0032	250	.9614	97.7	4.7
Skin Disorders SS (2)	M&F 37	—	718	7	1.81	.0097	.0025	385	.9522	96.4	7.2

* Basis of expected mortality: (Ref. 1) Prudential Assurance Co. (England) standard lives mortality 1957-1958;
(Ref. 2) N. Y. Life, Basic Select Tables (1955-60)
† "S" - Stardard, "SS" - Substandard

Endocrine and Metabolic

See Also

1. *1951 Impairment Study.* Chicago: Society of Actuaries (1954).
   - H17-H28 Glycosuria, found on examination (pp. 228-234).
   - H29 Blood sugar test, on examination (pp. 234-235).
   - H30-H39 Goitre, diffuse or nodular (pp. 236-241).
   - H40 Hypothyroidism, found on examination (pp. 241-242).
2. *1959 Build and Blood Pressure Study,* compiled and published by Society of Actuaries, Chicago (1960). See Volume I, "Mortality Experience According to Build," p. 45; Volume II, "Standard and Substandard Issues Combined," p. 7 and "Standard and Substandard Issues Separately," p. 63.

DIABETES MELLITUS

§901—DIABETES MELLITUS IN LIFE INSURANCE APPLICANTS

Reference: G. Goodkin, L. Wolloch, R. A. Gottcent, and F. Reich, "Diabetes-A Twenty Year Mortality Study," Trans. Assoc. Life Ins. Med. Dir. Amer., 58:217-269 (1974).

Subjects Studied: The series was comprised of 10538 diabetics (89 per cent male) who applied to the Equitable Life Assurance Society for insurance in the period from 1951 to 1970 and were followed to the anniversaries of their application in 1971. Insurance policies were issued to 2900 applicants of which 99.2 per cent were substandard. The other 7638 were declined for insurance either because they did not meet underwriting criteria (satisfactory diabetic status, general physical condition, build, blood pressure, family history, etc.), failed to complete underwriting requirements, or for non-medical reasons. Both declined and insured applicants were included in the study. Subjects were classed as diabetic if they were diagnosed as such by their attending physicians, if, at the time of application they were taking insulin or oral hypoglycemic agents in addition to a diet, or if the insurance record showed a history of diabetes confirmed by a physician's statement. Excluded from the study were individuals with a history of glycosuria without dietary treatment or medication, and those who had an abnormal glucose tolerance at the time of examination. Also excluded were diabetics who applied for Major Medical or Disability Income Insurance but who had not applied for life insurance. Age distribution of applicants within the indicated age groups:

Age at Application	Under 30	30-39	40-49	50-59	60 - up	Total	Ave. Age
No. Issued Cases	472	776	940	616	96	2900	41.2 yrs
No. Declined Cases	1615	1514	2001	1773	735	7638	42.2 yrs
Total Number	2087	2290	2941	2389	831	10,538	41.9 yrs
Per Cent	19.8%	21.7%	27.9%	22.7%	7.9%	100.0%	

Follow-up: In the total series 9919 out of 10538 cases, or 94.1 per cent, were successfully traced to the 1971 anniversary. All deaths were verified from a copy of the death certificate and both primary and secondary causes of death were recorded. The application or policy record was the unit of exposure; duplicate records on the same case were not eliminated.

Results: Mortality and survival data are presented by duration, all ages combined, in Tables 901a-b. The experience for applicants issued insurance was distinctly more favorable than that for the declined, the average EDR being 3.2 for the former and 16 for the latter. Mortality ratios varied in a somewhat irregular manner with duration of follow-up, but EDR increased to a maximum at 10-15 years and then decreased slightly at 15-20 years in both issued and declined cases. The 20-year cumulative survival ratio was 89.6 per cent for the group offered insurance and 68.5 per cent for those declined.

Table 901c shows comparative experience by age group averaged over the period of observation according to the known duration of the diabetic condition prior to application for insurance. As measured by the mortality ratio severity tends to increase with the duration of the diabetic history, but for a particular duration appears to be relatively more favorable for older persons. On the other hand, for all diabetic history durations together, the EDR index over the period of observation varies within narrow limits (averaging between 9.8 and 12 per 1000 per year), between ages 20 and 49 at time of application for insurance. For older age groups EDR tends to increase with age: 16 for age group 50-59; 25 for group aged 60 and older. Exposure was small at ages younger than 20 (only 12 deaths reported) and did not warrant breakdown according to duration of diabetic condition. However, in view of the youth of this class it is likely that short-term diabetic histories would predominate, for which the experience at other ages was shown to be more favorable.

When all ages were combined (Table 901d) excess mortality, measured either by mortality ratio or by EDR, also increased with duration of diabetes up to 15 years prior to application, with little change thereafter. This holds true for declined applicants as well as those issued insurance. Mortality ratios are consistently 2½ to 3 times greater on declined cases than on accepted. The EDR for durations up to 5 years prior to policy issue is low - 1.4 per 1000; for longer durations this function ranges between 5.6 and 6.6 per 1000. Excess deaths on declined cases increase with duration of diabetes, reaching and holding a level of about 25 extra deaths per 1000 for durations over 15 years.

DIABETES MELLITUS IN INSURANCE APPLICANTS

Table 901a Observed Data and Comparative Experience by Insurance Action and Duration of Follow-up
(Issued & Declined)

Insurance Action & Interval		Exposure Policy-Yrs	Deaths in Interval		Mortality Ratio		Survival Ratio		Excess Death Rate
No.	Start-End		Observed	Expected*	Interval	Cumulative	Interval	Cumulative	
i	t to t + Δt	E	d	d'	100 d/d'	100Σd/Σd'	100 p_i/p_i'	100 P/P'	1000(d-d')/E
	Issued								
1	0- 2 yrs	5563	19	11.36	167%	167%	99.7%	99.7%	1.4
2	2- 5	6646	28	24.85	113	130	99.8	99.6	0.5
3	5-10	7467	69	40.24	171	152	98.1	97.7	3.9
4	10-15	3476	59	27.74	215	168	95.5	93.3	9.0
5	15-20	698	16	10.37	154	167	96.0	89.6	8.1
All	0-20	23849	191	114.56	167	167	89.6	89.6	3.2
	Declined								
1	0- 2 yrs	14605	164	37.14	440	440	98.3	98.3	8.7
2	2- 5	17645	322	80.87	400	410	96.0	94.3	14
3	5-10	18398	495	116.20	425	420	90.0	84.9	21
4	10-15	7608	256	69.73	365	405	88.3	75.0	24
5	15-20	1583	50	22.14	225	395	91.4	68.5	18
All	0-20	59838	1287	326.08	395	395	68.5	68.5	16

Table 901b Derived Mortality and Survival Data

Insurance Action & Interval		Observed Rates				Expected Rates*			
		Ave. Ann. Mortality	Survival			Ave. Ann. Mortality	Survival		
No.	Start-End		Ave. Ann.	Interval	Cumulative		Ave. Ann.	Interval	Cumulative
i	t to t + Δt	$\bar{q}$ = d/E	$\bar{p}$	p_i	P	$\bar{q}'$ = d'/E	$\bar{p}'$	p_i'	P'
	Issued								
1	0- 2 yrs	.0034	.9966	.9932	.9932	.0020	.9980	.9960	.9960
2	2- 5	.0042	.9958	.9874	.9807	.0037	.9963	.9889	.9849
3	5-10	.0092	.9908	.9546	.9362	.0054	.9946	.9731	.9584
4	10-15	.0170	.9830	.9176	.8590	.0080	.9920	.9604	.9204
5	15-20	.0229	.9771	.8905	.7649	.0149	.9851	.9275	.8537
All	0-20	.0080	.9920	—	—	.0048	.9952	—	—
	Declined								
1	0- 2 yrs	.0112	.9888	.9777	.9777	.0025	.9975	.9950	.9950
2	2- 5	.0182	.9818	.9464	.9253	.0046	.9954	.9862	.9813
3	5-10	.0269	.9731	.8724	.8072	.0063	.9937	.9687	.9506
4	10-15	.0336	.9664	.8427	.6802	.0092	.9908	.9546	.9074
5	15-20	.0316	.9684	.8515	.5792	.0140	.9860	.9319	.8456
All	0-20	.0215	.9785	—	—	.0054	.9946	—	—

* Basis of expected mortality: Equitable Life Select & Ultimate Mortality Tables 1958-1963

§901—DIABETES MELLITUS IN LIFE INSURANCE APPLICANTS

Results (continued):

Table 901e gives the comparative experience for issued and declined cases by principal method of treatment of the diabetes. Among the accepted cases, mortality and survival are well within standard limits for patients treated by diet alone. Oral medication is associated with a definite excess mortality, but less marked than in all cases treated with insulin; mortality ratios of 153 and 225 per cent and EDR's of 2.8 and 5.0 extra deaths per 1000 per year, respectively. The mortality ratio of 305 per cent for diabetics issued insurance and with a daily insulin dosage of 50 units or more is higher than an average ratio of about 200 per cent for diabetics receiving a smaller insulin dosage. Among declined cases mortality ratios increase progressively with insulin dosage, but EDR remains virtually constant, reflecting an increase in the proportion of young diabetics, under age 20, in categories of successively higher insulin dosage (reported data which have not been reproduced in this abstract).

Experience categorized by build and blood pressure classes is summarized in Table 901f. Underweight diabetics exhibited the highest mortality ratio, 485 per cent, and the two overweight classes the lowest ratios 260 and 290 per cent, as compared to a ratio of 310 per cent for the majority of the cases with standard build, EDR again showed almost no variation by build class. Normotensive diabetics had a mortality ratio of 265 per cent and EDR of 8.2. All hypertensive categories were characterized by higher ratios and EDR values, both indices increasing with the level of systolic, diastolic, or both pressures in combination.

Comparative mortality by cause of declination is given in Table 901g. Causes of declination have been divided into two groups, one showing higher, the other lower mortality ratios and EDR's. Renal complications, evidenced by protein or casts in the urine, were associated with the highest excess mortality, a ratio of 935 per cent and 38 extra deaths per 1000 per year. Age at onset of diabetes was the cause of declination with the next highest mortality ratio, 910 per cent, but the EDR was less than 10 (most of these applicants gave a history of juvenile diabetes).

DIABETES MELLITUS IN INSURANCE APPLICANTS

Table 901c   Comparative Experience by Age & Known Duration of Diabetes Prior to Application (Issued and Declined Cases, All Policy Durations Combined)

Age & Known Duration of Diabetes	Number Alive	Exposure Policy-Yrs	Deaths during Interval	Expected Deaths*	Mortality Ratio	Ave. Ann. Mort. Rate	Est. 7-Yr Surv. Rate	Est. 7-Yr Surv. Index	Excess Death Rate
Years	ℓ	E	d	d'	100 d/d'	$\bar{q}=d/E$	$P=(1-\bar{q})^7$	100 P/P'	1000(d-d')/E
Age 1-19 yrs									
All Dur.	360	3022	12	2.68	450%	.0040	.9725	97.9%	3.1
Age 20-29 yrs									
Dur. 0-5	657	5714	35	5.86	595	.0061	.9578	96.4	5.1
5-10	451	3984	39	3.95	985	.0098	.9335	93.9	8.8
10-15	280	2524	46	2.60	1770	.0182	.8791	88.5	17
15-20	208	1723	28	1.76	1590	.0162	.8917	89.8	15
20 up	110	1046	18	1.10	1640	.0172	.8853	89.1	16
All Dur.	1706	14991	166	15.27	1090	.0111	.9246	93.1	10
Age 30-39 yrs									
Dur. 0-5	1078	9616	65	20.79	315	.0068	.9536	96.8	4.6
5-10	425	4113	35	9.41	370	.0085	.9417	95.7	6.2
10-15	235	2413	44	5.38	820	.0182	.8791	89.3	16
15-20	251	2326	46	5.08	905	.0198	.8695	88.2	18
20 up	268	2463	61	5.38	1130	.0248	.8386	85.2	23
All Dur.	2257	20931	251	46.04	545	.0120	.9187	93.3	9.8
Age 40-49 yrs									
Dur. 0-5	1695	12826	193	65.90	295	.0150	.8993	93.2	9.9
5-10	559	4731	85	25.17	340	.0180	.8808	91.4	13
10-15	212	1884	34	10.08	335	.0180	.8803	91.4	13
15-20	182	1645	36	9.04	400	.0219	.8565	89.0	16
20 up	233	1830	39	9.38	415	.0213	.8597	89.1	16
All Dur.	2881	22916	387	119.57	325	.0169	.8876	92.0	12
Age 50-59 yrs									
Dur. 0-5	1477	10323	225	106.84	210	.0218	.8567	92.2	11
5-10	445	3087	106	33.16	320	.0343	.7829	84.4	24
10-15	164	1183	46	11.36	405	.0389	.7573	81.0	29
15-20	119	888	40	9.44	425	.0450	.7242	78.0	34
20 up	110	704	28	6.70	420	.0398	.7523	80.4	30
All Dur.	2315	16185	445	187.50	235	.0275	.8224	89.3	16
Age 60-69 yrs									
Dur. 0-5	478	2769	103	48.67	210	.0372	.7667	86.8	20
5-10	165	1030	46	19.78	235	.0447	.7263	83.2	25
10-15	52	254	16	4.86	330	.0630	.6338	72.6	44
15-20	52	316	24	6.08	395	.0760	.5749	65.9	57
20 up	52	243	10	3.87	260	.0412	.7451	83.3	25
All Dur.	799	4612	199	83.26	240	.0431	.7344	83.4	25

* Basis of expected mortality: Equitable Life Select & Ultimate Mortality Tables 1958-1963

DIABETES MELLITUS

Table 901d Comparative Experience by Known Duration of Diabetes at Application and Insurance Action (All Ages & Policy Durations Combined)

Insur. Action Prior Duration of Diabetes	No. of Entrants	Exposure Policy-Yrs	Observed Deaths	Expected* Deaths	Mortality Ratio	Ave. Ann. Mort. Rate	Est. 7-Yr Surv. Rate	Est. 7-Yr Surv. Index	Excess Death Rate
	ℓ	E	d	d'	100 d/d'	$\bar{q} = d/E$	$P = (1-\bar{q})^7$	100 P/P'	1000(d-d')/E
Issued									
0- 5 yrs	1761	13931	89	69.54	128%	.0064	.9561	99.0%	1.4
5-10	579	4725	50	23.70	210	.0106	.9279	96.1	5.6
10-15	235	2255	22	8.26	265	.0098	.9337	95.8	6.1
15-20	183	1738	19	7.51	255	.0109	.9258	95.4	6.6
20 up	119	1087	11	4.67	235	.0101	.9313	96.0	5.8
Unknown	23	113	0	.88	0	.0000	1.0000	105.6	−7.8
All	2900	23849	191	114.56	167	.0080	.9453	97.8	3.2
Declined									
0- 5 yrs	3824	28979	539	180.03	300	.0186	.8768	91.6	12
5-10	1567	13036	262	68.46	385	.0201	.8675	90.0	15
10-15	756	6460	168	26.44	635	.0260	.8316	85.6	22
15-20	640	5246	155	23.97	645	.0296	.8109	83.7	25
20 up	654	5199	145	21.75	665	.0279	.8204	84.5	24
Unknown	197	918	18	5.43	330	.0196	.8706	90.7	14
All	7638	59838	1287	326.08	395	.0215	.8589	89.2	16

Table 901e Comparative Experience by Type of Treatment and Insurance Action (All Ages and Durations Combined)

Insurance Action & Treatment	No. of Entrants	Exposure Policy-Yrs	Observed Deaths	Expected Deaths*	Mortality Ratio	Ave. Ann. Mort. Rate	Est. 7-Yr Surv. Rate	Est. 7-Yr Surv. Index	Excess Death Rate
	ℓ	E	d	d'	100 d/d'	$\bar{q} = d/E$	$P = (1-\bar{q})^7$	100 P/P'	1000 (d-d')/E
Issued									
Diet only	625	5178	31	31.24	99%	.0060	.9588	100.0%	−0.1
Oral Medication	830	4572	37	24.20	153	.0081	.9447	98.0	2.8
Insulin <25u	234	2670	35	16.48	210	.0131	.9118	95.2	6.9
25-49u	642	6225	47	24.03	196	.0076	.9483	97.4	3.7
50u & up	392	3721	33	10.83	305	.0089	.9395	95.8	6.0
Unknown	1	2	0	0.00	0	.0000	1.0000	100.0	0.0
All insulin	1269	12618	115	51.34	225	.0091	.9379	96.5	5.0
Insulin & Medication	31	226	1	.99	101	.0044	.9694	100.0	0.0
Unknown Med.	145	1256	7	6.79	103	.0056	.9616	99.8	0.2
Declined									
Diet only	1034	8197	181	64.28	280	.0221	.8553	90.3	14
Oral Medication	1752	9187	173	63.25	275	.0188	.8754	91.9	12
Insulin <25u	550	5558	147	40.53	365	.0264	.8289	87.3	19
25-49u	1676	15324	354	66.80	530	.0231	.8491	87.6	19
50u & up	1377	12405	250	34.40	725	.0202	.8672	88.4	17
Unknown	104	488	6	1.70	355	.0123	.9170	94.0	8.8
All insulin	3707	33775	757	143.43	530	.0224	.8531	87.9	18
Insulin & Medication	71	440	5	1.49	335	.0114	.9231	94.5	8.0
Unknown Med.	1074	8239	171	53.63	320	.0208	.8635	90.3	14

* Basis of expected mortality: Equitable Life Select & Ultimate Mortality Tables 1958-1963

DIABETES MELLITUS IN INSURANCE APPLICANTS

Table 901f Comparative Experience by Build and Blood Pressure (Issued and Declined Cases, All Ages and Durations Combined)

Build or Blood Pressure Category	No. of Entrants	Exposure Policy-Yrs	Observed Deaths	Expected Deaths*	Mortality Ratio	Ave. Ann. Mort. Rate	Est. 7-Yr Surv. Rate	Est. 7-Yr Surv. Index	Excess Death Rate
	ℓ	E	d	d'	100 d/d'	$\bar{q} = d/E$	$P = (1-\bar{q})^7$	100 P/P'	1000(d-d')/E
Standard Build	6142	48754	760	245.68	310%	.0156	.8955	92.8%	11
Underweight	1316	12214	186	38.35	485	.0152	.8981	91.8	12
10-20% Overweight	852	6339	124	47.57	260	.0196	.8708	91.8	12
21% Overweight up	1634	10830	220	75.92	290	.0203	.8660	91.0	13
Blood Pressure									
S<140, D<90	6964	54123	706	264.25	265	.0130	.9122	94.3	8.2
S140-159, D<90	854	5849	154	46.06	335	.0263	.8296	87.7	18
S160 up, D<90	151	861	42	8.30	505	.0488	.7046	75.4	39
S<140, D90-99	150	1196	25	6.68	375	.0209	.8625	89.7	15
S140-159, D90-99	383	2456	75	17.94	420	.0305	.8048	84.7	23
S160 up, D90-99	222	1403	67	14.60	460	.0478	.7100	76.3	37
S<160, D100 up	114	716	13	4.70	275	.0182	.8796	92.1	12
S160 up, D100 up	300	1616	65	11.19	580	.0402	.7502	78.8	33

Table 901g Comparative Mortality by Reason for Declination (All Ages and Durations Combined)

Reason for Declination	No. of Entrants	Exposure Policy-Yrs	Observed Deaths	Expected Deaths*	Mortality Ratio	Excess Death Rate
	ℓ	E	d	d'	100 d/d'	1000(d-d')/E
Higher Risk						
Hypertension Alone	815	5225	134	39.33	340%	18
Hypertension + Non CV	432	2900	120	20.99	570	34
Other CV, Alone or Combination	577	3404	122	25.22	485	28
History of Coma, Shock, High Blood Sugar	195	2118	31	7.34	420	11
Albuminuria or Casts†	270	2025	86	9.20	935	38
Age of Onset Only●	303	2413	26	2.85	910	9.6
Miscellaneous Other Single Impairments	500	3844	114	20.11	565	24
Total Higher Risk	3092	21929	633	125.04	505	23
Lower Risk						
Build Not Standard	107	969	18	5.70	315%	13
High Urine or Blood Sugar□	1066	9161	147	36.23	405	12
Not Under Good Supervision	407	4990	91	25.37	360	13
Abnormal ECG Alone	88	758	20	6.87	290	17
Combination of Impairments■	259	2206	58	15.75	370	19
Non Medical Reasons	383	3102	55	17.33	315	12
Incomplete Data	2087	15540	218	72.53	300	9.4
Age of Applicant Only	149	1184	47	21.26	220	22
Total Lower Risk	4546	37910	654	201.04	325	12
Total Declination	7638	59839	1287	326.08	395	16

* Basis of expected mortality: Equitable Life Select & Ultimate Mortality Tables 1958-1963
† Albumin, casts, or other urinary findings other than glycosuria only, alone or in combination with other impairments excluding hypertension
● Age at onset of diabetes only, under 10 or over 60 years
□ At time of examination only
■ Combination of impairments excluding hypertension and albuminuria

DIABETES MELLITUS

§902–INSURED DIABETICS

References: (1) J. W. Barch, "Diabetes – A Continuing Mortality Study," Proc. Home Office Life Underwriters Assoc., 52:66-95 (1971).

(2) W. L. Bogardus, Panel Discussion, "Individual Life and Health Underwriting. 2. Diabetics," Trans. Soc. Actuaries, 25:D236-D240 (1973).

(3) J. W. Barch and J. L. Mast, Personal communication of additional data (1971-1973).

Subjects Studied: Policyholders insured by the Lincoln National Life Insurance Company from 1946 through 1965 from 10 through 64 years of age at time of application for insurance, traced to policy anniversaries in 1966 or to prior termination. Records underlying the data of the study indicated diabetes mellitus as a primary impairment; the possible existence of other impairments, accordingly, indicated heterogeneity in the subjects studied. To construct sub-groups with some degree of homogeneity for study purposes, all cases were classified into four groups according to criteria applicable at the time insurance was applied for:

(1) Cases without Complications (general cases). Exposed to Risk: 62238 policy years. Known diabetics under treatment by diet alone or by diet and insulin without complication of diabetes or major additional impairment;

(2) Cases with Complications. Exposed to Risk: 15008 policy years. Known diabetics under treatment with some complication of diabetes or having some history or finding of an additional major impairment;

(3) Miscellaneous Cases. Exposed to Risk: 10860 policy years.
    a. Known diabetics under treatment by diet and oral hypoglycemic agent,
    b. Applicants not classifiable as General or Complicated Cases;

(4) Selected Cases. Exposed to Risk: 13844 policy years. General cases under treatment by diet and insulin, presenting normal blood pressure and normal weight, and revealing no ratable evidence of poor control other than glycosuria and/or hyperglycemia (e.g., acidosis, insulin reactions, complications).

A fifth category comprising policyholders within the class of General Cases whose disease was diagnosed prior to age 20 was also reported on (see reference 2). The experience of this fifth group was presented with respect to durations subsequent to the first five policy years.

Follow-up: Policy records of the Lincoln National Life Insurance Company were used for follow-up and constituted the basis for counting deaths and numbers exposed to risk.

Results: (1) General Cases – Mortality and survival results for all durations combined according to age at issue of insurance are presented in Table 902a. A mortality ratio of 355 per cent was observed for the total experience. At the younger ages, mortality ratios are relatively high reaching 785 per cent for ages between 20 and 30 years (the ratio for ages under 20, however, is somewhat lower – 645 per cent). This function diminishes as the age at issue increases, declining to 215 per cent for age group 60-64 years. Seven-year survival indexes also decrease with age at issue, receding from 96.6 per cent for ages under 20 years to 86.9 per cent for the oldest ages (60-64 years). The excess death rate increases steadily from 5 per 1000 per year at issue ages 10 through 19 years to 20 per 1000 at ages 60-64 years. The average EDR for all ages combined is 9.7.

Experience by duration from commencement of coverage for all ages combined is given in Tables 902b-c. Mortality ratios and excess death rates tend to increase with duration. The former start at 245 per cent in the first two policy years and peak at 435 per cent in the interval extending over policy years 10 to 15, declining to 335 per cent in the following five years. Excess annual death rates increase from an average of 2.3 per 1000 over policy years 1 and 2 to 25 per 1000 in the last five years of policy duration.

INSURED DIABETICS WITHOUT COMPLICATIONS

Table 902a Comparative Experience by Age at Issue of Insurance, Cases without Complications, All Durations Combined

Age Group	Exposure Policy-Yrs	No. of Death Claims		Mortality Ratio	Est. 7-Yr Surv. Rate		Survival Index	Excess Death Rate
		Observed	Expected*		Observed	Expected*		
(Years)	E	d	d'	100 d/d'	P	P'	100 P/P'	1000(d-d')/E
10-19	4951	29	4.48	645%	.960	.9937	96.6%	5.0
20-29	15318	119	15.2	785	.947	.9931	95.3	6.8
30-39	18115	185	42.3	435	.931	.9838	94.6	7.9
40-49	16666	301	92.6	325	.880	.9617	91.5	13
50-59	6358	172	65.9	260	.825	.9294	88.8	17
60-64	830	30	13.8	215	.773	.8893	86.9	20
10-64	62238	836	234	355	.910	.9740	93.4	9.7

Table 902b Observed Data and Comparative Experience by Policy Duration, Cases without Complications, All Ages Combined

Interval		Exposure Policy-Yrs	No. of Death Claims		Mortality Ratio		Survival Ratio		Excess Death Rate
No.	Start-End		Observed	Expected*	Interval	Cumulative	Interval	Cumulative	
i	t to t + Δ t	E	d	d'	100 d/d'	100$\sum$d/$\sum$d'	100 p_i/p_i'	100 P/P'	1000(d-d')/E
1	0- 2 yrs	14228	56	22.8	245%	245%	99.5%	99.5%	2.3
2	2- 5	16652	119	44.4	270	260	98.7	98.2	4.5
3	5-10	19431	310	80.7	385	330	94.2	92.5	12
4	10-15	9442	264	60.4	435	360	89.6	82.9	22
5	15-20	2485	87	26.0	335	355	88.2	73.1	25

Table 902c Derived Mortality and Survival Data by Policy Duration, Cases without Complications

Interval		Observed Rates				Expected Rates*			
		Average Annual		Cumulative		Average Annual		Cumulative	
No.	Start-End	Mortality	Survival	Survival	Mortality	Mortality	Survival	Survival	Mortality
i	t to t + Δ t	$\bar{q} = d/E$	$\bar{p}$	P	Q	$\bar{q}' = d'/E$	$\bar{p}'$	P'	Q'
1	0- 2 yrs	.004	.996	.992	.008	.0016	.9984	.9968	.0032
2	2- 5	.007	.993	.971	.029	.0027	.9973	.9887	.0113
3	5-10	.016	.984	.896	.104	.0042	.9958	.9682	.0318
4	10-15	.028	.972	.778	.222	.0064	.9936	.9376	.0624
5	15-20	.035	.965	.651	.349	.0105	.9895	.8894	.1106

* Basis of expected mortality: Contemporaneous intercompany standard insurance experience

DIABETES MELLITUS

§902–INSURED DIABETICS

Results (continued):

Shown in Table 902d are mortality and survival results by age group, all policy years combined, according to the age at diagnosis and the duration of diabetes at time insurance was applied for. Where diagnosis of diabetes was made prior to age 50, mortality ratios tend to reach a peak when the diabetic condition has continued from 7 to 12 years following diagnosis (there is an excessive duplication of claims at durations 13-18 years for age group 40-49 years). On the basis of the foregoing, the author suggests that if serious complications have not become apparent by the time the disease has been present for 7-12 years, the most critical period may have passed, and subsequent complications may be less likely to occur.

The upper part of Table 902e shows experience, all ages and durations combined, for General Cases by build. The highest mortality ratio, 480 per cent, develops among underweights. Overweight and normal subjects experience about the same ratio, 325 to 330 per cent, but the author reports a higher mortality in overweight subjects after age adjustment.

(2) Cases with Complications – Experience under eight classes of complication is presented in Table 902f. Mortality ratios, averaging overall 560 per cent, range from 395 per cent for circulatory impairments other than a current finding or history of hypertension to 1290 per cent for albuminuria. The latter complication is also associated with the least favorable survival index (83.9 per cent) for an individual complication. Among all the complication subgroups by age at issue (not shown in table) mortality ratios are consistently higher at ages below 40 than at older ages. Here also, average yearly excess death rates, running from 12 to 26 per 1000 indicate that for albuminuria this function is the highest for any specific single complication.

(3) Miscellaneous Cases – The lower portion of Table 902e presents mortality and survival data (all ages and durations combined) for known diabetics treated by diet and oral hypoglycemic agent, and certain applicants of uncertain or undetermined diabetic condition. There is considerable diversity in experience under the several categories. Cases not classified by reason of incomplete information, by this circumstance a heterogeneous group, reveal the most adverse experience: mortality ratio of 470 per cent, a survival index (seven year estimate of mean) of 91.1 per cent and excess deaths of 13 per 1000 per year. The group of insureds composed of suspected diabetics indicates a mortality ratio of 215 per cent, and an EDR of 6.7 per 1000. Cases treated by oral agents alone or in combination with insulin showed more favorable experience: mortality ratio of 190 per cent, and an EDR of 3.7 per 1000. These may be compared with the corresponding indexes in Table 902a for all ages combined, which show a mortality ratio of 355 per cent and an EDR of 9.7 per 1000.

(4) Selected Cases – Table 902g presents experience of this classification, all policy years combined, in three subdivisions: according to age at issue of insurance; age at diagnosis of diabetes; and duration of diabetes at issue. Mortality ratios decline in both groupings based on age and lie in practically the same range – ratios in the age at issue class decrease from 390 per cent for ages 20-29 years to 275 per cent for age group 50-64 years, while ratios with respect to age at diagnosis decline from 370 to 220 per cent for the corresponding age groups. Average annual excess deaths per 1000 increase in both of these categories: by age at issue, from 3.0 to 19 per 1000; by age at diagnosis, from 7.0 to 15. Where, at time of issue, account is taken of the number of years elapsed since diagnosis, mortality ratios vary within the relatively narrow range 325 to 420 per cent for durations 7 years and longer; for shorter durations the ratio is 250 per cent. Excess death rates increase with duration, ranging from 6.0 for durations of 6 years or less to 21 for durations of 19 years and up. Survival indexes in all three classifications almost invariably diminish as age or duration increases.

The experience of Selected Cases by policy duration is presented in Tables 902h-i. Mortality ratios which average 325 per cent for the entire follow-up increase from 230 to 385 per cent in successive intervals through the 15th policy year and then recede to 295 per cent for the following five-year interval. Interval and cummulative survival ratios consistently decrease with policy duration, the former from 99.6 per cent at policy durations 0-2 years to 88.6 per cent in the 15-20 year interval. Excess death rates which average 2.1 per 1000 over the first two policy years increase to 24 per 1000 over policy durations 15-20 years.

INSURED DIABETICS WITHOUT COMPLICATIONS

Table 902d   Comparative Experience by Age at Diagnosis and Known Duration of Diabetes at Application, All Policy Years Combined

Age at Diagnosis	Duration of Diabetes	Exposure Policy-Yrs	No. of Death Claims		Mortality Ratio	Est. 7-Yr Surv. Rate		Survival Index	Excess Death Rate
			Observed	Expected*		Observed	Expected*		
		E	d	d'	100 d/d'	P	P'	100 P/P'	1000(d-d')/E
0-19 yrs	0- 6 yrs	4915	32	4.39	730%	.955	.9938	96.1%	5.6
	7-12	7002	64	6.97	920	.938	.9931	94.4	8.1
	13-18	4838	53	6.33	835	.926	.9909	93.4	9.6
	19 up	4225	44	11.6	380	.929	.9809	94.7	7.7
	All Durations	20980	193	29.3	660	.937	.9903	94.7	7.8
20-29	0- 6 yrs	5878	32	7.73	415	.963	.9908	97.1	4.1
	7-12	5596	66	12.6	520	.920	.9843	93.5	9.5
	13-18	2633	35	10.6	330	.911	.9722	93.7	9.3
	19 up	921	26	5.96	435	.818	.9556	85.6	22
	All Durations	15033	159	37.0	430	.928	.9829	94.4	8.1
30-39	0- 6 yrs	7828	68	25.8	265	.941	.9772	96.3	5.4
	7-12	4447	96	23.9	400	.858	.9630	89.1	16.
	13-18	1112	27	8.44	320	.842	.9481	88.8	17
	19 up	419	10	5.71	175	.844	.9084	93.0	10
	All Durations	13806	201	63.8	315	.902	.9681	93.2	9.9
40-49	0- 6 yrs	7570	134	50.4	265	.882	.9543	92.5	11
	7-12	1748	53	16.9	315	.806	.9343	86.3	21
	13-18	273	17	2.88	590	.638	.9285	68.7	52
	19 up	14	0	—	—	1.000	—	—	—
	All Durations	9605	204	70.2	290	.860	.9499	90.6	14
50-64	0- 6 yrs	2506	70	29.2	240	.820	.9212	89.0	16
	7-12	308	9	4.71	191	.813	.8977	90.5	14
	13 up	0	0	0	—	—	—	—	—
	All Durations	2814	79	33.9	235	.819	.9187	89.2	16
0-64	0- 6 yrs	28697	336	117	285	.921	.9718	94.8	7.6
	7-12	19101	288	65.3	440	.899	.9763	92.1	12
	13-18	8861	132	28.3	465	.900	.9779	92.1	12
	19 up	5579	80	23.5	340	.904	.9709	93.1	10
	All Durations	62238	836	234	355	.910	.9740	93.4	10

* Basis of expected mortality: Contemporaneous intercompany standard insurance experience

DIABETES MELLITUS

§902—INSURED DIABETICS

Results (continued):

(5) Cases with Juvenile Diagnosis (Under Age 20), Experience in First Five Policy Years Excluded. Experience for this group shown in Table 902j presents a quite different picture from that seen in all other groups without significant complications. Mortality ratios rise sharply with increase in total duration of the disease, peaking between 15 and 20 years following diagnosis at 1730 per cent of standard expected mortality. After this interval the ratios decline to 1580 per cent from the 18th through the 22nd year after diagnosis, diminishing thereafter to 415 per cent for years 36-48 following diagnosis. Excess death rates rise from an interval minimum of 3.2 per 1000 to a peak of 16 to 17 per 1000 during the intervals from 15 to 22 years following diagnosis, then fall to 9.9 per 1000 in the 21 to 25 year interval, and after that increase again to a maximum of 28 per 1000 in the last interval from 36 to 48 years after diagnosis. The trend of the 7-year survival index is the corresponding opposite of that for EDR, as is evident from a comparison of the last two columns of Table 902j.

In Table 902k experience for all ages and durations combined is presented for three groups according to insulin dosage. General Cases — classification (1) — show an apparent tendency for mortality ratio to increase with insulin dosage but no such tendency for EDR, the maximum of 13 extra deaths per 1000 being observed at the low insulin dosage of 1 to 30 units per day, and a corresponding minimum survival index of 91.4 per cent. Since these data are not age-adjusted the higher mortality ratios at the larger insulin dosage levels may be simply a result of a younger average age for the insulin groups as compared with the no-insulin group.

Selected Cases without complications and with best control (no glycosuria or hyperglycemia) show results similar to the preceding classification but somewhat more favorable, the mortality ratio averaging 305 per cent against the 355 per cent of the foregoing class. The other indexes are also relatively favorable. Selected cases with a history of glycosuria or hyperglycemia, indicating poorer control, show *less* favorable mortality at the *lower* insulin dosage of 1-30 units per day, with a mortality ratio of 520 per cent and EDR of 18 per 1000. These indexes are considerably higher than observed in the cases with best control and the same insulin dosage, and also are higher than they are when the insulin dosage exceeds 30 units per day, with or without best control. Cases with daily insulin dosage of 31 units up and glycosuria or hyperglycemia have a mortality ratio of 385 per cent, not greatly in excess of the mortality ratios of 305 and 360 per cent for selected cases with best control. The survival index and EDR are also similar at these higher insulin dosage levels.

INSURED DIABETICS WITH OR WITHOUT COMPLICATIONS

Table 902e Comparative Experience by Build and Other Factors, Cases without Known Complications

Category	Exposure Policy-Yrs	No. of Death Claims		Mortality Ratio	Est. 7-Yr Surv. Rate		Survival Index	Excess Death Rate
		Observed	Expected*		Observed	Expected*		
	E	d	d'	100 d/d'	P	P'	100 P/P'	1000(d-d')/E
Underweight	18296	210	43.7	480%	.922	.9834	93.8%	9.1
Normal weight	34905	442	134	330	.915	.9734	94.0	8.8
Overweight	9037	184	56.6	325	.866	.9569	90.5	14
Suspected Diabetes Mellitus	2851	36	16.8	215	.915	.9595	95.4	6.7
History Diabetes Mellitus	825	2	—	—	.983	—	—	—
Oral Agent†	3104	24	12.6	190	.947	.9719	97.4	3.7
Unclassified●	4080	68	14.4	470	.889	.9756	91.1	13

Table 902f Comparative Experience by Complication, Cases with Complications

Complication	Exposure Policy-Yrs	No. of Death Claims		Mortality Ratio	Est. 7-Yr Surv. Rate		Survival Index	Excess Death Rate
		Observed	Expected*		Observed	Expected*		
	E	d	d'	100 d/d'	P	P'	100 P/P'	1000(d-d')/E
Hypertension, current or history	1659	38	7.77	490%	.850	.9677	87.9%	18
Other circulatory	2259	46	11.7	395	.866	.9643	89.8	15
Albuminuria	2017	54	4.17	1290	.827	.9856	83.9	25
Other GU (not glycosuria)	946	16	3.83	420	.887	.9720	91.3	13
Respiratory	574	11	1.67	660	.873	.9798	89.1	16
Digestive	769	18	3.38	535	.847	.9696	87.4	19
Gen., Misc., extreme builds	2481	48	10.1	475	.872	.9718	89.7	15
Nonphysical	1405	22	4.55	485	.895	.9776	91.6	12
All Others/Combinations	2898	88	13.5	650	.806	.9678	83.3	26

* Basis of expected mortality: Contemporaneous intercompany standard insurance experience
† Cases treated by oral agents alone or in combination with insulin
● Cases not classified because information was incomplete

DIABETES MELLITUS

Table 902g Comparative Experience by Age and by Prior Duration of Diabetes,
Selected Cases without Complications

Age/Duration	Exposure Policy-Yrs	No. of Death Claims		Mortality Ratio	Est. 7-Yr Surv. Rate		Survival Index	Excess Death Rate
		Observed	Expected*		Observed	Expected*		
	E	d	d'	100 d/d'	P	P'	100 P/P'	1000(d-d')/E
Age at Issue								
20-29 yrs	1721	7	1.79	390%	.972	.9927	97.9%	3.0
30-39	5754	47	13.8	340	.944	.9833	96.0	5.8
40-49	4981	97	28.7	340	.871	.9604	90.7	14
50-64	1388	42	15.4	275	.806	.9249	87.2	19
Age at Diagnosis								
20-29 yrs	7017	67	18.1	370	.935	.9821	95.2	7.0
30-39	4377	72	20.0	360	.890	.9684	91.9	12
40-49	2089	44	17.1	255	.862	.9441	91.3	.13
50-64	361	10	4.50	220	.821	.9159	89.7	15
Duration of Diabetes at Issue								
0- 6 yrs	6987	70	27.9	250	.932	.9724	95.8	6.0
7-12	4415	76	18.2	420	.886	.9715	91.2	13
13-18	1908	32	9.85	325	.888	.9644	92.1	12
19 up	534	15	3.75	400	.819	.9519	86.1	21

Table 902h Observed Data and Comparative Experience by Policy Duration, Selected Cases
without Complications, All Ages Combined

Policy Interval		Exposure Policy-Yrs	No. of Deaths		Mortality Ratio		Survival Ratio		Excess Death Rate
No.	Start-End		Observed	Expected*	Interval	Cumulative	Interval	Cumulative	
i	t to t + Δt	E	d	d'	100 d/d'	100 $\sum$d/$\sum$d'	100 p_i/p_i'	100 P/P'	1000(d-d')/E
1	0- 2 yrs	2899	11	4.78	230%	230%	99.6%	99.6%	2.1
2	2- 5	3527	23	9.83	235	235	98.9	98.5	3.7
3	5-10	4399	69	19.7	350	300	94.5	93.0	11
4	10-15	2318	65	16.8	385	330	90.0	83.7	21
5	15-20	701	25	8.50	295	325	88.6	74.2	24
	0-20	13844	193	59.7	325	325		74.2	9.6

Table 902i Derived Mortality and Survival Data, Selected Cases without Complications

Interval		Observed Rates				Expected Rates*			
		Average Annual		Cumulative		Average Annual		Cumulative	
No.	Start-End	Mortality	Survival	Survival	Mortality	Mortality	Survival	Survival	Mortality
i	t to t + Δt	$\bar{q}$ = d/E	$\bar{p}$	P	Q	$\bar{q}'$ = d'/E	$\bar{p}'$	P'	Q'
1	0- 2 yrs	.004	.996	.992	.008	.0016	.9984	.9967	.0033
2	2- 5	.007	.993	.973	.027	.0028	.9972	.9884	.0116
3	5-10	.016	.984	.899	.101	.0045	.9955	.9665	.0335
4	10-15	.028	.972	.780	.220	.0072	.9928	.9319	.0681
5	15-20	.036	.964	.650	.350	.0121	.9879	.8768	.1232

* Basis of expected mortality: Contemporaneous intercompany standard insurance experience

INSURED DIABETICS WITHOUT COMPLICATIONS

Table 902j   Comparative Experience by Duration from Diagnosis, Juvenile onset cases without Complications (Diagnosed under Age 20), First Five Policy Years Excluded

Duration from Diagnosis	Exposure Policy-Yrs	No. of Deaths		Mortality Ratio	Est. 7-Yr Surv. Rate		Survival Index	Excess Death Rate
		Observed	Expected*		Observed	Expected*		
	E	d	d'	100 d/d'	P	P'	100 P/P'	1000(d-d')/E
6-13 yrs	1197	5	1.12	445%	.971	.9935	97.8%	3.2
12-16	1321	14	1.27	1100	.928	.9933	93.4	9.6
15-19	1782	31	1.79	1730	.884	.9930	89.2	16
18-22	1937	35	2.22	1580	.880	.9920	88.7	17
21-25	1767	20	2.46	815	.923	.9903	93.2	9.9
24-33	2958	49	6.14	800	.890	.9856	90.3	14
30-39	1567	41	6.18	665	.831	.9727	85.4	22
36-48	523	19	4.57	415	.772	.9404	82.1	28
6-48	13052	214	25.75	830	.891	.9863	90.3	14

Table 902k   Comparative Experience by Daily Insulin Dosage

Insulin Dosage	Exposure Policy-Yrs	No. of Death Claims		Mortality Ratio	Est. 7-Yr Surv. Rate		Survival Index	Excess Death Rate
		Observed	Expected*		Observed	Expected*		
	E	d	d'	100 d/d'	P	P'	100 P/P'	1000(d-d')/E
All Cases without Complications								
0 (Diet Alone)	11978	160	72.4	220%	.910	.9584	95.0%	7.3
All Insulin	50260	676	161.9	415	.910	.9776	93.0	10.2
1-30 units	15360	266	70.4	380	.885	.9684	91.4	13
31-60	26088	327	74.0	440	.915	.9803	93.4	9.7
61 up	8812	83	17.5	475	.936	.9862	94.9	7.4
Total	62238	836	234.3	355	.910	.9739	93.4	9.7
Selected Cases without Complications (Best Control, No Glycosuria or Hyperglycemia)†								
1-30 units	4766	74	25.0	295	.896	.9639	93.0	10
31-60	5575	67	22.0	305	.919	.9727	94.5	8.1
61 up	1212	15	4.19	360	.917	.9760	93.9	8.9
Total	11553	156	51.2	305	.909	.9694	93.8	9.1
Selected Cases without Complications (With History of Glycosuria or Hyperglycemia)●								
1-30 units	760	17	3.28	520	.854	.9702	88.0	18
31 up	1531	20	5.19	385	.912	.9765	93.4	9.7
Total	2291	37	8.47	435	.892	.9744	91.6	12

* Basis of expected mortality: Contemporaneous intercompany standard insurance experience
† Controlled diabetics (including those rated for amount of insulin)
● Minimal rating plus additional rating for glycosuria or hyperglycemia

DIABETES MELLITUS

§903—DIABETIC INSURED LIVES

Reference: P. S. Entmacher, "An Insurance-Clinical Dialogue on Diabetes," Trans. Assoc. Life Ins. Med. Dir. Amer., 55:205-212 (1971).

Subjects Studied: Diabetics accepted for life insurance by the Metropolitan Life Insurance Company between 1952 and 1965. There were 24,863 total years of life exposed to risk and 325 deaths. Exposures by age group at issue of coverage and by duration of insurance and deaths occurring in these subdivisions are indicated in Tables 903a-b. These diabetic applicants were free of known complications at the time of policy issue; cases were excluded if there was a significant ratable impairment other than diabetes.

Follow-up: Policy records of the Metropolitan Life Insurance Company were used for follow-up to January 1, 1971, and constituted the basis for counting deaths and numbers exposed to risk. There were 3,983 policy entrants, 15.6 per cent of whom were female. The average duration of follow-up was 6.2 years.

Results: Compared with that of standard lives insured in the same period, overall mortality experience was high — almost three and one-half times that of unimpaired risks. Mortality ratios, all durations combined, as shown in Table 903a, diminish as age at issue increases, declining from 590 per cent for age group 15-29 years to 200 per cent for ages 60-65 years. The number of excess deaths per 1000 (903a), however, increases through the entire age range: from 4 per 1000 per annum for ages at issue under 30 years to 15 per 1000 for age group 60-65 years. No clear trend in mortality ratio appears by duration from issuance of insurance coverage, mortality ratios ranging between 225 and 390 per cent, but EDR increases with duration (903b).

The principal causes of death experienced among the subject diabetics insured are presented in Table 903d. Of the total 325 deaths, cardiovascular-renal diseases accounted for nearly 70 per cent, with the cardiac deaths causing over half of them. Cancer accounted for about 10 per cent of the deaths, a smaller than average percentage for this age group in standard insureds. There was a relatively high frequency of accidents as a cause of death.

Table 903a   Comparative Experience by Age at Issue (Male and Female)

Age Group at Issue	Exposure Person-Yrs	Deaths Observed	Deaths Expected*	Mortality Ratio	Average Annual Mort. Rate	Estimated 5-Year Surv. Rate	Estimated 5-Year Surv. Index	Excess Death Rate
	E	d	d'	100 d/d'	$\bar{q} = d/E$	$P = (1-\bar{q})^5$	100 P/P'	1000(d-d')/E
15-29 yrs	7719	37	6.28	590%	.005	.976	98.0%	4.0
30-39 yrs	4710	47	8.17	575	.010	.951	95.9	8.2
40-49 yrs	7380	123	31.30	395	.017	.919	93.9	12
50-59 yrs	4382	98	38.30	255	.022	.893	93.3	14
60-65 yrs	672	20	9.90	200	.030	.860	92.6	15
15-65 yrs	24863	325	94.00	345	.013	.936	95.4	9.3

*Basis of expected mortality: Intercompany 1955-1960 Select Combined Male and Female

DIABETIC INSURED LIVES

Table 903b Observed Data and Comparative Experience by Duration — All Ages Combined (Male and Female)

Duration after Issue	Exposure	Deaths		Mortality Ratio		Survival Ratio		Excess
Start-End	Person-Yrs	Obs.	Exp.*	Interval	Cumulative	Interval	Cumulative	Death Rate
t to $t + \Delta t$	E	d	d'	$100\, d/d'$	$100\,\Sigma d/\Sigma d'$	$100\, p_i/p_i'$	$100\, P/P'$	$1000(d-d')/E$
0- 3 yrs	10755	88	25.30	350%	350%	98.3%	98.3%	5.8
3- 5	6108	77	22.70	340	345	98.2	96.5	8.9
5-10	6601	130	33.40	390	360	92.9	89.6	15
10-15	1215	22	9.82	225	350	95.1	85.2	10
15-20	184	8	2.74	290	345	86.3	73.5	29
0-20	24863	325	94.00	345	345		73.5	9.3

Table 903c Derived Mortality and Survival Data (Male and Female)

Duration after Issue	Observed Rates				Expected Rates*			
	Average Annual		Cumulative		Average Annual		Cumulative	
Start-End	Mortality	Survival	Survival	Mortality	Mortality	Survival	Survival	Mortality
t to $t + \Delta t$	$\bar{q} = d/E$	$\bar{p}$	P	Q	$\bar{q}' = d'/E$	$\bar{p}'$	P'	Q'
0- 3 yrs	.008	.992	.976	.024	.0024	.9976	.9928	.0072
3- 5	.013	.987	.951	.049	.0037	.9963	.9855	.0145
5-10	.020	.980	.861	.139	.0051	.9949	.9606	.0394
10-15	.018	.982	.786	.214	.0081	.9919	.9224	.0776
15-20	.043	.957	.629	.371	.0149	.9851	.8557	.1443

Table 903d Principal Causes of Death Among Insured Diabetics

Cause of Death	Number of Deaths	Per cent of All Causes	Cause of Death	Number of Deaths	Per cent of All Causes
Diabetic Coma	11	3.4%	Infections	12	3.7%
Cardiovascular-Renal			Cancer	30	9.2
Cardiac	180	55.4	External Causes		
Renal	25	7.7	Accidents	19	5.8
Cerebrovascular	15	4.6	Suicide	2	0.6
Arteriosclerosis	1	0.3	Other and Unknown	30	9.2
Total CVR	221	68.0	All Causes	325	100.0

* Basis of expected mortality: Intercompany 1955-60 Select Combined Male and Female

DIABETES MELLITUS IN INSUREDS

§904—DIABETES MELLITUS IN INSUREDS

Reference: "New York Life Single Medical Impairment Study—1972," unpublished report made available by J.J. Hutchinson and J.C. Sibigtroth (1973).

Subjects Studied: Policyholders of New York Life Insurance Company issued insurance in 1954-1970, followed to the 1971 policy anniversary. The experience is reported for cases who had been diagnosed as having diabetes. Different codes were used to distinguish cases being treated with insulin from all others. Further, the cases receiving insulin treatment were separated into those taking up to 25 units of insulin and those taking more than 25 units. Only substandard issues were studied; cases involving ratable impairments in addition to diabetes were excluded.

Follow-up: Insurance policy records formed the basis of entry, of counting policies, exposure and death claims, and of follow-up information.

Results: Comparative experience is given in Tables 904a-b for substandard cases, by sex and duration, all ages combined, separately for males treated with insulin (subclassified into less than 25 units, and 25 units up) and cases with other treatment. Among males treated with insulin, the mortality ratio for those taking less than 25 units showed no trend by duration, ranging between 132 and 196 per cent, with EDR highest (11 extra deaths per 1000) at 10-17 years. The mortality ratios for those taking 25 units or more, as compared with those being treated with less than 25 units of insulin, were higher throughout. At 10-17 years, the mortality ratio was 445 per cent and the EDR 22 per 1000. Among males receiving other treatment (not insulin), there was a tendency for the mortality ratio to be somewhat higher after ten years than in earlier years, with EDR highest, 26 per 1000, at 10-17 years. The male cumulative survival ratios at 17 years among cases treated with insulin were 90.1 and 81.1 per cent, respectively for those taking less than 25 units and those taking 25 units or more. For males receiving other than insulin treatment, the corresponding figure was 80.1 per cent.

The experience for females was much smaller than for males, and no breakdown by type of treatment was made. For all treatments combined, the mortality ratio among females appeared to be somewhat higher after five years, with EDR highest (12 extra deaths per 1000) at 10-17 years. The cumulative survival ratio at 17 years was 87.9 per cent.

From Table 904c, diabetic males taking insulin experienced an overall mortality ratio of 168 per cent for treatment up to 25 units and 335 per cent for insulin of 25 units or more. In the former group, the mortality ratio showed no definite trend by age, being highest at 725 per cent at ages 15-29. There was no excess mortality found in the age group 30-39, with only one death claim resulting from 1,113 policy years of exposure. The highest levels of EDR, slightly over 5 per 1000, were found in two different age groups, men 15 to 29 years, and men 50-59 years. In the group with higher insulin dosage, the mortality ratio was somewhat higher for males under entry age 40 than for subsequent ages. The EDR was highest (23 extra deaths per 1000) at ages 50-59. Among males receiving other than insulin treatment, the mortality ratio showed a downward trend, ranging from 750 per cent at ages 15-29 to 194 per cent at ages 50-59, in which age group the highest EDR (10 per 1000) was observed. The mortality ratio of 47 per cent in men age 60 up is based on a single death. The overall mortality ratio was 193 per cent.

The mortality ratios of females receiving all forms of treatment appeared somewhat higher at ages under 40, with EDR highest (8.6 extra deaths per 1000) at ages 50-59. The overall mortality ratio was 310 per cent.

From Table 904d, there was some increase in mortality in each of the various causes listed, except accidents and homicides. The major causes of death were found in diseases of heart and circulation, and "all other causes and unknown." The mortality ratio for these two categories were 260 and 445 per cent, respectively, with corresponding EDR of 2.3 and 2.4 per 1000. The 72 deaths from "all other causes and unknown" include 35 deaths due to diabetes, 10 deaths due to pneumonia and 8 deaths due to cerebrovascular accidents.

DIABETES MELLITUS

Table 904a   Observed Data and Comparative Experience by Sex, Treatment and Duration — Substandard Cases

Sex	Interval No.	Interval Start-End	Exposure Policy-Yrs	No. of Death Claims Observed	No. of Death Claims Expected*	Mortality Ratio Interval	Mortality Ratio Cumulative	Survival Ratio Interval	Survival Ratio Cumulative	Excess Death Rate
	i	t to t + Δ t	E	d	d'	100 d/d'	100 Σd/Σd'	100 p_i/p_i'	100 P/P'	1000(d-d')/E
Treatment - to 25 Units of Insulin										
Male	1	0- 2 yrs	2459	12	6.77	177%	177%	99.6%	99.6%	2.1
	2	2- 5	1904	17	9.63	177	177	98.8	98.4	3.9
	3	5-10	963	9	6.84	132	164	98.9	97.3	2.2
	4	10-17	318	7	3.58	196	168	92.6	90.1	11
Treatment - 25 Units of Insulin or More										
Male	1	0- 2 yrs	3127	10	3.79	265	265	99.6	99.6	2.0
	2	2- 5	3053	11	6.10	180	210	99.5	99.1	1.6
	3	5-10	2630	30	7.71	390	290	95.8	95.0	8.5
	4	10-17	1150	33	7.43	445	335	85.3	81.1	22
Other Treatment										
Male	1	0- 2 yrs	1156	5	3.00	167	167	99.7	99.7	1.7
	2	2- 5	1155	8	5.53	145	152	99.4	99.0	2.1
	3	5-10	1281	16	10.22	157	155	97.7	96.8	4.5
	4	10-17	544	22	7.73	285	193	82.8	80.1	26
All Treatments										
Female	1	0- 2 yrs	1263	4	1.36	295	295	99.6	99.6	2.1
	2	2- 5	1151	5	2.30	215	245	99.3	98.9	2.3
	3	5-10	846	8	2.17	370	290	96.6	95.5	6.9
	4	10-17	320	5	1.22	410	310	92.0	87.9	12

Table 904b   Derived Mortality and Survival Data

Sex	Interval No.	Interval Start-End	Observed Rates Average Annual Mortality	Observed Rates Average Annual Survival	Observed Rates Cumulative Survival	Observed Rates Cumulative Mortality	Expected Rates* Average Annual Mortality	Expected Rates* Average Annual Survival	Expected Rates* Cumulative Survival	Expected Rates* Cumulative Mortality
	i	t to t + Δ t	$\bar{q} = d/E$	$\bar{p}$	P	Q	$\bar{q}' = d'/E$	$\bar{p}'$	P'	Q'
Treatment - to 25 Units of Insulin										
Male	1	0- 2 yrs	.0049	.9951	.9903	.0097	.0028	.9972	.9945	.0055
	2	2- 5	.0089	.9911	.9640	.0360	.0051	.9949	.9795	.0205
	3	5-10	.0093	.9907	.9198	.0802	.0071	.9929	.9452	.0548
	4	10-17	.0220	.9780	.7871	.2129	.0113	.9887	.8732	.1268
Treatment - 25 Units of Insulin or More										
Male	1	0- 2 yrs	.0032	.9968	.9936	.0064	.0012	.9988	.9976	.0024
	2	2- 5	.0036	.9964	.9829	.0171	.0020	.9980	.9916	.0084
	3	5-10	.0114	.9886	.9281	.0719	.0029	.9971	.9772	.0228
	4	10-17	.0287	.9713	.7570	.2430	.0065	.9935	.9338	.0662
Other Treatment										
Male	1	0- 2 yrs	.0043	.9957	.9913	.0087	.0026	.9974	.9948	.0052
	2	2- 5	.0069	.9931	.9709	.0291	.0048	.9952	.9806	.0194
	3	5-10	.0125	.9875	.9117	.0883	.0080	.9920	.9421	.0579
	4	10-17	.0404	.9596	.6829	.3171	.0142	.9858	.8523	.1477
All Treatments										
Female	1	0- 2 yrs	.0032	.9968	.9937	.0063	.0011	.9989	.9978	.0022
	2	2- 5	.0043	.9957	.9808	.0192	.0020	.9980	.9919	.0081
	3	5-10	.0095	.9905	.9353	.0647	.0026	.9974	.9792	.0208
	4	10-17	.0156	.9844	.8377	.1623	.0038	.9962	.9534	.0466

*Basis of expected mortality: 1955-60 Select Basic Table

DIABETES MELLITUS IN INSUREDS

Table 904c   Comparative Experience by Sex, Age and Treatment — Substandard Cases, All Durations Combined

Sex	Age Group	Exposure Policy-Yrs	No. of Death Claims		Mortality Ratio	Ave. Ann. Mort. Rate	Est. 8-Yr Surv. Rate	Est. 8-Yr Surv. Index	Excess Death Rate
			Observed	Expected*					
		E	d	d'	100 d/d'	$\bar{q} = d/E$	$P = (1-\bar{q})^8$	100 P/P'	1000(d-d')/E
Treatment - to 25 Units of Insulin									
Male	15-29	919	6	0.83	725%	.0065	.9489	95.6%	5.6
	30-39	1113	1	1.94	52	.0009	.9928	100.7	−0.8
	40-49	1641	11	5.95	185	.0067	.9476	97.6	3.1
	50-59	1617	22	13.61	162	.0136	.8962	95.9	5.2
	60 up	354	5	4.49	111	.0141	.8924	98.8	1.4
	All Ages	5644	45	26.82	168	.0080	.9380	97.4	3.2
Treatment - 25 Units of Insulin Up									
Male	15-29	4889	19	4.64	410	.0039	.9693	97.7	2.9
	30-39	2956	25	6.03	415	.0085	.9343	95.0	6.4
	40-49	1345	15	6.51	230	.0112	.9142	95.0	6.3
	50-59	701	23	6.91	335	.0328	.7658	82.9	23
	60 up	69	2	0.94	215	.0290	.7903	88.2	15
	All Ages	9960	84	25.03	335	.0084	.9345	95.3	5.9
Other Treatment									
Male	15-29	458	3	0.40	750	.0066	.9486	95.5	5.7
	30-39	887	4	1.87	215	.0045	.9645	98.1	2.4
	40-49	1285	14	7.13	196	.0109	.9160	95.8	5.4
	50-59	1387	29	14.93	194	.0209	.8444	92.1	10
	60 up	119	1	2.15	47	.0084	.9347	108.1	−10
	All Ages	4136	51	26.48	193	.0123	.9054	95.3	5.9
All Treatments									
Female	15-29	1271	4	0.67	595	.0031	.9751	97.9	2.6
	30-39	785	5	0.86	580	.0064	.9502	95.9	5.3
	40-49	805	5	2.02	250	.0062	.9514	97.1	3.7
	50-59	611	8	2.73	295	.0131	.8999	93.3	8.6
	60 up	108	0	0.77	0	.0000	1.0000	105.9	−7.1
	All Ages	3580	22	7.05	310	.0061	.9519	96.7	4.2

Table 904d   Mortality by Cause of Death — Male and Female Combined

Cause	No. of Death Claims		Mortality Ratio	Excess Death Rate
	Observed	Expected†		
Malignant Neoplasms	24	20.35	118%	0.2
Diseases of the Heart & Circulatory System	87	33.58	260	2.3
Accidents and Homicides	12	11.74	102	0.0
Suicide	7	3.62	193	0.1
All Other Causes and Unknown	72●	16.09	445	2.4
Total	202	85.38	235	5.0

*Basis of expected mortality: 1955-60 Select Basic Table
† Distribution of total expected deaths by Intercompany Medically Examined Standard Issues 1965-70
● Includes 35 deaths due to diabetes, 10 deaths due to pneumonia and 8 deaths due to cerebrovascular accident

DIABETES MELLITUS

§905–NATURAL HISTORY OF DIABETES (JOSLIN CLINIC 1939-1963)

References: (1) T. Hirohata., B. MacMahon, and H. F. Root, "The Natural History of Diabetes. I. Mortality," Diabetes, 16:875-881 (1967).

(2) B. MacMahon, supplementary data in personal communication (1974).

Subjects Studied: 3853 patients selected from the extensive records of a private group diabetic clinic, the Joslin Clinic, Boston. Five cohorts were established with early diagnosis of diabetes mellitus (within one year of first Joslin Clinic visit), each cohort consisting of patients first seen over an 18-month period centered about July 1, 1939, 1944, 1949, 1954 and 1959 as "index years" of entry. Patients not resident in Massachusetts (about 30 per cent of the total) and non-whites were also excluded. All diagnoses were established by Dr. Elliott Joslin or Dr. Howard Root on the basis of typical symptoms such as polyuria and polydipsia, when present, glycosuria and abnormal "true glucose" levels (Somogyi-Nelson) in whole blood: 110 mg. per 100 ml. fasting, 150 at one hour and 110 at two hours of a standard glucose tolerance test. Such a test was seldom needed to establish diagnosis, since almost all patients had abnormally elevated fasting or random blood glucose levels. Distribution of patients by sex and age was as follows:

Age Group (Years)	0-19	20-39	40-59	60-79	80 up	Total
Male	252	305	832	465	17	1871
Female	247	200	811	695	29	1982
Total Number	499	505	1643	1160	46	3853
Per Cent	13.0%	13.1%	42.6%	30.1%	1.2%	100.0%

Follow-up: A variety of methods was employed including several mailings to patients, attempted telephone contacts with patients and referring physicians, search of death certificates, town directories and motor vehicle registrations. Follow-up to October 1, 1963 was obtained for 96.2 per cent of the subjects, most of the loss occurring after 1961 when periodic follow-up mailings to patients were temporarily discontinued.

Results: Presented in Tables 905a-b is the experience over the 25-year period of observation according to sex, age group and duration. The number of deaths from all causes among patients younger than age 40 at the first visit is small, and caution is called for in the interpretation of mortality and survival results. In juvenile diabetes (under age 20) excess mortality of females exceeds that of males, with a 25-year mortality ratio of 1080 versus 490 per cent, and EDR of 5.9 versus 4.2 extra deaths per 1000. The 25-year survival rates, however, were between 82 and 83 per cent in both sexes. Lower mortality ratios and excess death rates were found in the patients age 20-39 at diagnosis, and more favorable survival ratios, close to 88 per cent at 25 years. Although mortality ratios continued to decrease with age in the older patients, age 40-59, and 60-79, EDR's increased to 12, then to 13 extra deaths per 1000 in men, and to 16 and 29 in women. Both excess mortality and survival ratios were less favorable in females in almost all age/duration categories.

The trend in mortality ratios with duration in any age group was slightly upward, although subject to some irregular fluctuations at the younger ages in male diabetics. In the female diabetics the highest mortality ratios in patients under age 40 occurred in the first interval, up to five years after start of follow-up. Apart from this, mortality ratios showed little trend with duration in all four age groups of female patients. Excess death rates, on the other hand, did tend to increase with duration of the disease (despite some fluctuations of an apparently random character in the age groups under 40), while a progressive decrease was evident in the cumulative survival ratio.

Table 905c shows the experience on the same patients by entry cohort, sex and duration, all ages combined. In the male patients excess mortality appears to be distinctly higher in the 1939 cohort than in the 1944 and later cohorts, when corresponding durations are compared. In the 1939 cohort, after the first five years, the excess death rate was generally above 20 per 1000, except for a marked dip to 6.7 per 1000 from 10-15 years after entry. The mortality ratios also appear to be higher in the 1939 male cohort. It is difficult to discern a clear trend of excess mortality by entry cohort in female diabetics when corresponding intervals are compared, and the same is true for the survival ratios.

NATURAL HISTORY OF DIABETES (JOSLIN CLINIC 1939-1963)

Table 905a   Observed Data and Comparative Experience

Sex and Age	No. i	Interval Start-End t to t + Δt	Exposure Person-Yrs E	Observed d	Expected* d'	Mortality Ratio Interval 100 d/d'	Mortality Ratio Cumulative 100∑d/∑d'	Survival Ratio Interval 100 p_i/p_i'	Survival Ratio Cumulative 100 P/P'	Excess Death Rate 1000(d-d')/E
Male										
0-19 yrs	1	0- 5 yrs	1243.3	2	1.04	192%	192%	99.6%	99.6%	0.8
	2	5-10	830.7	4	0.86	465	315	98.1	97.7	3.8
	3	10-15	520.1	1	0.63	159	275	99.6	97.4	0.7
	4	15-20	335.4	7	0.49	1430	465	91.0	88.6	19
	5	20-25	122.3	2	0.24	835	490	92.9	82.4	14
		0-25 yrs	3051.8	16	3.26	490	490	82.4	82.4	4.2
20-39	1	0- 5 yrs	1493.1	4	3.88	103	103	100.0	100.0	0.1
	2	5-10	1192.6	8	4.56	175	142	98.5	98.5	2.9
	3	10-15	846.1	7	5.24	134	139	98.9	97.4	2.1
	4	15-20	588.3	15	5.75	260	175	92.2	89.8	16
	5	20-25	163.2	3	2.53	119	168	98.4	88.4	2.9
		0-25 yrs	4283.3	37	22.0	168	168	88.4	88.4	3.5
40-59	1	0- 5 yrs	3981.7	83	59.4	140	140	97.1	97.1	5.9
	2	5-10	2817.4	93	60.5	154	147	94.4	91.7	12
	3	10-15	1694.8	84	51.3	164	152	90.9	83.2	19
	4	15-20	809.7	52	34.2	152	152	88.1	73.5	22
	5	20-25	198.9	17	10.8	157	152	92.7	68.0	31
		0-25 yrs	9502.5	329	216	152	152	68.0	68.0	12
60-79	1	0- 5 yrs	2039.4	113	104	109	109	98.4	98.4	4.4
	2	5-10	1137.7	104	77.0	135	120	88.3	86.8	24
	3	10-15	472.8	50	42.5	118	119	91.9	79.8	16
	4	15-20	130.1	20	15.0	133	120	79.2	63.4	38
		0-20 yrs	3780.0	287	239	120	120	63.4	63.4	13
Female										
0-19 yrs	1	0- 5 yrs	1186.3	8	0.59	1360%	1360%	96.9%	96.9%	6.2
	2	5-10	845.3	3	0.44	680	1070	98.4	95.5	3.0
	3	10-15	630.0	1	0.40	250	840	99.5	95.0	1.0
	4	15-20	379.6	7	0.32	2200	1090	91.5	86.9	18
	5	20-25	172.5	2	0.20	1000	1080	95.1	82.6	10
		0-25 yrs	3213.7	21	1.95	1080	1080	82.6	82.6	5.9
20-39	1	0- 5 yrs	966.0	8	1.54	520	520	96.7	96.7	6.7
	2	5-10	750.8	3	1.59	189	350	99.0	95.7	1.9
	3	10-15	548.8	6	1.64	365	355	96.0	91.9	7.9
	4	15-20	333.3	2	1.53	131	300	99.2	91.1	1.4
	5	20-25	161.8	2	1.13	177	285	96.9	88.3	5.4
		0-25 yrs	2760.7	21	7.43	285	285	88.3	88.3	4.9
40-59	1	0- 5 yrs	3902.5	63	37.6	168	168	96.7	96.7	6.5
	2	5-10	2851.5	83	39.2	210	190	92.5	89.3	15
	3	10-15	1816.7	78	37.1	210	197	88.1	78.7	23
	4	15-20	851.3	64	25.3	255	205	80.6	63.5	45
	5	20-25	251.0	19	11.9	160	205	85.7	54.5	28
		0-25 yrs	9673.0	307	151	205	205	54.5	54.5	16
60-79	1	0- 5 yrs	3048.7	180	107	168	168	88.4	88.4	24
	2	5-10	1730.8	137	83.3	164	167	84.7	74.8	31
	3	10-15	809.8	85	58.1	146	162	81.2	60.8	33
	4	15-20	226.2	40	23.5	170	163	63.0	38.2	73
		0-20 yrs	5815.5	442	272	163	163	38.2	38.2	29

*Basis of expected mortality: Massachusetts Life Tables

DIABETES MELLITUS

Table 905b   Derived Mortality and Survival Data, Joslin Clinic Patients 1939-1963

| Sex and Age | Interval | | Observed Rates | | | | Expected Rates* | | | |
	No.	Start-End	Cumulative Survival	Interval Survival	Geom. Mean Ann. Surv.	Geom. Mean Ann. Mort.	Cumulative Survival	Interval Survival	Geom. Mean Ann. Surv.	Geom. Mean Ann. Mort.
	i	t to $t+\Delta t$	P	p_i	$\breve{p}$	$\breve{q}$	P'	p_i'	$\breve{p}'$	$\breve{q}'$
Male 0-19	1	0- 5 yrs	.992	.992	.998	.002	.9959	.9959	.9992	.0008
	2	5-10	.968	.976	.995	.005	.9908	.9949	.9990	.0010
	3	10-15	.959	.990	.998	.002	.9849	.9940	.9988	.0012
	4	15-20	.866	.903	.980	.020	.9777	.9927	.9985	.0015
	5	20-25	.797	.920	.983	.017	.9678	.9899	.9980	.0020
20-39	1	0- 5 yrs	.987	.987	.997	.003	.9870	.9870	.9974	.0026
	2	5-10	.954	.967	.993	.007	.9685	.9813	.9962	.0038
	3	10-15	.915	.959	.992	.008	.9396	.9701	.9939	.0061
	4	15-20	.803	.878	.974	.026	.8944	.9519	.9902	.0098
	5	20-25	.732	.911	.982	.018	.8278	.9255	.9846	.0154
40-59	1	0- 5 yrs	.900	.900	.979	.021	.9272	.9272	.9850	.0150
	2	5-10	.761	.845	.967	.033	.8302	.8954	.9781	.0219
	3	10-15	.590	.776	.951	.049	.7090	.8540	.9689	.0311
	4	15-20	.419	.709	.934	.066	.5703	.8044	.9574	.0426
	5	20-25	.285	.681	.926	.074	.4192	.7350	.9403	.0597
60-79	1	0- 5 yrs	.754	.754	.945	.055	.7660	.7660	.9481	.0519
	2	5-10	.464	.616	.908	.092	.5344	.6977	.9305	.0695
	3	10-15	.262	.565	.892	.108	.3285	.6147	.9073	.0927
	4	15-20	.106	.403	.834	.166	.1672	.5089	.8736	.1264
Female 0-19	1	0- 5 yrs	.967	.967	.993	.007	.9976	.9976	.9995	.0005
	2	5-10	.950	.982	.996	.004	.9951	.9975	.9995	.0005
	3	10-15	.942	.992	.998	.002	.9920	.9969	.9994	.0006
	4	15-20	.859	.911	.982	.018	.9880	.9959	.9992	.0008
	5	20-25	.811	.945	.989	.011	.9820	.9940	.9988	.0012
20-39	1	0- 5 yrs	.959	.959	.992	.008	.9921	.9921	.9984	.0016
	2	5-10	.940	.980	.996	.004	.9819	.9897	.9979	.0021
	3	10-15	.889	.946	.989	.011	.9673	.9852	.9970	.0030
	4	15-20	.862	.970	.994	.006	.9463	.9782	.9956	.0044
	5	20-25	.808	.937	.987	.013	.9152	.9672	.9934	.0066
40-59	1	0- 5 yrs	.922	.922	.984	.016	.9538	.9538	.9906	.0094
	2	5-10	.795	.863	.971	.029	.8902	.9333	.9863	.0137
	3	10-15	.632	.795	.955	.045	.8029	.9019	.9796	.0204
	4	15-20	.435	.688	.928	.072	.6852	.8535	.9688	.0312
	5	20-25	.291	.668	.922	.078	.5340	.7793	.9514	.0486
60-79	1	0- 5 yrs	.738	.738	.941	.059	.8344	.8344	.9644	.0356
	2	5-10	.483	.655	.919	.081	.6454	.7735	.9499	.0501
	3	10-15	.274	.567	.893	.107	.4509	.6986	.9308	.0692
	4	15-20	.097	.355	.813	.187	.2541	.5636	.8916	.1084

*Basis of expected mortality: Massachusetts Life Tables

NATURAL HISTORY OF DIABETES (JOSLIN CLINIC 1939-1963)

Table 905c   Comparative Experience by Cohort and Sex (All Ages Combined)

Sex and Cohort	Duration	Exposure	No. of Deaths		Cum. Survival		Mortality Ratio	Survival Ratio	Excess Death Rate
			Observed	Expected*	Observed	Expected*			
		E	d	d'	P	P'	100 d/d'	100 P/P'	1000(d-d')/E
Male									
1939	0- 5 yrs	993.0	28	20.7	.867	.8989	135%	96.4%	7.4
	5-10	834.0	39	19.6	.681	.7956	199	85.6	23
	10-15	672.0	21	16.5	.581	.7018	127	82.8	6.7
	15-20	550.0	27	14.5	.452	.6133	186	73.7	23
	20-25	400.5	20	11.2	.354	.5251	179	67.4	22
1944	0- 5 yrs	2020.9	36	36.2	.914	.9146	99	99.9	0.1
	5-10	1797.9	47	39.8	.801	.8197	118	97.7	4.0
	10-15	1541.2	54	39.0	.671	.7172	138	93.6	9.7
	15-20	1231.6	60	36.9	.520	.6152	163	84.5	19
1949	0- 5 yrs	1823.1	48	42.4	.875	.8883	113	98.5	3.1
	5-10	1532.0	60	42.4	.716	.7673	142	93.3	11
	10-15	1206.4	56	42.0	.562	.6456	133	87.1	12
1954	0- 5 yrs	1947.3	44	40.7	.893	.8978	108	99.5	1.7
	5-10	1656.6	61	41.3	.738	.7858	148	93.9	12
1959	0- 5 yrs	2035.1	55	39.1	.873	.9042	141	96.5	7.8
Female									
1939	0- 5 yrs	1308.2	42	25.3	.851	.9059	166%	93.9%	13
	5-10	1112.0	38	23.3	.716	.8076	163	88.6	13
	10-15	936.0	40	22.1	.574	.7132	181	80.5	19
	15-20	721.0	40	18.0	.432	.6217	220	69.5	31
	20-25	546.0	21	14.3	.355	.5438	147	65.3	12
1944	0- 5 yrs	1966.9	67	34.8	.842	.9103	193	92.5	16
	5-10	1658.0	64	33.5	.691	.8115	191	85.2	18
	10-15	1351.6	57	32.6	.555	.7179	175	77.3	18
	15-20	958.7	63	28.3	.398	.6160	225	64.6	36
1949	0- 5 yrs	2126.2	57	39.6	.872	.9087	144	96.0	8.2
	5-10	1798.2	67	40.9	.718	.8048	164	89.2	15
	10-15	1402.2	66	40.3	.562	.6978	164	80.7	18
1954	0- 5 yrs	1842.2	56	30.4	.856	.9205	184	93.0	14
	5-10	1461.8	59	27.1	.698	.8231	220	84.8	22
1959	0- 5 yrs	1968.0	52	31.8	.875	.9223	164	94.9	10

*Basis of expected mortality: Massachusetts Life Tables

DIABETES (JOSLIN CLINIC 1930-1959)

§906–DIABETES (JOSLIN CLINIC 1930-1959)

References: (1) I. I. Kessler, "Mortality Experience of Diabetic Patients - A Twenty-Six Year Follow-up Study," Am. J. Med., 51:715-724 (1971).

(2) I. I. Kessler, "Cancer Mortality among Diabetics," J. Natl. Cancer Inst., 44:673-686 (1970).

Subjects Studied: 21,447 white diabetic patients residing in Massachusetts first examined at the Joslin Clinic, Boston, between January 1930 and July 1956, who survived for at least one year beyond the date of their first clinic visit. There were 96,013 male person-years of exposure (44 per cent) and 122,313, female (56 per cent).

Follow-up: Subjects were followed to death or survival to the end of the follow-up period, January 1, 1960. Of the total population, 157, or 0.7 per cent, were lost to observation. Causes of death were investigated by a complete count of all deaths from cancer and accident so identified in clinic records. Deaths due to all other causes were estimated from review of death certificates in a 25 per cent random sample of the study group whose deaths were completely ascertained. From a comparison of the clinic and death certificate records it was further estimated that 1.9 per cent of cancer deaths among males and 2.9 per cent of those among females had been missed by this procedure.

Results: In Table 906a comparative mortality and survival experience is presented for six periods from 1931 through 1959. In the 29-year period, there were 4055 male deaths (43.4 per cent of male patients) and 6011 female (49.7 per cent). Mortality ratios among females increased consistently from 173 per cent in 1931-35 to 240 per cent in 1956-59. The increase among males (from 144 to 174 per cent) was less marked and the progression was interrupted by a reversal in 1941-45. The excess death rate averaged 17 extra deaths per 1000 per year for males and 27 per 1000 for females. The range of EDR, for males, was from 10 to 20 per 1000, and for females, from 17 to 33 per 1000. The progression in the case of males was irregular with the highest EDR's occurring both in 1936-40 and in 1956-59. Survival indexes reflected excess death rates: this function varied between 90 and 95 per cent for males and between 84 and 92 per cent for females.

In Table 906b comparative experience for all durations combined is presented for both sexes by attained age groupings. Among both males and females the greatest disparity with the general population in mortality rates is in age group 20 to 39 where the mortality ratio reaches 570 per cent for males and 745 per cent for females. The lowest ratios are at ages 80 years and over where they recede to 118 per cent and 145 per cent for males and females, respectively. Expressed as extra deaths per 1000, excess mortality is seen to rise steadily with advancing age for both sexes: male EDR's increase from 2.0 per 1000 at ages under 20 years to 29 per 1000 in the oldest age group, 80 and up; in the same age range female rates increase from 3.1 to 61 per 1000.

Comparative experience by cause of death is presented in Table 906c showing results on both the 25 per cent random sampling and the complete count bases. Mortality from diabetes mellitus was 3200 per cent that of the general population for males and 2300 per cent for females. Significant extra mortality but of a lower order is indicated for both sexes from coronary heart disease (CHD). When deaths due to diabetes and CHD were excluded, excess mortality virtually disappeared, the residual mortality ratio being 93 per cent for males and 109 per cent for females. Significantly reduced mortality ratios, below 100 per cent, were found in male diabetics who died of all types of cancer (mortality ratio 85 per cent), lung cancer (64 per cent), respiratory diseases other than tuberculosis (59 per cent), and accidental causes (77 per cent). On the other hand total cancer mortality in female diabetics was very close to that in the general population, while mortality due to respiratory tuberculosis and accidental causes was significantly elevated, with mortality ratios of 295 and 134 per cent, respectively. The only statistically significant increase in specific types of cancer was found in cancer of the pancreas, with a mortality ratio of 147 per cent in males and 215 per cent in females.

Comment: In another study of Joslin Clinic patients, Table 907c, age-specific cumulative survival ratios do show consistent improvement from earlier entry periods in the 1930's to the late 1950's, a trend not evident in the data, all ages combined, in Table 906a. The two reference articles of Kessler's study contain an exceptionally thorough analysis of cause of death and related factors in diabetics.

DIABETES MELLITUS

Table 906a   Comparative Experience by Time Period and Sex, All Ages Combined

| Sex and Time Period | Exposure Patient-Yrs | No. of Deaths | | Mortality Ratio | Ave. Ann. Mort. Rate | Est. 5-Yr Surv. Rate | Est. 5-Yr Surv. Index | Excess Death Rate |
		Observed	Expected*					
	E	d	d'	100 d/d'	$\bar{q} = d/E$	$P = (1-\bar{q})^5$	100 P/P'	1000(d-d')/E
Male								
1931-35	3165	111	77.1	144%	.035	.8365	94.6%	11
1936-40	7512	347	196.6	177	.046	.7894	90.1	20
1941-45	13191	460	328.0	140	.035	.8374	95.0	10
1946-50	21431	826	506.3	163	.039	.8216	92.6	15
1951-55	27907	1222	711.5	172	.044	.7994	91.0	18
1956-59	22807	1089	626.7	174	.048	.7830	90.0	20
All	96013	4055	2446.2	166	.042	.8059	91.7	17
Female								
1931-35	4832	193	111.3	173%	.040	.8156	91.6%	17
1936-40	10972	512	264.9	193	.047	.7874	89.0	23
1941-45	17814	849	416.0	205	.048	.7834	88.2	24
1946-50	27620	1291	587.8	220	.047	.7871	87.7	25
1951-55	34345	1666	749.6	220	.049	.7799	87.1	27
1956-59	26730	1500	619.3	240	.056	.7492	84.2	33
All	122313	6011	2748.9	220	.049	.7773	87.1	27

Table 906b   Observed Data and Comparative Experience by Age and Sex

| Sex and Time Period | Exposure Patient-Yrs | No. of Deaths | | Mortality Ratio | Ave. Ann. Mort. Rate | Est. 5-Yr Surv. Rate | Est. 5-Yr Surv. Index | Excess Death Rate |
		Observed	Expected*					
x to x + Δx	E	d	d'	100 d/d'	$\bar{q} = d/E$	$P = (1-\bar{q})^5$	100 P/P'	1000(d-d')/E
Male								
Under 20 yrs	6021	19	7.1	270%	.003	.9843	99.0%	2.0
20-39	17018	203	35.5	570	.012	.9418	95.2	9.8
40-59	38338	971	499.2	195	.025	.8796	93.9	12
60-79	32649	2484	1584.2	157	.076	.6732	86.3	28
80 up	1987	378	320.2	118	.190	.3480	83.8	29
All Ages	96013	4055	2446.2	166	.042	.8059	91.7	17
Female								
Under 20 yrs	6086	23	4.2	550%	.004	.9812	98.5%	3.1
20-39	15412	159	21.4	745	.010	.9495	95.6	8.9
40-59	40947	916	341.8	270	.022	.8930	93.1	14
60-79	56490	4251	1924.3	220	.075	.6763	80.4	41
80 up	3378	662	457.2	145	.196	.3361	69.5	61
All Ages	122313	6011	2748.9	220	.049	.7773	87.1	27

*Basis of expected mortality: Massachusetts annual Reports of Vital Statistics

DIABETES (JOSLIN CLINIC 1930-1959)

Table 906c Comparative Mortality by Cause of Death - Joslin Clinic Patients 1930-1959

Cause of Death	Male			Female		
	No. of Deaths		Mortality	No. of Deaths		Mortality
	Observed	Expected*	Ratio	Observed	Expected*	Ratio
	d	d′	100 d/d′	d	d′	100 d/d′
(25 per cent Random Sample)						
Diabetes Mellitus	312	9.89	3200%	651	28.14	2300%
Coronary Heart Disease	266	173.56	153	321	146.15	220
Other Heart Disease	61	90.05	68	118	140.16	84
Cerebrovascular Disease	58	52.04	111	111	92.04	121
Arteriosclerosis	15	9.42	159	16	15.05	106
Cirrhosis	12	9.09	132	4	6.33	63
Nephritis	20	14.09	142	25	21.41	117
Respiratory T.B.	11	12.12	91	15	5.08	295
Respiratory Disease	16	27.31	59	21	26.24	80
Peptic Ulcer	5	6.25	80	3	2.32	129
Gallbladder Disease	5	1.73	290	3	4.58	66
Prostate Disease	7	4.12	170	—	—	—
Other†	34	34.99	97	50	41.01	122
All Causes	943	574.5	164	1531	689.1	222
All Except Diabetes	631	564.6	112	880	660.9	133
All Except Diabetes & CHD	365	391.1	93	559	514.8	109
(Complete Count)						
Accidents	100	129.72	77%	146	109.20	134%
Cancer						
Stomach	51	57.84	88	47	54.54	86
Intestine	50	51.48	97	97	83.55	116
Rectum	18	28.07	64	27	27.76	97
Liver	15	16.27	92	35	28.17	124
Pancreas	30	20.41	147	48	22.51	215
Kidney	11	9.24	119	7	6.78	103
Bladder	14	18.09	77	7	11.52	61
Respiratory	46	71.74	64	25	19.71	127
Leukemia	14	12.45	112	13	12.36	105
Hodgkin's Disease	7	4.82	145	3	4.05	74
Prostate	46	42.46	108	—	—	—
Breast	—	—	—	88	100.41	88
Uterus	—	—	—	44	61.28	72
Ovary	—	—	—	27	28.01	96
All Other	56	87.66	64	76	68.88	110
Total Cancer	358	420.53	85%	544	529.53	103%

* Basis of expected mortality: Massachusetts annual Reports of Vital Statistics
† Excluding deaths due to accident or cancer, for which a complete count was made

DIABETES MELLITUS

§907–DIABETES (JOSLIN CLINIC 1930-1960)

Reference: P. S. Entmacher, H. F. Root, and H. H. Marks, "Longevity of Diabetic Patients in Recent Years," Diabetes, 13:373-377 (1964).

Subjects Studied: Diabetic patients treated at the Joslin Clinic in Boston in the period 1930-1958. There were 17654 men and women in the series representing a 50 per cent sample of the cases treated over the period. Experience was divided into three calendar periods, 1930-39, 1940-49 and 1950-58, to detect any trends developing. Entry of subjects into observation was based on date of first examination.

Follow-up: A variety of methods was employed in tracing subjects: communication with patients by correspondence and telephone, contacts with referring physicians, and searches of death certificates, town directories and motor vehicle registrations. In the series here presented follow-up was virtually complete, 98.8 per cent of the subjects being traced to the closing date. Half of the cases in the series were traced to the beginning of 1960 and the remaining ones to the beginning of 1961.

Results: In Table 907a, comparative mortality experience is presented at attained ages for male and female patients first seen from 1950 to 1958 and traced to January 1, 1961. Except for a relatively high mortality ratio of 265 per cent for females in age group 5-14 years, ratios increase to a peak between 25 and 34 years when they reach 735 per cent in the case of males and 1390 per cent for females. At older ages, these ratios diminish steadily to 160 and 240 per cent for male and female patients, respectively. Excess death rates per 1000 tend to increase with attained age - the progression is well defined for males but is quite irregular for females.

Mortality ratios are shown in Table 907b, by age and sex, the experience in patients first examined between 1950 and 1961 being compared with two different sets of expected rates: standard insurance risks and the general population. Since the mortality among standard insurance risks is lower than the general population, the mortality ratios based upon them are higher than those based upon general population mortality. Mortality ratios for female diabetics relative either to insurance or population standards are consistently higher than those for males. In both sexes the ratios are high at ages under 40 but decline progressively with advance in age. Even at ages over 50 the mortality of diabetic males is about three times as high as among standard insured male risks and about four times as high in the case of females.

In Table 907c, cumulative survival rates at the end of 10 and 20 years from commencement of treatment are shown by age group for patients first examined during the entry periods 1930-1939, 1940-1949, and 1950-1958 (10-year rates only). Such rates are shown, on one hand, for patients judged to have come under initial observation within one year of diabetes onset, and for those of all durations, on the other. It is clear that cases seen within a year of onset fare much better than the general run of cases - at the older ages, cumulative survival rates for first-year cases reaching 152 per cent of those for all durations. Also evident is the steady and substantial improvement in all age groups in the survival rates at the later periods contrasted with those at the earlier.

A comparison of mortality rates from the major causes of death among diabetics with those in the general population is presented in Table 907d. Mortality ratios for the diabetics are especially high in the vascular diseases, the elevation being more marked for females than for males. For all vascular diseases the mortality of males is about two and one-half times, and of females, about three and one-half times, that in the general population. For cerebral vascular disease, in both sexes, frequency is about double that of the general population. Renal vascular deaths show by far the greatest relative excess among diabetics - about seventeen times that in the general population in both sexes.

DIABETES (JOSLIN CLINIC 1930-1960)

Table 907a   Comparative Mortality Rates and Ratios by Sex and Attained Age
(Patients First Seen 1950-1958)

Attained Age	Male Diabetics				Female Diabetics			
	Ave. Ann. Mort. Rate		Mortality Ratio	Excess Death Rate	Ave. Ann. Mort. Rate		Mortality Ratio	Excess Death Rate
	Observed	Expected*			Observed	Expected*		
(Years)	$\bar{q}$	$\bar{q}'$	$100\,\bar{q}/\bar{q}'$	$1000(\bar{q}-\bar{q}')$	$\bar{q}$	$\bar{q}'$	$100\,\bar{q}/\bar{q}'$	$1000(\bar{q}-\bar{q}')$
5-14 yrs	.0009	.0005	180%	0.4	.0008	.0003	265%	0.5
15-24	.0054	.0012	450	4.2	.0008	.0006	133	0.2
25-34	.0103	.0014	735	8.9	.0153	.0011	1390	14
35-44	.0161	.0037	435	12	.0104	.0023	450	8.1
45-54	.0215	.0103	210	11	.0182	.0058	315	12
55-64	.0449	.0247	182	20	.0357	.0146	245	21
65-74	.0848	.0530	160	32	.0855	.0357	240	50

Table 907b   Mortality Ratios for Patients First Examined 1950-1961 by
Age and Standard Reference Basis

Sex	Reference Basis†	Mortality Ratios for Attained Age (Years)				
		20-29	30-39	40-49	50-59	60-74
Male	Insured Lives	810%	970%	470%	280%	300%
	General Population	690	670	310	180	170
Female	Insured Lives	930	1600	580	420	400
	General Population	880	950	380	290	240

Table 907c   Comparative Survival Rates by Entry Age for Patients with Early Diabetes (Diagnosed within 1 Year)
and All Durations of Diabetes

Survival Period and Entry Age	Cumulative Survival Rates for Various Entry Years								
	1930-1939			1940-1949			1950-1958		
	Duration Under 1 Yr	All Durations	Ratio	Duration Under 1 Yr	All Durations	Ratio	Duration Under 1 Yr	All Durations	Ratio
(Years)	P	P'	100 P/P'	P	P'	100 P/P'	P	P'	100 P/P'
Duration 10 Yrs									
Age 15-29	.875	.877	100%	.963	.919	105%	.994	.901	110%
30-44	.852	.816	104	.890	.863	103	.947	.840	113
45-59	.727	.631	115	.762	.676	113	.775	.712	109
60-74	.422	.341	124	.499	.408	122	.536	.407	132
Duration 20 Yrs									
Age 15-29	.752	.703	107%	.790	.732	108%	—	—	—
30-44	.663	.616	108	.707	.615	115	—	—	—
45-59	.345	.290	119	.434	.292	149	—	—	—
60-74	.079	.056	141	.117	.077	152	—	—	—

Table 907d   Comparative Mortality by Certain Causes of Death

Cause of Death	Mortality Ratio - Diabetics to General Population†	
	Male	Female
Total Vascular Disease	240%	340%
Ages 15-44	1220	1950
Ages 45-74	220	320
Heart Disease	200	320
Cerebral Vascular Disease	180	200
Renal Vascular	1780	1700
Cancer	150	160

*Basis of expected mortality: (general population) white males and females in New England (1949-51); (insured lives) 1946-49
Select Basic Tables, (adjusted for female mortality)

†Basis of expected mortality: (vascular diseases) white persons in New England (1949-51); (cancer) white persons in United
States (1950)

DIABETES MELLITUS

§908–DIABETES IN AN INDUSTRIAL POPULATION

Reference: S. Pell and C. A. D'Alonzo, "Factors Associated with Long-Term Survival of Diabetics," J. Am. Med. Assoc., 214:1833-1840 (1970).

Subjects Studied: Male diabetics, 370 under age 65, employed by the Du Pont Company, identified in a one year survey by the Medical Division of the company. Also identified were 38 female diabetics; because of the small number, these were omitted from the study. The male diabetics represented about one-half of one per cent of the male employees; female, about one-quarter of one per cent of the females. Age distribution of the males:

Occupational Class	to 25	25-34	35-44	45-54	55-64	Total	Median Age
			Age Group: Number and (Per Cent)				
Production	–	17(7.3)	69(29.6)	69(29.6)	78(33.5)	233(100.0)	49.8
Salaried	1(0.7)	17(12.4)	30(21.9)	49(35.8)	40(29.2)	137(100.0)	50.3
All Male Employees	1(0.3)	34(9.2)	99(26.7)	118(31.9)	118(31.9)	370(100.0)	50.1

For comparative purposes, in lieu of a standard experience for the "expected", a control group was formed from non-diabetic company employees selected to match the diabetics in age, sex, occupational class and area of residence.

Follow-up: The diabetic subjects and their controls were traced for the ten-year period from January 1957-December 1966. Of the 740 entrants, all but two were traced to death or the close of the follow-up period by means of company employment, or pension records, or upon inquiry of the Social Security Administration relative to survival.

Annual health examinations (biennial for employees under age 40) by company physicians provided information for studying association of diabetic mortality with insulin dosage, blood pressure, weight, frequency of albuminuria and glycosuria, and history of coronary heart disease.

Results: During follow-up 92 diabetics and 36 controls died, representing cumulative mortality rates of .254 and .097, respectively (yielding a ratio of 260 per cent); the ten-year survivorship ratio of diabetics to controls was 82.6 per cent. The annual average EDR was 17 per 1000. Rates and ratios and year-by-year experience for diabetics and the control group, all ages combined, are given in Tables 908a-b.

Tables 908c-d compare the experience of diabetics with that of control groups for each of six characteristics not related to severity of the diabetes. Comparison was not limited to matched pairs but to the relative experience under the diabetic and control groups. Mortality rates were increased in both diabetics and controls in the presence of hypertension, overweight and coronary heart disease, CHD (908d). Mortality ratio of hypertensive diabetics (relative to controls with comparable blood pressure) diminished with increase in severity of hypertension (908c). There was a similar tendency for overweight or the presence of CHD to bring about smaller mortality ratios when the diabetic group was compared with the control group exhibiting the same characteristic (overweight in these tables has been expressed both as per cent above "ideal" weight and as ponderal index - height divided by cube root of the weight). Excess mortality in terms of EDR showed relatively little change with respect to hypertension and overweight, but was more than doubled in CHD, although the latter increase was based on only four control deaths (908c).

The relative severity of diabetes at the younger ages is shown in Tables 908c-d for age on January 1, 1957, and in Tables 908e-f for age at diagnosis. Comparative mortality against matched controls is also given in Tables 908e-f for insulin dosage, glycosuria, and presence of albuminuria as indices of severity or complication of diabetes. Mortality ratio was increased for all of these indices, but EDR was increased only in the presence of glycosuria and albuminuria, not for cases with insulin dosage over 40 units (indicating a below-average age for this diabetic group).

Comment: Derivation of expected mortality from a matched control group in this carefully designed study presents advantages coupled with the disadvantage of random variability of annual distribution of control deaths and rates (Tables 908a-b). In life tables drawn from a large population q' would increase smoothly and there would be a corresponding even progression of d'. Data are also given in the article on comparative mortality by cause of death, which was found to be significantly increased for coronary heart disease and "all other" non-cardiovascular causes (including diabetes), and increased, but not significantly, for cerebrovascular disease, miscellaneous CV diseases, and cancer.

DIABETES IN AN INDUSTRIAL POPULATION

Table 908a   Diabetics and Non-diabetic Controls: Comparative Experience, All Ages Combined

No.	Start-End	No. Alive Start of Int. Diabetics	Diabetics	Controls*	Mortality Ratio Interval	Cumulative	Survival Ratio Interval	Cumulative	Excess Death Rate
i	t to t + Δt	ℓ	d	d′	100 d/d′	100 Q/Q′	100 p_i/p_i'	100 P/P′	1000(d-d′)/ℓ
1	0- 1 yr	370	6	2	300%	300%	98.9%	98.9%	11
2	1- 2 yrs	363	5	3	167	230	99.4	98.3	5.5
3	2- 3	358	3	2	150	210	99.7	98.0	2.8
4	3- 4	355	13	1	1300	350	96.6	94.7	34
5	4- 5	341	6	4	150	280	99.3	94.0	5.9
6	5- 6	335	14	3	465	325	96.5	90.7	33
7	6- 7	321	6	3	200	310	98.9	89.6	9.3
8	7- 8	315	18	7	255	295	96.0	86.1	35
9	8- 9	297	7	3	235	285	98.5	84.9	13
10	9-10	290	14	8	175	260	97.4	82.6	21
	0-10		92	36					17

Table 908b   Derived Mortality and Survival Data

No.	Start-End	Diabetic Experience Average Annual Mortality	Survival	Cumulative Survival	Mortality	Control Experience* Average Annual Mortality	Survival	Cumulative Survival	Mortality
i	t to t + Δt	$\bar{q}=d/\ell$	$\bar{p}$	P	Q	$\bar{q}'=d'/\ell$	$\bar{p}'$	P′	Q′
1	0- 1 yr	.016	.984	.984	.016	.005	.995	.995	.005
2	1- 2 yrs	.014	.986	.970	.030	.008	.992	.987	.013
3	2- 3	.008	.992	.962	.038	.005	.995	.982	.018
4	3- 4	.037	.963	.927	.073	.003	.997	.979	.021
5	4- 5	.018	.982	.910	.090	.011	.989	.968	.032
6	5- 6	.043	.957	.871	.129	.008	.992	.960	.040
7	6- 7	.019	.981	.854	.146	.008	.992	.953	.047
8	7- 8	.059	.941	.804	.196	.020	.980	.934	.066
9	8- 9	.024	.976	.785	.215	.009	.991	.925	.075
10	9-10	.049	.951	.746	.254	.024	.976	.903	.097

* Controls, matched by age, sex, occupation and location, selected at random from all company employees

DIABETES MELLITUS

Table 908c   Observed Data and Comparative Experience — All Diabetics and All Controls According to Various Characteristics

Group	No. of Entrants		No. of Deaths		Mortality Ratio		10-Year Surv. Ratio	Excess Death Rate
	Diabetics	Controls*	Diabetics	Controls*	Ave. Ann.	10-Yr Cum.		
	ℓ	ℓ'	d	d'	$100\ \breve{q}/\breve{q}'$	$100\ Q/Q'$	$100\ P/P'$	$1000(\breve{q}-\breve{q}')$
Occupation								
Production	226	225	60	24	275%	250%	81.6%	20
Salaried	144	145	32	12	295	275	84.2	17
Age (yrs) as of 1/1/57								
Under 45	133	135	20	3	720	675	86.5	15
45-54	119	114	31	11	295	270	81.5	20
55-64	116	121	41	22	220	198	77.8	24
Hypertensive Status								
Normotensive	144	193	29	14	305	285	85.7	16
Borderline	129	122	33	12	290	265	81.8	20
Hypertensive	83	42	30	10	163	151	83.3	18
Overweight								
<20 %	225	242	51	20	305	280	83.8	18
20-29 %	62	72	14	9	192	182	88.0	12
30+%	83	56	27	7	295	260	76.4	26
Ponderal Index								
13.1+	64	57	13	3	430	400	83.3	18
12.2-13.0	186	180	37	18	265	245	84.4	17
<12.2	147	127	42	15	270	245	80.3	21
Coronary Heart Dis.								
No	340	359	76	32	265	250	85.0	16
Yes	28	11	16	4	176	150	66.5	38

Table 908d   Derived Mortality and Survival Data (10-Year Experience)

Group	Diabetic Experience				Control Experience*			
	Cumulative		Geom. Mean Ann. Surv.	Geom. Mean Ann. Mort.	Cumulative		Geom. Mean Ann. Surv.	Geom. Mean Ann. Mort.
	Survival	Mortality			Survival	Mortality		
	P	Q	$\breve{p}$	$\breve{q}$	P'	Q'	$\breve{p}'$	$\breve{q}'$
Occupation								
Production	.727	.273	.9686	.0314	.891	.109	.9885	.0115
Salaried	.772	.228	.9745	.0255	.917	.083	.9914	.0086
Age (yrs) as of 1/1/57								
Under 45	.845	.155	.9833	.0167	.977	.023	.9977	.0023
45-54	.735	.265	.9697	.0303	.902	.098	.9897	.0103
55-64	.635	.365	.9556	.0444	.816	.184	.9799	.0201
Hypertensive Status								
Normotensive	.795	.205	.9773	.0227	.928	.072	.9926	.0074
Borderline	.738	.262	.9701	.0299	.902	.098	.9897	.0103
Hypertensive	.627	.373	.9544	.0456	.753	.247	.9720	.0280
Overweight								
<20%	.769	.231	.9741	.0259	.918	.082	.9915	.0085
20-29 %	.767	.233	.9738	.0262	.872	.128	.9864	.0136
30+%	.667	.333	.9603	.0397	.873	.127	.9865	.0135
Ponderal Index								
13.1+	.789	.211	.9766	.0234	.947	.053	.9946	.0054
12.2-13.0	.763	.237	.9733	.0267	.904	.906	.9900	.0100
<12.2	.707	.293	.9659	.0341	.880	.120	.9873	.0127
Coronary Heart Dis.								
No	.772	.228	.9745	.0255	.908	.092	.9904	.0096
Yes	.399	.601	.9122	.0878	.600	.400	.9502	.0498

* Controls, matched by age, sex, occupation and location, selected at random from all company employees

DIABETES IN AN INDUSTRIAL POPULATION

Table 908e Observed Data and Comparative Experience — Diabetics According to Various Characteristics and Matched Controls

Group	No. of Ent. Diab. or Cont.	No. of Deaths Diabetics	No. of Deaths Controls*	Mortality Ratio Ave. Ann.	Mortality Ratio 10-Yr Cum.	10-Year Surv. Ratio	Excess Death Rate
	ℓ or ℓ'	d	d'	100 q̆/q̆'	100 Q/Q'	100 P/P'	1000(q̆-q̆')
Daily Insulin Dosage							
None	185	48	22	235%	215%	83.7%	17
Under 40 units	101	27	11	270	245	81.7	20
40 units up	83	17	3	620	570	81.9	19
Age at Diagnosis							
25-34	75	10	3	355	340	89.8	11
35-44	105	31	9	500	440	74.8	29
45-54	109	30	11	305	275	80.1	21
55-64	50	19	11	190	172	78.8	24
Glycosuria							
0 or 1 result	140	36	17	230	210	84.2	17
2 or 3 results	108	29	11	295	270	80.7	21
4 or 5 results	87	24	6	455	405	76.9	26
Albuminuria							
0 or 1 result	245	55	25	235	220	86.1	15
2 or 3 results	90	34	9	450	380	67.9	37

Table 908f Derived Mortality and Survival Data

Group	Diabetic Experience Cumulative Survival	Diabetic Experience Cumulative Mortality	Diabetic Experience Geom. Mean Ann. Surv.	Diabetic Experience Geom. Mean Ann. Mort.	Control Experience* Cumulative Survival	Control Experience* Cumulative Mortality	Control Experience* Geom. Mean Ann. Surv.	Control Experience* Geom. Mean Ann. Mort.
	P	Q	p̆	q̆	P'	Q'	p̆'	q̆'
Daily Insulin Dosage								
None	.735	.265	.9697	.0303	.878	.122	.9871	.0129
Under 40 units	.726	.274	.9685	.0315	.889	.111	.9883	.0117
40 units up	.789	.211	.9766	.0234	.963	.037	.9962	.0038
Age at Diagnosis								
25-34	.861	.139	.9851	.0149	.959	.041	.9958	.0042
35-44	.696	.304	.9644	.0356	.931	.069	.9929	.0071
45-54	.719	.281	.9675	.0325	.898	.102	9893	.0107
55-64	.608	.392	.9515	.0485	.772	.228	.9745	.0255
Gylcosuria								
0 or 1 result	.738	.262	.9701	.0299	.876	.124	.9868	.0132
2 or 3 results	.724	.276	.9682	.0318	.897	.103	.9892	.0108
4 or 5 results	.715	.285	.9670	.0330	.930	.070	.9928	.0072
Albuminuria								
0 or 1 result	.772	.228	.9745	.0255	.897	.103	.9892	.0108
2 or 3 results	.610	.390	.9518	.0482	.898	.102	.9893	.0107

* Controls, matched by age, sex, occupation and location, selected at random from all company employees

DIABETES MELLITUS

§909—DIABETES IN NORWAY

Reference: K. Westlund, "Mortality of Diabetics," Life Insurance Companies' Institute for Medical Statistics at the Oslo City Hospitals (Report No. 13), Universitetsforlaget, Oslo (1969).

Subjects Studied: 3832 diabetic residents of Oslo after discharge from first hospitalization with this diagnosis, identified in the files of 13 departments of pediatrics or internal medicine over the period 1925-1955. There were 2288 females and 1544 males, a ratio of 1.48 to 1. More than 35000 observation years were distributed by attained age as follows:

Attained Age	<10	10-19	20-29	30-39	40-49	50-59	60-69	70-79	80 up	Total
Male	120	586	1082	1594	1976	2918	3442	1982	406	14106
Female	78	468	1026	1472	1864	3768	6196	4778	1284	20934
Total	198	1054	2108	3066	3840	6686	9638	6760	1690	35040
Per cent	0.5	3.0	6.0	8.8	11.0	19.1	27.5	19.3	4.8	100.0

Follow-up: Patients were traced (except for 17 lost to observation) until death or to the anniversary of discharge in 1961, at which time 9 per cent of the 1138 patients known to be still alive were resident outside of Oslo. Data with regard to time, place and cause of death were obtained from death certificates in the Central Bureau of Statistics.

Results: Table 909b presents comparative experience of subjects by sex and attained age during three periods: 1925-1940, 1941-1950, and 1951-1961. For the three periods together and attained ages combined, the mortality ratio for males was 355 per cent of that expected in the general Norwegian population, in the case of females, 285 per cent. In the three periods and for both sexes, mortality ratios were highest for attained ages under 50 years; average annual excess deaths per 1000 increased consistently with advancing age. Mortality ratios for quinquennial periods 1936-1940, 1941-1945, and 1946-1950 (not shown in Table 909b) encompassing World War II reveal a significant decrease during the war and a sharp post-war increase: ratios for males in the three quinquennia were 440, 340 and 540 per cent, respectively; for females, 600, 520 and 1070 per cent (expected *Oslo* mortality). A similar tendency can be discerned to some degree in the longer periods of Table 909b, except for all patients age 70 up and females under 30, who exhibited a decrease rather than an increase in mortality ratio from 1941-1950 to the last period, 1951-1961. The 5-year survival index revealed a consistent downward trend with increasing age in both sexes, and an upward trend from the earliest to the later periods, with a maximum in 1941-1950 among male patients, and a maximum in 1951-1961 among females (except ages 50-69).

Leading causes of death with some other causes showing high mortality ratios are shown in Table 909a below. Various forms of cardiovascular disease, including stroke, and diabetes were the leading causes of death in terms of numbers and EDR. Diabetes showed a mortality ratio of 4300 per cent in males and 2400 per cent in females. Other causes of death associated with a high ratio were cardiovascular diseases, tuberculosis, pneumonia, nephritis and GU diseases and cancer of the pancreas.

Table 909a   Excess Mortality by Cause of Death,* All Patients 1925-1961 (14106 Male Exposure Years, 20934 Female Exposure Years)

Cause of Death	Males				Females			
	No. of Deaths		Mortality Ratio	Excess Death Rate	No. of Deaths		Mortality Ratio	Excess Death Rate
	Observed	Expected†			Observed	Expected†		
	d	d′	100 d/d′	1000(d-d′)/E	d	d′	100 d/d′	1000(d-d′)/E
Diabetes Mellitus	112	2.6	4300%	7.8	196	8.2	2400%	9.0
Cor. Ht. Dis. & Sudden Death	245	54.4	450	14	368	78.3	470	14
Stroke	160	40.3	395	8.5	312	100.8	310	10
Other CV Disease	113	34.4	330	5.6	175	83.4	210	4.4
Tuberculosis	45	8.7	515	2.6	47	9.1	515	1.8
Pneumonia	79	16.5	480	4.4	113	43.2	260	3.3
Nephritis & G.U. Disease	53	16.5	320	2.6	72	12.3	585	2.9
Cancer of Pancreas	16	1.7	940	1.0	12	2.1	570	0.5
All Other	238	121.1	197	8.3	318	225.2	141	4.4
All Causes	1061	296.2	360	54	1613	562.6	285	50

* Revised cause of death per W.H.O. standards, after review of available records. This resulted in reduction of deaths attributed to diabetes from 891 to 308.

† Basis of expected mortality: contemporaneous Norwegian population rates

DIABETES IN NORWAY

Table 909b   **Comparative Experience by Period of Observation and Attained Age**

Sex and Period	Attained Age	Exposure Person-Yrs	Deaths		Mortality Ratio	Ave. Ann. Mort. Rate	Est. 5-Yr Surv. Rate	Est. 5-Yr Surv. Index	Excess Death Rate
			Observed	Expected*					
		E	d	d'	100 d/d'	$\bar{q}$ = d/E	P = $(1-\bar{q})^5$	100 P/P'	1000(d-d')/E
Male	5-29	533	10	1.6	625%	.0187	.9097	92.3%	16
1925	30-49	811	26	4.4	590	.0321	.8497	87.3	27
to	50-69	1498	119	27.9	425	.0794	.6611	72.6	61
1940	70 up	358	79	26.1	305	.2207	.2875	42.0	148
	All Ages	3200	234	60.0	390	.0731	.6841	75.2	54
1941	5-29	664	5	2.0	250	.0075	.9629	97.8	4.5
to	30-49	1115	22	5.4	405	.0197	.9052	92.7	15
1950	50-69	1842	124	29.3	425	.0673	.7058	76.5	51
	70 up	708	136	48.6	280	.1920	.3442	49.1	123
	All Ages	4329	287	85.3	335	.0663	.7096	78.4	47
1951	5-29	576	5	0.7	715	.0087	.9573	96.3	7.5
to	30-49	1644	39	4.2	930	.0237	.8868	89.8	21
1961	50-69	3020	240	47.0	510	.0795	.6610	71.5	64
	70 up	1321	256	99.9	255	.1937	.3407	50.5	118
	All Ages	6561	540	151.8	355	.0823	.6509	73.2	59
1925	5-29	1774	20	4.3	465	.0113	.9449	95.6	8.8
to	30-49	3569	87	14.0	620	.0243	.8840	90.2	20
1961	50-69	6360	483	104.2	465	.0759	.6738	73.2	60
	70 up	2387	471	174.6	270	.1973	.3332	48.7	124
	All Ages	14090	1061	297.1	355	.0753	.6761	75.2	54
Female	5-29	389	8	1.0	800%	.0206	.9012	91.3%	18
1925	30-49	808	28	3.6	780	.0346	.8384	85.7	30
to	50-69	2658	167	41.1	405	.0628	.7230	78.2	47
1940	70 up	900	180	60.6	295	.2000	.3276	46.4	133
	All Ages	4755	383	106.3	360	.0805	.6571	73.6	58
1941	5-29	626	8	1.1	725	.0128	.9377	94.6	11
to	30-49	1084	21	3.2	655	.0194	.9068	92.0	16
1950	50-69	3244	159	43.4	365	.0490	.7778	83.2	36
	70 up	1878	300	127.3	235	.1597	.4188	59.5	92
	All Ages	6832	488	175.0	280	.0714	.6904	78.6	46
1951	5-29	548	0	0.2	0	.0000	1.0000	100.2	−0.4
to	30-49	1443	20	2.5	800	.0139	.9326	94.1	12
1961	50-69	4062	210	45.3	465	.0517	.7669	81.1	41
	70 up	3283	512	234.3	220	.1559	.4284	62.0	85
	All Ages	9336	742	282.3	265	.0795	.6610	77.1	49
1925	5-29	1561	16	2.3	695	.0102	.9498	95.7	8.8
to	30-49	3336	69	9.3	740	.0207	.9008	91.3	18
1961	50-69	9965	536	129.8	415	.0538	.7585	81.0	41
	70 up	6061	992	422.2	235	.1637	.4092	58.7	94
	All Ages	20923	1613	563.6	285	.0771	.6696	76.8	50

*Basis of expected mortality: contemporaneous Norwegian population rates

DIABETES MELLITUS

§910–DIABETES IN SWEDEN

Reference: A. Grönberg, T. Larsson, and J. Jung, "Diabetes in Sweden. A Clinico-Statistical, Epidemiological and Genetic Study of Hospital Patients and Death Certificates," Acta Med. Scand., 183(Suppl. 477):1-275 (1967).

Subjects Studied: 3759 inpatients and outpatients in four medium-sized general hospitals in different counties of Sweden (Vänersborg, Växjö, Falun and Östersund). This was a retrospective study sponsored by the Medical Research Council of the Swedish Life Offices. The diagnosis was established by the presence of an elevated fasting blood glucose, above 110 mg. per 100 ml. (generally Hagedorn-Jensen method), or an abnormal oral glucose tolerance test (two-hour level exceeding the fasting level), in patients with typical symptoms or in asymptomatic patients with glycosuria. The four hospitals contributed data on 1680 male and 2079 female diabetics first registered in the period 1924-1957, with age distribution at the time of registration as follows:

	Age Under 10	10-19	20-29	30-39	40-49	50-59	60-69	70-79	80 up	Total
Male	58	166	177	182	234	317	325	197	24	1680
Female	69	121	127	130	210	459	599	337	27	2079
Total No.	127	287	304	312	444	776	924	534	51	3759
Distribution	3.4%	7.6%	8.1%	8.3%	11.8%	20.6%	24.6%	14.2%	1.4%	100.0%

Data were abstracted from the hospital records and analyzed in great detail. The distribution of patients is given in Table 910a by age at onset, sex and quinquennial period of duration of diabetes, with average attained age in each duration category. A summary of entries, deaths and transfers is given in Table 910b. Some of the characteristics of the patients at the time of first registration or first hospital study are given in Table 910c by classes of age at onset (0-14, 15-39, and 40 years up) and sex. About 30 per cent of the patients gave a family history of diabetes, and 87 per cent were first registered within five years of onset. In male patients 42 per cent exhibited diastolic hypertension (95 mm. or higher), but in females this rose to 74 per cent, because of the preponderance of maturity onset cases (age 40 up), and the very high prevalence of elevated diastolic readings in older females. The severity of juvenile diabetes is apparent from the fact that almost 100 per cent required treatment with insulin, over half of the patients exhibited glycosuria exceeding 25 grams per day, and the proportion of patients with a history of diabetic coma or pre-coma was several times higher than in the maturity-onset diabetics. Among diabetics age 40 and older 26 per cent of males and 40 per cent of females did not require treatment with insulin within five years of diagnosis. Of those who were put on insulin, less than one-third required a daily dosage exceeding 40 units.

Follow-up: The period from January 1, 1946 to December 31, 1955 was selected for follow-up. Information with regard to deaths and survivors was obtained by means of hospital records, population registers, and inquiries to officials of the home parishes where patients were resident. In the follow-up study 398 deaths were recorded in 16440 exposure-years on 3384 patients first registered prior to 1956. A separate study was made of death certificates and other information on all deaths in Sweden 1960-1963 in which diabetes was listed as the underlying (primary) or contributory cause of death.

Results: Mortality ratios, all ages combined, were practically the same for the two sexes: 143 per cent in the case of males, 140 per cent for females. In both males and females mortality at the younger attained ages was relatively high: under age 35 years mortality ratios reached 275 per cent in the case of men and 1060 per cent in the case of women. Ratios were materially lower for ages 35 and up, with a progressive decrease with advancing age in female diabetics from 175 per cent in those age 35-54 years to 102 per cent in the oldest age group. In male diabetics the mortality ratio was 143 per cent in patients age 35-54 years, rose to 175 per cent in those age 55-64, then fell to 133 and 125 per cent in those age 65-74 and 75 and up, respectively. The high mortality ratios at the younger ages are attributable in part to the small expected mortality rates; they contributed relatively little to the overall mortality ratio, all ages combined. Excess death rates were at a minimum in the age group 35-54 years, with an EDR of 1.9 per 1000 in men and 3.0 per 1000 in women. Higher EDR's were observed in both younger patients, 2.5 and 8.5 per 1000, respectively, in male and female diabetics, and in older patients, the maximum for males was 23 per 1000 in the oldest age group, and the maximum for females, 14 per 1000, occurring in those age 65-74 years. The general trend for EDR to increase with advancing age in many diseases did not apply to younger diabetics, under age 35. Estimated five-year survival indexes for all ages combined were about the same for male and female patients, 96.8 and 96.2 per cent, respectively. Within

DIABETES IN SWEDEN

Table 910a Distribution of 3759 Patients by Age at Onset of Diabetes, Sex, and Follow-up Duration during Observation Period 1946-1955, and Average Attained Age

Sex and Duration	Onset Age 0-14 yrs		Onset Age 15-39 yrs		Onset Age 40 up		All Onset Ages
	No. Entrants	Ave. Att. Age	No. Entrants	Ave. Att. Age	No. Entrants	Ave. Att. Age	No. Entrants
t to t+Δt	ℓ_t	$\bar{x}$	ℓ_t	$\bar{x}$	ℓ_t	$\bar{x}$	ℓ_t
Male							
0- 5 yrs	133	11.1	386	29.2	944	61.1	1463
5-10	126	16.0	252	34.8	469	63.4	847
10-15	121	20.4	173	38.8	212	64.4	506
15-20	87	25.0	124	42.8	101	67.4	312
20-25	48	30.4	71	47.0	37	70.9	156
25 up	33	—	69	—	12	—	114
All	548	—	1075	—	1775	—	3398
Female							
0- 5 yrs	125	10.6	251	29.0	1423	63.1	1799
5-10	115	15.7	186	33.5	782	64.9	1083
10-15	114	20.1	131	39.3	340	66.6	585
15-20	68	24.7	88	43.9	142	69.5	298
20-25	37	29.7	58	48.0	33	70.8	128
25 up	26	—	58	—	10	—	94
All	485	—	772	—	2730	—	3987

Table 910b Summary of Registration (Entries, Deaths, etc.) by Duration after Onset

Duration and Age	New Entries	Old Entries Continued	Total Entries	Deaths prior to 1/1/56	Moved but living 1/1/56	Still living after 1/1/56	Continued to later dur. per.	Total
t to t + Δt	ℓ_n	ℓ_o	$\ell_n+\ell_o$	d	ℓ_m'	ℓ_e'	ℓ_o'	$d+\ell_m'+\ell_e'+\ell_o'$
Duration								
0- 5 yrs	3262	0	3262	269	47	1111	1835	3262
5-10	235	1695	1930	147	25	867	891	1930
10-15	123	968	1091	96	14	470	511	1091
15-20	66	544	610	73	14	286	237	610
20-25	34	250	284	25	—	161	98	284
25 up	39	169	208	24	1	129	54	208
Age								
0 thru 14 yrs	352	681	1033	37	18	297	681	1033
15 thru 39	769	1078	1847	48	27	694	1078	1847
40 and up	2638	1867	4505	549	56	2033	1867	4505
Total	3759	3626	7385	634	101	3024	3626	7385

Table 910c Characteristics, Acute Complications, and Treatment of Diabetic Patients

Category	Male — Age at Onset				Female — Age at Onset			
	0-14 yrs	15-39 yrs	40 yrs up	Total	0-14 yrs	15-39 yrs	40 yrs up	Total
All Patients—No.	183	450	1047	1680	169	319	1591	2079
Mean Age Onset—Yrs	8.8	27.2	58.5	44.7	8.5	26.7	60.4	51.1
Family History Diabetes	40%	36%	27%	31%	33%	38%	24%	28%
Duration 0-5 Yrs—No.	133	386	944	1463	125	251	1423	1799
Glucosuria < 26 gm/day %	47%	46%	61%	60%	47%	40%	72%	66%
Hypertension Diastolic, 95 up %	18%	21%	62%	42%	24%	31%	94%	74%
Coma or Pre-coma History	14%	4%	1%	4%	23%	7%	3%	6%
On Insulin < 5 Yrs Dur.	97%	91%	64%	74%	98%	90%	60%	67%
Insulin 40 u (< 5 Yrs Dur.)	36%	45%	21%	31%	41%	45%	16%	24%

DIABETES MELLITUS

§910–DIABETES IN SWEDEN

Results (continued):

attained age groups under 75 years this survival index ranged from 92.7 to 99.1 per cent. Only for males age 75 years and older did the survival index fall outside this range, reaching 88.0 per cent (the corresponding female index was 99.2 per cent).

Presented in Table 910e is comparative mortality by age at onset, and by duration for the oldest age group, 40 years and up, and for all ages combined. Because of the lack of exposure data the only comparative index that could be used in this table was the mortality ratio. This decreased with advancing age in female diabetics, but in men the mortality ratio was 320 per cent for those age 0-19 years, 111 per cent for the next group, patients age 15-44 years, and 142 per cent for those age 40 and up. By duration from onset of diabetes the mortality ratio fluctuated over a relatively narrow range, within 15 years of onset, 120 to 141 per cent in males, and 110 to 140 per cent in females, then increased to higher levels at the longer durations. This increase with longer durations in diabetics is noteworthy because it is counter to the downward trend observed in most other diseases.

Table 910f contains follow-up data on morbidity, the prevalence of complications of diabetes during the earliest period of observation (0-5 years), a considerably later period, from 20 to 25 years after onset, and the average for all durations combined. The overall prevalence was slightly higher in females than in males: 17 versus 15 per cent for diabetic retinopathy, 15 versus 14 per cent for diabetic nephropathy, and 13 versus 12 per cent for diabetic neuropathy. Retinopathy had the lowest prevalence at all ages within five years of onset, nephropathy the corresponding highest prevalence in younger diabetics, under age 40, and neuropathy the highest in diabetics age 40 and older. There was a marked increase in prevalence of all of these complications with duration of the diabetes.

Comment: The reader who may be interested in the analysis of causes of death where diabetes was listed as a contributory cause should consult Chapter IV of this monograph, which also contains other detailed data on symptoms, morbidity, complications, genetics and the rating of diabetic risks in life and health insurance in Sweden. The authors note that oral anti-diabetic agents came into general use in Sweden after 1955 and were therefore applied to a slight extent, if at all, during the latter part of the observation period, 1946 to 1955, of this study.

DIABETES IN SWEDEN

Table 910d Comparative Experience by Sex and Attained Age

Sex and Attained Age	Exposure Person-Yrs	No. of Deaths		Mortality Ratio	Ave. Ann. Mort. Rate	Est. 5-Yr Surv. Rate	Est. 5-Yr Surv. Index	Excess Death Rate
		Observed	Expected*					
	E	d	d'	$100\,d/d'$	$\bar{q}=d/E$	$P=(1-\bar{q})^5$	$100\,P/P'$	$1000(d-d')/E$
Male								
0-34 yrs	2290	9	3.3	275%	.004	.980	98.8%	2.5
35-54 yrs	2387	15	10.5	143	.006	.969	99.1	1.9
55-64 yrs	1308	34	19.4	175	.026	.877	94.5	11
65-74 yrs	1117	56	42.1	133	.050	.773	93.7	12
75 yrs up	396	46	36.9	125	.116	.539	88.0	23
All Ages	7498	160	112.2	143	.021	.898	96.8	6.4
Female								
0-34 yrs	1813	17	1.6	1060%	.009	.954	95.8%	8.5
35-54 yrs	2024	14	8.0	175	.007	.966	98.5	3.0
55-64 yrs	2200	40	26.7	150	.018	.912	96.9	6.0
65-74 yrs	2195	103	71.4	144	.047	.786	92.7	14
75 yrs up	710	64	62.9	102	.090	.624	99.2	1.5
All Ages	8942	238	170.6	140	.027	.874	96.2	7.5

Table 910e Comparative Mortality by Sex, Age at Onset and Duration

Age at Onset	Duration from Onset	Males — Age at Onset			Females — Age at Onset		
		No. of Deaths		Mortality Ratio	No. of Deaths		Mortality Ratio
		Observed	Expected*		Observed	Expected*	
	t to $t+\Delta t$	d	d'	$100\,d/d'$	d	d'	$100\,d/d'$
0-19 yrs	All	7	2.2	320%	14	1.2	1170%
15-44 yrs	All	11	9.9	111	20	6.4	310
40 yrs up	0- 5 yrs	66	46.8	141	85	76.8	111
	5-10	36	27.5	131	57	47.3	121
	10-15	18	13.7	131	28	25.3	111
	15 up	22	12.1	182	34	13.6	250
	All	142	100.1	142	204	163.0	125
All Ages	0- 5 yrs	68	48.5	140%	87	79.1	110%
	5-10	36	30.0	120	57	47.5	120
	10-15	23	16.4	140	37	26.4	140
	15-20	19	9.5	200	38	12.7	300
	20 up	14	7.8	179	19	4.9	390
	All	160	112.2	143	238	170.6	140

Table 910f Late Complications During Observation Period

Complication and Duration Since Onset		Males — Age at Onset				Females — Age at Onset			
		0-14 yrs	15-39 yrs	40 yrs up	All Ages	0-14 yrs	15-39 yrs	40 yrs up	All Ages
Retinopathy	0- 5 yrs	0%	1%	5%	3%	0%	2%	7%	6%
	20-25 yrs	60	56	22	49	65	43	48	44
	All yrs	21	18	11	15	24	19	15	17
Nephropathy	0- 5 yrs	10	8	9	9	14	14	9	10
	20-25 yrs	44	25	16	29	51	33	30	38
	All yrs	23	13	12	14	27	18	12	15
Neuropathy	0- 5 yrs	2	3	14	10	2	3	12	10
	20-25 yrs	21	13	16	16	22	22	21	22
	All yrs	6	9	17	12	9	10	15	13

*Basis of expected mortality: Swedish population, males and females 1946-1955

DIABETES MELLITUS

§919–ABNORMAL BLOOD SUGAR IN INSUREDS

Reference: "New York Life Single Medical Impairment Study—1967," unpublished report made available by J.J. Hutchinson and J.C. Sibigtroth (1973).

Subjects Studied: Policyholders of New York Life Insurance Company issued insurance in 1949-1965, followed to the 1966 policy anniversary. These were cases in which the level of blood glucose was above normal value, fasting, post-prandial or in a glucose tolerance test, in the absence of a definite diagnosis of diabetes. Based on the degree of such blood glucose excess, certain policies were issued standard and others rated substandard. Both underwriting categories have been analyzed here. Policies involving a rating for any impairment other than abnormal blood glucose were excluded.

Follow-up: Insurance policy records formed the basis of entry, of counting policies, exposure and death claims, and of follow-up information.

Results: Comparative experience is given in Tables 919a-b for standard and substandard male cases by duration, all ages combined. Among standard cases, the mortality ratio showed an upward trend with duration ranging from 88 to 143 per cent, with an EDR of 3.7 per 1000 after 10 years. Among substandard cases, the mortality ratio showed no trend, being highest after 10 years at 158 per cent with an EDR of 7.6 per 1000. The cumulative survival ratio after 17 years was 93.7 per cent, compared to 97.2 per cent for standard cases.

Table 919c shows the corresponding experience by age group. Among standard male cases, the mortality ratio ranged from 135 per cent in two age groups under entry age 50, to 75 per cent for entry ages 50 up, with no excess mortality for the older ages. The estimated 8-year survival index ranged between 102.1 per cent at ages 50 and up and 98.7 per cent at ages 40-49. Among substandard cases, the highest mortality ratio of 230 per cent was observed for the age group 40-49, with an EDR of 6.1 per 1000. The estimated 8-year survival index was about normal for standard cases, but was irregular for substandard cases. The overall mortality ratios were 112 and 139 per cent, respectively.

Comparative mortality by major causes of death is given in Table 919d for male and female substandard cases combined. The major cause of death is found in diseases of heart and circulatory system, with a mortality ratio of 233 per cent and an EDR of 2.4 per 1000.

ABNORMAL BLOOD SUGAR IN INSUREDS

Table 919a Observed Data and Comparative Experience by Duration — All Ages Combined, Male Cases

Group	Interval No.	Interval Start-End	Exposure Policy-Yrs	No. of Death Claims Observed	No. of Death Claims Expected*	Mortality Ratio Interval	Mortality Ratio Cumulative	Survival Ratio Interval	Survival Ratio Cumulative	Excess Death Rate
	i	t to t + Δt	E	d	d'	100 d/d'	100 Σd/Σd'	100 p_i/p_i'	100 P/P'	1000(d-d')/E
Std	1	0- 5 yrs	5238	12	13.62	88%	88%	100.2%	100.2%	−0.3
	2	5-10	2649	15	12.71	118	103	99.5	99.8	0.9
	3	10-17	898	11	7.71	143	112	97.4	97.2	3.7
SStd	1	0- 5 yrs	2152	9	6.17	146%	146%	99.3%	99.3%	1.3
	2	5-10	849	6	5.25	114	131	99.5	98.9	0.8
	3	10-17	337	7	4.43	158	139	94.7	93.7	7.6

Table 919b Derived Mortality and Survival Data

Group	Interval No.	Interval Start-End	Observed Rates: Average Annual Mortality	Observed Rates: Average Annual Survival	Observed Rates: Cumulative Survival	Observed Rates: Cumulative Mortality	Expected Rates*: Average Annual Mortality	Expected Rates*: Average Annual Survival	Expected Rates*: Cumulative Survival	Expected Rates*: Cumulative Mortality
	i	t to t + Δt	$\bar{q}$ = d/E	$\bar{p}$	P	Q	$\bar{q}'$ = d'/E	$\bar{p}'$	P'	Q'
Std	1	0- 5 yrs	.0022	.9978	.9890	.0110	.0026	.9974	.9870	.0130
	2	5-10	.0056	.9944	.9614	.0386	.0047	.9953	.9638	.0362
	3	10-17	.0122	.9878	.8819	.1181	.0085	.9915	.9076	.0924
SStd	1	0- 5 yrs	.0041	.9959	.9795	.0205	.0028	.9972	.9860	.0140
	2	5-10	.0070	.9930	.9454	.0546	.0061	.9939	.9561	.0439
	3	10-17	.0207	.9793	.8164	.1836	.0131	.9869	.8715	.1285

Table 919c Comparative Experience by Age Group — All Durations Combined, Male Cases

Group	Age Group	Exposure Policy-Yrs	No. of Death Claims Observed	No. of Death Claims Expected*	Mortality Ratio	Ave. Ann. Mort. Rate	Est. 8-Yr Surv. Rate	Est. 8-Yr Surv. Index	Excess Death Rate
		E	d	d'	100 d/d'	$\bar{q}$ = d/E	P = (1 − $\bar{q}$)^8	100 P/P'	1000(d-d')/E
Std	<40	4743	11	8.13	135%	.0023	.9816	99.5%	0.6
	40-49	2743	17	12.57	135	.0061	.9519	98.7	1.6
	50 up	1299	10	13.34	75	.0076	.9404	102.1	−2.6
	All Ages	8785	38	34.04	112	.0043	.9661	99.7	0.5
SStd	<40	1279	0	2.17	0%	.0000	.0000	0 %	−1.7
	40-49	1387	15	6.52	230	.0108	.9164	95.2	6.1
	50 up	672	7	7.16	98	.0104	.9196	100.2	−0.2
	All Ages	3338	22	15.85	139	.0066	.9483	98.5	1.8

Table 919d Mortality by Cause of Death — Substandard Cases, Male and Female Combined

Cause	No. of Death Claims Observed	No. of Death Claims Expected†	Mortality Ratio	Excess Death Rate
Malignant Neoplasms	3	3.91	77%	−0.3
Diseases of the Heart and Circulatory System	15	6.44	233	2.4
Accidents and Homicides	2	2.25	89	−0.1
Suicide	1	0.69	145	0.1
All Other Causes & Unknown	1	3.09	32	−0.6
Total	22	16.38	134	1.6

* Basis of expected mortality: 1955-60 Select Basic Table
† Distribution of total expected deaths by Intercompany Medically Examined Standard Issues 1965-70

METABOLIC DISORDERS - LIPIDS

§950–MORTALITY RELATED TO SERUM CHOLESTEROL

Reference. K. Westlund and R. Nicolaysen, "Ten-Year Mortality and Morbidity Related to Serum Cholesterol," Scand. J. Clin. Lab. Invest., 30:Suppl. 127 (1972).

Subjects Studied: 3751 men age 40-49 who were actually at work in Oslo, Norway and had a check of their serum cholesterol. Subjects were enrolled from the records of about 20 industrial physicians in Oslo, and blood samples were analyzed at the Institute for Nutrition Research during the period April 1958 - June 1960. Through industrial medical records an attempt was made to discover all cases of the following conditions: myocardial infarction, angina pectoris, atherosclerosis obliterans, cerebrovascular events, diabetes mellitus, malignant tumor, urolithiasis, and cholecystitis. Serum blood cholesterol, blood pressure, and build measurements were used as predictors of total and coronary heart disease (CHD) mortality, as well as morbidity due to various cardiovascular causes.

Follow-up: The period to be covered was set to be exactly ten years from the date of the blood sample of each man. The industrial physician's record of each man was accordingly reviewed not less than one month after the expiry of the 10-year period. Of the 3751 men under study, 411 (11 per cent) left their places of work for reasons other than death in the course of the 10-year period. All 411 men, however were followed until death or the end of the observation period through population registers and Oslo hospital records (only 38 of the men had moved away from Oslo). The cause of death was determined for all deaths, and autopsy findings were reviewed whenever available.

Results: Of the 3751 subjects of the study, 190 died in the course of the 10-year period of observation. Observed deaths were compared with the expected number on the basis of population mortality rates for Norway and also for the city of Oslo. Relative to the latter, observed deaths from all causes among the subjects studied represented 74 per cent of those expected, and sudden deaths associated with coronary heart disease, 89 per cent. Compared with rates of death for the total population of Norway, observed mortality was 86 per cent for all causes combined and 104 per cent for such sudden deaths. The relatively favorable experience of the subjects studied may be attributable to the fact that the men examined were employed and excluded, on that account, chronically ill persons subject to greater risk of death.

In Table 950a comparative experience is displayed in relation to cholesterol, the mortality and survival rates and ratios being compared with the corresponding rates and ratios of men having a cholesterol level under 275 mg. per 100 cc. This comparison reveals the mortality ratio increased steadily from 59 per cent in men with the lowest cholesterol (under 200) to a maximum of 520 per cent in those with cholesterol 375 and up. The corresponding range in EDR was -1.3 to 13 extra deaths per 1000 annually, and in the 10-year survival ratio, 101.3 to 87.4 per cent. Correlation of mortality rates with serum cholesterol was remarkably close. In the 1629 men (43 per cent of the total) with serum cholesterol 275 and up the aggregate mortality ratio was 245 per cent and EDR, 4.6 per 1000. All of these mortality ratios and EDR values are based on age-adjusted geometric mean annual mortality rates.

Table 950b presents 10-year mortality rates for total deaths and those attributed to coronary heart disease (CHD), including sudden deaths, according to serum cholesterol, systolic blood pressure, diastolic pressure and weight/height relation to the average. All of these risk factors served as predictors, with mortality rates increasing with cholesterol, blood pressure, and relative weight for both CHD deaths and all causes. Comparative mortality and survival indices are omitted from this table, because the increase in mortality rates from one line to the next is readily apparent. The average cumulative mortality rates for the entire group were .051 (total) and .023 (CHD), and the mean annual rates were .0052 (total) and .0023 (CHD). Overweight was a weaker predictor factor for total and especially CHD mortality than cholesterol and blood pressure were. In the topmost categories of blood pressure and cholesterol the mortality rates were higher for both systolic and diastolic pressure ($\breve{q}_t$ .0188 and .0202, respectively) than for cholesterol ($\breve{q}_t$ .0166 at a serum level of 375 and up). However, there was a greater difference between mortality rates in the two lowest cholesterol categories than in the two lowest blood pressure categories.

MORTALITY RELATED TO SERUM CHOLESTEROL

Table 950a Comparative Experience by Cholesterol Level, Men Age 40-49

Serum Cholesterol	No. Alive at Start	No. of Deaths (10 Years)	10-Year Mort. Rate*	10-Year Surv. Rate	Ave. Ann. Mort. Rate	Mortality Ratio†	10-Year Surv. Ratio	Excess Death Rate
mg./100 ml.	ℓ	Σd	Q	P	$\breve{q}$	$100\,\breve{q}/\breve{q}'$	$100\,P/P'$	$1000(\breve{q}-\breve{q}')$
<275 (Control)	2122	68	.032	.968	.0032	—	—	—
Under 200	268	5	.019	.981	.0019	59%	101.3%	−1.3
200-224	411	12	.029	.971	.0029	91	100.3	−0.3
225-249	684	24	.035	.965	.0036	112	99.7	0.4
250-274	759	27	.035	.965	.0036	112	99.7	0.4
275-299	696	40	.058	.942	.0060	188	97.3	2.8
300-324	458	32	.070	.930	.0073	230	96.1	4.1
325-374	368	33	.089	.911	.0093	290	94.1	7.1
375 up	107	17	.154	.846	.0166	520	87.4	13
All 275 up	1629	122	.075	.925	.0078	245	95.6	4.6
Total	3751	190	.051	.949	.0052	162%	98.0%	2.0

Table 950b Total and CHD● Mortality, Men Age 40-49 by Cholesterol Level, Blood Pressure and Relative Weight, with 10 Years Follow-up

Category	Number of Men	Total Mortality				CHD● Mortality		
		No. of Deaths (10 Years)	10-Year*	Ave. Ann.		No. of Deaths (10 Years)	10-Year*	Ave. Ann.
	ℓ	d_t	$Q_t = d_t/\ell$	$\breve{q}_t$		d_c	Q_c	$\breve{q}_c$
Cholesterol (mg./100 ml.)								
Under 275	2122	68	.032	.0032		25	.012	.0012
275-324	1154	72	.063	.0065		26	.023	.0023
325-374	368	33	.089	.0093		20	.054	.0055
375 up	107	17	.154	.0166		15	.140	.0150
Systolic Pressure (mm.)								
Under 125	1481	58	.040	.0041		26	.018	.0018
125-144	1695	65	.038	.0039		34	.020	.0020
145-164	390	41	.101	.0106		17	.042	.0043
165 up	127	22	.163	.0176		8	.063	.0065
Diastolic Pressure								
Under 85	2296	86	.038	.0039		39	.017	.0017
85- 94	953	48	.049	.0050		23	.023	.0023
95-104	314	27	.083	.0086		13	.040	.0041
105 up	128	25	.185	.0202		10	.078	.0081
Weight/Height Relation								
Under +10%	2572	112	.044	.0045		51	.020	.0020
Overweight +10% to +25%	929	54	.058	.0060		26	.028	.0028
Overweight > +25%	182	19	.101	.0106		9	.049	.0050

* Age-adjusted rates, which may differ slightly from $\Sigma d/\ell$ in some entries
† Mortality rate for men with cholesterol under 275 used as a standard for comparison
● Deaths attributed to Coronary Heart Disease, including sudden deaths

METABOLIC DISORDERS - LIPIDS

§951—EFFECT OF CHOLESTEROL-LOWERING DIET ON CORONARY HEART DISEASE

Reference: M. Miettinen, O. Turpeinen, M. J. Karvonen, R. Elosuo, and E. Paavilainen, "Effect of Cholesterol-Lowering Diet on Mortality, from Coronary Heart-Disease and Other Causes. A Twelve-year Clinical Trial in Men and Women," Lancet, 2:835-878 (1972).

Subjects Studied: All male and female patients over 15 years of age in two mental institutions in Finland: the Kellokoski Hospital (K) and the Nikkilä Hospital (N). The study undertaken in 1958 was intended to determine the effect on coronary heart disease of a cholesterol-lowering diet. Patients with pre-existing CHD or other disease were not excluded. The experimental diet differed from the normal hospital diet in two important respects: ordinary milk was replaced by an emulsion of soybean oil in skim milk, and butter and ordinary margarine were replaced by a "soft" margarine with a high content of polyunsaturated fatty acids. The study was cross-over in design. In one of the hospitals a serum-cholesterol-lowering diet was introduced, and the other hospital using a normal diet served as the control. After six years the diets were reversed and the trial was continued for six more years. The number of subjects in the two hospitals during the diet and control periods and their median ages by sex were as follows:

			No. of Males	Median Age	No. of Females	Median Age
Hospital N	Diet Period (1)	1959-65	1003	50.1 yrs	2169	56.0 yrs
	Control Period (2)	1965-71	1022	50.2 yrs	1773	59.0 yrs
Hospital K	Control Period (1)	1959-65	880	47.5 yrs	1063	50.5 yrs
	Diet Period (2)	1965-71	1273	50.5 yrs	1429	53.2 yrs

Follow-up: Hospital records were utilized for all follow-up statistics on exposure and deaths. The underlying cause of death, assigned without knowledge of the hospital in which the patient belonged, was generally taken as that indicated on the death certificate, but was revised when necessary to conform to World Health Organization rules for selecting cause of death.

Results: Persons on the special diet had lowered mean serum-cholesterol levels in both hospitals and for the two sexes, with reduction from a control mean of 272 to 236 mg. per 100 ml. on the special diet. Analysis of subcutaneous fat samples obtained by needle biopsy showed a ratio of polyunsaturated to saturated fatty acids in the range 0.22 to 0.29 on the control diet, increasing to 1.42 to 1.78 on the special diet.

The experience in Tables 951a-b is divided by diet period, hospital and sex, but all mortality rates were adjusted by the authors to a common age distribution (that for all male patients). Entrants and exposure data are given in Table 951a, and deaths, average annual age-adjusted mortality rates and comparative indices in Table 951b. Mortality ratio, three-year survival index, and EDR are based on a comparison of the age-adjusted rates observed during the period of special diet with the corresponding rates found in the period of normal or control diet (subscript c). Mortality ratios of deaths from coronary heart disease (CHD) among patients on cholesterol-lowering diet to those on normal diet were lower in both hospitals and in the case of both males and females. Statistical tests indicated that for males the differences were highly significant in Hospital N and for the pooled experience of both hospitals. Due to the smaller population in Hospital K the difference was barely significant. The difference in CHD deaths for females in Hospital N was significant but was not in Hospital K over the two periods (due possibly to transfer of many chronic cases from Hospital K during the second or diet period), nor in the pooled female experience.

None of the other causes of death recorded, also shown in Table 951b, indicated any significant regular difference in mortality ratios over the two periods. Although differences in CHD mortality experience were significant, the differences in mortality from all causes were not because of the relatively large number of deaths apparently unaffected by diet and a slight tendency for mortality rates in deaths due to cancer and other causes during the diet period to exceed these rates in the control period.

Because of the nature of the subjects studied, death rates in both hospitals exceeded those found in the Finnish general population, the authors reporting a mortality ratio of 194 per cent in males and 264 per cent in females.

CHOLESTEROL-LOWERING DIET

Table 951a Entrants and Exposure (Person-Years) by Hospital and Diet Period

Hospital	Special Diet*				Control†			
	Male		Female		Male		Female	
	Entrants	Exposure	Entrants	Exposure	Entrants	Exposure	Entrants	Exposure
	ℓ	E	ℓ	E	ℓ	E	ℓ	E
N	1003 (1)	3531	2169 (1)	7426	1022 (2)	3636	1773 (2)	6741
K	1273 (2)	1878	1429 (2)	1943	880 (1)	1931	1063 (1)	2131
Total	2276	5409	3598	9369	1902	5567	2836	8872

Table 951b Comparative Experience, Special Diet vs. Normal (Control) by Cause of Death and All Causes (Mortality Rates Age-Adjusted)

Sex Cause of Death and Hospital	No. of Deaths/Period		Ave. Ann. Mort. Rate During Period		Mortality Ratio	Estimated 3-Yr Survival Rate		Est. 3-Yr Survival Index	"Excess" Death Rate
	Spec. Diet	Control	Spec. Diet	Control		Spec. Diet	Control		
	d	d_c	$\bar{q}=d/E$	$\bar{q}_c=d_c/E$	$100\,\bar{q}/\bar{q}_c$	P	P_c	$100\,P/P_c$	$1000(\bar{q}-\bar{q}_c)$
Male Patients									
Coronary Heart Disease									
N	20 (1)	52 (2)	.0057	.0130	44%	.9829	.9614	102.2%	−7.3
K	14 (2)	24 (1)	.0075	.0152	49	.9776	.9550	102.4	−7.7
Both	34	76	.0066	.0141	47	.9802	.9581	102.3	−7.5
Cerebrovascular Disease									
N	10 (1)	10 (2)	.0030	.0026	115	.9910	.9922	99.9	0.4
K	1 (2)	3 (1)	.0005	.0022	23	.9985	.9934	100.5	−1.7
Both	11	13	.0017	.0024	71	.9949	.9928	100.2	−0.7
Malignant Neoplasms									
N	10 (1)	18 (2)	.0028	.0045	62	.9916	.9865	100.5	−1.7
K	13 (2)	6 (1)	.0073	.0034	215	.9782	.9898	98.8	3.9
Both	23	24	.0050	.0040	125	.9850	.9880	99.7	1.0
Other Causes									
N	81 (1)	71 (2)	.0231	.0187	124	.9322	.9448	98.7	4.4
K	39 (2)	33 (1)	.0198	.0194	102	.9416	.9428	99.9	0.4
Both	120	104	.0215	.0190	113	.9368	.9440	99.2	2.5
All Causes									
N	121 (1)	151 (2)	.0346	.0388	89	.8996	.8880	101.3	−4.2
K	67 (2)	66 (1)	.0351	.0402	87	.8983	.8841	101.6	−5.1
Both	188	217	.0348	.0395	88	.8991	.8860	101.5	−4.7
Female Patients									
Coronary Heart Disease									
N	52 (1)	107 (2)	.0040	.0077	52	.9880	.9770	101.1	−3.7
K	21 (2)	22 (1)	.0065	.0081	80	.9805	.9758	100.5	−1.6
Both	73	129	.0052	.0079	66	.9844	.9764	100.8	−2.7
Cerebrovascular Disease									
N	27 (1)	30 (2)	.0023	.0022	105	.9931	.9934	100.0	0.1
K	6 (2)	5 (1)	.0021	.0019	111	.9937	.9943	99.9	0.2
Both	33	35	.0022	.0020	110	.9934	.9940	99.9	0.2
Malignant Neoplasms									
N	39 (1)	28 (2)	.0038	.0028	136	.9886	.9916	99.7	1.0
K	12 (2)	10 (1)	.0044	.0046	96	.9868	.9862	100.1	−0.2
Both	51	38	.0041	.0037	111	.9877	.9889	99.9	0.4
Other Causes									
N	208 (1)	235 (2)	.0210	.0194	108	.9382	.9428	99.5	1.6
K	50 (2)	28 (1)	.0177	.0113	157	.9478	.9664	98.1	6.4
Both	258	263	.0194	.0154	126	.9428	.9544	98.8	4.0
All Causes									
N	326 (1)	400 (2)	.0311	.0321	97	.9095	.9067	100.3	−1.0
K	89 (2)	65 (1)	.0307	.0259	119	.9106	.9242	98.5	4.8
Both	415	465	.0309	.0290	107	.9100	.9154	99.4	1.9

* Cholesterol-lowering experimental diet during period indicated in parentheses
† Normal Diet during period indicated in parentheses

§952–PROSPECTIVE STUDIES OF HYPERLIPIDEMIA

References: (1) J. Stamler and F. H. Epstein, "Coronary Heart Disease: Risk Factors as Guides to Preventive Action," Prev. Med., 1:27-48 (1972).

(2) R. Pelkonen, K. Penttinen, S. Koskinen, and E. A. Nikkilä, "Cardiovascular Mortality of 1600 Men: Effect of Serum Lipid Level, Smoking and Occupation – a Seven-Year Follow-up Study." 12ème Conference Internationale, Coopération Internationale pour les Assurances des Risques Aggravés. Paris: Societé Commerciale de Réassurance (1973), Vol. I (Part 2), pp. 247-260.

Subjects Studied: (1) 7594 white males age 30-59 and free of definite coronary heart disease (CHD) at entry, combined from six separate prospective studies in the United States: Framingham, Mass. residents; Albany, N.Y. civil servants; Chicago, Ill., two utility employee groups; Minneapolis – St. Paul, Minn. businessmen; Los Angeles, Calif., civil servants. These are independent prospective epidemiological studies designed to carry out follow-up of large groups for ten years or longer, correlating morbidity and mortality due to cardiovascular diseases, especially CHD, with the findings at periodic examinations. Data from these independent studies have been transmitted to a National Cooperative Pooling Project, so that the larger volume of pooled data could be processed statistically at a central unit. The subjects were classified in accordance with serum cholesterol level as well as other risk factors evaluated at the time of the initial examination.

(2) 2180 men aged 50-53 years, insured policyholders of the Salama Company, Helsinki, Finland, responded to an invitation to participate in a prospective study of cardiovascular disease. In the series 1661 had had both serum cholesterol and triglyceride levels determined at the time of the initial examination in 1965-1966, and these constituted the group reported. Additional data were presence of cardiovascular diseases, diabetes or hypertension, cigarette smoking, physical activity, and hypertension at time of entry.

Follow-up: (1) Personal contact, re-examination and other means were used to establish survival status, mortality and cause of death. The length of follow-up was ten years.

(2) Subjects were followed to 1972-73 (seven years) through policy records, and a check of the files of the Central Bureau of Statistics for death certificate information.

Results: Comparative ten-year experience for men in the National Cooperative Pooling Project is presented in Table 952a. The observed cumulative rates by cholesterol level and age group were adjusted to the U.S. 1960 population distribution for white males age 30-59 years, in the data presented in the article. In this series and in the Finnish men subjects in the three classes having the lowest serum cholesterol concentration were used to derive indices of comparative mortality and survival instead of expected rates taken from appropriate population life tables. Cumulative mortality and survival rates showed relatively little change in the Pooling Project series from the lowest category, cholesterol under 175 mg. per 100 ml. to the middle of seven categories, with cholesterol 225 to 249. In the range of these concentrations under 250 mg. per 100 ml. the average annual mortality ratio showed a minimum of 84 per cent and a maximum of 103 per cent. Some excess mortality was evident in the three categories comprising 32 per cent of the subjects with serum cholesterol 250 or above: mortality ratios of 140, 124 and 140 per cent respectively, and corresponding EDR's of 2.7, 1.6 and 2.7 per 1000. Although the difference is not large, men with cholesterol 250 and above did experience a significantly higher mortality than those with a lower serum cholesterol, under 250.

In the Finnish series the cholesterol and triglyceride categories were determined by dividing the total group into quintiles of nearly equal size. About 80 per cent of the Finnish men had a cholesterol 252 up, reflecting a considerably higher average serum cholesterol than in the U.S. men, only 32 per cent of whom had a cholesterol exceeding 249. The highest mortality was observed in the quintiles with the highest lipid levels: a mortality ratio 178 per cent in men with cholesterol 331 or above, and 191 per cent in men with triglyceride exceeding 167. The corresponding excess death rates were 8.0 and 8.7 per 1000, respectively. The next lower quintile for both cholesterol and triglyceride showed an excess mortality that did not exceed the limits of the apparently random fluctuations of mortality ratio and EDR in the control quintiles. The considerable effect of some other risk factors on the men in this series is shown in Table 952c. Men with "other cardiovascular disease" experienced a mortality ratio of 131 per cent and EDR of 3.0 per 1000 vs. men without cardiovascular disease at entry. For the risk factor hypertension the mortality ratio was 165 per cent and EDR 6.6 per 1000; for smokers the mortality ratio was 250 per cent and EDR 11 per 1000.

PROSPECTIVE STUDIES OF HYPERLIPIDEMIA

Table 952a   Comparative 10-Year Experience by Cholesterol Level, National Cooperative Pooling Project

| Level of Serum Cholesterol | No. of Men | No. of Deaths | Age Adjusted 10-Yr Rate | | 10-Yr Cum. Surv. Ratio* | Ave. Ann. Mort. Rate | Mortality Ratio* | Excess Death Rate |
			Mortality	Survival				
mg./100ml.	ℓ	d	Q	P	100P/P'	$\breve{q}$	100 $\breve{q}/\breve{q}'$	1000($\breve{q}$-$\breve{q}'$)
Under 175	658	41	.062	.938	100.3%	.0064	96%	−0.3
175-199	1186	78	.064	.936	100.1	.0066	99	−0.1
200-224	1594	122	.067	.933	99.8	.0069	103	0.2
225-249	1633	110	.055	.945	101.1	.0056	84	−1.1
250-274	1108	104	.090	.910	97.3	.0094	140	2.7
275-299	670	64	.080	.920	98.4	.0083	124	1.6
300 up	635	63	.090	.910	97.3	.0094	140	2.7

Table 952b   Comparative 7-Year Experience by Cholesterol and Triglyceride Levels, Finnish Men Age 50-53 Years

| Serum Level | No. of Men | No. of Deaths | 7-Yr Rates | | 7-Yr Cum. Surv. Ratio† | Ave. Ann. Mort. Rate | Mortality Ratio† | Excess Death Rate† |
			Mortality	Survival				
mg./100ml.	ℓ	d	Q	P	100 P/P'	$\breve{q}$	100 $\breve{q}/\breve{q}'$	1000($\breve{q}$-$\breve{q}'$)
Cholesterol								
102-251	330	22	.067	.933	100.2%	.0098	96%	−0.4
252-276	327	21	.064	.936	100.5	.0094	92	−0.8
277-300	328	25	.076	.924	99.2	.0113	111	1.1
301-330	331	24	.072	.928	99.6	.0107	105	0.5
331-553	332	40	.120	.880	94.5	.0182	178	8.0
All	1648	132	.080	.920	98.8	.0119	117	1.7
Triglyceride								
31-77	328	20	.061	.939	100.4%	.0090	94%	−0.6
78-100	340	29	.085	.915	97.8	.0127	132	3.1
101-126	330	16	.048	.952	101.8	.0071	74	−2.5
127-167	328	28	.085	.915	97.8	.0127	132	3.1
168-978	322	39	.121	.879	94.0	.0183	191	8.7
All	1648	132	.080	.920	98.4	.0119	124	2.3

Table 952c   Comparative 7-Year Experience by Various Risk Factors, Finnish Men Age 50-53 Years

| Risk Factor | No. of Men | No. of Deaths | 7-Yr Rates | | 7-Yr Cum. Surv. Ratio● | Ave. Ann. Mort. Rate | Mortality Ratio● | Excess Death Rate● |
			Mortality	Survival				
	ℓ	d	Q	P	100 P/P'	$\breve{q}$	100 $\breve{q}/\breve{q}'$	1000($\breve{q}$-$\breve{q}'$)
With CV Disease	975	86	.088	.912	97.9%	.0131	130%	3.0
No CV Disease	673	46	.068	.932	—	.0101	—	—
With Hypertension	451	50	.111	.889	95.5	.0168	165	6.6
No Hypertension	1001	69	.069	.931	—	.0102	—	—
Smokers	562	67	.119	.881	92.6	.0179	250	11
Non-Smokers	975	48	.049	.951	—	.0072	—	—

*Basis of expected mortality: average, cholesterol < 225; P' = .935 and $\breve{q}'$ = .0067
†Basis of expected mortality: average, cholesterol < 301; P' = .931 and $\breve{q}'$ = .0102;
  average, triglyceride < 127; P' = .935 and $\breve{q}'$ = .0096
●Basis of expected mortality: P and $\breve{q}$ in men without the risk factor

ENDOCRINE AND METABOLIC DISORDERS

§999–ENDOCRINE AND METABOLIC DISORDERS (MISCELLANEOUS)

References: (1) T. W. Preston and R. D. Clarke, "An Investigation into the Mortality of Impaired Lives During the Period 1947-63," J. Inst. Act., 92:27-74 (1966).
(2) A. Svensson and S. Astrand, "Substandard Risk Mortality in Sweden 1955-1965," Coopération Internationale pour les Assurances des Risques Aggravés. (See Rome Conference proceedings, 1969.)
(3) "New York Life Single Medical Impairment Study - 1972," unpublished report made available by J. J. Hutchinson and J. C. Sibigtroth (1973).

Subjects Studied: (1) Policyholders of Prudential Assurance Co., London, England, issued insurance 1947-1963 followed to 12/31/63. Both standard and substandard issues were included. Applicants with two or more ratable impairments were generally excluded.
(2) Insured lives reinsured with Sverige Reinsurance Co., Sweden, placed in force prior to 1955 and observed between anniversaries in 1955 and 1965.
(3) Policyholders of New York Life Insurance Co., issued insurance 1954-1970 followed to 1971 policy anniversary. Both standard and substandard issues were included. Applicants with more than one ratable impairment were excluded.

Follow-up: Insurance policy records formed the basis of entry, of counting policies, exposures and death claims, and of follow-up information.

Results: The Prudential Assurance and New York Life expected deaths were based on the experience of standard insured lives. The Swedish study used general population mortality; had comparison been made with the lower rates associated with selected insured lives, the mortality ratios and extra deaths reported would have been higher.

A high mortality was observed for diabetes cases in the Prudential Assurance and the Swedish Reinsurance studies. In the Prudential Assurance experience, the extra deaths per 1000 per year (EDR) increased with advancing age from 5.0 at ages under 30 to 8.7 at ages over 50. However, mortality ratios decreased with age: 835 per cent for ages under 30, 350 per cent for ages 30-50 and 174 per cent for ages over 50. The Swedish study combined all ages with an approximate average of 37 years, and produced an overall mortality ratio of 415 per cent and EDR of 11 per 1000. The presence of glycosuria at examination (as distinct from a definite diagnosis of diabetes) was accompanied by slight extra mortality in the various categories studied by Prudential Assurance. Mortality ratios were in the 130-150 per cent range and the EDR ranged from 1.0 to 2.3 per 1000.

Thyroid enlargement was studied by the New York Life but the experience was quite limited in the number of deaths observed. Non-toxic cases with operation produced a mortality ratio of 186 per cent, based on four death claims, and cases with toxicity unspecified but no operation, a ratio of 205 per cent (only five death claims). The Prudential Assurance mortality experience with a history of either toxic or non-toxic goiter was only slightly above the expected (8 and 10 death claims, respectively).

Underweight cases were studied by Prudential Assurance, separately for males and females. The mortality was very slightly elevated, the mortality ratios being 109 per cent for males and 112 per cent for females, and the EDR 0.4 per 1000 for both sexes. For overweights, the primary source of information was the Prudential Assurance study. Females experienced a mortality close to the standard. For males the mortality was somewhat above the standard. Mortality ratios were highest for entry ages 30-50: 153 per cent for overweights 20-30 per cent above the standard weight and 192 per cent for those who were more overweight. The corresponding EDR's were 1.1 and 1.9 per 1000. For ages over 50 the mortality ratios were substantially lower, but the EDR was 1.2 per 1000 for the 20-30 per cent overweight category and 3.0 per 1000 for heavier overweights. For ages under 30, the mortality ratio was 148 per cent and the EDR only 0.3 per 1000. The Swedish Reinsurance study reported the experience on overweights on an overall basis, with all ages, both sexes and all degrees of overweight combined. The mortality ratio was 134 per cent and the EDR 2.3 per 1000.

ENDOCRINE AND METABOLIC DISORDERS

Table 999 Comparative Experience, Three Series of Insureds

Disease/Category (Ref.)	Sex/Age		Policies in Force at Start ℓ	Exposure Policy-Yrs E	No. of Death Claims		Ave. Ann. Mort. Rate		Mortality Ratio	Est. 5-Yr Surv. Rate	Est. 5-Yr Surv. Index	Excess Death Rate
					Observed d	Expected* d'	Observed $\bar{q}=d/E$	Expected* $\bar{q}'=d'/E$	$100\,d/d'$	$P=(1-\bar{q})^5$	$100\,P/P'$	$1000(\bar{q}-\bar{q}')$
Diabetes S&SS† (1)												
Age under 30	M	25	395	1750	10	1.20	.0057	.0007	835%	.9718	97.5%	5.0
Age 30-50	M	41	751	3994	37	10.5	.0093	.0026	350	.9545	96.7	6.7
Age 50 up	M	53	213	1177	24	13.8	.0204	.0117	174	.9021	95.7	8.7
Diabetes SS (2)	M&F	37	–	7493	113	27.2	.0151	.0036	415	.9268	94.4	11
Glycosuria S&SS (1)												
No BSTT●	M	46	561	4365	32	24.4	.0073	.0056	131	.9639	99.1	1.7
BSTT Satisfactory	M	45	423	2647	18	11.8	.0068	.0045	152	.9665	98.8	2.3
Renal	M	42	305	1987	8	5.96	.0040	.0030	134	.9800	99.5	1.0
Thyroid Enlargement S&SS (3)												
Non-toxic, no operation	M&F	39	–	1969	5	6.06	.0025	.0031	83	.9874	100.3	-0.6
Non-toxic, with operation	M&F	40	–	670	4	2.15	.0060	.0032	186	.9705	98.6	2.8
Toxic, no operation	M&F	37	–	2157	6	5.09	.0028	.0024	118	.9862	99.8	0.4
Not stated, no operation	M&F	40	–	759	5	2.45	.0066	.0032	205	.9675	98.3	3.4
Non-toxic Goiter S&SS (1)	M	43	456	2390	10	8.44	.0042	.0035	118	.9793	99.7	0.7
Toxic Goiter S&SS (1)	M	42	491	2439	8	7.71	.0033	.0032	104	.9837	99.9	0.1
Underweight 20% or more S&SS (1)	M	45	6081	34349	172	158	.0050	.0046	109	.9752	99.8	0.4
	F	47	3906	29226	95	84.6	.0033	.0029	112	.9839	99.8	0.4
Overweight S&SS (1) Over Std. Wt.												
Age under 30 yrs 20% up	M	25	11900	53293	54	36.6	.0010	.0007	148	.9949	99.8	0.3
Ages 30-50 yrs 20%-30%	M	39	11284	70576	229	149	.0032	.0021	153	.9839	99.4	1.1
Ages 30-50 yrs 30% up	M	39	4116	24335	97	50.6	.0040	.0021	192	.9802	99.0	1.9
Age over 50 yrs 20%-30%	M	55	1454	9406	140	129	.0149	.0137	108	.9278	99.4	1.2
Age over 50 yrs 30% up	M	54	437	2771	44	35.7	.0159	.0129	123	.9231	98.5	3.0
Ages 30-50 yrs 20% up	F	41	2094	13981	23	24.3	.0016	.0017	95	.9918	100.0	-0.1
Age over 50 yrs 20% up	F	54	509	3401	26	24.3	.0076	.0071	107	.9624	99.7	0.5
Overweight SS (2)	M&F	44	–	4756	43	32.1	.0090	.0067	134	.9556	98.9	2.3

* Basis of expected mortality: (Ref. 1) Prudential Assurance Co. (England) standard lives mortality 1957-58; (Ref. 2) Sverige Reins. Co., population mortality,
  M or F (Sweden), 1956-60 and 1961-65; (Ref. 3) N. Y. Life, Basic Select Tables (1955-60)

† "S" = Standard, "SS" = Substandard

● BSTT = Blood sugar tolerance test

Author Index

Subject Index

Abstract (tabular), categories of, 6; comment, 6; description of, 5 to 6, 18, 19; follow-up, 6; reference, 6; results, 6; subjects studied, 6; text of, 6;
Accident, Cerebrovascular. *See* Stroke
Accidental death(s), aircraft and space, 42; choking on food, 42; drowning, 42; falls, 42; fire, 42; firearm, 42; industrial, 34, 36, 0-14; motor vehicle, 42; poisoning, 34, 35, 42; railway, 42; surgical and medical, 34, 42; water-transport, 42
Accidental and other risks, 42
Acid-fast stain in pulmonary tuberculosis, 136
Addiction Research Foundation-Toronto Clinic, 0-8
Addictions and intoxications, 35. *See also* Alcoholism
Advisory Committee to the Surgeon General of the Public Health Service, 38
Aetna Life Insurance Company, 97, 119, 120, 3-130, 3-141, 3-144, 3-150
Age and mortality, age groups, 18, 27-28; all ages, 26; central age, 18; individual age, 9, 18; median age, 18
Agonal rhythm, 115
Airway obstruction. *See* Pulmonary function
Albuminuria. *See* Proteinuria
Alcohol, effects of, 34
Alcoholic cardiomyopathy, 125, 126, 3-171
Alcoholics, clinic patients, 34, 35, 0-8; defined, 33; employee population, 34, 35, 0-2; hospitalized patients, 34, 35, 0-10, 0-12; insured lives, 34, 35, 0-4, 0-6. *See also* Alcoholism
Alcoholism, causes of death in, 35, 0-2, 0-6, 0-12; and cirrhosis of the liver, 34, 147, 148; description of, 33, 34; fatty liver in, 34, 147; mortality in, 34, 35, 0-2 to 0-13; prevalence of, 33; suicide in, 0-10, 0-12
Allergic and immune disorders, 157
Allergic rhinitis (hay fever), 158
Alveolar air, 132
Amebic dysentery, 147, 5-44
American Cancer Society, 39, 40, 41, 0-18, 0-30
American Cancer Society Studies, 24, 25, 32
American Lung Association, 136
American Public Health Association, 4-31
Amnesia in epilepsy, 66
Amputations, 160, 7-26
Amyotrophic lateral sclerosis, 70
Anemia, as a cause of congestive heart failure, 124; secondary, 160, 7-26
Anesthetic agents, 43, 0-36
Aneurysm(s), aortic, 123, 128; cerebral circulation, 61
Angina pectoris, arteriography in, 85, 3-34, 3-40; causes of, 77; cigarette smoking and, 40; in congenital aortic stenosis, 106; coronary artery bypass, in disabling, 3-66; description of, 77; mortality in, 84, 3-6, 3-10, 3-20, 3-28, 3-56, 3-66, 3-178; previous history of, as a risk factor in myocardial infarction, 83, 3-46; stable, unstable, and other terms, 77;

"tobacco angina," 40
Angiography, aorticorenal, 127; aortocranial, 63; coronary, 83, 3-34, 3-40; renal, 127
Angiosarcoma with exposure to polyvinyl chloride, 36
Annals of the New York Academy of Sciences, 34
Annuitants, 25
Antibiotics, effect on infectious diseases, 157; in skin disease, 161
Antihypertensive drugs, improved prognosis with use of, 97-99; in malignant hypertension, 97-98; in moderate and severe hypertension, 98-99; prognosis in hypertension prior to availability of, 91-95
Anxiety in neuroses, 73
Aorta, calcification of, 127, 128, 3-178; tortuosity of, 127, 3-178
Aortic diastolic murmur(s), 108, 109, 3-108
Aortic insufficiency (regurgitation), 104, 110-111, 3-122, 3-124, 3-126
Aortic stenosis, 104, 106, 108, 3-95, 3-124, 3-126
Aortic systolic murmur(s), 108, 109, 3-108
Aortic valve disease as a cause of angina pectoris, 77
Aortic valvular disease, 104, 110, 111, 3-124, 3-126
Aortography, 127
Apical diastolic murmur(s), 108, 109, 3-108
Apical systolic murmur(s), 108, 109, 3-108, 3-112, 3-114
Apoplexy. *See* Stroke
Armed Forces Institute of Pathology, 58
Army Institute of Pathology, 126
Arrythmias, deaths in the U.S., 115; after mitral valve replacement, 110; mortality in, 117-118; prevalence of, 115-117, 3-128 to 3-135; relation to the ECG, 113; as a risk factor in myocardial infarction, 83, 3-44, 3-46, 3-68
Arterial blood, in testing pulmonary function, 133, 134
Arteriogram (angiogram), aorticorenal, 127; aortocranial, 63; coronary, 83, 3-34, 3-40; renal, 127
Arteriosclerosis. *See* Atherosclerosis
Arthritis, osteo-, *See* Osteoarthritis; rheumatoid (atrophic, infectious), 160, 7-14; type unspecified, 160, 7-16
Arteriosclerotic heart disease. *See* Coronary heart disease
Asbestosis, 132; cigarette smoking and, 137; lung cancer in, 137; mortality in, 138; as occupational disease, 36, 132, 137
Ascites, in cirrhosis of the liver, 147, 5-34; in congestive heart failure, 124
Asthma, 131; as allergic disorder, 134, 4-2; bronchial, 4-2, 4-26; causes of death in, 135, 4-2; deaths in the U.S., 131, 134; description of, 134; mortality in, 135, 4-2, 4-26; in occupational diseases, 36; primary, 4-2; severity of attacks, 135
Ataxia(s), cerebellar, 68; in cerebral palsy, 66; Friedreich's, 68; locomotor (tabes dorsalis), 70; in multiple sclerosis, 67
Atherosclerosis (arteriosclerosis), and aortic

aneurysms, 128; and aortic calcification and tortuosity, 127, 3-178; association of various types, 125, 127; cerebrovascular, 63; cigarette smoking and, 39; coronary, 77; peripheral arterial occlusive disease, 125, 3-168, 3-178; of renal artery, 127
Atherosclerotic vascular disease in diabetes mellitus, 166
Athetosis in cerebral palsy, 66
Atrial arrhythmias following surgery for atrial septal defects, 106
Atrial (auricular) fibrillation, 114, 117
Atrial rhythm, (ECG), 116
Atrial septal defect, 104, 105, 106
Atrioventricular (AV) block, 116, 118, 3-136
Atrioventricular (AV) dissociation, 116
Azotemia as a complication of hypertension, 96, 98, 99

Backwash ileitis, 145
Bacterial endocarditis in congenital and valvular heart disease, 106, 107, 108, 111
Ballvalve prosthesis in mitral valvular disease, 110
Bellevue Hospital Pediatric and Adolescent Cardiac Clinic (New York), 110, 3-122
Bicuspid aortic valve, 107
Bigeminy, 114, 118, 3-135
Birth injury and cerebral palsy, 66
Bispebjerg Hospital, Copenhagen, 7-7
Bjork-Shiley aortic valve prosthesis, 111
Blalock-Taussig palliative operation for tetralogy of Fallot, 105, 3-92
Blindness, all causes, 71, 2-48; in sarcoidosis, 162
Blood and lymphatic system disorders, 156, 160, 7-2, 7-26
Blood pressure (arterial), casual reading, 87; control mechanisms, 88; excessive and, 88; high (elevated) reading, 87; kidney and, 88; lability (variability) of, 88; from life insurance examinations, 93; measurement of, 87; New York Heart Association classification, 87; normotensive (normal range), 87; physiological stimuli and, 88; as prognostic indicator, 87, 91-94, 3-80, 3-81, 3-90, 3-178; regulation of, 88. *See also* Hypertension
Blood pressure as an associated risk factor, in angina pectoris, 84, 3-28; in coronary heart disease, 3-16, 3-20, 3-34, 3-56; in early myocardial infarction, 82, 3-44, 3-48, 3-56; in stroke, 65; in survivors of acute myocardial infarction, 83, 3-28, 3-46, 3-48, 3-52, 3-56, 3-61
Blood sugar (glucose) elevated. *See* hyperglycemia
Blood urea nitrogen (BUN), in chronic renal failure, 153; in hypertension, 96; as indicator of azotemia or uremia, 153
Bone and joint disorders, 160, 7-26. *See also* Cancer, bone; Poliomyelitis
Bradycardia, 114
Brain, abscess of, 69; agenesis of, 68; congenital malformations of, 66, 68; cranial anomalies, 68; disorders in epilepsy, 66, 67; disorders of, 65 to 69; infections of, 68, 69; trauma, 69, 2-57

Brain tumor and optic neuritis, 71
Braunwald-Cutter aortic valve prosthesis, 111
Bristol Royal Infirmary, England, 3-101
Bronchiectasis, 131, 137, 4-26
Bronchitis, chronic. *See* Chronic bronchitis; cigarette smoking and, 39; other, 131
Bronchoscopy, in bronchiectasis, 135
Brooks Air Force Base, School of Aerospace Medicine, 3-141
Buerger's disease, 125
Build and Blood Pressure Study 1959, 29, 90 to 93, 95, 97, 121, 3-74, 3-153
Bundle branch block, in congenital heart disease, 105; mortality in, 118, 119, 3-138, 3-141; prevalence of, 116, 117; as a risk factor after myocardial infarction, 85, 3-68, 3-138
Bureau of Mines (1910), 4-12, 4-13
Bureau of Vital Statistics, 3-40
Byssinosis as an occupational disease, 36

Caesarean section, 6-1, 6-26
Cancer, 47 to 59, 1-4 to 1-103; causative factors in, 47; cellular anaplasia, 47; cellular autonomy, 47; deaths in the U.S., 47, 48; definition of, 47; distribution by stage (tables), 1-8, 109; excess mortality by age and sex, 51; family history of, 42; follow-up in, 1-5; histological type, 47; incidence and prevalence, 47, 48, 49, 1-8, 1-9; interpretation of findings, 56, 57; median survival time, 1-4; mortality trends in the U.S., 48; organization of data in *End Results in Cancer, Report No. 4,* 1-5; organization of results in tables, 1-6; overall 5-year survival experience, 50, 51, 52, 1-8, 1-9; as a public health problem, 47, 48; staging, 50, 1-5, 108; treatment, 50, 1-6
Cancer by site, blood (leukemia), 52, 1-78, 1-80, 1-82; bladder, 52, 55, 57, 1-55, 1-64; bone, 52, 54, 55, 1-88, 1-90; bone and soft tissues, 1-88 to 1-97; brain, 52, 54, 55, 57, 1-11, 1-14; breast, 52, 55, 57, 1-61, 1-76; cervix uteri, 52, 55, 57, 1-58, 1-70; colon, 52, 54, 57, 1-30, 1-48; connective tissue, 52, 54, 57, 1-88, 1-92; corpus uteri, 52, 55, 57, 1-59, 1-72; digestive tract, 1-25 to 1-53; endocrine system, 1-99 to 1-101; epithelioma, 1-102; esophagus, 52, 54, 55, 1-27, 1-42; eye, 52, 55, 57, 1-11, 1-12; gallbladder, 52, 54, 55, 1-29, 1-46; genitourinary tract, 1-54 to 1-77; Hodgkin's disease, 52, 1-79, 1-86; kidney, 52, 54, 57, 1-54, 1-62; larynx, 52, 54, 57, 1-16, 1-20; leukemia, acute, 52, 1-78, 1-80; leukemia, chronic, 52, 1-78, 1-82; lip, 52, 55, 57, 1-25, 1-32; liver, 52, 54, 1-29, 1-46; lung and bronchus, 52, 54, 55, 57, 1-17, 1-22; lymphatic system, 52, 1-79, 1-84 to 1-87; lymphosarcoma and other lymphomas, 52, 1-79, 1-84 to 1-87; melanoma, 52, 54, 57, 1-89, 1-94; mouth, 52, 54, 57, 1-25, 1-34; multiple myeloma, 52, 1-88, 1-90; nasopharynx, 52, 53, 1-16, 1-18; nervous system and sense organs, 1-11 to 1-15; nose and sinuses, 52, 54, 1-16, 1-18; ovary, 52, 54, 55, 1-59, 1-72; pancreas, 52, 54, 1-27, 1-42; penis, 52, 55, 57, 1-57, 1-68;

pharynx, 52, 54, 55, 57, 1-26, 1-36; prostate, 52, 54, 57, 1-56, 1-66; rectum, 52, 54, 57, 1-31, 1-52; respiratory tract, 1-16 to 1-23; recticular cell sarcoma, 1-79, 1-86; salivary gland, 52, 55, 57, 1-26, 1-40; stomach, 52, 54, 55, 57, 1-28, 1-44; testis, 52, 55, 57, 1-57, 1-68; thyroid gland, 52, 55, 57, 1-99, 1-100; tongue, 52, 54, 55, 57, 1-25, 1-32; vagina, 52, 54, 57, 1-60, 1-74; vulva, 52, 55, 57, 1-60, 1-74
Cancer localized, excess death rates, within 0-2 years, 51 to 53; within 2-5 years, 51 to 53; within 5-10 years, 53, 55 to 57; after 10 years, 56, 57
Cancer malignancy, grading (TNM system), 50
Cancer mortality associated with, alcoholism, 35; exposure to radioactive dusts, 37; occupational exposure, 37; smoking, 40, 0-20, 0-24, 0-27
Carcinogenic compounds in tobacco smoke, 39
Carcinoma(s), 47
Carcinoma of colon and ulcerative colitis, 146, 5-26, 5-28, 5-30
Cardiac catheterization studies in valvular heart disease, 108
Cardiac enlargement. *See* Heart enlargement
Cardiac failure. *See* Congestive heart failure
Cardiac transplant, 127, 128, 3-177
Cardiomegaly in rheumatic aortic regurgitation, 110. *See also* Heart enlargement
Cardiomyopathy, as a cause of angina pectoris, 77; deaths in the U.S., 123; description and classification, 125, 126; mortality in, 126, 3-168
Cardiovascular disease(s), 77 to 130, 3-1 to 3-179. *See also* Arrhythmias; Congenital heart disease; Coronary heart disease; Electrocardiographic (ECG) abnormalities; Hypertension; Valvular heart disease; *and other cardiovascular diseases*
Cardiovascular diseases and association with, bundle branch block (ECG), 119; ECG abnormalities, 122; intraventricular conduction delay (ECG), 119; left axis deviation (ECG), 119; left ventricular hypertrophy (ECG), 120; T wave abnormality (ECG), 121
Cardiovascular diseases as cause of death, in alcoholism, 35; in occupational diseases, 36, 0-16; in smoking, 40, 0-20, 0-24, 0-27
Cardiovascular diseases, long-term prospective study of, 124, 3-162
Cardiovascular-renal disease, family history of, 41, 42, 0-34
Casts (urinary), 151, 153, 154, 6-1, 6-26
Cataract, 71, 2-48
Cataract as an occupational disease, 36
Cerebral anastomosis technique, 63
Cerebral atherosclerosis, 63
Cerebral circulation, 62-63
Cerebral concussion, 69, 2-48
Cerebral demyelinating disease, 65
Cerebral embolism (embolus), 61, 64, 2-20
Cerebral hemorrhage, 61, 62, 64, 2-20, 2-48
Cerebral infarction, 63, 64, 2-12. *See also* Cerebrovascular disease
Cerebral occlusive disease, 62, 63, 2-4
Cerebral palsy, deaths in U.S., 62; descrip-

tion, 66; mortality by diagnostic type, 2-28; mortality by severity, 2-30
Cerebral vascular episodes, 62. *See also* Cerebrovascular disease
Cerebrovascular accident. *See* Stroke
Cerebrovascular disease, causes of death in, 62, 65, 2-2, 2-8, 2-12 to 2-23; cerebral circulation, 62, 63; cerebral embolism, 61, 64, 2-20; cerebral (intra-) hemorrhage, 61, 62, 64, 2-20, 2-40; cerebral infarction, 63, 64, 2-12; cerebral thrombosis, 61, 62, 2-8, 2-20; deaths in the U.S., 62; description of, 61; disability in, 62, 2-12, 2-16; excess mortality in hypertension, 90; extracranial arterial occlusion, 63, 64, 2-4; and hypertension, 61; incidence and prevalence of, 62, 2-10, 2-14 to 2-23; mortality in, 64, 65, 2-2 to 2-23; neurological status in, 64, 2-4, 2-8, 2-16; and optic neuritis, 71; recurrence rates in, 2-16, 2-22; stroke, 61 to 65, 2-2 to 2-23; subarachnoid hemorrhage, 61, 62, 64, 2-20; surgery in, 63, 64, 2-4; transient ischemic attack, 61, 63, 64, 2-22; trend, as a cause of death, 90, 100
Charity Hospital, New Orleans, 3-171
Chemical exposure in industry, 36
Chest disease(s). *See* Respiratory disease(s); Heart disease
Chest X-ray, abnormal appearance, heart and aorta, 127, 3-178; in bronchiectasis, 137; in chronic bronchitis, 135; in chronic obstructive pulmonary disease, 132; in emphysema, 132; normal, in hypertension, 95; in occupational diseases, 138; in pulmonary tuberculosis, 136; in valvular heart disease, 108
Children's Medical Center, Boston, 3-95
Children's Memorial Hospital, Chicago, 3-95
Cholecystectomy, 148, 5-38, 5-44
Cholecystitis, 148, 5-38, 5-44
Cholelithiasis (gallstones), 148, 5-38
Cholesterol level, serum (plasma), diet to lower, 171, 9-46; drug to lower, 3-61; as a mortality risk factor, 170, 171, 9-42; mortality study, Finland, 171, 9-46; mortality study, Norway, 170, 9-48; mortality study, pooled U.S., 171, 9-48; as a risk factor in coronary heart disease, 170, 171, 9-44
Cholesterol-lowering regimen, diet, 171, 9-46; drugs, 3-61
Cholinergic drugs, in treatment of myasthenia gravis, 161
Christie Hospital, England, 7-2
Chronic brain syndrome, 72
Chronic bronchitis, causes of death in, 135, 4-14; deaths in the U.S., 131; description of, 135; and emphysema, 134, 4-26; mortality in, 135, 4-14, 4-26
Chronic endocarditis, 107
Chronic obstructive pulmonary disease (COPD) (COLD), "blue bloater" type, 132; cigarette smoking and, 40; deaths in the U.S., 131; mortality in, 133, 134, 4-16, 4-18; "pink puffer" type, 132; pulmonary function in, 133, 4-16, 4-18; relation to emphysema, 132; severity indices of, 4-16, 4-18
Churchill Hospital, Oxford, England, 5-28
Cigarette smoke, composition of, 38, 39
Cigarette smoking, asbestos exposure and,

paroxysmal, 115; sinus, 114, 117; 3-128
Tay-Sachs disease, 68
Tetralogy of Fallot, 104, 105, 3-92
Texas Heart Institute, 3-42
Therapy, clinical trial, 7, 23; evaluation of results, 7, 31
Thiamine deficiency as a cause of congestive heart failure, 124
Thromboangiitis obliterans, 125
Thrombocytosis in polycythemia vera, 159
Thromboembolic complications of prosthetic heart valves, 111
Thrombosis, cavernous sinus, 69; cerebral, 61, 62, 2-8, 2-20; coronary, 77; intravascular, in polycythemia vera, 159. *See also* Cerebrovascular disease; Myocardial infarction
Thrombus, intracardiac, as a cause of endocarditis, 126
Thymoma and myasthenia gravis, 161, 7-20
Thyroid enlargement, 171, 9-50
Thyrotoxicosis, as a cause of heart failure, 124; as a cause of tachycardia, 113
Timed vital capacity (TVC), 130
"Tobacco angina," 40
Tobacco tar, 39
Tobacco use and consumption, 38
Toronto General Hospital, 2-44
Total lung capcity (TLC), 133
Total vital capacity, 132
Toxic agents, as environmental hazards, 37, 38; as occupational hazards, 36, 37; in tobacco smoke, 39
Toxic risks, 33, 35
Transient ischemic attack (cerebral), 61, 63, 64, 2-22
Transient situational disturbances, 71
Transposition of great vessels, 103, 104, 105, 107
Tremors, 71, 2-48
Triglyceride level, serum, 171, 9-48
Trudeau Sanatorium, New York, 136, 4-4
Tuberculin test, 136
Tuberculosis (TB), all types, 131-132, 157; family history of, 7-26; non-pulmonary, 157, 7-26; pulmonary, 136, 4-6, 4-11, 4-26. *See also* Pulmonary tuberculosis
Tuberculous menigitis, 68
Tumor, benign, 1-102
Tumor, malignant, 1-102. *See also* Cancer
Turner's Syndrome, 41

Ulcerative colitis, causes of death in, 146, 5-26, 5-28, 5-30, 5-32; in children, 46, 5-26, 5-30; colon cancer in, 146, 5-24 to 5-33; description of, 145; in first attack on relapse patients, 146, 5-28; in Mayo Clinic patients, 146, 5-24, 5-26; prognosis in, 146
Ullevål Hospital, Oslo, 0-12
Underweight, 171, 9-50
U.S. Bureau of Labor, 0-15
U.S. Department of Health, Education, and Welfare, 38, 103, 0-15, 0-22, 3-162. *See also* Framingham study, National Heart and Lung Institute, National Cancer Institute
U.S. Department of Labor (1913), 37
U.S. Public Health Service, 38, 0-15, 0-22, 3-162
University of Alabama Medical Center, 3-42
University of California, Cerebral Palsy Clinic, 2-28
University of Chicago Hospital, pulmonary function clinic, 133, 4-18
University of Helsinki Children's Hospital, Finland, 3-95
University of Manchester, England, 7-2
University of Manitoba, Canada, 3-136
University of Missouri School of Medicine, 2-14
University of Oregon Medical School, 3-66, 3-120
Upper respiratory tract, deaths in the U.S., 131, 137; diseases of, 137
Uremia as a cause of pericarditis, 126
Urinary abnormalities, 153, 154, 6-1 to 6-13, 6-26
Urinalysis, 153
Urine, casts in sediment of, in hypertension, 96; protein, in hypertension, 96; red cells, in hypertension, 96
Urine formation, 151
Urine sediment, 153, 6-1, 6-26
Uterine fibroma, 6-1
Vagotomy with pyloroplasty in peptic ulcer disease, 141
Valve failure in aortic valve replacement, 111
Valvular heart disease, 107-111, 3-116 to 3-127; aortic insufficiency (regurgitation), 108, 110, 3-122, 3-124; aortic stenosis, 108, 110, 3-124; causes of

death, 3-120, 3-124, 3-126; congenital aortic stenosis, 106, 3-95; congenital pulmonic stenosis, 107; deaths in the U.S., 104; diagnosis, 108; mitral insufficiency (regurgitation), 109, 3-120; mitral stenosis, 108-109, 3-116, 3-120; rheumatic, 104, 108
Valvular heart disease as a cause of congestive heart failure, 124
Valvuloplasty, closed mitral, in mitral stenosis, 109, 3-116
Valvulotomy, in congenital aortic stenosis, 106; in congenital pulmonic stenosis, 107
Varicose veins, 128, 3-178
Ventricular ectopic beats, 116
Ventricular hypertrophy, left. *See* Left ventricular hypertrophy
Ventricular premature beats, 114, 116, 117-118, 3-132, 3-134
Ventricular septal defect, 104, 105-106, 3-106
Vertebral-basilar arterial disease, 63, 64
Veterans Administration, 4, 64, 69, 72, 73, 82, 99, 0-22, 2-12, 2-36, 2-40, 2-54, 3-44, 3-46
Veterans Administration Cooperative Group on Antihypertensive Agents, 99
Violent death, 33, 35
Viral infection as a cause of pericarditis, 126
Virus diseases, 157
Vital staistics, 7

Wadsworth Veterans Administration Hospital, 2-12
Wandering pacemaker (ECG), 115
White blood cells in polycythemia vera, 159
William Slater Hospital, South Africa, 0-10
Williams-Steiger Occupational Safety and Health Act, 37
Withdrawals from follow-up study, 11, 12, 19
Wolff-Parkinson-White syndrome (ECG), 116
Work environment, 36, 37, 38
World Health Organization, 0-12

X-ray, chest. *See* Chest X-ray

Yale-New Haven Hospital, 137, 5-34

Zollinger-Ellison syndrome, 141